P9-DFA-523

Case Problems in Finance

Twelfth Edition

Edited by

W. Carl Kester

Mizuho Financial Group Professor of Finance

Richard S. Ruback

Willard Prescott Smith Professor of Corporate Finance

Peter Tufano

Sylvan C. Coleman Professor of Financial Management

All of Harvard Business School

Boston Burr Ridge, IL Dubuque, IA Madison, WI New York San Francisco St. Louis
Bangkok Bogotá Caracas Kuala Lumpur Lisbon London Madrid Mexico City
Milan Montreal New Delhi Santiago Seoul Singapore Sydney Taipei Toronto

CASE PROBLEMS IN FINANCE
Published by McGraw-Hill/Irwin, a business unit of The McGraw-Hill Companies, Inc., 1221 Avenue of the Americas, New York, NY, 10020. Copyright © 2005, 1997, 1992, 1987, 1981, 1975, 1972, 1969, 1962, 1959, 1953, 1949 by The McGraw-Hill Companies, Inc. All rights reserved. No part of this publication may be reproduced or distributed in any form or by any means, or stored in a database or retrieval system, without the prior written consent of The McGraw-Hill Companies, Inc., including, but not limited to, in any network or other electronic storage or transmission, or broadcast for distance learning.
Some ancillaries, including electronic and print components, may not be available to customers outside the United States.

This book is printed on acid-free paper.

1 2 3 4 5 6 7 8 9 0 DOW/DOW 0 9 8 7 6 5 4

ISBN 0-07-294551-6

Publisher: *Stephen M. Patterson*
Editorial assistant: *Meghan Grosscup*
Executive marketing manager: *Rhonda Seelinger*
Senior media producer: *Anthony Sherman*
Lead project manager: *Pat Frederickson*
Freelance project manager: *Rich Wright, Omega Publishing Services*
Senior production supervisor: *Rose Hepburn*
Director of design BR: *Keith J. McPherson*
Supplement producer: *Betty Hadala*
Senior digital content specialist: *Brian Nacik*
Cover design: *Jenny El-Shamy*
Typeface: *10.3/12 Times Roman*
Compositor: *Shepherd Inc.*
Printer: *R. R. Donnelley*

Library of Congress Cataloging-in-Publication Data

Case problems in finance / edited by W. Carl Kester, Richard S. Ruback, Peter Tufano.—
12th ed.
p. cm. — (The McGraw-Hill/Irwin series in finance, insurance and real estate)
ISBN 0-07-294551-6 (alk. paper)
1. Corporations—Finance—Case studies. 2. Business enterprises—Finance—Case studies
I. Kester, W. Carl. II. Ruback, Richard S., 1954- III. Tufano, Peter. IV. Irwin series in finance, insurance, and real estate

HG4026.C279 2005
658.15—dc22

2003069111

www.mhhe.com

To our families

The McGraw-Hill/Irwin Series in Finance, Insurance and Real Estate

Stephen A. Ross
Franco Modigliani Professor of Finance and Economics
Sloan School of Management
Massachusetts Institute of Technology
Consulting Editor

FINANCIAL MANAGEMENT

Benninga and Sarig
Corporate Finance: A Valuation Approach

Block and Hirt
Foundations of Financial Management
Eleventh Edition

Brealey and Myers
Principles of Corporate Finance
Seventh Edition

Brealey, Myers and Marcus
Fundamentals of Corporate Finance
Fourth Edition

Brooks
FinGame Online 4.0

Bruner
Case Studies in Finance: Managing for Corporate Value Creation
Fourth Edition

Chew
The New Corporate Finance: Where Theory Meets Practice
Third Edition

Chew and Gillan
Corporate Governance at the Crossroads: A Book of Readings
First Edition

DeMello
Cases in Finance

Grinblatt and Titman
Financial Markets and Corporate Strategy
Second Edition

Helfert
Techniques of Financial Analysis: A Guide to Value Creation
Eleventh Edition

Higgins
Analysis for Financial Management
Seventh Edition

Kester, Ruback, and Tufano
Case Problems in Finance
Twelfth Edition

Ross, Westerfield and Jaffe
Corporate Finance
Seventh Edition

Ross, Westerfield and Jordan
Essentials of Corporate Finance
Fourth Edition

Ross, Westerfield and Jordan
Fundamentals of Corporate Finance
Sixth Edition

Smith
The Modern Theory of Corporate Finance
Second Edition

White
Financial Analysis with an Electronic Calculator
Fifth Edition

INVESTMENTS

Bodie, Kane and Marcus
Essentials of Investments
Fifth Edition

Bodie, Kane and Marcus
Investments
Sixth Edition

Cohen, Zinbarg and Zeikel
Investment Analysis and Portfolio Management
Fifth Edition

Corrado and Jordan
Fundamentals of Investments: Valuation and Management
Third Edition

Farrell
Portfolio Management: Theory and Applications
Second Edition

Hirt and Block
Fundamentals of Investment Management
Seventh Edition

FINANCIAL INSTITUTIONS AND MARKETS

Cornett and Saunders
Fundamentals of Financial Institutions Management

Rose and Hudgins
Commercial Bank Management
Sixth Edition

Rose
Money and Capital Markets: Financial Institutions and Instruments in a Global Marketplace
Eighth Edition

Santomero and Babbel
Financial Markets, Instruments, and Institutions
Second Edition

Saunders and Cornett
Financial Institutions Management: A Risk Management Approach
Fourth Edition

Saunders and Cornett
Financial Markets and Institutions: A Modern Perspective
Second Edition

INTERNATIONAL FINANCE

Beim and Calomiris
Emerging Financial Markets

Eun and Resnick
International Financial Management
Third Edition

Levich
International Financial Markets: Prices and Policies
Second Edition

REAL ESTATE

Brueggeman and Fisher
Real Estate Finance and Investments
Twelfth Edition

Corgel, Ling and Smith
Real Estate Perspectives: An Introduction to Real Estate
Fourth Edition

Ling and Archer
Real Estate Principles: A Value Approach
First Edition

FINANCIAL PLANNING AND INSURANCE

Allen, Melone, Rosenbloom and Mahoney
Pension Planning: Pension, Profit-Sharing, and Other Deferred Compensation Plans
Ninth Edition

Crawford
Life and Health Insurance Law
Eighth Edition (LOMA)

Harrington and Niehaus
Risk Management and Insurance
Second Edition

Hirsch
Casualty Claim Practice
Sixth Edition

Kapoor, Dlabay and Hughes
Personal Finance
Seventh Edition

Williams, Smith and Young
Risk Management and Insurance
Eighth Edition

Introduction

Many readers might be experiencing the case method of instruction for the first time. Sometimes, the experience is a frustrating one, for cases typically end at the critical point, in the words of some, "just when they seem to be getting someplace." At that point, readers are left to make their own way. It might be helpful, therefore, to know from the outset what case problems are and what advantages we believe can be gained from their use.

The heart of case-method instruction is the use of problems to train students to discover, and then to fix in mind, ways of problem solving that are effective in that field of management. Appropriate use of theory and the acquisition of factual content and analytic skills are also important goals, but the main objective is an ability to handle different types of managerial problems intelligently.

The words *decisional* and *experiential* are sometimes used to contrast the case method with *expository* teaching. For example, most of the cases in this volume are descriptions of actual business situations. The facts are those known to some executive or other decision maker; they present an immediate financial problem needing resolution. Some cases emphasize the preliminaries of decision making—the difficulty of isolating and defining the crucial problem or of determining whether enough information is at hand to make an intelligent decision. The majority of cases, however, are action- and decision-oriented cases. They present reasonable alternative courses of action that might have been followed in the given situation. Sufficient information is given to place readers in the decision makers' positions. From this vantage point, students are challenged to analyze the problem and to decide on the course of action to be taken.

The cases themselves depict a wide range of financial problems and business situations. Reference to the Contents will show that problems have been drawn from most of the major areas covered in typical finance courses. Cases have been selected from a variety of industries and from different time periods. Cases are also included that illustrate different phases in the life cycle of businesses and problems associated with decline and distress as well as those that accompany prosperity. Although textbook readings that complement the cases provided here are easily assigned, this volume also includes a number of notes that have been developed specifically to support certain cases by providing students with essential background and technical materials.

Organization of the Book

The sequence of this book's major sections reflects our decision-oriented approach. As in prior editions, each section is organized as a progression. It begins with a comparatively simple case that establishes the main ideas of the section. The simple case is followed by a more challenging one in which a richer managerial context adds complexity to the analysis and the decisions to be made. By the end of each section, students encounter cases that compel them to reach far beyond the basics.

We begin in Part 1 with **Financing Current Operations.** This is a topic that is typically omitted from a first expository course in finance or might occur at the end of such a course. We begin with this topic because obtaining sufficient funds to maintain ongoing operations is the first responsibility of a financial manager. Although this subject is not glamorous, it enables students to focus on concrete problems of corporate financial management that require decisions. This part begins with a section that introduces students to elementary analytic skills such as financial ratio analysis and pro forma forecasting, which are necessary to the analysis of many other cases throughout the book. The rest of Part 1 engages students in a series of working capital management cases in which these basic skills are reinforced and students are introduced to various forms of short-term financing.

Working capital management and short-term financing naturally lead to a discussion in Part 2 of **Capital Structure, Long-Term Financing, and Risk Management.** The cases in this part begin with an exploration of **debt policy** and **long-term financing** decisions. In addition to an introduction to the determinants of optimal **capital structure,** students are introduced to a variety of **long-term financing instruments** (fixed- and floating-rate debt, equity, equity-linked securities, and so forth), **markets** and **institutions.** A newly revised and expanded section on **derivative instruments and risk management** is also included in Part 2. This section builds an understanding of how derivative instruments can be used in conjunction with other financial securities to achieve a particular liability structure with exposures to some external risk factors but not others. It also provides students with a broad conceptual foundation for understanding **options** as a metaphor for flexibility, which applies to a number of other areas of management such as valuing and selecting among projects and making certain kinds of operating decisions.

Part 3, **Valuation and Investment,** exploits the principles of finance established in Part 2 and the forecasting skills developed in Part 1 to build a valuation paradigm based on discounted cash flow and cost-of-capital concepts. The valuation skills built in **valuing and selecting investment opportunities** and **cost of capital and valuation** are then applied to a variety of major corporate finance problems found in the **advanced valuation** section. Cases in this section range from the valuation of complex projects and companies to valuing initial public offerings, highly leveraged transactions and real options. The volume concludes with six cases in Part 4 that provide a **Review and Synthesis** of the concepts covered throughout the whole collection of cases.

In this twelfth edition, 36 of the 69 cases and notes are new. Of these 36 cases and notes, 32 are completely new to this edition and 4 are updates of material that appeared in the eleventh edition. Most of the new cases were developed as part of a major renewal of the required finance curriculum at Harvard Business School. They reflect the changing financial environment as well as advances in the theory and practice of financial management. Nearly half of the cases included here are well-tested cases that continue to function effectively as vehicles for teaching finance fundamentals.

Using This Book

All of these cases are designed to provide a basis for class discussion; as such, they are not intended to illustrate correct or incorrect solutions to management problems. It need hardly be added that the discussion they provoke will move along more productive and realistic lines if students also have a standard finance text or reference book available and use it freely for expositions of models and background information not provided by this casebook. In addition, students will need to acquire proficiency in a number of analytic techniques useful in handling the quantitative aspects of case analysis. Several cases and problem sets appearing here have been included to provide some of that proficiency, but additional supplemental readings might also be useful depending on students' initial skill levels with respect to quantitative analytic techniques.

Case studies confront students with the necessity of making decisions, and this is perhaps their greatest value. Students cannot stop with an understanding of the facts and a listing of items that deserve consideration. Mastery of these matters is merely the jumping-off point for class discussion. To be effective, students must actually think the problem through to a decision, explain their analyses to classmates, and defend their ideas. The need to choose among balanced alternatives and to discuss the decision intelligently is a great force in learning. It helps to provide that elusive quality of judgment that must accompany an understanding of principles and theories if students of management are to become effective decision makers.

Since the cases present business situations that pose debatable action alternatives, they contain problems that can be narrowed but not settled by the usual techniques of financial analysis. Judgment must enter into the process of decision making, so unanimous agreement as to the best decision is neither expected nor desired. This ambiguity also contributes to the initial frustration of many students who have been working with purely scientific and technical problems in which a tight, strictly analytic approach can be expected to yield a single "right" conclusion.

When analyzing case problems, readers should not overlook intangible human factors. The choice between financial alternatives in many, if not all, cases depends in part on the decision maker's disposition for risk taking, and on other organizational and contextual matters.

Many of the cases included here also have important ethical dimensions to them. While these finance cases were not written primarily to raise ethical problems, such issues are of very real concern to business leaders and should not be overlooked. Richer discussions and better decision-making skills will be fostered through explicit attention to the ethical concerns that often accompany financing and investment decisions.

Working with cases might require more student time than normal textbook reading assignments coupled with problem sets. However, the satisfaction of handling problems that introduce the complexities involved in actual business decisions is normally sufficient to compensate for the extra time required.

W. Carl Kester

Richard S. Ruback

Peter Tufano

Acknowledgments

A considerable debt of thanks is owed to the many people and organizations who have contributed to the development of this collection of cases. Clearly, these cases could not have been written without the cooperation and generous sacrifices of time offered by scores of managers interviewed at those companies providing the decision-making settings. Sheer numbers and the need to respect confidentiality prohibit naming them all; but they know who they are, and it is our sincere hope that they will realize the full extent of our gratitude and derive some satisfaction from having had an impact on the education of students of finance around the world.

We wish to acknowledge our debt to past editors of this volume, whose pioneering work and sustaining influence have paved the way to this new edition. These include: Pearson Hunt, Charles M. Williams, James T. S. Porterfield, Leonard C. R. Langer, Robert F. Vandell, Alan B. Coleman, Frank L. Tucker, James E. Walter, Erich A. Helfert, Victor L. Andrews, David W. Mullins, Jr., J. Keith Butters, Scott P. Mason, William E. Fruhan, Jr., and Thomas R. Piper. Their continuing influence will be obvious to all who were users of prior editions of *Case Problems in Finance.*

Thirty current or former members of Harvard Business School's faculty authored, coauthored, or supervised the writing of cases used in this edition. In addition to those case authors who were also previous editors of this volume, we wish to thank Gregor M. Andrade, Paul Asquith, Malcolm P. Baker, George C. Chacko, Randolph B. Cohen, Joshua D. Coval, Mihir A. Desai, Benjamin C. Esty, Stuart C. Gilson, Robert R. Glauber, John P. Goldsberry III, Bruce C. Greenwald, Robin Greenwood, Samuel L. Hayes III, Simi Kedia, Timothy A. Luehrman, E. Scott Mayfield, Mark Mitchell, André F. Perold, Kevin R. Rock, Erik Stafford, Richard F. Vancil, and Luis M. Viceira for the use of cases for which they were author, coauthor, or supervisor. Sudhakar Balachandran of Columbia University, Zvi Bodie of Boston University, and Todd Pulvino of Northwestern University were coauthors of several cases included here, and we are most grateful for their contributions. Finally, we extend our sincere thanks to the many research associates who assisted in the writing of the cases in this volume under the supervision of faculty members, and to the MBA students at Harvard Business School whose many comments and insights helped us "season" the cases appearing here.

We are grateful to Harvard Business School's Division of Research and Faculty Development, which provided financial support for the development of the cases in this book, and to HBS Publishing for their considerable help and cooperation in the compiling of this volume. Carol Sweet, Amy Iakovou, Pat Hathaway, and Loni Turner at HBS Publishing were particularly helpful and deserve our warm thanks.

Most of all, we would like to express our special thanks and appreciation to Betsy Brink, Bridget Collins, Cristina Moody, and Julia Stevens for their invaluable assistance in the preparation of this volume. Their care and expertise in making revisions in the cases, assembling the manuscript, and taking care of all manner of tasks associated with the organization and production of this book has contributed greatly to its quality.

The editors assume full responsibility for the contents of this edition, but we are keenly aware of our obligation to our predecessors and colleagues.

W. C. K.

R. S. R.

P. T.

Contents

Part 1

Financing Current Operations

Introductory Exercises

Assessing a Firm's Future Financial Health

Assessing the long-term financial health of a company is an important task for management in its formulation of goals and strategies and for outsiders as they consider the extension of credit, long-term supplier arrangements, or an investment in the company's equity. History abounds with examples of firms that embarked upon overly ambitious programs and subsequently discovered that their portfolio of programs could not be financed on acceptable terms. The outcome frequently was the abandonment of programs in midstream, at considerable financial, organizational, and human cost.

It is the responsibility of management to *anticipate* future imbalance in the corporate financial system *before* its severity is reflected in the financials, and to consider corrective action before both time and money are exhausted. The avoidance of bankruptcy is an insufficient standard. Management must ensure the continuity of the flow of funds to all of its strategically important programs.

Figure I provides a conceptualization of the corporate financial system, with a suggested step-by-step process to assess whether it will remain in balance over the ensuing 2–3 years. The remainder of this note discusses each of the steps in the process and then provides an exercise on the various financial ratios that are useful as part of the analysis. The final section of the note demonstrates the relationship between a company's operating characteristics and its financial characteristics.

Step 1: Goals, Strategies, and Operating Characteristics and Step 2: Outlook for Firm Sales

The starting point for assessing a firm's long-term financial health must be a thorough investigation of (1) management's goals for the company and for each of the businesses (product markets) in which it chooses to compete; (2) the strategy planned for each product market; (3) the outlook for the market in terms of unit growth, product price, volatility, and predictability; (4) the main operating/technological/competitive/regulatory characteristics and risks; and (5) the outlook for the firm's sales.

The analyst is well-advised to devote substantial time exploring these areas as the corporate financial system is driven by the goals, strategies, market conditions, and the

This note is a rewritten version of an earlier note (HBS No. 297-063) and has been prepared as the basis for class discussion.

Copyright © 2002 President and Fellows of Harvard College. To order copies or request permission to reproduce materials, call 1-800-545-7685, write Harvard Business School Publishing, Boston, MA 02163, or go to http://www.hbsp.harvard.edu. No part of this publication may be reproduced, stored in a retrieval system, used in a spreadsheet, or transmitted in any form or by any means—electronic, mechanical, photocopying, recording, or otherwise—without the permission of Harvard Business School.

FIGURE I
The Corporate Financial System

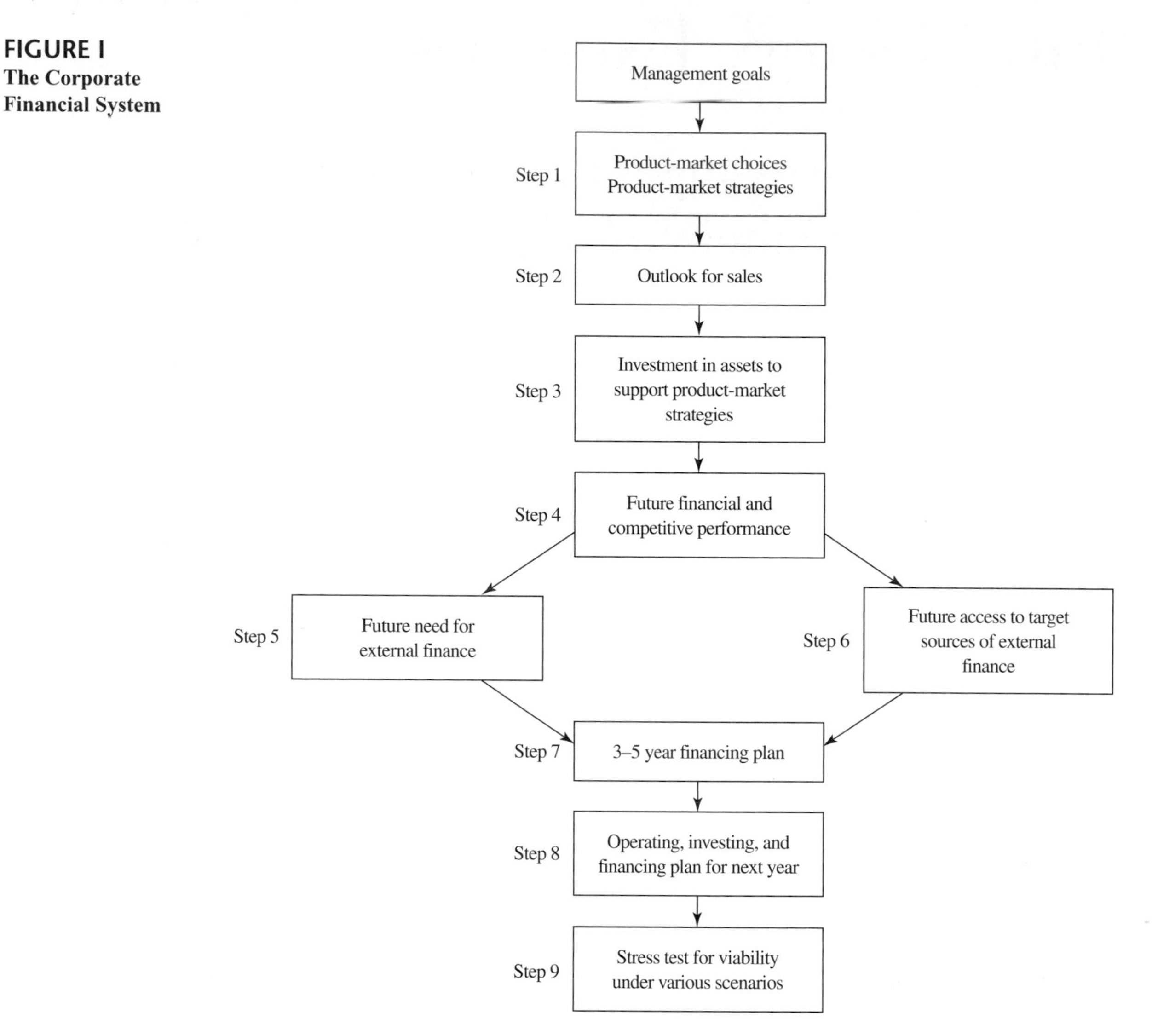

operating characteristics and risks. The firm's strategy and sales growth in each of its product-markets will largely determine the investment in assets needed to support these strategies; and the effectiveness of the strategies, combined with the response of competitors, will strongly influence the firm's competitive and profit performance and its resultant access to funds to finance the investment in the various type assets.

Step 3: Investments to Support the Product-Market Strategy(ies)

The product-market strategies inevitably require investments in accounts receivable, inventories, plant and equipment, and possibly, acquisitions. (They may also require heavy expenditures on research and development and/or high advertising and promotion expenditures to build market position. Because these expenditures are normally expensed, they will be discussed later as part of the section on performance.) Step 3 of the process is an attempt to estimate (1) the amounts that will be tied up in each of these asset types,

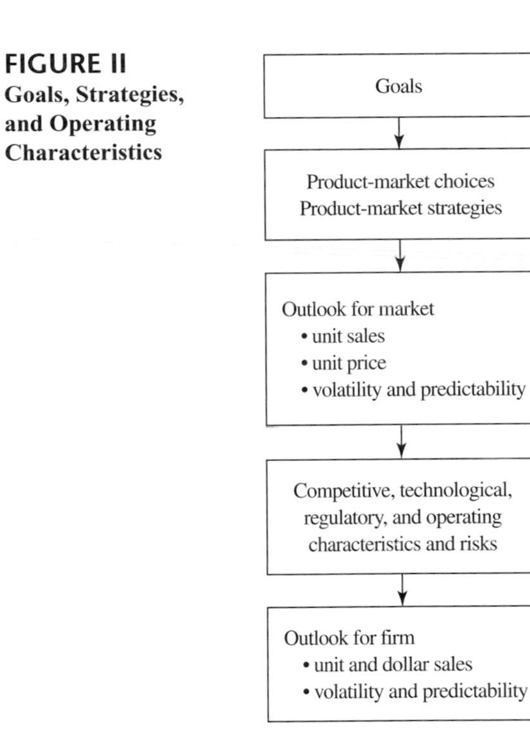

FIGURE II
Goals, Strategies, and Operating Characteristics

and (2) the level of total assets over the next 2–3 years. An analyst can make these estimates by studying the past pattern of the collection period, the days of inventory, and plant and equipment as a percent of cost of goods sold; and then applying a "reasonable value" for each to the sales forecast or the forecast of cost of goods sold.

Step 4: Future Profitability and Competitive Performance

Strong profitability is a necessity over the long run, for the level of profitability strongly influences (1) the company's access to debt finance; (2) the valuation of the company's common stock; (3) management's willingness to issue common stock; and (4) the company's "sustainable sales growth." Once again, a reasonable starting point is to analyze the past pattern of profitability, starting with a careful scrutiny of the underlying accounting choices and assumptions:

1. What has been the average level, trend, and volatility of profitability?
2. Is the level of profitability sustainable, given the outlook for the market and for competitive and regulatory pressures? (Figure III summarizes market and industry factors that can affect a firm's future profit performance.) Will profitability benefit from improving industry and competitive conditions?
3. Has management initiated major profit improvement programs?
4. Are there any "hidden" problems, such as suspiciously large levels or buildups of accounts receivable or inventories relative to sales, or a series of unusual transactions and/or accounting changes?
5. Is the company strong in terms of customer service, new product development, product quality, and management and employee retention and development? Is the current level of profitability at the expense of future growth and profitability?

FIGURE III
Sources of Downward Pressure on Profitability

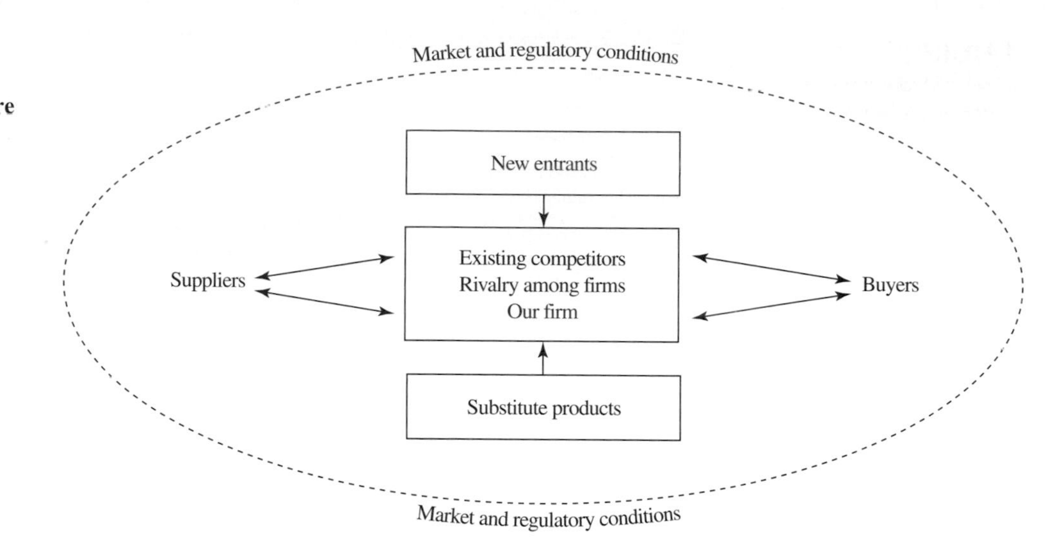

TABLE I
Assuming a 25% Increase in Sales ($ in millions)

Assets	1999		2000
Cash	$ 12	↑ 25%	$ 15
Accounts receivable	240	↑ 25%	300
Inventories	200	↑ 25%	250
Plant & equipment	400	↑ 25%	500
Total	$852		$1,065
Liabilities and Equity			
Accounts payable	$100	↑ 25%	$ 125
Accrued expenses	80	↑ 25%	100
Long-term debt	252	unchanged	252
Owners' equity	400	footnote[a]	442
Total	$852		$ 939
External financing need	0		126
Total	$852		$1,065

[a]It is assumed that the firm earns $60 million (a 15% return on beginning of year equity) and pays out $18 million as a cash dividend.

Step 5: Future External Financing Needs

Whether a company has a future external financing need depends on (1) its future sales growth, (2) the length of its cash cycle, and (3) the future level of profitability and profit retention. Rapid sales growth by a company with a long cash cycle (a long collection period + high inventories + high plant and equipment relative to sales) and low profitability/low profit retention is a recipe for an ever-increasing appetite for external finance, raised in the form of loans, debt issues, and/or sale of shares. Why? Because the rapid sales growth results in the rapid growth of an already large level of total assets. The increase in total assets is offset partially by an increase in accounts payable and accrued expenses, and by a small increase in owners' equity. However, the financing gap is substantial. For example, the company portrayed in Table I requires $126 million of additional external finance by the end of year 2000 to support the increase in total assets required to support 25% per year sales growth in a business that is fairly asset intensive.

TABLE II
Food Retailer—20% Increase in Sales

Assets	1999		2000
Cash	$ 12	↑ 20%	$ 14
Accounts receivable	0		0
Inventories	17	↑ 20%	20
Plant & equipment	80	↑ 20%	96
Total	$109		$130
Liabilities and Equity			
Accounts payable	$ 66	↑ 20%	$ 79
Accrued expenses	35	↑ 20%	42
Long-term debt	0		0
Owners' equity	8		9
Total	$109		$130
External financing need	0		0
Total	$109		$130

If, however, the company reduced its sales growth to 5% (and total assets, accounts payable, and accrued expenses increased accordingly by 5%), the need for additional external finance would drop from $126 million to $0.

High sales growth does *not* always result in a need for additional external finance. For example, a food retailer that extends no credit to customers, has only eight days of inventory, and does not own its warehouses and stores can experience rapid sales growth and not have a need for additional external finance *provided* it is reasonably profitable. Because it has so few assets, the increase in total assets is largely offset by a corresponding, spontaneous increase in accounts payable and accrued expenses.

Step 5 requires the development of pro forma income statements and balance sheets for each of the next 2–3 years to estimate (1) the dollar amount and timing of future external financing needs, (2) for how long the financing will be needed, (3) the confidence level in the forecasts, and (4) the deferrability of the underlying expenditures if the funds cannot be raised on acceptable terms.

Step 6: Access to Target Sources of External Finance

Having estimated the future financing need, management must identify the target sources (e.g., banks, insurance companies, public debt markets, public equity markets) and establish financial policies that will ensure access on acceptable terms:

1. How soundly is the company financed, given its level of profitability and cash flow, its level of business risk, and its future need for finance?
   a. How current is the company in its payment of suppliers?
   b. Is the company within its capacity to service the debt? What is the maturity structure of the existing debt?
   c. Is the company near to its borrowing limits according to restrictive covenants? Is it close to its internal policies in terms of debt levels and/or debt ratings?
   d. Are there any "hidden problems" such as unconsolidated subsidiaries with high debt levels or large contingent or unfunded liabilities?
2. Does the company have assured access to the debt markets? What are the target sources and what are their criteria for lending?
3. Does the company have assured access on acceptable terms to the equity markets? Is there a market for the shares? How many shares could be sold and at what price? Are management and/or the controlling shareholders(s) willing to issue additional shares?

4. Does the company have assets that could be sold to raise funds? At what price and how quickly could the assets be sold under ideal conditions? under adverse conditions?

Step 7: Viability of the 3–5 Year Plan

Are the company's goals, product-market strategies, investment requirements, and financing needs in balance with its financing capabilities over the 3–5 year planning period? What approximate mix of debt and equity must be raised to remain in compliance with the firm's debt policy?

Step 8: Current Year Financing Plan

How should the firm meet the current year's financing need? How should it balance the benefits of future financing flexibility (by selling equity now) and the hopes of realizing a higher share price by waiting to sell the equity (and therefore issuing debt now)?

Step 9: Stress Test under Scenarios of Adversity

Most 3–5 year financing plans work well if the expected scenario on which they are based in fact occurs. The test of the soundness of a 3–5 year plan is whether the continuity of the flow of funds to all strategically important programs can be maintained (or at least maintained as well as that of your competitors) even in times of adversity.

Figure IV is a somewhat more complete version of Figure I. Clearly, many of these questions require information beyond that contained in a company's published financial statements. Many require a thorough understanding of (1) the long-term goals and plans of management, (2) future industry structure and competitive behavior, (3) the competitive/technological/regulatory/operating characteristics of the industry and company, (4) the "availability" criteria of various sources of finance, and (5) the soundness of management. Analysis of the published financial statements and their footnotes is only *one part* of a complete analysis of a company's future financial health.

It is also clear that the evaluation of a firm's financial health can vary substantially, depending on the perspective of the individual making the evaluation. A bank or supplier considering the extension of seasonal credit may consider a company a very safe bet, whereas a long-term lender dependent on the health and profitability of that same company over a 15-year period may be very nervous.

The remainder of this note provides familiarity with the financial ratios that can be useful in answering some of the preceding questions. Exhibits 1 and 2 provide financial statements for 1995 and 1999 for a hypothetical company. The following section (Financial Ratios and Financial Analysis) presents four types of financial ratios and then asks a series of questions concerning the financial statements in Exhibits 1 and 2. Use the equations to answer two overall questions:

1. Has the financial condition of the company changed during the four-year period?
2. What are the most significant changes, as indicated by the financial ratios?

Financial Ratios and Financial Analysis

The two basic sources of financial data for a business entity are the income statement and the balance sheet. The income statement summarizes revenues and expenses over a period of time, e.g., for the year ending December 31, 1999. The balance sheet

FIGURE IV Corporate Financial System

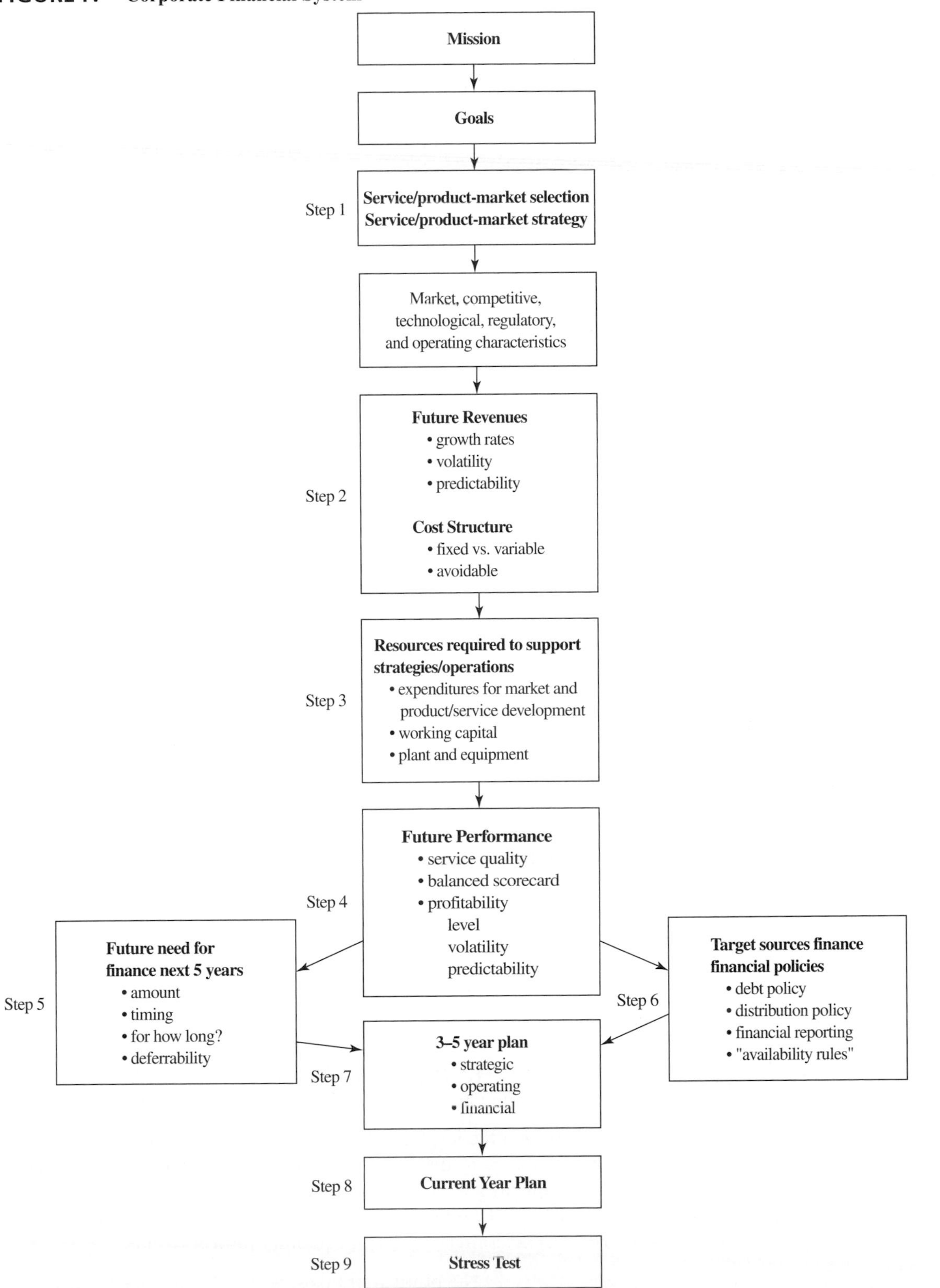

EXHIBIT 1
Magnetronics, Inc., Consolidated Income Statements for Years Ending December 31, 1995 and 1999 (thousands of dollars)

	1995	1999
Net sales	$32,513	$48,769
Cost of goods sold	19,183	29,700
Gross profit	$13,330	$19,069
Operating expenses	10,758	16,541
Interest expenses	361	517
Income before taxes	$ 2,211	$ 2,011
Federal income taxes	1,040	704
Net income	$ 1,171	$ 1,307

EXHIBIT 2
Magnetronics, Inc., Consolidated Balance Sheets at December 31, 1995 and 1999 (thousands of dollars)

	1995	1999
Cash	$ 1,617	$ 2,020
Accounts receivable	5,227	7,380
Inventories	4,032	8,220
Current assets	$10,876	$17,620
Net fixed assets	4,073	5,160
Total assets	$14,949	$22,780
Notes payable, banks	$ 864	$ 1,213
Accounts payable	1,615	2,820
Accrued expenses and taxes	2,028	3,498
Current liabilities	$ 4,507	$ 7,531
Long-term debt	2,750	3,056
Stockholders' equity	7,692	12,193
Total liabilities and stockholders' equity	$14,949	$22,780

is a list of what the business owns (its assets), what it owes (its liabilities), and what has been invested by the owners (owners' equity) at a specific point in time, e.g., *at* December 31, 1999.

From figures found on the income statement and the balance sheet, one can calculate the following types of financial ratios:

1. Profitability ratios
2. Activity ratios
3. Leverage ratios
4. Liquidity ratios

Profitability Ratios: How Profitable Is the Company?

Profitability is a necessity over the long run, for the level of profitability strongly influences (1) the company's access to debt finance, (2) the valuation of the company's common stock, (3) the company's willingness to issue common stock, and (4) the company's sustainable growth rate. One measure of the profitability of a business is profit as a percentage of sales, as determined by the profitability ratio equation:

$$\frac{\text{Net profit after taxes}}{\text{Net sales}}$$

The information necessary to determine a company's profit as a percentage of sales can be found in the company's ______________________________.

1. Magnetronics' profit as a percentage of sales for 1999 was $__________ divided by $__________, or __________%.
2. This represented an increase/decrease from __________% in 1995.
3. The deterioration in profitability resulted from an increase/decrease in cost of goods sold as a percentage of sales, and from an increase/decrease in operating expenses as a percentage of sales. The only favorable factor was the decrease in the __________.

Management and investors often are more interested in the return earned on the funds invested than in the level of profits as a percentage of sales. Companies operating in businesses requiring very little investment in assets often have low profit margins but earn very attractive returns on invested funds. Conversely, there are numerous examples of companies in very capital-intensive businesses that earn miserably low returns on invested funds, despite seemingly attractive profit margins.

Therefore, it is useful to examine the return earned on the funds provided by the shareholders and by the "investors" in the company's interest-bearing debt. To increase the comparability across companies, it is useful to use EBIAT (earnings before interest but after taxes) as the measure of return. The use of EBIAT as the measure of return also allows the analyst to compare the return on invested capital (calculated before the deduction of interest expense) with the company's estimated cost of capital to determine the long-term adequacy of the company's profitability.

4. Magnetronics had a total of $______________ of capital at year-end 1999 and earned before interest but after taxes (EBIAT) $______________ during 1999. Its return on invested capital is calculated as follows:

$$\frac{\text{Earnings before interest but after taxes (EBIAT)}}{\text{Owners' equity plus interest-bearing debt}}$$

In 1999 this figure was __________%, which represented an **increase/decrease** from the __________% earned in 1995.

From the viewpoint of the shareholders, an equally important figure is the company's return on equity. Return on equity is calculated by dividing profit after tax by the owners' equity.

$$\frac{\text{Profit after taxes}}{\text{Owners' equity}} = \text{Return on equity}$$

Return on equity indicates how profitably the company is utilizing shareholders' funds.

5. Magnetronics had $______________ of owners' equity and earned $______________ after taxes in 1999. Its return on equity was __________%, an **improvement/deterioration** from the __________% earned in 1995.

Management can "improve" (or "hurt") its return on equity in several ways. Each method of "improvement" differs substantially in nature. The analyst must look behind the return on equity figures and must understand the underlying causes of any changes. For example, did Return on Sales improve? Did the company's management of assets change? Did the company increase the use of borrowed funds relative to owners' equity? These three possible explanations are combined in the Du Pont system of ratio analysis:

$$\text{ROE} = \frac{\text{Net Income}}{\text{Sales}} \times \frac{\text{Sales}}{\text{Assets}} \times \frac{\text{Assets}}{\text{Equity}}$$

Activity Ratios: How Well Does a Company Employ Its Assets?

The second basic type of financial ratio is the activity ratio. Activity ratios indicate how well a company employs its assets. Ineffective utilization of assets results in the need for more finance, unnecessary interest costs, and a correspondingly lower return on capital employed. Furthermore, low activity ratios or a deterioration in the activity ratios may indicate uncollectible accounts receivables or obsolete inventory or equipment.

Total asset turnover measures the company's effectiveness in utilizing its total assets and is calculated by dividing total assets into sales:

$$\frac{\text{Net sales}}{\text{Total assets}}$$

1. Total asset turnover for Magnetronics in 1999 can be calculated by dividing $______________ into $______________. The turnover **improved/deteriorated** from _________ times in 1995 to _________ times in 1999.

It is useful to examine the turnover ratios for each type of asset, as the use of total assets may hide important problems in one of the specific asset categories. One important category is accounts receivables. The average collection period measures the number of days that the company must wait on average between the time of sale and the time when it is paid. The average collection period is calculated in two steps. First, divide annual credit sales by 365 days to determine average sales per day:

$$\frac{\text{Net credit sales}}{\text{365 days}}$$

Then, divide the accounts receivable by average sales per day to determine the number of days of sales that are still unpaid:

$$\frac{\text{Accounts receivable}}{\text{Credit sales per day}}$$

2. Magnetronics had $______________ invested in accounts receivables at year-end 1999. Its average sales per day were $______________ during 1999 and its average collection period was _________ days. This represented an **improvement/deterioration** from the average collection period of _________ days in 1995.

A third activity ratio is the inventory turnover ratio, which indicates the effectiveness with which the company is employing inventory. Since inventory is recorded on the balance sheet at cost (not at its sales value), it is advisable to use cost of goods sold as the measure of activity. The inventory turnover figure is calculated by dividing cost of goods sold by inventory:

$$\frac{\text{Cost of goods sold}}{\text{Inventory}}$$

3. Magnetronics apparently needed $______________ of inventory at year-end 1999 to support its operations during 1999. Its activity during 1999 as measured by the cost of goods sold was $______________. It therefore had an inventory turnover of _________ times. This represented an **improvement/deterioration** from _________ times in 1995.

A fourth and final activity ratio is the fixed asset turnover ratio, which measures the effectiveness of the company in utilizing its plant and equipment:

$$\frac{\text{Net sales}}{\text{Net fixed assets}}$$

4. Magnetronics had net fixed assets of $_____________ and sales of $_____________ in 1999. Its fixed asset turnover ratio in 1999 was _________ times, an **improvement/deterioration** from _________ times in 1995.
5. So far, we have discussed three measure of profitability: They are (a) ____________ ________________ (b) ______________________________ and (c) ____________ ________________. We have also discussed four activity ratios which measure the effectiveness of the company in utilizing its assets: They are (d) ____________ ______________ (e) __________________________ (f) ________________ __________ and (g) __________________________.
6. The deterioration in Magnetronics' operating profits as a percentage of total assets between 1995 and 1999 resulted primarily from __________________________
____
____
____
____
____

Leverage Ratios: How Soundly Is the Company Financed?

The third basic type of financial ratio is the leverage ratio. The various leverage ratios measure the relationship of funds supplied by creditors and the funds supplied by the owners. The use of borrowed funds by profitable companies will improve the return on equity. However, it increases the riskiness of the business and, if used in excessive amounts, can result in financial embarrassment.

One leverage ratio, the debt ratio, measures the total funds provided by creditors as a percentage of total assets:

$$\frac{\text{Total liabilities}}{\text{Total assets}}$$

Total liabilities include both current and long-term liabilities.

1. The total liabilities of Magnetronics as of December 31, 1999, were $_____________ or ________% of total assets. This represented an **increase/decrease** from ________% as of December 31, 1995.

Lenders—especially long-term lenders—want reasonable assurance that the firm will be able to repay the loan in the future. They are concerned with the relationship between total debt and the economic value of the firm. This ratio is called the total debt ratio at market.

$$\frac{\text{Total liabilities}}{\text{Total liabilities} + \text{Market value of the equity}}$$

The market value of equity is calculated by multiplying the number of shares outstanding of common stock times the market price per share.

2. The market value of Magnetronics' equity is $14,275,000 at December 31, 1999. Its total debt ratio at market was ___________________________.

A second ratio that relates the level of debt to economic value and performance is the times interest earned ratio. This ratio relates earnings before interest and taxes—a measure of profitability and of long-term viability—to the interest expense—a measure of the level of debt.

$$\frac{\text{Earnings before interest and taxes}}{\text{Interest expense}}$$

3. Magnetronics' earnings before interest and taxes were $_______________ in 1999 and its interest charges were $_______________. Its times interest earned was _________ times. This represented an **improvement/deterioration** from the 1995 level of _________ times.

A fourth and final leverage ratio is the number of days of payables. This ratio measures the average number of days that the company is taking to pay its suppliers of raw materials and components. It is calculated by dividing annual purchases by 365 days to determine average purchases per day:

$$\frac{\text{Annual purchases}}{\text{365 days}}$$

Accounts payable are then divided by average purchases per day:

$$\frac{\text{Accounts payable}}{\text{Average purchases per day}}$$

to determine the number of days purchases that are still unpaid.

It is often difficult to determine the purchases of a firm. Instead, the income statement shows cost of goods sold, a figure that includes not only raw materials but also labor and overhead. Thus, it often is only possible to gain a rough idea as to whether or not a firm is becoming more or less dependent on its suppliers for finance. This can be done by relating accounts payable to cost of goods sold,

$$\frac{\text{Accounts payable}}{\text{Cost of goods sold}}$$

and following this ratio over time.

4. Magnetronics owed its suppliers $_______________ at year-end 1999. This represented _________% of cost of goods sold and was an **increase/decrease** from _________% at year-end 1995. The company appears to be **more/less** prompt in paying its suppliers in 1999 than it was in 1995.
5. The deterioration in Magnetronics' profitability, as measured by its return on equity, from 15.2% in 1995 to 10.7% in 1999 resulted from the combined impact of ______
____
____
and ____
____.
6. The financial riskiness of Magnetronics **increased/decreased** between 1995 and 1999.

Liquidity Ratios: How Liquid Is the Company?

The fourth basic type of financial ratio is the liquidity ratio. These ratios measure a company's ability to meet financial obligations as they become current. The current ratio, defined as current assets divided by current liabilities,

$$\frac{\text{Current assets}}{\text{Current liabilities}}$$

assumes that current assets are much more readily and certainly convertible into cash than other assets. It relates these fairly liquid assets to the claims that are due within one year—the current liabilities.

1. Magnetronics held $_______________ of current assets at year-end 1999 and owed $_______________ to creditors due to be paid within one year. Its current ratio was _______________, an **improvement/deterioration** from the ratio of _______________ at year-end 1995.

The quick ratio, or acid test, is similar to the current ratio but excludes inventory from the current assets:

$$\frac{\text{Current assets} - \text{Inventory}}{\text{Current liabilities}}$$

Inventory is excluded because it is often difficult to convert into cash (at least at book value) if the company is struck by adversity.

2. The quick ratio for Magnetronics at year-end 1999 was _______________, an **improvement/deterioration** from the ratio of _______________ at year-end 1995.

A Warning

The calculated ratios are no more valid than the financial statements from which they are derived. The quality of the financial statements should be assessed, and appropriate adjustments made, before any ratios are calculated. Particular attention should be placed on assessing the reasonableness of the accounting choices and assumptions embedded in the financial statements.

The Case of the Unidentified Industries

The preceding exercise suggests a series of questions that may be helpful in assessing a company's future financial health. It also describes several ratios that are useful in answering some of the questions, especially if the historical trend in these ratios is examined.

However, it is also important to compare the actual absolute value with some standard to determine whether the company is performing well. Unfortunately, there is no single current ratio, inventory turnover, or debt ratio that is appropriate to all industries, and even within a specific industry, ratios may vary significantly among companies. The operating and competitive characteristics of the company's industry greatly influence its investment in the various types of assets, the riskiness of these investments, and the financial structure of its balance sheet.

Try to match the five following types of companies with their corresponding balance sheets and financial ratios as shown in Exhibit 3.

1. Electric utility
2. Japanese trading company
3. Aerospace manufacturer
4. Automobile manufacturer
5. Supermarket chain

In doing the exercise, consider the operating and competitive characteristics of the industry and their implications for (1) the collection period, (2) inventory turnover, (3) the amount of plant and equipment, and (4) the appropriate financial structure. Then identify which one of the five sets of balance sheets and financial ratios best matches your expectations.

EXHIBIT 3 Unidentified Balance Sheet

	A	B	C	D	E
Balance Sheet Percentages					
Cash	7.6%	2.7%	1.4%	7.2%	12.7%
Receivables	31.7	4.7	2.9	60.3	11.5
Inventories	5.3	2.0	23.0	8.7	48.1
Other current assets	1.2	3.0	1.8	7.3	0.0
Property and equipment (net)	30.2	66.6	49.9	4.3	25.0
Other assets	24.0	21.0	21.0	12.2	2.7
Total assets	100.0%	100.0%	100.0%	100.0%	100.0%
Notes payable	38.4%	4.2%	4.6%	50.8%	0.9%
Accounts payable	5.5	3.0	20.0	15.2	21.5
Other current liabilities	1.5	4.7	12.7	5.7	27.4
Long-term debt	17.4	30.0	37.5	22.7	8.1
Other liabilities	26.5	22.9	9.8	1.3	8.1
Owners' equity	10.7	35.2	15.4	4.3	34.0
Total liabilities and equity	100.0%	100.0%	100.0%	100.0%	100.0%
Selected Ratios					
Net profits/net sales	.04	.14	.02	.01	.05
Net profits/total assets	.03	.05	.06	.01	.03
Net profits/owners' equity	.29	.14	.41	.13	.10
Net sales/total assets	.78	.36	3.2	2.1	.67
Collection period (days)	149	48	3	106	63
Inventory turnover	11	10	10	23	1.1
Total liabilities/total assets	.89	.65	.85	.96	.66
Long-term debt/owners' equity	1.6	.85	2.4	5.3	.24
Current assets/current liabilities	1.0	1.0	.8	1.0	1.4
Quick ratio	.9	.9	.2	.9	.5

Tire City, Inc.

Jack Martin, Chief Financial Officer of Tire City, Inc., was preparing for a meeting with his company's bank later in the week. At that meeting, Mr. Martin intended to present a request that the bank grant Tire City a five-year loan to finance anticipated growth in the company and the expansion of the company's warehouse facilities.

In preparation for his meeting, Martin had gathered some recent financial statements for Tire City (see Exhibit 1).

Company Background

Tire City, Inc. (TCI) was a rapidly growing retail distributor of automotive tires in northeastern United States. Tires were sold through a chain of 10 shops located throughout eastern Massachusetts, southern New Hampshire, and northern Connecticut. These stores kept sufficient inventory on hand to service immediate customer demand, but the bulk of TCI's inventory was managed at a central warehouse outside Worcester, Massachusetts. Individual stores could be easily serviced by this warehouse, which could usually fill orders from individual stores within 24 hours.

For the year ended in December 1995, TCI had sales of $23,505,000. Net income for that period was $1,190,000. During the previous three years, sales had grown at a compound annual rate in excess of 20%. This record was a reflection of Tire City's reputation for excellent service and competitive pricing, which yielded high levels of customer satisfaction.

Past Relationship with MidBank

In 1991, TCI had borrowed funds from MidBank to build a warehouse. This loan was being repaid in equal annual installments of $125,000. At the end of 1995, the balance due on the loan was $875,000. Also, in 1991 TCI established a line of credit at MidBank. The company had not yet borrowed any money under this credit arrangement.

Current Financial Need

TCI had decided to expand its warehouse facilities to accommodate future growth. Indeed, the current warehouse facilities were practically bulging at the seams. During the next 18 months, TCI planned to invest $2,400,000 on its expansion, $2,000,000 of which would be spent during 1996 (no other capital expenditures were planned for 1996 and 1997). This expansion would fulfill the company's anticipated needs for several years. The warehouse construction project was expected to be completed in early

Professor W. Carl Kester prepared this case as the basis for class discussion rather than to illustrate either effective or ineffective handling of an administrative situation.

Copyright © 1997 by the President and Fellows of Harvard College. To order copies or request permission to reproduce materials, call 1-800-545-7685 or write Harvard Business School Publishing, Boston, MA 02163. No part of this publication may be reproduced, stored in a retrieval system, used in a spreadsheet, or transmitted in any form or by any means—electronic, mechanical, photocopying, recording, or otherwise—without the permission of Harvard Business School.

EXHIBIT 1
Financial Statements for Tire City, Inc.

For Years Ending 12/31	1993	1994	1995
INCOME STATEMENT			
Net sales	$16,230	$20,355	$23,505
Cost of sales	9,430	11,898	13,612
Gross profit	6,800	8,457	9,893
Selling, general, and administrative expenses	5,195	6,352	7,471
Depreciation	160	180	213
Net interest expense	119	106	94
Pre-tax income	1,326	1,819	2,115
Income taxes	546	822	925
Net income	$ 780	$ 997	$ 1,190
Dividends	$ 155	$ 200	$240
BALANCE SHEET			
Assets			
Cash	$ 508	$ 609	$ 706
Accounts receivable	2,545	3,095	3,652
Inventories	1,630	1,838	2,190
Total current assets	4,683	5,542	6,548
Gross plant & equipment	3,232	3,795	4,163
Accumulated depreciation	1,335	1,515	1,728
Net plant & equipment	1,897	2,280	2,435
Total assets	$ 6,580	$ 7,822	$ 8,983
LIABILITIES			
Current maturities of long-term debt	$ 125	$ 125	$ 125
Accounts payable	1,042	1,325	1,440
Accrued expenses	1,145	1,432	1,653
Total current liabilities	2,312	2,882	3,218
Long-term debt	1,000	875	750
Common stock	1,135	1,135	1,135
Retained earnings	2,133	2,930	3,880
Total shareholders' equity	3,268	4,065	5,015
Total liabilities	$ 6,580	$ 7,822	$ 8,983

1997. Therefore, TCI would not be able to deduct any depreciation on the new building in 1996. However, Mr. Martin was told by his accountant that in 1997, TCI could recognize a depreciation expense of 5% of the warehouse's total cost. The dollar value of TCI's depreciation expense on its other assets in 1996 and 1997 would be the same as it was in 1995.

The warehouse expansion project was designed so that disruption of the company's current operations would be minimized. However, management expected that by the end of 1996, TCI would temporarily have to decrease its inventories to a level of $1,625,000, significantly lower than the $2,190,000 shown on the balance sheet at the end of 1995. This cutback in inventories was expected to last only until the warehouse construction project was completed in early 1997. Mr. Martin had estimated that, by the end of 1997, inventory would rise back to the same proportional relationship to sales that it had in 1995.

Other than this temporary drop in inventory in 1996, the warehouse expansion was not expected to affect TCI's operations in any other material respects. Operating margins were expected to be consistent with recent past experience (the temporary drop in inventory would not affect cost of goods sold as a percent of sales, for example). Likewise, current accounts other than inventory were expected to maintain steady relationships to sales. Cash balances, for instance, would be maintained at a level of 3% of sales during the next two years. Although the Federal statutory marginal corporate tax rate was 35%, the average tax rate on TCI's pre-tax income had typically been higher than this due to miscellaneous local taxes. This higher overall level of taxation was expected to continue in the future at rates consistent with the most recent past experience. In view of this anticipated stability, Mr. Martin expected TCI's dividend payout policy to remain unchanged in the foreseeable future.

TCI had preliminary discussions with MidBank about borrowing money to finance the warehouse expansion and the growth of the business. The proposed terms of the financing called for taking down (i.e., borrowing) the loan in two separate parts on an as-needed basis: one in 1996 and one in 1997. The loan would be repaid in four equal annual installments. The first installment payment would take place one year after the construction of the warehouse was completed (i.e., in 1998). The interest rate was set at 10% per year.

Mr. Martin's Task

In preparation for his meeting, Mr. Martin intended to develop a set of pro forma financial statements for the company. He and his staff had projected a 20% increase in sales each year in 1996 and in 1997, from $23,505,000 to $28,206,000 and $33,847,000, respectively. Mr. Martin's first priority was to predict what the rest of the income statement and the balance sheet for the firm would look like at the end of 1996 and 1997.

Estimating Funds Requirements—Short-Term Sources of Funds

Butler Lumber Company

After a rapid growth in its business during recent years, the Butler Lumber Company in the spring of 1991 anticipated a further substantial increase in sales. Despite good profits, the company had experienced a shortage of cash and had found it necessary to increase its borrowing from the Suburban National Bank to $247,000 in the spring of 1991. The maximum loan that Suburban National would make to any one borrower was $250,000, and Butler Lumber had been able to stay within this limit only by relying very heavily on trade credit. In addition, Suburban was now asking that Butler Lumber secure the loan with its real property. Mark Butler, sole owner and president of Butler Lumber Company, was therefore looking elsewhere for a new banking relationship where he would be able to negotiate a larger and unsecured loan.

Butler had recently been introduced by a friend to George Dodge, an officer of a much larger bank, the Northrop National Bank. The two men had tentatively discussed the possibility that the Northrop Bank might extend a line of credit to Butler Lumber up to a maximum amount of $465,000. Butler thought that a loan of this size would more than meet his foreseeable needs, but he was eager for the flexibility that a line of credit of this size would provide. After this discussion, Dodge had arranged for the credit department of the Northrop National Bank to investigate Mark Butler and his company.

The Butler Lumber Company had been founded in 1981 as a partnership by Mark Butler and his brother-in-law, Henry Stark. In 1988 Butler bought out Stark's interest for $105,000 and incorporated the business. Stark had taken a note for $105,000, to be paid off in 1989, to give Butler time to arrange for the financing necessary to make the payment of $105,000 to him. The major portion of the funds needed for this payment was raised by a loan of $70,000, negotiated in late 1988. This loan was secured by land and buildings, carried an interest rate of 11%, and was repayable in quarterly installments at the rate of $7,000 a year over the next 10 years.

The business was located in a growing suburb of a large city in the Pacific Northwest. The company owned land with access to a railroad siding, and two large storage buildings had been erected on this land. The company's operations were limited to the retail distribution of lumber products in the local area. Typical products included plywood, moldings, and sash and door products. Quantity discounts and credit terms of net 30 days on open account were usually offered to customers.

HBS cases are developed solely as the basis for class discussion. Cases are not intended to serve as endorsements, sources of primary data, or illustrations of effective or ineffective management.

Copyright © 1991 President and Fellows of Harvard College. To order copies or request permission to reproduce materials, call 1-800-545-7685, write Harvard Business School Publishing, Boston, MA 02163, or go to http://www.hbsp.harvard.edu. No part of this publication may be reproduced, stored in a retrieval system, used in a spreadsheet, or transmitted in any form or by any means—electronic, mechanical, photocopying, recording, or otherwise—without the permission of Harvard Business School.

EXHIBIT 1
Operating Statements for Years Ending December 31, 1988–1990, and for First Quarter 1991 (thousands of dollars)

	1988	1989	1990	First Quarter 1991
Net sales	$1,697	$2,013	$2,694	$718[a]
Cost of goods sold				
Beginning inventory	183	239	326	418
Purchases	1,278	1,524	2,042	660
	$1,461	$1,763	$2,368	$1,078
Ending inventory	239	326	418	556
Total cost of goods sold	$1,222	$1,437	$1,950	$ 522
Gross profit	475	576	744	196
Operating expense[b]	425	515	658	175
Interest expense	13	20	33	10
Net income before taxes	$ 37	$ 41	$ 53	$ 11
Provision for income taxes	6	7	9	2
Net income	$ 31	$ 34	$ 44	$ 9

[a]In the first quarter of 1990 sales were $698,000 and net income was $7,000.

[b]Operating expenses include a cash salary for Mr. Butler of $75,000 in 1988, $85,000 in 1989, $95,000 in 1990, and $22,000 in the first quarter of 1991. Mr. Butler also received some of the perquisites commonly taken by owners of privately held businesses.

Sales volume had been built up largely on the basis of successful price competition, made possible by careful control of operating expenses and by quantity purchases of materials at substantial discounts. Much of the moldings and sash and door products, which constituted significant items of sales, were used for repair work. About 55% of total sales were made in the six months from April through September. No sales representatives were employed, orders being taken exclusively over the telephone. Annual sales of $1,697,000 in 1988, $2,013,000 in 1989, and $2,694,000 in 1990 yielded after-tax profits of $31,000 in 1988, $34,000 in 1989, and $44,000 in 1990.[1] Operating statements for the years 1988–1990 and for the three months ending March 31, 1991, are given in Exhibit 1.

Mark Butler was an energetic man, 39 years of age, who worked long hours on the job. He was helped by an assistant who, in the words of the investigator of the Northrop National Bank, "has been doing and can do about everything that Butler does in the organization." Other employees numbered 10 in early 1991, 5 of whom worked in the yard and drove trucks and 5 of whom assisted in the office and in sales.

As part of its customary investigation of prospective borrowers, the Northrop National Bank sent inquiries concerning Mark Butler to a number of firms that had business dealings with him. The manager of one of his large suppliers, the Barker Company, wrote in answer:

> The conservative operation of his business appeals to us. He has not wasted his money in disproportionate plant investment. His operating expenses are as low as they could possibly be. He has personal control over every feature of his business, and he possesses sound judgment and a willingness to work harder than anyone I have ever known. This, with a good personality, gives him a good turnover; and from my personal experience in watching him work, I know that he keeps close check on his own credits.

All the other trade letters received by the bank bore out this opinion.

[1]Sales in 1986 and 1987 amounted to $728,000 and $1,103,000, respectively; profit data for these years are not comparable with those of 1988 and later years because of the shift from a partnership to a corporate form of organization. As a corporation, Butler was taxed at the rate of 15% on its first $50,000 of income, 25% on the next $25,000 of income, and 34% on all additional income above $75,000.

EXHIBIT 2
Balance Sheets at December 31, 1988–1990, and March 31, 1991 (thousands of dollars)

	1988	1989	1990	First Quarter 1991
Cash	$ 58	$ 48	$ 41	$ 31
Accounts receivable, net	171	222	317	345
Inventory	239	326	418	556
Current assets	$468	$596	$776	$ 932
Property, net	126	140	157	162
Total assets	$594	$736	$933	$1,094
Notes payable, bank	$ —	$146	$233	$ 247
Notes payable, Mr. Stark	105	—	—	—
Notes payable, trade	—	—	—	157
Accounts payable	124	192	256	243
Accrued expenses	24	30	39	36
Long-term debt, current portion	7	7	7	7
Current liabilities	$260	$375	$535	$ 690
Long-term debt	64	57	50	47
Total liabilities	$324	$432	$585	$ 737
Net worth	270	304	348	357
Total liabilities and net worth	$594	$736	$933	$1,094

In addition to owning the lumber business, which was his major source of income, Butler held jointly with his wife an equity in their home. The house had cost $72,000 to build in 1979 and was mortgaged for $38,000. He also held a $70,000 life insurance policy, payable to his wife. She owned independently a half interest in a house worth about $55,000. Otherwise, they had no sizeable personal investments.

The bank gave particular attention to the debt position and current ratio of the business. It noted the ready market for the company's products at all times and the fact that sales prospects were favorable. The bank's investigator reported: "Sales are expected to reach $3.6 million in 1991 and may exceed this level if prices of lumber should rise substantially in the near future." On the other hand, it was recognized that a general economic downturn might slow down the rate of increase in sales. Butler Lumber's sales, however, were protected to some degree from fluctuations in new housing construction because of the relatively high proportion of its repair business. Projections beyond 1991 were difficult to make, but the prospects appeared good for a continued growth in the volume of Butler Lumber's business over the foreseeable future.

The bank also noted the rapid increase in Butler Lumber's accounts and notes payable in the recent past, especially in the spring of 1991. The usual terms of purchase in the trade provided for a discount of 2% for payments made within 10 days of the invoice date. Accounts were due in 30 days at the invoice price, but suppliers ordinarily did not object if payments lagged somewhat behind the due date. During the last two years, Butler had taken very few purchase discounts because of the shortage of funds arising from his purchase of Stark's interest in the business and the additional investments in working capital associated with the company's increasing sales volume. Trade credit was seriously extended in the spring of 1991 as Butler strove to hold his bank borrowing within the $250,000 ceiling imposed by the Suburban National Bank. Balance sheets at December 31, 1988–1990, and March 31, 1991, are presented in Exhibit 2.

The tentative discussions between George Dodge and Mark Butler had been about a revolving, secured 90-day note not to exceed $465,000. The specific details of the loan had not been worked out, but Dodge had explained that the agreement would involve the standard covenants applying to such a loan. He cited as illustrative provisions the requirement that restrictions on additional borrowing would be imposed, that net working capital would have to be maintained at an agreed level, that additional investments in fixed assets could be made only with prior approval of the bank, and that limitations would be placed on withdrawals of funds from the business by Butler. Interest would be set on a floating-rate basis at 2 percentage points above the prime rate (the rate paid by the bank's most creditworthy customers). Dodge indicated that the initial rate to be paid would be about 10.5% under conditions in effect in early 1991. Both men also understood that Butler would sever his relationship with the Suburban National Bank if he entered into a loan agreement with the Northrop National Bank.

Note on Bank Loans

Bank loans are a versatile source of funding for businesses. For example, these loans can be structured as short- or long-term, fixed- or floating-rate, demand or with a fixed maturity, and secured or unsecured. While each potential borrower's business is unique, reasons to borrow generally include the purchase of assets, including new fixed assets or entire businesses; repayment of obligations; raising of temporary or permanent capital; and the meeting of unexpected needs. Loan repayment generally comes from one of four sources: operations, turnover or liquidation of assets, refinancing, or capital infusion. This note describes traditional bank lending products, the role of the lending officer, credit evaluation, and the structuring of credit facilities and loan agreements. Specialized loan and credit products are described in the Appendix.

Traditional Commercial Bank Lending Products

While increased competition has forced banks to develop innovative credit facilities and financing techniques, traditional products, which include short-term, long-term, and revolving loans, continue to be the mainstay of commercial banking.

Short-Term Loans

Short-term loans, those with maturities of 1 year or less, comprise more than half of all commercial bank loans. Seasonal lines of credit and special-purpose loans are the most common short-term credit facilities. Their primary use is to finance working capital needs resulting from temporary buildups of inventory and receivables. Reflecting their use, repayment of short-term loans typically comes from the routine conversion of current assets to cash. These loans may be either secured or unsecured.

A seasonal line of credit is used by companies with seasonal sales cycles to finance periodic increases in current assets, such as inventory. The amount of credit made available is based on the borrower's estimated peak funding requirements. The borrower may draw on the seasonal line of credit as funds are required and repay the line as seasonal sales lead to liquidation of inventories. Interest accrues only on the amount of borrowing outstanding. A bank's commitments under lines of credit may exceed its ability to fund them all simultaneously, though simultaneous demand is unlikely to occur. So as not to have a legal obligation to lend its capital to a borrower in the rare case that demand for funds does exceed supply, the bank may structure this facility with a provision that allows the bank to terminate the facility at its option or provide funding subject to availability.

Businesses use special-purpose loans to finance, on a temporary basis, increases in current assets resulting from unusual or unexpected circumstances. Funding is based on the borrower's estimated needs, with the bank agreeing to fund either all or up to some percentage of the full amount. The credit facility is most likely to require full payment of accrued interest and principal at maturity, that is, a "bullet." The term for

Research Associate Susan L. Roth prepared this note under the supervision of Professor Scott P. Mason and with the assistance of the Citicorp Institute for Global Finance.

Copyright © 1991 by the President and Fellows of Harvard College.

Harvard Business School case 291-026.

such a loan is usually fixed and is determined by approximating the point in time when repayment can be made. The bank's principal risk with a special-purpose loan is default because of a change in the circumstances on which the repayment plan had been based. Therefore, from the bank's perspective, it is important that the source and timing of repayment be clear at the time of funding. Identifying alternatives to routine asset conversion as a source of repayment will further protect the bank.

Long-Term Loans

Introduced in the 1930s, long-term loans, or term loans, are relatively new in banking practice. Providing advantages in its flexibility to adapt to a borrower's special requirements, a term loan has the following characteristics:

- Original maturity of longer than 1 year
- Repayment provided from future earnings or cash flow rather than from short-term liquidation of assets
- Provisions of the loan arrangement detailed in and governed by a signed loan agreement between the borrower and the lender

Term loans are most often used for specific purposes such as purchase of fixed assets, acquisition of another company, or refinancing of existing long-term debt. The term loan may also be used in place of equity or a revolving credit facility to finance permanent working capital needs. The loan's amount and structure will closely match the transaction being financed. A term loan is typically fully funded at its inception, and principal and interest are repaid over a period of years from operating cash flows generated by the borrower. The tenor, or maturity, of term loans ranges from 1 to 10 years, with the average being from 2 to 5 years. Although the lender does not look to liquidation of the acquired assets as the primary source of funds for repayment, a term loan is likely to be secured. Most often, the security will be a claim on the assets purchased with the proceeds of the loan.

Revolving Loans

The revolving credit loan, a variation on the line of credit, has a commitment period often extending beyond 1 year, up to 3 or 4 years, and allows a business to borrow from a bank up to a maximum commitment level at any time over the life of a credit. The borrower's use of proceeds under a revolving loan tends to be not for an isolated transaction but to fund day-to-day operations, meet seasonal needs, or otherwise provide the borrower with a discretionary range of when and how much to borrow and when to repay the loan. Unlike a line of credit, a revolving loan is often used to finance permanent working capital needs when equity and trade credit are inadequate to support a company's sales volume.

Over the term of a revolving credit facility, the borrower has the right to repay a loan and later reborrow those funds. But this right to reborrow is effective only when the borrower is in compliance with the loan agreement's terms and conditions. The amount of commitment is based upon the value of the assets being funded as well as the borrower's creditworthiness. The borrower pays a commitment fee, based on the total amount of the revolving facility, to secure a formal commitment from the bank. Many revolving loans are structured to convert to term loans or to renew automatically at maturity. The latter structure, called an evergreen facility, automatically renews a revolving credit facility until either the bank or the borrower gives notice of termination. Like other credit facilities, a revolving line of credit may be secured or unsecured.

EXHIBIT 1
The Credit Proposal Memo

Source: Citicorp Institute for Global Finance.

The credit proposal memo and presentation typically includes the following information and analyses:

- Company background and relationship with the bank
- Purpose of the credit extension
- Financial statement analysis, cash flow projections, and debt service capacity
- Assessment of management process, strengths, and weaknesses
- Assessment of major risks, including impact of forecasted economic trends and the strength of competitors
- Analysis of repayment sources for all facilities and timing for those with a tenor, or maturity, of greater than one year
- Summary of loan structure and repayment terms
- Summary of key covenants and repayment terms of other instruments that might materially affect the position of the bank
- Statement of adherence to credit policy guidelines or explanation of exceptions
- Analysis of collateral
- Listing of noncredit products
- Trade or bank checkings
- Comment on trustee relationships

Role of the Loan Officer

"Banks succeed when the risks they assume are reasonable, controlled, and commensurate with their resources and credit competence. Lending officers, in turn, must accurately identify, measure, and manage risk if their banks are to succeed."[1]

The loan officer must balance two often conflicting responsibilities: those of a marketing officer and those of a credit officer. While budget pressures require the loan officer to develop new banking relationships, credit responsibilities require that these new relationships not sacrifice credit quality for short-term profits. "The costliest mistake that a bank management can make is to book unworthy loans in order to achieve budget goals."[2] The lending institution's credit policy should give loan officers guidelines to enable them to balance loan quality and quantity and achieve the bank's earnings objectives.

The lending institution and its shareholders expect loan officers to understand a credit thoroughly before approving the lending of the bank's capital. The credit proposal memo, described in Exhibit 1, includes the information and analyses used to evaluate a potential borrower's creditworthiness. Every commitment of a lending institution typically requires independent approval and the signatures of at least two senior lending officers, who are held directly accountable for the lending decision. Direct accountability is intended to make them more critical of any exceptions to the bank's credit policy.

Evaluating Creditworthiness

Before a bank agrees to commit its funds to a company, its loan officers analyze the prospective borrower to determine creditworthiness. Loan officers have a responsibility to "grasp the quantitative and qualitative details of each transaction thoroughly, analyze

[1]P. Henry Mueller, "Lending Officers and Lending," in *Bank Credit,* ed. Herbert V. Prochnow (New York: Harper & Row, 1981), p. 92.

[2]P. Henry Mueller, *Perspective on Credit Risk* (Robert Morris Associates, 1988), p. 18.

its variables, and make adequate allowance for their impact."[3] Evaluation of a borrower's ability and willingness to repay a loan at maturity involves financial analysis, including forecasting and sensitivity analysis, a qualitative assessment of management's character and capability, due diligence, and an identification and analysis of risk.

Financial Analysis

A thorough financial analysis requires preparation of the following:

- Year-to-year comparisons of financial statements
- Cash flow statements
- Liquidity analysis
- Capital structure analysis
- Projections and sensitivity analysis
- Estimation of asset values: market value and liquidation value
- Comparison of actual versus budgeted performance

A first step in the financial analysis of a potential borrower is a determination of the quality of earnings and the strength of the balance sheet. To make this determination, the credit officer analyzes financial, operating, and leverage ratios, and trends in revenues and expenses over time, and compares such ratios to industry averages, looking for positive and negative changes in the company's profitability and industry position.

The historical financial condition of a borrower, however, is an incomplete indication of creditworthiness. Because the loan will be approved or denied based on, among other essential criteria, an assessment of a borrower's ability to repay the loan from future cash flow generated by operations, an estimate of a borrower's future financial condition is important to the lending decision.

Pro forma financial and operating statements are prepared so that the lending officer may assess the borrower's potential to generate sufficient free cash flow to make interest and principal payments when due. These projections and the underlying assumptions must be tested under various scenarios to establish the borrower's sensitivity to change. While one cannot possibly test for every possible event, worst-case scenarios will indicate just how poorly the business can perform before the borrower defaults.

Qualitative Assessment

Credit evaluation also requires assessment of the character and capabilities of the persons to whom a loan may be extended, that is, the persons responsible for achieving the goals of the operating and financial plans. Lenders must determine the quality, breadth, and depth of the management team. Assessing its ability to implement operating and financial plans gives the lender insight into the management team's capability. Banks pay a high price for hasty credit decisions. Though gauging the integrity of a new customer takes time, integrity is a critical component of any lending decision. Management's interests should be aligned with the company's and with the bank's interests and expectations. Ownership and compensation systems indicate management's stake in the business.

Due Diligence

Due diligence is the process of going out and "kicking the tires" of the potential borrower. While time-consuming, it is an important aid to understanding better how the prospective borrower does business. Due diligence can include plant tours, trade checks, and inter-

[3] Mueller, "Lending Officers and Lending," p. 40.

views with the borrower's competitors, suppliers, customers, and employees. Comprehensive due diligence also includes reviews of employee relations, compensation and benefits, management's planned capital expenditures, other debt obligations, and management information systems and technology. An environmental audit may also be necessary. Due diligence should also uncover any contingent liabilities that may materially affect the borrower's ability to repay the loan at maturity. Unfunded pension liabilities, pending or threatened legal proceedings, and guarantees by the borrower are some examples of contingent liabilities.

Risk Assessment

Risk assessment is another component of the credit evaluation process. The credit officer must identify and analyze the key risks associated with a specific credit. Some risks are associated with the borrower and his or her business; with potential changes in the environment; and with cyclical activity and regulatory or other unanticipated developments. The loan officer must make judgments about future conditions that could affect a borrower's willingness and ability to repay the obligation. Determining potential risks and assessing their level of severity, the probability that they will occur, and the estimated costs associated with their occurrence are critical. The structure of the credit facility and loan agreement attempts to minimize risk.

Determining the Bank's Willingness and Ability to Lend

In addition to conducting a thorough credit evaluation, the loan officer must determine whether approving a loan application is in the bank's best interests and within regulatory capital and operating guidelines. A bank's ability to lend is restricted by banking regulations that limit the amount of loans that may be extended to any one borrower. A bank may also establish an internal limit ("house limit") on the amount lent to a single borrower. What influences a bank's willingness to lend are its earnings targets and portfolio objectives. A bank attempts to maintain diversification in its portfolio of loans and investments to reduce its exposure to risk. These targets and objectives shape a bank's loan origination and acquisition strategy. Thus a potential borrower must not only meet the lending institution's credit standards but also be within its target lending market and legal lending capacity.

Structuring the Credit Facility and Loan Agreement

Once creditworthiness is ascertained and the bank decides it is willing and able to extend credit to a company, the bank and the borrower can begin to structure an appropriate credit facility and loan agreement. The strength and the nature of a credit and the bank's credit policy help to determine the terms and conditions defined in a loan agreement.

Typically, short-term loans are not made pursuant to a loan agreement, or if so, the loan agreement is far less comprehensive than that used for long-term or revolving loans. The loan agreement discussed in this note applies to term and revolving loans and includes the following sections:

- Amount and terms of the credit facility
- Conditions precedent
- Representations and warranties
- Covenants of the borrower
- Events of default

Amount and Terms of the Credit Facility

This first section of a standard loan agreement describes how much and when the borrower may borrow, the interest provisions, repayment terms and additional fees, the intended use of loan proceeds, and any security interest taken by the bank.

The amount of a bank's commitment under a credit facility may be stipulated or based on a formula, for instance, a percentage of accounts receivable. The interest rate charged for use of those committed funds may be based on either a fixed or a floating rate. The use of a fixed or a floating interest rate, the method for determining the floating rate and reset periods, if applicable, and the method for computing accrued interest are negotiable factors. Interest can be computed on the basis of a 360- or a 365-day year. Computation using a 360-day year yields a higher effective rate for the borrower.

Additional fees the bank may charge include commitment and closing fees. The borrower pays a commitment fee to compensate the bank for its use of the bank's capital over the duration of the commitment. This fee typically ranges from .25% to .75% per year. The borrower may also pay a closing fee on the day the loan closes, that is, the date the loan's legal framework is in place. This payment compensates the bank for work done thus far in evaluating the borrower's creditworthiness and setting up a credit facility for it. In a competitive situation, this fee may be .25% to .375%; in a high-risk situation, it can be as much as 2.00% to 2.50% of the amount of the commitment. A penalty or default rate of interest may also be stipulated. Applied in the event that payments are not made when due, this rate is set high enough so that it would not be to the borrower's economic advantage to delay payments.

The option to prepay and the option to reduce the total commitment are provisions negotiated in this section of the loan agreement for term loans and revolving loans, respectively. These provisions distinguish most bank financing from alternative sources of funds. Under a revolving credit facility, the right to reduce the amount of the commitment is valuable to the borrower should the company's financing needs change. Reducing the amount of the commitment will reduce the commitment fee paid by the borrower, since it is based on the total commitment.

In the case of a term loan, the loan agreement may provide for full or partial prepayment of the loan at the borrower's discretion, with or without a premium or upon occurrence of certain events. The option to repay provides a route of escape from covenants that may become overly restrictive. Prepayment also works in favor of the borrower should the cost of other sources of funds decline significantly over the term of the loan, making refinancing more economical. Recognizing the value of this right, a borrower may agree to tighter covenants or a higher rate of interest than if locked in by prepayment restrictions.

A description of the use of loan proceeds is also included in this first section of the loan agreement to assure the bank that the borrower intends to use the loan proceeds in the manner understood by the bank.

An additional provision negotiated in this section of the loan agreement is the taking of collateral or guarantees to secure a loan. A claim on certain assets of the borrower can mitigate the bank's loss should the borrower default. Assets used as collateral are typically those purchased with the loan proceeds; levels of collateral are typically commensurate with the creditworthiness of the borrower. It is often to the bank's advantage to take as much security as possible against a loan.

If the borrower defaults on a secured loan, the bank has the right to take control of and liquidate the pledged assets. Funds from the liquidation are applied against the amount outstanding on the defaulted loan. If default is on an unsecured loan, the bank is only a general creditor of the business, and recovery of the principal is less likely.

Conditions Precedent

The conditions precedent are requirements the borrower must satisfy before the bank has a legal obligation to fund a commitment. These conditions may include any business transactions that must be completed or events that must have occurred. Other standard items in this section are the opinions of counsel, certificate of no defaults, the note, and resolutions of the borrower's board of directors authorizing the transaction. The condition precedent will also include a material adverse change clause encompassing both balance sheet condition and operations (income statement and prospects). This clause serves an important protective function for the lender in the case that a material adverse change occurs prior to funding and is not yet reflected in the financial statements.

Representations and Warranties

In considering a loan application, the lender relies on certain information furnished by the borrower and has thereupon made assumptions about the borrower's legal status, creditworthiness, and business position. It is upon these assumptions that the bank has agreed to lend money to the borrower. The representations and warranties section documents the information and assumptions relied upon. By executing the loan agreement, the borrower confirms the accuracy and truth of the information provided as of the date of execution. Misrepresentation constitutes an event of default. Principal representations and warranties include:

- Financial statements are correct, and there has been no material adverse change in the financial condition of the borrower
- The borrower is not subject to any litigation, pending or threatened, or party to a contract that could effect a material adverse change in the business position of the borrower
- Other facts pertinent to the credit judgment are correct
- No factual misstatement or omission in information furnished
- Due incorporation
- Continued existence
- The loan agreement will be legal, valid, and binding when signed
- No need for third-party consent
- Corporate authority
- No violation of existing agreements
- No violation of laws
- All tax returns have been filed; all taxes have been paid
- Collateral offered is owned by the borrower and free of liens

The material adverse change clause is designed to cover circumstances in which the borrower's ability to perform obligations under the loan agreement is thrown into doubt. With regard to the financial statements, the material adverse change clause is used to verify that there has been no material adverse change in the borrower's financial condition or operations since the date of the financial statements relied upon for the credit evaluation. This section may also contain a representation as to the accuracy of other information not included in the financial statements, including nonpublic information such as cash flow statements and projections, supplied by the borrower to the bank and fundamental to the credit decision.

The representations and warranties section also contains material adverse change standards with respect to actual or threatened legal proceedings where the outcome could significantly affect the strength of the borrower's credit standing in the eyes of the bank. These standards may also be broadened to include circumstances that may not be reflected immediately in the borrower's financial statements or result in litigation.

Covenants of the Borrower

Covenants are a heavily negotiated part of loan agreements. As representations and warranties verify certain statements by the borrower at the date of execution of the loan agreement, covenants carry forward the representations and warranties, and establish the borrower's ongoing obligation to maintain a certain status for the loan's duration. Covenants set minimum standards for a borrower's future conduct and performance and thereby reduce the risk that the loan will not be repaid. Violation of a covenant creates an event of default and gives the bank the right to refuse to make additional advances.

The use of certain covenants depends upon such factors as the nature of the borrower's business, the financial condition of the borrower, and the term of the loan. If credit risk is high, covenants may be tied directly to detailed financial projections provided by the borrower. If credit risk is low, a few general financial benchmarks may be sufficient. In any case, covenants should be no more restrictive than the policies any prudent manager would follow to maintain or build a solid credit rating, but they should be designed to give early warning of deterioration in the financial condition of the borrower. Covenants should also be drafted to allow for normal seasonal and cyclical variations of the borrower's business so that an event of default is not likely to occur.

Affirmative Covenants

Affirmative covenants stipulate actions the borrower must take and would normally take even if the loan were not in effect. Generally, they include the following:

- Application of loan proceeds to specified purpose
- Financial covenants
- Reporting requirements
- Compliance with laws
- Preservation of corporate existence
- Rights of inspection
- Maintenance of insurance
- Maintenance of properties
- Maintenance of records and books of account

As in the first section of the loan agreement, the borrower must assure the bank that the proceeds of the loan will be used in the manner the bank understood in its decision to extend credit.

Financial covenants are those based on information contained in the borrower's financial statements and focus on the borrower's financial position and overall operations. Financial covenants establish guidelines for operation of the borrower's business, carry forward the borrower's representations and warranties regarding its financial position, further help the bank to gather information about the borrower, and permit exercise of remedies upon default. Financial covenants establish minimum financial tests with which a borrower must comply. These tests can specify dollar amounts, such as (tangible) net worth and working capital, or ratios such as the current or quick ratios, net worth ratios, leverage ratio, and fixed-charge coverage ratio. Financial covenants should signal financial difficulty and be triggered long before liquidation or bankruptcy filing becomes necessary. They may be used like other affirmative and negative covenants to guide management decisions on an ongoing basis, or serve only as periodic tests.

To keep the bank informed of financial and operating performances, the borrower covenants that he or she will meet certain established reporting requirements and provide such information to the lender in a timely fashion. This information allows the bank's lending officer to monitor the borrower's financial condition and compliance with covenants.

Negative Covenants

The negative covenants tend to be more significant and more heavily negotiated than affirmative covenants because they place clear restrictions upon managerial decisions. These restrictions are intended to prevent management decisions that might impair the borrower's liquidity or solvency, or jeopardize the bank's claim against the borrower's earnings and assets.

Negative covenants typically include the following:

- Restrictions on mortgages, pledges, or other encumbrance of assets (negative pledge)
- Limitation on total indebtedness
- Restrictions on payment of cash dividends
- Restrictions on repurchase of shares
- Restrictions on mergers
- Restrictions on sale of assets
- Restrictions on sale subsidiaries
- Limitation on capital expenditure
- Restrictions on engaging in other businesses
- Restrictions on voluntary prepayment of other indebtedness
- Limitation on investment of funds
- Limitation on loans and advances
- Limitations on leasing arrangements

The negative pledge covenant is designed to prevent the borrower from creating liens on its assets or earnings for the benefit of other lenders. Its purpose is to provide a pool of assets that will be available for payment of unsecured creditors' claims equally, without preference of one over another in the event of default. The negative pledge is typically given to an unsecured creditor.

Restrictions on total indebtedness apply to a variety of debt instruments and often include capital lease obligations, deferred payment obligations, unfunded vested pension liabilities, guaranteed indebtedness, and indebtedness of others secured by property of the borrower. This restriction is usually stated as a specified amount or in the form of a ratio (total debt to total assets, to working capital, or to [tangible] net worth) and serves to limit the amount of additional indebtedness the borrower may incur over the term of the loan. The restriction may differ for short- and long-term obligations, and exceptions to the limit may be made for certain debt instruments such as subordinated debt.

In restricting the borrower's ability to merge or transfer a substantial part of its assets, the bank is ensuring the survival of the borrower's obligation. With reference to the sale or transfer of assets, those assets or subsidiaries fundamental to the bank's credit analysis should be specified as restricted from sale or transfer. Assets not involving the transfer of the borrower's business in or near its entirety should not be restricted by this covenant.

Restrictions on the use of funds for dividend payments, repurchase of shares, capital expenditures, or otherwise are included so that the bank may be further assured that cash will be available to make interest and principal payments when due. These restrictions and limitations also ensure the borrower's general adherence to its operating plan.

Events of Default

The events of default section describes circumstances in which the bank has the right to terminate the lending relationship. Situations leading to the declaration of an event of default include the following:

- Failure to pay interest or principal when due
- Inaccuracy in representations and warranties
- Failure to abide by a covenant
- Bankruptcy, liquidation, appointment of receiver
- Entry of a judgment in excess of a specified amount
- Impairment of collateral: invalidity of a guaranty or security agreement
- Failure to pay other indebtedness when due or perform under related agreements: cross-default and cross-acceleration
- Change of management or ownership
- Extraordinary circumstances
- Expropriation of assets
- Material adverse change

Upon the occurrence of an event of default, the most common remedy lenders exercise is the renegotiation of the loan agreement. In some cases, usually where the circumstances are considered less significant, the loan agreement provides the borrower a period of time, referred to as a cure or grace period, to correct its breach of a covenant. If the default is cured, the bank is then required to continue providing the loan to the borrower.

In the case where the default is not cured and the loan agreement is not negotiable, the bank may accelerate the loan and terminate the lending relationship. The bank may also set off the borrower's deposits against its obligation to repay the loan and exercise its right to foreclose on security covered under a security agreement.

The cross-default provision gives the bank the right to declare an event of default when the borrower is in default on another obligation. This provision is designed to prevent the bank from being placed at a disadvantage if competition to obtain repayment begins among the borrower's creditors, that is, the borrower has defaulted under another loan agreement and the lender is demanding payment.

Although banks rarely exercise the right to accelerate loan repayment, having this right substantially strengthens a lender's negotiating position with the borrower and other creditors of the borrower if problems are encountered with the loan. Acceleration is used sparingly by banks, since use by one could cause its invocation by other creditors and precipitate a bankruptcy.

Sale of Loans to Third Parties

No longer is the price of a loan set at the discretion of the loan officer guided by the lending institution. With increasing pressure to sell loans to third parties, the market is becoming the most influential factor in setting price.

Certain changes in the regulation of banks and in the business of commercial banking have precipitated increasing sales of loans. Regulatory changes, including new risk-based capital guidelines adopted by the Basle Committee on Banking Regulations and

Supervisory Practices on July 11, 1988, require banks to be better capitalized (tangible net worth as a percentage of total assets). This is costly and restricts lending capacity. In addition to the risk-based capital guidelines, regulations and internal bank lending policies restricting the amount of loans a bank can make to one borrower or group of borrowers often force banks to sell off all or a portion of the loans they originate.

Several vehicles facilitate the sale of loans, some allowing an originating bank to maintain partial ownership of the loan or responsibility for its management. Participations, syndications, and asset sales are all examples of underwriting activities undertaken by banks.

Participations

A participation loan is a single loan made to a large borrower by more than one lender. Participation loans are made when the lead lender cannot lend to a large borrower because of legal or internal lending limits restricting the amount of bank capital that can be loaned to one borrower or classification of borrowers. The lead bank originates the transaction and maintains responsibility for servicing the loan.

Many loan participations come about through correspondent banking relationships. A correspondent bank performs services for a bank in a market that is inaccessible to the other. Both banks must evaluate the creditworthiness of the borrower and independently decide to enter into the participation. While credit decisions are made independently, risk may not always be shared equally in participations. Some participations are structured on a last in, first out (LIFO) basis so that the originator, or first in, takes a larger portion of the risk associated with the participation loan.

Syndications

Syndications are similar to loan participations, except that the syndicate members lend directly to the borrower. An originating bank, called the lead bank or manager, arranges a credit facility for a large borrower. The bank then sells off portions of the loan to other lenders.

Syndication has been used increasingly for several reasons, including the ability to spread risk across lenders, to lend to large borrowers when the size of the individual credit is larger than legal or internal standards would allow, and to integrate the borrower's banking relationships. The syndicate members' obligations are separate; one lender is not responsible for the commitment of another; however, the rights and obligations of all the parties (the syndicate members and the borrower) are governed by one agreement, the syndicate loan agreement. Each participant in a syndication shares in the loan's risks and makes its own credit decision.

There are two types of syndicates: best-efforts and firm (or underwritten) commitment. In a best-efforts syndicate, the manager will market the loan under the agreed-upon terms and conditions, but if the syndication is not fully subscribed, the loan will not be made and the manager retains no legal obligation to the borrower. In a firm commitment syndicate, the lead bank agrees to make the loan regardless of its ability to syndicate it completely.

In a syndicate, a borrower pays certain fees in addition to interest on the loan: a commitment fee based on the amount of the credit and the undrawn portion; a management fee paid to the syndicate managers as compensation for assembling the syndicate and servicing the loan; and participation fees to syndicate participants based on the amount of their commitments. Participation fees range from .25% to 1.50% and are used to attract lending institutions to a syndicate. The agency fee paid to the bank servicing the loan can range from $5,000 a year for a routine transaction to $500,000 a year for a more complex transaction.

Asset Sale

A relatively recent development has been the sale of loans to third parties. An asset or loan sale is similar to a syndicate except that the lead bank initially takes the credit on its books and then sells off most or all of the credit, retaining little or nothing for its own portfolio. In this transaction, all risk from the sold portion is eliminated for the originating bank, and the loan is removed from its balance sheet. The bank earns a fee for its efforts in originating the loan. An asset sale typically occurs as a second phase to a syndication.

Appendix
Specialized Loans and Credit Products

Trade Finance Products

Trade finance products are specialized bank products designed to reduce the risks and uncertainties associated with commercial transactions by substituting the bank's credit risk for that of the purchaser of the goods. Thus, they facilitate trade.

When entering into trade finance credit arrangements, the bank evaluates the obligor's creditworthiness in much the same way it evaluates other short-term credits. The most common trade finance products are letters of credit and banker's acceptances.

Letters of Credit (L/C)

A letter of credit represents a conditional promise to pay and is generally non-negotiable. It substitutes the bank's credit for that of its customers by providing a guarantee of payment to the third party upon the satisfaction of certain conditions. This differs from the banker's acceptance, which, in effect, is payment.

In trade finance, a letter of credit is usually issued by the purchaser's bank, which agrees to pay the purchaser's obligation to a seller upon receiving proof that a specified delivery has been made. The bank has no obligation to delve into the content of the underlying commercial transaction (i.e., the sales agreement between the seller and buyer) except as specifically required by the terms of the L/C. The purchaser agrees to pay the bank the sales amount plus a fee.

The term of an L/C is generally related to the expected amount of time needed to complete the transaction. It may be revocable or irrevocable. A revocable L/C can be withdrawn, without notice to the beneficiary, at any time prior to actual performance of the transaction. An irrevocable L/C cannot be withdrawn before its expiration.

Stand-by letters of credit differ from trade L/Cs in that the issuing bank agrees to pay the L/C beneficiary only if its client defaults on payment to the beneficiary. So, in the above example, the seller would collect from the issuing bank only upon default of the purchaser.

Banker's Acceptances

A banker's acceptance represents the bank's commitment to pay a specific amount of money on a specific date. This commitment arises when the bank agrees to pay the obligations of a purchaser to enhance its creditworthiness. The commitment is created when a seller prepares a time draft[4] ordering a buyer to pay for goods purchased upon their receipt. Once signed and acknowledged by the purchaser and "accepted" by the purchaser's bank, the draft becomes a banker's acceptance. The liability accepted by the bank is called acceptance liability.

[4]A time draft is one that is due upon presentation and acceptance by the purchaser's bank after a specified period of time, e.g., 30 or 60 days.

The banker's acceptance is a short-term instrument generally with a duration of six months or less. The purchaser on whose behalf the banker's acceptance was accepted repays the bank under agreed-upon terms from the proceeds on the resale of the purchased goods. Since it is a negotiable instrument, the holder of a banker's acceptance may sell it to a third party or the bank, usually at a discount, to receive payment immediately. Thus, the banker's acceptance can be used as a form of accounts receivable financing.

Factoring

Factoring is a method of accounts receivable financing in which the lender purchases the borrower's receivables. By purchasing a firm's accounts receivable, the bank assumes certain risks and activities it does not have with typical accounts receivable financing, in which a lender lends money to a company based on its accounts receivable balance. Factoring gives the bank legal ownership of the receivables and therefore the risk of accounts receivable defaults. The credit and collection functions formerly handled by the company may be undertaken by the bank. A lender may provide factoring services on a discount or maturity basis.

Discount factoring is a service in which the seller of the receivables receives payment from the bank before their expected maturities. The amount the bank is willing to lend is based on the accounts receivable balance less discounts and estimated returns and bad debts. Interest is charged on the basis of the average daily balances owed.

Maturity factoring differs from discount factoring in that the lender performs the credit and collection functions and pays the borrower on invoice due dates. The factor receives a fee based on handling costs and estimated bad-debt risk.

Asset-Based Lending

Traditional loans may be secured by the assets of the borrower, and repayment is assumed to come from operating cash flow or conversion of current assets to cash. Asset-based loans differ from traditional loans in that the borrower's ability to repay the borrowed funds from operating cash flows is less predictable. A lender making an asset-based loan looks mainly to the value of the assets securing the loan for repayment of the obligation. Asset-based loans are made against accounts receivable, inventory, and equipment.

In lending against accounts receivable, the asset-based lender agrees, after careful analysis, to lend up to a certain percentage of the accounts receivable. The percentage of face value the lender lends against will be based upon the age, quality, and concentration of accounts receivable, keeping in mind the liquidation value should the borrower default. Generally the lender will lend up to 80% of face value of the qualifying receivables amount. Qualifying receivables is the total amount less nonconforming receivables.

The analysis of inventory is similar to the analysis of accounts receivable, where current information and ongoing monitoring are key to successful lending. The lender will identify the percentage of inventory in raw materials, work-in-process, and finished goods inventories that qualifies to be lent against based on their potential liquidation value. The advance rate against inventory is relatively low, sometimes 50% or less. This conservatism reflects the concerns for spoilage, technical obsolescence, and frequent deep discounts in disposing of inventories very quickly.

In lending against equipment, the asset-based lender has little concern for historical cost, fair market value, or replacement value. The lender instead wants to determine the value in a forced liquidation sale after related expenses, for instance, the cost of removing the equipment. Asset-based lenders will typically lend up to 80% of the forced sale value of machinery and equipment.

Toy World, Inc.

Early in January 1994, Jack McClintock, president and part owner of Toy World, Inc., was considering a proposal to adopt level monthly production for the coming year. In the past, the company's production schedules had always been highly seasonal, reflecting the seasonality of sales. Mr. McClintock was aware that a marked improvement in production efficiency could result from level production, but he was uncertain what the impact on other phases of the business might be.

Toy World, Inc. was a manufacturer of plastic toys for children. Its product groups included toy cars, trucks, construction equipment, rockets, spaceships and satellites, musical instruments, animals, robots, and action figures. In most of these product categories, the company produced a wide range of designs, colors, and sizes. Dollar sales of a particular product had sometimes varied by 30–35% from one year to the next.

The manufacture of plastic toys was a highly competitive business. The industry was populated by a large number of companies, many of which were short on capital and management talent. Since capital requirements were not large and the technology was relatively simple, it was easy for new competitors to enter the industry. On the other hand, design and price competition was fierce, resulting in short product lives and a relatively high rate of company failures. A company was sometimes able to steal a march on the competition by designing a popular new toy, often of the fad variety. Such items generally commanded very high margins until competitors were able to offer a similar product. For example, Toy World's introduction of a line of superhero action figures in 1991 had contributed importantly to that year's profits. In 1992, however, 11 competitors marketed similar products, and the factory price of the Toy World offering plummeted. In recent years, competitive pressures on smaller firms had also intensified due to an influx of imported toys produced by foreign toy manufacturers with low labor costs.

Company Background

Toy World, Inc. was founded in 1973 by David Dunton after his release from naval service. Before his military service, he had been employed as production manager by a large manufacturer of plastic toys. Mr. Dunton and his former assistant, Jack McClintock, established Toy World, Inc. with their savings in 1973. Originally a partnership, the firm was incorporated in 1974, with Mr. Dunton taking 75% of the capital stock and Mr. Clintock taking 25%. The latter served as production manager, and Mr. Dunton, as president, was responsible for overall direction of the company's affairs. After a series of illnesses, Mr. Dunton's health deteriorated, and he was forced to retire from active participation in the business in 1991. Mr. McClintock assumed the presidency at that time. In 1993, Mr. McClintock hired Dan Hoffman, a recent graduate of a prominent eastern technical institute, as production manager. Mr. Hoffman had worked during summers in the plastics plant of a large diversified chemical company and thus had a basic familiarity with plastics production processes.

Copyright © 1994 by the President and Fellows of Harvard College.
Harvard Business School case 295-073.

Company Growth

Toy World, Inc. had experienced relatively rapid growth since its founding and had enjoyed profitable operations each year since 1976. Sales had been approximately $8 million in 1993, and on the strength of a number of promising new products, sales were projected at $10 million for 1994. Net profits had reached $270,000 in 1993 and were estimated at $351,000 in 1994 under seasonal production. Tables A and B present the latest financial statements for the company. The cost of goods sold had averaged 70% of sales in the past and was expected to maintain roughly that proportion in 1994 under seasonal production. In keeping with the company's experience, operating expenses were likely to be incurred evenly throughout each month of 1994 under either seasonal or level production.

Expanding operations had resulted in a somewhat strained working capital position for Toy World, Inc. The year-end cash balance of $200,000 in 1993 was regarded as the minimum necessary for the operations of the business. The company had periodically borrowed from its primary bank, City Trust Company, on an unsecured line of credit. A loan of $752,000 was outstanding at the end of 1993. Mr. McClintock had been assured that the bank would be willing to extend a credit line of up to $2 million in 1994, with the understanding that the loan would be completely repaid and off the books for

TABLE A
Condensed Income Statements, 1991–1993 (thousands of dollars)

	1991	1992	1993
Net sales	$5,213	$6,167	$7,967
Cost of goods sold	3,597	4,440	5,577
Gross profit	$1,616	$1,727	$2,390
Operating expenses	1,199	1,542	1,912
Interest expense	68	75	85
Interest income	20	15	16
Profit before taxes	$ 369	$ 125	$ 409
Federal income taxes	125	43	139
Net profit	$ 244	$ 82	$ 270

TABLE B
Balance Sheet at December 31, 1993 (thousands of dollars)

Cash	$ 200
Accounts receivable	2,905
Inventory	586
Current assets	$3,691
Plant and equipment, net	1,176
Total assets	$4,867
Accounts payable	$ 282
Notes payable, bank	752
Accrued taxes[a]	88
Long-term debt, current portion	50
Current liabilities	$1,172
Long-term debt	400
Shareholders' equity	3,295
Total liabilities and shareholders' equity	$4,867

[a]The company was required to make estimated tax payments on the 15th of April, June, September, and December. In 1993 it elected to base its estimated tax payments on the previous year's tax. The balance of $88,000 was due on March 15, 1994.

at least a 30-day period during the year, and would be secured by the accounts receivable and inventory of Toy World. Interest on the line of credit would be charged at a rate of 9%, and any advances in excess of $2 million would be subject to further negotiations. Toy World's long-term debt, which had been raised years ago, had a fixed annual rate of interest of 9⅝% and was being amortized by payments of $25,000 in June and December of each year.

The company's sales were highly seasonal. Over 80% of annual dollar volume was usually sold between August and November. Table C shows sales by month for 1993 and projected monthly sales for 1994. Sales were made mainly to large variety store chains and toy brokers. Although the company quoted terms of net 30 days, most customers took 60 days to pay; however, collection experience had been excellent.

The company's production processes were not complex. Plastic molding powder, the principal raw material, was processed by injection molding presses and formed into the shapes desired. The toy sets were then assembled and packaged in cardboard cartons or plastic bags. Typically, all runs begun were completed on the same day, so that there was virtually no work in process at the end of the day. Purchases on net 30-day terms were made weekly in amounts necessary for estimated production in the coming week. Total purchases in 1994 were forecast at $3 million. It was the company's policy to retire trade debt promptly as it came due.

Mr. Hoffman, the production manager, believed the company would be able to hold capital expenditures during the next year to an amount equal to depreciation, although he had cautioned that projected volume for 1994 would approach the full capacity of Toy World's equipment.

Toy World Inc.'s practice was to produce in response to customer orders. This meant only a small fraction of capacity was needed to meet demand for the first seven months of the year. Ordinarily, not more than 25–30% of manufacturing capacity was used at any one time during this period. The first sizable orders for the Christmas business arrived around the middle of August. From August to December the workforce was greatly expanded and put on overtime, and all equipment was used 16 hours a day. In 1993 overtime premiums had amounted to $185,000. Whenever possible, shipments were made on the day an order was produced. Hence, production and sales amounts in each month tended to be equal.

As in the past, pro forma balance sheets and income statements based on an assumption of seasonal production had been prepared for 1994 and were presented to Mr. McClintock for his examination. These appear in Exhibits 1 and 2.

TABLE C
Monthly Sales Data (thousands of dollars)

	Sales 1993	Projected 1994
January	$ 64	$ 120
February	88	140
March	96	160
April	88	140
May	87	140
June	95	140
July	96	160
August	1,251	1,620
September	1,474	1,840
October	1,723	2,140
November	1,965	2,285
December	940	1,115

EXHIBIT 1 Pro Forma Balance Sheets under Seasonal Production, 1994 (thousands of dollars)

	Actual Dec. 31, 1993	Jan.	Feb.	Mar.	Apr.	May	June	July	Aug.	Sept.	Oct.	Nov.	Dec.
Cash[a]	$ 200	$ 878	$1,526	$1,253	$1,054	$ 915	$ 696	$ 527	$ 200	$ 200	$ 200	$ 200	$ 200
Accounts receivable[b]	2,905	1,060	260	300	300	280	280	300	1,780	3,460	3,980	4,425	3,400
Inventory[c]	586	586	586	586	586	586	586	586	586	586	586	586	586
Current assets	$3,691	$2,524	$2,372	$2,139	$1,940	$1,781	$1,562	$1,413	$2,566	$4,246	$4,766	$5,211	$4,186
Net plant and equipment[d]	1,176	1,176	1,176	1,176	1,176	1,176	1,176	1,176	1,176	1,176	1,176	1,176	
Total assets	$4,867	$3,700	$3,548	$3,315	$3,116	$2,957	$2,738	$2,589	$3,742	$5,422	$5,942	$6,387	$5,362
Accounts payable[e]	$ 282	$ 36	$ 42	$ 48	$ 42	$ 42	$ 42	$ 48	$ 486	$ 552	$ 642	$ 686	$ 334
Notes payable, bank[f]	752	0	0	0	0	0	0	0	433	1,741	1,745	1,677	942
Accrued taxes[g]	88	31	(23)	(162)	(251)	(305)	(394)	(448)	(352)	(271)	(126)	33	40
Long-term debt, current portion	50	50	50	50	50	50	50	50	50	50	50	50	
Current liabilities	$1,172	$ 117	$ 69	$ (64)	$ (159)	$ (213)	$ (302)	$ (350)	$ 617	$2,072	$2,311	$2,446	$1,366
Long-term debt[h]	400	400	400	400	400	400	375	375	375	375	375	375	350
Shareholder's equity	3,295	3,183	3,079	2,979	2,875	2,770	2,665	2,564	2,750	2,975	3,256	3,566	3,646
Total liabilities and equity	$4,867	$3,700	$3,548	$3,315	$3,116	$2,957	$2,738	$2,589	$3,742	$5,422	$5,942	$6,387	$5,362

a. Assumed maintenance of minimum $200,000 balance; includes excess cash in months when company is out of debt.
b. Assumed 60-day collection period.
c. Assumed inventories maintained at December 31, 1993, level for all of 1994.
d. Assumed equipment purchases equal to depreciation expense.
e. Assumed equal to 30% of the current month's sales and related to material purchases of $3,000,000 for 1994 as against sales of $10 million. This represents a 30-day payment period. Since inventories are level, purchases will follow seasonal production and sales pattern.
f. Plug figure.
g. Taxes payable on 1993 income are due on March 15, 1994. On April 15, June 15, September 15, and December 15, 1994, payments of 25% each of the estimated tax for 1994 are due. In estimating its tax liability for 1994, the company has the option of using the prior year's tax liability ($139,000) for its estimate and making any adjusting tax payments in 1995. Alternatively, the company could estimate its 1994 tax liability directly. Toy World planned to use its prior year's tax liability as its estimate and to pay $35,000 in April, June, September, and December.
h. To be repaid at the rate of $25,000 each June and December.

EXHIBIT 2 **Pro Forma Income Statements under Seasonal Production, 1994 (thousands of dollar)**

	Jan.	Feb.	Mar.	Apr.	May	June	July	Aug.	Sept.	Oct.	Nov.	Dec.	Total
Net sales	$ 120	$ 140	$ 160	$ 140	$ 140	$ 140	$ 160	$1,620	$1,840	$2,140	$2,285	$1,115	$10,000
Cost of goods sold[a]	84	98	112	98	98	98	112	1,134	1,288	1,498	1,600	780	7,000
Gross profit	$ 36	$ 42	$ 48	$ 42	$ 42	$ 42	$ 48	$ 486	$ 552	$ 642	$ 685	$ 335	$ 3,000
Operating expenses[b]	200	200	200	200	200	200	200	200	200	200	200	200	2,400
Interest expense	7	4	4	4	4	4	3	5	12	17	17	14	95
Interest income[c]	2	4	5	4	3	3	2	1	1	1	1	1	28
Profit (loss) before taxes	$(169)	$(158)	$(151)	$(158)	$(159)	$(159)	$(153)	$ 282	$ 341	$ 426	$ 469	$ 122	$ 533
Income taxes[d]	(57)	(54)	(51)	(54)	(54)	(54)	(52)	96	116	145	159	42	182
Net profit	$(112)	$(104)	$(100)	$(104)	$(105)	$(105)	$(101)	$ 186	$ 225	$ 281	$ 310	$ 80	$ 351

a. Assumed cost of goods sold equal to 70% sales.
b. Assumed to be same for each month throughout the year.
c. Toy World expected to earn a 4% annualized rate of return on average monthly cash balances.
d. Negative figures are tax credits from operating losses, and reduced accrued taxes shown on balance sheet. The federal tax rate on all earnings was 34%.

The Proposed Change to Level Production

Having experienced one selling season at Toy World, Mr. Hoffman was deeply impressed by the many problems that arose from the company's method of scheduling production. Overtime premiums reduced profits; seasonal expansion and contraction of the workforce resulted in recruiting difficulties and high training and quality-control costs. Machinery stood idle for seven-and-a-half months and then was subjected to heavy use. Accelerated production schedules during the peak season resulted in frequent setup changes on the machinery. Seemingly unavoidable confusion in scheduling runs resulted. Short runs and frequent setup changes caused inefficiencies in assembly and packaging as workers encountered difficulty relearning their operations.

For these reasons, Mr. Hoffman had urged Mr. McClintock to adopt a policy of level monthly production in 1994. He pointed out that estimates of sales volume had usually proved to be reliable in the past. Purchase terms would not be affected by the rescheduling of purchases. The elimination of overtime wage premiums would result in substantial savings, estimated at $225,000 in 1994. Moreover, Mr. Hoffman firmly believed that significant additional direct labor savings, amounting to about $265,000, would result from orderly production. But a portion of the savings would be offset by higher storage and handling costs, estimated at $115,000 annually.

Mr. McClintock speculated on the effect that level production might have on the company's funds requirements in 1994. He assumed that except for profits and fluctuations in the levels of inventories, accounts receivable, and accounts payable, funds inflows and outflows would be approximately in balance. To simplify the problem, Mr. McClintock decided to assume that gross margin percentages would not vary significantly by month under either method of production. That is, cost of goods sold would be 70% of sales in each of the 12 months under seasonal production and would be 65.1% of sales in each of the 12 months under level production. The increased storage and handling costs of $115,000 would be included in operating expenses.

SureCut Shears, Inc.

On April 28, 1996, Michael Stewart, senior loan officer at the Hudson National Bank of New York, was reviewing the credit file of SureCut Shears, Inc. in preparation for a luncheon meeting with the company's president and treasurer. David Fischer, treasurer of SureCut Shears, had recently informed Mr. Stewart that the company would be unable to liquidate its outstanding seasonal loan as initially anticipated. While agreeing to extend the outstanding $1.15 million loan, Mr. Stewart had suggested that he would like to stop by and discuss the company's recent progress when he was next in the vicinity of Savannah, Georgia, where SureCut Shears's home plant and offices were located.

SureCut Shears manufactured a complete line of household scissors and industrial shears. Its quality lines were distributed through wholesalers to specialty, hardware, and department stores located throughout the country. Cheaper products were sold directly to large variety chains. Although competition was severe, particularly from overseas companies, SureCut Shears had made profits in every year since 1958. Sales and profits had grown fairly steadily, if not dramatically, throughout the period.

Hudson National Bank had been soliciting the SureCut Shears account for several years prior to early 1995. After several unsuccessful calls, Mr. Stewart finally convinced the officers of SureCut Shears that association with a large New York bank offered several advantages not to be found with local banks. He was particularly pleased with the success of his efforts, because SureCut Shears historically held fairly sizable deposit balances in its principal banks.

The company had sufficient capital to cover its permanent requirements over the immediate future. Its short-term borrowings from banks were typically confined to the period July–December of each year, when additional working capital was needed to support a seasonal sales peak. As a matter of policy, the company attempted to produce at an even rate throughout the year, and this accounted in good part for the sizable need for seasonal funds.

In June 1995, Mr. Fischer arranged a line of credit of $3.5 million with the Hudson National Bank to cover requirements for the fall. At the time, he anticipated that the loan would be completely paid off by December 1995. He gave Mr. Stewart a pro forma estimate of the company's fund requirements over the coming 12-month period to support his request. (These estimates are shown in Exhibits 1 and 2.) In addition to these requirements, the forecast showed a need for about $1 million by June 1996. Mr. Fischer attributed this increase in funds requirements (no funds were needed in June 1995) to a plant modernization program. He explained that the program, requiring expenditures of $6 million, was about half completed and would be finished by August 1995. Efficiencies resulting from the modernization program, once completed, were expected to save about $900,000 per year before taxes in manufacturing costs.

Mr. Fischer called Mr. Stewart in early September 1995 to let him know that the company would require $350,000 more than had been initially requested to cover peak seasonal needs. Mr. Fischer explained that the main reason for the larger requirements was higher expenditures for modernization than had initially been estimated. Mr. Stewart informed Mr. Fischer that the bank would be happy to accommodate the additional loan requirements.

Copyright © 1996 by the President and Fellows of Harvard College.
Harvard Business School case 297-013.

EXHIBIT 1 **Pro Forma Income Statement, Fiscal 1996 (thousands of dollars)**

	Actual June 30, 1995	1995					1996							
		July	Aug.	Sept.	Oct.	Nov.	Dec.	Jan.	Feb.	Mar.	Apr.	May	June	Total
Sales	$30,135	$2,100	$2,700	$3,300	$4,500	$3,900	$3,300	$2,100	$2,100	$1,800	$1,500	$1,200	$1,500	$30,000
Cost of goods sold														
Materials and labor @ 60% of sales	18,081	1,260	1,620	1,980	2,700	2,340	1,980	1,260	1,260	1,080	900	720	900	18,000
Overhead (including depreciation $130)	3,560	300	300	300	300	300	300	300	300	300	300	300	300	3,600
	21,641	1,560	1,920	2,280	3,000	2,640	2,280	1,560	1,560	1,380	1,200	1,020	1,200	21,600
Gross profit	8,494	540	780	1,020	1,500	1,260	1,020	540	540	420	300	180	300	8,400
Selling and administrative expenses	3,240	270	270	270	270	270	270	270	270	270	270	270	270	3,240
Profit before taxes	5,254	270	510	750	1,230	990	750	270	270	150	30	(90)	30	5,160
Taxes	1,891	97	184	270	443	356	270	97	97	54	11	(32)	11	1,858
Profit after taxes	3,363	173	326	480	787	634	480	173	173	96	19	(58)	19	3,302
Dividends	1,495	0	0	300	0	0	300	0	0	300	0	0	600	1,500
Retained earnings	$ 1,868	$ 173	$ 326	$ 180	$ 787	$ 634	$ 180	$ 173	$ 173	$ (204)	$ 19	$ (58)	$ (581)	$ 1,802
Cumulative retained earnings	—	$173	$ 499	$ 679	$1,466	$2,100	$2,280	$2,453	$2,626	$2,422	$2,441	$2,383	$1,802	—

EXHIBIT 2 **Pro Forma Balance Sheets, Fiscal 1995 (thousands of dollars)**

	Actual June 30, 1995	1995						1996					
		July	Aug.	Sept.	Oct.	Nov.	Dec.	Jan.	Feb.	Mar.	Apr.	May	June
Cash	$ 2,121	$ 736	$ 736	$ 736	$ 736	$ 736	$1,139	$ 2,609	$ 3,179	$ 2,413	$ 2,235	$ 1,759	$ 727
Accounts receivable[a]	2,084	2,850	3,750	4,650	6,150	6,150	5,250	3,750	3,150	2,850	2,400	1,950	2,100
Inventories	8,106	8,372	8,312	7,894	6,758	5,981	5,563	5,862	6,161	6,640	7,298	8,135	8,793
Current assets	12,311	11,958	12,798	13,280	13,644	12,867	11,952	12,221	12,490	11,903	11,933	11,844	11,620
Net plant	24,564	26,059	27,554	27,554	27,554	27,554	27,554	27,554	27,554	27,554	27,554	27,554	27,554
Total assets	$36,875	$38,017	$40,352	$40,834	$41,198	$40,421	$39,506	$39,775	$40,044	$39,457	$39,487	$39,398	$39,174
Banks loans payable	$ 0	$ 1,000	$ 2,817	$ 3,253	$ 2,392	$ 628	$ 0	$ 0	$ 0	$ 0	$ 0	$ 0	$ 1,081
Accounts payable[b]	861	744	777	777	777	777	777	777	777	777	777	777	777
Taxes payable[c]	0	80	230	81	497	833	650	742	834	447	458	427	0
Misc. other	270	270	270	270	270	270	270	270	270	270	270	270	270
Current liabilities	1,131	2,094	4,094	4,381	3,936	2,508	1,697	1,789	1,881	1,494	1,505	1,474	2,128
Mortgage 8%	11,960	11,960	11,960	11,960	11,960	11,960	11,661	11,661	11,661	11,661	11,661	11,661	11,362
Common stock	11,500	11,500	11,500	11,500	11,500	11,500	11,500	11,500	11,500	11,500	11,500	11,500	11,500
Earned surplus	12,284	12,463	12,798	12,993	13,802	14,453	14,648	14,825	15,002	14,802	14,821	14,763	14,184
Total liab., net worth	$36,875	$38,017	$40,352	$40,834	$41,198	$40,421	$39,506	$39,775	$40,044	$39,457	$39,487	$39,398	$39,174

a. Assumes collections lag sales by 45 days.
b. Assumes 30-day payment period, in accordance with trade terms.
c. Estimated taxes are paid in four equal installments of $380,000 each in September, December, March, and June based on pro forma earnings calculated the previous June.

(continued)

EXHIBIT 2 *(concluded)*

	1995						1996					
	July	Aug.	Sept.	Oct.	Nov.	Dec.	Jan.	Feb.	Mar.	Apr.	May	June
Raw materials												
Opening balance	$ 810	$ 777	$ 777	$ 777	$ 777	$ 777	$ 777	$ 777	$ 777	$ 777	$ 777	$ 777
Plus: Purchases	744	777	777	777	777	777	777	777	777	777	777	777
Less: Trans. to work in progress	777	777	777	777	777	777	777	777	777	777	777	777
Closing balance	$ 777	$ 777	$ 777	$ 777	$ 777	$ 777	$ 777	$ 777	$ 777	$ 777	$ 777	$ 777
Work in Process												
Opening balance	$3,110	$3,110	$3,110	$3,110	$3,110	$3,110	$3,110	$3,110	$3,110	$3,110	$3,110	$3,110
Plus: Raw materials additions	777	777	777	777	777	777	777	777	777	777	777	777
Plus: Labor additions	778	778	778	778	778	778	778	778	778	778	778	778
Less: Trans. to finished goods	1,555	1,555	1,555	1,555	1,555	1,555	1,555	1,555	1,555	1,555	1,555	1,555
Closing balances	$3,110	$3,110	$3,110	$3,110	$3,110	$3,110	$3,110	$3,110	$3,110	$3,110	$3,110	$3,110
Finished Goods												
Opening balance	$4,186	$4,485	$4,425	$4,007	$2,871	$2,094	$1,676	$1,975	$2,274	$2,753	$3,411	$4,248
Plus: Work in process additions	1,555	1,555	1,555	1,555	1,555	1,555	1,555	1,555	1,555	1,555	1,555	1,555
Loss: Cost of goods sold	1,256	1,615	1,973	2,691	2,332	1,973	1,256	1,256	1,076	897	718	897
Closing balance	$4,485	$4,425	$4,007	$2,871	$2,094	$1,676	$1,975	$2,274	$2,753	$3,411	$4,248	$4,906
Total closing inventory	$8,372	$8,312	$7,894	$6,758	$5,981	$5,563	$5,862	$6,161	$6,640	$7,298	$8,135	$8,793

In January 1996, Mr. Fischer again contacted Mr. Stewart. He noted that sales had slackened considerably since his previous call. He attributed this decline largely to a retailing downturn then in progress, not to any special conditions affecting his company or the shears industry. Slackening in sales demand had created a need for additional short-term borrowing. Mr. Fischer believed that additional funds would be required until the company could adjust to the new economic conditions. He envisioned that this adjustment would probably not occur until mid-April 1996 or thereabouts. Once more, Mr. Stewart agreed to extend the necessary loan funds to SureCut Shears.

In early April 1996, Mr. Fischer phoned Mr. Stewart a third time to inform him that SureCut Shears would probably not be able to repay its outstanding short-term loan of $1.14 million before the seasonal upturn in funds requirements in June. Mr. Fischer explained that a further sales decline, occasioned by the retailing recession, was largely responsible for the company's inability to liquidate the loan as anticipated. In reply, Mr. Stewart noted that the bank preferred seasonal loans to be "off the books" for at least two months of the year but saw no reason why he would not be willing to renew SureCut Shear's outstanding loan. He nevertheless thought it advisable to explore whether the inability to repay the seasonal loan in 1996 might be caused by a permanent change in the nature of the company's loan needs, such as might be occasioned by the modernization program. Mr. Stewart consequently suggested a meeting for April 29 to discuss the company's recent progress.

In preparing for this meeting, Mr. Stewart carefully examined the various profit and loss statements and balance sheets that Mr. Fischer had submitted to the bank over the course of the previous nine months. (These data are shown in Exhibits 3 and 4.) He hoped this analysis might uncover the reasons for SureCut Shears's inability to repay its loan in accordance with original statements.

EXHIBIT 3 **Income Statements, 1995–1996 (thousands of dollars)**

	1995						1996		
	July	Aug.	Sept.	Oct.	Nov.	Dec.	Jan.	Feb.	Mar.
Sales	$2,070	$2,605	$3,080	$4,066	$3,373	$2,799	$1,758	$1,738	$1,498
Cost of goods									
Materials and labor	1,304	1,641	1,940	2,562	2,125	1,763	1,108	1,095	944
Overhead (incl. depreciation $130)	296	290	340	310	303	288	293	374	323
	1,600	1,931	2,280	2,872	2,428	2,051	1,401	1,469	1,267
Gross profit	470	674	800	1,194	945	748	357	269	231
Selling and administrative expenses	273	273	293	275	275	269	260	258	358
Profit before taxes	197	401	507	919	670	479	97	11	(27)
Taxes	67	136	172	312	228	163	33	4	(9)
Profit after taxes	130	265	335	607	442	316	64	7	(18)
Dividends	0	0	300	0	0	300	0	0	300
Retained earnings	$ 130	$ 265	$ 35	$ 607	$ 442	$ 16	$ 64	$ 7	$ (318)
Cumulative retained earnings	$ 130	$ 395	$ 430	$1,037	$1,479	$1,495	$1,559	$1,566	$1,248

EXHIBIT 4 **Balance Sheets, 1995–1996 (thousands of dollars)**

	1995							1996		
	June	July	Aug.	Sept.	Oct.	Nov.	Dec.	Jan.	Feb.	Mar.
Cash	$ 2,120	$ 957	$ 573	$ 702	$ 696	$ 830	$ 641	$ 1,133	$ 1,076	$ 688
Accounts receivable	2,084	2,837	3,644	4,395	5,651	5,526	5,573	3,958	3,169	2,867
Inventories	8,106	8,378	8,303	7,963	7,179	6,705	6,502	6,925	7,170	7,374
Current assets	12,310	12,172	12,520	13,060	13,526	13,061	12,716	12,016	11,415	10,929
Net plant	24,564	26,103	27,672	27,848	27,858	27,843	27,855	27,843	27,810	27,812
Total assets	$36,874	$38,275	$40,192	$40,908	$41,384	$40,904	$40,601	$39,859	$39,225	$38,741
Bank loans payable	$ 0	$ 1,270	$ 2,758	$ 3,677	$ 3,073	$ 1,879	$ 2,206	$ 1,303	$ 706	$ 1,148
Accounts payable	861	789	774	843	876	834	684	699	658	514
Taxes payable	0	67	204	(64)	290	552	306	357	360	(92)
Misc. other	269	275	317	284	290	275	269	266	260	258
Current liabilities	1,130	2,401	4,053	4,740	4,529	3,540	3,465	2,625	1,984	1,828
Mortgage 8%	11,960	11,960	11,960	11,960	11,960	11,960	11,661	11,661	11,661	11,661
Common stock	11,500	11,500	11,500	11,500	11,500	11,500	11,500	11,500	11,500	11,500
Earned surplus	12,284	12,414	12,679	12,708	13,395	13,904	13,975	14,073	14,080	13,752
Total liab., net worth	$36,874	$38,275	$40,192	$40,908	$41,384	$40,904	$40,601	$39,859	$39,225	$38,741

(continued)

EXHIBIT 4 (*concluded*)

	1995						1996		
	July	Aug.	Sept.	Oct.	Nov.	Dec.	Jan.	Feb.	Mar.
Raw Materials									
Opening balances	$ 810	$ 814	$ 757	$ 760	$ 793	$ 823	$ 778	$ 762	$ 753
Plus: Purchases	787	777	837	867	802	688	690	652	518
Less: Trans. to work in process	783	834	834	834	772	733	706	661	601
Closing balance	$ 814	$ 757	$ 760	$ 793	$ 823	$ 778	$ 762	$ 753	$ 670
Work in Process									
Opening balance	$3,110	$3,131	$3,196	$3,221	$3,224	$3,139	$3,037	$2,953	$2,781
Plus: Raw materials additions	783	834	834	834	772	733	706	661	601
Plus: Labor additions	789	789	772	789	748	789	789	688	646
Less: Trans. to finished goods	1,551	1,558	1,581	1,620	1,605	1,624	1,579	1,521	1,495
Closing balance	$3,131	$3,196	$3,221	$3,224	$3,139	$3,037	$2,953	$2,781	$2,533
Finished Goods									
Opening balance	$4,186	$4,433	$4,350	$3,982	$3,162	$2,743	$2,687	$3,210	$3,636
Plus: Work in process additions	1,551	1,558	1,581	1,620	1,605	1,624	1,579	1,521	1,495
Less: Cost of goods sold	1,304	1,641	1,949	2,440	2,024	1,680	1,056	1,095	960
Closing balance	$4,433	$4,350	$3,982	$3,162	$2,743	$2,687	$3,210	$3,636	$4,171
Total closing inventory	$8,378	$8,303	$7,963	$7,179	$6,705	$6,502	$6,925	$7,170	$7,374

Dell's Working Capital

Dell Computer Corporation had reported impressive growth for fiscal year 1996 with its sales up 52% over the prior year. Industry analysts anticipated the personal computer market to grow 20% annually over the next three years, and Michael Dell expected that his company, with its build-to-order manufacturing system, would continue its double-digit growth. Although Dell Computer had financed its recent growth internally, management needed a plan for financing the future growth.

Company Background

Dell Computer Corporation was founded in 1984 by then nineteen-year-old Michael Dell. The company designed, manufactured, sold, and serviced high performance personal computers (PCs) compatible with industry standards. Initially, the company purchased IBM compatible personal computers, upgraded them, then sold the upgraded PCs directly to businesses by mail order. Subsequently, Dell began to market and sell its own brand personal computer, taking orders over a toll free telephone line, and shipping directly to customers.

Selling directly to customers was Dell's core strategy. Sales were primarily generated through advertising in computer trade magazines and, eventually, in a catalog. Dell combined this low cost sales/distribution model with a production cycle that began after the company received a customer's order. This build-to-order model enabled Dell to deliver a customized order within a few days, something its competitors could not do. Dell was also the first in the industry to provide toll-free telephone and on-site technical support in an effort to differentiate itself in customer service.

Dell's Inventory Management

Dell built computer systems *after* the company received the customer's order. In contrast, the industry leaders built to forecast and maintained sizeable finished goods inventory in their stock or at their channel partners. Dell's build-to-order manufacturing process yielded low finished goods inventory balances. By the mid-1990s Dell's work-in-process (WIP) and finished goods inventory as a percent of total inventory ranged from 10% to 20%. This contrasted sharply with the industry leaders, such as Compaq, Apple, and IBM, whose WIP and finished goods inventory typically ranged from 50% to 70% of total inventory, not including inventory held by their resellers.

Dell maintained an inventory of components. The cost of individual components, such as processor chips, comprised about 80% of the cost of a PC. As new technology

Professor Richard S. Ruback and Research Associate Aldo Sesia prepared this case from published sources as the basis for class discussion rather than to illustrate either effective or ineffective handling of an administrative situation.

Copyright © 2000 by the President and Fellows of Harvard College. To order copies or request permission to reproduce materials, call 1-800-545-7685, write Harvard Business School Publishing, Boston, MA 02163, or go to http://www.hbsp.harvard.edu. No part of this publication may be reproduced, stored in a retrieval system, used in a spreadsheet, or transmitted in any form or by any means—electronic, mechanical, photocopying, recording, or otherwise—without the permission of Harvard Business School.

TABLE A
Days Supply of Inventory (DSI)[a]

Source: Dell Computer Corporation Fiscal 1993–1995 Annual Reports; casewriter estimates from Apple Computer, Compaq Computer, and IBM Fiscal 1992–1994 Annual Reports

	1993[b]	1994[b]	1995[b]
Dell Computer	55	33	32
Apple Computer	52	85	54
Compaq Computer	72	60	73
IBM	64	57	48

[a]DSI = (Net Ending Inventory)/(Quarterly COGS/90 Days)
[b]Dell's fiscal calendar ends in January; Apple's in September; Compaq and IBM's in December. The DSI for 1995 represents Dell's DSI for the quarter ended on 1/29/95, Apple's on 9/30/94, and Compaq's and IBM's on 12/31/94.

replaced old, the prices of components fell by an average of 30% a year.[1] Dell ordered components based on sales forecasts. Components were sourced from about 80 suppliers in the mid-1990s—down from a high of 200 or more. Dell issued "releases" for a certain amount of product from a supplier's inventory on a regular basis, depending upon the forecast.[2] Suppliers, many of whom had warehouses close to Dell's Austin, Texas, and Ireland plants, delivered parts to Dell, often on a daily basis.

As Michael Dell explained, "Other companies had to maintain high levels of inventory to stock reseller and retail channels. Because we built only what our customers wanted when they wanted it, we didn't have a lot of inventory taking up space and soaking up capital."[3] As such, Dell's supply of inventory was significantly lower than its competitors, providing a competitive advantage.

September 1990–August 1993

In 1990, Dell had only 1% of the U.S. PC market share.[4] Michael Dell anticipated that the fragmented PC industry was ready for a consolidation and that Dell was too small to survive a consolidation. At the time Michael Dell explained, "I realized we had to decide whether we should stay the size we were—and face the consequences—or go for big time growth. . . . Obviously, we went for growth—in one big leap."[5]

On September 10, 1990, in an attempt to capture sales from small businesses and first time consumers, Dell announced it was breaking from its direct-only business model and would begin to sell its PCs[6] through CompUSA (formerly SoftWarehouse Superstores). Over the next two and a half years, Dell expanded this indirect distribution channel by adding other mass market retailers (i.e., Staples, Inc.) and marketing its Precision line exclusively through Price Club. Additionally the company continued aggressive pursuit of foreign markets, relying on resellers to distribute Dell product when timing limitations or infrastructure obstacles complicated direct distribution. Annual sales increased by 268% within two years, compared to industry growth of 5%, and moved Dell into the top five in worldwide market share.[7] Exhibit 1 details sales growth for Dell and the PC industry.

[1]Anon, "Selling PCs like Bananas," *The Economist;* London, October 5, 1996, p. 63.

[2]Clare Goldsberry, "Computer Makers May Overcome JIT Troubles," *Plastics News,* August 15, 1994, p. 20.

[3]Michael Dell with Catherine Fredman, "Direct from Dell, Strategies That Revolutionized an Industry," 1999, p. 22.

[4]Jan Rivkin and Michael Porter, "Matching Dell," HBS case 799-158, June 6, 1999, p. 15.

[5]Michael Dell with Catherine Fredman, "Direct from DELL, Strategies That Revolutionized an Industry," 1999, p. 43.

[6]Systems sold through the retail channel were limited to certain predetermined configurations and were not customized.

[7]Jan Rivkin and Michael Porter, "Matching Dell," HBS Case 799-158, June 6, 1999, p. 15.

EXHIBIT 1
Dell's Annual Worldwide Sales Dollar Growth versus Industry

Source: Dell Computer Corporation Fiscal 1996 Annual Report; casewriter estimates from industry market share data from International Data Corporation

Calendar Year	Dell[a]	Industry
1991	63%	–2%
1992	126%	7%
1993	43%	15%
1994	21%	37%
1995	52%	31%

[a]Dell's fiscal year closes in alignment to calendar year stated

In August 1993, Dell reported a $76 million loss for the second quarter of 1993, its first loss. The loss was tied to $71 million in charges relating to the sell-off of excess inventory and the cost of scrapping a disappointing notebook computer line.[8] The company also took restructuring charges to consolidate European operations that had become redundant and inefficient. Dell's profit margin fell to 2% for the first quarter, ending May 2, 1993—well below the company's target of 5% that they had achieved or exceeded for 11 consecutive quarters. With $32 million in cash and cash equivalents, analysts thought Dell had enough cash and credit to last at least another year, but many wondered if the company had the resources to keep pace should the battle for market share intensify.[9]

> Like many companies, we were always focused on our profit and loss statement. But cash flow was not a regularly discussed topic. It was as if we were driving along, watching only the speedometer, when in fact we were running out of gas.[10]

September 1993–January 1996

Dell shifted its focus from exclusively growth to liquidity, profitability, and growth. It adopted company-wide metrics around the new focus, requiring each business unit to provide detailed profit and loss statements. In July 1994, less than a year after shifting the company's focus, Dell exited the low margin indirect retail channel where, CFO Tom Meredith noted, "We were losing our shirts."[11] Late in 1995, Dell instituted goals on ROIC (Return on Invested Capital) and CCC (Cash Conversion Cycle). Exhibit 2 presents Dell's CCC performance. The company took measures to improve its internal systems for forecasting, reporting, and inventory control. A new vendor certification program was put in place, reducing the number of suppliers, ensuring component quality, and improving delivery performance. Dell also brought in seasoned managers to lead the company during its next stage.

These changes, combined with Dell's re-entry into the notebook market, and its rapid introduction of computer systems based on Intel Corporation's new Pentium microprocessor chip, fueled the company's recovery. Dell's direct contact with customers helped it anticipate demand for newly developed Pentium-based systems and its low inventory of 386 and 486 technology made it less costly to move quickly to the new technology. Dell beat the competition to the marketplace with Pentium-based products and was the first in the

[8]Kyle Pope, "Dell Computer Posts Loss for Quarter, Backs Away from Forecast of Rebound," *Wall Street Journal,* August 18, 1993, p. B6.

[9]Peter Burrows and Stephanie Anderson Forest, "Dell Computer Goes into the Shop," *Business Week,* July 1993, p. 38.

[10]Michael Dell with Catherine Fredman, "Direct from DELL, Strategies That Revolutionized an Industry," 1999, p. 47.

[11]Rahul Jacob, "The Resurrection of Michael Dell, *Fortune,* September 18, 1995, p. 117.

EXHIBIT 2
Working Capital Financial Ratios for Dell

Source: Dell Computer Corporation fiscal 1993–1996 annual and quarterly reports

	DSI[a]	DSO[b]	DPO[c]	CCC[d]
Q193	40	54	46	48
Q293	44	51	55	40
Q393	47	52	51	48
Q493	55	54	53	56
Q194	55	58	56	57
Q294	41	53	43	51
Q394	33	53	45	41
Q494	33	50	42	41
Q195	32	53	45	40
Q295	35	49	44	40
Q395	35	50	46	39
Q495	32	47	44	35
Q196	34	47	42	39
Q296	36	50	43	43
Q396	37	49	43	43
Q496	31	42	33	40

[a]DSI (Days Sales of Inventory) = Net Inventory / (Quarterly COGS/90)
[b]DSO (Days Sales Outstanding) = Net Accounts Receivables / (Quarterly Sales/90)
[c]DPO (Days Payables Outstanding) = Accounts Payables / (Quarterly COGS/90)
[d]CCC (Cash Conversion Cycle) = DSI + DSO – DPO

industry to achieve volume production of systems with the 120 mhz Pentium processor.[12] Exhibit 3 presents Dell's percent of computer system sales by processor type.

In July 1995, Dell became the first manufacturer to convert its entire major product line to the Pentium technology.[13] By that time, in less than two years, the Pentium chip was at 133 MHz—the ninth upgrade. Dell was able to offer faster systems at the same price that rivals were marketing older Pentium technology. Because of its low finished goods inventory, Dell didn't have to dismantle PCs to replace the microprocessor when Intel Corporation discovered its Pentium chip was flawed in 1994. It was able to quickly manufacture systems with the "updated" Pentium chip, while others (i.e., Compaq) were still selling flawed systems from inventory. In a similar vein, Dell was able to begin shipping its Dell Dimension systems equipped with Microsoft Corporation's new Windows 95 operating system on August 25, 1995—the very day Microsoft launched the product. As a direct marketer, Dell was able to bring new component technology to the market within an average of 35 days—a third of the time it took competitors to move a new product through indirect channels.[14]

The Future

For its 1996 fiscal year, ended January 31, 1996, Dell reported revenue of $5.3 billion with net income of $272 million, or 5.1% of sales. Revenue was up 52% over the prior year compared with an industry increase of 31%. Exhibits 4 and 5 present Dell's Income Statement and Balance Sheet, respectively. Though favorable, the 1996 results suffered somewhat from component shortages. Michael Dell predicted the company's growth rate for the next year would again outpace the industry's growth.

[12]Anon, "Dell First to Ship Systems with New Pentium Processor," *PR Newswire,* April 19, 1995.

[13]Anon, "Dell Taking Orders for Factory-Installed Windows 95 on Dell Dimension Desktop PCs," *PR Newswire,* August 2, 1995.

[14]Judy Ward, "Runaway Horse: Michael Dell Wants to Rein In Growth: Shareholders Want Whip," *Financial World,* October 24, 1995, p. 36.

EXHIBIT 3
Percent of Dell Computer Systems Sales by Microprocessor

Source: Dell Computer Corporation Fiscal 1994–96 Annual Reports

Computer Systems	FY94	FY95	FY96
386 models	7%	0%	0%
486 models	92%	71%	25%
Pentium models	1%	29%	75%

EXHIBIT 4
Profit and Loss Statements for Dell Computer Corporation (millions of dollars)

Source: Dell Computer Corporation Fiscal 1996 Annual Report

Fiscal Year	1996	1995	1994	1993	1992
Sales	$5,296	$3,475	$2,873	$2,014	$890
Cost of Sales	4,229	2,737	2,440	1,565	608
Gross Margin	1,067	738	433	449	282
Operating Expenses	690	489	472	310	215
Operating Income	377	249	(39)	139	67
Financing & Other Income	6	(36)	0	4	7
Income Taxes	111	64	(3)	41	23
Net Profit	272	149	(36)	102	51

EXHIBIT 5
Balance Sheets for Dell Computer Corporation (millions of dollars)

Source: Dell Computer Corporation Fiscal 1994–1996 Annual Reports

	Year Ended		
	January 28, 1996	January 29, 1995	January 30, 1994
Current Assets:			
Cash	55	43	3
Short Term Investments	591	484	334
Accounts Receivables, net	726	538	411
Inventories	429	293	220
Other	156	112	80
Total Current Assets	1,957	1,470	1,048
Property, Plant & Equipment, net	179	117	87
Other	12	7	5
Total Assets	2,148	1,594	1,140
Current Liabilities:			
Accounts Payable	466	403	NA
Accrued and Other Liabilities	473	349	NA
Total Current Liabilities	939	752	538
Long Term Debt	113	113	100
Other Liabilities	123	77	31
Total Liabilities	1,175	942	669
Stockholders' Equity:			
Preferred Stock (Note a)	6	120	NA
Common Stock (Note a)	430	242	NA
Retained Earnings	570	311	NA
Other	(33)	(21)	NA
Total Stockholders' Equity	973	652	471
	2,148	1,594	1,140

[a] 1,190,000 shares of preferred stock converted to common stock in fiscal year 1996.

Hampton Machine Tool Company

On September 14, 1979, Jerry Eckwood, vice president of the St. Louis National Bank, was considering a loan request from a customer located in a nearby city. The company, Hampton Machine Tool Company, had requested renewal of an existing $1 million loan originally due to be repaid on September 30. In addition to the renewal of the existing loan, Hampton was asking for an additional loan of $350,000 for planned equipment purchases in October. Under the terms of the company's request, both loans, totaling $1.35 million, would be repayable at the end of 1979.

Since its establishment in 1915, Hampton Machine Tool Company had successfully weathered the severe cyclical fluctuations characteristic of the machine tool manufacturing business. In the most recent cycle Hampton had experienced record production and profitability during the mid- and late-1960s. Because Hampton's major customers included the military aircraft manufacturers and automobile manufacturers in the St. Louis area, the company's success in the 1960s reflected a strong automobile market and the heavy defense spending associated with the Vietnam War. Hampton rode the 1960s boom into the early 1970s. Hampton, along with the rest of the capital goods industry, experienced a severe decline in sales and profitability in the mid-1970s. Precipitous declines in the production of automobiles in St. Louis facilities reflected the 1973 oil embargo, subsequent increases in the price of gasoline, and the 1974–1975 recession. Massive reductions in defense spending in the post–Vietnam War period had a severe adverse impact on Hampton's other major customer segment, military aircraft manufacturers. Hampton's sales had bottomed out in the mid-1970s, and the several years prior to 1978 had seen a steady rebuilding of sales. Hampton's recovery was due primarily to three factors. First, military aircraft sales had increased substantially, reflecting both an expanding export market and a more benign domestic market. Second, though the automobile manufacturers in the area were not expanding, this segment of Hampton's market had at least stabilized. Finally, the adverse economic conditions in the mid-1970s had taken their toll in the regional capital goods industry. Consequently, Hampton's market share increased as many thinly capitalized competitors had been forced out of the industry. Hampton's recovery had suffered a mild setback, as 1978 sales were far below capacity. However, with a substantial backlog of firm sales orders, Hampton entered 1979 expecting its first year of capacity sales since 1972.

Hampton's conservative financial policies had contributed to its survival and success in the volatile capital goods industry. The company had traditionally maintained a strong working capital position as a buffer against economic uncertainty. As a result, the company had no debt on its balance sheet during the 10 years prior to December 1978. In a meeting in early December 1978, Benjamin G. Cowins, president of Hampton, requested the initial loan of $1 million to facilitate purchasing the stock of several dissident shareholders. While Hampton had some cash in excess of that required for normal operations, excess cash was not sufficient to effect the stock redemption. Therefore, Mr. Cowins had asked Mr. Eckwood for a loan from the St. Louis National Bank. The loan of $1 million was to be taken down at the end of December 1978. Hampton would make monthly interest payments at an interest rate of 1½% per month (approximately 18% on an annual basis) on the principal, which would be due at the end of September 1979. In support of this request, Mr. Cowins had submitted a forecast of

Copyright © 1980 by the President and Fellows of Harvard College.
Harvard Business School case 80–103.

EXHIBIT 1
Shipments at Selling Price (thousands of dollars)

		As Forecast Dec. 1978	Actual	As Forecast Sept. 1979
1979	January	$1,302	$ 861	
	February	1,872	672	
	March	1,635	1,866	
	April	1,053	1,566	
	May	1,293	873	
	June	1,479	1,620	
	July	1,488	723	
	August	1,797	507	
Eight months total		$11,919	$8,688	
	September	$ 1,299		$2,163
	October	1,347		1,505
	November	1,311		1,604
	December	2,298		2,265

monthly shipments for 1979 (see Exhibit 1), a balance sheet dated November 30, 1978 (first column of Exhibit 2), and documentation of Hampton's backlog of sales orders. Mr. Eckwood felt at the time that the documentation provided by Mr. Cowins was sufficient to support favorable action on the request. Furthermore, Hampton had traditionally kept its ample cash balances on deposit at the St. Louis National Bank, and the bank's management knew Mr. Cowins well. Mr. Cowins, then 58 years old, had succeeded his father-in-law as president of Hampton in 1963. He was widely respected in the business community as an energetic and successful executive. In mid-December 1978, Mr. Eckwood had approved the loan to Hampton.

Hampton took down the loan at the end of December 1978. The proceeds of the loan plus $2 million in excess cash were used immediately to repurchase 75,000 shares of Hampton's $10 par value stock from several dissident shareholders at an aggregate cost of $3 million.

After the loan was made, Mr. Cowins regularly sent the bank profit and loss statements and balance sheets documenting Hampton's financial condition. In preparing his analysis of Mr. Cowins's request, Mr. Eckwood focused on the documents presented in Exhibits 1, 2, and 3. In examining Hampton's financial statements, Mr. Eckwood recalled that Hampton's selling terms were 30 days net. Occasionally, a customer placing a large order would make an advance payment to help Hampton finance the construction of the machines ordered. Because Hampton's products were largely made to order, the construction period involved five to six months for some of the larger, more complex types of machines. Upon completion and shipment of orders against which advances had been paid, Hampton deducted the amount of the advance from the amount billed to the customer. Also, Mr. Eckwood understood that the company purchased its materials on terms of net 30 days.

In a letter to Mr. Eckwood, Mr. Cowins had made his request for the extension of the existing Hampton note until the end of the year plus an additional loan of $350,000 to finance equipment purchases. The additional loan would be needed by the end of October and would be payable at the end of the year, with monthly interest payments remaining 1½% of principal. In his letter, Mr. Cowins commented at some length on the company's financial condition, the reasons for the shortfall of actual from projected 1979 shipments, and Hampton's substantial backlog of firm sales orders. In addition, Mr. Cowins stated that he expected to be able to repay both loans in full by December 31, 1979. Mr. Cowins's letter is presented in full as Exhibit 4. Although Hampton would not need the additional $350,000 loan until the end of October, the maturity date of the existing note was fast approaching. Therefore, Mr. Eckwood needed to decide upon a response to Mr. Cowins's request.

EXHIBIT 2
Balance Sheets, 1978–1979 (thousands of dollars)

	1978		1979			
	Nov.	Dec.	Mar.	June	July	Aug.
Cash	$2,520	$ 491	$ 505	$1,152	$1,678	$1,559
Accounts receivable, net	1,245	1,863	1,971	1,893	1,269	684
Inventories	2,601	2,478	3,474	3,276	3,624	4,764
Current assets	6,366	4,832	5,950	6,321	6,571	7,007
Gross fixed assets	4,010	4,010	4,010	4,010	4,010	4,010
Accumulated depreciation	2,998	3,010	3,040	3,070	3,080	3,090
Net fixed assets	1,012	1,000	970	940	930	920
Prepaid expenses	62	40	39	24	24	42
Total assets	$7,740	$5,872	$6,959	$7,285	$7,525	$7,969
Notes payable, bank	—	$1,000	$1,000	$1,000	$1,000	$1,000
Accounts payable	$348	371	681	399	621	948
Accruals	561	777	849	678	585	552
Taxes payable[a]	150	74	373	354	407	479
Customer advance payments	840	1,040	1,040	1,566	1,566	1,566
Current liabilities	1,899	3,262	3,943	3,997	4,179	4,545
Common stock ($10 par value)	1,178	428	428	428	428	428
Surplus	4,363	2,182	2,588	2,860	2,918	2,996
Net worth	5,541	2,610	3,016	3,288	3,346	3,424
Total liabilities and net worth	$7,440	$5,872	$6,959	$7,285	$7,525	$7,969

a. Tax payments in 1979 include $75,000 due March 15 on underpayment of 1978 taxes and four equal payments of $181,000 due on the 15th of April, June, September, and December for estimated 1979 tax liability, with any underpayment of 1979 taxes due March 15, 1980.

EXHIBIT 3

Income Statements, 1978–1979 (thousands of dollars)

	Fiscal Year Ending 12/31/78	Dec. 1978	1979 Jan.	Feb.	Mar.	Apr.	May	June	July	Aug.	Eight Months Ending 8/31/79
Net sales	$7,854	$1,551	$861	$672	$1,866	$1,566	$873	$1,620	$723	$507	$8,688
Cost of Sales[a]	5,052	1,122	474	369	1,362	1,137	567	1,197	510	276	5,892
Gross profit	2,802	429	387	303	504	429	306	423	213	231	2,796
Selling and administrative expenses	1,296	248	103	61	205	172	96	130	87	66	920
Interest expense	—	—	15	15	15	15	15	15	15	15	120
Net income before taxes	1,506	181	269	227	284	242	195	278	111	150	1,756
Income taxes	723	87	129	109	136	116	94	133	53	72	842
Net income	$ 783	$ 94	$140	$118	$148	$126	$101	$ 145	$ 58	$ 78	$ 914
Dividends	$ 50	$ 25	—	—	—	—	—	$ 100	—	—	$ 100

a. Includes depreciation charges of $150,000 in 1978, $12,000 in December 1978, and $10,000 per month in 1979.

EXHIBIT 4

HAMPTON MACHINE TOOL COMPANY

East St. Louis, Illinois

September 12, 1979

Mr. Jerry Eckwood
Vice President
St. Louis National Bank
St. Louis, Missouri

Dear Mr. Eckwood:

I enclose the company's August 31 financial statements. While these statements show our cash balance as $1,559,000, you will note we have an obligation to a customer for cash advances of $1,566,000, and we expect to ship this order over the next three months. With respect to our note for $1,000,000 due September 30, we request that you renew it until the end of 1979. We also wish to borrow an additional $350,000 to be available at the end of October to be repaid by the end of the year with interest at the rate of 1½% per month on the principal. This additional loan is required to purchase certain needed equipment. At the end of the year, as you can see for yourself, we expect to be able to have enough cash on hand to retire our obligations in full.

For the past month or more we have been producing at capacity and expect to continue at this rate through the end of the year and beyond. On August 31, our backlog of unfilled orders amounted to about $16,500,000—approximately 90% of annual capacity. I should stress that these are firm orders from respected customers.

Despite our backlog, our shipment schedule has been upset, particularly the last several months, because we have had to wait on our suppliers for shipment of electronic control mechanisms. On August 31, we had seven machines with an accumulated cost of about $1,320,000 completed except for the installation of these electronic components. The components were finally received last week and will enable us to complete a number of machines in the next few weeks. After this imminent reduction in work in progress of about $1,320,000, the remainder of our work-in-progress inventories will probably remain stable for the foreseeable future because of our capacity rate of production.

We bought raw materials beyond our immediate needs in July and August to be assured of completing our orders scheduled to be shipped by the end of the year. We have accumulated about $420,000 worth of scarcer components above our normal raw materials inventories. The extra $420,000 will be used up by the end of the year, bringing our raw materials inventories back to normal levels for capacity production. Because we bought ahead this way, we expect to cut raw materials purchases to about $600,000 a month in each of the four remaining months of 1979.

Our finished goods inventories are, of course, negligible at all times since we ship machines within a day of completion.

Our revised shipment estimates (at selling price) are as follows:

September	$2,163,000
October	1,505,000
November	1,604,000
December	2,265,000
	$7,537,000

(continued)

EXHIBIT 4
(*concluded*)

The shipment estimates include the $2,100,000 order for the General Aircraft Corporation. We are now scheduled to ship against this order as follows: September, $840,000; October, $840,000; November, $420,000. Since we obtained a $1,566,000 advance from General Aircraft on this order, we will be due nothing on these shipments until their $1,566,000 credit with us is exhausted.

You will note the decline in our accrued expenses. As I mentioned to you last month when you visited us, we have been paying off commissions due to our three principal sales people (who are also large stockholders in the company). Last year when we needed funds to redeem part of our capital stock, these people agreed to defer their commissions until the funds could be more easily spared. In August, we paid off the last of these back commissions. This has been the principal cause of the decline in accruals, which, like prepaid expenses, normally do not change much from month to month. Assuming accruals will stay about the same as on August 31, our monthly outlay for all expenses other than interest and raw materials purchases should be around $400,000 per month.

Due to poor economic conditions and our desire to conserve cash, we have spent very little on new equipment in the last several years, and this has contributed somewhat to the difficulties we have had in maintaining production at a capacity rate this year. We feel that we should not further postpone replacing certain essential equipment if we are to avoid a possible major breakdown at an inconvenient time. Therefore, we think it necessary to purchase additional equipment costing $350,000 in October to maintain production efficiency. The proceeds from the additional loan we have requested will be used at the end of October to pay for this equipment. This equipment has an estimated life of eight years, an estimated net salvage value of zero, and the $350,000 purchase price will be depreciated on a straight-line basis.

Our tax people tell us that the equipment will qualify for a 10% investment tax credit (ITC). However, the tax savings of $35,000 will not affect our scheduled tax payments this year. We are scheduled to pay $181,000 in taxes on September 15 and to make another payment of the same amount on December 15. As I understand it, the ITC savings of $35,000 will reduce both our tax liability and the taxes payable on our balance sheet as well as increase reported earnings. However, the cash-flow impact of this savings will not be felt until March 1980 when we make our final settlement with the government on 1979 taxes.

Despite temporary bottlenecks that reduced shipments, our profits for the year to date have been quite satisfactory. With raw materials and components supply assured and the efficiency provided by the new equipment we plan to purchase, we feel confident we can meet our shipment forecasts for the rest of the year. Furthermore, the business that we expect to ship in the next four months is on our books on profitable terms. While our profit, as you know, varies with the item involved, our engineering estimates indicate that we expect to earn a profit before taxes and interest of about 23% of sales on these shipments. Even after taking into account our tax rate of 48% and the interest we must pay on our notes, 1979 looks like a very good year. Because of these good results and in view of our conservative dividend policy during the last several years of economic uncertainty, we plan to pay a dividend to our stockholders. Our dividend disbursements in 1979 have continued to be quite modest, and we want to be sure that those stockholders who stood by us last December have no cause to regret their action. Under the circumstances, we feel that a dividend of $150,000 payable in December is the least we can do in view of our high earnings and our stockholders' patient support.

If there is anything further you need to know, please do not hesitate to write or phone.

Sincerely yours,
(Signed) B. G. Cowins
President

Part 2

Capital Structure, Long-Term Financing, and Risk Management

Debt Policy and Long-Term Financing

E. I. du Pont de Nemours and Company (1983)

In early 1983, the management of E. I. du Pont de Nemours and Company (Du Pont) looked back on two decades of turbulence in the firm's operations. Difficulties in the 1970s and the mega-merger with Conoco had led the company to abandon its long-held policy of an all-equity capital structure. Following the Conoco acquisition in 1981, Du Pont's ratio of debt to total capital had peaked at 42%—the highest in the firm's history. The rapid escalation in financial leverage had cost Du Pont its cherished AAA bond rating. Du Pont had not regained the top rating despite a reduction in debt to 36% of capital by the end of 1982.

The operations of Du Pont had changed dramatically in the past 20 years. With the task of digesting Conoco under way, management faced an important financial policy decision—determining a capital structure policy appropriate for Du Pont in the 1980s. This decision would have implications for Du Pont's financial performance and possibly for its competitive position as well.

E. I. du Pont de Nemours and Company was founded in 1802 to manufacture gunpowder. By 1900, Du Pont had begun to expand rapidly through research and acquisitions. A technological leader in chemicals and fibers, the firm grew to be the largest U.S. chemical manufacturer. At the end of 1980, the firm ranked fifteenth on the Fortune 500 list of U.S. industrials. The 1981 merger with Conoco, Inc., a major oil company, elevated Du Pont to seventh place on the list of U.S. industrials.

Capital Structure Policy, 1965–1982

Historically, Du Pont had been well known for its policy of extreme financial conservatism. The company's low debt ratio was feasible in part because of its success in its product markets. Du Pont's high level of profitability allowed it to finance its needs through internally generated funds (see Exhibits 1 and 2 for selected financial data). In fact, financial leverage was actually negative between 1965 and 1970, since Du Pont's cash balance exceeded its total debt. Du Pont's conservative use of debt combined with its profitability and technological leadership in the chemical industry had made the company one of the few AAA-rated manufacturers. Du Pont's low-debt policy maximized its financial flexibility and insulated its operations from financing constraints.

In the late 1960s, competitive conditions in Du Pont's fibers and plastics businesses began to exert pressure on the firm's financial policy. Between 1965 and 1970, increases in industry capacity outstripped demand growth, resulting in substantial price declines.

Copyright © 1984 by the President and Fellows of Harvard College. Harvard Business School case 284-062.

As a result, Du Pont experienced decreases in gross margins and return on capital. Despite continued sales growth, net income fell by 19% between 1965 and 1970.

Three factors combined to intensify the pressure on Du Pont's financing policy in the mid-1970s. In response to competitive pressures, Du Pont in the early 1970s embarked on a major capital spending program designed to restore its cost position. The escalation of inflation ballooned the cost of the program to more than 50% over budget by 1974. Since capital spending was critical to maintaining and improving its competitive position, Du Pont was reluctant to reduce or postpone these expenditures. Second, the rapid increase in oil prices in 1973 pushed up Du Pont's feedstock costs and increased required inventory investment, while oil shortages disrupted production. Du Pont experienced the full impact of the oil shock in 1974; its revenues rose by 16% and costs jumped by 30%, causing net income to fall by 31%. Finally, the recession in 1975 had a dramatic impact on Du Pont's fiber business. Between the second quarter of 1974 and the second quarter of 1975, Du Pont's fiber shipments dropped by 50% on a volume basis. Net income fell by 33% in 1975. Over the period 1973–1975, Du Pont's net income, return on total capital, and earnings per share all fell by more than 50%.

Severe financing pressures resulted from the combination of inflation's impact on needed capital expenditures, cost increases driven by the escalation in oil prices, and recessionary conditions in the fiber business. The required investment in working capital and capital expenditures increased dramatically at a time when internally generated funds were shrinking. Du Pont responded to the financing shortfall by cutting its dividend in 1974 and 1975 and slashing working capital investment.

Since these measures were insufficient to meet the entire financing requirement, Du Pont turned to debt financing. With no short-term debt outstanding in 1972, the firm's short-term debt rose to $540 million by the end of 1975. In addition, in 1974, Du Pont floated a $350 million 30-year bond issue and a $150 million issue of 7-year notes. The former was Du Pont's first public long-term debt issue in the United States since the 1920s. As a result, Du Pont's debt ratio rose from 7% in 1972 to 27% in 1975, while interest coverage collapsed from 38.4 to 4.6 over the same period. Despite concern that the rapid increase in the company's debt ratio might result in a downgrading, Du Pont retained its AAA bond rating during this period. Had Du Pont abandoned its policy of financial conservatism, or was this a temporary departure from that policy forced by extraordinary financing pressures? In December 1974, Du Pont CEO Irving Shapiro stated, "We expect to use prudent debt financing over the long term."

Nonetheless, Du Pont moved quickly to reduce its debt ratio. Between 1976 and 1979, financing pressures eased. Capital expenditures declined from their 1975 peak as the spending program initiated in the early 1970s neared completion. Net income more than tripled during the period 1975–1979, helped by relatively moderate energy price increases and the economywide recovery from the 1974–1975 recession. Du Pont reduced the dollar value of its total debt in 1977, 1978, and 1979. By the end of 1979, Du Pont's debt had been pared to about 20% of total capital, and interest coverage had rebounded to 11.5 from 4.6 in 1975. Once again, the firm was well within the AAA-rated range. However, it was not apparent that the firm would return to the zero-debt policy of the past. In 1978, Richard Heckert, a Du Pont senior vice president, noted, "While we presently anticipate some further reduction in borrowings, we have considerable borrowing capacity and hence considerable flexibility."

An abrupt departure from maximum financial flexibility occurred in the summer of 1981. In July, Du Pont entered a bidding contest for Conoco, Inc., a major oil company and the fourteenth largest U.S. industrial. After a brief but frenetic battle, Du Pont succeeded in buying Conoco in August 1981. The price of almost $8 billion made the merger the largest in U.S. history and represented a premium of 77% above Conoco's preacquisition market value. With the acquisition, Du Pont virtually doubled its size and significantly increased its orientation toward undifferentiated commodity products. Both Du Pont's stock price and industry analysts responded negatively to the acquisition. Major concerns included the high price Du Pont had paid and the question of how Conoco would contribute to Du Pont's strategic objectives.

To finance the purchase of Conoco, Du Pont issued $3.9 billion in common stock and $3.85 billion in floating-rate debt. In addition, Du Pont assumed $1.9 billion of outstanding Conoco debt. The acquisition propelled Du Pont's debt ratio to nearly 40% from slightly over 20% at the end of 1980. Du Pont's bond rating was downgraded to AA, marking the first time in its history that the firm had fallen below the top rating.

The first year after the merger was a difficult one for Du Pont. Conoco's performance was hampered by declining oil prices in 1982, while an economic recession plagued the chemical industry. Although Du Pont's 1982 revenues were 2½ times 1979 sales, net income in 1982 fell below 1979 results; return on total capital was cut in half during this period, and earnings per share fell by 40%.

As Du Pont's management worked to frame and implement a coherent strategy for the merged company, they also got to work to repair the firm's extended financial condition. To reduce interest rate exposure, Du Pont refunded most of the firm's floating-rate debt with fixed-rate, long-term debt issues. Plans to reduce debt with the proceeds from the sale of $2 billion in Conoco coal and oil assets were frustrated by depressed energy prices. One analyst complained, "Du Pont managed to acquire Conoco at the peak of the oil cycle, and now they are looking at a tremendous glut of coal assets for sale that is going to make it very difficult to sell coal properties." Nevertheless, by the end of 1982, Du Pont had pared its debt ratio to 36% from the postmerger peak of 42%. Poor earnings in 1982 held interest coverage down to a near record low of 4.8. The firm retained its AA bond rating.

The increase in debt ratio accompanying the Conoco merger marked the second time in 10 years that Du Pont departed from its traditional capital structure policy. This, plus the fundamental changes in Du Pont's businesses, mandated the determination of a capital structure policy that would be feasible and appropriate for the years ahead.

Future Capital Structure Policy

Du Pont's financing policy had always been predicated on the notion of maximizing financial flexibility. This ensured that financing constraints did not interfere with the firm's competitive strategy. However, competitors differed widely from Du Pont and each other in their use of financial leverage (see Exhibit 3). Why should not Du Pont, like Dow Chemical and Celanese, reap the benefits of aggressive debt financing even if this resulted in a further reduction in its bond rating? (See Exhibit 4 for bond rating data.) Of course, electric utilities and telephone companies maintained high bond ratings despite aggressive use of debt (see Exhibit 4). While Du Pont's performance was more volatile than a company like AT&T, it was less volatile than many competitors and other industrial firms (see Exhibit 5).

In framing a debt policy, a key concern was how risky Du Pont's businesses were. The degree of business risk would help determine how much debt Du Pont could safely employ in its capital structure without unduly constraining its competitive strategy. The last 20 years had documented the increased volatility of Du Pont's basic businesses. Du Pont's competitive position and profitability had declined in many product lines. In many businesses, products were close to being undifferentiated commodities, and intense competition was common. Excess capacity and the economics of high-fixed-cost businesses pressured prices and profits. Moreover, Conoco competed in a volatile commodity business, a business in which Du Pont's management had little experience. The increased risk of Du Pont's operations argued for a relatively conservative capital structure.

Nonetheless, several factors suggested that the firm could pursue an aggressive debt policy. Du Pont was still the nation's largest chemical manufacturer, and large-scale economies were a common characteristic of chemical production processes. The firm remained the technological leader in the industry, and its success at R&D was second to none. Du Pont was pursuing capital spending programs designed to reduce costs in all business segments. The firm was widely diversified in terms of products and markets. In the past, Du Pont's economic muscle had often been constrained by aggressive antitrust policy, but the near-term future held some promise of a more benign regulatory environment. As for the impact of Conoco on Du Pont's business risk, some analysts thought the major diversification move would dampen the volatility of the firm's earnings. Edward Jefferson, who succeeded Irving Shapiro as Du Pont's chief executive officer, agreed, reasoning that the merger would "reduce the exposure of the combined companies to fluctuations in the price of energy."

Even with a recovery in gross margins, strong sales growth, and successful sales of Conoco assets, Du Pont would be forced to seek external financing each year from 1983 to 1987 (see Exhibit 6 for projections). The major reason was the need for a continued high level of capital expenditures. Capital spending was viewed as critical to Du Pont's future success because it was the key to minimizing the firm's cost position in existing products and launching new products swiftly and efficiently. In view of its importance, capital spending was essentially nondeferrable and often had to be increased rather than cut in bad times in order to redress the causes of poor performance.

Because of its large, nondeferrable financing needs, Du Pont was concerned about the cost and availability of financing (see Exhibit 7 for data on financing costs and volumes). Companies with high debt ratios and low bond ratings appeared to have some difficulty in obtaining debt financing in some years. However, firms rated A and above appeared to have little difficulty in raising funds. But compared with AAA-rated firms, the cost of debt financing was higher for A-rated firms, and the spread between A and AAA rates widened in high-interest-rate environments. In view of the importance and magnitude of Du Pont's projected financing needs, the firm was concerned about how the cost and availability of debt might affect its ability to pursue capital spending programs critical to its competitive position.

Capital Structure Policy Alternatives

One alternative for Du Pont was to restore its historical financial strength and AAA rating. Given Du Pont's substantial projected capital spending requirements, a return to zero debt was infeasible. A target ratio of debt to capital of 25% should be sufficient to ensure a high degree of financial flexibility and insulate Du Pont's competitive strategy from capital market conditions. However, achieving this debt ratio would not be easy (see Exhibit 8 for data on policy alternatives). Reducing the debt ratio from 36% in 1982 to 25% by the end of 1986 would require large equity issues in each year. Maintaining the target of 25% debt in 1987 would require additional large equity infusions. As of the end of 1982, Du Pont's stock price had yet to recover from the market's negative reaction to the Conoco merger, reinforced by the continuing recession. This raised questions concerning the terms and availability of the substantial new equity financing required to achieve a 25% debt ratio (see Exhibit 7 for equity issue data).

Although a conservative capital structure policy had the force of tradition, it was not clear that conservatism was appropriate for Du Pont in the 1980s. The cost of conservatism was clear (see Exhibit 8). Were Du Pont to abandon forever its historical conservatism and maintain a 40% target debt ratio, many measures of financial performance would benefit. For the recovery scenario projected in Exhibits 6 and 8, a high-debt policy generated higher projected earnings per share, dividends per share, and return on equity. No equity issues would be required through 1985. Equity issues in 1986 and 1987 would be much smaller than projected for the low-debt policy and thus might be more easily timed to take advantage of favorable market conditions. However, with higher financial leverage comes higher risk. In a pessimistic scenario (e.g., a recession), earnings per share and return on equity would suffer more severe declines with the high-debt policy. Other concerns were the availability of funds in all economic conditions with the high-debt alternative and the constraints limited availability might place on Du Pont's operations.

The Decision

The two decades drawing to a close in 1982 brought fundamental changes in Du Pont's businesses, culminating in the historic acquisition of Conoco. This acquisition also forced a dramatic departure from Du Pont's long-held capital structure policy. These changes both mandated and provided the opportunity for a fundamental reassessment of Du Pont's financing policy. In view of the escalation in Du Pont's debt ratio, the downgrading of its bond rating, and the negative stock market response to the Conoco merger, there was a considerable degree of uncertainty concerning Du Pont's financial policy. This underscored the importance of determining, committing to, and communicating a capital structure policy in the near future.

EXHIBIT 1 Selected Financial Data, 1965–1982 (millions of dollars except per share data)

Sources: Du Pont annual reports; Standard and Poor's Corporation.

	1965	1966	1967	1968	1969	1970	1971	1972
1. Sales	$2,999	$3,159	$3,079	$3,455	$3,632	$3,618	$3,848	$4,366
2. EBIT	767	727	574	764	709	590	644	768
3. Interest	2	4	7	7	10	11	15	20
4. Profit after taxes	407	389	314	372	356	329	356	414
5. Profit after taxes/Sales	13.6%	12.3%	10.2%	10.8%	9.8%	9.1%	9.3%	9.5%
6. After-tax return on total capital[a]	18.5%	16.6%	13.0%	14.2%	12.8%	11.1%	10.9%	12.1%
7. Return on equity	18.6%	16.8%	13.0%	14.6%	13.3%	11.8%	11.5%	12.7%
8. Earnings per share	$ 2.96	$ 2.83	$ 2.24	$ 2.66	$ 2.54	$ 2.29	$ 2.44	$ 2.83
9. Dividends per share	2.00	1.92	1.67	1.83	1.75	1.68	1.67	1.82
10. Average stock price	81.04	80.88	54.42	54.25	44.46	38.29	47.92	54.77
11. Average stock price/ Earnings per share	27.4	28.6	24.3	20.4	17.5	16.7	19.6	19.4
12. Market value/Book value	5.40	5.28	3.26	3.07	2.38	1.98	2.40	2.61
13. S&P 400 P/E	16.8	15.2	17.0	17.3	17.5	16.5	18.0	18.0
14. S&P 400 market value/ Book value	2.13	1.96	2.00	2.12	2.07	1.69	1.95	2.10

[a]After-tax return on total capital = (EBIT) (1 – Tax rate)/(All debt + Equity). Average stock price is average of year's high and low values. Per share data restated to be comparable with number of shares outstanding at December 31, 1982.

EXHIBIT 2 Selected Data Related to Funds Needs and Financial Strength, 1965–1982 (millions of dollars)

Source: Du Pont annual reports.

	1965	1966	1967	1968	1969	1970	1971	1972
Capital expenditures	$ 327	$ 531	$ 454	$ 332	$ 391	$ 471	$ 454	$ 522
Change in working capital[a]	—	(163)	121	102	154	135	(39)	63
Capital structure								
Short-term debt	$ 0	$ 0	$ 31	$ 57	$ 45	$ 56	$ 0	$ 0
	0%	0%	1.2%	2.1%	1.6%	1.9%	0%	0%
Long-term debt	$ 34	$ 58	$ 95	$ 150	$ 141	$ 160	$ 236	$ 240
	1.5%	2.4%	3.7%	5.5%	4.9%	5.3%	7.1%	6.8%
Equity	$2,190	$2,317	$2,409	$2,540	$2,685	$2,790	$3,095	$3,267
	98.5%	97.6%	95.1%	92.4%	93.5%	92.8%	92.9%	93.2%
Total capital	$2,224	$2,375	$2,535	$2,747	$2,871	$3,006	$3,331	$3,507
	100.0%	100.0%	100.0%	100.0%	100.0%	100.0%	100.0%	100.0%
Interest coverage	383.5	181.8	82	109.1	70.9	53.6	42.9	38.4
Bond rating (senior debt)	AAA	AAA	AAA	AAA	AAA	AAA	AAA	AAA

[a]Working capital investment is defined here as net working capital excluding cash, marketable securities, and short-term debt.

EXHIBIT 1 *(concluded)*

1973	1974	1975	1976	1977	1978	1979	1980	1981	1982
$5,964	$6,910	$7,222	$8,361	$9,435	$10,584	$12,572	$13,652	$22,810	$33,331
1,100	733	574	961	1,141	1,470	1,646	1,209	2,631	3,545
34	62	126	145	169	139	143	111	476	739
586	404	271	459	545	797	965	744	1,081	894
9.8%	5.8%	3.8%	5.5%	5.8%	7.5%	7.7%	5.4%	4.7%	2.7%
15.1%	9.0%	6.6%	9.7%	11.1%	13.7%	15.1%	10.9%	7.5%	6.6%
16.3%	10.7%	7.1%	11.4%	12.6%	16.7%	18.2%	13.1%	10.3%	8.2%
$ 4.01	$ 2.73	$ 1.81	$ 3.30	$ 3.69	$ 5.18	$ 6.23	$ 4.73	$ 5.81	$ 3.75
1.92	1.83	1.42	1.75	1.92	2.42	2.75	2.75	2.75	2.40
58.13	43.92	35.96	46.42	40.04	39.34	42.63	40.32	45.88	37.19
14.5	16.1	19.9	15.0	10.9	7.3	6.6	8.4	10.0	9.8
2.49	1.81	1.46	1.76	1.41	1.26	1.22	1.09	1.04	.83
13.4	9.4	10.8	10.4	9.6	8.2	7.1	8.4	8.5	10.4
1.89	1.34	1.31	1.46	1.33	1.20	1.17	1.26	1.22	1.16

EXHIBIT 2 *(concluded)*

1973	1974	1975	1976	1977	1978	1979	1980	1981	1982
$ 727	$1,008	$1,036	$ 876	$ 704	$ 714	$ 864	$1,297	$ 2,389	$ 3,195
278	561	(122)	20	243	341	438	17	2,046	(987)
$ 169	$ 320	$ 540	$ 259	$ 229	$ 258	$ 230	$ 393	$ 445	$ 319
4.2%	6.5%	10.3%	4.6%	4.0%	4.2%	3.5%	5.5%	2.6%	1.9%
$ 250	$ 793	$ 889	$1,282	$1,236	$1,058	$1,067	$1,068	$ 6,403	$ 5,702
6.2%	16.2%	16.9%	23.0%	21.4%	17.4%	16.1%	14.9%	37.0%	33.8%
$3,593	$3,782	$3,835	$4,032	$4,315	$4,761	$5,312	$5,690	$10,458	$10,850
89.6%	77.3%	72.8%	72.4%	74.6%	78.4%	80.4%	79.6%	60.4%	64.3%
$4,012	$4,895	$5,264	$5,573	$5,780	$6,077	$6,609	$7,151	$17,306	$16,871
100.0%	100.0%	100.0%	100.0%	100.0%	100.0%	100.0%	100.0%	100.0%	100.0%
32.4	11.8	4.6	6.6	6.8	10.6	11.5	10.9	5.5	4.8
AAA	AAA	AAA	AAA	AAA	AAA	AAA	AAA	AA	AA

EXHIBIT 3 Financial Data for Selected Chemical Companies, 1980 and 1982 (millions of dollars)

Source: Moody's Investors Service.

	Du Pont		Dow Chemical		Monsanto		Celanese	
	1980	1982	1980	1982	1980	1982	1980	1982
Sales	$13,652	$33,331	$10,626	$10,618	$6,574	$6,325	$3,348	$3,062
10-year compound annual sales growth rate	14.2%	22.5%	18.7%	16.0%	12.8%	11.0%	12.4%	7.4%
10-year compound annual EPS growth rate	7.5%	2.9%	19.9%	5.7%	8.3%	9.9%	8.9%	7.3%[a]
Net income	$ 744	$ 894	$ 805	$ 399	$ 149	$ 352	$ 122	$ (34)
Net income/Sales	5.4%	2.7%	7.6%	3.8%	2.3%	5.6%	3.6%	(1.1)%
Return on total capital	10.9%	6.6%	7.2%	7.9%	5.3%	8.3%	9.3%	(.3)%
Return on equity	13.1%	8.2%	18.1%	9.6%	5.5%	10.1%	11.2%	(1.2)%
Dividend payout	58.1%	64.0%	36.2%	101.7%	86.6%	45.2%	42.7%	42.7%[a]
Stock price/EPS[b]	8.4	9.9	7.6	13.7	13.7	8.3	6.3	6.7[a]
Market value/Book value[b]	109%	82.9%	138%	93.4%	72%	84.7%	67%	75.7%
Debt/Total capital	20.4%	35.7%	48.5%	42.7%	33.4%	24.5%	40.7%	42.9%
Interest coverage	10.9	4.8	2.2	1.6	2.8	7.1	4.5	3.8[a]
Bond rating (senior debt)	AAA	AA	A	A	AA	AA	A	BBB

[a]Celanese 10-year compound annual EPS growth rate, dividend payout ratio, stock price/EPS, and interest coverage use 1981 instead of 1982.
[b]Market value/book value and stock price/EPS are based on average of year's high and low stock prices.

EXHIBIT 4 Bond Rating Medians for 1979–1981

Source: Standard and Poor's Corporation.

	AAA	AA	A	BBB	BB	B
Industrial Corporations						
Interest coverage	18.25	8.57	6.56	3.82	3.27	1.76
Total debt/Capitalization	17.04%	23.70%	30.41%	38.62%	48.07%	58.77%
Electric Utilities						
Interest coverage	>4.00	3.25–4.25	2.50–3.50	<3.00	—	—
Total debt/Capitalization	<45%	42–47%	45–55%	>55%	—	—
Telephone Companies						
Interest coverage	>4.50	3.70–4.70	2.80–4.00	<3.00	—	—
Total debt/Capitalization	<40%	40–48%	48–58%	58–64%	—	—

EXHIBIT 5 Return on Total Capital

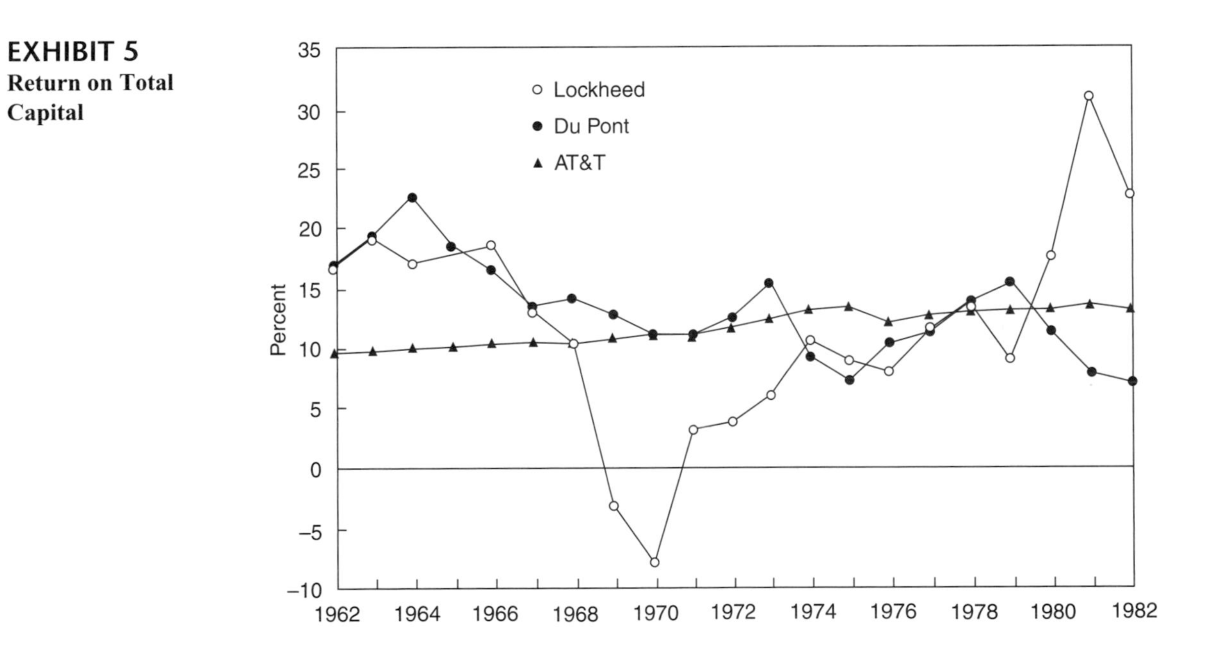

EXHIBIT 6 Financial Projections, 1983–1987 (millions of dollars)

Sources: Analysts' forecasts and casewriter's estimates.

	1983	1984	1985	1986	1987
Sources of Funds					
Net income	$1,009	$1,196	$1,444	$1,591	$1,753
Depreciation	2,101	2,111	2,212	2,396	2,667
Funds from operations	3,110	3,307	3,656	3,987	4,420
Assets sold	600	600	600	0	0
Decrease in cash	199	(200)	(200)	(150)	(150)
Other sources	74	135	135	135	135
Sources before new financing	$3,983	$3,842	$4,191	$3,972	$4,405
Uses of Funds					
Dividends	$ 571	$ 658	$ 794	$ 896	$ 964
Capital expenditures	2,767	3,386	4,039	4,202	4,667
Increase in net working capital[a]	973	414	594	587	650
Other	10	10	10	10	10
Total uses	$4,321	$4,468	$5,437	$5,695	$6,291
Net financing requirement	$ 338	$ 626	$1,246	$1,723	$1,886

Note: Assumptions are as follows: Sales are average of analysts' forecasts; average annual sales growth rate is 10%. EBIT recovers to 8.1% of sales by 1985. Net working capital (excluding cash) equals 13% of sales. Dividend payout ratio is 55%, and no dividend reductions are allowed. Net fixed assets equal 40% of sales. Depreciation is 15% of net fixed assets in the previous year.

a. Net working capital excludes cash, marketable securities and short-term debt.

EXHIBIT 7 Debt Financing Costs and Volumes, 1970–1982 (millions of dollars)

Sources: Salomon Brothers Inc., Bankers Trust Company, and Standard and Poor's Corporation.

	1970	1971	1972	1973	1974	1975	1976	1977	1978	1979	1980	1981	1982
Gross New Bond Issues by Industrials													
AAA debt					$1,650	$ 2,875	$ 700	$ 800	$ 275	$ 1,550	$ 1,750	$ 1,852	$ 543
AA debt					2,415	3,310	2,030	1,125	700	1,800	2,900	2,458	3,347
A debt					2,060	5,355	2,205	960	1,310	1,500	4,220	3,887	3,075
BBB debt					440	420	1,010	445	210	0	345	0	1,357
Common and Preferred Stock Issues													
Cash offerings	$9,200	$13,000	$13,100	$11,100	$7,400	$11,900	$13,300	$14,100	$14,600	$17,100	$28,600	$34,400	$38,700
Net[a]	6,800	13,500	13,000	9,100	4,300	10,500	10,300	6,800	(1,400)	(1,900)	18,200	12,000	16,400
Cash offerings by industrials	3,500	3,200	3,100	1,500	1,000	2,400	2,800	2,300	2,900	3,600	10,400	11,900	9,600
Maturity Distribution of New Debt Issues													
Medium-term						43%	30%	16%	21%	30%	44%	55%	62%
Long-term						57	70	84	79	70	56	45	38
Interest Rates													
90-day commercial paper	7.89%	5.12%	4.63%	8.11%	10.06%	6.41%	5.28%	5.45%	7.73%	10.72%	12.37%	15.15%	11.91%
New issue AAA debt	8.39	7.39	7.10	7.42	8.57	8.70	8.15	7.88	8.63	9.39	11.74	14.30	14.14
New issue AAA-AA spread	.26	.12	.10	.10	.20	.27	.17	.09	.14	.22	.44	.50	.38
New issue AAA-BBB spread	1.35	1.07	.71	.75	1.67	2.57	1.44	.79	.81	1.12	1.95	2.09	1.87
S&P 500 price/earnings ratio	16.5	18.0	18.0	13.4	9.4	10.8	10.4	9.6	8.2	7.1	8.4	8.5	10.4

[a]Stock offerings less stock repurchases.

EXHIBIT 8 Projected Financial Results under Two Financial Policy Alternatives, 1983–1987 (millions of dollars except per share data)

Sources: Analysts' forecasts and casewriter's estimates, based on assumptions of Exhibit 6.

	1983	1984	1985	1986	1987	1987 with 20% Lower EBIT
40% Debt Scenario						
Debt/Total capitalization	36.0%	37.1%	39.7%	40.0%	40.0%	40.0
Interest coverage[a]	3.67	3.88	3.95	3.89	3.86	3.09
Earnings per share	$4.20	$4.98	$ 6.02	$ 6.31	$ 6.62	$ 4.83
Dividends per share	$2.38	$2.74	$ 3.31	$ 3.56	$ 3.64	—
Return on total capital	7.9%	8.6%	9.3%	9.3%	9.2%	7.4%
Return on equity	9.0%	10.1%	11.5%	11.5%	11.4%	8.3%
New equity issues	$ 0	$ 0	$ 0	$ 704	$ 816	$ 816
Millions of shares sold[b]	0	0	0	11.7	13.0	13.0
25% Debt Scenario						
Debt/Total capitalization	33.8%	31.4%	28.2%	25.0%	25.0%	25.0%
Interest coverage[a]	3.91	4.60	5.57	6.23	6.17	4.94
Earnings per share	$4.13	$4.77	$ 5.41	$ 5.46	$ 5.60	$ 4.27
Dividends per share	$2.29	$2.49	$ 2.71	$ 2.72	$ 2.72	—
Return on total capital	7.9%	8.6%	9.3%	9.3%	9.2%	7.4
Return on equity	8.8%	9.8%	10.7%	10.4%	10.2%	7.8%
New equity issues	$ 398	$ 686	$1,306	$1,783	$1,271	$1,271
Millions of shares sold[b]	9.5	14.3	28.8	36.2	25.2	25.2

[a]Interest coverage is defined as EBIT/interest.

[b]Assumes new shares sold at a price-earnings ratio of 10.

Williams, 2002

"Tough times require tough decisions."

—Steven J. Malcolm, Williams Companies[1]

Steven J. Malcolm, the recently appointed president, chairman, and chief executive officer of Williams (The Williams Companies, Inc.) found himself making a number of tough decisions since taking the helm of Williams in early 2002. The Tulsa, Oklahoma, based Williams engaged in energy related businesses, including exploration and production, pipelines, energy trading, and for a while, telecommunications. The collapse of its telecommunications business, softness in the energy markets, and ongoing inquiries from regulators about its reporting and energy trading had put Williams under financial stress. Over the past six months, Williams had cut back on capital spending, planned more than a billion dollars of assets sales, slashed the firm's dividend by 95%, and raised financing in a variety of forms. Williams' priority was acknowledged to be "raising cash and access to cash."[2] In the summer of 2002, Malcolm was considering the latest in a series of decisions facing the beleaguered firm: whether to accept a secured credit agreement from Lehman Brothers and Berkshire Hathaway. Lehman Brothers was Williams' long-time financial advisor, and Berkshire Hathaway, run by the fabled investor Warren Buffett, had earlier bought pipeline assets from Williams and purchased $275 million of Williams' convertible preferred stock. The new agreement would provide Williams with funding of $900 million for one year. This one-year funding was backed by the assets of the former Barrett Resources Corporation, a company Williams had acquired in 2001, and was subject to a number of conditions. Exhibit 1 summarizes the terms of the proposed financing. Malcolm reflected on the proposed transaction and his first seven months as head of Williams.

Background on Williams

Williams had been a part of the Tulsa community since 1918, when Miller and David Williams relocated their pipeline construction business there from Arkansas. The company grew impressively from its beginnings, and many residents of Tulsa owed their fortunes to the performance of the company.[3] Williams engaged in many different types of energy activities, including the purchase, sale, transportation, and transmission

[1]Eileen O'Grady, "Williams Cos Gets $3.4 Bln from Asset Sales, Loans," *Bloomberg News,* August 1, 2002.

[2]Mark Johnson, "Williams Cos Debt Rating Is Reduced to Junk by S&P," *Bloomberg News,* July 23, 2002.

[3]Chip Cummins and Elliot Spagat, "Boom and Bust: At Williams Cos., Two Trendy Bets Yield Snake Eyes—Pipeline Concern Saw Future in Telecom, Energy Trades; Tulsa Is Burned but Loyal—Bake Goodies for the Bankers," *The Wall Street Journal,* September 5, 2002.

Post-doctoral fellow Robin Greenwood prepared this case under the supervision of Professors Joshua Coval and Peter Tufano. This case was developed from public sources. HBS cases are developed solely as the basis for class discussion. Cases are not intended to serve as endorsements, sources of primary data, or illustrations of effective or ineffective management.

Copyright © 2002 President and Fellows of Harvard College. To order copies or request permission to reproduce materials, call 1-800-545-7685, write Harvard Business School Publishing, Boston, MA 02163, or go to http://www.hbsp.harvard.edu. No part of this publication may be reproduced, stored in a retrieval system, used in a spreadsheet, or transmitted in any form or by any means—electronic, mechanical, photocopying, recording, or otherwise—without the permission of Harvard Business School.

of energy-related commodities (natural gas and liquids, crude oil, refined products, and electricity). It was also involved in exploration and refining, with several direct investments in international energy projects located in South America and Lithuania. More recently, the company had developed a large Energy Marketing and Trading business, which bought and sold a host of energy products and financial contracts on these products. This unit posted high profits between 1998 and early 2001, and as late as January 2001—before the collapse of its rival, Enron—Williams confidently predicted that this marketing and trading subsidiary would generate a minimum of $500 million in profits "under most market conditions."[4]

Part of Williams' growth during the 1990s could be attributed to the profitability of its telecommunications business. This business began in 1985, when Williams started to run optical fiber through old natural gas pipelines to deliver telecommunications services. Within a few years, they built one of the largest networks in the United States, and became the first firm to sell capacity to other phone companies. Williams sold this network in 1995 for $2.5 billion in cash to LDDS Worldcom. The remaining units formed the basis of WilTel Technology Ventures, which was later combined with other assets to form the Williams Communication Group (WCG). In October 1999, Williams listed WCG in an initial public offering (IPO) that raised approximately $680 million, in addition to $725 million raised through placements to private investors. Concurrent with the IPO, WCG raised $2.3 billion in debt, which was rated BB and BB-.[5] Finally, in early 2001, the Williams board approved the distribution of the remaining 398.5 million shares of WCG to Williams shareholders in the form of a tax-free dividend.

Exhibit 2 shows summary financial information for Williams and some of its rivals. Exhibit 3 shows financial information for the firm over the period from 1990 to mid-2002.

The Unfolding Situation in 2000–2001

Williams' problems began soon after the spinoff of WCG. The communications business had not fared well in the economic downturn, resulting in a well-publicized shakeout in the telecom sector. The biggest problem in the industry was oversupply: it was estimated that only 2 to 5% of the fiber optic lines in the United States were lit and carrying traffic—there were simply "too many people chasing too little business."[6] Bandwidth prices plummeted, with the monthly lease price of a T1 line between New York and London falling by more than 90% between 1998 and 2002.[7] Many firms reduced investment and laid off workers. For example, the telecom firms Nortel and Lucent cut

[4]"Williams Companies Sees Meeting, Exceeding '01 Estimate," Dow Jones News Service, January 3, 2001.

[5]Gracian Mack, "Williams Fiber Could Have Long-Term Glow," Redherring.com, October 2, 1999. Moody's, Standard & Poor's, and Fitch are three investment rating agencies. They evaluate the creditworthiness of bonds by judging the likelihood that a bondholder will receive the promised interest and principal payments. Bonds with high credit ratings are judged to have a high capacity to meet financial commitments. Lower ratings on bonds reflect a judgment that the investor runs the risk of failing to receive required payments of interest and principal. The top four classes of ratings (AAA/Aaa, AA/Aa, A/A, and BBB/Baa) are called "investment grade"; bonds rated below this (BB/Ba, B/B, CCC/Caa, etc.) are called speculative grade, non-investment grade, or sometimes "junk" bonds. The three firms use slightly different ratings symbols, with S&P and Fitch using ratings like BBB, and Moody's denoting these as Baa. Numbers following the rating (like B1 or B3) represent differences within grade, with 3s representing lower ratings than 1s.

[6]"Interview: Adam Quinton, Merrill Lynch, and Ivan Seidenberg, Verizon, Discuss the Telecom Industry," *CNBC: Market Week with Maria Bartiromo,* March 23, 2001 (Factiva).

[7]For example, the monthly leasing price of a DS-3 line between New York and London fell from over $80,000 to below $5,000 between January 1999 and June 2002 (source: Telegeography, http://www.telegeoraphy.com).

more than half of their staff between 2001 and 2002, and telecommunications giant WorldCom filed for bankruptcy protection in July 2002. During the first nine months of 2001, defaults in the telecommunications sector comprised the bulk of defaults in the speculative-grade bond market.[8] It became uncertain whether the newly independent, and debt-laden, Williams Communications could survive on its own under these conditions, and Williams took steps to support its former subsidiary.

Prior to the spinoff, Williams acknowledged that WCG's debt burden might prevent it from raising new funds. In March 2001, to strengthen WCG's capital structure, Williams converted a $975 million promissory note from WCG into 24.3 million newly issued shares of WCG equity, essentially replacing a debt investment in WCG with an additional equity state. Keith Bailey, then chairman of Williams Companies, Inc., stated that this would "enable Williams Communications to obtain the capital to fully execute its business strategy" and strengthen the balance sheet of the newly independent company.[9] Howard Janzen, Williams Communications president and CEO, said the agreement was a "key step" in preparation for the spinoff.[10] In addition, Williams provided indirect "credit support" for $1.4 billion of WCG's debt. These guarantees required Williams to make available proceeds of an equity issuance in the event of a WCG default or WCG's inability to raise financing to replace maturing debt. Under accounting rules, these obligations were treated as "off balance sheet," because they were contingent on actions by WCG, and thus did not appear as a liability on the firm's balance sheet. Williams would only be expected to perform on these obligations if WCG faced problems, which it soon did.

Financial conditions worsened in 2001, as news about problems in Enron Corporation's broadband unit and Global Crossing exposed significant weaknesses in the telecom sector. Although WCG had made the required interest payments, its inability to meet certain covenants constituted a breach of its lending agreements with its secured creditors.[11] On July 19, 2001, Moody's Investor Service downgraded WCG's unsecured debt rating from B2 to Caa1. In August, Standard & Poor's rating agency lowered WCG's corporate credit rating from BB- to B, reflecting "weakness in recent financial performance, lack of forward visibility, and exposure to customers whose risks are increasing."[12]

Following a disclosure by WCG that it might seek to reorganize under the U.S. bankruptcy code, Williams wrote off its investment in WCG in the third and fourth quarters of 2001. In addition, Williams took a one-time accounting charge of $1.3 billion related to guarantees and payment obligations it would be required to fulfill due to lingering ties to WCG.[13]

Ties to its former telecommunications subsidiary were not Williams' only problem. Following the collapse of Enron in late 2000 and early 2001, the future of energy trading was uncertain as market participants assessed their exposure to the former trading firm. In May 2002, one of Williams' competitors, El Paso Corp., announced it would curtail investment in, and exposure to, energy trading and instead concentrate on its natural gas business. Reliant Resources, another rival, said it would scale back its energy

[8]Quoted in Elizabeth Mooney, "Telecom Defaults Cramp Wireless Funding Options," *RCR Wireless News,* February 4, 2002. "Speculative grade" (also known as high-yield, non-investment grade or "junk") bonds are those with the weakest bond ratings, in particular, bonds with ratings of BB/Ba or worse.

[9]"Williams Makes Asset Pact," *The Journal Record,* March 1, 2001.

[10]Ibid.

[11]Ibid.

[12]"S&P—Williams Comm. Group Cut to 'B'—Outlook negative," *Market News International,* August 17, 2001.

[13]Estimated losses of $1,839 million attributable to WCG performance guarantees were partially offset by a $797.4 million benefit for income taxes. Williams reported a net loss from discontinued operations of $1,313 million in 2001.

trading after admitting impropriety in its trading practices. In June, Aquila Inc. dismissed its entire staff of 1,290 people in merchant wholesale energy.

In the second quarter of 2002, Williams Energy Marketing and Trading recorded its first loss in three years. Bill Hobbs, head of this unit, attributed the loss to a "curve shift" and the write-off of certain assets, although he admitted that business was getting more difficult: "We are operating in a mode where cash takes priority over earnings."[14]

Reflecting the firm's financial health, Moody's and Standard & Poor's downgraded the credit rating on Williams bonds three times, from Baa2 to B1.[15] In late July 2002, the yields on some of Williams' publicly traded bonds skyrocketed (see Exhibit 4). The deteriorating credit ratings and rising yields on Williams debt reflected the financial stress that the business was under. Williams executives had earlier claimed that if its credit ratings were to decline below investment grade (BBB or above), Williams' ability to participate in the energy marketing and trading business would be further limited. Hobbs, the CEO of Williams' trading unit, commented, "We have to get this credit issue resolved, otherwise we're just in a cash trading mode," i.e., the firm's traders would not be able to obtain credit from counterparties.[16] Obtaining credit was especially important when trading long-dated positions, such as "pre-pays" where counterparties pay in advance for energy products to be delivered sometimes years into the future.

Other challenges surfaced when on April 3, 2002, *The Wall Street Journal* reported that Williams Companies was facing an inquiry by the SEC about its financial reporting. State securities regulators opened a broad ranging investigation into the collapse of WCG.

Reflecting these troubles, Williams' stock price had also plummeted more than 90% in the past year, and was trading for $2.95 per share in late July 2002 (see Exhibit 5).

Despite Williams' many difficulties, its asset-based businesses, including its interstate natural gas pipelines, midstream operations, exploration, and production, all continued to meet performance expectations.[17] Between 2000 and 2001, Williams' revenues had increased $1.4 billion, due to higher gas and electric power trading margins, higher petroleum products revenues, and higher natural gas sales prices.

Time for Tough Decisions

Steven Malcolm, 53, was named CEO of the firm on January 21, 2002, and became chairman of the board in May. Malcolm was not new to Williams; he had joined the firm in 1984 and had previously served as its president and chief operating officer. He replaced the prior CEO and chairman, Keith Bailey, 59, who was retiring. On the day of Malcolm's announcement as CEO, Williams announced a regular dividend of $0.20 per share, with the press release noting that the company had paid a common stock dividend every quarter since 1974. This was the eighth dividend increase in 10 years, a streak that would soon be broken.

To raise cash, Williams made a number of important operating and financial decisions. Malcolm had a "four-pronged" plan that involved selling assets, reaching a resolution for its energy and trading book, managing and monitoring cash and businesses, and "right-sizing" Williams to reflect the new scope of operations. This plan was part

[14]Quoted in Williams Companies Conference Call, July 22, 2002. Financial Disclosure Wire.

[15]Moody's had downgraded Williams from Baa2 to B1 between May and July 2002. Standard & Poor's downgraded Williams from BBB to B+ between May and July 2002.

[16]Steven D. Jones, "Williams Cos. Finds Asset Sales Are Hard," *Dow Jones News Service,* May 31, 2002.

[17]Quoting Williams CEO Steve Malcolm in Williams teleconference call, July 22, 2002.

of Williams' broad self-described strategy to "live within its means."[18] This strategy was carried out throughout 2002.

One element of Williams' strategy was an aggressive program of asset sales. In December 2001, the firm announced that it would sell between $250 million and $750 million in assets during 2002. Actual asset sales outstripped this early estimate, and by May 2002, the firm had completed transactions selling $1.7 billion in assets, and announced its intention to sell an additional $1.5 to $3.0 billion over the next 12 months.[19] The day after announcing the extra planned asset sales, Williams' stock fell 10.6%. As examples of these sales, in July 2002, Williams announced plans to sell refineries in Tennessee and Alaska for an estimated $1 billion. Williams planned to sell other non-core assets, including all of its TravelCenters and its ethanol business. Williams even decided to sell its 123 piece corporate art collection, started by John Williams in the late 1960s.[20] Planned and completed asset sales are summarized in Exhibit 6.

Capital expenditures were a major use of Williams' cash, and their reduction was another part of Williams' plan. In December 2001, Williams announced that it planned to cut its 2002 capital spending by 25%, or $1 billion, to a total of $3 billion. Williams management aimed to cut its capital expenditure budget for 2003 from about $1.5–$2 billion to about $700 million per year.[21] Cutting investment was challenging, since much of it had been planned in the previous year, and some was required to maintain Williams' many assets. Nevertheless, Williams was able to reduce its capital expenditure needs in conjunction with its asset sales. For example, by selling its Kern River facility, Williams not only received cash and off-loaded some of its debt, but also shed responsibility for more than $1 billion in planned capital expenditures.

Third, Williams was in need of new financing. On December 19, 2001, *The Wall Street Journal* reported that Williams would be taking steps to bolster its balance sheet, which involved issuing $1 billion of equity-linked security called FELINE PACS. Issued in January 2002, these complicated securities consisted of a package consisting of senior debt securities (notes) and "equity purchase contracts." The notes had a nominal term of five years and paid 9% per annum in quarterly payments. The "equity purchase contract" element of the securities effectively required the holder to pay $25 to Williams in three years—probably by surrendering their notes—and to receive a number of shares of Williams' stock determined by the contract.[22] In a separate transaction, Williams sold preferred stock to Berkshire Hathaway, as described below.

Another part of Williams' strategy to raise cash was to reach "resolution" on its Williams Energy Marketing and Trading division, estimated by Williams to be worth $2.2 billion.[23] Williams publicly stated that it hoped to find a joint venture partner in the business; however, the complexity of negotiating and managing joint ventures made this difficult to accomplish.

As a final measure, in July 2002 Williams announced that it would cut its dividend by 95%, from 20 cents to 1 cent per share. The cut was expected to save the company

[18]"Williams CEO: Asset Sales Needed to Reach Solvency in Two Years," Inside F.E.R.C.'s Gas Market Report, September 27, 2002.

[19]"Round Two: Williams to Cut Costs, Sell Assets," *Gas Daily*, May 29, 2002.

[20]Tom Droege, "Embattled Tulsa, Okla.-Based Energy Company to Auction Its Art," *Tulsa World*, August 30, 2002.

[21]Williams Companies Conference Call, July 22, 2002, Financial Disclosure Wire.

[22]The holder would receive one share if the Williams share price was $41.25 or less in three years, but a smaller number of shares if the price of Williams was above $41.25.

[23]Williams estimate. Quoted in Williams Companies Conference Call, July 22, 2002. Financial Disclosure Wire.

about $95 million in the third quarter.[24] CEO Steve Malcolm explained, "Reducing our common stock dividend is one of a series of prudent and realistic steps we have taken and are taking to address our current business environment."[25]

Warren Buffett and Berkshire Hathaway

Billionaire Warren Buffett, the legendary "Oracle from Omaha," was the CEO of the insurance and holding company, Berkshire Hathaway (see Exhibit 7). A student of Benjamin Graham—the so-called father of value investing—Buffett had made a career buying assets at rock-bottom prices and holding them until they paid off. Oftentimes, he provided a "lifeline" to companies experiencing financial distress, such as the once bankrupt Fruit of the Loom. Most of his investments were long-term—Buffett claimed that he would not purchase a company for which he could not forecast the balance sheet in ten or twenty years. He summarized his investment strategy at an annual meeting: "Work out how much it will pay out from now until Judgment Day, then discount it back and buy it cheaper."[26]

Between 1997 and 2000, while many investors were pouring money into Internet stocks, Berkshire Hathaway stuck to more traditional businesses such as timber and insurance, claiming that the value of technology stocks had become "decoupled from the values of the businesses that underlay them."[27] Following the collapse of the Internet bubble, Buffett, who was flush with cash, began purchasing assets in the troubled energy industry. Buffett publicly announced that he might spend as much as $15 billion in this sector over the next few years.[28] Credit-crunched energy companies seeking cash found a ready buyer in Buffet when other alternatives were scarce. This was felt to be ideal for Buffett, who was said to like to be the "only buyer in the fire-sale."[29] Buffett started acquiring energy assets in 2000, when he took a controlling stake in Iowa based MidAmerican Energy for $1.24 billion.

In March 2002, MidAmerican purchased the 926 mile Kern River pipeline from Williams for $960 million in cash and debt, or approximately 8 times the expected cash flow of $120 million in 2002.[30] MidAmerican paid $450 million in cash to Williams and assumed debt of $510 million. The pipeline carried gas from Wyoming to California and was undergoing a massive expansion project aimed at doubling its capacity. As the new owner of the pipeline, MidAmerican would assume responsibility for a projected $1.26 billion in capital expenditures. Commenting on the deal, Buffett said "Williams has all the fundamentals in place—solid assets, strong demand for its products and a reputation for excellent customer service."[31] Malcolm said that the transaction with Berkshire would allow Williams to "reduce debt and increase cash

[24]Russel Ray, "Williams Cos. Credit Rating Is Downgraded to Junk Status," *Tulsa World,* July 23, 2002.

[25]Williams Conference Call, July 22, 2002.

[26]Berkshire Hathaway annual meeting, May 2002.

[27]Quoted from Warren Buffet's annual letter to shareholders of Berkshire Hathaway, 2000.

[28]Dan Moreau, "Buffett Uses Depressed Market to Mine Energy and Telecom Fields. Should You Try too?" *Investors Business Daily,* September 24, 2002.

[29]John Olson, energy analyst with Sanders Morris Harris Group. Quoted in Schlegel, Darrin, "Buffett Again Stirs Up Street; Energy Sector Full of Dry Holes? Not for This Billionaire," *Houston Chronicle,* November 15, 2002.

[30]Analyst estimate of $120 million from CSFB. Source: Williams Companies Company Update, Credit Suisse Equity Research, March 8, 2002.

[31]Ibid.

flow. [. . .] The sale of our Kern River system is an important building block in achieving the financial flexibility to expand our business now and in the future."[32]

Buffett also invested directly in Williams in early 2002. On March 17, 2002, one of Mid American's subsidiaries bought 1.47 million shares of Williams convertible preferred stock for $275 million, or $187.50 per share. The preferred stock paid a dividend of 9.875% per annum. The terms of the preferred stock allowed the holder to convert one share of preferred stock into 10 shares of Williams common stock at any time. (On March 27, the date the deal was closed, the price of Williams stock closed at $23.41 per share.) Commenting on the deal, Williams chairman Keith Bailey called it a "strong endorsement of our strategy and our future prospects for solid business performance."[33]

The Proposed Lehman-Berkshire Hathaway Deal

Williams had substantial amounts of short-term and long-term debt maturing in the second half of 2002 (see Exhibit 8). In addition, its credit and commercial paper facilities (firms held in reserve to raise additional short-term financing as needed) would need to be renewed (and presumably renegotiated) later in the year. On July 22, Williams identified cash on hand of about $450 million and one undrawn revolving credit facility (with a three-year term) for $700 million.[34]

One possible source of funding was the deal offered by a group of investors led by Warren Buffet's Berkshire Hathaway and by Lehman Brothers. Berkshire and Lehman offered to provide Williams with a one-year $900 million loan, which would provide temporary relief, and would result in a greater chance of Williams being able to secure a credit facility of $800 million.[35]

Under the proposal, Buffett and a subsidiary of Lehman Brothers would each advance Williams $450 million for a period of one year. The funds would go to Williams Production RMT (RMT), a wholly-owned subsidiary of Williams. The loan was guaranteed by Williams, Williams Production Holdings LLC, and certain RMT subsidiaries. RMT's major assets were the natural gas properties in the Rocky Mountain region, held by the former Barrett Resources Corporation, which Williams acquired in 2001 in a deal estimated to be worth $2.8 billion.

In addition to repayment of the principal in one year, Williams would be required to make a number of payments (see Exhibit 1). These included interest of about 5.8%, payable quarterly. An additional payment of 14% of the principal was to be paid in cash at maturity. Finally, the loan included a "deferred set-up fee" of at least 15%. If Williams did not sell the Barrett assets, it would owe 15% of the loan balance as part of this fee. If Williams were to sell its assets in Barrett, the fee would be increased to the larger of 15% of the loan balance or 15%–21% of the net sale price. The one-year loan also had a number of other terms. Accepting the terms of the deal would be another step to restoring liquidity at Williams. But the financing was not cheap. Malcolm pondered whether it was worth it.

[32]"The Williams Companies Announced Sale of Kern River Pipeline to MidAmerican Energy and of Midwestern Petroleum Pipeline to Its Energy Partners Subsidiary," Foster Natural Gas Report #2377, March 7, 2002.

[33]Quoted in "Williams Raises $275 Million in Sale of Cumulative Convertible Preferred Stock to Berkshire Hathaway Unit," *PR Newswire,* March 7, 2002.

[34]Williams Companies Conference Call, July 22, 2002, Financial Disclosure Wire.

[35]Howald, Gordon A. and Eric Cheng, "U.S. Equity Investment Research Comments," Credit Lyonnais Securities Inc., July 30, 2002.

EXHIBIT 1
Terms of the Proposed Short-Term Credit Agreement

Source: Summarized by casewriter from Williams Companies 10Q, September 30, 2002, and other public filings.

Lender:	**Lehman Brothers, Inc. and Berkshire Hathaway.**
Borrower:	Williams Production RMT Company (RMT), a subsidiary of Williams.
Maturity:	July 25, 2003
Initial Principal:	$900 million
Guaranties/Security:	The loan is guaranteed by Williams Companies as well as by certain subsidiaries. It is also secured by the capital stock and assets of RMT, which primarily consist of the oil and gas properties of Barrett Resources, which Williams acquired in 2001 for $2.8 billion.[a]
Required payments:	In addition to the repayment of principal, the borrower was required to make the following payments: (a) Williams owes cash interest payable quarterly at the Eurodollar rate plus 4% per annum, or about 5.8%. (b) Williams owes additional interest of 14% per annum, which is accrued and added to the principal balance, but not paid in cash until maturity. (c) Williams owes a "deferred set-up fee." This fee is equal to 15% of the loan amount if the majority of RMT's assets are not sold by the maturity date. If there is a sale, the fee would be the larger of 15% of the loan amount or 15%–21% of the purchase price less the indebtedness of RMT. (The latter percentage begins at 15% and steps up by 1% each 60 days to a maximum of 21%.)
Covenants:	Williams must: (1) maintain interest coverage ratio[b] of greater than 1.5 to 1; (2) maintain a fixed charge coverage ratio[c] of at least 1.15 to 1; (3) limit certain restricted payments, including redemption of capital stock of Williams; (4) limit capital expenditures in excess of $300 million (except for capital expenditures of borrower, RMT); (5) give the lenders attendance rights to all of its board of directors meetings, as well as any meetings of any committees of the board; (6) limit intercompany indebtedness, and (7) maintain parent liquidity[d] of at least $600 million, stepping up to $750 million over the year. If a default were to occur with respect to parent liquidity, Williams would have to, within two days, retain Lehman Brothers to sell RMT, with such a sale to be completed within 75 days. Liquidity projections to be provided weekly until the maturity date [. . .] In the event of a company sale, the loan was required to be prepaid in full.
Other pre-conditions to closing:	(1) On the Closing Date, Parent was required to borrow at least $5,000,000 under its $700,000,000 revolving credit facility. (2) The Chief Financial Officer of Williams had to certify that the Company was solvent and would continue to be solvent after giving effect to this loan.

[a]A secured loan is a loan backed by the assets of the borrower. The assets can be forfeited to the lender if the borrower fails to make payments on the loan, or meet other prespecified conditions.
[b]Interest coverage is the ratio of earnings before interest and taxes to interest expense.
[c]Fixed charge ratio is the ratio of earnings before interest and taxes, plus fixed charges before tax, divided by the fixed charges plus interest. The ratio indicates a firm's ability to satisfy fixed financing expenses, such as leases.
[d]Liquidity indicates the availability of cash and other short-term assets.

EXHIBIT 2 Selected Financial Data on the Williams Companies and Its Competitors ($ millions)

Source: Compustat

	The Williams Companies				Dynegy[a]				Dominion Resources				Murphy Oil			
	1998	1999	2000	2001	1998	1999	2000	2001	1998	1999	2000	2001	1998	1999	2000	2001
Revenue	7,452	8,593	10,110	11,035	14,258	15,430	29,445	42,242	6,086	5,520	9,260	10,558	1,694	2,037	4,614	4,467
EBITDA	1,481	1,619	2,673	3,389	243	343	1,130	1,517	1,825	2,027	2,705	3,030	218	398	684	769
Depreciation and amortization	646	742	832	798	113	129	389	454	734	716	1,176	1,245	213	215	228	255
Non-operating income and special items	(72)	107	583	(271)	128	124	331	153	426	91	95	126	5	24	38	32
Interest expense	515	668	1,010	787	83	95	281	279	612	574	1,024	997	18	28	30	39
Income tax expense	110	161	554	630	50	75	261	269	306	259	183	370	6	59	160	175
Minority interest and preferred dividends	(3)	(4)	(12)	68	17	17	64	25	63	18	2	0	0	0	0	0
Net Income	140	159	873	835	108	151	466	643	536	551	415	544	–14	120	306	331
Extraordinary items	(19)	60	(349)	(1,313)[b]	0	0	0	2	0	–255	21	0	0	0	–9	0
Net Income after extraordinary items	120	219	524	(478)	108	151	466	645	536	296	436	544	–14	120	297	331
Cash and marketable securities	503	2,527	1,606	1,301	28	45	86	218	426	280	360	730	28	34	133	83
Total current assets	3,532	6,517	15,477	12,938	2,117	2,805	10,150	9,507	2,285	2,192	5,866	5,354	437	593	817	599
Total assets	18,647	25,289	40,197	38,906	5,264	6,525	21,406	24,874	17,517	17,747	29,348	34,369	2,164	2,446	3,134	3,259
Current liabilities	4,439	5,772	16,804	13,495	2,026	2,539	9,405	8,555	3,519	2,999	7,592	7,478	381	488	745	560
Debt in current liabilities[c]	1,443	1,575	3,710	2,461	135	192	116	402	1,924	1,406	3,573	3,213	8	0	37	48
Deferred taxes	2,061	2,582	2,828	3,690	318	335	1,426	1,608	2,014	1,845	2,967	3,940	125	154	230	303
Long-term debt	6,366	9,235	10,342	9,501	1,247	1,534	3,733	4,324	5,456	7,321	10,486	13,251	333	393	525	521
Other liabilities	1,524	1,938	4,141	6,177	545	808	3,244	4,165	524	321	802	948	347	353	375	377
Total liabilities	1,725	2,508	3,581	3,134	4,136	5,216	17,808	18,652	11,512	12,486	21,847	25,617	1,186	1,388	1,875	1,761
Total shareholders' equity	4,257	5,761	6,082	6,044	1,128	1,309	3,598	6,222	6,005	5,261	7,501	8,752	978	1,057	1,260	1,498
Market value of equity	13,341	13,287	17,573	13,152	N/A[a]	N/A[a]	13,306	6,105	9,133	7,489	15,939	15,792	1,855	2,580	2,723	3,808
Cash flow from operations	613	1,534	594	1,783	251	9	438	811	1,207	1,255	1,343	2,414	321	369	748	636
Cash flow from investing activity	(2,040)	(1,970)	(2,337)	(3,543)	(295)	(319)	(1,304)	(3,413)	(650)	(1,542)	(2,597)	(4,193)	(381)	(349)	(619)	(642)
Capital expenditures	1,708	1,795	1,513	1,922	299	365	769	1,845	624	737	1,385	2,168	389	387	512	814
Cash flow from financing activity	1,809	880	2,012	2,047	50	327	907	2,734	(453)	141	1,334	1,905	65	(13)	(25)	(41)
Long-term debt/EBITDA	4.30	5.70	3.87	2.80	5.13	4.47	3.30	2.85	2.99	3.61	3.88	4.37	1.53	0.99	0.77	0.68
EBITDA interest coverage	2.88	2.42	2.65	4.31	41.03	2.56	1.22	4.05	2.48	3.18	1.98	2.71	167.50	7.76	13.30	17.42
LT Debt/(LT Debt + Equity)	0.32	0.41	0.37	0.42	N/A	N/A	0.22	0.41	0.37	0.49	0.40	0.46	0.15	0.13	0.16	0.12
Standard & Poor's Long-term Issuer Rating	BBB–	BBB	BBB	BBB+	BBB+	BBB+	BBB+	BBB+	A–	A–	BBB+	BBB+	A–	A–	A–	A–

[a]On June 4, 1998, NGC Corporation announced it changed its name to Dynegy. Dynegy merged with Illinova Corp on February 2, 2000.

[b]Williams recorded a write-off of $1.31 billion at the end of 2001. This includes a loss before income taxes of $271 million, estimated losses attributable to probable performance on WCG guarantee obligations of $1,839 million, and a benefit for income taxes of $797 million.

[c]Debt in current liabilities is the sum of short-term debt and the portion of long-term debt maturing within one year.

EXHIBIT 3 Williams Operating History and Capital Structure ($ millions)

Source: Compustat (1992–2001) and casewriter summary of June 30, 2002, 10-Q statement.

	1992	1993	1994	1995	1996	1997	1998	1999	2000	2001	Year to Date June 30, 2002
Revenue	$2,448	$2,438	$1,751	$2,856	$3,531	$4,410	$7,452	$8,593	$10,110	$11,035	$4,414
EBITDA	452	584	465	1,002	1,271	1,425	1,481	1,619	2,673	3,389	666
Depreciation and amortization	184	211	150	369	411	500	646	742	832	798	0
Non-operating income	66	170	78	50	45	22	(72)	107	583	(271)	490
Interest expense	162	166	146	278	360	405	515	668	1,010	787	483
Income tax expense	44	145	82	102	183	178	110	161	554	630	(81)
Minority interest and preferred	15	12	9	19	10	24	(3)	(4)	(12)	68	77
Net Income	114	220	156	284	352	341	140	159	873	835	(302)
Extraordinary items	10	0	82	1,019	0	(79)	(19)	60	(349)	(1,313)	(16)
Net income after extraordinary items	124	220	238	1,303	352	262	120	219	524	(478)	(318)
Cash and equivalents	212	64	36	90	115	81	503	2,527	1,606	1,301	773
Total current assets	743	627	1,457	1,344	1,890	2,256	3,532	6,517	15,477	12,938	12,374
Total assets	4,982	5,020	5,226	10,495	12,419	13,879	18,647	25,289	40,197	39,906	37,566
Current liabilities	978	733	1,474	2,050	2,199	3,027	4,439	5,772	16,804	13,495	12,493
Debt due within 1 year	165	54	890	320	329	734	1,443	1,575	3,710	2,461	2,347
Deferred taxes	571	625	663	1,568	1,627	1,719	2,061	2,582	2,828	3,690	3,421
Long-term debt	1,683	1,605	1,308	2,874	4,377	4,565	6,366	9,235	10,342	9,501	11,972
Other liabilities	232	334	276	816	795	996	1,524	1,938	4,141	6,177	4,062
Total liabilities	3,464	3,296	3,721	7,308	8,998	10,307	14,390	19,528	34,115	32,862	31,947
Total shareholder equity	1,518	1,724	1,506	3,187	3,421	3,572	4,257	5,761	6,082	6,044	5,618
Mkt value equity	1,802	2,506	2,276	4,456	5,887	9,109	13,341	13,287	17,573	13,152	1,524
Number of common shares (×1,000)	45,922	102,790	90,605	101,561	156,982	319,618	427,772	434,734	440,015	515,362	516,512
Cash flow from operations	254	350	368	829	710	920	613	1,488	506	1694	(872)
Income before extraordinary	128	232	165	299	362	351	147	162	873	835	(226)
Change in working capital	(47)	(35)	(136)	91	(64)	122	(212)	34	(248)	232	(647)[a]
Extraordinary items	0	0	179	0	0	(171)	(9)	0	(32)	(89)	(507)[b]
Depreciation, amortization, & other	173	153	160	438	412	618	687	1,292	(87)	715	508
Cash flow from investing	(511)	(277)	(427)	585	(1,420)	(1,271)	(2,040)	(5,276)	(4,165)	(4,994)	(717)
Net change in investments	(19)	0	81	75	(77)	(134)	(470)	(696)	(506)	(574)	(290)
Capital expenditure	(586)	(529)	(326)	(828)	(819)	(1,162)	(1,708)	(3,513)	(4,904)	(1,922)	(936)
Acquisitions and divestments	30	295	(55)	(831)	(306)	13	34	(88)	(726)	(1,343)	551
Other	64	(44)	(127)	2,168	(218)	13	105	455	620	(1,155)	(41)
Cash flow from financing	421	(220)	31	(1,359)	734	317	1,809	4,377	3,789	3,391	1,061
Net change in common stock	242	63	(387)	74	20	63	78	1,609	75	1,411	25
Net change in debt	264	(192)	152	(610)	609	453	1,681	2,886	3,262	1,095	840
Dividends	(83)	(89)	(94)	(119)	(158)	(182)	(261)	(264)	(266)	(341)	(207)
Other	(2)	(2)	360	(704)	263	(18)	310	146	717	1,226	403
Standard & Poor's long-term credit rating	BB+	BB+	BB+	BBB–	BBB–	BBB–	BBB–	BBB	BBB	BBB+	BBB

[a]Includes a decline in cash of $567 million due to an increase in accounts and notes receivable, and a decline in cash of $170 million due to increases in restricted cash, cash required to be on deposit by lenders.
[b]Payment obligations to Williams Communications Group, net of estimated tax loss.

EXHIBIT 4
Williams Bond Yields and Credit Ratings

Source: Datastream. The figure shows the yield on Williams 7⅝% debt issued in 1999 and maturing in 2019.

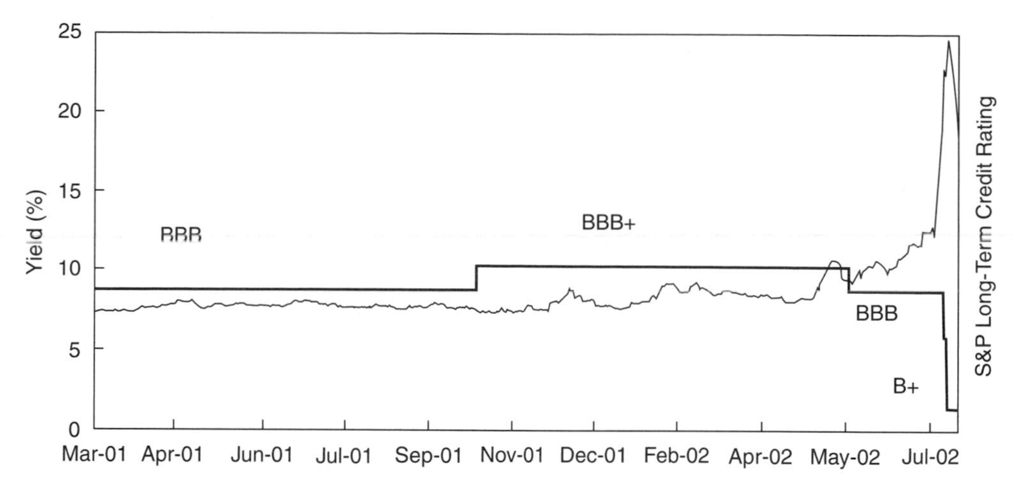

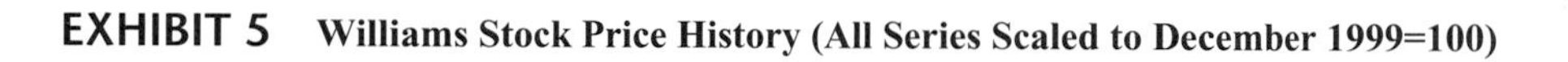

EXHIBIT 5 Williams Stock Price History (All Series Scaled to December 1999=100)

Source: Center for Research in Securities Prices (CRSP).

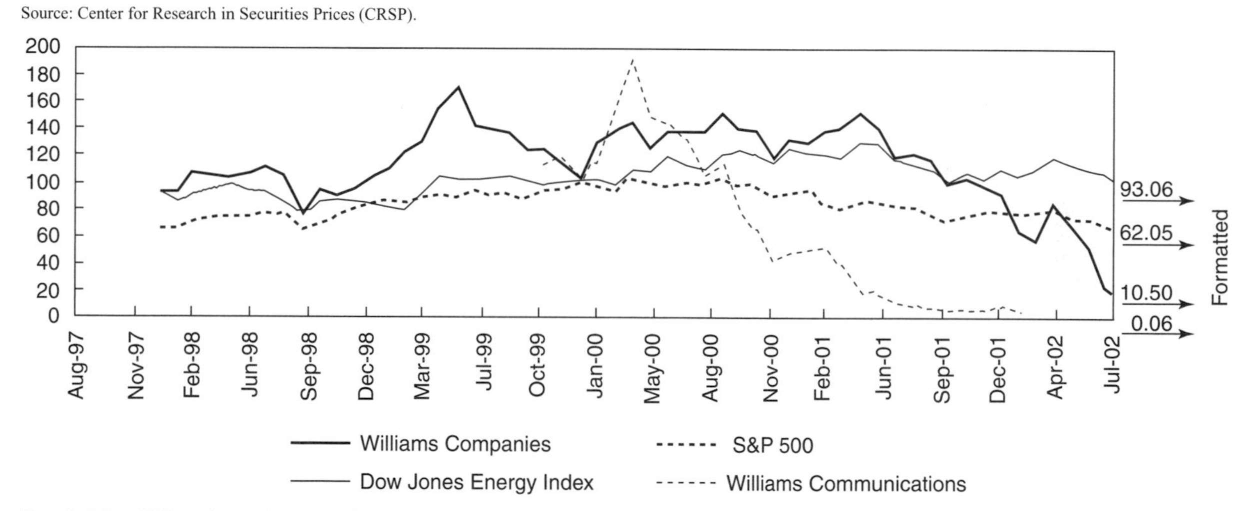

Notes: In dollars, Williams Companies closed at $2.95 on July 31, 2002. The graph shows the series scaled to December 1999=100. Williams Communications closed at $0.01. Relative values on July 31, 2002: (a)Dow Jones Energy Index=93.06, (b)S+P 500=62.05, (c)Williams=10.50, (d)Williams Communications=.06.

EXHIBIT 6 Williams Companies Asset Sales Announced Prior to July 30, 2002 ($ millions)

Source: Compiled by casewriter from listings on The Williams Companies Web page, <http://www.Williams.com>, accessed in October 2002.

Asset	Description	Purchaser	Date Announced	Closing Date	Transaction Value in Millions	Cash Proceeds in Millions	Debt Assumed in Millions
Completed:							
South Texas Gas Assets	Gas gathering/processing	Enbridge Inc.	10/11/01	01/04/02	$9	$9	
South Texas Gathering Systems	Gas gathering	Hurd Inv./Copano Energy	01/31/02	01/31/02	$6	$6	
Kern River Pipeline	Natural gas pipeline	MidAmerican/Berkshire Hathaway	03/07/02	03/27/02	$960	$450	$510
Williams Pipeline[a]	Refined products pipeline	Williams Energy Partners	03/08/02	04/11/02	$1,000	$674	
Wind River Reserves	Gas production	Undisclosed	04/01/02	04/01/02	$73	$73	
Gulf Properties	Offshore coastal leases	Energy Resource Tech/ Cal Dive	06/17/02	06/17/02	$6	$6	
Announced but not closed:							
South Texas Gas Assets	Regulated gas transmission	Enbridge Inc.	10/11/01		$41	$41	
Intention announced:							
Soda Ash	Soda ash mining operation		03/22/02				
Travel Centers	Retail marketing		05/22/02				
Bio-energy	Ethanol		05/22/02				
Memphis and Alaska refineries	Refineries		06/18/02				

[a]Remaining value of $326 million received in Class B units of limited partnership interest in WEG.

EXHIBIT 7
Financial Statements of Berkshire Hathaway, Inc. ($ millions)

Source: Berkshire Hathaway annual reports.

	1998	1999	2000	2001
Assets				
Cash and equivalents	$13,582	$3,835	$5,263	$5,313
Investments:				
Securities with fixed maturities	21,246	30,222	32,567	36,509
Equity securities and other	39,761	39,508	39,256	30,649
Receivables	7,224	8,558	11,764	11,926
Inventories	767	844	1,275	2,213
Investments in MidAmerican Energy Holdings Company	0	0	1,719	1,826
Assets of finance and financial products businesses	16,989	24,229	16,829	41,591
Property, plant, and equipment	1,509	1,903	2,699	4,776
Goodwill of acquired businesses	18,570	18,281	18,875	21,407
Other assets	2,589	4,036	5,545	6,542
Total assets	$122,237	$131,416	$135,792	$162,752
Liabilities and Shareholders' Equity				
Losses and loss adjustment expense	23,012	26,802	30,022	40,716
Unearned premiums	3,324	3,718	3,885	4,814
Accounts payable, accruals, and other liabilities	7,182	7,458	8,374	9,626
Income taxes	11,762	9,566	10,125	7,021
Borrowings under investment agreements and other debt	2,385	2,465	2,663	3,485
Liabilities of finance and financial products businesses	15,525	22,223	14,730	37,791
Minority interest	1,644	1,423	1,269	1,349
Total shareholders' equity	57,403	57,761	61,724	57,950
Total liabilities and shareholders equity	$122,237	$131,416	$132,792	$162,752
Statement of Cash Flows				
Cash from Operations	657	2,200	2,947	6,574
Cash from Investing	12,713	(12,598)	(2,271)	(11,694)
Cash From Financing	61	367	470	6,014
S&P Long-term domestic issuer credit rating	AAA	AAA	AAA	AAA
Market value of equity	100,246	95,424	75,286	82,880

EXHIBIT 8
Williams Debt Obligations Circa June 30, 2002 ($ millions)

Source: Williams 10Q Statement, June 30, 2002.

Maturity	Long-Term Debt	Short-Term Debt[a]
July 2002–June 2003	$1,636[b]	$711[c]
July 2003–December 2003	$434	
2004	$1,905	
2005	$255	
2006	$1,129	
2007	$1,520	
2008–2010	$491	
2011–2015	$2,119	
2016–2022	$1,608	
2023–2032	$2,513	
Total	$11,972	$711

[a]Williams also had access to an unused revolving credit facility of $700 million. This was a short-term debt facility that Williams had not yet accessed.
[b]A total of $500 million was expected to mature on July 31 and August 1, 2002.
[c]$300 million of this balance matured on July 31, 2002, with the remainder maturing in October.

EXHIBIT 9A Market Conditions: Monthly Issuance of Debt ($ billions) by Credit Rating, January 1997–July 2002

Source: Securities Data Corporation. Represents the proceeds of public debt offerings. For example, the dark line represents the monthly issuance volume of bonds rates BB.

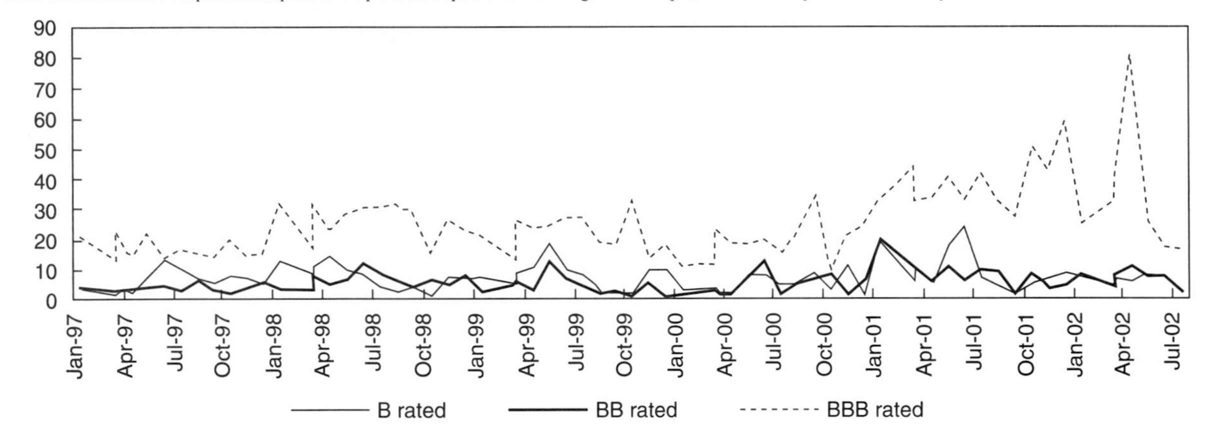

EXHIBIT 9B Interest Rates (in percent) for Long-Maturity Bonds, January 1997–July 2002

Source: Casewriter calculations from Lehman Brothers bond database and Federal Reserve Board.

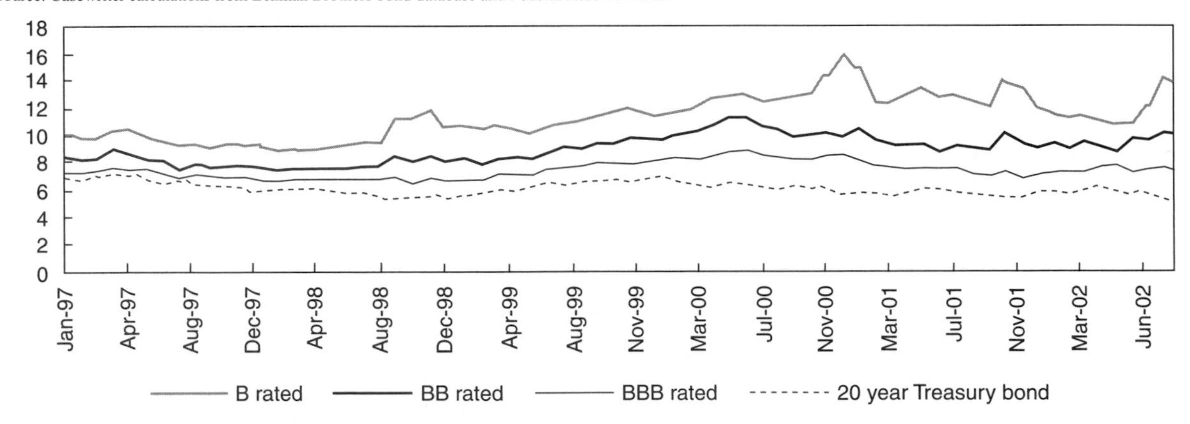

The Loewen Group, Inc. (Abridged)

In March 1999, John Lacey and the management team at the Loewen Group, Inc., had to decide what course of action to take in light of the company's imminent financial difficulties. On January 22, 1999, Lacey, a renowned turnaround specialist, was appointed chairman of Loewen, the second largest death care company in North America. Headquartered in Burnaby, British Columbia, Loewen owned over 1,100 funeral homes and more than 400 cemeteries in the U.S. and Canada; it also owned 32 funeral homes in the United Kingdom. The company had come a long way since its modest beginnings in Canada, where Ray Loewen, the founder (and, until recently, chairman and CEO), started out helping his father run the family funeral business in the late 1950s. During the last two decades, Loewen Group had grown explosively, mainly by acquiring small independent funeral homes and cemeteries in densely populated urban markets; in recent years the company had also acquired several large established funeral chains. Over the last five years alone, consolidated revenues had grown by nearly 30 percent a year, on average, from $303 million to over $1.1 billion.

Despite its impressive growth, the company faced a major financial crisis. It lost $599 million for 1998, compared to earning $43 million the previous year. Loewen's ongoing acquisitions program had been aggressively financed with debt. At year-end 1998, total debt stood at more than $2.3 billion—more than seven times the amount outstanding five years earlier. Loewen's common stock, which was simultaneously traded on the New York, Toronto, and Montreal stock exchanges, had ended the year at around $8 in New York, down from roughly $40 at the end of 1996.

Confronted with the company's mounting difficulties, in October 1998 the Board of Directors replaced Ray Loewen as CEO; soon thereafter, with the appointment of John Lacey, he was also replaced as chairman. The company also took some steps to raise profitability and cash flows. It consolidated various administrative functions at corporate headquarters and cut management overhead. It reviewed its pricing policies. Finally, it hired investment bankers to explore various financing options, including asset sales, strategic partnerships, and outside capital investments in the company. However, the company's situation continued to worsen, and in mid-February 1999 Standard & Poor's downgraded Loewen's public bonds from B+ to B–, its fourth downgrade in less than a year. Loewen's stock price dropped 38% that day. In addition, Loewen would almost surely violate certain covenants in its bank debt as a result of the company's 1998 financial performance, making it necessary to restructure the debt. Overall, in the twelve months prior to February 1999, Loewen's stock price fell by about 92%, to $1.93, and its bond prices fell by 30%.

This is an abridged version of an earlier case, The Loewen Group, Inc., HBS No. 201-062, which Professor Stuart Gilson prepared with the assistance of Research Associate Jose Camacho as the basis for class discussion rather than to illustrate either effective or ineffective handling of an administrative situation. Material in this case and in the original comes from published sources (public company documents and the general business press) and draws on research by David Gallo, Ian Reynolds, and Collin Roche (all HBS Class of 2000), as reported in their paper, "The Loewen Group: An Autopsy of a Chapter 11 Death Care Company."

Copyright © 2001 President and Fellows of Harvard College. To order copies or request permission to reproduce materials, call 1-800-545-7685, write Harvard Business School Publishing, Boston, MA 02163, or go to http://www.hbsp.harvard.edu. No part of this publication may be reproduced, stored in a retrieval system, used in a spreadsheet, or transmitted in any form or by any means—electronic, mechanical, photocopying, recording, or otherwise—without the permission of Harvard Business School.

Loewen had not yet missed any payments on its debt, and had approximately $30 million of cash on hand. However, this would not be sufficient to meet several large interest and principal payments that were due over the coming months. A payment default would only make negotiations with creditors more difficult, and increase the likelihood of bankruptcy. This possibility would no doubt weigh heavily on the managers' minds as they turned to the important task of restructuring the company's debts.

The Death Care Business

The primary activities of death care firms include the provision of funeral, burial, and cremation services, and related products like cemetery plots, caskets, urns, and gravesite markers. Funeral services and cemetery plots can be sold either on an "at-need" basis (i.e., at the time of death), or on a "prearranged" or "pre-need" basis. In the latter case, payment for a funeral service or cemetery plot is made in advance, and the proceeds are either held in trust or invested in an insurance policy (that names the death care firm as beneficiary).

In 1999 the death care industry was highly fragmented, with approximately 22,000 funeral homes and 9,600 commercial cemeteries in the U.S. Most of these were small family-owned concerns that served their local communities, where reputation and personal relationships were critically important in generating future business. The largest firms in the industry were, like Loewen, publicly traded, and had achieved this scale by acquiring hundreds of independent funeral homes and cemeteries. At the end of 1998, the four largest firms (Service Corporation, Loewen, Stewart Enterprises, and Carriage Services) collectively owned 2,986 funeral homes and 1,083 cemetery properties in the U.S., but this represented only 13.5% and 11.3%, respectively, of the U.S. market. (They also owned businesses outside the U.S.) Exhibit 1 provides financial data for the major firms in the industry and Exhibit 2 shows their stock price performance.

Aggregate revenues in the death care industry were relatively predictable. One reason was that death rates were largely driven by demographic factors that did not vary significantly from year to year. Since 1960, the number of deaths in the U.S. had increased at an annually compounded rate of 0.8% a year. Occasional large deviations from this rate were possible, however.[1] Another stabilizing influence on revenues was the historical lack of price competition in the industry. New entry into the funeral home business was extremely difficult, given how much weight most people placed on tradition and reputation when selecting a funeral home. New entry into the cemetery business was often limited by regulation, or by scarcity of land. Further, in the case of at-need sales, bereaved family members were rarely in a frame of mind to haggle over price.

This industry stability produced an exceedingly low business failure rate among funeral homes. According to Dun & Bradstreet, the average annual failure rate for funeral homes and crematoria—8 out of every 10,000—was less than one-tenth the rate for all U.S. businesses.

Pre-need Business

During the 1990s, pre-need sales of funeral services and cemetery plots had come to represent an increasing share of the death care business. The segment of the population that was most likely to buy on a pre-need basis—former Baby Boomers who were now in their 50s and 60s—was rapidly expanding. From the companies' perspective, pre-need sales provided a way to lock in sales growth and market share. A

[1]For example, the number of deaths in the U.S. actually declined in 1981 and 1982—by 0.6% and 0.2%, respectively—but then increased by 2.3% in 1983 due to the sudden onset of HIV-related illnesses. Source: F. B. Bernstein and Y. C. Nainzadeh, *Post Life Services,* Merrill Lynch, April 26, 1999.

large and increasing fraction of Loewen's revenues was derived from pre-need sales, particularly of cemetery plots; by 1998, $258 million (41%) of its funeral services revenues was from pre-need sales, as was $306 million (75%) of its cemetery revenues (up from 22% and 61%, respectively in 1995).

SCI was especially aggressive in marketing its pre-need business. At the end of 1998, SCI had a pre-need funeral backlog of $3.7 billion, compared to $410 million for Loewen, $819 million for Stewart Enterprises, and $225 million for Carriage Services.[2] (The backlog represented the total value of insurance policies outstanding that have been taken out to cover the costs of providing future services and products under pre-need sales contracts.) It was estimated that the total pre-need market in the U.S. was between $20 billion and $50 billion in size, measured by current backlog.[3]

Pre-need sales gave rise to cash flows in advance of rendering services. These funds were either invested in securities or in an insurance contract. Companies earned an investment return on monies that were paid to them in advance. The accounting for pre-need services was quite complicated. Standard industry practice was to defer recognition of revenues until services were delivered, but for pre-need sales of cemetery plots, the profit on the sale was usually as current income, although additional customer payments and expenses would not be received or incurred until well after that recognition.

Growth through Consolidation

Loewen Group and the other large public death care companies employed a dramatically different business model than traditional family-owned funeral homes. Traditional businesses had historically had to contend with high fixed operating costs, which limited profit margins. Fixed costs were high because a funeral home might typically perform only one or two services a week, yet have to employ an office receptionist and various back office staff full time. Similarly, essential assets like hearses and embalming equipment would sit around most of the time unused, tying up capital.

In the 1960s, Robert Waltrip, founder of Service Corporation (SCI), recognized the potential to realize enormous cost savings in the industry by buying up funeral properties in concentrated geographic areas, and eliminating redundant assets and overhead expenses. A cluster of funeral homes formed this way would only have to employ a single receptionist, for example, and could share hearses and other fixed assets. A typical cluster might include ten to twenty properties, located within a 30- to 60-mile radius. It was estimated that in an SCI-owned funeral home, fixed costs represented 54% of revenues on average, compared to 65% for the rest of the industry (although SCI homes were typically somewhat larger than average).[4] To avoid alienating local communities, SCI continued to operate acquired properties under the original name; no "SCI" sign or logo was displayed.

SCI's consolidation strategy had two other potential benefits. First, through increased buying power, the company might be able to obtain price concessions from suppliers (e.g., for caskets and embalming chemicals). In addition, managers of the acquired businesses would gain access to SCI's considerable financial resources and professional management practices. Thus SCI-owned funeral homes were also able to lower their variable costs, which were estimated to be 15% of revenues, versus 23% for the average U.S. funeral home.[5]

[2]Ibid.

[3]Data from the National Funeral Directors Association.

[4]See C. Schreiber and B. Esty, Service Corporation International, HBS Case No. 296-080 (July 24, 1996).

[5]Ibid.

The consolidation strategy had its critics, however. Over the years there had been recurring accusations in the news media that SCI and other funeral home consolidators reduced competition and charged excessive prices.[6]

Ray Loewen's Way

Ray Loewen's entry into the funeral home consolidation business began in 1969, when he purchased a funeral home in British Columbia after learning that the home's owner was thinking of selling out to SCI. (At the time, Loewen owned a single funeral home in Ontario.) Loewen foresaw that increasing numbers of funeral home directors, many of them in their 20s or 30s who had inherited the business from their parents, would be receptive to selling their businesses to pursue alternative careers or because a disproportionate fraction of their wealth was tied up in the business. Loewen approached the consolidation process differently from SCI. The few Canadian funeral directors who had sold their businesses to SCI appeared to be unhappy with SCI's approach of managing "from afar."[7] Loewen's self-described approach, in contrast, was to take a majority ownership stake in each acquired business, but to retain the same managers if possible, and to give them relative autonomy:

> You can't have a group of MBAs in a head office telling funeral directors how to work. They feel they know their craft and their community. So let's stress local management. If a man wants to retire—or do some estate planning—and he has a good operation, number one in his community, let's give him a good deal, allowing him to live well, ease up a bit, but remain with the firm that carries the family name.[8]

The seller often retained a small minority stake in the business, and might receive Loewen stock as partial payment. (SCI, in contrast, had a policy of acquiring full ownership of acquired properties, although the previous owners might be kept on in a management role.) After acquiring a business, Loewen Group would often provide financing for capital improvements and increased merchandising. However, the company eschewed aggressive sales tactics, the use of telemarketing, and negative advertising that was critical of competitors. Loewen believed such tactics undermined the industry's credibility. However, Loewen apparently spared no expense in courting independent funeral home and cemetery owners who were potential acquirees.

As Loewen Group continued to grow through acquisitions during the 1970s and 1980s, its demand for capital increased, and in mid-1987 it listed its shares on the Toronto Stock Exchange. (Three years later it also acquired a U.S. listing on Nasdaq.) In August 1987, Loewen paid $1.8 million for its first U.S. acquisition, on condition that the owner stay as manager for three years. "It was made clear," the owner said, "that if I did not wish to work, they did not wish to buy."[9] Shortly thereafter, Loewen acquired a small local chain of funeral homes in Fresno, California. Having achieved a foothold in the giant U.S. market, Loewen Group's growth escalated. Dozens, later hundreds, of new properties were added every year. Exhibit 3 shows acquisition premiums paid by Loewen and its competitors and Exhibit 4 presents summarized financial data over a ten-year period. By 1998, the company had properties in 48 U.S. states and eight Canadian provinces.

[6]For example, see Bruce Mohl, "Growth of Chains Has Led to Rise in Funeral Prices," *The Boston Globe,* August 28, 1995, p. 1. In 1998, the CBS investigative news program *60 Minutes* ran a report investigating allegations of over-charging by SCI.

[7]Kenneth Bagnell, "A Profitable Undertaking," *The Globe and Mail,* October 21, 1988, p. 128.

[8]Ibid.

[9]Ibid.

SCI's Hostile Takeover Offer

Described in the news media as "fierce competitors" and "archrivals," Loewen Group and SCI increasingly found themselves competing for properties in the same markets. In 1994, the two companies collided in the United Kingdom, where each sought to acquire the large British funeral company, Great Southern. SCI ultimately prevailed, paying almost $200 million.[10]

During 1996 SCI had made several informal acquisition proposals to Loewen, but all were declined. On September 17, 1996—the very day that Loewen's stock began trading on the New York Stock Exchange—SCI announced a formal offer to acquire all Loewen common stock for US$43 a share, which would value Loewen at about $2.5 billion. The offer was addressed to Ray Loewen personally, in a letter from SCI's president (Exhibit 5). At the close of the day of this announcement, Loewen stock traded at about US$40, below the proposed acquisition price, but significantly higher than the $33.75 closing price the day before.

Loewen's board of directors promptly rejected the offer. Ray Loewen believed the company's stock, which only two weeks earlier had traded around $30 a share, was significantly undervalued. He portrayed SCI's action as an attempt to eliminate an important, and more successful, competitor. One sympathetic expert described the situation as "This is an example of someone taking advantage of a company that is struggling."[11] Although within two weeks of its initial offer SCI increased its bid to $45 a share—and redirected its offer to Loewen's shareholders directly—Ray Loewen said the company's stock was worth at least $52 a share.

The stock price was depressed, he argued, because of a recent unfavorable jury verdict against the company in Mississippi. A funeral home operator had accused Loewen Group of reneging on an agreement to purchase two of his homes, plus certain insurance services. Although the properties were worth only a few million dollars, in November 1995 the jury found the company liable for damages of $500 million, including $400 million in punitive damages. Loewen's stock price fell by 15% on the day the verdict was announced, and its bonds were soon downgraded to speculative, or "junk," status.[12] To appeal the verdict, under Mississippi law the company would have had to post a bond equal to 125% of the award, or $625 million. For the year, the company reported an expense of $165 million to settle this and other lawsuits.

Loewen responded vigorously to SCI's informal approaches as well as to its formal offer. It filed an antitrust lawsuit in U.S. Federal court against SCI. (Soon thereafter a number of states, as well as the Canadian government, started their own antitrust investigations of the proposed acquisition.) Loewen also adopted lucrative severance packages, or "golden parachutes," for more than 70 of its senior executives.[13] And, perhaps most significantly, it accelerated its acquisition program.

In June 1996, Loewen, in partnership with the investment firm, The Blackstone Group, announced its plans to acquire the then-fourth-largest funeral service provider in the U.S., Prime Succession Inc. The total purchase price was $320 million, financed with $190 million of bank and public high-yield debt. A few months later, in a similar transaction, Loewen and Blackstone acquired Rose Hills cemetery, the largest cemetery in North America, for $285 million, of which $155 million was financed with

[10]Rachel Bridge, "SCI Set to Tie Up Southern Deal," *The Evening Standard,* August 8, 1994, p. 1.

[11]Mark S. Poert, "Smaller Firms Would Gain from 'Death-Care' Spiral," *Merger and Acquisitions Report,* September 23, 1996.

[12]Junk bonds, also known as *high-yield* or *below investment grade* bonds, are bonds that receive ratings lower than a BBB- by Standard & Poor's, or a Baa3 rating by Moody's.

[13]Loewen already had a "poison pill" shareholder rights plan in place before SCI made its offer.

debt. These transactions were complicated. After four years Loewen would have the option to buy Blackstone's equity stake (a "call"); but after six years, Blackstone would have the option to sell its stake to Loewen (a "put"). If Loewen bought out Blackstone, it would effectively pay an amount that would give Blackstone a 24% return per annum on its investment. If Blackstone exercised its option, Loewen would be obligated to pay Blackstone an amount of cash (or shares) that was determined by a EBITDA-multiple calculation of Blackstone's equity in the investment.

During all of 1996, Loewen acquired 159 funeral homes, 136 cemeteries, and two insurance companies, for total consideration of $620 million. By the beginning of 1997, it had entered into agreements to purchase $222 million of additional properties.

A relatively high percentage of the financing for these acquisitions came from issuing debt. The company's stated policy on debt financing was to maintain its long-term debt to equity ratio in the range of 1 to 1.5.[14] It expected that this ratio would move towards the top of the target range when it made more acquisitions, but it would endeavor to bring the ratio back down eventually through equity issues. At the end of 1996 Loewen's debt/equity ratio was 1.4:1.

In the first week of 1997, SCI suddenly dropped its bid for Loewen. In addition to concerns over the antitrust suit and Loewen's various takeover defenses, SCI cited Loewen's high debt financing costs as a major deterrent to proceeding with the offer. Special mention was made of the Prime Succession and Rose Hills transactions.

Distress

Loewen continued its aggressive growth strategy in 1997, acquiring 138 funeral homes, 171 cemeteries, and one insurance company, paying a total of $546 million. The year also marked the company's entry into the United Kingdom, where it acquired 32 funeral homes. Debt again played an important role in financing this growth, and for the full year, interest expense on long-term debt was $132 million, up from $93 million in 1996.

Loewen's businesses, however, performed less well than expected. The company attributed this in part to a decline in death rates, which negatively impacted all death care companies. Although Loewen's total funeral revenues increased by 9.5% during the year, its established funeral homes (i.e., those not acquired during the year) performed 3.2% fewer services than in 1996, and the gross margin earned by these properties declined from 40.8% to 38.7%. The company attributed most of the margin decline to an increase in reserves for doubtful accounts. The gross margin earned by Loewen's cemetery business also declined in 1997, from 31% to 28.2%. The company said this decline occurred in part because it reversed $3.7 million of sales (and $1.2 million of related costs) that it had reported in 1996 for transactions that were supposed to have taken place in 1997, but were never consummated. In addition, it took a $2.1 million write down for cemetery accounts receivable.

These trends worsened in 1998. Revenues and profits for the company's established funeral services and cemetery businesses continued to fall. In early October, it announced that earnings for the third quarter would likely be more than 30% below what analysts had forecasted—causing Loewen's stock price to fall 15% in a single day. Management blamed the shortfall on declining death rates, difficulties in integrating newly acquired assets, and problems in the cemetery business. By the end of 1998 Loewen's stock price had fallen to $8.44, from $25.75 at the start of the year.

[14]The Loewen Group Inc., Form 10-K, December 31, 1996. The ratio was calculated on the basis of book values.

New Management

In the second half of 1998, Loewen took a number of steps to address its problems. It severely cut back the pace of acquisitions. During all of 1998, it acquired only 89 funeral homes and 65 cemeteries, paying $278 million. It hired investment bankers to explore different options for raising cash and improving profitability. In July 1998, it sold its First Capital Life insurance subsidiary for $24 million, recording an accounting gain of about $5 million.

In October, following the company's third-quarter profit warning, Ray Loewen resigned as chief executive officer, and three months later he was replaced as chairman. Loewen had recently owned more than 18% of the company's common stock, but he had been forced to surrender almost his entire stake to the Canadian Imperial Bank of Commerce to settle a personal loan. Now the company's largest shareholder, the bank nominated John Lacey as Loewen Group's new chairman.

A graduate of Harvard Business School, John Lacey had built a reputation as a successful turnaround specialist. On the day that his appointment was announced, Loewen's stock price increased by 20% on the Toronto Stock Exchange. In previous assignments, Lacey had shown an ability to raise large amounts of cash through asset sales. For example, while at Oshawa Group, a Canadian grocery store chain, he negotiated the sale of the entire company for $1.5 billion. Following his appointment to Loewen, Lacey said: "My role over the last five or six years has been one of maximizing shareholder value. . . . I think what I do is look for opportunities to deliver value to the shareholders."[15]

Company Debt

By the end of the year, Loewen Group's long-term debt was the highest it had ever been, at $2.3 billion (including debt due within a year). The debt structure was complicated. For example, it owed approximately $540 million to a consortium of 25 Canadian and U.S. banks, led by the Bank of Montreal. It also had over $1.5 billion of publicly issued, senior guaranteed notes outstanding in nine different tranches.[16] About $875 million of the total long-term debt would mature in 1999.

Almost all of the debt was secured, or collateralized, by various assets of the company. If Loewen were liquidated, secured creditors would be entitled to receive the cash generated from the sale of the assets that secured their debt. In 1996, the banks and the note holders had agreed to share most of their security on a *pari passu* basis (i.e., in the event of liquidation, the two groups of creditors would have equal claim to the resulting cash proceeds).[17]

Loewen also had large contingent and other liabilities outstanding. This amount included $87.8 million owed to former owners of certain funeral and cemetery properties that Loewen had acquired. For tax reasons, the sellers had chosen to be paid in installments over several years, with $14 million due in each of the next two years. In return, they had signed contracts promising not to compete against Loewen during the life of the payments ("non-competition agreements").

[15]Drew Hasselback, "Lacey Joins Loewen for Another Selloff," *The Financial Post,* January 25, 1999, p. C02.

[16]A tranche is one class of a multiclass security or asset. The classes generally differ by risk profiles that are determined by differing maturity or priority of the claims on the underlying asset. In this case, the tranches of debt had differing maturities and seniority.

[17]The security consisted of accounts receivables and any related rights to receive payment, the capital stock of substantially all of Loewen's majority-owned subsidiaries, and a guarantee by each subsidiary that had pledged its stock.

The company's bank and public debt contained numerous covenants.[18] Among other things, the covenants limited the amount of debt and preferred stock that the company could issue and the dividends it could pay. Other covenants restricted the company's ability to sell assets, or required that proceeds from asset sales be used to retire debt. A covenant in Loewen's bonds stated that if ownership of the company's stock changed significantly, Loewen would have to offer to repurchase the bonds for 101% of their face value.

If Loewen violated a covenant or missed a scheduled interest or principal payment, an event of default would be declared. Creditors would then, after 30 days, have the right to accelerate their claims (i.e., all principal and accrued interest would become immediately due and payable). "Cross default" covenants in the debt ensured that if any one debt contract defaulted, all other contracts would be considered in default as well. In early 1999 Loewen was not in compliance with certain covenants in its bank debt. If it could not persuade its banks to waive the defaults, or renegotiate the covenants, the company might have no choice but to file for bankruptcy.

Bankruptcy

Corporate bankruptcy in the U.S. was governed by the U.S. Bankruptcy Code ("Code"). Chapter 11 of the Code dealt with reorganizations. If a company filed for Chapter 11,[19] it was allowed to conduct its regular business and propose a financial restructuring plan, without interference from creditors (e.g., secured creditors could not seize their collateral). A central presumption of the Code was that firms were worth more as going concerns than if shut down.[20] The bankruptcy case was overseen by a judge, who could hear appeals from creditors if they believed they were being unfairly treated. Creditors were also allowed to form committees to represent their interests in the case. Such committees could hire their own legal and financial advisors, and charge all professional fees to the company. The company also hired its own advisors.

To emerge from bankruptcy, management of the bankrupt firm (the "debtor") proposed a plan of reorganization to the creditors. The plan divided the firm's creditors and other financial claimholders into classes, and each class was asked to exchange its claims for new claims. Each class would vote separately on the proposed plan. If each class approved the plan by at least one-half in number and two-thirds in value, the judge would approve the plan and the firm would exit from Chapter 11. Minority creditors who voted against the plan would have to accept the will of the majority. The judge would determine whether the reorganization plan left the firm with a sensible new capital structure.

[18]A covenant is a promise by the borrower that certain acts will be performed and others refrained from. Typical covenants can require maintaining minimum working capital ratios, or interest coverage ratios. They can also place limits on significant asset purchases or sales.

[19]To initiate the bankruptcy procedure, Loewen's over 850 U.S. and 100 Canadian subsidiaries would probably each have to pay filing fees of $800 to the courts.

[20]In some countries, such as the United Kingdom, bankruptcy generally meant that the firm was liquidated or sold, and the proceeds were paid to creditors from most senior to most junior. In these countries, shareholders would only receive anything if there was enough value to make all creditors whole—which rarely happened.

Management had the exclusive right to propose the first plan. The law stated that a plan had to be proposed within 120 days of the bankruptcy filing, and confirmed within an additional 60 days. After this date the judge could allow other interested persons to file alternative plans. Most judges were willing to grant management extensions to the deadline, however. In practice, multiple extensions were often granted, and large complex cases might run for two or three years before an initial vote was taken.

In addition to being protected from creditors, firms benefited in other ways while they were in Chapter 11. They did not have to pay interest on their unsecured debt. They could cancel leases and other so-called "executory contracts," where both parties to the contract were still obligated to perform future services, such as the non-competes that Loewen had signed with acquired funeral homes. They could also borrow from new lenders through "debtor-in-possession financing," based on a provision of Chapter 11 giving new lenders to a bankrupt firm higher priority than the firm's pre-bankruptcy lenders.

If Loewen were to file for Chapter 11, its situation could be complicated by the fact that roughly 10% of its business was conducted in Canada.[21] A U.S. bankruptcy filing would almost certainly trigger a simultaneous bankruptcy filing in Canada. Canadian bankruptcy law was governed by the Companies' Creditors Arrangement Act (CCAA), which differed in some important ways from Chapter 11. For example, it was generally easier for creditors to remove management than in the U.S. In addition, management had only one chance to present a reorganization plan before the judge would order the firm liquidated. There was no provision for debtor-in-possession financing as in the U.S. If Loewen filed for bankruptcy in both countries, some kind of administrative protocol would have to be established for resolving potential conflicts between the two courts.

The Company's Options

John Lacey had relatively little time to develop a plan for dealing with the growing crisis. In December, the company suspended dividends for common shareholders. The company had $42 million of debt payments coming due in the first two weeks of April, and in early March it had still not reached an agreement with its banks on how to restructure their loans. Analysts publicly speculated that Loewen would soon start to sell some of its assets; one commented "Everyone is simply waiting for a liquidation of the assets."[22] However, raising large amounts of cash through asset sales could be difficult. The death care industry in general was feeling the effects of lower death rates, so there might be limited demand for Loewen's properties. Further, piecemeal sales of assets could take a long time, given the company's organizational complexity. Making a difficult situation even worse, regulators had recently suspended the licenses of sixteen of Loewen's funeral homes in Florida, after discovering certain accounting violations. Whether the full extent of the problem had been discovered remained to be determined.

[21] Loewen's U.S. assets were owned and operated by Loewen Group International Inc., a wholly owned subsidiary of the Canadian parent company.

[22] Will Edwards, "Funeral Service Unable to Find Buyer for Shares," Cincinnati Enquirer, November 27, 1999.

EXHIBIT 1 Selected Data on Loewen Group and Its Main Competitors (dollars in US$ millions, except for per share items)

Sources: Datastream, Compustat, and company annual reports.

	Loewen			Service Corp. International			Stewart Enterprises			Carriage Services		
	Dec 96	Dec 97	Dec 98	Dec 96	Dec 97	Dec 98	Oct 96	Oct 97	Oct 98	Dec 96	Dec 97	Dec 98
Sales	$899.4	$1,114.1	$1,136.2	$2,294.2	$2,468.4	$2,875.1	$433.4	$532.6	$648.4	$40.3	$77.4	$116.8
Gross profit	328.6	370.7	291.7	713.1	812.8	879.3	139.8	175.1	217.1	10.8	27.2	45.8
SG&A expense	76.7	99.5	125.2	63.2	66.8	66.8	14.1	15.4	16.6	2.5	5.3	7.6
Depreciation and amortization	56.8	71.4	88.5	108.7	125.2	160.5	21.7	18.0	21.1	3.6	7.8	11.4
Operating profit	195.1	199.8	78.0	541.2	620.8	651.9	104.0	141.8	179.4	4.7	14.1	26.7
Net interest expense	91.0	127.5	182.3	149.3	141.1	177.1	26.1	38.0	43.8	4.5	6.2	10.2
Taxes	29.1	2.7	(164.5)	148.6	205.4	176.4	30.8	36.7	23.1	0.1	3.7	7.5
Other miscellaneous income[a]	(11.1)	(26.9)	(659.2)[g]	22.0	59.4	43.6	4.1	0.4	(70.6)	(0.3)	0.1	0.5
Net income	63.9	42.7	(599.0)	265.3	333.8	342.1	51.3	67.4	41.9	(0.3)	4.3	9.5
Preferred dividends	8.9	9.5	8.9	0.0	0.0	0.0	0.0	0.0	0.0	0.6	0.9	0.6
Available for common[b]	55.0	33.2	(607.9)	265.3	374.6[i]	342.1	51.3	69.7	41.9	(0.4)	3.6	8.9
Earnings per share (reported)	0.97	$0.48	($8.22)	1.10	$1.36	$1.34	0.62	$0.76	$0.43	(0.19)	$0.33	$0.67
Assets	$3,496.9	$4,503.2	$4,673.9	$8,869.8	$10,514.9	$13,266.2	$1,365.9	$1,637.2	$2,048.9	$131.3	$277.9	$466.1
Short-term debt[c]	79.6	43.5	940.3	162.2	94.5	115.8	4.2	34.0	11.2	1.1	2.3	6.4
Long-term debt	1,428.6	1,750.4	1,393.9	2,221.2	2,634.7	3,764.6	515.9	524.4	913.2	43.3	126.0	216.2
Preferred stockholders' equity	157.1	157.1	157.1	0.0	—	—	0.0	—	—	17.3	14.0	1.7
Common stockholders' equity	891.1	1,383.1	748.3	2,235.3	2,726.0	3,154.1	547.4	819.6	839.3	57.0	98.6	200.4
Market value of equity	2,310.6	1,903.2	624.9	6,613.4	9,295.0	9,865.7	1,431.6	2,020.3	2,260.7	190.0	211.8	449.5
Number of funeral homes	956	1,070	1,151	3,377	3,685	4,066	308	401	558	76	120	166
Number of cemeteries	313	483	550	345	392	433	120	129	140	10	20	27
Interest coverage[d]	2.1	1.6	0.4	3.6	4.4	3.7	4.0	3.7	4.1	1.0	2.3	2.6
Bond rating	BB+	BB+	BB[h]	BBB+	BBB+	BBB+	NA	BBB	BBB	NA	NA	NA
Equity beta	0.81	0.63	1.18	0.93	0.58	0.65	1.19	1.30	1.31	NA	1.36	1.44
Price/earnings ratio	42.0	57.3	NM	24.9	24.8	28.8	27.9	29.0	54.0	(457.9)	58.8	50.4
Market/book ratio	2.6	1.4	0.8	3.0	3.4	3.1	2.6	2.5	2.7	3.3	2.1	2.2
Return on book equity[e]	6.2%	2.4%	–81.2%	11.9%	13.7%	10.9%	9.4%	8.5%	5.0%	–0.7%	3.7%	4.5%
Dividend payout ratio	20.6%	45.1%	NM	21.3%	18.7%	25.8%	5.4%	5.2%	14.0%	0.0%	0.0%	0.0%
CAGR Sales over 3 years[f]	44.2%	38.7	23.8	36.6%	30.2	20.3	33.4%	27.9	20.7	66.5%	78.7	68.9
Cash flow from operations	(46.9)	(160.7)	(124.5)	209.9	299.4	329.6	11.6	(15.2)	18.3	0.3	9.7	6.6
Cash flow from investing	(787.5)	(491.6)	(304.4)	(480.1)	(633.4)	(1,059.9)	(191.9)	(205.9)	(275.5)	(46.0)	(74.8)	(153.5)
Cash flow from financing	813.1	671.0	486.3	256.9	336.8	1,041.6	187.1	229.2	259.4	39.8	69.5	143.6

[a]Includes special and extraordinary expenses, net of tax. [b]Income after preferred dividends that is available to common shareholders. Preferred equity is senior to common equity, and so must be paid first. Available for common is the amount of income available after preferred equity dividends are made. [c]Current portion of long-term debt included in short-term debt line item. [d]Interest coverage is measured as operating profit divided by interest expense. [e]Return on equity is calculated as the end of period available for common divided by the end of period book value of equity. [f]Compound Annualized Growth Rate. [g]Represents asset impairment expense for a write-down of properties to fair value, including the company's investment in the Prime Succession and Rose Hills properties. [h]Loewen's debt was downgraded to B+ in January 1999 and to B– in February 1999. [i]SCI adds back an extraordinary expense of $40.8 million to net income to get available for common.

EXHIBIT 2 Stock Price History, 1990–1999 (US$)

Source: Datastream. Carriage Services first traded in August 1996 and is omitted from the figure for clarity.

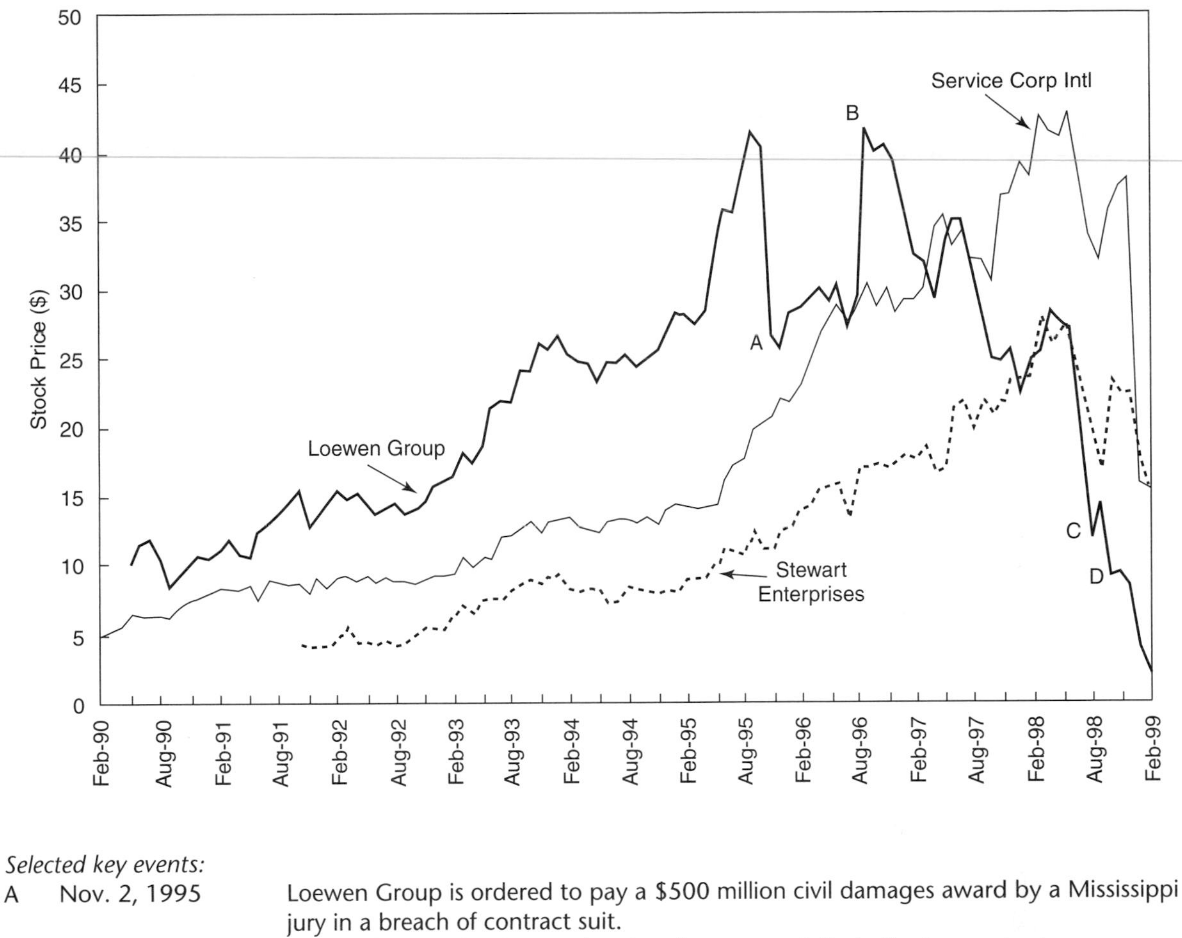

Selected key events:

A	Nov. 2, 1995	Loewen Group is ordered to pay a $500 million civil damages award by a Mississippi jury in a breach of contract suit.
B	Sep. 17, 1996	Service Corporation International makes an unsolicited offer to acquire Loewen.
C	Aug. 6, 1998	Loewen discloses that second-quarter earnings were 56% lower than last year.
D	Oct. 8, 1998	Ray Loewen is removed as CEO of Loewen Group, following company's announcement on previous day that third-quarter earnings will be less than 13 cents a share, versus analysts' consensus estimate of 19 cents a share.

EXHIBIT 3 Acquisitions by Major Death Care Companies, 1996–1998 (in US$ millions)

Source: F. B. Bernstein and Y. C. Nainzadeh, *Post Life Services,* Merrill Lynch, April 26, 1999.

	Revenues of Acquired Companies (1)			Amount Spent on Acquisitions (2)			Acquisition Revenue Multiple: (2) ÷ (1)		
Acquirer	1996	1997	1998	1996	1997	1998	1996	1997	1998
The Loewen Group	251.5	187.6	29.1	620.0	546.0	278.0	2.47×	2.91×	9.55×
Service Corp. Int'l	180.0	260.0	296.0	363.0	643.0	784.0	2.02×	2.47×	2.65×
Stewart Enterprises	68.8	77.8	109.1	179.0	184.5	266.3	2.60×	2.37×	2.44×
Carriage Services	28.6	42.8	51.9	69.1	118.3	158.7	2.42×	2.76×	3.06×

EXHIBIT 4 Historical Financial Information for Loewen, 1989–1998 (In US$ millions)

Sources: Datastream, Compustat, Bloomberg.

	1989	1990	1991	1992	1993	1994	1995	1996	1997	1998
Sales	$63.8	$117.6	$188.5	$231.5	$300.1	$417.5	$598.5	$899.4	$1,114.1	$1,136.2
Gross profit	25.5	47.2	72.2	87.4	114.5	159.0	225.4	328.6	370.7	291.7
EBITDA[a]	21.4	37.7	57.0	68.6	87.7	123.6	172.0	251.9	271.2	166.5
Operating profit	17.7	31.0	44.4	52.0	66.6	94.6	131.9	195.1	199.8	78.0
Interest expense	8.2	12.4	17.1	19.8	21.7	34.2	53.6	91.0	127.5	182.3
Special items	1.6	0.0	0.3	0.6	(1.3)	0.5	(195.1)[f]	(4.0)	(19.8)	(652.1)[g]
Pretax income	11.0	18.5	27.6	32.7	43.5	60.9	(116.8)	100.1	52.5	(756.4)
Taxes[b]	4.8	7.5	11.1	12.2	15.6	19.7	(47.2)	29.1	2.7	(164.5)
Minority interest	0.0	0.0	0.0	0.0	0.0	(2.7)	(7.1)	(7.1)	(7.1)	(7.1)
Net income	6.2	11.1	16.5	20.5	27.9	38.5	(76.7)	63.9	42.7	(599.0)
Preferred dividends	0.7	0.3	0.0	0.0	0.0	0.0	0.0	8.9	9.5	8.9
Available for common[c]	5.5	10.8	16.5	20.5	27.9	38.5	(76.7)	55.0	33.2	(607.9)
Dividends on common stock	0.0	0.0	0.6	1.1	1.7	2.9	2.4	11.4	15.0	7.5
Total assets	$163.4	$341.3	$446.1	$547.0	$748.5	$1,115.7	$2,263.0	$3,496.9	$4,503.2	$4,673.9
Total liabilities	94.9	207.1	249.0	301.4	423.7	704.6	1,648.3	2,448.7	2,962.9	3,768.5
Total debt due within one year	5.1	7.2	6.9	7.9	6.6	45.5	69.7	79.6	43.5	940.3
Long-term debt	79.7	172.1	217.0	251.5	334.4	471.1	864.8	1,428.6	1,750.4	1,393.9
Book value of common equity	59.9	134.3	197.1	245.7	324.8	411.1	614.7	891.1	1,383.1	748.3
Cash flow from operations[d]	7.2	14.0	28.7	35.2	47.2	43.2	10.2	(46.9)	(160.7)	(124.5)
Cash flow from investing[d]	(36.5)	(172.8)	(104.4)	(104.4)	(182.4)	(346.0)	(569.0)	(787.5)	(491.6)	(304.4)
Cash flow from financing[d]	46.5	14.4	91.2	60.5	139.8	313.5	586.0	813.1	671.0	486.3
Capital expenditures	3.1	8.6	14.0	12.6	20.7	39.8	36.1	72.6	85.3	62.7
Acquisition expenditures	36.0	159.7	78.4	83.2	147.6	265.6	487.9	619.6	546.5	252.6
Net proceeds from issuing equity	33.9	53.5	46.0	32.4	54.6	128.4	203.1	371.0	439.4	1.8
Net proceeds from issuing debt	14.0	91.7	37.2	28.3	84.2	172.9	381.2	455.2	253.5	508.1
Market value of equity	NA[h]	301.6	438.1	550.8	980.7	1,086.9	1,219.2	2,310.6	1,903.2	624.9
Market/book ratio	NA	2.2	2.2	2.2	3.0	2.6	2.0	2.6	1.4	0.8
Price/earnings ratio	NA	28.0	26.6	26.8	35.1	28.2	NM	42.0	57.3	NM
Interest coverage	2.2	2.5	2.6	2.6	3.1	2.8	2.5	2.1	1.6	0.4
Senior bond rating	-	-	-	-	BBB	BBB	BBB	BB+	BB+	BB[i]
Return on equity[e]	9.3%	8.0%	8.4%	8.4%	8.6%	9.4%	–12.5%	6.2%	2.4%	–81.2%
Dividend payout ratio	-	-	3.4%	5.2%	6.1%	7.5%	NM	20.6%	45.1%	NM
Year-end stock price	NA	$10.88	$13.38	$15.50	$25.38	$27.00	$25.31	$39.13	$25.75	$8.44
Number of shares (in mill.)	NA	27.7	32.7	35.5	38.6	40.3	48.2	59.0	73.9	74.0

NA: Not Available; NM: Not meaningful

[a]Earnings Before Interest, Taxes, Depreciation, and Amortization. [b]Loewen's combined Canadian Federal and Provincial tax rate was 45%. [c]Income after preferred dividends that is available to common shareholders. Preferred equity is senior to common equity, and so must be paid first. Available for common is the amount of income available after preferred equity dividends are made. [d]The cash flows from 1989 and 1990 are taken from SEC Form 20-F and converted from Canadian dollars into U.S. dollars using the average exchange rates of 1.1842 and 1.1667 Canadian dollars per U.S. dollar, respectively. Form 20-F is the form that foreign issuers must file instead of Form 10-K that domestic issuers must file with the SEC. [e]Return on equity is calculated as the end of period available for common divided by the end of period book value of equity. [f]Special charges, including legal expenses, from the settlements of two lawsuits. [g]Represents asset impairment expense for a write-down of properties to fair value and write-down of company's investment in Prime Succession and Rose Hills. [h]Loewen began trading in the United States in 1990. [i]Loewen's debt was downgraded to B+ in January 1999 and to B– in February 1999.

EXHIBIT 5

Letter to Raymond Loewen from William Heiligbrodt, SCI's President and Chief Operating Officer, September 17, 1996

Source: "Service Corporation International Announces a Proposed Business Combination with the Loewen Group Inc.," *PR Newswire,* September 17, 1996.

September 17, 1996

Mr. Raymond L. Loewen
Chairman of the Board and Chief Executive Officer
The Loewen Group Inc.

Dear Mr. Loewen:

As you know, I have tried to reach you several times since September 11. While your office has assured me that you received my messages, my calls have not been returned. In view of that, and in view of the importance of this matter, I am sending this letter.

I would like to discuss with you a combination of our two companies. The combination would involve a stock-for-stock exchange accounted for as a pooling which values Loewen Group at US$43 per share. We believe that this transaction can be structured in a manner that is tax-free to both companies . . .

I think you and your Board and stockholders would agree that our proposal is a generous one, resulting in the following premiums for Loewen Group stockholders:

— 48.9% above the price at which Loewen Group stock traded 30 days ago;
— 39.3% above the price at which Loewen Group stock traded one week ago; and
— 27.4% above the price at which Loewen Group stock is currently trading.

This represents an opportunity for your stockholders to realize excellent value, by any measure, for their shares. In addition, and importantly, since your stockholders would be receiving stock, they would continue to participate in Loewen Group's business as well as share in the upside of our business.

Thus, in essence, your stockholders would:

— continue their investment in our industry;
— get an immediate, and very significant, increase in the market value of their investment;
— get that immediate and substantial increase on an essentially tax free basis; and
— diversify their risk by participating in a much larger number of properties.

This is a "win-win" situation for you and your stockholders.

Finally, with respect to consideration, I would note also that our proposal is based on public information. After a due diligence review, we may be in a position to increase the consideration that your stockholders would receive. . . .

I would very much like to discuss any and all aspects of our proposal directly with you and your Board of Directors. We believe you and they will recognize the tremendous benefit to your stockholders of our proposal. Our proposal is conditioned upon approval of our Board and upon negotiation of mutually satisfactory agreements providing for a combination on a pooling basis.

We hope that after you meet with us, you will similarly determine that the transaction should be pursued. We look forward to hearing from you.

In view of the importance of this matter, we are simultaneously releasing this letter to the press.

Sincerely,

William Heiligbrodt
President and Chief Operating Officer
Service Corporation International

American Home Products Corporation

"I just don't like to owe money," said William F. Laporte when asked about his company's almost debt-free balance sheet and growing cash reserves.[1] The exchange took place in 1968, 4 years after Mr. Laporte had taken over as chief executive of American Home Products (AHP). The 13 subsequent years did not improve his opinion of debt financing. During Mr. Laporte's tenure as chief executive, AHP's abstinence from debt continued, while the growth in its cash balance outpaced impressive growth in both sales and earnings. At the end of 1980, AHP had almost no debt and a cash balance equal to 40% of its net worth. In 1981, after 17 years as chief executive, Mr. Laporte was approaching retirement, and analysts speculated on the possibility of a more aggressive capital structure policy.

Description of the Company

AHP's 1981 sales of more than $4 billion were produced by over 1,500 heavily marketed brands in four lines of business: prescription drugs, packaged (i.e., proprietary or over-the-counter) drugs, food products, and housewares and household products. Consumer products included a diversity of well-known brand names, such as Anacin, Preparation H, Sani-Flush, Chef Boy-Ar-Dee, Gulden's Mustard, Woolite, and the Ekco line of housewares. AHP's largest and most profitable business, prescription drugs, included sizable market shares in antihypertensives, tranquilizers, and oral contraceptives. AHP's success in these lines of business was built on marketing expertise. Whether the product was an oral contraceptive or a toilet bowl cleaner, "they sell the hell out of everything they've got," said one competitor.[2]

AHP's Corporate Culture

AHP had a distinctive corporate culture that, in the view of many observers, emanated from its chief executive. This culture had several components. One was reticence. A poll of Wall Street analysts ranked AHP last in corporate communicability among 21 drug companies. A second element of AHP's managerial philosophy was frugality and tight financial control. Reportedly, all expenditures greater than $500 had to be personally approved by Mr. Laporte even if authorized in the corporate budget.

Another important component of AHP's culture was conservatism and risk aversion. AHP consistently avoided much of the risk of new product development and introduction in the volatile drug industry. Most of its new products were acquired or licensed after their development by other firms or were copies of new products introduced by competitors. A substantial portion of AHP's new products were clever extensions of existing products. AHP thus avoided risky gambles on R&D and new product introductions and used its marketing prowess to promote acquired products and product extensions. When

[1] *Forbes,* September 1, 1968, p. 87.

[2] *The Wall Street Journal,* December 28, 1981, p. 1.

Copyright © 1983 by the President and Fellows of Harvard College. Harvard Business School case 283-065.

truly innovative products were introduced by competitors. AHP responded with "me-too" products and relied on its marketing clout to erode competitors' head starts.

Finally, an integral part of AHP's corporate philosophy was the firm's long-standing policy of centralizing complete authority in the chief executive. The current incumbent was described by a former colleague as a "brilliant marketer and tightfisted spender."[3] Mr. Laporte's management style was characterized as management from the top, unparalleled in any firm of comparable size. Though reticent in discussing operations, Mr. Laporte was emphatic in stating the objective underlying his use of this authority: "We run the business for the shareholders."[4] The author of a *Business Week* article on the firm commented, "One of the most common business platitudes is that a corporation's primary mission is to make money for its stockholders and to maximize profits by minimizing costs. At American Home, these ideas are a dogmatic way of life."[5]

AHP's Performance

This managerial philosophy produced impressive results. AHP's financial performance was characterized by stable, consistent growth and profitability. The firm had increased sales, earnings, and dividends for 29 consecutive years through 1981. This growth had been consistent and steady, ranging in recent years between 10% and 15% annually (see Exhibit 1 for a 10-year review of AHP's performance). Under Mr. Laporte's stewardship, AHP's return on equity had risen from about 25% in the 1960s to 30% in the 1980s. Because of its passion for parsimony, AHP had been able to finance this growth internally while paying out almost 60% of its annual earnings as dividends.

During Mr. Laporte's reign as chief executive, AHP's price-earnings ratio had fallen by about 60%, reflecting the marketwide collapse of price-earnings ratios of growth companies. Nonetheless, AHP's more than sixfold growth in earnings per share had pushed up the value of its stock by a factor of 3 during his tenure. AHP's stock was widely held by major institutional investors. Its popularity among investors reflected analysts' assessment of AHP's management. In the opinion of one analyst, "When you think of American Home Products, you think of the best-managed company in the whole pharmaceutical field."[6] Nevertheless, AHP's excess liquidity and low degree of leverage were criticized by many analysts. Others wondered whether it would be a good idea to tinker with success.

Capital Structure Policy

Many drug firms were relatively unleveraged, but none matched AHP's conservative capital structure. Because of AHP's diversified operations, it was difficult to find a truly comparable firm for comparative analysis. However, Warner-Lambert Company was about the same size as AHP and competed in roughly similar lines of business (see Exhibit 2 for a comparison of AHP and Warner-Lambert). Warner-Lambert had a debt ratio of 32%, and its bond rating was on the borderline between AAA and AA in 1980.

[3] *The Wall Street Journal*, December 28, 1981, p. 6.

[4] *HBS Bulletin*, January/February 1981, p. 123.

[5] *Business Week*, March 21, 1970, p. 76.

[6] David S. Saks, Wertheim & Co., quoted in *The Wall Street Journal*, January 7, 1981, p. 18.

For many years, analysts had speculated on the impact of a more aggressive AHP capital structure policy. An example of a pro forma recapitalization analysis is presented in Exhibit 3. This exhibit shows actual 1981 performance plus pro forma restatements of the 1981 results under three alternative capital structures: 30% debt, 50% debt, and 70% debt. As described in Exhibit 3, these restatements assume that AHP issued debt and used the proceeds plus $233 million of excess cash to repurchase stock in early 1981 at the then prevailing stock price of $30 per share. Though this approach is only one of several ways to achieve a higher debt ratio, it illustrates, in approximate terms, the impact of higher debt on AHP's financial performance.

In view of AHP's firmly rooted financial conservatism, it was premature to consider the details of a realistic recapitalization plan. However, the likely imminent retirement of the firm's strong-willed chief executive fueled speculation concerning an appropriate capital structure policy for AHP and the magnitude of the payoff from such a policy.

EXHIBIT 1 **Selected Financial Data for American Home Products Corporation, 1972–1981 (millions of dollars except per share data)**

	1972	1973	1974	1975	1976	1977	1978	1979	1980	1981
Sales	$1,587.1	$1,784.4	$2,048.7	$2,258.6	$2,471.7	$2,685.1	$3,062.6	$3,406.3	$3,798.5	$4,131.2
Cash	—	—	—	—	358.8	322.9	436.6	493.8	593.3	729.1
Total debt	—	—	—	—	7.8	10.3	13.7	10.3	13.9	16.6
Net worth	—	—	—	—	991.5	1,035.3	1,178.0	1,322.0	1,472.8	1,654.5
Total assets	1,042.0	1,126.0	1,241.6	1,390.7	1,510.9	1,611.3	1,862.2	2,090.7	2,370.3	2,588.5
Net income	172.7	199.2	225.6	250.7	277.9	306.2	348.4	396.0	445.9	497.3
Earnings per share . . .	$ 1.08	$ 1.25	$ 1.42	$ 1.58	$ 1.75	$ 1.94	$ 2.21	$ 2.51	$ 2.84	$ 3.18
Dividends per share . .	.59	.625	.777	.90	1.00	1.15	1.325	1.50	1.70	1.90
Percentages										
Annual growth in sales	—	12.4%	14.8%	10.2%	9.4%	8.6%	14.1%	11.1 %	11.7%	8.8%
Annual growth in EPS	—	15.7	13.6	11.3	10.8	10.9	13.9	13.6	13.1	12.0
Dividend payout	54.6%	50.0	54.7	57.0	57.1	59.3	60.0	59.8	60.0	59.7
After-tax profit margin	10.9	11.2	11.0	11.1	11.2	11.4	11.4	11.6	11.7	12.0
Return on equity	25.9	28.2	28.2	27.9	28.0	29.5	29.6	30.0	30.3	30.1

EXHIBIT 2
1980 Data for American Home Products Corporation and Warner-Lambert Company (millions of dollars except per share data)

	American Home Products Corporation	Warner-Lambert Company
Sales	$3,798.5	$3,479.2
5-year compound annual growth rate	11.0%	9.9%
Profit after taxes	$ 445.9	$ 192.7
5-year compound annual growth rate	12.2%	3.3%
Cash and equivalents	$ 593.3	$ 360.3
Accounts receivable, net	517.3	541.5
Inventory	557.3	645.8
Net property, plant, and equipment	450.5	827.1
Other	251.9	582.5
Total assets	$2,370.3	$2,957.2
Total debt	$ 13.9	$ 710.1
Net worth	1,472.8	1,482.7
Earnings per share	$ 2.84	$ 2.41
5-year compound annual growth rate	12.4%	3.0%
Dividends per share	$ 1.70	$ 1.32
5-year compound annual growth rate	13.6%	8.0%
Stock price (end of 1980)	$ 30	$ 20
Price-earnings ratio	10.6	8.3
Profit margin (Profit after taxes/Sales)	11.7%	5.5%
Return on equity	30.3%	13.0%
Percentage of total debt to total capital	.9%	32.4%
Interest coverage	436.6	5.0
Bond rating	AAA	AAA/AA[a]

a. Warner-Lambert's debt was rated AAA, but analysts felt the firm was close to being downgraded to AA.

EXHIBIT 3

Pro Forma 1981 Results for Alternative Capital Structure (millions of dollars except per share data)

	Actual 1981	Pro Forma 1981 for Varying Percentages of Debt to Total Capital		
		30%	50%	70%
Sales	$4,131.2	$4,131.2	$4,131.2	$4,131.2
EBIT[a]	954.8	922.2	922.2	922.2
Interest	2.3	52.7	87.8	122.9
Profit before taxes	952.5	869.5	834.4	799.3
Taxes	455.2	417.4	400.5	383.7
Profit after taxes	497.3	452.1	433.9	415.6
Dividends on preferred stock	.4	.4	.4	.4
Earnings available to common shareholders	496.9	451.7	433.5	415.2
Dividends on common stock	295.3	271.0	260.1	249.1
Average common shares outstanding	155.5	135.7	127.3	118.9
Earnings per share	$ 3.18	$ 3.33	$ 3.41	$ 3.49
Dividends per share	1.90	2.00	2.04	2.10
Beginning of Year after Recapitalization				
Cash and equivalents	$ 593.3	$ 360.3	$ 360.3	$ 360.3
Total debt	13.9	376.1	626.8	877.6
Net worth	1,472.8	877.6	626.9	376.1
Common stock price	$ 30	—	—	—
Aggregate market value of common stock	$4,665.0	—	—	—

a. EBIT is reduced in pro forma results because of the loss of interest income from the $233 million in excess cash used to repurchase stock.

Detailed Assumptions for Pro Forma Recapitalizations

1. Debt is assumed to be added to the capital structure by issuing debt and using the proceeds to repurchase common stock. All repurchases are assumed to be executed in January 1981.
2. Stock is assumed to be repurchased at a price of $30 per share, which was the prevailing stock price in early January 1981.
3. The minimum cash balance is assumed to be $360.3 million (equal to Warner-Lambert's 1980 cash balance); thus $233 million in excess cash is available for use in repurchasing stock.
4. A tax rate of 48% is used.
5. The common dividend payout ratio is 60%.
6. Interest rate on all debt in all recapitalizations is assumed to be 14% before tax.
7. Interest forgone on excess cash is assumed to be at a rate 14% before tax, so with recapitalization, EBIT falls by .14 times excess cash of $233 million or $32.6 million. Thus, pro forma EBIT is $922.2 million (actual EBIT of $954.8 million minus $32.6 reduction in interest from excess cash).

Details of Recapitalizations (millions of dollars)

	30% Debt	50% Debt	70% Debt
Excess cash	$233.0	$233.0	$ 233.0
Additional debt	362.2	612.9	863.7
Total repurchase	595.2	845.9	1,096.7
Reduction in common shares outstanding (million shares)	19.8	28.2	36.6

Debt Policy at UST Inc.

In December 1998, UST Inc.'s board of directors approved a plan to borrow up to $1 billion over five years to accelerate its stock buyback program.[1] For UST Inc., the leading producer of moist smokeless tobacco products and a company widely known for its conservative debt policy and high dividend payout (uninterrupted cash dividends since 1912), this announcement generated considerable attention on Wall Street. Investors eagerly awaited the subsequent actions of Vincent Gierer, Jr., UST's Chairman and CEO.

In 1997, UST had suspended its stock repurchase program, approved in 1996, because of legislative and legal issues confronting the tobacco industry.[2] In November 1998, the company signed the Smokeless Tobacco Master Settlement Agreement resolving its potential state Medicaid liability and reinstated its repurchase program.[3] Management believed that this agreement represented significant progress with respect to the legal and legislative matters confronting the company, permitting UST to proceed with its business strategy and potential recapitalization.

The Smokeless Tobacco Market

The U.S. smokeless tobacco industry generated $2 billion of retail revenue in 1998 with approximately 5 million consumers of moist smokeless tobacco and 7 million consumers of chewing tobacco including loose leaf, twist, plug, and dry. Moist smokeless tobacco consumption approximated 50% of the total. See Table A for a description of smokeless tobacco products. While decelerating recently, the USDA reported moist smokeless tobacco has been the fastest growing segment of the tobacco industry with volume increasing at a 3.7% annual growth rate over the past 17 years compared with a 2% annual decline in cigarette volume over the same period. A.C. Nielson reported that moist snuff volume grew 2.9% in 1997 and 1.2% in 1998.[4]

A number of factors contributed to the continued growth of the moist smokeless tobacco segment. The increased prevalence of smoking bans has led consumers to switch to smokeless tobacco to circumvent smoking restrictions. Consumers perceive that moist smokeless tobacco is less of a health risk than cigarettes. Smokeless tobacco is

[1]UST Inc. Press Release, "UST Increases First Quarter 1999 Dividend; Accelerates Stock Repurchase with $1 Billion to Be Borrowed Over 5 Years," December 10, 1998.

[2]"UST Stock Buybacks: Initiatives Planned for 1999," *Dow Jones News Service,* December 10, 1998.

[3]Merrill Lynch & Co., "UST Inc.," December 4, 1998.

[4]Data in this paragraph from Credit Suisse First Boston, "UST, Inc.: Still Chewing on the Story—Stay Tuned," August 27, 1999.

Professor Mark Mitchell prepared this case from published sources with the assistance of Janet T. Mitchell as the basis for class discussion rather than to illustrate either effective or ineffective handling of an administrative situation.

Copyright © 2000 by the President and Fellows of Harvard College. To order copies or request permission to reproduce materials, call 1-800-545-7685, write Harvard Business School Publishing, Boston, MA 02163, or go to http://www.hbsp.harvard.edu. No part of this publication may be reproduced, stored in a retrieval system, used in a spreadsheet, or transmitted in any form or by any means—electronic, mechanical, photocopying, recording, or otherwise—without the permission of Harvard Business School.

TABLE A Smokeless Tobacco Products

Source: Credit Suisse First Boston, "UST, Inc.: Still Chewing on the Story—Stay Tuned," August 27, 1999

Category	Definition	Use	Brand/(Manufacturer)
Snuff			
Dry	Powdered dry tobacco	Snorted through nose	(Conwood), (Swisher), (UST) & (B&W)
Moist	Fine, long, or powdered cut moist tobacco	Placed between lower lip and gum	Copenhagen (UST), Skoal (UST), Kodiak (Conwood), Silver Creek (Swisher) & Timber Wolf (Pinkerton)
Chewing Tobacco			
Loose Leaf	Moist tobacco which is cut into small strips	Placed between cheek and gum	Red Man (Pinkerton), Levi Garrett (Conwood) & Beech Nut (National)
Plug	Moist or dry tobacco compressed into a chunk	Placed between cheek and gum	Day's Work (Pinkerton), Red Man (Pinkerton), & Levi Garrett (Conwood)
Twist/Roll	Tobacco fashioned into a roll	Placed between cheek and gum	(Conwood)

less expensive to use than cigarettes based upon an average per-week usage measurement. Additionally, consumers have been shifting over time to moist smokeless tobacco from loose leaf chewing tobacco. While the consumer base remains primarily male (approximately 98%), smokeless tobacco use is no longer confined to the stereotypical blue collar or rural users as approximately 30% of users have attended some college. The overall moist smokeless tobacco market is expected to continue to grow at an annual rate of 1–3%, with a large portion of the growth expected in the price-value segment.[5]

Competitive Position

UST is the dominant producer of moist smokeless tobacco, or moist snuff, controlling approximately 77% of the market.[6] Exhibit 1 provides a description of UST's products and Exhibit 2 displays market share in the moist smokeless tobacco market from 1991 to 1998. Table B displays the 1998 market share of the top moist smokeless tobacco brands. UST was a driving force in the overall expansion of the moist smokeless tobacco market over the years, primarily through product innovations such as new forms and flavors. Historically, UST has been aggressive with its price increases, instituting almost annual, often twice annual, price increases over the past twenty-five years. Steadily increasing prices provided a solid boost to earnings and the company's stock price. Meanwhile, as UST expanded the category and continued to raise prices, smaller players eroded UST's market share primarily by cutting price.

Given UST's relatively significant share erosion in recent years, the investment community called upon management to take actions to compete more effectively against the value brands and stem the erosion of market share. Despite its history of expanding the overall smokeless tobacco industry through new product introductions and innovations, UST had been criticized recently for a reduction in innovation and tardiness of new product introductions and product line extensions. Inroads by smaller competitors, primarily in the value segment, led to missed earnings and lowered Wall

[5]Ibid.

[6]Ibid.

TABLE B
Smokeless Tobacco Brands (1998 Dollar Share)

Source: 1998 A.C. Nielson data

Copenhagen Fine Cut (UST)	29.9%
Skoal Fine Cut Wintergreen (UST)	11.8%
Kodiak Wintergreen (Conwood)	9.5%
Skoal Long Cut Wintergreen (UST)	9.4%
Copenhagen Long Cut (UST)	7.2%
Skoal Long Cut Straight (UST)	5.9%
Skoal Long Cut Mint (UST)	4.4%
Skoal Long Cut Cherry (UST)	2.9%
Skoal Bandits Wintergreen (UST)	2.2%
Skoal Long Cut Classic (UST)	2.0%
Skoal Long Cut Spearmint (UST)	1.8%
Skoal Fine Cut Straight (UST)	1.3%

Street expectations. A *Wall Street Journal* article in 1997 noted "The company's management, pleased with their dominant market share and keenly aware of the company's strong heritage, turned their noses at the smaller upstarts."[7] In fact, an alleged dispute over the company's course of action reportedly led to the resignation of two key executives. In February 1997, John J. Bucchignano, CFO, and Robert D. Rothenburg, President of the tobacco unit, resigned due to "philosophical differences about the strategic direction of the company."[8]

In 1997, rather than cut prices to counter the growth of value players, UST introduced its Red Seal brand tobacco to compete with the price-value brands and preserve pricing power and profitability of its premium brands.[9] Despite this new product, analysts felt that UST was too slow in responding to the threat of value competitors. At the time of its introduction, the value segment had already gained 9% market share, requiring Red Seal to compete against already successful value brands. Another 1997 product introduction, Copenhagen Long Cut, was introduced to combat Conwood's full-priced Kodiak brand. Conwood, through its promotion of "long-cut" brands, which are easier to use than fine cut products, had made strong inroads with young and new consumers. UST originally stood by its traditional Copenhagen Fine Cut, only succumbing to the pressure to introduce a competitive product after continuing market share losses. Rooster, introduced in 1998, was a new premium product packaged in a larger can, 1.5 ounce compared to the traditional 1.2 ounce, to provide more tobacco for the consumers' money.[10]

In addition to product introductions, UST renewed its focus on marketing and promotion. Due to restrictions on public advertising, UST focused its marketing expenditures on free samples, mail-in rebates, and promotional sales. In 1997 and 1998, the company implemented a number of marketing initiatives and promotions. For example, UST offered 4-for-3 pricing on selected products, increased couponing, expanded its sales force, provided retailer and wholesaler incentive programs, expanded outlets and/or markets for new products, executed selected per can discounts, used special commemorative lids, and repositioned certain Skoal products.[11]

[7] See Suein L. Hwang, "UST Stock Falls 12% as Firm Says Profit Won't Meet Expectations," *Wall Street Journal,* March 3, 1997.

[8] See Cathleen Egan, "UST Resignations Likely Turned on Battle vs. Private Labels," *Dow Jones News Service,* February 24, 1997.

[9] David Adelman, "UST(UST): No Surprises in 1Q Results; Retaining Underperform Rating," Morgan Stanley Dean Witter U.S. Investment Research, April 30, 1998.

[10] Credit Suisse First Boston, "UST, Inc.: Still Chewing on the Story—Stay Tuned," August 27, 1999.

[11] Ibid.

Litigation and Legislative Environment

Litigation and legislation are everyday occurrences in the tobacco industry. Smokeless tobacco manufacturers have historically faced less exposure to health related lawsuits than cigarette manufacturers. For example, UST had seven pending health related lawsuits (excluding the state Medicaid cases) at the end of 1998, compared to cases numbering in the hundreds filed against cigarette companies.[12] The lower exposure to health-related lawsuits is largely due to the fact that scientific evidence linking smokeless tobacco to cancer is less conclusive than studies researching cigarettes' tie to cancer, and snuff producers face no potential "secondhand" smoke litigation.

In 1998, the tobacco industry experienced a number of developments in the legal and political arena, most of which were viewed positively by the industry. In June, Congressional efforts to pass broad-based tobacco legislation unfavorable to the industry collapsed. In July, a U.S. District Court judge issued a ruling to "vacate" major portions of a 1993 EPA report classifying environmental tobacco smoke as a known human carcinogen.[13] In August, a federal appeals court ruled that "the FDA lacks jurisdiction to regulate tobacco products, and all of the FDA's regulations of tobacco products are invalid." Additionally, cigarette manufacturers won dismissal of several class-action lawsuits filed on behalf of smokers and labor union health care funds.[14]

Furthermore, in a landmark event for the tobacco industry, the industry agreed in November to settle state Medicaid lawsuits with a $206 billion settlement and a ban on advertising and promotions that appeal to youths. The settlement was negotiated among the four major cigarette manufacturers and eight states, but received unanimous approval of all 46 Attorneys General for states attempting to recover Medicaid costs for treating victims of tobacco related ailments. Separately, in November, UST negotiated and signed the Smokeless Tobacco Master Settlement Agreement to settle its Medicaid disputes. The agreement provided that UST pay $100 to $200 million, or $.015 to $.02 per can, over 10 years and agree to advertising and promotion restrictions, primarily aimed at reducing youth exposure. UST was the only major smokeless tobacco manufacturer to sign this agreement. Despite the major Medicaid state settlements, lawmakers are expected to continue to push for new laws to combat youth tobacco use, further restrict advertising, and empower the FDA to regulate nicotine as a drug. Other litigation against tobacco companies is expected to continue, especially suits filed by individuals. In addition to health related litigation, UST also faced a pending dispute at the end of 1998 whereby Conwood Co. alleged that UST had violated antitrust and advertising laws and participated in anti-competitive conduct.

Financial Results

UST has historically been one of the most profitable companies, not only in the tobacco sector, but also in corporate America. In 1997 and 1998, UST received accolades from *Forbes* which named UST the top company in terms of profitability. UST's five-year return on capital of 92.1% was nearly 20% higher than the 2nd ranked firm.[15] In a

[12]In 1986, UST prevailed with a unanimous jury verdict in the only moist smokeless tobacco liability lawsuit to make it through the trial process.

[13]See "Judge Rejects EPA Secondhand Smoke Report," *Association of Trial Lawyers of America,* 1998.

[14]See Alissa J. Rubin, "Judges Rule against FDA on Tobacco. U.S. to Appeal Decision That Bars Regulation," *Los Angeles Times,* August 15, 1998.

[15]*Forbes'* annual ranking of companies.

profitability study performed in 1998, John Dorfman of Dreman Value Management found UST the most profitable company as measured by return on equity, return on assets, and gross profit margin. Of 1,825 U.S. companies with a market value in excess of $500 million, only 15 companies passed a stringent test that included a minimum 40% return on equity, minimum 20% return on assets, and a gross profit margin of 20% or more. UST beat corporate icons such as Coca-Cola and Microsoft to attain the title of most profitable company.[16] UST's profitability stems from several factors including its commanding share of the moist smokeless tobacco market, premium product and strong name brand recognition, historical pricing flexibility, continued growth of moist smokeless tobacco, and limited market access by new competitors due to tobacco advertising restrictions.

Exhibit 3 presents summary financial information for the 11-year period from 1988 to 1998. Other than decreases in earnings and cash flow in 1997, UST posted continuous increases in sales, earnings, and cash flow over the entire period. Sales, earnings, and cash flow have grown at 10-year compound annual growth rates of 9%, 11%, and 12%, respectively. Concurrently, UST maintained enviable margins with average gross profit, EBITDA, EBIT, and net margins of 77%, 53%, 50%, and 31%, respectively. Annual return on equity averaged 89% and return on assets averaged 48%. Over this same period, UST provided a generous return of capital to investors, paying $2.2 billion in dividends and repurchasing $2.0 billion in stock.

While the vast majority of UST's operations revolve around the production of smokeless tobacco products, the company also produces and markets wine and premium cigars. Historically, UST has dallied modestly in operations outside of its core moist smokeless tobacco operations.[17] Such investments in non-core operations have traditionally provided returns far below those of the moist smokeless tobacco business. In 1998, smokeless tobacco contributed approximately 88% of revenues and 97% of operating profit. Wine and other businesses (cigars and international marketing of moist smokeless tobacco) contributed 10% and 2% of revenues, respectively, and 3% and 0% of operating profit, respectively. Exhibit 4 provides segment information for UST's operations from 1996 to 1998.

The Tobacco Industry

UST's 1998 financial performance relative to other tobacco companies is shown in Exhibit 5. Review of the operating statistics indicates UST compares very favorably to the other tobacco firms. UST's gross profit margin of 80% compares to a median of 28% for the group. Average return on assets of 54% and return on equity of 103% for UST compare to medians of 3.1% and 22.5% for the group. Furthermore, UST achieves these high returns with low financial leverage. UST's total debt to book capitalization is 17.6% compared to the group median of nearly 66%.

Standard & Poor's ("S&P") rates the debt of three of the six other tobacco companies as investment grade and two companies are rated BB, the highest level of speculative grade credit ratings. See Exhibit 6 for tobacco companies' S&P ratings and financial

[16]See John Dorfman, "Smokeless Tobacco Maker UST Tops Profitability Test," *Rocky Mountain News*, August 16, 1998.

[17]For example, UST purchased two Michigan television stations in 1980 (sold in 1985), acquired Heritage Health, a chain of alcohol and substance abuse centers, in 1986 (sold in 1988), bought 76% of the stock in Camera Platforms, a firm that leases camera cars to the movie industry, in 1990 (sold in 1995), and formed Cabin Fever Entertainment in 1988 to produce video and television programming (sold in 1998).

ratios. The favorable ratings are due primarily to the highly cash generative nature of the tobacco industry. S&P views the near-term outlook of the tobacco industry to be stable and the longer-term view to be less clear. Despite strong cash flows, the U.S. tobacco industry is characterized by legal challenges, declining volumes, marketing restrictions, taxes, discounting, and consolidation.[18]

UST has historically maintained an A-1 credit rating for its commercial paper. As UST increases its debt level, it will likely issue long-term debt, thereby increasing the average maturity of debt outstanding. S&P and the other rating agencies will review UST's overall corporate profile, pro-forma capital structure, and investment intentions to determine the appropriate senior debt rating for the company. S&P will consider, among other things, UST's cash flow generation and payment obligations, financial policies, market position and brand name recognition, geographic and product diversification, pricing power, industry dynamics, profitability margins and returns, capitalization ratios, and coverage ratios. The rating determination could have a significant impact on the cost of the recapitalization. See Exhibit 7 and Exhibit 8 for an overview of S&P's ratings criteria and key financial ratios.

Outlook

Once a Wall Street darling, research analysts in late 1998 have mixed views of UST's future, with a number of analysts maintaining "Neutral" ratings on the company. While UST has somewhat stabilized its market share, analysts remain concerned about the continued threat of price-value competitors and a softening smokeless tobacco market. Unlike cigarette companies who combat declining domestic consumption trends with offshore growth, UST has no immediate opportunity for international expansion. Historically lackluster performance of non-core operations creates some concern that management might use funds to over-invest in under-performing businesses. Additionally, public and political sentiment remains negative regarding the tobacco industry.

Despite the less than glowing outlook, the board of directors decided to borrow up to $1 billion to accelerate the company's stock repurchase program. Looking forward to 1999, Vincent Gierer and the UST management team face the task of implementing the major change in debt policy.

[18]See "Divergent Credit Trends for the Global Tobacco Industry," *Standard & Poor's* (September 22, 1999).

EXHIBIT 1 UST Inc. Product Information

Source: Credit Suisse First Boston research dated August 27, 1999.

Brands	Category	Introduction	% 1998 Sales	1998 Average Retail Cost per Can	Description	Competition
Copenhagen	Full Price	1822	48%	$3.13	Top selling brand in the industry. Straight-flavored. Copenhagen has a "made-date" on bottom of its container so consumers recognize that it is fresh. Both fine and long cut varieties. Long cut variety introduced in the first quarter of 1997.	Timberwolf (Swedish Match) and Redwood (Swisher)
Skoal Fine Cut	Full Price	1935	18%	$2.98	Second largest selling brand in the industry. Wintergreen and straight-flavored.	Kodiak (Conwood)
Skoal Long Cut	Full Price	1984	29%	$3.11	Available in six varieties: wintergreen, straight, mint, cherry, classic, and spearmint.	Kodiak (Conwood), Timberwolf (Swedish Match), and Silver Creek (Helme)
Skoal Bandits	Full Price	National introduction in 1983	3%	$3.10	Skoal packed in "tea bags" that are individual portion packs that make it easy to use and dispose.	Renegades (Swedish Match)
Red Seal	Price Value	Third Qtr 1997	1%	$1.29	Available in wintergreen and straight-flavors. Introduced in a 1.2 oz package.	Timberwolf (Swedish Match), Cougar, Redwood (Swisher), and Silver Creek (Helme)
Rooster	Full Price	Test marketed in Fourth Qtr 1997; National introduction in 1998	<1%	$2.44	Long-cut wintergreen and straight-flavored. Priced competitively to Copenhagen and Skoal but is packaged in a 1.5 oz can, offering consumers 25% more tobacco for their money.	Kodiak (Conwood)

EXHIBIT 2 Market Share Information for UST Inc.

Source: Credit Suisse First Boston Research dated August 27, 1999. Compiled from A. C. Neilson data and estimates.

	1991	1992	1993	1994	1995	1996	1997	1998	7 Yr. CAGR
Industry									
Premium Market Share %	99.0%	97.9%	97.2%	96.3%	94.9%	92.7%	90.9%	89.2%	(1.5%)
Price Value Market Share %	1.0%	2.1%	2.8%	3.7%	5.1%	7.3%	9.1%	10.8%	40.5%
UST									
Total Market Share %	86.2%	84.6%	85.1%	83.8%	81.7%	79.5%	78.2%	77.2%	(1.6%)
Increase/(Decrease)%		*(1.9%)*	*0.6%*	*(1.5%)*	*(2.5%)*	*(2.7%)*	*(1.6%)*	*(1.3%)*	
Premium Market Share %	86.2%	84.6%	85.1%	83.8%	81.7%	79.5%	78.2%	76.6%	(1.7%)
Price Value Market Share %	0.0%	0.0%	0.0%	0.0%	0.0%	0.0%	0.0%	0.6%	—
Conwood									
Total Market Share %	10.1%	11.3%	10.8%	11.1%	11.9%	12.8%	13.1%	13.2%	3.9%
Increase/(Decrease)%		*11.9%*	*(4.4%)*	*2.8%*	*7.2%*	*7.6%*	*2.3%*	*0.8%*	
Premium Market Share %	10.1%	11.3%	10.8%	11.1%	11.9%	12.2%	11.8%	11.6%	2.0%
Price Value Market Share %	0.0%	0.0%	0.0%	0.0%	0.0%	0.6%	1.3%	1.6%	—
Swedish Match									
Total Market Share %	1.8%	2.0%	1.0%	1.1%	1.4%	2.3%	3.0%	4.6%	14.3%
Increase/(Decrease)%		*11.1%*	*(50.0%)*	*10.0%*	*27.3%*	*64.3%*	*30.4%*	*53.3%*	
Premium Market Share %	1.8%	2.0%	1.0%	1.0%	0.8%	0.5%	0.3%	0.3%	(22.6%)
Price Value Market Share %	0.0%	0.0%	0.0%	0.1%	0.6%	1.8%	2.7%	4.3%	—
Swisher									
Total Market Share %	1.0%	2.1%	2.8%	3.6%	4.5%	4.9%	5.1%	3.8%	21.0%
Increase/(Decrease)%		*110.0%*	*33.3%*	*28.6%*	*25.0%*	*8.9%*	*4.1%*	*(25.5%)*	
Premium Market Share %	0.0%	0.0%	0.0%	0.0%	0.0%	0.0%	0.0%	0.0%	—
Price Value Market Share %	1.0%	2.1%	2.8%	3.6%	4.5%	4.9%	5.1%	3.8%	21.0%
Other Manufacturers									
Total Market Share %	0.9%	0.0%	0.3%	0.4%	0.5%	0.5%	0.6%	1.2%	4.2%
Increase/(Decrease)%		*(100.0%)*	*NM*	*33.3%*	*25.0%*	*0.0%*	*20.0%*	*100.0%*	
Premium Market Share %	0.9%	0.0%	0.3%	0.4%	0.5%	0.5%	0.6%	0.7%	(3.5%)
Price Value Market Share %	0.0%	0.0%	0.0%	0.0%	0.0%	0.0%	0.0%	0.5%	—

EXHIBIT 3 **Summary Financial Information for UST Inc. (in millions, except per-share data and ratios)**

Source: Company annual report for fiscal year ended December 31, 1998, and author's adjustments and calculations.

	1988	1989	1990	1991	1992	1993	1994	1995	1996	1997	1998	5-Yr CAGR	10-Yr CAGR
Summary Operating Data[a]													
Net Sales	$611.9	$673.9	$756.4	$898.4	$1,032.2	$1,097.5	$1,204.0	$1,305.8	$1,371.7	$1,401.7	$1,423.2	5%	9%
Gross Profit	437.3	488.4	564.6	670.9	775.4	851.1	952.0	1,043.6	1,098.9	1,109.8	1,139.7		
EBITDA	277.9	315.0	368.6	446.4	525.2	591.4	668.9	736.9	779.2	749.8	785.0	6%	11%
EBIT	260.2	298.4	349.0	423.8	500.8	564.8	640.7	707.8	750.9	719.3	753.3	6%	11%
Interest Expense (Income)	(1.1)	(3.2)	(3.2)	(2.3)	(1.9)	(2.0)	0.1	3.2	6.4	7.5	(2.2)		
Pretax Earnings	261.3	301.6	352.2	426.1	502.6	566.8	640.6	704.6	744.5	703.9	755.5		
Net Income	162.2	190.5	223.3	265.9	312.6	347.9	387.5	429.8	464.0	443.9	467.9	6%	11%
Free Operating Cash Flow	$135.2	$195.1	$217.8	$247.3	$267.9	$340.7	$399.2	$521.2	$456.4	$287.4	$429.5	5%	12%
Special Charges/ Non-Recurring Items (Gains)[b]	—	—	—	—	—	$(35.0)	—	—	-	$8.0	$21.0		
Basic Earnings per Share	$0.74	$0.87	$1.04	$1.26	$1.49	$1.67	$1.92	$2.21	$2.48	$2.41	$2.52	9%	13%
Diluted Earnings per Share	$0.71	$0.83	$0.99	$1.20	$1.43	$1.63	$1.88	$2.17	$2.44	$2.39	$2.50	9%	13%
Dividend per Share	$0.37	$0.46	$0.55	$0.66	$0.80	$0.96	$1.12	$1.30	$1.48	$1.62	$1.62	11%	16%
Dividend Payout Ratio	50%	53%	53%	52%	54%	58%	58%	59%	60%	67%	64%		
Balance Sheet and Cash Flow Data													
Cash and Cash Equivalents	$72.7	$54.6	$46.6	$41.5	$36.4	$25.3	$50.7	$69.4	$54.5	$6.9	$33.2		
Total Assets	$598.0	$630.2	$622.6	$656.5	$674.0	$706.2	$741.2	$784.0	$806.6	$826.4	$913.3		
Long-Term Debt	$21.8	$6.8	$3.1	-	-	$40.0	$125.0	$100.0	$100.0	$100.0	$100.0		
Total Debt	$30.8	$14.5	$4.8	$1.3	-	$40.0	$125.0	$200.0	$250.0	$110.0	$100.0		
Shareholders' Equity	$453.3	$482.3	$473.9	$482.9	$516.6	$463.0	$361.7	$292.8	$281.2	$436.8	$468.3		
Average Basic Shares Outstanding	220.6	219.8	215.2	211.6	209.8	208.5	202.0	194.4	187.4	183.9	185.5		
Working Capital	$221.1	$209.3	$197.2	$210.0	$249.0	$228.4	$221.2	$144.8	$144.0	$275.3	$309.9		
Capital Expenditures[c]	$20.8	$23.7	$37.2	$28.4	$30.1	$54.5	$23.7	$14.0	$36.7	$55.8	$35.5		
Dividends Paid	$81.7	$101.2	$118.3	$139.7	$168.0	$199.7	$225.7	$252.4	$277.3	$298.1	$301.1		
Share Repurchases	$67.4	$97.5	$151.3	$184.4	$212.6	$236.7	$298.8	$274.8	$237.8	$45.7	$151.6		

EXHIBIT 3 Continued

	1988	1989	1990	1991	1992	1993	1994	1995	1996	1997	1998	5-Yr CAGR	10-Yr CAGR
Stock Price Data													
High	$10.50	$15.38	$18.25	$33.88	$35.38	$32.75	$31.50	$36.00	$35.88	$36.94	$36.88		
Low	$6.00	$9.63	$12.38	$16.38	$25.38	$24.38	$23.63	$26.63	$28.25	$25.50	$24.56		
Year End	$10.25	$15.31	$18.25	$32.75	$32.00	$27.75	$27.88	$33.38	$32.38	$36.94	$34.88	5%	13%
Price/Earnings Ratio[d]	13.9x	17.6x	17.5x	26.0x	21.5x	16.6x	14.5x	15.1x	13.1x	15.3x	13.8x		
Market Equity[e]	$2,260.6	$3,366.0	$3,926.6	$6,930.0	$6,713.7	$5,785.0	$5,630.6	$6,487.2	$6,066.6	$6,794.0	$6,470.8		
Selected Growth Rates and Ratios												5-Yr Avg	10-Yr Avg
Sales Growth	7.2%	10.1%	12.3%	18.8%	14.9%	6.3%	9.7%	8.5%	5.0%	2.2%	1.5%		
Net Income Growth	23.9%	17.5%	17.2%	19.1%	17.5%	11.3%	11.4%	10.9%	8.0%	(4.3%)	5.4%		
Dividend Growth	23.3%	24.3%	19.6%	20.0%	21.2%	20.0%	16.7%	16.1%	13.8%	9.5%	0.0%		
Gross Profit Margin	71.5%	72.5%	74.6%	74.7%	75.1%	77.5%	79.1%	79.9%	80.1%	79.2%	80.1%	79.7%	77.3%
EBITDA Margin	45.4%	46.7%	48.7%	49.7%	50.9%	53.9%	55.6%	56.4%	56.8%	53.5%	55.2%	55.5%	52.7%
EBIT Margin	42.5%	44.3%	46.1%	47.2%	48.5%	51.5%	53.2%	54.2%	54.7%	51.3%	52.9%	53.3%	50.4%
Net Margin	26.5%	28.3%	29.5%	29.6%	30.3%	31.7%	32.2%	32.9%	33.8%	31.7%	32.9%	32.7%	31.3%
Return on Average Equity	38.0%	40.7%	46.7%	55.6%	62.5%	71.0%	94.0%	131.3%	161.7%	123.7%	103.4%	122.8%	89.1%
Return on Average Assets	28.3%	31.0%	35.6%	41.6%	47.0%	50.4%	53.5%	56.4%	58.3%	54.4%	53.8%	55.3%	48.2%
Long-Term Debt/ Capitalization	4.6%	1.4%	0.6%	0.0%	0.0%	8.0%	25.7%	25.5%	26.2%	18.6%	17.6%	22.7%	12.4%
Total Debt/ Capitalization	6.4%	2.9%	1.0%	0.3%	0.0%	8.0%	25.7%	40.6%	47.1%	20.1%	17.6%	30.2%	16.3%

[a]Before the cumulative effect of accounting changes. Excludes settlement charges and other special charges or non-recurring items. All net income adjustments apply a 40% tax rate.
[b]Author's estimates of pretax settlement charges and other special charges or nonrecurring items. Does not include effect of accounting changes.
[c]Additions for property, plant, and equipment net of dispositions.
[d]Based upon year-end stock price and basic earnings per share.
[e]Based upon average basic shares outstanding and year-end stock price.

EXHIBIT 4 Summary Financial Information (Segment Data) for UST Inc. (in millions)

Source: Company annual report for fiscal year ended December 31, 1998, and author's calculations.

	1996	% Total	1997	% Total	1998	% Total
Net Sales (unaffiliated customers)						
Tobacco	$1,167.5	*85.1%*	$1,181.8	*84.3%*	$1,245.6	*87.5%*
Wine	122.5	*8.9%*	145.0	*10.3%*	148.5	*10.4%*
Other	81.7	*6.0%*	74.9	*5.3%*	29.2	*2.1%*
Total Net Sales	$1,371.7		$1,401.7		$1,423.2	
Operating Profit						
Tobacco	$745.6	*97.6%*	$700.4	*96.3%*	$720.6	*96.8%*
Wine	17.9	*2.3%*	28.2	*3.9%*	22.1	*3.0%*
Other	0.1	*0.0%*	(1.3)	*(0.2%)*	1.7	*0.2%*
Total Operating Profit	$763.5		$727.3		$744.4	
Operating Profit Margin						
Tobacco	63.9%		59.3%		57.9%	
Wine	14.6%		19.4%		14.9%	
Other	0.1%		(1.7%)		5.9%	
Identifiable Assets at December 31						
Tobacco	$458.2	*56.8%*	$468.0	*56.6%*	$497.6	*54.5%*
Wine	194.9	*24.2%*	230.9	*27.9%*	277.2	*30.4%*
Other	91.6	*11.4%*	102.2	*12.4%*	87.2	*9.5%*
Corporate	61.9	*7.7%*	25.3	*3.1%*	51.3	*5.6%*
Total Identifiable Assets	$806.6		$826.4		$913.3	
Capital Expenditures (Gross)						
Tobacco	$29.2	*65.3%*	$29.4	*50.6%*	$27.7	*49.2%*
Wine	12.0	*26.9%*	20.1	*34.6%*	25.6	*45.6%*
Other	2.7	*6.0%*	6.1	*10.5%*	2.5	*4.4%*
Corporate	0.8	*1.8%*	2.5	*4.3%*	0.5	*0.8%*
Total Capital Expenditures	$44.7		$58.2		$56.3	
Depreciation						
Tobacco	$15.8	*56.2%*	$16.3	*54.0%*	$16.1	*51.3%*
Wine	8.9	*31.7%*	10.4	*34.6%*	12.0	*38.1%*
Other	1.8	*6.4%*	1.8	*6.1%*	1.7	*5.3%*
Corporate	1.6	*5.8%*	1.6	*5.3%*	1.7	*5.3%*
Total Depreciation	$28.1		$30.1		$31.4	

EXHIBIT 5 **Summary Financial Information for UST Inc. (in millions, except per share data and ratios)**

Source: Company financial statements and author's calculations and adjustments.

	Tobacco Product Manufacturers				Tobacco Leaf Merchants		
	UST Inc.	Philip Morris	North Atlantic Trading Co.	RJR Nabisco Holdings[i]	DiMon Inc.	Standard Commercial	Universal Corp
Summary Operating Data[a]							
Fiscal Year End	*Dec 31, 1998*	*Dec 31, 1998*	*Dec 31, 1998*	*Dec 31, 1998*	*June 30, 1995*	*March 31, 1998*	*June 30, 1998*
Net Sales	$1,423.2	$74,391.0	$93.1	$20,563.0	$2,171.8	$1,492.8	$4,287.2
Gross Profit	1,139.7	30,993.0	60.9	9,493.0	266.9	145.0	613.6
EBITDA[b]	785.0	15,501.0	36.3	3,602.0	200.2	85.8	329.5
EBIT[b]	753.3	13,811.0	29.1	2,467.0	156.7	65.3	278.4
Interest Expense (Income)	(2.2)	890.0	24.9	880.0	83.8	37.8	64.0
Pretax Earnings	755.5	12,921.0	4.2	1,455.0	72.9	37.1	231.3
Net Income	467.9	7,672.4	1.0	718.0	52.0	26.9	130.4
Free Operating Cash Flow	$429.5	$6,076.4	$14.5	$2,016.0	$52.5	$(61.3)	$110.2
Special Charges/Non-Recurring Items (Gains)[c]	$21.0	$3,834.0	–	$2,069.0	$16.9	–	$(16.7)
Basic Earnings per Share	$2.52	$3.16	$(7.09)[g]	$2.22	$1.17	$2.18	$3.71
Diluted Earnings per Share	$2.50	$3.14	$(7.09)[g]	$2.22	$1.16	$2.05	$3.68
Dividend per Share (Common)	$1.62	$1.68	–	$2.05	$0.66	–	$1.11
Dividend Payout Ratio	64%	53%	0%	92%	56%	0%	30%
Balance Sheet and Cash Flow Data							
Cash and Cash Equivalents	$33.2	$4,081.0	$2.8	$300.0	$18.7	$34.1	$79.8
Total Assets	$913.3	$59,920.0	$260.0	$28,892.0	$1,797.5	$839.5	$2,056.7
Long-Term Debt	$100.0	$12,615.0	$202.6	$9,982.0	$797.0	$197.1	$263.1
Total Debt	$100.0	$14,662.0	$215.6	$10,467.0	$1,079.5	$469.9	$849.6
Preferred Stock & Minority Interest	–	–	$39.3	$957.0	$0.5	$30.3	$31.7
Shareholders' Equity	$468.3	$16,197.0	$(15.4)	$7,809.0	$421.9	$149.6	$547.9
Average Basic Shares Outstanding	185.5	2,429.0	528.2	323.9	44.5	12.4	35.2
Working Capital	$309.9	$3,851.0	$42.0	$(259.0)	$706.4	$219.1	$328.8
Capital Expenditures[d]	$35.5	$1,804.0	$0.5	$576.0	$36.6	$9.7	$90.0
Stock Price Data							
Fiscal Year End	$34.88	$53.50	NA[h]	$29.69	$11.25	$15.94	$37.38
Price/Earnings Ratio[e]	13.8×	16.9×	NA[h]	13.4×	9.6×	7.3×	10.1×
Market Equity[f]	$6,470.8	$129,951.5	NA[h]	$9,614.4	$500.3	$197.3	$1,315.2

Selected Growth Rates and Ratios								Median (excl. UST)	Mean (excl. UST)
Sales Growth	1.5%	3.2%	10.2%	(0.5%)	2.2%	10.2%	4.2%		
Gross Profit Margin	80.1%	41.7%	65.4%	46.2%	12.3%	9.7%	14.3%	28.0%	31.6%
EBITDA Margin	55.2%	20.8%	39.0%	17.5%	9.2%	5.7%	7.7%	13.4%	16.7%
EBIT Margin	52.9%	18.6%	31.3%	12.0%	7.2%	4.4%	6.5%	9.6%	13.3%
Net Margin	32.9%	10.3%	1.1%	3.5%	2.4%	1.8%	3.0%	2.7%	3.7%
Return on Average Equity	103.4%	49.3%	NM	8.4%	12.5%	22.5%	25.6%	22.5%	23.7%
Return on Average Assets	53.8%	13.2%	0.4%	2.4%	2.7%	3.4%	6.5%	3.1%	4.8%
Long-Term Debt/Capitalization	17.6%	43.8%	89.4%	53.2%	65.4%	52.3%	31.2%	52.8%	55.9%
Total Debt/Capitalization	17.6%	47.5%	90.0%	54.4%	71.9%	72.3%	59.4%	65.7%	65.9%

[a]Before the cumulative effect of accounting changes and discontinued operations. Excludes settlement charges, special charges, and nonrecurring items. Net income adjustments generally apply a 40% tax rate.
[b]Excludes Other Income and Expense.
[c]Author's estimates of pretax settlement charges and other special charges or nonrecurring items. Does not include discontinued operations or effect of accounting changes.
[d]Additions of property, plant, and equipment net of dispositions.
[e]Based upon fiscal year-end stock price and basic earnings per share.
[f]Based upon average basic shares outstanding and fiscal year-end stock price.
[g]Includes impact of preferred stock dividends.
[h]North Atlantic Trading Company is privately held.
[i]RJR Nabisco Holdings spun its tobacco business (RJ Reynolds Tobacco) off to shareholders in 1999.

EXHIBIT 6 Key Financial Ratios for Tobacco Companies

Source: Data provided by Standard & Poor's to the casewriter.

	Tobacco Product Manufacturers			Tobacco Leaf Merchants				
Three years (1996–1998)	Philip Morris	North Atlantic Trading Co.[a]	RJR Nabisco Holdings	DiMon Inc.	Standard Commercial	Universal Corp	Tobacco Companies Median[b]	UST Inc.
Corporate Credit Rating	A	B+	BBB–	BB+	BB–	A–		
Outlook	Stable	Stable	Stable	Negative	Positive	Stable		
EBIT interest coverage (x)	11.2	1.3	2.5	2.6	3.3	3.5	3.0	101.5
EBITDA interest coverage (x)	12.7	1.6	3.7	3.3	5.4	4.4	4.1	105.6
Fund flow/total debt (%)	56.3	6.8	14.5	12.3	6.7	18.5	13.4	364.0
Free operating cash flow/total debt (%)	41.8	5.6	6.8	10.1	(2.6)	2.9	6.2	296.5
Return on capital (%)	38.4	11.8	10.3	13.4	6.6	16.9	12.6	140.6
Operating income/sales (%)	26.0	38.1	15.6	16.4	3.6	7.6	16.0	55.7
Total debt/capital (including ST debt) (%)	49.3	90.6	55.1	67.8	77.5	65.8	66.8	28.2

[a] Data for 1997–1998.

[b] Excludes UST Inc.

EXHIBIT 7
S&P Credit Ratings

Source: Standard & Poor's Corporate Ratings Criteria.

Long-Term Issue Credit Ratings

Investment Grade

AAA	Obligor's capacity to meet its financial commitment on the obligation is extremely strong.
AA	Obligor's capacity to meet its financial commitment on the obligation is very strong.
A	Somewhat more susceptible to adverse effects of changes in circumstances and economic conditions. However, obligor's capacity to meet financial commitment on obligation is still strong.
BBB	Adequate protection parameters. However, adverse economic conditions or changing circumstances are more likely to lead to a weakened capacity of the obligor to meet its financial commitment on the obligation.
Speculative Grade	
BB	Obligation faces major ongoing uncertainties or exposure to adverse business, financial, or economic conditions which could lead to obligor's inadequate capacity to meet its financial commitment on the obligation.
B	Obligor currently has capacity to meet its financial commitment on the obligation. Adverse business, financial, or economic conditions will likely impair obligor's capacity or willingness to meet financial commitment on the obligation.
Notes:	S&P's ratings of long-term speculative grade debt also includes CCC, CC, C, and D (default) with these grades displaying successively greater vulnerabilities to default. Plus (+) or minus (–) may be added to ratings AA to CCC to indicate relative standing within the major ratings definitions.

Short-Term Issue Credit Ratings

A-1	Obligor's capacity to meet its financial commitment on the obligation is strong. Within the category, certain obligations are designated with a (+) sign which indicates obligor's capacity is extremely high.
A-2	Somewhat more susceptible to the adverse effects of changes in circumstances and economic condition, however, obligor's capacity to meet financial commitment on obligation is satisfactory.
A-3	Exhibits adequate protection parameters. However, adverse economic conditions or changing circumstances are more likely to lead to a weakened capacity of obligor to meet its financial commitment on the obligation.
B	Regarded as having significant speculative characteristics. Obligor currently has the capacity to meet its financial commitment on the obligation; however, it faces major ongoing uncertainties which could lead to inadequate capacity to meet financial commitment on the obligation.
Notes:	S&P's ratings of short-term speculative grade debt also includes C and D (default).

EXHIBIT 8 Key Financial Ratios[a]

Source: Standard & Poor's *Credit Week,* July 28, 1999, and Standard & Poor's *The Outlook,* January 6, 1999.

Adjusted Key Industrial Financial Ratios—Senior Debt Ratings

Industrial Long-Term Debt	Investment Grade				Noninvestment Grade/Speculative		
Three-Years (1996–1998) Medians	**AAA**	**AA**	**A**	**BBB**	**BB**	**B**	**CCC**
EBIT interest coverage (x)	12.9	9.2	7.2	4.1	2.5	1.2	(0.9)
EBITDA interest coverage (x)	18.7	14.0	10.0	6.3	3.9	2.3	0.2
Fund flow/total debt (%)	89.7	67.0	49.5	32.2	20.1	10.5	7.4
Free operating cash flow/total debt (%)	40.5	21.6	17.4	6.3	1.0	(4.0)	(25.4)
Return on capital (%)	30.6	25.1	19.6	15.4	12.6	9.2	(8.8)
Operating income/sales (%)	30.9	25.2	17.9	15.8	14.4	11.2	5.0
Long-term debt/capital (%)	21.4	29.3	33.3	40.8	55.3	68.8	71.5
Total debt/capital (including ST debt) (%)	31.8	37.0	39.2	46.4	58.5	71.4	79.4

		Corporate Bond Yields						
Debt Yields—December 22, 1998	**U.S. Treasury**	**AAA**	**AA**	**A**	**BBB**	**BB+**	**BB/BB–**	**BB**
10–Year (%)	4.70	5.60	5.84	6.12	6.84	7.70	8.72	11.19
20–Year (%)	5.45	6.47	6.76	7.05	7.82	—	—	—

Formulas for Adjusted Key Industrial Financial Ratios

EBIT interest coverage = Earnings from continuing operations before interest and taxes/Gross interest incurred before subtracting capitalized interest and interest income

EBITDA interest coverage = Earnings from continuing operations before interest, taxes, depreciation and amortization/Gross interest incurred before subtracting capitalized interest and interest income

Funds from operations/Total debt = Net income from continuing operations + depreciation, amortization, deferred income taxes, and other noncash/long-term debt + current maturities, commercial paper, and other short-term borrowings

Free operating cash flow/Total debt = Funds from operations – capital expenditures – (+) the increase (decrease) in working capital (excluding changes in cash, marketable securities, and ST debt/long-term debt + current maturities, commercial paper, and other short-term borrowings

Pretax return on capital = EBIT + interest expense/average of beginning and ending year capital, including short-term debt, current maturities, long-term debt, noncurrent deferred taxes, and equity

Operating income/Sales = Sales minus cost of goods manufactured (before depreciation and amortization), SG&A, and R&D costs/Sales

Long-term debt/Capitalization = Long-term debt/Long-term debt + shareholders' equity (including preferred stock) + minority interest

Total debt/Capitalization = Long-term debt + current maturities, commercial paper, and other short-term borrowings/Long-term debt + current maturities, commercial paper, and other short-term borrowings + shareholders' equity (including preferred stock) + minority interest

[a]Note: Excludes discussion of operating lease equivalents as defined by S&P for simplification purposes.

Diageo plc

Ian Cray, Diageo plc's Treasurer, looked out of his office window onto the busy streets of London in October 2000. The London-based consumer goods company Diageo had recently announced its intention to sell its packaged food subsidiary, Pillsbury, to General Mills. Earlier in the year, Diageo also announced its intent to sell 20% of its Burger King subsidiary through an initial public offering during 2001, to be followed by a spin-off of the remainder of Burger King after December 2002. If these transactions took place, the firm would be focused exclusively on the beverage alcohol industry. As Diageo's business was restructured, it was an opportune time to rethink its financing mix.

On Cray's desk lay a novel report by Ian Simpson, Diageo's Director of Corporate Finance and Capital Markets, and Adrian Williams, the firm's Treasury Research Manager. Their analysis sought to *quantify* the textbook characterization of the tradeoff between the costs and benefits of different gearing, or leverage, policies. Built around a simulation model of the future cash flows of the company, their analysis attempted to understand the tax benefits of higher gearing versus the likelihood and severity of costly financial distress. While the analysis was still rough at points, the concepts and implementation were intriguing. Now that Diageo was rethinking its financial policies, the model could prove useful. Simpson, Williams, and Cray would soon meet to discuss its implications.

Diageo's Business

Diageo was formed in November 1997 from the merger of Grand Metropolitan plc and Guinness plc, two of the world's leading consumer product companies. The newly-merged firm was the seventh largest food and drink company in the world with a market capitalization of nearly £24 billion and annual sales of over £13 billion to more than 140 countries. The merger was ostensibly motivated by the desire to become the industry leader and expected cost savings of nearly £290 million per year due to marketing synergies, reduction in head office and regional office overhead expenses, and production and purchasing efficiencies.

Some investors had been critical of the merger. One equity analyst, who judged that the firm would underperform the market, wrote "Diageo is creating an entity that fails to learn from all the mergers and acquisitions in other consumer areas that found portfolio strength does not work."[1] Separately, Bernard Arnault, the CEO of LVMH, a French luxury goods and drinks company, tried to scuttle the deal, and replace it with a three way merger that included LVMH while "demerging" Pillsbury and Burger King. Arnault, already the largest shareholder, doubled his stake to 11% of the combined stock, but failed to change the terms of the merger.

[1] J. Wakely, A. Gowen, R. Newboult, F. Ramzan, "Diageo," Lehman Brothers, November 21, 1997.

Professors George Chacko and Peter Tufano and Research Associate Joshua Musher prepared this case. HBS cases are developed solely as the basis for class discussion. Cases are not intended to serve as endorsements, sources of primary data, or illustrations of effective or ineffective management.

Copyright © 2001 President and Fellows of Harvard College. To order copies or request permission to reproduce materials, call 1-800-545-7685, write Harvard Business School Publishing, Boston, MA 02163, or go to http://www.hbsp.harvard.edu. No part of this publication may be reproduced, stored in a retrieval system, used in a spreadsheet, or transmitted in any form or by any means—electronic, mechanical, photocopying, recording, or otherwise—without the permission of Harvard Business School.

While Diageo's name was not well known to the average consumer, its brands were among the most famous in the world. The firm was organized along four business segments. The largest was the Spirits and Wine business, which produced and marketed a portfolio of beverage alcohol such as scotch, vodka, gin, and tequila. Diageo's brands included Johnnie Walker, Smirnoff, J&B, Bailey's, Gordon's, Tanqueray, Cuervo, and Malibu. This division was not only the biggest (with revenues of £5 billion and the leading market share in the U.S. and U.K. markets) but also the fastest growing of Diageo's businesses, with sales growth of 8% for the year. More than 70% of sales and sales growth came from the Europe and North America markets. This segment enjoyed the largest profit margins of all of the segments, with 15% operating margins and growth in total operating profits of 15%. The high levels of operating profits reflected Diageo's strategy of concentrating on premium brands and pricing. (Exhibits 1 and 2 contain historical financial information for Diageo and its business segments.)

Diageo's second largest division was Guinness Brewing, which produced and sold beer to markets around the world. This segment, while substantially smaller in sales than the Spirits and Wine Division, was a close second to it in terms of operating profit growth rate. Due to the similarity in the products and distribution channels for these two businesses, Diageo was in the process of integrating them, which might result in cost reductions of £130 million annually.

Diageo's two remaining businesses were in packaged and fast foods. Its Pillsbury subsidiary was a leading producer of packaged food products. Its brands included Progresso, Green Giant, and Haagen Dazs. Diageo's fourth and smallest business segment was its Burger King subsidiary, which had sales of £941 million. Burger King operated a series of fast-food restaurants throughout the world, though the bulk of revenues came from North America.

Since the 1997 merger, Diageo's stock price performance had lagged versus broad market indices. (See Exhibit 3.) In September 2000, Paul Walsh, who had previously been the CEO of the Pillsbury subsidiary, was named the Group Chief Executive of Diageo. Walsh's new strategy involved focusing on "beverage alcohol, driving growth through innovation around our unrivalled portfolio of brands and providing an improved base for sustained profitable top line growth." To achieve this goal, Diageo agreed to sell Pillsbury to General Mills. Under the proposal, General Mills would pay Diageo $5.1 billion in cash plus 141 million newly issued shares of General Mills stock. The shares were worth approximately $5.4 billion and would result in Diageo owning approximately 33% of the new General Mills/Pillsbury business. In addition, Diageo management announced their intention to exit the fast food business through an initial public offering of Burger King. Walsh stated in July that "we are going to develop the option first of all to float 20 percent of Burger King. Then after 2002, we will potentially float the balance of 80 percent. . . . We can float 20 percent now without triggering a significant tax charge. There are tax regulations that say after 2002 we should be able to float the balance without incurring any taxes."[2]

With these actions, Diageo would concentrate solely on the beverage alcohol business. Continued growth could come from organic growth or from potential acquisitions. "Organic growth" might involve increased sales of existing products or product extensions, such as Smirnoff Ice, a blend of Vodka and lemon juice, or a new bottled version of Guinness. Ongoing capital expenditures to support organic growth as well as to modernize existing production facilities was projected to require about £ 400–500 million per year for the next five years.

Growth could also come from acquisitions, but the amount that Diageo might need was virtually impossible to estimate with much certainty. It was unclear which firms Diageo might be able to acquire, which other firms might bid for them, how much rival

[2]Bloomberg News Service, June 22, 2000.

bidders might be able and willing to spend, and how hotly contested the bidding might become. Diageo's major rivals in the alcoholic beverage industry, such as Bacardi, Allied Domecq, Seagrams, and Pernod Ricard, were not only potential rival bidders for firms and brands, but potential acquisition targets themselves in the consolidating beverage alcohol business. For example, Seagram's beverage unit was up for sale in autumn of 2000 and analysts guessed it might fetch $7 to $9 billion. Diageo was working on a joint bid for Seagrams with Pernod Ricard, which might commit Diageo to spend $3 to $5 billion. Smaller private firms and individual brands were also considered potential acquisition candidates at the right price. In an "expansion scenario," Diageo might spend as much as $6 to $8 billion for acquisitions in the next three years including Seagram's; a "minimalist" scenario might involve very little acquisition, and a "midrange" estimate was about $2.5 billion over five years. These were not official Diageo forecasts, but rather very rough guesses by the finance team. (See Exhibit 4 for comparable companies.) As part of its focus on shareholder value, Diageo was also an active seller of brands that did not fit into its growth strategy.[3]

In general, Diageo sought to be in a strong position to expand its beverage spirits business. While Diageo was already the world's largest beverage spirits firm, acquisitions could be integrated into its system, allowing Diageo to enjoy certain efficiencies and synergies. These benefits could arise from cost savings in manufacturing, procurement, and supply, or through savings in the distribution system and an enhanced ability to reach consumers. Acquisitions might be important in light of the industry consolidation, among both suppliers and distributors, in the alcoholic beverage business. It was therefore critical for the finance side of the business to be able to fund these opportunities, if and when they arose.

Diageo's Historical Capital Structure

In general, British firms tended to have more conservative financial policies than firms in other nations. Research showed that the book value of equity accounted for 42% of the total assets of the average U.K. firms (excluding financial service firms), as compared with 28% to 40% in other highly developed nations.[4] Both Guinness and Grand Metropolitan used reasonably little debt to finance themselves prior to the creation of Diageo. (See Exhibit 1.) This policy choice was reflected in the relatively high ratings on the bonds of the two firms, AA and A, respectively.[5] Rating agencies, like Standard

[3]For example, Diageo sold Dewar's Scotch whiskey and Bombay Gin to Bacardi for 1.2 billion pounds in early 1998. Approximately 500 million pounds of the cash payment was paid out to shareholders under the B-share program that began in February 1998. The 320 million pounds remaining after taxes went to pay down debt. Source: *The Financial Post,* March 31, 1998.

[4]R. Rajan and L. Zingales, "What Do We Know about Capital Structure? Some Evidence from International Data." *The Journal of Finance,* 50, (December 1995) 1421–1460. The study examined firms in the G-7 countries (the seven countries with the largest economies) which included the United States (with 34% equity as a percentage of assets), Japan (33%), Germany (28%), France (31%), Italy (33%), and Canada (40%). The calculation measured the book value of equity divided by total assets for each firm listed in the Global Vantage database.

[5]Debt ratings were generally broken down into two classes, Investment Grade (IG) and Non-Investment Grade (NIG). IG consists of debt with S&P ratings of BBB– and higher, while NIG were BB+ and lower. While many of the differences between individual ratings were small, NIG credits were considered to have significantly more risk and lower market liquidity for a few reasons. First, the higher credit risk required more time and expertise to value, and investors demanded higher promised returns. Second, regulations prohibited many institutional investors (such as money market mutual funds) from owning low-rated debt. Consequently, there was less money available to make the investments, shrinking the size of the market and reducing the bidding competition for the offered debt instruments. Together, these effects reduced the amount of money that weaker credits could raise, and increased the interest expense.

and Poor's and Moody's, assigned ratings to bonds to reflect the company's ability to make promised interest and principal payments on its debt.

When Guinness and Grand Met announced their merger, the companies were put on Credit Watch by one of the rating agencies due to the uncertainty about their new financial policies.[6] When the companies merged, management chose to retain the policies of the merged companies, in part to maintain the status quo, and in part because the policy "felt right." While Diageo could have increased its debt and let its debt rating fall to BBB (one level below its current A rating), the feeling was that this "seemed a bit risky." They also felt that there had been an implicit promise to the public when the individual companies had previously issued bonds. Diageo communicated its decision to investors and rating agencies in the merger announcement by stating "The enlarged group's policy will be to manage actively the capital structure so as to keep the interest cover ratio, in normal circumstances, within a band of five to eight times."[7] Once the merger was complete and policies disclosed, the rating agencies confirmed that the firm's debt would be rated A+, the rough average of the two predecessor firms.

Credit rating agencies use a long list of quantitative and qualitative factors to establish the creditworthiness of firms. The Treasury team, however, found that the firm's interest coverage ratio was probably a critical variable that determined its rating. Interest coverage was measured as Earnings Before Interest, Taxes, Depreciation, and Amortization (EBITDA) divided by Interest Payments. The Treasury team felt that Diageo could maintain its credit rating of A+ by maintaining interest coverage of 5 to 8 times. This was lower than required in some other industries to obtain an A+ rating, in part due to the stable nature of Diageo's portfolio of brands. (As a secondary target, they sought to keep EBITDA divided by Total Debt at about 30 to 35%.) If the firm's coverage were to fall below 5, it would risk a downgrade. The firm adjusted its coverage ratio in a lumpy fashion through a combination of debt issuance, repurchases, and other large transactions. Figure I, taken from an internal Diageo presentation, shows the firm's interest coverage over time, and the actions the firm took.

The strong debt rating afforded considerable benefits for Diageo in the capital markets. In general, the highest rated firms (known as Investment Grade firms) were able to raise financing more readily and paid lower promised yields than firms with weaker ratings. (See Exhibits 5 and 6.) The additional yield that lower-rated firms needed to pay on their debt (the credit yield spread) was calculated and reported widely. However, limitations on lower-rated firms' abilities to borrow were less well measured. The capital markets for highly rated international firms like Diageo were relatively deep. When the Treasury team was asked to speculate on its ability to raise funds, they guessed that as an A-rated borrower, they could probably raise additional debt of $8 billion in 12 months while maintaining the rating. If Diageo were rated BBB, it might be able to raise $5 to $8 billion, and if they were rated BB they could raise less than $5 billion over the same time. These were very rough unofficial estimates, which might vary over time. (In comparison, Diageo speculated that if their competitors were willing to sell assets and risk a credit rating downgrade, their two largest could each raise maybe $9 billion over this time, two others might be able to raise $3–$4 billion each, and a fifth $2–$2.5 billion.)

[6]A firm is placed on "CreditWatch" when it is exposed to material specific events or short-term trends that need special attention to evaluate, such as mergers, recapitalizations, voter referendums, regulatory action, or anticipated operating developments. A listing does not guaranty that the rating will change.

[7]Bloomberg News Service.

An additional benefit of a high rating was the ability to access short-term commercial paper borrowings at attractive rates. Short-term interest rates available through the commercial paper[8] (CP) market were up to 25 basis points below the London Inter-Bank Offer Rate (LIBOR), a rate that large banks quoted for short term unsecured loans. For comparison, the interest rate that A rated companies paid on 5-year bonds was typically LIBOR + 40 basis points, or 0.65% higher than the CP rates. Lower rated firms found it difficult to raise money in the commercial paper market, as this was an unsecured form of borrowing. Furthermore, the major holders of commercial paper (money market funds) were prohibited by regulation from holding more than 5% of their portfolios in low-rated short-term funds. Approximately 47% of Diageo's debt, about 3.2 billion pounds, was issued as short-term commercial paper with maturities of 6 months to one year. If Diageo's long-term debt were to be rated BBB, its ability to raise commercial paper might be severely limited.

The Corporate Treasury's Simulation-Based Model

One of Diageo's core philosophies, inherited from Grand Metropolitan, was the idea of "Managing for Value," a variant of "Economic Value Added." The idea was relatively simple—the return earned by a division should cover not only its operating expenses, but also the cost of the capital employed by the division.[9] While the mandate for Managing for Value came from the highest levels of Diageo, the Treasury team was charged with establishing the cost of capital for each of the 110 countries in which the firm operated. This was a very difficult task that kept them focused on calculating the pros and cons of various financing policies.

In December 1998, the Treasury team retreated to Drummuir, a resort in Scotland, to brainstorm about Diageo's financial policies. In particular, the staff considered new approaches in finance and rethought which treasury functions should be centralized, what the firm's risk footprint should be, how to calculate the cost of capital, and how to optimally structure the firm's balance sheet.

One of the more novel discussions revolved around the firm's funding policies. Finance textbooks and MBA programs often taught that a firm's gearing should reflect the tradeoff between the tax benefits of debt (modeled as tax shields) and the costs of financial distress. While the tax deductibility of interest on debt was easily modeled (Diageo's composite marginal tax rate was 27%), the costs of financial distress were more elusive. Textbooks depicted graphs of the stylized tradeoff between the tax shields and costs of financial distress, but it was much more difficult to examine this tradeoff rigorously in practice.

A long line of academic research attempted to measure the costs of financial distress. Financial difficulties gave rise to direct costs, including the costs for legal and financial advisors. Financial distress could also lead to indirect or strategic costs in three ways. First, competitors could attempt to take advantage of the situation by increasing their market share (for example, by starting a price war with the hope that the distressed firm

[8]Commercial paper is an unsecured promissory note, typically maturing within 270 days.

[9]Diageo instituted the philosophy through the bonus plan, which applied to the top three ranks of managers, more than 1,400 people in all. The plan was uncommon in three aspects. First, the bonus pool was benchmarked against the capital charges incurred by a division. Second, negative bonuses could be earned (penalized) when the capital charges were not covered. Finally, bonuses were paid into a "bonus bank" with a claw-back provision. Every year, an employee's bonus would be "paid" to his or her account. One-half of the balance was paid out immediately. The other half was held in escrow against potential future negative bonuses. This kept managers focused on long-term performance while meeting short-term goals.

just collapses). Second, customers might be less willing to purchase from the distressed firm, especially if the purchases are long-term in nature and might require future support (for example, warranty repairs). Third, management might focus on the financial crisis and not running the business, and the firm might forgo profitable investments for future cash flow. Recent research that quantified the average value loss of distressed firms influenced the Treasury team's thinking.[10] This data gave an indication of the cost of financial distress, but not its likelihood.

Simpson and Williams now felt they had most of the information they needed to roughly quantify the implications of the tradeoff between tax shields and the costs of distress. In order to do this, they would need to calculate their tax shields each year, as well as whether Diageo would get into financial distress in each year. To evaluate the likelihood of financial distress, they would have to model the firm's cash flow generation over time, over a broad range of market conditions.

A thorough review of historical results, as well as an audit by outside consultants, found that Diageo's operating cash flow or return on assets, as measured by EBIT/assets,[11] was driven by the fluctuations in sales and exchange rates. They calculated the historical time series of profitability by segment for Diageo as well as for a sample of comparable firms. (See Exhibit 7.) This distribution of profitability, especially for the beverage alcohol business, would give them some information on the future distribution of profitability. In general, all of Diageo's businesses, including the beverage alcohol business which it would retain, had relatively stable cash flows, which had allowed Diageo to take on a higher level of debt than other companies. Financial distress was determined by the financial policies of the company—in particular by its level of gearing and by the maturity of the debt it issued. (Interest payments on Diageo's short-term debt would be affected by interest rates.) With broad probability distributions and multiple gearing policies to consider, Simpson and Williams turned to Monte Carlo simulation analysis to help guide the process.

Monte Carlo analysis was a technique that physicists developed to help build the first nuclear weapons during the latter stages of the Second World War. This form of simulation was used to quantify uncertainty when the underlying problem was difficult or impossible to solve exactly, for example, when key parameters are random variables, and to understand the final distribution of outcomes, not just the expected value. Operating cash flow, exchange rates, and interest rates changed over time in a hard-to-predict fashion, and financial distress was a low probability, high significance "nonlinear" event. The simulation technique was a statistical analysis of multiple experiments or "trials." Each trial represented the results from one "realized" set of random draws of the different input variables. By keeping track of the output of each trial as well as the summary statistics, the user could construct a more precise distribution for the expected variability of the underlying model.

Simpson and Williams used spreadsheet programs to simulate the present value of taxes paid and financial distress costs paid, across a set of gearing policies. For each trial, earnings (EBIT) as a percentage of assets were forecast, by year, as a function of three

[10]See T. Opler, M. Saron, and S. Titman, "Designing Capital Structure to Create Shareholder Value." *Journal of Applied Corporate Finance,* 10 (1), Spring 1997, 21–32, and T. Opler, S. Titman, "Financial Distress and Corporate Performance," *Journal of Finance,* 49 (3), July 1994, 1015–1040. Over the period 1972–1991, the research studied industry-adjusted change in sales, operating income, and market value of highly levered firms in industries experiencing downturns. Industry downturns were defined as drops in sales and market values of 30% or greater. After controlling for industry performance, the studies found that highly levered firms lost an additional 14%, 12%, and 7% of sales, operating income, and market value relative to the average firm in the industry, and 26%, 27%, and 15% more than the least levered firms in their industry.

[11]Depreciation and amortization in this industry were relatively low, so EBIT and EBITDA were similar.

uncertainties: the return on assets for each geographical region, the currency exchange rates, and the interest rate paid on the firm's debt. Separately for each gearing policy, the model calculated the interest rate (as a rating-dependent credit spread over a base rate), and the total interest that the company would pay every year. The earnings and interest determined both the taxes paid, and the interest coverage ratio for the current period. The interest coverage ratio, in turn, established the current period debt rating. Diageo was assumed to be in financial distress when the interest coverage ratio was less than one. Economically, this was equivalent to a firm EBIT less than the interest payments, or that the firm would have to borrow money (or draw down reserves) to meet its debt obligations. A distress condition imposed a one-time permanent 20% reduction in the value of the firm. There was no provision in the model for issuing equity to pay down debt when coverage fell. However, when the interest coverage was too high, the firm issued a special dividend to "regear" itself back to the targeted coverage range.[12] The model assumed a constant year-end zero cash balance. An excess cash flow that the business generated (i.e., EBIT—interest—taxes—total dividends) was used to pay down the outstanding debt, while new debt was issued to finance a cash shortfall. Otherwise, assets were assumed to grow at the current interest rate. (See Exhibit 8 for a simplified flow chart of the analysis.)

Each trial was a 15-year sequence, which kept track of the firm's operating cash flows, interest payments, coverage, and distress on a semiannual basis. In any one trial, the firm might enjoy large tax shields from levering up, but never get into trouble. For some trials, however, the firm's cash flows might dip low enough to trigger distress and a 20% reduction in asset value. The model was run for 10,000 trials. Each trial calculated the present value of taxes paid and the cost of financial distress for each of the different debt policies. Once all trials were completed, the model generated statistical expectations for total tax paid and costs of financial distress under each of the different policies. See Figure II for the summary diagram from the analysis, which shows the average tax bill and costs of financial distress under a variety of interest coverage policies.

The Capital Structure Decision

Cray looked again at the value trade-off chart from the Monte Carlo analysis. Simpson and Williams had completed much of the analysis under the previous treasurer, so he could look at their work with fresh eyes. It was an interesting analysis that had the potential to help shape the capital structure of the restructured Diageo. However, he needed to make sure that it was robust enough to bring to attention of the Group Finance Director, Nick Rose, and ultimately to the Board of Directors. He reflected on his own concerns: He had always defined financial distress as "being unable to meet the expectations of the bondholders *and equity holders* of the firm."[13] He had spent a great deal of time making sure that firm's financial policies provided enough flexibility for Diageo to carry out its core strategy. Further, he appreciated that the firm had flexibility in some of its operating areas; for example, in times of stress, perhaps the firm would "tinker" with its £1 billion advertising budget. Cray wondered how these concerns might affect his interpretation of the analysis, and what he should recommend as the financial policy for Diageo looking forward.

[12]The model included regular dividend payments, which could be cut if cash flow after interest and tax payments were not large enough. Diageo's dividend policy was considered important to investors, and it was thought that the firm would have cut other expenditures, such as marketing or capital expenditures, or borrowed money, before cutting the dividend.

[13]Diageo's annual dividends were historically 4–5% of the firm's stock price, and the firm paid out about 70% of its net earnings. In absolute terms, the firm paid out £710 million in 1999.

EXHIBIT 1 **Grand Metropolitan, Guinness, and Diageo Financial Statements (£ Millions)**

Source: Diageo Annual Reports, Datastream.

	GrandMet CY 97 PF	Guinness CY 97 PF	FY 97 PF	FY 98	FY 99	FY 00
Sales	8,045	4,539	12,985	12,029	11,795	11,870
Operating costs	6,978	3,584	10,982	10,659	10,278	10,088
Interest payable (net)	153	81	268	360	324	363
Associates (net)	5	71	89	112	95	121
Other	(229)	(320)	(618)	478	94	(163)
Taxes	249	255	532	721	440	401
Net Income	441	370	674	879	942	976
Dividends			654	835	674	713

	See Note	FY98	FY99	FY00
Operating profits		1,866	1,966	2,043
Cash interest paid (net)		(258)	(432)	(405)
Taxes paid		(603)	(566)	(285)
Cash from Operations		1,005	968	1,353
Dividends from investments		120	58	64
Net capital sales (expenditures)		(370)	(444)	(488)
Net divestitures (acquisitions)		1,368	121	487
Cash from Investments		1,118	(265)	63
Management of liquid resources[a]		(600)	2,195	(219)
Dividends paid		(695)	(702)	(710)
Paid in capital from shares issued (repurchased)		(2,662)	(1,336)	(80)
New debt		2,097	(716)	(544)
Cash from Financing		(1,860)	(559)	(1,553)
Total Change in Cash		263	144	(137)

	GrandMet CY 97 PF	Guinness CY 97 PF	FY 97 PF	FY 98	FY 99	FY 00
Assets						
Cash and marketable securities	1,786	454	2,173	2,987	1,097	1,063
Accounts receivable	2,243	1,432	3,216	3,054	3,259	3,071
Inventory	995	1,909	2,374	2,236	2,202	2,139
Fixed assets	5,513	4,105	9,625	8,977	9,720	9,863
Total Assets	10,537	7,900	17,388	17,254	16,278	16,136
Liabilities and Owners' Equity						
Accounts payable	1,833	1,783	2,930	3,524	3,532	3,275
Short-term debt	1,730	1,289	2,293	4,724	3,905	3,066
Long-term debt	2,515	760	4,190	3,137	3,495	3,816
Other	463	167	674	705	753	694
Total Liabilities	6,541	3,999	10,087	12,090	11,685	10,851
Minority interests	416	131	530	535	567	574
Common stock	531	476	1,001	1,139	992	990
Retained earnings	3,049	3,294	5,770	3,490	3,034	3,721
Total Equity	3,996	3,901	7,301	5,164	4,593	5,285
Total Liabilities and Owners' Equity	10,537	7,900	17,388	17,254	16,278	16,136
Shares Outstanding	2,119[b]	1,877[b]		3,880	3,402	3,397
Market Value of Equity	12,565[b]	11,209[b]		27,548	22,538	20,144

Notes: Both Grand Metropolitan and Guinness reported year-end results on a calendar year basis. After the merger, Diageo established a fiscal year ending on June 30. The 1998 fiscal year overlaps calendar year 1997 by six months. Because the merger occurred before the GrandMet and Guinness fiscal years were over, and after the Diageo 1997 fiscal year was over, the 1997 results were pro forma. Historical pro forma cash flows were not required to be reported for GrandMet, Guinness, and Diageo for 1997, and were not calculated by Diageo after the merger.

[a]Liquid financial assets such as cash could be held in short- or long-term investments. A positive number in "Management of liquid resources" represented assets that were moved from short-term investments ("Cash") to longer-term investments, such as bank accounts that required withdrawal notices longer than one day.

[b]As of December 16, 1997, the day before the merger closed.

EXHIBIT 2
Diageo Segment Breakdown (£ Millions)

Source: Diageo Annual Reports

Turnover	CY 96 PF	FY 97 PF	FY 98	FY 99	FY 00
Class of business					
Spirits and Wine	5,830	5,692	5,327	4,929	4,971
Beer	2,262	2,259	2,176	2,234	2,146
Packaged Food	3,784	3,755	3,654	3,757	3,812
Restaurants	877	879	869	875	941
Associates and other[a]	687	400	3	0	0
Total	13,440	12,985	12,029	11,795	11,870
Geographical Area					
Europe	4,556	4,443	4,262	4,230	4,181
North America	5,790	5,718	5,619	5,656	5,639
Asia Pacific	1,260	1,226	915	777	886
Rest of World	1,147	1,198	1,230	1,132	1,164
Associates and other[a]	687	400	3	0	0
Total	13,440	12,985	12,029	11,795	11,870
Operating Profit	**CY 96 PF**	**FY 97 PF**	**FY 98**	**FY 99**	**FY 00**
Class of business					
Spirits and Wine	1,138	1,135	1,070	967	1,002
Beer	254	264	247	273	284
Packaged Food	412	423	447	478	492
Restaurants	161	160	179	185	202
Associates and other[a]	36	21	(1)	0	0
Total	2,001	2,003	1,942	1,903	1,980
Geographical Area					
Europe	543	552	534	594	585
North America	913	901	938	936	956
Asia Pacific	251	261	174	131	170
Rest of World	258	268	297	242	269
Associates and other[a]	36	21	(1)	0	0
Total	2,001	2,003	1,942	1,903	1,980

[a]An associate was an undertaking in which the group had a long-term equity interest and over which it exercises significant influence. The group's interest in the net assets of associates, other than goodwill, was included in investments in the group balance sheet. Joint arrangements where each party had its own separate interest in particular risks and rewards were accounted for by including the attributable share of the assets and liabilities, measured according to the terms of the arrangement. "Other" included discontinued operations.
1996 and 1997 results reflect the pro forma results for Grand Metropolitan and Guinness combined.

EXHIBIT 3
Diageo Stock Price and Scaled Financial Times Stock Exchange 100 Index, January 1998–July 2000

Source: Datastream

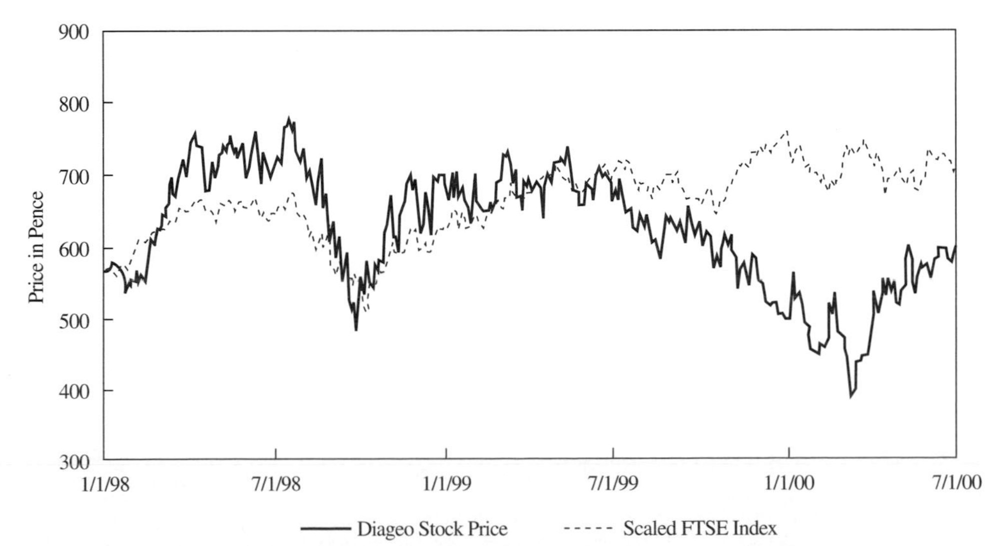

Note: The FTSE 100 Index was scaled to have the same starting value as Diageo's stock price on January 1, 1998.

EXHIBIT 4 Selected Financial Data on Companies with Which Diageo Compared Itself, as of Latest Annual Reporting Period before October 2000 (in local currency unless otherwise noted)

Sources: Bloomberg, Compustat, and GlobalVantage

		Alcohol		Beer			Beverage		Packaged Food				
Company	Diageo	Allied Domecq	Pernod Ricard	Anheuser Busch	Carlsberg	Heineken	Coca-Cola	Pepsico	Campbell Soup	General Mills	Heinz	Kellogg	Nestle
Domicile	U.K.	U.K.	France	U.S.	Denmark	Netherlands	U.S.	U.S.	U.S.	U.S.	U.S.	U.S.	Switzerland
Employees ('000)	72	40	14	24	18	37	37	118	22	11	47	15	231
Market capitalization (MM)	20,292	3,416	3,203	32,681	16,245	15,184	143,969	51,289	11,634	11,534	11,813	12,493	112,032
Market capitalization ($ MM)	30,720	4,970	3,210	32,681	2,327	15,219	143,969	51,289	11,634	11,534	11,813	12,493	69,988
Enterprise value[a] (MM)	27,113	4,780	4,388	37,804	23,727	15,955	150,196	54,334	14,725	14,794	15,925	14,627	124,904
Enterprise value ($ MM)	41,046	6,955	4,398	35,344	3,399	15,992	150,196	54,334	14,725	14,794	15,925	14,627	78,029
Price / Earnings ratio	20.8×	10.8×	13.7×	23.3×	14.0×	29.4×	59.2×	25.0×	16.3×	18.9×	13.3×	36.9×	23.7×
Market / Book ratio	4.3×	18.0×	1.6×	8.3×	1.6×	5.8×	15.1×	7.5×	84.9×	−39.9×	7.4×	15.4×	4.6×
Enterprise Value / EBIT[b]	13.7×	11.4×	11.8×	16.4×	14.2×	20.0×	31.3×	18.8×	11.3×	13.5×	11.8×	13.6×	15.8×
Interest Coverage[c]	5.0×	5.7×	10.4×	10.6×	4.1×	15.3×	15.5×	10.8×	7.3×	7.8×	6.2×	10.7×	7.4×
EBITDA / Total Debt[d]	34%	35%	40%	60%	40%	159%	84%	129%	48%	40%	40%	64%	85%
Book gearing[e]	59%	88%	36%	57%	42%	23%	40%	31%	96%	110%	72%	72%	34%
Market gearing[f]	25%	29%	27%	14%	32%	5%	4%	6%	21%	22%	26%	15%	10%
ROA[g]	15%	17%	39%	24%	10%	20%	24%	22%	29%	29%	19%	28%	18%
Credit rating[h]	A+	A–	NR	A+	BBB	AAA	A+	A	AA–	A+	A+	AA	AAA
Beta[i]	0.55	0.51	0.54	0.46	0.4	0.54	0.68	1.07	0.49	0.47	0.49	0.37	0.9
ROE[j]	22.3%	25.7%	22.3%	34.5%	11.6%	13.4%	27.1%	30.9%	383.9%	−986.2%	52.4%	39.7%	19.9%
Dividends Paid (MM)	713	116	0	545	256	125	1,580	784	382	328	514	389	1,693
CapEx (MM)	547	87	112	865	2,024	441	1,069	1,118	200	268	452	266	2,806
Exchange rate multiplier[k] to $	1.514	1.455	1.002	1	0.143	1.002	1	1	1	1	1	1	0.625

Notes: [a]Enterprise value is the market value of equity plus book value of short-term and long-term debt. [b]EBIT is the Earnings Before Interest and Taxes. [c]Interest coverage is defined as EBITDA/interest expense. [d]EBITDA is the Earnings Before Interest, Taxes, Depreciation, and Amortization. [e]Book gearing is defined as long-term plus short-term debt divided by the book value of capital (short-term plus long-term debt plus shareholder equity). [f]Market gearing is defined as long-term plus short-term debt divided by the book value of debt plus the market value of equity. [g]ROA is the Return on Assets, defined as the EBITDA/Assets. [h]Standard and Poor's rating. [i]Beta is calculated using weekly returns over the two-year period ending June 30, 2000. [j]Return on Equity. [k]The number of U.S. dollars = foreign currency × exchange rate.

EXHIBIT 4 Continued

	Restaurants		Consumer				Conglomerate	
Company	McDonalds	Tricon Global Restaurants	Colgate-Palmolive	Gillette	Philip Morris	Procter & Gamble	Seagram	Unilever
Domicile	U.S.	U.S.	U.S.	U.S.	U.S.	U.S.	U.S.	U.K.
Employees ('000)	314	210	37	40	137	110	34	255
Market capitalization (MM)	54,454	5,832	37,626	43,865	53,786	74,761	25,352	13,262
Market capitalization ($ MM)	54,454	5,832	37,626	43,865	53,786	74,761	25,352	21,374
Enterprise value[a] (MM)	61,706	8,340	40,416	48,594	68,254	86,887	33,229	16,239
Enterprise value ($ MM)	61,706	8,340	40,416	48,594	68,254	86,887	33,229	26,172
Price/Earnings ratio	28.0 ×	9.3 ×	40.1 ×	34.8 ×	7.0 ×	21.1 ×	1,690.1 ×	7.3 ×
Market/Book ratio	5.3 ×	–10.4 ×	20.5 ×	12.8 ×	3.5 ×	6.1 ×	2.1 ×	2.7 ×
Enterprise Value / EBIT[b]	19.2 ×	9.3 ×	25.8 ×	23.1 ×	5.0 ×	12.8 ×	47.9 ×	5.7 ×
Interest coverage[c]	9.9 ×	5.9 ×	8.5 ×	18.6 ×	14.1 ×	12.4 ×	2.4 ×	12.2 ×
EBITDA/Total Debt[d]	56%	51%	68%	53%	107%	74%	22%	121%
Book gearing[e]	41%	129%	60%	58%	49%	50%	39%	38%
Market gearing[f]	12%	30%	7%	10%	21%	14%	24%	18%
ROA[g]	19%	32%	26%	21%	25%	26%	5%	21%
Credit rating[h]	AA	BB	A	AA	A	AA	BBB–	A+
Beta[i]	0.81	0.42	1.29	1.03	0.34	0.37	1.02	0.77
ROE[j]	20.4%	–72.8%	47.2%	33.8%	48.7%	28.8%	1.0%	45.2%
Dividends paid (MM)	265	0	345	642	4,393	1,681	287	820
CapEx (MM)	1,868	470	373	932	1,749	3,018	607	865
Exchange rate multiplier[k] to $	1	1	1	1	1	1	1	1.612

Sources: Bloomberg, Compustat, and GlobalVantage

Notes: [a]Enterprise value is the market value of equity plus book value of short-term and long-term debt. EBIT is the Earnings Before Interest and Taxes. [c]Interest coverage is defined as EBITDA/interest expense. [d]EBITDA is the Earnings Before Interest, Taxes, Depreciation, and Amortization. [e]Book gearing is defined as long-term plus short-term debt divided by the book value of capital (short-term plus long-term debt plus shareholder equity). [f]Market gearing is defined as long-term plus short-term debt divided by the book value of debt plus the market value of equity. [g]ROA is the Return on Assets, defined as the EBITDA/Assets.[h]Standard and Poor's rating.[i]Beta is calculated using weekly returns over the two-year period ending June 30, 2000. [j]Return on Equity. [k]The number of U.S. dollars = foreign currency × exchange rate.

EXHIBIT 5 Selected Data on Bond Market for 5-Year Notes, October 31, 2000

Sources: Bloomberg, Securities Data Corporation, Standard and Poor's "Ratings Performance 1999; Stability and Transition."

Rating	Interest Rate (Pounds)	Interest Rate (Dollars)	Median Interest Coverage[a]	Issuing Firms with Rating	Average Monthly Issuance ($ Billion)	Minimum Monthly Issuance ($ Billion)	Maximum Monthly Issuance ($ Billion)
U.K. Government	5.56%	–	–	–	–	–	–
U.S. Government	–	5.83%	–	–	–	–	–
AAA	6.13%	6.76%	30.07	4%	3.64	0.53	11.08
AA	6.37%	6.81%	11.37	13%	3.25	0.00	23.63
A	6.76%	7.15%	8.34	25%	6.47	0.69	30.65
BBB	7.16%	7.57%	4.94	22%	1.76	0.09	8.73

Note: Monthly issuance data collected between January 1, 1998, and October 31, 2000, for dollar denominated bonds in the U.S. The global market for dollar denominated bonds was about half the size of the U.S. market. Issuers, however, tended to be higher rated firms or governments, and the individual issue sizes larger, relative to the U.S. market.
[a]Interest coverage defined as EBITDA/interest expense.

EXHIBIT 6 Diageo Liability Structure, June 30, 2000

Source: Diageo Annual Report

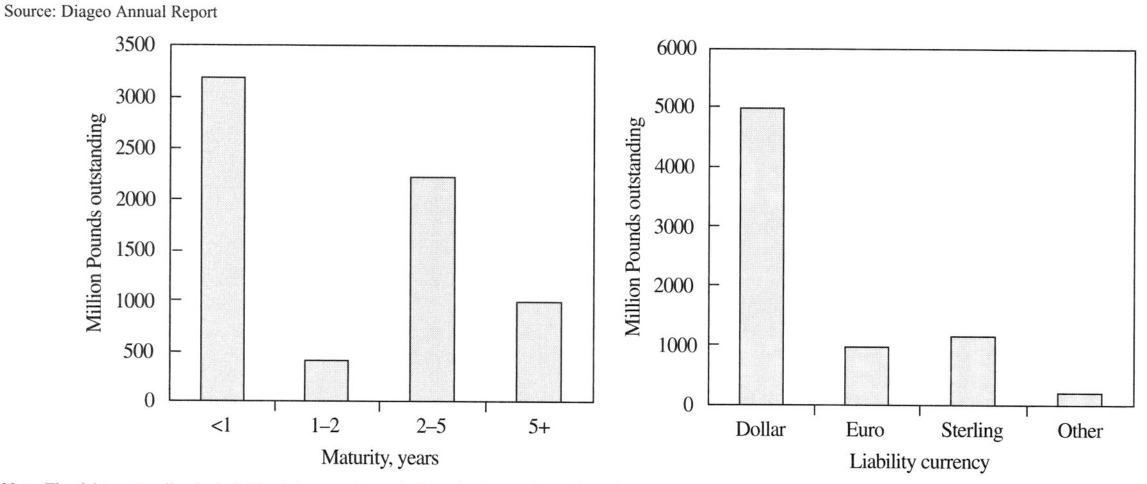

Note: The debt outstanding included bank loans and overdrafts, other borrowings, financial leases, and other long-term obligations.

EXHIBIT 7A Industry Returns on Assets (EBITDA/Assets), with Diageo Mix of Businesses

Source: Diageo

Industry	Firms in Composite	Average ROA	Max ROA	Median ROA	Min ROA	Volatility of Industry ROA[c]	Average of Firm Volatility[d]
Spirits	6	16.9%	24.2%	16.7%	12.6%	2.3%	3.4%
Beer	1	20.6%	27.2%	21.2%	14.3%	3.0%	–
Food	4	19.8%	25.8%	19.8%	12.5%	3.1%	3.6%
Fast Food	2	21.0%	29.6%	19.9%	14.1%	3.6%	4.4%
Weighted Average[a]	–	19.7%	26.7%	19.5%	16.3%	1.9%	–
Weighted Avg (Beverages)[b]	–	17.7%	24.9%	17.2%	15.1%	1.9%	–

[a]The Weighted Average weights the segment performance by the weight of that division within Diageo.
[b]The Weighted Avg (Beverages) uses weights that exclude the packaged and fast food categories.
[c]The ROA was calculated for the industry for each year in the sample. The volatility of industry ROA was calculated as the standard deviation of the time series.
[d]Calculated by taking the arithmetic average of the volatility (standard deviation) of each firm's ROA over the sample period.

EXHIBIT 7B
Median Industry Returns on Assets, 1950–1999

Source: Casewriter calculations based on Center for Research in Security Prices data with 239,126 observations over 50 years.

Industry	N	Mean ROA	Volatility
Food	155	15.4%	1.7%
Textiles/Printing	335	15.2%	2.0%
Retail	544	13.2%	2.2%
Transportation	266	14.3%	2.2%
Services	395	12.7%	2.2%
Chemicals	132	16.6%	2.4%
Financial Institutions	410	3.9%	2.5%
Extractive Industries	41	15.5%	2.8%
Utilities	194	11.7%	2.9%
Durable Manufacturing	1,187	14.2%	3.6%
Real Estate/Insurance	197	7.6%	3.8%
Pharmaceuticals	119	20.7%	4.8%
Computers	413	15.0%	4.8%
Mining/Construction	337	11.0%	5.0%

EXHIBIT 8 Simplified Flow Chart of Monte Carlo Simulation

Source: Diageo

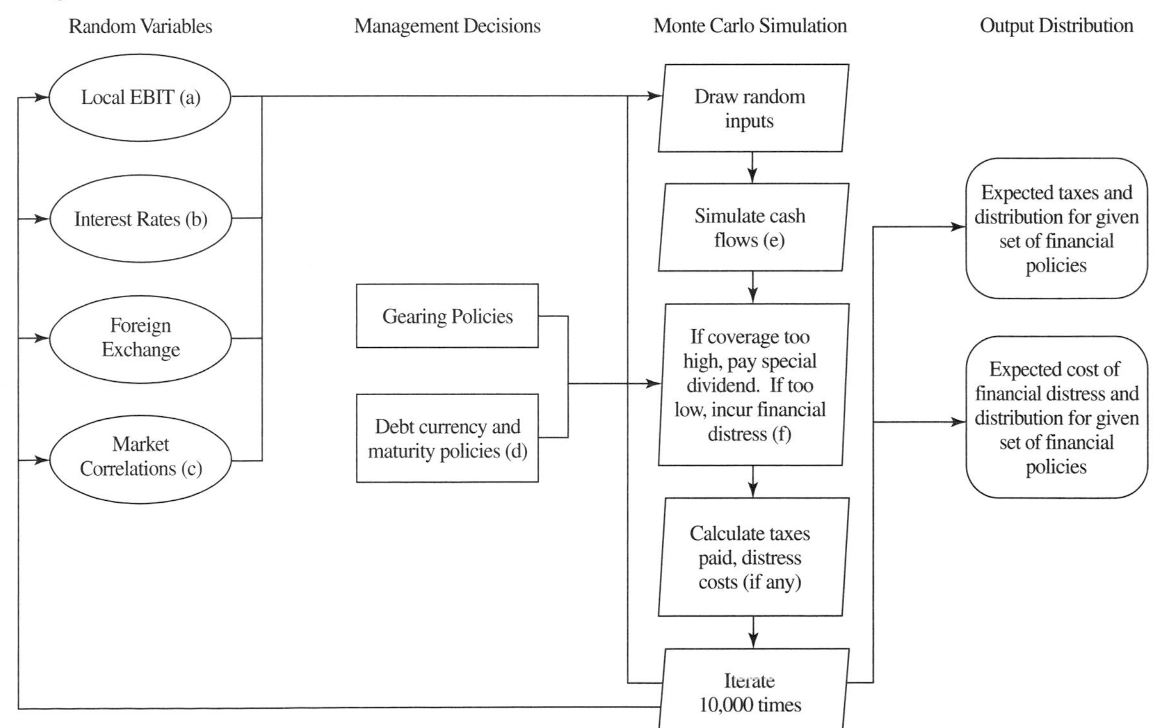

Notes:
[a]Local EBIT is calculated as (Assets) × (Simulated ROA), where ROA is the EBIT/Asset ratio.
[b]Interest rates are all linked to the U.S. interest rate. Credit spread for different ratings assumed fixed.
[c]Model assumes constant correlations between the random variables.
[d]Model assumes a constant currency and maturity mix of debt. All interest is charged on a floating-rate basis.
[e]The book value of assets is assumed to grow each year at the market interest rate, unless the firm is suffering from financial distress. The model does not allow for new equity issues. The return on the assets is assumed to average around 18%, with random fluctuations (normally distributed) with a standard deviation of 4%. The model did not include major investments (like acquisitions or divestitures).
[f]Financial distress is defined as the inability to pay interest from operating cash flow, or EBIT/Interest < 1. Distress gives rise to a 20% permanent reduction in firm value.

Hospital Corporation of America (A)

In January 1982, Hospital Corporation of America (HCA) faced a complex financial situation. Following a major acquisition in 1981, HCA's ratio of debt to total capital was approaching 70%, well in excess of its well-established target ratio of 60%. Interest coverage had dropped below its target of 3.0 to 2.4, the lowest level experienced since HCA was founded in 1968. Although some investors justified, even welcomed, HCA's more aggressive use of leverage, others were concerned. HCA's capital structure could cost the company its A bond rating. Mounting interest expense on the debt could also result in a decline in HCA's first-quarter earnings per share relative to that for a year ago. If it did, it would be the first such quarter-to-quarter decline in earnings per share in HCA's 13-year history. In light of these developments, HCA's management had to decide what, if anything, should be done about its capital structure and what specific steps should be taken in the near future to achieve the desired mix of debt and equity.

Early Development

Hospital Corporation of America was a proprietary hospital management company. It was founded in Nashville, Tennessee, by two physicians, Thomas F. Frist, Sr., and Thomas F. Frist, Jr., and by Jack C. Massey, a former pharmacist and former owner of Kentucky Fried Chicken. Beginning with only a single 150-bed hospital in 1968, HCA grew to become the nation's largest hospital management company. By 1981, HCA owned or managed 349 hospitals in the United States and overseas and had net operating revenues of $2.1 billion. Since its founding, revenues and earnings had grown at an annual rate of 32.2% and 32.6%, respectively. Pretax profit margins, averaging 9%, were the highest and most consistent among the major proprietary hospital chains. Recent financial statements and a 10-year summary of HCA's operations are presented in Exhibits 1–4.

The Proprietary Hospital Industry

Proprietary hospital management companies—that is, corporations that own and manage chains of hospitals on a for-profit basis—were a relatively new phenomenon in the $118 billion U.S. hospital-care business. The enactment of entitlement programs such as Medicare and Medicaid in 1965 stimulated demand for hospital services and virtually eliminated the tremendous bad-debt burden (i.e., weak accounts receivable) that had traditionally plagued the hospital industry. This created a valuable opportunity for private investors to build or acquire hospitals and operate them profitably. Tight control over costs, and efficiencies in such areas as staffing, purchasing, and hospital design, enabled hospital management companies to offer high-quality services at reasonable cost while achieving attractive profit margins.

With the ability to sell equity and other financial securities not generally available to nonprofit hospitals, proprietary hospital management companies expanded rapidly in the 1970s. While the number of hospitals operating in the United States actually declined steadily between 1975 and 1980 from a high of 7,200, the proprietary hospital

Copyright © 1983 by the President and Fellows of Harvard College. Harvard Business School case 283–053.

EXHIBIT 1
Consolidated Income Statements, 1979–1981 (millions of dollars except per share data)

	1979	1980	1981
Operating revenues	$1,043	$1,429	$2,406
Contractual adj. and doubtful accounts	143	197	343
Net revenues	901	1,232	2,064
Operating expenses	726	998	1,682
Depreciation and amortization	41	53	88
Interest expense	38	50	131
Income from operations	95	130	162
Other income	1	6	22
Income before income taxes	96	136	184
Provision for income taxes			
Current	28	44	49
Deferred	14	11	24
Net income	$ 54	$ 81	$ 111
Average number of common and common equivalent shares (millions)	41	47	50
Earnings per share	$ 1.34	$ 1.73	$ 2.23

Note: Figures may not add exactly because of rounding.

EXHIBIT 2
Consolidated Balance Sheets at December 31, 1979–1981 (millions of dollars)

	1979	1980	1981
Cash and cash equivalents	$ 30	$ 29	$ 50
Accounts receivable, net	149	214	363
Supplies	29	44	65
Other current assets	10	15	18
Current assets	218	303	498
Net property, plant, and equipment	802	1,187	2,066
Investments and other assets	40	81	188
Intangible assets	18	38	207
Total assets	$1,078	$1,610	$2,958
Accounts payable	$ 38	$ 58	$ 93
Dividends payable	2	3	4
Accrued liabilities	45	80	166
Income taxes payable	56	71	61
Current maturities of long-term debt	19	26	43
Current liabilities	160	238	367
Long-term debt	427	775	1,649
Deferred income taxes	74	85	117
Other liabilities	30	43	58
Total liabilities	691	1,141	2,191
Common stock (issued 52,210,645 shares in 1981; 45,378,375 shares in 1980; 19,456,634 shares in 1979)	19	45	52
Additional paid-in capital	157	144	342
Retained earnings	210	279	374
Shareholders' equity	387	469	768
Total liabilities and shareholders' equity	$1,078	$1,610	$2,958

Note: Figures may not add exactly because of rounding.

EXHIBIT 3 Ten-Year Historical Summary, 1972–1981 (millions of dollars except per share data and percentages)

	1972	1973	1974	1975	1976	1977	1978	1979	1980	1981
Summary of Operations										
Operating revenues	$ 173	$ 223	$ 298	$ 393	$ 506	$ 627	$ 797	$1,043	$1,429	$2,406
Interest expense	6	9	13	17	21	24	32	38	50	131
Income before income taxes	18	23	30	36	47	59	74	96	136	184
Net income	10	12	16	21	27	33	42	54	81	111
Average shares outstanding (millions)[a]	35	34	34	35	38	39	40	41	47	50
Earnings per share[a]	$ .30	$ .35	$ .45	$ .59	$ .71	$ .86	$ 1.05	$ 1.34	$ 1.73	$ 2.23
Cash dividends per share[a]	.02	.04	.05	.06	.09	.12	.17	.22	.27	.34
Dividend payout	6.7%	11.4%	11.1%	10.2%	12.7%	14.0%	16.2%	16.4%	15.6%	15.2%
Financial Position										
Total assets	$ 275	$ 321	$ 417	$ 508	$ 602	$ 709	$ 857	$1,078	$1,610	$2,958
Total debt	155	175	240	298	327	363	427	446	801	1,692
Shareholders' equity	91	107	121	142	186	215	252	387	469	768
Book value per share (year-end)	$ 2.69	$3.12	$3.53	$4.09	$4.89	$5.65	$ 6.57	$ 8.84	$10.33	$14.70
Average price-earnings ratio	33.7	18.1	7.3	8.0	9.2	8.6	10.9	11.8	15.9	18.5
Stock Performance										
High	$12.10	$9.90	$5.10	$7.10	$7.60	$9.00	$15.30	$19.90	$37.00	$50.70
Low	8.10	2.80	1.50	2.30	5.40	5.80	7.50	11.60	17.90	31.70
Selected Ratios										
Current ratio	1.3	1.4	1.2	1.5	1.5	1.4	1.4	1.4	1.3	1.4
Net profit margin	6.0%	5.5%	5.2%	5.3%	5.3%	5.3%	5.2%	5.2%	5.7%	4.6%
Return on beginning assets	5.3%	4.4%	4.9%	5.0%	5.3%	5.5%	5.9%	6.3%	7.5%	6.9%
Return on beginning equity	14.3%	13.4%	14.5%	17.0%	19.0%	17.9%	19.3%	21.5%	20.9%	23.7%
Asset turnover	.89	.81	.93	.94	1.00	1.04	1.12	1.22	1.33	1.50
Total debt/Total capital	63.1%	62.0%	66.4%	67.8%	63.7%	62.7%	62.9%	53.5%	63.1%	68.8%

[a] Average share figures include unexercised options. Per share earnings and dividends were computed based on average shares outstanding.

EXHIBIT 4 Key Statistics for HCA's Hospitals, 1972–1981

	1972	1973	1974	1975	1976	1977	1978	1979	1980	1981
Hospitals in Operation										
Owned and leased, U.S	46	53	56	62	68	72	81	88	144	188
Managed, U.S	2	4	6	8	15	21	26	45	56	146
Owned and managed, international	—	—	—	2	2	2	5	15	18	15
Total	48	57	62	72	85	95	112	148	188	349
Bed capacity	7,304	8,507	9,280	11,648	13,458	14,465	18,036	22,543	28,204	49,866
Occupancy rate (U.S.-owned only)	na	na	70%	66%	66%	66%	65%	68%	69%	68%
Sources of Revenues by Payer										
Cost-based										
Medicare	27%	27%	29%	30%	32%	33%	35%	36%	37%	38%
Medicaid	4	3	3	4	4	4	4	3	3	5
Blue Cross	8	9	8	7	5	5	5	4	4	3
Total cost-based	39%	39%	40%	41%	41%	42%	44%	43%	44%	46%
Charge-based	61	61	60	59	59	58	56	57	56	54
Total	100%	100%	100%	100%	100%	100%	100%	100%	100%	100%

na = not available.

EXHIBIT 5 **Comparative Data on Selected Publicly Held Hospital Management Companies, 1980–1981 (millions of dollars except per share data and percentages)**

	Hospital Corporation of America		Humana, Inc.		American Medical International, Inc.		National Medical Enterprises, Inc.		Lifemark	
	1980	1981	1980	1981	1980	1981	1980	1981	1980	1981
Summary of Operations										
Operating revenues	$1,429	$ 2,406	$1,392	$ 1,704	$ 766	$1,117	$ 723	$1,044	$ 203	$ 323
Interest expense	50	131	76	60	25	41	26	33	6	12
Income before income taxes	136	184	120	177	66	97	54	96	16	31
Net income	81	111	65	93	33	51	29	52	14	18
Earnings per share, primary	$ 1.73	$ 2.23	$ 1.53	$ 2.33	$ 1.23	$ 1.60	$ .91	$ 1.24	$ 1.77	$ 1.80
Cash dividends per share	27	.34	.35	.54	.38	.45	.20	.30	.33	.42
Dividend payout	15.6%	15.2%	22.9%	23.2%	30.9%	28.1%	22.0%	24.2%	18.6%	23.3%
Financial Position										
Total assets	$1,610	$ 2,958	$1,327	$ 1,502	$ 663	$ 984	$ 596	$ 867	$ 211	$ 387
Total debt	801	1,692	757	776	312	396	274	299	102	171
Preferred stock	—	—	66	64	—	—	5	5	—	—
Shareholders' equity	469	768	216	297	201	327	200	376	61	135
Book value per share	$10.33	$ 14.70	$ 5.97	$ 8.01	$ 7.36	$10.20	$ 5.47	$ 8.39	$ 7.56	$13.18
Average price-earnings ratio	15.9	18.5	11.9	16.3	18.3	16.9	8.2	15.6	16.1	10.3
Stock Performance										
High	$37.00	$ 50.70	$26.20	$ 46.38	$22.50	$32.50	$10.50	$27.25	$35.80	$28.10
Low	17.90	31.70	10.25	29.75	9.88	21.50	4.38	11.50	21.20	9.10
Bond rating[a]	A	A	NR	B+	Ba	NR	Ba	B+	Ba	BB+
Selected Ratios										
Current ratio	1.3	1.4	1.4	1.4	1.6	1.5	1.8	2.0	1.7	1.2
Net profit margin	5.7%	4.6%	4.6%	5.5%	4.3%	4.5%	4.1%	5.0%	6.9%	5.7%
Return on beginning assets	7.5%	6.9%	5.4%	7.0%	6.5%	7.7%	9.2%	8.7%	11.1%	8.7%
Return on beginning equity	20.9%	23.7%	38.1%	43.1%	21.3%	25.2%	27.0%	25.9%	40.3%	30.3%
Asset turnover	1.3	1.5	1.2	1.3	1.5	1.7	2.3	1.8	1.6	1.5
Total debt/Total capital	63.1%	68.8%	72.8%	68.2%	60.8%	54.8%	57.2%	44.0%	62.7%	55.9%
Hospitals in Operation										
Owned/managed	188	349	90	89	61	102	54[c]	57[c]	30	35
Bed capacity	28,204	49,866	16,765	16,431	6,117[b]	9,713[b]	6,593[c]	6,929[c]	3,546	4,563
Occupancy rate	69%[d]	68%[d]	58.9%	61.3%	60.6%[b]	na	na	na	na	na

EXHIBIT 5 Continued

Sources of Revenues by Payer										
Cost-based										
Medicare	37%	38%	39%	40%	45%	45%	42.1%	42.0%	—	—
Medicaid	3	5	5	5	7	7	12.6	12.7	—	—
Blue Cross	4	3	5	5	3	2	4.1	4.5	—	—
Total cost-based	44%	46%	49%	50%	55%	54%	58.8%	59.2%	44%	42%
Charge-based	56	54	51	50	45	46	41.2	40.8	56	58
Total	100%	100%	100%	100%	100%	100%	100%	100%	100%	100%
Growth Rates, 1976–1981										
Revenues		35.3%		41.1%		31.2%		47.0%		31.0%
Net income		32.4		54.6		46.1		52.7		40.9
Total assets		34.2		30.0		22.7		34.3		39.7
Hospitals in operation		30.1		6.8		13.4		18.7		11.7

Note: Fiscal year ends August 31 for Humana and American Medical International; December 31 for HCA and Lifemark; May 31 for National Medical Enterprises. NR = not rated; na = not available.

[a]Excludes convertibles.

[b]For owned hospitals only.

[c]Excludes long-term care facilities (i.e., nursing homes).

[d]U.S.-owned only.

EXHIBIT 6
HCA's Hospital Locations in the United States

EXHIBIT 7 Schedule of Outstanding Long-Term Debt, 1979–1981 (millions of dollars)

	1979	1980	1981
Mortgage notes and bonds, 6%–16½%, due through 1998	$288	$153	$ 176
Revenue bonds, 6¼%–13½%, due through 2011	63	102	134
Notes, debentures, and capitalized leases, 7%–16½%, due through 1999	75	227	281
Revolving credit and term loan agreements at prime or LIBOR, plus ½%–⅝%	—	168	515
Commercial paper and bank financing, 13¼% composite effective rate at December 31, 1981[a]	—	125	208
Convertible subordinated debentures:			
8¾%, due 1996, convertible at $43.50 per share	—	—	80
8¾%, due 2006, convertible at $41.17 per share	—	—	125
12%, due 1996, convertible at $62.30 per share	—	—	81
Guaranteed notes, 15½%, due 1988	—	—	50
Total	$427	$775	$1,649

Debt maturing in the next 5 years ($ millions):

1982	$ 34
1983	70
1984	71
1985	117
1986	163

[a]In 1980 and 1981 the company entered into revolving credit agreements with a group of banks, aggregating $160 million and $278 million, respectively. The lines were used to support commercial paper and other bank financing during these 2 years. Because of the availability of long-term financing under these agreements, the company classified the commercial paper issue under long-term debt.

EXHIBIT 8 Debt Issued in the U.S. Public Market by Industrial Corporations with Varying Credit Ratings, 1974–1981 (millions of dollars)

Source: Salomon Brothers Inc.

Credit Rating	1974		1975		1976		1977		1978		1979		1980		1981	
Aaa	$1,650	25.1%	$ 2,875	24.0%	$ 700	11.7%	$ 800	20.5%	$ 275	8.6%	$1,550	27.4%	$1,750	17.9%	$1,852	20.8%
Aa	2,415	36.7	3,310	27.7	2,030	33.8	1.125	28.9	700	21.8	1,800	31.8	2,900	29.7	2,458	27.7
A	2,060	31.3	5,355	44.7	2,205	36.8	960	24.6	1,310	40.8	1,500	26.5	4,220	43.2	3,887	43.7
Baa	440	6.7	420	3.5	1,010	16.8	445	11.4	210	6.5	0	0	345	3.6	0	0
Other ...	15	.2	9	.1	53	.9	567	14.6	713	22.3	809	14.3	549	5.6	690	7.8
	$6,580	100.0%	$11,969	100.0%	$5,998	100.0%	$3,897	100.0%	$3,208	100.0%	$5,659	100.0%	$9,764	100.0%	$8,887	100.0%

[c]Excludes long-term care facilities (i.e., nursing homes).
[d]U.S.-owned only.

Stone Container Corporation (A)

The first quarter of 1993 had been a trying one for the management of Stone Container Corporation, the United States's largest producer of cardboard containers and related paper products. In fact, it had been a tense 4 years since Stone's acquisition of Consolidated-Bathurst Inc. of Canada in March 1989. The accumulation of more than $3.3 billion of debt in connection with that acquisition had left the company highly leveraged relative to its rivals during a period of falling prices for paper and linerboard. Despite a strong bull market since the end of 1990, Stone's stock price was less than half its value at the time of the Consolidated-Bathurst acquisition. As the first quarter of 1993 drew to a close, Stone was preparing to report a first quarter loss of $0.91 per share, $0.76 higher than its loss in the same quarter of the previous year. Although it had not defaulted on its debt, it was drawing precariously close to the coverage and indebtedness covenants on its bank loans. Immediate steps would be necessary if Stone were to avoid default.

Company and Industry Background

In 1993, Stone Container Corporation was the paper and forest products industry's leading producer of containerboard and corrugated containers as well as kraft paper, bags, and sacks. Additionally, Stone Container held a major position in newsprint manufacturing and groundwood specialty papers. Stone Container also produced building products and wood pulp. With plants throughout the world, Stone Container employed 31,800 people. Sixty-nine percent of its sales came from the United States while Canada accounted for 16%, and Europe, 15%. Stone Container's 1992 sales totaled $5,520.7 million (see Exhibit 1). Other financial statements are provided in Exhibits 2 and 3. A ten-year historical summary of Stone's performance is provided in Exhibit 4.

The Paper and Forest Products Industry

In early 1993, the paper and forest products industry included a vast array of companies. Among them were Georgia-Pacific, the world's largest producer of paper and wood products; Scott Paper, the world's largest producer of sanitary tissue products; Weyerhauser, the world's largest private owner of softwood timber; and Stone Container, the industry leader in containerboard, corrugated containers, kraft paper, bags, and sacks. Other products made by industry participants included newsprint, packaging papers, paperboard, paper towels, lumber, logs, plywood, among many others.

Between 1986 and 1992 the paper and forest products industry grew from $61.6 billion in sales to $85.2 billion, a total increase just shy of 40%. In 1986, industry net profit was $2.85 billion. After exceeding $6 billion in 1988, industry net profits then fell to $.97 billion in 1992.[1]

[1] *Valueline,* July 23, 1993, p. 914.

Research Associate Kirk A. Goldman prepared this case under the supervision of Professor W. Carl Kester as the basis for class discussion rather than to illustrate either effective or ineffective handling of an administrative situation.

Copyright © 1997 by the President and Fellows of Harvard College. To order copies or request permission to reproduce materials, call 1-800-545-7685 or write Harvard Business School Publishing, Boston, MA 02163. No part of this publication may be reproduced, stored in a retrieval system, used in a spreadsheet, or transmitted in any form or by any means—electronic, mechanical, photocopying, recording, or otherwise—without the permission of Harvard Business School.

In general, most products in the paper industry have exhibited pronounced price cycles (see Exhibit 5). For example, during the seven-year period from 1985 to 1991, the price of a ton of unbleached kraft linerboard began at $270, rose progressively to $394, and then fell to $285 per ton. This cyclicality was amplified by the high degree of operating leverage inherent in the production of paper and paperboard, which was very capital intensive (roughly $1.30 in assets were required to produce $1.00 in sales). The economics of paper production dictated that plants be kept running at close to full capacity for as long as possible. When demand eased, producers generally preferred to cut prices rather than production.

Stone Container faced direct competition from Chesapeake Corporation, Willamette Industries, Temple-Inland, Union Camp Corporation, and Westvaco Corporation. Chesapeake Corporation produced primarily commercial tissues and kraft products, but also manufactured some corrugated containers, other packaging goods, and point-of-purchase displays. Willamette manufactured and sold pulp, uncoated white papers, paper bags, and corrugated containers as well as a variety of building materials. A large portion of Union Camp Corporation's 1992 sales were from uncoated white papers, kraft paper, and linerboard as well as other packaging products. Westvaco manufactured paper and paperboard as well as containerboard. Its plants also produced folding cartons, corrugated boxes, and food and beverage containers. See Exhibit 6 for a comparison of industry rivals.

No company competed directly with Stone Container in all product lines. However, each of these rivals manufactured a few products in common with Stone. For example, Westvaco used its bleached paperboard and containerboard to produce store displays and produce corrugated boxes that Stone also produced. But, unlike Stone Container, Westvaco was also a primary manufacturer of writing and printing papers. Similarly, Union Camp Corporation, which produced white papers, kraft papers, and linerboard, also derived 16% of its business from chemicals.

Early Company Background[2]

In 1888, at his mother's urging, Joseph Stone left his native Russia for a new beginning in the United States. After a brief stay in Philadelphia, Stone settled in Chicago, abandoned his position as a paper jobber in 1926 and, along with two of his sons, Norman and Marvin, created J.H. Stone & Sons with his lifetime savings of $1,500. They worked as jobbers for shipping supplies such as wrapping paper, bags, and tissues, out of a former wholesale grocery store in Chicago. Joseph Stone based his business strategy on high quality service at reasonable prices, with minimal capital tied up in inventory. During its first year, the business began to realize a profit. Joseph's third son, Jerome, entered the business and soon they began jobbing corrugated boxes.

The Great Depression changed J.H. Stone & Sons from jobbers to manufacturers. The National Recovery Act, signed in 1933 by President Roosevelt, outlawed price cutting. Previously, Stone and Sons had acquired their merchandise at a discount and passed some of the savings onto their customers. With this eliminated, Stone's customers would have to pay an unwanted premium for their services; hence, the move into manufacturing. In 1933, Stone purchased for $7,200 five pieces of obsolete equipment called "Big Betsy's" that converted corrugated sheets into boxes. Three years later, Stone acquired a used corrugator for $20,000. That same year, Joseph Stone passed away.

[2]The principal source for Stone Container's early history is "Stone Container Corporation," by Jordan Wankoff, *International Directory of Company Histories,* Adele Hast, editor (London: St. James Press, 1991), pp. 332–334.

In the ensuing years Stone & Sons grew significantly by way of acquisition, reaching sales of $1 million by 1939. Each time the family-owned company made an acquisition, it either paid entirely in cash or borrowed the money and repaid the loans early. Having witnessed the ravages of the Great Depression, it was the family's policy not to carry any significant debt for long periods of time. When it built a new plant in 1939, for example, it paid for the plant with a 20-year loan that it subsequently entirely repaid within 3 years.

During World War II, Stone & Sons carried a high war-priority rating. Consequently, the company did not suffer materials shortages. It contributed to the war effort by producing corrugated boxes to ship aid and arms overseas. In 1943, J.H. Stone & Sons acquired its first venture outside of Chicago by purchasing Light Corrugated Box Company of Philadelphia for $1.2 million. At this time, the three brothers brought in the first non-family general manager to run the plant.

After World War II, the company reincorporated as Stone Container Corporation. During the next several years, with Norman Stone as CEO, Stone Container continued to expand and diversify. It purchased mills that could produce jute linerboard and corrugated medium, two essential components in corrugated containers. To pay for these acquisitions, Stone borrowed $2 million. Consistent with long-standing company policy, however, the loan was repaid within a year.

In 1947, Stone Container issued 250,000 shares of stock in its initial public offering and became a publicly-owned company. With access to public capital markets, Stone widened its reach geographically in the 1950's by buying and building regional plants in Ohio, Indiana, Illinois, and Michigan (it was uneconomic to transport corrugated boxes more than about 125 miles). This expansion continued Stone's diversification in the paper industry, and by 1960 Stone was selling folding cartons, fiber cans, tubes, tags, and special paper packages, as well as corrugated containers and paperboard. The 1950s also saw Stone shifting its focus away from ordinary cardboard containers towards the production of more specialized containers that provided advertising on the exterior as well as simply a means of conveyance.

During the economic slowdown of the 1960's, Stone Container began an expansion into containers made from kraft linerboard. Kraft linerboard was lighter and stronger than jute linerboard. Because Stone previously had to purchase kraft linerboard, its profit margins were lower than they might have been if it had been more vertically integrated. Stone's involvement in the kraft market increased when it purchased a plant to produce kraft linerboard in 1961, and expanded further in subsequent years.

In 1975, Roger Stone, Marvin's son, became president of the company and chief executive officer four years later. Earlier in the 1970's Roger had been instrumental in refocusing the company on the sale of boxes to producers of nondurable consumer products such as foods, beverages, and toys.

Roger Stone's Acquisition Strategy

By 1979, depressed margins in the industry had prompted Stone Container to enter into merger negotiations with Boise Cascade. Boise offered the Stones $125 million in cash and stock to buy all of Stone Container's outstanding shares a sum more than twice the company's market value at that time. However, signs of an upswing in paper prices caused Stone to pull out of the deal and seek an acquisition of its own. Roger Stone's strategy was predicated on the notion that greater value could be created by buying up capacity from distressed producers during troughs in the industry cycle. This would enable Stone to acquire assets at favorable prices while avoiding the addition of expensive new capacity to the industry. Acquisitions were also a faster means of expansion: construction of a large new facility for producing paperboard could take 3 years to complete. As Roger Stone later commented, "We were willing to make that commitment [of capital to expand] when demand was down. That is when you should commit, when nobody else really wants to."[3]

In 1979, at a low point in the business cycle, Roger Stone expanded the Florence, South Carolina, linerboard plant at a cost of $55 million. Two years later, in 1981, Stone Container purchased an equity position in Dean-Dempsy Corporation. Using a highly leveraged acquisition strategy, Stone Container continued to increase its capacity very rapidly. In 1983, Stone Container bought the Continental Group's containerboard and brown-paper operations. Again, that year was bad for the industry and Continental was in serious need of cash. To finance the purchase, Stone took out a $600 million loan, which boosted its debt to 79% of total capital. It also had its first equity offering since its 1947 IPO, which dropped the family's ownership share from 57% to 49%. Containerboard prices then rose once again, allowing Stone to generate enough cash to pay off the bulk of its debt.

Two years after the Continental acquisition, Stone paid $457 million for containerboard and box-and-bag plants from Champion International Corporation. As part of this transaction, Stone gave Champion the right to purchase 12 to 14% of Stone's stock, potentially diluting further the family's equity to less than 40%. In 1987, Stone paid another $760 million for Southwest Forest Industries.

By this time, Stone had quintupled its annual production capacity to 4.8 million tons at one-fifth the normal cost of building new plants. It had borrowed heavily to achieve this expansion, however. To relieve some of its debt burden, Stone Container created a subsidiary, Stone Forest Industries, Inc., and sold a 51% interest in it in December of 1987 for $75 million in cash, along with $38 million of Stone Forest non-voting preferred stock. Additionally, Stone Forest assumed and repaid $100 million of Stone Container's bank indebtedness. With the paper industry again in a prosperous situation, Stone Container was able to handle its remaining debt obligations. Meanwhile the family's ownership share had been reduced further, to 30%.

Recent Investment and Financing

Even with the company heavily burdened by debt following its expansion in the mid-1980's, Roger Stone continued Stone Container's pattern of growth through highly leveraged acquisitions. In March of 1989, Stone Container bought Consolidated-Bathurst Inc. of Canada, Canada's fifth largest pulp and paper producer, for $2.7 billion. This acquisition made Stone Container the world's second largest producer of pulp, paper, and paperboard; a major player in the newsprint industry; and gave it entry to the European market through a U.K. subsidiary. This last feature was viewed by many analysts as particularly attractive given the coming integration of the European community. Unlike its previous acquisitions made during the troughs of industry cycles, however, Stone bought Consolidated-Bathurst near the peak of this cycle and paid a substantial 47% premium over market value for the company.

To finance the acquisition, Stone Container arranged a $3.3 billion bank credit facility. The credit facility included two eight-year term loans totaling $2.9 billion and two five-year revolving credit facilities that totaled $400 million. It used a portion of this credit to replace a $540 million credit facility that had been established the prior year. The rest of the borrowing was used to purchase Consolidated-Bathurst, pay the transactions costs associated with the acquisition, and refinance other debt of both Stone Container and Consolidated-Bathurst. Subsequent to the acquisition Consolidated-Bathurst was renamed Stone Consolidated.

[3]Wankoff, p. 334.

Over the years, Stone Container had grown increasingly dependent on the issuance of high-yield debt (i.e., "junk bonds") to finance its large acquisitions.[4] Stone initially financed the Consolidated-Bathurst purchase with short-term bank loans. At the time, it was planned that the company would refinance the loans by issuing high-yield bonds. Unfortunately the high-yield debt market developed serious liquidity problems before this could be accomplished. By August of 1989, amid a media and political bonanza, regulators forced many savings and loans banks to dump their junk bonds. Drexel Burnham stood on the verge of bankruptcy, and Michael Milken, its preeminent junk bond trader, was under indictment for various acts of securities fraud. This depressed an already slumping market (see Exhibit 7) and effectively eliminated Stone's intentions of refinancing its loans with high-yield bonds.

Later in 1989, Stone Container sold $330 million in noncore assets. But by 1990, it barely had sufficient cash to meet its debt obligations. Instead of resorting to the junk bond market, Stone Container had to pay substantial fees to refinance its revolving credit agreement with its bank lenders. Finally, in October of 1991, Stone reluctantly sold 9 million shares of stock for $175 million to raise much needed cash.

In 1992, Stone finally found room to maneuver within the public securities market. It began a process of refinancing and restructuring its debt using complex securities such as convertible exchangeable preferred stock and interest rate swaps. It also issued new subordinated debentures and notes at rates between 10¾% and 11%.

By the end of 1992, Stone Container Corporation owned or held interest in 136 manufacturing plants in 38 U.S. states, 27 in Canada, 15 in Germany, 14 in Mexico, two in both Belgium and France, and one in both the United Kingdom and the Netherlands. Additionally, Stone Container either owned wholly or held a majority share in 68 subsidiaries. Other affiliations (up to 50% ownership) included another 26 companies all around the globe. Total paperboard, paper, and pulp capacity amounted to 8.3 million tons per year. Against these assets, Stone had total long-term debt outstanding of more than $4.1 billion.

Developing a Financial Plan

The financial pressure on Stone had become severe by the first quarter of 1993. There seemed little doubt that paper prices would eventually recover as they had in the past, but how soon and by how much? During the twelve months ending March 1994, Stone would have to continue paying approximately $400 to $425 million in interest on its debt; make debt repayments of $365 million; and extend, refinance, or replace another $400 million in revolving credit facilities that were scheduled to terminate. Furthermore, it would continue to face difficulties remaining in compliance with coverage and total indebtedness covenants in its various credit agreements. Finally, the company was also required to make $100 million of new capital expenditures in order to be in compliance with new secondary-waste treatment regulations in Canada. All this had to be accomplished in a year in which Stone was likely to realize further pre-tax losses in the vicinity of $450 to $500 million.

In the first quarter of 1993, several alternatives were available to Stone Container for dealing with its financial situation:

1. Bank loan agreements could be renegotiated to extend their maturities and ease some of the binding covenants. This had been done successfully before in 1990. If the banks agreed, fees for the restructuring were likely to range between $70 and $80 million.

[4]Roger Stone was a classmate of Michael Milken at The Wharton School of The University of Pennsylvania. During the late 1970's and 1980's, Milken and his employer, Drexel Burnham Lambert, Inc., were widely credited with having created and dominated the U.S. junk bond market.

2. Assets could be sold for cash or, as had been done in 1987 with Stone Forest Industries, a significant equity interest in some of Stone's subsidiaries could be sold. Such sales might realistically raise $250 million to $500 million.
3. Intermediate-term senior notes could be sold to the public for purposes of repaying the bank debt. It was believed possible to underwrite up to $300 million of 5-year notes bearing a coupon in the 12% to 12½ range.
4. Up to $300 million of convertible subordinated notes might be sold for purposes of repaying senior bank debt. Such notes would likely bear a coupon of 8¾%, mature in 7 years, and be convertible into Stone's common stock at an effective conversion price 20% higher than the market price of Stone's common stock at the date of offering. Once determined, this conversion price would remain fixed through the life of the convertible. In March 1993, a 20% premium over market value would imply a conversion price of $18.00 per share, and a conversion ratio (shares of stock per $1,000 par value convertible bond) of 55.56.
5. Up to $500 million of common stock might be issued to the public with net proceeds to the company of approximately 95% of the offering price. The actual offering price would be determined by market conditions at the time of the offering itself. In March 1993, Stone's stock price was trading in the vicinity of $15 to $16 per share (stock price data are provided in Exhibit 8; additional capital market data are provided in Exhibit 9).

These alternatives were not necessarily mutually exclusive. More than one might be pursued over the course of the coming year. Whatever was decided, however, it was clear that Stone Container needed a comprehensive financial plan that would relieve the debt pressures confronting it now, see it through the rest of the paper-pricing cyclical trough, and restore it to some degree of financial stability.

EXHIBIT 1
Stone Container's Consolidated Statements of Operations (in millions except per share)

	Year Ended December 31,		
	1992	1991	1990
Net sales	$5,520.7	$5,384.3	$5,755.9
Cost of products sold	4,474.5	4,285.6	4,421.9
Selling, general, and administrative expenses	543.5	522.8	495.5
Depreciation and amortization	304.2	277.5	257.0
Equity (income) loss from affiliates	5.3	(1.1)	(7.4)
Total operating costs and expenses	5,327.5	5,084.8	5,167.0
Income from operations	193.2	299.5	588.9
Interest expense	(386.1)	(397.4)	(421.7)
Other, net	(7.3)	79.9	21.0
Income (loss) before income taxes	(200.2)	(18.0)	188.2
Provision (credit) for income taxes	(29.7)	31.1	92.8
Net income(loss)	(170.5)	(49.1)	95.4
Preferred stock dividends	(6.9)	-	-
Net income (loss) after preferred stock dividends	$(177.4)	$(49.1)	$95.4
Net income (loss) per common share[a]	$(2.50)	$ (0.78)	$1.56

[a]Amounts per common share have been adjusted for a 2% common stock dividend issued September 15, 1992.

EXHIBIT 2
Stone Container's Consolidated Balance Sheets (in millions)

	December 31,		
	1992	1991	1990
ASSETS			
Current assets:			
Cash and cash equivalents	$ 58.9	$64.1	$ 53.9
Accounts and notes receivable (less allowances of $19.3 and $15.6)	688.1	641.7	681.3
Inventories	785.1	820.9	761.9
Other	146.5	158.6	88.9
Total current assets	1,678.6	1,685.3	1,586.0
Property, plant, and equipment	4,936.5	4,826.6	4,455.1
Accumulated depreciation and amortization	(1,542.5)	(1,306.4)	(1,091.1)
Property, plant, and equipment—net	3,394.0	3,520.2	3,364.0
Timberlands	59.2	50.9	48.4
Goodwill	1,007.8	1,126.1	1,160.5
Other	542.4	520.4	531.1
Total assets	$6,682.0	$6,902.9	$6,690.0
LIABILITIES AND STOCKHOLDERS' EQUITY			
Current liabilities			
Notes payable	$ 33.0	$ 19.1	$ 24.8
Current maturities of long-term debt	184.8	108.5	386.9
Accounts payable	364.2	417.7	367.4
Income taxes	58.7	63.0	41.9
Accrued and other current liabilities	298.5	306.5	325.5
Total current liabilities	939.2	914.8	1,146.5
Senior long-term debt	2,501.6	2,851.1	2,537.6
Subordinated debt	1,019.2	622.0	671.7
Non-recourse debt of consolidated affiliates	584.3	573.3	471.2
Other long-term liabilities	152.7	105.4	105.2
Deferred taxes	242.6	263.9	262.7
Redeemable preferred stock of consolidated affiliate	36.3	31.1	26.6
Minority interest	2.3	3.8	8.0
Stockholders' equity:			
Series E preferred stock	115	—	—
Common stock	645.7	613.2	435.7
Retained earnings	595.0	832.8	926.7
Foreign currency translation adjustment	(147.2)	95.5	101.5
Unamortized expense of restricted stock plan	(4.7)	(4.0)	(3.4)
Total stockholders' equity	1,203.8	1,537.5	1,460.5
Total liabilities and stockholders' equity	$6,682.0	$6,902.9	$6,690.0

EXHIBIT 3
Stone Container's Consolidated Statements of Cash Flows (in millions)

	1992	1991	1990
Cash flows from operating activities			
Net loss	$(170.5)	$ (49.1)	$ 95.4
Adjustments to reconcile net loss to net cash provided by (used in) operating activities:			
Depreciation and amortization	304.2	277.5	257.0
Deferred taxes	(37.0)	21.6	58.6
Foreign currency transactions (gains) losses	15.0	(4.9)	(1.0)
Other—net	55.7	8.3	(7.6)
Changes in current assets and liabilities—net of investments for acquisitions and divestitures:			
Decrease (increase) in accounts and notes receivable—net	(66.6)	33.5	31.0
Decrease (increase) in inventories	10.5	(60.4)	25.6
Decrease (increase) in other current assets	9.2	(75.2)	3.2
Increase (decrease) in accounts payable and other current liabilities	(34.9)	59.2	(10.7)
Net cash provided by operating activities	85.6	210.5	451.5
Cash flows from financing activities			
Borrowings	1,024.8	753.0	280.2
Payments made on debt	(909.2)	(795.9)	(311.5)
Non-recourse borrowings of consolidated affiliates	40.0	155.5	235.0
Payments by consolidated affiliates on non-recourse debt	(13.6)	(34.4)	(42.4)
Proceeds from issuance of preferred stock	111.0	-	-
Proceeds from issuance of common stock	0.1	176.0	0.1
Cash dividends[a]	(30.7)	(44.7)	(43.0)
Net cash provided by financing activities	222.4	209.5	118.4
Cash flows from investing activities			
Capital expenditures:			
Funded by project financings	(79.1)	(219.8)	(245.2)
Other	(202.3)	(210.3)	(306.8)
Total capital expenditures	(281.4)	(430.1)	(552.0)
Payments made for businesses acquired	(27.2)	(18.9)	(44.8)
Proceeds from sales of assets	9.5	22.1	120.3
Other—net	(10.7)	13.8	(62.6)
Net cash used in investing activities	(309.8)	(413.1)	(539.1)
Effect of exchange rate changes on cash	(3.4)	3.3	0.2
Net cash flows			
Net increase (decrease) in cash and cash equivalents	(5.2)	10.2	31.0
Cash and cash equivalents, beginning of period	64.1	53.9	22.9
Cash and cash equivalents, end of period	$58.9	$64.1	$53.9

[a]Cash dividend payments were suspended in the third and fourth quarters of 1992.

EXHIBIT 4 Stone Container, 10-Year Historical Summary (dollars in millions except per share)

	Year Ends December 31,									
	1992	1991	1990	1989	1988	1987	1986	1985	1984	1983
Summary of Operations										
Net sales	5,520.7	5,384.3	5,755.9	5,329.7	3,742.5	3,232.9	2,032.3	1,229.1	1,244.4	655.8
Cost of products sold	4,474.5	4,285.6	4,421.9	3,893.8	2,618.0	2,347.8	1,564.6	944.1	924.9	526.0
Selling, general, and administrative expenses	543.5	522.8	495.5	474.5	351.1	343.8	241.2	157.0	147.6	83.4
EBITDA	502.7	575.9	838.5	961.4	773.4	541.3	226.5	128.0	171.9	46.4
Depreciation and amortization	304.2	277.5	257.0	237.1	148.1	138.7	92.3	67.8	64.4	34.2
Interest expense	386.1	397.4	421.7	344.7	108.3	131.1	85.3	63.3	59.3	24.9
Net income	(170.5)	(49.1)	95.4	285.8	341.8	161.3	35.4	3.8	33.7	(2.9)
Per share of common stock										
Net income (loss)	(2.50)	(0.78)	1.56	4.67	5.58	2.79	0.73	0.09	0.78	(0.09)
Dividends and distributions paid[a]	0.35	0.71	0.71	0.70	0.35	0.25	0.19	0.19	0.19	0.19
Price range of common shares—N.Y.S.E.										
High	32.63	26.00	25.25	36.38	39.50	39.83	20.00	13.17	14.42	15.00
Low	12.50	9.00	8.13	22.13	20.67	15.33	11.38	8.00	8.58	6.75
Average common shares outstanding (in millions)	71.0	63.2	61.3	61.2	61.3	57.9	48.8	42.3	43.1	33.8
Financial position at end of year										
Current assets	1,678.6	1,685.3	1,586.0	1,687.0	865.7	737.4	530.4	320.2	323.3	252.0
Current liabilities	939.2	914.8	1,146.5	1,072.6	408.3	334.9	203.4	165.1	164.4	104.0
Working capital	739.4	770.5	439.5	614.4	457.4	402.5	327.0	155.1	158.9	148.0
Property, plant, and equipment—(net)	3,394.0	3,520.2	3,364.0	2,977.9	1,276.0	1,300.0	924.4	642.6	657.7	689.1
Total assets	6,682.0	6,902.9	6,690.0	6,253.7	2,395.0	2,286.1	1,523.6	1,010.3	1,006.7	968.2
Long-term debt	4,105.1	4,046.4	3,680.5	3,536.9	765.1	1,070.5	767.0	493.3	482.8	548.2
Deferred taxes	242.6	263.9	262.7	185.6	140.3	120.4	69.9	49.2	55.8	38.0
Redeemable preferred stock	36.3	31.1	26.6	22.7	-	1.5	1.5	8.0	8.5	7.6
Minority interest	2.3	3.8	8.0	9.7	0.3	0.2	-	-	-	-
Stockholders' equity	1,203.8	1,537.5	1,460.5	1,347.6	1,063.6	740.3	481.8	294.7	295.1	270.3

EXHIBIT 4 Continued

Additional Information										
Paperboard, paper, and market pulp:										
Produced (thousands of short tons)	7,517	7,365	7,447	6,772	4,729	4,373	3,154	2,168	2,236	1,194
Converted (thousands of short tons)	4,373	4,228	4,241	3,930	3,344	2,998	2,495	1,530	1,439	767
Corrugated shipments (billion square feet)	51.67	49.18	47.16	41.56	34.47	32.09	25.95	15.19	14.46	8.58
Employees (end of year—in thousands)	31.2	31.8	32.3	32.6	20.7	18.8	15.5	9.4	9.0	8.9
Capital expenditures	281.4	430.1	552.0	501.7	136.6	105.7	63.3	47.1	41.9	21.0
Current ratio	1.8	1.8	1.4	1.6	2.1	2.2	2.6	1.9	2.0	2.4
Percent long-term debt/total capitalization	73.4%	68.8%	67.7%	69.3%	38.9%	55.4%	58.1%	58.4%	57.3%	63.4%
Return on beginning common stockholders equity	(11.5%)	(3.4%)	7.1%	26.9%	46.2%	41.8%	10.2%	1.1%	11.9%	(2.6%)
Pretax margin	(3.6%)	(0.3%)	3.3%	9.0%	14.7%	8.8%	2.9%	0.1%	4.4%	(1.3%)
Aftertax margin	(3.1%)	(0.9%)	1.7%	5.4%	9.1%	5.0%	1.7%	0.3%	2.7%	(0.4%)

[a]Cash dividend payments were suspended in the third and fourth quarters of 1992.

EXHIBIT 5 Constant-Dollar Kraft Paper and Linerboard Prices, 1980–1992 (1987 dollars)

Year	Price/Ton
1980	$523.0
1981	513.3
1982	441.5
1983	453.0
1984	439.6
1985	389.8
1986	438.6
1987	485.0
1988	495.7
1989	511.5
1990	516.3
1991	476.2
1992	454.9

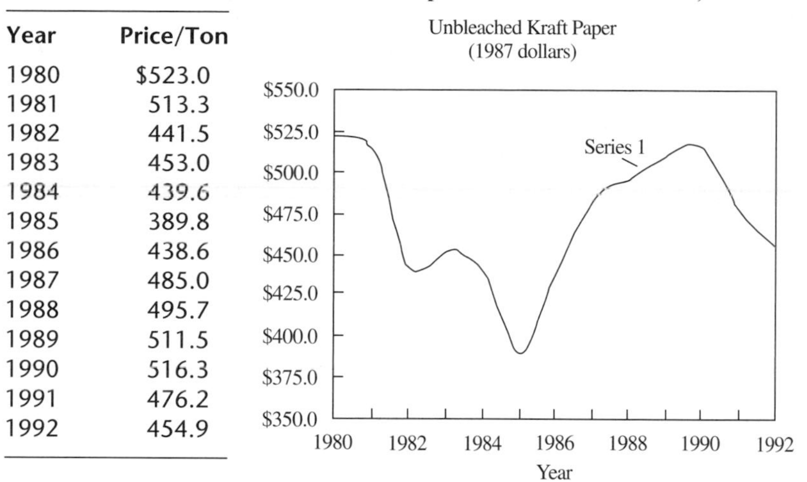

Year	Price/Ton
1980	$376.6
1981	361.2
1982	304.3
1983	332.6
1984	368.1
1985	270.1
1986	330.2
1987	380.0
1988	394.6
1989	377.9
1990	322.2
1991	285.7
1992	285.4

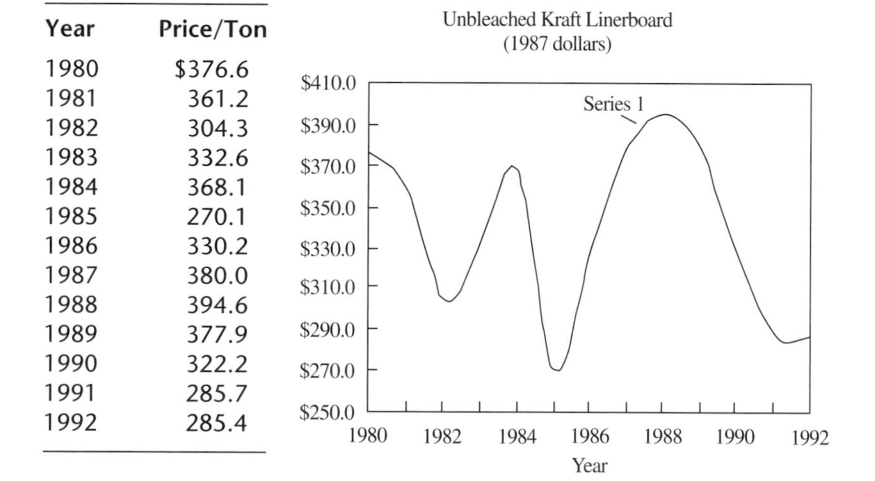

EXHIBIT 6 **Comparative Financial Data of Selected Competitors (end of 1992 fiscal years; in millions except per share data)**

	Stone Container Corp.	Chesapeake Corp.	Union Camp Corp.	Westvaco Corp.	Willamette Inds.
Sales	$5,520.7	$888.4	$3,064.4	$2,335.6	$2,372.4
Operating income	193.2	52.2	182.3	285.1	197.6
Interest expense	386.1	31.4	136.2	79.0	66.4
Net income	(177.4)	4.7	76.2	135.9	81.6
Number of shares outstanding	71.00	23.33	69.66	67.27	54.77
Earnings per share	2.50	0.17	1.10	2.06	1.52
Dividends per share	0.35	0.72	1.56	1.10	0.84
Capital expenditures	281.4	84.7	219.7	352.2	337.0
Depreciation	304.2	68.6	237.5	183.1	173.8
Current assets	1,628.6	211.8	1,023.9	671.5	481.0
Cash and short term investments	58.9	0.7	67.7	191.1	9.0
Total assets	6,682.0	958.9	4,739.1	3,703.9	2,527.4
Current liabilities	939.2	89.7	892.1	352.6	323.1
Total liabilities	5,478.2	958.9	4,739.1	3,703.9	2,527.4
Short-term debt	217.8	4.3	513.5	24.1	58.8
Long-term debt	4,105.1	382.8	1,289.7	1,055.5	843.6
Net worth	1,203.8	370.4	1,881.9	1,777.1	1,164.8
Total capitalization	5,526.7	757.5	3,685.1	2,856.7	2,067.2
Common share prices					
High	28.3	29.1	55.1	41.3	42.5
Low	15.0	18.3	40.1	32.0	29.0
Ending price-earnings ratio	-	120.6	41.9	17.9	27.1
Growth rates (5 years)					
Sales	11.3%	5.6%	5.3%	4.2%	10.6%
Net income	–	(31.1%)	(18.1%)	(1.4%)	(7.6%)
Total assets	23.9%	10.2%	10.2%	10.8%	16.1%
Financial ratios					
Return on sales	(3.1%)	0.5%	2.5%	5.8%	3.4%
Return on total capital	3.5%	4.4%	3.2%	6.6%	6.0%
Return on equity	(14.2%)	1.3%	4.1%	7.7%	7.0%
Current ratio	1.8	2.4	4.2	1.9	1.5
Debt to total capital	78.2%	51.1%	48.9%	37.8%	43.7%
Interest coverage	0.5	1.6	1.3	3.6	2.4

EXHIBIT 7 **New U.S. Public Bond Issues by Credit Rating**

Source: Securities Data Company, Inc.

	1988			1989			1990		
	Proceeds ($ billions)	% of Total	# of Issues	Proceeds ($ billions)	% of Total	# of Issues	Proceeds ($ billions)	% of Total	# of Issues
AAA	16.8	14.1	81	22.3	17.0	74	12.5	8.6	74
AA	21.1	17.7	139	24.0	18.3	169	35.2	30.7	148
A	30.2	25.3	209	31.4	24.0	208	32.6	28.4	243
BBB	14.1	11.8	100	12.4	9.5	82	13.2	11.5	93
Below BBB	37.1	31.1	205	41.0	31.2	221	21.1	18.5	142

	1991			1992			1993		
	Proceeds ($ billions)	% of Total	# of Issues	Proceeds ($ billions)	% of Total	# of Issues	Proceeds ($ billions)	% of Total	# of Issues
AAA	24.1	12.1	200	25.3	8.1	133	26.3	6.1	142
AA	34.3	17.2	246	40.1	12.9	237	56.4	13.1	332
A	74.1	37.2	706	88.9	28.6	687	125.1	29.1	930
BBB	22.5	11.3	188	45.8	14.7	308	60.0	13.9	400
Below BBB	44.3	22.2	253	110.5	35.6	744	162.5	37.8	1,402

EXHIBIT 8
Stone Container's Monthly Closing Stock Prices, 1989–1993 ($ per share, except index)

Stone Container Stock Price		S&P 500 Index	Stone Container Stock Price		S&P 500 Index
1989			**1991**		
January	31.859	297.47	January	13.109	343.93
February	31.625	288.86	February	14.344	367.07
March	29.531	294.87	March	15.563	375.22
April	30.516	309.64	April	16.547	375.34
May	28.922	319.05	May	21.328	389.83
June	24.875	317.98	June	21.203	371.16
July	26.719	346.08	July	20.594	387.81
August	31.375	351.45	August	21.453	395.43
September	28.547	349.15	September	18.500	387.86
October	25.609	340.36	October	22.297	392.45
November	24.016	345.99	November	19.609	375.22
December	23.406	353.40	December	25.375	417.09
1990			**1992**		
January	21.078	329.08	January	28.313	408.78
February	20.344	331.89	February	26.469	412.70
March	20.828	339.94	March	26.953	403.69
April	18.016	330.80	April	27.453	414.95
May	19.859	361.23	May	24.266	415.35
June	16.047	358.02	June	24.625	408.14
July	15.563	356.15	July	18.500	414.22
August	11.891	322.56	August	16.750	414.03
September	10.047	306.05	September	15.000	417.80
October	8.828	304.00	October	16.875	418.68
November	9.797	322.22	November	19.125	431.35
December	11.156	330.22	December	16.750	435.71
			1993		
			January	16.000	438.78
			February	15.375	443.38

EXHIBIT 9
Selected Interest Rates, 1990–1993

	Government Bonds		Corporate Bonds	
Interest Rate Data	Short Term	Long Term	Aaa	Baa
1990	7.51%	8.55%	9.32%	10.36%
1991	5.42	7.86	8.77	9.80
1992	3.45	7.01	8.14	8.98
January 1993	3.06	6.60	7.91	8.67
February 1993	2.95	6.26	7.71	8.39
March 1993	2.97	5.98	7.58	8.15
April 1993	2.89	5.97	7.46	8.14

MCI Communications Corporation (1983)

In April 1983, Wayne English, chief financial officer of MCI Communications Corporation, faced the problem of setting financial policy in an environment characterized by a large potential demand for external funding and great uncertainty concerning MCI's future. MCI, which provided long-distance telecommunications services in competition with AT&T, had seen its revenues grow from almost nothing in FY 1974 (ending March 31, 1974) to more than $1 billion in FY 1983. During that period, the company climbed from a loss of $38.7 million in FY 1975 to a profit of $170.8 million in FY 1983. In the last 2 years, its stock price had increased more than fivefold.

Nevertheless, the antitrust settlement between AT&T and the U.S. Department of Justice in January 1982 had significantly altered the economic landscape for MCI. The settlement, providing for the breakup of AT&T by early 1984, would affect MCI in two important ways. On the one hand, it offered the opportunity for greatly increased growth, since AT&T would be required, for the first time, to compete on equal quality-of-service terms with MCI. On the other hand, the settlement posed new uncertainties, since it promised to eliminate certain MCI cost advantages and to increase AT&T's competitive flexibility.

Even in the face of intensifying competition from AT&T, however, MCI was committed to extending the reach and capacity of its network. According to Brian Thompson, senior vice president for corporate development: "Economies of scale and scope are everything in this business. In the long term, the strategic high ground lies in owning your own facilities for basic call services and then leveraging off this to provide value-added services."

Company Background

MCI was organized in August 1968 under the leadership of William McGowan as the Federal Communications Commission (FCC) appeared willing to allow increased competition with AT&T in the long-distance market. In June 1971, the FCC formally adopted a policy of allowing qualified new companies to enter the market for specialized long-distance services, which consisted chiefly of *private line* (i.e., dedicated telephone line) services for large telephone users. By June 1972, MCI was ready to begin construction of its telecommunications network.

To provide the necessary funds, MCI sold 6 million shares of common stock to the public at $5 per share.[1] Net proceeds after expenses and commissions were $27.1 million. MCI also obtained a $64 million line of credit from a group of four banks headed by the First National Bank of Chicago and further loan promises of $6.45 million from private investors in the form of 7½% subordinated notes (with attached warrants) of up to 5-year maturities. The bank loans carried an interest rate of 3¾% above prime, plus a commitment fee of ½% per annum on the unborrowed balance.

[1]This and subsequent prices and numbers of shares have been adjusted for all stock splits on or before April 1, 1983.

Copyright © 1984 by the President and Fellows of Harvard College. Harvard Business School case 284–057.

Proceeds from these preferred offerings allowed MCI to retire its short-to-intermediate term bank debt and to issue longer-term debt. Leasing activity decreased and, in July 1980, MCI raised $50.5 million through the public sale of 20-year subordinated debentures.

In FY 1981, as the demand for investment funds intensified, the direction of MCI's financial policy shifted slightly from offerings of convertible preferreds to convertible debt. After obtaining $102.1 million in April 1981 through a straight subordinated debenture issue, MCI raised $98.2 million in August 1981 and $245.9 million in May 1982 with convertible debentures.

These convertible debentures carried forced conversion (i.e., *call*) provisions similar to those of the earlier preferred stock issues. As a result, MCI was able to force conversion of the May 1982 issue in December 1982 and of the August 1981 issue in February 1983. The consequent additions to common equity enabled MCI to take on a still greater debt burden. Thus, a straight debenture issue in September 1982 yielded $209.9 million, and a further convertible debenture in March 1983 produced almost $400 million.

In all, MCI raised about $1,050 million from the public sale of securities in FY1982 and FY1983. As with all MCI offerings, the initial issues were oversubscribed. Interest costs were relatively high (see Exhibit 7), but in the words of Mr. English, "Availability of funds [was] the paramount consideration"; cost was "secondary." Moreover, since profitability was increasing more rapidly than interest expense, interest coverage actually increased during this time. Considering the situation in 1975, and in comparison to other companies (see Exhibit 8), this was a remarkable achievement.

However, as details of the FCC s response to the AT&T antitrust settlement began to emerge, the resulting uncertainty cast doubt on MCI's continued ability to raise funds in these amounts. MCI would have to proceed with care, agility, and imagination.

The AT&T Antitrust Settlement and Other Developments

Historically, AT&T provided a necessary part of the MCI system—and its most serious competition. One part of AT&T—the local telephone operating companies (e.g., Illinois Bell, New England Telephone)—supplied MCI with connections to subscribers through their local telephone networks. MCI paid for these services at a rate negotiated in 1978, under the FCC's supervision, between MCI and the local telephone companies (predominantly AT&T subsidiaries). This charge was about $230 per month per access line, or $172.7 million a year by FY1983, MCI also used AT&T and other long-distance facilities to enable its customers to reach areas not already served by the MCI network. In FY1983, MCI paid at the standard commercial rate $137.2 million for these services.

MCI's principal competitor in the market for interstate long-distance services was AT&T's Long Lines division, with about 95% of the market in March 1983. AT&T Long Lines also reimbursed local operating companies for access lines, but at a rate about three times that charged MCI and the other competing carriers, such as GTE, Sprint, and ITT. This discrepancy was justified by the fact that MCI customers usually had to dial 20 digits to reach a long-distance number, compared with 11 digits (1, plus area code, plus 7-digit number) for an AT&T customer. Thus, AT&T Long Lines was expected to pay more for "superior access."

The settlement of the antitrust suit between AT&T and the Justice Department in January 1982 would separate AT&T from its local operating subsidiaries. AT&T would retain the Long Lines division and the intrastate long-distance facilities of the local companies. After separation occurred in January 1984, the long-distance operations would be consolidated in a new AT&T subsidiary named AT&T Communications. AT&T Communications would eventually compete on a more or less equal basis with MCI and the other long-distance companies (GTE, ITT, and so on). To ensure this result, the settlement required that by 1986 the newly independent local telephone companies provide *equal* quality of *access* to all competing long-distance providers. To implement equal access, a series of elections would be held in communities nationwide in which consumers would be asked to select a long-distance provider. Simultaneously, an FCC plan would phase out the differential in access charges between AT&T and its competitors by increasing the fees paid by MCI and others. Although equal access would be phased in over 2 to 3 years, the FCC plan in its original form called for an initial increase of about 80% in MCI access charges in 1984. Thus, on the one hand, MCI would eventually gain by acquiring equal access but, on the other hand, would immediately lose much of its existing cost advantage over AT&T.

The value of equal access to MCI was difficult to measure precisely. Some customers already enjoyed effectively equal access, since electronic switchboards had features that would automatically route calls via MCI lines whenever the usual 10- or 11-digit long-distance number was dialed. However, these tended to be large business customers who made up only a small fraction of MCI's revenue. A trial of equal access in part of Iowa led to an almost immediate increase in MCI's share of the long-distance market from less than 5% to about 20%. In this case, however, competition from MCI's non-AT&T competitors was not severe, and AT&T still paid more in access fees.

The impact of equalized access charges on market share was also difficult to judge. Under the FCC plan, AT&T's access pricing flexibility was expected to increase as deregulation of the long-distance market—the FCC's ultimate goal—proceeded. In principle, therefore, AT&T would be able to reduce its prices to prevent further erosion of its market share. In practice, however, it would make little economic sense for AT&T, with 95% of the market, to cut prices for the sake of preventing anything less than massive losses of market share to MCI and its other competitors. The outcome would depend on the direction taken by AT&T's management, which had been surprisingly aggressive in the past.

In the face of these uncertainties, it was difficult to predict MCI's growth in revenues and earnings in FY1984 and beyond. Forecasting the need for fixed and working capital was equally difficult; nevertheless, a consensus forecast is presented in Exhibit 9. Against these contingencies, MCI held about $550 million in cash in the spring of 1983. At the beginning of April 1983, its stock price stood at $47, and long-term interest rates had declined dramatically.

EXHIBIT 9 Baseline Forecast of Anticipated MCI Operating Characteristics for Years Ending March 31, 1983–1990 (millions of dollars)

Source: Casewriter's estimate based on security analysts' forecasts.

	1983	1984	1985	1986	1987	1988	1989	1990
1. Interstate long-distance market	$27,000	$29,800	$32,800	$36,000	$39,700	$43,600	$48,000	$52,800
2. MCI market share[a]	4.0%	6.2%	9.6%	13.5%	18.6%	19.8%	20.0%	20.0%
3. MCI revenues [(1) × (2)]	$ 1,073	$ 1,850	$ 3,160	$ 4,870	$ 7,380	$ 8,660	$ 9,600	$10,560
4. Access charges (% of sales)	16%	23%	29.5%	29.5%	29.5%	28.5%	27.5%	26.5%
5. Operating margin[b]	27.5%	20.5%	12.0%	12.0%	12.0%	13.0%	14.0%	15.0%
6. Operating earnings (EBIT) [(3) × (5)]	$ 295	$ 380	$ 390	$ 590	$ 890	$ 1,125	$ 1,345	$ 1,580
7. Interest paid	$ 75	$ 100	$ 100	$ 100	$ 100	$ 100	$ 100	$ 100
8. Other income	$ 21	$ 13	$ 3	$ 4	$ 4	$ 5	$ 5	$ 5
9. Provision for taxes	$ 70	$ 83	$ 58	$ 123	$ 206	$ 299	$ 400	$ 475
10. After-tax net income [(6) – (7) + (8) – (9)]	$ 171	$ 210	$ 235	$ 371	$ 588	$ 731	$ 850	$ 1,010
11. Increase in deferred taxes	$ 53	$ 65	$ 88	$ 106	$ 120	$ 140	$ 146	$ 140
12. Incremental investment factor	1.15	1.15	1.12	1.10	1.08	1.06	1.04	1.0
13. Capital expenditures for new capacity [Change in (3) × (12)]	$ 623	$ 890	$ 1,467	$ 1,881	$ 2,710	$ 1,357	$ 980	$ 960
14. Capital expenditures for replacement	—	—	—	$ 50	$ 50	$ 100	$ 100	$ 100
15. Total capital expenditures [(13) + (14)]	$ 623	$ 890	$ 1,467	$ 1,931	$ 2,760	$ 1,457	$ 1,080	$ 1,060
16. Depreciation	$ 104	$ 173	$ 272	$ 412	$ 601	$ 749	$ 800	$ 826
17. Net plant, equipment (end of year)	$ 1,324	$ 2,041	$ 3,236	$ 4,755	$ 6,914	$ 7,622	$ 7,902	$ 8,136
18. Additional working capital required	0	0	0	0	0	0	0	0

[a]This is total MCI revenue as a fraction of long-distance revenues and includes non-long-distance revenues. MCI's actual share of the interstate long-distance market would be slightly lower.

[b]Includes depreciation as a cost.

EXHIBIT 9 (*concluded*)

Assumptions Underlying the Forecasts

1. The interstate long-distance market, which amounted to about $27 billion in FY1983, would grow at 10% per year through FY1990.
2. MCI's revenues would increase from 4% of total long-distance revenues in FY1983, to 20% in FY1990. The increase would be rapid in the years immediately following the advent of *equal access,* but would subsequently slow down as AT&T began to defend its reduced share of the market, other competitors developed their networks, and the market itself adapted to the shock of competition. This pattern is shown on line 2. In each year, 10% of MCI revenues would come from other than long-distance growth. Thus, in FY1990, MCI was projected to hold 18% of the long-distance market. MCI's management was believed to be committed to a growth program of the dimensions shown on line 3 and would, if necessary, sacrifice profit margins to achieve it.
3. Access charges paid by MCI would almost double between FY1983 and FY1985. They would then taper off to about 26.5% of total revenues in FY1990. This was consistent with announced FCC intentions at the end of March 1983. However, there was a great deal of uncertainty in this area. AT&T currently paid access charges amounting to more than 50% of revenues, and reductions to the levels on line 4 would depend on the imposition of *direct* access charges on households and businesses. Legislation in Congress with a reasonable chance of passage forbade the imposition of such direct access charges.
4. MCI's operating margin (operating earnings as a fraction of revenues) would shrink under the dual pressure of higher access charges and increased competition from both AT&T and other long-distance suppliers. Ultimately, however, as access charges fell and the market stabilized, margins were expected to recover to a level of about 15%. Anticipated yearly margins are shown on line 5. However, as noted, these were subject to substantial uncertainty. In the best case, favorable regulatory and legislative action, coupled with restrained competitor behavior, might increase margins by as much as 7% (up to 22% of sales) from these levels. In an unfavorable situation, severe competition and high access charges could reduce margins by an equal amount.
5. Interest payments on MCI's outstanding debt were running at an annual rate of about $100 million at the end of FY1983 (for the year as a whole, interest payments were only $75 million because the debt level increased during the year) and, with no net change in indebtedness, would remain stable at this level through FY1990.
6. Other income, shown on line 8, represents interest on holdings of cash equivalents. As *excess* cash is used up, this figure is expected to decline to $3 million and then grow roughly with sales. This projection does not include interest on the proceeds of any future security offerings that are added temporarily to cash.
7. Provision for taxes, shown on line 9, amounts in 1984 to 25% of net income, which is below the 46% base rate because of investment tax credits and other special credits. As growth and investment slow in later years and reduce the available credits, taxes as a percentage of net income should increase.
8. Increases in deferred taxes, shown on line 11, accumulate at a rate related to present and past capital expenditures. As growth slows, so does the rate of accumulation of deferred tax credits.
9. In March 1983 each extra dollar of revenue required about $1.15 worth of investment in fixed plant and equipment. This factor was expected to fall to about $1.00 by FY1990, as improved electronic technology reduced equipment costs. The expected yearly pattern is shown on line 12. It was possible, however, that in the latter part of the period (post-FY1987) this factor would fall substantially below $1.00.
10. Replacement of older equipment would require the investments described on line 13.
11. Depreciation would be charged at an annual rate equal to 9.8% of the value at plant and equipment in place at the beginning of each year plus 4.9% of the value of total new investment.
12. No additions to working capital would be required throughout the period and any cash on hand at the end of FY1983 could be devoted to investment programs.
13. MCI would not penetrate the intrastate toll market.

Cox Communications, Inc. (1999)

Summer in Atlanta, Georgia, home of Cox Communications, Inc. (Cox), was usually quite warm, but the summer of 1999 was especially hot for Dallas Clement, Cox's 34-year-old treasurer. At the beginning of 1999, Clement and his team (Susan Coker and Mark Major, co-assistant treasurers) anticipated that Cox would be making several major acquisitions over the next three to five years, probably spending $7–$8 billion in the process. However, unexpectedly aggressive competition by rivals seeking to lock up valuable cable systems had brought a number of important properties into play sooner than expected. From a strategic viewpoint, Cox could not afford to lose these cable properties, especially those that could be combined with its existing systems to yield substantial market presence and attendant cost savings. By the beginning of July, the firm had already committed to over $7 billion in acquisitions to be completed by the end of the year, which would add over 1.6 million new subscribers in eight states. These deals would put stress on the firm's complicated balance sheet, requiring Clement's team to scramble to fund several years' of acquisitions in little more than six months.

Then, in mid-July, Cox learned that Gannett Co. would put its cable properties up for sale. Cox's parent, Cox Enterprises, Inc. ("CEI"), and Gannett were both approximately 100-year-old newspaper companies that had branched out into other communications businesses, including television and radio broadcasting, print media, production, and cable. There had been little indication that Gannett would sell its cable system, but the high prices being paid for cable subscribers apparently convinced Gannett to part with its cable assets. The Cox team estimated that, based on comparable recent transactions, Cox would need to bid about $2.7 billion to win the right to serve Gannett's 522,000 customers. With this acquisition and the others to which it had recently committed, Cox's subscriber base would grow 60% from the levels at the beginning of the year. This newest acquisition, however, would put even more pressure on the firm's funding ability, and Clement's team had to recommend how to fund it.

Clement's team had to figure out how much debt, equity, or equity-linked securities to issue, or how many of its appreciated non-strategic assets to sell, to fund these acquisitions. Their recommendation for funding the Gannett acquisition had to be consistent with the firm's long-run capacity to fund future activities. Specifically, they had to be mindful of the impact of their actions on the firm's investment-grade bond rating, which its board was keen to protect. At the same time, their recommendation had to respect the preferences of the Cox family, who owned more than two-thirds of Cox through their ownership of the privately held CEI, and who sought to maintain their super-majority ownership of Cox. The heat outside the Cox headquarters was nowhere as blistering as the heat within Clement's organization as his team worked late into the night.

Professors George Chacko and Peter Tufano and Research Associates Matthew Bailey and Joshua Musher prepared this case. HBS cases are developed solely as the basis for class discussion. Cases are not intended to serve as endorsements, sources of primary data, or illustrations of effective or ineffective management.

Copyright © 2000 President and Fellows of Harvard College. To order copies or request permission to reproduce materials, call 1-800-545-7685, write Harvard Business School Publishing, Boston, MA 02163, or go to http://www.hbsp.harvard.edu. No part of this publication may be reproduced, stored in a retrieval system, used in a spreadsheet, or transmitted in any form or by any means—electronic, mechanical, photocopying, recording, or otherwise—without the permission of Harvard Business School.

Cox Communications, Inc. and the Cable/Broadband Industry

Since its establishment in 1898 until 1962, Cox Enterprise's main business had been newspapers. The firm first entered the cable television business in 1962 with the purchase of cable systems in California, Oregon, Pennsylvania, and Washington. These cable systems carried television signals to homes via coaxial landlines, offering subscribers clear reception and new programming choices. By 1977, Cox's cable division operated in nine states and served 500,000 subscribers. By 1990, it served 1.5 million subscribers, and by the beginning of 1999, it was serving almost 3.7 million subscribers. In 1995, the cable business was partially spun off by CEI in the form of Cox Communications (Cox), with majority control and economic ownership retained by CEI.

Technological innovations, including the Internet, fiber optics, and wireless communications, as well as deregulation, made the late 1990s a period of tremendous change for cable operators. Cable operators spent billions of dollars replacing coaxial cables with fiber optic bundles, which provided 1000 times more capacity. This extra capacity allowed cable companies—now labeled "broadband" companies reflecting the breadth of services they offered—to provide consumers with pay-per-view and digital cable television services, high-speed Internet access, and digital telephony. Cable operators anticipated these and other new services (video-on-demand, interactive TV, video gaming, etc.) would drive much of the profit growth for at least the next several years. Increasing the breadth of services brought broadband companies into competition with a wider range of rivals, including satellite systems, telephone companies, and wireless companies, as part of the telecommunications convergence. Deregulation, in the form of the Telecommunications Reform Act of 1996, made this convergence possible by allowing cable operators and telephone companies to enter each other's businesses. While the traditional part of the cable industry was quite regulated, the growth of the broadband industry—and the competitive battles that would ensue—would take place in less-regulated territory.

Cox prided itself on delivering high-quality technology and services and was very aggressive in upgrading its network and introducing new services. By mid-1999, close to 60% of Cox's cable systems had been upgraded to 750 megahertz[1] (MHz) of capacity. Since analog video services took up only 550 MHz of capacity, this upgrade allowed Cox to offer high-speed Internet access to its cable television customers through Cox@Home, telephone service under the Cox Digital Telephone brand, and advanced digital television programming under the Cox Digital TV brand. Digital video was expected to drive the growth of Cox's core video revenues, which were otherwise anticipated to grow at an annual rate of 6%–8% for the next five years. This growth came from expected rate increases of 3%–5% and natural growth of the subscriber base. Revenues from high-speed Internet access and digital telephony, however, were anticipated to grow at significantly higher rates. (See Table A.) On an aggregate basis, these additional services were expected to raise operating cash flow growth from 8% to 15% annually. Not included in these estimates were additional services, such as Home Security Monitoring, that were still in the concept stage. Total capital expenditures, including those for network upgrades and expansion of services, were expected to be $1.3 billion in 2000 and close to $1.1 billion in 2001.

[1]Megahertz (MHz) in this context is a measure of bandwidth for high-speed digital data transfer. The bandwidth of a cable line is the maximum data speed that the line can transmit. Generally, the higher the bandwidth, the higher the maximum data transfer speed of the cable line. A 750 MHz line can transmit data at a rate of 750 million bits per second, where a bit is a 1 or a 0, representing one piece of information.

TABLE A
Gross Margins and Growth Rates for Cable Services

Source: Case writer estimates and Cox Communications, Inc.

	Monthly Cash Flow	Gross Margin[a]	Current Subscriber Penetration[b]	Target Penetration[c]
Analog TV	$30	75%	67%	67%
Digital TV	16–18	55	2	30
High-speed Internet	35–40	30	2	25
Digital telephony	55–60	55	1	25

[a]Gross margin is defined as revenue minus direct costs of the service.
[b]As a percentage of homes passed.
[c]Cox expected to reach these target levels within eight years.

Cable operators realized that they had to expand to spread the fixed costs of their operations and networks over as large a number of customers as possible. High *local* market share through consolidation led to tangible cost savings in the form of local scale economies, such as sharing the same cables and fleets of service technicians and vans. On a *national* scale, consolidation provided bargaining power when dealing with content providers, such as firms like HBO or Fox, that produced and distributed programming. Expansion also allowed cable operators to realize increasing returns by bundling services to more households.

As a result, Cox, as well as its competitors, rapidly expanded their customer bases via acquisitions. (See Exhibit 1 for some recent cable mergers and acquisitions, and Exhibit 2 for data on the largest operators that resulted.) For example, in 1995 Cox acquired Times Mirror Cable Television, which increased Cox's subscriber base by 1.3 million customers. In the first half of 1999 alone, Cox announced its intentions to purchase cable systems from Media General (April), merge with TCA Cable (May), and acquire certain AT&T cable properties. These acquisitions were expected to close by the end of 1999, but were by no means guaranteed to occur. They were contingent on regulatory approval, and the transfer of franchise rights by local communities. Obtaining the necessary approvals could take 3 to 15 months. These acquisitions would bring Cox's customer base to 5.5 million in 18 different states, making Cox the fifth-largest cable operator in the United States.

Competition among cable companies for customers had driven up the cost of new customers. Some analysts felt that the race became heated when Charter, owned by Paul Allen of Microsoft, purchased Marcus Cable in April 1998. As a result, while cable firms had paid approximately $2,000 per subscriber to expand their cable operations throughout most of the 1990s and as recently as 1998, this figure had risen to well over $4,000 per subscriber by 1999. With the number of available cable assets rapidly shrinking, incumbents in the industry had no choice but to pay these prices or face the prospect of becoming second-tier competitors.[2] Forrester Research estimated that the top five cable companies would serve 70% of subscribers in four years, up from around 56%.[3]

Achieving scale was expensive. The deals Cox announced in the first half of 1999, if consummated, would require nearly $7.6 billion in gross funding. Media General would cost $1.4 billion in cash, TCA would cost $4.1 billion ($2.0 billion in cash, $1.9 billion in Cox common equity, and $190 million in assumed debt), and AT&T would cost $2.1 billion (paid for with 50.3 million shares of AT&T. Cox, through subsidiaries, would acquire cable systems and other assets, including $750 million cash).

[2]Some of the recent acquisitions were swaps of subscribers being served by competing companies. The main reason for this was that there were economies associated with having clustered subscribers.

[3]T. Rhinelander, C. Mines, and K. Kopikis, "Cable's Multiservice Future," Forrester Research, February 1999.

The possible acquisition of Gannett's cable properties would make 1999 an extraordinary year for Cox. Gannett Co., founded in 1906 by Frank E. Gannett, was a diversified media company. Its 75 newspapers (including *USA Today,* the largest-selling daily newspaper in the United States) made it the nation's largest newspaper group, and its 21 television stations reached 17% of the United States. In 1995, the company had purchased Multimedia Inc., which gave Gannett cable systems in Indiana, Illinois, Kansas, North Carolina, and Oklahoma, and in 1999 reached about 522,000 subscriber households. Gannett's properties were attractive to Cox not only because of the number of subscribers, but also because they fit in well with its own strategy of concentrating subscribers in geographical areas to achieve economies of scale and scope. The Gannett systems, however, would not be cheap. Gannett would sell its cable properties by auction and Cox estimated that it would have to pay $2.7 billion, or over $5000 per subscriber, to win.

Financing Cox's Growth and the Gannett Acquisition

James Kennedy, the chairman of Cox's Board, and James Robbins, the firm's president and CEO, wrote in the annual report, "We constantly review potential growth opportunities and weigh them against a very clear litmus test: Will they create significant shareholder value? . . . Cox has the flexibility to [pursue these growth opportunities] in part because of our strong balance sheet." A key issue for Clement and his team to consider as they struggled with the current financing decision was how to retain sufficient financial flexibility to continue to fund planned and unexpected business opportunities.

Surely, funding the acquisitions would affect Cox's balance sheet. Even without the Gannett acquisition, internal cash flow would not be sufficient to fund the acquisitions that had been announced to date. Cox had financed its capital expenditures for network upgrades, acquisitions, capital investments, and new products through $1.9 billion from internal cash flow in conjunction with $1.9 billion of net issuance of debt, $370 million of equity (including its IPO in 1995), and $900 million from sales of non-strategic assets. The funding and asset sale choices were complicated by a variety of factors that Clement, Coker, and Major had to consider. In particular, the team was acutely aware of changing market conditions that could materially affect their ability to execute the transactions needed to fund the Gannett acquisition.

Issuing Common Shares

Cox could issue shares to the public for all or part of the required amount of funding. The firm's first and only share issuance had been almost four years earlier, in June 1995, when it raised a little under $400 million through public and private placements of equity. Any recommendation, however, to sell equity had to be mindful of the firm's unique ownership structure. CCI had two classes of common stock outstanding: class A shares were entitled to one vote each, and class C shares had supervoting privileges with 10 votes each. Neither class of common equity paid dividends. Through CEI, the Cox family owned 379.2 million out of 533.8 million class A shares, and all of the 27.6 million class C shares outstanding. After the anticipated issuance of 38.3 million shares as part of the TCA transaction in the next fiscal quarter, CEI would own 67.3% of Cox's common shares and would control 76.8% of Cox's voting stock.[4] The chairman and CEO of CEI, James Kennedy, was also the chairman of the board of Cox and was the grandson of CEI's founder.

[4]The number of shares was calculated on a fully diluted basis, assuming that 6.1 million outstanding stock options were exercised and that 5 million outstanding convertible preferred shares were converted. The convertible preferred shares had voting privileges, and did not receive dividends.

Cox had a number of financial objectives. The first was to double the size of the company every five years. The second was to preserve the family's economic ownership of Cox. The firm's initial public offering of Cox's equity in 1995 had allowed Cox to expand via acquisitions, but CEI did not want its ownership interests further diluted. To ensure that their interests as management were consistently aligned with those of the other shareholders, the family considered it appropriate to maintain a supermajority stake in conjunction with their control of the firm. This preference constrained the amount of equity financing Cox could undertake, as any equity issuance would have reduced the percentage ownership of CEI. Finally, there was a reluctance to increase the leverage of the firm, as discussed below.

Also on Clement's mind was his tactical ability to place a large block of Cox equity in the market. Charter Communications was expected to make its initial public offering in the fall. Because Charter and Cox appealed to similar investors, Clement was concerned that these investors would have less of an appetite for Cox shares after the Charter deal had been placed. Were he to issue equity, he might want to do so before Charter's IPO. Clement also had to consider overall market condition. The equity markets had enjoyed, for almost a decade, a long period of high returns as part of a prolonged economic expansion in the United States, but many pundits warned of an imminent correction in the markets. (See Exhibit 5.)

A minor consideration was the direct costs of an equity issue, including underwriting fees and expenses, which would likely be between 2%–3% of the amount raised. In addition, there might be some "market impact" of a large equity issue, as the market typically greeted new shares by reducing the price of the firm's outstanding equity (and thereby the price at which the new shares could be offered). Academic studies suggested that this response usually amounted to an additional 3%–4% reduction in the price of a firm's stock, although this discount varied across firms and over time.[5]

Issuing Debt or Borrowing

Alternatively, Cox could issue debt to fund the Gannett cable acquisition, whether in the form of a public debt issue or bank borrowing. The structure of the debt could take many forms determined by the source of the debt, the maturity structure, the level of cash coupons, and various options (such as the right to redeem or call the debt at par). Since 1995, Cox had raised $1.9 billion in debt. This debt had maturities ranging from 5 to 30 years, with yields ranging from 65 to 115 basis points above the yields on U.S. Treasury obligations of similar maturity.

The Cox executives, however, were concerned about increasing financial leverage. The Cox family was very conservative about the use of debt. Cox already had the highest level of debt financing of all the CEI subsidiaries. Furthermore, Cox had a publicly articulated goal of maintaining a high debt rating. Cox executives had stated, "We want to get the right balance of debt and equity. We obviously are continuing to be investment grade and that's important." Maintaining that rating required careful monitoring of several financial variables, the most important of which being Debt/EBITDA. Currently, Cox was targeting a Debt/EBITDA ratio of no greater than 5 going forward, the maximum that senior management felt would retain an investment-grade rating. Externally, the debt markets for companies rated investment grade seemed larger and more stable than for noninvestment grade firms.[6] Noninvestment grade firms could find it

[5]See Grinblatt, Mark, and S. Titman, "Financial Markets and Corporate Strategy," Irwin/McGraw-Hill, 1998, pp. 15–16 and the references therein for more information regarding the direct and indirect costs of issuing equity.

[6]An investment-grade rating was one of the four top ratings awarded by the national debt rating agencies.

difficult to obtain access to credit at times, as had happened in the late 1980s when Drexel, Burnham, Lambert, the premier underwriter of noninvestment grade debt, went out of business, and more recently during the Asian currency and Russian debt crises in 1998. Additionally, sub-investment grade debt cost more, as indicated by the BBB-to-BB yield spread versus the BBB-to-A spread. Such circumstances could severely limit future flexibility.

In addition to the risk that credit spreads might widen in the fall, Clement had to consider the fact that the 30-year Treasury yield had increased more than half a percent over the past six months. (See Exhibit 6 for current interest rates.)

The direct and indirect costs of a debt issuance would be less than that for issuing equity. Clement anticipated that the transaction costs would be less than 2%. Academic studies estimated the market impact of issuing debt (on Cox's stock price) to be around 1%–2%.[7]

Hybrid Security Issuance

Another possibility was to issue hybrid securities, which had characteristics of both debt and equity. The most common examples of this class are preferred stock or convertible bonds.[8] A more recent innovation in the hybrid market was "mandatory convertible" structures and "trust preferred" products that sought to combine the best features of both debt and equity. Many investment banks offered these products, but one particular variety that had recently been proposed to Clement was an equity-linked hybrid product developed by Merrill Lynch called FELINE Income PRIDES.[9]

This security had elements of both debt and equity. Each Income PRIDES was a unit consisting of (i) an obligation by the investor to purchase a fixed dollar amount of Cox's Class A Common Stock in three years, and (ii) preferred equity. Payments made by Cox to the preferred equity component of the Income PRIDES would be essentially deductible for tax purposes, but the security was treated like equity for financial reporting purposes due to the obligation of the holder to purchase equity in the future.

The legal structure that delivered this treatment was somewhat complicated.[10] Essentially, Cox would establish a legal entity (a Trust) that would issue preferred equity and common equity. Cox would purchase all the common equity and exercise full control of the Trust. The preferred equity of the Trust was bundled together with the purchase obligation described above and sold to investors as Income PRIDES.[11] For

[7]See Grinblatt, Mark, and S. Titman, "Financial Markets and Corporate Strategy," Irwin/McGraw-Hill, 1998, pp. 15–16 and the references therein for more information regarding the direct and indirect costs of issuing debt.

[8]A preferred stock pays a fixed dividend and has seniority between that of common equity and junior debt. Failure to pay dividends on preferred stock does not trigger bankruptcy, but sometimes leads to actions such as giving the preferred shareholders seats on the firm's board. A convertible bond is debt where the investor has the right to use the debt to purchase equity at a fixed price. In contrast, in mandatory convertible securities, the investor has the obligation to purchase equity in the future, although the price may not be set in advance.

[9]The description provided in this section of the FELINE PRIDES product issued by Cox and its associated structure has been greatly simplified, and at times deviates from the actual product, for pedagogical reasons. As with most hybrid products, there was a great deal of detail, critical to the accounting and tax treatment of the transaction, which this thumbnail description does not capture.

[10]This trust structure had been introduced first in an earlier set of products in the early to mid-1990s. These products went by many banks' acronym-labeled servicemarks such as MIPS, QUIPS, and TOPrS.

[11]Simultaneously with the issuance of the Income PRIDES, Cox issued FELINE Growth PRIDES and Capital Securities independent of the Income Prides. Growth PRIDES are similar to Income PRIDES except that instead of bundling the purchase obligation with a Capital Security, the purchase obligation is bundled with U.S. Treasury zero-coupon securities of the same maturity. There were also a few other contractual differences between Growth and Income PRIDES in terms of obligations/options retained by Cox and the holders of these securities.

example, an investor would pay $50 for an Income PRIDES unit and receive a 7% preferred dividend yield for three years, on a principal amount of $50. At the end of three years, the investor could satisfy the purchase obligation detailed above (to purchase the Class A Common Stock) by (a) exchanging the preferred equity for shares or (b) exchanging cash for shares. In either case, the number of shares Cox delivered to the Income PRIDES holder for this $50 varied depending on the market value of Cox's common shares at maturity. Generally, the higher the stock price in three years, the smaller the number of shares that the Income PRIDES holder would receive. (See Exhibit 7.)

After issuing the preferred equity, the Trust would use the proceeds to purchase new Cox debt. The 7% interest on this debt matched the payment terms of the preferred equity, so the Trust effectively served to pass through payments from Cox to the holders of the preferred equity. In effect, therefore, Cox would sell its debt to the Trust, which in turn would sell its preferred equity to investors. Cox would own the residual portion of the Trust through the Trust's common equity.

The financial reporting advantage of this structure to Cox was that its debt would not appear on the balance sheet as debt. Because Cox owned the Trust, Cox would have effectively issued debt to itself, which cancelled out when the two balance sheets were rolled up. Instead all that would appear on Cox's financial statements would be a line item for "Minority Shareholder Interest" reflecting the preferred equity issuance. This account would appear between debt and shareholders' equity on the balance sheet. For tax purposes, however, Cox would be able to deduct the interest payments it made on the debt issued to the Trust. Thus, for financial reporting purposes the FELINE Income PRIDES would appear to be equity, but for tax purposes the payments on the back-to-back debt would be treated like ordinary interest payments. Furthermore, ratings agencies would give equity credit to the debt due to the contractual obligation of investors in FELINE Income PRIDES to purchase Cox common stock in the future. Thus, the FELINE Income PRIDES allowed Cox to simultaneously issue debt and receive the tax benefits of deducting the interest payments, while receiving equity credit from ratings agencies and for accounting purposes.

Asset Sales

Cox could also sell, swap, or monetize some of the firm's non-strategic equity investments, as was anticipated with the AT&T transaction. For example, Cox held equity in Sprint PCS worth approximately $4.1 billion. Similarly, Cox held substantial equity investments in Discovery Communications ($2.5 billion), @Home ($1.5 billion), and Flextech ($300 million), along with smaller stakes in other firms. Simply selling these investments into the public markets would have meant a considerable tax burden for Cox.[12] Monetizing, or obtaining equivalent cash to, some of the non-strategic investments in a tax-efficient manner was an ongoing effort within the Cox Treasury.

Clement could sell some of these equity investments directly into the public market and use the proceeds to pay for some or all of the Gannett properties. One disadvantage of an outright sale was that Cox would have to pay taxes on the capital gains. Tax efficient disposals of these appreciated assets were also possible, such as in the AT&T transaction, where Cox had effectively swapped its AT&T shares for shares in AT&T subsidiaries that owned cable assets without triggering a taxable event. Through other types of monetizations, Cox might be able to receive the cash equivalent in value in these assets, yet defer the capital gains taxes from any sale for

[12]Cox faced a marginal tax rate of 35% on its gain on the sale of assets. The gain is the difference between the sale price of the assets and Cox's "tax basis," roughly the amount it had paid to acquire the assets less accumulated depreciation. The respective taxable bases were $0, $34 million, $7 million, and $48 million. Cox's shares in AT&T had a tax basis of zero.

a number of years.[13] There were a number of practical limitations, however. The Sprint PCS investment could not be sold or hedged until November. Additionally, the stakes in Sprint, @Home, and Flextech were large relative to average daily trading volumes in those stocks. Hence, actually trading these positions would be difficult.

Market Conditions

Apart from the policy issues surrounding the firm's capital structure choices, there were substantial execution concerns as well. As mentioned above, the team was worried that an IPO by its rival might make it harder for Cox to issue equity. More generally, there was considerable anxiety about the outlook for the markets in the fall. In the fall of 1998, the capital markets had almost melted down when Russia defaulted on part of its debt. The Dow Jones Industrial Average, a barometer equity market index, fell more than 10% in the following two weeks. Credit spreads (the difference between a corporate bond yield and an equivalent-maturity Treasury yield) roughly doubled over the next five months. For A-rated borrowers, spreads rose from 56 basis points to a high of 135 basis points, while for BBB-rated issuers, spreads increased from 95 basis points to 181 basis points.[14]

This had led to a dearth of debt issues in late 1998. While the markets recovered somewhat in the first part of 1999, more recent weakness in the bond markets had already led to the cancellation of some previously announced deals. For example, on May 21, Great Lakes Power Inc., a Canadian utility rated Baa3/BBB-, had postponed a $200 million 10-year issue, and further postponements of more than $1 billion of issuance had followed. Hardest hit were noninvestment grade issuers, and Internet and telecommunications companies.

The other major concern for the fall was the potential impact of Year 2000 issues. Many feared that computer systems that used two digits for tracking years would malfunction when the year 2000 began. While the risks for catastrophe seemed exaggerated, there was a real possibility that the markets would be inhospitable to new issues until some of the risks had been resolved.

The Recommendation

Regardless of whether Cox completed the acquisition of Gannett's cable operations, the other acquisitions of 1999 would materially change Cox's balance sheet. Any action Clement took would have to take into account ownership dilution on the one hand and the reaction of ratings agencies on the other. Additionally, Clement's team needed to evaluate the appropriate long-term financial policy for Cox and the specific financing of the potential Gannett acquisition and the other acquisitions Cox had recently announced in the context of this policy. Exhibit 8 shows various pro forma financial statements under different financing policies, with and without the Gannett purchase.

[13]See the case "Times Mirror Company PEPS Proposal Review" (Harvard Business School Case No. 296-089), written by Peter Tufano and Cameron Poetzscher, for more on the issue of equity monetizations.

[14]Source: Bloomberg.

EXHIBIT 1 Cost per Customer of Cable Acquisitions, 1994–1999

Source: Assorted Bloomberg News stories

Announcement Date	Acquirer	Seller	Total Value of Acquisition	Price Paid per Cable Customer
June 94	Comcast	Maclean Hunter	$1.27 billion	$2,300
October 95	Comcast	E. W. Scripps Co.	$1.49 billion	$1,900
April 98	Paul Allen	Marcus Cable	$2.78 billion	$2,200
June 98	Cox	TCI	$250.2 million	$2,176
June 98	AT&T	TCI	$59.4 billion	$2,700
July 98	Paul Allen	Charter	$4.5 billion	$3,750
October 98	Cox	Prime South Diversified[a]	$1.325 billion	$3,329
February 99	Adelphia	FrontierVision	$2.0 billion	$2,900
March 99	Adelphia	Century	$5.7 billion	$3,600
March 99	Adelphia	Harron Communications	$1.2 billion	$4,100
April 99	AT&T	Media One[b]	$62.5 billion	$4,700
April 99	Cox	Media General[c]	$1.4 billion	$5,380
May 99	Charter	Avalon Cable	$845 million	$3,250
May 99	Charter	Falcon	$3.6 billion	$2,250
May 99	Comcast	AT&T[d]	$3.4 billion	$4,500
May 99	Cox	TCA Cable TV[e]	$4.1 billion	$4,600
June 99	Comcast	Greater Media	$292 million	$3,700
June 99	Charter	Bresnan	$3.1 billion	$4,500
July 99	Cox	AT&T[f]	$2.15 billion	$4,350

[a]This deal included access to 105,000 hotels, together with interests in various nonconsolidated operations, and thus is not directly comparable to wholly residential transactions.
[b]Agreed to a swap of cable subscribers with MediaOne, including payment of cash.
[c]Agreed to buy cable systems covering 260,000 customers from Media General for $1.4 billion.
[d]As part of the deal Comcast also had an option to acquire from AT&T, in three years, additional cable systems covering between 1.0 million and 1.4 million subscribers for $4.8 billion to $6.7 billion. Comcast also agreed to supply AT&T-branded telephony in its cable systems, provided AT&T concluded telephony deals with two other non-AT&T cable companies.
[e]Merger with TCA Cable TV, serving 883,000 customers. TCA stock either converted into $62.50 cash, 0.7418 Cox shares plus $31.25 in cash, or 1.4836 Cox shares. Cox paid $4.1 billion.
[f]Cox and AT&T agreed that Cox would exchange its holding in AT&T for stock in AT&T subsidiaries that own cable TV systems. The swap consisted of 50.3 million AT&T shares (worth $2.8 billion), for which Cox acquired subsidiaries with approximately 495,000 customers and $750 million cash and other assets.

EXHIBIT 2 Comparative Financial Data for Major Cable Operators, 1998 (in millions of dollars, except ratios)

Source: Bloomberg Financial Analysis and Global Access

	AT&T	Cox	MediaOne	Time Warner	Comcast	Charter
Total assets	59,550	12,878	28,192	31,640	14,817	4,335
Equity market value[a](7/99)	178,390	20,436	45,111	90,571	26,839	NA
Debt book value	6,727	3,920	5,422	10,944	5,577	NA
Operating cash flow	10,309	666	5,517	1,845	1,078	30
Cable subscriber base[b]	15.5	6.0	NA	12.9	8.0	6.2
Net income/total assets	0.11	0.14	1.48	0.01	0.07	NM
ROE	26.0%	33.3%	235.3%	–6.0%	43.4%	NA
ROA	8.7%	13.1%	5.2%	0.5%	7.7%	–1.0%
Total liabilities/total assets	0.57	0.58	0.47	0.70	0.68	0.50
Debt-to-equity[c]	0.26	0.74	0.38	1.24	1.42	NA
Total debt/EBITDA[d]	0.6	5.1[e]	5.7	4.1	3.7	87.6
EBITDA interest coverage[f]	19.4	3.0	1.9	2.3	3.1	1.2
Bond rating	AA–/Aa3	A–/Baa2	BBB/Ba1	BBB/Baa3	BBB–/Baa3	NA
Equity beta	0.61	0.68	1.08	0.87	0.88	NA

[a]As of August 1999, Charter had not yet sold shares to the public.
[b]As of July 1999, the data for AT&T included the MediaOne subscriber base.
[c]As measured by the ratio of the book value of long-term debt to book value of shareholders' equity.
[d]Ratio of Total Debt to Earnings Before Interest, Taxes, Depreciation, and Amortization. This is a commonly used ratio for analysis of debt capacity.
[e]As reported by Cox on pro forma basis to credit agencies.
[f]EBITDA divided by the interest expense (for the same period) is a common ratio used for debt analysis. It approximates ability to repay on the basis of cash availability.

EXHIBIT 3 Financial Summary for Cox Communications (in millions of dollars unless noted)

Source: Bloomberg Financial Analysis and Global Access

	1996	1997	1998	99Q1	99Q2
Revenue	1,460	1,610	1,717	499	510
Cost of goods sold	468	496	540	168	159
Selling, general, and administrative	436	505	518	142	156
EBITDA	557	610	659	189	196
Depreciation and amortization	335	405	458	123	159
Nonoperating income (expense)	(104)	(193)	2,115	384	890
Interest expense	146	202	223	54	69
Income tax expense (refund)	23	(54)	883	144	352
Net income (loss)	(52)	(137)	1,271	251	506
Cash and marketable securities	42	28	31	90	23
Total current assets	165	377	197	265	210
Total assets	5,785	6,557	12,878	14,727	16,169
Current liabilities	250	245	336	334	362
Deferred taxes	294	722	2,887	3,668	4,152
Long-term debt	2,824	3,149	3,920	3,383	3,587
Other liabilities	155	84	359	485	439
Total liabilities	3,523	4,199	7,502	7,870	8,539
Total shareholders' equity	2,261	2,357	5,377	6,857	7,629
Capital expenditures	(579)	(708)	(809)	(225)	(277)
Cash flow from operations	309	555	666	176	18
Cash flow from investing activity	(552)	(1,108)	(1,600)	515	(292)
Cash flow from financing activity	246	539	937	(631)	207
Shares outstanding (all classes, millions)	540	541	545	555	555
Long-term debt / EBITDA[a]	5.1 ×	5.2 ×	5.9 ×	4.5 ×	4.6 ×
EBITDA interest coverage	3.8 ×	3.0 ×	3.0 ×	3.5 ×	2.9 ×
Free cash flow/long-term debt	–9.6%	–4.9%	–3.7%	–1.4%	–7.2%
Long-term debt/(long-term debt + equity)	55.5%	57.2%	42.2%	33.0%	32.0%
ROE (%)	–2.3%	–5.8%	23.6%	3.7%	6.6%
Price/book	2.76 ×	4.61 ×	3.64 ×	3.11 ×	2.72 ×
Debt-to-equity[b] (book value)	1.25 ×	1.34 ×	0.73 ×	0.49 ×	0.47 ×
Debt-to-equity (market value)	0.45 ×	0.29 ×	0.20 ×	0.16 ×	0.17 ×

[a]Source: Cox Communications. As reported pro forma numbers that include EBITDA of new acquisitions when debt is already on the balance sheet.
[b]As measured by the ratio of long-term debt to shareholders' equity.

EXHIBIT 4A Monthly Issuance of Nonconvertible Debt by Credit Rating, July 1988–July 1999

Source: Securities Data Corporation. Represents the face value of public offerings of nonconvertible debt. For example, the dark line represents the monthly issuance volume of bonds rated BBB.

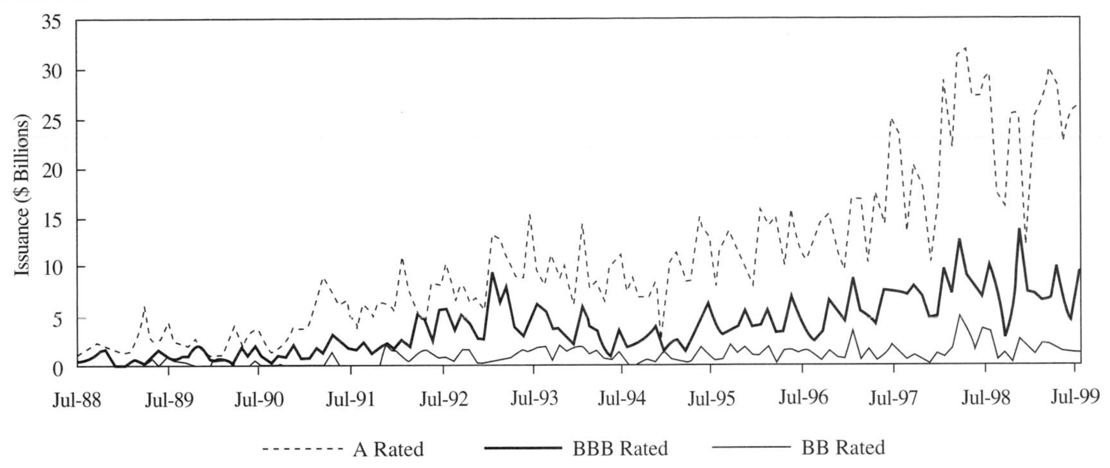

EXHIBIT 4B Credit Spreads for Long-Maturity Bonds, July 1992–July 1999

Source: Securities Data Corporation. Represents the face value of public offerings of nonconvertible debt. For example, the dark line represents the monthly issuance volume of bonds rated BBB.

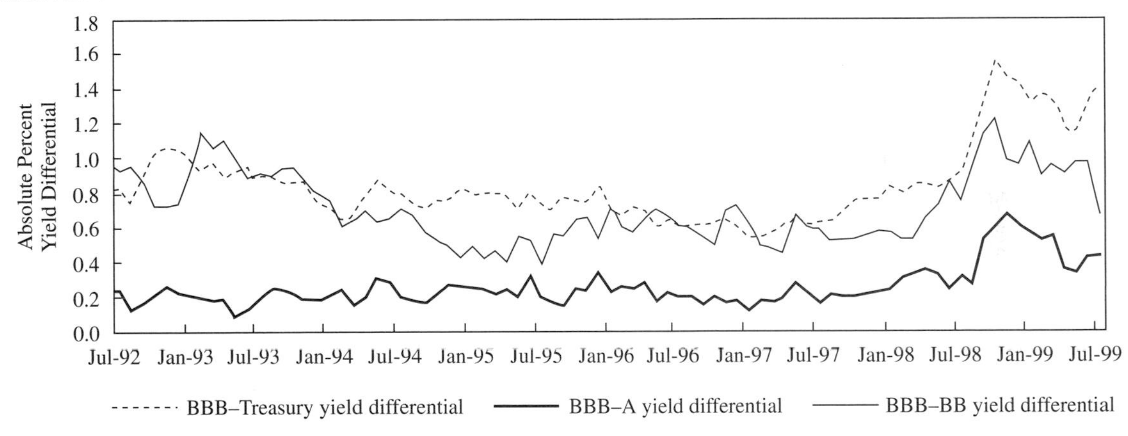

EXHIBIT 4C Supplementary Monthly Statistics for Exhibits 4A and 4B, July 1992–July 1999

Source: Securities Data Corporation

	A Issuance ($ MM)	BBB Issuance ($ MM)	BB Issuance ($ MM)	BBB–Treasury Spread (%)	BBB–A Spread (%)	BB–BBB Spread (%)
Minimum	2,628	791	100	0.54	0.09	0.38
Average	14,503	5,248	1,299	0.85	0.26	0.71
Maximum	32,007	14,149	5,126	1.57	0.68	1.23
Standard deviation	7,279	2,638	919	0.23	0.12	0.20
Standard deviation /Average	50%	50%	71%	44%	28%	27%

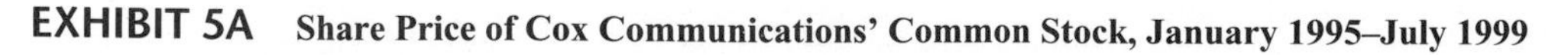

EXHIBIT 5A Share Price of Cox Communications' Common Stock, January 1995–July 1999

Source: Datastream International

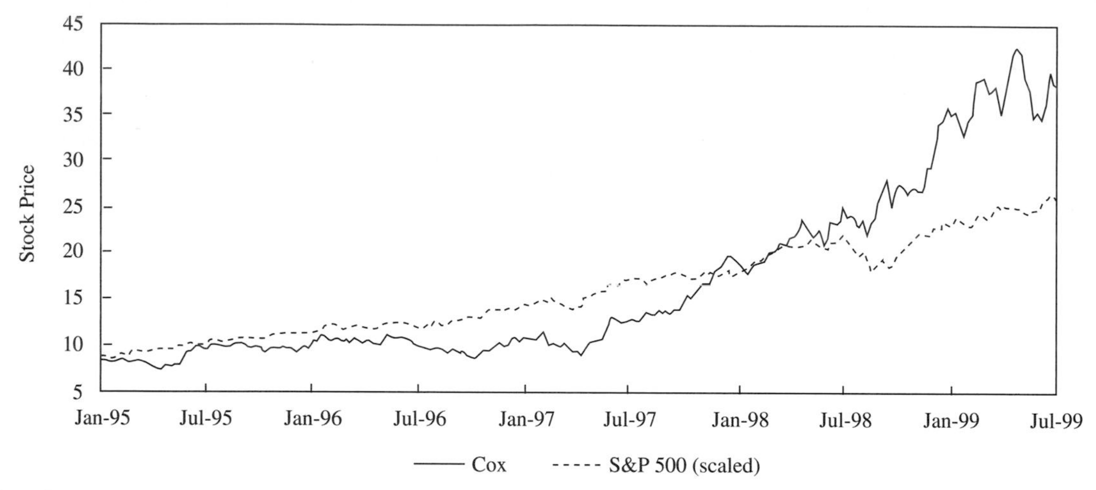

Note: These prices are corrected for stock splits. The price of Cox Communication Common stock as of 8/9/99 was $34.6875.

EXHIBIT 5B Historical Volatility of Cox Communications' Common Stock, June 1995–July 1999

Source: Bloomberg Financial Markets

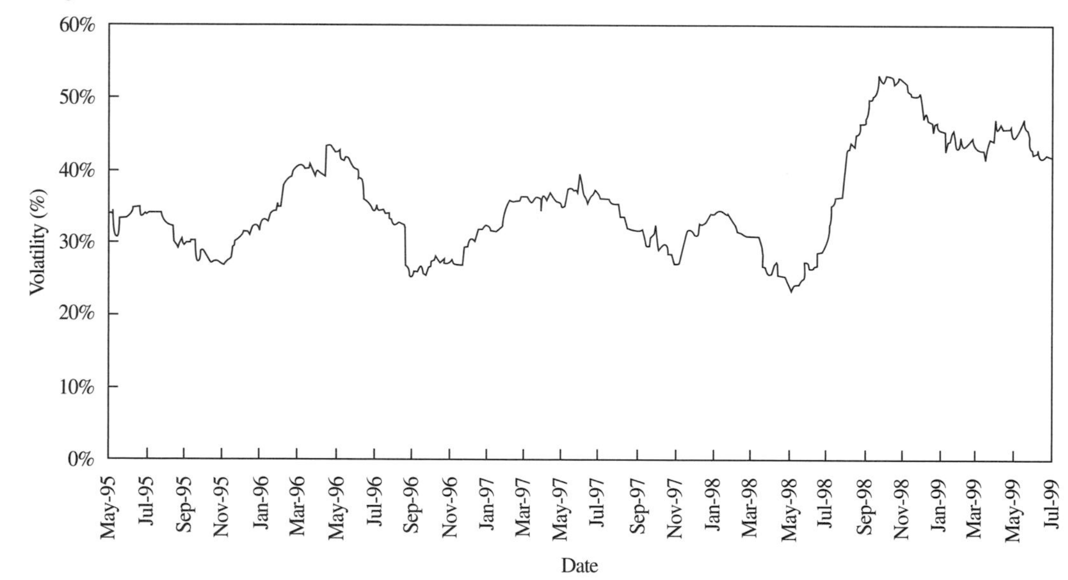

Note: The historical volatility is measured by the annualized standard deviation of the log of daily stock price returns over the previous 90 days. The historical volatility as of 8/9/99 was 42%. Implied volatilities on options on Cox Communications were about 47% as of 8/9/99.

EXHIBIT 6
Yields for Government and Corporate Bonds for July 15, 1999

Source: Bloomberg

	1 Year	2 Year	3 Year	5 Year	10 Year
Treasury bonds	5.38	5.64	5.70	5.83	5.83
U.S. Treasury strips	5.38	5.66	5.71	5.88	6.16
A-rated industrial bonds	5.99	6.33	6.44	6.70	6.93
BBB-rated industrial bonds	6.30	6.62	6.81	7.05	7.37
BB-rated industrial bonds	6.84	7.51	7.71	8.00	8.80

Note: All yields quoted on a semi-annual basis.

EXHIBIT 7
FELINE PRIDES Structure: Income PRIDES

Source: Cox Communications, Inc.

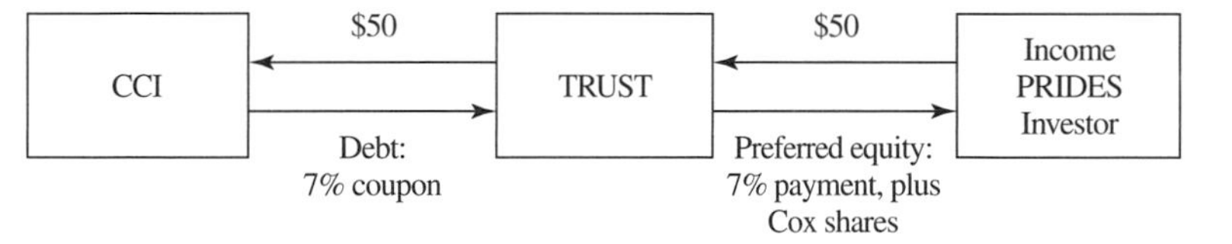

Under the Income PRIDES structure, the holders would receive a 7% cash payment for three years. At the end of the three years they were required to purchase a certain number of Cox's shares in exchange, at their option, for cash or their preferred equity in the Trust. The number of shares would be determined by Cox's share price in three years (S), as shown in the first column. The second column shows the number of shares delivered to the holder of a Feline PRIDE in three years, and the third column shows the value of the shares delivered in three years.

Simultaneous with the Income PRIDES offering, the Trust would buy the debt that Cox issued. The Cox debt would pay a 7% coupon per year.

Cox Share Price in 3 Years	Number of Cox Shares Delivered	Value of Cox Shares Delivered
S ≤ $34.6875	1.4414	1.4414 * S
$34.6875 < S < $41.7984	50/S	$50
S ≥ $41.7984	1.1962	1.1962 * S

EXHIBIT 8A Pro Forma Cash Flows[a] for Cox Communications If It Did Not Purchase Gannett, But If Other Proposed Acquisitions Were Undertaken (figures are in millions of dollars)

Source: Cox Communications, Inc.

	1999 E	2000 E	2001 E	2002 E	2003 E
OPERATING ACTIVITIES					
EBITDA Cox + Acquisitions	878	1,344	1,490	1,697	1,913
EBITDA Gannett	0	0	0	0	0
Interest Expense	(312)	(540)	(443)	(472)	(432)
TOTAL CASH FROM OPERATIONS[b]	566	804	1,047	1,225	1,481
INVESTING ACTIVITIES					
Acquisitions[c]	(2,673)	0	0	0	0
Gannett Acquisition	0	0	0	0	0
CapEx	(983)	(1,304)	(1,078)	(822)	(734)
Total Other	(122)	48	34	10	10
TOTAL CASH FROM INVESTMENTS	(3,778)	(1,256)	(1,044)	(812)	(724)
FINANCING ACTIVITIES					
Equity Issued	0	0	0	0	0
Monetization[d]	1,243	1,500	0	0	0
Beginning Debt	4,091	6,249	5,202	5,198	4,786
Maturing Debt		(431)	(341)	(200)	(277)
New Debt Financed (Retired)[e]	1,968	(617)	337	(212)	(480)
Ending Total Debt	6,249	5,202	5,198	4,786	4,029
TOTAL CASH FROM FINANCING	3,401	452	(4)	(412)	(757)
CONDENSED INCOME STATEMENT					
EBITDA	878	1,344	1,490	1,697	1,913
Depreciation	(197)	(261)	(216)	(164)	(147)
Interest	(312)	(540)	(443)	(472)	(432)
Taxes	(85)	30	10	10	10
Net Income	285	573	842	1,070	1,344
DEBT RATIOS					
Pro Forma Annualized EBITDA[f]	1,201	1,344	1,490	1,697	1,913
Leverage Ratio[g]	5.2 ×	3.9 ×	3.5 ×	2.8 ×	2.1 ×
EQUITY INTEREST					
Cox Family Economic Equity[h]	67.3%	67.3%	67.3%	67.3%	67.3%
Cox Family Voting Equity[i]	76.8%	76.8%	76.8%	76.8%	76.8%

[a]Assumes that planned monetizations of $500 million in 1999Q3 and $1.5 billion in 2000Q1 are implemented.

[b]As a result of significant accumulated tax losses to carry forward, Cox did not anticipate paying any cash taxes for the years shown here.

[c]This figure included $2.023 billion for cash portion of TCA merger, $1.4 billion for Media General acquisition, less $750 million in cash and other assets Cox was supposed to receive as part of the AT&T transaction.

[d]Monetization included $743 million raised in the first quarter, and $500 million scheduled for the third quarter of 1999. Both of these transactions were independent of the Gannett transaction. Cox also planned to raise $1.5 billion in 2000Q1 by monetizing a portion of the Sprint PCS position.

[e]Debt was treated as a plug, or balancing figure in this pro forma.

[f]Pro forma Annualized EBITDA is 4 × the Quarterly EBITDA results.

[g]Leverage ratio defined as the Ending Total Debt divided by the Pro Forma Annualized EBITDA.

[h]Economic equity was the percentage of the firm owned by the Cox family. Were the firm to be sold, they would receive this percentage of the proceeds. Calculation assumes maximum dilution from FELINE PRIDE conversion.

[i]Voting equity was the percentage of the firm controlled by the Cox family. They cast this percentage of the votes in any question that came before the shareholders.

EXHIBIT 8B **Pro Forma Cash Flows for Cox Communications If It Purchases Gannett by Issuing Debt (figures are in millions of dollars)**

Source: Cox Communications, Inc.

	1999 E	2000 E	2001 E	2002 E	2003 E
OPERATING ACTIVITIES					
EBITDA Cox + Acquisitions	878	1,344	1,490	1,697	1,913
EBITDA Gannett	0	151	163	176	190
Interest Expense	(312)	(540)	(657)	(667)	(640)
TOTAL CASH FROM OPERATIONS	566	955	996	1,207	1,463
INVESTING ACTIVITIES					
Acquisitions	(2,673)	0	0	0	0
Gannett Acquisition	0	(2,700)	0	0	0
CapEx	(983)	(1,334)	(1,103)	(847)	(759)
Total Other	(122)	48	34	10	10
TOTAL CASH FROM INVESTMENTS	(3,778)	(3,986)	(1,069)	(837)	(749)
FINANCING ACTIVITIES					
Equity Issued	0	0	0	0	0
Monetization	1,243	1,500	0	0	0
Beginning Debt	4,091	6,249	7,781	7,854	7,484
Maturing Debt		(431)	(341)	(200)	(277)
New Debt Financed (Retired)	1,968	1,962	414	(169)	(437)
Ending Total Debt	6,249	7,781	7,854	7,484	6,770
TOTAL CASH FROM FINANCING	3,401	3,031	73	(369)	(714)
CONDENSED INCOME STATEMENT					
EBITDA	878	1,495	1,653	1,873	2,103
Depreciation	(197)	(267)	(221)	(169)	(152)
Interest	(312)	(540)	(657)	(667)	(640)
Taxes	(85)	30	10	10	10
Net Income	285	718	785	1,047	1,322
DEBT RATIOS					
Pro Forma Annualized EBITDA	1,201	1,495	1,653	1,873	2,103
Leverage Ratio	5.2 ×	5.2 ×	4.8 ×	4.0 ×	3.2 ×
EQUITY INTEREST					
Cox Family Economic Equity	67.3%	67.3%	67.3%	67.3%	67.3%
Cox Family Voting Equity	76.8%	76.8%	76.8%	76.8%	76.8%

EXHIBIT 8C Pro Forma Cash Flows for Cox Communications If It Purchases Gannett by Issuing Equity (figures are in millions of dollars)

Source: Cox Communications, Inc.

	1999 E	2000 E	2001 E	2002 E	2003 E
OPERATING ACTIVITIES					
EBITDA Cox + Acquisitions	878	1,344	1,490	1,697	1,913
EBITDA Gannett	0	151	163	176	190
Interest Expense	(258)	(310)	(413)	(420)	(377)
TOTAL CASH FROM OPERATIONS	620	1,185	1,240	1,453	1,726
INVESTING ACTIVITIES					
Acquisitions	(2,673)	0	0	0	0
Gannett Acquisition	0	(2,700)	0	0	0
CapEx	(983)	(1,334)	(1,103)	(847)	(759)
Total Other	(122)	48	34	10	10
TOTAL CASH FROM INVESTMENTS	(3,778)	(3,986)	(1,069)	(837)	(749)
FINANCING ACTIVITIES					
Equity Issued	2,700	0	0	0	0
Monetization	1,243	1,500	0	0	0
Beginning Debt	4,091	3,495	4,797	4,625	4,010
Maturing Debt		(431)	(341)	(200)	(277)
New Debt Financed (Retired)	(785)	1,732	170	(415)	(700)
Ending Total Debt	3,495	4,797	4,625	4,010	3,033
TOTAL CASH FROM FINANCING	3,348	2,801	(171)	(615)	(977)
CONDENSED INCOME STATEMENT					
EBITDA	878	1,495	1,653	1,873	2,103
Depreciation	(197)	(267)	(221)	(169)	(152)
Interest	(258)	(310)	(413)	(420)	(377)
Taxes	(85)	30	10	10	10
Net Income	339	948	1,029	1,293	1,584
DEBT RATIOS					
Pro Forma Annualized EBITDA	1,201	1,495	1,653	1,873	2,103
Leverage Ratio	2.9 x	3.2 x	2.8 x	2.1 x	1.4 x
EQUITY INTEREST					
Cox Family Economic Equity	59.0%	59.0%	59.0%	59.0%	59.0%
Cox Family Voting Equity	69.9%	69.9%	69.9%	69.9%	69.9%

EXHIBIT 8D Pro Forma Cash Flows for Cox Communications If It Purchased Gannett with a Combination of Debt, Equity ($680 million), and PRIDES ($720 million) (figures are in millions of dollars)

Source: Cox Communications, Inc.

	1999 E	2000 E	2001 E	2002 E	2003 E
OPERATING ACTIVITIES					
EBITDA Cox + Acquisitions	878	1,344	1,490	1,697	1,913
EBITDA Gannett	0	151	163	176	190
Interest Expense	(310)	(473)	(580)	(591)	(521)
TOTAL CASH FROM OPERATIONS	568	1,022	1,074	1,283	1,582
INVESTING ACTIVITIES					
Acquisitions	(2,673)	0	0	0	0
Gannett Acquisition	0	(2,700)	0	0	0
CapEx	(983)	(1,334)	(1,103)	(847)	(759)
Total Other	(122)	48	34	10	10
TOTAL CASH FROM INVESTMENTS	(3,778)	(3,986)	(1,069)	(837)	(749)
FINANCING ACTIVITIES					
Equity Issued	1,400	0	0	0	0
Monetization	1,243	1,500	0	0	0
Beginning Debt	4,091	4,847	6,311	6,306	5,861
Maturing Debt		(431)	(341)	(200)	(277)
New Debt Financed (Retired)	566	1,895	336	(245)	(556)
Ending Total Debt	4,847	6,311	6,306	5,861	5,028
TOTAL CASH FROM FINANCING	3,399	2,964	(5)	(445)	(833)
CONDENSED INCOME STATEMENT					
EBITDA	878	1,495	1,653	1,873	2,103
Depreciation	(197)	(267)	(221)	(169)	(152)
Interest	(310)	(473)	(580)	(591)	(521)
Taxes	(85)	30	10	10	10
Net Income	287	786	863	1,123	1,440
DEBT RATIOS					
Pro Forma Annualized EBITDA	1,201	1,495	1,653	1,873	2,103
Leverage Ratio	4.0 ×	4.2 ×	3.8 ×	3.1 ×	2.4 ×
EQUITY INTEREST					
Cox Family Economic Equity	65.1%	65.1%	65.1%	63.0%	63.0%
Cox Family Voting Equity	75.0%	75.0%	75.0%	73.3%	73.3%

Compañia de Teléfonos de Chile

In April 1990, Claudio Garcia, the newly appointed senior executive vice president for finance and administration for Compañia de Teléfonos de Chile (CTC), found the telephone company in the middle of a challenging financial dilemma. CTC had embarked upon an aggressive expansion program that required substantial capital resources. The expansion program had been approved under Alan Bond, an Australian entrepreneur. The plan included reducing substantially the time needed to install telephone service and expanding capabilities to provide some of the latest high-tech capabilities that telecommunications had to offer.

However, because of significant personal financial difficulties, Mr. Bond sold his stake in the telephone company in April 1990. CTC was currently looking for new investors who could provide the necessary operating capital to continue its expansion. In seeking these investors, CTC had several options, but all had their drawbacks.

CTC could try to raise money from the local stock market. However, there were questions about whether there was sufficient capital in the market to finance fully CTC's needs. It could try to raise money from Chilean banks, but the small size of these banks and the legal restrictions they faced in being exposed to any one credit risk could prove problematic. Foreign commercial bankers had the necessary capital, but they shied away from making investments in Latin America—a region in which they faced massive loan write-offs from the debt crisis of the 1980s. Finally, CTC could also try to raise equity overseas through the listing of American Depository Receipts (ADRs), a step that likely would put its stock on the New York Stock Exchange. But this alternative also presented some substantial hurdles.

These, and many other questions, preoccupied Sr. Garcia as he considered how CTC's management might relax the financial constraints retarding CTC's growth.

Chile

The Country

In 1990, Chile was a country with a population of 12.9 million. Geographically, it was a long, thin country bounded by the Pacific Ocean on its west and the Andes Mountains along its east. These features made an extensive and reliable telephone network essential to the promotion of commerce within the country.

Since 1973, Chile had been ruled by Augusto Pinochet, a military general who had come to power in a coup over Salvador Allende, an elected Marxist leader who had ruled since 1970. In 1989, Pinochet put his continued leadership to a vote in a plebiscite—a vote that he lost. Though he promised an orderly transition of power, some observers questioned his sincerity. His long years in power, his vast control of the government through civil service appointments, and his complete dominance of the military forces made him a potent political force. Many wondered whether, once officially out of power, Pinochet might not continue to intervene in the governmental affairs of the country, or even stage another coup.

This case was prepared by Charles M. La Follette (MBA '92) under the supervision of Professors W. Carl Kester of Harvard Business School (Boston, MA, USA) and Enrique Ostale of Universidad Adolfo Ibañez (Santiago, Chile).

Copyright © 1992 by the President and Fellows of Harvard College. Harvard Business School case 293-015.

The Chilean Economy

The Chilean economy was largely based upon raw materials. The country was the world's largest exporter of copper and its third-largest producer (see Exhibit 1). Unlike its neighbors—Argentina, Bolivia, and Peru—Chile enjoyed a relatively stable economy. Inflation averaged 20.2% from 1984 to 1989.

Chile's history of debt payment was good. Unlike most of the Latin American region, Chile had never accumulated interest arrears on its $18 billion debt. Nevertheless, its image suffered in the financial community from being associated with Latin American economies in general. Throughout the 1980s, the total debt of Latin America had increased 76.9%. Interest arrears of the region had boomed 22-fold since 1983 (see Exhibit 2).

During the early 1980s, the debt-to-export ratio of the continent steadily increased from approximately 2-to-1 to nearly 4-to-1 by 1986. To many in the world's financial centers, it seemed that the region would never be able to earn its way out of financial distress. Exchange rates and other economic data for Chile are provided in Exhibit 3. Economic data on selected other Latin American countries are provided in Exhibit 4.

Company Background

CTC's Privatization

By the late 1980s, Chile did not have a broad telecommunications network. In fact, the country ranked only 12th out of 24 Latin American and Caribbean nations in the extensiveness of its telephone network (see Exhibit 5). Though it was a state-owned enterprise, CTC suffered from a mediocre record in servicing customer needs. Hundreds of thousands of potential customers had been on the waiting list for service for several years (see Exhibit 6).

In 1987 the government decided to address the country's telecommunications problems by privatizing CTC. It put the firm up to bid on the stipulation that the winning bidder would expand, modernize, and improve the telecommunications network, as well as provide some initial financial security to employees who might be let go in a reorganization.

Several firms made bids for the telephone network, including BellSouth, Bond Company, Alcatel Althsom N.V., Nippon Telegraph & Telephone Corp., Chase Manhattan, and Communicaciones Chile. Several of the bidders offered distressed Chilean debt securities as payment, seeking to perform a debt-for-equity swap for the company. But in the end, Alan Bond's firm won the day. Though lower in total value. Bond Company's all-cash bid of $114.8 million for 151 million shares (approximately 35% of total shares) of CTC was deemed more attractive than other, more creative financing bid structures. Bond Company subsequently acquired more shares that raised its ownership of CTC's stock to 49.5% by the end of 1988.

Bond Company immediately went to work on expanding the firm's operations. Soon after the acquisition, CTC embarked on an aggressive expansion mode to add 600,000 lines of service by the end of 1992. In addition, Bond Company's management began to implement a variety of other tactics that would further develop the company and make it one of the most modern telephone networks in South America. Among these goals were proposals to install a cellular service, implement new services such as paging and mobile radiocommunications, develop a high-speed data transmission network, advance towards full digitization of the network, improve the network maintenance and replacement program, introduce new value-added services, and operate a nationwide network of fiber optic and satellite transmission links.

Initial Setbacks

Unfortunately, the expansion and modernization program soon hit substantial difficulties. Many of these problems stemmed from the financial distress that began to afflict the Bond empire soon after its acquisition of CTC. Investors spanning the spectrum from American banks to local Chilean institutions began to shy away from CTC as an investment vehicle. By the late 1980s, the Bond Company found itself increasingly under pressure to sell substantial stakes in its holdings in order to meet debt obligations.

On April 11, 1990, Bond Company sold its stake of 365.5 million shares in CTC (along with an option to buy an additional 9.1 million shares) to Telefónica de España, S.A., the Spanish telephone company, for $392 million. Nevertheless, even after Alan Bond had sold his stake in CTC, investors continued for a while to associate the company with Bond's difficult financial situation.

In addition, Claudio Garcia—who had joined the firm in September 1989—soon learned that the development program might not meet its targets. In hiring an international telephone operating company as an outside consultant in December 1989, CTC's administration acknowledged that substantial changes needed to be made in the management of the expansion plan.

Financial Concerns

In light of CTC's pressing financial and operating problems, Telefónica chose to cut its dividend. Both as a state-owned enterprise and under Bond's ownership, CTC had paid cash dividends in the amount of 100% of its net income. In 1990, CTC lowered its dividend to 80% of net income for the year. Within each fiscal year, CTC had historically maintained a policy that required it to pay out 60% of each quarter's earnings to the shareholders through a dividend. (When paying out 100% of its earnings, the fraction paid out each quarter was 75% of that quarter's earnings.) This meant that it had a particularly large final dividend payout to make at the end of each year. Relevant financial statements for CTC are provided in Exhibits 7 and 8. CTC's dividend history is provided in Exhibit 9.

The lowered dividend did not solve all of CTC's financial problems, however. The company still faced an uphill struggle in sourcing capital externally to meet its substantial capital expenditure budget. Following Telefónica's takeover, this budget increased as a consequence of the decision to extend CTC's line expansion target to 1.7 million by 1996 (see Exhibit 10 for capital expenditures projected through 1996). In particular, there were well-voiced concerns at CTC about whether the company would be able to raise substantial funds from its home country.

The Local Stock Market

The local Chilean stock market was thinly capitalized. At a market capitalization of $11.6 billion as of March 31, 1990, the Chilean stock market was less than one third of 1% the size of the U.S. market, which had an estimated capitalization of $2.9 trillion. Chile's market was not even big by developing country standards. Its market ranked only 11th among the world's 32 developing country stock markets in market capitalization (see Exhibit 11).

Chile's stock market was open only between 10:30 AM and 11:15 AM, and again between 11:45 AM and 12:30 PM each business day. Odd lots of stock were traded only once a week by auction. Average daily trading in the market was only about $7–$8 million. Analysts estimated that a large Chilean company could expect to raise only about 1% of the total market capitalization of the market in any new offering. Trading data for CTC's stock is provided in Exhibit 12.

Chilean Banks

Commercial banks might also be constrained from providing CTC with the necessary capital. Chile's banking community was not particularly large. Only 3 of the world's 1000 largest banks were based in Chile. Even by Latin American standards, Chile had a small banking community—ranking fifth out of the nine largest bank centers in Latin America in terms of total assets (see Exhibit 13).

Under Chilean law, commercial banks could lend up to 25% of their capital and reserves to a single company if the loans were adequately secured by tangible assets. However, because covenants on CTC's outstanding debentures prohibited it from pledging assets to secure new debt without the approval of a majority of the debenture holders, Chilean banks were constrained to lend no more than 5% of their total capital and reserves to CTC. It was possible that CTC's financial needs would quickly top this limit.

Chilean Pension Funds

One of the most rapidly growing domestic pools of capital in Chile was private pension funds. However, regulations constrained the types of investments these funds could make. Although CTC's equity would normally have been an eligible investment for Chilean pension funds, the funds were prevented from investing in any company in which a single investor (other than the Chilean government) owned 45% of the stock or more. Thus, in April 1990, CTC was not an eligible investment for private Chilean pension funds.

The Overseas Capital Markets

American depository receipts, or ADRs, represented a new potential option for raising additional capital. ADRs are receipts traded in the United States that represent the shares of foreign companies. They allow U.S. investors to invest in foreign markets through securities denominated in dollars and traded on American exchanges. Though the actual shares are deposited in a custodian bank located in the issuer's home country, the instruments have proven to be convenient and trustworthy.

ADRs grew in popularity throughout the 1980s as institutional investors sought to diversify their portfolio risk across international boundaries. Their ADR holdings increased substantially during this period. Since 1987, the annual ADR trading volume on U.S. exchanges increased by an average of 23.8%, while trading of U.S. stocks grew by only 4.2%. In 1989 foreign companies raised $2.5 billion in new equity through ADRs. Exhibit 14 shows the growth of ADRs as a financial vehicle. Exhibit 15 shows the major institutional purchasers of ADRs.

Several different ADR programs were available. They differed primarily in the degree of financial reporting that a firm was willing to make to U.S. regulatory bodies. Level I ADRs provided the simplest method of accessing the U.S. capital markets. Level I ADRs were unlisted and traded by dealers in the over-the-counter market; the foreign company did not have to comply with U.S. generally accepted accounting principles (GAAP) or full Securities and Exchange Commission (SEC) disclosure requirements. In fact, Level I ADRs allowed non-U.S. companies to enjoy the benefits of a publicly traded U.S. security without having to alter their current reporting procedures at all.[1]

To list securities on U.S. exchanges, foreign issuers had to use sponsored Level II or Level III ADRs. Each level required different degrees of SEC registration and reporting, and adherence to U.S. GAAP.[2] A brief summary of the different requirements by

[1]Private Placement 144a ADRs was another method for entering the U.S. equity markets. In private placement ADRs, a private company could raise capital by placing ADRs with large institutional investors, again without registering with the SEC. However, this rule was not expected to become effective before June 1990.

[2]The Bank of New York, "American Depository Receipts and Privatizations," 1991, p. 5.

level is shown in Exhibit 16. Level III ADRs provided the most comprehensive (and expensive) means of entering the U.S. equity markets. Level III ADRs required full reporting of corporate data on a quarterly basis according to U.S. GAAP. In effect, in sponsoring a Level III ADR, foreign firms agreed to all of the reporting requirements with which listed domestic U.S. firms must comply.

Raising funds by issuing ADRs raised numerous problems for CTC. First, there was the potential problem that significant quantities of CTC's stock might flow back to the home market during market downturns—thereby causing disruptions, even suspensions, of trading in CTC stock on the Santiago Stock Exchange. Backflow could drive the price of the stock down and could lead to lower valuations in future stock offerings the company might pursue.

In addition, most ADRs came from companies domiciled in developed economies, not from companies in Latin America (see Exhibit 17). The appetite of U.S. investors for ADRs listed by a Latin American corporation had not been tested. Though there had recently been stock offerings for foreign telecommunication companies like Telefónica de España; Hongkong Telecommunications, Ltd.; Cable & Wireless Public Ltd., Co. (a U.K. company); and Telecom Corporation of New Zealand, Ltd., there might be perceptions of differences between the political risk of those countries and a country like Chile. In fact, there was no precedent to guide American institutional investors in evaluating a Chilean company, for there were no Chilean companies listed on the New York Stock Exchange.[3] In addition, given the recent questions about CTC's development program raised by an independent—and American—telephone company, there were some concerns about whether CTC could withstand the scrutiny of skeptical analysts in road shows across the United States.

Finally, there were questions about whether CTC could satisfy the arduous reporting requirements of a Level III ADR. Would it be worth paying for the increased administrative cost of fulfilling those reporting requirements? Where would it obtain the necessary skills to satisfy these requirements?

There were no easy answers to any of these questions. Nevertheless, it was imperative that Sr. Garcia devise a strategy to finance CTC's ambitious program of investment and growth, analyze the financing alternatives, and submit a plan soon to CTC's board of directors.

EXHIBIT 1

Copper Production and Export (thousands of tons)

Source: *Economist Pocket World in Figures* (London: Hutchinson Business Books, 1990), p. 35.

Top 5 Producers, 1988		Top 5 Exporters, 1988	
U.S.	1,857	Chile	976
USSR	1,380	Zambia	424
Chile	1,013	Canada	262
Japan	955	Zaire	198
Canada	529	Peru	147

[3]Also, there was no tax treaty in force between Chile and the United States. Chilean tax law provided for a 35% withholding tax on dividends paid to foreign shareholders. The 10% corporate tax on income from which dividends were paid was available to shareholders as a credit against the withholding tax, but that credit increased the base on which the withholding tax was imposed (thus, on CP 100 of dividends, foreign shareholders would pay a net withholding tax of CP 27.78 = .35 × CP 111.11 – .10 × CP 111.11).

EXHIBIT 2
Total Latin American Debt and Interest Arrears (millions of dollars)

Source: "External Debt of Developing Countries," in *World Debt Tables, 1990–1991* (Washington, D.C.: The World Bank, 1991), p. 142.

Year	Total Debt	Interest Arrears
1980	$242,535	$ 8
1983	360,999	1,198
1984	377,531	3,108
1985	389,974	2,463
1986	409,708	3,285
1987	445,122	8,393
1988	427,597	8,944
1989	422,188	16,722

EXHIBIT 3
Chilean Peso Exchange Rates and Economic Indicators

Source: Central Bank of Chile.

Chilean Peso/U.S. $ Exchange Rate				
Year Ended December 31	Year-End Rate	Average Rate[a]	High Rate	Low Rate
1985	183.86	163.03	183.86	129.43
1986	204.73	194.15	204.73	185.70
1987	238.14	221.09	238.14	205.18
1988	247.20	245.48	248.24	240.90
1989	297.37	297.34	297.37	245.84
1990	296.98[b]	na	na	na

Note: na = Not available.
[a]The average rate is calculated on the basis of month-end exchange rates.
[b]End of March 1990.

Selected Macroeconomic Indicators

Item	1979	1980	1981	1982	1983	1984	1985	1986	1987	1988	1989
GDP growth[a] (%)	8.3	7.8	5.5	–14.1	–0.7	6.3	2.4	5.7	5.7	7.4	10.0
Increase in Consumer Price Index (%)	38.9	31.2	9.5	20.7	23.1	23.0	26.4	17.4	21.5	12.7	21.40
Population (millions)[b]	10.9	11.1	11.3	11.3	11.7	11.9	12.1	12.3	12.5	12.7	12.90
Exports ($ millions)	3,835	4,705	3,837	3,706	3,831	3.651	3,804	4,199	5,224	7,052	8,190.40
Imports ($ millions)	4,191	5,469	6,513	3,643	2,845	3,288	2,956	3,099	3,994	4,833	
Current account surplus/deficit ($ millions)	–1,189	–1,971	–4,733	–2,304	–1,117	–2,111	–1,329	–1,137	–808	–167	–740
Total external debt ($ billions)	8.5	11.1	15.5	17.2	17.4	18.9	19.4	19.5	19.2	17.6	16.25
Debt service ratio to GDP[c] (%)	7.41	7.78	7.75	12.11	10.15	11.73	12.84	12.13	8.95	6.82	5.75
Exchange rate (pesos per $)[d]	38.00	39.00	39.00	73.57	87.07	128.24	183.66	204.73	238.14	247.20	297.37
Unemployment rate (%)	13.6	10.4	11.3	19.6	14.8	13.9	12.0	8.8	7.9	8.3	5.30

[a]Adjusted for inflation.
[b]Estimated as of June of each year.
[c]Includes mandatory amortization and interest payments on medium- and long-term debt and interest on short-term debt.
[d]Observed exchange rate as of December 31 of each year.

EXHIBIT 4 **Comparison of Macroeconomic Indicators for Selected Latin American Countries**

Source: *International Financial Statistics* (Washington D.C.: International Monetary Fund, April 1992).

	1985	1986	1987	1988	1989
Increase in Consumer Price Index					
Argentina	672.20%	90.00%	131.58%	342.73%	3,079.16%
Brazil	226.90	145.00	229.80	670.42	1,309.19
Colombia	24.00	18.90	23.30	26.10	25.65
Peru	163.40	78.00	85.96	666.16	3,398.50
Venezuela	11.40	11.50	28.16	29.46	84.27
Exports ($ millions)					
Argentina	$ 8,396.1	$ 6,852.2	$ 6,360.2	$ 9,134.8	$ 9,579.3
Brazil	25,639.0	22,349.0	26,224.0	33,789.0	34,383.0
Colombia	3,551.6	5,101.6	4,642.6	5,037.0	5,716.5
Peru	2,978.5	2,530.6	2,660.8	2,701.0	3,488.0
Venezuela	$ 14,438.0	$ 8,660.0	$ 10,577.0	$ 10,239.0	$ 13,310.0
Imports ($ millions)					
Argentina	$ 3,814.2	$ 4,724.1	$ 5,817.8	$ 5,321.6	$ 4,203.2
Brazil	$ 14,332.0	15,557.0	16,581.0	16,055.0	20,016.0
Colombia	4,140.9	3,861.6	4,321.9	5,001.8	5,004.1
Peru	1,835.0	2,908.8	3,562.3	3,348.0	2,749.2
Venezuela	$ 8,106.0	$ 8,504.0	$ 9,659.0	$ 12,726.0	$ 7,803.0
Current Account Surplus/Deficit ($ millions)					
Argentina	$ (952)	$ (2,859)	$ (4,235)	$ (1,572)	$ (1,305)
Brazil	(273)	(5,304)	(1,450)	4,159	1,025
Colombia	(1,809)	383	336	(216)	(195)
Peru	135	(1,077)	(1,481)	(1,091)	324
Venezuela	$ (3,334)	$ (2,693)	$ (2,709)	$ (4,302)	na
Total External Debt ($ millions)					
Argentina	$ 49,148.7	$ 51.422.0	$ 58,324.0	$ 58,803.0	$ 63,314.0
Brazil	106,472.8	111,045.0	121,174.0	113,469.0	115,096.0
Colombia	14,237.4	14,987.0	15,663.0	16,434.0	16,013.0
Peru	14,136.9	14,477.0	15,373.0	16,493.0	16,827.0
Venezuela	$ 34,692.8	$ 33,839.0	$ 34,833.0	$ 34,684.0	$ 33,194.0
GNP Growth (%)					
Argentina	–4.50%	5.60%	2.50%	–2.50%	–4.50%
Brazil	8.30	7.50	3.60	0.00	3.31
Colombia	3.10	5.80	5.40	4.10	3.40
Peru	2.40	9.17	8.26	–8.34	–11.65
Venezuela	1.30	6.34	4.51	6.11	–7.83
Population (millions)					
Argentina	30.33	30.74	31.14	31.53	31.93
Brazil	135.56	138.49	141.45	144.43	147.40
Colombia	28.62	29.19	29.73	30.24	32.53
Peru	19.70	20.21	20.73	21.26	21.79
Venezuela	17.32	17.79	18.27	18.76	19.25

Note: na = Not available.

EXHIBIT 5
Population per Telephone Line in 1986 for Latin American and Caribbean Nations (persons per line)

Source: *Economist Pocket World in Statistics* (London: Hutchinson Business Books, 1990), p, 125.

Country	Persons per line
Argentina	9.7
Bahamas	2.2
Barbados	3.3
Bolivia	41.4
Brazil	11.3
Chile	15.5
Colombia	13.0
Costa Rica	7.9
Cuba	18.9
Ecuador	27.4
El Salvador	38.1
Guatemala	62.0
Guyana	23.0
Honduras	86.6
Jamaica	205.0
Mexico	10.4
Neth. Antilles	4.0
Nicaragua	63.4
Panama	9.4
Paraguay	41.1
Peru	32.8
Trinidad and Tobago	11.0
Uruguay	7.6
Venezuela	11.3

EXHIBIT 6
CTC's Lines in Service and Waiting List

Source: Corporate documents.

	December 31,				
	1986	1987	1988	1989	1990[a]
Number of telephones	749,110	770,199	820,260	894,824	1,096,056
Telephones per 100 inhabitants	6.6	6.7	7.0	7.4	8.9
Number of lines installed	584,829	614,884	634,327	799,917	1,018,568
Lines in service	527,789	548,359	591,565	645,863	811,811
Applications pending	219,265	230,452	236,349	283,919	307,843
Digitalization (%)[b]	36.8	36.0	37.9	51.1	64.0
Automation (%)[c]	96.1	98.0	98.5	99.3	99.6
Local calls (millions)[d, e]	1,095	1,146	1,231	1,341	1,524
Local calls per line in service[e,f]	2,667	2,686	2,778	2,610	2,587

[a]Estimated.
[b]Percentage of lines installed and connected to digital exchanges.
[c]Percentage of lines installed and connected to automatic exchanges.
[d]Does not include calls made under CTC's "flat fee" charge system, or calls made from public telephones.
[e]Reflects information for the period ending the date indicated.
[f]Lines in service do not include lines that provide service on the "flat fee" charge system or that provide service from public telephones. Totals were calculated for each year on the basis of the monthly average of the number of lines in service during each year.

EXHIBIT 7

Consolidated Balance Sheets (Adjusted for general price-level changes and expressed in millions of *constant* 1990 Chilean pesos [CP], except number of shares)

Source: Corporate documents.

	1989	1988
Assets		
Current assets		
Cash and cash equivalents	CP 29,782	CP 27,770
Marketable securities	7,829	5,377
Accounts and notes receivable	31,094	16,722
Inventories	6,824	2,726
Other	743	1,587
Total current assets	76,272	54,182
Property, plant, equipment, net	295,440	216,796
Other assets	12,634	24,867
Total assets	CP 384,346	CP 295,845
Liabilities and shareholder's equity		
Current liabilities		
Bank borrowings	CP 11,232	CP 9,462
Current maturities of long-term debt	10,570	78
Accounts payable and accrued	46,012	28,029
Due to ENTEL	3,546	—
Other	3,481	159
Total current liabilities	74,841	37,728
Long-term liabilities		
Long-term debt	80,710	50,526
Accrued severance indem	4,971	5,142
Deferred income taxes	—	156
Total long-term liabilities	85,681	55,824
Shareholders' equity		
Common stock	200,560	195,694
Retained earnings	23,264	6,599
Total shareholders' equity	223,824	202,293
Total liabilities and shareholders' equity	CP 384,346	CP 295,845

EXHIBIT 8

Consolidated Statements of Income (adjusted for general price-level changes and expressed in millions of *constant* 1990 Chilean pesos [CP], except number of shares)

Source: Corporate documents.

	1988	1989
Operating revenues		
Tariff regulated services	CP 68,498	CP 82,676
Other	13,342	20,859
Total operating revenues	81,840	103,535
Operating costs and expense		
Oper. salaries and related	16,770	18,101
Depreciation and amort	12,088	13,868
Cost of ENTEL services	199	975
Other operating costs	11,339	16,031
Admin. and selling costs	9,836	11,371
Total operating costs and expenses	50,232	60,346
Operating income	31,608	43,189
Other income (expenses)		
Interest income	1,651	4,967
Net interest expense[a]	(3,961)	(2,226)
Purchasing power gain[b]	5,517	7,098
Other	(7,013)	(10,042)
Total other income, net	(3,806)	(203)
Income before income tax	27,802	42,986
Income tax[c]		
Current	1,479	(298)
Deferred	1,317	(3,322)
Net income	CP 25,006	CP 46,606

[a]Capitalized interest expense was CP 5,081 million in 1989 and CP 1,656 million in 1988, which gave rise to total (i.e., capitalized and noncapitalized) interest expense of CP 7,307 million and CP 5,617 million in 1989 and 1988, respectively.

[b]Purchasing power gains are noncash sources of earnings that reflect the effect of Chilean inflation on the monetary liabilities owed by CTC during each year, net of the loss resulting from the effect of inflation on monetary assets held.

[c]On January 14, 1989, the Chilean income tax was substantially changed. Among other changes, corporations were not subject to income tax beginning on January 1, 1989. Income taxes were payable by the shareholders on dividends received. In light of this change, the net liability for deferred taxes shown on the balance sheet as of December 31, 1988, was credited to income in 1989.

Subsequent Chilean legislation passed in the first half of 1990 introduced a corporate tax rate of 10% on income earned after January 1, 1990, with an increase in the rate to 15% for 1991, 1992, and 1993, and a decrease to 10% for the years 1994 and beyond.

EXHIBIT 9

CTC's Cash Dividend History[a] (Chilean pesos per share)

Source: Public documents.

	Interim	Final[b]	Total
1986	35.93	—	35.93
1987	17.14	25.56	42.70
1988	38.17	16.75	54.92
1989	46.02	9.06	55.08

[a]Chilean pesos are reflected at historical values, not at constant 1990 purchasing power values.

[b]The final dividend for each year is declared (and hence accrued) in April of each subsequent year.

EXHIBIT 10
CTC's Actual and Projected Capital Expenditures (millions of Chilean pesos)

Source: Corporate documents.

	Actual	
	1988	1989
For tariff-regulated services	CP 41,719	CP 79,325
For services not currently subject to tariff regulation	4,377	11,520
For new services requiring new concessions		6,422
Total	CP 46,096	CP 97,267

	Projected			
	1990	1991	1992	1993–1996
For tariff-regulated services	CP 100,602	CP 95,042	CP 77,458	CP 243,735
For services not currently subject to tariff regulation	4,963	4,380	3,413	10,880
For new services requiring new concessions	15,187	15,441	8,468	14,658
Total	CP 120,752	CP 114,863	CP 89,339	CP 269,273

EXHIBIT 11
World Stock Exchanges: Market Capitalization of Emerging Markets (millions of dollars)

Source: *Economist Book of Vital World Statistics* (London: Random Century House, 1991), p. 146.

	1989
Argentina	$ 4,225
Bangladesh	476
Brazil	44,368
Chile	9,587
Cote D'Ivoire	437
Colombia	1,136
Egypt	1,760
Greece	6,376
India	27,316
Indonesia	2,514
Jamaica	957
Jordan	2,162
Kenya	474
South Korea	140,946
Kuwait	9,932
Malaysia	39,842
Mexico	22,550
Morocco	621
Nigeria	1,005
Pakistan	2,457
Philippines	11,965
Portugal	10,618
Sri Lanka	471
Taiwan	237,012
Thailand	25,648
Trinidad and Tobago	411
Turkey	6,783
Uruguay	24
Venezuela	1,816
Zimbabwe	1,067

EXHIBIT 12 Trading Data for CTC's Stock[a]

Source: Public documents.

	Per Share (CP)[b]		Average Daily Number of Shares Traded (000s)[c]
	High	Low	
1989			
First quarter	188	149.5	135
Second quarter	207	172.5	342
Third quarter	206	173.75	202
Fourth quarter	200	169	383
1990			
First quarter	255	190	467

[a]Reported figures are for Series A shares only. CTC's capital is represented by no-par-value shares divided into two series (Series A and B). The rights of both series of shares are identical, except that the Series A shareholders as a class appoint six directors and the Series B shareholders as a class appoint one director. On December 31, 1989, there were 634,527,896 Series A shares issued and outstanding, and 67,552,376 Series B shares issued and outstanding.

[b]Chilean pesos are reflected at historical values; not at constant 1990 purchasing power values.

[c]Series A shares are traded principally on the Bolsa de Comercio de Santiago (the Santiago Stock Exchange). The shares are also listed on the Bolsa de Comercia do Valparaiso (the Valparaiso Stock Exchange) and are tradeable in a nascent electronic over-the-counter trading system. However, the Santiago Stock Exchange accounts for approximately 95% of the trading volume of CTC's shares in Chile.

EXHIBIT 13 Banking in Latin America

Source: *Economist Book of Vital World Statistics* (London: Random Century House, 1991), p. 148.

	Number of Banks in Top 1,000	Total Capital ($ millions)
Argentina	7	$ 3,159
Brazil	17	10,914
Chile	3	878
Colombia	1	94
Mexico	5	2,226
Panama	1	89
Peru	1	170
Uruguay	1	822
Venezuela	5	934

EXHIBIT 14 Selected Data on ADR Programs

Source: Philip Maher, "ADR Market Continued Growth in 1990, Riding Global Trend," *Investment Dealers' Digest,* February 1991, p. 12.

	1983	1984	1985	1986	1987	1988	1989
Total number of ADR programs	585	625	683	700	754	782	804
Number of ADR offerings	10	9	2	8	19	8	20
Total capital raised with ADRs ($ millions)	617	608	28	696	4,586	1,275	2,614

EXHIBIT 15
Top Institutional Holders of ADRs (July 1989)

Source: *Investment Dealers' Digest,* October 16, 1989.

	Amount ($ millions)
CIGNA	$980
Delaware Management	738
FMR	522
Manufacturers International	501
Capital Guardian	413
Wellington	386
California Public Management	369
INVESCO	239
Alliance Capital	232
IDS Financial	227
American Capital	206
Lazard Freres	198
J. P. Morgan	198
Scudder, Stevens	197
Dreman Value	182
Merrill Lynch Asset Management	181
Templeton	169
Pioneering Management	167
Newbold's Asset Management	143
Rosenberg Institute	143

EXHIBIT 16 Comparison of ADR Facilities

Sources: The Bank of New York, "American Depository Receipts and Privatizations," 1991; and J. P. Morgan, "American Depository Receipts for Chilean Companies: Benefitting from the U.S. Capital Markets," unpublished presentation materials.

Type of Program	Registration Requirements[a]	Disclosure Requirements	Type of U.S. Equity Offering[b]	Listing Possibilities	Typical Cost to Company
Unsponsored[c]	Form F–6	None	Rule 144A private placement	OTC/pinks	None
	Rule 12g3–2(b)	None		Bulletin board	None
Private placement	Rule 12g3–2(b)	Eurostyle	Rule 144A private placement	Various	$100,000 to $300,000
Sponsored					
Level I	Form F–6 Rule 12g3–2 (b)	None None	Rule 144A private placement	OTC/pinks Bulletin board	$5,000 to $20,000
Level II	Form F–6 20–F	None Detailed	Rule 144A private placement	NYSE AMEX NASDAQ	$200,000 to $400,000
Level III	F–1 20–F	Rigorous Detailed	Public offering	NYSE AMEX NASDAQ	$400,000 to $800,000

[a]The Securities Act of 1933 requires public securities to be registered with the Securities and Exchange Commission (SEC). Filing a Form F–6 registration statement complies with this requirement without substantial disclosure of information. Form F–1 requires financial information that is less than six months old and conforms to U.S. GAAP.

The Securities Exchange Act of 1934 requires companies listed on a major exchange to make regular filings of interim and annual reports to the SEC. A 20–F report requires detailed disclosure by foreign companies equivalent to a 10K report by domestic U.S. companies. Rule 12g3–2(b) of the 1934 Act permits exemption from such detailed disclosure by allowing foreign companies to file, on an ongoing basis, only that information that it is required to disclose in its country of domicile or that it distributes to any security holders outside the United States.

[b]Rule 144A permits restricted or nonpublic securities issued by foreign investors to be placed and traded privately among large, sophisticated institutional investors.

[c]No unsponsored programs have been initiated since 1983.

EXHIBIT 17
ADR Programs by Country of Origin (July 1989)

Source: *Investment Dealers' Digest,* October 16, 1989.

Percentage of Total ADR Programs by Country

	Number	Percentage
United Kingdom	197	23.0%
Australia	179	20.9
Japan	144	16.8
South Africa	91	10.6
Hong Kong	30	3.5
France	24	2.8
Germany	24	2.8
Netherlands	21	2.5
Italy	20	2.3
Other	127	14.8
Total	857	100.0%

Percentage Sponsored ADR Programs by Country

	Number	Percentage
United Kingdom	148	38.3%
Australia	80	20.7
Japan	19	4.9
Netherlands	18	4.7
France	14	3.6
Sweden	13	3.4
Norway	12	3.1
Mexico	11	2.9
Spain	8	2.1
Other	63	16.3
Total	386	100.0%

Dividend Policy at FPL Group, Inc. (A)

In the late afternoon of Thursday, May 5, 1994, Kate Stark, the electric utilities analyst at First Equity Securities Corporation, received an investment alert on one of the companies she followed. According to the report, Merrill Lynch's utilities analyst was downgrading FPL Group, Inc., Florida's largest electric utility. The report began:

> We are [lowering] the investment rating for FPL Group . . . due to our expectation that the Directors will choose not to raise the annual dividend from $2.48 at [the annual meeting on] Monday, May 9, FPL's shareholders face the possibility that the dividend is not entirely secure, as we believe FPL may seriously review its dividend policy at this time. . . . Management has suggested that it feels that its dividend payout is inappropriately high (in excess of 90% in 1993) given the increasing risks facing the industry. . . . When asked specifically what might be done about the high dividend payout levels, management suggested that there are two ways to address high payout levels: 1) a company can grow out of a high payout; 2) a company can cut its dividend . . . we expect the company to keep the dividend at the $2.48/share level through 1997.[1]

Although this analyst was predicting the dividend would not change, this was the first time Stark had seen one of her peers suggest the possibility of a dividend cut. Only three weeks earlier, Stark herself had issued a report on FPL Group with a "hold" recommendation based on the assumption that FPL would keep its dividend at $2.48 per share or increase it slightly. What concerned her, however, was the fact that FPL's stock price had fallen by more than 6% that day. While she could not be sure the drop was related to the report, she wondered what, if anything, she should say to her clients regarding FPL's stock and whether she should issue an updated report.

Electric Utility Industry

One can trace the history of the U.S. electric utility industry back to Thomas Edison's invention of the incandescent lamp in 1878. Electricity quickly became an important part of everyday life because of the ease with which it could be transported from one place to another and converted into other useful forms (mechanical power, light, etc.). Electricity—the flow of electrons—is created by forcing steam or water through a turbine lined with electromagnets, which induces electron movement. Once produced, electricity is transmitted through power lines and distributed to end users.

The concept of a public utility developed in the late nineteenth century to refer to a monopoly supplier of a "vital public service." The vital public service in this case was the generation, transmission, and distribution of electricity. In exchange for the monopoly right to supply electricity, power companies agreed to let government agencies regulate their prices and returns. By 1930, virtually every state had established a regulatory agency. In Florida, the Florida Public Service Commission not only regulated rates, returns, and capacity planning but also determined what nonutility businesses a utility could enter.

[1]Sanford Cohen and Daniel Ford, "FPL Group: Dividend Policy Review; Lowered Opinion," Merrill Lynch & Co., May 5, 1994, pp. 1, 3.

This case was prepared by Research Associate Craig F. Schreiber under the supervision of Professor Benjamin C. Esty. This case was prepared solely on the basis of public information without the participation of FPL Group, Inc.

Copyright © 1995 by the President and Fellows of Harvard College. Harvard Business School case 295–059.

The federal government's involvement in electric power began in earnest with the passage of the Federal Power Act in 1935. This act gave the Federal Power Commission (renamed the Federal Energy Regulatory Commission (FERC) in 1977) the authority to oversee wholesale electricity transactions (sales of electricity between utilities rather than to consumers). During that same year, Congress also passed the Public Utilities Holding Company Act (PUHCA), which gave the Securities and Exchange Commission (SEC) the authority to regulate utilities with interstate systems or substantial investments in assets not related to the generation, transmission, and distribution of electricity. To avoid direct SEC supervision, the industry had evolved into a large number of intrastate, and relatively undiversified, utility companies operating under extensive federal and state regulation.

Rise of Deregulation

During the 1970s and 1980s, deregulation eliminated or weakened the monopoly service rights and fixed-price systems common in such industries as trucking, airlines, banking, natural gas, and telecommunications. While the introduction of competition increased economic efficiency, there were often short-term costs in terms of layoffs and business failures. Although the electric utilities industry entered this era of deregulation at roughly the same time as these other industries, deregulation had proceeded at a somewhat slower pace. Nevertheless, regulatory changes had been chipping away at utilities' monopoly franchises in each of the industry's major segments since 1978.

Congress, responding to concerns about U.S. dependence on foreign oil and environmental damage resulting from burning fossil fuels (oil, gas, and coal) to produce electricity, passed the Public Utilities Regulatory Policies Act (PURPA) in 1978. The act encouraged the creation of power plants using renewable or nontraditional fuels such as geothermal, solar, and wind power and authorized FERC to regulate them. As long as these nonutility generators (known as "qualifying facilities," or QFs) met certain efficiency and size standards, the act required local utilities to buy all of their electrical output (see Exhibit 1).

Fourteen years later, Congress introduced competition into the second segment of the industry—transmission—with the passage of the National Energy Policy Act of 1992 (NEPA). This act required utilities to make their transmission systems available to third-party users at the same level of quality and cost enjoyed by the utilities themselves (see Exhibit 1). Prior to NEPA, a generator could sell power into another territory only if another utility agreed to transmit the power; after NEPA, a utility could demand access to another utility's transmission system. Shortly after NEPA took effect, legal disputes arose over transmission access. One of the first cases involved FPL (which controlled over 50% of Florida's transmission lines) and the Florida Municipal Power Agency. The municipal agency sued FPL for charging excessive rates and denying fair access to its transmission system. In October 1993, FERC interceded and ordered the two parties to negotiate a settlement; the negotiations were still going on as of May 1994.

One of the major concerns about the implementation of NEPA was whether there would be sufficient transmission capacity. Analysts generally agreed that existing capacity, combined with construction plans for new transmission lines, would be sufficient through the year 2002. But there was some doubt as to whether certain planned transmission line additions could be constructed due to health concerns regarding high-voltage electromagnetic radiation exposure and opposition to clear-cutting of large swaths of land.

Deregulation of the final segment of the industry—distribution—was just beginning in early 1994. Certain states, including California and Michigan, were either considering or experimenting with competition in the distribution of electricity. For example, on April 20, the California Public Utilities Commission released a proposal (the "blue book") to phase in "retail wheeling" beginning in 1996. California's commissioner said:

> If we ignore . . . the rapid change that is already upon us, we place California utilities and the state's economy at considerable risk. . . . Change isn't coming, it is not on the horizon, it is not around the corner, it is here before you now. . . . [The proposal will be a] godsend, compared to the slow death that utilities surely face if we ignore the change before us.[2]

Under retail wheeling, customers would be allowed to buy power from utilities other than the local monopoly supplier. The local utility would be required to open its transmission and distribution network to outside utilities wishing to sell power in that market (see Exhibit 1). At first, large industrial customers (primarily manufacturing plants) would get the right to choose their electricity suppliers from a range of competitive bids. Over time, the other major customer segments—commercial users (office buildings, retail shops, universities, etc.) and eventually residential users (households)—would also get the right to pick their electricity suppliers. According to the blue book, full retail wheeling would be in place by the year 2002.

In the week following the release of the blue book proposal, California's three largest utilities, Pacific Gas & Electric, Southern California Edison, and San Diego Gas & Electric, together lost over $1.8 billion of market value—an average of 8% each from the day of the announcement. This loss in market value occurred during a week when both the stock market and the S&P Electric Utilities Index were relatively flat.

Responding to the California proposal, a utility executive from Arizona commented: "What happens in California will create a domino effect across the country. . . . [Utility managers will] have to be prepared for competition from new as well as existing players in the market."[3]

While regulators in California were proposing a retail wheeling system, regulators in Michigan were already poised to experiment with such a system. In April 1994, they proposed a plan that would immediately allow several of the state's largest power users, including General Motors and Dow Chemical, to shop for power.[4] In the beginning, utilities with excess generating capacity would compete to serve the largest industrial and commercial customers. Eventually, utilities, or investors, might actually build new, dedicated generating plants to serve these customers.

Company Background

FPL Group's major subsidiary, Florida Power & Light Company (FP&L), was formed in 1925 through the consolidation of numerous electric and gas companies. The company enjoyed steady growth until the 1970s, when rising fuel costs and construction cost overruns—FP&L spent almost $1 billion rebuilding a faulty nuclear plant—reduced its profitability. At the same time, FP&L began experiencing operating problems, which manifested themselves through frequent power outages and increasing customer complaints about service.

[2]Anonymous, "California PUC Proposes Giving Ratepayers Access to Competitive Electric Market," *Electric Utility Week,* April 25, 1994, p. 6.

[3]Brad Altman, "Ratings Climate Just Turned Chillier for Electric Utilities, Agency Raters Say," *The Bond Buyer,* April 26, 1994, p. 5.

[4]Agis Salpukas, "Electric Utilities Brace for an End to Monopolies," *The New York Times,* August 8, 1994, pp. A1, D5.

To improve FPL Group's profitability, then Chairman Marshall McDonald decided to diversify into higher growth businesses and to establish a holding company structure to manage the new businesses. Over the next several years, FPL made four major acquisitions: Colonial Penn Life Insurance Company (an insurance company purchased for $566 million in 1985); Telesat Cablevision, Inc. (a cable television system purchased for $3.6 million in 1985); CBR Information Group Inc. (an information services company purchased for $54 million in 1986); and Turner Foods Corporation (a Florida citrus producer purchased for $47 million in 1988).[5] Besides the acquisitions, FPL Group established a real estate development subsidiary called Alandco and an alternative energy development subsidiary called ESI Energy.

To address the problems in operations, McDonald instituted a program of Japanese-inspired quality control. Before long, there were 1,700 quality control teams examining every aspect of the business for ways to improve operations. As a result, unscheduled downtime fell from 18% to 4%, and customer complaints fell by 60%.[6] Because of FPL's achievements, the Union of Japanese Scientists and Engineers awarded the company the prestigious Deming Prize for quality in 1989, making it the first non-Japanese company to receive that award. At the time, FPL was viewed as "one of the best-managed U.S. corporations."[7]

Despite the notoriety, the company still had some underlying problems. In 1986 the Nuclear Regulatory Commission (the federal regulator of nuclear power plants) put FPL's Turkey Point nuclear plant on its watch list for safety concerns.[8] Second, demand was growing faster in the late 1980s than expected and was projected to outstrip existing generating capacity in the near future. Third, Colonial Penn had lost more than $250 million since being acquired.[9] And finally, a 1988 survey indicated low employee morale largely due to burdens imposed by the quality management program.[10] As one manager later confided, "We definitely went overboard [with the quality program]."[11]

The Broadhead Era

These problems, combined with the growing prospect of competition, led FPL's board to select an industry outsider, James Broadhead, to succeed McDonald when he retired in 1989. Broadhead came to FPL from GTE, where he had been in charge of the telephone business—another industry that had recently been deregulated. Having seen one industry through deregulation, Broadhead's vision for the electric utility industry was one of full and open competition.

As soon as he arrived, Broadhead began developing a long-range strategic plan. The first step in the process was an "environmental scan." He formed employee teams and asked them to speculate about the industry's future in terms of technological requirements, regulation, and customer needs. From the scan, Broadhead concluded that FPL would need to have a commitment to quality and customer service, increase its focus on the utilities industry, expand capacity, and improve its cost position.

[5] *Moody's Public Utilities Manual* 1 (1993) 9:1, p. 2709.

[6] Robert Chapman Wood, "A Hero Without a Company," *Forbes*, March 18, 1991, p. 113.

[7] *International Directory of Company Histories* (Detroit: St. James Press, 1992), p. 624.

[8] Wood, "A Hero Without a Company," p. 114.

[9] Holt Hackney, "One Turkey Too Many," *Financial World*, May 1, 1990, p. 102.

[10] Wood, "A Hero Without a Company," p. 114.

[11] Betsy Wiesendanger, "Deming's Luster Dims at Florida Power & Light," *Journal of Business Strategy*, September/October 1993, p. 61.

Although he determined that a commitment to quality was essential, he believed the quality program needed to be scaled back. Paperwork had grown exponentially, and managers were spending too much time collecting and analyzing quality reports. Broadhead streamlined the quality process by cutting the number of quality teams, meetings, and reports.

Second, Broadhead wanted to renew FPL's focus on its core business. He said:

> Our long-term success is based on our core utility business. . . . We know a lot about generating, transmitting, distributing, selling, and conserving energy. Why venture away from that with the opportunities for growth that we face today?[12]

To reverse FPL's diversification program, Broadhead made plans to sell several of the nonutility businesses. After writing off $752 million (after-tax) in 1990 for losses at Colonial Penn (the bulk of the losses), Telesat Cablevision, and Alandco, Broadhead sold Colonial Penn in 1991 for an additional after-tax loss of $136 million. By 1994, FPL had written off and was trying to sell both Telesat Cablevision and Alandco.[13] However, FPL still owned three nonutility subsidiaries—ESI Energy, Turner Foods, and Qualtec Quality Services—which contributed 2% of total revenues.

At the same time, Broadhead commenced an aggressive capital expenditure program designed to meet projected demand into the next decade. FPL budgeted $6.6 billion, spread over five years, for the expansion. The various projects included building a new transmission line, refurbishing the oldest generating plant, improving operating efficiency at all plants, and buying a majority share in a coal-burning plant owned by The Southern Company (a utility based in Georgia). By 1994 operating efficiency had improved dramatically: nuclear plant availability had risen to 83% (compared to the industry average of 70%) and fossil fuel plant availability had risen to 89% (compared to 83% for the industry).[14] FPL funded this expansion through internal profits and by issuing $3.7 billion of long-term debt and $1.9 billion of common stock (see Exhibit 5).

To reduce costs, Broadhead reengineered the firm's budgeting and procurement procedures, flattened the organization, and reduced headcount by 30%; FPL eliminated 2,300 positions in 1991 (at an after-tax cost of $56 million) and another 1,700 positions in 1993 (at an after-tax cost of $85 million). These efficiency gains lowered operating and maintenance expense from 1.82¢ per kilowatt-hour (kWh) to 1.61¢ between 1990 and 1993.[15]

By early 1994, Broadhead's strategic redirection was showing signs of success. FPL was the largest utility in Florida (and the fourth largest in the country), provided power to 3.4 million customer accounts, and had a service territory covering almost 28,000 square miles (see Exhibit 2). Financially, 1993 had been a record year for FPL; not counting a one-time charge for layoffs related to the cost reduction program, net income was $514 million or $2.75 per share. Exhibits 3, 4a, 4b, and 5 present historical income statements, balance sheets, and cash flow statements for FPL Group.

While 1993 had been a good year, FPL expected 1994 to be even better due to decreasing capital expenditures and increasing sales (see Exhibit 6). Whereas capital

[12]Hackney, "One Turkey Too Many," p. 102.

[13]M. D. Luftig, et al., *FPL Group, Inc.—Company Report,* Kemper Securities Group, Inc., February 2, 1994, p. 3.

[14]Antonio N. Fins, "Feeling the Heat at a Florida Utility," *Business Week,* November 12, 1990, p. 94.

[15]Excludes expenses for fuel, purchased power, and conservation programs (e.g., free residential energy audits).

expenditures had totaled $5.8 billion during the past five years ($800 million under budget), they were expected to decline by 33% to $3.9 billion over the next five years. FPL's sales growth (measured in kilowatt-hours) had exceeded the national average over the past five years (3.4% annual growth versus 2.0%) and was expected to exceed the national average over the next five years as well (2.7% versus 1.8%).[16]

Recent Events in the Electric Utilities Industry

Several major events that had taken place over the past year had a large impact on the electric utilities industry. Foremost among them was the California proposal on retail wheeling. Although the Florida Public Service Commission was not considering retail wheeling as of May 1994, utility commissions in 23 states were considering various retail wheeling proposals. If and when the Florida regulators authorized retail wheeling, FPL would have many potential competitors. Florida had four major investor-owned utilities (including FPL), accounting for 73% of the state's generating capacity; 20 municipal and rural cooperative generating systems, accounting for about 24% of capacity; and 19 independent power producers (including 18 QF's), accounting for 3% of capacity.[17] In addition, there were several other large investor-owned utilities in neighboring states that might compete for Florida customers (see Exhibit 7).

Because of the changing competitive landscape, Standard & Poor's Ratings Group (S&P) announced a revision of its guidelines for evaluating investor-owned electric utilities in October 1993. Under the new system, S&P would include an evaluation of a utility's competitive position as part of its financial rating. According to the guidelines, S&P would now consider such factors as the prospects for customer and sales growth, revenue vulnerabilities and dependencies, rates by consumer class relative to competing utilities, adequacy of baseload and peaking capacity, fuel diversity, regulatory environment, and management's financial goals. Based on these criteria, S&P rated FPL's business position above average, placing it in the top 10% of investor-owned utilities.[18] Because of its competitive position and its improving financial performance, S&P had recently upgraded FPL's senior secured debt to "A-plus" and its senior unsecured debt to "single-A."[19]

Despite the improvement in its debt ratings, there was some concern about the company's interest expense given the 140-basis-point increase in long-term interest rates since September 1993 (see Exhibit 8). Historically, bond yields and utility stock prices moved in opposite directions, in part because investors viewed utility stocks with their high-dividend yields as bond surrogates, and in part because utilities had relatively high levels of debt and could not pass through all increases in interest expense to consumers. During this period of rising interest rates and increasing competition (from September 1993 to May 1994), FPL's stock price had fallen by 19.6%, while S&P's Electric Utilities Index had fallen by 22.1%. Compared to the market as a whole, FPL, like most utilities, was a low-beta stock. Over the prior year, its beta was 0.60.

[16]FPL Group Presentation, EEI Financial Conference, Coronado, California, October 31–November 2, 1994.

[17]Casewriter's estimates based on *Statistics of the Florida Electric Utility Industry 1992,* Division of Research & Regulatory Review, Florida Public Service Commission, September 1993, p. 18.

[18]Curtis Moulton, "Electric Utility Business Positions Detailed," *Standard & Poor's CreditWeek Reprint,* July 4, 1994, p. 2.

[19]Steven Stoll and Judith Waite, "Rating Update," *Standard & Poor's CreditWeek,* April 18, 1994, p. 66.

Investment Recommendation on FPL

As Stark sat in her office reviewing her file on FPL and the investment alert from Merrill Lynch, she wondered why FPL might want to cut its dividend. FPL management had stated that the company's payout ratio was too high, particularly given an uncertain and more competitive business environment. While it was true that FPL's payout ratio was at the high end for electric utilities, the industry was known for high payout ratios (see Exhibit 9). More importantly, Stark wondered why FPL would want to break its 47-year streak of dividend increases—a record that placed it first among all utilities and third among all publicly traded companies.

Dividend cuts were not common for utilities except in situations of financial trouble, and even then, they were not well received. She thought back to 1974 when Consolidated Edison Company of New York (Con Ed) surprisingly eliminated its dividend in the face of a hostile regulatory and macroeconomic environment. On the day after the announcement. Con Ed's stock price fell from $18 to $12 per share. More recently, in July 1992, Sierra Pacific Resources, a financially healthy utility in Nevada, cut its dividend by 39% in order to bring its payout ratio below 100%. The cut came during what turned out to be a record year in terms of profitability, not counting certain asset write-downs. The next day, its stock price fell by 23%. Within weeks of the announcement, shareholders filed a class-action suit against the firm for false and misleading financial statements, a suit that was finally settled in April 1994.[20] Given this series of events, Stark looked at the list of FPL's shareholders (see Exhibit 10) and wondered how they would respond to a dividend cut under somewhat similar circumstances. Would they react by suing the company, or would some of them actually prefer a lower dividend?

Because of the negative market reaction that normally accompanied dividend cuts and management's desire not to have to cut the dividend twice, dividend cuts tended to be large when they occurred. One benefit of a large cut, however, was that FPL could show strong dividend growth in the coming years. For example, if FPL were to cut its dividend payout ratio by as much as 30%, thereby putting it at the lower end of the industry in terms of payout ratios (see Exhibit 9), it could increase its dividend in future years faster than without the cut. The issue that puzzled Stark, however, was what FPL would do with the cash it was not paying out as dividends, a sum that might total as much as $150 million per year.

While a dividend cut was possible and would certainly lower the payout ratio quickly, she knew that FPL also had the option of growing out of its high payout ratio. As long as earnings increased at a faster rate than dividends, the payout ratio would fall. According to her numbers, if FPL slowed its dividend growth rate to 1% or so, the payout ratio would fall below 80% by 1998. If FPL kept its dividend at $2.48 per share, the payout ratio would fall below 80% a little sooner, perhaps by 1997.

As she flipped through her FPL file, Stark removed the proxy statement, dated March 22, 1994, for the upcoming annual meeting. At the meeting, shareholders would be asked to vote for directors, to ratify Deloitte and Touche as auditors, and to approve new annual and long-term incentive compensation plans. If approved, incentive compensation would be "based on achieving specific net income goals" rather than a range of financial and operating measures; the maximum bonus payout would be expanded from 100% of an officer's targeted bonus to 160% of the targeted bonus; and bonuses would be paid out in stock and cash in the ratio of 60/40, down from a ratio of 70/30. In addition, shareholders would vote on a proposal to change the voting rules for directors.

[20]Anonymous, "Sierra Pacific Resources Settles Class-Action Shareholder Lawsuit," *Electric Utility Week*, April 25, 1994, p. 4.

Deeper in the file, she came across several research reports put out by other utility analysts, including one that had been issued that day by Prudential Securities:

> We are lowering our rating on . . . FPL Group from a Buy to a Hold . . . We believe that dividend growth . . . will be limited by [FPL's] very high dividend payout ratio . . . We think that the answer for most companies will be to freeze the dividend for the next several years and hope that earnings grow.
>
> —Prudential Securities report, May 5, 1994

> A high dividend payout ratio and increasing competitive forces in the electric utility industry may make it difficult [for FPL] to increase the common dividend . . . Management's comments increase our confidence in our flat dividend expectation.
>
> —Donaldson, Lufkin & Jenrette report, March 24, 1994

> We are upgrading our investment recommendation on the share of FPL Group, Inc. to Buy from Hold . . . The improved outlook for earnings and declining financial pressures would appear to assure continuation of (dividend increases). However, we would not be surprised to see FPL Group reduce the rate of growth in the common dividend.
>
> —Salomon Brothers report, March 16, 1994

It still appeared that everyone, including Sanford Cohen, the author of today's investment alert, was expecting FPL either to increase its dividend slightly or to hold it at $2.48 per share. That morning, Stark had felt comfortable with her recommendation along the same lines. But the day's events made her question her assumptions. She had been watching her monitor to see how other analysts were responding to Cohen's report but had seen little news and no other predictions of a dividend cut.

As Stark sat in her office, she wondered if she should revise her investment recommendation. Given the 6% drop in price, this might be the time to change her recommendation from hold to buy. On the other hand, she might want to change her recommendation to sell if management's concern about the payout ratio stemmed from concerns about future earnings prospects. She knew she had to make a decision quickly—her major clients would likely call her that evening to get her opinion of the day's events in advance of the market's opening the following day.

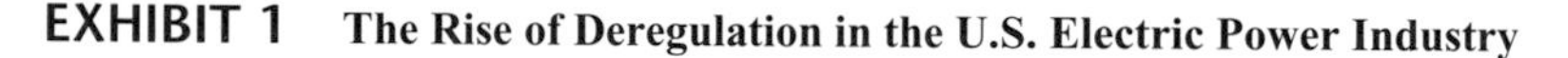

EXHIBIT 1 The Rise of Deregulation in the U.S. Electric Power Industry

Source: Casewriter's graphic.

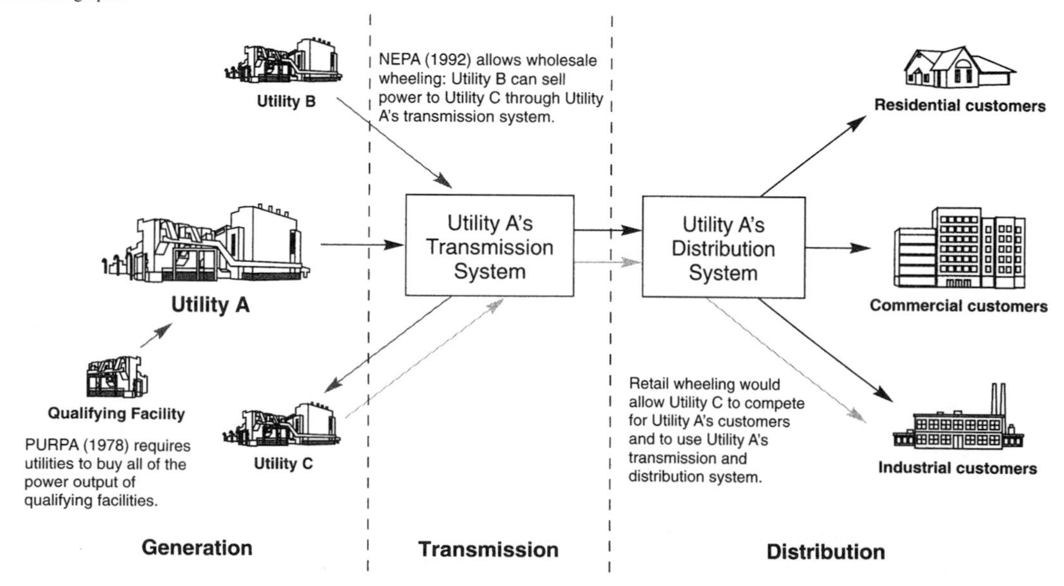

EXHIBIT 2
Florida Power & Light's Service Area, Generating Plans, and Bulk Transmission System

Source: FPL Group, Inc., 1991 Annual Report, p. 6 (as revised by the casewriter), and FPL Group, Inc., 1992 10-K Report, p. 9.

FP&L's service area covers 27,650 square miles and contains a population of 6.5 million people. During 1993, FP&L served approximately 3.4 million customer accounts. Florida is the fourth largest state in the United States and continues to experience substantial population growth. This growth is reflected in FP&L's service area, which includes six of the nation's ten fastest growing metropolitan areas—Naples, Fort Myers, Fort Pierce, Melbourne, Daytona Beach, and West Palm Beach.

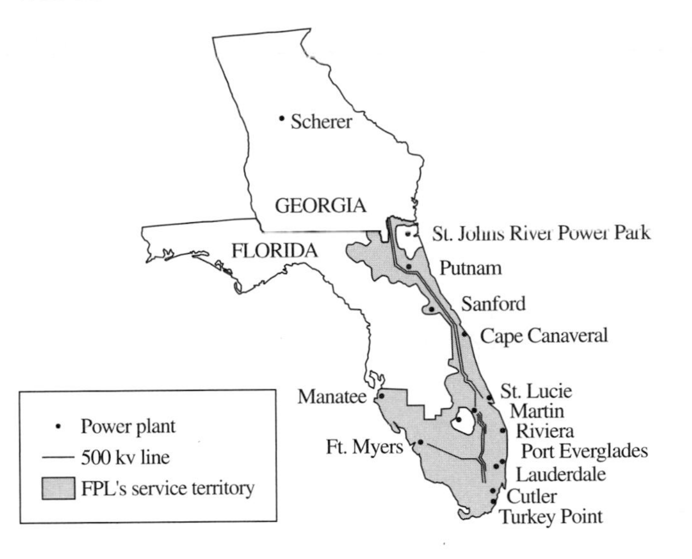

FP&L Capacity Resources

Name	Units	Capability (megawatts)
1. Manatee	2	1,566
2. Ft. Myers	2	504
3. Turkey Point	4	2,066
4. Cutler	2	207
5. Lauderdale	2	274
6. Port Everglades	4	1,142
7. Riviera	2	544
8. Martin	2	1,566
9. St. Lucie	2	1,553[a]
10. Cape Canaveral	2	734
11. Sanford	3	861
12. Putnam	2	448
13. St. Johns River	2	250[b]
14. Scherer	1	150[c]
Purchased Power		2,598
Peaking Units		1,892
Load Management		347
Total	32	16,702

[a]Represents FP&L's ownership of 100% of Unit 1 and 85% of Unit 2.
[b]Represents FP&L's 20% ownership of 624 MW units.
[c]Represents the first phase of FP&L's purchase of a 76% ownership interest in the 846 MW Scherer Unit 4.

EXHIBIT 3 FPL Group, Inc. Balance Sheet for the Years 1989–1993 (thousands of dollars)

Source: 1989–1993 annual reports for FPL Group, Inc.

	1989	1990	1991	1992	1993
Assets					
Property, plant and equipment					
Electric utility plant	$11,488,396	$12,184,176	$12,918,817	$13,534,791	$14,838,160
Construction work in progress	299,705	476,279	597,401	1,158,688	781,435
Other property	378,424	243,185	255,035	278,887	261,125
Less depreciation/amortization	4,087,780	4,481,736	4,690,403	5,106,066	5,591,265
	$ 8,078,745	$ 8,421,904	$ 9,080,850	$ 9,866,300	$10,289,455
Investments					
Utility special use funds	$ 201,217	$ 252,098	$ 291,632	$ 318,798	$ 378,774
Partnerships and joint ventures	0	168,571	236,090	296,593	368,724
Leveraged leases	0	134,174	139,008	144,398	155,449
Insurance/Banking assets	1,878,555	0	0	0	0
Other	287,678	19,060	61,222	62,952	82,045
	$ 2,367,450	$ 573,903	$ 727,952	$ 822,741	$ 984,992
Current assets					
Cash and cash equivalents	$ 61,220	$ 214,164	$ 170,211	$ 78,156	$ 152,014
Marketable securities	0	0	0	75,437	171,988
Receivables	573,171	492,503	513,937	516,585	504,597
Materials, supplies and fossil fuel	299,567	438,957	374,630	382,080	329,599
Recoverable storm costs	0	197,112	0	72,500	44,945
Other	118,284	43,818	45,419	58,418	48,214
	$ 1,052,242	$ 1,386,554	$ 1,104,197	$ 1,183,176	$ 1,251,357
Deferred debits and other assets					
Unamortized debt reacquisition costs	$ 0	$ 146,841	$ 150,601	$ 175,320	$ 302,561
Deferred litigation items of FPL	125,065	119,371	115,202	110,859	110,859
Deferred pension costs	0	45,918	51,640	0	0
Unamortized insurance policy acquisitions	250,434	0	0	0	0
Other	451,373	107,517	51,343	147,909	138,788
	$ 826,872	$ 419,647	$ 368,786	$ 434,088	$ 552,208
Total assets	$12,325,309	$10,802,008	$11,281,785	$12,306,305	$13,078,012

EXHIBIT 3 *(concluded)*

	1989	1990	1991	1992	1993
Capitalization and Liabilities					
Current liabilities					
Notes payable-commercial paper	$ 125,760	$ 48,814	$ 0	$ 0	$ 349,600
Current maturities of long-term debt	15,933	19,572	136,605	164,004	279,680
Accounts payable	335,509	357,904	389,562	411,369	323,282
Customers' deposits	187,875	189,648	201,014	215,435	216,140
Interest accrued	124,022	105,718	109,748	123,735	109,206
Income and other taxes	0	87,517	98,968	90,929	94,880
Deferred clause revenues	0	0	0	175	130,786
Other	0	127,225	171,061	172,069	335,043
	$ 789,099	$ 936,398	$ 1,106,958	$ 1,177,716	$ 1,838,617
Deferred credits/Other liabilities					
Accumulated deferred income taxes	$ 1,516,483	$ 1,538,645	$ 1,507,231	$ 1,718,388	$ 1,512,067
Deferred regular credit-income taxes	0	0	0	0	216,546
Unamortized investment tax credits	430,351	406,251	368,337	345,438	323,791
Capital lease obligations	0	74,887	279,657	324,198	271,498
Insurance/Banking liabilities	1,584,505	0	0	0	0
Other	583,972	319,804	501,216	393,080	517,653
	$ 4,115,311	$ 2,339,587	$ 2,656,441	$ 2,781,104	$ 2,841,555
Capitalization					
Common stock, $.01 par value	$ 1,333	$ 1,610	$ 1,708	$ 1,828	$ 1,901
Additional paid-in capital	1,780,392	2,566,844	2,886,113	3,312,903	3,589,994
Unearned compensation	279	(360,000)	(346,215)	(336,355)	(321,121)
Retained earnings	1,670,152	952,707	812,241	857,613	829,833
	$ 3,452,156	$ 3,161,161	$ 3,353,847	$ 3,835,989	$ 4,100,607
FPL preferred stock					
without sinking fund	$ 346,250	$ 346,250	$ 346,250	$ 421,250	$ 451,250
with sinking fund	173,050	165,950	150,150	130,150	97,000
Long-term debt	3,449,443	3,852,662	3,668,139	3,960,096	3,748,983
	$ 7,420,899	$ 7,526,023	$ 7,518,386	$ 8,347,485	$ 8,397,840
Total capital and liabilities	$12,325,309	$10,802,008	$11,281,785	$12,306,305	$13,078,012

EXHIBIT 4A FPL Group, Inc. Income Statement for the Years 1989–1993 (thousands of dollars)

Source: 1989–1993 Annual Reports for FPL Group, Inc.

	1989	1990	1991	1992	1993
Operating revenues					
Utility	$4,946,291	$4,987,690	$5,158,766	$5,100,463	$5,224,299
Nonutility	86,253	98,655	90,670	92,864	91,995
Total operating revenues	$5,032,544	$5,086,345	$5,249,436	$5,193,327	$5,316,294
Operating expenses					
Utility operations:					
Fuel/purchased power	$1,775,557	$1,927,233	$1,932,637	$1,829,908	$1,758,298
Operations and maintenance	1,194,871	1,243,583	1,276,244	1,203,474	1,251,284
Cost reduction program	0	0	90,008	0	138,000
Nonutility operation	85,101	102,179	69,469	74,195	70,256
Loss on discontinuing businesses	0	99,850	0	0	0
Depreciation and amortization	636,976	501,269	518,068	554,237	598,389
Taxes other than income taxes	408,320	451,494	485,962	497,739	526,109
	$4,100,825	$4,325,608	$4,372,388	$4,159,553	$4,342,336
Operating income	$ 931,719	$ 760,737	$ 877,048	$1,033,774	$ 973,958
Interest expense and other deductions (income)					
Interest and preferred stock dividends	$ 383,375	$ 393,074	$ 411,079	$ 410,152	$ 409,760
Allowance for funds used during construction	(21,623)	(25,424)	(34,044)	(57,782)	(66,238)
Other, net	(32,685)	(26,981)	(47,456)	(46,978)	(48,812)
	$ 329,067	$ 340,669	$ 329,579	$ 305,392	$ 294,710
Income taxes					
Current	$ 183,723	$ 66,632	$ 186,008	$ 147,961	$ 238,557
Deferred	2,086	55,261	(14,687)	113,472	11,942
	$ 185,809	$ 121,893	$ 171,321	$ 261,433	$ 250,499
Income from continuing operations	$ 416,843	$ 298,175	$ 376,148	$ 466,949	$ 428,749
Income (loss) from discontinued operations	16,494	(689,180)	(135,570)	0	0
Net Income (Loss)	$ 433,337	($ 391,005)	$ 240,578	$ 466,949	$ 428,749

Note: Preferred stock dividends result from intercompany transactions and are not tax deductible.

EXHIBIT 4B FPL Group, Inc. Earnings and Dividends Per Common Share, 1984–1993

Sources: FPL Group, Inc. annual reports, 1989–1993, Value Line, Inc., June 17, 1994.

Year	Earnings Per Share	Earnings Per Share before Extraordinary Items	Dividends Per Share	Average Shares Outstanding (in thousands)
1993	$2.30	$2.76	$2.47	186,413
1992	2.65	2.65	2.43	176,207
1991	1.48	2.66	2.39	162,553
1990	(2.86)	2.64	2.34	136,715
1989	3.12	2.99	2.26	131,544
1988	3.42	3.12	2.18	130,932
1987	3.10	2.69	2.10	129,959
1986	2.90	2.90	2.02	126,004
1985	3.11	3.11	1.94	119,696
1984	2.62	2.65	1.77	118,280

Note: "Earnings per share before extraordinary Items" excludes gains or losses from discontinued operations and charges relating to cost-reduction programs.

EXHIBIT 5 **FPL Group, Inc. Cash Flow Statement for the Years 1989–1993 (thousands of dollars)**

Source: 1989–1993 annual reports for FPL Group, Inc.

	1989	1990	1991	1992	1993
Cash flows from operating activities					
Net income (loss)	$410,416	($ 391,005)	$ 240,578	$ 466,949	$ 428,749
Depreciation and amortization	636,976	501,269	518,068	554,237	598,389
Increase (decrease) in deferred income taxes	31,325	47,912	(31,414)	211,156	10,225
Provision for refunds	38,650	10,257	0	0	0
(Increase) decrease in recoverable storm costs	0	0	0	(57,130)	12,184
Refund of revenues from tax savings rule	(37,692)	(22,960)	0	0	0
Deferrals under cost recovery clauses	(117,340)	(10,483)	120,772	(102,977)	138,949
Charges for discontinuing businesses	0	99,850	0	0	0
Increase (decrease) in accrued interest and taxes	(42,002)	49,962	15,481	5,948	(10,578)
Loss from discontinued operations	(16,494)	689,180	135,570	0	0
Other	59,129	78,813	194,466	(90,521)	89,058
Net cash provided by operating activities	$962,968	$1,052,795	$1,193,521	$ 987,662	$1,266,976
Cash flows from investing activities					
Capital and nuclear fuel expenditures	($836,493)	($1,038,740)	($1,343,931)	($1,390,930)	($1,247,661)
Sale of Colonial Penn	0	0	128,380	0	0
Net cash provided (used) by discontinued operations	58,488	(92,006)	(49,827)	0	0
Receipts from partnerships and leveraged leases	(90,667)	(96,894)	11,572	17,592	82,462
Other	(107,198)	(55,086)	1,427	(10,013)	34,365
Net cash used in investing activities	($975,870)	($1,282,726)	($1,252,379)	($1,383,351)	($1,130,834)
Cash flow from financing activities					
Unearned ESOP compensation	$ 0	($ 360,000)	$ 0	$ 0	$ 0
Issuance of FPL bonds and ether long-term debt	213,542	276,073	265,246	874,633	2,082,993
Issuance of FPL Group capital long-term debt	0	0	0	25,000	125,889
Issuance of preferred stock	0	0	0	125,000	190,000
Proceeds from FPL Group capital borrowings	0	260,000	0	0	0
Retirement of long-term debt and preferred stock	(193,890)	(141,892)	(360,372)	(699,614)	(2,648,170)
Issuance of common stock	73,124	796,491	318,341	422,626	276,287
Dividends on common stock	(297,861)	(323,919)	(392,000)	(430,716)	(461,639)
Sale of nuclear fuel	47,399	75	235,972	0	0
Increase (decrease) in notes payable—commercial paper	107,176	(76,946)	(48,814)	0	349,600
Other	8,478	(7,892)	(3,468)	(13,295)	22,756
Net cash provided (used) in financial activities	($ 42,032)	$ 421,990	$ 14,905	$ 303,634	($ 62,284)
Net increase (decrease) in cash and cash equivalents	($ 54,934)	$ 192,059	($ 43,953)	($ 92,055)	($ 73,858
Cash and cash equivalents at beginning of year	$ 77,039	$ 22,105	$ 214,164	$ 170,211	$ 78,156
Cash and cash equivalents at end of year	$ 22,105	$ 214,164	$ 170,211	$ 78,156	$ 152,014

EXHIBIT 6 **FPL Group—Financial Projections as of March 1994 (thousands of dollars)**

Sources: Donaldson, Lufkin & Jenrette Securities Corp., analyst report, May 1994; Salomon Brothers U.S. Equity Research, analyst report, March 16, 1994; Florida Power & Light Company 1994–1998 forecast and 1993 financial and statistical report.

	1992 Actual	1993 Actual	1994 Estimate	1995 Estimate	1996 Estimate	1997 Estimate	1998 Estimate	1993–1998 Annualized Growth
Florida Power & Light Company								
Electric sales (millions of kWh)	$69,290	$72,455	$74,411	$76,420	$78,484	$80,603	$82,779	2.7%
Customer accounts (thousands)	3,281	3,350	3,437	3,526	3,618	3,712	3,809	2.6
Total capacity (owned by FP&L, in megawatts)	16,627	16,697	17,559	17,563	18,030	18,051	18,051	1.6
Net income	$ 467	$ 429	$ 527	$ 557	$ 576	$ 596	$ 615	
Depreciation and amortization	554	598	665	711	741	778	795	
Capital expenditures	$ 1,270	$ 1,337	$ 901	$ 831	$ 743	$ 769	$ 624	
Maturing debt	152	11	2	81	101	4	185	
Preferred dividends	44	43	40	40	40	40	40	
Common dividends	431	461	—	—	—	—	—	
Average shares outstanding (millions)	176.2	186.4	191.5	192.1	192.1	192.1	192.1	
Capitalization ratios								
Long-term debt	48%	46%	46%	46%	45%	44%	44%	
Preferred stock	6	6	6	6	6	6	6	
Equity	46	47	48	48	50	50	50	

EXHIBIT 7 Investor-Owned Utilities in the Southeast United States in 1993

Sources: Value Line; annual reports; North American Utility Almanac (J. C. Bradford & Co., 1993 edition); Goldman Sachs Selected Electric Utility Industry Statistics (November 1994).

	FPL Group	Carolina Power	Duke Power	Florida Progress	SCANA Corp.	The Southern Co.	TECO Energy, Inc.
Electric subsidiaries	Florida Power and Light Company	Carolina Power and Light Company	Duke Power Co.	Florida Power Corp.	SC Electric and Gas Company	Alabama Power Co. Georgia Power Co. Gulf Power Co. (FL)	Tampa Electric Co.
Markets and customers							
Major markets	East/ South FL	East NC Northeast SC	Central NC Northwest SC	North Central FL	Southwest SC	Northwest FL, GA, and AL	Central FL
Total kWh produced (millions)	72,454.7	45,505.0	76.058.0	28,647.8	16,880.0	119,206.0	13,446.5
Customer mix (percent of sales)							
Residential	56.0%	33.0%	33.0%	47.0%	43.0%	32.0%	44.0%
Commercial	36.0	20.0	24.0	28.0	29.0	26.0	30.0
Industrial	4.0	26.0	28.0	12.0	20.0	27.0	10.0
Utility companies and other	4.0	21.0	15.0	13.0	8.0	15.0	16.0
Capital structure							
Long-term debt/Total capitalization	46.4%	48.2%	39.9%	48.7%	50.2%	45.1%	49.1%
Common stock/Total capitalization	47.3%	49.1%	50.9%	47.5%	47.0%	46.8%	48.3%
Total assets (millions)	$13,078	$8,194	$12,193	$5,639	$4,041	$25,911	$3,128
Profitability							
Return on common stock	12.5%	13.6%	13.2%	10.9%	12.6%	13.0%	14.3%
Earnings per share	$2.75	$2.23	$2.80	$2.26	$3.72	$1.57	$1.30
Cash flow per share	$5.85	$5.09	$5.80	$5.59	$6.02	$3.16	$2.70
Dividend per common share	$2.47	$1.66	$1.84	$1.95	$2.74	$1.14	$0.95
Dividend yield	6%	5%	5%	6%	6%	5%	4%
Payout ratio (all dividends)	91%	74%	68%	87%	74%	75%	73%
Capacity utilization							
Annual load factor[a]	57%	59%	60%	51%	57%	59%	n/a
Capacity margin[b]	8.6%	12.0%	14.3%	11.0%	7.9%	12.1%	13.8%
Percent of power purchased (1993 est.)	30.0%	11.0%	1.0%	15.0%	26.0%	7.0%	3.0%
Costs							
Operation/Maintenance costs/kWh	$0.0075	$0.0103	$0.0072	$0.0070	$0.0051	$0.0059	$0.0049
Busbar cost/kWh[c]	0.0366	0.0403	0.0317	0.0344	0.0293	0.0319	0.0368
Incremental generation cost/kWh[d]	0.0187	0.0154	0.0176	0.0182	0.0186	0.0115	0.0242
Transmission cost/kWh (1987)	0.0019	0.0009	0.0010	0.0010	0.0007	0.0008	0.0006
Rates (average realization per kWh)							
Residential	$0.0811	$0.0828	$0,0732	$0.0792	$0.0713	$0.0732	$0.0813
Commercial	0.0675	0.0694	0.0600	0.0581	0.0562	0.0704	0.0673
Industrial	0.0540	0.0549	0.0431	0.0479	0.0391	0.0451	0.0465

[a]Annual lead factor is the average level of capacity used by the utility.
[b]Capacity margin = (Total capacity – Peak load in summer)/Total capacity.
[c]Busbar cost is the unit output cost of electric power coming out of a generating plant before transmission and distribution.
[d]Incremental generation cost is the marginal cost to produce an additional kilowatt-hour.

EXHIBIT 8 FPL Group Stock Price and Interest Rates

Source: Datastream.

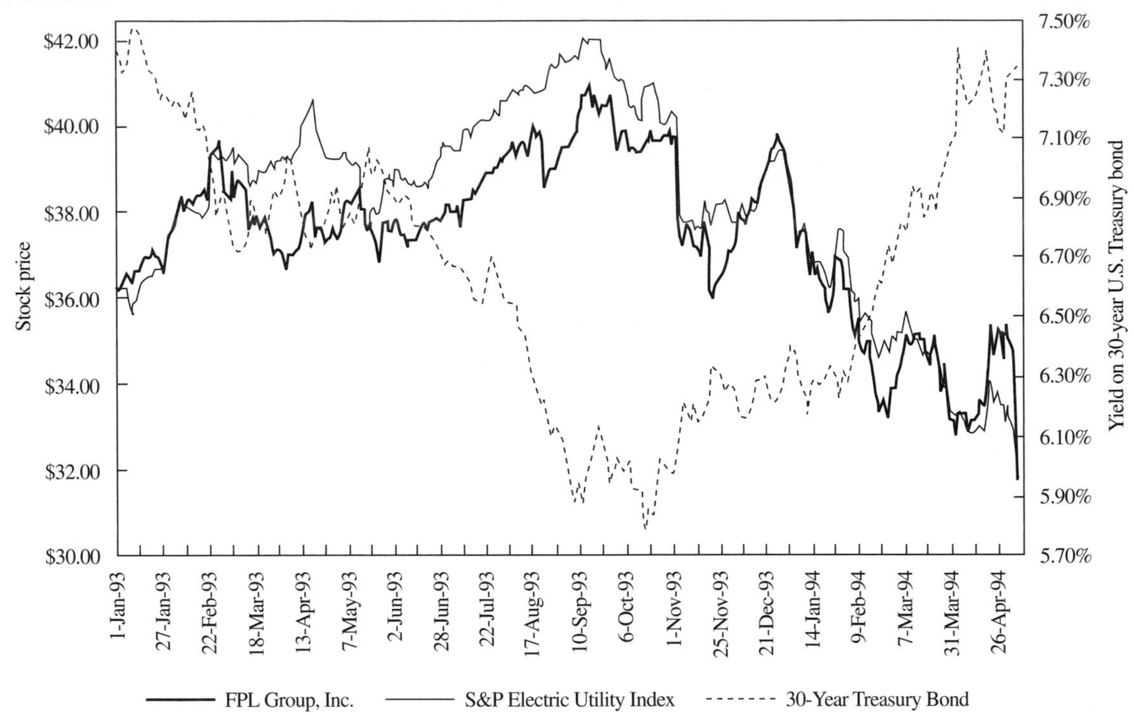

EXHIBIT 9 Dividends by Industry and for Electric Utilities, First Quarter 1994

Sources: *S&P Analysts' Handbook,* September 1994 Monthly Supplement; *Barron's,* May 16, 1994, p. 16.

S&P Industry Groups	Dividend Payout Ratio	Dividend Yield
Health care (drugs)	69.4%	4.1%
Household products	66.9	2.6
Tobacco	65.7	5.2
Publishing (newspapers)	58.0	2.5
Hardware and tools	53.6	2.8
Foods	45.7	2.7
Chemicals (specialty)	39.7	1.8
Cosmetics	39.4	1.9
Telecommunications (long distance)	39.3	2.3
Beverages (soft drinks)	38.2	1.7
Textiles	34.7	2.2
Regional banks	32.6	3.4
Aerospace/Defense	31.0	2.3
Retail (specialty)	29.7	0.9
Shoes	25.5	1.6
Hotel-Motel	25.4	0.9
Entertainment	23.9	0.7
Automobiles	20.6	1.9
Toys	16.0	0.8
Restaurants	15.1	0.8
Computer software/services	10.9	0.4
Electronics (semiconductors)	6.5	0.4
Airlines	deficit	0.1
Steel	deficit	0.9

EXHIBIT 9
(Concluded)

Sample of Electric Utility Companies	Dividend Payout Ratio	Dividend Yield
Texas Utilities	106.2%	9.6%
Oklahoma G&E	93.3	8.6
Potomac Electric	92.2	8.7
Houston Industries	90.9	10.0
Delmarva P&L	90.6	8.4
SCE Corp.	88.7	9.9
NY State E&G	88.0	9.3
Central & SW	87.2	7.9
Public Service of CO	87.0	7.7
Commonwealth Edison	84.2	7.1
Northern State Power	81.9	6.6
American Electric	81.4	8.6
Ohio Edison	81.1	9.0
Dominion Resources	79.4	6.5
Consolidated Edison	75.5	7.1
PacificCorp	74.5	6.5
Carolina P&L	72.3	7.1
Southern Company	71.5	6.5
Pacific G&E	71.3	8.5
Entergy	66.7	6.5
General Public Utilities	65.5	6.6
Duke Power	64.8	5.3
Centerior Energy	61.5	7.7
Philadelphia Electric	60.8	5.8

EXHIBIT 10
FPL Group Ownership Information, First Quarter 1994

Sources: FPL Group 1993 annual report and Proxy Statement (May 4, 1994), CDA/Spectrum, and casewriter estimates.

Type of Shareholder	Percent of Total Shares		Number of Shareholders
Individuals and other	51.9%		85,442
Institutions (total)	36.9		328
Pension funds/Universities		18.4%	
Mutual funds/Money managers		13.0	
Financial institutions		4.3	
Insurance companies		1.2	
ESOP (Fidelity Management is trustee)	11.1		
Insiders (officers and directors)	0.1		17
Total	100.0%		85,787
Number of shares outstanding at 12/31/93 (millions)	190.1		

Note: An ESOP (Employee Stock Ownership Plan) is a program administered by a third-party trustee to encourage employees to purchase stock in the company—often used as a retirement savings vehicle.

Ford Motor Company's Value Enhancement Plan (A)

On April 14, 2000, Ford Motor Co. announced a shareholder Value Enhancement Plan (VEP) to significantly recapitalize the firm's ownership structure. Ford had accumulated $23 billion in cash reserves, close to the company's largest ever cash position and significant relative to Ford's $57 billion equity market capitalization. Under the VEP, Ford would return as much as $10 billion of this cash to shareholders. In exchange for each share currently held, the plan would give stockholders one new share plus the choice of receiving $20 either in cash or additional new Ford common shares. Ford also announced that it would distribute ownership of its Visteon Corp. parts unit to shareholders.

Ford's share price had performed poorly over the previous year (Exhibit 1), and the proposal drew a positive reaction from analysts who had been urging the company for months to distribute cash to stockholders. Some hailed the VEP as the boldest step yet by Ford Chairman William Clay Ford Jr. and Chief Executive Officer Jacques Nasser to convince investors that they were undervaluing the world's No. 2 automaker.

However, the plan raised a number of questions for investors. Why was Ford proposing this transaction instead of a traditional share repurchase or a cash dividend? How did the interests of the Ford family factor into this decision, and what did the transaction imply about the future involvement of the family in the company? Why was Ford distributing such a significant amount of cash at this particular point in time? Did the distribution signal a change in the company's appetite for making acquisitions or future capital expenditures? If shareholders collectively elected to receive less than $10 billion in cash, how would Ford distribute the remaining cash?

Ford Motor Company

Headquartered in Dearborn, Michigan, Ford Motor Company was the world's largest producer of trucks and, after General Motors, the second-largest producer of cars and trucks combined. Ford also engaged in other businesses, including manufacturing automotive components and systems and financing and renting vehicles and equipment. The company had engaged in limited diversification in the 1950s and 1960s, but by the 1990s it had refocused attention on its automotive businesses and financial services. Ford also had grown significantly by acquisition. Recent major transactions included Ford's purchase of Hertz Corporation in 1987, Jaguar Cars in 1989, Volvo Cars in 1999, and Land Rover in early 2000.

Ford competed in an industry that was notoriously sensitive to the economic cycle. (See Exhibit 2 for the relationship between U.S. auto industry sales and GDP growth.)

Professor André F. Perold prepared this case. HBS cases are developed solely as the basis for class discussion. Cases are not intended to serve as endorsements, sources of primary data, or illustrations of effective or ineffective management.

Copyright © 2001 President and Fellows of Harvard College. To order copies or request permission to reproduce materials, call 1-800-545-7685, write Harvard Business School Publishing, Boston, MA 02163, or go to http://www.hbsp.harvard.edu. No part of this publication may be reproduced, stored in a retrieval system, used in a spreadsheet, or transmitted in any form or by means—electronic, mechanical, photocopying, recording, or otherwise—without the permission of Harvard Business School.

Car companies would see large swings in their cash flows as economic growth and the interest rates fluctuated. The industry was particularly badly hit during the oil crisis of the late 1970s and early 1980s when the United States experienced record double-digit inflation and treasury bills yielded almost 20%. In 1980, Chrysler was saved from bankruptcy by a government bailout that took the form of $1.5 billion of loan guarantees. Over the five years ending December 31, 1981, Ford's equity market value fell from $5.8 billion to $2.0 billion. It rebounded rapidly the next year—more than doubling—as economic conditions improved.

The history of Ford Motor Company dates back to its founding by Henry Ford and 11 investors in 1903. At that time, cars were custom made, unreliable, and costly novelties. Ford wanted to make them simple, inexpensive necessities. "The way to make automobiles is to make one automobile like another automobile, to make them all alike, to make them come through the factory just alike, just as one pin is like another pin when it comes from the pin factory," he said when the company was founded.[1] Unwavering in this vision, Henry Ford did not easily share control and, by 1906, he had acquired a majority position in the company's stock. In 1919, when the minority stockholders balked at building the giant (and expensive) River Rouge Plant in Dearborn, Michigan, Henry Ford bought them out. As a result, Ford, his wife, Clara, and their only son, Edsel, acquired full ownership. Ford would soon become the nation's third billionaire after Andrew Carnegie (steel) and John D. Rockefeller (oil). "Rockefeller at the height of his involvement in Standard Oil had owned no more than 27 percent of that company's stock. By contrast, Henry owned all of the Ford Motor Company, which gave him a power no other American industrialist had ever possessed."[2]

In January 1956, Ford Motor Company sold shares to the public. Until then, the Ford family and the Ford Foundation (formed in 1936) had been the company's sole stockholders. The Ford Foundation held by far the majority of the shares outstanding, although its holdings were non-voting Class A shares received upon the deaths of Edsel Ford in 1942 and Henry Ford in 1947. The Ford Foundation pressured the company to create a public market for Ford common shares so that it could sell its Ford shares and reduce its reliance on income received in the form of Ford dividends. Class A shares sold by the Ford Foundation became voting common shares. As shown in Exhibit 3, the Ford Foundation disposed of the last of these shares in 1973.

Going public also gave the company increased access to the capital markets. At that time, Ford was in the midst of a large research and development expenditure related to the Edsel, a car the company hoped would return it to parity with General Motors. The Edsel was introduced with great fanfare in 1957, but production was discontinued in 1959. Ford acknowledged a net loss of $350 million on a project that still ranks among the greatest flops in world business history.

The positions of chairman of the board and chief executive officer of Ford Motor Company were held by Ford family members, Henry Ford and his grandson, Henry Ford II, until Philip Caldwell assumed those roles in 1979. The family continued to be represented on the company's board of directors, and chairmanship of the board again came to be held by a family member when William Clay Ford, Jr. was appointed in January 1999. The composition of Ford's board of directors as of March 1, 2000, is shown in Exhibit 4. An abbreviated Ford family tree is shown in Exhibit 5.

In 1999, Ford recorded record net income of $7.2 billion on record revenues of $162.6 billion. Ford U.S. car and truck sales represented a 24.1% share of that market. The company had manufacturing facilities located in 25 countries on six continents,

[1]Source: Peter Collier and David Horowitz, *The Fords* (New York: Simon & Schuster, 1987, p. 49).

[2]Source: Ibid., p. 90.

and manufacturing employment represented about 80% of Ford's approximately 335,000 employees. Ford was now the world's most profitable auto company, and many believed the firm had achieved efficiencies that would enable it to sustain this position. Exhibit 6 provides selected financial information on Ford, while Exhibit 7 gives a breakdown of the company's cash flows. Exhibits 8 and 9 contain selected financial information on General Motors and DaimlerChrysler, respectively. Exhibit 10 provides auto company valuation information and interest rates as of April 14, 2000.

Ownership Structure

At the time of its initial public offering, Ford modified its structure of multiple share classes in order to preserve family control. In particular, Class B shares had special voting rights and could be owned only by Ford family members. As long as they owned a minimum number of Class B shares, the Ford family would retain 40% of the voting power. When Class B shares were sold outside the Ford family, they reverted to common stock. As shown in Exhibit 3, outstanding Class B shares declined by about 50% over the period 1956–2000 on a split-adjusted basis, but by much more in relation to total shares outstanding. Class B shares received the same per share dividends as paid on Ford's common shares.

As of February 2000, Ford had 1.15 billion common shares and 70.9 million Class B shares outstanding. The Ford family retained its 40% vote as long as it owned at least 60.7 million shares of the Class B stock. If Class B holdings fell between 33.7 million and 60.7 million shares, the family retained voting power of only 30%. Below 33.7 million Class B shares, all special privileges were lost.

Ford's special ownership structure meant that the interests of the Ford family would play a role in determining the company's financial policies. For example, institutional shareholders had for years urged Ford to conduct share repurchases over paying cash dividends. Yet, the family strongly preferred receiving dividends despite the fact that dividends were tax inefficient for many shareholders.[3] Cash dividends provided family members with liquidity without having to sell Class B shares and run the risk of diluting the family's control. Liquidity needs could be especially large in cases of divorce settlements or at times when Ford heirs died and large estate taxes had to be paid. In February 2000, there were 101 holders of Class B shares.

The Value Enhancement Plan

Under the terms of the Value Enhancement Plan, shareholders would exchange their existing common and Class B shares one-for-one for new Ford common and new Class B shares, respectively. In addition, all shareholders would receive either $20 per share in cash or the equivalent value in new Ford common shares based on Ford's stock price in late July 2000. For example, at a pre-distribution share price of $60 for existing common shares, new Ford shares would be worth $40. Stockholders thus would have the choice to receive $20 of cash or half a share of new Ford common. Shareholders also could elect to receive a combination of cash and new Ford common stock with an

[3]Shareholders were taxed on cash dividends at ordinary income rates, whereas gains realized on shares that were repurchased received capital gains treatment. For individual taxpayers in 2000, the highest U.S. federal tax bracket for ordinary income was 39.6% while long-term capital gains were generally taxed at a maximum rate of 20%. For the company, cash paid out in the form of dividends versus share repurchases was tax neutral since deductions were not allowed in either case.

aggregate value of $20. Shareholders who did not make an election would be treated as if they made a $20 all-cash election.

Ford officials said they thought 40% of shareholders would take the cash option. In the event that the cash option was oversubscribed, the $20-per-share payment would be distributed pro rata to ensure that the company distributed at most $10 billion. Dividends on new Ford shares would be reduced such that shareholders who elected stock only would get about the same dividend payment on their package of new shares as the quarterly $0.50 per share currently being paid.

The company later amended the VEP to offer shareholders a third option under which they could elect to receive a combination of cash and stock worth $20, where the relative cash/stock proportions would be chosen to allow shareholders to maintain the same percentage interest in the company as they had before the transaction. These proportions could only be determined once the shareholder elections had been received. This option was aimed at passive investors, including index funds, who invested in companies in proportions based on the market capitalization of their shares. Observers thought that 20% or more of Ford's shareholders might elect this option.

With respect to taxation, the company said that since shareholders receiving the cash distribution would suffer a "meaningful reduction" in their percentage ownership of the company, they would be taxed on that amount as a capital gain. Shareholders who received shares in lieu of cash would pay capital gains taxes on those shares only when they were sold.[4]

As part of the Value Enhancement Plan, Ford also announced that Visteon, its parts unit with $19 billion in revenues, would be spun off to shareholders. (The actual spin-off of Visteon would occur on June 28, 2000, and its market capitalization would be approximately $2 billion.) Visteon was the second-largest auto supplier, after Delphi Automotive Systems Corp., which General Motors Corp. had spun off to shareholders in 1999. The decision to spin off Visteon had been expected for months, but had met with opposition from U.S. employees represented by the United Auto Workers union. Protesters worried that it could mean fewer union jobs and lower wages. Strike plans were aborted after Ford agreed to keep Visteon workers on its payroll, guaranteeing wages and benefits under the current contract.

The Visteon part of the plan represented the second major spin-off of a Ford subsidiary in less than two years. In April 1998, Ford had distributed to shareholders its 80.7% interest in Associates First Capital valued at $26.6 billion.

Effect on Employee Savings Plans and Stock Options

Employees presently owned approximately 200 million shares of Ford common stock through various company savings plans for salaried and hourly employees. As with other shareholders, participants in these plans would receive cash by default if they did not make an election. However, any cash received for employees who made no election would be invested on their behalf in Ford common shares through open market purchases.

Employee stock options to buy Ford common shares would be adjusted as if the employees elected to receive all shares. For example, at an exchange rate of 1.5 new shares for each existing share, an employee who had an option to purchase 100 shares with a current exercise price of $30 would receive a new option to purchase 150 new shares with an exercise price of $20 per share. As of December 31, 1999, employees held options to purchase 75.3 million shares at an average exercise price of $32.66.

[4]The special tax treatment of the cash disbursement as a capital gain rather than ordinary income did not necessarily apply to shareholders owning more than 1% of Ford's shares outstanding or to shareholders who exercised control over corporate affairs.

Ford's Stated Rationale for the Recapitalization

Ford gave the following explanation for the recapitalization:[5]

> Ford believes the recapitalization will provide value, flexibility, liquidity, and alignment for Ford stockholders, and tie Ford management even more closely to the interests of Ford stockholders. Ford believes that its stock is undervalued, limiting, among other things, the Company's ability to use its stock for acquisitions or to attract, retain or incentivize employees. Ford believes the recapitalization will highlight its cash reserves and cash flow generating capacity, which have not been adequately reflected in its stock price.
>
> The recapitalization also will reshuffle ownership interests in the Company's revised capital structure, as Ford stockholders elect to increase or reduce their relative equity investment in the Company. Moreover, in Ford's judgment, certain objectives in the recapitalization, such as stockholder liquidity, could not be achieved as effectively through a conventional share repurchase. In particular, the recapitalization is responsive to the interests of stockholders who would ordinarily be disinclined to sell any portion of their existing Ford shares. The commitment to Ford of these long-term stockholders, which include current and retired employees, holders of Class B stock, and certain retail and institutional investors, is a source of strategic advantage to the Company. Finally, by allowing for the distribution of additional new common shares to holders of Class B stock, the recapitalization will more closely align the interests of all Ford stockholders.
>
> Executive officers of Ford generally are expected to elect to receive only stock in the recapitalization. More broadly, Ford's employee stock option and restricted stock programs will be adjusted to reflect the issuance of new shares in the recapitalization. As a consequence of the executive elections and the adjustments in the employee incentive plans, the recapitalization will tie Ford management's compensation even more closely to the performance of Ford's stock price.

In a company press release when the VEP was first announced, Chairman Bill Ford commented that "this innovative and unprecedented plan reflects our confidence in the outlook for our business and an absolute commitment to rewarding our shareholders. This action is indicative of the new mindset at Ford Motor Co. and our confidence in the future. It is shareholder-friendly because it offers all shareholders an option, the choice of cash or increased ownership." He added that by allowing the distribution of common shares to holders of Class B stock, the VEP would more closely align the interests of all Ford stockholders.

With respect to the Visteon spin-off, Mr. Ford said, "We believe independence for Visteon will result in it being a stronger competitor and is in the best long-term interest of both Visteon employees and Ford Motor Company shareholders." He said the separation would allow the automaker to focus on its core business and give Visteon a chance to build its client base outside Ford.[6]

Ford CEO and President Jacques Nasser said, "These pioneering actions will allow us to immediately reward our shareholders and accelerate our transformation into a leading consumer-focused company. Today's actions reflect our intense effort to transform and strengthen our overall business, unleash the spirit of the Ford team, better connect with customers, and reward shareholders while maintaining strategic flexibility."[7]

[5]Source: Ford SEC filings.

[6]Source: Company press release on April 14, 2000.

[7]Source: Ibid.

Immediate Outside Reaction

On Wall Street the reaction was generally very positive. Morgan Stanley auto analyst Stephen Girsky noted that "it is the first time in over a decade that Ford is returning excess cash to shareholders. It sends a message as to management's confidence in the future of the business."[8]

Girsky also noted that the deal rewarded shareholders much faster than would a traditional stock buyback, which could have taken as long as a year to execute without significantly affecting Ford's stock price. Companies conducting open market repurchases were in any event limited by SEC rules on any given day to repurchasing no more than 25% of average daily volume during the prior four weeks. Ford's average daily volume in March 2000 was 8.3 million shares. Alternative mechanisms for conducting share repurchases included fixed price tender offers (usually at a premium to prevailing prices) or auctions (at prices determined by the marketplace).

Goldman Sachs auto analyst Gary Lapidus said: "It's a powerful statement about the strength of Ford Motor Company's new business model. Great products, strong brands, shareholder and customer focused, Web-enabled, less asset intensive, less cyclical, and reinvesting capital for profitable growth, not for growth's sake." Lapidus also noted that Ford had not received much credit for its large cash position or its strong cash flow, which he estimated at $5 billion a year. He thought that Ford shares should be trading at $70 per share.[9] (Goldman Sachs had a relationship with Ford dating back to as early as the company's initial public offering and had advised Ford on the VEP transaction.)

Analysts further contended that the VEP avoided the difficulties a share buyback would have posed for the Ford family. By participating in a share repurchase, the family would have risked reducing its voting rights in the company. Mr. Ford had said that the family had agreed to take its portion of the distribution in the form of new Ford common shares, not cash. The family thus would have tens of millions of common shares to sell for liquidity purposes without reducing their holding of Class B shares.

Some analysts wondered whether the distribution of cash meant that Ford no longer would be spending heavily on acquisitions. Given the already significant consolidation in the global auto industry, the list of remaining acquisition candidates had grown shorter. Nevertheless, Mr. Nasser insisted during a press conference that the company would retain the flexibility to make more deals. Indeed, in June 2000, Ford would post the winning bid of $6.9 billion to purchase the troubled Korean auto manufacturer Daewoo Motor Company. (The deal ultimately was not consummated and Daewoo filed for bankruptcy in November 2000.)

In the stock market on April 14, 2000, investors initially welcomed the announcements. Ford shares rose 2% to $55.56 in morning trading on the New York Stock Exchange. But in a rapidly falling market, with the S&P 500 index down 5.8% for the day, Ford's shares closed down $3.07, or 5.6%, at $51.38.

Credit-rating agencies downgraded Ford's debt (from A+ to A) after the announcement of the VEP, warning that the restructuring reduced the company's ability to weather a downturn. But Ford officials said they expected this reaction and were comfortable with their new credit ratings.

[8]Source: "Ford Announces Shareholder Value Actions," Morgan Stanley research report, April 14, 2000.

[9]Source: Mark Yost, "Analysts Applaud Ford's Visteon Spinoff, $10 Billion Dividend," *Dow Jones Business News,* April 16, 2000.

Shareholder Objections

Certain Ford shareholders were quite critical about the structure of the transaction. In particular, Teachers Annuity and Insurance Association-College Retirement Equities Fund (TIAA-Cref) and the California Public Employees' Retirement System (Calpers), which owned 8.4 million and 6.5 million shares of Ford common stock, respectively, announced that they would oppose the VEP on the grounds that the transaction unfairly favored the Ford family over common shareholders.

In a proxy statement filed on July 18, 2000, TIAA-Cref and Calpers argued that:

> The Ford family would be able to maintain its 40-percent voting power with only 3.6 percent of the company's total equity after the transaction, versus the five-percent equity stake it currently holds. This is fundamentally at odds with the one share, one vote principle that constitutes perhaps the single most important tenet of good corporate governance. . . . Completion of the recapitalization would set an ominous precedent for the company to engage in similar restructurings going forward, in each case allowing the family to decrease its equity stake without giving up voting control. The establishment of such a precedent is clearly inimical to the interests of common shareholders and exposes the public to the risks of continuing dilution of their voting rights in the future.
>
> We are also skeptical of management's attempts to distinguish the present transaction from a stock dividend. The Class B shareholders will, in fact, receive shares of common stock in the recapitalization, in violation of the spirit (though not the letter) of the certificate's prohibition against the paying of common stock dividends on the Class B shares. We believe that common shareholders should, at a minimum, have the right to independently approve or reject a transaction that would result in the issuance of common shares to the Ford family.
>
> Finally, we note that Ford could have achieved the primary averred goal of the VEP—namely, the enhancement of shareholder value—through any number of mechanisms that avoided the VEP's dilutive effect on holders of the common stock. A straight stock repurchase or the declaration of a . . . dividend, for instance, could have satisfied investors and potentially reassured the market. Management made a conscious choice to pursue the VEP in lieu of such more basic alternatives, however, in an apparent attempt to preserve the Ford family's voting power.

Final Terms

On July 28, 2000, Ford announced that stockholders electing the share option would receive 0.748 new Ford common shares in lieu of $20 cash. This exchange rate was based on the $46.7317 volume-weighted average trading price of Ford common stock on the New York Stock Exchange during the five-day trading period ending July 28.

On Tuesday, August 1, Ford's shares closed at $46.875. Shareholders had to vote for or against the recapitalization proposal, and they had to elect the form in which to receive the distribution of $20 per share. The votes and elections were due the next day by 8:30 A.M.

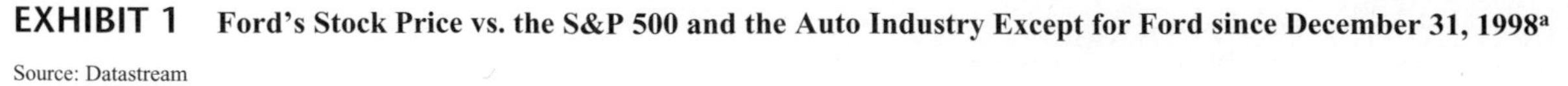

EXHIBIT 1 Ford's Stock Price vs. the S&P 500 and the Auto Industry Except for Ford since December 31, 1998[a]

Source: Datastream

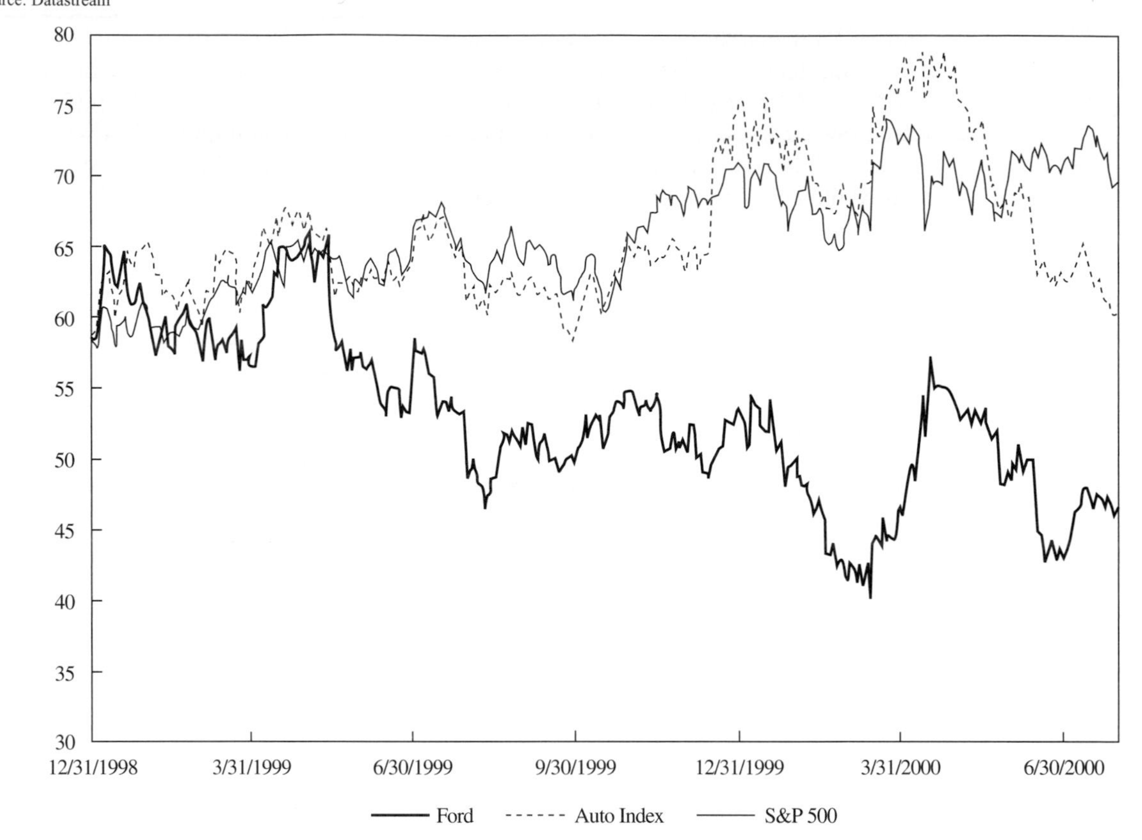

[a]The auto industry ex Ford is represented here by an equally-weighted index of General Motors, DaimlerChrysler, and Toyota stock returns. The starting S&P 500 and auto industry index levels are normalized to equal Ford's stock price on 12/31/98.

EXHIBIT 2 Growth in U.S. GDP and Big Three[a] Revenues, 1951–1999

Source: Datastream

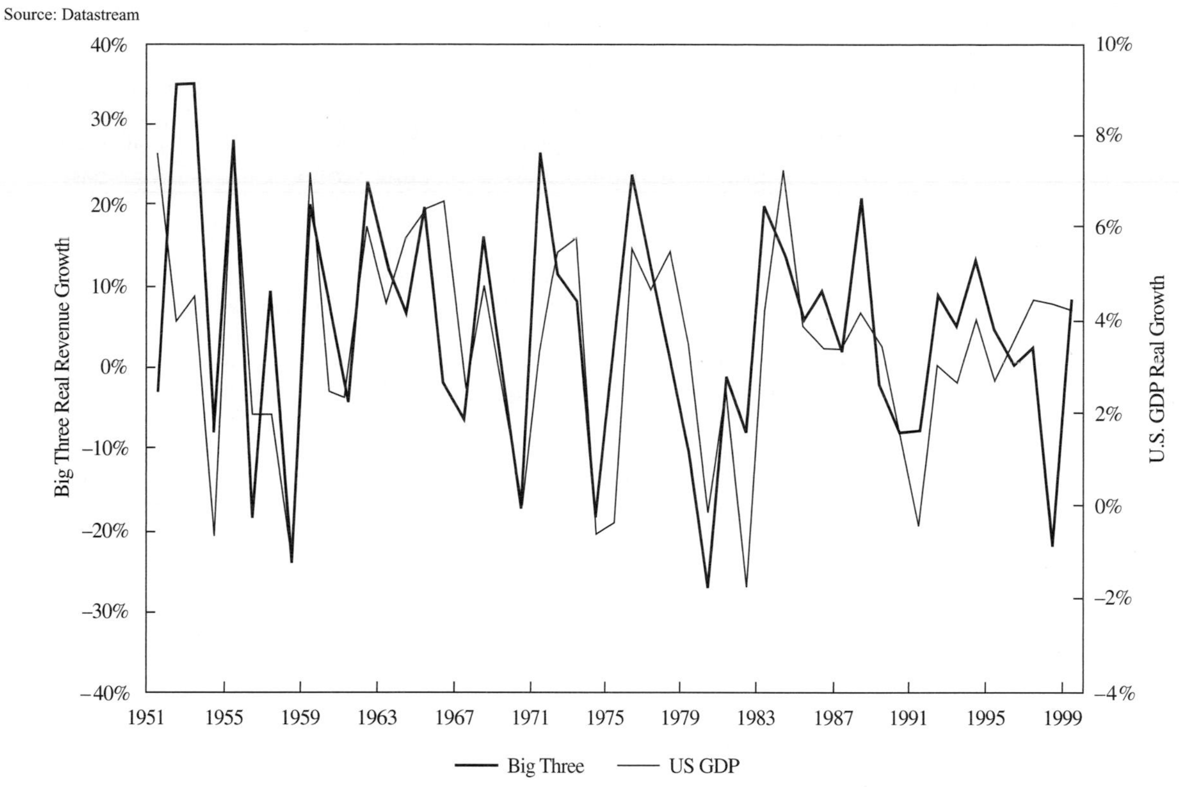

[a]The Big Three automakers were General Motors, Ford, and Chrysler (now DaimlerChrysler).

EXHIBIT 3 Ford Shares Outstanding, 1956–1999 (adjusted for stock splits)

Sources: Ford Motor Company annual reports and proxy statements; historical archives maintained by Elizabeth Adkins and James Sharon, Dearborn, Michigan; company investor relations.

Year	Total Shares Outstanding	Common Shares (Voting)	A Shares (Held by Ford Foundation, Non-voting)	B Shares (Held by Ford Family, Super-voting)	Common Shares Owned by Ford Family Board Members
1956	1,215,308,138	256,629,510	812,975,378	145,703,250	23
1957	1,225,925,325	270,078,323	812,975,378	142,871,625	1,625,625
1958	1,232,141,468	277,571,340	812,975,378	141,594,750	2,822,445
1959	1,234,384,088	371,137,298	721,659,128	141,587,663	1,650,353
1960	1,235,626,830	376,066,170	717,981,660	141,579,000	1,440,855
1961	1,237,900,478	467,862,728	628,470,788	141,566,963	839,745
1962	1,241,012,880	530,671,793	568,778,288	141,562,800	1,709,550
1963	1,244,410,335	581,380,729	522,405,281	140,624,325	1,215,596
1964	1,247,509,148	588,804,210	520,692,255	138,012,683	3,033,641
1965	1,250,714,430	674,903,081	437,812,504	137,998,845	2,888,010
1966	1,236,529,924	712,698,221	385,839,608	137,992,095	2,932,706
1967	1,233,429,671	733,178,790	363,052,755	137,198,126	2,964,150
1968	1,232,027,505	760,368,578	334,681,459	136,977,469	1,579,804
1969	1,229,813,168	790,385,501	302,459,231	136,968,435	1,557,709
1970	1,227,018,803	818,028,146	272,105,348	136,885,309	1,565,235
1971	1,172,092,826	846,098,708	189,462,195	136,531,924	918,956
1972	1,132,758,619	876,225,566	120,372,739	136,160,314	950,456
1973	1,115,889,941	904,308,480	75,480,334	136,101,128	883,496
1974	1,052,884,496	916,878,803		136,005,694	927,990
1975	1,060,925,006	925,261,121		135,663,885	968,096
1976	1,063,522,631	928,122,131		135,400,500	904,500
1977	1,069,687,422	937,929,591		131,757,831	738,324
1978	1,079,343,765	950,151,546		129,192,219	968,652
1979	1,084,753,620	959,332,149		125,421,471	747,351
1980	1,091,700,000	966,600,000		125,100,000	400,707
1981	1,085,400,000	971,100,000		114,300,000	492,120
1982	1,085,400,000	980,100,000		105,300,000	522,054
1983	1,098,000,000	1,009,200,000		88,800,000	288,426
1984	1,095,000,000	1,011,600,000		83,400,000	424,302
1985	1,116,600,000	1,033,800,000		82,800,000	470,796
1986	1,073,600,000	996,400,000		77,200,000	482,072
1987	1,015,000,000	939,600,000		75,400,000	238,114
1988	982,000,000	907,600,000		74,400,000	695,870
1989	945,600,000	874,800,000		70,900,000	733,230
1990	946,200,000	875,400,000		70,900,000	646,672
1991	966,000,000	896,000,000		70,900,000	855,296
1992	978,000,000	908,000,000		70,900,000	646,672
1993	998,000,000	928,000,000		70,900,000	1,080,282
1994	1,023,000,000	952,000,000		70,900,000	560,590
1995	1,160,000,000	1,089,000,000		70,900,000	1,262,366
1996	1,189,000,000	1,118,000,000		70,900,000	1,908,274
1997	1,203,000,000	1,132,000,000		70,900,000	1,987,399
1998	1,222,000,000	1,151,000,000		70,900,000	2,127,601
1999	1,222,000,000	1,151,000,000		70,900,000	2,317,054

EXHIBIT 4 Ford Motor Company Board of Directors as of March 1, 2000

Source: Ford Motor Company 1999 annual report.

Board Member	Age	Director Since	Share Ownership		Occupation
			Common	Class B	
Michael D. Dingman	68	1981	106,505	0	President and CEO of Shipston Group, Ltd.
Edsel B. Ford II	51	1988	245,680	5,633,928	Retired vice president of Ford Motor Company and president and chief operating officer of Ford Credit. Joined Ford in 1974 and held numerous positions in the Company's Ford and Lincoln-Mercury divisions.
William Clay Ford	74	1948	2,020,585	15,136,209	Retired chairman of Ford's Finance Committee. Employed with the Company since 1949. Held numerous executive positions and in 1978 became chairman of the board's Executive Committee. Elected to vice chairman of the board in 1980, retiring from that position in 1989.
William Clay Ford, Jr.	42	1988	188,239	3,300,320	Chairman of the Board of Directors since January 1999. Employed with the Company since 1979 and held a number of management positions at Ford. Named chairman of the board's Finance Committee in 1995.
Irvine O. Hockaday, Jr.	63	1987	19,815	0	President and CEO of Hallmark Cards, Inc.
Marie-Josée Kravis	50	1995	11,322	0	Senior fellow of the Hudson Institute Inc.
Ellen R. Marram	53	1988	23,465	0	President and CEO of efdex inc.
Jacques A. Nasser	52	1999	171,441	0	Named president and CEO of Ford in January 1999 after holding a variety of senior and global positions since joining the Company in 1968.
Dr. Homer A. Neal	57	1997	3,991	0	Director, University of Michigan ATLAS Project, professor of physics and interim president emeritus of the university.
Jorma J. Ollila	49	2000	2,000	0	Chairman and CEO of Nokia Corp.
Carl E. Reichardt	68	1986	23,298	0	Retired chairman and CEO of Wells Fargo & Company.
Robert E. Rubin	61	1999	5,000	0	Director, chairman of the executive committee and member of the Office of the Chairman, Citigroup, Inc. and former U.S. Secretary of the Treasury.
John L. Thornton	46	1996	21,118	0	President and co-chief operating officer of The Goldman Sachs Group, Inc.

EXHIBIT 5 Abbreviated Ford Family Tree

Source: Peter Collier and David Horowitz, *The Fords* (New York: Simon & Schuster, 1987).

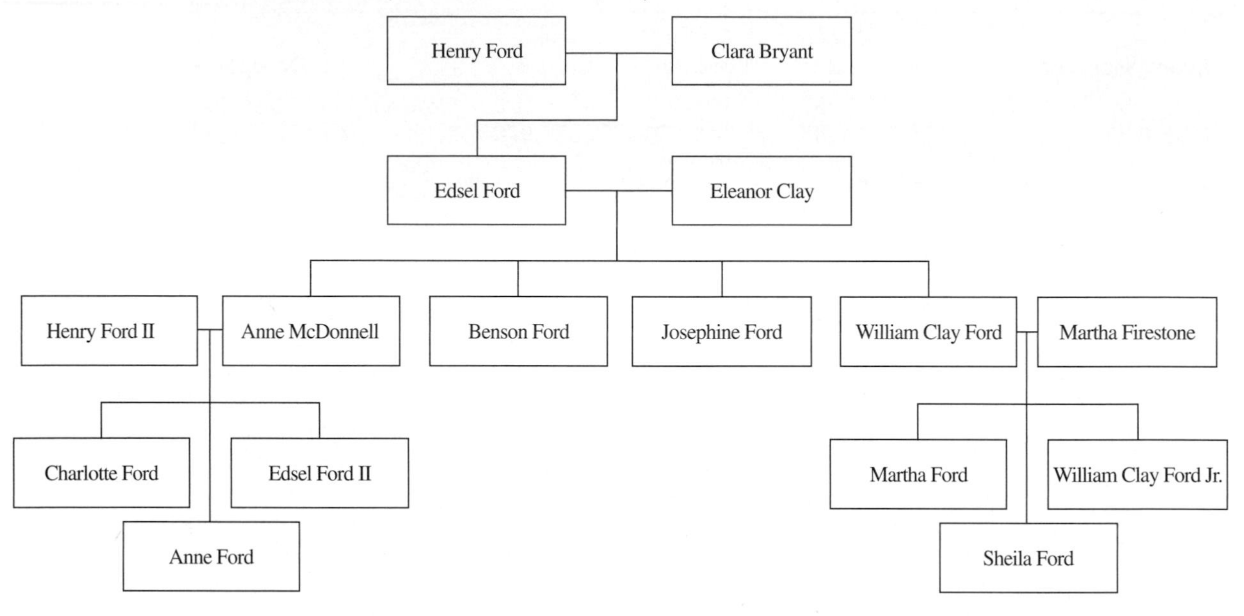

EXHIBIT 6 **Miscellaneous Ford Financial Information, 1986–1999 (consolidated, as of December 31, figures in $ millions except per share items)**

Sources: Company SEC filings and casewriter adjustments.

	1999	1998[a]	1997	1996	1995	1994	1993	1992	1991	1990	1989	1988	1987	1986
Selected Income Statement Items														
Total revenues	162,558	144,416	153,627	146,991	137,137	128,439	108,521	100,132	88,286	97,650	96,146	92,446	79,893	69,694
Automotive revenues	136,973	119,083	122,935	118,023	110,496	107,137	91,568	84,407	72,051	81,844	82,879	82,193	71,797	62,868
Gross profit	33,855	32,291	33,997	29,055	27,824	25,408	18,228	13,877	11,762	15,420	18,209	17,240	12,650	10,138
Depreciation and amortization	15,193	14,329	13,583	12,791	11,719	9,336	7,468	6,756	5,778	4,880	4,229	3,792	3,460	3,152
Operating profit	18,662	17,962	20,414	16,264	16,105	16,072	10,760	7,121	5,984	10,540	13,980	13,448	9,190	6,986
Pretax income	11,026	25,395	10,939	6,793	6,705	8,789	4,003	(127)	(2,587)	1,495	6,030	8,343	7,885	5,620
Income taxes	3,670	3,176	3,741	2,166	2,379	3,329	1,350	295	(395)	530	2,113	2,999	3,226	2,324
Net income	7,237	6,116	6,920	4,446	4,139	5,308	2,529	(502)	(2,258)	860	3,835	5,300	4,625	3,285
Selected Cash Flow Items														
Capital expenditures	10,274	10,407	9,675	10,410	10,456	9,470	6,814	5,790	5,847	7,163	6,767	4,782	3,612	3,353
Net common equity issued	(371)	(932)	295	192	(1,274)	715	394	1,325	-	-	(895)	(816)	(1,342)	(700)
Cash dividends	2,290	5,348	2,020	1,800	1,559	1,205	1,086	977	927	1,389	1,404	1,114	805	591
Selected Balance Sheet Items														
Cash and marketable securities	25,173	24,956	22,453	19,103	15,096	13,822	12,307	12,217	12,928	8,247	7,102	10,477	10,684	9,769
Net property, plant, and equipment	42,317	37,320	34,594	33,527	31,273	27,048	23,059	22,160	22,522	22,208	18,605	15,992	14,034	13,201
Automotive assets	105,181	88,744	85,079	79,658	72,772	68,639	61,737	57,170	52,397	50,824	45,819	43,128	39,734	34,021
Financial Services assets	171,048	148,801	194,018	183,209	170,511	150,983	137,201	123,375	122,032	122,839	115,074	100,239	76,260	59,211
Automotive long-term debt	10,542	8,713	7,047	6,495	5,475	7,103	7,084	7,068	6,539	4,553	1,137	1,336	2,058	2,467
Financial Services long-term debt	67,517	55,468	73,198	70,641	68,259	58,104	47,900	42,369	43,680	40,779	37,784	30,777	26,009	19,128
Shareholders' equity	27,537	23,409	30,734	26,762	24,547	21,659	15,574	14,753	22,690	23,238	22,728	21,529	18,493	14,860
Equity market capitalization	64,379	70,867	57,709	37,876	33,084	28,165	31,788	20,706	13,416	12,439	20,367	24,483	18,884	8,527
EPS (fully diluted)	5.86	4.86	5.62	3.64	3.33	4.44	2.10	(7.81)	(2.40)	0.92	4.06	5.40	4.46	3.03
Dividends per share	1.88	1.72	1.65	1.47	1.23	0.91	0.80	0.80	0.98	1.50	1.50	1.15	0.79	0.56

[a]1998 profits exclude a $15,955 million non-cash gain related to the spin-off to shareholders of Associates First Capital; 1998 dividends include a special $3.2 billion dividend paid in conjunction with the Associates First Capital spin-off.

EXHIBIT 7 Ford Motor Company Condensed Statement of Changes in Cash and Marketable Securities, 1986–1999 (consolidated, figures in $ millions)[a]

Sources: Company SEC filings and casewriter adjustments.

	1999	1998[b]	1997	1996	1995	1994	1993	1992	1991	1990	1989	1988	1987	1986
Net income	7,237	6,116	6,920	4,446	4,139	5,308	2,529	(502)	(2,258)	860	3,835	5,300	4,625	3,285
Depreciation and amortization	15,193	14,329	13,583	12,791	11,719	9,336	7,468	6,756	5,778	4,880	4,229	3,792	3,460	3,152
Decrease (increase) in net working capital[c]	5,856	8,348	9,723	6,999	4,446	6,065	2,606	5,730	7,874	1,426	(207)	761	6,003	5,648
Operating Cash Flow	28,286	28,793	30,226	24,236	20,304	20,709	12,603	11,984	11,394	7,166	7,857	9,853	14,088	12,085
Capital expenditures	(10,274)	(10,407)	(9,675)	(10,410)	(10,456)	(9,470)	(6,814)	(5,790)	(5,847)	(7,163)	(6,767)	(4,782)	(3,612)	(3,353)
Decrease (increase) in Financial Services receivables[d]	(23,645)	(21,088)	(25,735)	(22,174)	(25,689)	(27,337)	(19,001)	(6,656)	(239)	(6,620)	2,012	(13,368)	(15,561)	(12,216)
Net other investments	(6,363)	(801)	(666)	777	638	41	2,358	(365)	(2,097)	(13)	(4,516)	(145)	(4,549)	(907)
Investing Cash Flow	(40,282)	(32,296)	(36,076)	(31,807)	(35,507)	(36,766)	(23,457)	(12,811)	(8,183)	(13,796)	(9,270)	(18,295)	(23,722)	(16,476)
Net common equity issued	(371)	(932)	295	192	(1,274)	715	394	1,325	0	0	(895)	(816)	(1,342)	(700)
Cash dividends	(2,290)	(5,348)	(2,020)	(1,800)	(1,559)	(1,205)	(1,086)	(977)	(927)	(1,389)	(1,404)	(1,114)	(805)	(591)
Net increase (decrease) in debt	16,369	13,920	10,920	12,196	18,785	17,399	14,384	2,841	2,424	9,280	3,029	12,118	12,044	9,353
Financing activities, other	(1,495)	(1,634)	5	990	525	663	(2,748)	(3,073)	(27)	(116)	(2,691)	(1,953)	652	(492)
Financing Cash Flow	12,213	6,006	9,200	11,578	16,477	17,572	10,944	116	1,470	7,775	(1,960)	8,236	10,549	7,570
Net Change in Cash and Marketable Securities = Operating + Investing + Financing Cash Flows	217	2,503	3,350	4,007	1,274	1,515	90	(711)	4,681	1,145	(3,375)	(207)	915	3,179

[a]The accounting rules for marketable securities are somewhat complex. Depending on the type of security, and the purpose of the purchase, a purchase (or sale) will flow through either Operating or Investing Cash Flow. Changes to the account balances will, again, depending on the type and purpose of the security, flow through either the income statement, or a separate component of stockholders' equity. Because Ford treats marketable securities similar to cash (and most of the balance is treated as operational flows), this exhibit treats marketable securities as part of working capital. Consistent with this view, the purchase (sale) of, and changes in, marketable securities are included in the Operating Cash Flow statement, except for those explicitly listed in the SEC filings under Investing Cash Flow.

[b]1998 profits exclude a $15,995 million non-cash gain related to the spin-off to shareholders of Associates First Capital.

[c]The net change in current assets minus current liabilities. This includes adjustments for the effects of foreign currency exchange rate fluctuations.

[d]The account, Financial Services receivables, represents primarily the value of the outstanding loans and leases on the vehicle purchases (and leases) that the Financial Services division has financed. An increase in receivables suggests that the division has funded net new loans and leases.

EXHIBIT 8 **Miscellaneous General Motors Financial Information, 1986–1999 (consolidated, as of December 31, figures in $ millions except per share items)**

Sources: Company SEC filings.

	1999	1998	1997	1996	1995	1994	1993	1992	1991	1990	1989	1988	1987	1986
Selected Income Statement Items														
Total sales	176,558	155,445	178,174	164,013	168,829	154,951	138,220	132,429	123,056	124,705	126,932	123,642	101,782	102,813
Automotive sales	156,107	137,161	153,683	145,341	143,666									
Gross profit	30,904	24,988	31,954	26,238	28,779	25,497	20,266	15,743	14,688	17,230	19,946	19,146	14,578	13,615
Depreciation and amortization	12,318	11,147	11,803	7,145	12,021	10,251	9,442	8,959	7,916	7,362	7,168	7,081	6,112	6,594
Operating profit	18,586	13,841	20,151	19,093	16,758	15,246	10,824	6,784	6,772	9,868	12,778	12,065	2,569	1,431
Pretax income	9,047	4,944	7,714	6,620	9,776	8,353	2,575	(3,333)	(5,892)	(2,217)	6,398	6,735	3,491	2,644
Income taxes	3,118	1,636	1,069	1,723	2,844	2,695	110	(713)	(900)	(231)	2,174	2,103	(60)	(300)
Net income	6,002	2,956	6,698	4,963	6,881	4,901	2,466	(23,498)	(4,453)	(1,986)	4,224	4,856	3,551	2,945
Selected Cash Flow Items														
Capital expenditures	7,384	8,231	8,647	9,949	10,077	7,225	6,470	6,590	7,300	7,588	7,505	5,627	7,057	11,712
Net common issuance	(1,865)	(2,746)	(3,751)	229	(1,176)	1,185	594	5,549	2,497	14	(1,482)	(534)	422	(352)
Cash dividends	1,367	1,388	1,620	1,530	1,328	1,112	1,084	1,377	1,162	1,957	1,964	1,658	1,668	1,663
Selected Balance Sheet Items														
Cash and equivalents	12,140	10,276	22,984	22,262	16,643	16,076	17,962	15,275	10,092	7,821	10,213	10,181	7,744	7,315
Net property, plant, and equipment	38,523	37,176	34,567	37,504	37,740	34,780	34,225	35,350	36,826	36,145	33,995	31,931	32,040	30,376
Total assets[a]	274,730	246,688	221,767	216,965	217,123	198,599	188,201	191,013	184,326	180,237	173,297	164,063	168,102	146,222
Automotive assets	125,561	114,594	115,761	110,247	91,162	88,065	81,009	83,617	72,677	69,264	64,598	60,420	58,860	46,708
Financial Services assets	149,169	132,094	109,319	98,578	94,470	84,555	79,352	83,610	91,415	92,966	89,852	84,445	98,527	90,781
Total debt	129,697	114,871	93,027	85,300	83,324	73,730	70,441	82,952	94,022	95,634	93,425	88,130	85,797	80,604
Automotive long-term debt	7,415	7,118	5,491	5,192	5,968	6,082	6,218	6,857	6,405	4,615	4,255	4,243	3,949	4,007
Shareholders' equity	20,644	15,052	17,506	23,418	23,346	13,274	6,048	6,991	28,617	32,154	36,633	35,672	33,225	30,678
Equity market cap.	45,024	46,874	42,127	42,182	39,815	31,777	39,516	22,795	17,930	20,817	25,590	25,589	19,056	20,932
EPS (fully diluted)	9.18	4.18	8.62	6.02	7.21	5.15	2.13	(38.28)	(7.97)	(4.09)	6.33	7.17	5.03	4.11
DPS	2.00	2.00	2.00	1.60	1.10	0.80	0.80	1.40	1.60	3.00	3.00	2.50	2.50	2.50

[a]Total assets can differ from the sum of Automotive and Financial assets due to eliminations and other adjustments.

EXHIBIT 9 Miscellaneous DaimlerChrysler Financial Information, 1986–1999 (consolidated, as of December 31, figures in $ millions except per share items)

Sources: Company SEC filings.

	1999	1998[a]	1997	1996	1995	1994	1993	1992	1991	1990	1989	1988	1987	1986
Selected Income Statement Items														
Total sales	151,035	154,615	61,147	61,397	53,195	52,235	43,600	36,897	29,370	30,620	34,922	34,148	28,308	22,977
Gross profit	41,404	41,524	9,447	10,825	7,827	10,270	7,841	5,114	3,211	4,303	5,717	5,849	5,533	2,965
Depreciation and amortization	9,415	8,601	2,696	2,312	2,220	1,955	1,640	1,610	1,465	1,398	1,341	1,146	891	585
Operating profit	8,557	8,049	6,751	8,513	5,607	8,315	6,201	3,504	1,746	2,905	4,376	4,703	4,642	2,380
Pretax income	9,724	9,567	4,557	6,092	3,449	5,830	3,838	934	(810)	147	596	1,654	2,149	2,297
Income taxes	4,565	3,607	1,752	2,372	1,328	2,117	1,423	429	(272)	79	237	604	859	908
Net income	5,785	5,656	2,805	3,720	2,121	3,713	2,415	505	(538)	68	359	1,050	1,290	1,389
Selected Cash Flow Items														
Capital expenditures	29,657	19,659	7,150	5,429	4,109	4,024	2,995	2,289	2,348	2,262	1,665	1,690	1,975	2,061
Net common issuance	165	4,782	(2,130)	(241)	(1,047)	0	1,952	0	385	0	0	0	118	0
Cash dividends	2,395	7,572	1,096	963	710	399	281	225	169	269	268	225	219	176
Selected Balance Sheet Items														
Cash and equivalents	9,163	21,998	7,848	7,752	8,125	8,371	5,095	3,649	3,035	3,355	2,564	3,255	2,410	2,679
Net property, plant, and equipment	64,129	51,852	22,540	18,829	16,161	14,482	12,774	11,531	10,508	9,468	9,876	9,698	8,312	6,118
Total assets[b]	175,889	159,738	60,418	56,184	53,756	49,539	43,830	40,653	43,076	46,374	51,038	48,567	37,417	25,945
Automotive assets	101,424	103,513	44,483	41,251	38,358	36,001	32,492	25,144	23,050	22,218	21,670	19,718	17,472	11,482
Financial Services assets	74,466	56,225	19,599	17,721	17,835	16,648	14,251	17,548	21,280	24,702	30,090	28,750	25,277	21,028
Automotive long-term debt	4,431	4,247	2,258	1,709	2,215	2,098	2,516	3,707	3,506	3,898	3,249	3,314	3,333	2,334
Financial Services debt	60,509	43,189	6,748	5,475	7,643	5,552	4,355	9,727	11,474	15,094	13,753	13,315	10,885	9,100
Shareholders' equity	36,313	35,629	11,362	11,571	10,959	10,692	6,834	7,536	6,109	6,849	7,233	7,582	6,503	5,281
Equity market cap	78,254	96,228	22,815	23,183	20,855	17,398	18,836	9,469	3,435	2,838	4,239	6,002	4,894	5,345
EPS (fully diluted)	5.73	5.75	4.09	4.74	2.56	4.55	(3.81)	1.07	(1.64)	0.15	0.77	2.33	2.94	3.13
DPS	2.50	11.97	1.60	1.40	1.00	0.55	0.33	0.30	0.30	0.60	0.60	0.50	0.50	0.40

[a]In 1998, Chrysler Corporation merged with Daimler Benz to form DaimlerChrysler. Figures prior to 1998 are from Chrysler.
[b]Total assets can differ from the sum of Automotive and Financial assets due to eliminations and other adjustments.

EXHIBIT 10 Selected Auto Company Valuation Information and Interest Rates as of April 14, 2000

Sources: *The Value Line Investment Survey,* Yahoo!, *The Wall Street Journal,* Bulldogresearch, casewriter estimates.

	Ford	General Motors	DaimlerChrysler ADR	Toyota ADR	S&P 500
Stock price	$51.38	$82.06	$63.25	$101.81	$1,356.56
Beta[a]	0.81	0.93	0.80	0.55	1.00
Standard deviation[a]	31.6%	31.4%	32.7%	34.1%	19.6%
Earnings per share					
1995	3.58	7.28	NA	1.26	33.96
1999	5.86	8.53	6.25	2.05	48.17
Est. 2004	8.61	12.30	9.57	3.78	80.00
Growth in earnings per share					
1995–1999	13.1%	4.0%	NA	12.9%	9.1%
Est. 1999–2004	8.0%	7.6%	8.9%	13.0%	10.7%
Book value per share 1999	$22.65	$31.35	$39.40	$34.20	$200.35
Price/Earnings ratio on 1999 earnings	8.8x	9.6x	10.1x	49.7x	28.2x
Price/Book ratio on 1999 book value	2.3x	2.6x	1.6x	3.0x	6.8x

	Interest Rate
One-year U.S. Treasury bills	6.05%
30-year U.S. Treasury bonds	5.79%

[a]Estimated from weekly stock and index price changes over the previous three years. Stock price information for DaimlerChrysler is available since the merger in November 1998.

Marriott Corporation (A)

Over the next few years we will place special emphasis on enhancing our strong customer preference, increasing operating cash flow and reducing debt.

—Chairman's letter to shareholders,
Marriott Corporation *1990 Annual Report,* p. 3

Priorities for the next few years: Reduce our long-term debt to about $2 billion by the end of 1994, by maximizing cash flow and selling assets.

—Chairman's letter to shareholders,
Marriott Corporation *1991 Annual Report,* p. 5
[Third in a list of four priorities.]

J. W. Marriott, Jr., chairman of the board and president of Marriott Corporation (MC), had weathered difficult times in the last few years. The company his father had founded in 1927 had grown explosively during the 1980s, developing hotel properties around the world and selling them to outside investors while retaining lucrative long-term management contracts. However, the economic slowdown in the late 1980s and the 1990 real estate market crash left MC owning many newly developed properties for which there were no buyers, together with a massive burden of debt. As Marriott had promised in successive annual reports in recent years, the company was working to sell properties and reduce that burden, but progress was slow. Looking ahead to the end of 1992, three months away, financial results promised to be only slightly better than for 1991, although still a significant improvement over the low point reached in 1990. For the foreseeable future, MC's ability to raise funds in the capital markets would be severely limited.

But Marriott now faced a decision that had the potential to change this situation completely. He was considering a radical restructuring of the company proposed by Stephen Bollenbach, the new chief financial officer (CFO), under which the bulk of MC's service businesses would be split off from its property holdings—and debt. A new company would be created for the service businesses, with existing shareowners of MC receiving a share of stock in the new company to match each share they owned in the old one. The new company would have the financial strength to raise capital to take advantage of investment opportunities. The old one, valued for the chance of appreciation in its property holdings when the real estate market recovered, and not on the basis of earnings, would be under less pressure to sell properties at depressed prices.

Bollenbach had served as treasurer of MC in the early 1980s at the beginning of its period of rapid growth. After leaving in the middle of the decade, he had built a reputation for creating innovative financial structures in the hotel industry with the 1987 recapitalization of Holiday Corporation (later named Promus Companies, Inc.), and then with his rescue of Donald Trump's heavily indebted real estate holdings. Bollenbach returned to MC as CFO in February 1992. His proposed restructuring, called Project Chariot, reflected the imaginative and innovative thinking characteristic of the financial advisors who had contributed so much to MC's growth in the 1980s.

This case was prepared by Research Associate Charles A. Nichols III under the supervision of Professor Lynn Sharp Paine.

Copyright © 1993 by the President and Fellows of Harvard College. Harvard Business School case 394–085.

Project Chariot seemed like the perfect solution to the company's problems. Was it the right step to take now? MC's board of directors would be meeting soon, and Marriott needed to decide what to recommend.

Company and Industry Background[1]

Founding and Early Years

With 202,000 employees at the end of 1991, MC was ranked as the twelfth-largest employer in the United States.[2] The company traced its beginnings to 1927, when J. W. Marriott Sr. opened a small root beer stand in Washington, D.C. The business soon began to sell food and was renamed the Hot Shoppe restaurant. Working with his wife, Alice, Marriott Sr. saw the business grow throughout the 1930s and 1940s into a family-owned chain of 45 restaurants in nine states. The Marriotts also acquired contracts to run cafeterias and company kitchens, as well as to supply food to the airline industry. Growth and success were based upon a policy of careful attention to details and centralized and standardized operating procedures.

Initial Public Offering

MC went public in 1953, selling one-third of its shares. Although the company continued to sell stock to the public over the years, in 1992 the Marriott family still owned 25% of the company. In the first 5 years after the initial stock offering, it had doubled in size. In 1956 it opened its first hotel, in Washington, and in the next 8 years had grown to 120 Hot Shoppes and 12 hotels. J. W. Marriott Sr. resigned the position of president in 1964, passing it to his son J. W. Marriott Jr., then only 32. Under the son's leadership, MC abandoned the father's conservative financial policies. It turned to major borrowing to finance expansion that would maintain its historical 20% annual revenue growth rate. In the 1970s, MC began to use bank credit and unsecured debt instead of mortgages to finance development. According to new financial thinking developing in the company, borrowing was acceptable as long as cash flow was maintained at a sufficient multiple of interest charges. The company acquired restaurant chains and entered new businesses, such as theme park development and operation.

Joint Ventures

In 1978, MC embarked upon its first joint venture, constructing a group of hotels and then selling them to the Equitable Life Assurance Society, a major insurance company. Thus began a powerful growth strategy in which the company would plan and develop hotels, sell the properties to investors, and retain long-term management contracts. By 1980, following a 5-year period of 30% annual growth, 70% of MC's hotel rooms were owned by outside investors. MC possessed an enviable reputation for quality and reliability in service, and together with careful site selection procedures and hotel sizing, this reputation translated into occupancy rates 4–6% above industry averages. This gap had widened to more than 10% by 1992; when the industry average was only around 65%, MC's rate was 76–80%.[3]

[1]Much of the material in this section is based upon Keith F. Girard's, "What the Hell Happened to Marriott?" *Regardies,* April–May 1991, pp. 71–91.

[2]*Dun's Business Rankings,* 1993.

[3]Joseph J. Doyle, CFA, *Marriott Corporation,* Smith Barney Research Report (released December 18, 1992).

The Economic Recovery Tax Act of 1981 created new incentives for the ownership of real estate, which further fueled MC's hotel-developing activities. Its first real estate limited partnership, offered in that year, gave investors $9 in tax writeoffs for every $1 invested. Beginning in 1983, MC also branched out into the mid-price lodging market with "Courtyard" hotels, which were bundled into groups of 50 or more for limited partnership offerings. In 1985 scaled-down but full-service "compact hotels" for smaller city markets, as well as all-suite hotels and longer-term residence inns were introduced; MC entered the budget hotel market with "Fairfield Inns" in 1987. MC also continued to acquire restaurant chains, including Gino's in 1982 and Howard Johnson's in 1985, although its success in establishing a national business in this area was limited. In 1984 the company discontinued its theme park operations.

End of the Boom

In 1986 the Tax Reform Act ended most of the tax incentives for real estate investment, but MC, relying on the strong economy and its own reputation, continued its high-paced development activities. However, the market for its limited partnerships was drying up, and in 1989 the company experienced a sharp drop in income. It froze capital expenditures, which had increased threefold over the previous 6 years, sold off its airline in-flight catering business, and discontinued its restaurant operations. In 1990 the real estate market collapsed. MC's income plummeted and its year-end stock price fell by more than two-thirds, a drop of over $2 billion in market capitalization. For the first time, investor-owned Marriott hotels went bankrupt.

MC was saddled with large interest payments on properties it was unable to sell. Industry excess capacity led to low occupancy rates and deep discounting on room rates, resulting in large losses for many of MC's competitors and even bankruptcies in some cases. In 1991, MC intensified its focus on contract and management opportunities that required less capital outlay. These included captive food service markets such as hospitals, office buildings, and turnpike service plazas, as well as management of golf courses. The development and management of "life-care" community facilities for senior citizens was also a high-growth market that MC had entered, but capital constraints forced it to cut back on planned new construction.

Thus, the MC of September 1992 was a far cry from the real estate development engine of the 1980s. Capital spending had been reduced to an annual level of $350 million, only the amount necessary to maintain and refurbish the existing properties. While the company had improved its position from the low point in 1990, investors still regarded it at best as a company beset by the problems of a severely depressed industry, with several years of slow recovery ahead before it could begin to grow again. (See Table A for market statistics on MC.)

TABLE A
Market Statistics on Marriott Corporation, September 1992

Recent market price	$16.00
Estimated earnings per share	.75
Stock beta	1.30
Price/earnings ratio	
Marriott Corporation	21.30
S&P 500 Industrials (close of 3Q1992)	26.00
S&P Hotel/Motel (close of 3Q1992)	22.70

Sources: *Value Line* reports (September 4, 1992): MC annual statement: *S&P Analysts' Handbook.*

Corporate Culture

However, MC remained a company with many strengths, not least of which was a unique corporate culture built around the personality and values of the Marriott family, and especially of J. W. Marriott Sr., the founder. In every Marriott hotel lobby hung a painting of the two J. W. Marriotts: every Marriott hotel room contained a Gideon Bible, the Book of Mormon, and an authorized biography of J. W. Marriott Sr., a book commissioned and written in the 1970s and published in 1977.[4] The biography detailed the life of the founder, beginning with his roots in the Mormon frontier communities in Utah, his childhood and early struggles in difficult economic circumstances, and his work for several years as a missionary for his church. It described the source of his lifelong aversion to borrowing: the burden of debt on his family's sheep farm in Utah and the resulting foreclosure during the depression following World War I. The book closed with the picture of a wealthy and respected man, a leader in his church and active in politics and philanthropy.

In describing the growth of the MC, the book stressed the themes of careful attention to detail and organization, and above all of service to customers. But the organization itself was focused on the employees. On his retirement in 1964, in a letter to his son and successor, J. W. Marriott Sr. listed a number of "guideposts" in his management philosophy, including the principle that "People are No. 1—their development, loyalty, interest, team spirit."[5] And 9 years later, in introducing J. W. Marriott Sr. as a speaker to the employees at the opening of the Los Angeles Marriott, a company senior executive remarked, "Marriott believes that the customer is great, but you come first. Mr. Marriott knows that if he takes care of his employees, they'll take care of the customers."[6]

Project Chariot[7]

Under Project Chariot, MC would become two separate companies. The division would be effected by a special stock dividend, giving stockholders of MC a share of stock in the new company to match each share they held of MC. The new company, to be called Marriott International, Inc. (MII), would comprise MC's lodging, food, and facilities management businesses, as well as the management of its life-care facilities. Food management had become a major segment of MC's business. With nearly 3,000 accounts, it included as clients some of the largest corporations and educational institutions in the United States. The existing company, to be renamed Host Marriott Corporation (HMC), would retain MC's real estate holdings and its concessions on tollroads and in airports (see Exhibit 1 for details). The transaction would be conditioned upon a ruling from the Internal Revenue Service that the special dividend would be tax free to shareholders, and upon ratification by a majority of MC stockholders. The plan called for the distribution of the dividend by mid-1993.

Under the plan, MII and HMC would have separate management teams. J. W. Marriott Jr. would be chairman, president, and chief executive officer of MII; his brother Richard Marriott (currently vice chairman of MC) would be chairman of HMC; and Stephen Bollenbach (the current MC chief financial officer) would be HMC's president

[4]Robert O'Brien, *Marriott: The J. Williard Marriott Story* (Salt Lake City: Desert Book Company, 1977).

[5]Ibid., p. 266.

[6]Ibid., p. 8.

[7]Much of the material in this section is taken from Marriott Corporation Press Release, October 5, 1992, and from Mitch Hara, James Kirby, and Renee Noto, "Analysis of the Marriott Restructuring," a paper dated May 5, 1993, and written for the Harvard Business School Class on Corporate Restructuring.

and chief executive officer. The two companies would also have separate boards of directors, except that the two brothers would each serve on both boards. MII would have an ongoing contractual relationship with HMC similar to the current relationship between MC and owners of hotel properties managed by MC. Such contracts typically involved the payment by the property owners of an annual management fee of 2–3% of revenues. Similarly, MII would have the right to lease and operate the senior living facilities owned by HMC.

Under the spin-off, MII would have the right to purchase up to 20% of HMC's voting stock at market value in the event of a change in control of HMC. MII would also have right of first refusal if HMC offered its toll road and airport concessions for sale.

In the past several years. MC had reduced its work force significantly in response to its difficult economic situation. It was not expected that Project Chariot would lead to further cuts in the work force. After the division, MH would have 182,000 employees, and in 1992, on a projected pro forma basis, would have had $7.9 billion in sales and operating cash flow before corporate expenses, interest expense, and taxes of $408 million. HMC would have 23,000 employees, and 1992 projected pro forma sales of $1.8 billion, with operating cash flow before corporate expenses, interest expense, and taxes of $363 million. Under the plan, HMC would retain nearly all of MC's long-term debt of nearly $3 billion, although it would have access to a revolving line of credit of $600 million from MII through December 1997. However, MII itself would have very little long-term debt (see Exhibit 1).

Management Perspectives

Pure Plays

Dividing MC into two companies was consistent with the company's general strategy of separating property ownership from management operations. The theory was that added value came from finding investment opportunities and developing and managing hotels, not from the ownership of real estate. MC management had long felt that the financial markets undervalued the company's stock because of the difficulty investors had in distinguishing and separately valuing property ownership and management. Project Chariot offered investors the opportunity to participate in "pure plays" in the hotel management business and in hotel real estate investment business for longer-term appreciation.

Career Opportunities

In many ways, Project Chariot would offer attractive possibilities to Marriott's management. In the downsizing of the previous few years, many executive positions had been lost. MC had also seen the departure of fast-track executives who decided that their chances of rapid ascent in the organization and wealth accumulation were not as good as elsewhere. With two separate companies, there would now be twice as many top-level positions, and with MII poised for rapid growth, ambitious managers would be more likely to stay. Managers with stock holdings and options would also benefit personally from the expected increase in the value of the company's stock after the Project Chariot restructuring.[8]

[8]According to the MC March 1992 proxy statement, the Marriott family was deemed to control 25.75% (approximately 25.6 million shares) of common stock of MC. The holdings of all other directors, nominees, and executive officers amounted to approximately 300,000 shares. An additional 800,000 shares were set aside for executive officers under a restricted stock plan and deferred stock agreements, as well as approximately 2.8 million stock options (of which 1.1 million were currently exercisable) under a stock option plan.

Opportunities for HMC and MII

Because HMC would be valued more on the basis of the chance of appreciation in its property holdings than on expected income, the company would be under less pressure from investors to sell off hotels at distress prices. To the extent that HMC operated at a loss, the combined after-tax earnings of the two separate companies would be smaller than that of MC as a single entity, for HMC's losses would no longer offset MII's positive earnings. On the other hand, unburdened by debt, MII would have the ability to raise additional capital to finance growth, perhaps to participate in the consolidation of the hotel industry by purchasing the assets of competitors in financial difficulty. These new acquisitions would strengthen MII from a customer-service point of view.

Implications for Bondholders

While Project Chariot would very likely benefit stockholders in MC, the situation was quite different for bondholders. (See Exhibit 2 for a summary of MC's long-term debt.) Although MC management was confident that HMC would have the financial strength to make all payments of interest and principal on long-term obligations when due, the separation of the two companies would affect the security of MC debt holders. Bond rating agencies such as Moody's Investors Services (Moody's) and Standard and Poor's Corporation (S&P) were likely to lower the ratings on MC's long-term bonds to a level below investment grade. (See the Appendix for a discussion of bond ratings.) This development could force some institutional holders of MC debt to sell their holdings, since banks, insurance companies, and pension funds often operated under legal restrictions that limited the amount of non-investment-grade securities they could own. Fiduciaries managing such funds were also typically required by law to follow the "prudent person" rule in making investment decisions.

Legal Considerations

Covenants

MC's debt indentures contained the usual provisions but lacked so-called "event-risk" covenants that would have blocked the Project Chariot restructuring or required any measures to protect bondholders from its potentially adverse effects. Event-risk covenants had emerged in the 1980s when transactions such as leveraged buyouts (LBOs) had provided stockholders with large profits from tender offers at premium prices while creating large losses for bondholders in the reduced market value of their newly speculative investments. In response, bondholders began to insist on new covenants to promote them against the risk of the occurrence of such transactions.

These covenants provided that, on the occurrence of certain "triggering events," such as a merger or consolidation, a change in ownership, or a major distribution of cash or securities, the company might be required to redeem immediately all or a specified proportion of the debt, provide collateral, or increase the interest rate to market levels. Research revealed that in 1989, 30% of bonds issued included such covenants, with the securities of companies expected to be targets of takeovers more likely to be so protected.[9]

While event-risk covenants protected bondholders, they often did so at the cost of lower interest rates. With the collapse of the junk bond market in the early 1990s and the slowing of takeover and LBO activity, the use of such covenants decreased. None of MC's long-term debt indentures contained event-risk covenants, including the indentures under which MC issued $400 million of long-term bonds in April and May of 1992 (see Exhibit 2). These were now selling at 110, reflecting a general decline in market interest rates during 1992.

[9]Kenneth Lehn and Annette B. Poulsen, "Contractual Resolution of Bondholder–Stockholder Conflicts in Leveraged Buyouts," *Journal of Law and Economics* 24 (October 1991): 645–673.

Fraudulent Conveyance[10]

Several LBOs that became insolvent were attacked by creditors using the legal theory of "fraudulent conveyance." The doctrine of fraudulent conveyance, which dated to a sixteenth-century English statute, protected creditors from debtors who tried to shelter their wealth or avoid their debts by conveying their property to others. In some cases of failed LBOs, unsecured creditors attempted to recover funds from those benefiting from the LBO transaction, such as shareholders or advisors to the transaction. Because it was often difficult to prove intentional fraud by these parties, most LBO-related fraudulent conveyance actions were brought under the constructive fraud provisions of statutes such as the Federal Bankruptcy Code, the Uniform Fraudulent Conveyance Act, or the Uniform Fraudulent Transfers Act. According to section 548(a)(2) of the Bankruptcy Code, constructive fraud could be established when the debtor

1. received less than reasonably equivalent value for the property transferred: *and*
2. either
   a. was insolvent or became insolvent as a result of the transfer,
   b. retained unreasonably small capital after the transfer, or
   c. made the transfer with the intent or belief that it would incur debts beyond its ability to pay.

In the LBO situation, the tests of solvency and capitalization were the critical factors in determining constructive fraud.[11] Since courts excluded from consideration both intangible value created by a transaction and tangible value received by anyone other than the debtor (the corporation), LBOs failed the "reasonably equivalent value test" by their very nature.

LBO lawsuits were rarely successful. In large cases, plaintiffs almost always agreed to settlements averaging less than ten cents for each dollar of their claims.[12] A review of two dozen decisions found only five with a verdict for the plaintiffs, and federal appeals courts ruled for the defendants in virtually every key case considered between 1986 and 1992. Among the most favored defendants were "public shareholders who received most of the funds, but did not control the deal."[13]

Duties to Bondholders

U.S. courts had held that corporations have no responsibilities to safeguard the interests of bondholders other than those spelled out by the terms of the bond indenture. For example, in 1986 the Delaware Court of Chancery stated in *Katz v. Oak Industries:*

> Arrangements among a corporation, the underwriters of its debt, trustees under its indentures, and sometimes ultimate investors, are typically thoroughly negotiated and massively documented. The rights and obligations of the various parties are, or should be, spelled out in that documentation. The terms of the contractual relationship agreed to, and not broad concepts such as fairness, define the corporation's duty to bondholders.[14]

However, a more recent Delaware Chancery Court decision took the position that the duties of corporate boards of directors toward holders of corporate debt could be more extensive than simply to observe indenture provisions, particularly when the corporation was facing serious economic difficulties or bankruptcy. In such cases, very risky courses

[10]Material in this paragraph is taken from Timothy A. Luehrman and Lance L. Hirt, "Highly Leveraged Transactions and Fraudulent Conveyance Law," *The Continental Bank Journal of Applied Corporate Finance* 6, no. 1 (Spring 1993): 104–105.

[11]Ibid., pp. 106–107.

[12]Jack Friedman, "LBO Lawsuits Don't Pick Deep Pockets," *The Wall Street Journal,* January 27, 1993.

[13]Ibid.

[14]Cited in Lehn and Poulsen, p. 646.

of action could be beneficial to stockholders yet injurious to the interests of debt holders. In *Credit Lyonnais Bank N.V. v. Pathe Communications* (1991 WL 277613), the court imposed a duty on the board to respect "the community of interest that sustained the corporation, to exercise judgment in an informed, good faith effort to maximize the corporation's long-term wealth creating capacity."[15] A commentator noted that this decision altered the traditional approach in which "the board's duties to the company ran primarily to the stockholders, unless the company became insolvent, in which case the board's duty in some sense 'flipped' to creditors." In contrast, the new decision

> recognizes that there is no magic point at which duties should shift from stockholders to creditors. Instead, there is a continuum approaching insolvency in which the board's incentives become increasingly distorted and the creditor-stockholder conflict increases.[16]

The Delaware Chancery Court's decision in the *Credit Lyonnais* case was not based upon completely novel ideas about the legal responsibility of corporate leaders. As far back as 1932, E. Merrick Dodd Jr., in an article in the *Harvard Law Review,* noted that

> Despite many attempts to dissolve the corporation into an aggregate of stockholders, our legal tradition is rather in favor of treating it as an institution directed by persons who are primarily fiduciaries for the institution rather than for its members.[17]

However, Professor Dodd's view was far from the orthodox position of most financial economists and lawyers in 1990, who regarded managers as agents for the shareholders with responsibility primarily to protect and promote shareholders' interests.

Social and Economic Climate

As the junk bond market collapsed and many of its high-risk issues headed towards bankruptcy or renegotiation, public opinion regarding the acceptability of massive wealth transfers through financial engineering shifted. Although there were still defenders of such transactions, they were viewed with suspicion by large segments of the public who condemned them as paper transactions that contributed no real value to the economy. Junk bonds and real estate investments had left many financial intermediaries, such as commercial banks, pension funds, and life insurance companies, in financially shaky positions. Although commercial bank profits were starting to improve, the real estate market continued to languish as financial institutions shed nonperforming real estate loans, and residual fears dampened the enthusiasm of potential investors.

The Decision

Marriott wondered what he should recommend to the board of directors regarding Project Chariot. (See Exhibits 3–7 for relevant financial data.) He had been assured by legal counsel that the corporation was within its rights as a debtor to restructure itself in this way. Investment advisors had given him an opinion that the transaction was in the best interests of shareholders. His CFO, Bollenbach, was convinced that cash flows for HMC were more than adequate to cover debt service requirements. And surely, if public reaction were extremely negative, or if other difficulties arose, Project Chariot could be abandoned without significant loss. But with this transaction the company was entering new territory.

The board would be meeting soon, and Marriott needed to decide.

[15]Richard P. Swanson, Esq., "Directors' Duties to Creditors," p. 16.

[16]Ibid., p. 16.

[17]E. Merrick Dodd, Jr., "For Whom Are Corporate Managers Trustees?" *Harvard Law Review* XLV, no. 7 (May 8, 1932): 1162–1163.

EXHIBIT 1

Project Chariot: Division of Marriott Corporation into Marriott International, Inc. and Host Marriott Corporation (amounts are projected)

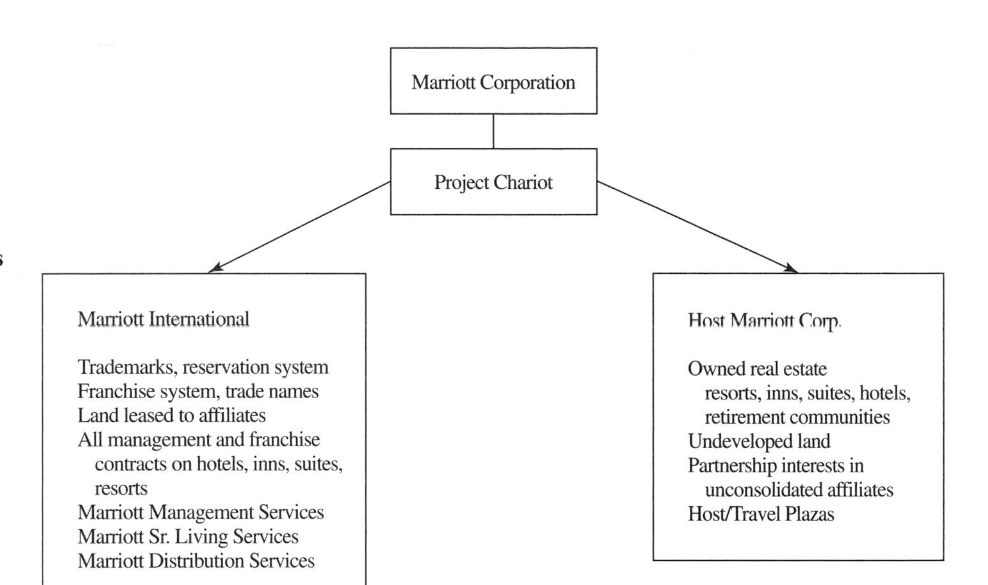

1992 Statistics[a]

	Marriott International	Host Marriott Corp.
EBIT	$259	$123
Interest	25	210
Net income	134	(49)
Preferred dividend	0	$17
Net income, common	$134	($66)
EPS	1.40	($0.69)
Total assets	$2,600	$4,600
Debt	400	2,000
Preferred stock	0	200
Common equity	800	600
Times interest	10.4	.59
Debt% book capital	67%	76%

[a]Millions of dollars, except per share data.

EXHIBIT 2

Marriott Corporation Long-Term Debt (millions of dollars)

Sources: MC Annual Statement; Moody's and S&P reports.

	1990	1991	Moody's	S&P
Secured notes, with an average rate of 8.6% at January 3, 1992, maturing through 2010	$ 175	$ 527	Baa3	BBB
Unsecured debt				
Senior notes, with an average rate of 9.3% at January 3, 1992, maturing through 2001[a]	1,198	1,323	Baa3[c]	BBB[c]
Debentures, 9.4%, due 2007	250	250	Baa3	BBB
Revolving loans, with an average rate of 5.3% at January 3, 1992, maturing through 1995[b] ...	1,780	676		
Other notes, with an average rate of 7.8% at January 3, 1992, maturing through 2015	209	193	Baa3	BBB
Capital lease obligations....................................	61	62		
	3,673	3,031		
Less current portion	(75)	(52)		
	$3,598	$2,979		

[a]Includes approximately $230 million (current valuation) of 8.25% Liquid Yield Option Notes, maturing in June 2006 for the face amount of $675 million and rated Ba1 (Moody's) and not rated by S&P.

[b]By year-end 1992, MC expected to have reduced its revolving loan borrowings by $500 million and its other debt by approximately $150 million.

[c]On April 29, 1992, MC issued $200 million of 10% 20-year senior notes, and on May 5, 1992, $200 million of 9.5% 10-year senior notes. Both issues were rated as Baa3 (Moody's) and BBB (S&P) and sold at yields in line with other Baa3 issues at the date of issue (see Exhibit A1 in Appendix).

EXHIBIT 3
Marriott Corporation Consolidated Statements of Income (millions of dollars except per share data)

Source: MC Annual Report.

	1989	1990	1991
Sales			
Lodging			
Rooms	$2,093	$2,374	$2,699
Food and beverages	1,082	1,146	1,194
Other	371	422	486
	3,546	3,942	4,379
Contract services	3,990	3,704	3,952
	7,536	7,646	8,331
Operating costs and expenses			
Lodging			
Departmental direct costs			
Rooms	481	554	628
Food and beverages	816	870	915
Other, including payments to hotel owners and net restructuring charges of $65 million in 1990 and $194 million in 1989	2,117	2,279	2,511
Contract services, including restructuring charges of $57 million in 1990 and $51 million in 1989	3,818	3,590	3,799
	7,232	7,293	7,853
Operating profit			
Lodging	132	239	325
Contract services, including $231 million gain on divestiture of airline catering business in 1989	403	114	153
Operating profits before corporate expenses and taxes	535	353	478
Corporate expenses, including restructuring charges of $31 million in 1990 and $811 million in 1989	(107)	(137)	(111)
Interest expense	(185)	(183)	(265)
Interest income	55	47	43
Income from continuing operations before income taxes	298	80	145
Provision for income taxes	117	33	63
Income from continuing operations	181	47	82
Discontinued operations, net of income taxes			
Income from discontinued operations	35	—	—
Provision for loss on disposal	(39)	—	—
	(4)	—	—
Net income	$ 117	$ 47	$ 82
Earnings (loss) per common share			
Continuing operations	$ 1.62	$ .46	$ .80
Discontinued operations	(.04)	—	—
	$ 1.58	$ .46	$ .80

EXHIBIT 4

Marriott Corporation Consolidated Balance Sheets (millions of dollars)

Source: MC Annual Report.

	1990	1991
Assets		
Current assets		
Cash and equivalents	$ 283	$ 36
Accounts receivable	654	524
Inventories, at lower of average cost or market	261	243
Other current assets	230	220
	1,428	1,023
Property and equipment	2,774	2,485
Assets held for sale	1,274	1,524
Investments in affiliates	462	455
Intangibles	494	476
Notes receivable and other	494	437
	$6,926	$6,400
Liabilities and Shareholders' Equity		
Current liabilities		
Accounts payable	$ 675	$ 579
Accrued payroll and benefits	305	313
Other payables and accruals	582	391
Notes payable and capital leases	75	53
	1,637	1,335
Long-term debt	3,598	2,979
Other long-term liabilities	388	351
Deferred income	312	232
Deferred income taxes	584	614
Convertible subordinated debt	—	210
Shareholders' equity		
Convertible preferred stock	—	200
Common stock, issued 105.0 million shares	105	105
Additional paid-in capital	69	35
Retained earnings	528	583
Treasury stock, 9.5 million and 11.4 million common shares, respectively, at cost	(295)	(244)
Total shareholders' equity	407	679
	$6,926	$6,400

EXHIBIT 5
Marriott Corporation Consolidated Statements of Cash Flows (millions of dollars)

Source: MC Annual Report.

	1989	1990	1991
Operating Activities			
Income from continuing operations	$ 181	$ 47	$ 82
Adjustments to reconcile to cash from operations			
Depreciation and amortization	186	208	272
Income taxes	41	18	27
Net restructuring charges	256	153	—
Proceeds from sale of timeshare notes receivable	—	—	83
Amortization of deferred income	(31)	(50)	(38)
Losses (gains) on sales of assets	(273)	(1)	3
Other	98	50	3
Working capital changes			
Accounts receivable	(100)	(76)	88
Inventories	(39)	(22)	63
Other current assets	(19)	(5)	13
Accounts payable and accruals	123	63	(47)
Cash from continuing operations	423	385	549
Cash from discontinued operations	86	(10)	3
Cash from operations	$ 509	$ 375	$ 552
Investing Activities			
Proceeds from sales of assets	$1,648	$ 990	$ 84
Less noncash proceeds	(258)	(15)	—
Cash received from sales of assets	1,390	975	84
Capital expenditures	(1,338)	(1,094)	(427)
Acquisitions	(242)	(118)	—
Other	(223)	(129)	(126)
Cash used in investing activities	(443)	(366)	(469)
Financing Activities			
Issuance of convertible preferred stock	—	—	$ 195
Issuances of long-term and convertible subordinated debt	873	1,317	815
Issuances of common stock	41	24	3
Repayments of long-term debt	(581)	(846)	(1,316)
Purchases of treasury stock	(280)	(294)	—
Dividends payments	(26)	(27)	(27)
Cash from (used in) financing activities	$ 27	$ 174	$ (330)
Increase (decrease) in cash and equivalents	93	183	(247)
Cash and equivalents, beginning of year	7	100	283
Cash and equivalents, end of year	$ 100	$ 283	$ 36

EXHIBIT 6 Marriott Corporation 10-Year Financial Summary (millions of dollars except per share data)

	1982	1983	1984	1985	1986	1987	1988	1989	1990[a]	1991
Reported sales growth		19%	21%	26%	29%	26%	13%	14%	1%	9%
Rate of general inflation		5	4	3	2	3	4	4	3	3
Real growth		14	17	23	27	23	9	10	(2%)	6
Increase in Marriott hotel rooms		11	11	10	16	32	14	14	12	7
Capital expenditures		$462	$627	$911	$821	$1,053	$1,359	$1,368	$1,094	$ 427
Asset Management										
Sales/total assets	.97	.95	.99	.99	1.02	1.09	1.11	1.16	1.10	1.30
Profitability										
Earnings per share	$ .41	$ .56	$ .74	$ .96	$ 1.16	$ 1.40	$ 1.59	$ 1.62	$ .46	$ .80
EBIT as % of sales	8.2%	8.2%	8.2%	8.4%	7.7%	7.3%	6.8%	6.4%	3.4%	4.9%
Net income as % of sales	4.7	4.8	4.9	4.6	4.1	3.8	3.5	2.4	0.6	1.0
Return on equity	20.0	20.0	22.1	22.1	20.6	22.2	30.4	23.8	9.7	18.3
Return on invested capital	8.5	7.6	7.5	7.4	6.3	6.4	6.7	5.7	3.9	6.5
Financial Leverage										
Long-term debt as % capital	54%	53%	48%	42%	47%	59%	61%	60%	68%	59%
Times interest earned	2.3	3.1	3.8	4.0	6.0	4.7	3.3	2.6	1.4	1.5
Senior debt rating	A2	A2	A2	A2	A2	A2	A3	A3	Baa2	Baa3
Valuation										
Share price	$11.70	$ 14.25	$ 14.70	$ 21.58	$ 29.75	$ 30.00	$ 31.63	$ 33.38	$ 10.50	$ 16.50
Earnings per share	.41	.56	.74	.96	1.16	1.40	1.59	1.62	.46	.80
Dividends per share	.06	.08	.09	.11	.14	.17	.21	.25	.28	.28
Price/earnings ratio	29	25	20	22	26	21	20	21	23	21
Market/book ratio	3.0	3.1	2.8	3.3	3.9	4.4	4.8	5.5	2.4	3.3

[a]Operating results in 1990 included pretax restructuring charges and writeoffs, net of certain nonrecurring gains, of $153 million related to continuing operations. Operating results in 1989 included pretax restructuring charges and writeoffs of $256 million related to continuing operations, a $231 million pretax gain on the transfer of the airline catering division, and a $39 million after-tax charge recorded in conjunction with the planned disposal of the restaurant division.

EXHIBIT 7 Unconsolidated Affiliates

Marriott Corporation held ownership positions ranging from 1% to 50% in 267 hotels. This financial interest was reported as a $445 million "Investment in Affiliates," under either the cost or equity method of accounting (depending on the percent ownership). Marriott held management contracts and ground leases on these properties, and it provided limited guarantees on the debt of some of the properties in the form of a commitment to advance additional amounts to affiliates, if necessary, to cover certain debt requirements. Such commitments were limited to $349 million. Marriott Corporation's pretax income from affiliates was $97 million in 1991 and included management fees, net of direct costs, $81 million; ground rental income, $18 million; interest income, $19 million; and equity in net losses, ($21 million). Pretax income from affiliates was $47 million in 1986.

In 1991 the affiliates reported sales of $1,855 million, down slightly from the $1,900 million reported in 1990. Operating expense before interest totaled $2,076 million in 1991 versus $2,082 million in 1990.

Operating Results of Unconsolidated Affiliates (millions of dollars)

	1986	1990	1991	1992
Sales	$889	$1,801	$1,855	$1,900
Cash operating expenses		1,709	1,729	1,735
Depreciation	811	344	347	347
EBIT	$ 78	($252)	($221)	($182)
Interest expenses	213			
Net loss	($135)			

Balance Sheets of Unconsolidated Affiliates at December 31 (millions of dollars)

Assets	1986	1991	1992	Liabilities & Equity	1986	1991	1992
Current	$ 194	$ 158	$ 204	Current liabilities	$ 154	$ 445	$1,464
Noncurrent	2,721	4,842	4,589	Long-term debt	2,377	4,233	3,162
Total	$2,915	$5,000	$4,793	Other liabilities	242	565	694
				Equity	142	(243)	(527)
				Total	$2,915	$5,000	$4,793

Marriott Corporation Pretax Income from Unconsolidated Affiliates (millions of dollars)

	1986	1990	1991	1992
Management fees, net of cost		$76	$81	$82
Ground rents	$63	17	18	19
Interest income		21	19	16
Equity in net loss	(16)	(16)	(21)	(24)
Total	$47	$98	$97	$93

Appendix
Explanation of Bond Ratings[18]

Since the early 1900s, bonds have been assigned quality ratings that reflect their probability of going into default. The two major rating agencies are Moody's Investors Service (Moody's) and Standard & Poor's Corporation (S&P). These agencies' rating designations are shown in Exhibit A1. The AAA and AA bonds are extremely safe. A and BBB bonds are strong enough to be called investment grade bonds, and they are the lowest-rated bonds that many banks and other institutional investors are permitted by law to hold, BB and lower bonds are speculations, or junk bonds; they have a significant probability of going into default, and many financial institutions are prohibited from buying them.

Bond Rating Criteria

Although the rating assignments are judgmental they are based on both qualitative and quantitative factors, some of which are listed below:

1. Debt ratio.
2. Times-interest-earned ratio.
3. Fixed charge coverage ratio.
4. Current ratio.
5. Mortgage provisions: Is the bond secured by a mortgage?
6. Subordination provisions: Is the bond subordinated to other debt?
7. Guarantee provisions: Some bonds are guaranteed by other firms.
8. Sinking fund: Does the bond have a sinking fund to ensure systematic repayment?
9. Maturity: Other things the same, a bond with a shorter maturity will be judged less risky than a longer-term bond.
10. Stability: Are the issuer's sales and earnings stable?
11. Regulation: Is the issuer regulated, and could an adverse regulatory climate cause the company's economic position to decline?
12. Antitrust and legal: Are any antitrust actions or lawsuits pending against the firm that could erode its position?
13. Overseas operations: What percentage of the firm's sales, assets, and profits are from overseas operations, and what is the political climate in the host countries?
14. Environmental factors: Is the firm likely to face heavy expenditures for pollution-control equipment?
15. Pension liabilities: Does the firm have unfunded pension liabilities that could pose a future problem?
16. Labor unrest: Are there potential labor problems on the horizon that could weaken the firm's position?
17. Resource availability: Is the firm likely to face supply shortages that could force it to curtail operations?
18. Accounting policies: Conservative accounting policies are a plus factor in bond ratings.

[18]Based on Eugene F. Brigham and Louis C. Gapenski, *Financial Management*, 5th ed. (New York: The Dryden Press, 1988), pp. 545–547. Data on bond yield have been added.

Representatives of the rating agencies have consistently stated that no precise formula is used to set a firm's rating—all the factors listed, plus others, are taken into account, but not in a mathematically precise manner. Statistical studies have borne out this contention, for researchers who have tried to predict bond ratings on the basis of quantitative data have had only limited success, indicating that the agencies do indeed use a good deal of subjective judgment when establishing a firm's rating.

EXHIBIT A1
Comparison of Bond Ratings

	Moody's	S&P	Yields[a]
High quality	Aaa	AAA	7.80%
	Aa	AA	8.07
Investment grade	A	A	8.26
	Baa	BBB	8.72
Junk bonds substandard	Ba	BB	9.04
	B	B	10.81
Speculative	Caa	CCC	—
	C	D	—

Note: Moody's and S&P use "modifiers" for bonds rated below AAA. S&P uses a plus and minus system; thus, A+ designates the strongest A-rated bonds, and A– the weakest. Moody's uses a 1, 2, or 3 designation, with 1 denoting the strongest and 3 the weakest; thus, within the AA category, Aa1 is the best, Aa2 is average, and Aa3 is the weakest.
[a]Yields of corporate bonds with 10-year maturities as at September 28, 1992.

EXHIBIT A2
Bond Ratings of Industrial Corporations (1987–1989 Medians)

	AAA	AA	A	BBB	BB	B	CCC
Times interest earned	12.0	9.1	5.5	3.6	2.3	1.0	.8
Long-term debt as percent of capital ...	12%	19%	30%	38%	51%	66%	62%

Derivative Instruments and Risk Management

Introduction to Derivative Instruments

A derivative is a financial instrument, or contract, between two parties that derives its value from some other underlying asset or underlying reference price, interest rate, or index. Common derivatives include options, forward contracts, futures contracts, and swaps. Common underlying assets include interest rates, exchange rates, commodities, stocks, stock indices, bonds, and bond indices. Derivatives are created and traded in two interlinked markets—organized exchanges at the national and regional level, and an international network of dealers and end-users in which transactions are executed privately, that is, "over the counter" (OTC).

Over recent decades, financial markets have been marked by increased volatility. As foreign exchange rates, interest rates, and commodity prices continue to experience sharp and unexpected movements, it has become increasingly important that corporations exposed to these risks be equipped to manage them effectively. Risk management, the managerial process that is used to control such price volatility, has consequently risen to the top of financial agendas. And in the hot spot are these so-called derivatives. Furthermore, as these instruments have become more readily available, their application has extended beyond traditional risk management to the more opportunistic realm of speculation. In both applications, derivatives represent powerful tools by which institutions and individuals alike can significantly affect their financial security and viability.

Derivatives are used by a variety of entities such as corporations, commercial banks, and individual and institutional investors to reduce or "lay off" various risks, including the aforementioned interest rate risk, foreign currency risk, commodity price risk, and investment risk. Exhibit 1 provides results of a survey on the uses of derivatives by chief financial officers. For example, a chief financial officer (CFO) of a company heavily exposed to foreign exchange fluctuations often exploits the foreign exchange forward market to shield the company's balance sheet from currency depreciation. Similarly, a grain producer might use a forward contract to hedge against price depreciation in, say, wheat or soybeans. Through the use of a put option, an investor can establish a limit on the potential loss on an investment. On the other end of the application spectrum, an entity can trade derivatives for purely speculative purposes. Broadly, holders of derivatives securities, as well as their counterparties, can achieve goals ranging from risk management to speculation. The derivatives themselves help allocate economic risks efficiently by transferring risks between parties such that each holds the risks it is better able or more willing to bear.

This case was prepared by Research Associate Kendall Backstrand under the supervision of Professor W. Carl Kester.

Copyright © 1995 by the President and Fellows of Harvard College. Harvard Business School case 295–141.

This note provides a conceptual basis for understanding the fundamental properties and applications of common derivative products that give rise to their use in financial management. Each of three major families of derivative instruments—options, forwards and futures, and swaps—is discussed in the separate sections that follow.

Options

Common Terminology

Options are derivative instruments that can be used as a means of speculation or investment as well as hedging or risk management. Options written on both financial and physical assets have been traded for many years in dealer markets. However, it was not until 1973, when the Chicago Board of Trade formed the Chicago Board Options Exchange (CBOE), that organized public markets for options began to appear. Exchanges were then established to trade options written on assets such as individual stocks, stock indices, commodities, foreign currencies, and Treasury bonds.

An option is a contract between the buyer (or holder) of the option and the seller (or writer) of the option. This contract gives the buyer of the option the *right* to buy (or sell) an asset from (to) the seller of the option. The seller, on the other hand, is *obligated* under the terms of the option contract to perform. Plainly stated, an option contract defines the rights of the buyer and the obligations of the seller. The option to buy an asset is known as a *call* option, and the option to sell an asset is known as a *put* option. An example of a call and put option written on a particular company's common stock, that of Microsoft Corporation, is provided in Table A.

The specified asset involved in the option contract is referred to as the *underlying asset* on which the option is written. The specified price at which the asset may be bought or sold in the future is known as the *exercise,* or *strike, price.* Purchasing or selling the asset in the future through the option contract is referred to as *exercising* the option, and the specified date on or before which the option may be exercised is called the *expiration date,* or *maturity date.* So-called *American*-style options are contracts that may be exercised at any time prior to maturity, whereas *European*-style options are contracts that may be exercised only at maturity.

The options on Microsoft's stock shown in Table A were American options. A holder of the call option could have purchased Microsoft's stock at $60 per share by exercising the call option on or before April 15, 1995. Likewise, a holder of the put option could have sold Microsoft's stock at $60 per share by exercising the put option on or before April 15, 1995.

Option contracts have a *market,* or *premium, value,* and an *intrinsic value.* The market value of the option is simply the price at which a buyer and seller are willing to enter into an option contract. More specifically, it is the up-front cash premiums that the buyer must pay the seller in order to claim the rights of that particular option contract. As shown in Table A, the market value of the call option on Microsoft's stock was $7.50 per option as of the end of trading on November 30, 1994. Likewise, the market value of

TABLE A
Options Traded on Microsoft's Stock, November 30, 1994 (dollars per share)

Stock (asset) price	$64.125
Exercise price	$60
Maturity date	April 15, 1995
Call option price (premium)	$7.50
Put option price (premium)	$2.125

the put option on Microsoft's stock was $2.125. Because standard option contracts are contracts to buy or sell 100 shares at a time, an investor would actually have had to pay $750.00 to buy a standard call option contract on Microsoft's stock, and $212.50 to buy a standard put contract.

The intrinsic value of an option can be thought of as the price a rational investor would pay for an option if it were about to mature instantly. Because an option contract gives the holder the right to exercise but not the obligation, the intrinsic value of an option can never be less than zero. This is true because if the option is never exercised by the holder, it simply expires worthless.

If, for instance, the price of Microsoft's stock had fallen to $55 per share, the owner of the call option described in Table A would not have elected to exercise the option to buy at $60 per share. An investor wishing to own Microsoft's stock, in this case, would have been better off buying it directly on the stock exchange at $55 per share. Thus, at a stock price of $55 per share, the intrinsic value of a call option with an exercise price of $60 would have been zero, representing a worthless position for the holder of the call.

In general, the intrinsic value of a call option is always the greater of zero and the difference between the current market price of the underlying asset and the option's exercise price. In the case of a call option, this intrinsic value will be positive when the market price of the asset exceeds the exercise price of the option, and zero otherwise. At $64.125 per share, the call option on Microsoft's stock had a positive intrinsic value of $64.125 less $60, or $4.125. The call option holder could have bought Microsoft's stock for less than its actual market value. The opposite is true in the case of a put option: Sensible investors would not sell a put option's underlying asset at the put's exercise price unless that exercise price were above the asset's market value. Thus, the intrinsic value of a put option is always the greater of zero and the difference between the put's exercise price and the current market price of the underlying asset.

An option is said to be *in-the-money* when its intrinsic value is positive and *out-of-the-money* when it is zero. That is, a call option is in-the-money when its underlying asset's market price is above the exercise price; it is out-of-the-money when the opposite occurs. The converse is true for a put option: When the exercise price is above (below) the underlying asset's market price at maturity, the put is considered in-the-money (out-of-the-money). As the term suggests, an *at-the-money* option describes an option when its exercise price exactly equals the underlying asset's market price. Again using the Microsoft example, the terms described in Table A constitute an in-the-money call option and an out-of-the-money put option. If the exercise price were $64.125, or the stock price were $60, both options would be at-the-money. If the market price of an underlying asset is far above (below) the exercise price of a call (put) option, then the option is said to be *deep-in-the-money.* If the opposite is true, it is said to be *deep-out-of-the-money.* A deep-in-the-money position at maturity is the most desirable outcome for either a call or put option.

Graphical representation of an option's intrinsic value is useful to illustrate its total payoff. Payoff diagrams for both put and call options written on the same underlying asset with the same exercise price are provided in Figure I, where K = Exercise price, and P = Premium.

Determinants of Option Value

Notice in Table A that each option's market value is greater than its intrinsic value. This will always be true for options that have some time remaining before maturity. A graph of a call option's market, or premium, value relative to intrinsic value is shown in Figure II, where

$$K = \text{Exercise price}$$

FIGURE I
Payoff Diagrams

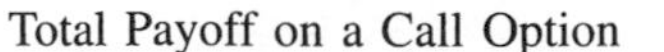

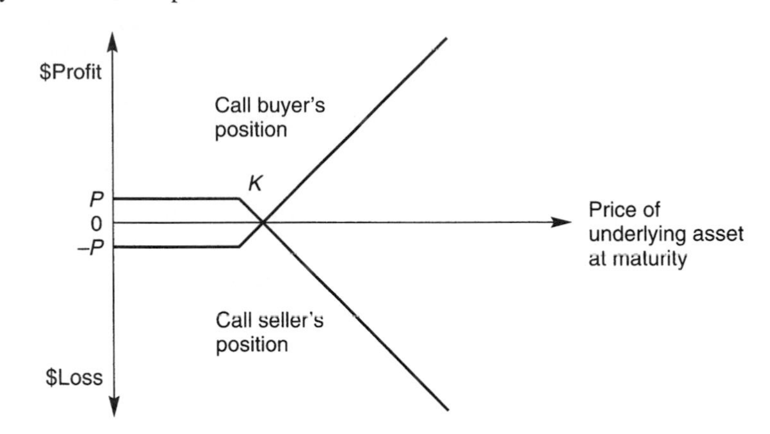

FIGURE II
Call Option Premium in Relation to Intrinsic Value

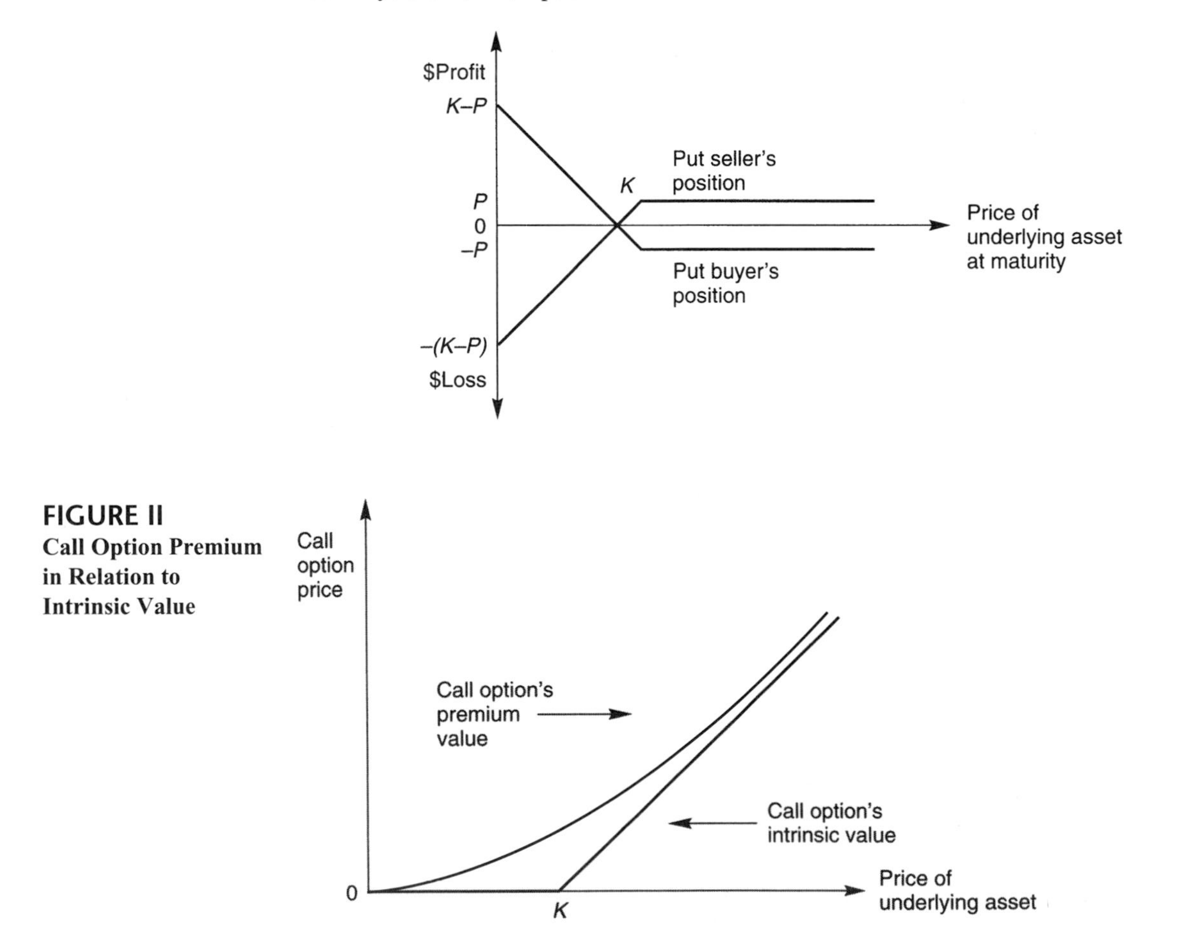

How much greater the premium value is over the intrinsic value depends on several factors. In general, for generic American-style call and put options, the premium value depends upon the following six determinants: underlying asset price, exercise price, the risk-free rate of return, volatility of the asset price, time to expiration, and expected cash distributions, if any. Their respective effects on option value are briefly described below.

Asset Price

For an American or European call option, the higher the price of the underlying asset, the greater the option's intrinsic value and the more likely it will remain above the option's exercise price at expiration. Hence, the higher the asset price, the greater will be the call option's premium, other things held constant. The opposite is true for American and European put options: the higher the value of the underlying asset, the lower the put option's intrinsic value and premium, other things held constant.

Exercise Price

An increase in a call option's exercise price *decreases* both the intrinsic value of the option and the likelihood that the option will be worth anything at maturity. Consequently, the higher an American or European call option's exercise price, the lower its premium value will be, other things held constant. Again, the opposite is true of a put option: A higher exercise price *increases* the put option's intrinsic value, other things held constant, and would be reflected in a higher premium.

Interest Rates

Because buyers of options do not pay or receive the option's exercise price until later, if ever, interest rates play a role in the determination of option premium value. Specifically, an increase in the interest rate lowers the present value of the cash exercise price expected to be paid or received in the future. For a call option, a rise in interest rates means the future cash payment of its exercise price is worth less in present value terms, implying greater option value for the holder. Hence, the value of an American or European call option increases as interest rates rise, holding other factors constant. In contrast, a rise in interest rates lowers the present value of the cash that a put option holder might receive in the future upon exercising the put. Consequently, American and European put option premiums decline as interest rates rise, other things being equal.

Volatility of the Asset Price

Other factors held constant, the more volatile the underlying asset price, the more valuable the option. Again, this is true because of the asymmetrical construct between an option's potential upside gains and downside losses (see Figure I). The holder of a call option experiences unlimited potential gains as the price of the asset increases. At the same time, however, the call option holder effectively limits loss by simply not exercising the option if the asset's price falls below the option's exercise price. The holder of a put, although only experiencing limited potential gains (the maximum gain being obtained when the asset price is zero upon maturity, implying an intrinsic value exactly equal to the option's exercise price), can also limit loss by simply not exercising the put if the asset's price rises above the put's exercise price. In short, the more volatile the asset price, the greater the chance the holder of either a put or call option has of realizing a gain without equally increasing the chance of incurring a large loss. Thus, higher expected volatility in the underlying asset's price enhances both American and European option values, other things being equal.

Time to Expiration

American and European call options increase in value when the time remaining to expiration is further away. This positive influence derives from two sources. First, in connection with the interest rate effect, the longer the time before expiration when the exercise payment will be made, the lower the discounted present value of that cash payment. Second, in connection with the volatility effect, the more time there is before expiration, the more likely it is that a large price change will occur and dramatically increase the value of the option. Consequently, so long as there is time remaining before expiration, an option's premium will exceed its intrinsic value. Provided there are no cash distributions to owners of a call option's underlying asset (see below), it follows that a call option should not be exercised before maturity, because doing so would sacrifice the value attributable to time.

American put option value is also positively affected by time to expiration. Because of the asymmetry between potential gains and losses from holding a put option, more time before expiration increases the chance that the put will mature in the money. Although the proceeds to be received from the future exercise of the put will have a lower present value as time to expiration increases, other things constant, this negative influence will not generally outweigh the positive influence associated with price volatility unless interest rates are high. When this is so, American put option holders might find it in their best interests to exercise their puts prematurely and reinvest the cash proceeds.

For European put options, the time to expiration can have either a positive or negative influence on prices depending on which of two effects dominate. When a European put is in the money, a longer time to expiration will tend to have a negative influence on premium value because the expected receipt of cash proceeds from exercising the put is farther in the future. However, if the European put is deep-out-of-the-money, a long time to expiration will tend to enhance option value. This is because more time provides a greater opportunity for the stock price to drop far enough to make the put valuable at expiration. Of course, the stock price could rise as well, but as in the case of call options, losses on the downside can be limited by simply not exercising the put.

Cash Distributions

Some assets, notably many common stocks, have cash distributions associated with them. A cash dividend paid on an underlying stock decreases the value of a call option, other things held constant. The reason is that cash dividends reduce the market price of the stock on the day the stock goes *ex dividend* (i.e., begins to trade without rights to any cash dividends previously declared on the stock; shareholders of record just prior to the ex dividend date are entitled to the cash dividends, but holders of call options on that stock are not). As the price of a stock declines when it goes ex dividend, so too will the value of a call option on the stock, other things remaining constant. The opposite is true for a put option: the holder of the put option, as well as the owner of the stock, benefit from cash dividends in that the stock owner receives a cash payout and the put holder obtains increased option value when the stock's price declines upon going ex dividend.

A summary of the effect each of the preceding factors has on American option value is illustrated in Table B.

TABLE B
Summary of Factors Determining American Option Value[a]

	Call Option	Put Option
Asset price	+	–
Exercise price	–	+
Interest rates	+	–
Volatility of the asset price	+	+
Time to maturity	+	+[b]
Cash distributions	–	+

[a]The + and – signs indicate the nature of the effect each factor has on the value of the option.
[b]As discussed above, time to maturity could have either a positive or negative influence on European put option value.

Put-Call Parity

Consider again the Microsoft put and call options described in Table A. Notice that, in addition to being written on the same stock, these options had identical exercise prices and maturity dates. Given their similar characteristics, it seems logical that the market values of the call and put would have been related to one another in a predictable way. That is, as the price of Microsoft's stock changed, the prices of the options should also have changed, but in such a way that an astute investor could not have bought one and sold another so as to lock in a visually riskless profit. Should such an *arbitrage* opportunity develop, the very act of exploiting it ought to set buy and sell transactions in motion that will ultimately ensure a kind of parity between put and call prices.

This is, in fact, the case. A condition known as *put-call parity* describes the relationship that a put and call option written on the same stock with the same exercise price and maturity date must sustain if there are to be no riskless arbitrage opportunities.[1] Specifically, put-call parity states that the difference in price between a call option and a put option with the same terms should equal the price of the underlying asset less the present discounted value of the exercise price. This relationship can be described as follows:

$$V_c - V_p = P_a - X$$

where

V_c = the price of a call option
V_p = the price of a put option
P_a = the price of the underlying asset
X = present discounted value of the underlying asset's exercise price

Another way to interpret this relationship is to say that someone owning a call option while having simultaneously written (sold) a comparable put option on the same asset should, at all times, be in a position equivalent to someone who purchased the underlying asset with a pure-discount (i.e., zero-coupon) loan having a face value equal to the option's exercise price and maturing at the option's expiration date. The value of these two options must be equal because each investor would realize identical payoffs at the time of maturity. You can demonstrate this to yourself by constructing payoff diagrams such as those shown in Figure I for each of these two positions. As you will observe, the payoff in both cases is equivalent to owning stock purchased on "margin" (that is, purchased partly with borrowed proceeds).

Consider what could be done if this relationship were not true. For illustrative purposes, assume that the options on Microsoft's stock shown in Table A were European options. Suppose further that the call option on Microsoft's stock shown in Table A actually sold for $8.50 instead of $7.50. At the time, short-term interest rates were about 6% annually (equivalent to a compound daily rate of 1.6 basis points, or 0.016%). Under these conditions, strict put-call parity would *not* have held:

$$(\$8.50 - \$2.125) > (\$64.125 - \$58.709)$$

$$\$6.375 > \$5.414$$

where

$8.50 = assumed market value of the call option
$2.125 = market value of the put option
$64.125 = market value of Microsoft's stock
$58.709 = current value of a pure-discount loan maturing on April 15 at a value of 60

[1] Strictly speaking, put-call parity as described above applies only to European options because, unlike American options, they cannot be exercised prior to the expiration date.

Upon observing such a discrepancy, an astute trader would have executed the following transactions:

November 30, 1994	**Per Share Cash Proceeds**
1. Write (sell) a call option on Microsoft's stock	$8.50
2. Buy a put option on Microsoft's stock	(2.125)
3. Borrow $58.709 at a daily compound rate of interest of 0.016%	58.709
4. Purchase Microsoft's stock at $64.125	(64.125)
Net proceeds	$0.959

April 15, 1995	
a. If Microsoft's stock was worth more than $60 per share, then:	
1. Deliver the stock to the call option owner	—
2. Receive $60 from the call option owner	$60.00
3. Use the proceeds from the exercise of the call option to repay the loan	(60.00)
Net proceeds	$0.00
b. If Microsoft's stock was worth less than $60 per share, then:	
1. Exercise the put by delivering the stock to the put writer	—
2. Receive $60 from the put writer	$60.00
3. Use the proceeds from exercising the put to repay the loan	(60.00)
Net proceeds	$0.00

Notice that regardless of what happened to the price of Microsoft's stock, the trader would have received $60 on April 15, 1995, which is exactly sufficient to repay the loan with interest. Thus, the residual net proceeds of $0.959 per share from the November 30, 1994, transactions represent an immediate, riskless profit involving no commitment of the trader's own capital. Notice too that such an arbitrage profit would have been virtually immaterial at the call option's actual price of $7.50. If call or put option prices deviated substantially from levels dictated by the put-call parity relationship, transactions similar to those described above would drive prices up or down until the arbitrage opportunity was eliminated.

Applications

Options can be used to insure against various risks as well as to bet on various market movements. Risk management, or insurance, is often achieved through, for example, the purchase of put options. Assume a company expects to receive some foreign currency and is concerned that the currency will depreciate against its home currency. To limit its losses, the company might elect to purchase an at-the-money put option written on the exposed currency. Buying such a put option would, in effect, limit the company's loss associated with currency depreciation to the amount of the put premium. In effect, by buying a put option, the company buys insurance against currency depreciation. The cost of this insurance is the put premium. By insuring against loss in this way, however, the company also gives up some of the potential gains it might realize from currency appreciation in that it must pay a cash premium to buy the put.

Speculative positions can also be achieved by using options. A directional position is taken when a company or individual uses options to bet on a belief that the underlying asset price will move in one particular direction. If an entity believes that the British pound will appreciate, for example, then it could buy a call option written on the pound (i.e., go "long" British pounds). Because the currency could easily move in the "wrong" direction, (i.e., contrary to one's prior beliefs), buying currency call options does not secure a profit, nor does this transaction cover an already exposed position. But still, because of the inherent asymmetry of potential upside gains and downside losses, the holder stands to gain quite a bit, while potentially losing only the amount of the premium paid for the call option. This would be a more powerful way to speculate on the pound's movement than simply buying the currency in the spot market because, for a given amount of dollars, considerably more currency can be controlled through the purchase of relatively inexpensive option contracts than can be done by buying pounds outright on the spot foreign exchange market (a standard option contract on British pounds would provide an investor with a call option on £62,500 for a price in the vicinity of $1500; the same amount of currency might cost $95,000 to $100,000 on the spot market).

Forwards and Futures

Forwards and futures, like options, are derivative securities that can be used as a means of hedging or risk management, as well as to speculate. Predating any other derivative instrument, the privately traded forward contract serves as the foundation for its more standardized exchange-traded variant, the futures contract. While these two contracts are viewed and traded quite differently, they both operate under the same essential framework. Specifically, both the forward and the futures contract are defined by an obligation of the buyer and the seller both to perform under the specified terms of the contract. In this respect, forward and futures contracts differ fundamentally from option contracts. Because options give the owner the right but not the obligation to exercise the option, option contracts provide owners with asymmetric payoff patterns that are well suited to insuring against loss under certain circumstances. Because forwards and futures provide an obligation to transact at a prespecified future price, they are better suited for true "hedging" activities in which transacting parties wish to lock in future prices without risk. Figure III provides a payoff diagram of a generic forward contract to illustrate and distinguish these particular forms of derivative securities from options. (Note that F = Forward price.)

FIGURE III
Total Payoff on a Forward Contract

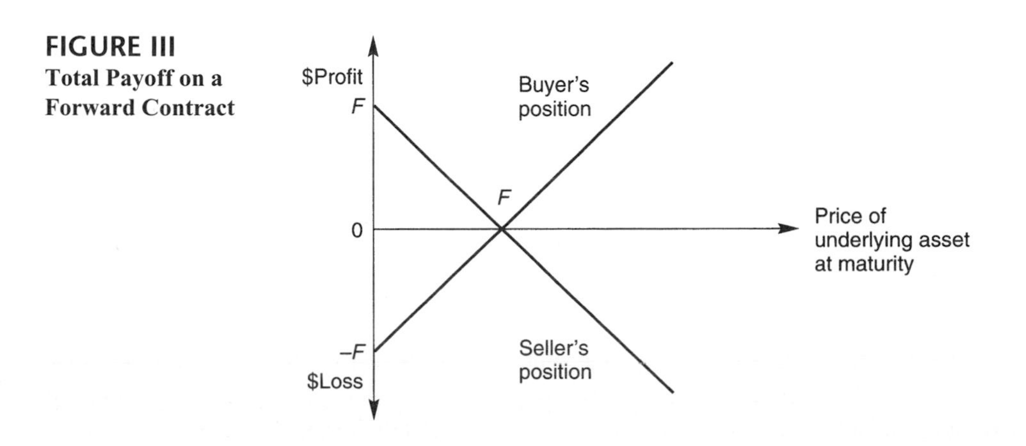

Forward Contracts

In contrast to exchange-traded derivatives, forward contracts are not standardized products. Instead, forward contracts are OTC derivatives that can be tailored to meet specific user needs. The underlying assets of these contracts include traditional agricultural or physical commodities, currencies (referred to as foreign exchange forwards), and interest rates (referred to as forward rate agreements or FRAs). A forward transaction typically involves a contract, most often with a bank, under which both the buyer (or holder) of the contract and the seller (or writer) of the contract are obligated to execute a transaction at a prespecified price on a prespecified date. That is, the seller is *obligated* to deliver a specified asset to the buyer on a specified date in the future. Likewise, the buyer is *obligated* to pay the seller a specified price (the forward price) upon delivery. If, at maturity, the actual spot market price is higher than the forward contract's exercise price, the contract holder makes a profit and the seller suffers a loss; if the spot price is lower, the contract seller makes a profit and the buyer suffers a loss. In any event, one party's gain is the other party's loss.

Normally, a forward contract's exercise price is fixed at inception at a level that makes the contract's value zero in the eyes of both the buyer and the seller. That is, ignoring risk aversion, both sides of the transaction would be roughly indifferent between entering into the contract at the specified exercise price or remaining unhedged. However, as the value of the underlying asset changes throughout the life of the contract, the value of the forward contract as seen by the buyer and the seller also changes. Specifically, the value changes for the benefit of one party and at the expense of the other. This property of the forward contract makes it a "zero-sum game" for the buyer and the seller.

To illustrate this zero-sum characteristic, consider a forward contract written on some specified asset with a forward exercise price for the asset of $50. Now imagine how a sudden upswing in the asset's price to $55 will affect both parties' views of the value of the contract. The party on the sell side of the forward contract views the contract to have lost value because the price at which he or she is obligated to sell the asset ($50) is now below that which could be received in the spot market ($55). In contrast, the party on the buy side of the contract sees this change as positive because, as the spot price of the asset increases, there is a better chance that the forward exercise price will be below the prevailing spot market price in the future when the forward contract matures and the asset is to be delivered. If this market condition persists until the specified delivery date, the seller's loss of $5 ($55–$50) equals the buyer's gain.

To summarize, both the buyer and the seller of a forward contract view their positions as having zero initial value. The agreed-upon forward price for the underlying asset is the contract price that fulfills this initial condition: that is, the forward price is determined so as to eliminate any initial value for either party. Subsequent changes in the spot market price of the underlying asset will lead to equal but opposite gains on the part of the buyer and seller.

Cost of Carry, Arbitrage, and Forward Prices

To understand how the correct forward price is determined, one must first appreciate the concepts of *cost of carry* and, again, *arbitrage.* Simply stated, the cost of carry is the opportunity cost that would be borne by an investor if the asset underlying a forward contract were actually bought and held rather than the forward contract itself. In the simplest possible case, this would essentially be the cost of money; that is, the opportunity cost of tying up one's money in the asset in question, thereby foregoing its use in other investments. For some underlying assets, however, ownership requires storage and the incurrence of *storage costs* (e.g., rental of space in a grain silo, rental of vault space, insurance costs). Storage costs, if any, add to the cost of carry.

Offsetting some of the cost of carry are cash payouts on the underlying asset (e.g., cash interest payments on debt securities or cash dividend payments on shares of stock) and so-called *convenience yields.* A convenience yield is the value that might be associated with actually owning, and therefore being able to use, the asset in question rather than simply having a future claim on that asset. A manufacturer that uses a lot of copper, for example, might wish to own a fairly sizable inventory of copper to assure that shortages are not experienced as demand for output fluctuates. Likewise, heavy users of fuel oil will often prefer to own oil itself rather than oil futures to safeguard against unanticipated interruptions in supply.

Consider now an asset such as gold, which provides no cash payouts, and capital market conditions in which the 1-year yield on Treasury bills is 10%. For simplicity, assume further that under current market conditions, the convenience yield on gold equals storage costs. Under these simplified conditions, the cost of carry on gold is simply the cost of money. If someone were to purchase gold with cash in the spot market for \$375 per ounce and hold it for a year, money would be tied up for a year, thereby imposing an opportunity cost on the investors of 10%, or \$37.50—resulting in a total cost of \$412.50 per ounce of gold by the time it is used or sold 1 year later.

This opportunity cost could be avoided if the investor elected instead to enter into a forward contract that would oblige him or her to pay cash for gold a year later, but not before. What would be a fair price to agree to pay 1 year later? In principle, the investor should be happy to pay any price less than or equal to \$412.50, for at such prices, the investor should be no worse off, and possibly better off, than buying gold and holding it for a year. Similarly, the party writing the forward contract should be happy to sell the contract at any price equal to or greater than \$412.50, for such prices would permit the writer to buy and hold gold for a year, thus eliminating the risk of future price changes in the spot market, while also at least covering his or her cost of carry. The interests of both the buyer and the seller can be met at their mutual breakeven price of $\$412.50 = \$375 \times (1 + .10)$.

This pricing equilibrium implies the following simple formula for determining the forward price of an asset:

$$F_n = S(1 + c)^n$$

where

F_n = the forward price of an asset n years into the future
S = the current spot price for the asset
c = the annual cost of carry, expressed as a fraction of the asset's spot price (e.g., .01, .05, etc.)
n = years to maturity

Because c is composed of several different costs and yields, the forward price can also be expressed more fully as

$$F = S(1 + r_f + s - i - v)^n$$

where

r_f = the riskless rate of return
s = storage costs
i = cash yield
v = convenience yield

All are expressed as annual costs or yields as a fraction of the spot price.

Forward contracts in which the forward price is established at inception, according to the above formula, will have an initial value of zero. Notice that any other forward price would lead to a potential arbitrage opportunity. Suppose, for example, that a forward contract on gold such as that described above was struck at a below-market forward price of $400 per ounce. This being the case, and assuming ample supplies of gold in storage, arbitrageurs could lock in a riskless profit by simultaneously buying that which is relatively "cheap" (gold in the forward market) and selling that which is relatively "expensive" (gold in the spot market).

Specifically, an arbitrageur would:

	Per Ounce Cash Proceeds
1. Borrow some gold and sell it (i.e., "short" gold)	$375.00
2. Invest the proceeds of the sale for 1 year at 10%	(375.00)
3. Enter into a 1-year forward contract to purchase gold at $400.00/oz.	—
Net proceeds	$0.00

One year later, the same arbitrageur would:

	Per Ounce Cash Proceeds
1. Collect the proceeds from the 1-year investment	$412.50
2. Use the proceeds to execute the forward agreement to buy gold at $400/oz.	(400.00)
3. Deliver the gold to the party from whom it was originally borrowed	—
Net proceeds	$12.50

In effect, market arbitrageurs would make a riskless profit of $12.50 per ounce of gold on zero net investment. This arbitrage opportunity arises because the forward price is too low given the current spot price and the cost of carry. To eliminate this arbitrage opportunity, forward and/or spot prices for gold must adjust until the forward price formula shown above is satisfied.

Notice that if a forward contract's underlying asset does not have a significant cash payout relative to the cost of money, and/or if storage costs significantly exceed convenience yields, the cost of carry will be positive and the current forward price will be greater than the spot price. This premium of the forward price over the spot price is known as *contango.* Typical examples of assets with low or no cash payouts are stock indices and foreign exchange.[2] The opposite will be true if there are large cash payouts or when the convenience yield is especially high (a common occurrence for many commodities when supply conditions in the spot market become quite tight). Under these

[2]In the particular case of foreign exchange, the forward price must take account of two interest rates because two currencies are involved. "Shorting" one currency implies borrowing it at prevailing interest rates in that currency, while investment in the other currency will take place at that other currency's prevailing interest rates. The formula for determining the forward exchange rate between a domestic currency *(d)* and a foreign currency *(f)* is as follows:

$$F = S \times (1 + R^d)/(1 + R^f)$$

where

F = forward rate of exchange, expressed as units of domestic currency per unit of foreign

S = spot market rate of exchange, expressed as units of domestic currency per units of foreign

R^d = domestic interest rate

R^f = foreign interest rate

conditions, the forward price will be below the spot price, a condition known as *backwardation.* Notice too that, regardless of how high or low the forward price is relative to the spot price at the time the forward contract is established, the forward price eventually converges with the spot price as the time to delivery shortens to zero. This is because the cost of carry in an asset necessarily becomes less as the time to delivery approaches.

Futures Contracts

Futures contracts, unlike forwards, trade on organized exchanges. They are traded in three primary areas: agricultural commodities, metals and petroleum, and financial assets. While commodity futures have been traded since the 1860s, financial futures were first traded in 1972 with the advent of the foreign currency future. Since then, financial futures have been established for various debt instruments, stock market indices, and foreign currencies.

The basic form of the futures contract mirrors that of the forward contract: Both parties are obligated under the terms of the contract to deliver a specified asset or pay the specified price of the asset on the contract maturity date. In addition, the futures contract entails the following two obligations, both of which help to minimize the default (or credit) risk inherent in forward contracts.

1. The value of the futures contract is "settled" (i.e., paid or received) at the end of each trading day. In the language of the futures markets, the futures contract is *cash settled,* or *marked-to-market,* daily. The marked-to-market provision effectively reduces the performance period of the contract to a day, thereby minimizing the risk of default.
2. Both buyers and sellers are required to post a performance bond called *margin.* At the end of each trading day, gains and losses are added to and taken away from the margin account, respectively. The margin account must remain above an agreed-upon minimum or the account will be closed. The margin provision prevents the depletion of accounts, which, in turn, largely eliminates the risk of default.

With these additional features in mind, a futures contract can be thought of as a connected series of 1-day forward contracts in which the forwards are settled and restruck daily until the specified maturity date. By definition, a futures contract is an agreement between the seller of the contract and the buyer of the contract in which the seller is obligated to deliver a specified asset to the buyer on a specified date in the future and the buyer is obligated to pay the seller the then prevailing futures price upon delivery. The nature of marked-to-market defines the "then prevailing futures price" simply as the then prevailing spot price. Therefore, upon final settlement of a futures contract that has reached maturity, the only profit and loss incurred is that associated with the last day's market movement.

Applications

The two generic uses for forwards and futures are speculation and hedging. As an example of forward market speculation assume an investor expects the dollar price of the Japanese yen to fall dramatically over the next 90 days. Foreign currency markets allow such an investor to bet on his or her expectations. First, the investor sells yen forward at the prevailing forward spot rate. After 90 days, assuming the yen depreciated as expected, the investor then purchases yen in the spot market for delivery on the forward contract. If all goes well, the forward price at which the investor sells yen will exceed the future spot price at which he or she buys, and a profit will result from the difference. Of course, if the opposite is true and the yen strengthens against the dollar, the investor will lose the difference between the future spot rate and the forward price.

Hedging, unlike speculation, is a tactic used to avoid or limit risk. Forward and futures contracts are commonly used for this purpose. For example, assume an investor will hold some specified asset for 1 year and is fearful of price depreciation over the holding period. To hedge against price depreciation by locking in a known value today, the investor could sell a forward contract written on the asset; that is, he could sell the asset forward, just as the investor in the previous speculation example sold the yen forward. In doing so, the investor covers his or her "long" position in the asset with a "short" position (the forward sale). Losses that might occur on the long position will be offset by gains on the short position, and vice versa. In this way, uncertainty about the future market value of the asset in question can be eliminated.

Swaps

A swap is any agreement to a future exchange of one asset for another, one liability for another, or more specifically, one stream of cash flows for another. The most common swaps include currency swaps, in which one currency is exchanged for another at prespecified terms on one or more prespecified future dates, and interest rate swaps, in which one type of interest payment (e.g., interest payments that float with LIBOR[3]) is exchanged for another (e.g., fixed interest payments) at one or more prespecified future dates. Like other derivative securities, these swaps (as well as more sophisticated swaps not addressed in this note) are used by various entities such as corporations, banks, and investors to hedge risk or to speculate, in the expectation of making a profit. As a tool of risk management, swaps offer considerable flexibility and cost savings to their users. The boom in swaps transactions since the early 1980s is testament to the growing demand for flexible and standardized risk management products.

Although its origins can be traced back to the 1970s, the swap market did not publicly exist until 1981 when currency swaps were first introduced. U.S. interest rate swaps followed in 1982 as rising interest rate volatility necessitated a flexible means by which companies with floating interest rate exposures could hedge such risk. As swap markets grew, swaps became common adjuncts to financings, particularly cross-border financings, as a way to help companies lower their funding costs. They did so by enabling companies to source capital in whatever market or currency it was found to be cheapest (e.g., floating-rate Swiss francs), and then to convert the resulting liability into whatever form made most sense (e.g., fixed-rate dollars). Today it is a common practice of major borrowers to analyze funding opportunities in light of relative pricings for new debt issues and swaps across global markets.

Like a forward or futures contract, a swap is a private agreement between two parties in which both parties are *obligated* to exchange some specified cash flows at periodic intervals for a fixed period of time. In contrast to a forward or futures contract, a swap agreement generally involves multiple future points of exchange. The cash flows of a swap may be fixed in advance, or adjusted for each settlement date by reference to some specified interest rate, such as LIBOR, or other market yield. Although it is convenient to describe swaps as involving an outright exchange of cash flows at the so-called *settlement dates,* in practice, it is generally the case that a *difference check* is simply paid by whichever party in the swap is obligated to pay more cash than is to be received at that settlement date. For example, consider a fixed-for-floating interest rate swap agreement that requires one party to pay a fixed rate of interest of 9% a year on $100 million of principal in exchange for receiving from a counterparty interest equal to LIBOR plus

[3]LIBOR stands for the London Interbank Offered Rate. It is the interest rate offered by banks for dollar deposits in the London market. It is frequently used as a base interest rate for dollar loans.

½% on $100 million. If, at the first settlement date, LIBOR is equal to 7.5%, the party paying a fixed rate would owe the floating-rate counterparty a net payment of $1 million: [.09 – (.075 + .005)] × $100 million. If, at the next settlement date, LIBOR had risen to 9%, the fixed-rate party would receive a net cash payment of $.5 million from the floating rate counterparty: [.09 – (.09 + .005)] × $100 million. All of these settlements would be carried out by a financial intermediary such as an investment or commercial bank.

Also, like forward or futures contracts, swaps are priced so as to have zero value at inception. As interest rates or exchange rates change, the swap agreement then takes on positive value for whichever party becomes a net recipient of cash, and negative value for the counterparty that is the net payer of cash. In a sense, a swap agreement can be thought of as a prepackaged bundle of forward contracts, and its cash flows can be decomposed into the equivalent cash flows of these individual forward contracts.

Currency Swaps

In its simplest form, a currency swap is an agreement between two parties to exchange a given amount of one currency for another and to repay these currencies with interest in the future. As an example, consider one party, Global Enterprises, Inc. (Global) that has borrowed 200 million Swiss francs (SF) at 6% and wishes to transform this liability into dollars. At the same time, the World Financial Institution (WFI), which actively manages the currency mix of its debt portfolio in light of changing economic conditions, wishes to convert a $100 million obligation bearing 8% interest into a Swiss franc liability. Both companies' obligations have a 4-year maturity and are rated AAA. The prevailing spot exchange rate between the Swiss franc and the U.S. dollar is SF 2.00/$1.

Given these "matching," or opposite, hedging needs, a mutually satisfactory swap could be arranged in which Global agrees to pay 8% dollar interest to WFI for 4 years plus $100 million at maturity, and WFI agrees to pay Global 6% Swiss franc interest for 4 years plus SF 200 million at maturity. In this way, each borrower would have its debt service to its respective lender exactly covered, and each would be left with a payment stream in the currency of its choice. Figure IV illustrates this arrangement and the cash flows entailed.

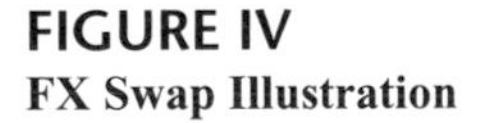
FIGURE IV
FX Swap Illustration

Swap Diagram

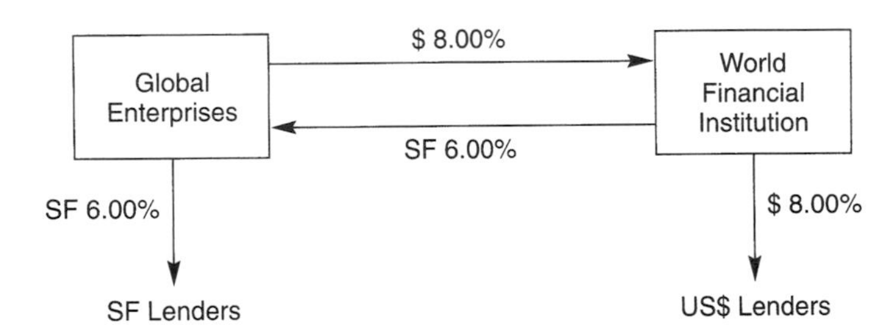

Swap Cash Flow Diagram (millions)

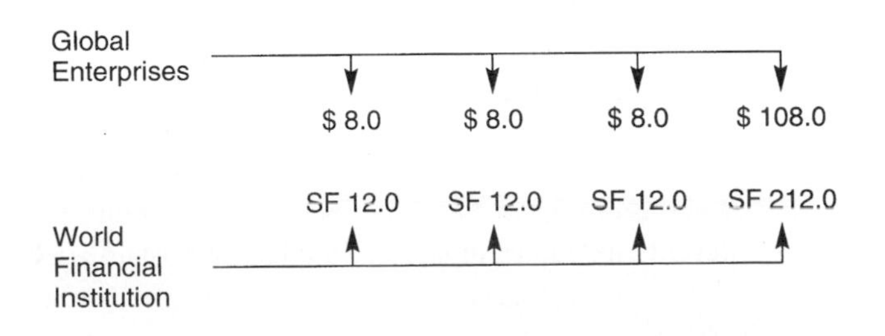

TABLE C
Selected Swap Rates, December 16, 1985[a]

	3 Years		5 Years	
	Pay	Receive	Pay	Receive
U.S. dollars	8.79%	8.97%	9.42%	9.58%
British sterling	11.49	11.70	11.45	11.66
Japanese yen	7.12	7.28	7.02	7.17
Swiss francs	5.10	5.35	5.35	5.60
Deutsche marks	5.80	6.10	6.45	6.75

[a]All quotes are fixed annual rates against six-month dollar LIBOR, and quoted from the swap dealer's perspective. That is, the bank is willing to pay British sterling at a fixed annual rate of 11.49% in exchange for receiving six-month dollar LIBOR, and to receive British sterling at a fixed annual rate of 11.70% in exchange for paying six-month dollar LIBOR.

In practice, one party in a swap agreement seldom makes payments directly to the counterparty. When parties to a swap are matched directly, a financial institution usually intermediates the agreement, guaranteeing each party that payments in the needed currency will continue uninterrupted even if the counterparty defaults. The intermediary is paid a fee for acting as guarantor.

The most common swap arrangement is one in which the intermediary itself acts as the swap counterparty to its corporate clients. Major international banks make a market in currency swaps by quoting bid and offer rates for payments in various currencies for various maturities. The bid rate and the offer rate are the fixed rates of return in a specified currency that a bank is willing to pay a corporate client in exchange for receiving six-month dollar LIBOR, or to receive from a corporate client in exchange for paying six-month dollar LIBOR. For example, foreign currency swap rates being quoted by Morgan Guaranty, Ltd. in London on December 16, 1985, are shown in Table C.

The bank earns a profit on swap transactions by realizing the spread between its bid and offer rates on six-month dollar LIBOR. Notice that by relating any two quotes to dollar LIBOR, fixed swap rates can be quoted between any two currencies. For instance, using the quotes in Table C, the bank would be willing to pay yen for 3 years at a fixed annual rate of 7.12% in exchange for receiving deutsche marks for 3 years at a fixed annual rate of 6.10%, and to receive yen at a fixed annual rate of 7.28% in exchange for paying deutsche marks at a fixed annual rate of 5.80%.

Applications

Currency swaps, like other derivative instruments, are often used by corporations, banks, and government entities to hedge foreign exchange risk on both assets and liabilities. In this capacity, a currency swap functions much like a series of long-dated forward foreign exchange contracts.

One of the most common applications of currency swaps is their use in conjunction with debt issues. Companies sometimes find that they can source capital especially cheaply by selling debt denominated in a foreign currency. At the same time, however, they may wish to avoid the exchange rate risk associated with such foreign currency debt. A currency swap allows such companies to capture the low-cost capital while avoiding exchange rate risk. In effect, currency swaps allow corporate financial officers to uncouple the market in which financial execution takes place from the currency of the liability that they ultimately incur. In addition to transforming new debt, swaps are also flexible tools for companies to transform the currency denomination of existing debt. To cite a well-known example of such an application, the World Bank pursues a swap program to fine-tune its liability structure by actively swapping into and out of different currencies to achieve the lowest possible debt costs.

TABLE D
Interest Rate Swap Quotes[a]

Years	Bid	Offer
3	8.79%	8.97%
5	9.21	9.36
7	9.48	9.63

[a]Rates are quoted from the bank's perspective. Thus, the bank is willing to pay a fixed rate of interest of 8.79% in exchange for receiving six-month LIBOR for 3 years, and to receive 8.97% in exchange for paying six-month LIBOR for 3 years.

Interest Rate Swaps

An interest rate swap is a derivative transaction in which an asset or liability with a floating rate of interest can be converted into a fixed-rate instrument, or vice versa. Like a currency swap, an interest rate swap is a counterparty transaction in which the respective positions of two counterparties with equal but opposite needs are exchanged.

Principal payments are not exchanged in interest rate swaps. This is because the dollar value of the principal remains the same throughout the contract for both the fixed-rate asset or liability and the floating-rate asset or liability. The agreed "notional" principal is only used as a basis for calculating the fixed- and floating-rate payment streams. These payments are made, or more commonly netted by the use of a difference check, on specified periodic settlement dates. While the fixed rate of interest is set for the life of the contract, the floating interest rate is set at the beginning of each interval and typically based on three- or six-month LIBOR.

An example of a typical U.S. dollar-denominated interest rate swap might involve a company that wants to convert a portion of its fixed-rate debt to floating rate, perhaps because it has acquired some assets generating cash flows that will vary directly with short-term interest rates. To achieve this conversion, the company's treasurer could call a swap dealer at a major bank to obtain quotes on interest rate swaps. As with currency swaps, dealers in interest rate swaps typically make a market in six-month LIBOR. That is, swap dealers quote a bid rate, which is the fixed rate of interest the bank will pay in exchange for receiving six-month LIBOR (i.e., the "price" at which the bank stands ready to "buy" six-month LIBOR), and an offer rate, which is the fixed rate of interest the bank is willing to accept as payment in exchange for paying six-month LIBOR (i.e., the "price" at which the bank stands ready to "sell" six-month LIBOR). Swap rate quotes made in London by Morgan Guaranty, Ltd. on December 16, 1985, are shown in Table D.

Given these quotes, a company wishing to get out of fixed-rate debt into floating-rate debt for, say, 5 years could do so by agreeing to pay the bank six-month LIBOR in exchange for receiving fixed-rate payments of 9.21%, which could then be used to cover a portion of the interest on its outstanding fixed-rate debt obligations.[4]

Applications

Interest rate risk is the leading reason that corporations use swaps. They are typically used to insure against loss in value of existing corporate liabilities and assets due to unexpected changes in interest rates. For example, a corporation that has recently taken on a substantial amount of debt might want to adjust the duration of its debt to match better the duration of its expected cash inflows, thereby reducing the exposure of the corporation's market value to interest rate risk.

[4]In practice, the bid rate by the bank may not cover precisely the fixed rate of interest that the company must pay to its debt holders. When this occurs, an adjustment is made by adding or subtracting an appropriate number of basis points to the fixed rate paid and six-month LIBOR received.

In addition to hedging, corporations often use interest rate swaps to reduce debt costs. There are three principal ways by which these swaps might provide cost savings: (1) speculating on market movements, (2) exploiting arbitrage opportunities, and (3) reducing transactions costs. A corporation can speculate on the direction of interest rates by swapping in and out of fixed- and floating-rate agreements in hopes of achieving lower borrowing rates. Of course, this sort of speculation can result in higher borrowing costs if interest rates move in an adverse direction.

A corporation might also reduce borrowing costs by exploiting arbitrage opportunities arising from an ability to source either fixed- or floating-rate debt at particularly attractive rates in one market compared to another. A company wishing to issue fixed-rate debt might, for example, discover that it can command unusually low rates in the Eurodollar floating-rate note market. The company can exploit this opportunity by issuing the floating-rate notes, thus securing the low-cost funds, and then entering into an interest rate swap that would convert the floating-rate debt to fixed rate. In this respect, like currency swaps, interest rate swaps enable corporate treasurers to uncouple the market in which they source funds from the desired interest rate structure of their debt obligations. In the early days of the swap market, funding could be obtained at savings of as much as 50 basis points given the significant arbitrage opportunities that were then available. Today, due to more integrated capital markets, arbitrage savings are rarer and more commonly below 20 basis points.

Finally, transaction costs of an interest rate swap are relatively lower than those of its predecessor, the interest rate forward contract (forward rate agreements), due to the standardized nature of the swap market. Thus, interest rate swaps represent an attractive risk management and cost-savings tool for an increasingly wide range of market participants.

Basis Rate Swaps

A basis rate swap is essentially an interest rate swap in which both interest rates are floating. In effect, a basis rate swap allows a borrower or investor to exchange cash flows determined by one floating interest rate for cash flows determined by another floating interest rate. For example, a corporation could transform a loan based on six-month LIBOR to the same loan based on one-month commercial paper rates.

A basis rate swap can be thought of as two interest rate swaps paired together. One of the pair would be a floating-for-fixed swap, and the other would be an exchange of the fixed rate with another floating rate. For example, a company could swap a six-month LIBOR obligation for a fixed rate, and then swap the fixed rate with another counterparty for another floating-rate obligation based upon commercial paper rates. The basis rate swap conveniently rolls into one transaction what would otherwise be two using conventional fixed-for-floating interest rate swaps.

EXHIBIT 1
Survey of the Use of Derivatives by CFOs

Source: *Institutional Investor*, CFO forum, February 1993.

A. Percent of affirmative answers to the question: What kind of derivatives, if any, does your company use?	
Foreign exchange forwards	64.2%
Interest rate swaps	78.9
Foreign exchange options	40.4
Oil and energy-linked swaps	11.9
Other commodity-linked swaps	14.7
Exchange-traded interest rate futures and options	29.1
Exchange-traded foreign exchange futures and options	11.0
Exchange-traded equity futures and options	10.1
OTC interest rate futures and options	13.8
Equity-linked swaps	4.6
Equity swaps	2.8
B. Percent of affirmative answers to the question: For what purpose does your company use derivatives?	
To hedge floating rate debt	52.7%
To hedge commercial paper issuance	23.2
To create synthetic floating-rate debt at a lower cost	35.7
To create synthetic fixed-rate debt at a lower cost	43.8
To access capital markets globally	15.2
To hedge investments overseas	36.6
To achieve strategic liability management	40.2

Glossary

American option See **Option.**

Arbitrage Profiting from price differences on the same security, currency, or commodity traded in two or more markets.

At-the-money Term used to describe an option contract that has an exercise price equal to the current market price of the underlying asset.

Backwardation Pricing situation in which forward and futures prices are higher for those contracts expiring in the near future than those expiring farther out.

Bid/ask spread Difference between the bid price (the highest price a prospective buyer is prepared to pay for a particular security) and the ask price (the lowest price a prospective seller is willing to accept for the same security).

Call option See **Option.**

Contango Pricing situation in which forward and futures prices get progressively higher as maturities get progressively longer.

Cost of carry Out-of-pocket costs incurred while an investor has an investment position.

Deep-in/out-of-the-money Call option whose exercise price is well below the current market price of the underlying asset **(deep-in-the-money)** or well above the current market price of the underlying asset **(deep-out-of-the-money).** The situation would be exactly opposite for a put option.

Default (credit) risk Financial risk that a debtor will fail to make timely payments of interest and principal as they come due, or to meet some other provision of a financial agreement.

Derivative instrument Financial instrument whose value is based on that of another underlying security.

Difference check Form of direct, one-way payment upon settlement of a financial contract.

European option See **Option.**

Ex-dividend The absence of the right to receive a cash dividend payment already declared on a stock.

Exercise price Price at which some security underlying a derivative instrument can be purchased or sold on or before the contract's maturity date.

Expiration date See **Maturity date.**

Forward contract Privately traded contract to buy or sell a specific amount of some underlying asset at a specified price on a specified future date.

Futures contract Standardized exchange-traded contract to buy or sell a specific amount of some underlying asset at a specified price on a specified future date.

Guarantor Entity that takes on a contingent liability by assuming the responsibility for payment of a debt or performance of some obligation if the party primarily liable fails to perform.

Hedging The reduction of risk by eliminating the possibility of future gains or losses (e.g., by buying or selling forward and futures contracts).

Insurance The reduction of risk by the purchase of contingent claims (e.g., put options, call options, guarantees, insurance policies) that offset future losses by paying off under those circumstances in which losses are expected to be incurred.

In-the-money Term used to describe an option contract that has an exercise price below the current market price of an underlying asset in the case of a call option, and above the current market price of the underlying asset in the case of a put option.

Intrinsic value For call options, the greater of zero and the difference between the market value of the call's underlying asset and its exercise price. For put options, the greater of zero and the difference between the put's exercise price and the market value of its underlying asset.

London Interbank Offered Rate (LIBOR) Rate that the most creditworthy international banks dealing in Eurodollars charge each other for large loans.

Margin Amount of cash an investor deposits with a broker when borrowing from the broker to buy securities. If the price of the security purchased "on margin" falls, the broker will require the investor to put up more "margin" by making additional cash deposits.

Mark-to-market Adjust the recorded value of a security or portfolio to reflect actual current market values.

Market value (or price) The price at which willing buyers and sellers trade similar items in a free and open market.

Maturity date Date on which payment on some financial contract becomes due and payable. In the case of options, the maturity date is the final date on which the option owner can buy or sell the underlying asset.

Option The right, but not the obligation, to buy or sell some specified underlying asset for a specified price on (or before) a specified date.

- **Call option** Gives its buyer the right to buy some underlying asset at a fixed price on or before a specified date in the future.
- **Put option** Gives its buyer the right to sell some underlying asset at a fixed price on or before a specified date in the future.
- **American option** Option that can be exercised on or before the expiration date.
- **European option** Option that can be exercised only on the expiration date.

Option premium Price an option buyer must pay an option seller for an option contract.

Out-of-the-money Term used to describe an option contract that has an exercise price above the current market price of the underlying asset in the case of a call option, and below the current price of the underlying asset in the case of a put option.

Over-the-counter (OTC) Market in which securities transactions are conducted through a telephone and computer network connecting dealers in stocks and bonds, rather than on the floor of an organized exchange.

Put-call parity Relationship between put and call option prices that, if held in parity, prevents arbitrage opportunities.

Put option See **Option.**

Settlement date Date by which an executed order must be settled, either by a buyer paying for the securities with cash or by a seller delivering the securities and receiving the proceeds of the sale for them.

Speculation Assumption of risk in anticipation of gain, but often implying a higher than average possibility of loss.

Spot price Current delivery price of some physical commodity or financial asset traded in the spot market.

Strike price See **Exercise price.**

Swap Exchange of one asset or liability with particular terms and conditions for another asset or liability with different terms and conditions for a specified period of time.

Transaction costs Cost of buying or selling a security, which consists mainly of the brokerage commission, the dealer markdown or markup, or fee (as would be charged by a bank).

Zero-coupon security Security that makes no periodic interest payments but instead is sold at a deep discount from its face value.

Sally Jameson: Valuing Stock Options in a Compensation Package (Abridged)

Sally Jameson, a second-year MBA student at Harvard Business School, was thrilled but confused. It was late May 1992, graduation was approaching, and she had finally landed the job of her choice. She had just finished an early morning telephone conversation with Bob Marks, the MBA recruiting coordinator at Telstar Communications, a large, publicly held multinational company. Mr. Marks had offered Ms. Jameson a unique position in operations at Telstar, and from the description, it sounded exactly like the job that she wanted. Since her first interview with Telstar, she had been very impressed with the company and its people. While Ms. Jameson was certain that she would accept the job, there was still one unsettled, yet crucial, matter—her compensation.

During the conversation with Marks, Jameson had asked what her compensation package would be.

> **Marks:** "Well, Sally, we are all very impressed with you and would like to offer you a starting salary of $50,000. In addition, you will also receive a signing bonus."
> **Jameson:** "The base salary is a little below what I had expected. Is that negotiable?"
> **Marks:** "I'm afraid not. That's the same starting package all MBAs get. However, you will receive a bonus upon accepting our offer. You can receive $5,000 in cash, or choose stock options instead."
> **Jameson:** "I'm not too familiar with stock options. Could you explain to me what they are?"
> **Marks:** "Sure. Executives at Telstar have been eligible to receive stock options for years. The goal was to tie management's compensation more closely to increases in shareholder value. Although our stock has performed erratically over the last ten years, the board continues to believe that stock options are the best form of incentive compensation. Because the options represent the right to buy Telstar stock at a set price, after a set period of time, management has an incentive to take actions to move the stock price upward. Several months ago, we had a consulting firm examine our compensation structure. They recommended that we extend eligibility for stock options to all employees as part of our new incentive-based compensation plans. Thus, the two MBAs that we hope to hire this year will be the first employees who will be offered stock options. Given that this is an experiment, we decided to give MBAs a choice between cash or options."
> **Jameson:** "How much are these options worth?"
> **Marks:** "To tell you the truth, I'm not really sure. All I know are the details: each of the 3,000 options you'll be granted allows you to buy one share of Telstar stock at $35.00 per share at the time of your fifth anniversary with the firm.[1] Yesterday, our stock, which pays no dividend and is not expected to pay one in the foreseeable future, closed at $18.75. Should you leave at any point before your fifth year, you lose the options. You can't take them with you.

[1]Casewriter's note: Stock options of this sort would more typically have been written with a strike price equal to or just slightly above the current price.

Professor Peter Tufano and Research Associate Michael Lewittes prepared this case. HBS cases are developed solely as the basis for class discussion. Certain details have been disguised. Cases are not intended to serve as endorsements, sources of primary data, or illustrations of effective or ineffective management.

Copyright © 1993 President and Fellows of Harvard College. To order copies or request permission to produce materials, call 1-800-545-7685, write Harvard Business School Publishing, Boston, MA 02163, or go to http://www.hbsp.harvard.edu. No part of this publication may be reproduced, stored in a retrieval system, used in a spreadsheet, or transmitted in any form or by any means—electronic, mechanical, photocopying, recording, or otherwise—without the permission of Harvard Business School.

"I have been told by our legal staff that these incentive stock options meet the IRS code for special treatment—that means you won't pay any taxes on the options until you actually exercise them and then sell the shares. At that point, your gains on the shares (equal to the difference between their fair market value at that time and $35.00) will be taxed at either ordinary tax rates or at capital gains rates, depending on whether you've held the stock for less than or more than one year after exercising the option. If you choose the cash signing bonus, it is taxed at ordinary tax rates.[2] It's your choice, Sally, but just between you and me, I'd take the cash bonus. Telstar stock is only at $18.75; it doesn't seem to me that these options are worth the paper that they're printed on. I think it's just another example of consultants trying to justify their fees. You do what you think is best; either way, though, I need to know by tomorrow if you accept the offer and, if you do, which compensation package you'd prefer."

While Bob Marks seemed to prefer the cash bonus, Sally Jameson was less sure. Taking out her *Wall Street Journal,* she noticed that both short-term and long-term Telstar options were traded (see Exhibit 1). From an online financial database, she got a graph of Telstar's common stock price and a plot of the historical volatility of the stock price as measured by the annualized standard deviation of the stock's returns (see Exhibits 2 and 3). She also found data on government bill, note, and bond yields that would be useful in her analysis (see Exhibit 4).

As she thought about the problem, she decided to approach it in two steps: first, she would attempt to determine what the options were worth, assuming she stayed at Telstar for at least five years. Then, she would consider other issues, including the likelihood that she might not stay at Telstar that long.

EXHIBIT 1
Listed Telstar Options Quotations as of Close of Market—May 27, 1992

Source: *Wall Street Journal,* May 28, 1992.

Strike Price	Calls Expiration Date (1992)			Puts Expiration Date (1992)		
	June 20	July 18	Oct. 17	June 20	July 18	Oct. 17
$17.50	1.4375	1.8750	2.5000	.1875	r	1.0625
$20.00	.1875	.5000	1.3125	1.3750	r	r
$22.50	r[a]	.1250	.5625	r	3.5000	r

[a] r = not traded

Long Term Call Options: Expiration Date	Strike Price	Option Price
Jan. 22, 1994	$12.50	7.7500
Jan. 22, 1994	$17.50	4.6250
Jan. 22, 1994	$20.00	3.7500

[2]In May 1992, Ms. Jameson's marginal tax rate would have been 28%. The maximum marginal tax rate was 31%. The capital gains tax rate was 28%.

EXHIBIT 2
Stock Price of Telstar Common Stock, 1/4/82 through 5/27/92[a]

Source: Compiled from Thomson Financial Datastream.

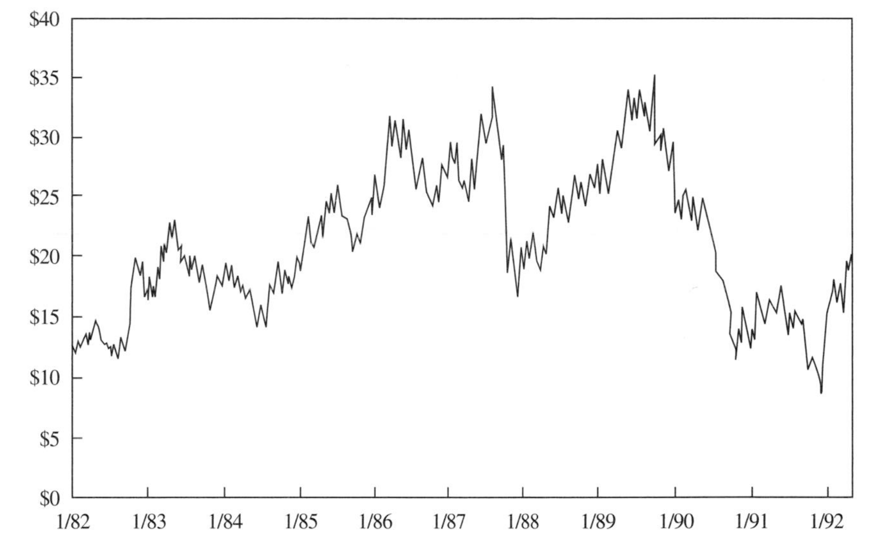

[a]Stock price has been adjusted for stock splits and dividends. On May 27, 1992, Telstar stock closed at $18.75 per common share.

EXHIBIT 3
Volatility of Telstar Common Stock, 1982 through May 27, 1992[a]

Source: Calculated by case writer.

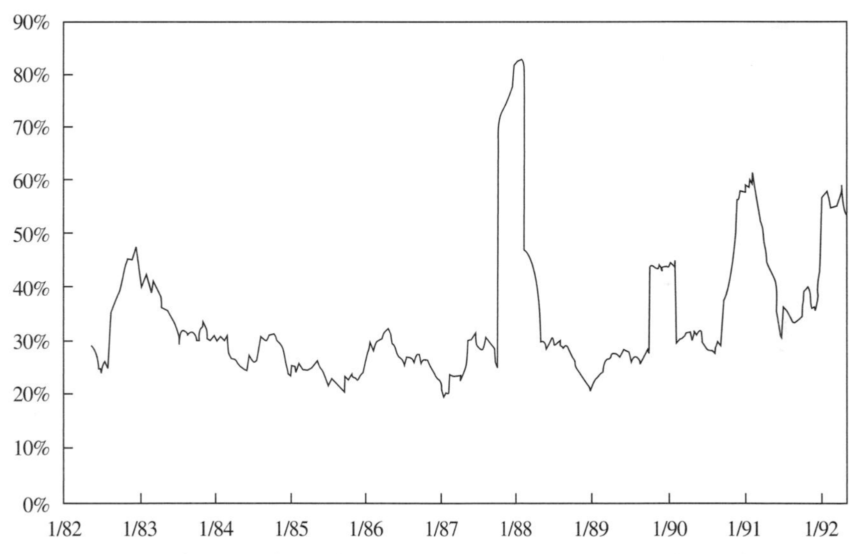

[a]Volatility measured by the annualized standard deviation of daily stock returns measured over the prior ninety days.

EXHIBIT 4
Treasury Security Yields as of May 27, 1992[a]

Source: Calculated from Thomson Financial Datastream.

	Annualized Treasury Bill and Bond Yields
1-month	3.70%
2-month	3.72%
3-month	3.69%
6-month	3.81%
1-year	4.02%
2-year	5.25%
5-year	6.02%
7-year	7.08%
10-year	7.41%
30-year	7.89%

[a]Rates all quoted on a bond equivalent yield basis.

Student Educational Loan Fund, Inc. (Abridged)

The situation facing Rick Melnick in the fall of 1995 reminded him of the cases he had studied as a student in the MBA Class of 1992 at Harvard Business School (HBS). As one of his many responsibilities as Associate Director of Financial Management at HBS, Melnick oversaw the School's Student Educational Loan Fund (SELF), a tax-exempt, separately incorporated but related unit of HBS. SELF had been established in 1961 to fund loans to HBS students. In response to student desires, the SELF board of directors proposed a new policy for the program. Under the new plan, students would receive monthly-paid, fixed-rate loans instead of the traditional semi-annually-paid, variable-rate loans that had been offered since SELF's inception. On his desk, Melnick had proposals from two banks on a variety of schemes to fund the new loans. There was no lack of financial products available, including swaps, caps, floors, and swaptions. In deciding among these alternatives, Melnick felt that he needed to consider the overall goal of SELF, in addition to economic and other business criteria.

The HBS MBA Program and Alternative Sources of Student Loans

Tuition for the two-year MBA program at HBS was $42,000 for the Class of 1996, with an additional $4,700 for education materials. Health insurance and living and personal expenses added several thousand dollars more to the cost of the program. The cost of the program coupled with the loss of income during the two years forced 52% of students to obtain some form of student loan, and the average loan balance at graduation was projected to be $45,372.[1]

There were many sources of loans available to students.[2] The Federal government, through the U.S. Department of Education's Student Financial Assistance Programs, offered several types of subsidized and unsubsidized student loans, including Stafford and Perkins loans. The terms and eligibility requirements of these loans varied, although generally they were available only to U.S. citizens and permanent residents who were not in default of previous federal government student loans. Stafford loans allowed students who were U.S. citizens or permanent residents to borrow up to $18,500 annually. Up to $8,500 of this was subsidized in the case of students demonstrating financial need; no interest accrued on subsidized loans during the student's enrollment and until six months after graduation. The interest rate on Stafford loans was reset on

[1]Includes loans from all sources.

[2]Regardless of the source of the loan, interest payments on student loans were not tax deductible under United States tax law, in contrast to mortgage interest payments.

Professor Peter Tufano and Charles M. Williams Fellow Cameron Poetzscher prepared this case. HBS cases are developed solely as the basis for class discussion. Cases are not intended to serve as endorsements, sources of primary data, or illustrations of effective or ineffective management. This case is an abridged version of an earlier case, Student Educational Loan Fund, Inc., HBS No. 296-046.

Copyright © 2001 President and Fellows of Harvard College. To order copies or request permission to reproduce materials, call 1-800-545-7685, write Harvard Business School Publishing, Boston, MA 02163, or go to http://www.hbsp.harvard.edu. No part of this publication may be reproduced, stored in a retrieval system, used in a spreadsheet, or transmitted in any form or by any means—electronic, mechanical, photocopying, recording, or otherwise—without the permisson of Harvard Business School.

July 1 each year, based on the 13-week T-bill rate; the maximum rate was capped at 8.25%. The upfront fee on Stafford loans was 4%. Level monthly repayments commenced six months after graduation and extended for up to 10 years.[3]

Perkins loans were lower cost loans, reserved for U.S. citizens or permanent residents with extreme loan needs and high education debt levels. There were government-imposed, university-wide limits on the total funds available for Perkins loans, and they were generally available only to students in the second year of the MBA program. Up to $5,000 could be borrowed annually under the Perkins program. The interest rate on Perkins loans was fixed at 5%, and there were no upfront fees. Level monthly repayments commenced 10 months after graduation and extended over 10 years.

Student loans were also available from U.S. commercial banks, although these too were usually restricted to U.S. citizens and permanent residents. The terms of bank loans varied widely. Typically, they allowed students to borrow an amount equal to the cost of education minus other financial aid. A co-applicant was sometimes required for loans over $7,500. Loan approval was based on the credit history and repayment ability of the student and co-applicant. The interest rate on these loans was not subsidized by either the Federal government or HBS, and was typically 1.5%–2.0% above prime, with upfront fees of 5%–10%. Some bank loans required students to pay interest while enrolled in school, while others accrued interest and capitalized it at graduation. Monthly repayments extended over 10 to 25 years.[4]

HBS Student Loans

In addition to these external loan sources, HBS students could also borrow money from the School itself. The HBS Student Loan Program allowed students to borrow up to $25,000, provided that their total MBA-related debt would not exceed $62,000 at graduation. The $25,000 limit had been established in 1994 in an attempt to limit the exposure of HBS to defaults by students with high loan balances. U.S. citizens and permanent residents were required to exhaust government borrowing sources before applying for HBS loans. Unlike the other loans, HBS loans were not restricted to U.S. citizens or permanent residents but instead were available to students of several foreign countries. Many of these foreign students found it hard to obtain loans in their home countries, where education was often free or significantly cheaper than in the United States and therefore there were few established sources of student financial aid.

A satisfactory credit history was required to receive an HBS loan, and the school reserved the right to check the credit histories of applicants. However, unlike bank loans, no co-applicant was needed. The Financial Aid Office at HBS was responsible for processing and approving applications for HBS loans. After a student was approved for an HBS student loan, he or she signed a promissory note. The loan funds were then advanced by HBS and applied against the student's term bill, the largest item on which was tuition. Funds in excess of the outstanding balance of charges on the student's term bill were remitted directly to the student via check a number of weeks after the promissory note was signed. Additional funds could be advanced throughout the student's enrollment in the MBA program, subject to the student's continuing to meet loan eligibility requirements. Students typically borrowed at the beginning of each semester.

[3]Depending on the lender, monthly repayments either (i) were calculated using the 8.25% maximum interest rate and then fixed prior to the first repayment for the entire term of the loan or (ii) were calculated using the prevailing interest rate and then fixed each July 1 for the following 12 months only. HBS used the former method.

[4]Monthly repayments on bank loans either (i) were calculated using the initial interest rate and fixed prior to the first repayment for the entire term of the loan or (ii) were calculated using the prevailing interest rate and fixed until any subsequent interest rate change.

Interest accrued on HBS loans from the date on which the promissory note was signed. However, no interest payments were required while a student was enrolled in the MBA program, so all interest accrued during this period was capitalized at graduation.[5] Repayments on HBS loans were made in up to 10 semi-annual installments, commencing six months after graduation and continuing for up to five years. The principal repayment required at each installment increased according to a predetermined schedule that did not vary as a function of the original principal amount outstanding, except for the final payment. Accordingly, large HBS loans involved a final balloon payment that was often a significant percentage of the original amount borrowed, while loans for smaller amounts were often repaid in less than five years. Students were permitted to prepay HBS loans at any time with no penalty.

See Exhibit 1 for a summary and comparison of the alternative student loans. See Exhibit 2 for sample amortization schedules for HBS loans of different sizes.

SELF

HBS loans were made from funds that were originally contributed by donors to the school for the exclusive purpose of making loans. Since the 1960s, the annual aggregate value of HBS loans made had grown rapidly as the student body had become increasingly diverse. SELF was originally set up to accommodate this rapid expansion. By purchasing HBS student loans at graduation each year, SELF freed up donor loan funds for use by incoming students. SELF bought many, but not all, of the loans outstanding under the HBS loan program. In a typical year, SELF bought from HBS approximately 225 loans, with an average balance that had recently ranged from $15,000 to $22,000. See Exhibit 3 for SELF's financial statements.

For each loan that SELF bought, it paid HBS the outstanding balance of the loan (principal plus accrued interest) and received the right to all future cash flows from the loan. The process remained transparent to students, however. Harvard University's central student billing office in the Holyoke Center continued to administer the loans, sending bills to students and collecting payments. Any payments received by Holyoke from SELF-owned loans were consolidated and remitted to SELF monthly by check. SELF was dependent on the Holyoke Center for all data on outstanding HBS student loans, which at times made it challenging for SELF to obtain the data it desired.

Interest rates were reset twice a year, in late May and late November, based on SELF's cost of capital over the preceding six months.[6] This was calculated as the weighted average of SELF's cost of debt, based on credit lines established with its bank, and its cost of equity, which had been arbitrarily set at 10% for the past several years.[7] However, SELF voluntarily sought to moderate the interest rate it charged students, and thus the interest rate on HBS student loans showed less volatility than SELF's cost of capital. For example, when the prime rate had been 18%, students had been charged only 12%.

The ability of students to prepay, or default on, their loans made it difficult to predict SELF's cash inflows. Students often made large prepayments in the first quarter of

[5]That is, accrued interest was added to the original principal to obtain a new ("capitalized") principal amount, on which future interest calculations would be based.

[6]For example, the interest rate set in early June 1995 was based on SELF's cost of capital from November 1994 through April 1995. This interest rate was used to calculate the interest charge that was applied to HBS student loans for the subsequent July 1995–December 1995 half-year. This interest charge appeared on statements mailed in early December 1995 for payment by December 31, 1995. The interest charge was calculated on a simple, not compound, basis.

[7]It was difficult for SELF to determine its cost of equity given the different sources of funds it relied on. One benchmark was the returns on the Harvard University endowment, which were 11.8%, 16.4%, and 8.4% for FY 1992, FY 1993, and the first nine months of FY 1994, respectively.

the year, coinciding with yearly bonuses. For example, on past occasions when Wall Street had experienced a record year, the overall amount of prepayments had jumped significantly.[8] It was extremely difficult to obtain accurate or comprehensive data on prepayment patterns, but Melnick had managed to compile some limited estimates for selected recent classes, as shown in Exhibit 4. Also, HBS students occasionally defaulted on their HBS loans. Net loan write-offs (defaults), which had averaged about 1.4% over the past few years, varied from year to year and represented a sustained delay in repayment or a permanent failure to pay.

The New HBS Student Loans

While many students had taken advantage of HBS loans over the years, there was some dissatisfaction on the part of students with the terms of the loans. Melnick and some members of SELF's board of directors believed there were several reasons for this. Requiring payments semi-annually rather than monthly resulted in larger payments that did not coincide with the regular pattern of cash inflows from salaries, necessitating more complex financial planning on the part of students. Melnick believed that this contributed to a higher rate of delinquency. The increasing size of the payments over time, particularly the large balloon payment at the end, was difficult for other financial institutions to understand and evaluate; this often made it more difficult for students to be approved for housing and other loans.

With this in mind, Melnick had proposed a new set of terms for the HBS loans. His proposal envisioned a mortgage-like structure, with equal monthly payments over five years and a fixed interest rate set in advance.[9] Students would still be permitted to make prepayments at any time without penalty. For example, using the capitalized balances shown in Exhibit 2 and assuming a loan term from July 1996 to June 2001 and a fixed interest rate of 9%, the monthly payments would be $111.55 for the $5,000 loan and $446.19 for the $20,000 loan.[10]

Funding SELF

To finance the purchase of student loans each year, SELF had historically relied on lines of credit at its two banks. These lines were identical. At the time of the case, each provided a commitment of up to $7.5 million. Interest on the loans was charged at the prime rate, and interest payments were required monthly. See Exhibit 5 for capital markets data as of November 1995 and Exhibit 6 for historical interest rates.

SELF was required to maintain compensating cash balances equal to 5% of the unused part of the commitment; these compensating balances earned no interest for SELF. SELF was also required to maintain a debt to net worth ratio of not more than four to one. SELF was permitted to drawn down and repay the lines at will, without penalty. This ability was critical for SELF, given the large and erratic prepayments it received from its borrowers. SELF used the two credit lines identically, borrowing in equal amounts as required, and repaying in equal amounts as loan repayments and prepayments were received from students.

[8]Placement data for the HBS Class of 1995 were: Consulting, 38%; Investment Banking, 17%; Manufacturing, 20%; Other Service Industries, 25%.

[9]The interest rate would still vary during a student's enrollment in the MBA program; only after graduation would the rate be fixed.

[10]The proposal actually entailed monthly repayments commencing six months after graduation (i.e., 12/96 or 1/97) and extending for five years from that date; different assumptions are used in the example above purely for purposes of comparison with the traditional loans.

These credit lines were secured by the assets of SELF (i.e., the loans receivable from students) but were non-recourse to Harvard University.[11] However, the University issued a "comfort letter" to the two banks, stating that it would maintain a specified minimum amount of equity in SELF.[12] The credit lines had a term of one year, and thus had to be renewed annually. This had never been a problem in the past.

With the impending switch to the new fixed-rate, mortgage-style HBS student loans, Melnick had asked his banks to outline several interest rate derivative products that could be combined with the existing prime-based loan in order to address the mismatch between SELF's new loans and its funding. Representative quotes for some of these products, including fixed-for-floating swaps, caps, floors, and basis swaps, are outlined in Exhibit 7.

A fixed-for-floating swap was a contract where SELF and the bank would exchange a fixed interest rate for a floating rate. In this instance, SELF would pay a fixed rate of interest (5.76%) on a "notional principal" in return for receiving a floating rate of interest (LIBOR) on the same notional principal. By combining this type of swap with LIBOR-based floating rate debt, it would effectively transform that debt into fixed rate debt.[13] In practice, the payments would be *netted,* with SELF paying the bank if LIBOR is less than 5.76%, and the bank paying SELF if LIBOR exceeded 5.76%. SELF would not be required to make any up-front payments to enter into this swap.

Purchasing a cap would give SELF the right, but not the obligation, to receive the excess of a floating interest rate over the fixed cap rate. For example, if SELF bought a 6% cap on 1-month U.S. Dollar LIBOR on $10 million notional principal, it would receive ($\frac{1}{12}$) × (LIBOR − 6%) × $10 million in any month in which LIBOR exceeded 6%. (If LIBOR were below 6%, SELF would receive no payments.) By buying a cap, a borrower whose interest payments were tied to LIBOR could set an upper limit or cap on its borrowing costs. Parties who bought caps were required to pay money up-front to enter into this option; for the 6% cap, this would cost 1.52% of the notional principal amount.

A floor was an option which paid its holder the difference if LIBOR fell below a preset amount. Often borrowers sold floors, and by doing this, gave their counterparty (its bank) the right, but not the obligation, to receive the excess of a fixed floor rate over a floating interest rate. For example, if SELF *sold* a 6% floor on 1-month U.S. Dollar LIBOR on $10 million notional principal, SELF would have to *pay* ($\frac{1}{12}$) × (6% − LIBOR) whenever LIBOR was below 6% in a month. By selling a floor, a borrower whose interest payments were tied to LIBOR could set a lower limit or floor on its borrowing costs. Parties who sold floors received money up-front to enter into this option contract; for the 6% floor, SELF would receive 2.12% of the notional principal amount. Often, a borrower would buy a cap and sell a floor to constrain its interest payments within a prespecified band.

Entering a basis swap would obligate SELF to exchange one floating rate for another. For example, SELF could enter into a basis swap to exchange Prime for LIBOR. Each month it would pay the current LIBOR rate and receive the Prime Rate less 2.80%. As with the fixed-floating swap, the payments would be netted and no money would change hands at the initiation of the swap. By combining a basis swap with its Prime-based borrowings, SELF could transform its loan into a LIBOR-based floating rate borrowing.

[11] Harvard University was rated Aaa/AAA.

[12] A "comfort letter" is a declaration of intent or assurance by one party to a contract, or an auditor or other entity with knowledge of that party, to another party to the contract.

[13] "Notional principal" is the amount of "principal" used for calculating the periodic "interest" payments due to each party. Unlike the principal on a traditional loan, it is not exchanged at the commencement of the swap contract. The notional principal could amortize according to various methods. The rates given in Exhibit 7 reflect "mortgage-style amortization" which would match the SELF loans, where the principal declined as it would under a mortgage with equal monthly payments.

SELF could bundle its existing bank loans with one or more of these contracts in order to transform its current Prime-based borrowing into another type of borrowing. At any time, SELF could prepay its Prime-based loan without penalty, but cancelling the derivative contracts might be more complicated. SELF could effectively "cancel" the derivative contracts in three ways. The first involved marking-to-market the outstanding value of the contract (calculating its present value) and then either paying to or receiving from its counterparty the present value of the remaining portion of the contract at then-prevailing interest rates. While the bank was not contractually required to agree to this, it almost always did. Second, SELF could enter the exact opposite contract with its original counterparty, which would result in a net exposure each month of zero. Third, SELF could enter the opposite contract with another counterparty, and then, subject to approval by the original counterparty, assign the original contract to the new counterparty, effectively removing SELF from the picture.

EXHIBIT 1 Alternative Student Loan Programs

Source: "MBA Financial Aid: Overview and Instructions," HBS, 1995–1996.

	Stafford	Perkins	Bank	HBS (Traditional)
Eligibility	U.S. citizens and permanent residents	U.S. citizens and permanent residents	U.S. citizens and permanent residents	U.S. citizens and permanent residents; citizens of Australia, Canada, Mexico, New Zealand, and most West European countries
Limits:				
Annual	$8,500 (subsidized) $18,500 (total)	$5,000	Education cost minus other financial aid	N/A
Aggregate	$138,500 (total)	$30,000	Education cost minus other financial aid	$25,000
Other	N/A	Subject to availability, given government-imposed, university-wide funding limits	Subject to bank's discretion	Total MBA-related debt at graduation must be no more than $62,000
Fees	4%	None	5–10%	None
Interest rate	Reset each July 1 based on recent 13-week T-Bill rate plus 3.1%; capped at 8.25%	5% fixed	Varies (typically prime plus 1.5%–2.0%)	Reset every 6 months based on SELF's cost of capital
Repayments:				
Commence	6 months after graduation	6–9 months after graduation	Varies (usually up to 6 months after graduation)	6 months after graduation
Style	Level monthly payments, subject to adjustment at each interest rate change	Level monthly payments	Varies (usually level monthly payments, fixed for the lifetime of the loan, or adjusted with interest rate changes)	Semi-annual; principal amortization increases gradually, culminating in final balloon payment
Loan maturity (maximum)	10 years	10 years	10–25 years	5 years

EXHIBIT 2
Amortization Schedule for Traditional HBS Loans

Source: SELF, Inc.

Date	Interest Rate[a]	Repayment			Ending Balance
		Interest	Principal	Total	
09/95 (Beg. SY)[b]					$5,000[c]
06/96 (Graduation)	9.0%			0	5,374[d]
12/96	8.5	228	750	978	4,624
06/97	8.0	185	750	935	3,874
12/97	8.5	165	1,000	1,165	2,874
06/98	9.0	129	1,000	1,129	1,874
12/98	9.5	89	1,500	1,589	374
06/99	10.5	20	374	393	0

Date	Interest Rate[a]	Repayment			Ending Balance
		Interest	Principal	Total	
09/95 (Beg. SY)[b]					$20,000[c]
06/96 (Graduation)	9.0%				21,494[d]
12/96	8.5	914	750	1,664	20,744
06/97	8.0	830	750	1,580	19,994
12/97	8.5	850	1,000	1,850	18,994
06/98	9.0	855	1,000	1,855	17,994
12/98	9.5	855	1,500	2,355	16,494
06/99	10.5	866	1,500	2,366	14,994
12/99	11.5	862	2,000	2,862	12,994
06/00	12.0	780	2,000	2,780	10,994
12/00	11.0	605	2,500	3,105	8,494
06/01	10.5	446	8,494	8,940	0

[a]Interest rate applied to period ending at the specified date. Interest rates are hypothetical.
[b]Assumed borrowing date.
[c]Amount initially borrowed.
[d]Interest accrued from 9/95 to 6/96 is capitalized at 6/96.

EXHIBIT 3 SELF Financial Statements ($ thousands)

Source: SELF, Inc.

	At or for Year Ended June 30,		
	1993	1994	1995
Balance Sheet:			
Assets:			
Cash and cash-compensating balances[a]	$626	$885	$814
Principal and accrued interest receivable	13,258	12,277	11,523
Less: reserve for delinquent notes and related interest[b]	(847)	(520)	(429)
Net notes receivable	12,412	11,757	11,095
Receivable from Harvard University[c]	556	646	624
Total assets	$13,594	$13,288	$12,533
Liabilities and Net Worth:			
Notes payable and accrued interest	$10,568	$9,855	$8,687
Paid-in capital	3,338	3,338	3,338
Accumulated surplus (deficit)	(312)	95	508
Total liabilities and net worth	$13,594	$13,288	$12,533
Income Statement:			
Interest income	$870	$974	$929
Interest expense	533	536	630
Net interest income	337	438	298
Provision for delinquent notes[d]	1,081	854	861
Bad debt recoveries[d]	663	845	1,007
Net bad debt expense	418	9	(146)
Administrative expenses	16	22	31
Excess (deficiency) of revenue over expenses	$(96)	$407	$413
Cash Flow Statement:			
Cash flows from operating activities:			
Excess of revenue over expenses	$(96)	$407	$413
Net bad debt expense	418	9	(146)
Write-off of notes and interest receivable[e]	(785)	(1,039)	(685)
Recoveries of notes and interest receivable[e]	523	704	739
Loans purchased from Harvard University	(5,303)	(3,349)	(3,205)
Loans repaid (net of write-offs and recoveries)	3,938	4,354	3,971
Other changes in operating working capital	524	(122)	42
Net cash provided by operating activities	(782)	963	1,129
Cash flows from financing activities:			
Increase in notes payable	5,010	6,315	4,555
Principal repayments	(4,899)	(7,019)	(5,754)
Net cash used by financing activities	111	(704)	(1,199)
Net increase (decrease) in cash	$(671)	$259	$(70)

[a]SELF is required by its banks to maintain cash-compensating balances equivalent to 5% of the unused portion of its bank loan commitments. These balances were $516,000, $258,000, and $318,000 in 1993, 1994, and 1995, respectively.

[b]SELF establishes a reserve against 50% of the principal and 100% of the accrued interest due on notes receivable for which at least $250 is at least 90 days overdue. Notes are written off if they remain delinquent for five consecutive quarters.

[c]Principal and interest repayments on notes receivable that have been collected by Harvard University on behalf of SELF but not yet remitted to SELF.

[d]Accounting provisions and recoveries.

[e]Cash write-offs and recoveries.

EXHIBIT 4
Principal Balance on SELF Loans for Recent HBS Classes

Source: SELF, Inc.

Class	Borrowers	Original Principal	Scheduled Balance (12/31/94)	Actual Balance[a] (12/31/94)
1991	209	3,793,194	2,186,694	1,061,732
1992	250	5,210,899	3,960,899	2,239,035
1993	242	5,302,767	4,697,767	3,665,726
1994	214	3,359,643	3,199,143	2,724,509

[a]Including prepayments and defaults.

EXHIBIT 5
U.S. Capital Markets Data, November 21, 1995

Source: compiled from BLOOMBERG.

Maturity	U.S. Treasuries[a]	AAA[b]	AA[b]	A[b]	BBB[b]
3-month	5.52%	5.90%	6.03%	6.06%	6.13%
6-month	5.50	5.89	6.03	6.06	6.12
1-year	5.45	5.83	5.93	6.08	6.14
2-year	5.49	5.79	5.80	5.93	6.08
3-year	5.56	5.92	5.94	5.98	6.27
5-year	5.69	6.05	6.12	6.30	6.39
10-year	5.95	6.31	6.36	6.54	6.79
30-year	6.27	6.85	6.88	7.04	7.37
Other Interest Rates					
One-month LIBOR:	5.82%				
Prime rate:	8.75%				

[a]U.S. Treasury bills, notes, and bonds
[b]Composite rates for debt of industrial companies rated AAA, AA2, A2, and BBB2, respectively.

EXHIBIT 6 Historical Interest Rates, 1/86–11/95[a]

Source: Compiled from BLOOMBERG.

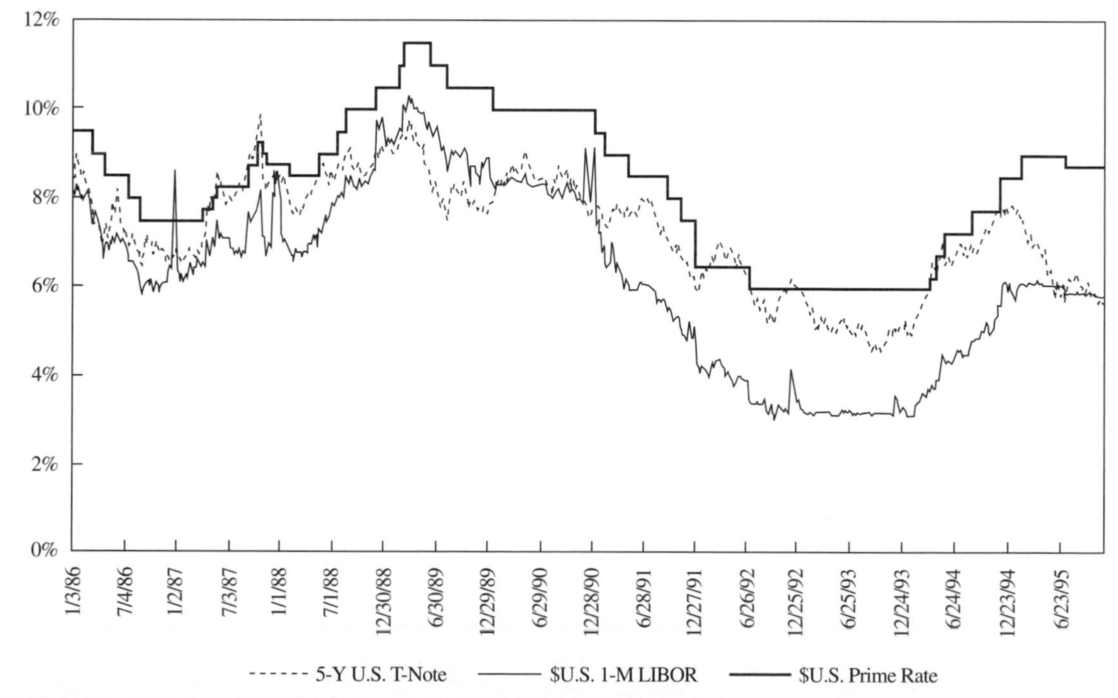

[a]On 11/21/95, the 5-year T-Note, 1-month LIBOR, and prime rates were 5.69%, 5.82%, and 8.75%, respectively.

EXHIBIT 7
Representative Terms of Selected Financial Instruments, November 21, 1995

Source: SELF, Inc.

Swaps

Notional amount:	$10 million
Floating rate:	1-month $U.S. LIBOR[a]
Maturity:	5 years
Payment frequency:	Monthly
SELF receives:	1-month $U.S. LIBOR[a]
SELF pays:	5.76% per annum

Caps/Floors

Notional amount:	$10 million
Floating rate:	1-month $U.S. LIBOR[a]
Maturity:	5 years
Payment frequency:	Monthly

Premium paid by/to SELF:[b]

Rate	Cap	Floor
4%	NQ	0.22%
5%	NQ	0.81%
6%	1.52%	2.12%
7%	0.90%	3.98%
8%	0.55%	6.13%
9%	0.34%	NQ
10%	0.22%	NQ

NQ = not quoted

Basis Swap

Notional amount:	$10 million
Maturity:	5 years
Payment frequency:	Monthly
SELF pays:	1-month $U.S. LIBOR[a]
SELF receives:	Prime[c]—2.80% per annum

[a]The rate prevailing on the first day of the month was used to determine the payment occurring at the end of that month.
[b]First number shows upfront premium (as a percentage of initial notional principal) paid by SELF to purchase a cap at the given rate; second number shows premium received by SELF to sell a floor at the given rate. "NQ" indicates "not quoted."
[c]The weighted average daily $U.S. prime rate.

Arley Merchandise Corporation

In the fall of 1984, the Arley Merchandise Corporation was considering how to raise $5 million to repay debt and position itself for future growth. The company was a leading privately owned manufacturer of curtains, draperies, and bedcoverings. It had enjoyed 32 years of continuous profitability. Present management of Arley had increased their ownership of the company's common stock following a December 31, 1981, leveraged buyout of shares owned by a founder of the company for almost $8 million in cash and notes. Arley's three senior officers currently owned 54.4% of the outstanding shares in approximately equal proportions. The investment firm that participated in the leveraged buyout owned 19.3% of the stock. The balance of the shares (26.3%) were owned in smaller blocks of less than 5%.

Arley's decision to raise new financing followed a two-year period of sharply increasing earnings. For the fiscal year ending June 1982, Arley had earned $.15 per share. In the two subsequent years, earnings per share had surged to $.41 and $1.03, respectively (see Exhibit 1).

While the company desired to raise capital through an initial public offering of shares, it was not anxious to do so while earnings per share were rising at a rate in excess of 150% per year. Instead, Arley's owners hoped to fully demonstrate the earning power of the company *before* bringing it public in order to achieve a more attractive selling price for the firm's shares. Unfortunately, just as the company's income statements began to reflect its full earning power, investor enthusiasm for new issues of common stock of small firms was rapidly receding (see Exhibit 2).

The dollar volume of new issues of common stock of small firms during the first 10 months of 1984 fell to 30% of the level it had reached in the prior year. While this volume was still significant by historical standards, there was little reason to believe that the downward spiral was any more likely to flatten out or reverse than continue in its present direction. The mid-1970s era demonstrated just how fickle the new equity issue market could become for small firms. During the interval from 1973 through 1979 the market for new equity issues of small firms effectively disappeared (see Exhibit 3).

Arley and its investment bankers had been discussing some innovative financing alternatives that would allow the company to sell its stock at a price high enough to be acceptable to the current owners of the business but not so high as to make it unmarketable for the underwriters. Exhibit 4 indicates that the common stocks of large established firms in the home furnishings industry were trading at prices equal to 8 or 9 times annual earnings. Exhibit 4 also shows other financial information for firms in this industry. A new public offering of the common stock of a small firm in this industry (such as Arley) would presumably be priced on a pro forma basis (assuming the new capital structure for Arley) at a price/earnings ratio below the level of more seasoned firms.

Professor William E. Fruhan prepared this case. HBS cases are developed solely as the basis for class discussion. Cases are not intended to serve as endorsements, sources of primary data, or illustrations of effective or ineffective management.

Copyright © 1987 President and Fellows of Harvard College. To order copies or request permission to reproduce materials, call 1-800-545-7685, write Harvard Business School Publishing, Boston, MA 02163, or go to http://www.hbsp.harvard.edu. No part of this publication may be reproduced, stored in a retrieval system, used in a spreadsheet, or transmitted in any form or by any means—electronic, mechanical, photocopying, recording, or otherwise—without the permission of Harvard Business School.

Arley's current owners felt that any price less than $8 per share was unacceptable, while Arley's investment bankers did not feel that a price above $6.50 per share would represent an acceptable underwriting risk given existing conditions in the financial markets.

The price gap that had to be bridged was about $1.50 per share. Several alternatives for bridging the gap were considered, each of which included some form of money-back guarantee to an investor purchasing a newly issued Arley share. The money-back guarantee might take several forms. It could be $8 per share in cash, $8 per share in Arley notes, or $8 per share in market value of Arley common or preferred stock as of the date the guarantee was utilized. The point in time at which the money-back guarantee might be exercised was also an issue under consideration. It might take effect, for example, at the end of one year, at the end of two years, at the end of five years, or at the end of 10 years. Alternatively, the guarantee could be exercisable continuously over some time period rather than on a specific date. While the potential variations in the design of the proposed security seemed unlimited, Arley's investment banker recommended the following terms for the offering:

750,000 *units* consisting of
750,000 *shares* of common stock

and

750,000 *rights* to sell common stock

Each unit would consist of one share of common stock and one right to sell common stock, each right entitling the holder to sell to the company one share of common stock at $8, subject to adjustment, during a 15 business day period beginning two years from the date of issuance. The company may pay for the common stock in cash or an equivalent amount of the company's senior subordinated notes due 10 years from the date of issuance, as the company may specify by notice to the holders of the rights no later than 60 days prior to the commencement of the rights period. In the event notes were offered as payment in whole or in part for shares of common stock, cash would nevertheless be paid if the aggregate value of the common stock to be repurchased by the company were not more than $1 million. The common stock and rights included in the units were separately transferable immediately upon issuance at the option of the holder.

The notes, if issued, would bear interest payable quarterly at 128% of the 10-year Treasury rate determined as of the date of the notice. The notes may be redeemed at the option of the Company, in whole or in part, at any time after two years from the date of issuance at redemption prices declining from 106% of par at the end of two years to 100% of par at the end of five years. The notes would be subject to a mandatory sinking fund commencing four years from the date of issuance, calculated to retire 75% of the notes prior to maturity. The notes would be subordinated to all senior indebtedness (as defined) of the company ($14,310,000 at September 21, 1984).

The sale of the units at $8 per unit would raise a total of $5,054,000 net of underwriting discounts and expenses associated with the offering. The proceeds of the offering would be utilized to repay bank debt currently borrowed at the prime rate (12.5%).

Around the date of the proposed Arley offering, low-rated straight debt was trading in a yield range of 14%–16% (see Exhibit 5). Convertible subordinated debentures were trading at interest rates equal to about 70% of the rate appropriate for straight debt of equivalent bond ratings. Convertible debt also carried a conversion premium of about 20% (see Exhibit 5). Baa-rated debt of industrial firms was yielding about 115% of 10-year Treasury debt, a figure somewhat below the average ratio for the past two or three years (see Exhibit 6). Ninety-day Treasury bills were yielding approximately 10% (see Exhibit 7).

EXHIBIT 1 **Historical Financial Data, 1980–1984 (thousands of dollars except per-share data)**

	Fiscal Year Ending					First Quarter Ending	
	June 30, 1980	June 30, 1981	June 30, 1982	June 24, 1983	June 22, 1984	September 23, 1983	September 21, 1984
Income Statement Data							
Net sales	$36,658	$40,015	$46,830	$49,968	$67,561	$14,101	$17,348
Cost of goods sold	28,078	29,453	35,652	36,070	46,861	9,689	11,670
Gross profit	8,580	10,562	11,178	13,898	20,710	4,412	5,678
Selling, shipping, and administrative expenses	6,195	6,785	8,351	8,819	10,478	2,426	3,056
Interest expense	268	301	1,011	1,911	1,841	358	580
Income before taxes	2,117	3,476	1,816	3,168	8,391	1,628	2,042
Net income	$902	$1,742	$945	$1,667	$4,167	$814	$1,021
Weighted average shares outstanding	8,945	8,945	6,500	4,055	4,055	4,055	4,094
Earnings per share	$.10	$.19	$.15	$.41	$1.03	$.20	$.25
Dividends per share[a]	0	0	0	0	0	0	0
Balance Sheet Data							
Working capital	$8,690	$9,847	$9,774	$10,131	$11,039	—	$10,607
Total assets	15,424	18,672	20,684	22,944	29,173	—	39,977
Total long-term debt (less current maturities)	2,334	1,892	10,673	9,520	6,761	—	9,248
Redeemed stock	—	—	(7,796)	—	—	—	—
Stockholders' investment	7,805	9,737	2,888	4,553	8,720	—	10,290

[a]Arley had paid no dividends in the past and did not anticipate paying any dividends in the foreseeable future.

EXHIBIT 2
Underwritten Initial Public Equity Offering of Small U.S. Firms 1983–1984 (millions of dollars)

Source: *Venture Capital Journal.*

	Number of Issues Underwritten	Index of Offerings for 1983 Dollars Underwritten	Number of Issues Underwritten	Index of Offerings for 1983 Dollars Underwritten
January	19	$163	43	$353
February	26	345	24	147
March	42	432	27	141
April	29	268	19	89
May	42	349	23	135
June	68	932	16	96
July	75	772	20	109
August	64	678	22	188
September	56	396	16	110
October	53	467	16	79
Total 10 months	$474	$4,802	226	$1,447

Note: Small firms are defined as having less than $10 million of net worth prior to their initial public equity offerings.

EXHIBIT 5 Corporate Offerings of Straight Debt and Convertible Debt, October–November 1984 (millions of dollars)

Source: Moody's Bond Survey; *Investment Dealers' Digest.*

Offering Date	Amount Sold	Issuer	Maturity	Bond Rating	Yield	Conversion Premium
Straight Debt						
10/23/84	$1,200	Occidental Petroleum	10-year	Ba2	14.5%	
10/23/84	50	Horn & Hardart	7-year	B1	14.5	
10/23/84	30	MacLeod-Stedman	7-year	B3	15.5	
10/23/84	58	Showboat, Inc.	20-year	B3	15.8	
10/25/84	70	Cannon Group	10-year	B2	15.4	
10/30/84	200	Chrysler Financial	15-year	Ba2	13.0	
11/02/84	115	Elsinore Finance	15-year	B2	15.5	
11/08/84	180	Lear Petroleum	10-year	B1	14.5	
Convertible Debt						
10/05/84	$100	Lorimar	20-year	B2	8.9%	20%
10/05/84	175	Texas Eastern	25-year	Baa3	12.0	28
10/05/84	60	SCM	25-year	Ba1	10.0	16
10/05/84	30	Mobile Comm. Corp. of America	20-year	B1	11.0	26
10/11/84	55	Wetterau	20-year	Baa3	9.3	20
10/15/84	25	Richardson Electric	20-year	B2	9.9	17
10/24/84	75	First Boston	25-year	A3	9.3	20
11/01/84	50	Communications Industries	25-year	Ba2	9.0	19
11/02/84	35	Insilco Corp.	26-year	Baa3	9.0	25

EXHIBIT 6
Yields on Long-Term Baa Industrial Bonds versus 10-Year Treasury Bonds, January 1982–October 1984

	Yield to Maturity		
	Long-Term Baa	10-Year Treasury	Baa/Treasury
1/82	16.75%	13.93%	1.20
2/82	17.00	14.19	1.20
3/82	17.00	13.99	1.22
4/82	17.25	14.17	1.22
5/82	16.75	13.81	1.21
6/82	16.75	13.69	1.22
7/82	17.00	14.32	1.19
8/82	16.63	13.63	1.22
9/82	15.25	12.77	1.19
10/82	13.38	11.05	1.21
11/82	13.38	11.05	1.21
12/82	13.50	10.69	1.26
1/83	13/13	10.31	1.27
2/83	13/13	10.75	1.22
3/83	12.75	10.24	1.25
4/83	12.75	10.59	1.20
5/83	11.88	10.18	1.17
6/83	12.50	10.79	1.16
7/83	12.75	10.89	1.17
8/83	13.75	11.67	1.18
9/83	13.88	11.92	1.16
10/83	13.25	11/39	1.16
11/83	13.50	11.71	1.15
12/83	13.38	11.58	1.16
1/84	13.38	11.76	1.14
2/84	13.25	11.59	1.14
3/84	13.88	12.04	1.15
4/84	14.00	12.43	1.13
5/84	14.75	12.78	1.15
6/84	16.00	13.78	1.16
7/84	15.50	13.75	1.13
8/84	14.75	12.85	1.15
9/84	14.63	12.76	1.15
10/84	14.38	12.40	1.16

EXHIBIT 7
Interest Rates, November 14, 1984

Source: Compiled from datastreams.

Bond Type	Effective Annual Yield
Treasury Obligations	
1 year	10.25%
2 year	11.14%
3 year	11.41%
5 year	11.83%
10 year	12.15%
Corporate Bonds	
Aaa-rated	12.22%
Aa-rated	12.55%
A-rated	12.94%
Baa-rated	13.83%
Ba-rated	not reported

The Pension Plan of Bethlehem Steel (2001)

(We are) deeply concerned that there is a pension crisis in America that threatens the financial strength and solvency of many corporations, cities, states and even our federal government.

—Ryan Labs, Inc.[1] newsletter

Anita Cavell grabbed the pension reports she photocopied in Baker Library—many of which, like the above, foretold of impending doom—and ran off to her afternoon class at Harvard Business School (HBS). Although she was just 28 years old and decades from retirement, Cavell suddenly developed a keen interest in pensions. It was October 16, 2001—the day after Bethlehem Steel, her father's pension plan sponsor and his employer for 36 years, filed for bankruptcy protection. Cavell's father planned to retire within months and was counting on Bethlehem Steel for annual pension income roughly equal to 40% of his current yearly wages. It was hard-earned income he now feared he might never see.

Under normal circumstances, Cavell thought, her father's fears, probably shared by many of Bethlehem Steel's 100,000 current and future pensioners, might have attracted public concern. But circumstances were anything but normal. The world was rapt with the monumental tragedies of Tuesday morning, September 11, 2001, and that day's continuing aftermath around the world. An already fragile U.S. economy reacted dramatically to the news of that day. All U.S. financial markets closed indefinitely on September 11 for the first time since World War II. When markets reopened September 17, the Dow Jones Industrial Average lost 7% of its value in one of the largest one-day losses in its 105-year history. Similarly, the broader S&P 500 index closed down 5% on September 17. Confirming signs of economic weakness, the Federal Reserve cut its benchmark U.S. short-term interest rate on October 3, for the tenth time in 2001. This "discount rate" was slashed to 2.0%, a rate unseen since 1958. Understandably, Bethlehem Steel's news on October 15 did not capture national attention.

Cavell knew she couldn't do much about the condition of the markets or of Bethlehem Steel. However, she decided to focus on something she *could* do—help her father—by evaluating the financial outlook for her father's retirement income.

[1]Ryan Labs was a New York City–based registered investment advisor specializing in asset management, liability consulting and research, and trademarked a pension fund Liability Index. More information is available at <http://www.ryanlabs.com>.

Dean's Research Fellow Akiko M. Mitsui prepared this case under the supervision of Professor Peter Tufano and Boston University Professor Zvi Brodie. This case was developed from published sources and uses a disguised protagonist. HBS cases are developed solely as the basis for class discussion. Cases are not intended to serve as endorsements, sources of primary data, or illustrations of effective or ineffective management.

Copyright © 2002 President and Fellows of Harvard College. To order copies or request permission to reproduce materials, call 1-800-545-7685, write Harvard Business School Publishing, Boston, MA 02163, or go to http://www.hbsp.harvard.edu. No part of this publication may be reproduced, stored in a retrieval system, used in a spreadsheet, or transmitted in any form or by any means—electronic, mechanical, photocopying, recording, or otherwise—without the permission of Harvard Business School.

Employment-Based Pensions in the United States

Historical Background

Pensions were designed to provide incomes to retired workers. Government-sponsored pensions were the most prevalent form of pensions worldwide. In several countries such as the United States, United Kingdom, the Netherlands, Japan, and Switzerland, employer-sponsored pensions for former workers played important roles in supplementing government pensions. (See Exhibit 1, Samples of Worldwide Pension Structures.)

In the United States, the government-sponsored Social Security program was not introduced until 1935. However, employer-sponsored pension programs dated back to the 19th century and supported retired public workers such as teachers, police officers, and fire fighters. American Express Company established the first U.S. corporate pension plan in 1875, and was followed by utilities, banks, railroads, and manufacturing companies.

Government tax and income policies fostered the growth of private pensions in the early- and mid-1900s. Since the 1920s, a corporation could generally deduct its contributions to a pension fund from taxable income, and assets in a pension fund could grow tax-free. In the 1940s, pension plans enabled employers to effectively increase employee compensation without violating the wage and price controls in effect during World War II.[2] After World War II, organized labor bargained for private pensions, starting with a 1946 grievance filed by the steelworkers' union against Inland Steel.

In the latter half of the 1900s, the government introduced funding and reporting standards for private pensions. In addition, insurance from the Pension Benefits Guaranty Corporation (PBGC), a federal agency, was mandated for certain types of pension plans sponsored by companies.

In 2000, 67 million U.S. workers, or 45% of the workforce, participated in employer-sponsored pension plans.[3] Financial assets of employment-based pension funds were substantial, when compared both with the market values and assets of individual companies (see Exhibit 2), and with total financial assets in the United States. For instance, out of the $6.1 trillion total value of pension assets in the United States as of September 30, 2001, $2.7 trillion was invested directly in corporate equities, an amount that represented almost one-fourth of the $11.9 trillion market value of U.S. corporations at that date.[4] (See Exhibit 3, U.S. Pension Assets by Fund Type and Asset Category.)

Pension Plan Terminology

A pension *plan* was a contractual arrangement under which benefits were paid to retired workers. An employer who committed to pay pension benefits was a plan *sponsor.* A current or former employee who was eligible for benefits was a plan *participant.* A pension *fund* or *trust* was an entity that was legally separate from the employer, and which held and invested funds to pay benefits to participants.

Defined Benefit (DB) Plans

In a defined benefit (DB) plan, the plan sponsor committed to make fixed monthly payments, similar to annuities, to plan participants (and often to surviving spouses) from retirement until death. For each year of employment, participants earned future

[2]Richard M. Steinberg, Ronald J. Murray, and Harold Danker, *Pensions and Other Employee Benefits: A Financial Reporting and ERISA Compliance Guide,* 4th ed. (New York: John Wiley & Sons, 1993), p. 4.

[3]U.S. Census Bureau and Bureau of Labor Statistics, *Annual Demographic Survey March Supplement Table NC8: Pension Plan Coverage of Workers by Selected Characteristics: 2000* (November 2001).

[4]Federal Reserve System, *Flow of Funds Accounts 3rd Qtr. 2001* Tables L.1, L.119, L.120, L.213 (Washington: December 7, 2001).

benefits according to a plan formula that typically was a function of salary and length of service, and subject to a vesting schedule.[5] The benefits that participants earned by any given date were the sponsor's long-term liabilities, which linked DB plans intimately to corporate financial policy. Sponsors were obligated to pay benefits earned by a vested employee after the employee reached normal retirement age, whether the employee retired from the sponsor firm or left the firm before retirement due to job change or termination. A discount rate and other assumptions (such as mortality and retirement ages) were applied to pension liabilities to estimate their present value.

DB plans operated as *funded* plans or as *pay-as-you-go* plans. In a funded plan, the sponsor regularly contributed funds to a legally separate pension trust so that the trust's assets would equal or exceed the present value of the plan's liabilities. While the trust assets served as collateral for the firm's pension liabilities to participants, gains and losses on these assets did not affect participants, since their benefits were defined. Investment performance did affect the sponsor. If fund assets grew in value, the sponsor's next contribution to match the plan's liabilities would decrease and vice versa.

Alternatively, defined benefit plans operated as *pay-as-you-go* plans. In these plans, sponsors simply paid pension benefits to participants from funds available when the payments were due.

Defined Contribution Plans[6]

In contrast to a defined benefit plan, in a defined contribution (DC) plan the sponsor did not promise retirees pre-calculated benefits, but instead arranged for pre-determined contributions to individual employee accounts. Depending on the plan, the contributions to employees' accounts were made by employees themselves and/or by the employer. An employee usually had some choice of how to invest funds in his or her individual account, and gains and losses were reflected in the account balances. If an employee resigned from the company or was terminated, the employee's contributions to the individual account, plus any gains or losses, were still owned by the employee. Any employer contributions to the individual account were also available to the employee, subject to vesting rules. At retirement age, employees received their final account balances. Thus, a DC plan, by design, was always "fully-funded," which meant that the pension fund's assets equaled its liabilities. Retirees generally received final account balances as lump sums.

Almost 75% of DC plan assets at year-end 2000 were in 401(k) plans, which were named after the section of U.S. tax law that permitted employees to contribute a portion of their wages to their individual accounts on a pre-tax basis. Corporations often made tax-deductible contributions to 401(k) accounts to match a portion of employees' contributions. From the introduction of 401(k) plans in the early-1980s through 2001, DC plans accounted for most of the growth in new privately sponsored retirement plans. (See Exhibit 4, Number of Privately Sponsored DB, DC, and 401(k) Plans, 1975–2000.)

[5]Vesting referred to the time period that an employee had to work with the pension plan sponsor before the employee had a right to claim benefits that were earned. U.S. tax laws required employees to be eligible for 100% of their earned benefits after five to seven years of service. A formula for a typical defined benefit plan might have provided 1.5% of an employee's average income over the final five years of employment for each year of employment with the sponsor, with 100% vesting after five years and pension payments starting at age 65. Assuming that a 45-year-old employee with 20 years of service with the sponsor resigned, and that this person's average annual salary over the last five years was $100,000, in 20 years, at age 65, this fully vested employee would receive annual defined benefit pension payments of 1.5% × 20 (service years) × $100,000, or $30,000 per year until death.

[6]Technically speaking, DC plans were not pension plans, but were retirement savings plans.

Regulation and Valuation of Basic Corporate DB Plans

Legally, corporations were not required to provide pensions to employees. If offered, however, pension plans and sponsoring firms were subject to complex rules and regulations that differed according to plan type. The following discussion focuses on rules for basic DB plans sponsored by corporations in the United States. Pension plans for state or local government employees were not subject to these rules. In addition, DC plans and plans that offered "non-basic" benefits, such as healthcare or supplemental executive benefits, were subject to different rules.

Employee Retirement Income Security Act of 1974 (ERISA)

In 1963, the Studebaker auto company shocked the American public when it shut down without enough money to pay the pensions earned by the company's 4,000 workers. Reacting to this and other similar instances, the U.S. Congress passed the Employee Retirement Income Security Act (ERISA), which was enacted in 1974. ERISA fundamentally changed the way in which corporations were required to operate pension plans and introduced several forms of protection for pension plan participants.

Funding Requirements

ERISA required basic-benefit corporate DB plans to operate as fully funded plans, so that collateral was available to pay retirement benefits. ERISA granted such plans favorable tax treatment, but applied heavy penalties against sponsors with underfunded plans.

Officially, there were no limits to a sponsor's contributions to its pension fund. However, all assets in a pension trust were earmarked solely to pay pension benefits, even any assets that exceeded liabilities. The only way an employer could use excess pension assets for non-pension use was to terminate the plan, pay all accrued benefits, and revert excess cash back to the company. Indeed, in the early 1980s, due to strong equity market performance and high interest rates, several corporate pension plans became significantly overfunded, and corporate raiders in some cases acquired companies, terminated overfunded pension plans and paid off the accrued benefits to reclaim excess pension cash. In one celebrated case, the takeover of The Great Atlantic and Pacific Tea Company, Inc. (which owned the A&P grocery chain) appeared to be executed solely to tap into A&P's overfunded pension plan.[7] Such takeovers became so notorious that a blockbuster 1980s Hollywood movie, *Wall Street,* was based on the "greed is good" character Gordon Gekko in just such a pension/takeover scheme. From 1980 to 1986, almost 1,500 defined benefit pension plans with assets of over $36 billion were terminated. Companies recaptured $19 billion from these plans.[8]

PBGC Insurance

In addition to introducing minimum funding requirements, ERISA further protected DB plan participants by creating a new government agency, the Pension Benefit Guaranty Corporation (PBGC). PBGC insurance became mandatory for all basic-benefit DB plans, which were also the only plans eligible for PBGC insurance. In some ways, PBGC was similar to another government agency, the Federal Deposit Insurance Corporation (FDIC), which guaranteed deposits at U.S. banks. When an overfunded insured plan was terminated, all benefits earned by employees were paid by the plan and

[7]Lynn Asinov, "Excess Pension Assets Lure Corporate Raiders," *The Wall Street Journal,* September 11, 1985.

[8]Marcia Parker, "Goodyear Using Pension Surplus to Reduce Debt," *Crain's Cleveland Business,* September 18, 1998.

PBGC had little to do with it. However, upon termination of an underfunded insured plan, PBGC became the trustee of the plan by taking the plan's assets and paying the participants' benefits when they retired. Upon retirement, participants of PBGC-trusteed plans were guaranteed to receive the benefits they earned as of the plan's termination date. However, the benefits were subject to a limit of $40,705 per year per participant for plans taken over by the PBGC in 2001, or whatever greater limit was possible from the plan's assets. In ERISA's early years, even if a sponsor company with the ability to fully fund its underfunded, insured plan decided to terminate the plan, PBGC took over and made up the deficits.

PBGC charged yearly insurance premiums to plan sponsors and did not use federal tax dollars for operations. PBGC charged sponsors a flat-rate $1 per participant insurance premium in 1974 when PBGC was created. The flat rate was changed to $2.60 in 1979 and to $8.50 in 1986. From 1987, premiums included flat-rate and variable-rate charges. In 2001, premiums were $19 per plan participant, plus $9 per year for every $1,000 that a plan's liabilities exceeded its assets. PBGC's premium income did not always leave PBGC in strong financial shape relative to its expenses and possible future plan takeovers. (See Exhibit 5 for selected PBGC data and Exhibit 6 for historical PBGC claims.)

Revised Termination Criteria for PBGC-Insured Plans

In response to perceived abuses[9] in terminations of both overfunded and underfunded insured plans, the government introduced restrictions on plan terminations in 1986. To discourage terminations of overfunded insured plans, an employer was required to pay a 10% penalty tax on money reclaimed from the plans. (Reclaimed pension assets were also added to the sponsor's gross income subject to regular income tax.) In addition, starting in 1987, sponsors could not take tax deductions for contributions to plans that were over 150% funded.[10] Terminations of overfunded pensions continued unabated, however, and the penalty tax on reversions was increased to 50% in 1990.[11]

The government also introduced restrictions on terminations of underfunded plans. Under the new rules, an underfunded insured plan could not be terminated unless the sponsor company had filed for bankruptcy or the PBGC decided that the plan caused financial distress to the sponsor. After termination, the sponsor was technically liable to the PBGC for the plan's full unfunded liability, plus interest.[12] As a practical matter, however, the PBGC recovered only a very small fraction of the unfunded liabilities of underfunded, terminated plans.[13]

[9]For instance, LTV Steel Corp. filed for bankruptcy protection in 1986 and terminated its insured pension plans, leaving PBGC with over $2 billion of LTV's unfunded pension liabilities. Then LTV created new pension plans that were similar to the terminated plans. In 1990 the U.S. Supreme Court ruled that LTV staged the bankruptcy to pass its onerous pension liabilities on to PBGC. The Court required LTV to restore the original plans and take responsibility for $1.8 billion of remaining unfunded liabilities. LTV emerged from bankruptcy in 1993 and filed for bankruptcy protection again in 2000.

[10]The tax-exempt limit increased to 155% in 1999, 160% in 2001, 165% in 2002, 170% in 2003, and would be repealed in 2004.

[11]Under some circumstances, such as for a company that is in Chapter 7 bankruptcy liquidation or for a company that replaces the terminated plan with a new one, this 50% penalty tax on reverted assets could be reduced to 20%.

[12]To collect an unfunded liability, PBGC could assert a tax lien against the company for up to 30% of the company's net worth. Net worth was measured by PGBC as of any date within 120 days prior to the plan termination date, and could be based on the sponsor's equity market value or any other reasonable measure of net worth as determined by PBGC. Certain liens, such as those for taxes and unpaid wages, are priority claims under U.S. bankruptcy law, and must be paid in full before creditors can collect general unsecured claims.

[13]PBGC Corporate Policy and Research Division.

Fiduciary Duties and Asset Management

ERISA required a sponsor to appoint fiduciaries to control and manage pension plan operations, administration, and assets. A fiduciary could be an executive of the sponsor company, but in the role of fiduciary, a fiduciary's legal duties were to:

- Manage assets *solely in the interest of participants* and according to the plan document, and
- Diversify plan assets to minimize risk of large losses from any one investment, considering asset risk/return ratios, and the portfolio's liquidity relative to cash flow needs of the plan.

ERISA did not fully specify the requirements for either of these fiduciary duties. However, one notable specification required that no more than 10% of a pension fund's assets could be invested in the stock and other marketable securities of the sponsor company.[14] In aggregate, U.S. DB pension funds allocated approximately 55% of their assets in equities and mutual funds, 29% in bonds, and 16% in other assets at year-end 2000. (See Exhibit 3 for more details.)

Reporting, Disclosure, and Valuation Protocols

ERISA subjected DB plans to extensive reporting and disclosures to several government agencies, including the U.S. Department of Labor (DOL), PBGC, and the Internal Revenue Service (IRS). ERISA also required sponsors to release annual reports to employees about their plans. Separately, FASB (Financial Accounting Standards Board) accounting guidelines required sponsors to report pension costs, pension income, and net pension assets/liabilities in the company's annual financial reports. DOL, IRS, PBGC, and FASB each applied different methodologies for valuing assets and liabilities. These methodologies were notoriously complex, but a few basic protocols are highlighted below.

Asset Valuation

Pension assets were recorded at fair market value, the price at which assets could be exchanged between willing buyers and willing sellers. Alternatively, assets were valued at actuarial value, or 80–120% of fair market value. Finally, FAS 87, the FASB accounting standard required for company balance sheets and income statements, permitted the use of market-related value. Market-related value either was fair market value or was based on a smoothed average of fair market values over the prior 2–5 years. Market-related value also permitted smoothing over time of large yearly losses or gains on pension assets. Market-related value was compared with plan liabilities to calculate a pension plan's funding status and expenses on company financial statements, which partially protected reported corporate results from volatile returns on pension assets.

Liability Valuation

The valuation of pension plan liabilities was essentially a two-step process—calculation of future cash payments and discounting them to present value. Numerous assumptions, which were determined by an actuary specifically for each pension plan, were used to estimate timing and amounts of payments. For example, *timing* of cash flows was affected by average participant age, the employee-to-retiree ratio, average retirement age, and retiree life expectancies. The *amounts* of future cash flows were affected by employee turnover and wage increases.

Liabilities were also valued by separately estimating cash flows as if the plan would terminate or as if the plan would continue indefinitely. On a terminating basis, often

[14]DC funds such as 401(k) plans and employee stock ownership plans were not subject to this limit.

called the accumulated benefit obligation (ABO) method, liabilities included only those benefits already earned by employees. Liabilities measured for an ongoing plan, often called the projected benefit obligation (PBO) method, additionally considered projected wage increases and future years of service expected from employees.

The second step in pension liability valuation—the selection of a discount rate—was perhaps the most debated, most important, and least standardized factor affecting pension valuations. (See Exhibit 7.) Some discount rates were based on 30-year U.S. Treasury bond rates, a practice that caused uproar in the pension industry in late 2001 after continued declines in these rates. (See Exhibit 8, Selected Market Data.) Some argued that discount rates should reflect market rates at which plan liabilities could be settled, i.e., a "settlement rate." To settle liabilities, firms often bought long-term annuities that provided cash flows equaling future pension payments from highly rated insurance companies. The rates on such annuities were similar to long-term, AA-rated corporate bond rates, which many companies thus used to approximate settlement rates.

In addition to the debate over Treasury rates or market settlement (long-term AA-rated corporate bond) rates, agencies differed over whether to apply recent rates or historical average rates.

The U.S. Steel Industry and Bethlehem Steel

The 1997–2001 American Steel Crisis

U.S. market conditions following the September 11, 2001, terrorist attacks and valuation techniques required for DB pension plans negatively affected all DB plan sponsors. However, the situation was especially sensitive for traditional U.S. steel companies, which already were distressed, typically had large DB pension plans, and whose market demand was highly correlated with economic activity.

The American steel crisis was triggered in 1997, after financial turmoil in Asia and slowing world economies resulted in dramatic reduction in steel demand. Global overcapacity and overproduction led to the lowest world steel prices in 20 years toward the end of 2001, of approximately $200 per ton for basic traded hot-rolled band (a basic flat-sheet product). These factors, combined with the strength of the U.S. dollar, high labor costs, and aging equipment, made it difficult for U.S. steel producers to compete in the domestic market against lower-priced imports. An influx of steel from countries such as Russia, Japan, The Republic of Korea, Brazil, and Canada resulted.[15]

Major integrated U.S. steel producers, such as U.S. Steel and Bethlehem Steel, also faced domestic competition from newer technologies. Minimills, which emerged in the 1960s, used scrap metal and non-unionized labor to remain competitive with import prices. Furthermore, the older, integrated steel companies incurred "legacy costs"—contractual obligations to pay pension and health benefits to retirees. These obligations became part of union contracts long before minimills emerged as a competitive threat. Few, if any, minimills incurred such costs.[16]

From January 1, 1999, to October 15, 2001, 24 U.S. steel companies, responsible for 35 million out of 124 million tons of total U.S. steelmaking capacity and 53,000 employees, filed for bankruptcy protection.[17] In October 2001, the U.S. steel industry employed just over 200,000, the lowest number ever recorded by the U.S. Bureau of Labor

[15] U.S. Department of Commerce, *U.S. Industry and Trade Outlook 2000: Steel Mill Products* (2001).

[16] Standard & Poors, *Industry Surveys, Metals: Industrial* (July 12, 2001).

[17] OECD, "Follow Up Special Meeting at High Level on Steel Issues, U.S. Government Report" (Paris: December 17, 2001); United Steelworkers of America, "Steel Companies Filing for Bankruptcy, 1997–2001" (December 10, 2001).

Statistics. Employment totaled 515,500 when data was first collected in 1939; the number peaked at 726,100 in 1953.[18]

Industry Response

In response to the domestic steel crisis, the U.S. industry sought trade protection, encouraged worldwide negotiations to cut capacity, and attempted to consolidate. All three strategies gained momentum in late 2001. The U.S. International Trade Commission was expected to recommend that President Bush impose tariffs on several imported steel products. The world's steelmakers agreed to meet in Paris by year-end to discuss management of global steel oversupply. Finally, it was rumored that U.S. Steel might propose to take over three bankrupt, integrated steelmakers if the government paid for unfunded portions of the firms' pension and retiree health plans. While bankrupt U.S. steel firms were responsible for supporting 600,000 retirees, their unfunded pension and retiree health plan liabilities were estimated to be $3 billion to $12 billion.[19]

Bethlehem Steel

Bethlehem Steel Corporation (NYSE:BS) was the second largest U.S. integrated steel producer with $4.2 billion in sales and approximately 14,700 employees in 2000. The company was a symbol of the success and subsequent troubles of the integrated steel industry in the United States.

The company began as Saucona Iron in Bethlehem, Pennsylvania, in 1857, rolling iron railroad rails. It was incorporated in 1904 and was renamed Bethlehem Steel.[20] The company's profile in 2001 highlighted its long history:

> For 97 years, Bethlehem Steel has provided the steel to build, transport, and defend America. Its products have produced enduring structures such as the Golden Gate Bridge, U.S. Supreme Court Building, Chicago's Merchandise Mart, and much of New York City's skyline. A major producer of armaments for the military, Bethlehem Steel's workforce in World War II numbered about 300,000. In addition to its steel plants, Bethlehem had shipyards on both U.S. coasts that delivered a ship a day (1,121 in total) to the Allied war effort. The Company's support of the military continues today as it was the sole supplier of armor plate steel for the repair of the USS Cole.

Bethlehem Steel had been a component of the S&P 500 and its forerunner since 1918. However, the steel crisis greatly affected the firm, which had the highest labor costs in the industry. Despite attempts to streamline costs, the souring market conditions, an eroding financial position, and additional loss of clients after the September 11, 2001, tragedies forced Bethlehem Steel to file for bankruptcy protection on October 15, 2001. With 11 million tons of steelmaking capacity at stake, Bethlehem Steel became the largest of the bankrupt U.S. steel companies. The stock price closed at $8.38 at year-end 1999 but only at $0.22 on October 16, 2001. The company's equity market value fell from $1.1 billion to $29 million over the same period, which resulted in Bethlehem Steel's elimination from the S&P 500 index, and threatened its listing on the New York Stock Exchange. One issue of the company's bonds, which traded on September 14, sold at 31% of face value.[21]

Bethlehem Steel's pension and retiree health plans appeared to play a large role in the company's condition. Chairman and CEO Robert S. Miller commented: "The major

[18]Standard & Poors, *Industry Surveys, Metals: Industrial* (July 12, 2001).

[19]Len Boselovic, "U.S. Steel Pushes Tariffs to Fund Retiree Liabilities Pitch Comes Same Day Allegheny Technologies Lays Off 520 Workers," *Pittsburgh Post-Gazette,* December 11, 2001; and Leslie Wayne, "Parched, Big Steel Goes to Its Washington Well," *The Sunday New York Times,* January 20, 2002.

[20]Bethlehem Steel Corporation, "Corporate Profile," <www.bethsteel.com> (December 11, 2001).

[21]Bloomberg.

issues facing Bethlehem . . . include . . . unfair trade practices and relatively high levels of steel imports. We are also grappling with high employment costs due to significant legacy obligations and productivity issues."[22]

The company's employment costs were predicted to be 37% of sales in 2001. Employment costs included $48 per ton of steel in legacy costs for pension and retiree health plan expenses out of a total average company production cost of $484 per ton of steel.[23] The bankruptcy filing listed $4.2 billion in company assets, $4.5 billion in liabilities, and negative stockholders' equity of $300 million at September 30, 2001. Liabilities included $540 million of unfunded pension liabilities and $1.8 billion of unfunded retiree health plan liabilities. (The health plan was not insured by PBGC and, like most retiree health plans, was a pay-as-you-go plan.) The assets of Bethlehem Steel's pension plan were invested approximately 70% in equities and equity mutual funds as of year-end 2000.

The numbers reported in the bankruptcy filing were calculated using FAS 87 guidelines. Using market interest rates and fair market asset values as of September 30, 2001, Bethlehem Steel estimated unfunded pension liabilities to be $1.85 billion and unfunded retiree healthcare liabilities to be $3 billion. With these estimates, the company's total liabilities as of September 30 would have ballooned to $6.75 billion, increasing negative net worth to over $2.5 billion. The September 30 deficits existed despite the company's claim that "it has always met or exceeded the minimum pension funding requirements under ERISA."[24] (See Exhibit 9, Selected Financial Data, Bethlehem Steel, and Exhibit 10, Estimated Data, The Pension Plan of Bethlehem Steel and Subsidiaries.)

The company noted that it expected to continue operating the health and pension plans while under Chapter 11, but that if the company filed for Chapter 7 liquidation, it would be likely that the plans would be terminated.[25]

Anita Cavell

It was time for Cavell to "crack the case." She reflected upon one of her many readings, in which four U.S. Congressmen warned the U.S. Treasury Secretary of the effects of current market conditions on pension plans. "The historic low rate of 30-year Treasury bonds . . . [has] potential to create a major crisis for defined benefit [pension] plan sponsors and their employees," the Congressmen wrote. From this comment and others, Cavell knew she would have to apply current interest rates, and other current market conditions, to value her father's pension plan.

Cavell was also deeply engaged in thought about some of the broader issues surrounding defined benefit pensions, a topic that she had previously considered to be rather dull. Was it the economic condition of the company that threatened her father's pension plan, or vice versa? What was the effect of all the ERISA rules—funding, PBGC insurance, reporting, asset management—on the current status of her father's pension plan? Was pension funding an issue specific to Bethlehem Steel, or was it possibly part of a much broader industry, national, or international matter? If she were the CEO of Bethlehem Steel, what could she do to protect both the interests of the company shareholders and the interests of its many loyal employees?

[22]Robert S. Miller, "Letter to Shareholders of Bethlehem Steel," October 15, 2001, <www.bethsteel.com> (December 10, 2001).

[23]Bethlehem Steel, 8-K, 10-K, and financial reports. 10-K reports filed March 9, 2000, and January 31, 2001. Available from Securities Exchange Commission,<http://www.sec.gov> (December 14, 2001).

[24]Bethlehem Steel, "Managing Legacy Costs," 2000 Annual Review <www.bethsteel.com> (December 14, 2001).

[25]Bethlehem Steel, "Employee Benefit Q&A," November 2 and December 10, 2001, <www.bethsteel.com> (December 14, 2001).

EXHIBIT 1 Samples of Worldwide Pension Structures[a]

Sources: Colin Gillion, John Turner, Clive Bailey and Denis Latiulippe, "*Social Security Pensions: Development and Reform*" (Geneva: International Labour Organization, 2000); HSBC, "Strategy Ideas, Pension Problems: A Global Special," November 26, 2001; International Labour Office, "Social Security: Issues, Challenges and Prospects," International Labour Conference, 89th Session 2001; OECD, "Private Pension Systems: Regulatory Policies," Working Paper AWP 2.2; OECD, "Private Pension Systems and Policy Issues," Private Pensions Series No. 1; OECD, "Financial Market Trends No. 73," June 1999; OECD, "Institutional Investors Statistical Yearbook 2001"; Eurostat, "Statistics on Pension Funds" Theme 4 - 29/2001; Federal Reserve Board, "Flow of Funds Third Quarter 2001," December 7, 2001; U.S. Social Security Administration, "Social Security Programs Throughout the World, 1999"; Casewriter interpretations.

	Government Social Security Pensions			Occupational/Employer Sponsored Pensions				Pers. Savings
Country	Basic Pension Benefits Are Based on Prior Wage or Are Flat-Rate for All Workers?/ Normal Retirement Age	Average Pension Benefit as a % of Disposable Income in 1992 or Average Pension Benefit as a % of Average Earnings in 1996	Employee + Employer Contributions to Government Pensions as % of Labor Costs, 1998	Private Employer-Sponsored Pension Plans	Occupational Pensions Are Primarily DB or DC?/Is Pre-Funding Required or Can Plans Be Pay-As-You-Go?	Financial Assets of Occupational Pension Funds 1999 (US$ Billion)/ Pension Assets as % of GDP 1999	Investment Management Requirements/Actual Allocations 1999	Household Savings Rates as a % of Disposable Household Income, 2000
Canada	Flat rate and wage based/65	32% of average earnings	5 + 6	Voluntary	Pre-funding required	$310/48%	Max. 5% real estate, 10% in own company, 30% in shares of one company/Actual 41% debt, 27% equities, 32% other	3.9
Finland	Flat rate and wage based/65	49% of average earnings	6 + 21	Mandatory	100% DB/ Pre-funding required	$60 (2000)/ 50%	Max 30% equities, 5% unlisted shares, 40% real estate, 30% in own company/Actual 69% bonds, 9% equities, 22% other	1.7
France	Wage based/60	83% of disposable income	9 + 28	Voluntary	Majority DC/ Pay as you go	$64 (2000)/ 5%	Min. 50% in EU gov't bonds/ Actual 1998 83% debt, 10% equities, 7% other	15.8
Germany	Wage based/65	54% of average earnings	17 + 17	Voluntary	DC/Pay as you go[b]	$63/3%	Max. 20–25% equities, 15–20% property, 10% own company/ Actual (1998) 76% debt, 10% equities, 14% other	9.8
Japan	Flat rate/65	24% of disposable income	7 + 7	Required if co. has >15 employees	100% DB/ Most pre-funded, but not required	$937/21%	Trustee must exercise "care, loyalty" and asset-liability match considered./Actual (1998) 48% debt, 23% equities, 29% other	11.3
Rep. of Korea	Wage based/65	40% of average earnings	4 + 9	Mandatory	DC/Pre-funding not required	$14/3%		16.6

EXHIBIT 1 *(concluded)*

	Government Social Security Pensions			Occupational/Employer Sponsored Pensions				Pers. Savings
Country	Basic Pension Benefits Are Based on Prior Wage or Are Flat-Rate for All Workers?/ Normal Retirement Age	Average Pension Benefit as a % of Disposable Income in 1992 or Average Pension Benefit as a % of Average Earnings in 1996	Employee + Employer Contributions to Government Pensions as % of Labor Costs, 1998	Private Employer-Sponsored Pension Plans	Occupational Pensions Are Primarily DB or DC?/Is Pre-Funding Required or Can Plans Be Pay-As-You-Go?	Financial Assets of Occupational Pension Funds 1999 (US$ Billion)/ Pension Assets as % of GDP 1999	Investment Management Requirements/Actual Allocations 1999	Household Savings Rates as a % of Disposable Household Income, 2000
The Netherlands	Flat rate/65	78% of disposable income	23 + 14	Voluntary	Almost 100% DB/Most pre-funded	$449/113%	Max 5% own co. & assets to be diversified/Actual 30% debt, 47% equities 23% other	7.6
Switzerland	Wage based/ 63 women, 65 men	91% of disposable income	10 + 10	Mandatory	DB and DC/ Pre-funding required	$267 (1998)/ 102%	Actual 26% bonds, 21% equities, 53% other	8.8
United Kingdom	Flat rate and wage based/ 60 women, 65 men	49% of disposable income	8 + 9	Voluntary	Pre-funding required	$1,226/85%	Max. 10% in any one mutual fund and 25% with one fund manager, 5% own company/ Actual 71% equities, 29% other (2000)	5.0
United States	Wage based/ 65–67	38% of average earnings	7 + 7	Voluntary	DB and DC; Majority DC/ Most require pre-funding	$6,901 ($4,674 corp. plans, $2,227 gov't employee)/ 75%	DB plans: Assets must be diversified and max. 10% in own corp./Actual 44% equities, 27% debt, 12% mutual funds, 17% other (Sept. 2001)	1.0

[a]Pension structures are difficult to compare across countries due to different financial, regulatory, and labor conditions. This exhibit is designed to provide a general sense of comparability only, and nothing should be inferred from any missing data, nor should the data be considered up-to-date in all circumstances.

[b]Germany uses a "book-reserve" system, whereby pension benefits earned each year are charged on a book basis to company financial statements, but are not necessarily funded.

EXHIBIT 2 U.S. Corporate Pension Funds by Total Pension Assets, Dec. 31, 2000[a]

Sources: 2002 Nelson Information Directory of Plan Sponsors; Compustat; Casewriter interpretations.

Sponsor Company	Total U.S. Pension Fund Assets[a,b] ($ mil.)	U.S. Defined Benefit Pension Assets[b] ($ mil.)	U.S. Defined Benefit Pension Liabilities[b] (PBO, $ mil.)	Total Assets of Sponsor ($ mil.)	Equity Market Value of Sponsor ($ mil.)
1 General Motors	$104,881	$85,263	$86,042	$303,100	$27,923
2 Verizon Comm.	85,756	55,225	33,136	164,735	135,460
3 General Electric	76,656	49,757	28,535	437,006	476,115
4 Lucent Tech.	75,185	45,262	26,113	48,792	103,434
5 IBM	66,548	44,594	37,539	88,349	148,146
6 SBC Commun.	63,518	40,814	25,577	98,651	161,715
7 Ford Motor Co.	60,000	54,544	50,200	284,421	44,716
8 Boeing Co.	53,900	42,856	29,102	42,028	55,198
9 AT&T Corp.	37,718	21,863	13,063	242,223	64,863
10 Lockheed Martin	36,000	22,738	18,524	30,349	14,632
11 E.I. DuPont	31,484	20,314	17,763	39,426	50,213
12 DaimlerChrysler AG	31,445	24,373	20,539	187,088	42,141
13 BellSouth Corp.	31,368	19,406	12,264	50,925	76,635
14 ExxonMobil Corp.	25,819	14,575	18,714	149,000	301,238
15 Qwest Commun.	23,401	13,594	9,470	73,501	68,352
16 Raytheon Company	22,550	13,821	10,469	26,777	10,373
17 United Tech. Corp.	20,730	13,119	12,232	25,364	36,978
18 Honeywell Int'l.	20,000	12,264	10,132	25,175	38,195
19 Citigroup	19,948	9,899	9,176	902,210	256,447
20 United Airlines	18,300	8,511	9,252	24,355	2,046
21 Northrop Grumman	17,150	11,763	9,121	9,622	5,981
22 Philip Morris Inc.	16,964	13,018	10,785	79,067	97,191
23 Delta Air Lines	16,751	10,398	9,263	21,931	6,174
24 BP	20,900	9,070	5,546	143,938	181,753
25 Procter & Gamble	15,491	1,691	2,627	34,194	74,761
26 Royal Dutch Shell	15,459	6,678	5,405	73,499	129,865
27 Bank of America	15,165	8,652	8,011	642,191	74,025
28 Prudential Ins. Co.	15,055	9,797	n/a	n/a	private co.
29 United Parcel Serv.	14,701	7,661	4,547	21,662	66,663
30 P G & E Corp.	14,061	7,808	5,405	35,291	7,268
31 Eastman Kodak Co.	13,355	9,170	7,291	14,212	11,438
32 Alcoa, Inc.	13,050	9,790	8,270	31,691	28,995
33 Minn. Mining & Manuf.	12,719	8,965	8,273	14,522	47,728
34 American Airlines	12,655	5,731	6,434	26,213	5,959
35 Chevron Texaco	12,200	4,225	3,836	41,264	54,129
36 World Bank	12,000	11,000	n/a	n/a	private co.
37 U.S. Steel Group	11,990	9,312	6,291	8,711	1,598
...					
66 Bethlehem Steel	**7,171**	**5,735**	**6,060**	**5,467**	**231**

[a]Some data in Total U.S. Pension Fund Assets column may be latest available as of September 2001.

[b]Data in these columns were derived from 10-Ks, which use FASB valuation guidelines. Liabilities are based on Projected Benefit Obligations (PBOs), and assets may be fair market or market-related values.

EXHIBIT 3 U.S. Pension Assets by Fund Type and Asset Category

Source: Federal Reserve Board, "Flow of Funds Report Third Quarter 2001," December 7, 2001; Casewriter's interpretations. Numbers may not add up due to rounding.

	Corporate-Sponsored Funds (9/30/01)		State and Local Government-Sponsored Funds (9/30/01)		Total (9/30/01)	
	$, Billions	%	$, Billions	%	$, Billions	%
Equities	$1,591	39%	$1,100	53%	$2,692	44%
Debt instruments	822	20	806	39	1,628	27
Mutual fund shares	706	17	0	0	706	12
Cash	244	6	62	3	306	5
Insurance contracts	440	11	0	0	440	7
Miscellaneous assets	235	6	109	5	345	6
Total	**$4,039**	**100%**	**$2,078**	**100%**	**$6,117**	**100%**

	Corporate-Sponsored Funds as of 12/31/00			
	Defined Benefit		Defined Contribution	
	$, Billions	%	$, Billions	%
Equities	$1,009	49%	$993	41%
Debt instruments	595	29	223	9
Mutual fund shares	122	6	716	29
Cash	125	6	113	5
Insurance contracts	112	5	349	14
Miscellaneous assets	100	5	50	2
Total	**$2,062**	**100%**	**$2,444**	**100%**

EXHIBIT 4 Number of Privately Sponsored DB, DC, and 401(k) Plans, 1975–2000

Sources: U.S. Department of Labor, Pension Benefits Welfare Administration, "Private Pension Plan Bulletin, Abstract from 1997 Form 5500 Reports" and "Abstract from 1993 Form 5500 Reports"; Pension Benefits Guaranty Corporation; Casewriter's interpretations.

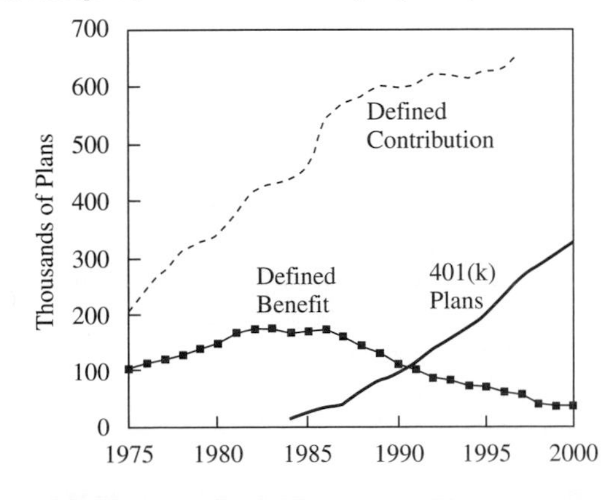

Defined contribution line includes 401(k) plans, 403(b) plans, employee stock ownership plans, and profit-sharing plans.

Latest available data for number of total DC plans is for 1997.

EXHIBIT 5 PBGC Net Assets, Premiums, and Insured DB Plan Funding Status, 1980–2000

Sources: Pension Benefits Guaranty Corporation Data Books; Pension Welfare Benefits Admin.; Casewriter's interpretations.

Year	PBGC Net Asset (Liability) Position[a], $ Mil	Total Underfunding of Plans That Are "Reasonably Possible"[b] to Terminate, $ Mil	PBGC Insurance Premiums Charged to Plan Sponsors, per Participant	PBGC Insurance Premiums Charged per $1,000 of Underfunded Amount of Plan and Maximum Premium per Participant	Total PBGC Insurance Premiums Collected, $ Mil	Aggregate Funding Ratio of All Insured Plans
1980	$ (104)	n/a	$ 2.60	None	$ 76	114%
1981	(190)	n/a	2.60	None	87	134
1982	(322)	n/a	2.60	None	93	147
1983	(517)	n/a	2.60	None	95	144
1984	(445)	n/a	2.60	None	94	152
1985	(1,298)	n/a	2.60	None	94	153
1986	(3,826)[c]	n/a	8.50	None	215	145
1987	(1,481)	n/a	16.00	None	283	133
1988	(1,451)	n/a	16.00	$6, max. $34	482	137
1989	(1,001)	n/a	16.00	$6, max. $34	620	130
1990	(1,781)	$ 8,000	16.00	$6, max. $34	679	132
1991	(2,340)	13,000	19.00	$9, max. $53	764	120
1992	(2,568)	12,360	19.00	$9, max. $53	875	115
1993	(2,621)	13,060	19.00	$9, max. $53	890	110
1994	(1,043)	18,230	19.00	$9, max. $53	955	104
1995	(123)	14,560	19.00	$9, max. $53+	838	112
1996	993	22,470	19.00	$9, max. $53+	1,146	102
1997	3,700	20,730	19.00	$9, no max.	1,067	111
1998	5,353	15,380	19.00	$9, no max.	966	111
1999	7,237	17,500	19.00	$9, no max.	902	n/a
2000	9,971	3,790	19.00	$9, no max.	807	n/a

[a]PBGC's net asset/liability position is the difference between PBGC's total assets and total liabilities.
[b]Value of reasonably possible terminations is underfunded amount of pension plans at below-investment grade rated firms.
[c]1986 figure includes $1.8 billion in liabilities from LTV Corp. that were later returned to LTV by a Supreme Court ruling.

EXHIBIT 6 Largest PBGC Claims[a] and Claims by Industry, 1975–2000

Source: Pension Benefits Guaranty Corporation 2000 Data Book; Casewriter's interpretations.

Companies with Largest Claims	Claims, $Mil	Year(s) of Plan Terminations	% of Total Claims
Pan American Air	$ 841.1	1991, 1992	13%
Eastern Airlines	552.7	1991	9
Wheeling Pitt Steel	495.2	1986	8
Sharon Steel	290.8	1994	5
LTV Republic Steel	221.9	1986	3
Kaiser Steel	221.6	1987, 1988	3
CF&I Steel	187.6	1992	3
Allis-Chalmers (Manuf.)	185.7	1985, 1986	3
Uniroyal Plastics	149.9	1992	2
Blaw-Knox (Manuf.)	121.3	1992, 1994	2
Top 10 total	**$3,268.0**		**51%**
All other total	**$3,180.7**		**49%**

Total Claims by Industry	Total Claims, $Mil	% of Total Claims
Agriculture, Mining & Construction	$ 128	2%
Primary Metals Manufacturing	1,887	29
Other Manufacturing	2,139	33
Air Transportation	1,473	23
Other Transport & Utilities	193	3
Wholesale and Retail Trade	248	4
Finance, Insurance, & Real Estate	23	0
Services	359	6
Total	**$6,449**	**100%**

[a]Claims are the excess of plan liabilities over plan assets. With the exception of LTV (1986), numbers may not account for money later recovered by PBGC from plan sponsors. Recoveries, if any, were generally no more than 5% of claims.

EXHIBIT 7 Simplified Samples of Liability, Discount Rate and Asset Valuation Guidelines for U.S. DB Pension Plans

Source: Casewriter

	PBGC	IRS—ERISA "RPA 94"	FASB "FAS 87"
Liability measurement	Accumulated benefits (ABO-type)	Accumulated benefits (ABO-type)	Projected benefits (PBO)
Base rate for discount rate	85% of 30-year Treasury bond rate	90–105% of 30-year Treasury bond rate	Long-term, AA- or better-rated corporate bond rate
Measurement date for base rate	Last month-end rate before the start of the pension plan's accounting year	Wtd. avg. of rates at end of calendar year: 40% weight for prior year-end rate, 30% for 2-yr. ago rate, 20% for 3-yr. ago rate, 10% for 4-yr. ago rate	Most recent year-end rate
One major use of discounted liability value using this discount rate	To measure the funding status of a plan for PBGC insurance-premiums. Additional premiums are required if fund liabilities exceed assets.	To compute "funding ratio" (assets:liabilities). Ratio will reveal: (a) minimum that sponsor *must* contribute to meet funding rules and (b) maximum that sponsor *can* contribute on a tax-deductible basis.	To specify the plan's net assets/liabilities reported on the sponsor company's annual balance sheet, and to calculate part of annual pension cost/income for sponsor company income statement.
Rate on 12/31/00 for plans w/ Jan.–Dec. accounting yr	5.51% (85% of 6.48%, 30-yr. T-bond rate at year-end 1999)	6.27%= 1.05*[(.4*6.48)+(.3*5.09)+(.2*5.93)+(.1*6.64)] weighted T-bond rates at year-end 1996–1999.	Mean used by S&P 500 firms at YE 2000: 7.5% Moody's AA Corporate Bond Yield, 12/31/00: 7.48%
Asset valuation method	Actuarial value = 80% to 120% of fair market value	Fair market value	Market-related value = fair market value or value based on smoothed average of prior 2–5 years' fair market values. Also smooths large annual gains or losses in asset values resulting from investment returns on assets.

EXHIBIT 10 Estimated Data, The Pension Plan of Bethlehem Steel and Subsidiaries

Sources: IRS 5500 filings, 1999 and 2000; Ryan Labs; Casewriter's interpretations

ASSETS at Fair Market Values Plan year = Jan. 1–Dec. 31 $ Millions	Dec. 31, 2000	Other Data, Dec. 31, 2000	Dec. 31, 1999
CASH	214		216
FIXED INCOME SECURITIES			
Government securities	633		598
Corporate debt	613	Portfolio	604
International bonds	249	Modified Duration	234
TOTAL, FIXED INCOME SECURITIES EQUITIES	1,494	5.21 years	1,436
Corporate stocks	2,301		2,462
Bankers Trust Equity Index Fund	1,568		1,971
Putnam International Trust	149	Portfolio Beta	162
TOTAL, CORPORATE EQUITIES	4,017	1.00 to S&P 500	4,595
TOTAL ASSETS	5,725		6,247

Projected Liabilities (PBO Basis)[a] as of Year-End 2000 ($ millions)

Year	2001	2002	2003	2004	2005	2006	2007	2008	2009	2010	2011	2012
Payments due, nominal	585	583	582	581	581	579	577	575	573	569	564	557
Year	2013	2014	2015	2016	2017	2018	2019	2020	2021	2022	2023	2024
Payments due, nominal	549	540	529	517	504	488	471	453	434	415	395	375
Year	2025	2026	2027	2028	2029	2030	2031	2032	2033	2034	2035	2036
Payments due, nominal	356	337	320	302	285	268	251	234	218	202	186	171
Year	2037	2038	2039	2040	2041	2042	2043	2044	2045			
Payments due, nominal	156	142	129	117	105	94	84	75	67			

PV of Projected Liabilities (PBO) @PBGC rate, 5.51%	$7,907	Modified Duration[b]	11.42
PV of Projected Liabilities (PBO) @IRS rate, 6.27%	7,299	Modified Duration[b]	10.88
PV of Projected Liabilities (PBO) @AA Corp. Bond Rate, 7.48%	6,482	Modified Duration[b]	10.09
PV of Projected Liabilities (PBO) @FAS87 rate used by company 8%	6,179	Modified Duration[b]	9.78

Other Information as of January 1, 2000

		Approx. share of benefits due
Total plan participants	99,723	
Active (employed) participants	15,840	26%
Retired and beneficiaries receiving benefits	68,803	70
Terminated vested	15,080	4
Weighted average age of active participants	49 years	
Weighted average retirement age	60 years	
Weighted average years of service	22 years	

[a]Liabilities in this exhibit estimate a Projected Benefit Obligation (PBO), which adds liabilities earned to date and liabilities that are expected to be earned in the future through wage increases and additional years of employment. After discounting to present value, an Accumulated Benefit Obligation (ABO) could be assumed to be roughly equal to 92% of the PBO in this case.

[b]Duration represents approximate % change in value/nominal change in yield, and is expressed in years. In approximation, the formula for Macaulay duration is: $\Delta P \approx -P*(D/[1+Y])*\Delta Y$, where P is price, D is Macaulay duration, and Y is the yield expressed in decimal form. The expression D/(1+Y), or modified duration, is also a commonly used basic measure of bond sensitivity to interest rates.

Tiffany & Company (1993)

In July 1993, Tiffany & Company concluded an agreement with its Japanese distributor, Mitsukoshi Ltd., that would fundamentally change its business in Japan. Under the new agreement, Tiffany's wholly owned subsidiary, Tiffany & Company Japan Inc. (Tiffany–Japan), assumed management responsibilities in the operation of 29 Tiffany & Company boutiques previously operated by Mitsukoshi in its stores and other locations in Japan. Tiffany looked forward to the new arrangement, as it was now responsible for millions of dollars in inventory that it previously sold wholesale to Mitsukoshi, resulting in enhanced revenues in Japan derived from higher retail prices. It was also apparent, however, that fluctuations in the yen/dollar exchange rate would now affect the dollar value of its Japanese sales, which would be realized in yen. Since Japanese sales were large and still growing, it seemed evident such fluctuations could have a substantial impact on Tiffany's future financial performance.

Company Background

Founded in New York in 1837, Tiffany & Company was an internationally renowned retailer, designer, manufacturer, and distributor of luxury goods. The famous blue-box company found its initial success in fine jewelry, most notably diamonds, but had since expanded its product line to include timepieces, china, crystal, silverware, and other luxury accessories. In the fiscal year ending January 31, 1993 (FY 1992), Tiffany earned $15.7 million on revenues of $486.4 million and had total assets of $419.4 million. Recent financial statements are provided in Exhibits 1 and 2. An historical summary of operations is provided in Exhibit 3.

After more than a century of independence, Tiffany was acquired by Avon Products, Inc. in 1979. For the next several years, Avon, a nationwide door-to-door cosmetics marketer, worked to expand Tiffany's product line to reach beyond its traditional affluent customer base to the larger middle market. While this diversification strategy resulted in enhanced sales for Tiffany from $84 million in 1979 to $124 million in 1983, operating expenses as a percentage of sales grew inordinately from 34% to 43% in 1978 and 1983, respectively. Avon soon realized that Tiffany's traditional market niche was substantially different than its own and, in 1984, decided to put the company up for sale. The most attractive offer came from Tiffany's own management, who agreed to buy back Tiffany's equity and the Fifth Avenue store building for a total of $135.5 million. In what ultimately took the form of a leveraged buyout (LBO), the terms of the deal distributed virtually all of the equity shares to three key investor groups. Management ended up with 20% of total equity shares. Investcorp, the Bahrain- and London-based merchant bank that backed management in the deal, received 49.8% of total equity shares. The third player, General Electric Credit Corporation (GECC), ended up with 25.7% of total equity shares. It was

This case was prepared by Research Associate Kendall Backstrand under the supervision of Professor W. Carl Kester.

Copyright © 1994 by the President and Fellows of Harvard College. Harvard Business School case 295–047.

through an $85 million credit arrangement with GECC that management was able to refinance a substantial portion of the purchase price.[1]

The aftermath of the LBO was marked by very tight free cash flow coupled with significant growth potential on the horizon. After the company had once again become profitable and realizing that the company's growth prospects demanded more cash than could be generated internally, in 1987, management offered Tiffany stock to the public at approximately $15 a share (adjusted for a subsequent stock split). In 1989, Mitsukoshi purchased 1.5 million shares of Tiffany's common stock from GECC.[2] As of January 31, 1993, Mitsukoshi owned approximately 14% of Tiffany stock, the largest percentage of any single institutional investor. Three other institutional investors collectively owned approximately 26% of the stock, followed by all Tiffany executive officers and directors as a group at 4.9%.

In 1993, Tiffany was organized into three distribution channels: U.S. retail, direct marketing, and international retail. U.S. retail included retail sales in Tiffany-operated stores in the United States and wholesale sales to independent retailers in North America. The 16 stores in this channel accounted for 50% of total sales in FY 1992. Direct marketing, representing the smallest channel of distribution, consisted of corporate and catalog sales. In FY 1992, its sales represented 18% of Tiffany's total sales. International retail, which included retail sales through Tiffany-operated stores and boutiques, corporate sales, and wholesale sales to independent retailers and distributors, primarily in the Far East and Europe, accounted for 32% of total sales in FY 1992. Jewelry sales from all three channels accounted for 65% of 1993 sales, making jewelry the most significant product line. Exhibit 4 provides financial results of Tiffany's domestic and foreign operations.

The past several years for Tiffany were marked by a trend of international expansion, beginning in 1986 when it opened a flagship retail store in London. Additional flagship stores were then opened in Munich and Zurich in 1987 and 1988, respectively. In 1990, the Zurich store was expanded. Stores were opened in Hong Kong at the Peninsula Hotel and at the Landmark Center in August 1988 and March 1989, respectively. Taipei saw the opening of a store in 1990, as did Singapore (at the Raffles Hotel), Frankfurt, and Toronto in 1991. Also in 1991, the London store was expanded. In 1992, Tiffany opened five new boutiques in Japan, and two new boutiques were opened by an independent retailer in Korea. Early 1993 saw continued international growth, with the opening of two more boutiques in Japan, a second store in Singapore's Ngee Ann City, two boutiques by independent retailers in Saipan and the Philippines, and the expansion of the Peninsula Hotel store in Hong Kong.

Exhibit 5 shows the growth in the number of Tiffany stores and boutiques around the world from 31 to 79, implying a 250% increase from 1987 to 1993. These 79 retail locations included 16 stores in the United States, 56 stores in the Far East, 6 stores in Europe, and 1 store in Canada, all of which ranged in size from 700 to 13,000 gross square feet, with a total of approximately 127,000 gross square feet devoted to retail purposes.

[1] This included a $75 million secured revolving credit facility; a $10 million, 16% subordinated note due in 1992; and common stock warrants to purchase approximately 25% of the company's equity on a fully diluted basis.

[2] Prior to Mitsukoshi's purchase of Tiffany's common stock from GECC, Tiffany and Mitsukoshi entered into an agreement by which Mitsukoshi agreed not to purchase in excess of 19.99% of Tiffany's issued and outstanding common shares. This agreement would expire on September 31, 1994.

Tiffany's worldwide capital expenditures were $2.28 million in FY 1992, compared with $41.4 million in FY 1991. These expenditures were primarily for the opening of new stores and boutiques and the expansion of existing stores. Management anticipated capital expenditures to drop further to $18.0 million in FY 1993 before rebounding to approximately $25.0 million in FY 1994. Management also expected to open four or five new stores per year in the foreseeable future.[3] To support future expansion plans, and fluctuations in seasonal working capital needs, management planned to rely upon internally generated funds and a $100 million noncollateralized revolving credit facility available at interest rates based upon Eurodollar rates, a prime rate, certificate of deposit rates, or money market rates.[4] As in the past, cash dividends were expected to be maintained at a relatively moderate level, which would permit the company to retain a majority of its earnings.

Impetus for Change in the Japanese Operations

While Tiffany found new market potential across the globe, nowhere was it as promising as in Japan, where Tiffany's sales accounted for only 1% of the $20 billion Japanese jewelry market. The thriving Japanese economy of the late 1980s and very early 1990s stimulated a booming demand for certain types of expensive and glamorous Western goods. Among these were Tiffany products, principally those of the fine jewelry line marketed toward older women. However, as the Japanese economy finally slowed and Japanese consumers became more cautious in their spending, the demand for Tiffany's luxury items also slumped. In response to soft consumer demand in Japan, Mitsukoshi cut back on Tiffany inventory levels. Mitsukoshi's wholesale purchases from Tiffany-Japan declined from 23% of Tiffany's total sales in FY 1991 to 15% in FY 1992. Declining wholesale shipments were also accompanied by a small decline in gross margin from 49.4% in FY 1991 to 48.7% in FY 1992. Despite lackluster consumer demand in the first half of FY 1993, however, Tiffany continued to believe that Japanese sales had attractive long-run growth potential. It was for this reason that Tiffany sought greater control over its future in Japan and ultimately decided to restructure its Japanese operations.

From 1972 through July 1993, Mitsukoshi acted as the principal retailer of Tiffany products in Japan, purchasing selected goods from Tiffany–Japan on a wholesale basis. Mitsukoshi sold the products on a retail basis to the Japanese consumer, realizing profits in the form of relatively higher retail prices. Since the wholesale transactions were denominated entirely in dollars, fluctuations in the yen/dollar exchange rate did not represent a source of volatility for Tiffany's expected cash flows. Instead, Mitsukoshi bore the risk of any exchange rate fluctuations that took place between the time it purchased the inventory from Tiffany and when it finally made cash settlement. Typically, Tiffany merchandise sold by Mitsukoshi was priced at a substantial premium (100% in some cases) over the domestic U.S. retail price for such merchandise.[5]

[3]Due to the significant number of Tiffany boutiques already operating in Japan, future openings there were expected to occur only at a very modest rate, if at all, in the near-term future.

[4]Tiffany's business was seasonal in nature, with the fourth quarter typically representing a proportionally greater percentage of annual sales, income from operations, and net income. In FY 1992, net sales totaled $107,238,000, $120,830,000, $105,897,000, and $152,431,000 for the first, second, third, and fourth quarters, respectively. Management expected this pattern to continue in the future.

[5]Tiffany management believed that a retail price reduction in Japan of 20% to 25% would likely result in a substantial increase in unit volume of jewelry sales.

The new agreement between the two companies, however, fundamentally changed both companies' financial situations. In repurchasing the merchandise previously sold by Tiffany to Mitsukoshi, Tiffany–Japan assumed new responsibility for establishing yen retail prices, holding inventory in Japan for sale, managing and funding local advertising and publicity programs, and controlling local Japanese management.[6] Mitsukoshi, on the other hand, would no longer be an independent retailer of Tiffany products but would still receive fees equaling 27% of net retail sales in compensation for providing boutique facilities, sales staff, collection of receivables, and security for store inventory.[7]

With greater control over retail sales in its Japanese operations. Tiffany looked forward to long-run improvement in its performance in Japan despite continuing weak local economic conditions. However, increased sales and profits were not the only changes that Tiffany could anticipate as a result of the new agreement. Tiffany now faced the risk of foreign currency fluctuations previously borne by Mitsukoshi. Past history warned Tiffany that the yen/dollar exchange rate could be quite volatile on a year-to-year, and even month-to-month, basis. Exhibit 6 illustrates the significant strengthening of the yen against the dollar during the 10 years ending in 1993. While a continuation of this strengthening would enhance the dollar value of Tiffany's yen-denominated cash inflows, there was the distinct possibility that the yen might eventually become overvalued and crash suddenly, just as the U.S. dollar did in 1985. Indeed, there was some evidence that the yen was overvalued against the dollar in 1993 (see Exhibit 7).

Hedging to Manage Foreign Exchange Risk

The possibility of sharp, unexpected movements in the yen/dollar exchange rate had prompted Tiffany's management to study the desirability of engaging in a program to manage exchange rate risk. To reduce exchange rate risk on its yen cash flows, Tiffany had two basic alternatives available to it. One was to enter into forward agreements to sell yen for dollars at a predetermined price in the future. The other was to purchase yen put options. The terms at which Tiffany could purchase forward contracts and put options, along with other financial market data, are shown in Exhibit 8.

Before committing Tiffany to a hedging program, management wanted to be sure it understood what the potential risks and rewards were for each of these so-called "derivative" instruments. Perhaps more importantly, it was essential to determine whether or not a risk management program was appropriate for Tiffany, what its objectives should be, and how much, if any, exposure should be covered.

[6]The repurchase of inventory by Tiffany necessitated the reversal of $115 million in sales and related gross profit previously recognized on merchandise sold to Mitsukoshi. Accordingly, Tiffany recorded a $57.5 million reserve to provide for product returns, which reduced the second fiscal quarter's (ended July 31, 1993) net income by approximately $32.7 million, or $2.07 per share. Of the $115 million of sales being reversed, only $52.5 million of inventory held in Mitsukoshi boutiques was actually repurchased during the month of July 1993 (Mitsukoshi agreed to accept a deferred payment on $25 million of this repurchased boutique inventory, which was to be repaid in yen on a quarterly basis with interest of 6% per annum over the next 4½ years). Approximately $62.5 million of Tiffany & Company inventory maintained in Mitsukoshi warehouses would be repurchased throughout the period ending February 28, 1998. Payment for this warehouse inventory was to be made in yen 40 days following actual receipt of the inventory.

[7]Fees were reduced to 5% on certain high-value jewelry items repurchased from Mitsukoshi. Tiffany–Japan would also pay Mitsukoshi incentive fees equal to 5% of the amount by which boutique sales increase year-to-year, calculated on a per-boutique basis. In Tokyo, Tiffany boutiques could be established only in Mitsukoshi's stores, and Tiffany-brand jewelry could be sold only in such boutiques (though Tiffany–Japan reserved the right to open a single flagship store in Tokyo).

EXHIBIT 1
Consolidated Income Statements (thousands of dollars)

Annual Income Statements

	Years Ended January 31,	
	1992	**1993**
Net sales	$491,906	$486,396
Cost of goods sold	248,897	249,363
Gross profit	243,009	237,033
Selling, general, and administrative expenses	180,939	209,140
Provision for uncollectible accounts	1,012	1,152
Income/(loss) from operations	61,028	26,741
Interest expense and financing costs	6,337	7,231
Other income	375	415
Income/(loss) before income taxes	55,066	19,925
(Benefit)/provision for income taxes	23,261	4,213
Net income/(loss)	$ 31,805	$ 15,712

Second Quarter Income Statements (thousands of dollars)

	Six Months Ended July 31,	
	1992	**1993**[a]
Net sales	$228,068	$223,714
Product return for Japan realignment	0	(115,000)
	228,068	108,714
Cost of goods sold	119,481	117,486
Cost related to product return for Japan realignment	0	(57,500)
Gross profit	108,587	48,728
Selling, general, and administrative expenses	92,578	99,792
Provision for uncollectible accounts	458	906
Income/(loss) from operations	15,551	(51,970)
Other expenses, net	3,453	3,410
Income/(loss) before income taxes	12,098	(55,380)
(Benefit)/provision for income taxes	5,106	(23,867)
Net income/(loss)	$ 6,992	$ (31,513)

[a]Data reflect the loss in net income for the second fiscal quarter ending July 31, 1993, due to the repurchase.

EXHIBIT 2
Consolidated Balance Sheets (thousands of dollars)

	July 31, 1993	Years Ended January 31, 1992	1993
Assets			
Current Assets			
Cash and short-term investments	$ 6,665	$ 3,972	$ 6,672
Accounts receivable, less allowances of $4,170 and $7,293	51,432	51,687	51,378
Income tax receivable	10,630	—	—
Inventories	247,891	213,435	224,151
Prepaid expenses	14,058	12,777	10,107
Total current assets	$330,676	$281,871	$292,308
Property and equipment, net	$ 96,320	$ 88,975	$ 94,454
Deferred income taxes	21,205	5,047	5,723
Other assets, net	26,204	18,989	25,770
Total assets	$474,405	$394,882	$418,255
Liabilities and Stockholders' Equity			
Current Liabilities			
Short-term borrowings	$ 24,235	$ 43,566	$ 22,458
Accounts payable and accrued liabilities	98,497	66,781	61,919
Income taxes payable	0	7,371	2,679
Merchandise and other customer credits	6,029	4,687	5,318
Total current liabilities	$128,761	$122,405	$ 92,374
Long-term trade payable	$ 26,472	—	—
Reserve for product return	31,768	—	—
Long-term debt	101,500	50,000	101,500
Deferred income taxes	0	7,957	3,858
Postretirement benefit obligation	14,510	11,960	13,560
Other long-term liabilities	$ 1,921	$ 2,521	$ 2,157
Shareholders' Equity			
Common stock, $.01 par value; authorized 30,000 shares, issued 15,660 and 15,620	$ 157	$ 159	$ 156
Additional paid-in capital	69,969	67,927	69,553
Retained earnings	107,002	129,364	140,705
Foreign currency translation adjustments[a]	(7,655)	2,680	(5,608)
Total stockholders' equity	$169,473	$200,130	$204,806
Total liabilities and shareholders' equity	$474,405	$394,973	$418,255

[a]The accounting for foreign exchange translation gains and losses is governed by the Statement of Financial Accounting Standards #52 (FASB #52). Under this accounting method, all foreign assets and liabilities are translated at the exchange rate prevailing on the balance sheet date. Equity accounts are translated at historical rates. Income statement items are translated at either the prevailing rate on the date that a sale or purchase occurred, or a weighted average of exchange rates for the appropriate period. An important provision in FASB #52 is that translation gains and losses are *not* flowed through the income statement. Instead, they are booked directly to a separate equity account such as "Foreign Currency Translation Adjustments" or "Cumulative Translation Adjustment." Only if and when an asset is sold or liquidated does the realized translation gain or loss move from the translation adjustment account to flow through the income statement.

EXHIBIT 3 **Historical Summary (thousands of dollars except per share amounts)**

	January 31,					
	1988	1989	1990	1991	1992	1993
Summary of operations						
Net sales	$230,488	$290,344	$383,964	$455,712	$491,906	$486,396
Income/(loss) from operations	33,691	44,193	60,977	67,806	61,028	26,741
Interest expense and financing costs	2,174	826	2,578	4,475	6,337	7,231
Income/(loss) before income taxes	31,194	43,032	58,387	63,475	55,066	19,925
Net income/(loss)	$ 16,176	$ 24,901	$ 33,305	$ 36,661	$ 25,470	$ 15,712
Capital expenditures	$ 1,895	$ 9,680	$ 14,040	$ 24,835	$ 41,385	$ 22,754
Depreciation and amortization	1,118	1,634	3,455	5,487	8,134	11,425
Common shares outstanding	12,570	15,370	15,560	15,670	15,870	15,620
Income/(loss) per share	$ 1.17	$ 1.62	$ 2.13	$ 2.34	$ 20.1	$ 1.00
Cash dividends per share	—	$ 0.10	$ 0.18	$ 0.26	$ 0.28	$ 0.28
Dividend payout (%)	0.0%	6.0%	8.0%	11.0%	14.0%	28.0%
Financial position						
Net working capital[a]	$ 66,772	$ 89,082	$127,074	$162,265	$203,032	$220,813
Inventories	70,778	103,771	142,545	173,964	213,435	224,151
Total assets	126,669	162,648	237,061	307,268	394,882	419,355
Total debt	—	7,253	32,565	49,272	93,566	123,958
Shareholders' equity	71,621	99,193	135,568	176,183	200,039	204,806
Book value per share	$ 5.70	$ 6.29	$ 8.71	$ 11.24	$ 12.61	$ 13.11
Average annual P/E	14.5	14.3	19.8	16.9	24.2	34.0
Stock price						
High	$ 27.30	$ 29.70	$ 61.30	$ 53.80	$ 57.50	$ 52.90
Low	$ 9.70	$ 14.00	$ 26.00	$ 27.50	$ 32.60	$ 23.00
Equity beta (β)						1.35
Selected ratios						
Current ratio	2.4	2.5	2.5	2.3	2.3	3.2
Net profit margin (%)	7.3%	8.6%	8.7%	8.0%	6.5%	3.2%
Return on assets (%)	13.0%	15.0%	14.0%	12.0%	8.0%	4.0%
Return on equity (%)	23.0%	25.0%	25.0%	21.0%	16.0%	8.0%
Asset turnover	1.82	1.79	1.62	1.48	1.25	1.16
Total debt/total capital (%)	0.0%	4.0%	14.0%	16.0%	24.0%	30.0%

[a]Excluding short-term borrowings.

EXHIBIT 4
Domestic and Foreign Operations (thousands of dollars)

	Years Ended January 31,	
	1992	1993
Domestic		
Net sales	$439,055	$414,558
U.S.	316,282	326,828
Export	122,773	87,730
Income/(loss) from operations	98,229	73,559
Identifiable assets	278,730	287,127
Foreign		
Net sales	52,851	71,838
Income/(loss) from operations	3,888	2,381
Identifiable assets	116,152	132,228

EXHIBIT 5 Worldwide Retail Locations

	Tiffany's Subsidiary Companies					Independent		
	North America and Europe			Pacific Rim				
End of Fiscal Year	U.S.	Canada	Europe	Japan	Elsewhere	Mitsukoshi	Others	Total
1987	8	0	2	0	0	21	0	31
1988	9	0	3	0	1	21	0	34
1989	9	0	5	0	2	24	0	40
1990	12	0	5	0	3	27	0	47
1991	13	1	7	0	4	38	2	65
1992	16	1	7	7	4	36	4	75
1993	16	1	6	37	5	8	6	79

EXHIBIT 6
Yen/Dollar Exchange Rates (end of period)

Year/Month	Yen/Dollar	Year/Month	Yen/Dollar
1983	231.70	1992	
1984	251.60		
1985	200.25	January	125.55
1986	158.30	February	129.15
1987	121.25	March	132.92
1988	125.05	April	133.30
1989	143.80	May	127.75
1990	135.75	June	125.87
1991		July	127.20
January	131.45	August	123.08
February	132.95	September	120.07
March	140.60	October	123.45
April	136.38	November	124.75
May	138.45	December	124.86
June	137.90	1993	
July	137.42	January	124.80
August	136.85	February	118.00
September	132.85	March	116.65
October	130.60	April	111.60
November	130.08	May	107.25
December	124.90	June	106.35

End-of-Year Exchange Rates

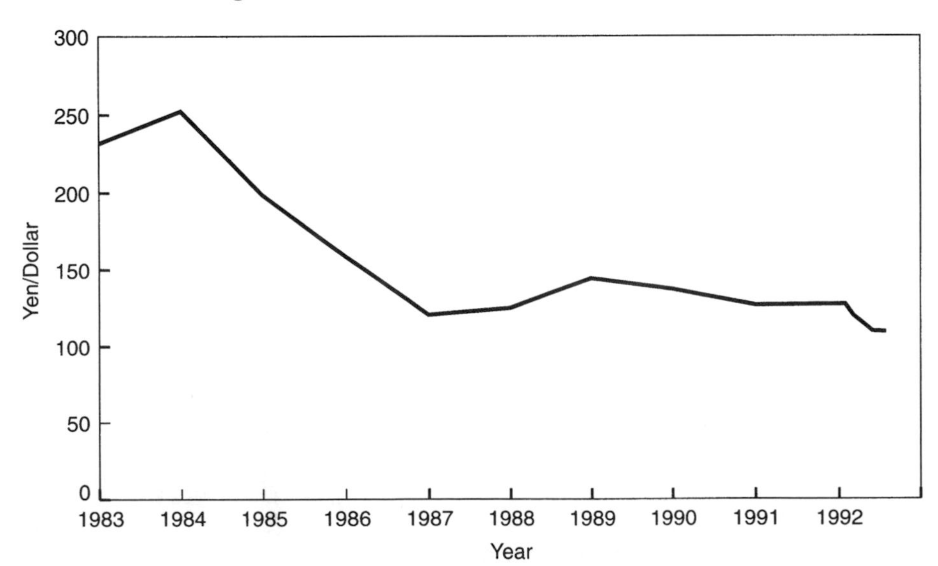

EXHIBIT 7
Japanese Yen: Percent Over-/Under-Valued versus U.S. Dollar[a]

Source: Currency and Bond Market Trends (Merrill Lynch, October 1994), p. 22.

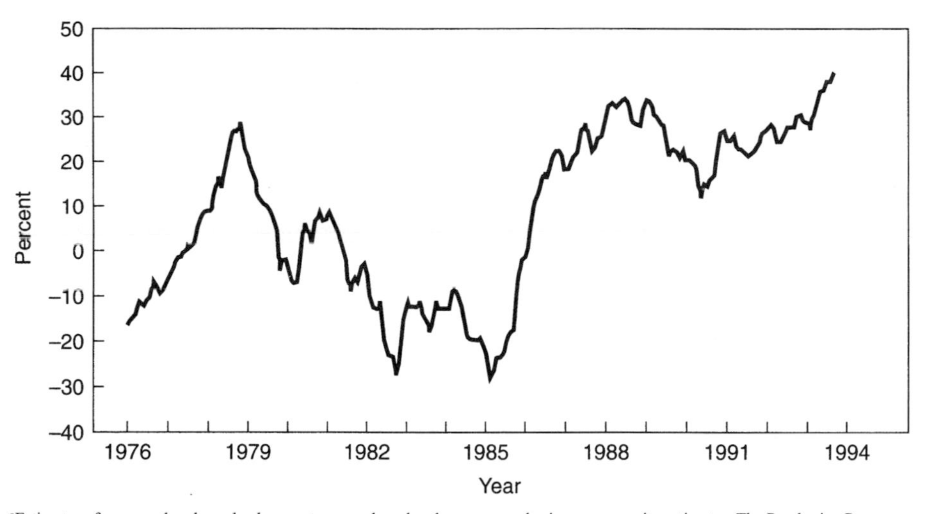

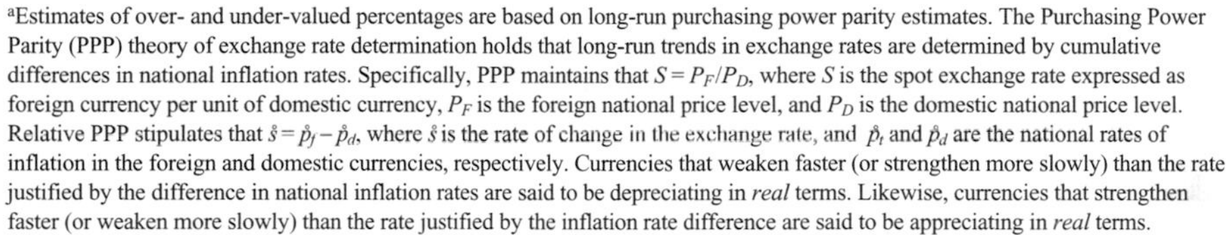
[a]Estimates of over- and under-valued percentages are based on long-run purchasing power parity estimates. The Purchasing Power Parity (PPP) theory of exchange rate determination holds that long-run trends in exchange rates are determined by cumulative differences in national inflation rates. Specifically, PPP maintains that $S = P_F/P_D$, where S is the spot exchange rate expressed as foreign currency per unit of domestic currency, P_F is the foreign national price level, and P_D is the domestic national price level. Relative PPP stipulates that $\mathring{s} = \mathring{p}_f - \mathring{p}_d$, where $\mathring{s}$ is the rate of change in the exchange rate, and $\mathring{p}_t$ and $\mathring{p}_d$ are the national rates of inflation in the foreign and domestic currencies, respectively. Currencies that weaken faster (or strengthen more slowly) than the rate justified by the difference in national inflation rates are said to be depreciating in *real* terms. Likewise, currencies that strengthen faster (or weaken more slowly) than the rate justified by the inflation rate difference are said to be appreciating in *real* terms.

EXHIBIT 8
Selected Financial Market Data (end of month)

A. Interest Rates

1993 Eurodollar Interest Rates (percentage)

	One Month	Three Months	Six Months	One Year
January	3.1250	3.2500	3.3750	3.6875
February	3.1250	3.1250	3.2500	3.5000
March	3.1250	3.1875	3.3125	3.5625
April	3.0625	3.1250	3.2500	3.5000
May	3.1875	3.3125	3.4375	3.8125
June	3.1250	3.2500	3.5000	3.6875

1993 Euroyen Interest Rates (percentage)

	One Month	Three Months	Six Months	One Year
January	3.5000	3.4375	3.3750	3.3125
February	3.2188	3.2813	3.2188	3.2188
March	3.5313	3.4063	3.4063	3.4063
April	3.2188	3.2188	3.2813	3.3125
May	3.2500	3.2500	3.3438	3.4375
June	3.1875	3.1875	3.1876	3.2501

B. 1993 Yen/Dollar Exchange Rates (yen per dollar)

	Spot	Forward	
		One Month	Three Months
January	124.800	124.845	124.865
February	118.000	118.015	118.025
March	116.650	116.665	116.675
April	111.600	111.605	111.605
May	107.250	107.255	107.230
June	106.350	106.355	106.330

C. June 1993 Yen/Dollar Foreign Currency Option Prices (100ths of a cent per yen; each option contract is for ¥6,250,000)

Strike	Month of Maturity			Strike	Month of Maturity		
Price	July	August	September	Price	July	August	September
Calls				*Puts*			
87.0				87.0			0.36
89.0				89.0			0.54
90.0				90.0	0.25	0.50	0.92
91.0			3.32	91.0			1.04
91.5				91.5		0.85	
92.0	1.54		2.52	92.0	0.57	1.07	1.44
92.5				92.5	0.94	1.12	1.63
93.0	1.02			93.0	1.16		
93.5			2.22	93.5	1.22		2.06
94.0	0.94	1.46	1.99	94.0	1.26		
94.5	0.66	1.15		94.5			
95.0	0.59	1.21	1.33	95.0			
96.0		0.70	0.93	96.0			
97.0		0.55	0.78	97.0			
98.0			0.59	98.0			

United Grain Growers Limited (A)

"Everybody talks about the weather, but nobody does anything about it."

In late 1998, Brian Hayward, Peter Cox, George Prosk, and Mike McAndless pored over a colorful PowerPoint presentation that outlined the risks faced by their firm, United Grain Growers Limited (UGG). The graphs and numbers in the consulting report quantified a point they knew well: that the agriculture business was risky. The four men were the CEO, CFO, Treasurer, and Risk Manager, respectively, of Winnipeg-based UGG, one of the oldest grain distributors in Canada. A grain distributor helped farmers sell their grain by providing storage and sorting facilities, and transportation services.

UGG management had commissioned a study of the firm's risks because, as Hayward put it, his first responsibility was to "make sure we're in business tomorrow." The small Canadian firm had embarked on a modernization program to position itself in the deregulating Canadian agricultural industry. Its grain distribution revenues were largely determined by the amount of grain it handled, so anything that affected the quantity of grain shipped had a material impact on the firm's revenues, profits, and cash flow. Events of the prior two years showed how the firm's future could be threatened by unexpected risks, and UGG's management and Board of Directors were keen to understand these risks in light of their strategic importance. A recent Canadian regulatory guideline also recommended that Boards be held responsible for the "identification of the principal risks of the corporation's business and ensuring the implementation of appropriate systems to manage these risks."

Working with senior line managers, the risk consulting division of Willis Corroon, a leading insurance broker, had quantified the potential likelihood and severity of the six most material risks to UGG. The greatest risk was the impact of weather on the size of the harvest. The report suggested that, on average, once every ten years, UGG might face adverse weather that could reduce after-tax profits by as much as 11 million dollars,[1] or about 70% of its 1998 earnings. UGG's management needed to figure out the implications of this analysis, and what—if anything—should or could be done about the weather.

Grain Distribution

Agriculture—and in particular the grain industry—was one of civilization's oldest industries. Despite advances that had doubled yields per acre in the last 40 years, the industry had always been quite volatile, characterized by boom and bust cycles. This volatility had its roots in the forces of supply and demand in the global market. Grain supplies were variable due to natural forces such as pests, disease, and weather. While farmers could apply a variety of treatments to control insects or protect against disease,

[1]All dollar figures represent Canadian dollars. UGG's 1999 fiscal year began August 1, 1998.

Professors Peter Tufano and Stuart Gilson and Research Associate Joshua Musher prepared this case.
HBS cases are developed solely as the basis for class discussion. Cases are not intended to serve as endorsements, sources of primary data, or illustrations of effective or ineffective management.

Copyright © 2001 President and Fellows of Harvard College. To order copies or request permission to reproduce materials, call 1-800-545-7685, write Harvard Business School Publishing, Boston, MA 02163, or go to http://www.hbsp.harvard.edu. No part of this publication may be reproduced, stored in a retrieval system, used in a spreadsheet, or transmitted in any form or by any means—electronic, mechanical, photocopying, recording, or otherwise—without the permission of Harvard Business School.

they could do little to affect the weather. A late season frost or extremes in rainfall would affect the amount and/or quality of the crop harvested. As a result, grain supply was subject to large fluctuations. In conjunction with fluctuations in demand, this led to erratic grain prices and revenues. (See Exhibit 1.)

To assure supplies of agricultural products, reduce price fluctuations, and support the agricultural industry, many governments regulated the farming sector to some degree. In Canada, regulation varied by type of grain. Farmers sold wheat, barley, and oats ("Board grains") to the Canadian Wheat Board[2] (CWB), a government-mandated monopsony that essentially guaranteed a floor price that farmers received. Farmers sold other (non-board) grains at market prices. Grain distributors like UGG were important intermediaries between the farmer and the end market. Farmers typically hauled their grain to local or regional distribution centers called grain elevators. At these elevators, grain was stored by grade, then aggregated into larger lots going to specific buyers or export facilities, providing for logistical economies of scale. These services were also provided at export terminals. Approximately two-thirds of the grain that UGG shipped out of its country elevators was sent to its own export terminals. On average, about 70% of Canadian grain was exported, although this fell to only about 60% of the 1999 harvest.

Distributors charged farmers a handling fee for these services. Annually each distributor filed maximum tariffs, which may subsequently be discounted, but not exceeded. For UGG, average revenue for Board grains, including the local grain elevators and terminal handling, fell from around $23 per tonne[3] in 1998, to $19 per tonne in 1999. (See Exhibit 2.) The CWB also allocated the railcars which moved the grain from the elevators to the customer.[4] This system tended to stabilize (but also limit) distributors' market shares. In 1998, the three largest distributors were Saskatchewan Wheat Pool, Agricore, and UGG, with 30%, 25%, and 15% market shares, respectively. For non-regulated (non-Board) grains, UGG performed similar services and received an average gross margin of $17 and $19 per tonne in 1998 and 1999, respectively.

In legal terms, distributors served as the CWB's agent in handling board grains, but as principal for transactions with farmers on non-Board grains. As the CWB's agent, UGG did not have exposure to price fluctuations while the grain was in its custody. For non-board grains, however, UGG was the legal owner who assumed price risk for grains it held.[5] Distributors like UGG could and often did use commodity futures markets to hedge themselves against short-term fluctuations in non-Board grain prices.

The Canadian agriculture industry was under pressure from several directions. Many farmers disagreed with CWB policies and its monopsony power, and there was open debate about its future. The government, while trying to remove global trade barriers,[6] was deregulating at home. In 1995, it repealed legislation that kept grain transportation costs fixed (and low) for many years, and was currently reviewing other details of the grain transportation and distribution systems. Meanwhile, the market was demanding more specialized products such as malting barley, which required more specific contracting in advance of planting.

[2]The CWB was initially formed in 1919 to transition the grain industry to peacetime production at the end of World War I. Following a period of dormancy, it was revived in 1935 when the Great Depression threatened the financial stability of the industry.

[3]A metric tonne, 1000 kilograms or about 2200 pounds, was equivalent to approximately 36.7 bushels of wheat or durum, 45.9 bushels of barley, or 64.8 bushels of oats.

[4]Allocations had typically been driven by historical market share. Annual adjustments of two percentage points were based on service factors such as reliability and quality control. These policies have since evolved periodically and one was currently under review.

[5]Other risks, for both Board and non-Board grains, included quality risk (e.g., the protein content of the grain might be lower than anticipated) and spoilage.

[6]Government subsidies, estimated at $540 billion worldwide in 1998, provided a significant cushion to farmers.

United Grain Growers

UGG was established in 1906 by special legislation passed by the Canadian Parliament—the United Grain Growers Act. For the first 87 years of its existence, it was a cooperative, owned and operated by farmers for their mutual benefit. In 1993, UGG restructured itself as a public corporation and issued limited voting common shares on the Toronto Stock Exchange, in part to raise capital for strategic initiatives that would broaden the firm beyond its initial function as a grain distributor. Despite this change in legal form, UGG retained its strategic goal of "Meeting Farmers' Business Needs." Twelve of its 15 Board members were selected by farmer customers, with three elected by the common shareholders.

Recognition of two trends in the Canadian agricultural industry formed the basis for UGG's strategic vision. As described in its 1998 Annual Report, "The first is the shift towards a business environment driven more by commercial forces and less by government intervention. The second major trend is the rapid integration of technology—and biotechnology in particular—into mainstream agriculture." UGG designed a two-pronged strategy to respond to these trends: to modernize its grain handling business and to provide farmers with services beyond grain handling.

Grain Handling and Merchandising was the core division within UGG. The most tangible sign of modernization was the replacement of many small grain elevators that had dotted the Canadian landscape for a century. Between 1994 and 1999, UGG consolidated 224 scenic wooden elevators into 128 larger facilities. Older vintage wooden elevators could hold from 3000 to 8000 tonnes of grain and load perhaps 10 to 15 railcars at once, while upgraded wooden elevators could load between 18 and 25 railcars. Newer concrete high throughput (HTP) elevators had 15,000 to 40,000 tonnes of capacity and could load 25 to 100 or more railcars with grain at one time. This could cut UGG's operating costs by 8% and decrease its average shipping costs.[7] By 1998, 13 HTP elevators had been built at an average cost of $9 million each, with annual operating expenses of $1.25 million (of which approximately 75% were fixed costs) over their anticipated 50-year life. Another seven or eight were needed to complete the network, which was expected within three years. Another 15 elevators would be upgraded at an average cost of $3 million each and a further 48 of the old elevators closed. The initiative also included upgrading the logistics systems to reduce the frequency of imperfect deliveries by half, further reducing handling costs.

The second major initiative was to diversify UGG's operations by expanding its three other divisions: Crop Production Services, Livestock Services, and Farm Business Communications. Crop Production Services, which sold farm supplies such as fertilizer, proprietary seed, and consulting advice, was the largest of these three divisions. The business was highly seasonal, with most of the sales and profit coming in the spring during planting season. An aggressive acquisition program, including eight purchases of local retail distributors in fiscal 1998 alone, supplemented internal growth. Livestock Services manufactured and sold feed and animal breeding stock with superior production economics. Nutritionists also helped formulate custom feed diets to maximize animal growth rates. The Crop Production Services and Livestock Services divisions both offered financing programs for farmers who were trying to expand their own operations. The Farm Business Communications division provided one-stop shopping for information that farmers needed, such as farm magazines and a Web-site with updated market and weather information, as well as grain marketing tips. Recognizing the growing importance of technology (biotechnology in particular) in agriculture, UGG modified its

[7]For comparison, a fully loaded tractor-trailer could carry about 40 tonnes of grain, while one railcar could carry between 85 and 100 tonnes of grain. Loading a unit train of 100 railcars at one time could reduce shipping costs by as much as 20%.

strategic direction somewhat in 1995. The company began to seek out alliances and partnerships with "upstream" research companies, as well as "downstream" food processors—in effect, forming a *de facto* vertical integration through alliance. Since 1993, when it derived about 70% of its income from grain operations, UGG spent about $65 million on acquiring and building its non-grain handling businesses. By 1998, these divisions accounted for about half of operating income.

UGG could carry out its strategic plan if it had internal resources and access to external funds sufficient to fund its growth strategy. These initiatives had already cost $175 million, and Cox expected to spend another $150 million in the next two years to build the new HTP elevators, upgrade the existing elevators, and fund the expansion of the Crop Production Services and Livestock Services divisions. The expansion included acquiring retail outlets, building new seed treatment and feed mill facilities, as well as funding working capital needs.[8]

These large investments required more capital than the UGG could internally generate as a cooperative, and were the primary motivation for UGG's Initial Public Offering of 1.22 million shares at $8.00 each, which raised $9.8 million in 1993.[9] Two subsequent public equity offerings raised another $39 million in total, but total equity market capitalization remained small. Only one equity analyst followed the company, and management felt that the firm's volatile earnings and lack of a dedicated investor base contributed to what they believed was a relatively high cost of equity (or conversely, undervalued stock).

UGG's management determined that cash flows could support a debt to asset leverage ratio of 55%, and decided to raise funds through debt. UGG turned to banks for approximately half of its long term fixed asset financing, and in 1996 arranged for a ten-year loan of $100 million at an effective interest rate of 8.87%. In addition to using short-term bank financing for approximately 60% of its residual working capital requirements, in 1995 UGG began raising cash by a method called "securitizing." Essentially, UGG sold amounts receivable due from the CWB (for the grain UGG had bought on the CWB's behalf) and receivables due from farmers (for crop-input purchases). In 1998, UGG securitized a total of $173 million ($204 million in 1996) under two different $150 million facilities.[10] The securitization program reduced the amount of inventory and receivables that UGG had to finance, both on an absolute basis, and as a percentage of sales.

The Industry Climate

Events in the mid-1990s challenged UGG's strategic initiatives. In 1995, the government began reviewing the industry regulations. When it partially deregulated the transportation system, the railroads began consolidating routes. UGG had to take a $12.5 million

[8]The Crop Production Services division required significant working capital due to the seasonal nature of the business. Inventory was generally sold on credit during a six-week period in the spring. Farmers would generally pay in the fall when the crops were sold.

[9]The IPO raised $8.8 million net of fees and issue costs. This amount excluded $20.5 million of equity (6.85 million shares) issued in exchange for patronage interest owed to co-op members. Patronage interest was the distribution of profits paid to cooperative members. These distributions had been retained for several years to provide another source of financing to the company.

[10]UGG remained responsible for delivering the grain and collecting the funds. However, it was responsible for only a very limited proportion of any outstanding balance that a customer failed to pay. Securitization was a means of off-balance sheet funding. The description was due to the accounting treatment, where neither the assets (e.g., inventory subject to the sales) nor the corresponding liability (e.g., the accounts payable used to purchase the inventory) appeared on the balance sheet. In most cases, this lowered the ratio of debt to assets, financing costs and, in Canada, the capital taxes that were based on the amount of the firm's equity and debt.

charge for a three-year program to close 93 country elevators on routes that were going to be abandoned. The government commission also recommended major changes to the CWB. One of the reforms allowed distributors to set their own tariffs within limits. Later that year, a poor harvest contributed to low inventories and sales volume, and four out of the five major distributors lost money in the handling business. Low inventories contributed to higher grain prices, and farmers planted seven million more acres of cereals to compensate. Acreage in non-cereal grains such as canola, UGG's main proprietary seed product, fell by four million acres.[11] As a consequence, operating income from the Crop Production Services division fell about 50%.

These industry-wide economic strains, coupled with the attraction of UGG's modernized grain handling assets, prompted two of UGG's competitors, Alberta Pool and Manitoba Pool Elevators, to initiate a joint hostile takeover bid for UGG in January 1997. The bidders first purchased 1.6 million shares in the open market to acquire a 13% stake in the firm. They then offered to purchase the remaining shares at $13.75 per share, valuing the firm at $169 million, a 34% premium over the average stock price immediately before they began to acquire shares. They then bought another 1.98% of the stock on the open market, and entered into a "lock-up" agreement with one of UGG's other shareholders, which gave the Pools control over approximately 22% of UGG's common shares. UGG's investment advisors characterized the bid as "inadequate," as it failed to reflect the investments made by UGG in the past few years. UGG's board threatened to trigger a recently adopted "shareholder rights plan" (commonly known as a "poison pill") in defense. Under this plan, if a party acquired 15% or more of the company's stock, each shareholder (other than the would-be acquirer) would be able to purchase, at a 50% discount to market price, approximately 8.5 additional common shares for every share held, unless the acquirer complied with the bid provisions of the plan. This would have substantially diluted the share ownership of the non-complying bidder. The public exchange between UGG and the potential acquirers became acrimonious but the takeover attempt was ultimately defeated in March 1997 when a Canadian judge ruled that UGG was free to trigger its poison pill. Rather than suffer substantial dilution of their existing investment, the bidders withdrew their offer.[12] Subsequently, the two bidders merged to form Agricore.

In the aftermath of the takeover attempt, and consistent with its drive to form alliances, UGG formed a strategic alliance with Archer Daniels Midland Company (ADM), one of the largest food processors in the United States and a major customer of UGG. Under the alliance, ADM would gain "a secure grain supply for its processing operations" and UGG could "plan more efficiently for future transportation and grain handling demands, and increase market share."[13] ADM paid approximately $113 million to acquire a 42% stake in the outstanding common shares of UGG. After several years of working together, UGG also formalized a partnership with Marubeni Corporation, one of Japan's leading oilseed-crushing firms, on October 1, 1997. As part of the agreement, Marubeni purchased 750,000 newly issued shares at $16 per share (the market price for UGG stock was $14) in a private placement, giving it 4.5% ownership in UGG.[14] (See Exhibits 3 and 4.)

[11]For non-proprietary grains, farmers usually saved some of their harvested grain to use as seed.

[12]The firm spent approximately $2.2 million to respond to the hostile takeover offer.

[13]UGG Annual Report, 1997, page 8.

[14]UGG issued 4,828,320 shares to ADM in August 1997, after approval by UGG shareholders in a special meeting held on July 17, 1997, when the stock was trading at $14.55. ADM also converted a debenture it purchased from UGG in May 1997 into an additional 2,207,250 shares. Both of these transactions were executed at $16 per share, valuing the firm's equity at $269 million. In September, UGG repurchased 3,908,650 shares, also at $16 per share. Including the ADM, Marubeni, and repurchase transactions, UGG netted $61 million in new capital.

The Willis Report

While UGG had a long-standing risk management function, this subject received increasing interest in the firm throughout the 1990s. In 1992, shareholders of a U.S. agricultural cooperative successfully sued their directors because the firm did not hedge its grain risk when prices were falling.[15] The Dey Report, a 1994 regulatory recommendation from the Toronto Stock Exchange, charged Canadian Boards of Directors with the responsibility to understand the major risks faced by their firms, and have procedures for managing those risks.[16] Several "derivatives disasters," including the revelations of trading losses by rogue traders at Orange County in 1994, Barings Bank in 1995, and Sumitomo Corporation in 1996, brought risk management activities into the public focus. This emerging interest in risk management prompted UGG to participate in a benchmarking review of best risk management practices in its Treasury department. The Audit Services department, which reported directly to the Audit Committee of the Board of Directors, also felt a need to establish internal corporate-wide controls and reporting protocols on risk related matters.

Concurrently Cox and McAndless were discussing the concept of a significantly broader application of traditional risk management processes with one of its insurance consultants. Their objective was to better identify and evaluate all of UGG's risks (business as well as its traditionally insurable risks). Willis welcomed the opportunity to participate in the project. They had specialized resources available to analyze and evaluate the risks faced by businesses, to advise on how best to manage those risks, as well as where to purchase insurance to cover them. Willis was willing and able to provide the rigorous analysis of risks that UGG sought. Moreover they were willing to assist in facilitating the consolidated, corporate-wide risk identification and ranking process which was a necessary precursor to quantitative analysis. This analysis offered UGG a potential opportunity to structure a more comprehensive arrangement of its insurance through a single policy covering multiple risks. It might also enable the firm to adopt a standard approach to risk management, which would help UGG spend time and money where the benefits of risk reduction or opportunity were greatest.

On February 11, 1997, twenty UGG senior managers and other employees met for an onsite risk brainstorming session facilitated by Willis. Their first task was to identify the risks the firm faced. (See Exhibit 5.) The next task was to rank them, by polling the group, in relative importance to the firm. The risks were consolidated into twenty-five categories, and finally prioritized into groups of six for quantitative analysis. Once this process was complete, Willis focused its attention on the first group of six which included commodity price risk, inventory management risk (spoilage and obsolescence), customer and supplier counterparty risk, accounts receivable and credit risk, environmental risks, and weather risk.

Willis assembled a team of specialists from several departments to analyze the various risks. The team included several actuaries,[17] a statistician, and a marketer who understood

[15]Paul H. Brane et al. v. Porter E. Roth et al., First Court of Appeals, Indiana, February 28, 1992.

[16]Similar guidelines were recommended in both the U.S. ("Report of the National Commission on Fraudulent Financial Reporting," 1987, also known as the Treadway Report), and the U.K. ("Report of the Committee on the Financial Aspects of Corporate Governance," 1992, also known as the Cadbury Report).

[17]An actuary applies statistics and financial theory to solve insurance and pension problems such as what premiums to charge, or how much money needs to be invested to cover future liabilities.

insurance markets. The methodology used depended on the amount of information available. Large data sets, such as the weather or commodity prices, were analyzed with statistical methods. Risks where significant data was available, such as credit risk, were analyzed with traditional actuarial data. When hard data was lacking, as was the case for environmental and counterparty risk, the team surveyed experts in the field to get informed estimates of the potential liability. The data collection and analysis was conducted over an 18-month period, punctuated by delays as UGG management focused on other urgent business matters.

For each of the top six risks, the Willis team had to summarize the distribution of the size and severity of UGG's potential losses. They used a measure called "Earnings at Risk" (EaR), which had been developed by the financial community, to describe aggregate risks. EaR expressed a "worst-case" loss, set against a benchmark of expected profit, within a specified confidence or probability level. For example, a 95% EaR of $5.6 million implied that, 5% of the time or once every twenty years, the firm would fall short of its earnings target by more than $5.6 million.[18] The advantage of EaR was the simplicity of aggregating multiple risks into a single number.[19] (See Exhibit 6.)

Analyzing the weather risk presented a challenge to Ken Risko, the statistician, ironically because there was too much data. Risko had 70 years of monthly information on the average temperature, low temperature, and precipitation for approximately 160 weather stations covering UGG's territory, and data on yields for 5 different relevant crops. Using spreadsheets to analyze the data with regression techniques, he found that the four variables, precipitation in June and July and the average temperature in February and September, explained approximately 85% of the variation in crop yields. These results appeared valid to agriculture experts. The modeled yields, in turn, explained approximately 94% of the variability of UGG's grain handling earnings. (See Exhibit 7.)

Willis needed to communicate complex information without resorting to tables of numbers and pages of explanations and caveats. It also needed to convey the meaning and limits of the statistical analysis. Willis used this opportunity to test a new tool under development called CHARM (Comprehensive Holistic All Risk Model). CHARM generated graphical output in several formats to highlight the various aspects of each risk. The most general format was a probability distribution showing the probability of incurring a loss as a function of the size of the dollar loss. This was usually implemented either in cumulative form (i.e., to show the probability of losing at least a certain amount) or as a distribution (i.e., to show the probability of a specific outcome), though one could be inferred from the other. (See Exhibit 8.) The presentation concluded with CHARM's translation of the statistical distribution into a demonstration of how risk management might impact the volatility of UGG's operating income. The results convinced Cox that he had the information to do something to improve the firm's risk management performance and potentially reduce UGG's long term cost of risk. (See Exhibit 9.)

[18]The financial community pioneered the concept as Value at Risk. VaR was generally stated as the largest amount that an institution estimated its portfolio might fall in value due to changing market conditions, within a specified probability. It could also be expressed as a probability that the losses would exceed a specific amount. Using the example above, the firm would lose less than $5.6 million (relative to its benchmark) in 19 out of 20 years. However, there was also a 5% chance in any one year that the firm would lose more than $5.6 million.

[19]Multiple risks, in general, do not add in a simple manner because the correlation between events must be considered. Events with a negative correlation tend to offset one another, and even positively correlated events that are imperfectly correlated with one another tend to occur at different times.

What to Do about the Weather?

Five of the six risks that Willis analyzed could be managed through traditional methods. Environmental risk was generally controlled using property and liability insurance and well-defined and executed operating procedures, which also applied to containing inventory risk. Credit and counterparty risks were controlled with credit limits, a diverse customer and supplier base, and aggressive monitoring of the ability and willingness to fulfill their commitments. These credit and other financial risk management programs were all well-established and supervised by Prosk. The Marketing and Transportation Division managed the firm's exposure to grain price fluctuations using financial contracts such as commodity futures and options, and by establishing and monitoring position limits in concert with Cox and Hayward.[20]

One of the largest risks presented in the analysis was the weather, which UGG could not manage because historically there had been no financial products that would effectively mitigate the risk. Several firms were attempting to fill this gap with new products and services. One recent innovation was weather derivatives, a new class of financial instrument offered by a few pioneering firms. Typically custom written, these contracts were structured to pay a specified amount of money as a function of a particular weather characteristic. For example, Boston's Logan Airport purchased an option that paid when winter snowfall exceeded a specific amount. A more common implementation used "degree-days" (defined as the average daily temperature minus 65 degrees Fahrenheit) as the underlying variable. The contract would then pay the difference between the realized number of degree-days and the contracted number of degree-days, multiplied by a predetermined dollar figure. These markets were still emerging, however, and the contracts were illiquid with large bid-ask spreads.

Willis, however, believed they might be able to find an insurer willing to write a contract to protect UGG. Such a contract might bundle UGG's existing risks (property and casualty and environmental) with its risk due to poor weather. Initially, the Willis and UGG team thought that it would be easier to link the contract to verifiable weather conditions, much like weather derivative contracts. UGG would need to pay a premium for this insurance, and negotiations would likely revolve around the extent to which the insurer would provide UGG with coverage.

As Cox and his team were reviewing the alternatives, disaster struck in the form of a poor macroeconomic environment. An Asian currency crisis caused a general weakness in commodity markets. The CWB, faced with low prices and poor demand, was having difficulty marketing the recent crop. Despite a 27% increase in non-board grain shipments, CWB shipments for the first half of fiscal year 1999 were down 45%, costing UGG approximately $5.0 million in lost after tax profit. This experience prompted the team to realize that it may be better to link the coverage directly to the quantity of grain handled in Canada rather than just the consequences of adverse weather. But, Cox wondered, would the insurers be interested in providing "unconditional volume protection" and at what price?

[20]A futures contract was a commitment to buy (or sell) a commodity at a fixed price in the future, and could be used to lock in prices. An option gave the holder the right to buy (or sell) a commodity at a fixed price in the future.

EXHIBIT 1
Historical Yields and Total Production of Canadian Wheat, 1908–1998

Source: Statistics Canada

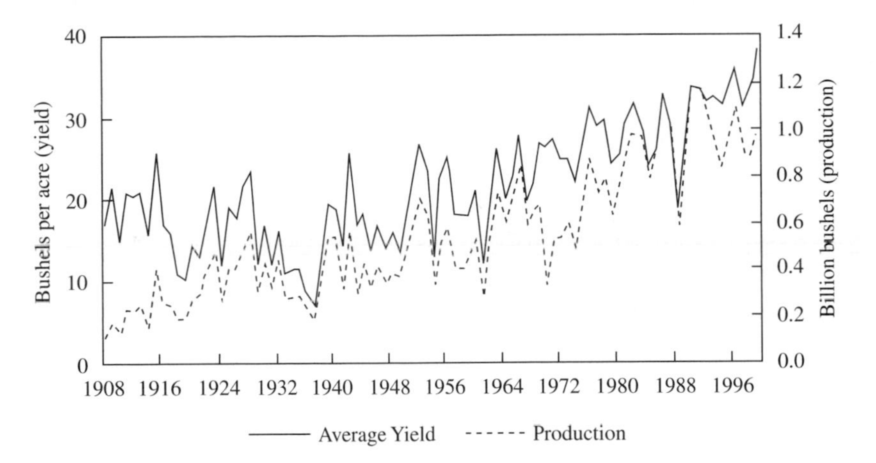

EXHIBIT 1B
Historical Wheat Prices,[a] 1993–1998 (Canadian dollars per tonne)

Source: Datastream

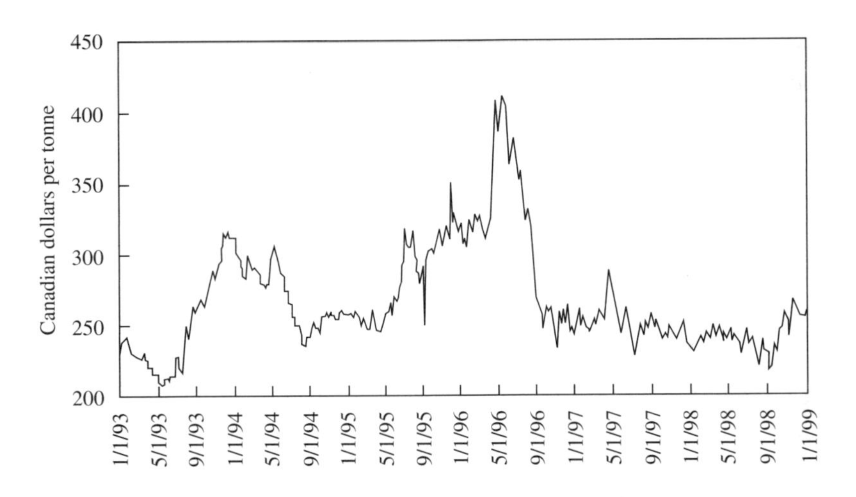

EXHIBIT 2 Representative Tariffs, CWB Shipments, and UGG Market Share, 1988–1998 ('000 tonnes unless otherwise noted)

Sources: UGG, company reports, Canadian Grain Commission, and casewriter estimates.

Fiscal Year	Country Elevator Shipments[a, b]	Terminal Elevator Shipments[b]	Total Number of Country Elevators	Number of High Throughput Elevators	Total Country Elevator Capacity[b]	Average Country Elevator Capacity[b]	Country Elevator Turnover	UGG Country Market Share	Representative Wheat Tariff[c, d]	Representative Malt Barley Tariff[c, e]
1990	4,841	2,163	276	0	1,149	4.16	4.21 x	16.2%	$8.40	$10.20
1991	5,869	3,785	269	0	1,145	4.26	5.13 x	15.2%	8.65	10.55
1992	5,411	3,861	266	0	1,134	4.26	4.77 x	12.8%	8.51	10.30
1993	5,333	3,150	252	3	1,125	4.46	4.74 x	13.3%	8.53	10.12
1994	5,679	3,127	224	6	1,099	4.91	5.17 x	14.4%	8.42	9.73
1995	6,222	3,599	220	8	1,069	4.86	5.82 x	18.3%	8.57	9.94
1996	5,164	2,626	173	10	973	5.62	5.31 x	16.8%	8.93	12.84
1997	5,346	3,192	152	12	864	5.68	6.19 x	14.6%	9.10	13.12
1998	4,987	3,064	145	16	823	5.68	6.06 x	14.9%	9.37	13.01

[a]Country elevators were located in the provinces and acted as local gathering and storage facilities. Terminal elevators were export facilities, which generally loaded the grains onto ships.

[b]In thousands of tonnes.

[c]Realized tariffs in dollars per tonne at country elevators. Tariffs were rough weighted averages over the three provinces where UGG operated. They were for country elevation, and did not include fees for services such as cleaning, inspection, or storage, or for any terminal handling. The tariffs for individual provinces could vary as much as +/– 15% from the average.

[d]Wheat, a so-called Board grain, was marketed through the Canadian Wheat Board.

[e]UGG directly marketed malt barley to customers. It was responsible for the marketing; it decided when to buy, when to sell, and where the malt barley went (e.g., UGG terminals), depending on the farmer supply and customer demand. As a consequence, UGG was able to earn higher, but more volatile, net tariffs.

EXHIBIT 3A Historical Income Statements for UGG, 1993–1998 (in millions of Canadian dollars)

Source: Company reports.

	1993	1994	1995	1996	1997	1998
Sales and revenue from services	1,049.0	1,217.4	1,736.5	1,969.9	1,921.3	1,887.3
Gross profit and revenue from services[a]	151.8	158.1	188.5	203.2	220.0	229.7
Selling, general, and administrative expenses	123.7	132.6	158.0	163.0	165.3	169.1
Depreciation and amortization	13.0	12.9	15.4	16.1	16.3	17.2
Net operating income	16.1	12.6	15.2	24.1	38.5	43.3
Unusual and extraordinary items and discontinued operations	0.4	(2.0)	(12.5)	0.0	(4.5)	0.0
Interest and securitization expense[b]	6.4	8.8	14.9	16.0	13.7	11.4
Taxes	2.1	1.6	(4.9)	2.2	11.2	15.6
Net income	7.0	0.2	(7.4)	5.9	9.1	16.3

[a]This was the gross value of the total services provided by UGG (e.g., inspection, cleaning, distribution, storage, and logistical arrangements for grain, and distribution for other products). It was calculated as sales minus the direct costs of goods sold. The costs of providing the services (or generating the sales) were not subtracted.
[b]Securitization expense was the interest paid on CWB inventories that were securitized.

EXHIBIT 3B Historical Balance Sheet for UGG, 1993–1998 (in millions of Canadian dollars)

Source: Company reports.

	1993	1994	1995	1996	1997	1998
Cash and equivalents	18.1	22.1	42.2	48.1	69.3	46.9
Accounts receivable and prepaid expenses	117.2	175.9	116.4	97.8	93.6	88.3
Inventories (net of securitizations)[a]	175.7	190.0	187.5	181.4	121.7	136.2
Plant, property, and equipment	141.5	158.2	182.1	190.3	193.3	226.3
Other assets	15.9	17.8	16.1	13.9	11.2	17.5
Total assets	468.4	564.0	544.3	531.4	489.2	515.2
Short-term debt	210.4	226.8	218.4	165.7	85.1	46.4
Accounts payable	52.1	81.3	79.3	86.2	93.4	83.5
Dividends payable	1.2	3.7	3.8	3.8	4.3	5.3
Deferred income taxes	49.4	53.1	46.5	41.9	44.8	45.3
Long-term debt	28.7	64.6	65.6	100.1	100.2	100.0
Total liabilities	341.9	423.5	413.7	397.7	327.9	280.6
Total shareholders' equity	126.5	140.5	130.6	133.7	161.3	234.6
Total liabilities and equity	468.4	564.0	544.3	531.4	489.2	515.2
Assets securitized[b]	0	0	110.7	203.7	217.7	173.2

[a]Securitized receivables and inventory held on behalf of the CWB was not included in UGG receivables and inventory as the lender technically held the title to them. Because neither the asset nor the associated financing was recorded on the balance sheet, this type of funding was referred to as "off-balance sheet."
[b]To correct for the distortion of "off-balance sheet" financing, rating agencies typically added back the balance of the securitized assets to both the assets and liabilities of the company when calculating financial ratios and ability to repay debt. Bank covenants typically did not make this adjustment.

EXHIBIT 5 Selected List of Risks Identified by UGG Management during On-Site Meeting, February 11, 1997

Source: UGG

Business interruption	Employee liability	Pension plan performance
Cargo/marine exposure	Employee performance/fidelity	Process compliance/execution
Civil disturbance	Environmental	Product liability
Commodity basis/price[a]	Foreign exchange	Product performance
Competition	Head office catastrophe	Quebec separates from Canada
Consumer preferences	Industrial espionage	R&D ventures
Contractual non-performance	Intellectual property	Regulatory (CWB, transportation)
Credit/receivables	Interest rates	Stock market crash
Counterparty	Inventory	Strategic planning
Directors & officers exposure	Labor strike	Technology (choice, use of)
Data accuracy	Leverage (too much or too little)	Transportation
Disease/spoilage	Loss of key personnel	Unionization
Computer system failure	Mergers and acquisitions	Weather
Employee injury	Major property exposure	

[a]Basis risk is the risk that the price of the commodity being held diverges from the price of the commodity hedged. For example, the protein content of the grain held in storage may differ from the protein content specified by the hedge contract. The relative price difference might widen or narrow, causing a gain or loss even though the grain is otherwise hedged.

EXHIBIT 6 Analysis of the First Six Risks That Willis Reviewed (in millions of Canadian dollars)

Source: UGG and Willis reports, casewriter estimates.

Risk	Definition	Earnings at Risk[a]	Method to Manage Risk
Weather	Impact on harvested yields	11.5	None
Environmental Liability	Inadvertent release of toxic substances to external environment	2.5	Insurance/control
Counterparty	Failure of another company, such as a supplier, to meet contractual obligations, such as delivery of inventory to sell.	4.3	Diversification/due diligence/contracts
Credit	Failure of another company to pay money owed to UGG	1.6	Diversification/due diligence/contracts
Inventory	Spoilage of inventory	2.2	Operational control, insurance
Commodity	Price falls while holding in inventory	11.9	Futures and options

[a]Figures are at 90% confidence or probability level, except for commodities, which were calculated at the 95% confidence level. The figures represent that there was a 90% (or 95%) probability that the largest loss would be less than the stated number.

EXHIBIT 7

All-Wheat Yield in Saskatchewan and the July Precipitation for 1960 through 1992

Source: Casewriter estimates based on data from UGG and Willis.

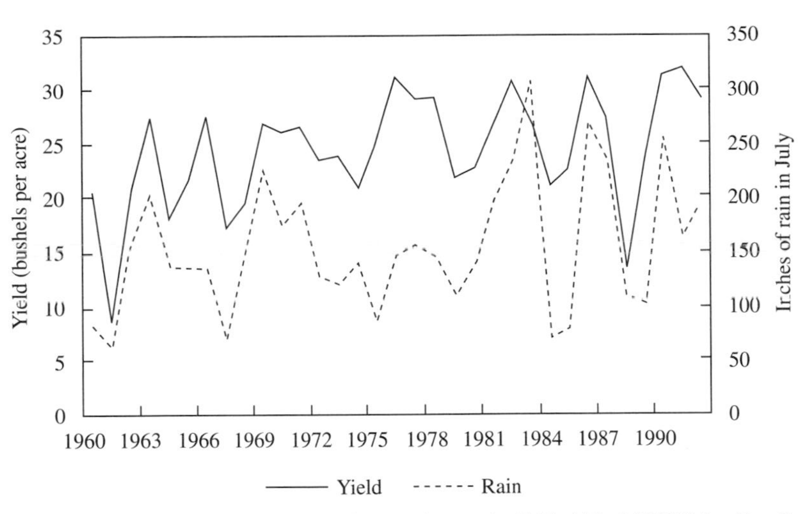

Note: The yield depends on the rain according to the regression equation Yield = 15.5 + 0.0577 * Rain, with an R-squared of 43%. The t-statistics for the intercept and slope were 7.8 and 4.8, respectively.

EXHIBIT 8

CHARM plot showing the probability distribution of earnings with and without the impact of the weather. When the weather risk is removed, the variation in EBIT is smaller, as shown by the lighter curve, though the expected value is the same.

Source: UGG and Willis Corroon

Probability Density

$45,125

$27,775

66,475 61,025 55,575 50,125 44,675 39,225 33,775 28,325 22,875 17,425 11,975 6,525

EBIT (000's)

Excluding Weather Impact — Including Weather Impact

EXHIBIT 9

Potential Impact of Integrated Risk Program on Historical Operating Income, 1985–1998 (in millions of Canadian dollars)

Source: UGG and Willis Corroon.

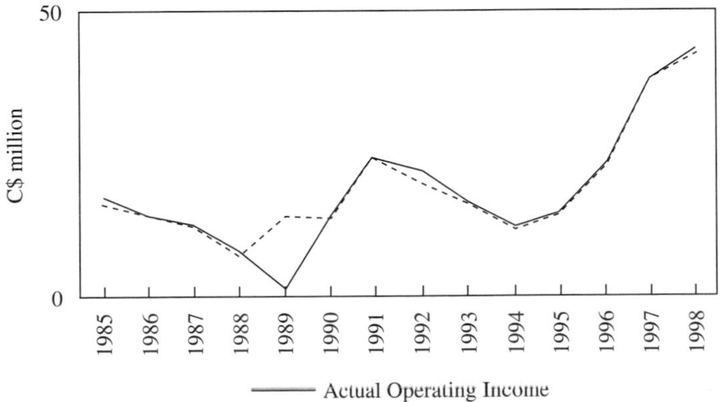

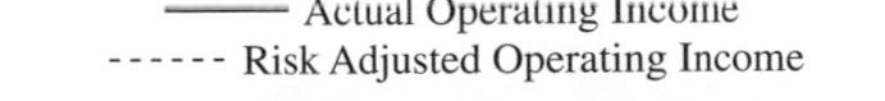

Note: A major drought reduced the 1988 grain harvest, which was marketed in 1989, by about 20%.

Part 3

Valuation and Investment

Valuing and Selecting Investment Opportunities

Valuing Capital Investment Projects

1. Growth Enterprises, Inc. (GEI) has $40 million that it can invest in any or all of the four capital investment projects, which have cash flows as shown in Table A below.

TABLE A
Comparison of Project Cash Flows* ($ thousands)

Project	Type of Cash Flow	Year 0	Year 1	Year 2	Year 3
			Year of Cash Flow		
A.	Investment	($10,000)			
	Revenue		$21,000		
	Operating expenses		11,000		
B.	Investment	($10,000)			
	Revenue		$15,000	$17,000	
	Operating expenses		5,833	7,833	
C.	Investment	($10,000)			
	Revenue		$10,000	$11,000	$30,000
	Operating expenses		5,555	4,889	15,555
D.	Investment	($10,000)			
	Revenue		$30,000	$10,000	$5,000
	Operating expenses		15,555	5,555	2,222

*All revenues and operating expenses can be considered *cash* items.

Each of these projects is considered to be of equivalent risk. The investment will be depreciated to zero on a straight-line basis for tax purposes. GEI's marginal corporate tax rate on taxable income is 40%. None of the projects will have any salvage value at the end of their respective lives. For purposes of analysis, it should be assumed that all cash flows occur at the *end* of the year in question.

This case was prepared as the basis for class discussion rather than to illustrate either effective or ineffective handling of an administrative situation. Problem 1 appears in the case, "Introduction to Investment Evaluation Techniques" (HBS case no. 285-115) by Professor Dwight B. Crane and was revised for inclusion in this case. Problems 3 and 4 appear in the case, "Investment Analysis and Lockheed Tri Star" (HBS case no. 291-031) by Professor Michael E. Edleson and were also revised for inclusion in this case.

Copyright © 1997 by the President and Fellows of Harvard College. To order copies or request permission to reproduce materials, call 1-800-545-7685 or write Harvard Business School Publishing, Boston, MA 02163. No part of this publication may be reproduced, stored in a retrieval system, used in a spreadsheet, or transmitted in any form or by any means—electronic, mechanical, photocopying, recording, or otherwise—without the permission of Harvard Business School.

A. Rank GEI's four projects according to the following four commonly used capital budgeting criteria:
   (1) Payback period.
   (2) Accounting return on investment. For purposes of this exercise, the accounting return on investment should be defined as follows:

$$\frac{\text{Average annual after-tax profits}}{(\text{Required investment})/2}$$

   (3) Internal rate of return.
   (4) Net present value, assuming alternately a 10% discount rate and a 35% discount rate.

B. Why do the rankings differ? What does each technique measure and what assumptions does it make?

C. If the projects are independent of each other, which should be accepted? If they are mutually exclusive (i.e., one and only one can be accepted), which one is best?

2. Electronics Unlimited was considering the introduction of a new product that was expected to reach sales of $10 million in its first full year, and $13 million of sales in the second year. Because of intense competition and rapid product obsolescence, sales of the new product were expected to remain unchanged between the second and third years following introduction. Thereafter, annual sales were expected to decline to two-thirds of peak annual sales in the fourth year, and one-third of peak sales in the fifth year. No material levels of revenues or expenses associated with the new product as expected after five years of sales. Based on past experience, cost of sales for the new product was expected to be 60% of total annual sales revenue during each year of its life cycle. Selling, general, and administrative expenses were expected to be 23.5% of total annual sales. Taxes on profits generated by the new product would be paid at a 40% rate.

   To launch the new product, Electronics Unlimited would have to incur immediate cash outlays of two types. First, it would have to invest $500,000 in specialized new production equipment. This capital investment would be fully depreciated on a straight-line basis over the five-year anticipated life cycle of the new product. It was not expected to have any material salvage value at the end of its depreciable life. No further fixed capital expenditures were required after the initial purchase of equipment.

   Second, additional investment in net working capital to support sales would have to be made. Electronics Unlimited generally required 27¢ of net working capital to support each dollar of sales. As a practical matter, this buildup would have to be made by the *beginning* of the sales year in question (or, equivalently, by the end of the previous year). As sales grew, further investments in net working capital ahead of sales would have to be made. As sales diminished, net working capital would be liquidated and cash recovered. At the end of the new product's life cycle, all remaining net working capital would be liquidated and the cash recovered.

   Finally, Electronics Unlimited expected to incur tax-deductible introductory expenses of $200,000 in the first year of the new product's sales. These costs would not be recurring over the product's life cycle. Approximately $1.0 million had already been spent developing and test marketing the new product. These expenditures were also one-time expenses that would not be recurring during the new product's life cycle.

   A. Estimate the new product's future sales, profits, and cash flows throughout its five-year life cycle.
   B. Assuming a 20% discount rate, what is the product's net present value? (Except for changes in net working capital, which must be made before the start of each

sales year, you should assume that all cash flows occur at the end of the year in question.) What is its internal rate of return?

C. Should Electronics Unlimited introduce the new product?

3. You are the CEO of Valu-Added Industries, Inc. (VAI). Your firm has 10,000 shares of common stock outstanding, and the current price of the stock is $100 per share. There is no debt; thus, the "market value" balance sheet of VAI appears as follows:

VAI Market Value Balance Sheet

Assets	$1,000,000	Equity	$1,000,000

You then discover an opportunity to invest in a new project that produces positive net cash flows with a present value of $210,000. Your total initial costs for investing and developing this project are only $110,000. You will raise the necessary capital for this investment by issuing new equity. All potential purchasers of your common stock will be fully aware of the project's value and cost, and are willing to pay "fair value" for the new shares of VAI common.

A. What is the net present value of this project?

B. How many shares of common stock must be issued, and at what price, to raise the required capital?

C. What is the effect, if any, of this new project on the value of the stock of the existing shareholders?

4. Lockheed Tri Star and Capital Budgeting[1]

In 1971, the American aerospace company, Lockheed, found itself in Congressional hearings seeking a $250 million federal guarantee to secure bank credit required for the completion of the L-1011 Tri Star program. The L-1011 Tri Star Airbus was a wide-bodied commercial jet aircraft with a capacity of up to 400 passengers, competing with the DC-10 trijet and the A-300B airbus.

Spokesmen for Lockheed claimed that the Tri Star program was economically sound and that their problem was merely a liquidity crisis caused by some unrelated military contracts. Opposing the guarantee, other parties argued that the Tri Star program had been economically unsound and doomed to financial failure from the very beginning.

The debate over the viability of the program centered on estimated "break-even sales"—the number of jets that would need to be sold for total revenue to cover all accumulated costs. Lockheed's CEO, in his July 1971 testimony before Congress, asserted that this break-even point would be reached at sales somewhere between 195 and 205 aircraft. At that point, Lockheed had secured only 103 firm orders plus 75 options-to-buy, but they testified that sales would eventually exceed the break-even point and that the project would thus become "a commercially viable endeavor." Lockheed also testified that it hoped to capture 35%–40% of the total free-world market of 775 wide bodies over the next decade (270–310 aircraft). This market estimate had been based on the optimistic assumption of 10% annual growth in air travel. At a more realistic 5% growth rate, the total world market would have been only about 323 aircraft.

[1]Facts and situations concerning the Lockheed Tri Star program are taken from U. E. Reinhardt, "Break-Even Analysis for Lockheed's Tri Star: An Application of Financial Theory," *Journal of Finance* 27 (1972), 821–838, and from House and Senate testimony.

Costs

The preproduction phases of the Tri Star project began at the end of 1967 and lasted four years after running about six months behind schedule. Various estimates of the initial development costs ranged between $800 million and $1 billion. A reasonable approximation of these cash outflows would be $900 million, occurring as follows:

End of Year	Time "Index"	Cash Flow ($ millions)
1967	t=0	–$100
1968	t=1	–$200
1969	t=2	–$200
1970	t=3	–$200
1971	t=4	–$200

According to Lockheed testimony, the production phase was to run from the end of 1971 to the end of 1977 with about 210 Tri Stars as the planned output. At that production rate, the average unit production cost would be about $14 million per aircraft.[2] The inventory-intensive production costs would be relatively front-loaded, so that the $490 million ($14 million per plane, 35 planes per year) annual production costs could be assumed to occur in six equal increments at the end of years 1971 through 1976 (t=4 through t=9).

Revenues

In 1968, the expected price to be received for the L–1011 Tri Star was about $16 million per aircraft. These revenue flows would be characterized by a lag of a year to the production cost outflows; annual revenues of $560 million could be assumed to occur in six equal increments at the end of years 1972 through 1977 (t=5 through t=10). Inflation-escalation terms in the contracts ensured that any future inflation-based cost and revenue increases offset each other nearly exactly, thus providing no incremental net cash flow.

Deposits toward future deliveries were received from Lockheed customers. Roughly one-quarter of the price of the aircraft was actually received two years early. For example, for a single Tri Star delivered at the end of 1972, $4 million of the price was received at the end of 1970, leaving $12 million of the $16 million price as cash flow at the end of 1972. So, for the 35 planes built (and presumably, sold) in a year, $140 million of the $560 million in total annual revenue was actually received as a cash flow two years earlier.

Discount Rate

Experts estimated that the cost of capital applicable to Lockheed's cash flows (prior to Tri Star) was in the 9%–10% range. Since the Tri Star project was quite a bit riskier (by any measure) than the typical Lockheed operation, the appropriate discount rate was almost certainly higher than that. Thus, 10% was a reasonable (although possibly generous) estimate of the appropriate discount rate to apply to the Tri Star program's cash flows.

[2]This figure excludes preproduction cost allocations. That is, the $14 million cost figure is totally separate from the $900 million of preproduction costs shown in the table above.

Break-Even Revisited

In an August 1972 *Time* magazine article, Lockheed (after receiving government loan guarantees) revised its break-even sales volume: "[Lockheed] claims that it can get back its development costs [about $960 million] and start making a profit by selling 275 Tri Stars."[3] Industry analysts had predicted this (actually, they had estimated 300 units to be the break-even volume) even prior to the Congressional hearings.[4] Based on a "learning curve" effect, production costs at these levels (up to 300 units) would average only about $12.5 million per unit, instead of $14 million as above. Had Lockheed been able to produce and sell as many as 500 aircraft, this average cost figure might even have been as low as $11 million per aircraft.

A. At originally planned production levels (210 units), what would have been the estimated value of the Tri Star program as of the end of 1967?

B. At "break-even" production of roughly 300 units, did Lockheed break even in terms of net present value?

C. At what sales volume would the Tri Star program have reached true economic (as opposed to accounting) break-even?

D. Was the decision to pursue the Tri Star program a reasonable one? What effects would you predict the adoption of the Tri Star program would have on shareholder value?

[3] *Time* (August 21, 1972), 62.

[4] Mitchell Gordon, "Hitched to the Tri Star—Disaster at Lockheed Would Cut a Wide Swathe," *Barron's* (March 15, 1971), 5–14.

Merck & Company: Evaluating a Drug Licensing Opportunity

Rich Kender, Vice President of Financial Evaluation & Analysis at Merck, was working with his team to decide whether his company should license Davanrik, a new drug with the potential to treat both depression and obesity. The small pharmaceutical concern that developed the drug, LAB Pharmaceuticals, lacked the resources to complete the lengthy approval process, manufacture the compound, and market the drug. LAB had approached Merck with an offer to license the compound. Under this agreement, Merck would be responsible for the approval of Davanrik, its manufacture, and its marketing. The company would pay LAB an initial fee, a royalty on all sales, and make additional payments as Davanrik completed each stage of the approval process.

Merck

In 2000, Merck & Co., Inc., was a global research-driven pharmaceutical company that discovered, developed, manufactured, and marketed a broad range of human and animal health products, directly and through its joint ventures, and provided pharmaceutical benefit management services (PBM) through Merck-Medco Managed Care. Since 1995, Merck had launched 15 new products including Vioxx™ for the treatment of osteoarthritis, Fosamax™ for the treatment of osteoporosis, and Singulair™ for treating asthma. The Company earned $5.9 billion on 1999 sales[1] of $32.7 billion, about a 20% increase from 1998. Exhibits 1 and 2 contain Merck's Income Statement and Balance Sheet.

A handful of Merck's most popular drugs, Vasotec™, Mevacor™, Prinivil™, and Pepcid™, generated $5.7 billion in worldwide sales. The patents for these drugs, however, would expire by 2002.[2] Once the patents expired, Merck anticipated that the sales of these drugs would decline substantially as generic substitutes became available. The only way to counter the loss of sales from drugs going off patent was to develop new drugs and constantly refresh the company's portfolio. The company develops new compounds primarily through internal research, but complements this through initiatives with biotechnology companies to ensure Merck is on the leading edge of select therapeutic categories.

[1]Including $15.2 billion in Medco (PBM) sales.

[2]Deutsche Bank Equity Analyst Report, January 2000.

David Krieger (MBA '00) and Professor Richard S. Ruback prepared this case. HBS cases are developed solely as the basis for class discussion. Cases are not intended to serve as endorsements, sources of primary data, or illustrations of effective or ineffective management.

Copyright © 2000 President and Fellows of Harvard College. To order copies or request permission to reproduce materials, call 1-800-545-7685, write Harvard Business School Publishing, Boston, MA 02163, or go to http://www.hbsp.harvard.edu. No part of this publication may be reproduced, stored in a retrieval system, used in a spreadsheet, or transmitted in any form or by any means—electronic, mechanical, photocopying, recording, or otherwise—without the permission of Harvard Business School.

Davanrik

LAB Pharmaceuticals originally developed Davanrik to treat depression. Antidepressant drugs work by affecting certain parts of the central nervous system. Various receptors in the human brain, when stimulated or blocked, create or inhibit various moods. The serotonin system controls nervousness, depression, insomnia, hunger, sexual dysfunction, nausea, and headaches. Through a combination of chemical compounds, the receptors in this system of cells can be stimulated or blocked to treat a patient with one or more of the given symptoms.[3] Davanrik seemed not only to stimulate the receptor that promotes antidepression, but also to block the receptor that causes hunger.

At the time of LAB's offer, Davanrik was in pre-clinical development, ready to enter the three-phase clinical approval process required for pharmaceuticals in the United States. In Phase I, the drug is given to a small number of healthy volunteers to test for safety. This usually takes about 1½ years. In Phase II, a larger number of patients are tested to determine if the drug is effective in treating a certain condition and to measure potential side effects. This usually takes about 2½ years. Finally, in Phase III, a large number of patients are tested for safety and efficacy. This phase takes about 3 years to complete. Exhibit 3 summarizes the FDA approval process.

LAB Pharmaceuticals specializes in developing compounds for the treatment of neurological disorders. While the company was only 15 years old and though it had a few drugs in Phase II and Phase III testing, none had successfully completed the FDA approval process. In fact, the FDA had recently denied approval of another of LAB's compounds that had completed all three phases of clinical testing; LAB's stock price fell by over 30% in response to this decision. As a result, LAB was hesitant to issue additional equity to finance the testing of Davanrik and was seeking a larger pharmaceutical company to license the drug and provide LAB with some much-needed cash. The licensee would design, administer, and fund the clinical testing of the compound, its manufacturing, and its marketing. The licensor, LAB, would receive an initial payment followed by additional payments as Davanrik completes each clinical testing phase. LAB would also receive a royalty on the eventual sales of Davanrik.

Davanrik's Potential Cash Flows

Rich Kender assembled a team to evaluate the potential profitability of Davanrik. Senior researchers evaluated scientific aspects of the compound, and marketers evaluated the market size, potential competition, and requirements to successfully launch the drug. Meanwhile, manufacturing managers determined the capital required to produce the drug, and people in Kender's own department built a financial analysis of the licensing decision.

The evaluation team determined the costs and likelihood of completing each stage of the FDA approval process along with a forecast of profitability of the drug if it successfully completed the approval process. Overall, the approval process was expected to consume about seven years. LAB obtained a patent on the product which is estimated to have a remaining life, including all possible extensions, of 17 years. Therefore, the product would have a 10 year period of exclusivity, beginning in 7 years.

[3]From The Merck Manual of Diagnosis and Therapy, Section 15, Chapter 189 (Mood Disorders).

Phase I

Davanrik would be administered to 20–80 healthy people to determine if the drug was safe enough to continue into the efficacy stages of clinical testing. Phase I would take two years to complete. It was expected to cost $30 million, including an initial $5 million fee to LAB for licensing the drug. There was a 60% chance that Davanrik would successfully complete Phase I.

Phase II

In this phase, Davanrik would be given to 100–300 patient volunteers to determine its efficacy for treating depression and/or weight loss and to document any side effects. To complete the efficacy tests, Davanrik would have to demonstrate a statistically significant impact on patients suffering from depression, obesity, or both. The Merck team estimated a 10% probability that Phase II would show that Davanrik would be efficacious for depression only, a 15% probability for weight loss only, and a 5% probability that it would be efficacious for both depression and weight loss at the same time.[4] Like Phase I, Phase II would require two years of clinical testing to complete. Phase II was expected to cost $40 million, including a $2.5 million licensing milestone payment to LAB.[5]

Phase III

In Phase III, Davanrik would be administered to 1000–5000 volunteers to determine safety and efficacy in long term use. Because of the number of volunteers and nature of testing, this was the most costly of the phases and was expected to take three years to complete. The costs and probabilities of success depended on the outcome from Phase II. If Davanrik was effective for only depression, Phase III trials would cost $200 million including a $20 million payment to LAB, and have an 85% chance of success. If it was effective for weight loss only, it would cost $150 million (including a $10 million LAB payment), and have a 75% chance of success. If, however, it was efficacious for both weight loss and depression, more specialized trials would be required to determine efficacy for the dual indication. The total cost of the Phase III clinical tests for the two separate indications together with the dual indication was expected to be $500 million, including a $40 million licensing payment to LAB, and had a 70% chance of successful outcome. Under this scenario, there was a 15% chance of a successful outcome for depression only, and a 5% chance of a successful outcome for weight loss only. The probability of complete failure of the dual indications or either separate indication was only 10%.

Davanrik had substantial potential profits, especially if it was effective as a treatment for both depression and weight loss. If the drug were approved only for the treatment of depression, it would cost $250 million to launch, and had a commercialization present value of $1.2 billion.[6] If Davanrik were only approved for weight loss, it would cost $100 million to launch, and would have a PV of $345 million. However, if Merck could launch the product with claims for both indications, it would cost $400 million to launch and have a PV of $2.25 billion.

[4]According to the FDA, a pharmaceutical must prove dual indications in addition to proving each indication separately if it wants to be able to claim therapeutic effects for people suffering from both disorders.

[5]All cash flows are expressed as after-tax present values discounted to time zero, including capital expenditures.

[6]This PV was calculated as the after-tax present value of 10 years' worth of cash flows from the drug discounted back to today. It was believed that after 10 years, the drug had very little value to the company since it would be off its patent by then (and thus a terminal value of zero was used in the calculation).

EXHIBIT 1
Consolidated Statement of Income and Retained Earnings

Source: 1999 Merck & Co. Annual Report.

	Year Ended December 31,		
	1999	1998	1997
Sales	32,714.0	26,898.2	23,636.9
Costs, Expenses, and Other Materials and Production	17,534.2	13,925.4	11,790.3
Marketing and Administrative	5,199.9	4,511.4	4,299.2
Research and Development	2,068.3	1,821.1	1,683.7
Acquired Research	51.1	1,039.5	0
Equity Income from Affiliates	(762.0)	(884.3)	(727.9)
Gains on Sales of Businesses	0	(2,147.7)	(213.4)
Other (income) Expense, Net	3.0	499.7	342.7
	24,094.5	18,765.1	17,174.6
Income Before Taxes	8,619.5	8,133.1	6,462.3
Taxes on Income	2,729.0	2,884.9	1,848.2
Net Income	5,890.5	5,248.2	4,614.1
Basic Earnings per Common Share	2.51	2.21	1.92
Earnings per Common Share Assuming Dilution	2.45	2.15	1.87
Retained Earnings Balance, January 1	20,186.7	17,291.5	14,772.2
Net Income	5,890.5	5,248.2	4,614.1
Common Stock Dividends Declared	(2,629.3)	(2,353.0)	(2,094.8)
Retained Earnings Balance, December 31	23,447.9	20,186.7	17,291.5

EXHIBIT 2
Consolidated Balance Sheet

Source: 1999 Merck & Co. Annual Report.

	Year Ended December 31,	
	1999	1998
Assets		
Current assets		
Cash and cash equivalents	2,021.9	2,606.2
Short-term investments	1,180.5	749.5
Accounts receivable	4,089.0	3,374.1
Inventories	2,846.9	2,623.9
Prepaid expenses and taxes	1,120.9	874.8
Total current assets	11,259.2	10,228.5
Investments	4,761.5	3,607.7
Property, plant, and equipment (at cost)		
Land & buildings	4,725.0	3,892.8
Machinery, equipment, and office furnishings	7,385.7	6,211.7
Construction in progress	2,236.3	1,782.1
	14,347.0	11,886.6
Less allowance for depreciation	4,670.3	4,042.8
	9,676.7	7,843.8
Goodwill and other intangibles	7,584.2	8,287.2
Other assets	2,353.3	1,886.2
	35,634.9	31,853.4
Liabilities and Stockholders' Equity		
Current liabilities		
Accounts payable and accrued liabilities	4,158.7	3,682.1
Loans payable and current portion of long-term debt	2,859.0	624.2
Income tax payable	1,064.1	1,125.1
Dividends payable	677.0	637.4
Total current liabilities	8,758.8	6,068.8
Long-term debt	3,143.9	3,220.8
Deferred income taxes and noncurrent liabilities	7,030.1	6,057.0
Minority interests	3,460.5	3,705.0
Stockholders' equity		
Common stock	29.7	29.7
Other paid-in capital	5,920.5	5,614.5
Retained earnings	23,447.9	20,186.7
Accumulated other comprehensive income (loss)	8.1	(21.3)
	29,406.2	25,809.6
Less treasury stock, at cost	16,164.6	13,007.8
Total stockholders' equity	13,241.6	12,801.8
	35,634.9	31,853.4

EXHIBIT 3 Compound Success Rates by Stage

Source: PhRMA, based on data from Center for the Study of Drug Development, Tuft University, 1995.

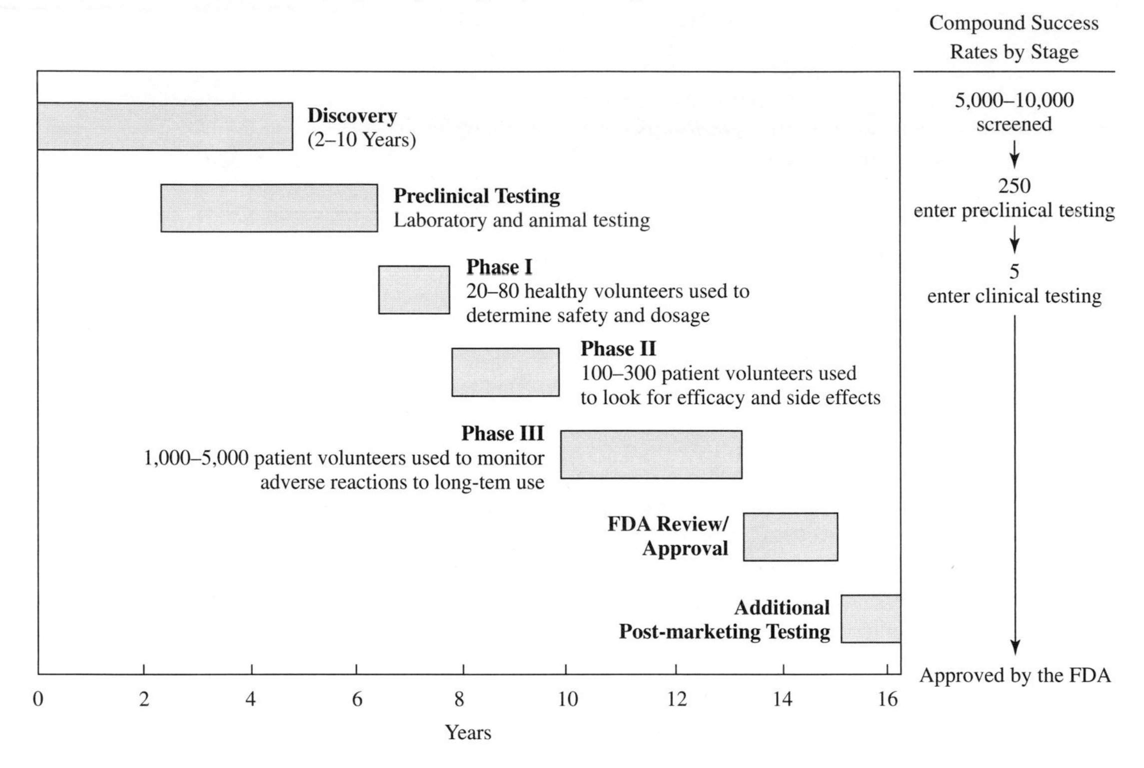

Tree Values

Joe Smith, a forest owner in southern New Hampshire, sought Karen Bennett's help after receiving an unsolicited but attractive offer from a local businessman for some of his timber. Ms. Bennett, a forest resource specialist with the University of New Hampshire Cooperative Extension, provided non-industrial private forest owners with advice on managing their forests. Ms. Bennett had visited Mr. Smith and walked his property with him. She aimed to help Mr. Smith understand the alternatives available to him so that he could make an informed decision about whether he should cut his trees.

Earning Potential of Trees

Mr. Smith inherited the woodland from his father. He always considered the forestland an asset but, aside from occasionally checking on the prices of land in the region, he had given little thought to the value of his holding. The logger who approached Mr. Smith about a timber sale proposed cutting the trees that were 12″ DBH (diameter at breast height, i.e., 4½ feet above ground) and larger, leaving more space for the smaller trees to grow. He said this selective harvest would leave the smaller, fastest growing trees to provide for future harvests.

On her visit to Mr. Smith, Ms. Bennett observed that the acreage included a variety of New England hardwoods, including Sugar Maples, Paper Birches, Red Maples, and Red Oaks. Although Mr. Smith was curious about the value of individual trees, Ms. Bennett explained that foresters usually think and talk in terms of total board feet of a forest area rather than the price of individual trees. Timber is a high volume business, and prices for standing timber (or stumpage prices) were given in dollars per thousand board feet (MBF). Stumpage prices varied according to species, property location, tree size and quality, and ease of access. Current prices for Red Oak in central New Hampshire ranged from $40–$1200 per MBF, and prices for Sugar Maples were $90–$900 per MBF.[1]

Ms. Bennett explained that the value of a tree depended on the volume of usable lumber that could be cut from it, and also on the tree's quality, or grade. As trees grew larger their volume increased, and larger trees provided more board feet of lumber. Exhibit 1 contains information on average hardwood volumes. For example, a 12″ DBH tree would yield about 60 board feet of lumber; a 14″ DBH tree would provide about 110 board feet. Trees smaller than about 12″ DBH had little commercial value except as firewood. The rate of physical growth of trees could vary widely because of differences in sites and conditions. In general, a good quality hardwood tree growing on a

[1] *NHTOA Quarterly Forest Product Market Report,* 1st Quarter 2000 (January–March).

Research Associate Kathleen S. Luchs prepared this case under the supervision of Professor Richard S. Ruback as the basis for class discussion rather than to illustrate either effective or ineffective handling of an administrative situation.

Copyright © 2000 by the President and Fellows of Harvard College. To order copies or request permission to reproduce materials, call 1-800-545-7685, write Harvard Business School Publishing, Boston, MA 02163, or go to http://www.hbsp.harvard.edu. No part of this publication may be reproduced, stored in a retrieval system, used in a spreadsheet, or transmitted in any form or by any means—electronic, mechanical, photocopying, recording, or otherwise—without the permission of Harvard Business School.

well managed site in New England would grow about 2″ in diameter in ten years, while lower quality trees on inferior or unmanaged sites might grow at only half that rate.[2]

In addition to physical size, a tree's value also depended on its quality. As trees grew larger they provided not just more lumber, but also better quality lumber, especially if the trees had sufficient growing space and few defects such as knots or wormholes. The U.S. Forest Service had a system of log grades for assessing timber quality but there was no law requiring the use of this system. Individual mills often defined their own standards and some foresters used a system of tree grades to value a stand. Whatever method was used to measure the quality of timber, a tree's value increased significantly as its quality improved.[3] Quality or tree grade increases peaked for most New England hardwoods at around 20 inches DBH, although a tree continued to grow in diameter.[4] Trees could be a similar size and provide about the same board feet of lumber, but their value could be very different depending on the grade of that lumber. Exhibit 2 presents average hardwood prices by tree grade.

Tree values also depended on increases in timber prices. Prices of hardwood timber had steadily increased over the last 20 years and would likely continue to do so. One authority estimated that prices for New England hardwoods were currently increasing 1–3% above the rate of inflation.[5]

Woodland Management

Like many New England woodlands, Mr. Smith's forest was "middle aged," with most of the trees around 50 to 60 years old, most likely having grown on former farmland. Although there were as many as 300 trees per acre on the property, most of these trees had no commercial use except for firewood because of their species, size, or quality. Ms. Bennett estimated that on the 40 acres of forestland there were about 60 crop trees per acre. The crop trees were about evenly divided between 12″ DBH and 14″ DBH trees. While the site was favorable, the land had not been actively managed, and many of the trees were crowded. The size and current condition of the crop trees meant they were mostly tree grade 4. The smaller trees in the forest were not necessarily younger than the larger trees. Some of them were simply slow growing because of genetics, stress, disease, or poor growing conditions.

Ms. Bennett suggested that if Mr. Smith was interested in improving his forestland, he should consider thinning, including cutting about half of the 12″ and 14″ trees. Selecting and cutting the lower quality trees would eliminate competition. Such thinning would allow the better quality trees to grow as much as 2″ in diameter over 10 years. Exhibit 3 shows that these trees were also more likely to move into the next tree grade. Mr. Smith would need to hire a private forester to select which trees to thin and to develop an overall management plan for his forest.

[2]Gary Gof and Peter Smallidge, "Tree Value: A Basis of Woodland Management," <http://www.dnr.cornell.edu/ext/forestrypage/publications%20&%20articles/proceedings/sawtimber_economics_goff.htm>

[3]Robert R. Morrow, "Tree Value: A Basis for Woodland Management," An Extension Publication of the Department of Natural Resources, New York State College of Agriculture and Life Sciences at Cornell University, Ithaca, New York, vol. 19, no. 4 (Fall 1981).

[4]Mark J. Ducey, "How Fast Do Quality Hardwoods Grow?" Proceedings for Tree Investment Workshop, Caroline A. Fox Research and Demonstration Forest, Hillsborough, NH, Oct. 15 and 29, 1999.

[5]Ibid.

EXHIBIT 1
Average Hardwood Volumes

Source: Karl Davies, "The Myth of Low Tree Value Growth Rates," *Massachusetts Woodland Steward*, vol. 29, no. 4 (Fall 1999) and additional information provided by author.

DBH (inches)	Number of 16 ft Logs	Board Feet/Tree
10	0.50	20
11	0.75	40
12	1.00	60
13	1.25	85
14	1.50	110
15	1.75	145
16	2.00	180
17	2.25	230
18	2.50	280
19	2.50	315
20	2.50	350
21	2.50	385
22	2.50	430

EXHIBIT 2
Average Hardwood Stumpage Prices by Tree Grade

Source: New Hampshire Forest Market Report 1998–1999, University of New Hampshire Cooperative Extension; additional values estimated by case writer.

Tree Grade	$MBF
4	40
3	120
2	260
1	445
Veneer	845

EXHIBIT 3
Probabilities of Tree Grade Increases with Each 2″ Growth in DBH

Source: Estimates provided by Karl Davies based on his research and paper "Grade Value Increase Rates for Northeastern Timber Species" (Second draft). A first draft of this paper is available at <http://www.daviesand.com/Papers/Economics/GVI_Rates/index.html.>

Tree Grade Change	4 to 3	3 to 2	2 to 1	1 to Veneer
Trees on unthinned, unmanaged forestland	60%	50%	40%	10%
Trees on thinned, managed forestland	80%	70%	60%	20%

The Super Project

In March 1967, Crosby Sanberg, a financial analysis manager at General Foods Corporation, told a casewriter, "What I learned about incremental analysis at the Business School doesn't always work." He was convinced that under some circumstances sunk costs were relevant to capital project evaluations. He was also concerned that financial and accounting systems did not provide an accurate estimate of incremental costs and revenues, and that this was one of the most difficult problems in measuring the value of capital investment proposals. Mr. Sanberg used the Super project as an example.[1]

Super was a new instant dessert, based on a flavored, water-soluble, agglomerated powder.[2] Although four flavors would be offered, it was estimated that chocolate would account for 80% of total sales.

General Foods was organized along product lines in the United States, with foreign operations under a separate division. Major U.S. product divisions included Post, Kool-Aid, Maxwell House, Jell-O, and Birds Eye. Financial data for General Foods are given in Exhibits 1, 2, and 3.

The $200,000 capital investment project request for Super involved $80,000 for building modifications and $120,000 for machinery and equipment. Modifications would be made to an existing building, where Jell-O was manufactured. Since available capacity of a Jell-O agglomerator would be used in the manufacture of Super, no cost for the key machine was included in the project. The $120,000 machinery and equipment item represented packaging machinery.

The Market

A Nielsen survey indicated that powdered desserts constituted a significant and growing segment of the total dessert market, as shown in Table A. On the basis of test market experience, General Foods expected Super to capture a 10% share of the total dessert market. Eighty percent of this expected Super volume would come from growth in total market share or growth in the powders segment, and 20% would come from erosion of Jell-O sales.

Production Facilities

Test market volume was packaged on an existing line, inadequate to handle long-run requirements. Filling and packaging equipment to be purchased had a capacity of 1.9 million units on a two-shift, five-day workweek basis. This represented considerable excess capacity, since 1968 requirements were expected to reach 1.1 million units, and the national potential was regarded as 1.6 million units. However, the extra capacity resulted from purchasing standard equipment, and a more economical alternative did not exist.

[1]The name and nature of this new product have been disguised to avoid the disclosure of confidential information.

[2]Agglomeration is a process by which the processed powder is passed through a steam bath and then dried. This fluffs up the powder particles and increases solubility.

Copyright © 1967, 1995 by the President and Fellows of Harvard College.

Harvard Business School case 112-034. This case was written by Richard F. Vancil.

TABLE A
Dessert Market, August–September 1966 Compared with August–September 1965

Desserts	Market Share Aug.–Sept. 1966	Change from Aug.–Sept. 1965	
		Share Points	Volume (%)
Jell-O	19.0%	3.6	40.0
Tasty	4.0	4.0	(new)
Total powders	25.3	7.6	62.0
Pie fillings and cake mixes	32.0	–3.9	(no change)
Ice cream	42.7	–3.4	5.0
Total market	100.0%		13.0

Capital Budgeting Procedure

The General Foods Accounting and Financial Manual identified four categories of capital investment project proposals: (1) safety and convenience; (2) quality; (3) increased profit; and (4) other. Proposal procedures and criteria for accepting projects varied according to category (Exhibit 4). In discussing these criteria, Mr. Sanberg noted that the payback and return guidelines were not used as cutoff measures and added:

> Payback and return on investment are rarely the only measures of acceptability. Criteria vary significantly by type of project. A relatively high return might be required for a new product in a new business category. On the other hand, a much lower return might be acceptable for a new product entry which represented a continuing effort to maintain leadership in an existing business by, for example, filling out the product line.

Super fell into the third category, as a profit-increasing project. Estimates of payback and return on funds employed were required for each such project requiring $50,000 or more of new capital funds and expense before taxes. The payback period was the length of time required for the project to repay the investment from the date the project became operational. In calculating the repayment period, only incremental income and expenses related to the project were used.

Return on funds employed (ROFE) was calculated by dividing 10-year average profit before taxes by the 10-year average funds employed. Funds employed included incremental net fixed assets plus or minus related working capital. Start-up costs and any profits or losses incurred before the project became operational were included in the first profit and loss period in the financial evaluation calculation.

Capital Budgeting Atmosphere

A General Foods accounting executive commented on the atmosphere within which capital projects were reviewed:

> Our problem is not one of capital rationing. Our problem is to find enough good solid projects to employ capital at an attractive return on investment. Of course, the rate of capital inputs must be balanced against a steady growth in earnings per share. The short-term impact of capital investments is usually an increase in the capital base without an immediate realization of profit potential. This is particularly true in the case of new products.
>
> The food industry should show a continuous growth. A cyclical industry can afford to let its profits vary. We want to expand faster than the gross national product. The key to our capital budgeting is to integrate the plans of our eight divisions into a balanced company plan which meets our overall growth objectives. Most new products show a loss in the first two or three years, but our divisions are big enough to introduce new products without showing a loss.

Documentation for the Super Project

Exhibits 5 and 6 document the financial evaluation of the Super project. Exhibit 5 is the summary appropriation request prepared to justify the project to management and to secure management's authorization to expend funds on a capital project. Exhibit 6 presents the backup detail. Cost of the market test was included as "Other" expense in the first period, because a new product had to pay for its test market expense, even though this might be a sunk cost at the time capital funds were requested. The "Adjustments" item represented erosion of the Jell-O market and was calculated by multiplying the volume of erosion times a variable profit contribution. In the preparation of this financial evaluation form, costs of acquiring packaging machinery were included, but no cost was attributed to Jell-O agglomerator capacity to be used for the Super project, because the General Foods Accounting and Financial Manual specified that capital project requests be prepared on an incremental basis:

> The incremental concept requires that project requests, profit projections, and funds-employed statements include only items of income and expense and investment in assets which will be realized, incurred, or made directly as a result of, or are attributed to, the new project.

Exchange of Memos on the Super Project

After receiving the paperwork on the Super project, Mr. Sanberg studied the situation and wrote a memorandum arguing that the incremental approach advocated by the manual should not be applied to the Super project. His superior agreed with the memorandum and forwarded it to the corporate controller with the covering note contained in Appendix A. The controller's reply is given in Appendix B.

Appendix A Memos to Controller

To: J. C. Kresslin, Corporate Controller

From: J. E. Hooting, Director, Corporate Budgets and Analysis

March 2, 1967

Super Project

At the time we reviewed the Super project, I indicated to you that the return on investment looked significantly different if an allocation of the agglomerator and building, originally justified as a Jell-O project, were included in the Super investment. The pro rata allocation of these facilities, based on the share of capacity used, triples the initial gross investment in Super facilities from $200,000 to about $672,000.

I am forwarding a memorandum from Crosby Sanberg summarizing the results of three analyses evaluating the project on an

1. Incremental basis
2. Facilities-used basis
3. Fully allocated facilities and costs basis

Crosby has calculated a 10-year average ROFE using these techniques. Please read Crosby's memo before continuing with my note.

* * *

Crosby concludes that the fully allocated basis, or some variation of it, is necessary to understand the long-range potential of the project.

I agree. We launch a new project because of its potential to increase our sales and earning power for many years into the future. We must be mindful of short-term consequences, as indicated by an incremental analysis, but we must also have a long-range frame of reference if we are to really understand what we are committing ourselves to. This long-range frame of reference is best approximated by looking at fully allocated investment and "accounted" profits, which recognize fully allocated costs, because in fact, over the long run all costs are variable unless some major change occurs in the structure of the business.

Our current GF preoccupation with only the incremental costs and investment causes some real anomalies that confuse our decision making. Super is a good example. On an incremental basis the project looks particularly attractive because, by using a share of the excess capacity built on the coattails of the lucrative Jcll-O project, the incremental investment in Super is low. If the excess Jell-O capacity did not exist, would the project be any less attractive? In the short term, perhaps yes because it would entail higher initial risk; but in the long term, it is not a better project just because it fits a facility that is temporarily unused.

Looking at this point from a different angle, if the project exceeded our investment hurdle rate on a short-term basis but fell below it on a long-term basis (and Super comes close to doing this), should we reject the project? I say yes, because over the long run, as "fixed" costs become variable and as we have to commit new capital to support the business, the continuing ROFE will go under water.

In sum, we have to look at new project proposals from both the long-range and the short-term point of view. We plan to refine our techniques of using a fully allocated basis as a long-term point of reference and will hammer out a policy recommendation for your consideration. We would appreciate any comments you may have.

To: J. E. Hooting, Director, Corporate Budgets and Analysis

From: C. Sanberg, Manager, Financial Analysis

February 17, 1967

Super Project: A Case Example of Investment Evaluation Techniques

This will review the merits of alternative techniques of evaluating capital investment decisions using the Super project as an example. The purpose of the review is to provide an illustration of the problems and limitations inherent in using incremental ROFE and payback, and thereby provide a rationale for adopting new techniques.

Alternative Techniques

The alternative techniques to be reviewed are differentiated by the level of revenue and investment charged to the Super project in figuring a payback and ROFE, starting with incremental revenues and investment. Data related to the alternative techniques are summarized at the end of this memo.

Alternative 1. Incremental Basis

Method

The Super project as originally evaluated considered only incremental revenue and investment, which could be directly identified with the decision to produce Super. Incremental fixed capital ($200M) basically included packaging equipment.

Result

On this basis, the project paid back in 7 years with a ROFE of 63%.

Discussion

Although it is General Foods' current policy to evaluate capital projects on an incremental basis, this technique does not apply to the Super project. The reason is that Super extensively utilizes existing facilities, which are readily adaptable to known future alternative uses.

Super should be charged with the "opportunity loss" of agglomerating capacity and building space. Because of Super, the opportunity is lost to use a portion of agglomerating capacity for Jell-O and other products that could potentially be agglomerated. In addition, the opportunity is lost to use the building space for existing or new product volume expansion. To the extent there is an opportunity loss of existing facilities, new facilities must be built to accommodate future expansion. In other words, because the business is expanding, Super utilizes facilities that are adaptable to predictable alternative uses.

Alternative 2. Facilities-Used Basis

Method

Recognizing that Super will use half of an existing agglomerator and two thirds of an existing building, which were justified earlier in the Jell-O project, we added Super's pro rata share of these facilities ($453M) to the incremental capital. Overhead costs directly related to these existing facilities were also subtracted from incremental revenue on a shared basis.

Result

A ROFE of 34% results.

Discussion

Although the existing facilities utilized by Super are not incremental to this project, they are relevant to the evaluation of the project because, potentially, they can be put to alternative uses. Despite a high return on an incremental basis, if the ROFE on a project were unattractive after consideration of the shared use of existing facilities, the project would be questionable. Under these circumstances, we might look for a more profitable product for the facilities.

In summary, the facilities-used basis is a useful way of putting various projects on a common ground for purposes of *relative* evaluation. One product using existing capacity should not necessarily be judged to be more attractive than another practically identical product that necessitates an investment in additional facilities.

Alternative 3. Fully Allocated Basis

Method

Further recognizing that individual decisions to expand inevitably add to a higher overhead base, we increased the costs and investment base developed in Alternative 2 by a provision for overhead expenses and overhead capital. These increases were made in year 5 of the 10-year evaluation period, on the theory that, at this point, a number of decisions would result in more fixed costs and facilities. Overhead expenses included manufacturing costs, plus selling and general and administrative costs on a per unit basis equivalent to Jell-O. Overhead capital included a share of the distribution system assets ($40M).

Result

A ROFE of 25% results.

Discussion

Charging Super with an overhead burden recognizes that overhead costs in the long run increase in proportion to the level of business activity, even though decisions to spend more overhead dollars are made separately from decisions to increase volume and provide the incremental facilities to support the higher volume level. To illustrate, the Division-F1968 Financial Plan budgets about a 75% increase in headquarters' overhead spending in F1968 over F1964. A contributing factor was the decision to increase the sales force by 50% to meet the demands of a growing and increasingly complex business. To illustrate further, about half of the capital projects in the F1968 3-year Financial Plan are in the "nonpayback" category. This group of projects comprised largely "overhead facilities" (warehouses, utilities, etc.), which are not directly related to the manufacture of products but are necessary components of the total business activity as a result of the cumulative effect of many decisions taken in the past.

The Super project is a significant decision that will most likely add to more overhead dollars, as illustrated above. Super volume doubles the powdered dessert business category; it increases the Division businesses by 10%. Furthermore, Super requires a new production technology: agglomeration and packaging on a high-speed line.

Conclusions

1. The incremental basis for evaluating a project is an inadequate measure of a project's worth when existing facilities with a known future use will be utilized extensively.
2. A fully allocated basis of reviewing major new product proposals recognizes that overheads increase in proportion to the size and complexity of the business and provides the best long-range projection of the financial consequences.

Alternative Evaluations of Super Project (thousands of dollars)

	1. Incremental Basis	2. Facilities-Used Basis	3. Fully Allocated Basis
Investment			
Working capital	$267	$267	$267
Fixed capital			
Gross	200	653	672
Net	113	358	367
Total net investment .	380	625	634
Profit before taxes[a]	239	211	157
ROFE	63%	34%	25%
Jell-O Project			
Building	$200 × ⅔ = $133		
Agglomerator	640 × ½ = 320		
	$453		

Note: Figures based on 10-year averages.
[a]Assumes 20% of Super volume will replace existing Jell-O business.

Appendix B Controller's Reply

To: Mr. J. E. Hooting, Director, Corporate Budgets and Analysis

From: Mr. J. C. Kresslin, Corporate Controller

Subject: Super Project

March 7, 1967

On March 2 you sent me a note describing Crosby Sanberg's and your thoughts about evaluating the Super project. In this memo you suggest that the project should be appraised on the basis of fully allocated facilities and production costs.

In order to continue the dialogue, I am raising a couple of questions below.

It seems to me that in a situation such as you describe for Super, the real question is a *management decision* as to whether to go ahead with the Super project or not go ahead. Or to put it another way, on the basis of our current knowledge, are we or are we not better off in the aggregate if we use half of the agglomerator and two thirds of an existing building for Super?

It might be assumed that, for example, half of the agglomerator is being used and half is not and that a minimum economically sized agglomerator was necessary for Jell-O and, consequently, should be justified by the Jell-O project itself. If we find a way to utilize it sooner by producing Super on it, aren't we better off in the aggregate, thus rendering the different ROFE figure for the Super project by itself somewhat irrelevant? A similar point of view might be applied to the portion of the building. Or if we charge the Super project with half an agglomerator and two thirds of an existing building, should we then go back and relieve the Jell-O projects of these costs in evaluating the management's original proposal?

To put it another way, since we are faced with making decisions at a certain point in time on the basis of what we know, I see very little value in looking at the Super project all by itself. Better we should look at the total situation before and after to see how we fare.

As to allocated production costs, the point is not so clear. Undoubtedly, over the long haul, the selling prices will need to be determined on the basis of a satisfactory margin over fully allocated costs. Perhaps this should be an additional requirement in the course of evaluating capital projects, as we seem to have been surprised at the low margins for "Tasty" after allocating all costs to the product.

I look forward to discussing this subject with you and with Crosby at some length.

EXHIBIT 1
Consolidated Balance Sheet of General Foods Corporation at April 1, 1967 (millions of dollars)

Cash	$ 20
Marketable securities	89
Receivables	180
Inventories	261
Prepaid expenses	14
Current assets	564
Land, buildings, equipment (at cost, less depreciation)	332
Long-term receivables and sundry assets	7
Goodwill	26
Total assets	$929
Notes payable	$ 22
Accounts payable	86
Accrued liabilities	73
Accrued income taxes	57
Current liabilities	238
Long-term notes	39
3 ⅜% debentures	22
Other noncurrent liabilities	10
Deferred investment tax credit	9
Total liabilities	318
Common stock issued	164
Retained earnings	449
Common stock held in treasury, at cost	(2)
Stockholders' equity	611
Total liabilities and stockholders' equity	$929
Common stock—no. of shares outstanding at year-end	25,127,007

EXHIBIT 2
Common Stock Prices of General Foods Corporation, 1958–1967

	Low	High
1958	$24	$ 39¾
1959	37⅛	53⅞
1960	49⅛	75½
1961	68⅝	107¾
1962	57¾	96
1963	77⅝	90½
1964	78¼	93¼
1965	77½	89⅞
1966	62¾	83
1967	65¼	81¾

EXHIBIT 3 **Summary of Statistical Data of General Foods Corporation, Fiscal Years 1958–1967 (millions of dollars except assets per employee and figures on a share basis)**

	1958	1959	1960	1961	1962	1963	1964	1965	1966	1967
Earnings										
Sales to customers (net)	$1,009	$1,053	$1,087	$1,160	$1,189	$1,216	$1,338	$1,478	$1,555	$1,652
Cost of sales	724	734	725	764	769	769	838	937	965	1,012
Marketing, admin., and general expenses	181	205	236	261	267	274	322	362	406	449
Earnings before income taxes	105	115	130	138	156	170	179	177	185	193
Taxes on income	57	61	69	71	84	91	95	91	91	94
Net earnings	$ 48	$ 54	$ 61	$ 67	$ 72	$ 79	$ 84	$ 86	$ 94	$ 99
Dividends on common shares	24	28	32	35	40	45	50	50	53	55
Retained earnings—current year	24	26	29	32	32	34	34	36	41	44
Net earnings per common share[a]	$ 1.99	$ 2.21	$ 2.48	$ 2.69	$ 2.90	$ 3.14	$ 3.33	$ 3.44	$ 3.73	$ 3.93
Dividends per common share[a]	1.00	1.15	1.30	1.40	1.60	1.80	2.00	2.00	2.10	2.20
Assets, Liabilities, and Stockholders' Equity										
Inventories	$ 169	$ 149	$ 157	$ 189	$ 183	$ 205	$ 256	$ 214	$ 261	$ 261
Other current assets	144	180	200	171	204	206	180	230	266	303
Current liabilities	107	107	126	123	142	162	202	173	219	238
Working capital	$ 206	$ 222	$ 230	$ 237	$ 245	$ 249	$ 234	$ 271	$ 308	$ 326
Land, buildings, equipment, gross	203	221	247	289	328	375	436	477	517	569
Land, buildings, equipment, net	125	132	148	173	193	233	264	283	308	332
Long-term debt	49	44	40	37	35	34	23	37	54	61
Stockholders' equity	287	315	347	384	419	454	490	527	569	611
Stockholders' equity per common share[a]	$11.78	$12.87	$14.07	$15.46	$16.80	$18.17	$19.53	$20.99	$22.64	$24.32
Capital Program										
Capital additions	$ 28	$ 24	$ 35	$ 40	$ 42	$ 57	$ 70	$ 54	$ 65	$ 59
Depreciation	11	14	15	18	21	24	26	29	32	34
Employment Data										
Wages, salaries, and benefits	$ 128	$ 138	$ 147	$ 162	$ 171	$ 180	$ 195	$ 204	$ 218	$ 237
Number of employees (000s)	21	22	22	25	28	28	30	30	30	32
Assets per employee ($ 000s)	$ 21	$ 22	$ 23	$ 22	$ 22	$ 23	$ 24	$ 25	$ 29	$ 29

Note: Column totals may not add exactly because of rounding.

[a]Per share figures calculated on shares outstanding at year-end and adjusted for 2-for-1 stock split in August 1960.

EXHIBIT 4 Criteria for Evaluating Projects by General Foods Corporation

Source: The General Foods Accounting and Financial Manual.

The basic criteria to be applied in evaluating projects within each of the classifications are set forth in the following schedule:

Purpose of Project	Payback and ROFE Criteria
a. Safety and Convenience:	
1. Projects required for reasons of safety, sanitation, health, public convenience, or other overriding reason with no reasonable alternatives. Examples: Sprinkler systems, elevators, fire escapes, smoke control waste disposal, treatment of water pollution, etc.	Payback—return on funds projections not required but the request must clearly demonstrate the *immediate* need for the project and the lack or inadequacy of alternative solutions.
2. Additional nonproductive space requirements for which there are no financial criteria. Examples: Office space, laboratories, service areas (kitchens, rest rooms, etc.)	Requests for nonproductive facilities, such as warehouses, laboratories, and offices should indicate the advantages of owning rather than leasing, unless no possibility to lease exists. In those cases where the company owns a group of integrated facilities and wherein the introduction of rented or leased properties might complicate the long-range planning or development of the area, owning rather than leasing is recommended. If the project is designed to improve customer service (such as market-centered warehouses), this factor is to be noted on the project request.
b. Quality:	
Projects designed primarily to improve quality.	If payback and ROFE cannot be computed, it must be clearly demonstrated that the improvement is identifiable and desirable.
c. Increased Profit:	
1. Projects justified primarily by reduced costs.	Projects with a payback period *up to ten years* and a ten year return *on* funds as *low as 20%* PBT are considered worthy of consideration, provided (1) the end product involved is believed to be a reasonably permanent part of our line or (2) the facilities involved are so flexible that they may be usable for successor products.
2. Projects designed primarily to increase production capacity for an existing product.	Projects for a proven product where the risk of mortality is small, such as coffee, Jell-O gelatin, and cereals, should assure a payback in *no more than ten years* and a ten-year PBT return on funds of *no* less than 20%.
3. Projects designed to provide facilities to manufacture and distribute a new product or product line.	Because of the greater risk involved, such projects should show a high potential return on funds (not less than a ten-year PBT return of 40%). The payback period, however, might be as much as *ten years* because of losses incurred during the market development period.*
d. Other	
This category includes projects which by definition are excluded from the three preceding categories. Examples: standby facilities intended to insure uninterrupted production, additional equipment not expected to improve profits or product quality and not required for reasons of safety and convenience, equipment to satisfy marketing requirements, etc.	While standards of return may be difficult to set, some calculation of financial benefits should be made where possible.

*These criteria apply to the United States and Canada only. Profit-increasing capital projects in other areas in categories c1 and c2 should offer at least a ten-year PBT return of 24% to compensate for the greater risk involved. Likewise, foreign operation projects in the c3 category should offer a ten-year PBT return of at least 48%.

EXHIBIT 5 Capital Project Request Form of General Foods Corporation

Source: General Foods.

NY 1292-C 10-64
PTD. In USA

"Super" Facilities 66-42
Division & Location

Jell-O Division — St. Louis
Division & Location

December 23, 1966
Date

New Request [X] Supplement [ ]

Expansion-New Product
Purpose

[X] A
[ ] R

Project Description
To provide facilities for production of Super, chocolate dessert. This project included finishing a packing room in addition to filling and packaging equipment.

Summary of Investment	
New Capital Funds Required	$200M
Expense Before Taxes	– –
Less: Trade-In or Salvage, If Any	– –
Total This Request	$200M
Previously Appropriated	– –
Total Project Cost	$200M

Financial Justification	
ROFE (PBT Basis) - 10 Yr. Average	62.9
Payback Period	6.83 Yrs.
Not Required	☐
* Based on Total Project Cost and Working Fund of	$510M

Estimated Expenditure Rate	
Quarter Ending Mar. F19 67	$160M
Quarter Ending June F19 68	40M
Quarter Ending F19	
Quarter Ending F19	
Remainder	

Other Information	
Major ☐ Specific Ordinary ☐ Blanket ☐	
Included in Annual program Yes ☐ No ☐	
Percent of Engineering Completed	80%
Estimated Start-Up Cost	$15M
Estimated Start-Up Date	April

Level of Approval Required

☐ Board ☐ Chairman ☐ Exec. V.P. ☐ Gen. Mgr.

For Division Use—Signatures	
Name & Title	Date

Signatures		Date
Director Corp. Eng.		
Director B&A		
General Manager		
Exec. Vice President		
President		
Chairman		

EXHIBIT 5 ***(concluded)***

INSTRUCTIONS FOR CAPITAL PROJECT REQUEST FORM NY 1292-A

The purpose of this form is to secure management's authorization to commit or expend funds on a capital project. Refer to Accounting and Financial Manual Statement No. 19 for information regarding projects to which this form applies.

NEW REQUEST–SUPPLEMENT—Check the appropriate box.

PURPOSE—Identify the primary purpose of the project in accordance with the classifications established in Accounting and Financial Statement No. 19, i.e., Sanitation, Health and Public Convenience, Non-Productive Space, Safety, Quality, Reduce Cost, Expansion—Existing Products, Expansion—New Products, Other (specify). Also indicate in the appropriate box whether the equipment represents an addition or a replacement.

PROJECT DESCRIPTION—Comments should be in sufficient detail to enable Corporate Management to appraise the benefits of the project. Where necessary, supplemental data should be attached to provide complete background for project evaluation.

SUMMARY OF INVESTMENT

New Capital Funds Required—Show gross cost of assets to be acquired.

Expense Before Taxes—Show incremental expense resulting from project.

Trade-In or Salvage—Show the amount expected to be realized on trade-in or sale of a replaced asset.

Previously Appropriated—When requesting a supplement to an approved project, show the amount previously appropriated even though authorization was given in a prior year.

FINANCIAL JUSTIFICATION

ROFE—Show the return on funds employed (PBT basis) as calculated on Financial Evaluation Form NY 1292-C or 1292-F. The appropriate Financial Evaluation Form is to be attached to this form.

Not Required—Where financial benefits are not applicable or required or are not expected, check the box provided. The nonfinancial benefits should be explained in the comments.

In the space provided, show the sum of The Total Project Cost plus Total Working Funds (line 20, Form NY 1292-C, or line 5, Form NY 1292-F) in either of the first three periods, whichever is higher.

ESTIMATED EXPENDITURE RATE—Expenditures are to be reported in accordance with accounting treatment of the asset and related expense portion of the project. Insert estimated quarterly expenditures beginning with the quarter in which the first expenditure will be made. The balance of authorized funds unspent after the fourth quarter should be reported in total.

OTHER INFORMATION—Check whether the project is a major, specific ordinary, or blanket, and whether or not the project was included in the Annual Program. Show estimated percentage of engineering completed; this is intended to give management an indication of the degree of reliability of the funds requested. Indicate the estimated start-up costs as shown on line 32 of Financial Evaluation Form NY 1292-C. Insert anticipated start-up date for the project; if start-up is to be staggered, explain in comments.

LEVEL OF APPROVAL REQUIRED—Check the appropriate box.

EXHIBIT 6 Financial Evaluation Form of General Foods Corporation (thousands of dollars)

Source: General Foods.

NY 1292-C 10-64
PTD. In USA

Jell-O	St. Louis	The Super Project	67-89	
Division	*Location*	*Project Title*	*Project No.*	*Supplement No.*

Date

Project Request Detail	1st Per.	2nd Per.	___ Per.	___ Per.	___ Per.
1. Land	$				
2. Buildings	80				
3. Machinery & Equipment	120				
4. Engineering					
5. Other (Explain)					
6. Expense Portion (Before Tax)					
7. Sub Total	$200				
8. Less: Salvage Value (Old Asset)					
9. Total Project Cost*	$200				
10. Less: Taxes on Exp. Portion					
11. Net Project Cost	$200				

*Same as Project Request

Return of New Funds Employed—10-Yr. Avg.	PBT (C ÷ A)	PBT (B ÷ A)
A - New Funds Employed (Line 21)	$380	$380
B - Profit Before Taxes (Line 35)		$239
C - Net Profit (Line 37)	$115	
D - Calculated Return	30.2%	62.0%

Part Year Calculation for First Period	
Part Year Calculation for First Period	– Yrs.
Number of Full Years to Pay Back	6.00 Yrs.
Part Year Calculation for Last Period	0.83 Yrs.
Total Years to Pay Back	6.83 Yrs.

Funds Employed	1st Per. F 68	2nd Per. F 69	3rd Per. F 70	4th Per. F 71	5th Per. F 72	6th Per. F 73	7th Per. F 74	8th Per. F 75	9th Per. F 76	10th Per. F 77	11th Per.	10-Yr. Avg.
12. Net Project Cost (Line 11)	$200	200	200	200	200	200	200	200	200	200		
13. Deduct Depreciation (Cum.)	19	37	54	70	85	98	110	121	131	140		
14. Capital Funds Employed	$181	163	146	130	115	102	90	79	69	60		113
15. Cash												
16. Receivables	124	134	142	157	160	160	169	169	178	178		157
17. Inventories	207	222	237	251	266	266	281	281	296	296		260
18. Prepaid & Deferred Exp.												
19. Less Current Liabilities	(2)	(82)	(108)	(138)	(185)	(184)	(195)	(195)	(207)	(207)		(150)
20. Total Working Funds (15 Thru 19)	329	274	271	264	241	242	255	255	267	267		267
21. Total New Funds Employed (14 + 20)	$510	437	417	394	356	344	345	334	336	327		380
Profit and Loss												
22. Unit Volume (in thousands)	1100	1200	1300	1400	1500	1500	1600	1600	1700	1700		1460
23. Gross sales	$2200	2400	2600	2800	3000	3000	3200	3200	3400	3400		2920
24. Deductions	88	96	104	112	120	120	128	128	136	136		117
25. Net Sales	2112	2304	2496	2668	2880	2880	3072	3072	3264	3264		2803
26. Cost of Goods Sold	1100	1200	1300	1400	1500	1500	1600	1600	1700	1700		1460
27. Gross Profit	1012	1104	1196	1288	1380	1380	1472	1472	1564	1564		1343
Gross Profit % Net Sales												
28. Advertising Expense	1100	1050	1000	900	700	700	730	730	750	750		841
29. Selling Expense												
30. Gen. and Admin. Cost												
31. Research Expense												
32. Start-Up Costs	15											2
33. Other (Explain) Test Mkt.	360											36
34. Adjustments (Explain) Erosion	180	200	210	220	230	230	240	240	250	250		250
35. Profit Before Taxes	$(643)	(146)	(14)	168	450	450	502	502	564	564		239
36. Taxes	(334)	(76)	(7)	87	234	234	261	261	293	293		125
36A. Add: Investment Credit	(1)	(1)	(1)	(1)	(1)	(1)	(1)	(1)	–	–		(1)
37. Net Profit	(308)	(69)	(6)	82	217	217	242	242	271	271		115
38. Cumulative Net Profit	$(308)	(377)	(383)	(301)	(84)	133	375	617	888	1159		
39. New Funds to Repay (21 less 38)	$818	814	800	695	440	211	(30)	(283)	(552)	(832)		

See Accounting & Financial Manual Policy No. 19 for Instructions.

INSTRUCTIONS FOR PREPARATION OF FORM NY 1292-C FINANCIAL EVALUATION

This form is to be submitted to Corporate Budget and Analysis with each profit-increasing capital project request requiring $50,000 or more of capital funds and expense before taxes.

Note that the ten-year term has been divided into eleven periods. The first period is to end on the March 31st following the operational date of the project, and the P & L projection may thereby encompass any number of months from one to twelve, e.g., if the project becomes operational on November 1, 1964, the first period for P & L purposes would be 5 months (November 1, 1964 through March 31, 1965). The next nine periods would be fiscal years (F'66, F'67, etc.) and the eleventh period would be 7 months (April 1, 1974 through October 30, 1974). This has been done primarily to facilitate reporting of projected and actual P & L data by providing for fiscal years. See categorized instructions below for more specific details.

PROJECT REQUEST DETAIL—*Lines 1 through 11* show the breakdown of the Net Project Cost to be used in the financial evaluation. *Line 8* is to show the amount expected to be realized on trade-in or sale of a replaced asset. *Line 9* should be the same as the "Total Project Cost" shown on Form NY 1292-A, Capital Project Request. Space has been provided for capital expenditures related to this project which are projected to take place subsequent to the first period. Indicate in such space the additional costs only; do not accumulate them.

EXHIBIT 6 *(continued)*

FUNDS EMPLOYED

Capital Funds Employed—Line 12 will show the net project cost appearing on *line 11* as a constant for the first ten periods except in any period in which additional expenditures are incurred; in that event show the accumulated amounts of *line 11* in such period and in all future periods.

Deduct cumulative depreciation on *line 13*. Depreciation is to be computed on an incremental basis, i.e., the net increase in depreciation over present depreciation on assets being replaced. In the first period depreciation will be computed at one half of the first year's annual rate; no depreciation is to be taken in the eleventh period. Depreciation rates are to be the same as those used for accounting purposes. *Exception:* When the depreciation rate used for accounting purposes differs materially from the rate for tax purposes, the higher rate should be used. A variation will be considered material when the first full year's depreciation on a book basis varies 20% or more from the first full year's depreciation on a tax basis.

The ten-year average of Capital Funds Employed shall be computed by adding *line 14* in each of the first ten periods and dividing the total by ten.

Total Working Funds—Refer to Financial Policy No. 21 as a guide in computing new working fund requirements. Items which are not on a formula basis and which are normally computed on a five-quarter average shall be handled proportionately in the first period. For example, since the period involved may be less than 12 months, the average would be computed on the number of quarters involved. Generally, the balances should be approximately the same as they would be if the first period were a full year.

Cash, based on a formula which theorizes a two weeks' supply (2/52nds), should follow the same theory. If the first period is for three months, two-thirteenths (2/13ths) should be used; if it is for 5 months, two-twenty-firsts (2/21sts) should be used, and so forth.

Current liabilities are to include one half of the tax expense as the tax liability. The ten-year averages of Working Funds shall be computed by adding each line across for the first ten periods and dividing each total by ten.

PROFIT AND LOSS PROJECTION

P & L Categories (Lines 22–34)—Reflect only the incremental amounts which will result from the proposed project; exclude all allocated charges. Include the P & L results expected in the individual periods comprising the first ten years of the life of the project. Refer to the second paragraph of these instructions regarding the fractional years' calculations during the first and eleventh periods.

Any loss or gain on the sale of a replaced asset (see *line 8*) shall be included in *line 33*.

As indicated in the caption Capital Funds Employed, no depreciation is to be taken in the eleventh period.

The ten-year averages of the P & L items shall be computed by adding each line across for the eleven periods (10 full years from the operational data) and dividing the total by ten.

Adjustments (Line 34)—Show the adjustment necessary, on a before-tax basis, to indicate any adverse or favorable incremental effect the proposed project will have on any other products currently being produced by the corporation.

Investment Credit is to be included on *line 36-A*. The Investment Credit will be spread over 8 years, or fractions thereof, as an addition to PAT.

RETURN ON NEW FUNDS EMPLOYED—Ten-year average returns are to be calculated for PAT (projects requiring Board approval only) and PBT. The PAT return is calculated by dividing average PAT *(line 37)* by average new funds employed *(line 21)*; the PBT return is derived by dividing average PBT *(line 35)* by average new funds employed *(line 21)*.

PAYBACK YEARS FROM OPERATIONAL DATE

Part Year Calculation for First Period—Divide number of months in the first period by twelve. If five months are involved, the calculation is 5/12 = .4 years.

Number of Full Years to Payback—Determined by the last period, excluding the first period, in which an amount is shown on *line 39*.

Part Year Calculation for Last Period—Divide amount still to be repaid at the end of the last full period *(line 39)* by net profit plus the *annual* depreciation in the following year when payback is completed.

Total Years to Payback—Sum of full and part years.

NetFlix.com, Inc.

In July 2000, Reed Hastings, chairman and CEO of NetFlix.com, Inc., faced a critical decision. Three months earlier, following one of the worst episodes on record for the NASDAQ market, NetFlix had submitted its S-1 filing for its initial public offering (IPO).[1] As a result of the market downturn, many Internet companies had been forced to withdraw their IPOs. Investment bankers indicated to Hastings that NetFlix would need to show positive cash flows within a twelve-month horizon in order to have a successful offering. Hastings knew that NetFlix was at a crucial stage. With revenues doubling every six months, NetFlix was enjoying tremendous success. But continued success depended on the company's ability to sustain triple-digit growth for the foreseeable future. Soon, Hastings would have to decide whether or not to proceed with the company's anticipated IPO.

Hastings asked Barry McCarthy, the chief financial officer, to reevaluate the cash flow requirements of the company's current business plan, to suggest modifications that would improve the company's projected cash flows, and to make a recommendation on whether the company should go forward with its planned offering. As McCarthy reviewed the existing NetFlix business model, he considered possible changes that might allow the company to proceed with its planned IPO and yet sustain the type of future growth that would be necessary for the company to achieve its long-run objectives. McCarthy was acutely aware of the company's current financing need, but he worried about the effect that changes to the business plan might have on the company's current operations.

The Company

NetFlix.com, Inc., was founded in 1997 by Reed Hastings and Marc Randolph. NetFlix operated an Internet-based unlimited rental subscription service for digital video disc (DVD) formatted movies. The DVD provided a new technology for storing and playing movies with image and sound quality exceeding that of traditional videocassettes. A DVD was similar in size to an audio compact disc and was capable of holding an entire feature-length film, as well as additional information such as subtitles in different languages, additional shorter videos about the making of the film or other related subject matter, and information about the actors, director, and producers. With its high quality and additional features, the new DVD technology provided an attractive alternative to

[1]After reaching a historical high of 5,048 on March 10, 2000, the NASDAQ Composite Index had fallen 25% to 3,794 by April 18, 2000, the day of the NetFlix S-1 filing.

Professor E. Scott Mayfield prepared this case. HBS cases are developed solely as the basis for class discussion. Cases are not intended to serve as endorsements, sources of primary data, or illustrations of effective or ineffective management.

Copyright © 2000 President and Fellows of Harvard College. To order copies or request permission to reproduce materials, call 1-800-545-7685, write Harvard Business School Publishing, Boston, MA 02163, or go to http://www.hbsp.harvard.edu. No part of this publication may be reproduced, stored in a retrieval system, used in a spreadsheet, or transmitted in any form or by any means—electronic, mechanical, photocopying, recording, or otherwise—without the permission of Harvard Business School.

traditional videocassettes for the home video market. By combining the superiority of the new DVD technology with the convenience of the Internet, NetFlix provided a new way to select and to rent home movies.

Randolph managed production of the NetFlix web site, including the features, functionality, and content on the site. Randolph believed that consumers were often frustrated in their efforts to select and view movies at traditional video stores because of limited selections and a focus on new release movies. With its unlimited "virtual" shelf space for stocking videos, the NetFlix web site focused on improving the experience of selecting a movie to watch by providing an intelligent interface for browsing, searching, and evaluating potential movies. The NetFlix web site also integrated movies currently showing in theaters by providing the ability to check local listings and show times, as well as the ability to view movie trailers on its web site. In addition, the NetFlix web site kept track of each subscriber's preference for various types of movies and provided an individualized predicted rating for all of the movies on the web site.

Since launching its web site in April 1998, NetFlix had experienced rapid growth. Revenues had grown from $1.4 million in 1998 to $5.0 million in 1999. The number of full-time employees increased from 46 in December 1998 to 270 in December 1999. By March 31, 2000, NetFlix had over 120,000 paying subscribers. Typical of most Internet startups, however, NetFlix had not yet earned a profit, reporting net losses of $11.1 and $29.8 million in 1998 and 1999, respectively. Exhibit 1 and Exhibit 2 provide annual financial statements for 1998 and 1999. Exhibit 3 provides quarterly operating results for 1999.

The NetFlix business model focused exclusively on the new DVD format technology. Management had four main reasons for focusing on this specific segment of the home video market.

- DVD players were the fastest growing segment of the video player market. Because of the rapid adoption of the new DVD technology, sales were forecast to grow at a 49% compound annual rate over the next five years.[2] Exhibit 4 provides a comparison of DVD player and videocassette recorder sales during the first five years after their respective introductions.
- Because of their small size, light weight, and durability, DVDs could be distributed to subscribers on a cost effective basis via regular U.S. mail. Including the costs associated with processing the order, McCarthy estimated the round-trip cost of shipping a DVD to a subscriber and back to NetFlix to be about $1.00.
- In order to promote sales of DVD players, manufacturers were willing to include NetFlix promotional offers with their packaging materials at essentially no cost, which allowed customer acquisition costs to be kept to a minimum. Management had negotiated agreements with most of the leading DVD manufacturers, including Sony, Toshiba, Panasonic, and RCA. These manufacturers accounted for over 90% of the DVD players sold in the United States in 1999.
- Management believed that early adopters of DVD technology were likely to have a computer with an already existing Internet connection and were likely to be willing to conduct commerce over the Internet.

Hastings viewed NetFlix as a combination of a traditional video store, such as Blockbuster or Hollywood Video, and a subscription cable TV service, such as HBO, Cinemax, or Showtime. By paying a single monthly subscription fee ranging from $15.95 to $19.95, a NetFlix subscriber could rent an unlimited number of DVDs each

[2]Paul Kagan Associates, Inc., as cited in NetFlix S-1 filing.

month and could keep a DVD as long as desired.[3] Because NetFlix did not impose a specific date on which a DVD was to be returned, subscribers did not have to worry about paying additional fees for videos that were returned late. In order to attract new subscribers to the NetFlix web site, NetFlix distributed coupons for a free month of service with new DVD players. The costs associated with these free months of service to new subscribers made up the majority of sales and marketing expenses. In 1999 alone, NetFlix recorded over $16.4 million in sales and marketing expense.

Once a subscriber had signed up for the free month of service, the objective was to get the subscriber to convert from free- to paid-status and then to retain that subscriber for as long as possible. In order to study the effect of the subscription fee on conversion and retention rates, management had tested a variety of different price points. Based on analyses of data from these market tests, McCarthy believed that his company's ability to retain subscribers was comparable to that of successful subscription cable services. McCarthy estimated that approximately 70% of new subscribers converted to paid-status and that 40% of subscribers that converted to paid-status continued to subscribe after six months. McCarthy expected retention rates for subscribers that subscribed more than six months to be quite high.

Because the NetFlix business model focused on the acquisition and retention of individual subscribers, McCarthy projected future NetFlix financing requirements using a subscriber model. First, McCarthy modeled the expected cash flows from a newly acquired subscriber, including the subscription fees paid, the expected number of discs rented, the costs associated with shipping and disc acquisition, and any other cash flows that varied directly with the acquisition or loss of an individual subscriber. Second, McCarthy modeled the likelihood that any given subscriber would be retained over the forecast horizon. And last, McCarthy used the projected number of future new subscribers together with the number of existing subscribers to forecast the company's expected aggregate cash flows.

The Marquee Queue

A key aspect of the NetFlix business model was the "Marquee Queue" concept. The "Marquee Queue" allowed a subscriber to have several movies on hand for viewing at all times. A subscriber's queue was simply a list of all the movies that the subscriber had selected, but that had not yet been sent to the subscriber. After logging on to the NetFlix web site, a new subscriber would browse the virtual aisles and select movies that he or she wanted to watch. These movies would be used to build the subscriber's queue. The NetFlix web site made it easy for the subscriber to edit the queue, such that the list could be arranged in the desired order. NetFlix would then ship the DVDs at the top of the queue to the subscriber.

NetFlix allowed a subscriber to have up to four DVDs in his or her possession at one time. Once a subscriber had viewed a movie and returned the DVD to NetFlix, the next DVD in the queue was automatically sent to the subscriber. In this way, a subscriber could always have movies in his or her possession for immediate viewing.

[3]Since launching its web site, management had tested a variety of different pricing plans. From February 1999 through October 1999, NetFlix generated most of its revenues from individual DVD rentals and associated shipping charges. In September 1999, NetFlix launched its subscription rental service for a fixed monthly fee of $15.95. Under this plan, subscribers could rent up to four DVDs per month. In February 2000, NetFlix modified its subscription rental service to provide unlimited rentals for a fixed monthly fee of $19.95. At that time, existing subscribers were migrated to the unlimited rental service at their original fee of $15.95.

Conclusion

Knowing that NetFlix had a limited time frame in which to assemble a "critical mass" of subscribers, McCarthy considered the effect that entering into revenue-sharing agreements with movie studios might have on projected NetFlix cash flows. He also wondered whether the major movie studios that had already signed agreements with Blockbuster would be willing to sign similar agreements with a relatively new Internet startup such as NetFlix. Considering the enormous growth requirements facing NetFlix, McCarthy was concerned that revenue-sharing agreements alone might not free up enough working capital to allow for a successful offering later in the year. McCarthy also considered whether NetFlix could afford to continue offering a free month of service in order to attract potential new subscribers. At the same time, he wondered whether the company could afford not to do so.

EXHIBIT 1
Income Statements for NetFlix.com, Inc. (thousands of dollars)

Source: Company reports.

	Year Ended December 13,	
	1998	1999
Revenues	1,339	5,006
Cost of revenue	1,311	4,373
Gross profit	28	633
Operating expenses:		
Product development	3,857	7,413
Sales and marketing	4,815	16,424
General and administrative	1,358	2,085
Stock-based compensation	1,151	4,742
Total operating expenses	11,181	30,664
Operating loss	(11,153)	(30,031)
Other income (expense)		
Interest and other income, net	114	924
Interest expense, net	(42)	(738)
Net loss	(11,081)	(29,845)

EXHIBIT 2
Balance Sheets for NetFlix.com, Inc. (thousands of dollars)

Source: Company reports.

	Year Ended December 31,	
	1998	1999
Assets		
Current assets		
Cash and cash equivalents	1,061	14,198
Short-term investments	–	6,322
Prepaids and other current assets	635	720
Total current assets	1,696	21,240
Rental library, net	2,011	8,695
Property and equipment, net	1,062	4,499
Deposits and other assets	80	339
Total assets	4,849	34,773
Liabilities and Shareholders' Equity		
Current liabilities		
Notes payable	1,000	625
Current portion of capital lease obligations	579	571
Accounts payable	3,063	5,334
Accrued liabilities	1,640	3,211
Deferred revenue	118	471
Total current liabilities	6,400	10,212
Capital lease obligations	172	811
Note payable	—	3,959
Total liabilities	6,572	14,982
Mandatorily redeemable conv. pref stock	6,321	51,819
Shareholders equity (deficit):		
Convertible preferred stock	4	4
Common stock	3	7
Additional paid-in capital	8,100	16,087
Deferred stock-based compensation	(4,711)	(6,841)
Accumulated deficit	(11,440)	(41,285)
Total shareholders' equity (deficit)	(8,044)	(32,028)
Total liabilities and shareholders' equity (deficit)	4,849	34,773

EXHIBIT 3
Quarterly Operating Results for NetFlix.com, Inc. (thousands of dollars)

Source: Company reports.

	Quarter Ended			
	March 31 1999	June 30 1999	Sept. 30 1999	Dec. 31 1999
Revenues	847	854	1,170	2,135
Cost of revenue	663	670	1,276	1,764
Gross profit	184	184	(106)	371
Operating expenses				
Product development	1,324	1,533	2,106	2,450
Sales and marketing	1,954	2,930	4,994	6,546
General and administrative	532	553	404	596
Stock-based compensation	787	1,203	1,500	1,252
Total operating expenses	4,597	6,219	9,004	10,844
Operating loss	(4,413)	(6,035)	(9,110)	(10,473)
Interest and other income, net	74	112	351	387
Interest expense, net	(165)	(129)	(149)	(295)
Net loss	(4,504)	(6,052)	(8,908)	(10,381)

EXHIBIT 4 Historical and Projected Unit Sales, Average Unit Price, and Household Penetration Rates for Videocassette Recorders and Digital Video Disc Players during the First Five Years after Introduction[a]

Source: Consumers Electronics Manufacturer's Association.

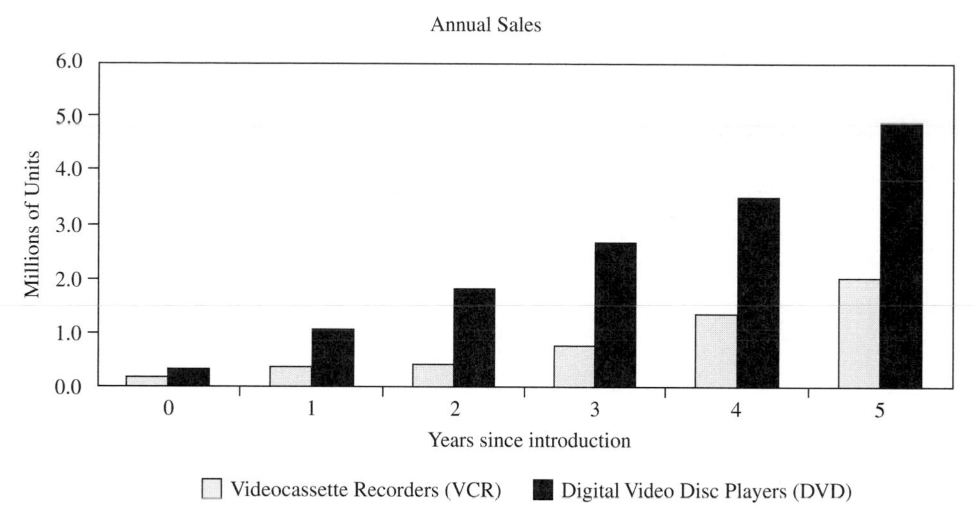

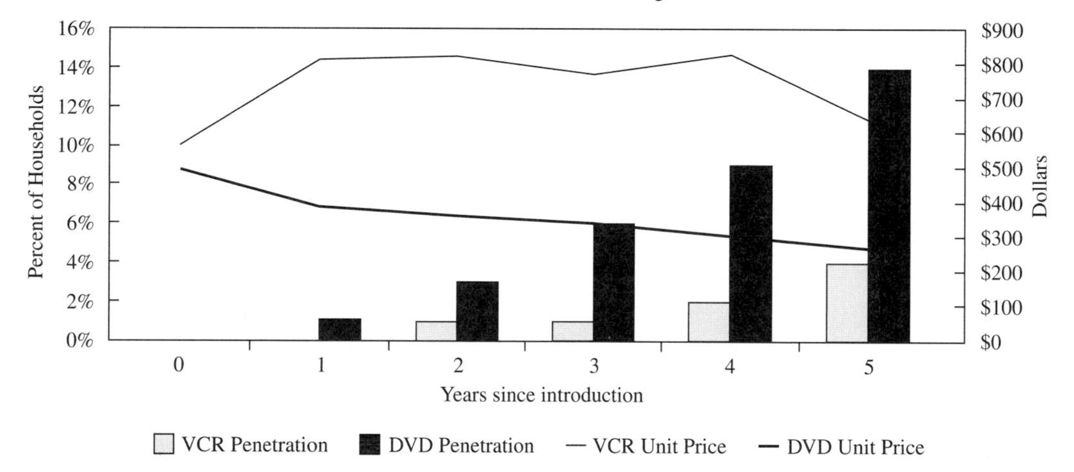

[a]Unit sales are sales to dealers. Consumer sales are estimated to be about 60% of dealer sales. For DVD players, years 3, 4, and 5 are forecasted values.

EXHIBIT 5
Rental Library (thousands of dollars)

Source: Company reports.

	As of December 31,	
	1998	1999
Rental library	2,186	10,882
Less accumulated depreciation	(175)	(2,187)
Rental library, net	2,011	8,695

A-Rod: Signing the Best Player in Baseball

Introduction

In December of 2000 Alex Rodriguez, perhaps the best young player in baseball, became a free agent. Tom Hicks, the Chairman of Southwest Sports Group; Mike Cramer, the President and COO of Southwest Sports Group; and Doug Melvin, the General Manager of the Texas Rangers, faced a major long-term investment decision. They were on the verge of offering Rodriguez a 10-year contract to leave the Seattle Mariners and play shortstop for the Rangers. Rodriguez became a free agent at the end of the 2000 season and was able to negotiate freely with any of the 30 teams in Major League Baseball. Hicks, Cramer, and Melvin knew that the bidding would be fierce, and believed the competition was willing to offer contracts well over $100 million. They wanted to offer a contract that would be accepted, but only if it was at a price that was justified financially.

Alex Rodriguez

At the age of 17, Alex Rodriguez became the first overall pick in the 1993 Major League Draft. He broke into Major League Baseball one year later, and quickly developed into one of the game's best players, exhibiting a rare combination of stellar offense and defense. By his third full season in the majors, Rodriguez won a batting title and became just the third man in baseball history to hit 40 home runs and steal 40 bases in the same year. He also set the American League record for home runs by a shortstop.[1] (See Table A.)

TABLE A
Alex Rodriguez Key Offensive Statistics

Source: *www.espn.com* accessed on May 5, 2002

Year	Team	Batting Avg.	Home Runs	RBI	Stolen Bases
1996	Seattle	.358	36	123	15
1997	Seattle	.300	23	84	29
1998	Seattle	.310	42	124	46
1999	Seattle	.285	42	111	21
2000	Seattle	.316	41	132	15

[1]Major League Index of Player Pages (ML-IPP)

Professor Randolph B. Cohen and Jason Wallace prepared this case. HBS cases are developed solely as the basis for class discussion. Cases are not intended to serve as endorsements, sources of primary data, or illustrations of effective or ineffective management.

Copyright © 2002 President and Fellows of Harvard College. To order copies or request permission to reproduce materials, call 1-800-545-7685, write Harvard Business School Publishing, Boston, MA 02163, or go to http://www.hbsp.harvard.edu. No part of this publication may be reproduced, stored in a retrieval system, used in a spreadsheet, or transmitted in any form or by any means—electronic, mechanical, photocopying, recording, or otherwise—without the permission of Harvard Business School.

Aside from his superb playing ability, Rodriguez possessed intangible qualities that made him a crowd favorite. He was young, handsome, articulate, and humble, which, in combination with his Hispanic background, allowed him to have a broad appeal among fans worldwide. At 25 years old in 2000, he was young enough for the team that signed him to have confidence that he would still be in his prime at the end of a lengthy contract. Most important of all, Hicks, Cramer, and Melvin all believed Rodriguez to possess the kind of leadership and desire to win that would make the whole team better.

Major League Baseball

In 2000, Major League Baseball consisted of 30 teams, split between the National and American Leagues. The leagues and their members were parties to a Major League Agreement, which governed matters concerning MLB teams.

Team revenue was derived from three primary sources:

1. *Local revenues* consist of ticket sales, local television, radio and cable rights, ballpark concessions, parking, and team sponsorships.
2. *Central Fund revenues* serve as a receipt and disbursement fund for central transactions that were shared equally by the 30 teams. It primarily consisted of national television contracts and licensing arrangements.
3. *Revenue sharing* transfers a portion of local revenues from high-revenue teams to low-revenue teams.[2]

Revenue sharing was created as a result of the Collective Bargaining Agreement that became effective on January 1, 1997. The agreement called for each team to contribute a portion of its local revenues, a percentage that peaked at 20% in 2000, to a pool. Once the pool was accumulated, 75% of the proceeds were distributed equally to all teams. The remaining 25% were distributed to teams whose total revenue was below the average revenue for all teams based on the extent to which that team's revenue was below the average.[3]

MLB teams differed greatly in their local revenue, which made up the vast majority of MLB's total revenue. In 2000, the Montreal Expos had approximately $13 million of local revenue, versus $190 million for the New York Yankees (Exhibit 1). Most other professional sports leagues pooled a much larger percentage of television rights and distributed them equally among all the teams. In Major League Baseball, however, most television and radio rights were negotiated and sold locally to each individual team.[4] Since the 30 Major League teams were located in cities of varying size, the local broadcast revenues that accrued to each team varied a great deal.

From 1996 to 2000, salaries accounted for a little over 50% of total league expenses.[5] Other expenses for each team included costs for player development (minor league salaries, team expenses, and scouting), transportation, road-meal expenses, salaries for coaches and trainers, player disability insurance, stadium expenses, front office expenses, ticket office and promotion expenses, and other administrative expenses.[6] Most types of operating expenses are fixed costs that vary little from team to team. But salaries vary tremendously across the teams (Exhibit 1). Higher levels of

[2]The Report of the Independent Members of the Commissioner's Blue Ribbon Panel, p. 15

[3]Cleveland Indians 10-K filing, March 31, 1999

[4]Report of the Blue Ribbon Panel, p. 18

[5]Derived from various sources from *Forbes* (April 16, 2001), baseball-almanac.com (accessed on September 6, 2002), and Report of the Blue Ribbon Panel on Baseball Economics (July 2000)

[6]*Baseball and Billions,* Andrew Zimbalist, p. 59

local revenue enabled large media market teams and teams with better stadiums to pay higher salaries and attract the best players. This led to strong on-field performance and further increased fan enthusiasm and hence, local revenues. Under free agency, which began in 1976, star players who improved team quality and attracted fans could successfully demand to be compensated for the revenue they helped generate. The rapid increase in the salaries of top players explained why average player salaries grew much faster than minimum salaries (Exhibit 2).

The Texas Rangers

The history of the Texas Rangers dated to 1971, when the owner of the Washington Senators received approval to move the team to Arlington, Texas, and rename them the Texas Rangers.[7] The team was part of the American League and played in the four-team West division. From the team's inception in Texas through 1994, they played in Arlington Stadium, which held 42,000 people after a 1976 renovation. In 1994, the team moved into a new 49,200-seat stadium, The Ballpark at Arlington (Exhibit 3). The Rangers played 81 of each season's 162 games at The Ballpark. The stadium cost $191 million to build and was financed in a public/private partnership between the Rangers and the city of Arlington. $135 million came from the issuance of municipal bonds with the remainder coming from the sale and lease of luxury suites, loans guaranteed by the Rangers, and the concessions contract.[8] The Rangers maintained, operated, and kept all revenues from the games held there (other than the revenue to cover the lease payment).[9]

Ownership changed hands several times over the years, including an ownership stint by an investor group that included George W. Bush before he became President. Southwest Sports Group purchased the team in January 1998 for $250 million. Tom Hicks formed Southwest Sports Group in 1998 as a sports entertainment company for the purpose of holding the Rangers and other sports-related properties. The holdings of Southwest Sports Group included the Dallas Stars of the National Hockey League, the Rangers, Mesquite Championship Rodeo, and one-half stakes in the Frisco Roughriders Minor League Baseball team and the Center Operating Company, which constructed and operated American Airlines Center, the home of the Stars. Southwest Sports was also a joint venture partner with Fox Sports and Colorado Studios in Lone Star Mobile Productions. Mr. Hicks is also Chairman and a founding partner of Hicks, Muse, Tate & Furst, a Dallas-based leveraged-buyout firm.

Mr. Hicks' pursuit of Rodriguez was part of a formula for the Rangers that had been successfully implemented with the Stars. The plan was to spend considerable resources on talent to upgrade the quality of the team. It was likely this would result in short-term losses. Soon, though, a championship caliber team would fill the seats and significantly boost profits and franchise value in the long term. When Hicks bought the Stars for $84 million in 1995, they were struggling, having finished in fifth place in their division. Hicks and his management team were very aggressive in trading for and signing top-flight players. The team improved dramatically, as they finished first in their division and won the Stanley Cup championship in 1999. They were also able to build American Airlines Center, a state-of-the-art arena outfitted with considerable high-revenue luxury box and club seating. By 2000, the team had tripled revenues and was on well on its way to becoming the top team in the NHL in revenue. This, along with the Stars' very healthy operating profit margins, had led to a tripling of the value of the franchise.

[7] *www.rangers.mlb.com* accessed on May 5, 2002

[8] *www.rangers.mlb.com* accessed on May 5, 2002

[9] *www.rangers.mlb.com* accessed on May 5, 2002

In pursuit of Rodriguez, Mr. Hicks and his team spent a lot of time in the fall of 2000 with Rodriguez and his agent, Boras. Top Stars player Mike Modano showed Rodriguez the town and discussed the organization's commitment to winning. This was not just a contract negotiation; it was an all-out effort to sell Rodriguez on the future of the Rangers. At the end of the recruitment process, the Rangers' management had several issues to consider. First, they had to determine how much to offer Rodriguez. They also needed to determine what incremental benefits Rodriguez had to bring the Rangers in order for the investment to be worthwhile.

Rodriguez and Revenue

When determining how much to offer Rodriguez, the negotiating team needed to form an opinion of the tangible benefits that Rodriguez would bring the franchise. They evaluated how quickly they would see results, and if they could rely upon them every year over the contract life. The most obvious benefit would be increased attendance. Baseball's history had consistently shown that winning teams drew more fans. Baseball experts felt that although most star players would in a normal year add only a game or two to a team's win total, a player of Rodriguez's rare talents could enable a team to win perhaps eight additional games in a typical year. The Rangers drew an average of 35,000 fans per game for the 80 home games of the 2000 season, so the capacity utilization of their stadium was about 71%—there was room in the stadium for the new fans a better team might draw. Recent historical trends had shown that fans, on average, spent $2.50 on parking and concessions and an additional $1.80 on merchandise. Average ticket prices were $18. The extraordinary skill of Rodriguez would also likely increase the Rangers' probability of making the playoffs. Reaching the American League Championship Series could add about $10 million of incremental revenue and reaching the seventh game of the World Series could add over $20 million in incremental revenue.

The wide appeal of Rodriguez would also likely make the Rangers more attractive to potential sponsorship partners. Sponsorship revenue for teams with relatively new ballparks could account for 7% to 10% of total local revenue. Rodriguez's presence would also likely increase the team's television and radio audience, but due to long-term fixed-fee deals with local broadcasters, it was not clear that the Rangers would directly benefit from this. It also needed to be kept in mind that the Rangers would not be able to keep all of the incremental revenue that Rodriguez generated. Due to the Rangers' relatively high level of revenue, they were a net payer into Major League Baseball's revenue sharing arrangement laid out in the most recent Collective Bargaining Agreement.

The negotiating team also considered the many intangible benefits that Rodriguez could bring to the Rangers. His signing would demonstrate a commitment to winning and to being a first-class organization. They believed that this would help with future free agent signings and would prevent their own young players from signing with other teams. Rodriguez could add significantly to the visibility of the franchise and enhance their ability to negotiate future projects for the franchise, including a new state-of-the-art spring training facility. They believed that even after Rodriguez retired, his value and presence would still stay with the team. Hicks and Cramer felt that the long-term presence of a legendary player could turn an ordinary franchise into a franchise that was one of a select group of baseball "crown jewels." These franchises, such as the Boston Red Sox and Los Angeles Dodgers, could carry price tags $100 or $200 million higher than similar franchises that lacked their prestige and glamour **(**Exhibit 4**).** Ultimately Hicks, Cramer, and Melvin believed that the incremental revenue that Rodriguez generated, combined with the intangible benefits, could substantially increase the long-term franchise value of the Rangers.

The Texas Rangers generally used an 8% discount rate for calculating comparable numbers.

The Contract

Hicks, Cramer, Melvin, and their organizations spent hours analyzing how much they could pay Rodriguez. Their latest internal proposal was a 10-year contract that would have a nominal value of $252 million. If the proposed contract was put forth to Rodriguez and accepted, it would break new ground for its size. The next highest paid player was Kevin Brown, whose annual salary averaged $15 million as a pitcher for the Los Angeles Dodgers. The proposed contract would also dwarf Rodriguez's prior contract with the Mariners that had paid him less than $4 million a year. The size of the contract would be slightly larger than the $250 million that Southwest Sports Group paid for the entire franchise in 1998. Large as it was, the Rangers felt their offer was appropriate under the circumstances. They had learned that offers were outstanding to Yankees shortstop Derek Jeter and to slugger Manny Ramirez for over $18 million per season, and that hard-hitting Carlos Delgado had been offered in excess of $17 million annually. While these were all excellent players, the Rangers felt Rodriguez was considerably more valuable and would cost commensurately more. Additionally, it was important to note that because Rodriguez was so young, his abilities justified a 10-year contract beginning in 2001. The Rangers' fans would know that their star player was committed to the team for the long haul, and this in turn would likely lead to increased loyalty and enthusiasm among the fans.

The contract would have two basic pieces, a base salary and a signing bonus.[10] The signing bonus was to be $10 million, paid evenly over the first five years of the contract. The contract called for a portion of each year's compensation to be deferred for 10 years at a 3% interest rate. The payout schedule can be seen in Exhibit 5. The annual salary and prorated signing bonus would not be the only expenses related to the contract. Since the proposed contract was guaranteed for 10 years, it must be paid regardless of Rodriguez's performance or time out for injury. The Rangers planned to purchase contract insurance in the event that Rodriguez had a career-ending injury. Contract insurance for a contract of this magnitude would require a premium each year of approximately 10% of that year's contract value.

The negotiating team also believed that the right way to examine the financial attractiveness of the contract was only to consider that portion of his salary and insurance premium that would compensate for the extra tangible and intangible benefits he brought to the team. The Rangers had to have a shortstop, and the price of an average shortstop was increasing every year; so they believed the true "cost" of his contract was only the incremental amount that was meant to be payment for the "Rodriguez factor." The average salary of all the starting shortstops in Major League Baseball for 2000 was a little over $3 million.[11] Nomar Garciaparra, the fine Red Sox shortstop, would be paid $7.25 million for next season.

Now it was time for a decision. Additional team statistics are available in Exhibit 6. If they put forth a contract for $252 million, they were confident it would be accepted. Could they financially justify that high a price? Should they offer less? And if they did, how much lower could they go before another team outbid them?

[10]The contract would also include nominal bonuses for milestones such as All Star appearances and MVP awards.

[11]CBS Sportsline.com accessed on May 5, 2002

EXHIBIT 1
Fiscal Year 2000

Source: Adapted from *Forbes* (April 16, 2001), baseball-almanac.com (accessed on September 6, 2002), and Report of the Blue Ribbon Panel on Baseball Economics (July 2000)

Team	Total Revenue	Local Revenue %	Player Payroll
New York Yankees	$192,400,000	98.9%	$92,538,260
New York Mets	$162,000,000	94.1%	$79,509,776
Atlanta Braves	$145,500,000	92.9%	$84,537,836
Cleveland Indians	$142,900,000	94.2%	$75,880,971
San Francisco Giants	$138,800,000	69.8%	$53,737,826
Seattle Mariners	$138,300,000	84.7%	$58,915,000
Los Angeles Dodgers	$131,300,000	88.9%	$88,124,286
Texas Rangers	$126,500,000	87.4%	$70,795,921
Boston Red Sox	$125,700,000	89.7%	$77,940,333
Baltimore Orioles	$124,000,000	91.8%	$81,447,435
Houston Astros	$122,200,000	72.3%	$51,289,111
Detroit Tigers	$120,800,000	66.0%	$58,265,167
Colorado Rockies	$119,100,000	89.8%	$61,111,190
Chicago Cubs	$112,400,000	87.1%	$60,539,333
St. Louis Cardinals	$110,500,000	84.7%	$61,453,863
Arizona Diamondbacks	$109,100,000	89.9%	$81,027,333
Anaheim Angels	$94,400,000	72.7%	$51,464,167
Chicago White Sox	$92,600,000	71.3%	$31,133,500
San Diego Padres	$84,000,000	72.3%	$54,821,000
Tampa Bay Devil Rays	$81,300,000	86.6%	$62,765,129
Toronto Blue Jays	$80,300,000	68.2%	$46,238,333
Philadelphia Phillies	$79,200,000	66.8%	$47,308,000
Cincinnati Reds	$77,800,000	58.4%	$46,867,200
Oakland Athletics	$74,700,000	53.9%	$31,971,333
Kansas City Royals	$72,600,000	53.8%	$23,433,000
Pittsburgh Pirates	$70,400,000	51.7%	$28,928,333
Milwaukee Brewers	$69,600,000	54.8%	$36,505,333
Florida Marlins	$67,300,000	60.5%	$20,072,000
Minnesota Twins	$58,000,000	33.9%	$16,519,500
Montreal Expos	$53,900,000	24.5%	$34,807,333

Note: Local revenue % are as of fiscal year 1999

EXHIBIT 2
Major League Baseball Player Salary Information

Source: *Charleston Gazette*, 13 December 2001

Season	Minimum Salary	Average Salary
2000	$200,000	$1,895,630
1999	$200,000	$1,611,166
1998	$170,000	$1,398,831
1997	$150,000	$1,336,609
1996	$122,667	$1,119,981
1995	$109,000	$1,110,766
1994	$109,000	$1,168,263
1993	$109,000	$1,076,089
1992	$109,000	$1,028,667
1991	$100,000	$851,492
1990	$100,000	$597,537
1989	$68,000	$497,254
1988	$62,500	$438,729
1987	$62,500	$412,454
1986	$60,000	$412,520
1985	$60,000	$371,571
1984	$40,000	$329,408
1983	$35,000	$289,194
1982	$33,500	$241,497
1981	$32,500	$185,651
1980	$30,000	$143,756
1979	$21,000	$113,558
1978	$21,000	$99,876
1977	$19,000	$76,066
1976	$19,000	$51,501
1975	$16,000	$44,676
1974	$15,000	$40,839

EXHIBIT 3
Texas Rangers Home Attendance Information

Source: *www.rangers.siegler.net* accessed on May 5, 2002 Note: The 1994 and 1995 seasons were shortened by a players' strike

Year	Games	Total Attendance	Average	Capacity
1993	79	2,244,616	28,413	42,000
1994	62	2,503,198	40,374	49,200
1995	72	1,985,910	27,582	49,200
1996	80	2,889,020	36,113	49,200
1997	80	2,945,244	36,816	49,200
1998	81	2,927,409	36,141	49,200
1999	80	2,771,469	34,643	49,200
2000	80	2,800,147	35,002	49,200

EXHIBIT 4
Estimated Franchise Values

Source: *Forbes* (April 16, 2001)

Team	Value	2000 Revenue	Multiple
New York Yankees	$635,000,000	$192,400,000	3.3×
New York Mets	$454,000,000	$162,000,000	2.8×
Atlanta Braves	$407,000,000	$145,500,000	2.8×
Los Angeles Dodgers	$381,000,000	$131,300,000	2.9×
Cleveland Indians	$372,000,000	$142,900,000	2.6×
Texas Rangers	$342,000,000	$126,500,000	2.7×
Boston Red Sox	$339,000,000	$125,700,000	2.7×
Baltimore Orioles	$335,000,000	$124,000,000	2.7×
Colorado Rockies	$334,000,000	$119,100,000	2.8×
San Francisco Giants	$333,000,000	$138,800,000	2.4×
Seattle Mariners	$332,000,000	$138,300,000	2.4×
Houston Astros	$318,000,000	$122,200,000	2.6×
Detroit Tigers	$290,000,000	$120,800,000	2.4×
Chicago Cubs	$247,000,000	$112,400,000	2.2×
Arizona Diamondbacks	$245,000,000	$109,100,000	2.2×
St. Louis Cardinals	$243,000,000	$110,500,000	2.2×
Chicago White Sox	$213,000,000	$92,600,000	2.3×
Pittsburgh Pirates	$211,000,000	$70,400,000	3.0×
Milwaukee Brewers	$209,000,000	$69,600,000	3.0×
Anaheim Angels	$198,000,000	$94,400,000	2.1×
Cincinnati Reds	$187,000,000	$77,800,000	2.4×
San Diego Padres	$176,000,000	$84,000,000	2.1×
Toronto Blue Jays	$161,000,000	$80,300,000	2.0×
Philadelphia Phillies	$158,000,000	$79,200,000	2.0×
Tampa Bay Devil Rays	$150,000,000	$81,300,000	1.8×
Oakland Athletics	$149,000,000	$74,700,000	2.0×
Kansas City Royals	$138,000,000	$72,600,000	1.9×
Florida Marlins	$128,000,000	$67,300,000	1.9×
Minnesota Twins	$99,000,000	$58,000,000	1.7×
Montreal Expos	$92,000,000	$53,900,000	1.7×

Note: Value is the value of the team, without deduction for debt, other than stadium debt.

EXHIBIT 5
Rodriguez Proposed Contract

Source: *http://rangers.siegler.net/roster/arodriguez.html* accessed on May 5, 2002

Year	Base Salary	Signing Bonus	Amount Deferred
2001	$21 million	$2 million	$5 million in 2011
2002	$21 million	$2 million	$4 million in 2012
2003	$21 million	$2 million	$3 million in 2013
2004	$21 million	$2 million	$3 million in 2014
2005	$25 million	$2 million	$4 million in 2015
2006	$25 million		$4 million in 2016
2007	$27 million		$4 million in 2017
2008	$27 million		$3 million in 2018
2009	$27 million		$3 million in 2019
2010	$27 million		$3 million in 2020

EXHIBIT 6 Team Statistics

Sources: Adapted from Baseballstats.net (accessed on May 5, 2002), baseball-almanac.com (accessed on September 6, 2002), and U.S. Census Bureau (populations between 1990 and 2000 are interpolated)

Team	Attendance	Player Payroll	Population	Wins
		1990		
Anaheim Angels	2,555,688	$21,405,390	14,531,529	80
Atlanta Braves	980,129	$11,429,334	2,959,500	65
Baltimore Orioles	2,415,189	$ 7,982,084	6,726,395	76
Boston Red Sox	2,528,986	$21,968,333	5,455,403	88
Chicago Cubs	2,243,791	$13,768,500	8,239,820	77
Chicago White Sox	2,002,357	$10,461,000	8,239,820	94
Cincinnati Reds	2,400,892	$15,519,166	1,817,569	91
Cleveland Indians	1,225,240	$14,595,000	2,859,644	77
Detroit Tigers	1,495,785	$18,170,167	5,187,171	79
Houston Astros	1,310,927	$17,313,000	3,731,029	75
Kansas City Royals	2,244,956	$22,046,282	1,582,874	75
Los Angeles Dodgers	3,002,396	$20,948,461	14,531,529	86
Milwaukee Brewers	1,752,900	$18,277,000	1,607,183	74
Minnesota Twins	1,751,584	$13,872,300	2,538,776	74
Montreal Expos	1,373,087	$21,907,668	3,208,970	85
New York Mets	2,732,745	$21,172,073	19,565,441	91
New York Yankees	2,006,436	$20,215,750	19,565,441	67
Oakland Athletics	2,900,217	$23,092,000	6,277,525	103
Philadelphia Phillies	1,992,484	$13,510,167	5,893,019	77
Pittsburgh Pirates	2,049,908	$14,749,000	2,394,811	95
San Diego Padres	1,856,396	$16,598,334	2,498,016	75
San Francisco Giants	1,975,528	$21,940,709	6,277,525	85
Seattle Mariners	1,509,727	$12,288,167	2,970,300	77
St. Louis Cardinals	2,573,225	$19,577,000	2,492,348	70
Texas Rangers	2,057,911	$12,672,333	4,037,282	83
Toronto Blue Jays	3,885,284	$17,019,001	3,898,933	86
		1991		
Anaheim Angels	2,416,236	$31,782,501	14,715,741	81
Atlanta Braves	2,140,217	$18,923,500	3,074,770	94
Baltimore Orioles	2,552,753	$14,627,334	6,814,563	67
Boston Red Sox	2,562,435	$32,767,500	5,491,773	84
Chicago Cubs	2,314,250	$26,813,120	8,331,592	77
Chicago White Sox	2,934,154	$16,730,437	8,331,592	87
Cincinnati Reds	2,372,377	$25,369,166	1,833,732	74
Cleveland Indians	1,051,863	$18,070,000	2,868,263	57
Detroit Tigers	1,641,661	$23,736,334	5,214,097	84
Houston Astros	1,196,152	$11,156,000	3,824,883	65
Kansas City Royals	2,161,537	$28,122,662	1,602,193	82
Los Angeles Dodgers	3,348,170	$32,916,664	14,715,741	93
Milwaukee Brewers	1,478,729	$24,398,000	1,615,422	83
Minnesota Twins	2,293,842	$22,331,000	2,581,779	95
Montreal Expos	934,742	$20,208,500	3,231,923	71
New York Mets	2,284,484	$32,590,002	19,728,883	77
New York Yankees	1,863,733	$27,615,835	19,728,883	71
Oakland Athletics	2,713,493	$36,332,500	6,353,709	84
Philadelphia Phillies	2,050,012	$20,073,332	5,922,563	78
Pittsburgh Pirates	2,065,302	$23,064,667	2,391,199	98
San Diego Padres	1,804,289	$22,585,001	2,529,598	84
San Francisco Giants	1,737,478	$30,839,333	6,353,709	75
Seattle Mariners	2,147,905	$16,126,834	3,028,746	83
St. Louis Cardinals	2,448,699	$21,435,001	2,503,474	84
Texas Rangers	2,297,720	$19,184,500	4,155,734	85
Toronto Blue Jays	4,001,527	$27,538,751	3,977,070	91

EXHIBIT 6 (*Continued*)

Team	1992			
	Attendance	Player Payroll	Population	Wins
Anaheim Angels	2,065,444	$32,584,670	14,899,952	72
Atlanta Braves	3,077,400	$35,853,321	3,190,040	98
Baltimore Orioles	3,567,819	$23,963,719	6,902,730	89
Boston Red Sox	2,468,574	$42,138,665	5,528,142	73
Chicago Cubs	2,126,720	$32,374,664	8,423,364	78
Chicago White Sox	2,681,156	$30,180,333	8,423,364	86
Cincinnati Reds	2,315,946	$35,429,559	1,849,896	90
Cleveland Indians	1,224,094	$9,323,339	2,876,881	76
Detroit Tigers	1,423,963	$28,222,167	5,241,022	75
Houston Astros	1,211,412	$14,916,500	3,918,737	81
Kansas City Royals	1,867,689	$31,968,586	1,621,512	72
Los Angeles Dodgers	2,473,266	$42,050,166	14,899,952	63
Milwaukee Brewers	1,857,351	$29,953,168	1,623,661	92
Minnesota Twins	2,482,428	$27,272,834	2,624,782	90
Montreal Expos	1,669,127	$16,050,854	3,254,876	87
New York Mets	1,779,534	$44,009,334	19,892,326	72
New York Yankees	1,748,737	$34,902,292	19,892,326	76
Oakland Athletics	2,494,160	$48,029,667	6,429,892	96
Philadelphia Phillies	1,927,448	$25,451,334	5,952,108	70
Pittsburgh Pirates	1,829,395	$36,228,647	2,387,588	96
San Diego Padres	1,721,406	$27,689,604	2,561,179	82
San Francisco Giants	1,560,998	$33,240,600	6,429,892	72
Seattle Mariners	1,651,367	$26,373,334	3,087,192	64
St. Louis Cardinals	2,418,483	$28,714,502	2,514,600	83
Texas Rangers	2,198,231	$26,228,500	4,274,186	77
Toronto Blue Jays	4,028,318	$49,427,166	4,055,206	96
	1993			
Anaheim Angels	2,057,460	$27,444,899	15,084,164	71
Atlanta Braves	3,884,720	$47,206,416	3,305,309	104
Baltimore Orioles	3,644,965	$29,253,066	6,990,898	85
Boston Red Sox	2,422,021	$46,164,788	5,564,512	80
Chicago Cubs	2,653,763	$36,005,976	8,515,136	84
Chicago White Sox	2,581,091	$42,115,723	8,515,136	94
Cincinnati Reds	2,453,232	$41,641,387	1,866,059	73
Cleveland Indians	2,177,908	$16,690,997	2,885,500	76
Detroit Tigers	1,971,421	$38,038,498	5,267,948	85
Houston Astros	2,084,618	$30,130,233	4,012,592	85
Kansas City Royals	1,934,578	$40,164,878	1,640,830	84
Los Angeles Dodgers	3,170,393	$33,529,000	15,084,164	81
Milwaukee Brewers	1,688,080	$25,635,387	1,631,900	69
Minnesota Twins	2,048,673	$27,127,768	2,667,785	71
Montreal Expos	1,641,437	$17,622,040	3,277,829	94
New York Mets	1,873,183	$40,822,667	20,055,768	59
New York Yankees	2,416,942	$46,588,791	20,055,768	88
Oakland Athletics	2,035,025	$35,351,334	6,506,076	68
Philadelphia Phillies	3,137,674	$28,695,858	5,981,652	97
Pittsburgh Pirates	1,650,593	$24,318,667	2,383,976	75
San Diego Padres	1,375,432	$12,842,333	2,592,761	61
San Francisco Giants	2,606,354	$36,342,322	6,506,076	103
Seattle Mariners	2,052,638	$33,311,042	3,145,638	82
St. Louis Cardinals	2,844,977	$24,190,667	2,525,726	87
Texas Rangers	2,244,616	$35,959,690	4,392,638	86
Toronto Blue Jays	4,057,947	$51,935,034	4,133,343	95

EXHIBIT 6 (*Continued*)

Team	Attendance	Player Payroll	Population	Wins
		1994		
Anaheim Angels	1,512,622	$24,528,385	15,268,375	47
Atlanta Braves	2,539,240	$44,100,972	3,420,579	68
Baltimore Orioles	2,535,359	$38,711,487	7,079,065	63
Boston Red Sox	1,775,818	$36,337,937	5,600,882	54
Chicago Cubs	1,845,208	$32,546,333	8,606,908	49
Chicago White Sox	1,697,398	$40,144,836	8,606,908	67
Cincinnati Reds	1,897,681	$41,458,052	1,882,222	66
Cleveland Indians	1,995,174	$31,705,667	2,894,119	66
Detroit Tigers	1,184,783	$41,118,509	5,294,874	53
Houston Astros	1,561,136	$33,092,500	4,106,446	66
Kansas City Royals	1,400,494	$40,667,375	1,660,149	64
Los Angeles Dodgers	2,279,355	$38,837,526	15,268,375	58
Milwaukee Brewers	1,268,399	$24,786,857	1,640,139	53
Minnesota Twins	1,398,565	$25,053,237	2,710,788	53
Montreal Expos	1,276,250	$18,771,000	3,300,782	74
New York Mets	1,151,471	$30,903,583	20,219,211	55
New York Yankees	1,675,556	$47,512,342	20,219,211	70
Oakland Athletics	1,242,692	$34,574,000	6,582,260	51
Philadelphia Phillies	2,290,971	$31,143,000	6,011,197	54
Pittsburgh Pirates	1,222,520	$21,503,250	2,380,365	53
San Diego Padres	953,857	$13,774,268	2,624,343	47
San Francisco Giants	1,704,608	$42,260,538	6,582,260	55
Seattle Mariners	1,104,206	$28,463,110	3,204,084	49
St. Louis Cardinals	1,866,544	$29,622,052	2,536,852	53
Texas Rangers	2,503,198	$32,399,097	4,511,090	52
Toronto Blue Jays	2,907,933	$42,265,168	4,211,480	55
		1995		
Anaheim Angels	1,748,680	$34,702,577	15,452,587	78
Atlanta Braves	2,561,831	$47,023,444	3,535,849	90
Baltimore Orioles	3,098,475	$48,739,636	7,167,233	71
Boston Red Sox	2,164,410	$38,157,750	5,637,252	86
Chicago Cubs	1,918,265	$36,797,696	8,698,680	73
Chicago White Sox	1,609,773	$40,750,782	8,698,680	68
Cincinnati Reds	1,837,649	$47,739,109	1,898,386	85
Cleveland Indians	2,842,745	$40,180,750	2,902,738	100
Detroit Tigers	1,180,979	$28,663,667	5,321,800	60
Houston Astros	1,363,801	$33,614,668	4,200,300	76
Kansas City Royals	1,233,530	$31,181,334	1,679,468	70
Los Angeles Dodgers	2,766,251	$36,725,956	15,452,587	78
Milwaukee Brewers	1,087,560	$17,407,384	1,648,378	65
Minnesota Twins	1,057,667	$15,362,750	2,753,791	56
Montreal Expos	1,309,618	$13,116,557	3,323,735	66
New York Mets	1,273,183	$13,097,944	20,382,653	69
New York Yankees	1,705,263	$58,165,252	20,382,653	79
Oakland Athletics	1,174,310	$33,372,722	6,658,444	67
Philadelphia Phillies	2,043,598	$30,333,350	6,040,741	69
Pittsburgh Pirates	905,517	$17,665,833	2,376,753	58
San Diego Padres	1,041,805	$25,008,834	2,655,925	70
San Francisco Giants	1,241,500	$33,738,683	6,658,444	67
Seattle Mariners	1,643,203	$37,984,610	3,262,530	79
St. Louis Cardinals	1,756,727	$28,679,250	2,547,978	62
Texas Rangers	1,985,910	$35,888,726	4,629,542	74
Toronto Blue Jays	2,826,483	$42,233,500	4,289,617	56

EXHIBIT 6 (*Continued*)

Team	1996			
	Attendance	Player Payroll	Population	Wins
Anaheim Angels	1,820,521	$25,140,142	15,636,799	70
Atlanta Braves	2,901,242	$53,797,000	3,651,119	96
Baltimore Orioles	3,646,950	$55,127,855	7,255,400	88
Boston Red Sox	2,315,231	$38,516,402	5,673,621	85
Chicago Cubs	2,219,110	$32,605,000	8,790,452	76
Chicago White Sox	1,676,403	$44,827,833	8,790,452	85
Cincinnati Reds	1,861,428	$43,696,946	1,914,549	81
Cleveland Indians	3,318,174	$47,686,907	2,911,356	99
Detroit Tigers	1,168,610	$17,955,500	5,348,725	53
Houston Astros	1,975,888	$29,613,000	4,294,154	82
Kansas City Royals	1,435,997	$19,980,250	1,698,787	75
Los Angeles Dodgers	3,188,454	$37,313,500	15,636,799	90
Milwaukee Brewers	1,327,155	$11,701,000	1,656,616	80
Minnesota Twins	1,437,352	$21,254,000	2,796,794	78
Montreal Expos	1,616,709	$17,264,500	3,346,688	88
New York Mets	1,588,323	$24,890,167	20,546,095	71
New York Yankees	2,250,877	$61,511,870	20,546,095	92
Oakland Athletics	1,148,380	$22,524,093	6,734,627	78
Philadelphia Phillies	1,801,677	$30,403,458	6,070,285	67
Pittsburgh Pirates	1,332,150	$16,994,180	2,373,141	73
San Diego Padres	2,187,886	$33,376,026	2,687,506	91
San Francisco Giants	1,413,922	$34,646,793	6,734,627	68
Seattle Mariners	2,723,850	$43,131,001	3,320,976	85
St. Louis Cardinals	2,654,718	$38,730,666	2,559,103	88
Texas Rangers	2,889,020	$41,330,028	4,747,993	90
Toronto Blue Jays	2,559,573	$28,778,577	4,367,753	74
	1997			
Anaheim Angels	1,767,330	$46,684,364	15,821,010	84
Atlanta Braves	3,464,488	$53,111,000	3,766,389	101
Baltimore Orioles	3,711,132	$64,611,399	7,343,568	98
Boston Red Sox	2,226,136	$40,611,351	5,709,991	78
Chicago Cubs	2,190,308	$30,791,000	8,882,224	68
Chicago White Sox	1,864,782	$41,849,500	8,882,224	80
Cincinnati Reds	1,785,788	$38,206,000	1,930,712	76
Cleveland Indians	3,404,750	$58,865,056	2,919,975	86
Detroit Tigers	1,365,157	$20,985,500	5,375,651	79
Houston Astros	2,046,781	$34,932,500	4,388,008	84
Kansas City Royals	1,517,638	$33,868,149	1,718,106	67
Los Angeles Dodgers	3,319,504	$48,472,321	15,821,010	88
Milwaukee Brewers	1,444,027	$26,564,840	1,664,855	78
Minnesota Twins	1,411,064	$32,197,500	2,839,797	68
Montreal Expos	1,497,609	$18,010,500	3,369,641	78
New York Mets	1,766,174	$34,985,330	20,709,538	88
New York Yankees	2,580,325	$73,389,577	20,709,538	96
Oakland Athletics	1,264,218	$7,879,889	6,810,811	65
Philadelphia Phillies	1,490,638	$31,102,439	6,099,830	68
Pittsburgh Pirates	1,657,022	$15,124,166	2,369,530	79
San Diego Padres	2,089,333	$32,765,172	2,719,088	76
San Francisco Giants	1,690,869	$43,067,378	6,810,811	90
Seattle Mariners	3,192,237	$46,298,970	3,379,422	90
St. Louis Cardinals	2,634,014	$50,224,167	2,570,229	73
Texas Rangers	2,945,228	$44,591,013	4,866,445	77
Toronto Blue Jays	2,589,297	$48,964,833	4,445,890	76

EXHIBIT 6 (*Continued*)

Team	Attendance	Player Payroll	Population	Wins
		1998		
Anaheim Angels	2,519,280	$54,190,500	16,005,222	85
Atlanta Braves	3,360,860	$61,840,254	3,881,658	106
Baltimore Orioles	3,684,650	$77,320,921	7,431,735	79
Boston Red Sox	2,314,704	$59,547,000	5,746,361	92
Chicago Cubs	2,623,194	$51,061,000	8,973,996	90
Chicago White Sox	1,391,146	$37,855,000	8,973,996	80
Cincinnati Reds	1,793,649	$20,707,333	1,946,875	77
Cleveland Indians	3,467,299	$56,843,441	2,928,594	89
Detroit Tigers	1,409,391	$23,318,980	5,402,577	65
Houston Astros	2,458,451	$48,354,000	4,481,863	102
Kansas City Royals	1,494,875	$35,610,000	1,737,424	72
Los Angeles Dodgers	3,089,222	$60,731,667	16,005,222	83
Milwaukee Brewers	1,811,593	$37,254,036	1,673,094	74
Minnesota Twins	1,165,976	$22,027,500	2,882,800	70
Montreal Expos	914,909	$8,317,500	3,392,594	65
New York Mets	2,287,948	$58,710,665	20,872,980	88
New York Yankees	2,955,193	$73,963,698	20,872,980	114
Oakland Athletics	1,232,343	$18,585,114	6,886,995	74
Philadelphia Phillies	1,715,722	$29,922,500	6,129,374	75
Pittsburgh Pirates	1,560,950	$13,695,000	2,365,918	69
San Diego Padres	2,555,874	$53,081,166	2,750,670	98
San Francisco Giants	1,925,364	$48,339,715	6,886,995	89
Seattle Mariners	2,651,511	$44,845,014	3,437,868	76
St. Louis Cardinals	3,195,691	$47,608,948	2,581,355	83
Texas Rangers	2,927,399	$62,755,368	4,984,897	88
Toronto Blue Jays	2,454,303	$37,618,500	4,524,027	88
		1999		
Anaheim Angels	2,253,040	$53,345,297	16,189,433	70
Atlanta Braves	3,284,901	$79,831,599	3,996,928	103
Baltimore Orioles	3,432,099	$78,948,641	7,519,903	78
Boston Red Sox	2,446,277	$75,260,656	5,782,730	94
Chicago Cubs	2,813,854	$55,544,648	9,065,768	67
Chicago White Sox	1,349,151	$24,535,000	9,065,768	75
Cincinnati Reds	2,061,324	$38,891,007	1,963,039	96
Cleveland Indians	3,468,436	$73,341,692	2,937,212	97
Detroit Tigers	2,026,491	$36,979,666	5,429,502	69
Houston Astros	2,706,017	$58,064,000	4,575,717	97
Kansas City Royals	1,506,068	$17,442,000	1,756,743	64
Los Angeles Dodgers	3,098,042	$76,607,247	16,189,433	77
Milwaukee Brewers	1,701,790	$43,576,575	1,681,333	74
Minnesota Twins	1,202,829	$15,795,000	2,925,803	63
Montreal Expos	772,737	$18,140,250	3,415,547	68
New York Mets	2,726,008	$72,503,334	21,036,423	96
New York Yankees	3,293,659	$92,440,955	21,036,423	98
Oakland Athletics	1,434,632	$24,562,547	6,963,178	87
Philadelphia Phillies	1,825,337	$32,116,500	6,158,919	77
Pittsburgh Pirates	1,638,023	$24,532,420	2,362,307	78
San Diego Padres	2,523,538	$46,487,179	2,782,251	74
San Francisco Giants	2,078,365	$46,016,934	6,963,178	86
Seattle Mariners	2,915,908	$47,001,254	3,496,314	79
St. Louis Cardinals	3,235,833	$46,337,129	2,592,481	75
Texas Rangers	2,774,501	$81,676,598	5,103,349	95
Toronto Blue Jays	2,163,486	$49,972,300	4,602,163	84

EXHIBIT 6 (*Continued*)

Team	2000			
	Attendance	Player Payroll	Population	Wins
Anaheim Angels	2,066,982	$51,464,167	16,373,645	82
Atlanta Braves	3,234,304	$84,537,836	4,112,198	95
Baltimore Orioles	3,153,397	$81,447,435	7,608,070	74
Boston Red Sox	2,625,333	$77,940,333	5,819,100	85
Chicago Cubs	2,789,511	$60,539,333	9,157,540	65
Chicago White Sox	1,947,799	$31,133,500	9,157,540	95
Cincinnati Reds	2,577,371	$46,867,200	1,979,202	85
Cleveland Indians	3,456,278	$75,880,971	2,945,831	90
Detroit Tigers	2,438,617	$58,265,167	5,456,428	79
Houston Astros	3,020,581	$51,289,111	4,669,571	72
Kansas City Royals	1,564,847	$23,433,000	1,776,062	77
Los Angeles Dodgers	2,880,242	$88,124,286	16,373,645	86
Milwaukee Brewers	1,573,621	$36,505,333	1,689,572	73
Minnesota Twins	1,000,760	$16,519,500	2,968,806	69
Montreal Expos	926,272	$34,807,333	3,438,500	67
New York Mets	2,820,530	$79,509,776	21,199,865	94
New York Yankees	3,227,657	$92,538,260	21,199,865	87
Oakland Athletics	1,728,885	$31,971,333	7,039,362	91
Philadelphia Phillies	1,612,769	$47,308,000	6,188,463	65
Pittsburgh Pirates	1,748,908	$28,928,333	2,358,695	69
San Diego Padres	2,423,149	$54,821,000	2,813,833	76
San Francisco Giants	3,318,800	$53,737,826	7,039,362	97
Seattle Mariners	3,148,317	$58,915,000	3,554,760	91
St. Louis Cardinals	3,336,493	$61,453,863	2,603,607	95
Texas Rangers	2,800,075	$70,795,921	5,221,801	71
Toronto Blue Jays	1,819,919	$46,238,333	4,680,300	83

Note: Colorado, Florida, Tampa Bay, and Arizona are not included as they were not in existence for the whole time period.

Ocean Carriers

In January 2001, Mary Linn, Vice President of Finance for Ocean Carriers, a shipping company with offices in New York and Hong Kong, was evaluating a proposed lease of a ship for a three-year period, beginning in early 2003. The customer was eager to finalize the contract to meet his own commitments and offered very attractive terms. No ship in Ocean Carrier's current fleet met the customer's requirements. Linn, therefore, had to decide whether Ocean Carriers should immediately commission a new capesize carrier that would be completed two years hence and could be leased to the customer.

Ship Operations

Ocean Carriers Inc. owned and operated capesize dry bulk carriers that mainly carried iron ore worldwide. This type of vessel ranged in size from 80,000 deadweight tons to 210,000 deadweight tons of cargo carrying capacity. Capesize carriers were too large to transit the Panama Canal and therefore had to sail around Cape Horn to travel between the Atlantic and Pacific Oceans. In January 2001, there were 553 capesizes in service in the world.

Ocean Carriers' vessels were mostly chartered on a "time charter" basis for a period such as one year, three years, or five years, although the spot charter market was used on occasion. The company that chartered the ship was called the "charterer." The charterer paid Ocean Carriers a daily hire rate for the entire length of the contract, determined what cargo the vessel carried, and controlled where the vessel loaded and unloaded. The company, in turn, supplied a seaworthy vessel that complied with international regulations and manned the vessel with a fully qualified and certified crew.

Operations also included ensuring adequate supplies and stores were onboard, supplying lubricating oils, scheduling repairs, conducting overall maintenance of the vessel, and placing all insurances for the vessel. For a new ship coming on line in early 2003, operating costs were expected to initially average $4,000 per day, and to increase annually at a rate of 1% above inflation. Charterers were not charged a daily rate for the time the vessel spent in maintenance and repair, although operating costs were still incurred. Initially, 8 days a year were scheduled for such work. The time allotted to maintenance and repairs increased to 12 days per year after five years of operation, and to 16 days a year for ships older than 10 years.

The company had a policy of not operating vessels older than 15 years. Every five years, international regulations mandated that a special survey be undertaken to ensure seaworthiness as defined by international regulations. By the fifteenth year, the maintenance required to comply with the special surveys was very costly. Exhibit 1 shows the

Angela Chao (HBS MBA 2001) and Research Associate Kathleen Luchs prepared this case under the supervision of Professor Erik Stafford. HBS cases are developed solely as the basis for class discussion. Cases are not intended to serve as endorsements, sources of primary data, or illustrations of effective or ineffective management.

Copyright © 2001 President and Fellows of Harvard College. To order copies or request permission to reproduce materials, call 1-800-545-7685, write Harvard Business School Publishing, Boston, MA 02163, or go to http://www.hbsp.harvard.edu. No part of this publication may be reproduced, stored in a retrieval system, used in a spreadsheet, or transmitted in any form or by any means—electronic, mechanical, photocopying, recording, or otherwise—without the permission of Harvard Business School.

EXHIBIT 1
Capital Expenditures Anticipated in Preparation for Special Surveys

2007	2012	2017	2022	2027
$300,000	$350,000	$750,000	$850,000	$1,250,000

Source: Company estimates

capital expenditures anticipated in preparation for the special surveys. These outlays were considered capital expenditures, which would each be depreciated on a straight-line basis over a 5-year period. To avoid the larger expenditures for older ships, the company planned to sell the vessel into the secondhand market, or "scrap" the vessel just before the third special survey. When scrapped, the vessel was demolished and its steel was sold to demolition yards. The company estimated the scrap value to be $5M at the end of the fifteenth year.

Supply of Capesizes

Daily hire rates were determined by supply and demand. The number of ships available equaled the number of vessels in service the previous year plus any new ships delivered minus any scrappings and sinkings. When the market demand for shipping capacity was high, owners would keep a vessel in operation as long as possible. Conversely, when market demand was low, scrapping rose. Supply was also affected by the increases in size and efficiency the newer ships offered. As ships got bigger, faster, and more fuel efficient, fewer ships were needed to carry the same amount of cargo. Moreover, there had been very few scrappings in recent years, and most of the capacity of the worldwide fleet of capesizes was fairly young. Exhibit 2 shows the capesize fleet by age category as of December 2000. Exhibit 3 shows the number of new capesize vessels by expected delivery date.

Estimates of future orders for vessels were not entirely reliable, especially projections spanning more than two or three years in the future. If sentiment was optimistic on market conditions, more vessels would be added to the order book. If the market outlook was poor, then vessels would be cancelled or converted to other types of vessels. A capesize took approximately 10 months to build, but contracts were signed to secure a berth place approximately two years before delivery and over one year before steel cutting for the vessel. "Delivery" referred to when the vessel was complete and delivered from the shipyard to the owner.

Market Conditions

The demand for dry bulk capesizes was determined by the world economy, especially its basic industries. Over 85% of the cargo carried by capesizes was iron ore and coal. Production and demand for these products increased in a strong economy. Changes in trade patterns also affected the demand for capesizes. For example, if a Western European country decided to switch its supply of iron ore from the United States to Australia, the demand for capesizes would increase since the distance between Europe and Australia is greater than the distance between Western Europe and the United States.

Spot charter rates tended to fluctuate more widely than time charter rates, i.e., the highs were higher and the lows were lower in the spot market. Therefore, when the market was high, ship owners sought time charters to lock in the high rates for as long a period as possible while the charterers preferred to trade in the spot market to avoid

EXHIBIT 2
Capesize Fleet by Age Category as of December 2000

Source: Company estimates

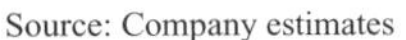

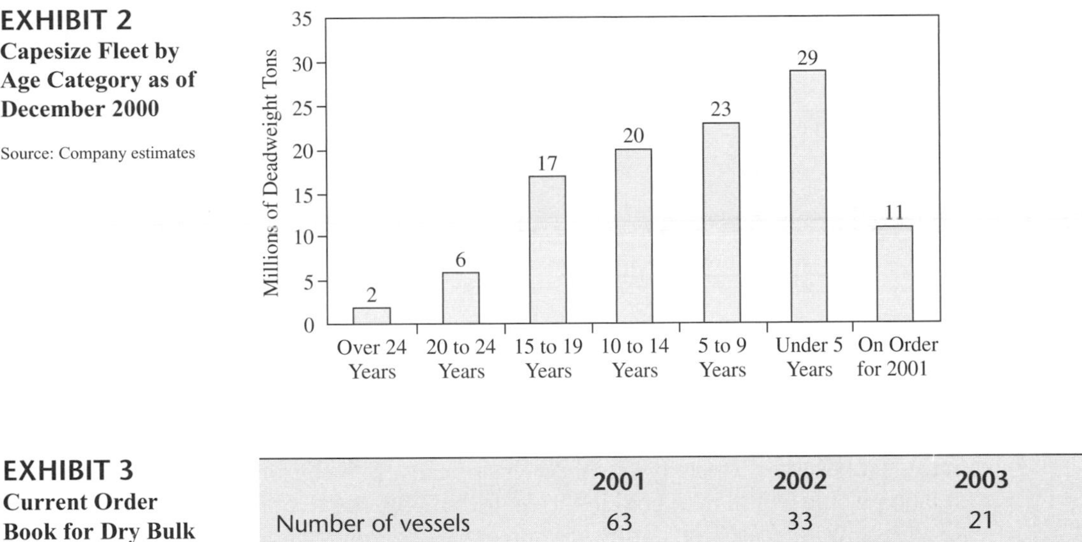

EXHIBIT 3
Current Order Book for Dry Bulk Capesizes by Delivery Date

Source: Company documents

	2001	2002	2003	2004
Number of vessels	63	33	21	9

EXHIBIT 4 Daily Hire Rate Adjustment Factor for Dry Bulk Capesizes Based on Age of Vessel

Source: Company estimates

Over 24 Years	20 to 24 Years	15 to 19 Years	10 to 14 Years	5 to 9 Years	Under 5 Years
0.65	0.75	0.80	1.00	1.05	1.15

having to pay high daily rates any longer than necessary. Because Ocean Carriers' vessels were relatively new and a bit larger than the industry average, they earned a premium to the market. For example, new ships generally earned a 15% premium in daily hire rates relative to the industry-wide average, while ships over 25 years old typically received a 35% discount from the industry average. Exhibit 4 shows average adjustments to daily hire rates for 3-year time charters based on the age of the ship.

The average prevailing spot market rate at the time was $22,000 per day.[1] With Australian production in iron ore expected to be strong and Indian iron ore exports expected to take off in the next few years, Linn took an optimistic view of the long-term market demand for capesizes. However, she also considered that 63 new vessels were scheduled for delivery in 2001 and that imports of iron ore and coal would probably remain stagnant over the next two years. Linn therefore anticipated that spot rates would fall in 2001 and 2002. In 2003, however, Linn was aware that Australian and Indian ore exports would begin, and that these new supplies would significantly increase trading volumes. Demand for capesizes would likely increase with these higher trading volumes, possibly boosting prices. Exhibit 5 provides data on some demand drivers, fleet size, and average daily hire rates over time.

[1]This was the current spot rate for a 10–14 year old ship. Newer ships commanded a higher daily rate, and older ships received a lower rate.

EXHIBIT 5 Worldwide Iron Ore Vessel Shipments, Fleet Size, and Average Daily Hire Rates for Capesize Charters, 1994–2001

Source: Company documents

	1994	1995	1996	1997	1998	1999	2000	2001E
Iron ore vessel shipments	375	397	385	424	420	410	440	436
Fleet size	NA	NA	NA	540	523	523	552	612
Avg. spot rate	$16,851	$20,149	$11,730	$14,794	$10,105	$ 9,427	$22,575	
Avg. 3-yr charter rate	$18,250	$18,544	$14,079	$16,063	$13,076	$12,626	$15,344	

Linn enlisted the services of a shipping-industry consulting firm to help her forecast daily hire rates for a new capesize. Worldwide iron ore vessel shipments and charter rates had been very strongly associated historically. The consulting group felt that this relation would continue to hold in the future, and based its forecast of charter rates off of long-term forecasts for worldwide iron vessel shipments. The long-term forecast for worldwide iron ore vessel shipments was for 2% annual growth during 2002 to 2005, and then dropping to 1.5% thereafter. Exhibit 6 shows the forecast of daily hire rates that was prepared for Linn.

Newbuilding

The charterer currently in negotiations with Ocean Carriers for a three-year time charter starting in 2003 had offered a rate of $20,000 per day with an annual escalation of $200 per day. The expected rate of inflation was 3%.

The vessels in Ocean Carriers' current fleet could not be committed to a time charter beginning in 2003 because the ships either were already leased during that period or were too small to meet the customer's needs. Moreover, there were no sufficiently large capesizes available in the secondhand market. Ocean Carriers had to decide immediately if it should commission a new 180,000 deadweight ton ship for delivery in early 2003. The ship would cost $39 million, with 10% of the purchase price payable immediately and 10% due in a year's time. The balance would be due on delivery. A new ship would be depreciated on a straight-line basis over 25 years. In addition, Linn expected to make a $500,000 initial investment in net working capital, which she anticipated would grow with inflation.

Linn was also confident that the charterer would honor his proposed contract with Ocean Carriers if the company agreed to the terms. While there is always a risk that the charterer would stop paying before the end of the contract or terminate the contract early, Linn considered that the risk was small. Ocean Carriers had long established relationships with its charterers and only contracted with reputable charterers.

The proposed contract, though, was only for three years, and it was Linn's responsibility to decide if future market conditions warranted the considerable investment in a new ship.

EXHIBIT 6 **Forecasted Daily Time Charter Rates for New Capesize Vessel**

Source: Company documents

Age of Ship	Event Year	Calendar Year	Iron Ore Shipments (Millions of Tons)	% Growth	Avg Daily Charter Rate	% Growth	Adjustment Factor for Hire Rate	Adjusted Daily Hire Rate	Expected Daily Hire Rate
	0	2000	440	7.3%	15,344	21.5%			
	1	2001	436	–0.9%	14,747	–3.9%			
	2	2002	445	2.0%	15,072	2.2%			
1	3	2003	454	2.0%	15,403	2.2%	1.15	17,713	20,000
2	4	2004	463	2.0%	15,742	2.2%	1.15	18,103	20,200
3	5	2005	472	2.0%	16,088	2.2%	1.15	18,501	20,400
4	6	2006	479	1.5%	16,273	1.2%	1.15	18,714	18,714
5	7	2007	486	1.5%	16,460	1.2%	1.05	17,283	17,283
6	8	2008	493	1.5%	16,650	1.2%	1.05	17,481	17,481
7	9	2009	501	1.5%	16,841	1.2%	1.05	17,682	17,682
8	10	2010	508	1.5%	17,035	1.2%	1.05	17,886	17,886
9	11	2011	516	1.5%	17,231	1.2%	1.05	18,092	18,092
10	12	2012	524	1.5%	17,429	1.2%	1.00	17,428	17,428
11	13	2013	532	1.5%	17,629	1.2%	1.00	17,628	17,628
12	14	2014	540	1.5%	17,832	1.2%	1.00	17,831	17,831
13	15	2015	548	1.5%	18,037	1.2%	1.00	18,036	18,036
14	16	2016	556	1.5%	18,245	1.2%	1.00	18,243	18,243
15	17	2017	564	1.5%	18,454	1.2%	0.80	14,762	14,762
16	18	2018	573	1.5%	18,667	1.2%	0.80	14,932	14,932
17	19	2019	581	1.5%	18,881	1.2%	0.80	15,104	15,104
18	20	2020	590	1.5%	19,098	1.2%	0.80	15,278	15,278
19	21	2021	599	1.5%	19,318	1.2%	0.80	15,454	15,454
20	22	2022	608	1.5%	19,540	1.2%	0.75	14,654	14,654
21	23	2023	617	1.5%	19,765	1.2%	0.75	14,823	14,823
22	24	2024	626	1.5%	19,992	1.2%	0.75	14,993	14,993
23	25	2025	636	1.5%	20,222	1.2%	0.75	15,166	15,166
24	26	2026	645	1.5%	20,455	1.2%	0.75	15,341	15,341
25	27	2027	655	1.5%	20,690	1.2%	0.65	13,448	13,448

Whirlpool Europe

By the spring of 1999, Whirlpool Corporation (WHR:NYSE), the worldwide leader in the home appliance industry, had nearly ten years experience selling to the European market and had grown its European market share to a sizeable 13%. Whirlpool Europe's chief financial officer and its vice president of logistics were evaluating an investment in an enterprise resource planning (ERP) system. Named *Project Atlantic,* the system would re-organize the information flow in all of Whirlpool Europe. If successful, the project would improve operating effectiveness and efficiency in Whirlpool's sales and marketing, operations and logistics, and finance areas. The cost of the project, however, would be substantial, and would include the direct costs of the system and the personnel that would be required to complete the complex implementation. Senior management had quantified the costs and benefits, and now needed to evaluate them.

Company Background

In 1989, Whirlpool Corporation entered the European market, paying $470 million to purchase a 53% stake in the appliance division of Dutch-based Philips Electronics. The companies formed a joint venture firm named Whirlpool International BV (WIBV) and one year later, launched a dual-branding program which added the Whirlpool name to the Philips product lines. In July 1991, Whirlpool purchased Philips' 47% stake for $600 million to become the sole owner of WIBV. Over time, Whirlpool developed three pan-European brands to differentiate its product line: Whirlpool, Bauknecht, and Ignis. Other regional brands like Laden, sold exclusively in France, were also created. By fiscal 1998, Whirlpool Europe was third in market share with $2.4 billion in sales.

Whirlpool Europe manufactured products based on sales budgets or forecasts, and then held them as finished goods inventory. European manufacturing operated 11 plants, ten located in Europe and one in Africa. Each plant produced a specific product line across all brands. Exhibit 1 provides a plant listing. Unique country requirements, such as language, products attribute preferences, and electrical specifications resulted in multiple stock-keeping units (SKUs) for the same model. In total, Whirlpool Europe manufactured 6,900 SKUs. Orders moved from manufacturing to one of two central distribution centers and then on to one of 12 regional distribution centers before reaching the customer.

In each major European market, a country sales office—responsible for sales generation and forecasting, order processing and fulfillment, billing and cash collection—was the primary interface with customers. Whirlpool Europe operated many stand-alone

Research Associate Aldo M. Sesia, Professor Sudhakar Balachandran of Columbia University, and Professor Richard S. Ruback prepared this case. HBS cases are developed solely as the basis for class discussion. Cases are not intended to serve as endorsements, sources of primary data, or illustrations of effective or ineffective management.

Copyright © 2001 President and Fellows of Harvard College. To order copies or request permission to reproduce materials, call 1-800-545-7685, write Harvard Business School Publishing, Boston, MA 02163, or go to http://www.hbsp.harvard.edu. No part of this publication may be reproduced, stored in a retrieval system, used in a spreadsheet, or transmitted in any form or by any means—electronic, mechanical, photocopying, recording, or otherwise—without the permission of Harvard Business School.

information systems that were developed by individual plants, distribution centers, or sales offices specifically to meet their own business requirements. Information could not be easily shared across functions or organizations, and was often inconsistent and irreconcilable. The sales organization, for example, had to access as many as 13 independent inventory systems to view inventory across the supply chain.

There were two types of customers: consumers who purchased stand-alone appliances for their homes and contractors who purchased built-in appliances for new home construction or kitchen remodeling.

Success in the consumer market depended on product quality, price, and availability. Whirlpool Europe estimated that its distribution centers had the product that matched the customer's demand 79% of the time. If the product was unavailable, the customer had to either wait or switch to another product. Often, the lack of immediate availability resulted in lost sales.

Kitchen remodeling in Europe generally involved the installation of new cabinets along with built-in appliances. Installation often occurred only a few weeks after the kitchen was ordered by the homeowner. Whirlpool estimated that this segment of the market would grow to about 25% of kitchen appliance sales. To supply the built-in appliances to this market, Whirlpool would have to deliver its appliances within ten days of being ordered by the contractor. Under its current inventory and information systems, Whirlpool was unable to reliably satisfy the contractors' required delivery time.

Project Atlantic

Description

The goal of Project Atlantic was to design and implement an enterprise resource planning (ERP) system that would allow Whirlpool Europe to better serve its consumer market for stand-alone appliances and contract market for built-in appliances and, at the same time, reduce its inventory by 12 days of sales. These competing goals would be accomplished through an information system that would allow a country sales office to view product throughout the supply chain, thereby increasing the efficiency of the distribution process. Project Atlantic was expected to provide some integration with suppliers and to increase inventory visibility across the supply chain. This would enable the company to improve product availability and have a substantially lower inventory level. In addition, the ERP system would allow Whirlpool to build products to specific orders from contractors.

Whirlpool Corporation took a phased approach to implementation of its ERP systems, beginning in North America, Brazil, and select central European countries. Project Atlantic would focus on the remaining European countries. With ERP, Whirlpool Europe's disparate information systems would be retired and replaced with a single computing architecture for all of Europe. The company planned to install a standard or so-called "off-the-shelf" ERP system, without any modifications, requiring the company to change many of its operating processes.[1] Employee acceptance of change was therefore critical for success.

The project would be managed under country groupings called Waves. Exhibits 2A and 2B detail the Wave groupings and implementation schedules.

[1]The company identified seven top-level operational processes, of which 74 sub-processes were determined to be impacted by ERP.

Benefits

Working Capital Reduction

The company had 51 days sales of inventory (DSI).[2] Of the 51 days, approximately eight days were reserved and allocated units, nine were in transit, and three were obsolete. The ERP system would enable Whirlpool to make its supply chain more transparent and efficient, thereby eliminating the reserved, allocated, and obsolete units, and reducing the in-transit time. After a statistical study of its inventory, Whirlpool Europe developed a theoretical model target inventory level of 29 days. Project Atlantic was forecasted to reduce 12 days of inventory in each Wave—over half of the difference between its actual inventory and the theoretical model inventory. Exhibit 3 shows data for 1997 including DSI by Wave. Exhibit 4 details the yearly percent DSI reduction in DSI by Wave.

Revenue and Gross Margin Increase

A primary goal of the ERP system was to increase product availability by making the supply chain more visible and by integrating sales forecasting and inventory management. The company's targeted product availability was 92%. The projections assumed that the ERP system and process changes would enable the company to realize an increase in unit sales equal to 25% of the improvement in product availability. Those incremental sales would contribute to increasing the profitability of Whirlpool Europe. Exhibit 3 includes 1997 data on product availability, units, revenue, and margins by Wave. Exhibit 4 details the projected timing of the product availability improvements.

The company's ability to evaluate profitability at a product line, account, or order level was hindered by the lack of an integrated information system. Decisions on prices, for example, were sometimes made with incomplete or dated information. By installing ERP, the company forecasted a 0.25% gross margin increase by the second year after implementation. To forecast the impact, the company used 1997 revenue as the baseline to apply the gross margin increase for each year of cash flow projections. Exhibit 5 presents the projected improvements by year and by wave.

Other Cost Savings

The ERP system was expected to substantially simplify the processing and management of customer orders. An 18% reduction in the 79 order desk employees at an average cost of $40,000 per year per employee was expected once the system was implemented. The ERP system would also simplify the accounting function and result in a 15% reduction in the 60 finance employees. The expected cost saving was $45,000 per year for each employee that was eliminated.

The ERP system was also anticipated to generate other cost savings. Whirlpool paid about $40 annually for each square meter of warehouse space. With the reduction in inventory from the implementation of the ERP system, warehouse space could be reduced by 15% (7,200 square meters). Also, customers returned 3% of units they purchased, which cost Whirlpool about $30 per unit returned. ERP was expected to reduce the number of returned units by eliminating shipping errors. The ERP system was also forecast to reduce bad debt expense and information system expenses. Exhibit 6 details these anticipated savings.

[2]DSI = (Ending Inventory) / (COGS/Days in Period)

Costs

Capital Expenditures

The company would need to spend $4.3 million in 1999 for capital equipment, $8.6 million in 2000, $6.9 million in 2001, and $4.1 million in 2002. It would cost $600,000 and $300,000 for software licenses in 1999 and 2000, respectively. The capital equipment would be depreciated in equal amounts over five years.

Implementation

Implementation required extensive employee training; creation, testing, and documentation of new business processes; and, of course, installation of the ERP software. Implementation of each Wave would require an average of 50 current Whirlpool employees working with external consultants at an expected cost of $45,000 for each employee. According to forecast, the company would need 19 consultants in 1999, nine in 2000, seven in 2001, and four in the following year, at an average monthly cost per consultant of $15,400.

To ensure compliance with the project plan, the company planned to put a three-person task force in place beginning in July 2000 through June 2004, at an annual cost of $600,000.

Ongoing Operational

Beginning in 2003, when all Wave implementations were completed, the cost to manage and maintain the new information systems was forecasted to be $3 million annually. However, because each Wave was scheduled to go on-line at a different time, costs would begin early in the program. Beginning in 1999, the company expected to incur $600,000 in annual expense, which would increase by an additional $600,000 each subsequent year through 2003, reaching $3,000,000 annually.

License maintenance fees were forecasted to begin in 2000 at a cost of $100,000 and increase an additional $100,000 each year through 2003, reaching $400,000 annually. These costs would continue until the system was replaced.

Cost of Capital and Taxes

Whirlpool Europe used a 9% cost of capital to discount the ERP project and faced a 40% tax rate.

EXHIBIT 1
Whirpool Europe's Manufacturing Sites

Source: Company documents.

Location	Products
Amiens France	Washers and Dryers
Norrkoping Sweden	Microwave Ovens
Poprad Slovakia	Washers
Neunkirchen Germany	Dishwashers
Schorndorf Germany	Washers
Cassinetta Italy	Refrigerators and Cooking Appliances
Naples Italy	Washers
Siena Italy	Chest Freezers
Trento Italy	Refrigerators and Freezers
Isithebe South Africa	Refrigerators and Freezers

EXHIBIT 2A
Project Atlantic Implementation Groupings[a]

Source: Company documents.

Wave West	Wave South	Wave Central	Wave North
Belgium	Italy	Czech Republic	Denmark
France	Portugal	Hungary	Finland
Netherlands	Spain	Poland	Ireland
Plus: Warehouse		Slovakia	Norway
Mgt and Physical Dist.			Sweden
			United Kingdom

[a]Austria, Germany, and Switzerland were not part of Project Atlantic.

EXHIBIT 2B
Wave Implementation Schedule

Source: Company documents.

	West	South	Central	North
Start Date:	MAY 1999	MAY 2000	MAR 2001	JAN 2002
End Date:	APR 2000	FEB 2001	DEC 2001	AUG 2002

EXHIBIT 3 **1997 Data for Whirlpool Europe**

Source: Company documents.

Wave	DSI	Product Availability	Units Sold	Revenue (000s US$)	Margin (000s US$)
West	45	73.5%	2,271,139	477,784	58,859
South	51	83.1%	1,415,949	283,549	46,241
Central	67	76.8%	977,665	185,625	43,678
North	55	83.2%	1,443,156	280,901	29,818

EXHIBIT 4
Improvements in DSI and Availability by Year and Wave

Source: Company documents.

	Improvements by Year by Wave					
Wave	2000	2001	2002	2003	2004	2005
West	25%	40%	35%			
South		35%	40%	25%		
Central			40%	40%	20%	
North				40%	40%	20%

EXHIBIT 5
Margin Improvements by Year by Wave

Source: Company documents.

	Cumulative Margin Improvements by Year by Wave					
Wave	**2000**	**2001**	**2002**	**2003**	**2004**	**2005**
West	0.06%	0.25%	0.25%	0.25%	0.25%	0.25%
South		0.10%	0.25%	0.25%	0.25%	0.25%
Central			0.13%	0.25%	0.25%	0.25%
North				0.13%	0.25%	0.25%

EXHIBIT 6 Forecasted Other Expense Savings by Year (000s US$)

Source: Company documents.

	2000	2001	2002	2003	2004	2005	2006	2007
Order Desk Headcount	0	190	411	442	474	506	537	569
Finance Headcount	81	135	216	324	405	405	405	405
Warehouse Space	18	72	155	230	274	288	288	288
Bad Debt Expense	102	512	922	1,024	1,024	1,024	1,024	1,024
Information Systems	420	840	840	1,280	1,280	1,280	1,280	1,280
	621	1,749	2,544	3,300	3,457	3,503	3,534	3,566

Health Development Corporation

Mr. Paul Couturier, the CEO of Health Development Corporation (HDC), was negotiating the sale of his company in the spring of 2000. The Company, which owned and managed health clubs in the Greater Boston area, had retained a local investment firm, Kaufman & Co., to solicit bids. They received several bids from national or regional health club companies seeking to establish themselves in the Boston area. The bids were lower than expected, largely because of the way the bidding companies considered HDC's ownership of Lexington Club's real estate. Like most health clubs, HDC generally leased their health club real estate but in 1999, HDC had taken advantage of an opportunity to purchase the Lexington Club at what Paul Couturier thought was a very attractive price. He was surprised that HDC's ownership of the Lexington Club seemed to be reducing the company's offering price and was mulling his alternatives.

The Company

HDC owned nine health and fitness clubs in the Greater Boston area. It also operated three other facilities under management contracts, including Shad Hall at the Harvard Business School. As Exhibits 1 and 2 demonstrate, the Company had realized rapid growth between 1994 and 1999, almost doubling its revenue and tripling its operating margin.

Much of HDC's success came from its three largest clubs located in Boston suburbs near the Route 128 beltway. Each of these clubs offered a range of services, including fitness, personal training, tennis, swimming, and childcare. The Wellesley Center, located in Wellesley, MA, was a 75,000 square foot facility that had over 4500 members. Its projected annual revenue was in excess of $6.3 million for the year 2000. The Lexington Club, located in Lexington, MA, was a 62,000 square foot facility that had over 4000 members with projected annual revenue in excess of $3.9 million for the year 2000. The Colonial Club, located in Lynnfield, MA, near the intersection of Routes 128 and 95, was a 55,000 square foot facility that had over 2500 members with projected annual revenue in excess of $2.7 million for the year 2000.

The Company continued to expand during 1999, adding the Franklin Club in Franklin, MA, and the Andover Club in Andover, MA. The Andover Club required a substantial capital investment to convert it from a tennis-only facility into a multi-purpose facility. The Company anticipated that the new facilities would not be profitable for about two years after their acquisition. The startup costs of the two new facilities were expected to reduce operating profits by about $400,000 in the year 2000.

Professor Richard S. Ruback prepared this case. HBS cases are developed solely as the basis for class discussion. Cases are not intended to serve as endorsements, sources of primary data, or illustrations of effective or ineffective management.

Copyright © 2000 President and Fellows of Harvard College. To order copies or request permission to reproduce materials, call 1-800-545-7685, write Harvard Business School Publishing, Boston, MA 02163, or go to http://www.hbsp.harvard.edu. No part of this publication may be reproduced, stored in a retrieval system, used in a spreadsheet, or transmitted in any form or by any means—electronic, mechanical, photocopying, recording, or otherwise—without the permission of Harvard Business School.

The Opportunity to Purchase the Lexington Club Real Estate

Until the spring of 1999, HDC leased the building and 9 acres of land that housed the Lexington Club. The lease terms of health clubs are generally linked to the revenue generated by the facility. HDC's lease payments for the Lexington Club were about 23.5% of its revenue. With anticipated revenue of about $3.9 million in the year 2000, the projected lease payment was about $925,000. The revenue and the lease payments were expected to grow at about 5% a year.

In 1999, HDC had the option to purchase the Lexington Club real estate for $6.5 million. The Company had not purchased real estate in the past for two reasons. First, as a small privately held company, HDC preferred to use its limited capital to add, expand, or enhance clubs. Second, leasing property allowed the company to reduce its risk by keeping real estate costs proportional to revenue. In the case of the Lexington property, however, HDC management determined that the lease payments were substantially greater than the costs of owning the real estate. After attempting unsuccessfully to renegotiate the lease payments downward, HDC decided to purchase the Lexington Club property. The Company financed the Lexington Club purchase with $750,000 of excess cash and a mortgage for $5,750,000 at an interest rate of 8.75%.

The Offers to Purchase

Kaufman & Company solicited bids for HDC in February 2000. In exchange for signing a confidentiality agreement, potential bidders received an information memorandum that provided a detailed description of the Company, its operations, and its financial results. Potential bidders were also given the opportunity to visit the health clubs and to interview management. Five potential buyers submitted bids.

HDC, with the advice of Kaufman & Co., decided to focus on the bid by Town Sports International (TSI). TSI had a large share of the New York health club market, with 67 clubs, but only five clubs in the Boston market. TSI shared many of HDC's operating philosophies, making it an ideal fit with HDC. TSI's offer price was the highest of the initial offers and the potential synergies between TSI and HDC made Kaufman confident that the highest final bid would also come from TSI. Nevertheless, HDC was disappointed with the initial offer price and hoped that negotiations would substantially improve the offer.

In negotiations, TSI revealed that it viewed the Lexington purchase as a negative, and would have been willing to pay the same or a higher multiple of EBITDA if HDC did not own the real estate. HDC argued that the Lexington purchase was clearly a value increasing decision, and therefore should increase the equity value of the Company. The math, however, undeniably supported TSI's position. The valuation projected HDC's year 2000 earnings before taxes, interest, depreciation, and amortization (EBITDA). A multiple of about five times was applied to the EBITDA to determine the total enterprise value, and the debt of the Company was subtracted to determine the equity value of the Company. Exhibit 3 shows that the real estate purchase reduced excess cash by $750,000 and added $5.75 million in debt. This $6.5 million was greater than five times the resulting increase in EBITDA.

Paul Couturier and Kaufman & Company began to assess alternative structures. One choice was to sell the Lexington real estate to another entity that would in turn lease it back to the potential buyer. According to TSI's operating model, which set benchmark operating cost ratios, the projected lease payment for the Lexington Club could not exceed $525,000. Given current interest rates, HDC believed they could obtain a ten-year mortgage at an 8.5% interest rate but that would require the lease payments to increase to 110% of the mortgage payment. This arrangement seemed to have the potential to meet the concerns of TSI and maximize the value to the HDC shareholders, but it was going to be difficult to structure.

EXHIBIT 1 Income Statement for Health Development Corporation

Source: Company reports.

	Year Ended December 31,								
	1994	1995	1996	1997	1998	1999	2000[a]	2001[a]	2002[a]
Total Revenue	8,316	9,957	12,584	13,636	14,549	16,162	19,324	21,311	22,809
Club Operating Expenses	5,779	6,990	8,837	9,337	9,877	10,885	13,130	14,313	15,092
Gross Profit	2,537	2,967	3,747	4,299	4,672	5,277	6,194	6,998	7,717
Rent and Other Expenses[b]	1,831	2,226	2,869	2,842	2,771	2,299	2,275	2,375	2,510
Depreciation and Amortization	363	426	517	619	682	1,058	1,233	1,466	1,452
Operating Income	343	315	361	838	1,219	1,920	2,687	3,157	3,755
Net Interest Expense	17	3	(22)	(28)	(36)	480	975	1,094	1,061
Non-Recurring Expenses[c]	0	36	52	186	40	(6)	0	0	0
Pre-Tax Income	325	279	331	680	1,216	1,445	1,712	2,062	2,694
Income Taxes	146	126	158	333	499	660	729	798	1,032
Net Income	179	153	173	347	716	785	982	1,264	1,662
Expense Adjustments:									
Non-Recurring Items	0	36	52	(3)	40	(6)	0	0	0
Directors' Wages and Fees	42	40	83	78	64	74	91	96	102
Professional Fees	24	44	68	140	143	123	126	130	130
Terminated Operations	0	0	0	236	41	0	0	0	0
Contributions and Other Items	0	2	3	4	41	28	17	19	22
Adjusted Pre-Tax Income	391	400	537	1,135	1,544	1,665	1,946	2,307	2,948
Adjusted EBITDA[d]	771	830	1,032	1,726	2,190	3,202[e]	4,152	4,867	5,460
EBITDA Margin	9.3%	8.3%	8.2%	12.7%	15.1%	19.8%	21.5%	22.8%	23.9%

[a]Projections include only current HDC properties, and include no assumptions regarding additional future acquisitions.
[b]Includes Rent, Insurance, Real Estate Taxes, and other Tax Expenses.
[c]Includes $50,000 in claim settlement in 1996; $189,000 in losses on a club termination in 1997; $40,000 in purchase financing costs in 1998.
[d]Figure includes $80,000 and $528,000 of losses for the company's new Andover facility for 1999 and 2000, respectively.
[e]Does not reflect a full year of ownership of HDC's Lexington facility, which would result in an additional $200,000 of EBITDA if annualized.

EXHIBIT 2
Balance Sheets for Health Development Corporation

Source: Company reports.

	As of September 30, 1999
Assets	
Current assets	
Cash and Marketable Securities	997
Accounts Receivable	226
Inventory	21
Prepaid and Other Current Items	127
Total Current Assets	1,371
Property, Plant, and Equipment	
Property and Equipment	12,047
Construction in Progress	1,320
Total Property, Plant, and Equipment	13,367
Less: Accumulated Depreciation	(3,349)
Net Property and Equipment	10,018
Other Assets	716
Total Assets	12,105
Liabilities and Shareholders' Equity	
Current Liabilities	
Accounts Payable	135
Accrued Expenses	1,250
Prepaid Membership Fees	1,888
Current Portion of Long-Term Debt	210
Other Current Liabilities	39
Total Current Liabilities	3,522
Long-Term Debt	6,704
Other Long-Term Liabilities	682
Total Liabilities	10,908
Shareholders' Equity	
Common and Preferred Stock	9
Paid-In Capital	718
Retained Earnings	470
Total Shareholders' Equity	1,197
Total Liabilities and Equity	12,105

EXHIBIT 3
Value of HDC with Owned and Leased Lexington Real Estate

Source: Casewriter estimates.

	Lexington Real Estate	
	Owning	Leasing
Adjusted Pre-Tax Income (excluding Lexington Real Estate)	2,612	2,612
Cost of Lexington Real Estate		
Interest	504	0
Depreciation	162	0
Lease Cost	0	925
Adjusted Pre-Tax Income	1,946	1,687
Interest (excluding Lexington)	471	471
Depreciation (excluding Lexington)	1,071	1,071
Lexington Real Estate Interest	504	0
Lexington Real Estate Depreciation	162	0
EBITDA	4,154	3,229
Multiple	5×	5×
Value of Operations	20,770	16,145
Plus:		
Excess Cash	0	750
Total Enterprise Value	20,770	16,895
Less:		
Corporate Debt (excluding Lexington)	1,917	1,917
Lexington Real Estate Debt	5,750	0
Equity Value	13,103	14,978

Cost of Capital and Valuation

Diversification, the Capital Asset Pricing Model, and the Cost of Equity Capital

Risk as Variability in Return

The rate of return an investor receives from holding a stock for a given period of time is equal to the dividends received plus the capital gains in the period divided by the initial market value of the security:

$$R = \frac{\text{Dividends} + (\text{Ending price} - \text{Beginning price})}{\text{Beginning price}}$$

Alternatively, return can be viewed as the dividend yield plus the percentage capital appreciation:

$$R = \text{Dividend yield} + \text{Percentage capital appreciation}$$

Suppose an investor buys one common share of Du Pont for $100 on January 1. Over the year, he or she receives $4 in dividends and sells the share for $108 on December 31. The return on this investment is 12%:

$$R_{\text{Du Pont}} = \frac{\$4 + (\$108 - \$100)}{\$100} = \frac{\$12}{\$100} = .12$$

or

$$R_{\text{Du Pont}} = 4\%\text{ dividend yield} + 8\%\text{ appreciation} = 12\%$$

If the ending price is $85, the return is –11%.

The return on any security can be viewed as the cash the security holder receives (including liquidation at the end of the period) divided by the initial investment. Investing in a savings account that offers a 5% interest rate results in an annual return of 5%:

$$R_{\text{Savings account}} = \frac{\$5 + (\$100 - \$100)}{\$100} = .05$$

There is an important difference, however, between investing in a savings account and investing in common stocks. The investor knows before committing any funds that the savings account will earn a return of 5%. The actual return will not differ from the expected return of 5%. Thus, savings accounts are considered a safe, or risk-free, security.

On the other hand, an investor who expects a return of 12% on Du Pont's common shares may be disappointed or pleasantly surprised. The actual return on Du Pont may

Copyright © 1976 by the President and Fellows of Harvard College. Harvard Business School case 276–183.

FIGURE I
Risk as Variability in Return

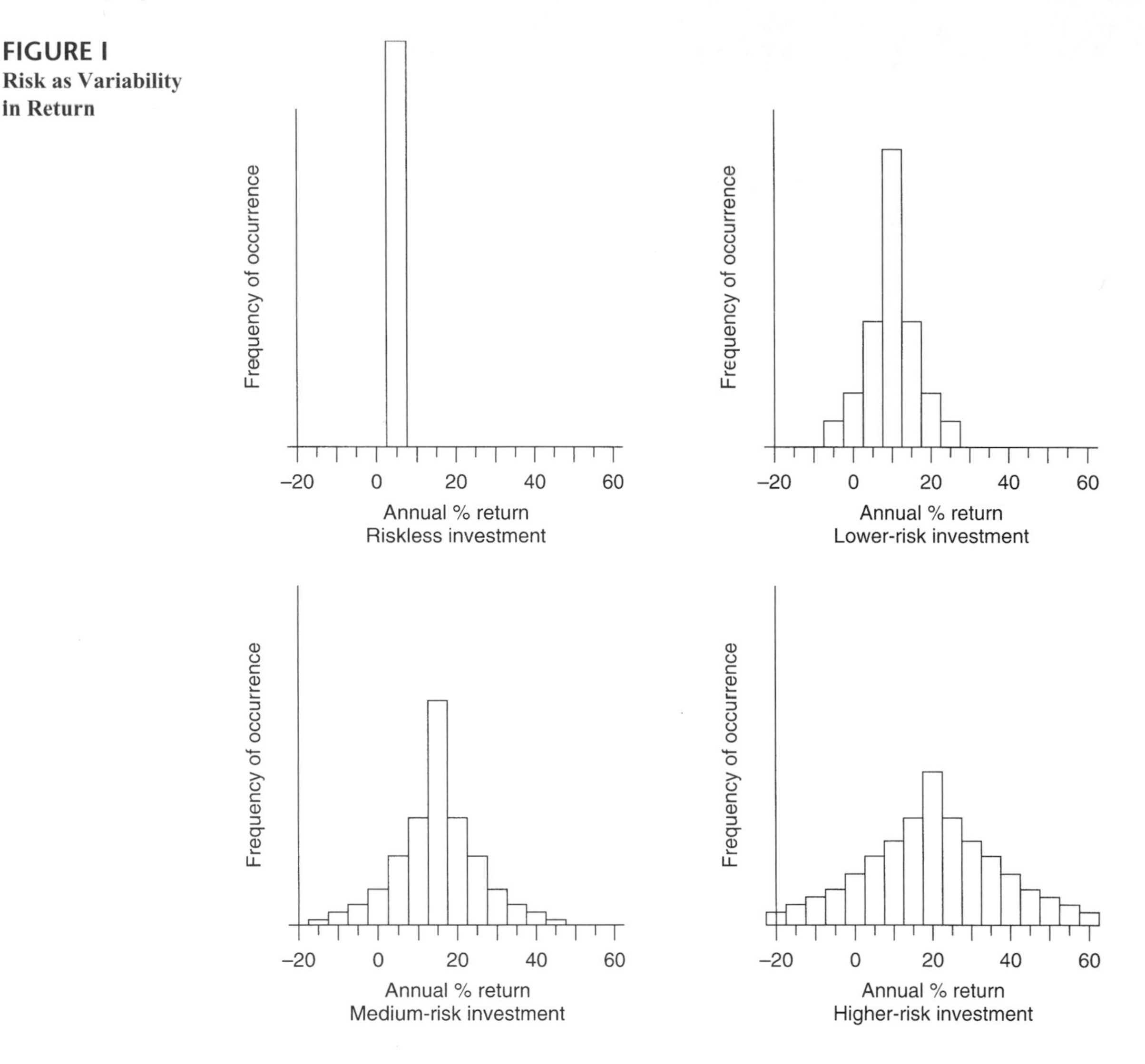

be less than or greater than 12%, since (1) Du Pont may change its dividend and, more important, (2)the market price at the end of the period may differ from the anticipated price. Actual returns on common stock vary widely from year to year. An investor committing funds at the beginning of any period cannot be confident of receiving the average or expected return.

In general, an investment with actual returns that are not likely to depart from the expected or average return is considered a low-risk investment. One with quite volatile returns from year to year is said to be risky. Thus, risk can be viewed as variability in return (see Figure I).

Risk Reduction through Diversification

Risky stocks can be combined in such a way that the combination of securities, called a portfolio of securities, is less risky than any one of the component individual stocks. Consider the example outlined in Table A. Suppose we have two firms located on an isolated Caribbean island. The chief industry on the island is tourism. Company A manufactures and sells suntan lotion. Its sales, earnings, and cash flows are highest during

TABLE A
Example of Risk Reduction through Diversification

	Weather Conditions	Return on Stock $A = R_A$
Company A: Suntan lotion manufacturer	Sunny year	33%
	Normal year	12
	Rainy year	–9
	Weather Conditions	**Return on Stock $B = R_B$**
Company B: Disposable umbrella manufacturer	Sunny year	–9%
	Normal year	12
	Rainy year	33

Returns on a Portfolio (R_p) Consisting of 50% invested in Stock A and 50% in Stock B:
$R_p = .50\ (R_A) + .50\ (R_B)$

	Weather Conditions	Return on the Portfolio = R_P
Portfolio containing A and B	Sunny year	.50 (33%) + .50 (–9%) = 12%
	Normal year	.50 (12%) + .50 (12%) = 12%
	Rainy year	.50 (–9%) + .50 (33%) = 12%

sunny years. Thus, its stock does well in sunny years and poorly in rainy years. Company B manufacturers and sells disposable umbrellas. Returns on its stock reflect its higher earnings in rainy years. In purchasing stock in either A or B, an investor is subject to considerable risk or variability in return. For instance, the investor's return on the stock of company B will vary from 33% to –9%, depending on weather conditions.

Suppose, however, that instead of buying only one security, the investor puts half of his or her funds in stock A and half in stock B. The possible returns on this portfolio of securities are calculated in Table A. If a recession occurs, a \$50 investment in stock A loses \$4.50, while \$50 invested in stock B returns \$16.50. The total return on \$100 invested in the portfolio is 12%:

$$\frac{-\$4.50 + \$16.50}{\$100}$$

Note that the return on this portfolio is 12% regardless of which weather condition prevails.

Combining these two risky securities yields a portfolio with a certain return. Since we are sure of earning 12% on the portfolio, it is a very low-risk investment, comparable to a risk-free security such as a savings account. This example demonstrates risk reduction through diversification. By diversifying the investment over both firms, the investor creates a portfolio that is less risky than its two component stocks.

Total risk elimination is possible in this example because there is a perfect negative relation between the returns on stock A and B. In practice, such a perfect relation is very rare. Most firms' securities tend to move together, and therefore complete elimination of risk is not possible. However, as long as there is some lack of parallelism in the returns of securities, diversification will always reduce risk. Since companies' fortunes, and therefore their stocks' returns, do not move completely in parallel, investment in a diversified portfolio composed of many securities is less risky than investment in a few individual stocks.

FIGURE II
Elimination of Unsystematic Risk through Diversification

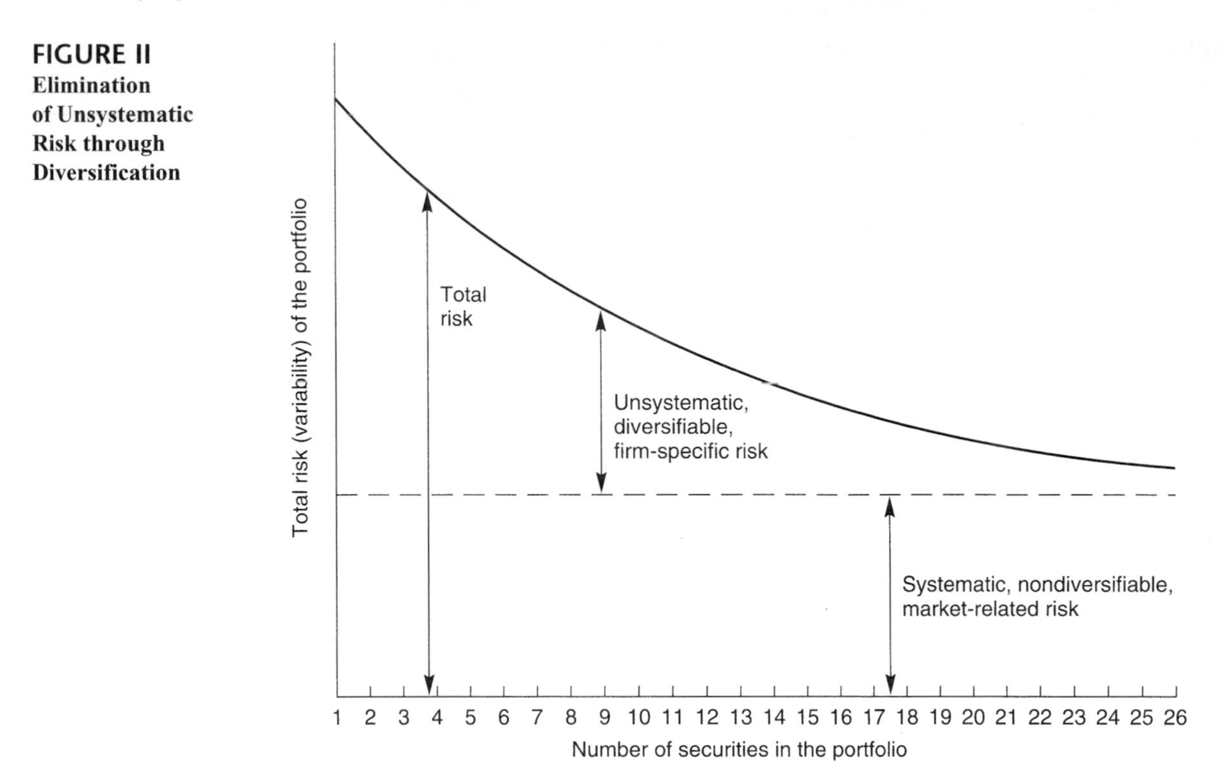

Systematic and Unsystematic Risk

Combining securities into portfolios reduces risk. When combined with other securities, a portion of a stock's variability in return is canceled by complementary variations in the returns of other securities. Some firms represented in the portfolio may experience unanticipated adverse conditions (e.g., a wildcat strike). However, this may well be offset by the unexpected good fortune of other firms in the portfolio. Nevertheless, since to some extent stock price (and returns) tend to move in concert, not all variability can be eliminated through diversification. Even investors holding diversified portfolios are exposed to the risk inherent in the overall performance of the stock market (for instance, the stock market crash of October 1987). Thus, it is convenient to divide a security's total risk into that portion that is peculiar to a specific firm and can be diversified away (called unsystematic risk) and that portion that is market-related and nondiversifiable (called systematic risk):

$$\text{Total risk} = \underset{\substack{\text{(diversifiable risk,} \\ \text{firm-specific)}}}{\text{Unsystematic risk}} + \underset{\substack{\text{(nondiversifiable risk,} \\ \text{market-related)}}}{\text{Systematic risk}}$$

Figure II illustrates the reduction of total risk as securities are added to a portfolio. Unsystematic risk is virtually eliminated in portfolios of 30 or 40 securities drawn from industries that are not closely related. Because the remaining systematic risk is market related, diversified portfolios tend to move in tandem with the market. The popular market indices (the Dow Jones Industrial Average, the S&P 500, and the New York Stock Exchange Index, for instance) are themselves diversified portfolios and tend to move in parallel. Thus, there is a close correspondence between swings in the returns of any diversified portfolio and in the returns on market indices such as the Dow. Examples of systematic and unsystematic risk factors are listed in Table B.

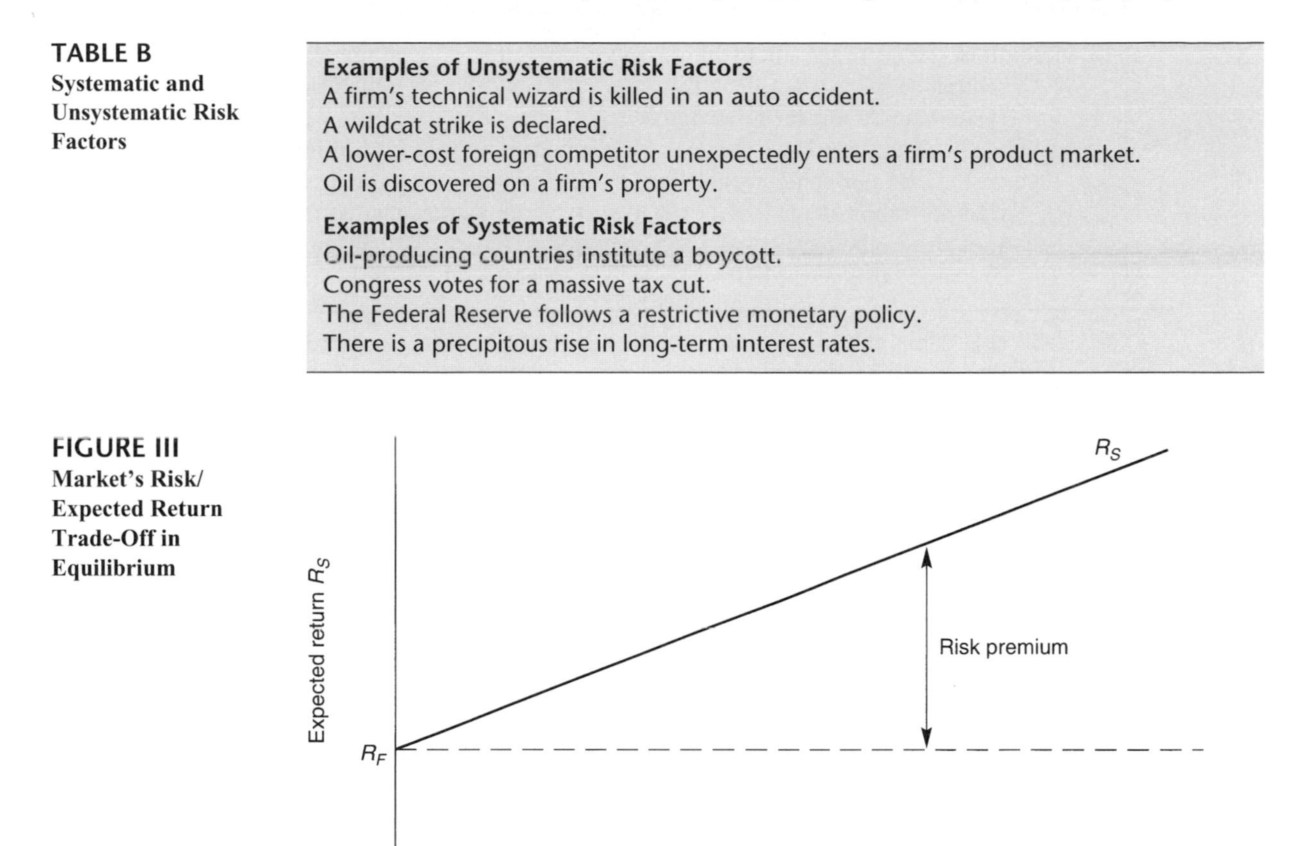

TABLE B
Systematic and Unsystematic Risk Factors

Examples of Unsystematic Risk Factors
A firm's technical wizard is killed in an auto accident.
A wildcat strike is declared.
A lower-cost foreign competitor unexpectedly enters a firm's product market.
Oil is discovered on a firm's property.

Examples of Systematic Risk Factors
Oil-producing countries institute a boycott.
Congress votes for a massive tax cut.
The Federal Reserve follows a restrictive monetary policy.
There is a precipitous rise in long-term interest rates.

FIGURE III
Market's Risk/ Expected Return Trade-Off in Equilibrium

Risk, Return, and Market Equilibrium

Investors are risk-averse and must be compensated for taking risk. Thus, risky securities are priced by the market to yield a higher expected return than low-risk securities. This extra reward, called the risk premium, is necessary to induce risk-averse investors to hold risky securities. In a market dominated by risk-averse investors, there must be a positive relation between risk and expected return to achieve equilibrium. The expected return on a risk-free security (such as a Treasury bill) is the risk-free rate. The expected return on risky securities can be thought of as this risk-free rate plus a premium for risk:

$$R_S = R_F + \text{Risk premium}$$

The market's risk/return trade-off is illustrated in Figure III.

The Capital Asset Pricing Model (CAPM)

The capital asset pricing model (CAPM) represents an idealized view of how the market prices securities and determines expected returns. It provides a measure of the risk premium and a method for estimating the market's risk/expected return curve.

In the CAPM, investors hold diversified portfolios to minimize risk. Because they hold portfolios consisting of many securities, events peculiar to specific firms (i.e., unsystematic risk) have a negligible impact on their overall return. Only a small fraction of an investor's funds are invested in each security. Furthermore, variations in returns from one security will, as likely as not, be canceled by complementary variations in the returns of other securities. Therefore, the only risk to which investors are sensitive is systematic, or market-related, risk.

Since unsystematic risk can be eliminated simply by holding large portfolios, investors are not compensated for bearing unsystematic risk. Investors holding diversified portfolios are exposed only to systematic, market-related risk. Therefore, the relevant risk in the market's risk/expected return trade-off is systematic risk, not total risk. The investor is rewarded with a higher expected return for bearing systematic, market-related risks. Only systematic risk is relevant in determining the premiums for bearing risk. Thus, the model predicts that a security's return is related to that portion of risk that cannot be eliminated by portfolio combination.

An individual investor who invests in only one stock is still exposed to both systematic and unsystematic risk. However, he or she is rewarded in terms of a higher expected return only for the systematic risk he or she bears. There is no reward for bearing unsystematic risk, since it can be eliminated by adequate diversification.

The CAPM provides a convenient measure of systematic risk. This measure, called beta (β), gauges the tendency of a security's return to move in parallel with the overall market's return (e.g., the return on the S&P 500). A stock with a beta of 1 tends to rise and fall the same percentage as the market (i.e., the S&P 500 index). Thus, $\beta = 1$ indicates an average level of systematic risk. Stocks with $\beta > 1$ tend to rise and fall by a greater percentage than the market. They have a high level of systematic risk and are very sensitive to market changes. Similarly, stocks with $\beta < 1$ have a low level of systematic risk and are less sensitive to market swings.

These results determine the risk/expected return trade-off under the CAPM. In general,

$$R_S = R_F + \text{Risk premium}$$

If the CAPM correctly describes market behavior,

$$R_S = R_F + \beta_S(R_M - R_F)$$

The expected return on a security (R_S) is equal to the risk-free rate plus a risk premium. With the CAPM, the risk premium is β multiplied by the return on the market (R_M) minus the risk-free rate. Alternatively, the relation can be expressed in terms of the risk premium (i.e., the return over and above the risk-free rate):

$$\begin{aligned} R_S - R_F &= \beta_S(R_M - R_F) \\ &= \text{Risk premium for security } S \end{aligned}$$

Thus, the risk premium on a stock (or portfolio or any security) varies directly with the level of systematic risk, β. This risk/expected return trade-off with the CAPM is called the security market line (SML) and is illustrated graphically in Figure IV.

One perhaps counterintuitive aspect of the determination of expected returns with the CAPM can be illustrated with a simple example. Consider a firm engaged in oil exploration. The return (denoted R_A) to the shareholders in such a firm is very variable. If oil is found, the return is very high. If no oil is discovered, shareholders lose their entire investment and the return is negative. The stock's total risk level is very high. However, much of the variability in return is generated by factors independent of the returns on other stocks (i.e., the return on the market). This risk is unique to the firm and is therefore unsystematic risk. Since the stock's return is not closely related to the return on the market as a whole, it contributes little to the variability of a diversified portfolio. Its unsystematic risk can be diversified away by holding large portfolios. Nevertheless, the costs of exploration and the price of oil are related to the general level of economic activity. As a result, the stock does contain some systematic, market-related risk. Most of its total risk is unsystematic risk, however, associated with the chances of finding oil.

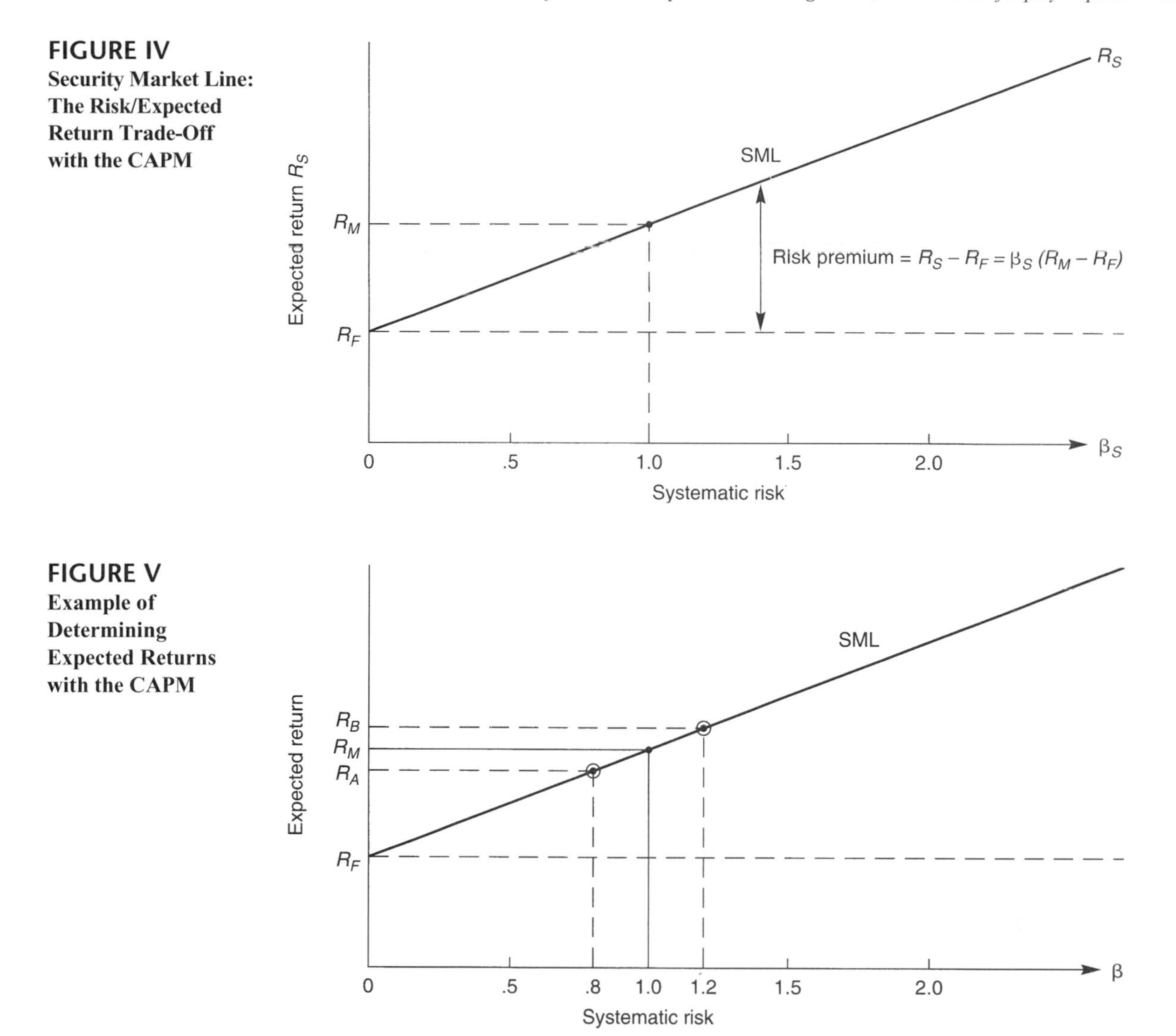

FIGURE IV
Security Market Line: The Risk/Expected Return Trade-Off with the CAPM

FIGURE V
Example of Determining Expected Returns with the CAPM

Although the firm's stock is very risky in terms of total risk, it has a low level of systematic risk. Its beta might be .8. The market will therefore price this stock to yield a relatively low expected return. From the viewpoint of investors holding large portfolios, it is a low-risk security. Its expected return is denoted R_A in Figure V. Note that the return on this stock (R_A) is less than the return on the average stock in the market (R_M).

In contrast, consider a firm that manufactures computers. As a large stable firm, its total variability in return might be less than that of the oil exploration firm. However, its sales, earnings, and therefore stock returns are closely related to changes in overall economic activity. The return on its stock is very sensitive to changes in the return on the market as a whole. Therefore, its risk cannot be eliminated by diversification. When combined with other securities in a diversified portfolio, changes in its return tend to reinforce swings in the returns of the other securities. It has a relatively high level of systematic risk and a beta of perhaps 1.2. Viewed as an individual security, it appears less risky (in terms of total risk) than the oil exploration firm. Nevertheless, because of its high level of nondiversifiable risk, the market considers it the riskier security. Therefore, it is priced to yield a high expected return. Its return is labeled R_B in Figure V. Such counterintuitive examples are rare, however. Most firms with high total risk also have high betas (and vice versa).

TABLE C
Summary of the Determination of Expected Returns with the CAPM

1. Total risk is defined as variability in return.
2. The investor can reduce risk by holding a diversified portfolio.
3. The total risk of a security can be divided into unsystematic and systematic risk.
   a. Risk that can be eliminated through diversification is called unsystematic risk. It is associated with events unique to the firm and independent of other firms.
   b. The risk remaining in a diversified portfolio is called systematic risk. It is associated with the movement of other securities and the market as a whole.
4. If the CAPM correctly describes market behavior, investors hold diversified portfolios to minimize risk.
5. Since investors hold diversified portfolios with the CAPM, they are exposed only to systematic risk. In such a market, investors are rewarded in terms of a higher expected return only for bearing systematic, market-related risk. There is no reward associated with unsystematic risk because it can be eliminated through diversification. Thus, relevant risk is systematic or market-related risk, and it is measured by beta.
6. The risk/expected return trade-off with the CAPM is called the security market line (SML). Securities are priced such that:

   $$R_S = R_F + \text{Risk premium, or } R_S = R_F + \beta_S(R_M - R_F)$$

   Thus, the SML gives us an estimate of the expected return on any security, R_S.

In summary, if the CAPM correctly describes market behavior, the relevant measure of a security's risk is its market-related or systematic risk (measured by beta). If a security's return has a strong positive relation with the return on the market (i.e., has a high beta), it will be priced to yield a high expected return (and vice versa). Since unsystematic risk can be easily eliminated through diversification, it does not increase a security's expected return. The market cares only about systematic risk. These results are summarized in Table C.

Application of the CAPM to Corporate Finance: Estimating the Cost of Equity Capital

The CAPM provides insight into the market's pricing of securities and the determination of expected returns. It has clear applications in investment management and in corporate finance. The cost of equity capital, k_E, is the expected (or required) return on a firm's common stock. The firm must be expected to earn k_E on the equity-financed portion of investments to keep the price of its stock from falling. If the firm cannot expect to earn at least k_E, funds should be returned to the shareholders, who can earn k_E on marketable securities of the same risk level. Since k_E involves the market's expectations, it is difficult to measure. The CAPM can be used by financial managers to obtain an estimate of k_E.

The CAPM provides a conceptual framework for determining the expected return on common stocks, and it can be used to estimate firms' cost of capital. If the CAPM correctly describes market behavior, the market's expected return on a common stock is given by the security market line (SML):

$$R_S = R_F + \beta_S(R_M - R_F)$$

The expected return on a firm's stock is, by definition, its cost of equity capital. Therefore, in terms of cost of capital, the SML is

$$k_E = R_F + \beta_S(k_M - R_F)$$

TABLE D **Betas for Selected Firms in Four Industries**

Electric Utilities		Airlines		Computer Hardware		Computer Software	
Company	**β**	**Company**	**β**	**Company**	**β**	**Company**	**β**
American Electric Power	.75	AMR Corp.	1.25	AST Research	1.50	Adobe Systems	1.80
Baltimore Gas & Electric	.80	Delta	1.20	Apple Comp.	1.10	Borland International	1.60
Consolidated Edison	.75	Northwest	1.75	Compaq	1.25	Computer Assoc.	1.55
Duke Power	.75	UAL	1.60	Digital Equip.	1.05	Intuit	1.85
FPL Group	.75	US Air Group	1.55	Hewlett-Packard	1.10	Microsoft	1.20
Niagara Mohawk	.80			IBM	.90	Novell Inc.	1.40
Ohio Edison	.80					Oracle	1.45
Pacific Gas & Electric	.75						

where

$k_E = R_S$ = Firm's cost of equity capital
$k_M = R_M$ = Cost of equity for the market as a whole (or for an average firm in the market)
β_S = Beta of the firm's stock

Thus, to estimate k_E we need estimates of R_F, the risk-free rate; $k_M = R_M$, the expected return on the market as a whole; and β_S, the level of systematic risk associated with the firm's stock.

R_F can be estimated as the average or expected rate of return on Treasury bills in the future. In recent years, this rate has ranged between 3% and 9%. A reasonable estimate might be 6% per year.

The market risk premium is the difference between the return on the market, k_M, and the risk-free rate, R_F. The expected risk premium in the future is difficult to estimate. A common approach is to assume that investors expect returns in the future to be about the same as returns in the past. The average annual market risk premium (large company equities versus long-term Treasury bonds) was 7.4% in the period 1926–1995.[1]

The stock's beta, β_S, can be estimated by linear regression.[2] Betas are also available from many brokerage firms and investment advisory services. Furthermore, one can get an intuitive estimate simply by observing the stock's reaction to swings in the market as a whole. Finally, a rough guess at beta can be made by noting the tendency of the firm's earnings and cash flows to move in parallel with the earnings and cash flows of other firms in the economy.

Betas for selected firms in four industries are presented in Table D. Despite relatively high degrees of operating and financial leverage, electric utilities have very stable earnings streams. Swings in the earnings and stock returns of utilities are modest relative to swings in the earnings and returns of most firms in the economy. Therefore, electric utilities have a low level of systematic risk and low betas.

At the other extreme, airline revenues are closely tied to passenger miles, which are in turn very sensitive to changes in economic activity. This basic variability in revenues is amplified by high operating and financial leverage. The result is earnings and returns that show wide variations relative to swings in the earnings and returns of most firms. Thus, airlines have high betas.

[1] *Stocks, Bonds, Bills, and Inflation—1996 Yearbook: Market Results for 1926–1995* (Chicago, Ibbotson Associates, 1996).

[2] The estimated regression equation is $R_S - R_F = \alpha + \beta_S(R_M - R_F) + e$. Given past values of R_F, R_S, and R_M, the regression yields estimates of alpha. α (which should be zero), and the stock's beta. β_S.

TABLE E Examples of Estimating the Cost of Equity Capital Using the CAPM

Assumptions	*SML*		
$R_E = .09$ = risk-free rate	$k_E = R_F + \beta\,(k_M - R_F)$		
$R_M - R_F = .08$	$= .09 + \beta(.08)$		
Consolidated Edison	**Delta Airlines**	**Digital Equipment**	**Adobe**
$\beta_{Consolidated} = .75$	$\beta_{Delta} = 1.20$	$\beta_{DEC} = 1.05$	$\beta_{Adobe} = 1.80$
$k_E = .06 + .75(.07)$	$k_E = .06 + 1.20(.07)$	$k_E = .06 + 1.05(.07)$	$k_E = .06 + 1.80(.07)$
$= .11$	$= .14$	$= .13$	$= .19$

Estimates of the cost of equity capital for four firms are presented in Table E. Plugging the assumed values of R_F, k_M, and β into the SML generates estimates of k_E. As expected, the low-risk utility has an estimated cost of equity below that of the other three firms.

The assumed value of k_M represents a major potential source of error in these estimates. High and low estimates of k_M can be used to generate a reasonable range of estimates of k_E. The estimation of β also introduces error into the estimate of k_E.

The CAPM and Risk-Adjusted Discount Rates

The CAPM provides a conceptual framework for determining the k_E appropriate for a subsidiary's capital budgeting decisions. Assume that the holding company described in Figure VI has no debt outstanding. The parent company owns all the equity in its subsidiaries, and the holding company's stock is publicly traded.[3] Such a firm can be viewed as a portfolio of assets. Its stock's beta is a weighted average of the betas associated with the riskiness of each subsidiary industry. Suppose that the parent company's beta is 1. However, the appropriate cost of equity capital for capital budgeting purposes is not the k_E derived from the beta of the holding company's stock. The cost of equity capital used to evaluate investment proposals for a subsidiary should reflect the risk associated with the industry in which that subsidiary operates. Thus, while the holding company's beta of 1 yields a k_E of 13%, investments in the utility subsidiary should be evaluated using a lower k_E, since the utility industry is less risky than the other subsidiary industries. Therefore, the market's expected (or required) return is lower for investments in the utility subsidiary. Since the airline industry is risky, a higher k_E should be used in capital budgeting for an airline subsidiary.

Application of the firm's overall k_E to the individual subsidiaries would result in poor decisions. Good projects in the utility subsidiary would be rejected, while poor projects in the airline subsidiary would be accepted. When the cost of equity capital used in a subsidiary's capital budgeting decisions reflects the risk associated with that subsidiary's line of business, this ensures that project returns are measured against the returns shareholders would expect to receive on alternative investments of corresponding risk.

How can we estimate the beta appropriate for a subsidiary? An obvious approach is to use the beta on similar independent firms operating in the same industry. The resulting estimates of k_E reflect the risk level of the industry and are therefore appropriate

[3]The cost of equity is appropriate to evaluate capital investment only when the firm is all equity-financed. The note "Leveraged Betas and the Cost of Equity" explains how to estimate the cost of capital for firms that are financed with debt.

FIGURE VI
Corporate Structure of a Holding Company with Three Subsidiaries

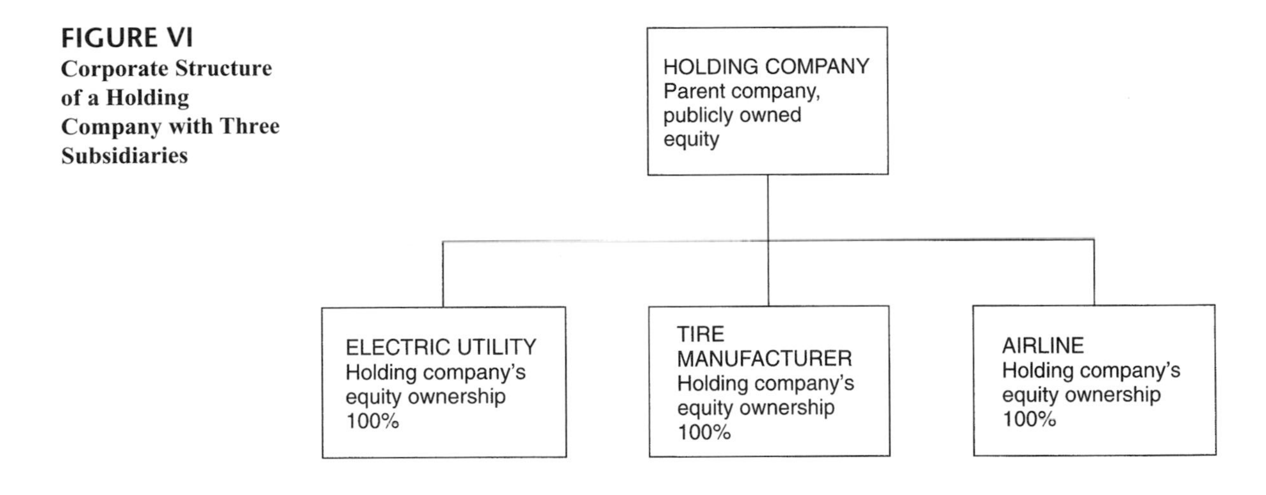

for investment decisions concerning a subsidiary operating in the same industry. If there are no independent firms in the industry, an intuitive estimate of beta can be made. This estimate would reflect the degree to which the subsidiary's earnings and cash flows tend to move in concert with other firm's earnings and cash flows.

Conclusion and Caveats

The CAPM is widely applied in investment management and corporate financial management. Although some of the model's assumptions are clearly unrealistic, empirical tests demonstrate that there is a strong relation between returns and risk as measured by beta. However, the nature and stability of the relations predicted by the SML are not fully supported by these tests. Furthermore, application of the CAPM requires estimating $k_M - R_F$, the market risk premium, and R_F, the risk-free rate. The estimates of beta are also subject to error. Thus, the CAPM should not be relied upon as the sole answer to cost-of-capital determination.

Nevertheless, the model has much to say about the way returns are determined in the securities market. The cost of equity capital is inherently difficult to measure. The shortcomings of the CAPM appear less severe than those of alternative methods of estimating the cost of equity capital (for instance, the dividend growth model). Though imperfect, the CAPM represents an important approach to this difficult task. Using the CAPM in conjunction with more traditional approaches, corporate financial managers can develop realistic, useful estimates of the cost of equity capital.

Cost of Capital at Ameritrade

In mid-1997, Joe Ricketts, Chairman and CEO of Ameritrade Holding Corporation, wanted to improve his company's competitive position in deep-discount brokerage[1] by taking advantage of emerging economies of scale. The success of the strategy required Ameritrade grow its customer base. The growth would require substantial investments in technology, to improve service and capacity, and in advertising, to increase customer awareness. The strategy would require large expenditures relative to Ameritrade's existing capital. In order to evaluate whether the strategy would generate sufficient future cash flows to merit the investment, Ricketts needed an estimate of the project's risk.

Company Background

Formed in 1971, Ameritrade has been a pioneer in the deep-discount brokerage sector. Not only did Ameritrade help create the deep discount market, but it also was the first to offer many new services that changed the way individual investors managed their portfolios. Ameritrade, for example, was the first to offer automated touch-tone phone trading (1988), online Internet trading[2] (1994), a personal digital assistant to access trades (1995), and online program investing for individual investors (1996).

The average return on equity during 1975 to 1996 was 40%, as all years, except two, posted a positive return. Recent returns on equity were much higher, with each of the most recent five years having larger returns than the 40% average.

In March 1997, Ameritrade (NASDAQ: AMTD) raised $22.5 million in an initial public offering allowing the company to continue its long tradition of adopting the latest advances in technology, and to substantially increase advertising to build its brand and improve market share.

Revenue Sources

Exhibit 1 displays Ameritrade's income statement for the fiscal years 1995–1997, and Exhibit 2 presents the balance sheet for 1996 and 1997.

Ameritrade's two primary sources of revenue were from transaction and net interest. Transaction revenues consisted of brokerage commissions, clearing fees, and payment for order flow, which were cash payments received by Ameritrade for routing orders to execution agents. Interest revenues were generated by charging customers on debt balances

[1]Deep-discount brokers offer no-frills execution of equity and fixed income transactions for a minimal fee.

[2]In 1995 Ameritrade acquired K. Aufhauser & Company, which in 1994 launched the first Internet trading site.

Professors Mark Mitchell and Erik Stafford prepared this case with the assistance of Research Associates Jose Camacho and Aldo Sesia as the basis for class discussion rather than to illustrate either effective or ineffective handling of an administrative situation.

Copyright © 2000 by the President and Fellows of Harvard College. To order copies or request permission to reproduce materials, call 1-800-545-7685, write Harvard Business School Publishing, Boston, MA 02163, or go to http://www.hbsp.harvard.edu. No part of this publication may be reproduced, stored in a retrieval system, used in a spreadsheet, or transmitted in any form or by any means—electronic, mechanical, photocopying, recording, or otherwise—without the permission of Harvard Business School.

maintained in brokerage accounts and the investment of customers' cash segregated in compliance with federal regulations in short-term marketable securities. Interest revenues were offset by interest payments to customers based on credit balances maintained in brokerage accounts.

Virtually all of Ameritrade's revenues were directly linked to the stock market. Investors generally curtailed trading activity and their borrowing in response to sustained downward movements in the stock market. For example, trading activity declined more than 20% in 1988 following the stock market crash of October 19, 1987. A substantial decline in the stock market could therefore lead to a steep decline in Ameritrade's brokerage commissions and net interest revenues.

Full-service brokers were less sensitive to market movements than deep-discount brokers like Ameritrade. Full-service brokers received asset management fees, which partially shielded the revenue stream from market declines. Moreover, most full-service brokerage firms such as Merrill Lynch diversified their revenue stream by engaging in investment banking activities such as mergers and security underwritings.

Planned Investments and the Cost of Capital

Ricketts planned to grow Ameritrade's revenues by targeting self-directed investors. Ricketts decided Ameritrade's mission was "to be the largest brokerage firm worldwide based on the number of trades."

Ricketts' strategy called for price cutting, technology enhancements, and increased advertising. First, Ameritrade would reduce commissions from $29.95 to $8.00 per trade for all Internet market orders. There were currently no major players in this price range although many customers were price sensitive. To ensure competitors such as Charles Schwab and E*Trade did not follow Ameritrade's lead and try to compete on price, Ameritrade would have to become the low cost provider of reliable online brokerage services. State of the art technology was the only way to prevent system outages and move towards the goal of 100% reliability. Therefore, up to $100 million would be budgeted for technology enhancements, which also would increase trade execution speed—an important attribute to individual investors. Finally, Ameritrade's advertising budget would be increased to $155 million for the 1998 and 1999 fiscal years combined.

In order to gauge the financial impact of the advertising program and the investment in physical plant and technology, there needed to be some accounting for the project's risk. The plan would only create value if the investment returned more than it cost. Surely the providers of capital would demand a return that reflected the riskiness of the investment. Joe Ricketts strongly believed that his role as CEO was to maximize shareholder value. If the expected returns on investment were greater than the cost of capital, he was going to invest, even if there was a chance of bankrupting the firm. Ricketts felt that the expected return on investment was very high, on the order of 30% to 50%. But, he also knew that some members of his management team were not nearly as optimistic as he was, estimating the expected investment returns at only 10% to 15%. But what was the cost of capital?

Recently, a CS First Boston analyst report employed a discount rate of 12% when evaluating Ameritrade. The CFO at Ameritrade often used a 15% discount rate, while there were some managers at Ameritrade who felt that the borrowing cost of 8–9% was the appropriate rate by which to discount the future profit estimates. There was also the issue of the type of business that Ameritrade was in. Was Ameritrade a discount brokerage firm or instead a technology/Internet firm? A recent analyst report from ABN-AMRO valued Ameritrade on a comparables basis using Internet firms such as Yahoo, Mecklermedia, and Netscape. In addition, E*Trade management continued to insist that E*Trade, while deriving all of its revenues from brokerage operations, was not a brokerage firm, and thus should not be valued as such.

Joe Ricketts hired a consultant to provide a cost of capital estimate that could be used in evaluating Ameritrade's upcoming investments. Exhibits 3–6 provide information that was considered in estimating the cost of capital for Ameritrade.

EXHIBIT 1 **Consolidated Annual Income Statements for the Fiscal Year Ending in September**

Source: Ameritrade Annual Report, 1997.

	1997	1996	1995
Net Revenues			
Transaction Income	$ 51,936,902	$ 36,469,561	$ 23,977,481
Net Interest	18,193,946	11,477,878	8,434,584
Other	7,107,492	6,391,314	2,607,538
Total Net Revenues	77,238,340	54,338,753	35,019,603
Expenses Excluding Interest			
Employee Compensation	19,290,808	14,049,642	8,481,977
Commissions and Clearance	3,320,262	2,530,642	2,516,796
Communications	5,623,468	3,685,535	2,352,590
Occupancy and Equipment Cost	5,422,839	2,889,654	1,626,725
Advertising and Promotion	13,970,834	7,537,265	4,842,392
Provision for Losses	59,000	148,014	1,428,663
Amortization of Goodwill	363,002	363,002	94,152
Other	7,763,014	4,717,406	2,846,280
Total Expenses Excluding Interest	55,813,227	35,921,160	24,189,575
Income Before Income Taxes	21,425,113	18,417,593	10,830,028
Taxes	7,602,964	7,259,248	3,798,881
Net Income	$ 13,822,149	$ 11,158,345	$ 7,031,147
EPS	$ 1.00	$ 0.87	$ 0.55
Shares Outstanding	13,768,889	12,813,823	12,813,823

EXHIBIT 2 **Consolidated Annual Balance Sheets for the Fiscal Year Ending in September**

Source: Ameritrade Annual Report, 1997.

	1997	1996
ASSETS		
Cash & Cash Equivalents	$ 53,522,447	$ 15,767,170
Cash & Investments Segregated in Compliance with Federal Regulations	319,763,921	175,668,497
Receivable from Brokers, Dealers, & Clearing Organizations	17,823,640	15,096,862
Receivable from Customers & Correspondents	325,407,147	166,075,055
Furniture, Equipment, & Leasehold Improvements	8,709,923	3,746,178
Goodwill	6,346,763	6,709,765
Equity Investments	7,597,972	7,157,783
Other Investments	5,000,000	5,000,000
Deferred Income Taxes	39,314	444,378
Other Assets	13,145,616	6,013,544
Total Assets	$ 757,356,743	$ 401,679,232
LIABILITIES & STOCKHOLDERS' EQUITY		
Liabilities:		
Payable to Brokers, Dealers, & Clearing Organizations	1,404,999	1,193,479
Payable to Customers & Correspondents	666,279,440	356,942,970
Accounts Payable and Accrued Liabilities	19,252,931	7,221,008
Notes Payable to Bank	–	4,853,000
Income Taxes Payable	3,430,279	806,711
Total Liabilities	690,367,649	371,017,168
Stockholders' Equity:		
Class A Common Stock	131,534	114,494
Class B Common Stock	13,644	13,644
Additional Paid in Capital	23,297,506	809,665
Retained Earnings	43,546,410	29,724,261
Total Stockholders' Equity	66,989,094	30,662,064
Total Liabilities & Stockholders' Equity	$ 757,356,743	$ 401,679,232

EXHIBIT 3 Capital Market Return Data (Historical and Current)

Source: Yields are from Datastream, historical data are from Ibbotson Associates, *SBBI 2000 Yearbook.*

Prevailing Yields on U.S. Government Securities (August 31, 1997)	
	Annualized Yield to Maturity
3-Month T-Bills	5.24%
1-Year Bonds	5.59%
5-Year Bonds	6.22%
10-Year Bonds	6.34%
20-Year Bonds	6.69%
30-Year Bonds	6.61%

Historic Average Total Annual Returns on U.S. Government Securities and Common Stocks (1950–1996)		
	Average Annual Return	**Standard Deviation**
T-Bills	5.2%	3.0%
Intermediate Bonds[a]	6.4%	6.6%
Long Term Bonds[b]	6.0%	10.8%
Large Company Stocks[c]	14.0%	16.8%
Small Company Stocks[d]	17.8%	25.6%

Historic Average Total Annual Returns on U.S. Government Securities and Common Stocks (1929–1996)		
	Average Annual Return	**Standard Deviation**
T-Bills	3.8%	3.3%
Intermediate Bonds[a]	5.4%	5.8%
Long Term Bonds[b]	5.5%	9.2%
Large Company Stocks[c]	12.7%	20.3%
Small Company Stocks[d]	17.7%	34.1%

[a]Portfolio of U.S. Government bonds with maturity near 5 years.
[b]Portfolio of U.S. Government bonds with maturity near 20 years.
[c]Standard and Poor's 500 Stock Price Index.
[d]A subset of small cap stocks traded on the NYSE (1926–1981); Dimensional Fund Advisor's Small Company Fund (1982–1997).

EXHIBIT 4 Selected Data for Comparable Firms

Source: Compustat; Standard & Poor's; company public filings

	Debt/Value (Market Values)		Debt/Value (Book Values)		
Firm Name *(Industry)*	**Current**	**Avg 1992–1996**	**Current**	**Avg 1992–1996**	**Brokerage Revenues (%)**
A G Edwards *(Investment Services)*[a]	0.00	0.00	0.00	0.00	57
Bear Stearns *(Investment Services)*	0.60	0.50	0.69	0.60	35
Charles Schwab Corp *(Discount Brokerage)*	0.05	0.08	0.25	0.30	82
E*Trade *(Discount Brokerage)*	0.00	NA	0.00	NA	95
Lehman Brothers *(Investment Services)*	0.79	NA	0.80	0.79[b]	13
Mecklermedia *(Internet)*	0.00	0.00[b]	0.00	0.00[b]	0
Merrill Lynch & Co *(Investment Services)*	0.57	0.52	0.77	0.65	37
Morgan Stanley Dean Witter *(Investment Services)*	0.57	0.53	0.70	0.63	12
Netscape *(Internet)*	0.00	NA	0.00	NA	0
Paine Webber *(Investment Service)*	0.51	0.53	0.63	0.58	46
Quick & Reilly Group *(Discount Brokerage)*	0.00	0.00	0.00	0.00	81
Raymond James Financial *(Investment Services)*	0.05	0.04	0.07	0.06	51
Waterhouse Investor Srvcs *(Discount Brokerage)*	NA	0.38	NA	0.70[c]	99
Yahoo *(Internet)*	0.00	NA	0.00	NA	0

[a]Investment Services includes brokerage, asset management, investment banking, and trading.
[b]Indicates average over 1993–1996.
[c]Indicates average over 1992–1995.

EXHIBIT 5
Stock Price Data for Discount Brokers

Source: Center for Research on Security Prices, University of Chicago.

Ameritrade				
Date	Shares	Price	Dividend	Stock Split
31-Mar-97	13,153	15.625	-	
30-Apr-97	13,153	12.500	-	
30-May-97	13,153	14.000	-	
30-Jun-97	14,518	15.750	-	
31-Jul-97	14,518	15.375	-	
29-Aug-97	14,518	18.813	-	

Charles Schwab				
Date	Shares	Price	Dividend	Stock Split
30-Sep-87	29,121	15.875	-	
30-Oct-87	29,121	7.875	-	
30-Nov-87	29,121	6.625	-	
31-Dec-87	25,388	6.000	-	
29-Jan-88	25,388	6.500	-	
29-Feb-88	25,388	9.000	-	
31-Mar-88	25,388	7.375	-	
29-Apr-88	25,388	7.625	-	
31-May-88	25,388	6.875	-	
30-Jun-88	25,294	7.250	-	
29-Jul-88	25,294	7.500	-	
31-Aug-88	25,294	6.750	-	
30-Sep-88	25,328	6.750	-	
31-Oct-88	25,328	7.500	-	
30-Nov-88	25,328	6.750	-	
30-Dec-88	25,354	6.750	-	
31-Jan-89	25,354	10.250	-	
28-Feb-89	25,354	8.625	-	
31-Mar-89	25,354	8.875	-	
28-Apr-89	25,354	10.125	-	
31-May-89	25,354	11.750	0.030	
30-Jun-89	25,352	11.000	-	
31-Jul-89	25,352	16.500	0.030	
31-Aug-89	25,352	15.750	-	
29-Sep-89	25,386	14.000	-	
31-Oct-89	25,386	13.000	0.030	
30-Nov-89	25,386	12.500	-	
29-Dec-89	25,332	13.875	-	
31-Jan-90	25,332	13.500	0.030	
28-Feb-90	25,332	15.250	-	
30-Mar-90	25,332	17.000	-	
30-Apr-90	25,332	15.125	0.030	
31-May-90	25,332	15.750	-	
29-Jun-90	25,099	15.250	-	
31-Jul-90	25,099	13.625	0.030	
31-Aug-90	25,099	12.625	-	
28-Sep-90	25,255	11.375	-	
31-Oct-90	25,255	12.625	0.040	
30-Nov-90	25,255	11.875	-	
31-Dec-90	24,464	11.375	-	
31-Jan-91	24,464	16.000	0.040	
28-Feb-91	24,464	18.250	-	
28-Mar-91	24,464	20.250	-	
30-Apr-91	24,464	18.125	0.040	

EXHIBIT 5
(*Continued*)

Charles Schwab				
Date	**Shares**	**Price**	**Dividend**	**Stock Split**
31-May-91	24,464	22.500	-	
28-Jun-91	24,435	24.750	-	
31-Jul-91	24,435	27.500	0.050	
30-Aug-91	24,435	28.375	-	
30-Sep-91	25,596	31.125	-	
31-Oct-91	25,596	37.750	0.060	
29-Nov-91	25,596	32.750	-	
31-Dec-91	38,394	30.375	-	3 for 2
31-Jan-92	38,394	31.875	0.040	
28-Feb-92	38,394	33.250	-	
31-Mar-92	38,479	34.625	-	
30-Apr-92	38,479	28.500	0.060	
29-May-92	38,479	28.875	-	
30-Jun-92	38,626	23.500	-	
31-Jul-92	38,626	24.625	0.060	
31-Aug-92	38,626	22.500	-	
30-Sep-92	38,149	18.000	-	
30-Oct-92	38,149	20.250	0.060	
30-Nov-92	38,149	24.875	-	
31-Dec-92	37,741	26.125	-	
29-Jan-93	37,741	30.250	0.060	
26-Feb-93	37,741	32.375	-	
31-Mar-93	37,741	36.500	-	
30-Apr-93	37,741	32.750	0.075	
28-May-93	37,741	35.250	-	
30-Jun-93	56,612	28.500	-	3 for 2
30-Jul-93	56,612	29.000	0.050	
31-Aug-93	56,612	32.875	-	
30-Sep-93	57,625	34.500	-	
29-Oct-93	57,625	34.625	0.050	
30-Nov-93	57,815	31.875	-	
31-Dec-93	57,815	32.375	-	
31-Jan-94	57,815	29.500	0.070	
28-Feb-94	57,815	27.500	-	
31-Mar-94	57,815	26.875	-	
29-Apr-94	57,815	28.375	0.070	
31-May-94	57,815	30.250	-	
30-Jun-94	57,114	24.750	-	
29-Jul-94	57,114	26.750	0.070	
31-Aug-94	57,114	30.750	-	
30-Sep-94	56,829	29.625	-	
31-Oct-94	56,829	35.375	0.070	
30-Nov-94	57,325	31.875	-	
30-Dec-94	57,325	34.875	-	
31-Jan-95	57,325	40.000	0.090	
28-Feb-95	57,325	44.375	-	
31-Mar-95	85,988	32.250	-	3 for 2
28-Apr-95	85,988	34.250	0.060	
31-May-95	85,988	35.000	-	
30-Jun-95	85,896	43.875	-	
31-Jul-95	85,896	46.125	0.080	
31-Aug-95	87,061	46.625	-	
29-Sep-95	174,122	29.000	-	2 for 1

EXHIBIT 5
(*Continued*)

Charles Schwab				
Date	**Shares**	**Price**	**Dividend**	**Stock Split**
31-Oct-95	174,122	22.875	0.040	
30-Nov-95	174,678	24.250	-	
29-Dec-95	174,678	20.125	-	
31-Jan-96	174,678	25.125	0.040	
29-Feb-96	174,678	25.500	-	
29-Mar-96	174,678	25.875	-	
30-Apr-96	174,032	24.500	0.040	
31-May-96	174,032	24.250	-	
28-Jun-96	174,989	24.500	-	
31-Jul-96	174,989	24.125	0.050	
30-Aug-96	174,989	25.000	-	
30-Sep-96	175,166	23.000	-	
31-Oct-96	175,166	25.000	0.050	
29-Nov-96	175,166	30.250	-	
31-Dec-96	175,173	32.000	-	
31-Jan-97	175,173	37.500	-	
28-Feb-97	175,173	37.500	0.050	
31-Mar-97	175,173	32.000	-	
30-Apr-97	175,068	36.625	-	
30-May-97	175,068	40.625	0.050	
30-Jun-97	175,813	40.500	-	
31-Jul-97	176,422	47.000	-	
29-Aug-97	176,422	42.750	0.050	

E*Trade				
Date	**Shares**	**Price**	**Dividend**	**Stock Split**
30-Aug-96	29,393	10.500	-	
30-Sep-96	29,539	13.188	-	
31-Oct-96	29,539	11.125	-	
29-Nov-96	29,539	10.938	-	
31-Dec-96	29,545	11.500	-	
31-Jan-97	29,545	17.625	-	
28-Feb-97	29,545	24.000	-	
31-Mar-97	30,440	18.000	-	
30-Apr-97	30,440	15.000	-	
30-May-97	30,440	17.625	-	
30-Jun-97	30,958	19.625	-	
31-Jul-97	30,958	30.500	-	
29-Aug-97	30,958	32.125	-	

Quick & Reilly				
Date	**Shares**	**Price**	**Dividend**	**Stock Split**
31-Jan-84	6,318	17.625	-	
29-Feb-84	6,318	15.000	0.050	
30-Mar-84	6,318	14.875	-	
30-Apr-84	6,318	17.125	-	
31-May-84	6,318	17.375	-	
29-Jun-84	6,318	18.000	0.050	
31-Jul-84	6,318	14.750	-	
31-Aug-84	6,318	18.000	0.050	
28-Sep-84	6,318	17.000	-	
31-Oct-84	6,318	17.875	-	
30-Nov-84	6,318	15.250	0.050	

EXHIBIT 5
(*Continued*)

Quick & Reilly				
Date	Shares	Price	Dividend	Stock Split
31-Dec-84	6,318	15.500	-	
31-Jan-85	6,318	23.375	-	
28-Feb-85	6,318	23.750	0.110	
29-Mar-85	6,318	23.125	-	
30-Apr-85	6,318	20.625	-	
31-May-85	6,318	22.625	0.060	
28-Jun-85	6,318	24.000	-	
31-Jul-85	6,318	24.125	-	
30-Aug-85	6,318	22.875	0.060	
30-Sep-85	6,318	20.125	-	
31-Oct-85	6,318	22.250	-	
29-Nov-85	6,318	25.500	0.060	
31-Dec-85	6,318	32.500	-	
31-Jan-86	6,318	36.375	-	
28-Feb-86	6,318	39.125	0.170	
31-Mar-86	6,318	39.000	-	
30-Apr-86	6,318	30.375	-	
30-May-86	11,149	33.375	0.070	
30-Jun-86	11,149	35.500	-	
31-Jul-86	11,149	29.000	-	
29-Aug-86	11,149	28.750	0.070	
30-Sep-86	11,149	23.875	-	
31-Oct-86	11,149	32.125	-	
28-Nov-86	11,149	29.500	0.070	
31-Dec-86	11,149	26.750	-	
30-Jan-87	11,149	36.125	-	
27-Feb-87	11,149	36.875	0.200	
31-Mar-87	11,149	36.000	-	
30-Apr-87	16,724	21.375	-	3 for 2
29-May-87	16,724	21.500	0.055	
30-Jun-87	9,477	19.250	-	
31-Jul-87	9,477	20.250	-	
31-Aug-87	9,477	24.625	0.055	
30-Sep-87	9,477	23.000	-	
30-Oct-87	9,477	12.125	-	
30-Nov-87	9,477	11.625	0.055	
31-Dec-87	9,477	12.500	-	
29-Jan-88	9,477	12.625	-	
29-Feb-88	9,477	13.500	0.180	
31-Mar-88	9,452	12.250	-	
29-Apr-88	9,452	12.625	-	
31-May-88	9,452	11.500	0.060	
30-Jun-88	9,452	11.875	-	
29-Jul-88	9,452	11.500	-	
31-Aug-88	9,452	11.250	0.060	
30-Sep-88	9,452	11.750	-	
31-Oct-88	9,452	11.750	-	
30-Nov-88	9,452	11.500	0.060	
30-Dec-88	9,452	10.875	-	
31-Jan-89	9,452	15.000	-	
28-Feb-89	9,452	13.750	0.060	
31-Mar-89	9,452	13.250	-	
28-Apr-89	9,452	13.000	-	

EXHIBIT 5
(Continued)

Quick & Reilly				
Date	**Shares**	**Price**	**Dividend**	**Stock Split**
31-May-89	9,452	16.125	0.060	
30-Jun-89	9,452	14.000	-	
31-Jul-89	9,452	16.500	-	
31-Aug-89	9,452	17.000	0.060	
29-Sep-89	9,452	16.750	-	
31-Oct-89	9,452	15.750	-	
30-Nov-89	9,452	14.875	0.060	
29-Dec-89	9,452	13.625	-	
31-Jan-90	9,452	12.000	-	
28-Feb-90	9,452	13.625	0.130	
30-Mar-90	9,452	13.250	-	
30-Apr-90	9,452	13.000	-	
31-May-90	9,452	15.250	0.070	
29-Jun-90	9,452	14.000	-	
31-Jul-90	9,452	13.500	-	
31-Aug-90	9,452	11.375	0.070	
28-Sep-90	9,452	10.375	-	
31-Oct-90	9,452	9.750	-	
30-Nov-90	9,452	10.125	0.070	
31-Dec-90	9,437	10.250	-	
31-Jan-91	9,437	13.125	-	
28-Feb-91	9,437	16.125	0.070	
28-Mar-91	9,210	18.875	-	
30-Apr-91	9,210	17.500	-	
31-May-91	9,210	17.750	0.070	
28-Jun-91	9,452	17.000	-	
31-Jul-91	9,452	19.625	-	
30-Aug-91	9,452	20.625	0.070	
30-Sep-91	9,210	19.250	-	
31-Oct-91	9,210	20.375	-	
29-Nov-91	9,210	20.000	0.070	
31-Dec-91	9,220	27.750	-	
31-Jan-92	9,220	27.500	-	
28-Feb-92	9,220	28.500	0.180	
31-Mar-92	9,292	28.625	-	
30-Apr-92	9,292	21.500	-	
29-May-92	9,292	21.500	0.080	
30-Jun-92	9,292	21.000	-	
31-Jul-92	9,292	20.125	-	
31-Aug-92	9,292	19.625	0.080	
30-Sep-92	9,884	20.125	-	
30-Oct-92	9,884	21.000	-	
30-Nov-92	9,884	25.375	0.080	
31-Dec-92	9,884	24.750	-	
29-Jan-93	9,884	27.000	-	
26-Feb-93	9,884	26.000	0.220	
31-Mar-93	9,824	27.125	-	
30-Apr-93	9,824	25.125	-	
28-May-93	9,824	26.125	0.100	
30-Jun-93	10,315	28.875	1.443	
30-Jul-93	10,623	30.750	-	
31-Aug-93	10,623	35.000	0.100	
30-Sep-93	10,643	36.250	-	
29-Oct-93	10,643	35.875	-	

EXHIBIT 5
(Continued)

Quick & Reilly				
Date	**Shares**	**Price**	**Dividend**	**Stock Split**
30-Nov-93	10,678	34.250	0.100	
31-Dec-93	11,212	35.750	1.788	
31-Jan-94	10,678	35.375	-	
28-Feb-94	11,238	28.375	0.270	
31-Mar-94	11,238	25.625	-	
29-Apr-94	11,238	26.375	-	
31-May-94	11,238	26.875	0.120	
30-Jun-94	11,168	25.375	-	
29-Jul-94	11,168	24.750	-	
31-Aug-94	11,121	29.250	0.120	
30-Sep-94	11,121	25.875	-	
31-Oct-94	11,111	25.750	-	
30-Nov-94	11,111	24.750	0.120	
30-Dec-94	11,111	28.375	-	
31-Jan-95	11,075	30.875	-	
28-Feb-95	11,075	35.000	0.290	
31-Mar-95	11,075	35.500	-	
28-Apr-95	11,075	40.625	-	
31-May-95	11,075	47.000	-	
30-Jun-95	16,613	36.625	0.150	3 for 2
31-Jul-95	16,613	38.500	-	
31-Aug-95	16,613	37.375	0.100	
29-Sep-95	16,613	45.875	-	
31-Oct-95	24,920	23.750	-	3 for 2
30-Nov-95	24,952	25.375	0.070	
29-Dec-95	24,952	20.500	-	
31-Jan-96	25,056	23.250	-	
29-Feb-96	25,056	26.250	0.080	
29-Mar-96	25,056	29.500	-	
30-Apr-96	25,056	30.500	-	
31-May-96	25,056	33.875	0.070	
28-Jun-96	25,056	32.500	-	
31-Jul-96	25,178	28.375	-	
30-Aug-96	25,178	29.250	0.080	
30-Sep-96	25,178	26.500	-	
31-Oct-96	25,178	26.250	-	
29-Nov-96	25,178	28.375	0.080	
31-Dec-96	25,178	29.875	-	
31-Jan-97	25,173	36.625	-	
28-Feb-97	25,173	35.000	0.190	
31-Mar-97	37,760	20.875	-	3 for 2
30-Apr-97	37,760	22.125	-	
30-May-97	37,760	23.000	0.060	
30-Jun-97	38,606	23.250	-	
31-Jul-97	38,664	26.250	-	
29-Aug-97	38,664	34.250	0.060	

Waterhouse Investor Services				
Date	**Shares**	**Price**	**Dividend**	**Stock Split**
29-May-87	2,572	6.938	-	
30-Jun-87	2,572	8.000	-	
31-Jul-87	2,572	8.250	-	
31-Aug-87	2,572	7.500	-	

EXHIBIT 5
(*Continued*)

Waterhouse Investor Services				
Date	**Shares**	**Price**	**Dividend**	**Stock Split**
30-Sep-87	2,572	8.000	-	
30-Oct-87	2,572	6.250	-	
30-Nov-87	2,572	6.000	-	
31-Dec-87	2,572	5.250	-	
29-Jan-88	2,572	4.500	-	
29-Feb-88	2,482	4.750	-	
31-Mar-88	2,482	6.000	-	
29-Apr-88	2,482	5.875	-	
31-May-88	2,482	6.250	-	
30-Jun-88	2,482	5.000	-	
29-Jul-88	2,482	3.500	-	
31-Aug-88	2,482	3.250	-	
30-Sep-88	2,482	4.000	-	
31-Oct-88	2,482	3.375	-	
30-Nov-88	2,482	3.500	-	
30-Dec-88	2,482	2.750	-	
31-Jan-89	2,482	3.750	-	
28-Feb-89	2,472	3.750	-	
31-Mar-89	2,472	4.750	-	
28-Apr-89	2,472	4.250	-	
31-May-89	2,420	5.000	-	
30-Jun-89	2,420	6.000	-	
31-Jul-89	2,420	6.000	-	
31-Aug-89	2,419	5.750	0.120	
29-Sep-89	2,419	5.625	-	
31-Oct-89	2,419	5.375	-	
30-Nov-89	2,417	5.000	-	
29-Dec-89	2,417	4.500	-	
31-Jan-90	2,417	4.375	-	
28-Feb-90	2,420	3.750	-	
30-Mar-90	2,420	4.250	-	
30-Apr-90	2,420	4.375	-	
31-May-90	2,572	4.250	-	
29-Jun-90	2,572	4.750	-	
31-Jul-90	2,572	4.625	-	
31-Aug-90	2,377	4.375	0.150	
28-Sep-90	2,377	4.250	-	
31-Oct-90	2,377	4.000	-	
30-Nov-90	2,370	3.750	-	
31-Dec-90	2,370	3.625	-	
31-Jan-91	2,370	3.750	-	
28-Feb-91	2,320	4.500	-	
28-Mar-91	2,320	6.125	-	
30-Apr-91	2,320	7.000	-	
31-May-91	2,320	8.250	-	
28-Jun-91	2,900	8.000	-	5 for 4
31-Jul-91	2,900	10.375	-	
30-Aug-91	2,943	10.750	0.160	
30-Sep-91	2,943	14.250	-	
31-Oct-91	2,943	14.000	-	
29-Nov-91	2,943	15.500	-	
31-Dec-91	2,943	27.500	-	
31-Jan-92	2,943	26.500	-	
28-Feb-92	4,415	21.750	-	3 for 2

EXHIBIT 5
(Continued)

Waterhouse Investor Services				
Date	Shares	Price	Dividend	Stock Split
31-Mar-92	4,466	25.375	-	
30-Apr-92	4,466	20.625	-	
29-May-92	4,466	21.750	-	
30-Jun-92	4,466	17.125	-	
31-Jul-92	4,466	17.625	-	
31-Aug-92	4,466	13.750	0.200	
30-Sep-92	4,847	14.375	-	
30-Oct-92	4,847	15.625	-	
30-Nov-92	4,847	20.750	-	
31-Dec-92	4,847	20.500	-	
29-Jan-93	4,847	25.250	-	
26-Feb-93	4,847	24.375	-	
31-Mar-93	6,071	20.500	-	5 for 4
30-Apr-93	6,071	18.500	-	
28-May-93	6,071	27.250	-	
30-Jun-93	6,072	33.500	-	
30-Jul-93	6,072	33.000	-	
31-Aug-93	6,072	42.625	0.250	
30-Sep-93	6,072	50.125	-	
29-Oct-93	6,072	47.250	-	
30-Nov-93	9,108	25.750	-	3 for 2
31-Dec-93	9,150	21.250	-	
31-Jan-94	9,150	21.250	-	
28-Feb-94	9,150	20.500	-	
31-Mar-94	9,150	17.625	-	
29-Apr-94	9,150	16.000	-	
31-May-94	9,150	15.250	-	
30-Jun-94	9,150	13.375	-	
29-Jul-94	9,150	13.000	-	
31-Aug-94	9,150	17.000	0.200	
30-Sep-94	9,150	14.125	-	
31-Oct-94	9,150	16.125	-	
30-Nov-94	9,150	14.250	-	
30-Dec-94	9,154	12.250	-	
31-Jan-95	9,154	14.500	-	
28-Feb-95	9,154	17.375	-	
31-Mar-95	9,154	16.125	-	
28-Apr-95	9,154	15.625	-	
31-May-95	9,154	17.500	-	
30-Jun-95	9,154	23.000	-	
31-Jul-95	9,154	27.625	-	
31-Aug-95	9,154	28.625	0.250	
29-Sep-95	11,442	25.500	-	5 for 4
31-Oct-95	11,442	19.750	-	
30-Nov-95	11,442	19.750	-	
29-Dec-95	11,452	24.750	-	
31-Jan-96	11,452	23.625	-	
29-Feb-96	11,452	24.625	-	
29-Mar-96	11,452	33.375	-	
30-Apr-96	11,452	36.250	-	
31-May-96	11,458	36.625	-	
28-Jun-96	11,458	37.125	-	
31-Jul-96	11,501	37.625	-	
30-Aug-96	11,501	37.375	0.220	
30-Sep-96	11,501	37.875	-	

EXHIBIT 6 **Stock Return Data for Investment Service Firms, Internet Firms, and the Aggregate Stock Market**

Source: Center for Research on Security Prices, University of Chicago.

Date	AG Edwards	Bear Stearns	Lehman Bros	Meckler-media	Merrill Lynch	Morgan Stanley Dean Witter	Netscape	Paine Webber	Raymond James	Yahoo	VW NYSE, AMEX, & Nasdaq[a]	EW NYSE, AMEX, & Nasdaq[a]
31-Jan-84	0.026040				–0.013280			–0.042860	0.040000		–0.012910	0.005760
29-Feb-84	–0.111680				–0.167330			–0.175370	–0.102560		–0.039170	–0.053810
30-Mar-84	–0.042290				–0.019140			0.073300	–0.050000		0.013450	0.007100
30-Apr-84	0.012050				–0.011710			0.080510	–0.067670		0.002730	–0.019420
31-May-84	–0.017860				–0.044780			–0.113730	–0.072580		–0.052350	–0.050770
29-Jun-84	0.100610				0.119790			0.084960	–0.043480		0.023590	0.013800
31-Jul-84	0.016670				–0.076280			–0.090160	0.018180		–0.020350	–0.047450
31-Aug-84	0.178140				0.304570			0.189190	0.214290		0.112570	0.089620
28-Sep-84	–0.032710				–0.077820			–0.105300	–0.029410		0.000390	0.000270
31-Oct-84	0.024150				0.023630			0.029790	0.015150		0.000130	–0.020890
30-Nov-84	–0.066040				–0.091290			–0.041320	–0.179100		–0.010620	–0.031410
31-Dec-84	–0.017170				–0.013700			–0.046550	–0.054550		0.023790	0.005050
31-Jan-85	0.331610				0.277780			0.431820	0.430770		0.085730	0.122760
28-Feb-85	–0.007780				–0.023190			–0.022220	0.027030		0.017000	0.047140
29-Mar-85	–0.036860				–0.085820			0.026620	0.013160		–0.001930	–0.008530
30-Apr-85	–0.094260				–0.034290			–0.123810	–0.025970		–0.002180	–0.011290
31-May-85	0.085970				0.089360			0.065220	0.013330		0.055870	0.022930
28-Jun-85	0.102500				0.011720			–0.040140	0.039470		0.017190	0.003470
31-Jul-85	–0.064640				0.040930			–0.092530	0.017720		–0.000540	0.019510
30-Aug-85	–0.036590				–0.052240			–0.038430	0.025000		–0.004800	–0.003410
30-Sep-85	–0.132490				–0.141730			–0.049180	–0.048780		–0.039650	–0.056140
31-Oct-85	0.088240				0.100920			0.008620	0.000000		0.044570	0.018960
29-Nov-85	0.099100	–0.103450			0.127500			0.197440	0.256410		0.069270	0.053270
31-Dec-85	0.141800	0.193590			0.022300			0.003580	0.015920		0.043060	0.029130
31-Jan-86	0.039710	0.156760			0.152730			0.107140	0.288890		0.009860	0.043400
28-Feb-86	0.149310	0.130840			0.036590			0.068390	0.103450		0.072840	0.062360
31-Mar-86	0.083990	0.128720			0.012230			0.036360	0.171880		0.053880	0.047720
30-Apr-86	–0.086830	0.065640			–0.102720	0.051150		–0.137430	–0.100000		–0.008060	0.015840
30-May-86	0.026070	0.003620			–0.008080	0.013420		0.051530	–0.007410		0.050810	0.036630
30-Jun-86	–0.066370	–0.168520			–0.054610	–0.062910		–0.116500	–0.040600		0.014300	0.008960
31-Jul-86	–0.067630	–0.141920			–0.039710	–0.070670		–0.010990	–0.187500		–0.059690	–0.073610
29-Aug-86	0.104660	0.160310			0.145110	0.149050		0.175930	0.038460		0.066390	0.022110
30-Sep-86	–0.094340	–0.145530			–0.052810	–0.119400		–0.015590	–0.092590		–0.079140	–0.060490
31-Oct-86	0.151040	0.217050			0.195120	0.160830		0.172690	0.081630		0.049440	0.024620
28-Nov-86	–0.022620	–0.057320			–0.074050	–0.030890		–0.075210	–0.056600		0.015170	–0.006280

EXHIBIT 6 *(Continued)*

Date	A G Edwards	Bear Stearns	Lehman Bros	Meckler-media	Merrill Lynch	Morgan Stanley Dean Witter	Netscape	Paine Webber	Raymond James	Yahoo	VW NYSE, AMEX, & Nasdaq[a]	EW NYSE, AMEX, & Nasdaq[a]
31-Dec-86	−0.040740	−0.102160			−0.075950	−0.129190		−0.063200	−0.026800		−0.026540	−0.034530
30-Jan-87	0.334950	0.318180			0.198630	0.112910		0.178570	0.319590		0.128370	0.116820
27-Feb-87	0.000000	−0.022990			−0.015430	−0.048610		−0.033540	0.289060		0.047630	0.074950
31-Mar-87	0.044950	−0.024650			−0.002920	0.036500		−0.003500	0.261940		0.023240	0.033090
30-Apr-87	−0.122380	−0.121020			−0.152050	0.005280		−0.084210	−0.116400		−0.017130	−0.019610
29-May-87	−0.023900	−0.028990			−0.041380	0.020320		−0.061150	−0.101800		0.005220	0.000710
30-Jun-87	−0.104650	0.022090			0.010870	−0.003440		0.020490	−0.031200		0.043830	0.022010
31-Jul-87	0.073390	−0.007350			0.100360	0.023490		0.052210	−0.062070		0.044050	0.034700
31-Aug-87	0.027180	0.103700			0.032570	0.069370		0.023050	0.169120		0.037230	0.015590
30-Sep-87	−0.071130	0.080270			−0.031750	0.023730		−0.029960	−0.142640		−0.020740	−0.015510
30-Oct-87	−0.337840	−0.400000			−0.357380	−0.337560		−0.474900	−0.352940		−0.224870	−0.270850
30-Nov-87	−0.174420	−0.145830			−0.153060	−0.163930		−0.021760	−0.113640		−0.072900	−0.052300
31-Dec-87	0.033330	0.023900			0.091460	0.148460		−0.128790	−0.038450		0.070410	0.027940
29-Jan-88	0.080650	0.144580			0.072630	−0.019510		0.113040	0.137600		0.045340	0.078110
29-Feb-88	0.062390	0.157890			0.062500	0.168660		0.109690	−0.035290		0.051610	0.062010
31-Mar-88	−0.035460	−0.054550			−0.064360	0.055560		−0.078010	0.089270		−0.017060	0.034370
29-Apr-88	0.029410	0.019420			0.000000	0.106880		−0.038460	−0.067420		0.011000	0.015250
31-May-88	−0.042860	−0.085710			0.031750	−0.086240		0.032320	−0.048190		0.000940	−0.017020
30-Jun-88	0.159400	0.093750			0.113990	0.275100		0.070310	−0.008610		0.051390	0.048480
29-Jul-88	−0.006490	−0.067310			0.013950	0.004720		−0.036500	0.025640		−0.007180	0.000550
31-Aug-88	−0.039220	−0.041240			−0.050460	−0.015720		0.038180	−0.050000		−0.027940	−0.023710
30-Sep-88	0.084080	0.028670			0.039020	−0.003190		0.036760	0.017370		0.037280	0.018700
31-Oct-88	−0.006330	0.084210			0.051640	0.051280		−0.028370	0.157630		0.017650	−0.011780
30-Nov-88	−0.057320	0.029130			−0.049550	−0.036700		−0.065400	−0.069770		−0.016400	−0.036700
30-Dec-88	0.042970	−0.038100			−0.090050	0.053970		0.015750	0.105000		0.020800	0.019540
31-Jan-89	0.169930	0.178220			0.270830	0.078310		0.116280	0.193180		0.065940	0.063130
28-Feb-89	−0.044690	0.001010			−0.037190	0.032400		0.028060	0.051430		−0.016360	0.002790
31-Mar-89	−0.038830	0.025420			−0.047210	0.006110		−0.047620	−0.009090		0.021550	0.017030
28-Apr-89	−0.006130	−0.041320			0.040540	−0.055060		0.014290	0.018350		0.048530	0.030680
31-May-89	0.154320	0.068710			0.060610	0.137630		0.070700	0.090090		0.039650	0.027370
30-Jun-89	−0.003420	0.034190			−0.061730	−0.017010		−0.026490	0.069420		−0.004980	−0.008330
31-Jul-89	0.178380	0.107440			0.232460	0.110000		0.258500	0.147290		0.077720	0.031610
31-Aug-89	0.087160	0.034850			−0.039430	0.062610		0.016430	−0.013510		0.022280	0.019290
29-Sep-89	0.008270	−0.083970			−0.108210	−0.063830		−0.160430	0.009590		−0.001750	0.004470
31-Oct-89	−0.148150	−0.075000			−0.025100	−0.069580		−0.121020	−0.122450		−0.029380	−0.050950
30-Nov-89	0.103260	−0.034950			−0.086580	0.050940		−0.014200	0.015500		0.017850	−0.008220

EXHIBIT 6 *(Continued)*

Date	A G Edwards	Bear Stearns	Lehman Bros	Meckler-media	Merrill Lynch	Morgan Stanley Dean Witter	Netscape	Paine Webber	Raymond James	Yahoo	VW NYSE, AMEX, & Nasdaq[a]	EW NYSE, AMEX, & Nasdaq[a]
29-Dec-89	–0.096750	0.009430			–0.004740	–0.071810		0.000000	–0.061070		0.018280	–0.012170
31-Jan-90	–0.115380	–0.028040			–0.133330	–0.077370		–0.037040	–0.012360		–0.070050	–0.045810
28-Feb-90	0.055900	0.060770			0.000000	0.029540		0.038770	0.148760		0.014980	0.015750
30-Mar-90	0.137410	–0.038460			–0.033330	0.008200		0.044780	0.075400		0.024150	0.022040
30-Apr-90	–0.104170	–0.020000			–0.034480	0.028460		–0.042860	–0.013420		–0.028160	–0.026720
31-May-90	0.203490	0.179290			0.138550	0.129220		0.119700	0.118910		0.088870	0.046650
29-Jun-90	–0.007920	–0.009170			–0.047620	0.024650		0.013420	–0.036590		–0.004300	0.005380
31-Jul-90	–0.058820	–0.083330			0.061110	–0.163230		–0.066230	0.000000		–0.009380	–0.027290
31-Aug-90	–0.081460	–0.097780			–0.132280	–0.068180		–0.113190	–0.101270		–0.091730	–0.109790
28-Sep-90	–0.268570	–0.142860			–0.091460	–0.121950		–0.096770	–0.116340		–0.053870	–0.080490
31-Oct-90	0.046880	–0.097220			–0.046980	–0.012630		–0.151790	–0.048000		–0.012420	–0.056330
30-Nov-90	0.119400	0.124920			0.107140	0.092780		0.126740	0.084030		0.065980	–0.036650
31-Dec-90	0.095730	0.125000			0.070970	0.025940		0.037740	0.144500		0.029540	–0.003870
31-Jan-91	0.202450	0.135800			0.186750	0.101150		0.054550	0.074830		0.049040	0.085250
28-Feb-91	0.168370	0.142610			0.172590	0.184870		0.319310	0.219240		0.075690	0.133650
28-Mar-91	0.136940	0.125000			0.218340	0.177300		0.197370	0.270830		0.028780	0.077820
30-Apr-91	0.019310	0.034190			0.089610	–0.015060		0.054950	0.057380		0.003350	0.031020
31-May-91	0.075760	0.094630			0.086090	0.087560		–0.041460	0.063950		0.040590	0.030340
28-Jun-91	–0.099720	–0.128000			–0.064020	–0.103110		–0.142080	–0.041090		–0.044240	–0.034500
31-Jul-91	0.198820	0.110090			0.081430	0.161200		0.095540	0.034290		0.046830	0.034920
30-Aug-91	0.025220	–0.014880			0.018180	0.029970		0.081630	0.038670		0.026910	0.028570
30-Sep-91	0.202900	0.016950			0.148810	0.063490		0.118920	0.114260		–0.011060	0.008670
31-Oct-91	0.076310	0.058330			0.072540	0.081290		0.202900	0.105260		0.017720	0.023860
29-Nov-91	–0.126870	–0.039760			–0.067630	–0.016170		–0.152610	–0.125540		–0.037270	–0.025390
31-Dec-91	0.299660	0.182610			0.231770	0.197180		0.335070	0.217820		0.107040	0.036450
31-Jan-92	–0.056110	0.066180			–0.031710	–0.110040		–0.016040	–0.165530		–0.001650	0.149480
28-Feb-92	–0.066430	0.080000			–0.019650	–0.008850		0.080430	–0.003500		0.013290	0.052010
31-Mar-92	–0.088760	–0.077420			–0.015660	–0.013390		–0.045450	0.128840		–0.023680	–0.014120
30-Apr-92	–0.163220	–0.006990			–0.109090	–0.110860		–0.142860	–0.135510		0.013850	–0.032890
29-May-92	0.098770	0.006690			–0.004080	0.050690		0.049140	–0.086490		0.006520	0.005500
30-Jun-92	–0.078430	–0.022220			0.041240	–0.024330		0.023670	–0.014910		–0.019240	–0.039700
31-Jul-92	–0.006130	–0.045450			0.019800	0.097260		0.069360	0.006020		0.039930	0.027280
31-Aug-92	0.043460	–0.014290			–0.030580	–0.075180		–0.135350	–0.071860		–0.020760	–0.024440
30-Sep-92	–0.071430	0.016260			0.020150	–0.051850		–0.106920	–0.113030		0.012420	0.011930
30-Oct-92	0.115380	0.024000			0.093830	0.031250		0.140850	0.116790		0.010900	0.016320
30-Nov-92	0.166670	0.100390			0.095710	0.075560		0.197280	0.209150		0.040190	0.067730

EXHIBIT 6 *(Continued)*

Date	A G Edwards	Bear Stearns	Lehman Bros	Meckler-media	Merrill Lynch	Morgan Stanley Dean Witter	Netscape	Paine Webber	Raymond James	Yahoo	VW NYSE, AMEX, & Nasdaq[a]	EW NYSE, AMEX, & Nasdaq[a]
31-Dec-92	–0.063840	0.045110			–0.014490	0.051890		0.010360	–0.032430		0.017540	0.035650
29-Jan-93	0.089950	–0.014390			0.098740	0.015700		0.035900	0.137650		0.012330	0.066740
26-Feb-93	–0.019420	–0.005840			0.046650	0.022080		–0.054650	–0.137930		0.005450	–0.007910
31-Mar-93	0.080200	0.081480			0.045870	0.110500		0.089470	0.043660		0.025010	0.030880
30-Apr-93	–0.050690	0.089040			–0.010530	–0.064450		–0.072460	0.005490		–0.025510	–0.012760
28-May-93	–0.052430	0.133330			0.079430	0.102300		0.136460	0.038250		0.029420	0.037950
30-Jun-93	0.051550	0.050280			0.069310	0.051440		0.073730	0.003370		0.005130	0.011970
30-Jul-93	0.063730	0.026600			0.074070	0.019890		0.034330	–0.057890		–0.000760	0.014100
31-Aug-93	0.010140	0.039900			0.118970	0.179360		0.067220	0.154410		0.039340	0.040400
30-Sep-93	0.082570	0.042110			0.010310	0.049770		0.019530	0.087380		0.000610	0.025790
29-Oct-93	0.046610	–0.111110			–0.007400	–0.096260		–0.099620	–0.035710		0.018040	0.040090
30-Nov-93	–0.032390	0.018180			–0.063230	–0.084010		–0.088510	–0.027780		–0.017350	–0.024370
31-Dec-93	–0.032970	–0.016850			–0.074380	–0.013940		0.014080	–0.050000		0.019450	0.016120
31-Jan-94	0.016300	0.114290			0.073210	0.121910		0.097220	0.064960		0.031330	0.048920
28-Feb-94	–0.048130	–0.106670			–0.094710	–0.156850		–0.097050	–0.070920		–0.024090	–0.009490
31-Mar-94	–0.190340	–0.098270		–0.045050	–0.083080	–0.039400		–0.047010	–0.048550		–0.045740	–0.046020
29-Apr-94	–0.013990	0.083330		0.000000	–0.010070	–0.037110		–0.007410	–0.040320		0.009830	–0.010820
31-May-94	0.071770	0.019820		0.905660	0.063860	–0.025560		–0.007760	–0.003030		0.009500	–0.000270
30-Jun-94	–0.080000	–0.165640	–0.166670	–0.128710	–0.102560	–0.048120		–0.053030	–0.016950		–0.027380	–0.026570
29-Jul-94	0.014490	–0.051470	0.050000	–0.011360	0.046430	0.065930		0.032000	–0.068970		0.030410	0.015470
31-Aug-94	0.150000	0.141090	0.039680	–0.275860	0.115490	0.155460		0.015190	0.185190		0.042830	0.036790
30-Sep-94	–0.086210	–0.123290	–0.092310	–0.031750	–0.147690	–0.109320		–0.115380	–0.026250		–0.018650	0.004500
31-Oct-94	0.013700	0.015630	0.050850	–0.311480	0.143830	0.052310		0.060870	–0.032260		0.014870	–0.002400
30-Nov-94	–0.060000	–0.029230	–0.037100	–0.071430	–0.034920	–0.091010		–0.098690	–0.041670		–0.037070	–0.040570
30-Dec-94	0.043480	–0.016000	–0.008400	0.410260	–0.059210	–0.002110		0.100920	–0.026090		0.012750	–0.012860
31-Jan-95	0.020830	0.081300	0.152540	–0.181820	0.030910	0.019070		0.000000	0.095710		0.020550	0.027710
28-Feb-95	0.224490	0.136840	0.069120	0.155560	0.119450	0.120580		0.166330	0.163930		0.039620	0.027990
31-Mar-95	–0.016000	–0.013330	–0.006900	0.730770	0.036590	0.004750		–0.071940	–0.023100		0.026970	0.018740
28-Apr-95	0.039770	0.114860	0.083330	0.566670	0.070590	0.031540		0.062020	0.014490		0.024880	0.025980
31-May-95	–0.010930	0.038180	0.015380	0.517730	0.038680	0.095320		0.160290	0.050000		0.034160	0.020500
30-Jun-95	0.000660	0.055560	0.107590	0.411210	0.117020	0.077180		–0.044300	0.059320		0.030840	0.048690
31-Jul-95	0.088890	0.035090	0.017140	–0.006620	0.057140	0.023720		0.086090	0.122580		0.040670	0.055180
31-Aug-95	–0.005100	–0.061020	0.064040	0.126670	0.042970	0.038860		–0.055120	0.011490		0.009340	0.030380
29-Sep-95	0.098050	0.042420	–0.015870	–0.112430	0.084600	0.116550	0.262630	0.025970	–0.007270		0.036390	0.025990
31-Oct-95	–0.042250	–0.075580	–0.064520	–0.373330	–0.112000	–0.099790	0.408000	0.120250	–0.011490		–0.011150	–0.040580

EXHIBIT 6 (*Continued*)

Date	A G Edwards	Bear Stearns	Lehman Bros	Meckler-media	Merrill Lynch	Morgan Stanley Dean Witter	Netscape	Paine Webber	Raymond James	Yahoo	VW NYSE, AMEX, & Nasdaq[a]	EW NYSE, AMEX, & Nasdaq[a]
30-Nov-95	0.065100	0.101890	0.042530	0.510640	0.004680	−0.008620	0.571020	0.011070	0.052330		0.042970	0.017200
29-Dec-95	−0.115740	−0.086210	−0.060770	−0.098590	−0.081080	−0.065220	0.005420	−0.101120	−0.056570		0.015400	0.009780
31-Jan-95	0.052360	0.157230	0.205880	−0.185550	0.120290	0.185740	0.181650	0.037500	0.035290		0.028090	0.033290
29-Feb-96	−0.034830	0.060870	−0.032200	−0.155880	0.013190	−0.015750	−0.379000	−0.036390	0.005680		0.016050	0.031540
29-Mar-96	0.032370	0.020620	0.080810	0.090910	0.054230	0.109330	−0.186270	0.106920	0.021240		0.011200	0.024120
30-Apr-96	−0.055280	0.015150	−0.051400	0.333330	−0.006170	−0.030290	0.469880	−0.051140	0.005560		0.025130	0.057330
31-May-96	0.090430	0.014180	−0.032510	0.156250	0.077430	−0.014930	0.115780	0.053650	0.005520	−0.058820	0.026720	0.061050
28-Jun-96	0.064780	−0.020730	0.010200	0.094590	0.005790	−0.007580	−0.085400	0.085710	−0.001320	−0.250000	−0.007660	−0.030600
31-Jul-96	0.009220	−0.047620	−0.065660	−0.172840	−0.068330	−0.004070	−0.365460	−0.115790	−0.077350	−0.142860	−0.053390	−0.078620
30-Aug-96	0.022830	0.045560	−0.084320	0.044780	0.014490	−0.020510	−0.104430	−0.012140	0.119760	0.090280	0.032220	0.044770
30-Sep-96	0.045890	−0.005350	0.224850	0.028570	0.075510	0.041880	0.310950	0.018180	0.041500	0.082800	0.052990	0.028970
31-Oct-96	0.025750	0.016130	−0.028990	−0.034720	0.066410	0.013570	−0.045820	0.119050	0.005150	−0.070590	0.013940	−0.019970
29-Nov-96	0.046030	0.170370	0.161190	0.165470	0.146620	0.196520	0.262710	0.154260	0.164100	−0.031650	0.065730	0.024770
31-Dec-96	0.081120	0.013640	0.077250	−0.024690	0.015580	−0.049900	0.017900	0.041290	0.065550	−0.111110	−0.011350	−0.001420
31-Jan-97	0.011150	0.076230	0.007970	0.050630	0.032210	0.003500	−0.334070	0.280000	0.070540	0.992650	0.053040	0.061720
28-Feb-97	0.044120	0.055000	0.065140	0.337350	0.144730	0.105030	−0.231020	−0.089580	0.034880	−0.107010	−0.000880	−0.010430
31-Mar-97	−0.128730	−0.125000	−0.130110	−0.135140	−0.105470	−0.069310	0.032190	−0.134100	−0.050040	−0.070250	−0.044390	−0.047880
30-Apr-97	0.138210	0.161900	0.162390	0.062500	0.110920	0.077870	−0.099790	0.203540	0.108700	0.213330	0.042460	−0.021390
30-May-97	0.060710	0.070490	0.207650	−0.245100	0.115790	0.075250	0.092380	0.048530	0.176470	−0.054950	0.071250	0.085170
30-Jun-97	0.156360	0.051920	−0.012200	−0.012990	0.125000	0.046820	0.084570	−0.014080	−0.001640	0.093020	0.044200	0.044240
31-Jul-97	−0.011700	0.199270	0.231480	0.065790	0.181340	0.220960	0.144250	0.148210	0.057080	0.602840	0.076310	0.048620
29-Aug-97	−0.059170	−0.031400	−0.121600	−0.006170	−0.124050	−0.082240	0.085180	−0.043550	0.002160	0.053100	−0.036450	0.027020

[a]"VW (EW) NYSE, AMEX & Nasdaq" represents the value-weighted (equal-weighted) index of all U.S. publicly traded firms.

Pioneer Petroleum Corporation

One of the critical problems confronting management and the board of Pioneer Petroleum Corporation in July 1991 was the determination of a minimum acceptable rate of return on new capital investments. The company's basic capital budgeting approach was to accept all proposed investments with a positive net present value when discounted at the appropriate cost of capital. At issue was how the appropriate discount rate would be determined.

The company was weighing two alternative approaches for determining a minimum rate of return: (1) a single cutoff rate based on the company's overall weighted average cost of capital, and (2) a system of multiple cutoff rates that reflected the risk-profit characteristics of the several businesses or economic sectors in which the company's subsidiaries operated. The issue had assumed increased importance because of management's decision to extend the use of the cutoff rate to the evaluation of existing operations and investments. It was planned to evaluate divisional managers on the basis of their net profits after the deduction of a charge for capital employed by the division.

Pioneer Petroleum had been formed in 1924 through the merger of several formerly independent firms operating in the oil refining, pipeline transportation, and industrial chemicals fields. Over the next 60 years, the company integrated vertically into exploration and production of crude oil and marketing refined petroleum products, and horizontally into plastics, agricultural chemicals, and real estate development. It was restructured in 1985 as a hydrocarbons-based company, concentrating on oil, gas, coal, and petrochemicals. Pioneer was one of the primary producers of Alaskan crude, and in 1990, Alaska provided 60% of Pioneer's domestic petroleum liquids production. Pioneer was also one of the lowest-cost refiners on the West Coast and had an extensive West Coast marketing network. Pioneer's Alaskan crude production provided all of the crude oil for its West Coast refining and marketing operations. This integration required collaboration and coordination among divisions to optimize overall performance and to decrease overall risk.

In 1990 total revenues exceeded $15.6 billion and net income was over $1.5 billion. (See Exhibit 1 for a financial summary of recent operations.) Volatile oil prices were a major concern for Pioneer. In 1990, for example the price of West Texas Intermediate crude during the first quarter was $21.80 per barrel, and it reached a low of about $15.50 in mid-June. With the Iraqi invasion of Kuwait, crude prices rose to more than $40 per barrel, but they fell to about $25 per barrel as the year ended. The average price of West Texas Intermediate crude during 1990 was about $24.50 per barrel. The management of Pioneer emphasized the importance of operational and financial flexibility to respond to these price swings.

Pioneer spent about $3.1 billion on capital expenditures in 1990 and forecasted capital expenditures of almost $4.5 billion in 1991. Some of these expenditures, like the addition of a sulfur recovery facility and the improvement of a coker, allowed the refineries to process the heavy Alaskan crude oil more efficiently. These types of investments had provided good returns, and the light product yield in Pioneer's refineries was substantially higher than the industry average. Pioneer also invested in exploration and development, as it replaced all its 1990 production with new reserves. Most of this

Copyright © 1991 by the President and Fellows of Harvard College, Harvard Business School case 292–011.

exploration was in the lower 48 states and the Gulf of Mexico. Investments were also directed to environmental projects, and Pioneer anticipated spending an additional $3 billion in the next 5 years to meet the new standards of the 1990 Clean Air Act amendments and the California Air Resources Board's regulations. These environmental regulations also provided opportunities for Pioneer to capitalize on its strengths. Pioneer's gasolines were among the cleanest burning in the industry, and its chemical unit produced about one-third of the world's supply of methyl tertiary butyl ether (MTBE), which was used to make cleaner-burning gasolines. The market for MTBE had been growing, and the new regulations were expected to lead to even higher growth. Also, Pioneer's SMOGMAN service centers specialized in state-required smog checks and related repairs.

Weighted Average Cost of Capital

The company's weighted average cost of capital was calculated in three steps: first, the expected future target proportions of debt and equity in the company's capital structure were estimated; second, costs were assigned to each of these capital components; third, a weighted average cost of capital was calculated on the basis of these proportions and costs (see Table A).

There was a general consensus in management on the future mix of debt and equity in Pioneer's capital structure. A firm policy had been adopted that debt should represent approximately 50% of total capital (defined as total debt plus book equity) to balance the competing objectives of enhancing the returns to shareholders and maintaining financial flexibility. The company was committed to using its dividend and stock repurchase program to maintain appropriate financial leverage. Cash dividends increased by 10% in both 1990 and 1991. Its debt was A rated.

Assigning an after-tax cost to debt was straightforward. Pioneer's investment bankers, Steven, Mitchell, O'Hara, forecasted early in 1990 that the company's future debt issues would require a coupon of 12%, assuming continuation of its debt policy and A rating. At a 34% tax rate, this represented a 7.9% after-tax cost.

The cost of equity had been more difficult to conceptualize or to estimate. After prolonged debate, Pioneer decided to use the current earnings yield on the stock as the cost of both new equity and retained earnings. Advocates pointed out that no dilution of earnings per share would occur if the company earned at least this return on new equity. With earnings per share estimated at $6.15 in 1990 and a market price of $63, cost of equity had been set at 10%.

Divisional Costs of Capital

The alternative proposed by the supporters of multiple cutoff rates in lieu of a single companywide rate involved determining the cost of capital for each division. The divisional rate would reflect the risks inherent in each of the economic sectors or industries

TABLE A 1990 Weighted Average Cost of Capital Calculation

Source	Target Proportion of Future Capital Components	Estimated Future After-Tax Cost	Weighted Cost
Debt	.50	7.9%	4.0%
Equity	.50	10.0	5.0
			9.0%

in which the company's principal operating subsidiaries worked. For example, the divisional cost of capital for production and exploration was 20%, and the divisional cost of capital for transportation was 10%. All the other divisional rates fell within this range. The suggestion was that these multiple cutoff rates determined the minimum acceptable rate of return on proposed capital investments in each of the main operating areas of the company and represented the rate charged to each of the various profit centers for capital employed. However, there were still areas of ambiguity. For example, it was unclear whether all environmental projects would have the same discount rate or the discount rate corresponding to the division.

The divisional cost of capital would be calculated using a weighted average cost of capital approach for each operating sector. The calculations would follow three steps: first, an estimate would be made of the usual debt and equity proportions of independently financed firms operating in each sector. Several such independents competed against each of the company's affiliates. Second, the costs of debt and equity given these proportions and sectors would be estimated in accordance with the concepts followed by the company in estimating its own cost of capital. Third, these costs and proportions would be combined to determine the weighted average cost of capital, or minimum acceptable rate of return, for net present value discounting purposes in each sector.

These multiple hurdle or discount rates had been calculated for several periods in the past, and it invariably turned out that their weighted average, when weighted according to the company's relative investment in each sector, exceeded the company's actual overall average cost of capital. The difference was attributed to the fact that the divisional cost of capital overlooked the risk diversification benefits of many investments undertaken by Pioneer Petroleum. As compared to nonintegrated enterprises operating in any given branch, a vertically and horizontally integrated firm such as Pioneer Petroleum enjoyed some built-in asset diversification and important captive markets between certain of its vertically integrated parts. For example, the risks associated with a refinery investment by an integrated company like Pioneer Petroleum were much less than for an identical investment made by an independent. It was proposed that this diversification premium be allocated back and deducted from the multiple subsidiary discount rates as calculated previously in proportion to the relation between the investment in each subsidiary and the company's total assets.

The Management Discussion

As management and the board of Pioneer Petroleum began their latest review of the alternatives of using single or multiple minimum acceptable cutoff rates, the officers of the operating subsidiaries were asked to restate their positions.

Those supporting the use of a single target rate contended that the stockholders of Pioneer Petroleum expected the company to invest their funds in the highest return projects available. They suggested that, without exception, the affiliates backing multiple rates were those that were unable to compete effectively for new funds when measured against the corporate group's actual cost of capital. Furthermore, it was not obvious that the categories suggested by the advocates of multiple rates were very helpful in grouping projects according to their riskiness. For example, recent experience in tankers had been disastrous for many companies, and yet tanker investments would be initiated by the transportation division and would therefore be subjected to an unrealistically low hurdle rate.

The proponents of multiple divisional hurdle rates argued that a single company-wide cost of capital subsidized the higher-risk divisions at the expense of the lower-risk divisions. Because the cost of capital was too high for the low-risk divisions, too few low-risk investments were made. In the high-risk divisions too much investment occurred because the hurdle rate was too low. As evidence, proponents of multiple rates noted that Pioneer was the only major company that continued to invest heavily in exploration and development, and that it lagged behind its competitors in marketing and transportation investment. The proponents also argued that the companywide cost of capital was too low, and that investments should be required to earn at least as much as an investment in common stocks. The average return since 1980 on the S&P index of common stocks of 16.25% substantially exceeded the 9% companywide cost of capital (see Exhibit 2). If Pioneer was serious about competing over the long run in industries with such disparate risk-profit characteristics, it was absolutely essential to relate internal target rates of return to the individual businesses.

EXHIBIT 1 **Financial Summary, 1983–1990**

	1983	1984	1985	1986	1987	1988	1989	1990
Sales ($ millions)	$20,397	$20,268	$18,594	$12,687	$14,182	$15,259	$13,417	$15,646
Net income ($ millions)	1,133	326	(297)	428	923	1,211	1,542	1,555
Earnings per share	$ 3.38	$ 2.27	$ .86	$ 1.65	$ 3.41	$ 4.43	$ 5.59	$ 6.15
Dividends per share	1.75	1.50	1.20	2.00	2.00	2.00	2.20	2.45
Return on book equity	15.9%	13%	4.8%	11.4%	19.6%	21.2%	26.3%	25%
Beta								.8

EXHIBIT 2 **Information on U.S. Capital Markets, 1980–1990**

	1980	1981	1982	1983	1984	1985	1986	1987	1988	1989	1990
Yields on newly issued Aa industrials	11.8%	14.0%	13.4%	11.9%	12.9%	11.4%	9.4%	9.7%	9.9%	9.5%	9.4%
Yields on 90-day T-bills	11.2	14.7	10.5	8.8	9.9	7.7	6.2	5.5	6.4	3.4	7.8
Realized returns on S&P 500 index of common stocks	32.4	–4.9	21.4	22.5	6.3	32.2	18.5	5.3	16.8	31.5	–3.2

Leveraged Betas and the Cost of Equity

A stock's expected return, its dividend yield plus expected price appreciation, is related to risk. Risk-averse investors must be compensated with higher expected returns for bearing risk. One source of risk is the financial risk incurred by shareholders in a firm that has debt in its capital structure. The objective of this note is to delineate a methodology for measuring the risk associated with financial leverage and estimating its impact on the cost of equity capital.

Financial Leverage and Risk

The presence of debt in a firm's capital structure has an impact on the risk borne by its shareholders. In the absence of debt, shareholders are subjected only to basic business or operating risk. This business risk is determined by factors such as the volatility of a firm's sales and its level of operating leverage. As compensation for incurring business risk, investors require a premium in excess of the return they could earn on a riskless security such as a Treasury bill. Thus, in the absence of financial leverage, a stock's expected return can be thought of as the risk-free rate plus a premium for business risk.

The addition of debt to a firm's capital structure increases the risk borne by its shareholders. One course of additional risk is the increased risk of financial distress (e.g., bankruptcy). A second source is the effect of financial leverage on the volatility of shareholders' returns. The fixed obligations associated with debt amplify the variations in a firm's operating cash flows. The result is a more volatile stream of shareholders' returns. For investors to hold the shares of firms with debt in their capital structures, they must be compensated for the additional risk generated by financial leverage. The additional risk premium associated with the presence of debt in a firm's capital structure is the financial risk premium.

The expected return on a firm's stock is the risk-free rate plus a premium for risk:

$$\text{Expected return} = \text{Risk-free rate} + \text{Risk premium}$$

The risk premium consists of a premium for business risk and a premium for financial risk:

$$\text{Expected return} = \begin{matrix}\text{Risk-free} \\ \text{rate}\end{matrix} + \begin{matrix}\text{Business risk} \\ \text{premium}\end{matrix} + \begin{matrix}\text{Financial risk} \\ \text{premium}\end{matrix}$$

This relation can be expressed in symbols:

$$R_S = R_F + BRP + FRP$$

Thus, the expected return on a firm's stock can be decomposed into three components. These components are: (1) the return on a riskless security, R_F; (2) a premium reflecting the firm's basic business (or operating) risk in the absence of financial leverage, *BRP;* and (3) a premium for the additional risk created by the existence of debt in a firm's capital structure, *FRP.* This relation is illustrated graphically in Exhibit 1. The capital asset pricing model (CAPM) provides a methodology for measuring these risk premiums and estimating the impact of financial leverage on expected returns.

Copyright © 1988 by the President and Fellows of Harvard College. Harvard Business School case 288–036.

The Effect of Financial Leverage on Beta

The CAPM is an idealized representation of the manner in which capital markets price securities and thereby determine expected returns.[1] Since the CAPM models the risk/expected return trade-off in the capital markets, it can be used to examine the impact of financial leverage on expected returns.

In the CAPM, systematic (or market-related) risk is the only risk relevant in the pricing of securities and the determination of expected returns. Systematic risk is measured by beta (β). The CAPM provides a measure of a stock's risk premium employing beta, which facilitates the estimation of the stock's expected return. In general,

$$R_S = R_F + \text{Risk premium}$$

If the CAPM correctly describes market behavior,

$$R_S = R_F + \beta\,(R_M - R_F)$$

A stock's expected return is equal to the risk-free rate, R_F, plus a premium for risk. With the CAPM, the risk premium is beta times the expected return on the market, R_M, minus the risk-free rate. This basic CAPM expression is known as the security market line, the SML.

If a firm has no debt in its capital structure, the stock's risk premium consists solely of a business risk premium. The stock's beta therefore reflects the systematic risk inherent in the firm's basic business operations. With no financial leverage, this beta is the stock's unlevered beta, β^U. This unlevered beta is the beta the stock would have if the firm had no debt in its capital structure.

The presence of debt in a firm's capital structure results in additional risk. The systematic risk inherent in the firm's basic business operations is amplified by financial leverage. With financial leverage, the beta on a firm's stock reflects both business and financial risk. This beta is called a levered beta, β^L. Employing a levered beta in the CAPM expression, the SML measures both the business risk premium and the financial risk premium. The beta published by various investment advisory services reflects *both* the business and the financial risk experienced during the time period over which the beta was determined.

Under the assumptions of the CAPM there is a simple relation between levered and unlevered betas:

$$\beta^L = \beta^U(1 + D/E)$$

Alternatively,

$$\beta^U = \frac{\beta^L}{1 + D/E}$$

A stock's levered beta is equal to its unlevered beta multiplied by a factor that includes the firm's ratio of debt to equity, *D/E*. Therefore, a stock's beta (and its expected return) increases as its debt ratio increases. The increase in beta reflects the additional systematic risk generated by financial leverage. The resulting increase in expected return reflects the increase in the financial risk premium required by investors as compensation for additional risk.[2]

[1]For a more complete description of the CAPM, see the note "Diversification, the Capital Asset Pricing Model, and the Cost of Equity Capital."

[2]This relation is only valid when the firm's debt does not have any systematic risk. It would be inappropriate to use this approach when the firm has risky debt outstanding.

These results can be employed to estimate the impact on expected return of a change in a firm's capital structure. The approach is illustrated in Exhibit 2. Assuming the firm currently employs debt in its capital structure, its observed beta will be the levered beta associated with its current ratio of debt to equity. The beta the stock would have if the firm changed its debt ratio can be estimated by a two-step procedure. The first step involves unlevering the stock's beta. Given its current debt ratio, *D/E,* and its current beta, β^L, its unlevered beta, β^U, can be calculated from the foregoing equation. The second step consists of relevering the stock's beta to reflect a change in capital structure. Given β^U and the new hypothetical debt ratio, *D/E,* the other equation presented can be used to calculate the stock's new levered beta, β^L. This levered beta is an estimate of the beta the stock would have if the debt ratio changed to that employed in the second stage of the procedure. The resulting estimate of beta can then be plugged into the familiar CAPM expression presented earlier, the security market line, to estimate the stock's expected return associated with the proposed debt ratio.

An example of levering and unlevering beta and expected return is presented in Exhibit 3 for General Electric (GE). An increase in GE's ratio of debt to equity from approximately .05 to .33 would result in an increase in its beta from 1.15 to 1.46. The increase in financial risk would result in an increase in the financial risk premium required by investors. Therefore, the estimated expected return on GE's stock rises from about 14% to roughly 16%. Similarly, a decrease in GE's debt ratio would decrease its beta and expected return.

The Decomposition of Expected Return into the Risk-Free Rate, Business Risk Premium, and Financial Risk Premium

The CAPM can be employed to decompose a stock's expected return into its basic components. This can be accomplished by combining the equation relating levered and unlevered beta and the basic CAPM expression, the SML. The general and CAPM versions of this decomposition are

$$\text{Expected return} = \begin{matrix}\text{Risk-free}\\ \text{rate}\end{matrix} + \begin{matrix}\text{Business risk}\\ \text{premium}\end{matrix} + \begin{matrix}\text{Financial risk}\\ \text{premium}\end{matrix}$$

$$R_S = R_F + \beta^U(R_M - R_F) + \beta^U(D/E)(R_M - R_F)$$

Alternatively,

$$R_S = R_F + \beta^U(R_M - R_F) + (\beta^L - \beta^U)(R_M - R_F)$$

Thus, the expected return on a stock can be decomposed into (1) the risk-free rate, (2) a business risk premium preset with no debt in the firm's capital structure (i.e., $D/E = 0$), and (3) the additional risk premium created by the existence of debt in the capital structure. With no debt in a firm's capital structure, the expected return on its stock consists only of the first two components. The effects of financial leverage are captured entirely in the third component. With the CAPM, this third component, the financial risk premium, is simply the increase in its beta, $\beta^L - \beta^U$, caused by financial leverage, multiplied by the risk premium on the market as a whole, $R_M - R_F$. Additional debt amplifies the systematic risk inherent in a firm's basic business operations and drives up the beta and expected return on its stock.

The example presented in Exhibit 4 demonstrates the use of these concepts to decompose the expected returns on two stocks, Procter & Gamble (P&G) and Colgate-Palmolive. P&G's business (or operating) risk is somewhat greater than Colgate's. Colgate's unlevered beta is .88. versus .92 for P&G, leading to a business risk premium of

6.16% for Colgate compared with 6.44% for P&G. Colgate's basic business risk is amplified by the higher level of debt in its capital structure, however, resulting in a financial risk premium which is roughly .70 percentage points more than P&G's. Thus, Colgate's overall risk premium—business risk premium plus financial risk premium—is actually larger than P&G's. Consequently, Colgate's levered beta and the expected return on its stock reflect its higher level of business and financial risk relative to P&G.

An example of the decomposition of the expected return on GE's stock at different debt ratios is presented in Exhibit 5. Note that changing the firm's debt ratio affects only its financial risk premium. As expected, the financial risk premium, the levered beta, and the expected return on GE's stock all increase with additional financial leverage.

Application to Corporate Finance

The CAPM facilitates the examination of the impact of financial leverage on expected returns. It therefore has an important application to corporate finance. A firm's cost of equity capital, k_E, is the expected (or required) return on the firm's stock. If the firm cannot expect to earn at least k_E on the equity-financed portion of its investments, funds should be returned to its shareholders, who can earn k_E on other securities of the same risk level in the financial marketplace. The CAPM can be used by financial managers to obtain an estimate of k_E and to examine the impact on k_E of financial leverage.

A firm's cost of equity capital is by definition the expected return on its stock. Since the basic CAPM expression, the security market line, yields estimates of expected returns, it can also be used to estimate costs of equity capital. Similarly, the CAPM concepts and techniques relating expected returns and financial leverage can be applied in examining the impact of financial leverage on the cost of equity capital. *The results presented earlier can be applied directly simply by recognizing that R_S, a stock's expected return, is equal to k_E, its cost of equity capital.*

To apply these concepts requires as inputs the risk-free rate, R_F, the expected return on the market as a whole, R_M, the stock's beta, and the ratio of debt to equity, D/E. As with any CAPM application, R_F can be estimated as the return on Treasury bills or bonds, and R_M can be estimated as the expected return on the Standard and Poor's Index of 500 Stocks. Betas can be estimated by linear regression and are also published by various investment advisory services. In estimating the debt ratio, the CAPM approach assumes that market values of debt and equity are employed. By definition, market values reflect the current values of debt and equity. In contrast, book values represent values prevailing in the past when the securities were issued. In addition, betas are themselves market-determined variables. Nevertheless, for convenience, book value debt ratios are often used in practice.

To examine the relation between the cost of equity capital and financial leverage, the estimated inputs are simply plugged into the equations presented earlier. The resulting expected returns are, by definition, costs of equity capital. The approach demonstrates that a firm's cost of equity is positively related to the level of debt in its capital structure, and the increment to the cost of equity generated by financial leverage can be estimated in the manner described earlier.

Conclusion

The capital asset pricing model is based upon extremely simple and clearly unrealistic assumptions. Empirical studies demonstrate that, consistent with the CAPM, there is a strong relation between stock returns and risk as measured by beta. Studies also generally support the relation between returns and financial leverage posited by the CAPM. However, these studies are by no means conclusive in establishing the validity of the CAPM. The application of the CAPM is also limited by problems associated with the model's inputs. Use of the model requires ad hoc estimates of several inputs, and the betas employed are subject to substantial estimation errors.

Thus, the CAPM should not be viewed as a wholly reliable method of estimating the cost of equity and examining the impact of financial leverage. However, in view of the deficiencies in alternative approaches, the CAPM represents a useful tool that managers may apply to an inherently difficult area of corporate finance. Finally, an alternative approach relating expected returns and financial leverage is outlined briefly in the Appendix.

Appendix

The CAPM methodology described in this note incorporates the implicit assumption that the firm's cost of debt is equal to the risk-free rate. An alternative approach that relaxes this restrictive assumption is presented in this Appendix. This more general approach examines the relation between the cost of equity capital and financial leverage. This relation expressed in cost of equity terms is

$$k_E^L = k_E^U + (k_E^U - k_D)\ D/E$$

where

k_E^L = levered cost of equity capital
k_E^U = unlevered cost of equity
k_D = cost of debt
D/E = ratio of debt to equity

In this equation k_E^U is the cost of equity if the firm has no debt in its capital structure. Therefore, k_E^U reflects the risk-free rate and a premium for business risk. The second term on the right-hand side of the equation captures the impact of financial leverage—the financial risk premium. With additional debt, the increase in the levered cost of equity is related to the difference between the unlevered cost of equity and the cost of debt. Solving for k_E^U, the equation becomes

$$k_E^U = \frac{k_E^L + k_D(D/E)}{1 + D/E}$$

Thus, given estimates of k_E^L, k_D, and D/E, the firm's unlevered cost of equity, k_E^U, can be calculated. The value of k_D will change with the degree of leverage in the firm's capital structure. Thus, the schedule of debt cost versus leverage must be known to estimate a new equity capital cost at a new debt ratio. To estimate the levered cost of equity associated with some new debt ratio, k_E^U, the new k_D, and the proposed D/E can be used as inputs in the previous equation.

This alternative approach can be employed in a manner analogous to that described previously. The equations can be manipulated to yield estimates of the cost of equity associated with various debt ratios and to decompose the cost of equity into its components. The advantage of this approach is that it is not tied exclusively to the assumptions of the CAPM. Specifically, it avoids the assumption that the firm's cost of debt is the risk-free rate. The advantage of the CAPM approach is the simple methodology it provides for levering and unlevering betas.

EXHIBIT 1
The Relation between a Firm's Financial Leverage and the Expected Return on Its Stock

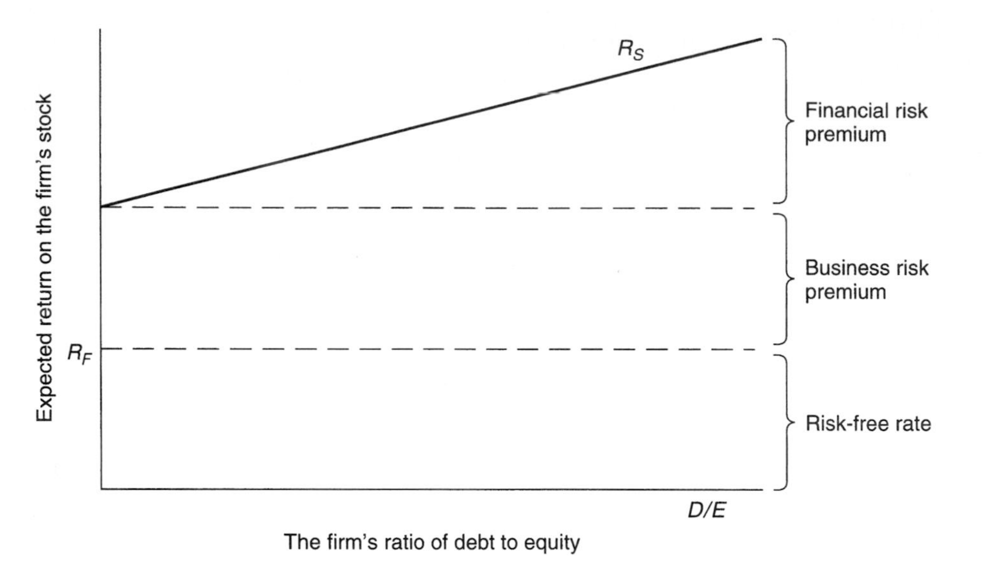

EXHIBIT 2
The Relation of Expected Return and Financial Leverage with the CAPM

Definitions:

R_S = stock's expected return
R_M = expected return on the market
D/E = firm's ratio of debt to equity
β^L = (levered) beta on the stock of a firm if $D/E > 0$
β^U = (unlevered) beta on the stock of the same firm if $D/E = 0$

CAPM equations:

Security market line (SML): $R_S = R_F + \beta(R_M - R_F)$
Levering beta: $\beta^L = \beta^U(1 + D/E)$

Unlevering beta: $\beta^U = \dfrac{\beta^L}{1 + D/E}$

To estimate the impact of a change in capital structure:

Step 1: Estimate the unlevered beta.
Given: current D/E and current estimated β^L.

Unlever the beta by solving: $\beta^U = \dfrac{\beta^L}{1 + D/E}$

Step 2: Estimate the levered beta associated with the new D/E.
Given: β^U from Step 1 and the new D/E.
Lever the beta by solving: $\beta^L = \beta^U(1 + D/E)$

The estimated beta for the new debt ratio is then used in the SML equation to estimate the expected return associated with the new D/E.

EXHIBIT 3 Sample Analysis of the Impact on Expected Return of Financial Leverage with the CAPM, General Electric Company

Assumptions:

$R_M = 13\%$; $R_F = 6\%$

GE's current $D/E = .05$

Current $\beta_{GE}^{L} = 1.15$

Unlevering GE's beta:

$$\beta_{GE}^{U} = \frac{\beta_{GE}^{L}}{1 + D/E} = \frac{1.15}{1 + 0.5} = 1.10$$

CAPM:

	Levering Beta	Security Market Line (SML)
Equations:	$\beta_{GE}^{L} = \beta_{GE}^{U}(1 + D/E)$	$R_S = R_F + \beta_{GE}(R_M - R_F)$
Example: Proposed $D/E = 0.50$	$\beta_{GE}^{L} = 1.10\ (1 + 50) = 1.65$	$R_S = 6\% + 1.65\ (13\% - 6\%) = 17.6\%$

Summary results:

Debt Ratio	GE's Beta	GE's Expected Return, R_S
Currently, $D/E = .05$	1.15	14.0%
Unlevered, $D/E = 0$	1.10	13.7%
Proposed, $D/E = .33$	1.46	16.2%
Proposed, $D/E = .50$	1.65	17.6%

EXHIBIT 4 Sample Decomposition of Expected Return, Procter & Gamble Company and Colgate-Palmolive Company

	Procter & Gamble		Colgate-Palmolive
Unlevering betas:			
Debt ratio	$D/E = .14$		$D/E = .31$
Levered beta	$\beta^L_{PG} = 1.05$		$\beta^L_{CG} = 1.15$
To unlever beta		$\beta^U = \frac{\beta^L}{1 + D/E}$	
Unlevered beta	$\beta^U_{PG} = .92$		$\beta^U_{CP} = .88$

Expected return calculation and decomposition:
Assumptions: $R_M = 13\%$; $R_F = 6\%$
Definitions: BRP = business risk premium; FRP = financial risk premium

	Procter & Gamble		Colgate-Palmolive	
Expected return decomposition:	$R_{PG} = R_F + \beta^U_{PG}(R_M - R_F)$	$+ (\beta^L_{PG} - \beta^U_{PG})(R_M - R_F)$	$R_{CP} = R_F + \beta^U_{CP}(R_M - R_F)$	$+ (\beta^L_{CP} - \beta^U_{CP})(R_M - R_F)$
Substituting assumed values:	$R_{PG} = 6\% + .92\,(13\% - 6\%)$	$+ (1.05 - .92)(13\% - 6\%)$	$R_{CP} = 6\% + .88\,(13\% - 6\%)$	$+ (1.15 - .88)(13\% - 6\%)$
Results:	$13.35\% = 6\% + 6.44\%$	$+.91$	$14.05\% = 6\% + 6.16\%$	$+ 1.89\%$
	$R_{PG} = R_F + BRP_{PG}$	$+ FRP_{PG}$	$R_{CP} = R_F + BRP_{CP}$	$+ FRP_{CP}$

EXHIBIT 5
Sample Decomposition of Expected Return at Various Debt Ratios, General Electric Company

	From Exhibit 3:	
	Debt Ratio	**GE's Beta**
Assumptions:		
$R_M = 13\%$	Currently, $D/E = .05$	$\beta^L_{GE} = 1.15$
$R_F = 6\%$	Unlevered, $D/E = 0$	$\beta^U_{GE} = 1.10$
	Proposed, $D/E = .33$	$\beta^L_{GE} = 1.46$
	Proposed, $D/E = .50$	$\beta^L_{GE} = 1.65$
Expected return decomposition:		
	$R_{GE} = R_F + BRP_{GE}$	$+ FRP_{GE}$
	$R_{GE} = R_F + \beta^U_{GE}(R_M - R_F)$	$+ (\beta^L_{GE} - \beta^U_{GE})(R_M - R_F)$
Example:		
Proposed $D/E = .50$	$R_{GE} = 6\% + 1.10(13\% - 6\%)$	$+ (1.65 - 1.10)(13\% - 6\%)$
	$17.55\% = 6\% + 7.70\%$	$+ 3.85\%$
Summary results:		

Debt Ratio	$R_{GE} = R_F + BRP_{GE} + FRP_{GE}$
Currently, $D/E = .05$	$14.05\% = 6\% + 7.70\% + .35\%$
Unlevered, $D/E = 0$	$13.70\% = 6\% + 7.70\% + 0\%$
Proposed, $D/E = .33$	$16.22\% = 6\% + 7.70\% + 2.52\%$
Proposed, $D/E = .50$	$17.55\% = 6\% + 7.70\% + 3.85$

Marriott Corporation: The Cost of Capital (Abridged)

In April 1988, Dan Cohrs, vice president of project finance at the Marriott Corporation, was preparing his annual recommendations for the hurdle rates at each of the firm's three divisions. Investment projects at Marriott were selected by discounting the appropriate cash flows by the appropriate hurdle rate for each division.

In 1987, Marriott's sales grew by 24% and its return on equity (ROE) stood at 22%. Sales and earnings per share had doubled over the previous 4 years, and the operating strategy was aimed at continuing this trend. Marriott's 1987 annual report stated:

> We intend to remain a premier growth company. This means aggressively developing appropriate opportunities within our chosen lines of business—lodging, contract services, and related businesses. In each of these areas, our goal is to be the preferred employer, the preferred provider, and the most profitable company.

Cohrs recognized that the divisional hurdle rates at Marriott would have a significant impact on the firm's financial and operating strategies. As a rule of thumb, increasing the hurdle rate by 1% (for example, from 12% to 12.12%), decreased the present value of project inflows by 1%. Because costs remained roughly fixed, these changes in the value of inflows translated into changes in the net present value of projects. Figure I shows the substantial impact of hurdle rates on the anticipated net present value of projects. If hurdle rates increased, Marriott's growth would be reduced, as once profitable projects would no longer meet the hurdle rates. Conversely, if hurdle rates decreased, Marriott's growth would accelerate.

Marriott also considered using the hurdle rates to determine incentive compensation. Annual incentive compensation constituted a significant portion of total compensation, ranging from 30% to 50% of base pay. Criteria for bonus awards depended on specific job responsibilities but often included the earnings level, the ability of managers to meet budgets, and overall corporate performance. There was some interest, however, in basing the incentive compensation, in part, on a comparison of the divisional return on net assets and the market-based divisional hurdle rate. The compensation plan would then reflect hurdle rates, making managers more sensitive to Marriott's financial strategy and capital market conditions.

Company Background

Marriott Corporation began in 1927 with J. Willard Marriott's root beer stand. Over the next 60 years, the business grew into one of the leading lodging and food service companies in the United States. Marriott's 1987 profits were $223 million on sales of $6.5 billion. See Exhibit 1 for a summary of Marriott's financial history.

Marriott had three major lines of business: lodging, contract services, and restaurants. Exhibit 2 summarizes its line-of-business data. Lodging operations included 361 hotels,

This case was prepared by Professor Richard S. Ruback

Copyright © 1989 by the President and Fellows of Harvard College. Harvard Business School case 289–047.

FIGURE I
Typical Hotel Profit and Hurdle Rates

Source: Casewriter's estimates.

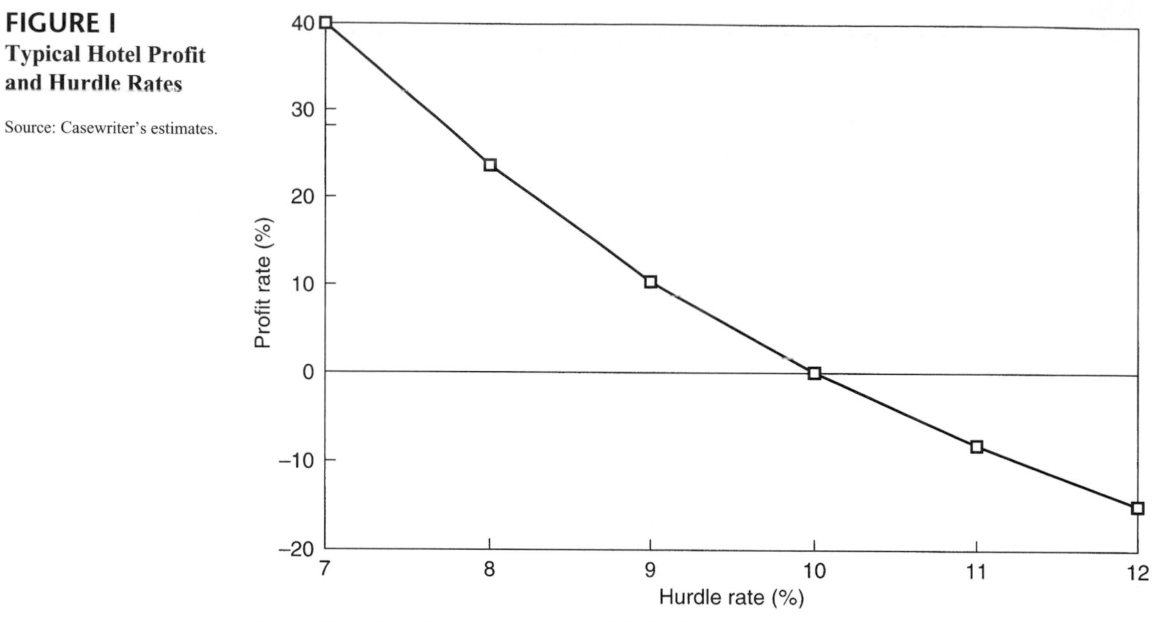

Note: Profit rate for a hotel is its net present value divided by its cost.

with more than 100,000 rooms in total. Hotels ranged from the full-service, high-quality Marriott hotels and suites to the moderately priced Fairfield Inn. Lodging generated 41% of 1987 sales and 51% of profits.

Contract services provided food and services management to health-care and educational institutions and corporations. It also provided airline catering and airline services through its Marriott In-Flite Services and Host International operations. Contract services generated 46% of 1987 sales and 33% of profits.

Marriott's restaurants included Bob's Big Boy, Roy Rogers, and Hot Shoppes. Restaurants provided 13% of 1987 sales and 16% of profits.

Financial Strategy

The four key elements of Marriott's financial strategy were:

- Manage rather than own hotel assets.
- Invest in projects that increase shareholder value.
- Optimize the use of debt in the capital structure.
- Repurchase undervalued shares.

Manage Rather Than Own Hotel Assets

In 1987, Marriott developed more than $1 billion worth of hotel properties, making it one of the ten largest commercial real estate developers in the United States. With a fully integrated development process, Marriott identified markets, created development plans, designed projects, and evaluated potential profitability.

After development, the company sold the hotel assets to limited partners, while retaining operating control as the general partner under a long-term management contract. Management fees typically equaled 3% of revenues plus 20% of the profits before depreciation and debt service. The 3% of revenues usually covered the overhead cost of managing the hotel. Marriott's 20% of profits before depreciation and debt service often required it to stand aside until investors earned a prespecified return. Marriott also guaranteed a portion of the partnership's debt. During 1987, 3 Marriott hotels and 70 Courtyard hotels were syndicated for $890 million. In total, the company operated about $7 billion worth of syndicated hotels.

Invest in Projects That Increase Shareholder Value

The company used discounted cash flow techniques to evaluate potential investments. The hurdle rate assigned to a specific project was based on market interest rates, project risk, and estimates of risk premiums. Cash flow forecasts incorporated standard companywide assumptions that instilled some consistency across projects. As one Marriott executive put it:

> Our projects are like a lot of similar little boxes. This similarity disciplines the pro forma analysis. There are corporate macro data on inflation, margins, project lives, terminal values, percent of sales required to remodel, and so on. Projects are audited throughout their lives to check and update these standard pro forma template assumptions. Divisional managers still have discretion over unit-specific assumptions, but they must conform to the corporate templates.

Optimize the Use of Debt in the Capital Structure

Marriott determined the amount of debt in its capital structure by focusing on its ability to service its debt. It used an interest-coverage target instead of a target debt-to-equity ratio. In 1987, Marriott had about $2.5 billion of debt, 59% of its total capital.

Repurchase Undervalued Shares

Marriott regularly calculated a "warranted equity value" for its common shares and was committed to repurchasing its stock whenever its market price fell substantially below that value. The warranted equity value was calculated by discounting the firm's equity cash flows by its equity cost of capital. It was checked by comparing Marriott's stock price with that of comparable companies using price/earnings ratios for each business and by valuing each business under alternative ownership structures, such as a leveraged buyout. Marriott had more confidence in its measure of warranted value than in the day-to-day market price of its stock. A gap between warranted value and market price, therefore, usually triggered repurchases instead of a revision in the warranted value by, for example, revising the hurdle rate. Furthermore, the company believed that repurchases of shares below warranted equity value were a better use of its cash flow and debt capacity than acquisitions or owning real estate. In 1987, Marriott repurchased 13.6 million shares of its common stock for $429 million.

The Cost of Capital

Marriott measured the opportunity cost of capital for investments of similar risk using the weighted average cost of capital (WACC):

$$\text{WACC} = (1 - \tau)\bar{r}_D(D/V) + \bar{r}_E(E/V)$$

where D and E are the market value of the debt and equity, respectively, $\bar{r}_D$ is the pretax cost of debt, $\bar{r}_E$ is the after-tax cost of equity, and V is the value of the firm. ($V = D + E$), and τ is the corporate tax rate. Marriott used this approach to determine the cost of capital for the corporation as a whole and for each division.

To determine the opportunity cost of capital, Marriott required three inputs: debt capacity, debt cost, and equity cost consistent with the amount of debt. The cost of capital varied across the three divisions because all three of the cost-of-capital inputs could differ for each division. The cost of capital for each division was updated annually.

TABLE A
Market-Value Target Leverage Ratios and Credit Spreads for Marriott and Its Divisions

	Debt Percentage in Capital	Fraction of Debt at Floating	Fraction of Debt at Fixed	Debt Rate Premium Above Government
Marriott	60%	40%	60%	1.30%
Lodging	74	50	50	1.10
Contract services	40	40	60	1.40
Restaurants	42	25	75	1.80

TABLE B
U.S. Government Interest Rates, April 1988

Maturity	Rate
30-year	8.95%
10-year	8.72
1-year	6.90

Debt Capacity and the Cost of Debt

Marriott applied its coverage-based financing policy to each of its divisions. It also determined for each division the fraction of debt that should be floating-rate debt based on the sensitivity of the division's cash flows to interest rate changes. The interest rate on floating-rate debt changed as interest rates changed. If cash flows increased as the interest rate increased, using floating-rate debt expanded debt capacity.

In April 1988, Marriott's unsecured debt was A rated. As a high-quality corporate risk, Marriott could expect to pay a spread above the current government bond rates. It based the debt cost for each division on an estimate of the division's debt cost as an independent company. The spread between the debt rate and the government bond rate varied by division because of differences in risk. Table A provides the market-value target leverage rates, the fraction of the debt at floating rate, the fraction at fixed rates, and the credit spread for Marriott as a whole and for each division. The credit spread was the debt rate premium above the government rate required to induce investors to lend money to Marriott.

Because lodging assets, like hotels, had long useful lives, Marriott used the cost of long-term debt for its lodging cost-of-capital calculations. It used shorter-term debt as the cost of debt for its restaurant and contract services divisions because those assets had shorter useful lives.

Table B lists the interest rates on fixed-rate U.S. government securities in April 1988.

The Cost of Equity

Marriott rccognized that meeting its financial strategy of embarking only on projects that increased shareholder values meant that it had to use its shareholders' measure of equity costs. Marriott used the capital asset pricing model (CAPM) to estimate the cost of equity. The CAPM, originally developed by John Lintner and William Sharpe in the early 1960s, had gained wide acceptance among financial professionals. According to the CAPM, the cost of equity, or equivalently, the expected return for equity, was determined as

$$\text{Expected return} = R = \text{Risk-free rate} + \beta \times (\text{Risk premium})$$

where the risk premium is the difference between the expected return on the market portfolio and the riskless rate.

The key insight in the CAPM was that risk should be measured relative to a fully diversified portfolio of risky assets such as common stocks. The simple adage "Don't put all your eggs in one basket" dictated that investors could minimize their risks by holding assets in fully diversified portfolios. An asset's risk was not measured as its individual risk. Instead, the asset's contribution to the risk of a fully diversified or market portfolio was what mattered. This risk, usually called systematic risk, was measured by the beta coefficient (β).

Betas could be calculated from historical data on common stock returns using simple linear regression analysis. Marriott's beta, calculated using monthly stock returns during the 1983–1987 period, was 1.11.

Two problems limited the use of the historical estimates of beta in calculating the hurdle rates for projects. First, corporations generally had multiple lines of business. A company's beta, therefore, was a weighted average of the betas of its different lines of business. Second, leverage affected beta. Adding debt to a firm increased its equity beta even if the riskiness of the firm's assets remained unchanged, because the safest cash flows went to the debt holders. As debt increased, the cash flows remaining for stockholders became more risky. The historical beta of a firm, therefore, had to be interpreted and adjusted before it could be used as a project's beta, unless the project had the same risk and the same leverage as the firm overall.

Exhibit 3 contains the beta, leverage, and other related information for Marriott and comparable companies in the lodging and restaurant businesses.

To select the appropriate risk premium to use in the hurdle rate calculations, Mr. Cohrs examined a variety of data on the stock and bond markets. Exhibit 4 provides historical information on the holding-period returns on government and corporate bonds and the S&P 500 Composite Index of common stocks. Holding-period returns were the returns realized by the security holder, including any cash payment (e.g., dividends for common stocks, coupons for bonds) received by the holder plus any capital gain or loss on the security. As examples, the 5.23% holding-period return for the S&P 500 Composite Index of common stocks in 1987 was the sum of the dividend yield of 3.20% and the capital gain of 2.03%. The –2.69% holding-period return for the index of long-term U.S. government bonds in 1987 was the sum of the coupon yield of 7.96% and a capital gain of –10.65%.[1]

Exhibit 5 provides statistics on the spread between the S&P 500 Composite returns and the holding-period returns on Treasury bills, U.S. government bonds, and high-grade, long-term corporate bonds.

Mr. Cohrs was concerned about the correct time interval to measure these averages, especially given the high returns and volatility of the bond markets shown in Exhibits 4 and 5.

[1]Cash payments are assumed to be invested in the respective securities monthly.

EXHIBIT 1 Financial History of Marriott Corporation (millions of dollars except per share amounts)

Source: Company reports.

	1978	1979	1980	1981	1982	1983	1984	1985	1986	1987
Summary of Operations										
Sales	$1,174.1	$1,426.0	$1,633.9	$1,905.7	$2,458.9	$2,950.5	$3,524.9	$4,241.7	$5,266.5	$6,522.2
Earnings before interest expense and income taxes	107.1	133.5	150.3	173.3	205.5	247.9	297.7	371.3	420.5	489.4
Interest expense	23.7	27.8	46.8	52.0	71.8	62.8	61.6	75.6	60.3	90.5
Income before income taxes	83.5	105.6	103.5	121.3	133.7	185.1	236.1	295.7	360.2	398.9
Income taxes	35.4	43.8	40.6	45.2	50.2	76.7	100.8	128.3	168.5	175.9
Income from continuing operations[a]	48.1	61.8	62.9	76.1	83.5	108.4	135.3	167.4	191.7	223.0
Net income	54.3	71.0	72.0	86.1	94.3	115.2	139.8	167.4	191.7	223.0
Funds provided from cont. operations[b]	101.2	117.5	125.8	160.8	203.6	272.7	322.5	372.3	430.3	472.8
Capitalization and Returns										
Total assets	$1,000.3	$1,080.4	$1,214.3	$1,454.9	$2,062.6	$2,501.4	$2,904.7	$3,663.8	$4,579.3	$5,370.5
Total capital[c]	826.9	891.9	977.7	1,167.5	1,634.5	2,007.5	2,330.7	2,861.4	3,561.8	4,247.8
Long-term debt	309.9	365.3	536.6	607.7	889.3	1,071.6	1,115.3	1,192.3	1,662.8	2,498.8
Percent to total capital	37.5%	41.0%	54.9%	52.1%	54.4%	53.4%	47.9%	41.7%	46.7%	58.8%
Shareholders' equity	418.7	413.5	311.5	421.7	516.0	628.2	675.6	848.5	991.0	810.8
Per Share and Other Data										
Earnings per share										
Continuing operations[a]	$ .25	$ .34	$ .45	$ .57	$ .61	$ .78	$ 1.00	$ 1.24	$ 1.40	$ 1.67
Net income	.29	.39	.52	.64	.69	.83	1.04	1.24	1.40	1.67
Cash dividends	.026	.034	.042	.051	.063	.076	.093	.113	.136	.17
Shareholders' equity	2.28	2.58	2.49	3.22	3.89	4.67	5.25	6.48	7.59	6.82
Market price at year-end	2.43	3.48	6.35	7.18	11.70	14.25	14.70	21.58	29.75	30.00
Shares outstanding (in millions)	183.6	160.5	125.3	130.8	132.8	134.4	128.8	131.0	130.6	118.8
Return on avg. shareholders' equity	13.9%	17.0%	23.8%	23.4%	20.0%	20.0%	22.1%	22.1%	20.6%	22.2%

[a]The company's theme park operations were discontinued in 1984.
[b]Funds provided from continuing operations consist of income from continuing operations plus depreciation, deferred income taxes, and other items not currently affecting working capita .
[c]Total capital represents total assets less current liabilities.

EXHIBIT 2 Financial Summary by Business Segment 1982–1987 (millions of dollars)

Source: Company reports.

	1982	1983	1984	1985	1986	1987
Lodging						
Sales	$1,091.7	$1,320.5	$1,640.8	$1,898.4	$2,233.1	$2,673.3
Operating profits	132.6	139.7	161.2	185.8	215.7	263.9
Identifiable assets	909.7	1,264.6	1,786.3	2,108.9	2,236.7	2,777.4
Depreciation	22.7	27.4	31.3	32.4	37.1	43.9
Capital expenditures . .	371.5	377.2	366.4	808.3	966.6	1,241.9
Contract Services						
Sales	$ 819.8	$ 950.6	$1,111.3	$1,586.3	$2,236.1	$2,969.0
Operating profit	51.0	71.1	86.8	118.6	154.9	170.6
Identifiable assets	373.3	391.6	403.9	624.4	1,070.2	1,237.7
Depreciation	22.9	26.1	28.9	40.2	61.1	75.3
Capital expenditures . .	127.7	43.8	55.6	125.9	448.7	112.7
Restaurants						
Sales	$ 547.4	$ 679.4	$ 707.0	$ 757.0	$ 797.3	$ 879.9
Operating profit	48.5	63.8	79.7	78.2	79.1	82.4
Identifiable assets	452.2	483.0	496.7	582.6	562.3	467.6
Depreciation	25.1	31.8	35.5	34.8	38.1	42.1
Capital expenditures . .	199.6	65.0	72.3	128.4	64.0	79.6

EXHIBIT 3 Information on Comparable Hotel and Restaurant Companies

Source: Casewriter estimates.

Company and Nature of Business	Arithmetic Average Return[a]	Equity Beta[b]	Market Leverage[c]	1987 Revenues ($ billions)
Marriott Corporation (Owns, operates, and manages hotels, restaurants, and airline and institutional food services)	10.57%	1.11	41%	6.52
Hotels				
Hilton Hotels Corporation (Owns, manages, and licenses hotels; operates casinos)	17.16	0.76	14	0.77
Holiday Corporation (Owns, manages, and licenses hotels and restaurants; operates casinos)	32.89	1.35	79	1.66
La Quinta Motor Inns (Owns, operates, and licenses motor inns)	–5.19	0.89	69	0.17
Ramada Inns, Inc. (Owns and operates hotels and restaurants)	10.57	1.36	65	0.75
Restaurants				
Church's Fried Chicken (Owns and franchises restaurants and gaming businesses)	1.79	1.45	4	0.39
Collins Foods International (Operates Kentucky Fried Chicken franchise and moderately priced restaurants)	24.32	1.45	10	0.57
Frisch's Restaurants (Operates and franchises restaurants)	45.83	0.57	6	0.14
Luby's Cafeterias (Operates cafeterias)	15.50	0.76	1	0.23
McDonald's (Operates, franchises, and services restaurants)	23.93	0.94	23	4.89
Wendy's International (Operates, franchises, and services restaurants)	7.76	1.32	21	1.05

[a]Calculated over the period 1983–1987.

[b]Estimated using 5 years of monthly data over the 1983–1987 period.

[c]Book value of debt divided by the sum of the book value of debt plus the market value of equity.

EXHIBIT 4

Annual Holding-Period Returns for Selected Securities and Market Indexes, 1926–1987

Source: Casewriter estimates based on data from the University of Chicago's Center for Research in Security Prices.

Years	Arithmetic Average	Standard Deviation
Short-Term Treasury Bills		
1926–1987	3.54%	0.94%
1926–1950	1.01	0.40
1951–1975	3.67	0.56
1976–1980	7.80	0.83
1981–1985	10.32	0.75
1986	6.16	0.19
1987	5.46	0.22
Long-Term U.S. Government Bond Returns		
1926–1987	4.58%	7.58%
1926–1950	4.14	4.17
1951–1975	2.39	6.45
1976–1980	1.95	11.15
1980–1985	17.85	14.26
1986	24.44	17.30
1987	–2.69	10.28
Long-Term, High-Grade Corporate Bond Returns		
1926–1987	5.24%	6.97%
1926–1950	4.82	3.45
1951–1975	3.05	6.04
1976–1980	2.70	10.87
1981–1985	18.96	14.17
1986	19.85	8.19
1987	–0.27	9.64
Standard and Poor's 500 Composite Stock Index Returns		
1926–1987	12.01	20.55
1926–1950	10.90	27.18
1951–1975	11.87	13.57
1976–1980	14.81	14.60
1981–1985	15.49	13.92
1986	18.47	17.94
1987	5.23	30.50

EXHIBIT 5
Spreads between S&P 500 Composite Returns and Bond Rates, 1926–1987

Source: Casewriter estimates based on data from the University of Chicago's Center for Research in Security Prices.

Years	Arithmetic Average	Standard Deviation
Spread between S&P 500 Composite Returns and Short-Term U.S. Treasury Bill Returns		
1926–1987	8.47%	20.60%
1926–1950	9.89	27.18
1951–1975	8.20	13.71
1976–1980	7.01	14.60
1981–1985	5.17	14.15
1986	12.31	17.92
1987	–0.23	30.61
Spread between S&P 500 Composite Returns and Long-Term U.S. Government Bond Returns		
1926–1987	7.43%	20.78%
1926–1950	6.76	26.94
1951–1975	9.48	14.35
1976–1980	12.86	15.58
1981–1985	–2.36	13.70
1986	–5.97	14.76
1987	7.92	35.35
Spread between S&P 500 Composite Returns and Long-Term, High-Grade Corporate Bonds		
1926–1987	6.77%	20.31%
1926–1950	6.06	26.70
1951–1975	8.82	13.15
1976–1980	12.11	15.84
1981–1985	–3.47	13.59
1986	–1.38	14.72
1987	5.50	34.06

Lex Service PLC—Cost of Capital

On November 25, 1993, the directors of Lex Service PLC received a memorandum from G. Lionel Harvey, the company's deputy chief executive, concerning the approaching board meeting on December 2. Attached to the memo was a report by the L.E.K. Partnership, a London-based consulting firm, concerning Lex's cost of capital. The report and its implications for management were to be discussed at this board meeting.

Recent developments at Lex had focused top management's attention on the company's capital budgeting procedures and its cost of capital. Between 1991 and 1993, various sales of subsidiaries and other assets had provided Lex with more than £340 million of funds. During this same period, approximately £132.5 million of this amount had been used to pay for a string of new acquisitions in the automotive distribution and leasing businesses.[1] Since Lex employed discounted cash flow analysis to help evaluate the worth of its investment opportunities, the question of what rate of return to demand on its investments had come squarely to the forefront as it implemented its acquisition program.

Company Background

At the time of its public incorporation in 1928, what was then known as Lex Garages Limited consisted of a single garage located on the corner of Lexington and Brewer streets in London. More than 60 years later, Lex Service PLC had become the leading company in automotive distribution and leasing in the United Kingdom. In 1992, Lex earned £90 million on total revenues of £911 million, and had total assets of £420 million. In 1993, the company expected to earn in excess of £80 million on revenues of approximately £1.2 billion. Recent financial statements are provided in Exhibits 1 and 2.

Originally an operator of a small group of parking garages and petrol stations, in 1945 Lex began to expand its automotive activities through a series of acquisitions of companies holding distribution franchises for various British, European, and American car manufacturers. Perhaps the most significant acquisition was made in the late 1950s, when Lex obtained from the Volvo Car Corporation the exclusive franchise to import and distribute Volvo cars in the United Kingdom. Over the next few decades this importership came to be regarded as one of the ultimate success stories within the U.K. automotive industry. In the early 1970s, Lex began to diversify into other service businesses in the United Kingdom, marking its second series of acquisitions. These areas of business included transportation and leasing, as well as hotel management from which it subsequently withdrew.

[1]Most of the balance was used to repay about £197 million of debt, leaving the company with very little financial leverage as it approached the end of 1993.

Professor W. Carl Kester and Research Associate Kendall Backstrand prepared this case as the basis for class discussion rather than to illustrate either effective or ineffective handling of an administrative situation.

Copyright © 1996 by the President and Fellows of Harvard College. To order copies or request permission to reproduce materials, call 1-800-545-7685, write Harvard Business School Publishing, Boston, MA 02163, or go to http://www.hbsp.harvard.edu. No part of this publication may be reproduced, stored in a retrieval system, used in a spreadsheet or transmitted in any form or by any means—electronic, mechanical, photocopying, recording, or otherwise—without the permission of Harvard Business School.

After Britain's 1973–1974 economic recession, however, Lex realized the dangers of its sole dependence on local markets and launched an international diversification strategy. Lex forecasted attractive growth potential in the United States, which led to its third series of U.S.-based acquisitions, including those of luxury hotels, vehicle parts distributors, and electronic components distributors. The latter was initiated m 1981, when Lex acquired Schweber Electronics, the third largest electronic components distributor in the United States. This acquisition provided the foundation for Lex's new core business. By the end of 1983, Lex was structured around two principal groups—Lex Automotive and Lex Electronics Worldwide. Lex Electronics accounted for approximately 30% of Lex's total sales, and nearly 90% of this was contributed by Schweber in the United States.

Recent Developments

The U.K. car and truck market hit a decade low in 1991. As a result, Lex's sales were badly affected, and the company reported a loss of £3 million compared with a profit of £5 million in 1990. However, in 1991 Lex implemented a new business strategy that refocused the company's efforts on its core competence in automotive distribution and leasing. In doing so, Lex engaged in several transactions that strengthened the balance sheet, providing the resources necessary to expand its traditional businesses.

In September 1991, Lex sold its electronics businesses to Arrow Electronics, Inc., the second largest electronic component distributor in the world. Lex received $109 million (approximately £58 million) in cash along with 6.8 million shares of Arrow's common stock valued at £57 million at the time of the sale. Then in February 1992, Lex sold its European electronic component distribution businesses to Arrow for £33 million, £21 million of which was received in cash and the remainder in an Arrow debenture which would earn interest at 12%. By May 1993, Lex had sold nearly all of its shares in Arrow Electronics for gross proceeds of £116.8 million.

In the face of the same challenging market conditions, Volvo Car Corporation deemed it necessary to gain greater control over its marketing in the United Kingdom, its second largest market. In March 1992, Volvo ended its 33-year-long import agreement with Lex four years before the scheduled termination date. Upon relinquishing the franchise to Volvo, Lex realized £100 million for the value in the concession.[2] Lex's stock fell 30% to 205 pence per share in response to the news. While it was clear that this market reaction reflected a major loss in Lex's value, it was also clear that the cash received would provide Lex with more internal funds to finance future growth initiatives.

Immediately following the termination of its Volvo import agreement, Lex acquired the Swan National Motor Group, the retail motor distribution arm of Swan National Limited, for a total consideration of £44 million. In March 1993, the company acquired Lucas Autocentres, which operated high-quality fixed-price auto service centers in the United Kingdom, for £13.1 million in cash, and in July 1993, it acquired the Arlington Motor Group for £48.6 million in cash. Arlington operated a series of truck and van distributorships.

Finally, Lex reentered the profitable auto importing business by acquiring a controlling interest in the U.K. importership, Hyundai Car (U.K.), in September 1993. Lex bought a 50.1% interest in the business from I.M. Group, which owned the Hyundai franchise.[3] The

[2]Of the £100 million, £20 million was received in cash on completion of the sale and three sterling loan notes of £26 million, £26 million, and £28 million were payable on 1 January, 1993, 1994, and 1995, respectively.

[3]As part of this transaction, Lex and I.M. Group exchanged call and put options, respectively, covering the remaining 49.9% interest in the joint venture exercisable in December 1991 for not more than £22 million.

acquisition gave Lex management control of a three-year rolling contract that Hyundai Car (U.K.) held with the Hyundai Motor Company of Korea. In addition, Lex acquired from I.M. Group 49% of I.M. Finance, which offered retail finance to Hyundai customers and wholesale finance to Hyundai dealers. The total cost of these acquisitions amounted to £16 million.

Two Major Lines of Business

Subsequent to these 1992–1993 transactions, Lex Services's businesses consisted of two fundamental halves: automotive distribution and contract hire (vehicle leasing and finance). As shown in Exhibit 3, automotive distribution was carried out chiefly through wholly or majority owned subsidiaries, the largest of which was the Lex Retail Group. Contract hire, on the other hand, was conducted primarily through "associated" enterprises that were jointly owned with Lombard North Central PLC, a part of the National Westminster Bank. Lex and Lombard each owned 50% of Lex Vehicle Leasing (auto leasing), Transfleet (truck leasing), and Harvey (fork-lift truck leasing). Lex managed these businesses on a day-to-day basis while Lombard provided funding to support their fleet investments. For accounting purposes, the contract-hire joint ventures were consolidated into the accounts of Lombard. Lex's share of the results of these associated undertakings was included in its consolidated income statement, and its share of their net assets (total assets net of all liabilities, i.e., net worth) was included in its consolidated balance sheet. Total capital actually employed in each of these major lines of business is shown in Exhibit 4.

In addition to these operating halves of its businesses, Lex was also a substantial holder of property not required for operating purposes. Such "investment" property might be obtained when, for example, a dealer outgrew its premises and moved to a larger location, leaving Lex in possession of the original land and buildings. Since these holdings were not required for current operations, they were reclassified as investment properties that might be sold. In 1992, £4.5 million of land and buildings were sold, and at least £5.0 million of such property was expected to be disposed of in 1993. L.E.K. estimated that Lex possessed investment property with a book value of £31.4 million in mid-1993. L.E.K also estimated, however, that the current market value of this property was approximately 23% below book value (see Exhibit 4).

Lex's Cost of Capital

Lex engaged the L.E.K. Partnership to undertake a thorough analysis of its cost of capital. In executing this assignment, L.E.K. ultimately provided not one but several estimates of capital costs that might be used as discount rates in Lex's capital budgeting process. One approach taken by L.E.K. was to estimate capital costs for the entire Lex Group treated as a consolidated entity. Another approach made use of financial data about several different independent companies, each specializing in one of the lines of business in which Lex participated, in order to develop individual cost of capital estimates for Lex's various divisions. Common to both approaches was the use of the so-called "Capital Asset Pricing Model," or "CAPM" for short.

The Capital Asset Pricing Model

The CAPM was originally developed by John Lintner of the Harvard Business School and William Sharpe of Stanford University in the early 1960s. The model first received practical application as a means of evaluating the performance of investment fund managers, but was soon applied as a means of estimating discount rates intended for use in capital budgeting systems. By the 1980s, it was in widespread use among finance professionals.

Briefly, the CAPM stipulates that investors' required rate of return on a risky investment is the sum of a risk-free interest rate and a risk premium. The risk premium compensates investors for the risks they bear in committing their money to an investment with uncertain returns. The CAPM formula is generally written as:

$$R_S = R_F + \beta \times (R_M - R_F),$$

where:

R_S = investors' expected return on a risky asset;
R_F = risk-free rate;
β = beta; a measure of the asset's riskiness (including both business risk and financial risk); and
R_M = expected return on a well diversified portfolio of capital assets (most commonly approximated by the so-called "market portfolio" of stocks).

The fundamental concept underlying the CAPM was that sensible, risk-averse investors would diversify their holdings of risky assets in order to diminish their exposure to unexpected changes in the value of any one of those risky assets. Consequently, the riskiness of an individual asset, according to CAPM, should be measured relative to a fully diversified portfolio of risky assets such as common stocks. In other words, an asset's risk was not simply the volatility of its returns on an individual basis (i.e., its "total risk"). Rather, it was the asset's contribution of risk to a fully diversified portfolio that mattered (i.e., its "systematic" or "non-diversifiable" risk). The risk premium in the CAPM—$\beta \times (R_M - R_F)$—was the *quantity* of risk times the *price* of risk where, loosely speaking, β captured the quantity of risk and $(R_M - R_F)$ reflected the price of risk.

Implementing the CAPM typically requires use of both historical and contemporary capital market data. Some of the data collected by L.E.K. and discussed in their report are described below.

Risk-Free Rate

The risk-free rate is generally proxied by current yields on default-free government securities. In the United Kingdom, the government issued both ordinary fixed-rate bonds and, since 1981, inflation-indexed bonds. In November 1993, the yields on various U.K. government bonds were as follows:

TABLE A
Prevailing Yields to Maturity on U.K. Government Bonds, September 1993

	Non-Indexed Bonds	Inflation Indexed Bonds
Short-term gilts (less than 5 year maturities)	6.3%	3.4%
Medium-term bonds (between 5 and 15 year maturities)	6.8	3.4
Long-term bonds (more than 15 year maturities)	7.2	n.a.

Equity Risk Premium ($RM_M - RF_F$)

The equity risk premium in CAPM is the extra rate of return above the risk-free rate that an investor requires for making an investment in the market portfolio. Because this cannot easily be observed directly, L.E.K. recommended relying upon the historic spread in returns on the market portfolio and government bonds.

In its report, L.E.K. observed that the average equity market premium over (non-indexed) long-term gilts had varied considerably over time. Between 1966 and 1979, for example, it was 2.7%. Between 1979 and 1992, it averaged 8.0%. The average over this entire time period (1966–1992) was 5.3%. Other direct estimates of the arithmetic average returns on U.K. gilts and equities spanning a longer time period are as follows:

TABLE B
Historic Average Total Annual Returns on U.K. Gilts and Equities

Source: Barclays de Zoete Wedd Securities Limited. *The BZW Equity-Gilt Study*, 39th edition, January 1994.

	Average Nominal Returns	Standard Deviation
Short-term gilts		
1919–1993	5.47%	4.37%
1946–1993	7.20	4.46
Medium- to long-term gilts		
1919–1993	6.74	13.20
1946–1993	7.14	14.39
Equities		
1919–1993	14.68	25.74
1946–1993	16.63	28.94

For comparison purposes, the realized holding-period returns for U.S. equities and government securities are shown in Table C.

TABLE C
Historic Average Total Annual Returns on U.S. Government Bills, Bonds, and Equities

Source: Ibbotson Associates. *Stocks, Bonds, Bills and Inflation 1995 Yearbook* (Chicago 1995).

	Average Nominal Returns	Standard Deviation
U.S. treasury bills	3.7%	3.3%
Intermediate-term government bonds	5.3	5.7
Long-term government bonds	5.4	8.8
Equities[a]	12.4	20.3

[a]For large company stocks

Beta

Using five years of monthly returns on Lex's stock and the Financial Times Stock Exchange Index of 100 Stocks (FTSE-100), and simple linear regression techniques, Lex's β was estimated to be 1.23.[4] This estimate reflected Lex's gearing (or leverage) during the period in which the beta was measured. Although Lex's gearing had dropped considerably in recent months due to debt repayments following asset sales, its debt-to-total capital ratio had been in the 35% to 40% range on a market-value basis during most of the five-year period used to estimate Lex's beta.

Because debt obligations generally convey a safer stream of cash flows to lenders than that received by equity investors, the use of debt elevates the systematic risk borne by equity. Thus, when a company has some debt in its capital structure, the "equity betas" estimated directly from stock returns will be higher than the so-called "asset-betas," which reflect the systematic risk of *total* returns on the assets in question. The asset beta can be conceived of as a value-weighted average of the company's debt beta and equity beta as follows:

$$\beta_A = (D / V)\beta_D + (E / V)\beta_E$$

where:

β_A = asset beta
β_D = debt beta
β_E = equity beta
D = market value of debt
E = market value of equity
V = total market value (D+E)

[4]Casewriter's estimate.

If interest and principal payments expected on the debt are fairly safe, the beta of the debt can be considered to be approximately zero ($\beta_D = 0$). Under this assumption the relationship between the levered equity beta and the underlying asset (or unlevered) beta can be reduced to:

$$\beta_A = \frac{E}{V}\beta_E$$

Lex's 1993 leverage (gearing) ratios, on both book- and market-value bases, are shown in Exhibit 4. Lex's recent actual leverage was below management's future target levels, however. For the consolidated company, management anticipated that the future target book-value debt-equity ratio would be at least 15% and might be as high as 30%. Within this range of modest leverage, it was believed that Lex's pre-tax cost of debt would be approximately 8.4% under prevailing capital market conditions. In 1993, Lex's *marginal* corporate tax rate was 33%. Due to factors such as deferred taxes and the utilization of tax-loss carryforwards associated with Arrow Electronics, among other factors, Lex's effective *average* corporate tax rate on consolidated pre-tax income was approximately 18%.

Divisional Capital Costs

In its report to management, L.E.K. also estimated individual *asset* betas for Lex's major divisions. Since these were not independently owned companies with separately observable market returns on equity, L.E.K. made these estimates by reference to a set of comparable companies that specialized in each division's line of business. The comparable companies and the average estimated asset beta for each of Lex's divisions are shown in Exhibit 5. The target debt-equity ratios for each division are shown in Exhibit 6.

Employing Cost of Capital Estimates

Lex's asset sales in recent years had released a considerable amount of capital, which was now available for redeployment in new businesses. New opportunities were being identified and evaluated on a regular basis. Although estimating the cost of capital was but one aspect of investment analysis, it was an essential step that had to be taken soon if Lex were to make the best possible use of its capital.

The L.E.K. Partnership's report raised a number of important issues concerning how one should estimate Lex's cost of capital and how such estimates should be used. Of concern to Lex's top management and its board of directors was whether L.E.K.'s approach made good sense, gave reasonable results, and whether or not one or multiple estimates of capital costs (i.e., one for each division) should be used for valuation and capital budgeting purposes.

EXHIBIT 1
Consolidated Annual Income Statements (millions of pounds, except per share data)

Source: Annual reports.

Year Ending December 26	1992	1991
Turnover		
Continuing operations	£ 620.2	£ 598.6
Acquisitions	163.0	—
	783.2	598.6
Discontinued Operations	127.5	722.2
Total turnover	910.7	1,320.8
Cost of sales	(777.9)	(1,114.0)
Gross profit	132.8	206.8
Net operating expenses	(121.8)	(189.6)
Operating profit		
Continuing operations	2.7	0.5
Acquisitions	1.6	—
	4.3	0.5
Discontinued operations	6.7	6.7
Total operating profit	11.0	17.2
Income from interests in associated undertakings	21.6	0.8
Discontinued operations:		
Profit on sale of, and other gains in, Arrow Electronics, Inc. shares	15.0	—
Termination and sale of businesses	63.7	(50.6)
Interest payable and similar charges	(4.3)	(17.5)
Profit/(loss) before taxation	107.0	(50.1)
Taxation on profit/(loss)	(16.5)	(3.4)
Profit/(loss) after taxation	90.5	(53.5)
Dividends	(10.0)	(9.4)
Retained profit/(loss) for the financial year	£ 80.5	£ (62.9)
Earnings per ordinary share after extraordinary items[a] (pence)	96.7p	(57.4)p
Earnings per ordinary/share before extraordinary items[a] (pence)	18.3p	15.7 p
Dividends per ordinary share (pence)	10.6p	10.0 p
Stock price, December 31, 1992 (pence)	278p	202 p
Average number of ordinary shares outstanding (millions)	93.6	93.2

[a]Extraordinary items consist chiefly of revenues and costs from the sale of discontinued operations, and gains on the sale of Arrow Electronics shares.

EXHIBIT 2

Consolidated Balance Sheets (millions of pounds)

Source: Annual reports.

Year Ending December 26	1992	1991
Fixed Assets		
Tangible assets		
Land and buildings	£ 133.7	£ 131.0
Vehicles, plant, and machinery	17.3	6.9
Fixtures, fittings, tools, and equipment	6.3	7.4
	157.3	145.3
Investments	86.1	74.5
Associated undertakings[a]	243.4	219.8
Current assets		
Stocks	75.3	151.8
Debtors	83.4	72.8
Cash at bank and in hand	17.7	15.3
	176.4	239.9
Creditors: amounts falling due within one year		
Bank loans and overdrafts	4.0	5.6
Creditors[b]	117.1	209.3
	121.1	214.9
Net current assets	55.3	25.0
Total assets less current liabilities	298.7	244.8
Creditors: amounts falling due after more than one year		
Bank and other loans	22.4	66.6
Creditors	0.7	0.9
	23.1	67.5
Provisions for liabilities and charges	20.0	9.5
Net assets	255.6	167.8
Capital and reserves		
Called up share capital	24.4	24.4
Share premium account	69.1	68.9
Revaluation reserve	19.9	25.0
Profit and loss account	142.2	49.5
Shareholders' funds	255.6	167.8

[a]Figures shown represent the book value of Lex's investment share in the net assets (total assets less loans and goodwill) of its associated companies. See Exhibit 3 for a listing of associated companies.

[b]Amounts owed to creditors are comprised chiefly of accounts payable to trade creditors, taxes payable, and accruals and deferred income.

EXHIBIT 3

Principal Subsidiary and Associated Undertakings, 1993

Source: Annual reports.

Principal subsidiary undertakings

Automotive distribution
Lex Retail Group Limited
Dan Perkins Limited
Gilbert Rice Limited
Gilldale Limited
Graham Motors (SNM) Limited
Hyundai Car (UK) Limited (Lex Group effective holding 50.1%)
Hyundai Finance Holdings (UK) Limited
Lex Brooklands Limited
Lex Mead Limited
Lex Tillotson Limited
Sellers & Batty (Peterborough) Limited
Seltra SA (France)
Shaw & Kilburn Limited
SNM Cars Limited
Specialist Cars (SNM) Limited
Target Motors (SNM) Limited
The S.M.T. Sales & Service Company Limited

Principal associated undertakings

	Lex Group Effective Holding in Ordinary Share Capital
Automotive distribution	
Campbell Automotive Group Inc. (USA)	50%
Contract hire and vehicle finance	
Lex Vehicle Leasing Limited	50%
Transfleet Services Limited	50%
Harvey Plant Limited	50%
Lex Systems Leasing Limited	50%
I.M. Finance Limited	49%
VOCS Contract Hire Limited	49%

EXHIBIT 4 Capital Employed and Gearing Ratios by Line of Business, 1993 (millions of pounds, except percentages and ratios)

Source: Based on L.E.K. Partnership. "Lex Service PLC: Cost of Capital" (London: November 25, 1993).

	1993 Capital Employed			Equity Market/ Book Ratio	1993 Debt/Capital Ratio	
	Debt	Equity	Total		Book	Market
Automotive distribution[a]	£ 6.4	£ 189.1	£ 195.5	1.26	3.3%	2.6%
Contract hire[b]	457.2	99.0	556.2	1.35	82.2	77.4
Property[c]	0.0	31.4	31.4	.77	0.0	0.0
Total	463.6	319.5	783.1			

[a]Figures shown include Lex's 50% interest in the Campbell Automotive Group.

[b]Figures shown for contract hire are the values of *total* debt and *total* equity for each associate company. Lex's percentage equity ownership position in each of these associates is shown in Exhibit 3. Lex has not guaranteed the borrowings of any of its associated joint ventures. However, both Lex and Lombard have agreed to ensure that the total assets of each U.K. contract hire company will at all times at least equal its total liabilities.

[c]Figures shown are for real estate owned by Lex Services but currently not used in automotive distribution and, therefore, available for redeployment. Sale of such real estate would give rise to non-trading profits or losses in the period in which it was sold.

EXHIBIT 5 Asset Betas of Comparable Companies

Source: Based on L.E.K. Partnership. "Lex Service PLC: Cost of Capital" (London: November 25, 1993).

Automotive Distribution		Property	
Evans Halshaw Holdings P.L.C.	.54	Bradford Property	.94
Vardy Reg P.L.C.	.65	British Land Co. P.L.C.	.66
Appleyard Group P.L.C.	.81	Brixton	.66
Quicks Group P.L.C.	.72	Capital & Counties P.L.C.	.49
Perry Group P.L.C.	.55	Frogmore Estates P.L.C.	.97
Lookers P.L.C.	.51	G. Portland	.71
Trimoco Motor Group Ltd.	.53	Land Sec.	.65
Dagenham Motors Ltd.	.59	MEPC P.L.C.	.72
Average	.61	H.W. Peel & Co. Ltd.	.33
		Slough Estates P.L.C.	.72
Lex Vehicle Leasing			
T. Cowie P.L.C.	.40	Average	.68
Jessups P.L.C.	.28		
Dawson Group P.L.C.	.54		
Average	.41		

EXHIBIT 6 Target Debt-Equity Ratios

Source: Based on L.E.K. Partnership. "Lex Service PLC: Cost of Capital" (London: November 25, 1993).

	Book-Value Target Range			Equity Market/	Market-Value Target Range		
	Minimum	Midpoint	Maximum	Book Ratio	Minimum	Midpoint	Maximum
Consolidated Company	.15	.225	.30	1.24	.12	.18	.24
Automotive	.10	.185	.27	1.26	.08	.15	.21
Contract Hire[a]	6.60	6.60	6.60	1.35	4.89	4.89	4.89
Property	1.00	1.00	1.00	.77	1.30	1.30	1.30

[a]Figures shown for Contract Hire represent a value weighted average of the individual target debt-equity ratios for Lex Vehicle Leasing, Transfleet Service, and Harvey Plant.

Sampa Video, Inc.

Sampa Video, Inc. was the second largest chain of videocassette rental stores in the greater Boston area, operating 30 wholly owned outlets. Begun in 1988 as a small store in Harvard Square catering mostly to students, the company grew rapidly, primarily due to its reputation for customer service and an extensive selection of foreign and independent movies. These differentiating factors allowed Sampa Video to compete directly with the leader in the industry, Blockbuster Video. But unlike the larger rival, Sampa had no ambitions to grow outside of its Boston territory. Exhibit 1 contains summary financial information on the company as of their latest fiscal year-end.

In March 2001, Sampa Video was considering entering the business of home delivery of movie rentals. The company would set up a web page where customers could choose movies based on available in-store inventory and pick a time for delivery. This would put Sampa in competition with new Internet-based competitors, such as Netflix.com that rented DVDs through the mail and Kramer.com and Cityretrieve.com that hand delivered DVDs and videocassettes.

While it was expected that the project would cannibalize the existing operations to some extent, management believed that incremental sales would be substantial in the long run. The project would provide customers the same convenience as Internet-based DVD rentals for the wider selection of movies available on videocassettes. Sampa also planned to hand deliver DVDs. The company expected that the project would increase its annual revenue growth rate from 5% to 10% a year over the following 5 years. After that, as the home delivery business matured, the free cash flow would grow at the same 5% long-term rate as the videocassette rental industry as a whole. Exhibit 2 contains management's projections for the expected incremental revenues and cash flows achievable from the project.

Sampa management's major concern was the significant up-front investment required to start the project. This consisted primarily of setting up a network of delivery vehicles and staff, developing the website, and some initial advertising and promotional efforts to make existing customers aware of the new service. Management estimated these costs at $1.5 million, all of which would be incurred in December 2001, as the service would be launched in January 2002.[1]

Management was debating how to assess the project's debt capacity and the impact of any financing decisions on value. In thinking about how much debt to raise for the project, two options were being considered. The first was to fund a fixed amount of debt, which would be either kept in perpetuity or paid down gradually. The second alternative was to adjust the amount of debt so as to maintain a constant ratio of debt to firm value. Exhibit 3 contains information on market conditions as well as management's assumptions regarding the project's expected cost of debt.

Professor Gregor Andrade prepared this case. HBS cases are developed solely as the basis for class discussion. Cases are not intended to serve as endorsements, sources of primary data, or illustrations of effective or ineffective management.

Copyright © 2001 President and Fellows of Harvard College. To order copies or request permission to reproduce materials, call 1-800-545-7685, write Harvard Business School Publishing, Boston, MA 02163, or go to http://www.hbsp.harvard.edu. No part of this publication may be reproduced, stored in a retrieval system, used in a spreadsheet, or transmitted in any form or by any means—electronic, mechanical, photocopying, recording, or otherwise—without the permission of Harvard Business School.

[1]For the purposes of this exercise, it is assumed that all start-up costs would have been capitalized, and depreciated over time. In reality, some of these costs would have been capitalized (e.g., investment in delivery vehicles) while others would have been expensed immediately (e.g., advertising costs).

EXHIBIT 1
Summary Financial Information on Sampa Video, Inc., 2000 (in thousands of dollars)

Source: Casewriter estimates.

	FY 2000
Sales	22,500
EBITDA[a]	2,500
Depreciation	1,100
Operating Profit	1,400
Net Income	660

[a]EBITDA is the Earnings Before Interest, Taxes, Depreciation, and Amortization.

EXHIBIT 2
Projections of Incremental Expected Sales and Cash Flows for Home Delivery Project 2002–2006 (in thousands of dollars)

Source: Casewriter estimates.

	2002E	2003E	2004E	2005E	2006E
Sales	1,200	2,400	3,900	5,600	7,500
EBITD[a]	180	360	585	840	1,125
Depreciation	(200)	(225)	(250)	(275)	(300)
EBIT	(20)	135	335	565	825
Tax Expense	8	(54)	(134)	(226)	(330)
EBIAT[a]	(12)	81	201	339	495
CAPX[b]	300	300	300	300	300
Investment in Working Capital	0	0	0	0	0

[a]EBITD is the Earnings Before Interest, Taxes, and Depreciation. EBIAT is the Earnings Before Interest and After Taxes. Taxes calculated assuming no interest expense.
[b]Annual capital expenditures of $300,000 were in addition to the initial $1.5 million outlay, and are assumed to remain constant in perpetuity.

EXHIBIT 3
Additonal Assumptions

Source: Casewriter estimates.

Risk-Free Rate (R_f)	**5.0%**
Project Cost of Debt (R_d)	6.8%
Market Risk Premium	7.2%
Marginal Corporate Tax Rate	40%
Project Debt Beta (β_d)	0.25
Asset Beta for Kramer.com and Cityretrieve.com	1.50

Capital Cash Flows: A Simple Approach to Valuing Risky Cash Flows

1. Introduction

The most common technique for valuing risky cash flows is the Free Cash Flow method. In that method, interest tax shields are excluded from the Free Cash Flows and the tax deductibility of interest is treated as a decrease in the cost of capital using the after-tax weighted average cost of capital (WACC). Because the weighted average cost of capital is affected by changes in capital structure, the Free Cash Flow method poses several implementation problems in highly leveraged transactions, restructurings, project financings, and other instances in which capital structure changes over time. In these situations, the capital structure has to be estimated and those estimates have to be used to compute the appropriate weighted average cost of capital in each period. Under these circumstances, the Free Cash Flow method can be used to correctly value the cash flows, but it is not straightforward.

This paper presents an alternative method for valuing risky cash flows. I call this method the Capital Cash Flow (CCF) method because the cash flows include all of the cash available to capital providers, including the interest tax shields. In a capital structure with only ordinary debt and common equity, Capital Cash Flows equal the flows available to equity—net income plus depreciation less capital expenditure and the increase in working capital—plus the interest paid to debtholders. The interest tax shields decrease taxable income, decrease taxes, and thereby increase after-tax cash flows. In other words, Capital Cash Flows equal Free Cash Flows plus the interest tax shields. Because the interest tax shields are included in the cash flows, the appropriate discount rate is before-tax and corresponds to the riskiness of the assets.

Although the Free Cash Flow and Capital Cash Flow methods treat interest tax shields differently, the two methods are algebraically equivalent. In other words, the Capital Cash Flow method is a different way of valuing cash flows using the same assumptions and approach as the Free Cash Flow method. The advantage of the Capital Cash Flow method is its simplicity. Whenever debt is forecasted in levels instead of as a percent of total enterprise value, the Capital Cash Flow method is much easier to use because the interest tax shields are easy to calculate and easy to include in the cash flows. The Capital Cash Flow method retains its simplicity when the forecasted debt levels and the implicit debt-to-value ratios change throughout the forecast period. Also, the expected asset return depends on the riskiness of the asset and therefore does not change when capital structure changes. As a result, the discount rate for the Capital Cash Flows does not have to be re-estimated every period. In contrast, when using the FCF method, the after-tax weighted average cost of capital (WACC) has to be re-estimated every period. Because the WACC depends on value-weights, the value of the firm has to be estimated simultaneously. The CCF method avoids this complexity so that it is especially useful in valuing highly levered firms whose debt is usually forecasted in levels and whose capital structure changes substantially over time.

The Capital Cash Flow method is closely related to my work on valuing riskless cash flows (Ruback (1986)) and to Stewart Myers' work on the Adjusted Present Value (APV) method (Myers (1974)). In my paper on riskless cash flows, I showed that the interest tax shields associated with riskless cash flows can be equivalently treated as increasing cash flows by the interest tax shield or as decreasing the discount rate to the after-tax riskless rate. The analysis in this paper presents similar results for risky cash flows; namely, risky cash flows can be equivalently valued by using the Capital Cash Flow method with the interest tax shields in the cash flows or by using the Free Cash Flow method with the interest shields in the discount rate.

The Adjusted Present Value method is generally calculated as the sum of Free Cash Flows discounted by the cost of assets plus interest tax shields discounted at the cost of debt. It results in a higher value than the Capital Cash Flow method because it assigns a higher value to interest tax shields. The interest tax shields that are discounted by the cost of debt in the APV method are discounted by the cost of assets explicitly in the CCF method and implicitly in the Free Cash Flow method. Stewart Myers suggested the term "Compressed APV" to describe the CCF method because the APV method is equivalent to CCF when the interest tax shields are discounted at the cost of assets. However, most descriptions of APV suggest discounting the interest tax shields at the cost of debt (Taggart (1991) and Luehrman (1997)).

The Adjusted Present Value method treats the interest tax shields as being less risky than the assets because the level of debt is implicitly assumed to be a fixed dollar amount. The intuition is that interest tax shields are realized roughly when interest is paid so that the risk of the shields matches the risk of the payment. This matching of the risk of the tax shields and the interest payment only occurs when the level of debt is fixed. Otherwise, the risk of the shields depends on both the risk of the payment *and* systematic changes in the amount of debt. Because the risk of a levered firm is a weighted average of the risk of an unlevered firm and the risk of the interest tax shields, the presence of less risky interest tax shields reduces the risk of the levered firm. As a result, a tax adjustment has to be made when unlevering an equity beta to calculate an asset beta.

The Capital Cash Flow method, like the Free Cash Flow method, assumes that debt is proportional to value. The higher the value of the firm, the more debt the firm uses in its financial structure. The more debt used, the higher the interest tax shields. The risk of the interest tax shields therefore depends on the risk of the debt as well as the changes in the level of the debt. When debt is a fixed proportion of value, the interest tax shields will have the same risk as the firm, even when the debt is riskless. Because the interest tax shields have the same risk as the firm, leverage does not alter the beta of the firm. As a result, no tax adjustment has to be made when calculating asset betas.

The primary contributions of this paper are to introduce the Capital Cash Flow method of valuation, to demonstrate its equivalency to the Free Cash Flow method, and to show its relation to the Adjusted Present Value method. The Capital Cash Flow method has been used in teaching materials to value cash flow forecasts, in Kaplan and Ruback (1995) to value highly levered transactions, and in Hotchkiss, Gilson, and Ruback (1998) to value firms emerging from Chapter 11 reorganizations.[1] Also, finance textbooks contain some of the ideas about the relation between the discount rate for interest tax shields, unlevering formulas, and financial policy. This paper provides the basis for the applications of Capital Cash Flows and highlights the linkages between the three methods of cash flow valuation.

Although the focus of this paper is on cash flow methods that yield estimates of total enterprise value, the results have implications for the Equity Cash Flow and Residual Income methods. In the Equity Cash Flow method, the free cash flows to equity are discounted at the cost of equity capital. That method is equivalent to the Free

[1]Teaching materials include Ruback (1989, 1995a, 1995b) and Holthausen and Zmijewski (1996).

Cash Flow method and has the same drawbacks.[2] The cost of equity capital, like the weighted average cost of capital, changes as leverage changes and requires a simultaneous estimation of the equity-to-value ratios and the value whenever the debt is forecasted in levels. In those situations, the Capital Cash Flow method is a simpler approach. Similarly, as Lundholm and O'Keefe (2000) stress, the Residual Income approach is equivalent to the Free Cash Flow method as long as consistent assumptions are used—including the assumption that the discount rate consistently incorporates the assumed debt policy. Thus, the Residual Income approach does not mitigate the valuation issues addressed in this paper.

Section 2 of this paper describes the mechanics of the Capital Cash Flow method, including the calculation of the cash flows and the discount rate. Section 3 shows that the Capital Cash Flow method is equivalent to the Free Cash Flow method through an example and then with a more general proof. Section 4 relates the Capital Cash Flow and the Adjusted Present Value methods and shows that the difference between the two methods depends on the implicit assumption about the financial policy of the firm. I also show that the assumption about financial policy has implications regarding the impact of taxes on risk and thereby determines the approach used to transform equity betas into asset betas.

2. Mechanics of Capital Cash Flow Valuation

The present value of Capital Cash Flows is calculated by discounting the CCFs by the expected asset return, K_A. This section details the calculation of the CCFs in Section 2.1 and explains the calculations of K_A in Section 2.2. An example is presented in Section 2.3.

2.1 Calculating Capital Cash Flows

Capital Cash Flows include all of the cash flows that are paid or could be paid to any capital provider. By including cash flows to all security holders, CCFs measure all of the after-tax cash generated by the assets. Since CCFs measure the after-tax cash flows from the enterprise, the present value of these cash flows equals the value of the enterprise.

Figure I summarizes the calculation of Capital Cash Flows. The calculations depend on whether the cash flow forecasts begin with net income (NI) or earnings before interest and taxes (EBIT).

The Net Income Path

Net income includes any tax benefit from debt financing because interest is deducted before computing taxes. The interest tax shields therefore increase net income. Available cash flow is net income plus cash flow adjustments and non-cash interest. Cash flow adjustments include those adjustments required to transform the accounting data into cash flow data. Typical adjustments include adding depreciation and amortization because these are non-cash subtractions from net income. Non-cash interest occurs when the interest is paid in kind by issuing additional debt instead of paying the interest in cash. These non-cash interest payments are deducted from net income like cash interest but are not a cash outflow and therefore must be added to net income to calculate cash flow available.

Capital expenditures are subtracted from net income because these cash outflows do not appear on the income statement and thus are not deducted from net income. Subtracting the increases in working capital transforms the recognized accounting revenues and costs into cash revenues and costs. The label "available cash flow" often appears in projections and measures the funds available for debt repayments or other

[2]See Ruback (1995b) and Esty (1999) for a discussion of the relation between the Free Cash Flow and Equity Cash methods.

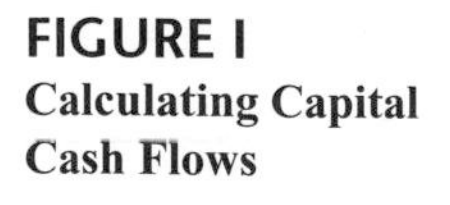

FIGURE I
Calculating Capital Cash Flows

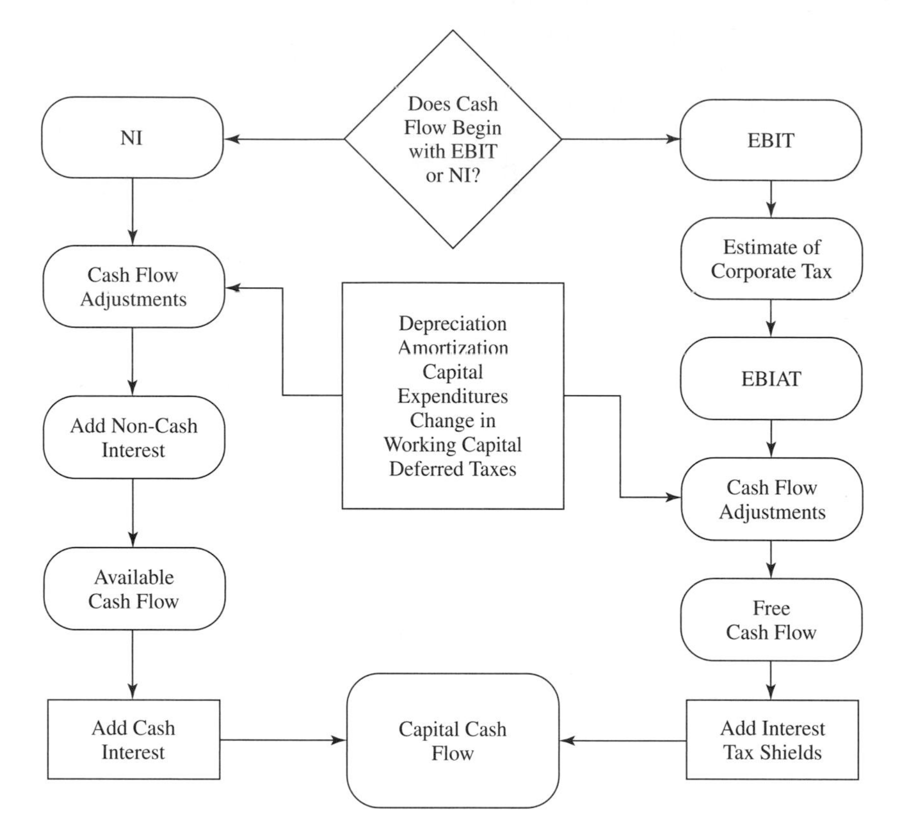

corporate uses. Capital Cash Flow is computed by adding cash interest to available cash flow so that cash flows represent the after-tax cash available to all cash providers.

The EBIT Path

When cash flow forecasts present EBIT instead of net income, corporate taxes have to be estimated to calculate earnings before interest and after taxes (EBIAT). Typically the taxes are estimated by multiplying EBIT by a historical marginal tax rate. EBIAT is then adjusted using the cash flow adjustments that transform the accounting data into cash flow data. EBIAT plus cash flow adjustments equals Free Cash Flow, which is used to compute value using the after-tax weighted average cost of capital (WACC). Free Cash Flows equal Capital Cash Flows less the interest tax shields. Interest tax shields, therefore, have to be added to the Free Cash Flows to arrive at the Capital Cash Flows. The interest tax shields on both cash and non-cash debt are added because both types of interest tax shields reduce taxes and thereby increase after-tax cash flow.

The EBIT path should yield the same Capital Cash Flows as the net income path. In practice, however, the net income path is usually easier and more accurate than the EBIT path. The primary advantage of the net income path is that it uses the corporate forecast of taxes, which should include any special circumstances of the firm. Taxes are rarely equal to the marginal tax rate times taxable income. The EBIT path involves estimating taxes, usually by assuming a constant average tax rate. This ignores the special circumstances of the firm and adds a likely source of error.

2.2 Calculating the Expected Asset Return

The appropriate discount rate to value Capital Cash Flows (CCFs) is a before-tax rate because the tax benefits of debt financing are included in the CCFs. The pre-tax rate should correspond to the riskiness of the CCFs. One such discount rate is the pre-tax weighted average cost of capital:

$$\text{Pre-tax WACC} = \frac{D}{V}K_D + \frac{E}{V}K_E \tag{2.1}$$

where D/V is the debt-to-value ratio, E/V is the equity-to-value ratio, and K_D and K_E are the respective expected debt and equity returns. Using the pre-tax WACC as a discount rate is correct, but there is a much simpler approach. If expected returns in (2.1) are determined by the Capital Asset Pricing Model (CAPM):

$$K_D = R_F + \beta_D R_P \tag{2.2}$$

$$K_E = R_F + \beta_E R_P \tag{2.3}$$

where R_F is the risk-free rate, R_P is the risk premium, and β_D and β_E are the debt and equity betas, respectively. Substituting (2.2) and (2.3) into (2.1) yields:

$$\text{Pre-tax WACC} = \frac{D}{V}(R_F + \beta_D R_P) + \frac{E}{V}(R_F + \beta_E R_P). \tag{2.4}$$

Simplifying:

$$\text{Pre-tax WACC} = R_F + \left(\frac{D}{V}\beta_D + \frac{E}{V}\beta_E\right)R_P. \tag{2.5}$$

The beta of the assets, β_U, is a weighted average of the debt and equity beta:

$$\beta_U = \frac{D}{V}\beta_D + \frac{E}{V}\beta_E. \tag{2.6}$$

Substituting (2.6) into (2.5) provides a simple formula for the pre-tax WACC, which is also labeled as the Expected Asset Return, K_A:

$$K_A = \text{Pre-tax WACC} = R_F + \beta_U R_P \tag{2.7}$$

Note that the pre-tax expected asset return depends only on the market-wide parameters for the risk-free rate, R_F, and the risk premium, R_P, and on the unlevered asset beta, β_U. The debt-to-value and equity-to-value ratios are *not* in (2.7). K_A, therefore, does *not* depend on capital structure and does *not* have to be recomputed as capital structure changes. This means that the debt-to-value and equity-to-value ratios do *not* have to be estimated to use the Capital Cash Flow valuation method. This eliminates much of the complexity encountered when applying the FCF method.

The discount rate for the Capital Cash Flows is simple to calculate regardless of the capital structure. It takes two steps. First, estimate the asset beta, β_U. The asset beta is usually estimated using equation (2.6) by multiplying the equity beta (β_E) by the equity-to-value ratio and adding an estimate of the debt beta multiplied by the debt-to-value ratio. Second, use β_U, together with the risk-free rate, R_F, and the risk premium, R_P, to compute the expected asset return, K_A. For example, if the equity beta is 1.25, the debt beta is 0.25, and the equity-to-value ratio is 0.75, the asset beta is $0.75 \times 1.25 + 0.25 \times 0.25 = 1.0$. With an asset beta of 1.0, an assumed risk free rate to equal 10% and an assumed risk premium of 8%, the expected asset return is $10\% + 1.0 \times 8\% = 18\%$.

2.3 Numerical Example

Table A contains a numerical example that demonstrates the Capital Cash Flow method. The example assumes an initial investment of $100,000 to be depreciated equally over three years. Panel A details the assumptions. The asset beta is assumed to equal 1.0 in all three years.[3] The forecasted expected pre-tax operating profits are \$50,000 in year one, \$60,000 in year two, and \$70,000 in year three. The risk-free rate is assumed to be 10%, the risk premium is assumed to be 8%, and the tax rate is assumed to be 33%. The debt is assumed to be risky, with a debt beta of 0.35 in the first year, 0.30 in the second year, and 0.25 in the third year. The project is financed with debt so that the initial debt is \$100,000 at the beginning of year one, \$50,000 at the beginning of year two, and \$20,000 at the beginning of year three.

The Capital Cash Flow is calculated by following the net income path. The cash flow available is equal to net income plus noncash adjustments. CCF is calculated by adding the expected interest to the cash flow available.

The value of the Capital Cash Flows is calculated using the expected asset return. The easiest way to calculate the asset return is to use the asset beta in the CAPM. Using a risk-free rate of 10%, an asset beta of 1.0, and a risk premium of 8% yields an expected asset return of 18%. The asset return does not depend on leverage because it is a pre-tax cost of capital. It remains constant even though the leverage changes through time. As Panel B of Table A shows, discounting the CCFs at the expected asset return results in a value of \$136,996.

3. The Relation between Capital Cash Flow and Free Cash Flow Valuation

3.1 Numerical Example

Panel C of Table A presents a Free Cash Flow valuation of the same cash flows valued using Capital Cash Flows in Panel B. The Free Cash Flows are calculated from EBIT, which is reduced by the hypothetical taxes on EBIT to determine EBIAT. Adding the non-cash adjustments to EBIAT results in Free Cash Flows.

TABLE A
An Example of Capital Cash Flow and Free Cash Flow

Panel A: Assumptions				
Market parameters				
Riskless debt rate =	10%			
Risk premium =	8%			
Tax rate =	33%			
		year 1	year 2	year 3
Asset Beta		1.00	1.00	1.00
Debt Beta		0.35	0.30	0.25
Expected Cash Flows				
Operating Profit		50,000	60,000	70,000
Less: Depreciation		33,333	33,333	33,333
EBIT		16,667	26,667	36,667
Less: Expected Interest (#1)		12,800	6,200	2,400
Pre-tax Income		3,867	20,467	34,267
Less: Taxes		1,276	6,754	11,308
Net Income		2,591	13,713	22,959

[3]The equivalency of the CCF and FCF methods does not depend on a constant asset beta. The asset beta could change each year. In practice, however, the asset beta is related to the assets of the company and thus is assumed to be constant unless the asset composition changes.

TABLE A
(Continued)

Non-cash Adjustments (#2)	43,333	43,333	43,333
Cash Flow Available	45,924	57,046	66,292
Beginning Debt	100,000	50,000	20,000

Panel B: Capital Cash Flow Valuation

	year 1	year 2	year 3
Cash Flow Available	45,924	57,046	66,292
Plus: Expected Interest (#1)	12,800	6,200	2,400
Capital Cash Flow	58,724	63,246	68,692
Cost of Assets (#3)	18.0%	18.0%	18.0%
Discount Factor	0.8475	0.7182	0.6086
Present Value of CCFs	49,766	45,422	41,808
Total Enterprise Value	136,996		

Panel C: Free Cash Flow Valuation

	year 1	year 2	year 3
EBIT	16,667	26,667	36,667
Less: Tax on EBIT	5,500	8,800	12,100
EBIAT	11,167	17,867	24,567
Non-Cash Adjustments (#2)	43,333	43,333	43,333
Free Cash Flows	54,500	61,200	67,900
Capitalization			
Total Enterprise Value (#4)	136,996	102,932	58,214
Debt	100,000	50,000	20,000
WACC Calculations			
Debt			
Percent	73.0%	48.6%	34.4%
After-tax cost (#5)	8.6%	8.3%	8.0%
Contribution (#6)	6.3%	4.0%	2.8%
Equity			
Percent	27.0%	51.4%	65.6%
Equity beta (#7)	2.76	1.66	1.39
Cost (#8)	32.1%	23.3%	21.1%
Contribution (#9)	8.7%	12.0%	13.9%
WACC	14.9%	16.0%	16.6%
Discount Factor	0.8702	0.7501	0.6431
Present Value of FCFs	47,426	45,905	45,665
Total Enterprise Value	136,996		

Note #1: Expected Interest is calculcated using the Expected Cost of Debt from the CAPM (riskfree rate plus the debt beta times the risk premium).
Note #2: Noncash adjustments include depreciation plus $10,000 of other adjustments.
Note #3: Expected asset return is calculated using the assumed asset beta in the CAPM with the assumed riskless debt rate and risk premium.
Note #4: Total Enterprise Value is the present value of the remaining cash flows.
Note #5: After-tax cost of debt is the Expected Cost of Debt times (1-tax rate).
Note #6: Debt contribution is the After-tax Expected Cost of Debt times the percent debt.
Note #7: Equity is determined by levering the asset beta ((asset beta - debt beta contribution)/percent equity).
Note #8: Cost of equity is calculcated using the CAPM as the riskfree rate plus the equity beta times the risk premium.
Note #9: Equity contribution is the cost of equity times the percent equity.

The Free Cash Flows are valued using the after-tax weighted average cost of capital (WACC). The WACC has two components: the after-tax cost of debt and the levered cost of equity. The after-tax cost of debt depends on the assumed riskiness of the debt with the cost of debt calculated as its CAPM expected return using (2.2). The levered cost of equity is calculated by levering the asset beta to determine the levered equity beta. Because the fraction of debt is not the same each year, the WACC and its components need to be recomputed each year.

The formula for levering the asset or unlevered beta is:

$$\beta_E = \left(\beta_U - \frac{D}{V}\beta_D\right) / \frac{E}{V} \tag{3.1}$$

which requires information on the value of the firm to compute the percentage of debt and equity in the capital structure.[4] Generally, an iterative or dynamic programming approach is used to solve for a consistent estimate of enterprise value.[5] However, because the value is already computed in Panel B, that value can be used to compute the debt and equity proportions. Based on the implied equity-to-value ratio of 27.0% in the first year, the asset beta of 1.0, and the debt beta of 0.35, the implied equity beta is 2.76. Using the CAPM and the assumed market parameters, the expected cost of equity is 32.1% in the first year. Weighting the expected after-tax cost of debt and the expected cost of equity by their proportions in the capital structure results in a WACC of 14.9% for the first year.

The capital structure changes in each period because the ratio of the value of the remaining cash flows and the amount of debt outstanding does not remain constant throughout the life of the project. Repeating the process of valuing the enterprise, determining the debt and equity proportions, unlevering the asset beta, and estimating the equity cost of capital according to the CAPM results in a weighted average cost of capital of 16.0% for the second year and 16.6% for the third year. These after-tax WACCs rise as the percentage of debt in the capital structure, and the corresponding amount of the interest tax shields, fall.

Total Enterprise Value is calculated by discounting the FCFs by the after-tax WACCs. Since the after-tax WACCs change, the discount rate for each period is the compounded rate that uses the preceding after-tax WACCs. The resulting value of the Free Cash Flows is $136,996, exactly the same value as obtained in the Capital Cash Flow calculations in Panel B of Table A.

3.2 Proof of Equivalency

This section shows that the Capital Cash Flow method is equivalent to the Free Cash Flow method. To keep the analysis simple, assume the asset being valued generates a constant pre-tax operating cash flow. This cash flow is before tax but after cash adjustments such as depreciation, capital expenditures, and changes in working capital. The after-tax operating cash flow equals earnings before interest and after-tax plus the cash flow adjustments and equals Free Cash Flow, FCF, that measures the cash flow of the firm if it were all equity financed.

The value, V_{FCF}, is calculated using the Free Cash Flow method by discounting the free cash flows by the after-tax WACC:

$$V_{FCF} = \frac{FCF}{WACC} \tag{3.2}$$

[4]This formula is derived in Section 4.2 of this paper.

[5]See Esty (1999) for an explanation of the iterative technique and a project finance application of that approach.

where V is the value of the project being valued. WACC, the after-tax weighted average cost of capital, is defined as:

$$\text{WACC} = \frac{D}{V}K_D(1-\tau) + \frac{E}{V}K_E \tag{3.3}$$

with D and E equal to the market value of debt and equity, respectively; τ is the tax rate, $K_D(1-\tau)$ is the after-tax expected cost of debt, and K_E is the expected cost of equity.

The Capital Cash Flow is the expected cash flow to all capital providers with its projected financing policy, including any benefits of interest tax shields from its financial structure. Since Free Cash Flow measures the cash flow assuming a hypothetical all equity capital structure, Capital Cash Flow is equal to Free Cash Flow plus interest tax shields:

$$\text{CCF} = \text{FCF} + \text{Interest Tax Shield} = \text{FCF} + \tau K_D D \tag{3.4}$$

where $\tau K_D D$ is the interest tax shield calculated as the tax rate [τ] times the interest rate on the debt [K_D] times the amount of debt outstanding, D.

Value is calculated using the Capital Cash Flow method, V_{CCF}, by discounting the Capital Cash Flows by the expected return on assets. The expected asset return is measured using the Capital Asset Pricing Model and the asset beta (β_U) of the project being valued:

$$V_{CCF} = \frac{\text{FCF} + \tau K_D D}{R_F + \beta_U R_P} \tag{3.5}$$

where R_F is the risk-free rate and R_P is the risk premium.

The goal is to show that the value obtained using FCFs and WACC is the *same* as the value obtained using CCFs and K_A. In other words, the goal is to show that (3.2) is identical to (3.5). Combining (3.2) and (3.3):

$$V_{FCF} = \frac{\text{FCF}}{K_D \frac{D}{V}(1-\tau) + \frac{E}{V}K_E} \tag{3.6}$$

In (3.6) K_E and K_D are measured using the Capital Asset Pricing Model according to (2.2) and (2.3). By substituting the equality between the pre-tax WACC and the cost of assets from (2.7):

$$V_{FCF} = \frac{\text{FCF}}{(R_F + \beta_U R_P) - \tau K_D \frac{D}{V}} = \frac{\text{FCF}}{K_A - \tau K_D \frac{D}{V}} \tag{3.7}$$

Multiplying both sides by the denominator on the right-hand side of (3.7) yields:

$$V_{FCF}(K_A) - \tau K_D D = \text{FCF} \tag{3.8}$$

Rearranging terms by adding $\tau K_D D$ to both sides and dividing by the cost of assets shows that:

$$V_{FCF} = \frac{\text{FCF} + DK_D}{K_A} = V_{CCF} \tag{3.9}$$

which is identical to (3.5). Thus, this proof shows that the FCF approach in (3.2) and the CCF approach of (3.5) will, when correctly applied, result in identical present values for risky cash flows.[6]

[6]Taggart (1991) analyzes the impact of personal taxes on the Free Cash Flow approach and shows that the corporate tax rate is the only tax rate that explicitly enters the valuation equation. The algebraic equivalence of the Capital Cash Flow and Free Cash Flow implies that the corporate tax rate is also the only tax rate in the Capital Cash Flow valuation equation.

3.3 Choosing between Capital Cash Flows and Free Cash Flow Methods

The proof in Section 3.2 shows that the Capital Cash Flow method and the Free Cash Flow method are equivalent because they make the same assumptions about cash flows, capital structure, and taxes. When applied correctly using the same information and assumptions, the two methods provide identical answers. The choice between the two methods, therefore, is governed by ease of use. The ease of use, of course, is determined by the complexity of applying the method and the likelihood of error.

The form of the cash flow projections generally dictates the choice of method. In the simplest valuation exercise, when the cash flows do not include the interest tax shields and the financing strategy is specified as broad ratios, the Free Cash Flow method is easier than the Capital Cash Flow method. To apply the FCF method, the discount rate can be calculated in a straightforward manner using prevailing capital market data and information on the target capital structure. Because that target structure does not (by assumption) change over time, a single weighted average cost of capital can be used to value the cash flows. This type of valuation often occurs in the early stages of a project valuation before the detailed financial plan is developed. When the goal is to get a simplified "back-of-the-envelope" value, the FCF method is usually the best approach.

When the cash flow projections include detailed information about the financing plan, the Capital Cash Flow method is generally the more direct valuation approach. Because such plans typically include the forecasted interest payments and net income, the CCFs are simply computed by adding the interest payments to the net income and making the appropriate non-cash adjustments. These cash flows are valued by discounting them at the expected cost of assets. This process is simple and straightforward even if the capital structure changes through time. In contrast, applying the Free Cash Flow method is more complex and more prone to error because, as illustrated in Section 3.1 and Panel C of Table A, firm and the equity value have to be inferred to apply the FCF method. Also, the CCF method can easily incorporate complex tax situations. Therefore, in most transactions, restructurings, leverage buyouts, and bankruptcies, the CCF method will be the easier to apply.

4. Capital Cash Flows and Adjusted Present Value

Both Capital Cash Flows and Adjusted Present Value can be expressed as:

$$\text{Value} = \text{Free Cash Flows Discounted at } K_A + \text{Interest Tax Shields Discounted at } K_{ITS}$$

where K_{ITS} is the discount rate for interest tax shields. For both methods, the discount rate for the Free Cash Flows is the cost of assets (K_A), which is generally computed using the CAPM with the beta of an unlevered firm. The methods differ in K_{ITS}, the discount rate for interest tax shields: the APV method generally uses the debt rate; the CCF method uses the cost of assets, K_A. APV assigns a higher value to the interest tax shields so that values calculated with APV will be higher than CCF valuations.[7]

[7] Inselbag and Kaufold (1997) present examples of Free Cash Flow and APV valuations that result in identical values for debt policies with both fixed debt and proportional debt. This occurs because they infer the equity costs that result in equivalence in their FCF valuations instead of obtaining discount rates from the CAPM.

TABLE B
Percentage Differences between APV Values and CCF Values (V_{APV}/V_{CCF})

Tax Shield/ All Equity Value[2]	Ratio of Expected Asset Return to Debt Rate (K_A/K_D)[1]		
	1.25	1.50	1.75
10%	2%	5%	7%
15%	3%	7%	10%
20%	4%	8%	13%

Note #1: Calculations assume perpetual cash flows and interest tax shields.
Note #2: All Equity Value is the Free Cash Flows discounted at the cost of assets.

To gauge how much higher APV valuations are relative to CCF valuations, Table B calculates the difference in values assuming perpetual cash flows and interest tax shields. I define the value of the interest tax shields in the CCF valuation as a proportion, γ, of the all equity value. The ratio of V_{APV} to V_{CCF} becomes:

$$\frac{V_{APV}}{V_{CCF}} = \frac{1 + \gamma\left(\frac{K_A}{K_D}\right)}{1 + \gamma} \tag{4.1}$$

Table B presents the percentage differences between the APV and CCF valuations. For example, if $K_D = 10\%$ and $K_A = 15\%$, the ratio of the expected asset return to the expected debt return is 1.5, locating it in the middle column of Table B. If the tax rate is 36% and the debt is 42% of the all equity value, the value of the interest tax shield is about 15% of the all equity value, locating it in the middle row of Table B. In this example, therefore, the APV approach would provide a discounted cash flow value that is 7% higher than the CCF value.

In the CAPM framework, the discount rate for the interest tax shields should depend on the beta of the interest tax shields:

$$K_{ITS} = \text{Risk free rate} + \beta_{ITS} * \text{Risk Premium} \tag{4.2}$$

When debt is assumed fixed, Section 4.1 shows that the beta of the interest tax shields equals the beta of the debt. This implies that the appropriate discount rate for the interest tax shields is the debt rate, which is the rate used in the APV method. It also implies that the interest tax shields reduce risk so that a tax effect should appear when unlevering equity betas. When debt is assumed proportional to value, Section 4.2 shows that the beta of the interest tax shields is equal to the unlevered or asset beta. This implies that the appropriate discount rate is the cost of assets, which is the rate used in the CCF method. It also implies that taxes have no effect on the transformation of equity betas into asset betas. Debt could also be a linear function of firm value with both fixed and proportional components. Section 4.3 shows that the beta of the interest tax shields with a linear debt policy is a value-weighted average of the interest tax shield betas for the fixed and proportional debt policies described in sections 4.1 and 4.2, respectively.

4.1 Fixed Debt Policy

When debt is perpetual and fixed as a dollar amount, D, which does not change as the value of the firm changes, the value of the interest tax shields is:

$$V_{ITS,t} = \frac{\tau \overline{K}_D D}{K_{D,t}} \tag{4.3}$$

where $\bar{K}_D$ is the fixed yield on the debt, $K_{D,t}$ is the cost of debt in period t from (2.2), and τ is the tax rate. The value of the debt can change through time if $\bar{K}_D$ is fixed and the cost of debt changes. Assuming $\bar{K}_D$ is the fixed yield,

$$V_{D,t} = \frac{D\bar{K}_D}{K_{D,t}} \tag{4.4}$$

Substituting (4.4) into (4.3), the value of the interest tax shield at time t therefore can be expressed as:

$$V_{ITS,t} = \tau V_{D,t} \tag{4.5}$$

The beta of the interest tax shields, β_{ITS}, equals:

$$\beta_{ITS} = \frac{Cov(V_{ITS,t}, R_M)}{V_{ITS,t-1} Var(R_M)} \tag{4.6}$$

Substituting (4.5) into (4.6) and simplifying,

$$\beta_{ITS} = \frac{Cov(V_{D,t}, R_M)}{V_{D,t-1} Var(R_M)} = \beta_D \tag{4.7}$$

The beta of the interest tax shields is therefore equal to the beta of the debt when the debt is assumed to be a fixed dollar amount.[8,9] If the debt is assumed to be riskless, the interest tax shields will also be riskless. If the debt is risky, the interest tax shields will have the same amount of systematic risk as the debt. This result shows that the practice of discounting interest tax shields by the expected return on the debt is appropriate when the debt is assumed to be a fixed dollar amount.

The assumption of fixed debt and the result that the beta of interest tax shields equals the debt beta implies that leverage reduces the systematic risk of the levered assets. The value of a levered firm (V_L) exceeds the value of an unlevered or all equity firm (V_U) by value of the interest tax shields from the debt of the levered firm (V_{ITS}):

$$V_L = V_U + V_{ITS} \tag{4.8}$$

Equation (4.8) holds in each time period and abstracts from differences between levered and unlevered firms other than taxes. Also, the analysis assumes strictly proportional taxes. I assume that interest is deductible and that interest tax shields are realized when interest is paid.

The beta of the levered firm, β_L, is a value-weighted average of the unlevered beta, β_U, and the beta of the interest tax shields, β_{ITS}:

$$\beta_L = \frac{V_U}{V_L}\beta_U + \frac{V_{ITS}}{V_L}\beta_{ITS} \tag{4.9}$$

When the beta of the interest tax shields equals the debt beta, equation (4.9) simplifies to:

$$\beta_L = \beta_U - \tau\frac{D}{V_L}(\beta_U - \beta_D) \tag{4.10}$$

[8]When debt is assumed to be fixed in value instead of a fixed dollar amount, the beta of the interest tax shields is zero regardless of the debt beta.

[9]If the debt is not perpetual, the beta of the interest tax shields would equal the beta of the debt when the interest payment and principle payments have the same beta.

The beta of a levered firm, β_L, can also be expressed as a value weighted average of the debt and equity of the levered firm:

$$\beta_L = \frac{E}{V_L}\beta_E + \frac{D}{V_L}\beta_D \tag{4.11}$$

Where E is the equity of the levered firm, β_E is the equity beta, and β_D is the debt beta. Setting (4.10) equal to (4.11):

$$\frac{E}{V_L}\beta_E + \frac{D}{V_L}\beta_D = \beta_L = \beta_U - \tau\frac{D}{V_L}(\beta_U - \beta_D) \tag{4.12}$$

which can be simplified as:

$$\beta_E = \left(\beta_U - \frac{D}{V_L}(\beta_D + \tau(\beta_U - \beta_D))\right) / \frac{E}{V_L} \tag{4.13}$$

Thus the equity beta is equal to the asset beta less the proportion of debt borne by the debt holder and the reduction due to the tax effect and scaled by leverage. The equity beta is reduced by the tax effect because the government absorbs some of the risk of the cash flows. With fixed debt, the interest tax shields portion of the cash flows are insulated from fluctuations in the market value of the firm.

When the debt is riskless, the beta of the debt is zero. Therefore, (4.13) simplifies to:

$$\beta_E = \frac{E + D(1-\tau)}{E}\beta_U \tag{4.14}$$

Equation (4.14) is the standard unlevering formula that correctly includes tax effects when the debt is assumed to be fixed and assumes a zero debt beta. In the next subsection I show that when debt is assumed to be proportional to firm value, taxes do not appear in the unlevering formula.

4.2 Proportional Debt Policy

When the value of debt is assumed to be proportional to total enterprise value, the firm varies the amount of debt outstanding in each period so that:

$$V_D = \delta V_U \tag{4.15}$$

where δ is the proportionality coefficient and V_U is the value of the unlevered firm. The value of the interest tax shields is the tax rate times the value of the debt so that

$$V_{ITS} = \tau V_D = \tau\delta V_U \tag{4.16}$$

Substituting (4.16) into the definition of the beta of the interest tax shields from (4.6):

$$\begin{aligned} \beta_{ITS} &= \frac{Cov(V_{ITS,t}, R_M)}{V_{ITS,t-1}Var(R_M)} \\ &= \frac{Cov(\tau\delta V_{Ut}, R_M)}{\tau\delta V_{U,t-1}Var(R_M)} \\ &= \frac{Cov(V_{U,t}, R_{M,t})}{V_{U,t-1}Var(R_M)} \\ &= \beta_U \end{aligned} \tag{4.17}$$

The equality between the beta of the interest tax shields and the beta of the unlevered firm implies that the rate used to discount the interest tax shields is equal to K_A, the unlevered or asset cost of capital.[10]

The equality between the betas for the interest tax shields and the assets also implies that there is no levering/unlevering tax effect. From (4.9) the beta of a levered firm is a weighted average of the beta of the unlevered firm and the beta of the interest tax shields. Since the asset beta equals the interest tax shield beta, the beta of the levered firm equals the beta of the unlevered firm. To calculate the beta of levered equity, (4.13) can be restated as:

$$\beta_E = \left(\beta_U - \frac{D}{V}\beta_D\right) / \frac{E}{V} \tag{4.18}$$

This result means that tax terms should not be included when applying the Capital Cash Flow or Free Cash Flow methods.[11]

4.3 Choosing between Capital Cash Flows and Adjusted Present Value Methods

Section 4.2 shows that the difference between the Capital Cash Flow and the Adjusted Present Value methods is the implicit assumption about the determinants of leverage. CCF (and equivalently FCF) assumes that debt is proportional to value; APV assumes that debt is fixed and independent of value. Debt cannot literally be strictly proportional to value at all levels of firm value. For example, when a firm is in financial distress, the option component of risky debt increases, thereby distorting the proportionality. Nevertheless, Graham and Harvey (1999) report that about 80% of firms have some form of target debt-to-value ratio, and that the range around the target is tighter for larger firms. That suggests that the CCF approach is more appropriate than the APV approach when valuing corporations.

There are circumstances when the fixed debt assumption is more accurate. These cases typically involve some tax or regulatory restriction on debt, such as industrial revenue bonds that are fixed in dollar amounts. Luehrman (1997) presents an example of APV valuation in which debt is assumed to be a constant fraction of *book* value. To the extent that book value does not respond to market forces, a fraction of book value is a fixed dollar amount.

In practice, valuations are often performed on forecasts that make assumptions about debt policy. When that policy is characterized as a target debt-to-value ratio, the proportional policy seems more accurate. In project finance or leveraged buyout situations, however, the forecasts typically are characterized as a changing dollar amount of debt in each year. These amounts can, of course, be characterized as a changing percentage of value or as a changing dollar amount through time. It isn't obvious from the forecasts themselves whether the assumption of proportional debt or fixed debt is the better description of debt policy. The answer in these circumstances depends on the likely dynamic behavior. If debt policy adheres to the forecasts regardless of the evolution of value through time, the fixed assumption is probably better. Alternatively, if debt is likely to increase as the firm expands and value increases, then the proportional assumption is probably better.

[10]Harris and Pringle (1985) also show that the interest tax shields should be discounted by the pre-tax weighted average cost of capital when debt is assumed to be proportional to value.

[11]Kaplan and Ruback (1995) incorrectly used tax adjustments to unlever observed equity betas to obtain asset betas when applying the Capital Cash Flow method. Correcting this error does not meaningfully change the results of Kaplan and Ruback (1995).

Debt policy can of course be more complex than either an exclusively fixed debt or proportional debt policy, and whatever the debt policy, valuation depends on that policy. For example, debt policy can include a fixed component and a component that is proportional to value:

$$V_D = V_F + \delta V_U \tag{4.19}$$

Such a linear debt policy could occur in a project finance application where a fixed amount of debt is subsidized or guaranteed by a government agency and the remaining debt is roughly proportional to the value of the project.

The valuation of cash flows from a project with a linear debt policy such as (4.19) will combine features of the fixed debt and proportional debt policies. The beta of the interest tax shields for the linear debt policy, for example, is a value-weighted average of the beta with a fixed debt policy (4.7) and the beta with a proportional debt policy (4.17) with the value-weights equal to the relative values of the fixed and proportional debt components:

$$\begin{aligned} \beta_{ITS} &= \frac{Cov(\tau V_{D,t}, R_M)}{\tau V_{Dt-1} Var(R_M)} \\ &= \frac{Cov(\tau V_{Ft} + \delta V_{Ut}, R_M)}{\tau V_{Dt-1} Var(R_M)} \\ &= \frac{V_{Ft-1}}{V_{Dt-1}} \beta_D + \frac{\delta V_{Ut-1}}{V_{Dt-1}} \beta_A \end{aligned} \tag{4.20}$$

The value of a project with a linear capital structure could be valued by valuing the interest tax shields using the pre-tax expected return implied by the beta of the interest tax shields from (4.20) and adding that value to the value of the free cash flows:

$$V_{APV} = \frac{FCF}{K_A} + \frac{\tau K_D D}{K_{ITS}}, \tag{4.21}$$

where D is the amount of debt including the fixed and proportional component and K_{ITS} is calculated using the CAPM with β_{ITS} from (4.21).

The value of the project can also be valued more simply adding the value of the fixed interest tax shields to the CCF value:

$$V_{CCF} = \frac{FCF + \tau K_D D_P}{K_A} + \frac{\tau K_D D_F}{K_D}, \tag{4.22}$$

where D_P and D_F are the amount of proportional debt and fixed debt, respectively. The first term on the right-hand side of (4.22) is the formula for the CCF value when the debt is proportional to value (3.9). The discount rate for the interest tax shields from the proportional debt is the expected asset return for the same reasons it is the correct rate for the proportional interest tax shields discussed in Section 4.2. In short, interest tax shields are proportional to the value of the debt so that when debt is proportional to value, the interest tax shields will have the same risk as the value of the firm.

The second term on the right-hand side of (4.22) is the value of the interest tax shields associated with the fixed portion of the linear debt policy. The discount rate for the interest tax shields from the fixed portion is the expected debt rate for the same reason that it is the correct rate for the fixed interest tax shields discussed in Section 4.1. When the amount of debt is fixed, the interest tax shields are also fixed, and the value of the interest tax shields will vary as the value of the debt varies. The fixed interest tax shields therefore will have the same risk as the fixed debt.

Equation (4.22) is consistent with the generally accepted approach of identifying project cash flows with different risk characteristics and valuing those components at an expected return that reflects their risk. In Hochkiss, Gilson, and Ruback (2000), for example, the value of firms emerging from bankruptcy is valued as the capital cash flow value of their continuing operations plus the value of their fixed net operating losses discounted at a debt rate. The different risk characteristics of the interest tax shields in (4.22) arise because of the combination of fixed and proportional debt in the linear debt policy. Similarly, Miles and Ezzel (1980, 1983) model the debt policy as mixed through time with fixed debt in the first period and proportional debt in subsequent periods.

The best approach to estimating the value of interest tax is to model the debt policy, and then appropriately value resulting interest tax shields using the corresponding discount rate. As an example, Arzac (1996) recognizes that excess available cash flow is typically used to repay senior debt after a leveraged buyout and suggests a "recursive APV approach" to value the transactions. In most corporate circumstances, however, the valuation, at least at its initial stage, will not have the information to model the debt policy in detail and with precision. The practical alternatives may be to simply choose between the APV approach with its assumed fixed debt policy and the CCF (or equivalent FCF) approach with its assumed proportional debt policy.

Beyond the Graham and Harvey (1999) evidence that most corporations have target debt ratio, theories of debt policy generally suggest that debt changes as value changes. For example, in the static tradeoff between tax benefits and bankruptcy costs, doubling the operations of a firm would double its value, in turn doubling the tax benefits of debt financing and bankruptcy costs so that the amount of debt would also double. Thus, for most applications, the proportional debt assumption appears to be a more accurate description of corporate behavior. That means that the Capital Cash Flow or the equivalent FCF method of valuation will generally be preferred to APV and that asset beta calculations should not include tax adjustments.

5. Conclusions

This paper presents the Capital Cash Flow (CCF) method of valuing risky cash flows. The CCF method is simple and intuitive. The after-tax capital cash flows are just the before-tax cash flows to both debt and equity, reduced by taxes including interest tax shields. The discount rate is the same expected return on assets that is used in the before-tax valuation. Because the benefit of tax deductible interest is included in the cash flows, the discount rate does not change when leverage changes.

The CCF method is algebraically equivalent to the popular method of discounting Free Cash Flows by the after-tax weighted average cost of capital. But in many instances, the Capital Cash Flow method is substantially easier to apply and, as a result, is less prone to error. The ease of use occurs because the Capital Cash Flow method puts the interest tax shields in the cash flows and discounts by a before-tax cost of assets. The cash flow calculations can generally rely on the projected taxes, and the cost of assets does not generally change through time even when the amount of debt changes. In contrast, when applying the Free Cash Flow method, taxes need to be inferred, and the cost of capital changes as the amount of debt changes.

The Capital Cash Flow method is closely related to the Adjusted Present Value method. Adjusted Present Value is generally calculated as the sum of operating cash flows discounted by the cost of assets plus interest tax shields discounted at the cost of debt. The interest tax shields that are discounted by the cost of debt in the APV method are discounted by the cost of assets in the Capital Cash Flow method. The Adjusted Present Value method results in a higher value than the Capital Cash Flow method because it treats the interest tax shields as being less risky than the firm as a whole because the level of debt is implicitly assumed to be a fixed dollar amount. As a result, a tax adjustment is made when unlevering an equity beta to calculate an asset beta. In contrast, the Capital Cash Flow method, like the FCF method, makes the more economically plausible assumption that debt is proportional to value. The risk of the interest tax shields therefore matches the risk of the assets.

Beyond introducing the Capital Cash Flow method, demonstrating its conceptual equivalence to the Free Cash Flow method, and showing its relation to the Adjusted Present Value method, this paper makes the more general point that the financial policy affects the choice of valuation technique. A proportional debt policy, for example, implies that interest tax shields are valued at the cost of assets and that taxes do not affect the measure of risk that goes into calculating the discount rate. In contrast, when the amount of debt is fixed, interest tax shields are valued at the expected return of debt and taxes do affect the measure of risk. Furthermore, the debt policy need not be exclusively proportional or fixed, and, as an example, I provide a Capital Cash Flow valuation for a linear debt policy that has both fixed and proportional components. Whatever the debt policy, valuation depends on that policy and the challenge is to value the cash flows using an approach that consistently incorporates the assumption about debt policy.

References

Arzac, E. R., 1996, "Valuation of Highly Leveraged Firms," *Financial Analysts Journal,* 52 (July/August), 42–49.

Esty, B. C., 1999, "Improved Techniques for Valuing Large-Scale Projects." *The Journal of Project Finance,* 5 (Spring 1999), 9–25.

Gilson, S. C., E. S. Hotchkiss, and R. S. Ruback, 2000, "Valuation of Bankrupt Firms," *Review of Financial Studies,* 13, 43–74.

Graham, J. R. and C. R. Harvey, 2001, "The Theory and Practice of Corporate Finance: Evidence from the Field," 60 (May/June), 187–243.

Harris, R. S. and J. J. Pringle, 1985, "Risk-Adjusted Discount Rates—Extensions from the Average-Risk Case," *Journal of Financial Research,* 8 (Fall), 237–244.

Holthausen, R. W. and M. E. Zmijewski, 1996, "Security Analysis: How to Analyze Accounting and Market Data to Value Securities," working paper and teaching material, The Wharton School and University of Chicago.

Inselbag, I. and H. Kaufold, 1997, "Two DCF Approaches for Valuing Companies under Alternative Financing Strategies and How to Choose between Them," *Journal of Applied Corporate Finance,* 10 (Spring), 114–122.

Kaplan, S. N. and R. S. Ruback, 1995, "The Valuation of Cash Flow Forecasts: An Empirical Analysis," *The Journal of Finance,* 50 (September), 1059–1093.

Kaplan, S. N. and R. S. Ruback, 1996, "The Market Pricing of Cash Flow Forecasts: Discounted Cash Flow vs. the Method of Comparables," *Journal of Applied Corporate Finance,* 8 (Winter), 45–60.

Luehrman, T. A., 1997, "Using APV: A Better Tool for Valuing Operations," *Harvard Business Review,* 75 (May–June), 145–154.

Miles, J. A. and J. R. Ezzell, 1980, "The Weighted Average Cost of Capital, Perfect Capital Markets, and Project Life: A Clarification," *Journal of Financial and Quantitative Analysis,* 15 (September), 719–730.

Miles, J. A. and J. R. Ezzell, 1985, "Reformulating Tax Shield Valuation: A Note," *Journal of Finance,* 40 (December), 1485–1492.

Miller, M. H., 1977, "Debt and Taxes," *Journal of Finance,* 32 (March), 261–276.

Myers, S. C., 1974, "Interactions of Corporate Financing and Investment Decisions—Implications for Capital Budgeting," *The Journal of Finance,* 29, 1–25.

Ruback, R. S., 1986, "Calculating the Market Value of Riskless Cash Flows," *Journal of Financial Economics,* 15 (March), 323–339.

Ruback, R. S., 1989, "Teaching Note for RJR Nabisco," Harvard Business School Case No. 289-057.

Ruback, R. S., 1995a, "Technical Note for Capital Cash Flow Valuation," Harvard Business School Case No. 295-069.

Ruback, R. S., 1995b, "Technical Note for Introduction to Cash Flow Valuation Methods: Harvard Business School Case No. 295-155.

Taggart, R. A., 1991, "Consistent Valuation and Cost of Capital Expressions with Corporate and Personal Taxes," 20 (Autumn), 8–20.

Advanced Valuation

Radio One, Inc.

Radio One (Nasdaq: ROIA, ROIAK), the largest radio group targeting African-Americans in the country, had achieved tremendous success by purchasing underperforming radio stations, changing them to urban formats, and using its programming, marketing, and operating skills to cut unnecessary costs. Under the leadership of Alfred Liggins III, chief executive officer and president, the company posted consistent, above-average, same-station broadcast revenue and cash flow growth, and grew from 7 stations in 1995 to 28 in 1999.

In October 1999, two of the nation's largest owners of radio stations—Clear Channel Communications Inc. (NYSE: CCU) and AMFM Inc (NYSE: AFM)—announced plans to merge. Scott Royster (HBS '92), chief financial officer and executive vice president of Radio One, knew that the Federal Communications Commission (FCC) would require Clear Channel to divest some of its radio assets after the proposed merger. The divestitures were an opportunity for Radio One to acquire 12 established urban stations in the top 50 markets. Acquiring those stations would more than double the size of Radio One and help build its national platform. Liggins and Royster had to decide if Radio One should purchase the stations and how much to offer.

The Company

Radio One was founded by Liggins's mother, Catherine Hughes, who learned the radio business while teaching at Howard University. In 1980, Hughes and her husband raised money to purchase WOL-AM in Washington, D.C., for just under $1 million.[1] Hughes changed the format from R&B music and public affairs to talk radio.[2] To save money, the Hugheses themselves became radio personalities. As a result, Cathy Hughes became known as a hard-hitting political analyst and spokesperson. (Exhibit 1 contains brief biographies of the Radio One executives.)

In 1987, Hughes purchased WMMJ-FM in Washington for about $7.5 million and began to broadcast a new musical format targeting African-Americans. In 1992 and 1993, Hughes acquired four stations in Baltimore, Maryland, for $6.4 million and in

[1] Broadcasting & Cable, "Mother/Son Makes Radio One," August 30, 1999. The Hugheses were the beneficiaries of a now defunct FCC regulation that allowed the sale of financially distressed radio assets to minorities at below-market prices.

[2] Ibid.

High Tech Fellow Pauline Fischer and Professor Richard Ruback prepared this case solely as the basis for class discussion. HBS cases are not intended to serve as endorsements, sources of primary data, or illustrations of effective or ineffective management.

Copyright © 2000 President and Fellows of Harvard College. To order copies or request permission to reproduce materials, call 1-800-545-7685, write Harvard Business School Publishing, Boston, MA 02163, or go to http://www.hbsp.harvard.edu. No part of this publication may be reproduced, stored in a retrieval system, used in a spreadsheet, or transmitted in any form or by any means—electronic, mechanical, photocopying, recording, or otherwise—without the permission of Harvard Business School.

1995 purchased WKYS-FM in Washington for $34.0 million—the largest acquisition in the company's history at the time. WKYS-FM presented an exciting opportunity because the station had been No. 1 in its markct but had fallen to No. 13 by the time of the acquisition.

Also in 1995, Liggins discovered an opportunity to introduce a new radio station to the Atlanta, Georgia, market. Liggins believed that the Atlanta market and its growing African-American population provided a profitable opportunity. But Hughes and the other members of Radio One's board of directors thought that the company needed to focus on its newly acquired stations. Sure in his convictions, Liggins formed a separate company to purchase an Atlanta station for approximately $5 million. In June 1995, Radio One of Atlanta introduced WHTA-FM.

By the end of 1996, WKYS had achieved a No. 2 ranking in Washington, and one of the acquired Baltimore stations, WERQ-FM, had become the No. 1 station in its market. By 1998, Liggins's Atlanta-based WHTA was ranked No. 4.[3] The WHTA affiliate and its sister station WAMJ-FM were later purchased by Radio One and became wholly owned subsidiaries of the company in March 1999. (Exhibit 2 summarizes Radio One's acquisition activity.)

Corporate Strategy

Radio One's strategy was to "provide urban-oriented music, entertainment, and information to a primarily African-American audience in as many major markets as possible."[4] Hughes and Liggins believed that radio broadcasting primarily targeting African-Americans had significant growth potential. As Exhibit 3 summarizes, African-Americans were the largest minority group in the United States and were expected to experience 60% faster population growth than the general population between 1995 and 2010. African-Americans also experienced 150% faster income growth between 1980 and 1995, and listened to the radio on average 24% longer than the general population.[5]

Radio One pursued a clustering strategy within each market by acquiring two or more stations that targeted different demographic segments within the African-American population. In Detroit, for example, the company owns WDTJ-FM, targeting the 18–34 demographic, WDMK-FM, targeting the 25–54 demographic, and WCHB-AM, a talk radio station targeting the 35–64 demographic. To build clusters, Radio One acquired underperforming stations in the top 50 African-American markets.[6] Liggins and Royster worked together to cut costs and create efficiencies. Radio One centralized certain functions, including finance, accounting, legal, human resources management, information systems, and overall program management. The programming itself was left to local managers with strong oversight from the company's vice president of programming.

Liggins and the company's sales executives worked to convert audience share ratings into advertising revenue. Although minority-targeted advertising dollars lagged behind those of the general population, Radio One was able to use its multiple stations to sell more advertising by targeting the African-American market. Power ratios, calculated as revenue share divided by audience share, indicated how much of the total radio advertising dollars in a particular market was being captured by a particular station relative to its audience share. Historically, advertisers had not been willing to pay as much

[3]Company reports.

[4]Ibid.

[5]The company estimated that African-Americans listened to the radio for 27.2 hours per week and the general population listened for 22.0 hours per week.

[6]Radio One also made acquisitions in existing markets where expanded coverage was desirable and in new markets where they believed it was advantageous to have a presence.

to target the largely African-American urban listeners because their income generally lagged behind listeners to mainstream radio stations, resulting in power ratios substantially less than one. Radio One, however, was able to increase the power ratios of most of its stations by demonstrating to advertisers that the growing African-American population purchased more of certain goods and services than the general population despite their lower average income.

Exhibit 4 summarizes rising power ratios for urban radio, and Exhibit 5 details Radio One's turnaround record.

Performance

Liggins assumed day-to-day control of Radio One in 1997 and led the company to its initial public offering in May 1999. In its 1999 fiscal year, ended December 31, 1999, Radio One recorded $81.7 million in net revenue, defined as revenue from local and national advertising less agency commissions—equivalent to an average annual growth rate of 51% over three years. Broadcast cash flow (BCF), which equals operating income before depreciation, amortization, local marketing arrangement fees, and corporate expenses, reached $37.4 million—a 56% average annual growth rate over three years. After-tax cash flow equaled $16.3 million—a 125% increase since 1998. During 1999, Radio One's same station net broadcast revenue and broadcast cash flow both increased almost 40%. Exhibits 6 and 7 present Radio One's Income Statements and Balance Sheets for 1997 through 1999.

The Radio Industry

Although the FCC historically imposed tight controls on the radio industry, it began to relax its rules in the 1990s. In 1992, the FCC relaxed existing regulations to allow one company to own two FM stations in one market or 36 stations nationwide (18 AM and 18 FM). The Telecommunications Act of 1996 lifted nearly all of the limitations on ownership.[7] Significant consolidation occurred within a few years of the passage of the Act, which allowed stations to realize economies of scale through pricing power, capacity utilization, and cost reduction.

Radio had always been attractive to advertisers because it was the only medium that reached audiences at work and in the car.[8] Consolidation enhanced the appeal of radio advertising because broadcasters that controlled numerous radio assets could deliver TV-like reach and offer attractive "packages" to advertisers.[9] These packages included sale of advertising inventory across their "network" of stations. Rather than making sales on a station-by-station basis, network sales allowed the transfer of an advertisement from one station to the next, thereby ensuring that each was fully using its advertising capacity. The highly competitive radio network business doubled following the passage of the Act, reaching over $1 billion in early 1999.[10]

Consolidation significantly decreased expenses as companies enjoyed cost savings from programming syndication and purchasing from vendors, reduction in duplicate staffing in markets where multiple stations were owned, and the creation of national representation agreements.

[7]The Act reserved power in the FCC to approve or deny all applications for ownership of stations.

[8]Radio grew its share of all ad spending in 1999 to 8.2% from 7.5% in 1998 and 6.4% in 1992. Radio had consistently taken market share from all other traditional media.

[9]Credit Suisse First Boston, Radio One, Inc., Equity Research Report dated March 9, 2000.

[10]Morgan Stanley Dean Witter, Radio One, Inc., Equity Research Report dated March 14, 2000.

Clear Channel Opportunity

In 1999, Clear Channel was the nation's largest radio station operator, owning over 500 stations domestically and two internationally.[11] In the fall of 1999, Clear Channel petitioned the FCC to purchase the second-largest station group, fellow Texas-based competitor AMFM Inc., for $17.4 billion in stock and $6.1 billion in assumed debt. If consummated, the merger would create the largest radio company in the world in terms of revenue and number of stations.[12] The combined company would own over 830 stations in both large and mid-sized markets across the country. Although the Act of 1996 relaxed the national ownership cap, it retained a limit on the number of stations owned by a single entity in a particular market.[13] As a result, Clear Channel would have to divest nearly 100 stations in 37 markets where it overlapped with AMFM. The proposed divestiture was the largest in the history of the industry; gross proceeds were predicted to reach $4.3 billion.

The divestitures were a potentially attractive opportunity for Radio One to enter new markets. Some of the stations were similar to Radio One's urban format and had management teams with strong positions in their markets. At least 25 of the 100 stations for sale were urban format; 12 of those were in the top 50 African-American markets. The station in Los Angeles, the fourth-largest African-American market in the United States, presented an especially attractive opportunity for Radio One. If it acquired the 12 stations from Clear Channel, Radio One would draw more African-American listeners than any other radio broadcaster and cover more African-American households than any other media vehicle targeting that audience, including that of BET Holdings—a media company targeting the African-American audience largely through its cable asset, Black Entertainment Television (BET).[14]

Consolidation had substantially increased the purchase price of radio stations. In 1990, for example, broadcast FM stations sold for roughly 10–12x BCF; by 1999, they sold for 18–20x BCF. Minority-owned and women-owned ventures were most affected by the increase because they had traditionally lacked access to the amount of capital necessary to purchase stations. The FCC, under the leadership of Chairman William Kennard, took affirmative steps to ensure that these industry dynamics did not preclude broad participation in the broadcast radio market by advocating the sale of at least some of the divested stations to minorities and women. Clear Channel, in a concerted effort to include these groups in sale negotiations, met with interested civic, political, and business leaders from the African-American and Hispanic communities. Only Radio One, however, had the experience and access to capital to purchase a significant group of stations.

[11]Clear Channel also owned 24 television stations and was the nation's largest outdoor advertising company based on total advertising display inventory of 133,097 domestically and 422,060 internationally.

[12]Bill Carter, "The Leader in U.S. Radio to Buy No. 2," *New York Times,* October 5, 1999.

[13]The FCC's ownership limitations depended on the size of the city and other broadcasting assets owned. For example, in New York a company could own as many as eight stations, while in a smaller city it was limited to owning six. If a company also owned a television station in a city, ownership was limited to seven radio stations; if two television station were owned, there was a six radio station ownership limit. The FCC also ordered stations to be divested if one company controlled more than 40% of the radio revenues in a city. Source: Bill Carter, "The Leader in U.S. Radio to Buy No. 2," *New York Times,* October 5, 1999.

[14]Company estimated that it reached nearly 8 million African-Americans on a weekly basis, compared with just 2.1 million reached by BET's cable station during evening hours during the same time period.

Conclusion

Liggins and Royster realized that the Clear Channel/AMFM divestiture was an unprecedented growth opportunity for their company. Urban stations, particularly those in the top 50 markets, rarely became available. Liggins and Royster, therefore, decided that Radio One should attempt to purchase 12 of the Clear Channel stations in the top 50 markets. The resulting larger national footprint would bring greater advertising revenue and serve as a more meaningful platform for the company's planned expansion into other forms of media, including cable, the recording industry, and the Internet.

Royster was uncertain how much the company should be willing to pay for the stations. Infinity Broadcasting paid $1.4 billion, or about 21.5x 2000 BCF to acquire 18 stations from Clear Channel[15] and Cox Radio paid about $380 million, or about 18.4x 2000 BCF for 7 of the stations.[16] The 12 stations Radio One targeted were of similar quality to those purchased by Infinity, and thus Royster anticipated offering at least 20x BCF.

In the weeks following Clear Channel's divestiture announcement, Radio One's stock increased from the mid-$40s to as high as $97 per share. At $97 per share, Radio One was trading at nearly 30x's forward BCF. Exhibit 8 shows that the 30x multiple was substantially greater than the typical trading multiple for radio companies. Royster and Liggins attributed the stock price gains to the market's expectation that Radio One would submit a bid, and by early March 2000 analysts were speculating on the scope of Radio One's acquisition. In addition, Royster and Liggins were in negotiations with Davis Broadcasting for the purchase of 1 station in Charlotte, North Carolina, and 5 stations in Augusta, Georgia; and with Shirk, Inc. and IBL, LLC for the purchase of 3 stations in Indianapolis, Indiana. The proposed acquisitions, therefore, would add 21 stations.

Royster projected the performance of Radio One's stations and the 21 targeted stations. Those projections are contained in Exhibit 9. In addition to the information in Exhibit 9, Royster recognized that each targeted station would require about $100,000 of capital expenditures each year. Also, Radio One would have to provide the stations with their initial working capital because the working capital of the targeted stations would not be sold to Radio One in the proposed asset sale.

Liggins and Royster wanted to gauge the purchase price range that would make sense. They wanted Radio One's offer price to be preemptive but not dilutive. At one extreme, to be preemptive, the price would have to exceed the stand-alone cash flow value of the targeted stations. At the other extreme, to avoid dilution, Radio One could afford to pay up to its 30x multiple.

[15]Prudential Securities, Infinity Broadcasting, Equity Research Consumer Services Report dated May 16, 2000.

[16]Credit Suisse First Boston, Cox Radio Inc., Equity Research Report dated March 25, 2000.

EXHIBIT 1 Executive Biographies[a]

Catherine L. Hughes, 53, became chairperson of the board of directors and secretary of Radio One in 1980 and was chief executive officer of Radio One from 1980 to 1997. Hughes was one of the founders of Radio One's predecessor company in 1980. Starting in 1980, Hughes worked in various capacities for Radio One, including president, general manager, general sales manager, and talk-show host. She began her career in radio as general sales manager of WHUR-FM—the Howard University urban-contemporary radio station. Ms. Hughes was also the mother of Alfred Liggins, Radio One's chief executive officer, president, treasurer, and director.

Alfred C. Liggins III, 35, became chief executive officer in 1997, and president, treasurer, and a director of Radio One in 1989. Liggins joined Radio One in 1985 as an account manager at WOL-AM. In 1987, he was promoted to general sales manager and promoted again in 1988 to general manager overseeing Radio One's other markets. Liggins was a graduate of the Wharton School of Business/Executive M.B.A. Program.

Scott R. Royster, 36, became executive vice president of Radio One in 1997 and chief financial officer in 1996. Prior to joining Radio One, he served as an independent consultant to Radio One. From 1995 to 1996, Royster was a principal at TSG Capital Group, LLC—a private equity investment firm located in Stamford, Connecticut, which became an investor in Radio One in 1987. Royster also served as an associate and later a principal at Capital Resource Partners—a private capital investment firm in Boston, Massachusetts—from 1992 to 1995. Scott Royster was a graduate of Duke University and Harvard Business School.

Mary Catherine Sneed, 49, was named Radio One's chief operating officer in January 1998 and general manager of Radio One of Atlanta in 1995. Prior to joining Radio One, she held various positions with Summit Broadcasting, including executive vice president of the Radio Division and vice president of operations from 1992 to 1995. Ms. Sneed was a graduate of Auburn University.

Linda J. Eckard, 43, was named general counsel of Radio One in January 1998 and assistant secretary of Radio One in April 1999. Prior to this, Ms. Eckard represented Radio One as outside counsel from July 1995 until assuming her role as general counsel. Ms. Eckard was a partner in the Washington, D.C., office of Davis Wright Tremain LLP from August 1997 to December 1997. Prior to this, Ms. Eckard was a shareholder of Roberts & Eckard, P.C.—a firm she co-founded in April 1992. Ms. Eckard was a graduate of Gettysburg College, the National Law Center at George Washington University, and the University of Glasgow. Ms. Eckard was admitted to the District of Columbia Bar and the Bar of the United States Supreme Court.

Steve Hegwood, 39, was vice president of programming for Radio One and program director of WKYS-FM since 1995. From 1990 to 1995, Hegwood was program director of WJLB-FM in Detroit, Michigan.

[a]SEC Form 10-K for fiscal year ended December 31, 1999.

EXHIBIT 2 Radio One's Acquisition Strategy

Source: Adapted from numerous SEC 10-K Filings.

	Number of Stations		
Market	**FM**	**AM**	**Year(s) of Acquisition**
Washington, DC	2	2	1980, 1987, 1995, 1998
Baltimore, MD	2	2	1992, 1993
Philadelphia, PA	1		1997
Detroit, MI[a]	2	2	1998
Atlanta, GA	2		1999
Cleveland, OH	1	1	1999
St. Louis, MO	1		1999
Richmond, VA	7		1999
Boston, MA	1		1999
TOTAL	**19**	**7**	

[a]One station is located in Kingsley, Michigan.

EXHIBIT 3 African-American Demographic Information

Source: Adapted from company reports

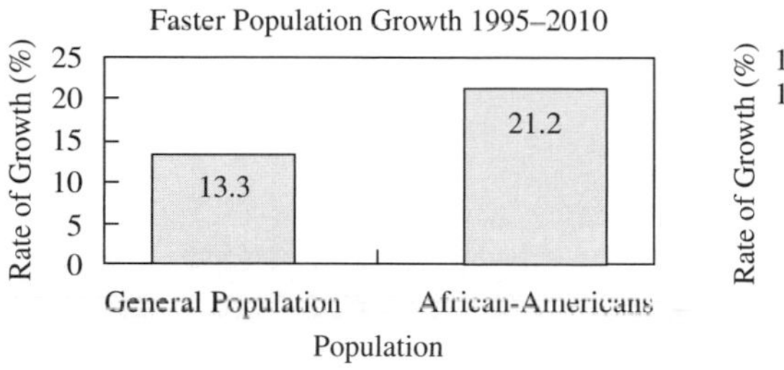

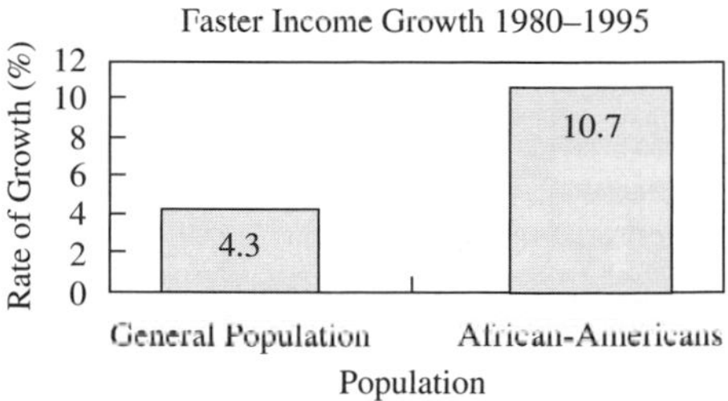

Key Demographic Statistics

60% faster population growth
Largest minority group in the United States
Population projected to reach 40MM by 2010
150% faster income growth than general population

EXHIBIT 4 Rising Urban Format Power Ratios 1991–2002[a]

Source: Adapted from company reports

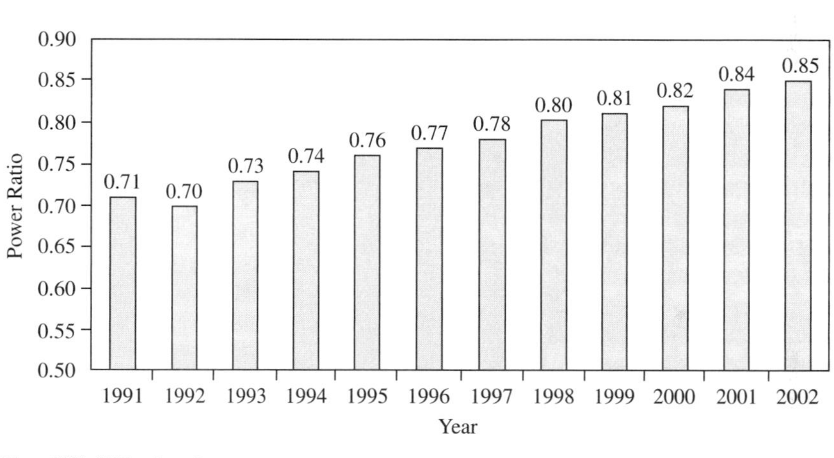

[a]Years 2000–2002 estimated

EXHIBIT 5 Radio One's Turnaround Record

Source: Adapted from company reports

	Cost(mm)	96BCF	Multiple	99BCF	Multiple
Washington, DC	$46.2	$6.3	7.3×	$14.9	3.1×
Baltimore	$13.7	$3.3	4.2×	$11.8	1.2×
Philadelphia	$20.0	$0.2	100×	$ 1.7	11.8×
Atlanta	$13.5	$1.2	11.2×	$ 6.9	2.0×

EXHIBIT 6 Radio One, Inc., and Subsidiaries—Consolidated Statements of Operations

	1997	1998	1999
Revenue			
Broadcast revenue, including barter revenue of $1,010,000, $644,000, and $1,821,000, respectively	$36,955,000	$52,696,000	$93,260,000
Less: Agency commissions	4,588,000	6,587,000	11,557,000
Net broadcast revenue	$32,367,000	$46,109,000	$81,703,000
Operating Expenses			
Program and technical	$ 5,934,000	$ 8,015,000	$13,576,000
Selling, general and administrative	12,914,000	16,486,000	30,683,000
Corporate expenses	2,155,000	2,800,000	4,155,000
Stock-based compensation	—	—	225,000
Depreciation and amortization	5,828,000	8,445,000	17,073,000
Total operating expenses	$26,831,000	$35,746,000	$65,712,000
Operating income	$ 5,536,000	$10,363,000	$15,991,000
Interest expense, including amortization of deferred financing costs	8,910,000	11,455,000	15,279,000
Other income, net	415,000	358,000	2,149,000
(Loss) income before (benefit) provision for income taxes and extraordinary item	$ (2,959,000)	$ (734,000)	$ 2,861,000
(Benefit) Provision for income taxes	—	(1,575,000)	2,728,000
(Loss) income before extraordinary item	$ (2,959,000)	$ 841,000	$ 133,000
Extraordinary item			
Loss on early retirement of debt	1,985,000	—	—
Net (loss) income	$ (4,944,000)	$ 841,000	$ 133,000
Net loss applicable to common shareholders	$ (6,981,000)	$ (2,875,000)	$ (1,343,000)
Basic and diluted loss per common share			
Loss before extraordinary item	$ (.53)	$ (.31)	$ (.08)
Net loss	$ (.74)	$ (.31)	$ (.08)
Weighted average shares outstanding			
Basic and diluted	9,392,000	9,392,000	16,137,000
Other Data:			
Broadcast cash flow	$13,519,000	$21,608,000	$37,444,000
EBITDA (before non-cash compensation)	$11,364,000	$18,808,000	$33,289,000
After-tax cash flow	$ 2,869,000	$ 7,248,000	$16,303,000
Capital expenditures	$ 2,035,000	$ 2,236,000	$ 3,252,000

EXHIBIT 7 Radio One, Inc., and Subsidiaries—Consolidated Balance Sheets

Source: Company reports

	1997	1998	1999
Assets			
Current assets:			
Cash and equivalents	$ 8,500,000	$ 4,455,000	$ 6,221,000
Investments, available for sale	—	—	256,390,000
Trade accounts receivable, net of allowance for doubtful accounts of $1,243,000 and $2,429,000, respectively	$ 8,722,000	12,026,000	19,833,000
Prepaid expenses and other	315,000	334,000	1,035,000
Deferred income taxes	—	826,000	984,000
Total current assets	$ 17,537,000	$ 17,641,000	$284,463,000
Property and equipment, net	4,432,000	6,717,000	15,512,000
Intangible assets, net	54,942,000	127,639,000	218,460,00
Other assets	2,314,000	1,859,000	9,101,000
Total assets	$ 79,225,000	$153,856,000	$527,536,000
Liabilities and Stockholder Equity			
Current liabilities:			
Accounts payable	$ 258,000	$ 1,190,000	$ 1,663,000
Accrued expenses	$ 3,029,000	3,708,000	6,941,000
Income taxes payable	—	143,000	1,532,000
Total current liabilities	$ 3,287,000	$ 5,041,000	$ 10,136,000
Long-term debt and deferred interest, net of current portion	74,954,000	131,739,000	82,626,000
Deferred income tax liability	—	15,251,000	14,518,000
Total liabilities	$ 78,241,000	$152,031,000	$107,280,000
Commitments and contingencies			
Senior cumulative redeemable preferred stock:			
Series A, $.01 par value, 140,000 shares authorized, 84,843 shares issued and outstanding	9,310,000	10,816,000	—
Series B, $.01 par value, 150,000 shares authorized, 124,467 shares issued and outstanding	13,658,000	15,868,000	—
Stockholders' equity:			
Common stock—Class A, $.001 par value, 30,000,000 shares authorized, 0 and 17,221,000 shares issued and outstanding	—	—	17,000
Common stock—Class B, $.001 par value, 30,000,000 shares authorized, 1,572,000 and 2,867,000 shares issued and outstanding	—	2,000	3,000
Common stock—Class C, $.001 par value, 30,000,000 shares authorized, 3,146,000 and 3,184,000 shares issued and outstanding	—	3,000	3,000
Accumulated comprehensive income adjustments	—	—	40,000
Additional paid-in capital	—	—	446,400,000
Accumulated deficit	(21,989,000)	(24,864,000)	(26,207,000)
Total stockholders' (deficit) equity	$(21,984,000)	$ (24,859,000)	$420,256,000
Total liabilities and stockholders' equity	$ 79,225,000	$153,856,000	$527,536,000

EXHIBIT 8 Radio Industry Trading Multiples as of March 2000 Based on 2001E Forecasts

Source: Credit Suisse First Boston, Radio One, Inc., Equity Research Report, March 9, 2000, and casewriter estimates.

Ticker	Company	BCF[a]	EBITDA[a]	After-Tax Cash Flow[b]	Asset Beta[c]
BBGI	Beasley Broadcasting Group	11.8	13.7	15.4	NA
CBS	CBS	15.1	15.8	22.3	1.06
AFM	AMFM Inc	14.7	15.4	14.4	0.96
CITC	Citadel Communications	14.6	15.7	21.7	0.68
CCU	Clear Channel Communic.	17.2	17.9	20.1	0.65
CXR	Cox Radio	17.4	18.7	24.2	0.27
CMLS	Cumulus Media	17.7	19.2	37.2	0.83
EMMS	Emmis Broadcasting	11.0	12.0	13.2	0.55
ETM	Entercom Communications	16.6	17.7	21.1	0.30
HBCCA	Hispanic Broadcasting	42.1	44.5	59.7	1.23
INF	Infinity Broadcasting	18.8	19.4	26.9	0.82
ROIA	Radio One	22.1	24.2	36.5	0.82
SGA	Saga Communications	9.9	11.4	14.5	0.26
WOM	Westwood One	24.4	25.3	38.6	1.29
	AVERAGE	**18.1**	**19.4**	**26.1**	**0.75**

[a]BCF & EBITDA: Adjusted Market Value Multiple to 2001

[b]After-Tax Cash Flow: Current Price as a Multiple of 2001

[c]Asset betas are equity betas adjusted for leverage by multiplying the equity beta by the equity-to-value ratio and adding the debt beta (assumed to equal 0.25) times the debt-to-value ratio.

EXHIBIT 9 Radio One, Inc. Actual and Projected Financial Performance of Existing Markets and Potential New Markets

Source: Adapted from company reports

	Pro Forma		Projected			
	1999	2000	2001	2002	2003	2004
Gross Revenue—Existing Markets						
Washington	32,221	34,812	37,597	41,357	45,492	50,042
Baltimore	25,162	26,952	29,108	32,019	35,221	38,743
Philadelphia (WPHI)	6,239	7,277	8,151	8,966	9,863	10,849
Philadelphia (WPLY)	8,978	9,500	10,450	11,495	12,645	13,909
Detroit	8,309	11,075	12,736	14,010	15,130	16,341
Atlanta	15,811	17,584	19,782	21,760	23,936	26,330
Cleveland	2,415	5,488	6,311	6,942	7,497	8,097
St. Louis	—	1,028	2,056	2,467	2,837	3,064
Richmond	10,713	13,226	15,210	17,492	19,241	20,780
Boston	—	3,401	4,081	4,693	5,162	5,575
Existing Gross Revenue	109,848	130,343	145,482	161,201	177,024	193,730
Gross Revenue—Potential New Markets[a]						
Charlotte	1,002	1,250	2,250	3,250	4,250	4,700
Augusta	2,708	2,750	3,200	3,400	3,600	3,800
Indianapolis	5,173	5,814	6,600	8,200	9,500	11,000
Los Angeles	38,626	41,117	45,221	49,517	54,221	59,372
Miami	1,501	1,634	1,634	2,043	2,553	3,191
Cleveland	13,370	13,750	15,000	16,500	17,750	19,000
Houston	36,618	39,547	43,502	47,852	52,638	57,743
Dallas	4,756	6,120	8,500	11,700	13,500	15,188
Greenville	4,614	4,864	5,418	5,750	6,250	6,500
Raleigh	12,118	13,538	15,163	16,679	18,347	20,182
New Markets Gross Revenue	120,486	130,384	146,488	164,891	182,609	200,676

	Pro Forma		Projected			
	1999	2000	2001	2002	2003	2004
Direct Expenses—Existing Markets						
Washington	(4,098)	(5,080)	(5,486)	(5,790)	(6,369)	(7,006)
Baltimore	(3,232)	(4,018)	(4,339)	(4,483)	(4,931)	(5,424)
Philadelphia (WPHI)	(800)	(1,078)	(1,207)	(1,255)	(1,381)	(1,519)
Philadelphia (WPLY)	(921)	(1,078)	(1,207)	(1,379)	(1,517)	(1,669)
Detroit	(818)	(1,483)	(1,705)	(1,961)	(2,118)	(2,288)
Atlanta	(2,080)	(2,436)	(2,741)	(3,046)	(3,351)	(3,686)
Cleveland	(166)	(632)	(727)	(972)	(1,050)	(1,134)
St. Louis	—	(163)	(326)	(345)	(397)	(429)
Richmond	(1,607)	(1,982)	(2,279)	(2,449)	(2,694)	(2,909)
Boston	—	(484)	(581)	(657)	(723)	(781)
Existing Gross Expenses	(13,722)	(18,434)	(20,598)	(22,337)	(24,531)	(26,845)
Direct Expenses—Potential New Markets[a]						
Charlotte	(150)	(189)	(313)	(435)	(549)	(607)
Augusta	(406)	(357)	(379)	(402)	(426)	(452)
Indianapolis	(519)	(607)	(702)	(882)	(1,078)	(1,257)
Los Angeles	(5,155)	(5,496)	(6,045)	(6,619)	(7,248)	(7,938)
Miami	—	—	—	—	—	—
Cleveland	(1,707)	(1,650)	(1,800)	(1,980)	(2,130)	(2,280)
Houston	(4,479)	(4,746)	(5,220)	(5,742)	(6,317)	(6,929)
Dallas	(547)	(825)	(1,063)	(1,463)	(1,688)	(1,898)
Greenville	(566)	(603)	(672)	(729)	(791)	(858)
Raleigh	(1,565)	(1,770)	(1,982)	(2,180)	(2,398)	(2,638)
ROI Direct Expenses	(15,094)	(16,243)	(18,176)	(20,432)	(22,624)	(24,857)
Net Revenue—Existing Markets						
Washington	28,123	29,732	32,111	35,567	39,123	43,036
Baltimore	21,930	22,934	24,769	27,536	30,290	33,319
Philadelphia (WPHI)	5,439	6,199	6,944	7,711	8,482	9,330
Philadelphia (WPLY)	8,057	8,422	9,243	10,116	11,127	12,240
Detroit	7,491	9,592	11,031	12,048	13,012	14,053
Atlanta	13,731	15,148	17,041	18,714	20,585	22,644
Cleveland	2,249	4,856	5,584	5,970	6,448	6,964
St. Louis	—	865	1,730	2,122	2,440	2,635
Richmond	9,106	11,244	12,931	15,043	16,547	17,871
Boston	—	2,917	3,500	4,036	4,440	4,795
Existing Net Revenue	96,126	111,909	124,884	138,863	152,494	166,887
Net Revenue—Potential New Markets[a]						
Charlotte	852	1,061	1,937	2,815	3,701	4,093
Augusta	2,302	2,393	2,821	2,998	3,174	3,348
Indianapolis	4,654	5,207	5,898	7,318	8,422	9,743
Los Angeles	33,471	35,621	39,176	42,898	46,973	51,436
Miami	1,501	1,634	1,634	2,043	2,553	3,191
Cleveland	11,663	12,100	13,200	14,520	15,620	16,720
Houston	32,139	34,802	38,282	42,110	46,321	50,814
Dallas	4,209	5,295	7,438	10,238	11,813	13,289
Greenville	4,048	4,261	4,746	5,021	5,459	5,642
Raleigh	10,553	11,769	13,181	14,499	15,949	17,544
New Markets Net Revenue	105,392	114,143	128,313	144,460	159,985	175,820

EXHIBIT 9 (*Continued*)

	Pro Forma		Projected			
	1999	2000	2001	2002	2003	2004
Operating Expenses—Existing Markets						
Washington	13,480	13,827	14,864	15,734	16,316	16,807
Baltimore	9,860	10,260	11,030	11,737	12,121	12,425
Philadelphia (WPHI)	3,779	3,957	4,254	4,618	4,926	5,240
Philadelphia (WPLY)	5,815	3,622	3,743	3,791	3,853	3,875
Detroit	6,421	6,578	7,071	7,495	7,776	8,032
Atlanta	6,799	7,503	8,066	8,393	8,716	8,994
Cleveland	1,774	3,791	4,075	4,234	4,451	4,667
St. Louis	—	1,440	1,548	1,912	2,199	2,358
Richmond	5,914	7,648	8,222	9,627	10,319	10,709
Boston	—	2,243	2,411	2,783	2,998	3,137
Existing Operating Expenses	53,842	60,869	65,284	70,324	73,675	76,244
Operating Expenses—Potential New Markets[a]						
Charlotte	665	1,023	1,249	1,461	1,659	1,781
Augusta	1,361	1,584	1,669	1,758	1,851	1,949
Indianapolis	2,954	3,206	3,463	3,848	4,255	4,639
Los Angeles	14,448	15,621	16,176	16,584	17,581	18,642
Miami	510	584	584	862	1,224	1,313
Cleveland	4,862	4,600	4,700	4,958	5,101	5,149
Houston	10,129	10,592	11,046	11,469	11,850	12,035
Dallas	4,012	4,195	4,938	5,238	5,500	5,900
Greenville	1,919	1,928	2,071	1,945	1,922	1,574
Raleigh	5,516	5,769	5,981	6,627	7,077	7,561
New Markets Operating Expenses	46,376	49,102	51,877	54,750	58,020	60,543
BCF—Existing Markets						
Washington	14,866	15,904	17,246	19,833	22,808	26,229
Baltimore	11,846	12,673	13,738	15,799	18,169	20,894
Philadelphia (WPHI)	1,658	2,242	2,689	3,092	3,556	4,090
Philadelphia (WPLY)	2,500	4,800	5,500	6,325	7,274	8,365
Detroit	1,069	3,013	3,959	4,553	5,236	6,021
Atlanta	6,933	7,645	8,975	10,321	11,869	13,650
Cleveland	470	1,066	1,510	1,737	1,997	2,297
St. Louis	—	–575	182	209	241	277
Richmond	3,192	3,596	4,709	5,415	6,228	7,162
Boston	—	674	1,090	1,254	1,442	1,658
Existing BCF	42,534	51,038	59,598	68,538	78,820	90,643
BCF—Potential New Markets[a]						
Charlotte	187	38	688	1,354	2,042	2,312
Augusta	941	809	1,152	1,240	1,323	1,399
Indianapolis	1,700	2,001	2,435	3,470	4,167	5,104
Los Angeles	19,023	20,000	23,000	26,314	29,393	32,794
Miami	991	1,050	1,050	1,181	1,329	1,878
Cleveland	6,800	7,500	8,500	9,563	10,519	11,571
Houston	22,009	24,210	27,236	30,641	34,471	38,780
Dallas	197	1,100	2,500	5,000	6,313	7,389
Greenville	2,129	2,333	2,675	3,076	3,538	4,068
Raleigh	5,037	6,000	7,200	7,872	8,871	9,982
New markets BCF	59,014	65,041	76,436	89,711	101,966	115,277
Total BCF	101,548	116,079	136,034	158,249	180,786	205,920
Corporate Expenses	6,000	6,000	6,900	7,935	9,125	10,494
EBITDA	95,548	110,079	129,134	150,314	171,661	195,426
Non-cash Compensation	225	0	0	0	0	0
Depreciation and amortization[b]	107,520	107,520	107,500	107,500	107,500	107,500
EBIT	(12,197)	2,559	21,634	42,814	64,161	87,926

[a]Potential acquisitions in Charlotte and Augusta were from Davis Broadcasting; in Indianapolis from Sturk, Inc., and IBL, LLC; and the remaining potential acquisitions were from Clear Channel Communications, Inc.

[b]Includes about $90 million of tax deductible depreciation and amortization in each year beginning 2001 and ending in 2015, as a result of the potential acquisitions.

EXHIBIT 10
Corporate and Government Bond Rates as of March 1, 2000

Source: Federal Reserve Statistical Release; Bloomberg

Government Bond Yields	
Maturity	**Rate**
3 months	5.36
6 months	5.68
1 year	5.84
3 years	6.14
5 years	6.19
10 years	6.28
30 years	6.35

Corporate Bonds (10-Year Maturity)	
Rating	**Rate**
AAA	7.1
AA	7.18
A	7.34
BBB	7.7
BB	9.1
B	9.68

American Chemical Corporation

In June 1979, American Chemical Corporation announced a tender offer for any and all shares of the Universal Paper Corporation. American was one of the largest diversified chemical companies in the United States (see Exhibit 1). Universal was a large paper and pulp company (see Exhibit 2).

Universal's management opposed the takeover and, among other things, sued in federal court to have the tender offer blocked on grounds that American's acquisition of Universal would violate the Clayton Act of the U.S. antitrust laws. Both firms engaged in the production of sodium chlorate. Universal alleged that its acquisition by American would substantially reduce competition in the sodium chlorate business, particularly in the southeastern U.S. market, where the two firms were competitors. The U.S. government joined Universal in seeking a preliminary injunction to stop American's tender offer. Though it denied the allegations, American prevented a preliminary injunction by agreeing to divest its sodium chlorate plant located near Collinsville, Alabama, in the event it acquired Universal. American subsequently was successful in acquiring over 91% of Universal's shares.

In October 1979, American began looking for a buyer for the Collinsville plant. A number of potential buyers were approached, including the Dixon Corporation, a specialty chemicals company. After lengthy negotiations, Dixon agreed to purchase the net assets of the Collinsville plant from American for $12 million, subject to approval by its board of directors.

The Market for Sodium Chlorate

Sodium chlorate ($NaClO_3$) was a chemical produced by the electrolytic decomposition of salt ($NaCl$) according to the chemical formula

$$NaCl + 3H_2O + \text{energy} \rightarrow NaClO_3 + 3H_2$$

Sodium chlorate was sold either as a white crystalline solid or in a 25% water solution.

Approximately 85% of the sodium chlorate produced in the United States was sold to the paper and pulp industries, where it was used in the bleaching of pulp. Sodium chlorate was reacted with salt ($NaCl$) and sulfuric acid (H_2SO_4) to produce a bleaching agent, chloride dioxide (ClO_2), according to the formula

$$NaClO_3 + NaCl + H_2SO_4 \rightarrow \tfrac{1}{2}Cl_2 + ClO_2 + Na_2SO_4 + H_2O$$

Chloride dioxide was the active ingredient actually used by paper and pulp producers to bleach pulp. The remaining 15% of the sodium chlorate produced in the United States was used in soil sterilants, in oxidizers for use in uranium mining, and in producing various chemicals, including sodium chlorite, potassium chlorate, and ammonium perchlorate.

Sales of sodium chlorate had grown rapidly during the 1970s, from 220,000 tons in 1970 to an expected 435,000 tons in 1979 (see Exhibit 3). Sales increased by approximately 8.6% per year during the period 1970–1974 but then declined 12% in 1975 when pulp production decreased during the recession. Demand improved during the subsequent recovery, and sales grew by more than 10% per year between 1975 and 1979.

Copyright © 1980 by the President and Fellows of Harvard College. Harvard Business School case 280-102.

Demand for sodium chlorate from pulp producers was expected to continue increasing at 8–10% per year. While pulp production was projected to increase at a slower annual rate of about 3–4%, pulp producers' use of sodium chlorate was expected to grow more rapidly because use of sodium chlorate (and the active ingredient chloride dioxide) helped solve their plant effluent problems. Other uses of sodium chlorate also were expected to grow at about 8–10% per year.

Capacity additions had not kept pace with sales growth during the 1970s (see Exhibit 3). Though sales had increased by over 95% between 1970 and 1979, capacity had increased by less than 70% during this period. The resulting tight markets in 1973–1974 and 1977–1978 caused a substantial improvement in profit margins between 1970 and 1979, even though production costs also increased greatly during this period. These tight markets and cost increases had caused prices for sodium chlorate to increase rapidly beginning in 1973 (see Exhibit 3).

In late 1979, there were a dozen domestic producers of sodium chlorate (see Exhibits 4 and 5). The market was dominated by large diversified chemical companies (Hooker, Pennwalt, American, and Kerr-McGee). However, a number of paper and pulp companies (Georgia-Pacific and Universal) had integrated backward into the production of sodium chlorate. In addition, two firms (Brunswick and Southern) specialized in producing sodium chlorate. The three largest producers accounted for over 55% of domestic capacity.

The majority of sodium chlorate plants were located in the southeastern United States (see Exhibit 4), where approximately two-thirds of the product was consumed due to the high regional concentration of pulp and paper mills. Freight costs represented a significant portion of delivered sodium chlorate costs, and plants tended therefore to be located within 800 miles of their principal markets. Market concentration was slightly higher in the southeastern market than in the total U.S. market. The three largest producers accounted for approximately 59% of the southeastern market.

In addition to existing producers, two firms had announced plans to enter the sodium chlorate business in 1980. Union Chemicals Corporation was constructing a 40,000-ton plant in Gainsville, Georgia, and Louisiana Paper Company was building a 35,000-ton plant in Greenville, Mississippi. This increase in industry capacity was expected to reduce margins and decrease capacity utilization during 1980 and 1981. However, as sales and productive capacity achieved a closer balance, prices and margins were expected to improve once again. It should be noted that the selling price necessary to obtain a 15% return on investment on a newly constructed 40,000-ton sodium chlorate plant was estimated to be $420 per ton in 1979.

The Collinsville Plant

American's plant in Collinsville, Alabama, had the capacity to produce 40,000 tons of sodium chlorate per year. Sodium chlorate was produced by the electrolysis of sodium chloride brine in electrolytic cells called D cells, which used graphite electrodes. The facility consisted of 20 cell tanks (or groups of cells) that were operated batchwise. They were filled with saturated brine and then electrolized to an endpoint. Graphite was consumed in the process. The resulting fluid was chemically treated to precipitate impurities, which were discarded. The remaining sodium chlorate solution was either shipped as a fluid or crystallized to a white solid.

The plant had been consistently profitable during the period 1974–1979 (see Exhibit 6). Operating profits had ranged from a low of $817,000 in 1975 to a high of $4,845,000 in 1978. Net assets had grown from $4,619,000 in 1974 to $5,414,000 in 1979. Though the ratio of operating profits to net assets had dropped to 16.9% in 1975, it equaled 90.0% in 1978 and averaged 54.3% during the 1974–1979 period.

The major cost of production was electric power. The Collinsville facility needed approximately 7,000 kilowatt-hours (kWh) to produce a ton of sodium chlorate, and power costs accounted for 55–60% of manufacturing costs. Salt, graphite, and other variable costs typically represented another 20%, and labor and maintenance costs accounted for the remaining 20% of manufacturing costs.

Electric power was purchased from the Tennessee Valley Authority (TVA), whose hydroelectric power plants historically had been a source of cheap electric power. During the early 1970s, TVA's rates had been as much as 50% less than the rates of other electric utilities. However, as the region's power demands grew, TVA was finding it necessary to supplement its hydroelectric power plants with more expensive fossil fuel plants. TVA also was facing increasing pressure from consumer groups to allocate the more expensive power of fossil fuel plants to industrial users instead of residential users. As a result, the Collinsville plant's cost of power had increased from $.019 per kWh in 1977 to $.025 per kWh in 1979.

Capital expenditures at the Collinsville plant had ranged from $200,000 to $500,000 per year between 1973 and 1979 and were primarily for maintenance and pollution control. In late 1979, the plant was basically in compliance with all environmental regulations. Future capital expenditures were expected to range from $475,000 to $600,000 per year.

American had supported a research and development program that was expected to reduce costs at its sodium chlorate plants. New sodium chlorate plants increasingly were using metal electrodes (instead of graphite electrodes), which eliminated graphite costs and also reduced power needs by approximately 30%. However, the graphite electrodes at American's plants at Collinsville and Wenatchee, Washington, were not convertible at an acceptable cost to commercially available metal electrodes. American's research group therefore was working on a permanent laminate (or coating) that could be applied to the graphite electrodes in American's plants. Use of this laminate would eliminate graphite costs and was expected to reduce power needs by 15–20%. Development was approximately 40% complete, and scale-up to a pilot plant was scheduled for March 1980. American expected that the laminate could be installed at the Collinsville plant at a one-time cost of about $2.25 million, which could be depreciated over a period of 10 years. Installation at Collinsville was scheduled for December 1980.

Proposed Sale of the Collinsville Plant to the Dixon Corporation

The Dixon Corporation was a specialty chemicals company that produced a number of chemicals for sale primarily to the paper and pulp industry. Its principal products included sulfuric acid, aluminum sulfate, and liquid sulfur dioxide. As described earlier, sulfuric acid was used together with sodium chlorate to produce chloride dioxide, which was the active ingredient used to bleach pulp. Sulfuric acid also was used in the manufacture of other chemicals, steels, rayon, and detergents and in oil refining. Aluminum sulfate was used as a coagulant and purifying agent in the treatment of industrial and municipal waste. Dixon sold liquid sulfur dioxide to the paper and pulp industry for use in bleaching pulp, though it also was used to produce hydrosulfites for use in textile dyeing. The firm's principal plant was located in Calhoun, Georgia, and its sales were concentrated in the southeastern United States. Dixon's sales had grown rapidly and the firm had been consistently profitable (see Exhibit 7).

Acquisition of the Collinsville plant fit well with Dixon's strategy of supplying chemicals to the paper and pulp industry. Sodium chlorate would complement Dixon's existing product lines. Dixon already did business with some of the Collinsville plant's major customers. Sodium chlorate, therefore, could be marketed largely through Dixon's existing sales group.

In evaluating the plant's purchase, Dixon prepared the pro forma financial statements shown in Exhibit 8. These figures analyzed the plant's future profitability given its unlaminated graphite electrodes and in the absence of the operating economies that might be realized from installing laminated electrodes. Industry overcapacity was expected to push margins down in the short run. However, Dixon expected that sodium chlorate prices would increase on average at 8% per year. Power costs (per kWh) were projected to increase more rapidly, at 12% per year. Selling expenses could be reduced by marketing sodium chlorate through Dixon's existing sales force. Dixon also expected to write up the value of the Collinsville plant, which would increase its depreciation charges.[1]

As part of the sale agreement, American agreed to provide ongoing technical support to the Collinsville plant. American would keep Dixon informed concerning development of the laminated electrodes and make this technology available to Dixon. However, Dixon would have to pay for all costs associated with installation of the laminated electrodes.

The $12 million purchase price was to be financed entirely with debt capital. It was to be financed in part by privately placing $8 million in 15-year mortgage bonds with two insurance companies. These bonds would carry an 11.25% interest rate. The sinking fund provision on these bonds would retire $800,000 of bonds each year beginning the sixth year. The remainder of the $12 million purchase price was to be financed by having Dixon issue American a $4 million note to be paid off in equal amounts over 5 years. The note also carried an 11.25% interest rate.[2]

This financing package would temporarily increase Dixon's debt-to-total-capital ratio to approximately 47%. Though the firm had almost no debt immediately prior to the proposed acquisition, Dixon had relied more heavily on debt capital in the past. However, use of this much debt would initially raise the debt ratio above the firm's target debt ratio of about 35%.

[1]Net working capital accounted for $1.4 million of the $12 million purchase price (Exhibit 6). Dixon planned to allocate the $10.6 million balance of the $12 million purchase price to the Collinsville plant. The plant would be depreciated over 10 years on the straight-line method of depreciation to a zero residual value. This relatively short life was permitted for tax purposes because it corresponded to the anticipated remaining physical life of the plant.

[2]Market interest rates were as follows:

Short-term Treasury bills:	10.5%
Long-term Treasury bonds:	9.5%
Long-term AA corporate bonds:	10.25%
Long-term A corporate bonds:	10.75%
Long-term BBB corporate bonds:	11.25%

EXHIBIT 1 **Financial Statements for American Chemical and Other Selected Large Chemical Companies, 1974–1978 (millions of dollars except per share data)**

	American Chemical					Allied Chemical					Dow Chemical				
	1974	1975	1976	1977	1978	1974	1975	1976	1977	1978	1974	1975	1976	1977	1978
Sales	$4,828	$4,671	$4,805	$5,235	$5,490	$2,216	$2,333	$2,630	$2,923	$3,268	$4,938	$4,888	$5,652	$6,234	$6,888
Net income	323	198	212	251	349	151	116	117	135	120	558	616	613	566	575
Earnings per share	$ 7.60	$ 4.66	$ 4.98	$ 5.91	$ 8.20	$ 5.43	$ 4.17	$ 4.52	$ 4.93	$ 4.25	$ 3.18	$ 3.33	$ 3.30	$ 3.01	$ 3.16
Dividends per share	1.00	1.25	1.50	1.65	1.80	1.53	1.80	1.80	1.85	2.00	.60	.75	.95	1.15	1.30
Dividend yield	5.3%	5.7%	4.3%	5.0%	4.1%	6.3%	5.4%	4.5%	4.5%	7.1%	2.5%	1.7%	2.3%	4.5%	5.6%
Common stock prices															
High	$ 23	$ 30	$ 36	$ 46	$ 48	$ 54	$ 42	$ 45	$ 51	$ 45	$ 35	$ 48	$ 57	$ 44	$ 31
Low	10	17	21	30	32	23	27	33	39	28	25	27	38	25	22
Closing	19	22	35	33	44	28	33	40	44	28	28	46	43	27	25
Closing P/E ratio	2.5	4.7	7.0	5.6	5.4	5.2	7.9	8.8	8.9	6.6	8.8	13.8	13.0	9.0	7.9
Total capitalization	$2,014	$2,109	$2,198	$2,465	$2,527	$1,550	$1,839	$1,959	$2,279	$2,467	$3,498	$4,316	$5,118	$5,889	$6,793
% debt	44%	37%	37%	29%	39%	28%	34%	33%	36%	38%	37%	36%	37%	40%	43%
% preferred stock	—	—	—	—	20%	—	—	—	—	—	—	—	—	—	—
% common stock	56%	63%	63%	71%	41%	72%	66%	67%	64%	62%	63%	64%	63%	60%	57%
Beta			1.20					1.43					1.25		
Interest coverage[a]	6.3	3.9	4.1	4.3	6.7	9.2	5.7	5.2	5.4	4.9	10.6	8.2	6.5	4.9	4.4
Bond rating[b]			BBB/A					A/A					A/Aa		

	Du Pont					Monsanto					Union Carbide				
	1974	1975	1976	1977	1978	1974	1975	1976	1977	1978	1974	1975	1976	1977	1978
Sales	$6,910	$7,221	$8,361	$9,435	$10,584	$3,498	$3,625	$4,270	$4,595	$5,019	$5,320	$5,665	$6,346	$7,036	$7,870
Net income	404	272	459	545	787	323	306	366	276	303	530	382	441	385	394
Earnings per share	$ 2.74	$ 1.81	$ 3.10	$ 3.69	$ 5.39	$ 9.35	$ 8.63	$10.05	$ 7.46	$ 8.29	$ 8.69	$ 6.23	$ 7.15	$ 6.05	$ 6.09
Dividends per share	1.83	1.42	1.75	1.92	2.42	2.30	2.55	2.75	3.03	3.18	2.18	2.40	2.50	2.80	2.80
Dividend yield	6.0%	3.2%	3.7%	4.8%	5.8%	5.9%	3.4%	3.2%	5.4%	6.8%	5.3%	3.9%	4.0%	6.8%	8.2%
Common stock prices															
High	$ 60	$ 45	$ 54	$ 45	$ 46	$ 70	$ 81	$ 100	$ 89	$ 60	$ 46	$ 67	$ 77	$ 62	$ 43
Low	28	29	39	35	33	39	41	76	52	44	32	40	56	40	34
Closing	31	42	45	40	42	41	76	88	58	47	41	61	62	41	34
Closing P/E ratio	11.3	23.2	14.5	10.8	7.8	4.4	8.8	8.8	7.8	5.7	4.7	9.8	8.7	6.8	5.6
Total capitalization	$4,874	$5,085	$5,772	$6,127	$6,394	$2,396	$2,942	$3,349	$3,668	$4,115	$3,752	$4,485	$5,212	$5,750	$5,997
% debt	16%	17%	22%	21%	17%	25%	29%	27%	28%	30%	26%	30%	32%	30%	28%
% preferred stock	5%	5%	4%	4%	4%	—	—	—	—	—	—	—	—	—	—
% common stock	79%	78%	74%	75%	79%	75%	71%	73%	72%	70%	74%	70%	68%	70%	72%
Beta			1.22					1.43					1.05		
Interest coverage[a]	9.5	4.1	6.0	6.1	9.5	11.4	9.1	8.4	7.0	6.5	14.0	8.4	7.0	5.0	4.9
Bond rating[b]			AAA/Aaa					AA/Aa					A/Aa		

[a]Defined as EBIT/interest.

[b]Standard and Poor's rating/Moody's rating.

EXHIBIT 2 Financial Statements for Universal Paper and Other Selected Large Paper Companies, 1974–1978 (millions of dollars except per share data)

	Universal Paper					Crown Zellerbach					International Paper				
	1974	1975	1976	1977	1978	1974	1975	1976	1977	1978	1974	1975	1976	1977	1978
Sales	$1,867	$1,902	$2,136	$2,248	$2,525	$1,172	$1,767	$2,136	$2,318	$2,467	$3,042	$3,081	$3,541	$3,669	$4,150
Net income	149	109	154	168	191	125	75	98	109	112	263	218	254	234	234
Earnings per share	$ 3.60	$ 2.63	$ 3.72	$ 4.06	$ 4.61	$ 5.06	$ 3.01	$ 3.88	$ 4.34	$ 4.39	$ 5.95	$ 4.93	$ 5.60	$ 4.98	$ 4.94
Dividends per share	.75	.75	.75	.85	1.00	1.75	1.80	1.80	1.83	1.90	1.75	2.00	2.00	2.00	2.00
Dividend yield	6.3%	3.9%	2.5%	2.8%	3.6%	7.5%	5.1%	4.0%	5.6%	6.2%	5.6%	3.5%	2.9%	4.6%	5.5%
Common stock price															
High	$ 17	$ 21	$ 34	$ 36	$ 38	$ 40	$ 41	$ 49	$ 45	$ 38	$ 56	$ 62	$ 80	$ 70	$ 49
Low	10	12	18	24	26	20	24	36	32	29	32	35	58	39	35
Closing	12	19	30	30	28	24	36	43	34	31	36	58	69	44	37
Closing P/E ratio	3.4	7.1	8.1	7.4	6.0	4.7	12.0	11.6	7.8	7.1	6.1	11.8	12.3	8.8	7.5
Total capitalization	$1,349	$1,620	$1,787	$1,938	$2,018	$1,220	$1,290	$1,345	$1,446	$1,647	$2,207	$2,801	$3,093	$3,303	$3,407
% debt	30%	29%	32%	32%	33%	33%	33%	31%	30%	34%	33%	41%	34%	32%	28%
% preferred stock	—	—	—	—	—	1%	1%	1%	1%	1%	—	—	—	—	—
% common stock	70%	71%	68%	68%	67%	66%	66%	68%	69%	65%	67%	59%	66%	68%	72%
Beta			1.52					1.03					1.43		
Interest coverage[a]	6.8	5.0	6.8	7.4	8.2	8.1	4.5	5.3	5.7	4.7	11.1	5.4	5.1	4.7	5.3
Bond rating[b]			A/Aa					A/A					AA/Aa		

	Mead Corporation					Kimberly-Clark					St. Regis Paper				
	1974	1975	1976	1977	1978	1974	1975	1976	1977	1978	1974	1975	1976	1977	1978
Sales	$1,526	$1,245	$1,599	$1,822	$2,322	$1,439	$1,484	$1,585	$1,726	$1,911	$1,471	$1,395	$1,642	$1,996	$2,300
Net income	82	53	89	98	121	95	103	121	131	149	105	96	91	107	127
Earnings per share	$ 3.27	$ 2.05	$ 3.61	$ 4.10	$ 5.12	$ 4.10	$ 4.41	$ 5.21	$ 5.60	$ 6.36	$ 4.76	$ 4.27	$ 3.82	$ 3.36	$ 3.94
Dividends per share	.60	.80	.89	.98	1.21	1.48	1.60	1.80	2.20	2.60	1.25	1.43	1.55	1.66	1.74
Dividend yield	9.2%	6.6%	4.4%	4.7%	6.8%	6.5%	4.4%	4.1%	5.1%	6.4%	7.3%	4.5%	4.2%	5.6%	6.4%
Common stock price															
High	$ 13	$ 13	$ 23	$ 24	$ 34	$ 35	$ 37	$ 47	$ 48	$ 50	$ 37	$ 35	$ 31	$ 39	$ 35
Low	8	9	12	18	17	19	24	36	37	39	18	20	34	29	26
Closing	9	12	21	22	23	25	37	44	43	41	19	34	39	31	28
Closing P/E ratio	2.8	5.9	5.8	5.4	4.5	6.1	8.4	8.4	7.7	6.4	4.0	8.0	10.2	9.2	7.1
Total capitalization	$ 826	$ 880	$ 965	$1,071	$1,171	$1,030	$1,086	$1,196	$1,347	$1,435	$1,127	$1,189	$1,296	$1,694	$1,791
% debt	34%	35%	33%	38%	36%	24%	21%	20%	20%	19%	33%	29%	26%	31%	30%
% preferred stock	6%	6%	5%	4%	1%	—	—	—	—	—	—	—	—	—	—
% common stock	60%	59%	62%	58%	63%	76%	79%	80%	80%	81%	67%	71%	74%	69%	70%
Beta			2.16					.99					1.14		
Interest coverage[a]	4.6	2.9	4.5	4.7	5.3	9.1	8.3	10.0	10.1	10.5	7.6	7.2	6.1	5.6	5.9
Bond rating[b]			A/A					AA/Aa					NR		

[a]Defined as EBIT/interest.

[b]Standard and Poor's rating/Moody's rating; NR = not rated.

EXHIBIT 3
Sales and Capacity of Sodium Chlorate Producers in the United States, 1970–1979

	Sales of Sodium Chlorate (tons)	Domestic Capacity (tons)	Average Price (dollars/ton)
1970	220,000	270,000	$129
1971	260,000	300,000	136
1972	280,000	300,000	144
1973	300,000	320,000	152
1974	310,000	335,000	188
1975	270,000	355,000	243
1976	345,000	370,000	295
1977	380,000	385,000	367
1978	410,000	420,000	392
1979	435,000[a]	455,000	413[a]

[a]Expected.

EXHIBIT 4
Domestic Producers of Sodium Chlorate

Producer	Capacity (tons)	Plants	Capacity (tons)
Hooker Chemical Corporation	114,000	Columbus, Miss.[a]	65,000
		Taft, La.[a]	40,000
		Niagara Falls, N.Y.	9,000
Pennwalt Corporation	72,000	Calvert City, Ky.[a]	37,000
		Portland, Ore.	26,000
		Tacoma, Wash.	9,000
American Chemical Corporation	65,000	Collinsville, Ala.[a]	40,000
		Wenatchee, Wash.	25,000
Kerr-McGee Corporation	63,000	Hamilton, Miss.[a]	33,000
		Henderson, Nev.	30,000
International Minerals & Chemicals Corporation	40,000	Orrington, Me.	40,000
Olin Corporation	20,000	McIntosh, Ala.[a]	20,000
ERCO Corporation	20,000	Monroe, La.[a]	20,000
Universal Paper Corporation	20,000	Rome, Ga.[a]	20,000
Georgia-Pacific Corporation	15,000	Plaquemine, La.[a]	15,000
Brunswick Chemical Company	11,000	Brunswick, Ga.[a]	11,000
Southern Chemicals Corporation	10,000	Reigelwood. N.C.[a]	6,000
		Butler, Ala.[a]	4,000
Pacific Eng. and Prod. Co. of Nevada	5,000	Henderson, Nev.	5,000
U.S. total	455,000		455,000
Southeastern U.S. total			311,000

[a]Plants serving the southeastern U.S. market.

EXHIBIT 5 **Financial Statements of Selected Sodium Chlorate Producers, 1974–1978 (millions of dollars except per share data)**

	Pennwalt					Kerr-McGee					Inter. Minerals & Chemicals				
	1974	1975	1976	1977	1978	1974	1975	1976	1977	1978	1974	1975	1976	1977	1978
Sales	$ 641	$ 714	$ 777	$ 835	$ 921	$1,550	$1,799	$1,955	$2,165	$2,072	$ 859	$1,303	$1,260	$1,280	$1,364
Net income	27	33	35	42	45	116	131	134	119	118	70	166	135	108	120
Earnings per share	$ 2.81	$ 3.25	$ 3.56	$ 4.23	$ 4.54	$ 4.64	$ 5.15	$ 5.19	$ 4.61	$ 4.57	$3.59	$ 9.91	$ 7.73	$ 6.09	$ 6.61
Dividends per share	1.24	1.36	1.54	2.25	2.05	.85	1.00	1.19	1.25	1.25	.57	1.38	2.10	2.45	2.60
Dividend yield	7.4%	4.6%	4.9%	5.2%	6.7%	1.4%	1.4%	1.8%	2.7%	2.6%	1.9%	5.3%	5.9%	6.4%	7.4%
Common stock prices															
High	$ 26	$ 30	$ 38	$ 39	$ 43	$ 93	$ 95	$ 83	$ 75	$ 53	$ 41	$ 49	$ 42	$ 44	$ 44
Low	15	17	27	32	32	47	60	61	45	40	21	31	33	35	34
Closing	17	28	33	39	33	72	70	68	47	48	39	38	41	41	35
Closing P/E ratio	6.0	8.6	9.3	9.2	7.3	15.5	13.6	13.1	10.2	10.5	10.9	3.8	5.3	6.7	5.3
Total capitalization	$ 371	$ 441	$ 469	$ 500	$ 524	$ 851	$1,091	$1,325	$1,433	$1,533	$ 577	$ 781	$ 990	$1,083	$1,161
% debt	28%	34%	33%	34%	31%	19%	20%	24%	21%	17%	42%	38%	37%	36%	32%
% preferred stock	—	—	—	—	—	—	—	—	—	—	10%	4%	2%	1%	1%
% common stock	72%	66%	67%	66%	69%	81%	80%	76%	79%	83%	48%	58%	61%	63%	67%
Beta			1.33					1.06					.81		
Interest coverage[b]	2.9	3.3	3.8	4.1	4.2	19.4	17.1	10.8	8.4	6.4	5.5	11.6	8.4	5.5	6.3
Bond rating[c]			A/A					AA/Aa					NR/A		

	Georgia-Pacific					Brunswick Chemical					Southern Chemicals				
	1974	1975	1976	1977	1978	1974	1975	1976	1977	1978	1974	1975	1976	1977	1978
Sales	$2,432	$2,359	$3,038	$3,675	$4,403	$ 1.9	$ 2.1	$ 3.0	$ 4.0	$ 4.3	$ 1.7	$ 2.0	$ 2.7	$ 3.6	$ 3.9
Net income	164	148	215	282	302	.20	.15	.37	.71	.79	.10	(.05)	.28	.74	.73
Earnings per share	$ 1.74	$ 1.54	$ 2.12	$ 2.54	$ 2.93	$ .40	$ .30	$ .74	$ 1.42	$ 1.58	$ .61	$ (.24)	$ 1.38	$ 3.69	$ 3.66
Dividends per share	.47	.49	.70	.83	1.03	.10	.10	.15	.35	.40	—	—	—	.30	.30
Dividend yield	3.1%	1.9%	2.1%	3.5%	4.5%	[a]	[a]	[a]	2.9%	3.5%	[a]	[a]	[a]	1.2%	1.3%
Common stock prices															
High	$ 27	$ 30	$ 37	$ 37	$ 33	[a]	[a]	[a]	$ 13	$ 14¼	[a]	[a]	[a]	$ 28	$ 31
Low	13	16	26	25	24	[a]	[a]	[a]	7½	9	[a]	[a]	[a]	11	20
Closing	15	26	37	28	24	[a]	[a]	[a]	12	11½	[a]	[a]	[a]	25	23
Closing P/E ratio	8.6	16.9	17.4	11.0	8.2	[a]	[a]	[a]	8.5	7.3	[a]	[a]	[a]	6.7	6.4
Total capitalization	$1,935	$2,150	$2,045	$2,541	$2,878	$ 1.8	$ 1.9	$ 2.1	$ 2.6	$ 3.2	$ 1.6	$ 1.5	$ 1.8	$ 2.4	$ 3.0
% debt	45%	42%	22%	29%	29%	33%	30%	25%	19%	15%	50%	50%	41%	28%	21%
% preferred stock	—	—	—	—	—	—	—	—	—	—	—	—	—	—	—
% common stock	55%	58%	78%	71%	71%	67%	70%	75%	81%	85%	50%	50%	59%	72%	79%
Beta			1.50			[a]	[a]	[a]	1.10		[a]	[a]	[a]	1.20	
Interest coverage[b]	4.3	4.4	8.1	9.9	9.3	6.7	5.0	12.3	47	53	3.5	.4	9.0	22	24
Bond rating[c]			AA/Aa					NR					NR		

[a]Stock not publicly traded.
[b]Defined as EBIT/interest.
[c]Standard and Poor's rating/Moody's rating; NR = not rated.

EXHIBIT 6 Financial Statements for the Collinsville Plant, 1974–1979 (thousands of dollars)

	1974	1975	1976	1977	1978	1979[a]
Operating Data						
Sales (tons)	36,899	30,819	37,464	40,076	39,790	38,507
Average price ($/ton)	$ 188	$ 243	$ 295	$ 367	$ 392	$ 413
Sales	$ 6,937	$ 7,489	$11,052	$14,708	$15,598	$15,903
Variable costs						
Power	2,935	3,395	4,631	5,530	6,173	6,759
Graphite	354	369	545	653	689	714
Salt and other	693	800	1,047	1,274	1,307	1,385
Total variable costs	3,982	4,564	6,223	7,457	8,169	8,858
Fixed costs						
Labor	590	608	646	739	924	1,072
Maintenance	143	201	220	272	235	237
Other	474	659	902	1,063	509	1,107
Total fixed costs	1,207	1,468	1,768	2,074	1,668	2,416
Total manufacturing costs	5,189	6,032	7,991	9,531	9,837	11,274
Depreciation	433	394	402	391	384	399
Selling	114	92	126	155	181	204
R&D	105	154	207	274	351	429
Total other costs	652	640	735	820	916	1,032
Operating profit	$ 1,096	$ 817	$ 2,326	$ 4,357	$ 4,845	$ 3,597
Percent of Sales Ratios						
Power costs	42.3%	45.3%	41.9%	37.6%	39.6%	42.5%
Variable costs	57.4	60.9	56.3	50.7	52.4	55.7
Fixed costs	17.4	19.6	16.0	14.1	10.7	15.2
Manufacturing costs	74.8	80.5	72.3	64.8	63.1	70.9
Operating profit	15.8	10.9	21.0	29.6	31.1	22.6
Accounts receivable	10.1	10.4	10.2	9.9	10.1	10.2
Inventories	3.7	7.3	6.2	4.4	4.1	4.1
Accounts payable	5.8	6.3	5.6	5.3	5.1	5.5
Net assets	66.6	64.5	47.0	35.2	34.5	34.0
Asset Data						
Accounts receivable	$ 701	$ 779	$ 1,128	$ 1,456	$ 1,575	$ 1,622
Inventories	254	544	681	647	639	651
Net property, plant, and equipment	4,066	3,978	4,003	3,853	3,964	4,014
Total assets	5,021	6,301	5,812	6,956	6,178	6,287
Accounts payable	402	472	619	780	795	873
Net assets	$ 4,619	$ 4,829	$ 5,193	$ 5,176	$ 5,383	$ 5,414
Operating profit/net assets	23.7%	16.9%	44.8%	84.2%	90.0%	66.4%

[a]Expected.

EXHIBIT 7 **Financial Statements for Dixon Corporation, 1975–1979 (thousands of dollars except per share data)**

	1975	1976	1977	1978	1979[a]
Income Statements					
Sales	$19,128	$23,830	$28,348	$34,770	$42,259
Cost of goods sold	14,085	16,889	19,950	24,467	29,185
Selling and administrative	1,952	2,308	2,824	3,291	4,436
Research	325	388	593	682	716
Interest	400	320	240	160	80
Taxes	1,125	1,878	2,285	2,932	3,818
Profit after taxes	$ 1,241	$ 2,047	$ 2,456	$ 3,238	$ 4,024
Earnings per share	$ 1.13	$ 1.86	$ 2.23	$ 2.94	$ 3.66
Dividends per share	.20	.30	.40	.40	.50
Balance Sheets					
Cash and marketable securities	$ 385	$ 357	$ 556	$ 1,273	$ 2,996
Other current assets	4,208	5,016	5,939	7,267	8,917
Property, plant, and equipment	7,436	7,895	8,354	8,842	8,918
Total assets	$12,029	$13,268	$14,849	17,382	$20,831
Current liabilities	$ 2,314	$ 2,836	$ 3,402	$ 4,138	$ 5,113
Debt (including current maturity)	5,000	4,000	3,000	2,000	1,000
Stockholders' equity	4,715	6,432	8,447	11,244	14,718
Total liabilities and equity	$12,029	$13,268	$14,849	$17,382	$20,831
Stock price range	$ 7–14	$ 8–22	$ 19–30	$ 25–40	$ 35–45
Closing stock price	9	20	27	38	40[b]
Beta			1.06		
Bond rating			NR		

NR = not rated.
[a]Expected.
[b]October 30, 1979.

EXHIBIT 8 **Pro Forma Financial Statements for the Collinsville Plant, 1979–1984 (thousands of dollars)**

	1979[a]	1980	1981	1982	1983	1984
Operating Data						
Sales (tons)		32,000	35,000	38,000	38,000	38,000
Average price ($/ton)		$ 415	$ 480	$ 520	$ 562	$ 606
Sales		$13,280	$16,800	$19,760	$21,356	$23,028
Variable costs						
Power		6,304	7,735	9,386	10,526	11,780
Graphite		645	791	875	940	992
Salt and other		1,285	1,621	1,753	1,836	1,956
Total variable costs		8,234	10,147	12,014	13,302	14,728
Fixed costs						
Labor		1,180	1,297	1,427	1,580	1,738
Maintenance		256	277	299	322	354
Other		1,154	1,148	1,179	1,113	1,153
Total fixed costs		2,590	2,722	2,905	3,015	3,245
Total manufacturing costs		10,824	12,869	14,919	16,317	17,973
Selling		112	125	138	152	168
R&D		451	478	508	543	591
Depreciation		1,060	1,110	1,160	1,210	1,270
Total other costs		1,623	1,713	1,806	1,905	2,029
Operating profit		$ 833	$ 2,218	$ 3,035	$ 3,134	$ 3,026
Percent of Sales Ratios						
Power costs		47.5%	46.0%	47.5%	49.3%	51.2%
Variable costs		62.0	60.4	60.8	62.3	64.0
Fixed costs		19.5	16.2	14.7	14.1	14.1
Manufacturing costs		81.5	76.6	75.5	76.4	78.0
Operating profit		6.3	13.2	15.4	14.7	13.1
Accounts receivable		10.0	10.0	10.0	10.0	10.0
Inventories		4.5	4.5	4.5	4.5	4.5
Accounts payable		5.5	5.5	5.5	5.5	5.5
Net assets		84.5	65.2	53.7	47.5	41.8
Asset Data						
Accounts receivable	$ 1,622	$ 1,328	$ 1,680	$ 1,976	$ 2,136	$ 2,303
Inventories	651	598	756	889	961	1,036
Net property, plant, and equipment	10,600	10,025	9,440	8,840	8,230	7,560
Total assets	12,873	11,951	11,876	11,705	11,327	10,899
Accounts payable	873	730	924	1,087	1,175	1,267
Net assets	$12,000	$11,221	$10,952	$10,618	$10,152	$9,632
Operating profit/Net assets		7.4%	20.3%	28.6%	30.9%	31.4%

Note: These pro forma financial statements were based on the following assumptions: (1) Continued use of *unlaminated* graphite electrodes. (2) Though excess industry capacity would hold price increases to less than an 8% annual rate in 1980, by 1984 the average annual price increase over the period 1979–1984 was assumed to equal 8%. (3) Power costs per kWh would increase 12% per year. (4) Depreciation would increase because Dixon would have written up the value of the Collinsville plant to $10.6 million.

[a]Expected.

Adecco SA's Acquisition of Olsten Corporation

In the summer of 1999, John Bowmer, Adecco's CEO, faced a tough situation. Adecco SA, one of the world's leading staffing companies, was in the midst of attempting to acquire the staffing operations of Olsten Corporation. Eighteen months earlier, Bowmer had first made contact with Olsten's CEO at that time, Frank Liguori, and a member of the board of directors, Josh Weston. But now, the negotiations with Olsten had come to a standstill, and Olsten had received an offer from a competitor. Bowmer did not know what price the other suitor for Olsten had offered or how Stuart Olsten, the son of Olsten's founder, was leaning. He decided to talk directly to his friend Weston to remove the deadlock in the negotiations. In preparation for this conversation, Felix Weber, the CFO of Adecco, reviewed his team's valuation of Olsten. Adecco needed not only to ascertain the right price to bid for Olsten, but also to address the more "emotional" needs of the seller. Though the negotiations looked promising, the entrance of a new bidder had made them complicated.

Bowmer and Weber were well aware of the importance of the Olsten acquisition for Adecco's strategy. Adecco was a global leader in employment services and had grown rapidly through acquisitions and organic growth since its creation through a merger in 1996. Adecco's global corporate strategy targeted market leadership as a key goal. Bowmer made this point in clear terms: "An important part of Adecco's global strategy is to become the number one or two staffing service firm in each of the major markets globally." The acquisition of Olsten would enable Adecco to increase its share of the large U.S. market from 6% to 10%, making it the number one staffing company in the country.

Given the strategic importance of the Olsten acquisition, Weber pondered over his valuation model. Coming up with a right price was critical, in particular, as Adecco was not alone anymore in its interest in acquiring Olsten. Vedior, a Dutch company and Adecco's rival in Europe, was also in talks with Olsten. Bowmer reflected on the role of the Olsten family, who held 67% of the voting power in Olsten through its control of supervoting Class B shares.[1] Though Edward A. Blechschmidt had taken over as CEO in February 1999, Stuart Olsten was the chairman of the board and would no doubt have an important say in the matter. Bowmer hoped that he could talk directly with Weston to establish what was important to both parties and come to an agreement on the price and address the concerns of major shareholders.

[1]Supervoting stock has voting rights greater than common stock, which is usually characterized by one share one vote.

Professors Simi Kedia and Peter Tufano prepared this case. This case was developed from published sources. HBS cases are developed solely as the basis for class discussion. Cases are not intended to serve as endorsements, sources of primary data, or illustrations of effective or ineffective management.

Copyright © 2001 President and Fellows of Harvard College. To order copies or request permission to reproduce materials, call 1-800-545-7685, write Harvard Business School Publishing, Boston, MA 02163, or go to http://www.hbsp.harvard.edu. No part of this publication may be reproduced, stored in a retrieval system, used in a spreadsheet, or transmitted in any form or by any means—electronic, mechanical, photocopying, recording, or otherwise—without the permission of Harvard Business School.

The Staffing Industry

The staffing industry had first appeared in the mid-twentieth century, but its role evolved over time. Initially, staffing firms provided mostly unskilled work in the industrial sector or short-term replacements for sick or temporarily-absent workers, earning them the nickname "temp firms." Over time, staffing firms began to place more skilled workers in all sectors of the economy and for much longer assignments than in the past. They also broadened their activities to provide firms with permanent placement, payroll, outplacement, and other managed services. Reflecting these changes, the "staffing industry" shed its old label of "temp firms." Rather than providing stand-in workers, they now provided firms with just-in-time flexible workforces. With this change, staffing companies sought to become long-term business partners, serving as valuable intermediaries between employees and employers.

The global staffing industry grew at an extraordinary 13% per annum on average between 1987 to 1999. Two general factors were responsible for this growth rate. First, economic expansion of the late 1980s and subsequent contraction encouraged companies to carefully scrutinize operating costs and introduce more flexible cost structures. In the past, employing temporary workers involved lower direct costs, though legislation (particularly in Europe) aimed at establishing the right of temps to earn at least as much as full time employees had reduced this advantage. Yet, by employing temporary workers, companies could still reduce the idle time of permanent workers, shift wages from semi-fixed to variable costs, and adjust their cost structures for just-in-time staffing, especially when faced with seasonality, and economic and product cycles. Client companies also used staffing companies to save on the indirect costs of hiring, finding, assessing, and training workers. (See Exhibit 1.) Second, the staffing industry's growth also reflected changes in the "professional" segment of the labor market. For many reasons, short-term assignments became more acceptable to professionals in information technology (IT), accountancy, engineering, sales, finance, legal, medical, energy, automotive, and purchasing segments of the labor market. These professionals apparently valued the ability to deepen their specialization, broaden their work experiences, and build more flexible careers. The professional segment of the staffing industry facilitated this trend.

The staffing industry was fragmented with the top five companies in the world accounting for 27% of the market. (See Exhibit 2 for the size of major world markets, and Exhibit 3 for the major global companies and their market shares.) The industry had been consolidating rapidly over the past few years. In 1998, there were a total of 514 acquisitions announced worldwide, sharply higher than the 105 in 1994. This trend towards consolidation had been spurred by increasing globalization of the client companies. Whereas big business was a small fraction of total staffing revenues in the early 1990s, it had risen to approximately 50% by 1999. By consolidating, staffing firms moved from being local service providers to having a national presence and being global players. It allowed staffing firms to provide a full range of consistent services in all countries in which global clients operated, as well as to leverage investment in infrastructure like IT, and to exploit economies of scope.

Substantial economies of scale and scope were possible with consolidation. Large staffing companies brought together employees and employers and became thriving labor exchanges. As the staffing firm increased in size and catered to more employers, employees were attracted to the firm and its large pool of employers. Similarly, with size and a larger pool of employees, more employers were attracted to the firm. Increases in size and market share thus substantially reduced the costs of selling and recruiting for the staffing company and, therefore, increased margins. Adecco's historical estimates indicated a strong relationship between its profitability and national market share, as well as a relationship between growth and returns. (See Exhibits 4 and 5.)

In addition, the large sums that staffing agencies were spending on internal information technology systems made size an advantage. Adecco's internally developed Xpert system was a state-of-the-art evaluation and testing tool, and its MAX Adia Office Automation & Design (TM) system integrated the results of Adecco's skills testing with personal attributes and work history to automatically match available candidates with customer requirements. MAX also tracked the performance of temporary personnel and provided quality reports to their customers.

The U.S., by far the largest staffing market, had a compound annual growth rate of 17% from 1993 to 1998. The specialized services area, including IT, accounting, and legal staffing, had not only the highest growth rates (see Exhibit 6), but also the highest gross margins. This trend of high margins and high growth in the specialized services was expected to continue in the future, especially in IT due to system conversion needs for the year 2000. However, growth rates in general staffing were projected to decline in the short run. Specialized staffing was characterized by higher margins, with net income as a percentage of sales being 4.9% in 1997 for the U.S. in comparison to 2.2% for generalized staffing.

Adecco SA

Formed in 1996 from the merger of the Swiss firm Adia SA with the French firm Ecco, Swiss-based Adecco SA was the world's largest staffing company by 1999. Adecco had grown rapidly, increasing annual sales from 6.4 billion Swiss Francs (CHF) in 1996 to CHF 15.3 billion in 1998 and operating over 3,000 offices in 52 countries. Net income before amortization of goodwill[2] increased from CHF 240 million in 1996 to CHF 406 million in 1998, and Adecco shareholders enjoyed nearly a quadrupling of their share values in the time since the firm's inception. Adecco outperformed its peers over this period and was the first firm in the industry to be certified by the International Organization for Standardization (ISO). (See Exhibit 7 for Adecco financials and Exhibit 8 for its stock performance.) It was the market leader in France, Canada, Switzerland, Australia, and Spain, and was second in the U.S. and U.K. Only in the Benelux countries and Japan was it fourth or fifth in the market.

Adecco's success was the result of a consistent strategy aimed at making Adecco the "employer of choice" and the "supplier of choice." (See Exhibit 9.) The first goal of this three-pronged strategy was rapid growth to be achieved both organically as well as through acquisitions. This sales growth had resulted in higher total return to shareholders. (See Exhibit 5.)

Along with increasing growth rates, gaining national market share was an important goal for Adecco. John Bowmer said, "We will be number one or two in market share in the 11 biggest national markets, and we will work to attain a 20% share of each market." This strategy, he said, was "not ego or vanity but. . . good business sense," citing the fact that historically EBIT margins increased with market share. (See Exhibit 4.) Employers preferred dealing with fewer staffing firms who were able to provide services in different regional and national markets, because it was less expensive and guaranteed "consistent service." One-third of Adecco's contracts were with large national or multinational firms with multiple sites. While these arrangements carried lower gross margins, overhead costs were also correspondingly lower. While the average cost of services in the U.S. was 15–20% for the placement in small companies, they amounted to only 5 to 10% for large contract business.

[2]Goodwill arose when a firm acquired another company for a price in excess of book value. This difference was amortized and "expensed" on a firm's income statement, although its was a non-cash charge.

The third driver of Adecco's strategy was an emphasis on its high-value business segments. Adecco was a diversified staffing company with 88% of its worldwide sales coming from general staffing and the remaining 12% from IT and other specialized staffing. (See Exhibit 10.) In specialized staffing, characterized by higher margins, Adecco operated a number of well established brands like AOC (accounting), Jonathan Wren (finance and banking), Ajilon and Computer People (both IT), TAD and Roevin (engineering and technical), and Econova/Lee Hecht Harrison (outplacement).

Achieving the number one market position in the large U.S. market was high on the goals of Adecco's board. In December 1998, the board had met to discuss potential acquisitions that would enable Adecco to increase market share in the U.S. Olsten was on top of the list, although this position was not undisputed. The Chairman of Adecco suggested that it might be preferable to invest heavily in Internet human resource companies that provided staffing services through the Internet, rather than through physical offices. He also wondered whether it might be prudent to delay the acquisition. He believed that Olsten's value was more likely to fall than rise over time, given the problems it faced, and he was concerned that it might lose market share in the wake of the merger.

Olsten Corporation

William Olsten founded Olsten Corporation, a $5 billion home health care and staffing firm, in 1950. After stints as a produce buyer, soap seller, and restauranteur, he went into the staffing business, placing his sister and his wife as the firm's first temps. The firm grew rapidly and went public in 1967. By 1998, the company was the third largest staffing company in the world with global staffing revenues of $3.1 billion, and U.S. revenues of $2.4 billion. It was operating in 14 countries with 1,500 offices and had a global market share of 3.9%. It also had sizeable presence in the fast-growing IT area, which accounted for 12–14% of total staffing revenues.

The Olsten family continued to play an important role in the firm through its ownership of Class B stock, which was entitled to ten votes per share versus one vote for each share of common stock. In 1999, there were about 68 million common shares and 13 million Class B shares outstanding. The Olsten family owned 16% of the firm, but controlled 66% of the votes cast in corporate matters.

In the 1970s, Olsten extended its temporary staffing expertise into home health care. Olsten Health Services in the United States and Canada provided home care management and coordination for the managed care community along with home infusion and other therapies. In 1993, Olsten acquired Lifetime Corporation, the then largest provider of home health. In 1998, Olsten repurchased home health offices it had sold to Columbia/HCA for approximately $30 million. By that year, Health Services accounted for about 27% of Olsten's total revenues.[3]

Olsten also aggressively expanded its staffing business outside the U.S. After the death of William Olsten in 1991, his son, Stuart Olsten, directed this initiative. A series of acquisitions from 1994 to 1997 substantially increased Olsten's presence in Europe and Latin America, and in total Olsten invested approximately $150 million in these acquisitions.[4]

[3]The percentage of sales from health care increased slightly if total company sales did not include franchise and subcontractor sales, as was Adecco's practice.

[4]Among others, Olsten acquired or purchased majority stakes in Office Angels in the U.K.; in Norsk Personal AS (the second-largest staffing company in the Nordic area); Alegro Vikarservice ApS (Denmark); OFFiS Unternehmen fur Zeitarbeit GmbH & Co. KG (Germany's third-largest staffing firm); Kontorsjouren AB (Sweden's third-largest staffing firm); Dataset OY (Finland); and Sogica SA (France and Spain); and various majority investments in South America.

Although Olsten was the largest provider of home health services in the U.S., this business had become increasingly difficult. In 1997, the government had reduced reimbursements through its Medicare interim payment system, and managed-care organizations were also cutting payments for home nursing. Several health-care subsidiaries faced both civil and criminal investigations for Medicare fraud, and over a thousand health companies closed for financial reasons. Olsten launched a comprehensive restructuring and recovery plan for its health care business in 1997, the efficiencies of which were expected to materialize in 1998 and 1999. In October 1998, Olsten paid $4.5 million to settle a federal Medicare fraud investigation involving Quantum Health Resources,[5] and in March 1999, it pled guilty to other federal and state investigations relating to its home health division, incurring special charges of $61 million. Further on March 30, 1999, the company announced plans to take a special charge during the first quarter of 1999, aggregating $46 million as part of the ongoing restructuring of business units. Of this, approximately $22 million was for compensation and severance costs, $16 million was for asset write-offs, and $8 million was for integration costs.

The company faced other challenges as well. Completing the purchase of its European subsidiaries was proving more expensive than anticipated. In some of these subsidiaries, Olsten had acquired a 51% stake, planning to fund its purchase of the balance out of cash flow and additional equity raised once the anticipated appreciation in share price materialized. Under these agreements, Olsten might need $100–$150 million to complete the Sogica earnout,[6] $50–$100 million for the Norsk earnout, and $15–$20 million to complete earnouts of minority interest in Latin America. The Sogica payment was contractually due in March 2000, and the Norsk buyout depended on the intentions of the Norsk minority shareholders. (They had the right to sell their stake at any time based on a third party value evaluation.) Additional staffing services in France and health service units in the U.S. were purchased in the first six months of 1999 for $15 million in cash. Minority interest was estimated to be around 6% of Olsten's enterprise value.

Olsten's debt rose over this period, increasing from $461 million in December 1997 to $606 million in January 1999 and to $746 million by July 1999. The long-term debt of $746 million included a revolving credit line agreement with a consortium of 11 banks. As of July 1999, Olsten had drawn down $344 million of the $400 million credit line. This agreement was scheduled to expire in 2001, thus its classification as long-term debt. The credit agreement was subject to a number of affirmative covenants (e.g., Olsten had to provide audited financial statements), negative covenants (e.g., Olsten was restricted in selling assets and issuing debt), and financial covenants (e.g., Olsten had to maintain certain financial ratios). In May 1999, the company's revolving credit agreement was amended to revise provisions related to the maintenance of various financial ratios and covenants. In 1996, Olsten was required to maintain an EBIT/Interest Expense ratio of at least 5, and a Debt/EBITDA ratio of at most 2.5. The banks voluntarily amended these covenants in April 1999, requiring Olsten to maintain an EBIT/Interest ratio of at least 3 and a Debt/EBITDA ratio of at most 3.75. Any failure on the part of Olsten to observe these covenants or adhere to the credit agreement would constitute an event of default. Banks were unwilling to increase Olsten's credit lines, and it was unlikely that the obligations in 2000 could be met through internal cash flow generation.

As a consequence, Olsten performance lagged behind other firms in the staffing industry and its stock price declined sharply. (See Exhibit 11 for Olsten financial statements.) Olsten's board and management came to appreciate the position of the firm,

[5]An infusion therapies company Olsten had acquired in 1996.

[6]In an "earnout," an acquirer agrees to pay the seller a contingent payment well after the deal is consummated. The payment is based on the subsequent performance, typically accounting performance, of the acquired entity.

and in particular its need to finance the repurchase of minority interests and earnouts in 2000. As a consequence, they were actively looking for alliances or mergers by the end of 1998.

Adecco's Initial Approach to Olsten

The Adecco management team selected Olsten from among a number of potential acquisitions because of its fit with Adecco. The staffing business of Olsten complemented Adecco's business in the U.S. Whereas Adecco operated mostly in the western part of the U.S., Olsten was dominant in the East. Outside the U.S., Olsten had significant presence in Scandinavia, Latin America and Germany, where Adecco's market share was small. Olsten's sizeable presence in the specialty IT business would allow Adecco to increase market share in this segment. Finally, Adecco management felt that the cultures of the two companies were compatible, making Olsten a desirable acquisition.

In early talks held in December 1998, Adecco expressed its interest in acquiring Olsten. Bowmer and Weber were in complete agreement that they did not want to acquire the troubled home health care business and the preliminary offer was for Olsten's staffing business. Though initially, Stuart Olsten, the Olsten board, and their financial advisors did not want to separate the businesses, they had become reconciled to this as the negotiations progressed. Olsten had also indicated that a successful offer (for the company including healthcare) would be above $20 a share even though the share price was trading much below that, recently at $7.38. This target price was partly based on the share price of $32, above which the stock had briefly traded in 1996. (See Exhibit 12 for Olsten stock price.)

As talks proceeded, Olsten and Adecco agreed that the home health care unit would be spun off as a separate company to the current shareholders of Olsten as part of the acquisition. On February 10, 1999, Adecco made an offer for Olsten's staffing business. In March, Olsten employed Solomon Smith Barney Inc. and later, Warburg Dillon Read LLC, to review strategic options and Adecco's offer. Stuart Olsten indicated that a successful offer would have to value the staffing business at a minimum of $16 a share, higher than the $11 being offered by Adecco. By April, Olsten and Adecco had executed a confidentiality agreement and Adecco commenced due diligence.

The negotiations between Adecco and Olsten took a turn for the worse with the emergence on the scene of Vedior, a large Dutch staffing company, which also showed an interest in acquiring the staffing business of Olsten. In late June, Warburg Dillon Read, on behalf of Olsten, was in talks with both Goldman Sachs, on behalf of Adecco, and with the investment bankers of Vedior. By early July, Adecco and Vedior submitted competing non-binding proposals for the acquisition of Olsten's staffing business. On July 9 and July 14, a special committee of the board of directors of Olsten, consisting of Blechschmidt, Stuart Olsten, and four other directors, met to review both offers. The board of Olsten was scheduled to meet on July 22, 1999, to consider the sale of Olsten. Bowmer and Weber knew they had to convince Josh Weston and Stuart Olsten, in particular. Though Weber was not interested in getting involved in a bidding war with Vedior over Olsten, he decided to reexamine his valuation model given the importance of Olsten for Adecco's U.S. strategy.

Over the last few years, Adecco had made many large acquisitions of personnel services businesses, including TAD, Delphi Group plc, and Career Staff Ltd. The acquisition activity had allowed them to develop their "Pentagon Approach" to valuation that had been hailed for its success by Wall Street. The Pentagon Approach was a simple five-step method for valuing target businesses. It involved (1) valuing the target business as-is;

(2) valuing the business with all synergies less any costs of integration; (3) adding any potential gains from Adecco's cross-border financing strategy; (4) adding any potential gains from reduced tax liability accruing from Adecco's ownership of the business; and (5) finally determining the suitable price to be paid.

The estimated synergies from combining the two businesses, as well as the resulting integration costs, were methodically determined for each country and for the various specialties. Olsten's staffing business could be merged with a U.S. subsidiary of Adecco SA. Adecco estimated that integration of Olsten's North American operations would lead to significant synergies, 50% of which would be realized in 2000 and the full potential to be realized thereafter. However, based on their experience, there were also likely to be significant one-time costs of integrating the two businesses in the U.S. In valuing Olsten's non-U.S. operations, Adecco assumed no synergies nor integration costs. Adecco's pro forma forecast of Olsten's staffing business, incorporating all synergies and integration costs in line with the second step of the Pentagon Approach, are presented in Exhibit 13. The cash flows were expected to grow at 5% per annum after the ten-year period modeled.

Adecco's policy was to finance internal growth through cash generated from operations while financing external growth through a mix of debt and equity. In the case of Olsten, Adecco expected to finance 30–40% of the total price through equity and the rest with debt. Weber anticipated raising additional equity, bringing the capital structure to 80% equity (at market value) and 20% debt, which is what was applied for WACC. Adecco, rated BBB+, faced an average long-term borrowing rate in U.S. dollars of approximately 7%. Bowmer and Weber felt comfortable with Adecco's ability to raise debt financing for the Olsten acquisition at this rate.[7]

Based on tax treaties between the U.S. and Switzerland, the parent company, Adecco SA, was entitled to receive royalty payments of about 1–2% of gross revenues for marketing and corporate services provided. These royalties paid by the U.S. subsidiary would be considered as expenses in the estimation of the firm's U.S. tax liability. These royalties would be treated as income for the parent Adecco and taxed accordingly, at the Swiss corporate tax rate of 9%. The valuation analysis in Exhibit 13 did not incorporate this factor into the projected cash flows.

It had been the policy of Adecco not to pay the full estimated value of the acquiring business. This was driven by the conviction that a part of the value being created was from synergies unique to Adecco and from Adecco's ability to leverage its global position to create additional value from financing and taxation.

Bowmer thought about the stalemate in the negotiations. He not only had to decide what Adecco should offer to pay for Olsten's staffing business, but he also had to convince Josh Weston and Stuart Olsten that it was in the best interest of Olsten shareholders to accept Adecco's offer. He hoped that he would be able to learn about the issues and choices before the Olsten board and how best to address them.

[7] It was tentatively agreed that Adecco would assume $750 million of Olsten debt. Adecco would then decide whether to retain, refinance, or repay the debt.

EXHIBIT 1
Survey Results on Firm's Use of Employment Companies

Source: Adecco. Survey conducted by McKinsey/Deloitte Touche.

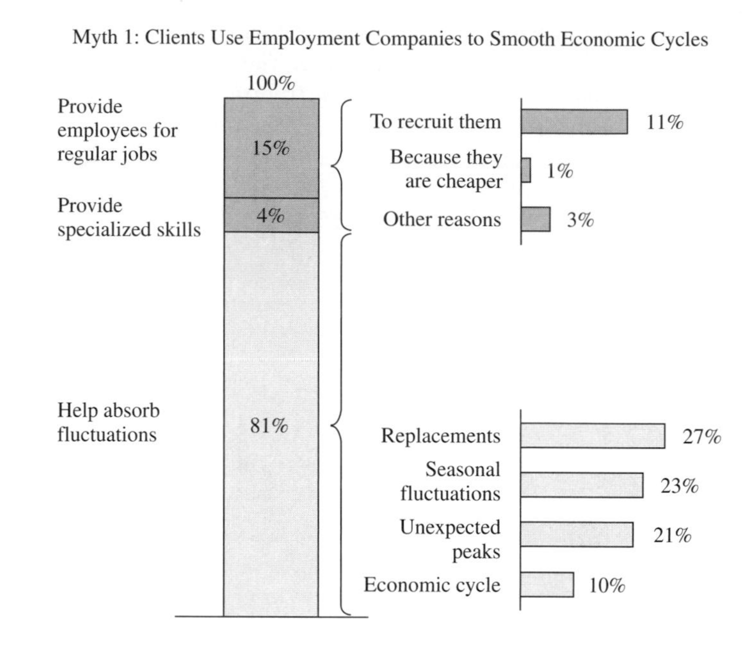

EXHIBIT 2
Global Staffing Market Share, 1998

Sources: Baird Business Services, Adecco estimates.

	Industry Size (Billions $)	Adecco Share (%)	Olsten Share (%)
U.S.	72	5.5	4.2
U.K.	17	4.5	0.9
France	12	29.4	3
Japan	12	8	0
Netherlands	7	6	0
Switzerland	2	3.0	0
Other European[a]	7	39.8	20.6

[a]Includes Belgium, Germany, Spain, and Scandinavia.

EXHIBIT 3
Global Market Shares Based on 1998 Revenues

Source: ABN Amro Research, Adecco estimates.

	Global Market Share (%)	No. of Countries	No. of Offices
Adecco	8.2	52	3000
Manpower	8.1	50	3000
Olsten	3.9	14	1500
Randstand	3.4	11	1616
Kelly	3.1	19	1800
Vedior	3.0	8	1301
Interim Service	2.5	12	1350

EXHIBIT 4
Relationship between Gross EBIT Margin and Market Share for Adecco

Source: Adecco. (Points on the chart represent countries where Adecco operated.)

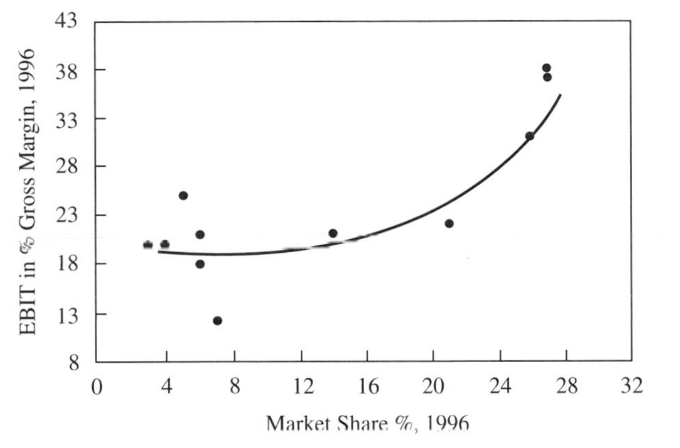

EXHIBIT 5
Shareholder Return and Sales Growth for Adecco (1997–1998)

Source: Adecco. (Points on the chart represent countries where Adecco operated.)

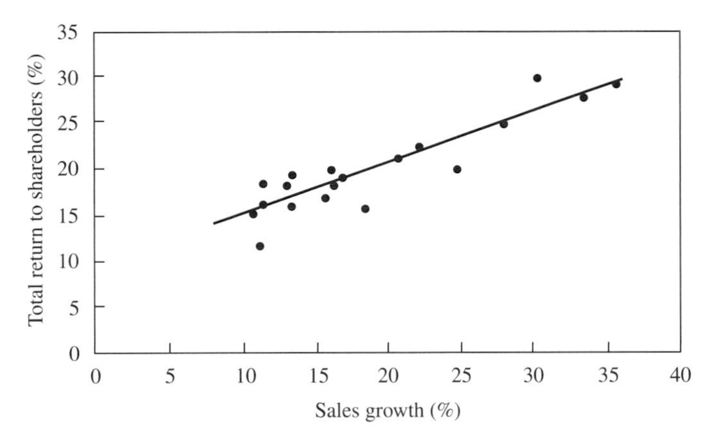

EXHIBIT 6
Growth Rates for U.S. Staffing Industry and Selected Segments, 1993–1998

Source: Stephens Inc.

	Annual Growth Rates (Year over Year Percentages)					
Industry Segment	**1993**	**1994**	**1995**	**1996**	**1997**	**1998**
Total Temporary Help	17	24	16	14	16	15
Medical	3	6	9	5	10	11
Professional/Special	33	33	25	25	26	25
Technical/IT	12	25	30	27	27	25
Office/Clerical	13	22	12	9	10	9
Industrial	32	29	11	7	10	10

EXHIBIT 9
Adecco's Strategic Goals

Source: Adecco.

Our Strategy Has Been Consistent

Growth beyond market
- Organic growth 50% above market
- Acquisitions and organic growth

Market leadership
- No 1 or No 2 in all major markets with 20% market share
- Quality/Cost enhancement through Technology

Optimized business mix
- Specialty business focus
- Evolution from staffing to HR services

Employer of Choice
Supplier of Choice

EXHIBIT 10
1998 Pro Forma Segment Shares for Adecco and Targeted Olsten Staffing Business

Source: Adecco estimates.

	% of Adecco Sales	% of Olsten Sales
General staffing	88.3	82.6
IT	5.2	13.4
Other Specialties	6.5	3.9

EXHIBIT 11A
Olsten Consolidated Income Statement ($ millions)

Sources: Olsten Annual Report, unaudited 10Q dated July 4, 1999.

	1996	1997	1998	July 4, 1999[b]
Revenue	3,378	4,113	4,603	2,447
Cost of services sold	2,422	3,017	3,501	1,848
Gross Profit	956	1,096	1,102	598
Selling general and administrative expenses	768	915	1,050	639
Net interest expense	12	21	30	20
Merger and other non-recurring charges	80	0	0	0
Income before taxes and minority interest	95	160	21	(60)
Taxes	39	63	8	(16)
Income before minority interest	56	98	13	(44)
Minority interest[a]	2	5	9	4
Net income	55	93	4	(49)

[a]Olsten did not own 100% of all its subsidiaries. Minority interest was the income attributable to the other (minority) shareholders in these businesses.

[b]The numbers are for the six months ending July 4, 1999.

EXHIBIT 11B Olsten Consolidated Balance Sheet ($ millions, except number of shares)

Sources: Olsten Annual Report, unaudited 10Q dated July 4, 1999.

	1997	1998	July 4, 1999
ASSETS			
Current assets			
Cash	85	54	15
Receivables, less allowance for doubtful accounts	847	1,006	1,147
Prepaid expenses and other current assets	91	134	141
Total current assets	1,023	1,194	1,303
Fixed assets, net	186	233	238
Net intangibles, principally goodwill	534	614	596
Other assets	7	18	10
Total assets	1,750	2,059	2,146
LIABILITIES			
Current liabilities			
Accrued expenses	152	196	198
Payroll and related taxes	86	144	155
Accounts payable	56	143	135
Insurance costs	41	36	42
Total current liabilities	335	519	529
Long-term debt	461	606	746
Other liabilities	112	111	105
SHAREHOLDERS' EQUITY			
Class A Common Stock $0.10 par values	7	7	7
Class B Common Stock $0.10 par value	1	1	1
Additional paid in capital	447	447	448
Retained earning	391	377	322
Accumulated other comprehensive income	(4)	(10)	(11)
Total Shareholders' Equity	842	823	767
Total Liabilities plus Shareholder Equity	1,750	2,059	2,146
Class A Shares Outstanding (110,000,000 authorized)	68,151,708	68,253,080	68,276,817
Class B Shares Outstanding (50,000,000 authorized)	13,157,617	13,071,560	13,066,003

EXHIBIT 11C Olsten's Consolidated Statement of Cash Flows ($ millions)

Sources: Olsten Annual Report, unaudited 10Q dated July 4, 1999.

	1996	1997	1998	July 4,1999[a]
OPERATING ACTIVITIES:				
Net income	55	93	4	(49)
Depreciation and amortization	44	56	69	40
(Increase) decrease in net operating assets	(113)	(63)	(15)	(126)
Net cash provided (used) by operations	(14)	85	59	(135)
INVESTING ACTIVITIES:				
(Increase) decrease in plant, property and equipment	(41)	(71)	(90)	(40)
(Acquisitions) disposal of subsidiaries and businesses	(136)	(150)	(107)	(15)
(Increase) decrease in other investments	0	9	0	0
Net cash provided (used) by investments	(177)	(211)	(197)	(54)
FINANCING ACTIVITIES:				
Net increase (decrease) in debt	188	128	124	160
Dividends paid to shareholders	(20)	(23)	(18)	(7)
Issuance of common stock, net	21	2	0	0
Net cash provided (used) by financing	189	108	106	154
Effect of exchange rate on cash	0	(3)	0	(3)
Net change in cash or equivalents	(2)	(21)	(31)	(39)
Cash payments for interest expense	15	24	29	21

[a]The numbers are for the six months ending July 4, 1999.

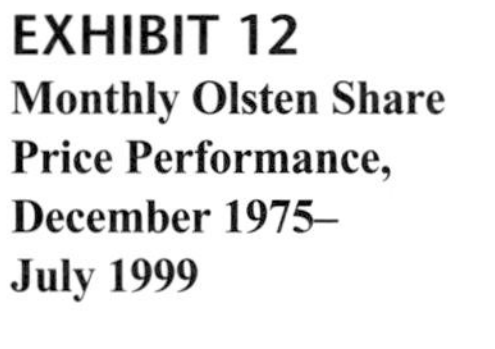

EXHIBIT 12
Monthly Olsten Share Price Performance, December 1975–July 1999

Source: Datastream.

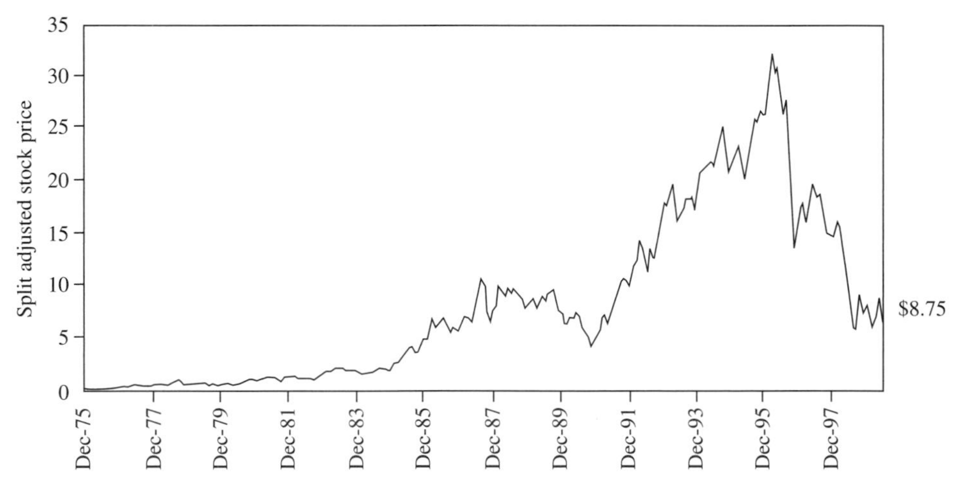

EXHIBIT 13 Selected Pro Forma Financial Statement Items for Olsten's Staffing Business, 1998–2009 ($ millions)

Source: Adecco and casewriter's estimates.

	1998A	1999	2000	2001	2002	2003	2004	2005	2006	2007	2008	2009
Revenues	3,097	3,506	3,607	3,979	4,393	4,779	5,196	5,653	6,156	6,709	7,317	7,981
Cost of goods sold	2,417	2,766	2,825	3,096	3,409	3,694	4,004	4,354	4,738	5,159	5,623	6,133
SG&A	517	611	593	616	671	737	803	875	954	1,042	1,138	1,241
Depreciation expense	25	37	40	42	45	49	54	58	63	68	74	83
Operating income	138	91	149	224	267	299	335	367	401	440	482	523
Income taxes[a]	45	30	49	74	88	98	110	122	132	145	159	173
EBIAT[b]	93	61	100	150	179	201	225	246	269	295	323	351
SELECTED ASSETS												
Operating cash[c]	53	35	36	40	44	48	52	57	62	67	73	80
Accounts receivable	553	554	590	651	718	781	850	924	1,007	1,097	1,196	1,305
Other current assets	30	27	30	35	41	48	52	57	62	67	74	80
Other operating assets[d]	16	29	42	58	77	97	106	115	125	137	149	163
Gross PPE	198	249	305	364	426	493	568	649	737	833	938	1,053
Net property plant and equipment	173	188	203	220	238	255	276	299	325	353	384	415
SELECTED LIABILITIES												
Total current liabilities	359	331	341	376	415	452	491	534	582	634	691	754
Other non-interest liabilities[d]	113	107	110	121	134	95	103	112	122	133	145	158

[a]Income taxes have been calculated as 33% of operating income assuming no interest expense.
[b]EBIAT was earning before interest and after taxes. It was calculated as operating earnings less taxes. These earnings were consolidated earnings for Olsten's staffing business and included minority interest.
[c]Operating cash was the cash that was required to operate the business.
[d]The category "non-interest liabilities" is not included in "total current liabilities." Similarly, the category "other operating assets" is not included in "other current assets."

EXHIBIT 14
Securities Market Data for Selected U.S. Staffing Companies ($ millions)

Sources: Calculated by casewriter from data from Datastream and the Center for Research in Security Prices.

	Year End	Book Value of Debt	Market Value of Equity	Equity Beta[a]
Kelly[b]	1996	42	1,028	
	1997	55	1,145	
	1998	48	1,137	0.58
Manpower[b]	1996	128	2,668	
	1997	261	2,832	
	1998	258	1,988	0.88
Olsten	1996	330	1,201	
	1997	461	1,220	
	1998	606	599	0.98

[a]Equity betas were calculated over the period 1996 to 1998.
[b]Kelly and Manpower were large U.S. firms which operated exclusively in the staffing business.

EXHIBIT 15
Ten-Year Interest Rates as of July 14, 1999

Source: Bloomberg.

	Interest Rate
U.S. Treasury coupon bonds	5.76%
AA rated bonds	6.56%
BBB rated bonds	7.14%

Cooper Industries, Inc.

In May 1972, Robert Cizik, executive vice president of Cooper Industries, Inc., was reviewing acquisition candidates for his company's diversification program. One of the companies, Nicholson File Company, had been approached by Cooper Industries 3 years earlier but had rejected all overtures. Now, however, Nicholson was in the middle of a takeover fight that might provide Cooper with a chance to gain control.

Cooper Industries

Cooper Industries was organized in 1919 as a manufacturer of heavy machinery and equipment. By the mid-1950s, the company was a leading producer of engines and massive compressors used to force natural gas through pipelines and oil out of wells. Management was concerned, however, over its heavy dependence on sales to the oil and gas industries and the violent fluctuation of earnings caused by the cyclical nature of heavy machinery and equipment sales. Although the company's long-term sales and earnings growth had been above average, its cyclicality had substantially dampened Wall Street's interest in the stock. (Cooper's historical operating results and financial condition are summarized in Exhibits 1 and 2.)

Initial efforts to lessen the earnings volatility were not successful. Between 1959 and 1966, Cooper acquired (1) a supplier of portable industrial power tools, (2) a manufacturer of small industrial air and process compressors, (3) a maker of small pumps and compressors for oil field applications, and (4) a producer of tire-changing tools for the automotive market. The acquisitions broadened Cooper's markets but left it still highly sensitive to general economic conditions.

A full review of Cooper's acquisition strategy was initiated in 1966 by the company. After several months of study, three criteria were established for all acquisitions. First, the industry should be one in which Cooper could become a major factor. This requirement was in line with management's goal of leadership within a few distinct areas of business. Second, the industry should be fairly stable, with a broad market for the products and a product line of "small-ticket" items. This product definition was intended to eliminate any company that had undue profit dependence upon a single customer or several large sales per year. Finally, it was decided to acquire only leading companies in their respective market segments.

The new strategy was initially implemented with the acquisition in 1967 of the Lufkin Rule Company, the world's largest manufacturer of measuring rules and tapes. Cooper acquired a quality product line, an established distribution system of 35,000 retail hardware stores throughout the United States, and plants in the United States, Canada, and Mexico. It also gained the services of William Rector, president of Lufkin, and Hal Stevens, vice president of sales. Both were extremely knowledgeable in the hand tool business and had worked together effectively for years. Their goal was to build through acquisition a hand tool company with a full product line that would use a common sales and distribution system and joint advertising. To do this, they needed Cooper's financial strength.

Copyright © 1974 by the President and Fellows of Harvard College, Harvard Business School case 274–116.

Lufkin provided a solid base to which two other companies were added. In 1969 the Crescent Niagara Corporation was acquired. The company had been highly profitable in the early 1960s but had suffered in recent years under the mismanagement of some investor-entrepreneurs who had gained control in 1963. A series of acquisitions of weak companies with poor product lines eroded the company's overall profitability until, in 1967, a small loss was reported. Discouraged, the investors wanted to get out, and Cooper—eager to add Crescent's well-known and high-quality wrenches, pliers, and screwdrivers to its line—was interested. It was clear that some of Crescent's lines would have to be dropped and inefficient plants would have to be closed, but the wrenches, pliers, and screwdrivers were an important part of Cooper's product policy.

In 1970, Cooper further expanded into hand tools with the acquisition of the Weller Electric Corporation. Weller was the world's leading supplier of soldering tools to the industrial, electronic, and consumer markets. It provided Cooper with a new, high-quality product line and production capacity in England, West Germany, and Mexico. (Information on the three acquisitions is provided in Exhibit 3.)

Cooper was less successful in its approach to a fourth company in the hand tool business, the Nicholson File Company. Nicholson was on the original "shopping list" of acceptable acquisition candidates that Mr. Cizik and Mr. Rector had developed, but several attempts to interest Nicholson in exploring merger possibilities had failed. The Nicholson family had controlled and managed the company since its founding in 1864, and Paul Nicholson, chairman of the board, had no interest in joining forces with anyone.

Nicholson File Company

But Nicholson was too inviting a takeover target to be overlooked or ignored for long. A relatively poor sales and profit performance in recent years, conservative accounting and financial policies, and a low percentage of outstanding stock held by the Nicholson family and management all contributed to its vulnerability. Annual sales growth of 2% was far behind the industry growth rate of 6% per year, and profit margins had slipped to only one-third those of other hand tool manufacturers. In 1971, Nicholson common stock was trading near its lowest point in many years and well below its book value of $51.25. Lack of investor interest in the stock was reflected in its low price-earnings ratio of 10–14, which compared with 14–17 times earnings for other leading hand tool companies. The stock was clearly selling on the basis of its dividend yield, with only limited hopes for capital appreciation. (Exhibits 4 and 5 show Nicholson's operating results and balance sheets.)

What made Nicholson so attractive was its basic competitive strength—strengths that the family-dominated management had not translated into earnings. The company was one of the largest domestic manufacturers of hand tools and was a leader in its two main product areas. Nicholson held a 50% share of the $50 million market for files and rasps, where it offered a broad, high-quality line with a very strong brand name. Its second product line, hand saws and saw blades, also had an excellent reputation for quality and held a 9% share of this $200 million market. Only Sears, Roebuck and Company and Disston, Inc., had larger market shares.

Nicholson's greatest asset, however, was its distribution system. Forty-eight direct salesmen and 28 file and saw engineers marketed its file, rasp, and saw products to 2,100 hardware wholesalers in the United States and Canada. These wholesalers in turn sold to 53,000 retail outlets. Their efforts were supported by heavy advertising and promotional programs. Overseas, the company's products were sold in 137 countries through 140 local sales representatives. The company seemed to have all the necessary strengths to share fully in the 6–7% annual sales growth forecast for the industry.

The Raid by H. K. Porter Company

Cooper was not alone in its interest in Nicholson. H. K. Porter Company, a conglomerate with wide-ranging interests in electrical equipment, tools, nonferrous metals, and rubber products, had acquired 44,000 shares of Nicholson stock in 1967 and had been an attentive stockholder ever since. On March 3, 1972, Porter informed Nicholson management of its plan to tender immediately for 437,000 of Nicholson's 584,000 outstanding shares at $42 per share in cash. The offer would terminate on April 4 unless extended by Porter; and the company was unwilling to acquire fewer shares than would constitute a majority.

Nicholson management was alarmed by both the proposal and the proposer. The company would contribute less than one-sixth of the combined sales and would clearly be just another operating division of Porter. It was feared that Porter's quest for higher profits might lead to aggressive cost cutting and the elimination of marginal product lines. Nicholson's Atkins Saw Division seemed especially vulnerable in view of its low profitability.

Loss of control seemed both painful and likely. The $42 cash offer represented a $12 premium over the most recent price of the stock and threatened to create considerable stockholder interest. The disappointing performance of the stock in recent years would undoubtedly increase the attractiveness of the $42 offer to Nicholson's 4,000 stockholders. And the Nicholson family and management owned only 20% of the outstanding shares—too few to ensure continued control.

Immediately after learning of the Porter tender offer, Mr. Cizik and Mr. Rector approached the Nicholson management with an offer of help. It was clear that Nicholson had to move immediately and forcefully; the first ten days of a tender offer are critical. Messrs. Cizik and Rector stressed that Nicholson must find a better offer and find it fast. Indeed, Cooper would be willing to make such an offer if Nicholson's management and directors would commit themselves to it—now.

Nicholson was not ready for such decisive action, however, and three days passed without any decision. With each day the odds of a successful counteroffer diminished. Finally, the Cooper officers decided the risks were too great and that Porter would learn of Cooper's offer of help and might retaliate. Cooper's stock was depressed, and it was possible that an angry Porter management might strike for control of Cooper. The offer was withdrawn.

By late March, the situation was increasing in seriousness. Management of Nicholson moved to block the raid. It personally talked with the large shareholders and made a strong public statement recommending against the offer. But announcements by Porter indicated that a substantial number of Nicholson shares were being tendered. It was no longer a matter of whether or not to be acquired. The issue was, by whom!

Management sought to find an alternative merger that would ensure continuity of Nicholson management and operating independence. Several companies had communicated with Nicholson in the wake of the Porter announcement, but no one other than Cooper had made a specific proposal. This was largely due to their reluctance to compete at the price levels being discussed or to enter into a fight with Porter.

Finally, on April 3, agreement was reached with VLN Corporation on the terms of a merger with VLN. VLN was a broadly diversified company with major interests in original and replacement automotive equipment and in publishing. Under the VLN merger terms, one share of new VLN cumulative convertible preferred stock would be exchanged for each share of Nicholson common stock. The VLN preferred stock would pay an annual dividend of $1.60 and would be convertible into five shares of VLN common stock during the first year following the merger, scaling down to four shares after the fourth year. The preferred stock would be callable at $50 per share after the fifth year and would have liquidating rights of $50 per share. (See Exhibit 6 for a financial summary of VLN.)

Nicholson management, assured of continued operating independence, supported the VLN offer actively. In a letter to the stockholders, Paul Nicholson pointed out that (1) the exchange would be a tax-free transaction, (2) the $1.60 preferred dividend equaled the current rate on the Nicholson common stock, and (3) a preferred share was worth a minimum of $53.10 (VLN common stock had closed at $10.62 on the day prior to the offer). He felt confident that the necessary majority of the outstanding common stock would be voted in favor of the proposed merger when it was brought to a vote in the fall. (Under Rhode Island law, a simple majority was sufficient to authorize the merger.[1])

Porter quickly counterattacked by pointing out to Nicholson stockholders that VLN common stock had recently sold for as low as $4⅝, which would put a value in the first year of only $23.12 on the VLN preferred stock. Furthermore, anyone who converted into VLN common stock would suffer a sharp income loss, since VLN had paid no common dividends since 1970.

Nicholson's stockholders were thus presented with two very contradictory appraisals of the VLN offer. Each company based its argument on some stock price, either the highest or the lowest, that would make the converted preferred stock compare favorably or not with the $42 cash offer.

Opportunity for Cooper?

Mr. Cizik and his staff were still attracted by the potential profits to be realized from Nicholson. It was felt that Nicholson's efforts to sell to every market segment resulted in an excessive number of products, which held down manufacturing efficiency and ballooned inventories. Cooper estimated that Nicholson's cost of goods sold could be reduced from 69% of sales to 65%.

The other major area of cost reduction was Nicholson's selling expenses. There was a substantial overlap of Nicholson's sales force and that established by Cooper for its Lufkin-Weller-Crescent hand tool lines. Elimination of the sales and advertising duplications would lower selling, general, and administrative expenses from 22% of sales to 19%.

There were other possible sources of earnings, but they were more difficult to quantify. For instance, 75% of Nicholson's sales were to the industrial market and only 25% to the consumer market. In contrast, sales by Cooper's hand tool group were distributed between the two markets in virtually the exact opposite proportions. Thus, sales increases could be expected from Nicholson's "pulling" more Cooper products into the industrial markets and vice versa for the consumer market. Also, Cooper was eager to use Nicholson's strong European distribution system to sell its other hand tool lines.

The battle between Porter and VLN seemed to provide Cooper with an unexpected, second opportunity to gain control of Nicholson. Porter had ended up with just 133,000 shares tendered in response to its offer—far short of the 249,000 shares

[1]Nicholson File was incorporated in Rhode Island. Under Rhode Island corporation law, a merger can be voted by shareholders holding a majority of the common stock outstanding. For reasons specific both to the laws of Rhode Island and to the Nicholson situation, dissenting stockholders of Nicholson would not be entitled to exercise the rights of dissent and would be forced to accept the exchange offer.

needed to give it majority control.[2] Its slate of directors had been defeated by Nicholson management at the Nicholson annual meeting on April 21. Tom Evans, president of Porter, now feared that Nicholson might consummate the merger with VLN and that Porter would be faced with the unhappy prospect of receiving VLN preferred stock for its 177,000 shares of Nicholson stock. Mr. Evans knew that the VLN stock had been a lackluster performer and might not show any significant growth in the near term. Furthermore, the $1.60 dividend rate seemed low in relation to current market yields of 7% on straight preferred stocks and 6.5% on intermediate-term U.S. Treasury bonds. Finally, he feared that it would be difficult to sell a large holding of VLN stock, which traded in small volume on the American Stock Exchange.

On the other hand, a merger of Cooper and Nicholson would allow Mr. Evans to convert his Nicholson shares into either common stock or convertible preferred stock of Cooper. This was a much more attractive alternative, assuming that an acceptable exchange rate could be set. Mr. Evans anticipated that earnings should rebound sharply from the cyclical downturn in 1971 and felt that Cooper stock would show significant price appreciation. Furthermore, Cooper stock was traded on the New York Exchange, which provided substantial liquidity. At a private meeting in late April, Mr. Evans tentatively agreed to support a Cooper–Nicholson merger on the condition that he receive Cooper common or convertible securities in a tax-free exchange worth at least $50 for each Nicholson share he held.

Mr. Cizik was now faced with the critical decision of whether to move for control. Cooper had acquired 29,000 shares of Nicholson stock during the preceding month in the open market—in part to build some bargaining power but largely to keep the loose shares out of the hands of Porter. Still uncommitted, however, were an estimated 50,000–100,000 shares that had been bought by speculators in the hope of an escalation of acquisition offers. Another 150,000–200,000 shares were unaccounted for, although Mr. Cizik suspected that a considerable number would go with the recommendation of Nicholson management. (Exhibit 7 shows Mr. Cizik's best estimate of the distribution of Nicholson stock in early May.) His hopes for gaining 50.1% of the Nicholson shares outstanding depended upon his gaining support of at least 86,000 of the shares still either uncommitted or unaccounted for.

If he decided to seek control, it would be necessary to establish both the price and the form of the offer. Clearly, the terms would have to be sufficiently attractive to secure the shares needed to gain majority control.

Mr. Cizik also felt that the terms should be acceptable to the Nicholson management. Once the merger was complete, Cooper would need to work with the Nicholson family and management. He did not want them to feel that they and other Nicholson stockholders were cheated by the merger. As a matter of policy, Cooper had never made an "unfriendly" acquisition, and this one was to be no exception. The offer should be one that would be supported by the great majority of the stockholders.

However, the price and the form of the payment had to be consistent with Cooper's concern that the acquisition earn a satisfactory long-term return and improve the trend of Cooper's earnings per share over the next 5 years. (A forecast of Cooper's earnings per share is shown in Exhibit 8.) The company anticipated making additional acquisitions, possibly on an exchange of stock basis, and maintenance of a strong earnings pattern and stock price was therefore important. On May 3, the common stock of Cooper and Nicholson closed at $24 and $44, respectively.

[2]Porter needed 292,584 shares to hold 50.1% majority control. It already owned 43,806 shares and needed, therefore, an additional 248,778 shares.

EXHIBIT 1 Condensed Operating and Stockholder Information. Cooper Industries, Inc., 1967–1971 (millions of dollars except per share data)

	1967	1968	1969	1970	1971
Operations					
Net sales	$ 198	$ 206	$ 212	$ 226	$ 208
Cost of goods sold	141	145	154	164	161
Depreciation	4	5	4	4	4
Selling and administrative expenses	23	25	29	29	29
Interest expense	1	2	3	4	3
Income before taxes and extraordinary items	29	29	22	24	11
Income taxes	14	15	11	12	5
Income before extraordinary items	15.2	13.9	10.6	12.4	5.6
Preferred dividend	1.0	.9	.9	.9	.9
Net income applicable to common stock	$ 14.2	$ 13.0	$ 9.7	$ 11.5	$ 4.7
Common Stock					
Earnings per share before extraordinary items	$ 3.34	$ 3.07	$ 2.33	$ 2.75	$ 1.12
Dividends per share	1.20	1.25	1.40	1.40	1.40
Book value per share	16.43	17.26	18.28	19.68	18.72
Market price	23–59	36–57	22–50	22–35	18–38
Price-earnings ratio	7–18	12–19	9–22	8–13	16–34

EXHIBIT 2 Balance Sheet at December 31, 1971, Cooper Industries, Inc. (millions of dollars)

Cash	$ 9	Accounts payable	$ 30
Accounts receivable	49	Accrued taxes	3
Inventories	57	Long-term debt due	5
Other	2	Current liabilities	38
Current assets	117	Long-term debt[a]	34
Net plant and equipment	47	Deferred taxes	4
Other	8	Preferred stock	11
Total assets	$172	Common equity (4,218,691 shares outstanding)	85
		Total liabilities and net worth	$172

[a]Maturities of long-term debt are $5.5 million, $6 million, $4 million, $2 million, and $2 million in the years 1972 through 1975, respectively.

EXHIBIT 3
Summary of Cooper Industries' Recent Acquisitions (millions of dollars)

	Year Preceding Acquisition by Cooper				
	Sales	Net Income	Book Value	Acquisition Price Paid	Form of Transaction
Lufkin Rule Company	$22	$1.4	$15	$20.6	Convertible preferred
Crescent Niagara Corporation	16	(.04)	4.9	12.5	Cash
Weller Electric Corporation	10	.9	4.4	14.6	Common stock

EXHIBIT 4 Condensed Operating and Stockholder Information, Nicholson File Company, 1967–1971 (millions of dollars except per share data)

	1967	1968	1969	1970	1971
Operations					
Net sales	$ 48.5	$ 49.1	$ 53.7	$ 54.8	$ 55.3
Cost of goods sold	32.6	33.1	35.9	37.2	37.9
Selling, general, and administrative expenses	10.7	11.1	11.5	11.9	12.3
Depreciation expense	2.0	2.3	2.4	2.3	2.1
Interest expense	.4	.7	.8	.8	.8
Other deductions	.3	.1	.2	.2	.2
Income before taxes	2.53	1.85	2.97	2.42	2.02
Taxes[a]	.60	.84	1.31	.88	.67
Net income	$ 1.93	$ 1.01	$ 1.66	$ 1.54	$ 1.35
Percentage of Sales					
Cost of goods sold	67%	67%	67%	68%	69%
Selling, general, and administrative expenses	22	23	21	22	22
Income before taxes	5.2	3.8	5.5	4.4	3.7
Stockholder Information					
Earnings per share	$ 3.19	$ 1.65	$ 2.88	$ 2.64	$ 2.32
Dividends per share	1.60	1.60	1.60	1.60	1.60
Book value per share	45.66	48.03	49.31	50.20	51.25
Market price	33–46	35–48	29–41	25–33	23–32
Price-earnings ratio	10–14	21–30	10–14	9–13	10–14

[a]The ratio of income taxes to income before taxes has been reduced primarily by the investment tax credit and by the inclusion in income of equity in net income of partially owned foreign companies, the taxes for which are provided for in the accounts of such companies and not in the tax provision of Nicholson. It was estimated that the average tax rate would be 40% in future years.

EXHIBIT 5 Balance Sheet at December 31, 1971, Nicholson File Company (millions of dollars)

Cash	$ 1	Accounts payable	$ 2
Accounts receivable	8	Other	2
Inventories[a]	18	Current liabilities	4
Other	1	Long-term debt	12
Current assets	28	Common stock	31
Investment in subsidiaries	3	Total liabilities and net worth	$47
Net plant and equipment	16		
Total assets	$47		

[a]Inventories in the amount of $11.8 million are priced at cost on the last-in, first-out method. The estimated replacement cost exceeds the carrying amounts by $9.2 million. The remaining inventories are priced at the lower of cost on the first-in, first-out method or market.

EXHIBIT 6
Condensed Operating and Stockholder Information, VLN Corporation, 1967–1971 (millions of dollars except per share data)

	1967	1968	1969	1970	1971
Operations					
Net sales	$ 45	$ 97	$ 99	$ 98	$ 100
Net income	1.97	3.20	3.20	1.13	2.98
Financial Position					
Current assets	$ 25	$ 46	$ 49	$ 41	$ 46
Current liabilities	6	11	15	10	13
Net working capital	19	35	34	31	33
Long-term debt	10	18	16	15	17
Shareholders' equity	21	36	40	39	41
Stockholder Information					
Earnings per share	$ .78	$ .61	$ .53	$ .27	$ .54
Dividends per share	—	—	—	.20	—
Shareholders' equity per share	8.23	9.64	10.00	9.24	9.69
Market price range	6–17	10–18	7–18	4–10	5–8
Price-earnings ratio	8–22	16–30	13–34	$15–37	9–15

EXHIBIT 7
Estimated Distribution of Nicholson File Company Stock

Shares supporting Cooper		
H. K. Porter	177,000	
Cooper Industries	29,000	206,000
Shares supporting VLN		
Nicholson family and management	117,000	
Owned by VLN	14,000	131,000
Shares owned by speculators		50,000–100,000
Shares unaccounted for		197,000–147,000
Total Nicholson shares outstanding		584,000

EXHIBIT 8
Five-Year Forecast of Cooper Industries' Earnings, Excluding Nicholson File Company, 1972–1976

	1972	1973	1974	1975	1976
Net income available to common stockholders ($ millions)	$11.0	$11.9	$12.8	$13.8	$15.0
Number of shares outstanding (millions)	4.21	4.21	4.21	4.21	4.21
Primary earnings per share	$ 2.61	$ 2.83	$ 3.04	$ 3.27	$ 3.56

Note: Forecasts are casewriter's estimates.

Interco

On August 8, 1988, Interco's board of directors met to discuss, among other matters, a merger proposal from City Capital Associates Limited Partnership. City Capital had offered $64 per common share of Interco on July 28, 1988, and had raised that offer to $70 per share on the morning of August 8. At this board meeting, Interco's financial advisors, Wasserstein, Perella & Co., established a valuation range of $68–$80 per common share of Interco and presented its evaluation of the offer. Given its valuation, Wasserstein Perella advised the Interco board (see Exhibit 1) that the $70 per share offer was inadequate and not in the best interests of the company and its shareholders. The board of directors voted to reject the City Capital offer.

The Company

Founded in December 1911, the International Shoe Company was established as a footwear manufacturing concern and remained so until the early 1960s. In 1966 the company was renamed Interco to reflect the changing character of its business. It had grown into a major manufacturer and retailer of a wide variety of consumer products and services. Among the most well known of the Interco brands were Converse and Florsheim shoes, Ethan Allen furniture, and London Fog rain gear.

Interco's various operations were substantially autonomous and were supported by a corporate management staff in St. Louis, Missouri. The company's philosophy had historically been to acquire companies in related fields and to provide their existing management teams with the incentives to expand their businesses, while relieving them of such routine support functions as financial and legal requirements. Nearly half of Interco's growth had come through acquisition. The company continually sought entities that would complement the existing Interco companies. Additional criteria used in screening and selecting acquisition candidates included the presence of highly skilled managers, and products that had established leadership positions in their respective markets.

Equity analysts viewed Interco as a conservative company that was finally "overcapitalized." With a current ratio of 3.6 to 1 and a debt-to-capitalization ratio, including capitalized leases, of 19.3% on February 29, 1988, Interco had ample financial flexibility. This flexibility had allowed the company to repurchase its common shares and make acquisitions as opportunities arose.

Operating Divisions

Interco was organized in four major operating divisions:

- Apparel Manufacturing
- General Retail Merchandising
- Footwear Manufacturing and Retailing
- Furniture and Home Furnishings

As listed in Exhibit 2, there were numerous independent companies within these four operating divisions.

This case was prepared by Research Associate Susan L. Roth under the supervision of Professor Scott P. Mason.

Copyright © 1991 by the President and Fellows of Harvard College. Harvard Business School case 291–033.

Apparel Manufacturing

This group consisted of 11 apparel companies that designed, manufactured, and distributed a full range of branded and private-label sportswear, casual apparel, outer garments, and headwear for men and women. Apparel brands included Le Tigre, Sergio Valente, and Abe Schrader. Distribution was national in scope to department stores, specialty shops, and other retail units, including discount chains.

General Retail Merchandising

This group operated 201 retail locations in 15 states. General retailing included large do-it-yourself home improvement centers, general merchandise discount stores, men's specialty apparel shops, and specialty department stores. Over the prior few years, general retail had been greatly scaled back; it was now dominated largely by Central Hardware, a do-it-yourself home improvement chain that emphasized customer service and a broad selection of products.

Footwear Manufacturing and Retailing

This division designed, manufactured, and distributed men's and women's footwear principally in the United States, Australia, Canada, and Mexico. The group operated 778 retail shoe stores and leased shoe departments in 42 states and in Australia. Interco's two major footwear operations, Converse Inc. and the Florsheim Shoe Co., commanded leading positions in their respective markets: athletic shoes and men's traditional footwear.

Furniture and Home Furnishings

This group manufactured, distributed, and retailed quality wood and upholstered furniture and home furnishings. Furniture brands included Broyhill, Lane, Ethan Allen, and Hickory Chair. In recent years, furniture had expanded through acquisitions and increasing profitability to dominate Interco's net income. At the end of fiscal year 1988, Interco was the largest furniture manufacturer in the world.

Strategic Repositioning Program

Interco's goals included long-term sales and earnings growth, increased return on corporate assets, and most important, improved return on shareholders' equity. To achieve these goals, Interco took a four-pronged approach that included (1) improving the profitability of existing operations, (2) divesting underperforming assets, (3) making acquisitions that had the potential for better-than-average returns and growth, and (4) employing opportunistic financial strategies such as share repurchases and the prudent use of borrowing capacity.

With these goals established, Interco began a strategic repositioning program in 1984 aimed at improving overall corporate performance. As part of this initiative, Interco accelerated its efforts to divest underperforming assets and reposition itself in markets offering superior growth opportunities and profitability. The program resulted in a substantial change in Interco's mix of sales, as shown in Table A. In fiscal 1988 the furniture and footwear groups together accounted for 60% of corporate sales, with apparel and general retail accounting for the rest. This was a reversal of the sales distribution in fiscal 1984.

TABLE A Percent of Sales by Operating Group, 1988 and 1984

Source: Interco annual report, February 29, 1988.

	1988	1984
Apparel	24%	33%
General retail	16	26
Footwear	27	21
Furniture	33	20

Recent Financial Performance

Overall corporate performance for fiscal year 1988 was positive, with sales and net income increasing 13.4% and 15.4%, respectively, over 1987 levels. This performance was attributable largely to the contributions of the furniture and home furnishings and footwear groups, as well as a decrease in Interco's effective tax rate. Due to the Tax Reform Act of 1986, the company's effective tax rate in 1988 was 42.8%, versus 47.1% in fiscal 1987. Growth in earnings moved Interco further toward its goal of a 14–15% return on equity; 1988's ROE of 11.7% was up from 9.7% in fiscal 1987.

The furniture and home furnishings group had an outstanding year in 1988, earning an operating profit of $149.1 million, versus $123.8 million in fiscal 1987, and achieving sales of $1.11 billion, compared to $967.4 million in 1987. Favorable demographic trends in family formations made the outlook for this group positive despite its exposure to cyclical fluctuations in housing starts and interest rates.

Showing the largest percentage gains for fiscal year 1988, sales for the footwear group increased 34.2%, and operating profits soared nearly 77%. These earnings were supported by the performance of Converse, acquired in September 1986, which had a record year in sales and earnings in 1988.

Despite multiple restructuring efforts, including divestiture of underperforming assets, the apparel manufacturing and general retail divisions remained ongoing problems, due largely to a change in the nature of these businesses. In calendar year 1987, a variety of problems continued to plague the U.S. apparel manufacturing industry. Consumer spending was lower than anticipated, imports from countries with lower labor costs continued to flow into the United States, and department stores increasingly emphasized private-label goods at the expense of manufacturers of branded apparel. In response to an intensely competitive retailing industry and a drop-off in consumer spending, retailers implemented heavy promotion and deep-discounting programs in 1987 and into 1988. As a result, sales had been advancing at a moderate pace, with earnings declining at a more rapid rate. Industry experts were forecasting moderate industry growth in the absence of any significant economic downturn.

Interco's general retail merchandising and apparel manufacturing groups turned in less than stellar performances in fiscal 1988. The former group's operating profits fell 3.7% on a modest increase in sales over the comparable 1987 period. The latter group earned operating profits of $20.2 million after an $11.6 million restructuring charge, compared to $47.3 million in 1987, on sales that slipped only slightly from 1987 levels.

The Takeover Bid

Interco management and Wall Street analysts believed that the apparel group's performance would continue to weaken Interco's overall operations and cause the equity markets to undervalue its common stock. Exhibits 3 and 4 give the history of Interco's common stock price. After the stock market crash of October 1987, Interco had accelerated its share repurchase program with the board of directors' authorization to buy back up to 5 million shares. By the end of fiscal year 1988, more than 4 million shares of common stock had been repurchased at a total cost of $152.3 million.

Given that Interco was widely viewed in the investment community as a potential takeover target, Harvey Saligman, Interco's chairman and CEO, contacted Wasserstein, Perella & Co. to discuss potential defensive measures aimed at maintaining Interco's independence. To deter any unwanted third-party acquisition, the board voted on July 11, 1988, to amend Interco's shareholder rights plan, making any hostile takeover of the company prohibitively expensive. Exhibit 5 describes Interco's shareholder rights plan in more detail.

Determined to improve the return on shareholders' investment and to deter a third-party acquisition further, on July 15, 1988, Interco announced plans to restructure. The apparel group's performance for the quarter ended May 31, 1988, continued to be poor, with a 13.4% decline in sales from the comparable 1987 quarter. The proposed restructuring would involve the sale of the apparel segment, a special dividend, and/or a stock repurchase. Interco retained two investment banking firms, Goldman, Sachs & Co. and Wasserstein, Perella & Co., to explore strategic alternatives and to sell the apparel manufacturing division and possibly other assets. Saligman's restructuring plan was aimed at "narrow[ing] the focus of Interco's business and improv[ing] the price of its shares."[1]

But a takeover attempt could not be avoided. City Capital had already accumulated 8.7% of Interco's common stock, and on July 27, 1988, it proposed a merger with Interco. Pursuant to this proposal, City Capital offered to buy all of Interco's common shares that it did not already own at a price of $64 per share. City Capital also advised the board of its willingness to negotiate the terms of the proposal, including price. In response, the Interco board expanded Wasserstein, Perella's mandate as financial advisor. Its advisory services would now include delivering an opinion on the fairness of City Capital's offer and valuing and recommending other alternatives.[2] How much Interco was worth was a question its board of directors would have to consider in evaluating alternatives to a merger with City Capital.

City Capital Associates Limited Partnership

City Capital Associates Limited Partnership was led by two Washington, D.C., businessmen, Steven M. Rales and his brother Mitchell. The Rales brothers had been involved in multiple acquisitions, either through Danaher Corporation, a publicly owned company they controlled, or through one of their other partnerships. These acquisitions had included Western Pacific Industries, Inc., Chicago Pneumatic Tool Co., Mohawk Rubber Co., and Master Shield, Inc. The brothers' acquisition focus had been on undervalued targets with strong market niches. With the completion of eight medium-sized acquisitions, Danaher had grown since 1981 from a small real estate trust into a diversified conglomerate of manufacturing companies. Due in part to the acquisitions and the use of tax loss carryforwards, Danaher Corp.'s earnings had increased sixfold, from $2.9 million in 1984 to $19 million in 1987.

The Rales brothers had formed City Capital with the sole purpose of acquiring Interco. As disclosed in a Securities and Exchange Commission filing, it was their intention, after completing the acquisition, to sell Interco's apparel businesses and to consider selling parts of the footwear and general retailing businesses. In this same filing, the Rales brothers indicated that they would consider paying more than $64 per common share for Interco.

On the morning of August 8, 1988, City Capital raised its offer for Interco to $70 per share and stated its willingness to increase the price per share further should a review of more-detailed company information so warrant. Under the assumption of 37.5 million fully diluted shares outstanding, the offer had an indicated value of over $2.6 billion. The offer was conditional upon, among other things, the board's redemption of the

[1]Francine Schwade, "Interco Receives Bid from Rales Group for Takeover Value at $2.26 Billion," *The Wall Street Journal,* July 29, 1988, p. 4.

[2]Interco had retained Wasserstein, Perella pursuant to a unique compensation contract that offered a substantial contingency fee of $3.7 million payable to Wasserstein. Perella once City Capital rescinded its offer and only if a recapitalization was completed. Wasserstein, Perella would receive $1.8 million for its services with or without this contingency fee. See George Anders and Francine Schwadel, "Wall Streeters Helped Interco Defeat Raiders But at a Heavy Price," *The Wall Street Journal,* July 7, 1990, p. A1.

newly amended rights plan or the invalidation of those rights pursuant to the proposed merger. Before raising the value of its offer for Interco, City Capital had arranged the required $2.5 billion in financing. Drexel Burnham Lambert, Inc., City Capital's financial advisor, had stated that it was "highly confident" it could raise up to $ 1.375 billion of debt and/or equity for the $70-per-share proposal. Additional bank financing, including a $1.1 billion credit facility arranged by Chase Manhattan Corp., would provide the remainder of the necessary funding.

Evaluation of the Takeover Bid

The original agenda for Interco's board meeting on August 8, 1988, largely focused on a previously announced restructuring plan that included selling the company's faltering apparel group, paying a special dividend, and/or repurchasing shares of common stock. However, with City Capital already owning a sizable portion of Interco's stock, Saligman and the board of directors recognized the urgency of responding to the Rales brothers' offer. To arrive at a conclusion, the board members would spend much of the August 8 board meeting discussing Wasserstein, Perella's evaluation of the $64-per-share City Capital offer, and other proposed alternatives. The two key alternatives consisted of a friendly merger and a restructuring of the company. Under both scenarios, it was assumed that key managers, including Saligman, would remain with the company. Before any decision could be made on City Capital's offer or any of the strategic alternatives, however, it was important for the board to assess Interco's value as determined by Wasserstein, Perella. Historical financial statements are provided in Exhibits 6 and 7. Business segment information is given in Exhibit 8.

As the financial advisor to Interco, Wasserstein, Perella prepared a number of analyses that resulted in a valuation range for the company of $68–80 per share. Specifically, discounted cash flow analysis, comparable transaction analysis, and premiums paid analysis were used to determine that City Capital's offer of $70 per share was inadequate and not in the best interests of Interco and its shareholders. Exhibits 9–13 provide significant assumptions that Wasserstein, Perella relied on in determining its expert opinion on Interco's value. Exhibit 14 gives then-current market interest rates.

At Interco's board meeting on August 8, 1988, Wasserstein, Perella informed the board of its analysis of City Capital's offer. Interco's board of directors voted to reject the $70-per-share bid the same day.

EXHIBIT 1 Board of Directors as of May 16, 1988

Source: Notice and proxy statement, May 16, 1988.

Harvey Saligman	Chairman of the board and chief executive officer (CEO) of Interco
Harry M. Krogh	President and chief operating officer (COO) of Interco
Ronald L. Aylward	Vice chairman of the board of Interco
R. Stuart Moore	Vice president of Interco; president of The Lane Company, Inc., a subsidiary of Interco
Mark H. Lieberman	Vice president of Interco; president of Londontown, a division of Interco
Richard B. Loynd	Vice president of Interco; chairman of the board of Converse, Inc., a subsidiary of Interco
Charles J. Rothschild, Jr.	Vice president of Interco; chairman of the board of Megastar Apparel Group, a division of Interco
Zane E. Barnes	Chairman of the board, president, CEO, and director of Southwestern Bell Corporation, engaged in the general telecommunications business
Donald E. Lasater	Chairman of the board, CEO, and director of Mercantile Bancorporation, Inc., a bank holding company, and chairman of the board and director of Mercantile Bank National Association
Lee M. Liberman	Chairman of the board, president, CEO, and director of Laclede Gas Company, a gas public utility
Robert H. Quenon	President, CEO, and director of Peabody Holding Company, Inc., which is engaged in coal mining and sales
William E. Cornelius	President, CEO, and director of Union Electric Company, an electric public utility
Marilyn S. Lewis	Civil leader and volunteer
Thomas H. O'Leary	Vice chairman of the board and director of Burlington Northern, Inc., a holding company with transportation, energy, and natural resources concerns

As of April 15, 1988, all directors, nominees, and officers of Interco as a group (24 persons) beneficially owned 1.14% of the outstanding shares of Interco's common stock.

EXHIBIT 2 Subsidiaries

Source: Lotus One Source.

Abe Schrader Corp.	Golde's Department Stores, Inc.
Big Yank Corp.	Grand Entry Hat Corp.
Bowen Shoe Co., Inc.	Highland House, Inc.
Broyhill Furniture Industries, Inc.	Highland Transport, Inc.
Campco Holdings, S.A.	Hy-Test, Inc.
Campus Pacific, Ltd.	Interco Subsidiary, Inc.
Central Hardware Co.	Keith O'Brien Investment Co.
Clayton Operations, S.A.	Lane Co., Inc.
College-Town, Inc.	Lease Management, Inc.
Converse, Inc.	Julius Marlow Holdings, Ltd.
Delmar Sportswear, Inc.	L. J. O'Neill Shoe Co.
Ethan Allen, Inc.	ORC Financial Ag
Factory Outlet Co.	Patriot Investment Co.
Fine's Men's Shops, Inc.	Queen Casuals, Inc.
Florsheim, Inc.	Senack Shoes, Inc.
Florsheim Shoe Store Co. of Hawaii	Sky City Stores, Inc.
Florsheim Shoe Store Co.—Midwest	Stuffed Shirt, Inc.
Florsheim Shoe Store Co.—Northwest	United Shirt Distributors, Inc.
Florsheim Shoe Store Co.—South	Walton Road Management Co.
Florsheim Shoe Store Co.—West	

EXHIBIT 3
Common Stock Price History (monthly)

Source: Interactive Data Corporation.

Month-End Prices (adjusted for stock splits)	
1986	
31-Jan-86	$35.125
28-Feb-86	39.000
31-Mar-86	39.250
30-Apr-86	39.625
30-May-86	43.500
30-Jun-86	47.188
31-Jul-86	41.375
29-Aug-86	43.750
30-Sep-86	40.000
31-Oct-86	43.750
28-Nov-86	44.125
31-Dec-86	36.875
1987	
30-Jan-87	39.750
27-Feb-87	42.625
31-Mar-87	44.125
30-Apr-87	39.625
29-May-87	40.125
30-Jun-87	45.375
31-Jul-87	51.250
31-Aug-87	53.250
30-Sep-87	47.500
30-Oct-87	36.000
30-Nov-87	30.000
31-Dec-87	32.250
1988	
29-Jan-88	37.125
29-Feb-88	42.000
31-Mar-88	42.000
29-Apr-88	41.125
31-May-88	43.875
30-Jun-88	44.750
29-Jul-88	68.500

EXHIBIT 4
Common Stock Price History (Daily)

Source: Interactive Data Corporation.

Daily Closing Prices

Date	Price	Date	Price
02-May-88	$40.250	21-Jun-88	43.125
03-May-88	41.500	22-Jun-88	43.750
04-May-88	41.000	23-Jun-88	43.625
05-May-88	41.625	24-Jun-88	43.500
06-May-88	40.625	27-Jun-88	43.625
09-May-88	40.875	28-Jun-88	44.000
10-May-88	41.750	29-Jun-88	44.000
11-May-88	41.625	30-Jun-88	44.750
12-May-88	42.000	01-Jul-88	44.625
13-May-88	42.125	04-Jul-88	N.A.
16-May-88	42.250	05-Jul-88	45.375
17-May-88	42.000	06-Jul-88	44.500
18-May-88	41.500	07-Jul-88	44.625
19-May-88	40.625	08-Jul-88	45.000
20-May-88	40.625	11-Jul-88	45.250
23-May-88	40.375	12-Jul-88	45.375
24-May-88	41.500	13-Jul-88	46.375
25-May-88	42.500	14-Jul-88	49.000
26-May-88	42.625	15-Jul-88	54.375
27-May-88	41.250	18-Jul-88	54.500
30-May-88	N.A.	19-Jul-88	58.375
31-May-88	43.875	20-Jul-88	58.125
01-Jun-88	43.500	21-Jul-88	57.875
02-Jun-88	42.875	22-Jul-88	57.250
03-Jun-88	44.125	25-Jul-88	58.000
06-Jun-88	43.250	26-Jul-88	58.875
07-Jun-88	42.000	27-Jul-88	59.375
08-Jun-88	43.875	28-Jul-88	67.750
09-Jun-88	43.375	29-Jul-88	68.500
10-Jun-88	43.375	01-Aug-88	68.875
13-Jun-88	43.500	02-Aug-88	67.625
14-Jun-88	43.625	03-Aug-88	67.000
15-Jun-88	42.500	04-Aug-88	67.375
16-Jun-88	42.875	05-Aug-88	68.250
17-Jun-88	43.625	08-Aug-88	72.500
20-Jun-88	43.250		

EXHIBIT 5 **Shareholder Rights Plan**

On September 23, 1985, Interco's board of directors adopted a shareholder rights plan designed to deter unsolicited takeover bids by creating the threat of substantial dilution for any person or group attempting an unfriendly merger with Interco.

The original plan was amended on July 11, 1988, by the board of directors. At that time, the directors were aware that Interco's common stock was under accumulation and were suspicious of a third-party acquisition offer for the company.[a] Changes in the purchase price per share and certain triggering provisions, otherwise known as poison pill shareholder rights, made the takeover defense more onerous. Specifically, the amended rights plan declared that it would issue a dividend of one share purchase right per share of common stock. The amended rights plan also gave the board sole discretion to lower certain triggering percentages such that the massive dilutive effects of the plan would come into play when a person or group acquired as little as 15% of the shares of Interco's stock.

At Interco's board meeting on August 8, 1988, the board approved "golden parachute" severance agreements for Interco's senior executives, to be triggered upon an acquisition by a third party, including City Capital. According to an SEC filing, the golden parachute severance agreements were valued at $16.3 million and covered 17 top executives at Interco. Lump-sum payments, including $2.2 million to Harvey Saligman, would be made under certain conditions if the company was taken over.

[a]As claimed in Civil Action No. 10111, the Second Amended and Consolidated Class Action Complaint, as filed in the Court of Chancery of the State of Delaware in and for New Castle County, p. 16.

EXHIBIT 6 Interco's Consolidated Balance Sheets (thousands of dollars except per share data)

Source: Annual reports and 10-Q reports.

	February 28,			May 31,	
	1986	**1987**	**1988**[a]	**1987**	**1988**
Current assets					
Cash	$ 16,856	$ 16,631	$ 20,849	$ 29,700	$ 19,622
Marketable securities	127,341	63,747	11,033	57,789	16,366
Receivable, net	402,225	446,755	486,657	431,743	460,759
Inventories	647,116	733,907	805,095	786,792	872,135
Prepaid expenses and other current assets	22,547	25,614	35,665	25,622	44,959
Total current assets	$1,215,815	$1,286,654	$1,359,299	$1,331,646	$1,413,840
Property, plant, and equipment					
Land	26,770	32,266	32,525	—	—
Buildings and improvements	437,812	465,811	471,787	—	—
Machinery and equipment	320,256	364,499	380,402	—	—
	784,838	862,576	884,714	868,670	890,887
Less accumulated depreciation	343,018	377,226	405,215	386,762	412,332
Net property, plant, and equipment	441,820	485,350	479,499	481,908	478,555
Other assets	99,238	153,383	146,788	149,170	146,878
Total assets	$1,756,893	$1,925,387	$1,985,586	$1,962,724	$2,039,273
Current Liabilities					
Notes payable	$ —	$ 68,840	$ 70,517	$ 97,297	$ 146,016
Current maturities of long-term debt and capital lease obligations	9,647	11,915	8,172	9,288	8,900
Accounts payable and accrued expenses	184,032	216,365	239,513	278,847	292,051
Income taxes	12,699	17,327	4,402	15,294	5,463
Total current liabilities	$ 249,587	$ 358,226	$ 373,343	$ 400,726	$ 452,430
Long-term debt, less current maturities	127,409	135,019	257,327	133,403	255,279
Obligations under capital leases, less current maturities	56,495	50,546	41,813	49,270	40,032
Other long-term liabilities	43,249	55,381	61,766	56,410	63,484
Shareholders' equity					
Preferred stock, no par value	66,027	61,795	57,113	61,285	36,721
Common stock, $3.75 stated value	163,765	163,643	155,088	155,088	155,088
Capital surplus (41,356,847 shares issued	104,205	98,246	44,539	49,149	32,117
Retained earnings	1,027,895	1,099,006	1,179,964	1,111,527	1,194,884
	1,361,892	1,422,690	1,436,704	1,377,049	1,418,810
Less 5,173,811 treasury shares	81,739	96,475	185,367	54,134	190,762
Total shareholders' equity	1,280,153	1,326,215	1,251,337	1,322,915	1,228,048
Total liabilities and net worth	$1,756,893	$1,925,387	$1,985,586	$1,962,724	$2,039,273

[a]February 29, 1988.

EXHIBIT 7 Interco's Consolidated Statement of Earnings (thousands of dollars)

Source: Annual reports and 10-Q reports.

	Years Ended February 28,			First Quarter Ended May 31,	
	1986	1987	1888[a]	1987	1988
Income:					
Net sales	$2,832,384	$2,946,902	$3,341,423	$781,421	$778,107
Other income	36,140	32,175	29,237	6,293	6,864
	2,868,524	2,979,077	3,370,660	787,714	784,971
Costs and expenses:					
Cost of sales	1,932,258	2,000,423	2,284,640	522,759	522,942
Selling, general, and administrative expenses	681,886	712,861	799,025	199,145	201,129
Interest expense	25,523	28,082	33,535	7,351	9,179
	2,639,667	2,741,366	3,117,200	735,438	733,067
Earnings before income taxes	228,857	237,711	253,460	52,276	51,904
Income taxes	109,008	111,937	108,457	25,276	25,762
Net earnings	$ 119,849	$ 125,774	$ 145,003	$ 26,514	$ 30,689
Operating income[b]	218,240	233,618	257,758	53,334	54,219
Operating cash flow[c]	267,756	287,133	319,275	—	—

[a]For the year ended February 29, 1988.
[b]Operating income equal to the sum of earning before income taxes and interest expense less other income.
[c]Operating cash flow equal to the sum of operating income and depreciation expense.

EXHIBIT 8 **Business Segment Information**

Source: Annual reports and 10-Q reports.

	Years Ended February 28,			First Quarter Ended May 31,	
	1986	1987	1988	1987	1988
Net sales to unaffiliated customers					
Apparel	$ 907,833	$ 817,660	$ 813,198	$160,339	$138,836
General retail	461,785	498,324	532,251	148,138	149,209
Footwear	558,286	663,521	890,411	209,535	226,672
Furniture	904,480	967,397	1,105,563	263,409	263,390
Total	$2,832,384	$2,946,902	$3,341,423	$781,421	$778,107
Operating earnings					
Apparel	$ 66,716	$ 47,269	$ 20,240	$ (670)	$ (247)
General retail	32,085	40,610	39,101	14,136	12,498
Footwear	48,475	52,136	92,204	15,777	19,700
Furniture	105,111	123,766	149,090	38,319	32,196
Total	$ 252,387	$ 263,781	$ 300,635	$ 67,562	$ 64,147
Other income	$ 36,140	$ 32,175	$ 29,237	$ 6,293	$ 6,864
Corporate expense	(34,147)	(30,163)	(42,877)	(14,228)	(9,928)
Earnings before interest and taxes	254,380	265,793	286,995	59,627	61,083
Interest expense	(25,523)	(28,082)	(33,535)	(7,351)	(9,179)
Earnings before income taxes	$ 228,857	$ 237,711	$ 253,460	$ 52,276	$ 51,904
Identifiable assets at year end					
Apparel	$ 456,972	$ 465,601	$ 425,350		
General retail	234,004	248,639	252,195		
Footwear	291,292	497,706	595,861		
Furniture	618,980	640,106	688,853		
	$1,601,248	$1,852,052	$1,962,259		
Corporate assets	155,645	73,335	23,327		
Total	$1,756,893	$1,925,387	$1,985,586		
Depreciation expense					
Apparel	$ 11,965	$ 12,123	$ 12,521		
General retail	8,294	9,079	9,681		
Footwear	8,286	10,638	13,107		
Furniture	20,971	21,675	26,208		
Capital expenditures					
Apparel	$ 13,433	$ 8,869	$ 9,220		
General retail	6,169	8,167	10,735		
Footwear	8,114	7,486	9,236		
Furniture	27,278	24,720	36,188		

EXHIBIT 9
Summary of the Takeover Offer

Source: Adapted with minor modifications in terminology from Wasserstein, Perella & Co. presentation to the Interco Board of Directors, August 8, 1988. Civil Action No. 10111, filed in the Court of Chancery of the State of Delaware in and for New Castle County, Exhibit 23.

City Capital Associates, L.P. Offer	
Date	August 8, 1988
Price per share	$70.00
Premium to stock one-day prior[a]	17.9%
Premium to stock one-month prior	59.1%
Premium to 52-week low	137.3%
Premium to 52-week high	17.2%
Value of equity	$2,622.8MM
Net debt	318.5MM
Value of firm	$2,941.3MM

	Value of Firm as a Multiple of:			Value of Equity as a Multiple of:	
	Sales	Operating Cash Flow	Operating Income	Net Income	Book Value
Year ending 2/29/88	0.9x	9.2x	11.4x	18.1x	2.2x
Estimate of year ending 2/28/89	0.9	8.8	10.7	17.0	2.2

[a] Premiums based on stock prices as of July 27, 1988.

EXHIBIT 10
Premiums Paid Analysis

Source: Wasserstein, Perella & Co. presentation to the Interco Board of Directors, August 8, 1988. Civil Action No. 10111, filed in the Court of Chancery of the State of Delaware in and for New Castle County, Exhibit 23.

		Average Premium Paid over Stock Price			
	# Deals[a]	1 Day	4 Weeks	52-Week Low	52-Week High
1st Quarter 1988	19	62.3%	95.5%	159.5%	16.7%
2nd Quarter 1988	9	68.6	91.3	182.8	31.5
3rd Quarter 1988[b]	12	36.5	49.9	181.3	2.6
1988	40	56.0	80.9	171.3	15.8
Rales		17.9	59.1	137.3	17.2

[a]Wasserstein, Perella & Co. selected tender offers.
[b]Selected tender offers from the months of July and August.

EXHIBIT 11 Comparable Transaction Analysis
Purchase Price Multiples by Business Segment
Furniture Manufacturing Companies

Source: Wasserstein, Perella & Co. presentation to the Interco Board of Directors, August 8, 1988. Civil Action No. 10111, filed in the Court of Chancery of the State of Delaware in and for New Castle County, Exhibit 23.

			Purchase Price Multiples[a]				
Announcement Date	Acquiror/Target	Aggregate Price ($MM)[a]	Net Income	Book Value[b]	Sales	Operating Income	Operating Cash Flow
12/14/87	La-Z-Boy/Kincaid	$ 63.5	22.0x	2.1x	0.8x	11.7x	8.1x
11/17/86	INTERCO/Lane	523.7	19.3	2.8	1.6	11.1	9.6
08/12/86	Chicago Pacific/ General Mills Furniture	89.3	14.1	1.8	1.0	12.0	9.9
06/03/86	Masco/Henredon	260.9	31.6	2.6	2.1	20.3	15.8
08/08/88	Rales Proposal	$2,941.3	18.1	2.2	0.9	11.4	9.2

[a]Sales, operating income, and operating cash flow multiples adjusted for the value of net debt outstanding.
[b]Book value adjusted for intangibles.

EXHIBIT 11 Footwear Manufacturing Companies

Source: Wasserstein, Perella & Co. presentation to the Interco Board of Directors, August 8, 1988?? Civil Action No. 10111, filed in the Court of Chancery of the State of Delaware in and for New Castle County, Exhibit 23.

			Purchase Price Multiples[a]				
Announcement Date	Acquiror/Target	Aggregate Price ($MM)[a]	Net Income	Book Value[b]	Sales	Operating Income	Operating Cash Flow
04/25/88	NIKE/Cole Haan	$ 95.0	36.2x	N.M.	1.5x	14.1	12.2
06/03/87	Moacq/Morse Shoe	312.5	2.5	1.8	0.5	13.0	9.2
03/10/87	Reebok/AVIA	191.0	40.6	6.7	2.1	24.6	23.3
09/18/86	Reebok/Rockport	146.1	30.7	N.M.	1.7	26.0	23.9
07/31/86	INTERCO/Converse	202.7	37.1	1.8	0.9	24.7	18.2
08/08/88	Rales Proposal	$2,941.3	18.1	2.2	0.9	11.4	9.2

[a]Sales, operating income, and operating cash flow multiples adjusted for the value of net debt outstanding.
[b]Book value adjusted for intangibles.

Apparel Companies

Source: Wasserstein, Perella & Co. presentation to the Interco Board of Directors, August 8, 1988. Civil Action No. 10111, filed in the Court of Chancery of the State of Delaware in and for New Castle County, Exhibit 23.

			Purchase Price Multiples[a]				
Announcement Date	Acquiror/Target	Aggregate Price ($MM)[a]	Net Income	Book Value[b]	Sales	Operating Income	Operating Cash Flow
04/28/88	Wesray/William Carter	$ 157.4	N.M.	1.6x	0.8x	24.0x	13.7x
02/02/88	Salant/Manhattan Indus.	129.7	N.M.	1.4	0.4	N.M.	N.M.
03/17/86	W Acquisition/Warnco	504.7	21.0x	2.5	0.9	10.6	9.2
11/04/85	West Point Pepperall/ Cluett, Peabody	551.9	19.6	1.5	0.6	10.6	9.2
08/08/88	Rales Proposal	$2,941.3	18.1	2.2	0.9	11.4	9.2

[a]Sales, operating income, and operating cash flow multiples adjusted for the value of net debt outstanding.
[b]Book value adjusted for intangibles.

Central Hardware Division

Source: Wasserstein, Perella & Co. presentation to the Interco Board of Directors, August 8, 1988. Civil Action No. 10111, filed in the Court of Chancery of the State of Delaware in and for New Castle County, Exhibit 23.

			Purchase Price Multiples[a]				
Announcement Date	Acquiror/Target	Aggregate Price ($MM)[a]	Net Income	Book Value[b]	Sales	Operating Income	Operating Cash Flow
06/24/88	Management Group/ Payless Cashways	$1,189.4	22.0x	2.3x	0.6x	13.1x	9.2x
08/08/88	Rales Proposal	$2,941.3	18.1	2.2	0.9	11.4	9.2

[a]Sales, operating income, and operating cash flow multiples adjusted for the value of net debt outstanding.
[b]Book value adjusted for intangibles.

EXHIBIT 11 Value Ranges by Business Segment

Source: Wasserstein, Perella & Co. presentation to the Interco Board of Directors, August 8, 1988, Civil Action No. 10111, filed in the Court of Chancery of the State of Delaware in and for New Castle County, Exhibit 23.

Business Segment	1988 Sales	Multiple Range	Value Range	Median Value
Apparel	$ 813.2	.4–.9	$ 325.3–$ 731.9	$ 569.2
General retail	532.3	.6–.6	319.4–319.4	319.4
Footwear	890.4	.5–2.1	445.2–1,869.8	1,335.6
Furniture	$1,105.6	.8–2.1	884.5–2,321.8	1,437.3
			$1,974.4–$5,242.9	$3,661.5

Business Segment	1988 Operating Income	Multiple Range	Value Range	Median Range
Apparel	$ 20.2	10.6–24.0	$ 214.1–$ 484.8	$ 214.1
General retail	39.1	13.1–13.1	512.2–512.2	512.2
Footwear	92.2	13.0–26.0	1,198.6–2,397.2	2,268.1
Furniture	$ 149.1	11.1–20.3	1,655.0–3,026.7	1,766.8
			$3,579.9–$6,420.9	$4,761.2

Business Segment	1988 Operating Cash Flow	Multiple Range	Value Range	Median Value
Apparel	$ 32.7	9.2–13.7	$ 300.8–$ 448.0	$ 300.8
General retail	48.8	9.2–9.2	448.9–448.9	448.9
Footwear	105.3	9.2–23.9	968.8–2,516.7	970.7
Furniture	$ 175.3	8.1–15.8	1,419.9–2,769.7	1,709.2
			$3,138.4–$6,183.3	$3,429.6

EXHIBIT 12 Discounted Cash Flow Analysis

Source: Adapted with minor modifications in terminology from Wasserstein, Perella & Co., presentation to the Interco Board of Directors, August 8, 1988. Civil Action No. 1011, filed in the Court of Chancery of the State of Delaware in and for New Castle County, Exhibit 23.

Assumptions	Furniture Group	Footwear Group	Apparel Group	Retail Group	Total
Sales growth[a]	7.7%	6.3%	7.1%	7.6%	7.2%
Operating margin range[b]	13.1%–14.1%	9.1%–10.4%	6.4% 7.0%	6.5%–7.5%	9.2%–10.1%
Capital expenditures[c]	1x	1x	1x	1x	1x
Increase in working investment[d]	12.5%	12.5%	12.5%	7.5%	11.6%
Tax rate					41.0%

	Multiple of Cash Flow in Year 10		
	14.0x	15.0x	16.0x
Terminal value ($millions)	$4,746.0	$5,085.0	$5,424.0
Implied stock price			
Discount rate			
10.0%	$ 80.00	$ 84.00	$ 88.00
11.0	74.00	77.00	81.00
12.0	68.00	72.00	75.00
13.0	63.00	66.00	69.00

[a]10-year annual compound growth rate.
[b]Projected operating margin in 1989 and in 1998.
[c]As a multiple of depreciation.
[d]As a percent of the change in sales in 1994 forward.

EXHIBIT 13 Reference Range—Retain Core Companies Case (millions of dollars except per share data)

Source: Wasserstein, Perella & Co. presentation to the Interco Board of Directors, August 8, 1988. Civil Action No. 1011, filed in the Court of Chancery of the State of Delaware in and for New Castle County, Exhibit 23.

Segment	Range
Furniture group	$1,525–$1,750
Footwear group	775–900
Total	2,300–2,650
After-tax divestiture proceeds	588–639
Net corporate adjustments[a]	(335)–(273)
Range	2,553–3,016
Per share range[b]	68.00–80.00+

[a]Accounts for net debt, overfunded pension, and miscellaneous other assets that include real estate, which could be understated.
[b]Based on 37.5 million fully diluted shares outstanding.

EXHIBIT 14
Indexes of Monthly Adjusted Closing Prices 1980–1988; Actual Daily Closing Prices, July–August 1988; and Market Interest Rates, August 1988

Source: Interactive Data Corp.

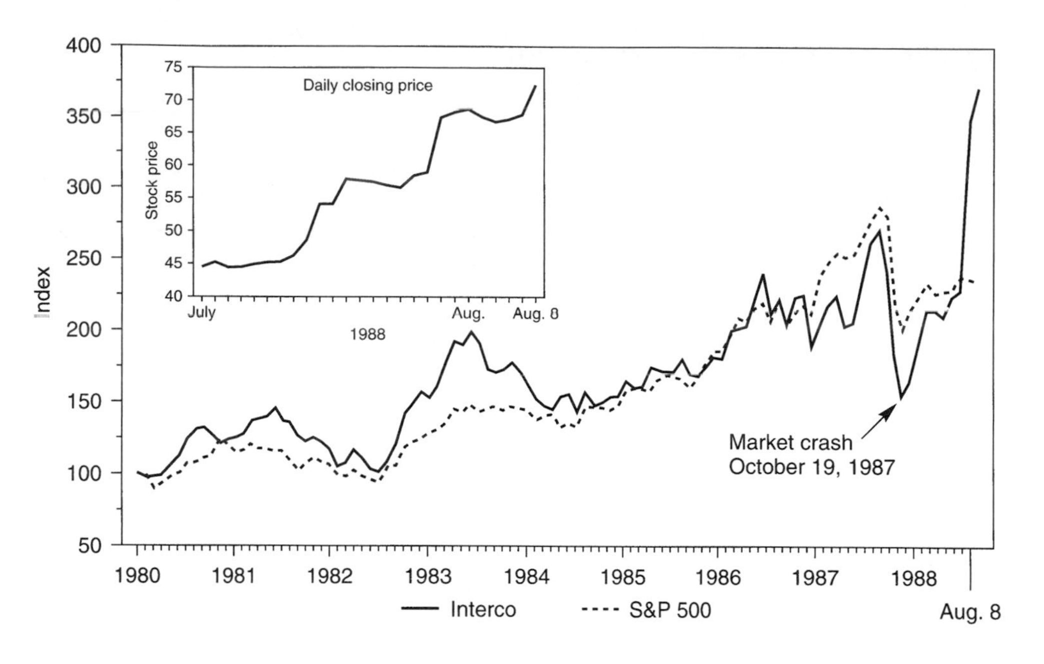

Market Interest Rates

Source: Salomon Brothers, Inc.

Yield curve at August 4, 1988	
1-year Treasury bills	7.83%
7-year Treasury bonds	8.87
10-year Treasury bonds	9.01
30-year Treasury bonds	9.10
Corporate bond rates at August 5, 1988 (industrial companies)	
10-year AAA	9.50%
10-year AA	9.65
10-year A	9.80
10-year BBB	10.10

Eskimo Pie Corporation (Abridged)

In early 1991, Reynolds Metals, the makers of aluminum foil and other aluminum products, decided to sell its holding of Eskimo Pie, a marketer of branded frozen novelties. Reynolds had few interests outside its aluminum and packaging business, and the Eskimo Pie Corporation, with roughly $47 million in sales, accounted for less than 1% of Reynolds revenues. Reynolds planned to use the proceeds from the sale of Eskimo Pie to fund investments in its core aluminum business. Eskimo Pie was 84% owned by Reynolds Metals, and 4% owned by the Reynolds Foundation. The remaining 12% of the Eskimo Pie was held by various Reynolds family members and a small group of outside investors.

Goldman Sachs, a New York investment banking firm, was retained to assist with the sale of Eskimo Pie. Goldman estimated that the sale price of Eskimo Pie would be about 1.2 times 1990 sales, or about $57 million. Nestlé Foods paid a comparable multiple for Drumstick, another ice cream novelty company, in 1990. Goldman organized an auction for Eskimo Pie, and Nestlé was the highest of six bidders with a price of $61 million.

Mr. David Clark, President of Eskimo Pie Corporation, recognized that the sale of Eskimo Pie to Nestlé would mean the end of its independence. Nestlé was likely to consolidate its ice cream novelty businesses by eliminating Eskimo Pie's headquarters and management staff. He had struggled to find a way to keep the company independent since he first learned of the sale. But Clark had been unable to raise sufficient funds to purchase Eskimo Pie in a leveraged buyout, and the sale to Nestlé seemed inevitable.

The Eskimo Pie Corporation

Background

Eskimo Pie, a chocolate covered bar of vanilla ice cream, was the first ice cream novelty. Its history appears on the Eskimo Pie box:

> Genuine Eskimo Pie . . .
>
> One day working in a confectionery store to supplement his teaching income, Christian K. Nelson became puzzled by a little boy's indecision between a chocolate candy bar and a scoop of ice cream. When questioned, the freckle-faced boy replied, "I want 'em both but I only got a nickel."
>
> With a clever hunch and a little ingenuity, Mr. Nelson found a way to combine the two ingredients in what would become America's first chocolate-covered ice cream bar. The little boy got his wish and Mr. Nelson founded a corporation on the success of the Eskimo Pie product.

This case derives from an earlier case, "Eskimo Pie Corporation," HBS No. 293-084, prepared by Professor Richard S. Ruback and Research Associate Dean Mihas (MBA '92). This version was prepared by Professor Richard S. Ruback. HBS cases are developed solely as the basis for class discussion. Cases are not intended to serve as endorsements, sources of primary data, or illustrations of effective or ineffective management.

Copyright © 2001 President and Fellows of Harvard College. To order copies or request permission to reproduce materials, call 1-800-545-7685, write Harvard Business School Publishing, Boston, MA 02163, or go to http://www.hbsp.harvard.edu. No part of this publication may be reproduced, stored in a retrieval system, used in a spreadsheet, or transmitted in any form or by any means—electronic, mechanical, photocopying, recording, or otherwise—without the permission of Harvard Business School.

Christian Nelson, age 27, began trying to make chocolate stick to ice cream in 1920 while operating an ice cream and confectionery store in Iowa. After months of experimentation, Nelson discovered that cocoa butter made the chocolate adhere to the ice cream. He introduced his product as the "I-Scream-Bar" in 1921. One year later, Mr. Nelson formed a partnership with Russell Stover and the product was renamed Eskimo Pie.

Because the lack of refrigeration made centralized production and distribution impossible, Eskimo Pie licensed rights to make and distribute the Eskimo Pie bar according to Mr. Nelson's recipe. By the spring of 1922, licenses had been sold to 2,700 manufacturers across the country. Sales were averaging one million Eskimo Pies a day and soared to two million a day by early summer. Russell Stover, Nelson's business partner, designed a tin foil wrapper, which added to the product's glamour and provided a mechanism to collect royalties. U.S. Foil Company (which was later renamed Reynolds Metal Company) manufactured the printed wrappers around the clock to satisfy demand.

In spite of the popularity of Eskimo Pies, the Eskimo Pie Corporation was not financially successful. Eskimo Pie had difficulty collecting royalties both because the company lacked a reliable accounting system and because of patent infringers. By the summer of 1923, it was estimated that over a billion Eskimo Pies had been sold and yet the firm could not pay its debt of $100,000. Nelson sold Eskimo Pie to the U.S. Foil Company, and in 1924 Eskimo Pie Corporation became a subsidiary of U.S. Foil Company.[1] Nelson was paid a small fraction of a cent in royalties on every Eskimo Pie sold thereafter.

1991 Operations

Eskimo Pie had two lines of business in 1991. The first was the licensing of the Eskimo Pie brand products and the sublicensing of Welch's and Heath brand products. The second was a manufacturing operation that produced and distributed ingredients and packaging for the dairy industry. Table A presents the sales breakdown of these businesses. The company was also engaged in intensive research and product development efforts to extend its product lines. Eskimo Pie had a total of 130 employees.

Exhibit 1 presents historical financial information for Eskimo Pie from 1987 to 1990, and Exhibit 2 contains summary of cash flows from 1989 and 1990.

Licensing

Eskimo Pie granted exclusive territorial licenses for the manufacture, distribution, and sale of Eskimo Pie brand products through a national network of about 20 dairy product manufacturers. Eskimo's licensees agreed to maintain the strict quality standards, and Eskimo maintained the right to inspect all premises used for the manufacture and handling of Eskimo products. The licensees are Eskimo Pie's direct customers, and the

TABLE A
Sales by Business Line

	Year Ended December 31,		
Business	1989	1990	1991
Licensing			
Eskimo Pie	58%	59%	56%
Welch's and Heath[a]	14	14	24
Flavors, packaging and other	28	27	20

[a]Heath products included only in 1991.

[1]Stover sold his share for $30,000 in 1923. Stover went on to develop a nationwide candy business. After the sale of Eskimo Pie to U.S. Foil, Nelson was employed by Eskimo Pie and retired as a vice president in 1961. His significant inventions include the use of dry ice to store ice cream and machinery that automated the production of ice cream novelties. Mr. Nelson died on March 8, 1992, at the age of 98.

top 10 licensees account for over 75% of revenues. Carnation was Eskimo Pie's largest licensee and manufacturer with territorial licenses to 11 western states.

Payment to Eskimo Pie by licensees was embedded in the price paid for ingredients and packaging supplied by Eskimo Pie rather than as a royalty payment based on units sold. If a licensee elected to use outside parties for certain ingredients and packaging, the licensee then paid Eskimo Pie a trademark license fee.

Eskimo Pie also sublicensed the manufacture and distribution of frozen novelties under established brand names of other food companies. Sublicensing had been an important component of Eskimo Pie's strategy since 1975 when it developed the Nestlé Crunch Bar and sublicensed its manufacture and distribution. Shortly after it acquired Carnation, Nestlé terminated the sublicensing arrangement in 1986.

In 1991 Eskimo Pie licensed frozen novelties for Welch's and Leaf Incorporated, who owns the Heath brand name. Under the arrangements, Eskimo Pie had the exclusive authority to grant sublicenses for the manufacture and sale of these products similar to the way it did for its own Eskimo Pie brand products. Eskimo Pie purchased the base ingredients from the food companies and re-sold them, along with packaging, to sublicensees. Approximately 80% of the Eskimo Pie brand licensees were also licensees for Welch's and/or Heath products.

Eskimo Pie provided centralized marketing for Eskimo Pie, Welch's, and Heath brand products. The majority of marketing expenses were spent on retail advertising and promotions; the balance went to regional consumer promotions using television and coupon campaigns. One or more of the company's Eskimo Pie brand products were found in 98% of all U.S. grocery stores, and Eskimo Pie enjoyed one of the highest consumer brand name recognition levels in the industry. Exhibit 3 shows the distribution and market share of Eskimo Pie products (including Heath and Welch's) during the 1987–1991 period.

Manufacturing

Eskimo Pie operated three plants in the United States. These plants manufactured key ingredients and packaging used by licensees, such as the proprietary chocolate coating, *Midnite Sun,* that gave Eskimo Pie products their distinctive flavor. The plants also produced generic ingredients and packaging sold both to licensees and non-licensees in the dairy industry. The plants employ a total of 46 hourly workers at an average hourly wage of $10.06. The plants also employed 18 salaried employees.

Product Innovation

Eskimo Pie's new product program was successful: ten products introduced since 1987 were being actively marketed and sold in 1991. Eskimo Pie was the first to market a sugar-free frozen dairy novelty bar made with NutraSweet and held a patent on that product's coating. The introduction of *Sugar Freedom Eskimo Pie* products in 1987 was largely responsible for the growth of Eskimo Pie's unit market share from 2.3% in 1987 to 5.3% in 1991. As of 1991, the *Sugar Freedom Eskimo Pie* products were leading the Eskimo Pie line. The company was also the first to introduce a fat-free frozen novelty product made with Simplesse, a patented fat substitute. By the end of 1991, Eskimo Pie was test marketing a fat-free ice cream sandwich and expected to introduce a *Fat Freedom Eskimo Pie* line in the spring of 1992.

The Frozen Novelty Industry

The frozen novelty industry in 1991 was highly fragmented with over 400 brands representing sales of $1.3 billion. During the 1980s, major food companies such as General Foods, Mars, and Coca Cola entered the frozen novelties business. This

TABLE B
1991 Leading Frozen Novelty Brands

Brand	Company	Unit Share
Popsicle	Unilever	7.6%
Klondike	Empire of Carolina	5.4
Eskimo Pie	Eskimo Pie	5.3
Snickers	Mars	4.8
Weight Watchers	H. J. Heinz	4.3

transformed the industry's structure of low growth, little advertising, and few participants into a rapidly growing industry. Industry revenues went from $590 million in 1980 to $1.5 billion by 1987. The number of ice cream novelty brands, 100 in 1980, expanded to over 500 by 1987. Advertising expenditures increased from less than $2 million to $75 million per year during this period. Exhibit 4 presents the frozen novelties sales trends.

By the late 1980s, the industry began to consolidate, with many of the larger companies exiting or significantly reducing their commitment to the frozen novelty business. By 1991, advertising expenditures had been reduced to about $25 million, and the market growth had slowed significantly. Table B shows the top five frozen novelties as ranked by unit market share in 1991.

Nestlé's Offer

Reynolds retained Goldman Sachs to sell Eskimo Pie because of its long-standing relationship with Reynolds and because it represented Nestlé in its Drumstick acquisition. David Clark was directed to work with the Goldman Sachs team that arrived in April 1991 to prepare a sales strategy and the documentation required by buyers. Clark and his staff cooperated reluctantly, recognizing that Eskimo Pie would be unlikely to continue its 70 year history of operating as a stand-alone company in Richmond and that its corporate staff would be unlikely to retain their positions. Exhibit 6 presents the projected income statements that Goldman collected.

Eskimo Pie's management and Wheat First Securities, a Richmond, Va., investment banking firm, formed a group to attempt a private buyout. This group obtained $20 million in credit and contributed another $15 million in equity, but the bid was rejected early on when higher offers came in. The buyout proposal could not secure additional financing because of the generally tight credit environment and the unpopularity of high yield debt financed LBOs. Also, Eskimo Pie could not use secured borrowing because the business was not asset intensive.

Goldman contacted several potential buyers. Many expressed interest but were concerned that Eskimo Pie's licensing approach to the business diverged from the more traditional integrated manufacturing and marketing approach. Reynolds received six offers for Eskimo Pie. Nestlé Foods was the highest bidder at $61 million, and Reynolds began negotiating the specifics of the sale in mid-1991.

Negotiations between Reynolds and Nestlé progressed slowly because of two complications. First, Nestlé, a Swiss company, wanted to tailor the transaction to take advantage of its tax conditions. Second, Eskimo Pie discovered in the third quarter of 1991 that a small quantity of cleanup solvents, inks and oils were disposed of at its New Jersey plant. The company contacted the regulatory authorities, and conducted testing to determine the extent of any contamination. Although Eskimo Pie did not expect cleanup costs to exceed $300,000, Nestlé remained cautious.

The Proposed Initial Public Offering

As the end of fiscal year 1991 approached, it was becoming apparent that Eskimo Pie was going to have a record year. Sales were higher than anticipated and operating margins had improved. In addition, Eskimo had also accumulated a $13 million cash reserve. David Clark contacted Wheat First again, searching for an alternative to the Nestlé acquisition that would keep Eskimo Pie independent. Any solution would have to provide Reynolds with as much cash as the proposed acquisition.

Wheat First proposed the initial public offering of Reynolds' shares. Reynolds had dismissed this possibility early on, at the advice of Goldman Sachs. Goldman argued that a public offering would be worth less than a private sale because of the potential for synergies with an acquiring firm. The fact that Nestlé, with its potential synergies in its Carnation and Drumstick units, had submitted the highest bid seemed to confirm Goldman's reasoning. Wheat First, however, had two reasons to think that its initial public offering might yield more than the sale to Nestlé. First, as Exhibit 5 shows, the new issues market was hot, and the number of new issues and their dollar value soared. Second, Wheat First was working with an updated forecast, and it projected a more promising outlook. The forecasted 1991 net income in Exhibit 6 is $2,893,000; actual results were going to be closer to $4,000,000. And forecasted sales in 1991 were projected at about $57 million; actual sales would be about $61 million. Capital expenditures were expected to be less than $1 million in 1992.

Wheat First proposed a two-step transaction. First, Eskimo Pie would pay out a $15 million or $4.52 per share special dividend. The $15 million dividend would be funded by the $13 million in cash that Eskimo Pie had accumulated and another $2 million in debt. The second step of the transaction was an initial public offering of up to 100% of the existing Eskimo Pie common shares. Wheat First suggested offering 3.3 million secondary shares with the option to offer 10–15% more shares. This "Green Shoe"[2] clause would provide cash to pay off the $2 million loan and provide over $2 million in working capital.

Wheat First estimated that the offering price would be between $14 and $16 a share. Exhibit 7 shows the proceeds from the initial public offerings at the two offering prices. At $16 a share, the firm and Reynolds obtained more from the IPO than from the Nestlé bid of $61 million. Furthermore, even at an offering price of $14, the IPO equalled the Nestlé offer, without the complications and conditions that Nestlé wanted to attach to its purchase of Eskimo Pie. Exhibit 8 shows that price earnings ratios for comparable companies such as Ben & Jerry's and Dreyer's Grand Ice Cream were about 30×. The S&P 500 was trading at 25× earning at the time.

Wheat First had not done business with Reynolds, and Goldman Sachs advised Reynolds Metals against the initial public offering. Goldman argued a deal with Nestlé was more certain, and they remained skeptical that an initial offering could yield as much as the private sale. The sale to Nestlé was likely to be closed soon, especially in light of the potential public offering. An initial public offering would take several months to complete, and Reynolds would risk changes in market conditions that would cool off the IPO market. Furthermore, an offering the size of the proposed Eskimo Pie deal would be one of Wheat First's largest. Wheat First and the management of Eskimo Pie stressed that with a public offering, the sale of Eskimo Pie by Reynolds would be made much easier, without complicated negotiations and compromises. In addition, an independent Eskimo Pie would stay in Richmond, which allowed Reynolds to get liquidity while saving a local company and local jobs.

[2]A "Green Shoe" clause in an underwriting agreement provides the issuer the opportunity to issue additional shares for distribution.

EXHIBIT 1 Historical Financial Information

Source: Eskimo Pie Prospectus, p. 10.

	Year Ended December 31,			
	1987	1988	1989	1990
Income Statement Data (in thousands):				
Net sales[a]	$30,769	$36,695	$46,709	$47,198
Cost of goods sold	21,650	25,635	31,957	31,780
Gross profit[a]	9,119	11,060	14,752	15,418
Advertising and sales promotions	4,742	4,241	5,030	5,130
General and administrative	6,068	5,403	6,394	7,063
Operating income (loss)	(1,691)	1,416	3,328	3,225
Interest income	308	550	801	1,004
Interest expense	(88)	(107)	(88)	(67)
Other income (expense)-net[b]	1,738	(77)	(108)	(20)
Income taxes	96	729	1,511	1,616
Net income	$ 171	$ 1,053	$ 2,422	$ 2,526
Balance Sheet Data (in thousands):				
Cash	$ 5,550	$ 8,109	$10,723	$13,191
Working capital	9,342	11,107	10,830	$11,735
Total assets	20,857	23,006	26,159	29,518
Long-term debt	1,269	1,094	919	744
Stockholders' equity	16,162	17,215	18,215	19,496
Per Share Data:				
Weighted average number of common shares outstanding	3,316	3,316	3,316	3,316
Net income per share	$ 0.05	$ 0.32	$ 0.73	$ 0.76
Cash dividend per share	—	—	$ 0.40	$ 0.40

[a]Beginning in 1991 the Company increased prices for products and assumed responsibility for advertising and sales promotion costs previously shared with licensees. This change in business practice accounts for approximately one-half of the increase in net sales for 1991 with a similar impact on 1991 gross profit.
[b]Includes the gain on sale of building of approximately $1,700,000 in 1987.

EXHIBIT 2 Cash Flow Summary

Source: Eskimo Pie Prospectus, p. F-4.

	Year Ended December 31,	
	1989	1990
Operating activities:		
Net income	$ 2,422	$ 2,526
Depreciation	1,006	1,352
Amortization	175	118
Deferred income taxes	250	(58)
Pension liability and other	(154)	(156)
Decrease (increase) in receivables	1,212	(734)
Decrease (increase) in inventories and prepaid expenses	(524)	(51)
Increase (decrease) in payables to parent	2,065	(621)
Increase (decrease) in accounts payable and accrued expenses	143	3,006
Net cash provided by operating activities	6,595	5,382
Investing activities		
Capital expenditures[a]	(2,358)	(1,311)
Other	(121)	(101)
Net cash used in investing activities	(2,479)	(1,412)
Financing activities		
Cash dividends	(1,327)	(1,327)
Principal payments on long-term debt	(175)	(175)
Net cash used in financing activities	(1,502)	(1,502)
Increase (decrease) in cash and cash equivalents	2,614	2,468
Cash and cash equivalents at beginning of year	8,109	10,723
Cash and cash equivalents at end of year	$10,723	$13,191

[a]Capital expenditures in 1989 are principally related to equipment acquired for use by licensees and, in 1990, an expansion of an ingredients manufacturing facility.

EXHIBIT 3 Distribution and Market Share of Eskimo Pie, Heath, and Welch's Frozen Novelties

Source: Eskimo Pie Prospectus, p. 4.

	1987	1988	1989	1990	1991
Distribution of at least one Eskimo product at U.S. grocery stores	76.3%	78.1%	91.2%	95.6%	97.9%
Unit market share of Eskimo products	3.3	3.9	5.7	6.8	7.5

EXHIBIT 4 Industry Information for Frozen Novelties

Source: 1980–87 Nieldsen; 1988–90 IRI

Year	Industry Revenues (millions)	Units Sold (millions)	% Change in Sales	Average Price	Advertising Spending (millions)
1980	$ 590	N/A	N/A	N/A	$ 2
1981	680	N/A	15.3%	N/A	4
1982	770	457	13.2	$1.69	17
1983	940	525	22.1	1.79	23
1984	1,100	577	17.0	1.90	32
1985	1,300	643	18.2	2.02	44
1986	1,400	681	7.7	2.06	77
1987	1,500	717	7.1	2.09	38
1988	1,355	637	–9.7	2.13	26
1989	1,332	623	–1.7	2.19	40
1990	1,321	590	–0.8	2.24	21

EXHIBIT 5 Initial Public Offerings, Volume in $ Billions, by Quarter

Source: Securities Data Corp.

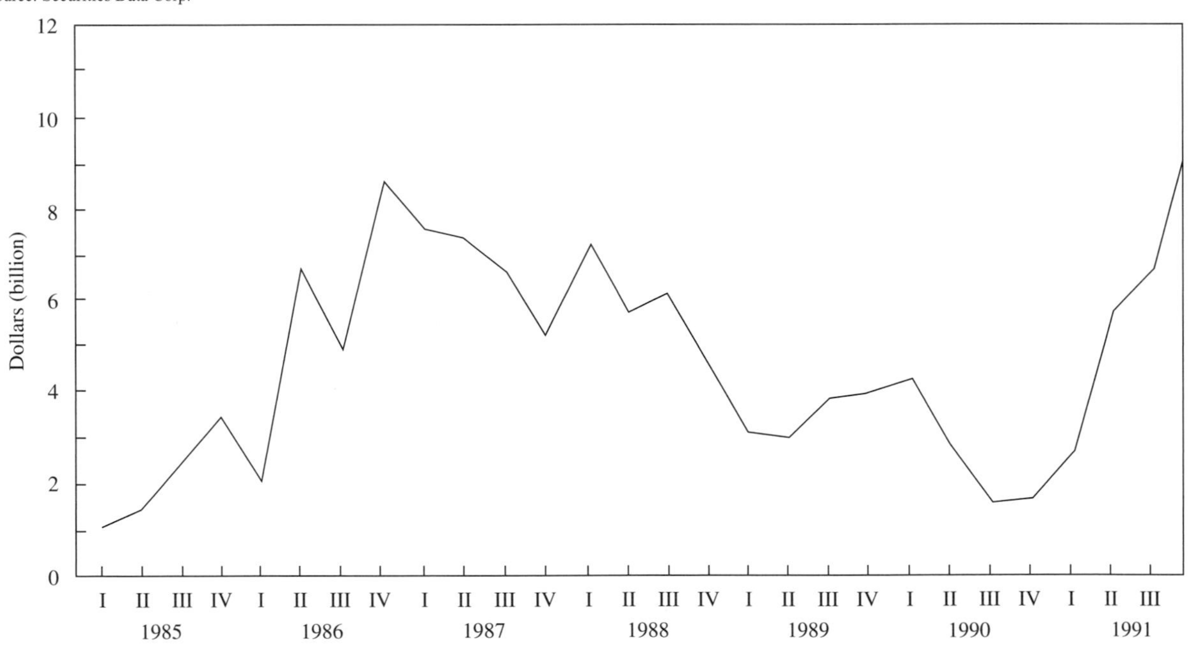

EXHIBIT 6

Projected Income Statements for Eskimo Pie by Goldman Sachs[a]

Source: Goldman Sachs

	Year Ended December 31,		
	1991	**1992**	**1993**
Net Sales	$56,655	$59,228	$59,961
Operating expenses	52,610	54,755	55,337
Operating income	4,045	4,473	4,624
Interest income	828	890	1,058
Interest expense	52.5	38.5	24.5
Pretax income	4,821	5,324	5,657
Income taxes	1,928	2,130	2,263
Tax rate	40.00%	40.00%	40.00%
Net income	$2,893	$3,195	$3,394
Margin	5.1%	5.4%	5.7%
Earning per share	$0.87	$0.96	$1.02
Average shares outstanding	3,316	3,316	3,316

[a]Adjusted for 2.5 to 1.0 stock split in March 1992.

EXHIBIT 7

Hypothetical Proceeds from an Initial Public Offering

Source: Casewriter estimates

Total for firm:		
Offer price	$ 14.00	$ 16.00
Special dividend	4.52	4.52
Total per share	$ 18.52	$ 20.52
Shares outstanding[a]	3,316	3,316
Total proceeds[a]	$61,412	$68,044
1991 Net income[a]	$ 3,749	$ 3,749
Implied P/E multiple	12.38	14.15
Reynolds' Proceeds:		
Shares owned[a]	2,789	2,789
Per share proceeds:		
Stock price	14.00	16.00
Special dividend	4.52	4.52
Total per share	18.52	20.52
Total for holdings[a]	51,645	57,222

[a]Units are in thousands.

EXHIBIT 8A Description of Comparable Companies

Source: Moody's, 1990.

Ben & Jerry's Homemade, Inc. makes super premium ice cream in unique and regular flavors and markets its ice cream through supermarkets, grocery stores, convenience stores, and restaurants, as well as franchised Ben & Jerry ice cream parlors and company-owned ice cream parlors.

Dreyer's Grand Ice Cream, Inc. engages in the manufacture and distribution of ice cream and other frozen dairy products.

Empire of Carolina, Inc. engages in designing, manufacturing, and marketing plastic toys, seasonal decorative items, and buttons for the apparel industry. The company also manufactures and distributes foreign novelty products, chocolate, and confectionery products, and sells proprietary frozen systems and packaging.

Steve's Homemade Ice Cream, Inc. engages in the marketing, sale, and distribution of Steve's ice cream as "super premium" pre-packaged pints, primarily to supermarkets, grocery stores, gourmet shops, delicatessens, and convenience stores. The company is also engaged in franchising and licensing Steve's Ice Cream stores, which are operated by independent owners. Through Swensen's Inc. subsidiary, the company owns, develops, and franchises ice cream shops and limited menu restaurants featuring Swensen's premium ice cream.

Hershey Foods Corporation and its subsidiaries are engaged in the manufacture, distribution, and sale of consumer food products. The Corporation, through its Hershey Chocolate USA, Hershey International, and Hershey Pasta Group divisions, and its subsidiary Hershey Canada, Inc. produces and distributes a broad line of chocolate, confectionery, and pasta products, as well as other consumer food products. On August 25, 1988, the Corporation acquired from Cadbury Schweppes Inc. and Cadbury Schweppes plc ("Cadbury") certain assets and liabilities of Cadbury's U.S. confectionery operations ("Peter Paul/Cadbury").

Tootsie Roll Industries, Inc. is engaged in the manufacture and sale of candy. The company's products are sold under the registered trademarks: "Tootsie," "Tootsie Rolls," "Tootsie Pops," "Tootsie Pop Drops," "Tootsie Roll Flavor Rolls," "Charms," "Mason Dots," and "Mason Crows."

EXHIBIT 8B Information about Comparable Companies as of December 31, 1991

Source: Standard & Poor's, Compustat, and casewriter estimates.

Company	Sales	Cash Flow[a]	Operating Income[b]	Net Income	Book Value of Equity	Market Value of Equity	Total Debt
Ben & Jerry's	97.0	6.7	10.2	3.7	26.3	110.1	2.8
Dreyer's Grand Ice Cream	354.9	24.1	37.0	15.9	113.1	534.0	44.3
Empire of Carolina, Inc.	243.1	16.8	37.4	8.8	45.1	51.4	89.8
Steve's Homemade Ice Cream	35.1	2.7	3.9	1.8	11.1	37.4	3.1
Hershey Foods Corp.	2,899.2	292.3	463.0	219.5	1,335.3	4,002.5	282.9
Tootsie Roll Inds.	207.9	32.5	47.2	25.5	152.8	728.8	0.0

[a]Net Income before extraordinary items plus depreciation and amortization.
[b]Before extraordinary items.

EXHIBIT 8C **Monthly Stock Returns for the S&P 500 Composite and for Comparable Companies**

Source: Standard & Poors, Research Insight.

	Ben & Jerry's	Dreyer's	Empire of Carolina Inc	Steve's Ice Cream	Hershey Foods	Tootsie Roll	S&P 500
Jan-88	−0.0517	0.1509	0.0677	0.9000	0.0561	0.0122	0.0404
Feb-88	0.0909	−0.0492	0.1212	−0.1842	0.0301	−0.0763	0.0418
Mar-88	0.1500	0.0259	0.0541	0.0323	−0.0660	0.0141	−0.0333
Apr-88	−0.0580	0.1513	0.0282	−0.0625	−0.0303	0.0443	0.0094
May-88	−0.0462	0.0073	−0.0750	0.1000	−0.0248	0.0509	0.0032
Jun-88	0.0484	0.1304	0.0541	0.1818	0.0591	−0.0183	0.0433
Jul-88	0.0000	−0.0256	0.0282	0.0256	0.000	0.0370	−0.0054
Aug-88	−0.0308	−0.0658	0.1750	−0.0250	−0.0284	−0.0357	−0.0386
Sep-88	0.0318	0.0845	−0.1277	−0.1026	0.0526	0.0101	0.0397
Oct-88	0.1462	0.1299	−0.0707	−0.0571	0.0950	0.0408	0.0260
Nov-88	−0.1544	0.0115	0.0000	−0.0909	−0.0804	−0.0863	−0.0189
Dec-88	−0.0635	0.0682	0.3421	0.1000	0.0400	0.0320	0.0147
Jan-89	0.0848	−0.0426	0.0220	0.3939	−0.0144	−0.0750	0.0711
Feb-89	−0.0781	−0.1000	0.1923	0.0761	−0.0029	−0.0721	−0.0289
Mar-89	−0.0678	−0.0864	−0.0161	0.0505	0.0443	0.0372	0.0208
Apr-89	0.1636	0.0811	−0.1784	0.0000	0.0708	0.0628	0.0501
May-89	−0.0156	0.2125	0.0600	−0.1277	0.0150	0.0546	0.0351
Jun-89	−0.0476	0.0103	0.1132	0.0976	0.1572	0.0666	−0.0079
Jul-89	0.1167	0.0918	0.3241	0.0444	0.0566	0.0931	0.0884
Aug-89	−0.0149	0.2056	0.0577	0.0000	−0.0516	0.0444	0.0155
Sep-89	0.0152	−0.0698	0.1273	−0.0426	0.0000	0.0229	−0.0065
Oct-89	−0.1194	−0.1583	0.1629	−0.1000	0.0379	−0.0451	−0.0252
Nov-89	0.0339	0.1584	−0.0694	0.0741	0.0130	0.0727	0.0165
Dec-89	0.0328	−0.0513	−0.2836	−0.0460	0.0399	−0.0086	0.0214
Jan-90	−0.1587	−0.0811	−0.1875	−0.1566	−0.1115	−0.0719	−0.0688
Feb-90	0.0189	0.1765	−0.2051	0.3000	−0.0841	0.0590	0.0085
Mar-90	0.0370	0.0833	0.1613	−0.0769	0.0948	0.0244	0.0243
Apr-90	−0.0714	0.0154	0.3056	−0.2619	0.0158	0.0386	−0.0269
May-90	0.3077	0.1591	−0.2979	0.0645	0.0913	0.1689	0.0920
Jun-90	0.0147	0.0654	0.1212	−0.3636	0.0750	0.0129	−0.0089
Jul-90	0.0870	−0.0245	−0.1892	0.0714	0.0266	−0.0114	−0.0052
Aug-90	−0.2267	−0.1006	−0.1500	−0.1778	−0.0065	−0.2052	−0.0943
Sep-90	−0.0948	−0.0140	−0.0196	−0.4324	−0.0493	0.0235	−0.0512
Oct-90	−0.0095	0.0213	0.0000	−0.0476	−0.0450	−0.0036	−0.0067
Nov-90	0.0577	0.2569	0.0000	0.7000	0.0210	0.1000	0.0599
Dec-90	0.0727	−0.0422	−0.1200	−0.2647	0.0714	0.0599	0.0248
Jan-91	0.0848	0.1047	0.2046	−0.0800	0.0600	0.0215	0.0415
Feb-91	0.0938	0.1368	−0.0566	0.1304	0.0088	0.0991	0.0673
Mar-91	0.1000	0.0944	−0.0800	0.1154	0.0251	0.0875	0.0222
Apr-91	−0.0260	−0.1017	0.2174	0.3103	−0.0184	0.0363	0.0004
May-91	0.0667	0.0094	0.2143	−0.1974	0.0991	0.0225	0.0386
Jun-91	−0.0375	0.0766	−0.0441	−0.0492	−0.0712	−0.0110	−0.0479
Jul-91	0.2857	0.0000	−0.0154	−0.0345	0.0276	0.1114	0.0449
Aug-91	0.1515	−0.0174	0.1875	0.9643	0.0059	0.0178	0.0197
Sep-91	0.1491	−0.0425	0.1053	−0.1273	−0.0716	0.0208	−0.0191
Oct-91	0.0458	0.0093	0.2143	0.6250	0.0611	0.0622	0.0119
Nov-91	0.0146	0.0734	0.0392	−0.2821	−0.0729	0.0364	−0.0439
Dec-91	0.0648	0.1897	−0.2642	0.8214	0.1678	0.1453	0.1116

EXHIBIT 9
Selected Financial Market Data, November 1991

Source: Federal Reserve Bulletin, S&P Bond Guide.

I. Treasury Yields	
90 day	4.56%
Six months	4.61
One year	4.64
Five years	6.62
Ten years	7.42
Thirty years	7.92
II. Corporate Borrowing Rates	
Long-term Bond Yields	
AA	8.74%
A	9.27
BBB	9.56
BB	11.44
B	14.68
Floating Rates	
Prime rate	7.50%
Prime commercial paper (6 months)	4.76

Netscape's Initial Public Offering

August 8, 1995, had taken an unexpected turn for Netscape Communications Corporation's board of directors. Earlier that morning, the day before the company's scheduled initial public offering (IPO), Netscape's lead underwriters proposed to the board a 100% increase in the original offering price, from $14 to $28 per share. This recommendation came in response to the remarkable oversubscription for Netscape's shares, which had already prompted the underwriters to increase the number of shares to be offered from 3.5 million to 5 million. Under the current proposal, a company with a net book value of just over $16 million that had yet to turn a profit was suddenly valued at over $1 billion.

The board faced a pricing dilemma within the context of an extremely unpredictable industry. While its members wanted to be responsive to Wall Street's current zeal, they also wanted to make sure that the fundamentals of Netscape justified such a dramatic increase in valuation.

Netscape Communications

Founded in April 1994, Netscape Communications Corporation provided a comprehensive line of client, server, and integrated applications software for communications and commerce on the Internet and private Internet Protocol (IP) networks. These products enabled the growing network of servers on the World Wide Web to communicate through multimedia, including graphics, video, and sound. Designed with enhanced security code, these software products provided the confidentiality required to execute financial transactions and to sell advertisements on the Internet and private IP networks.

The company's most popular product, Netscape Navigator, was the leading client software program that allowed individual personal computer (PC) users to exchange information and conduct commerce on the Internet. Navigator featured a click-and-point graphical user interface that enabled users to navigate the Internet by manipulating icons and windows rather than by using text commands. With the user-friendly interface as a guide, Navigator offered a variety of Internet functions, including Web browsing, file transfers, news group communications, and e-mail. Initially shipped in December 1994, Netscape Navigator generated 49% and 65% of total revenues for the quarters ended March 31, 1995, and June 30, 1995, respectively.

Netscape's server software provided enterprises with the basic capabilities necessary for creating and operating Web server "sites," or places on the Web where browsers could visit. Incorporating both browser and server functions, the company's integrated applications software programs were designed to provide enterprises with the capability to manage large-scale commercial sites on the Internet. Such applications enabled these enterprises to conduct full-scale electronic commerce through a seamless system. Together, server and integrated applications software accounted for 36% of total revenues in the first quarter of 1995, and 28% of total revenues in the second. Of these revenues, the majority were generated by one of Netscape's three server products, Netscape Commerce Server.[1]

[1]Bundled packages of Netscape Navigator and Netscape Commerce Server accounted for about 10% of total revenues in the first quarter, while their contribution in the second quarter was immaterial.

This case was prepared by Research Associate Kendall H. Backstrand under the supervision of Professor W. Carl Kester.

Copyright © 1996 by the President and Fellows of Harvard College. Harvard Business School case 296–088.

Revenues from Netscape's server and integrated applications products were expected to increase as a percentage of overall revenues in the future.

In addition to product revenues, Netscape generated service revenues, which were attributable to fees from consulting, maintenance, and support services. These revenues amounted to approximately 5% and 7% of total revenues for the quarters ended March 31, 1995, and June 30, 1995, respectively.

Financial Performance

Netscape had incurred total losses of $4.3 million on total revenues of $16.6 million for its first two operating quarters ending June 30, 1995. The company expected to continue to operate at a loss for the foreseeable future. Exhibits 1 and 2 provide Netscape's financial statements since its incorporation in April 1994.

Operating activities for the six months ended June 30, 1995, had generated $7.3 million in cash. Cash flows from financing activities of $20.5 million were primarily attributable to the net proceeds of $17.3 million from the issuance of Series C Preferred Stock and borrowings of $2.2 million under a debt facility agreement. Cash used in investment activities of $22.1 million related to $16.6 in short-term investments and $5 million in capital expenditures. At the end of the second quarter of 1995, Netscape's principal sources of liquidity were $8.9 million in cash and the $16.6 million in short-term investments. The company expected total capital expenditures for 1995 of approximately $12 million.

Industry Background

The demand for Netscape's products had evolved out of the development of the Internet in the late 1960s. The Internet was a global network designed to facilitate communication between some 35,000 computer networks using the enabling code termed Internet Protocol. According to International Data Corporation (IDC), in mid-1995 there were approximately 57 million Internet users. Of those 57 million users, IDC estimated that approximately 8 million were accessing information on the World Wide Web.

Engineered in the early 1990s, the Web was a technology that linked one bit of information on the Internet with another so that users could share "webs" of ideas. The Web consisted of a network of Web servers, which posted information in a common format described by the Hypertext Markup Language (HTML). Internet users were able to access information on the Web by implementing the appropriate Hypertext Transfer Protocol (HTTP). Because it necessitated complex coding, the Web had remained largely undiscovered by nontechnical users who simply wanted to browse, a popular pastime that came to be dubbed "surfing the Net."

Netscape's Entrance

Meanwhile, at the University of Illinois at Urbana-Champaign, a group of computer science students working at the National Center for Supercomputing Applications (NCSA) developed the graphical software program that gave rise to the notion of "surfing." Named NCSA Mosaic, the software program enabled nontechnical users to access and retrieve information on the Web. The Mosaic code organized Web information into neat collections of graphical electronic menus on which users could simply click-and-point to browse their contents.

In April 1993, the founders of Mosaic, under the leadership of then senior Marc Andreessen, began distributing the software for free to anyone who had the technical means to retrieve it electronically. The superb results of this strategy—2 million Mosaic users within 1 year—made for more than cocktail conversation among high-tech gurus in California's Silicon Valley. Jim Clark, the founder of Silicon Graphics, Inc. (known for its workstations that turned data into 3-D computer images), was among those who were impressed not only by Mosaic itself but by the broader vision of its creator, Andreessen.

After hearing that Andreessen had moved to Silicon Valley in early 1994, Clark sent him an e-mail asking if they might meet to discuss the future of Mosaic. This exchange and subsequent discussions formed the launching pad for Mosaic Communications, which was shortly renamed Netscape Communications Corporation. In addition to dropping the Mosaic name, Netscape paid Spyglass (the company that had engaged in an exclusive licensing arrangement with the University of Illinois) a one-time $2.4 million fee for the rights to certain Mosaic code. With the original code, Clark's management experience and $3 million in seed money, and Andreessen's vision and technical expertise, Netscape made its entrance into the highly dynamic Internet market.

Netscape entered the broad Internet market via the Web browser market, where it faced two challenges: (1) it had to set a new industry standard, and (2) it had to make money. The former challenge was the immediate concern. To set a new standard, Netscape had to create a program that would destroy Mosaic, which in 1994 wielded 60% of the Web browser market. The rival program was initially named Mozilla and then renamed Netscape Navigator at the time of its debut in December 1994. Using the same "give away today and make money tomorrow" strategy that Andreessen's team had used to popularize Mosaic, Netscape had succeeded in capturing 75% of the Web browser market by the spring of 1995. Mosaic, under the guise of Spyglass, trailed far behind with 5% of the market. Having set the industry standard, Netscape was poised to make money by selling server software to companies that wanted marketing access to potential consumers.

The Competitors

Netscape was the indisputable leader of its kind. As the Internet community and its demands continued to increase, however, so did the multitude of competitors. Netscape faced potential competition from PC and UNIX software vendors and on-line service providers, which were new entrants in the Web browser, server, and service markets. Financial information on the following competitors is provided in Exhibit 3.

Spyglass, Inc., with its Enhanced Mosaic Web browser technology, was Netscape's nearest competitor. However, while Spyglass marketed the only current rival product to Netscape's Navigator, it did so to a distinctly different market. Instead of focusing on the commercial browser market dominated by Netscape, by mid-1995, Spyglass had honed its strategy on the code market. As a code vendor, Spyglass produced the code and then sold it to other software companies wanting to incorporate it into their own programs. Spyglass also sold the computer code for creating server software. By employing this strategy, Spyglass attempted to capture the corporate market, which would ultimately compete with Netscape on the end-user front. Microsoft, for example, was among Spyglass' licensees and a rising competitor for Netscape.

As the de facto gatekeeper of computing, Microsoft was perhaps the most formidable of Netscape's competitors in the long term. In August 1995, the powerful PC software company was only weeks away from releasing its long-awaited Windows 95 operating system, which included a rival browser it had created from Spyglass code. The Microsoft browser would allow Windows users to access Microsoft Network, the company's proprietary on-line service, and would also offer broader Internet access. Further, Microsoft was scheduled to release its server software in mid-1996.

The on-line computer service providers also had made strides recently to move into Netscape's market. For example, both America Online and Prodigy had created independent browsers. Compuserve had licensed Spyglass software code for its recently released Web browser software. In mid-1995, these three on-line services had a total of approximately 8–9 million subscribers. As the on-line market became increasingly threatened by the rising popularity of the Web and its access providers, it was imperative that these companies compete for Netscape's market if they hoped to participate in the unfolding future of on-line commerce and communication.

Initial Public Offerings (IPOs)

Young, rapidly growing companies facing intense competition typically raise equity capital in two broad ways. One way is through a private equity transaction, and the other is through a public offering of stock. A private transaction involves direct negotiations with various financial or nonfinancial institutions. In such a case, a company raises money from these various entities, which then own a portion of that company in the form of its privately held shares of stock or other securities convertible into stock. Given the absence of a liquid market, these private investors must negotiate the terms of the sale with known buyers to whom they wish to sell their stakes in the company.

A public issue entails the sale of a company's equity to the public at large. The stock trades on public markets (either organized exchanges such as the New York Stock Exchange or over-the-counter markets such as the NASDAQ), provided that the issue has been registered with the Securities and Exchange Commission (SEC). An example of a public issue is an initial public offering (IPO), in which a company issues a portion of its stock to the public for the first time. Companies find it desirable to "go public" when their equity capital needs increase to the point where the opportunity cost of remaining private and compensating investors for the lack of liquidity becomes too great relative to the lower cost of capital derived from liquid public markets.

While the monetary benefits of going public are potentially sizable, so too are the associated costs. The total costs are comprised of ongoing costs associated with being a publicly traded company and one-time costs associated with the IPO itself. Specifically, ongoing costs result from the need to report timely information to investors and regulators. One-time costs, which are attributable to direct costs (legal, auditing, and underwriting fees) and indirect costs (management time invested in the process, and the dilution associated with selling shares at an offering price that is, on average, below the price prevailing in the market shortly after the IPO), reflect the time and financial commitments associated with the IPO process.

The human capital resources involved in the process of an initial public offering include the company's founders and senior management, the underwriters, and institutional investors. If the company had received venture capital in the early stages of its development, a characteristic referred to as "venture-backed," the venture capitalists are often intimately involved in the IPO process as well as the company's operations. By creating liquidity and market-determined prices for the stock, going public creates the potential for substantial financial rewards for all of the parties involved.

The "Going Public" Process

In the United States, companies issuing stock to the public for the first time typically use what is known as a "firm commitment contract."[2] This contract describes the relationship between the issuing firm and the investment bankers underwriting the offering. Specifically under the contract, the underwriters first commit to bear the risk of the issue by purchasing the shares offered, less an underwriting discount. The underwriters

[2]Another type of contract between the issuer and the underwriters is known as a "best efforts" contract. Unlike a firm commitment, in which the underwriters assume risk, a best efforts contract only requires the investment bankers to make their best efforts to sell the minimum number of shares. In the event there is insufficient demand to fully subscribe the minimum number of shares, the issue is withdrawn. This type of contract is typically used in smaller, more speculative offerings.

then guarantee to deliver the proceeds of the sale (net of commission) to the issuing company, whether or not the offer is fully subscribed. In the event of weak demand or undersubscription, the underwriters are allowed to sell the remaining shares at a lower price. Such action is referred to as "breaking the syndicate," as the syndicate of underwriters is originally formed to stabilize the market price immediately following the offering. On the other hand, in the event of strong demand or oversubscription at the time of the offering, the underwriters can sell additional shares, called an overallotment option or "greenshoe," amounting to as much as 15% of the total shares offered.

At times, the IPO market is characterized as a "hot issue" market because of the high returns earned by initial buyers of the shares. Such desirable returns occur as a result of either underpricing or oversubscription of a company's shares. This was the experience of Boston Chicken, which saw heavy initial demand and an unprecedented increase of 143% in the company's stock price after its IPO in November 1993. In Boston Chicken's case, this value increase was sustained over time. Not all companies experience a similar result, however. Snapple, for example, saw its stock price explode in after-market trading following its December 1992 IPO, only to lose this premium value over time. In yet another recent IPO, that of PixTech in July 1995, the company's stock price fell nearly 15% after the first day of trading following the offering. Clearly, not all companies have the good fortune of offering their stocks to the public during hot issue markets as indicated by such disparate outcomes.

Netscape's IPO

In response to its growing capital needs, in early 1995, Netscape began to explore the option of raising money through an initial public offering. The IPO market in the first half of 1995 had generated proceeds totaling nearly $12 billion for some 300 companies, which saw their stock prices increase on the first day of trading by an average of 20%. This outstanding momentum was largely attributable to venture-backed high-technology stock offerings (which recently represented well over half of all venture-backed IPOs), particularly those related to the Internet. (A 5-year history of the IPO market is illustrated in Exhibit 4; a chart illustrating IPO waves for the past 25 years is shown in Exhibit 5; and information on several recent Internet-related IPOs is provided in Exhibit 6.) In the spring of 1995, Netscape decided that the time was right to initiate an initial offering of its stock, despite its limited track record. The principal reasons for going public were to fund expected future growth, to stockpile cash reserves for potential acquisitions, and to gain visibility and credibility within the industry.

Netscape's Financing History

Since Clark's initial investment, Netscape had been injected with various forms of investment capital. Clark himself contributed an additional $1.1 million in the fall of 1994. At the same time, the Silicon Valley venture capital firm of Kleiner, Perkins, Caufield & Byers invested $5 million. The third and largest round of financing came in April 1995 from Adobe Systems and five other media companies. This final private placement of stock totaled $18 million and was orchestrated by Morgan Stanley. At the time of the IPO, Clark, Kleiner Perkins, and the group of media companies owned the largest stakes of Netscape's equity at 24%, 11%, and 11%, respectively. The company's president and CEO, James Barksdale, held shares amounting to 10% of total equity.

The IPO Team

The principal parties involved in the IPO of Netscape included the founders and the senior management team; the venture capitalists at Kleiner Perkins; and the investment bankers at Morgan Stanley and Hambrecht & Quist (H&Q), the co-underwriters of the

IPO. In addition to the lead underwriters, there were 26 other investment banks in the syndicate to help create a market for Netscape's shares. They all had agreed to pay the final offering price, less underwriting fees, to Netscape in the event investors withdrew their orders. Auditors, lawyers, and insurers also provided necessary services.

Netscape's cofounders and senior management were intimately involved in the IPO process, both from a practical and financial perspective. Since Netscape was not generating profits, the lure for Netscape's recently formed senior management team was not high salaries but rather preferred stock that could be converted into shares of common stock when Netscape went public. Clark and Barksdale, as well as others on the management team, including the vice president of technology, Andressen, stood to gain millions on paper in the face of a highly oversubscribed IPO within a "hot issue" market.

The lead underwriters were engaged in the IPO process from the very beginning. The investment bankers from these firms were responsible for everything from doing the initial "due diligence" to issuing the final prospectus, which stipulated the final offering price of the shares. If the proposed $28-per-share price was approved by the board, the underwriters would earn $9.8 million, or a 7% sales commission on every share sold to initial investors.[3]

Going Public

On July 17, 1995, Morgan Stanley and H&Q issued a preliminary prospectus, or an offering circular, suggesting it might offer 3.5 million Netscape shares priced at $12 to $14 per share. This preliminary offering price was based on the future business prospects of Netscape and the Internet industry in general, financial and operating information of Netscape, and stock price-related data and other financial and operating information of competitors.

The next and final step before the offering was the "road show," in which management and underwriters made presentations to potential major investors throughout the world. The purpose of a road show was largely to stimulate interest among institutional investors. Clark and Barksdale joined the underwriters for a two-week road show, which entailed traveling to 20 cities and talking to about 2,000 institutional investors. A road show also enabled underwriters to gauge the interest of institutional investors for purposes of determining the final offering price. Upon returning from the road show, the Morgan Stanley underwriters called some of the investors they had previously visited to assess their current interest in terms of price and quantity of shares. The response was overwhelmingly favorable, yet only indicated potential demand. Such potential would not be realized until the orders in the "book" were translated into purchase orders when trading began on the day of the offering. Despite this uncertainty, however, the investment bankers from Morgan Stanley and H&Q felt confident enough to recommend doubling the offering price proposed in the preliminary prospectus.

The Board Decision

The time had come when Clark and the other Netscape board members had to approve or reject their underwriters' vote of high confidence. In going over the new valuation of the company, the board struggled to disregard the wild speculation surrounding what

[3]This commission value does not account for the potential exercise of the overallotment option. At 750,000 shares, this option would generate an additional $1,470,000 at $1.96 per share. Clearly, the underwriters would benefit from any demand for shares in excess of the original 5 million being considered.

had been called the hottest IPO of the year. Indeed, Netscape had commercialized the young world of cyberspace, causing a flood of enthusiasm on Wall Street greater than that experienced by the biotech industry in the 1980s and early 1990s. Much like the then unchartered biotech industry, however, the future commercial size of cyberspace was unknown. Perhaps most unavoidable in the minds of the board members, the subscription for such a hot stock had the potential of reaching many times 5 million shares by the time of the offering the next morning. Still, Netscape had a negative bottom line and parents who had watched the Regenerons of the IPO world make painful mistakes.[4] Perhaps the investment community would react similarly to Netscape's decision to raise the price, interpreting such an increase as unjustifiably opportunistic. The board's responsibility was thus to determine the appropriateness of the proposed increase in price after balancing the potential risks and rewards that might accompany such a move.

EXHIBIT 1
Consolidated Income Statement for Netscape Communications Corporation

	Inception (April 4 to December 31, 1994)	Six Months Ended June 30, 1995
Revenues		
Product revenues	$ 378,490	$15,580,258
Service revenues	317,381	1,045,133
Total revenues	695,871	16,625,391
Cost of revenues		
Cost of product revenues	114,777	1,222,045
Cost of service revenues	104,313	513,767
Total cost of revenues	219,090	1,735,812
Gross profit	476,781	14,889,579
Operating expenses		
Research and development	2,031,986	6,115,152
Sales and marketing	2,813,689	9,256,066
General and administrative	1,669,193	3,693,005
Property rights agreement and related charges	2,486,688	500,000
Total operating expenses	9,001,566	19,564,223
Operating loss	(8,524,775)	(4,674,644)
Interest income	55,238	495,583
Interest expense	(308)	(128,655)
Net loss	$(8,469,845)	$(4,307,716)
Net loss per share	$ (0.26)	$ (0.13)
Shares used in computing net loss per share	32,256,307	33,000,751

[4]Regeneron Pharmaceuticals, Inc., a pharmaceutical company developing treatments for diseases of the central nervous system, had raised its offering price and the number of shares to be sold subsequent to its successful road show, only to be met with a discounted stock price after disappointed investors withdrew their orders. In addition to being negative publicity for Regeneron itself, the Regeneron experience was thought to have been a catalyst for the subsequent closing of the window for biotech IPOs at large.

EXHIBIT 2

Consolidated Balance Sheets for Netscape Communications Corporation

	December 31, 1994	June 30, 1995
Assets		
Cash and short-term equivalents	$3,243,510	$ 8,868,436
Short-term investments	—	16,567,300
Accounts receivable	701,649	8,277,869
Other current assets	67,284	804,971
Total current assets	4,012,443	34,518,576
Property and equipment, net	2,447,098	6,761,045
Deposits and other assets	699,100	1,251,582
Total assets	$7,158,641	$42,531,203
Liabilities and Stockholders' Equity		
Accounts payable	$ 855,068	$ 4,607,174
Accrued compensation and related liabilities	527,340	1,075,066
Other accrued liabilities	667,503	1,897,819
Deferred revenues	2,575,145	14,963,843
Current portion of long-term obligations	725,000	725,000
Installment notes payable	—	551,449
Total current liabilities	5,350,056	23,820,351
Long-term obligations	725,000	725,000
Installment notes payable	—	1,511,331
Total liabilities	6,075,056	26,056,682
Preferred stock, $0.0001 par value	701	901
Common stock, $0.0001 par value	451	1,514
Additional paid-in capital	9,552,278	39,683,666
Notes receivable from stockholders	—	(638,065)
Deferred compensation	—	(9,812,151)
Accumulated deficit	(8,469,845)	(12,777,561)
Accumulated translation adjustment	—	16,217
Total stockholders' equity	1,083,585	16,474,521
Total liabilities and stockholders' equity	$7,158,641	$42,531,203

EXHIBIT 3 **Comparative Information on Potential Competitors (for year ended June 30, 1995; thousands of dollars except per share data)**

	Netscape[a]	America Online, Inc.	Microsoft Corp.	Spyglass, Inc.
Net revenues	$17,321	$394,290	$5,937,000	$ 9,084
Operating expenses	30,521	413,584	3,899,000	6,745
Operating income (loss)	(13,200)	(19,294)	2,038,000	2,339
Interest expense	(129)	—	—	—
Net income (loss)	(12,778)	(33,647)	1,453,000	1,509
Earnings per share	(0.39)	(0.99)	2.32	0.41
Weighted average shares outstanding	33,001	33,986	627,000	3,788
Capital expenditures	7,618	57,751	495,000	824,609
Depreciation, depletion, and amortization	918	11,136	269,000	161,303
Current assets	34,519	132,856	5,620,000	37,372
Cash and short-term investments	25,436	64,050	4,750,000	34,556
Total assets	42,531	406,464	7,210,000	39,963
Current liabilities	23,820	133,312	1,347,000	2,718
Total liabilities	26,057	188,520	1,877,000	4,368
Net worth	$16,475	$217,944	$5,333,000	$35,595
Current ratio	1.45	1.00	4.17	13.75
Debt/total capital	0.18	0.08	—	—
Common stock price (close)	N/A	22.00	90.38	14.31
P/E ratio	N/A	N/A	39.00	34.90
Equity beta[b]	N/A	0.73	0.72	N/A

[a]Netscape's financial data reflects the company's performance since inception in April 1994. Netscape did not begin to ship products or earn significant product revenues until December 1994.

[b]Bloomberg estimates based on weekly data for the year ended June 30, 1995.

EXHIBIT 4 **Historical Data of the IPO Market**

	1990	1991	1992	1993	1994
All IPOs					
Number of companies	166	352	477	604	510
Total dollar amount offered (in $ billions)	$ 4.75	$16.01	$22.76	$30.74	$17.98
Average % gain after first day of trading	10.3%	11.6%	9.4%	11.7%	8.1%
Venture-Backed IPOs					
Number of companies	42	122	152	165	136
Average age of companies	6	6	6	7	7
Total dollar amount offered (in $ billions)	$ 1.19	$ 3.90	$ 4.58	$ 4.86	$ 3.35
Average offering size (in $ millions)	28.3	32.0	29.1	29.6	24.8
Average offering valuation (in $ millions)	$109.3	$118.5	$101.7	$100.5	$ 86.8

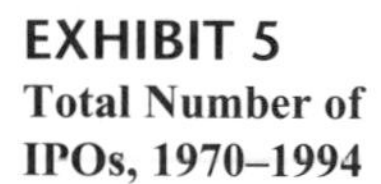

EXHIBIT 5
Total Number of IPOs, 1970–1994

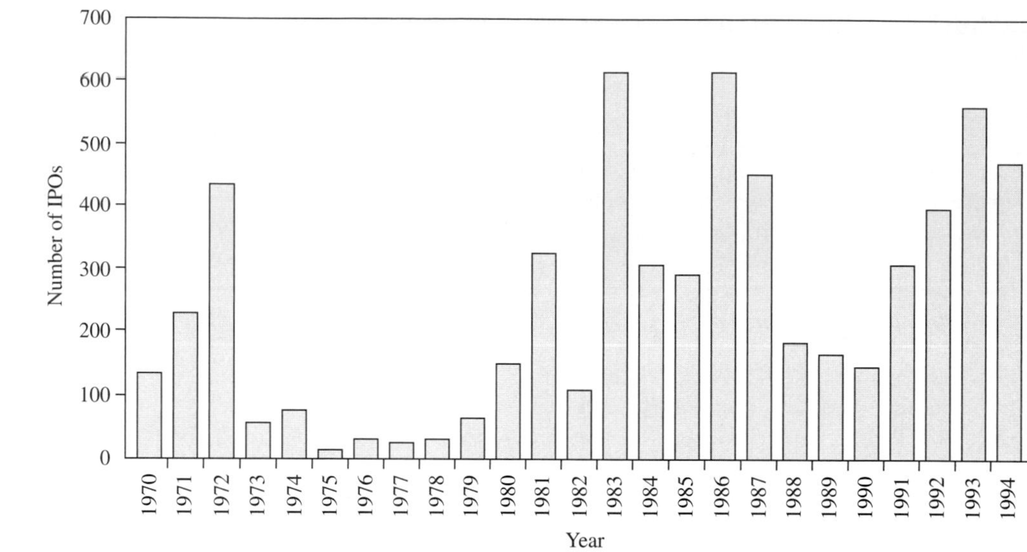

EXHIBIT 6 **Information on Internet-Related IPOs (for the respective fiscal year preceding the IPO)**

	Netcom Online Communication Services, Inc. (year ended 12/31/93)	Performance Systems International, Inc. (year ended 12/31/94)	Spyglass, Inc. (year ended 9/30/94)	Uunet Technologies Inc. (year ended 12/31/94)
Financial Data				
Net revenues	$2,411,600	$15,214,000	$3,629,392	$12,413,863
Operating costs and expenses	2,169,600	19,876,000	2,272,662	19,387,821
Operating income	242,000	(4,662,000)	751,520	(6,973,958)
Interest expense	(3,400)	(731,000)	—	(76,232)
Net income	227,300	(5,342,000)	1,331,262	(6,948,759)
Earnings per share	$ 0.04	$ (0.26)	$ 0.39	$ (0.35)
Weighted average shares outstanding	6,300,600	20,395,000	3,448,952	20,029,824
Capital expenditures	1,027,600	2,536,000	208,567	5,897,309
Depreciation, depletion, and amortization	156,900	3,183,000	68,034	1,010,027
Current assets	235,500	5,564,000	3,254,562	6,192,629
Cash and short-term investments	75,500	3,358,000	1,450,651	4,649,737
Total assets	1,347,000	17,055,000	5,296,727	12,024,575
Current liabilities	789,300	7,118,000	1,406,727	5,755,418
Total liabilities	802,300	11,721,000	3,056,727	6,422,085
Net worth	$ 544,700	$ 5,334,000	$2,240,000	$ 5,602,490
IPO Data				
Date of IPO	12/14/94	5/8/95	6/27/95	5/25/95
Price per share offered	$ 13.00	$ 12.00	$ 17.00	$ 14.00
Number of shares offered	1,850,000	4,370,000	2,000,000	4,725,000
% of total equity sold	28%	17%	40%	17%
% change in stock price after first day of trading	+31%	+27%	+60%	+96%
Price per share on August 8, 1995	$ 36.375	$ 22.00	$ 49.25	$ 46.25

Gulf Oil Corporation—Takeover

On the morning of March 5, 1984, George Keller of the Standard Oil Company of California (Socal) still had not made up his mind about how much to bid. The stakes were high. For sale was Gulf Oil Corporation, the most doddering of the seven sisters. But the price was high as well. Determined to depart in dignity, Gulf management made clear that it would not consider any bid below $70 per share, a considerable premium over the $43 price at which Gulf had traded during the close of 1983, when the sale of Gulf was a remote possibility.

Bidding against Mr. Keller were some who were willing to pay $70 and more. Included in the confidential auction in Pittsburgh with Standard Oil of California were members of the Atlantic Richfield Company (ARCO) and bankers from Kohlberg, Kravis, Roberts & Co., specialists in leveraged buyouts.

Mr. Keller felt the bid from Kohlberg, Kravis was the one to beat, since it came essentially from Gulf itself. This proposal allowed Gulf to become a private firm by tendering for the shares of its public stock. The undeniable attraction of the offer lay in its preservation of the name, the assets, and the jobs of Gulf Oil, until management found a long-term solution.

The challenge from ARCO was far less threatening. If ARCO offered more than $75 per share, its debt-to-total-capital ratio would exceed 60%, an uncomfortably high level. Socal, in contrast, had a debt-to-total-capital ratio that was so low that the banks were queuing up to lend money to it. The banks were so anxious to lend Socal $14 billion that the potential loan was oversubscribed by 30%.

The profusion of bank credit meant that Mr. Keller could safely bid $79, $80, or even higher. The opportunities created by the acquisition were enormous, but so were the risks of betting the whole company on them. With one stroke, Socal could ensure itself access to vast quantities of high-quality light oil. Overnight, Socal could virtually double its reserves and give the next generation of management something with which to work.

An appraisal of the value of the opportunities offered by the Gulf deal required, of course, an idea of how the two companies (Exhibit 1) would perform as a unit. A pro forma balance sheet (Exhibit 2) showed that the combined firm would have a considerable amount of financial leverage. While manageable in the short run, the debt would have to be reduced over the next few years.

The most direct way of accomplishing this reducing was to sell some of Gulf's assets. Another way, Mr. Keller felt, was to make use of funds Gulf currently spent on exploration and development.[1] These funds amounted to over $2 billion in 1983 (Exhibit 3). The only question was whether, by using funds that had been earmarked for the search for more oil, the long-run viability of the new enterprise would be sacrificed at the expense of financial expediency. After all, if investing in new sources of oil were worthwhile before Gulf's acquisition, it would be just as worthwhile afterwards. An opposite point of view, however, was that if Socal purchased Gulf, its reserves would be so large that Gulf's contribution to the exploratory effort could safely be discontinued.

[1]Exploration and development is a time-consuming effort. For an on-shore site, it generally takes 4 years between the time the lease is acquired until the field comes on-stream. Having been developed, the field is productive for another 7–10 years.

Copyright © 1984 by the President and Fellows of Harvard College. Harvard Business School case 285–053.

Aside from the question of how to reduce the takeover debt, there was the issue of the tax cost of the acquisition. Although the tax considerations were complex,[2] it was felt that the tax benefits and costs nearly offset each other.[3] The decision, therefore, of how much to bid depended solely upon the economic benefits of the acquisition. At times, those benefits seemed almost incalculable. As Mr. Keller said, "But it's like a 100-year mining project. A straight rate of return analysis would prevent you from doing it. The decision has to be a little glandular."[4]

The Takeover

While the seeds for Gulf's demise were sown over the course of a decade, the event that precipitated the emergency meeting in Pittsburgh on March 5, 1984, was far more recent. The decision to sell the company was made in response to a takeover attempt by Boone Pickens, Jr., the chief executive officer of Mesa Petroleum Company.

Boone Pickens had a long string of successes in targeting undervalued oil companies, beginning in 1969. In 1982, the year prior to its attempt on Gulf, Mesa tendered for two companies: Cities Service, and General American Oil of Texas. In both cases, Mesa failed to gain control but made a substantial profit in reaching an accommodation with the target. In the case of Cities Service, Mesa sold back the stock it acquired through the tender offer for a gain of $31.5 million. In the case of General American, Mesa received $15 million for withdrawing its tender offer and another $42.4 million when it sold the shares accumulated in open market purchases to a higher bidder.

On August 11, 1983, Mr. Pickens and a consortium of experienced investors began purchasing shares of Gulf Oil for $39. Two months later, the Gulf Investors' Group, as the consortium called itself, had spent $638 million and had acquired about 9% of all the Gulf shares outstanding at an average cost of approximately $43 per share.

The share purchases were totally unexpected. Mesa Petroleum was a small company compared to Gulf. If Mr. Pickens intended to acquire control of Gulf, the deal would require borrowing at least $10 billion, many times the magnitude of Mesa's net worth. To put the effort in perspective, 4 years before, the largest takeover was $1 billion, and that involved the conglomerate United Technologies. What Mr. Pickens was attempting was as audacious as it was unprecedented.

What contributed to the surprise was the opinion of many that the time for oil megamergers had passed. Within a few years, Occidental Petroleum had acquired Cities Service; U.S. Steel had bought Marathon Oil; Du Pont had taken over Conoco; and Elf Aquitane had gained control of Texasgulf. The political sentiment was that these takeovers, costing tens of billions of dollars, were not in the public interest. Senator Bennett Johnston (D. La.) put the principle forcefully: "When a few merge, it's one

[2]Advice concerning the tax aspects of this transaction was provided by the law firm of Simpson Thacher & Bartlett.

[3]It was expected that the acquisition would be structured as a liquidating sale of Gulf's assets. Under the Tax Equity and Fiscal Responsibility Act of 1982 (TEFRA), the treatment of such a sale held both benefits and drawbacks for the acquiring company. On the positive side, no gain was recognized by the acquired company on the sale of its assets. More important, the acquiring company was allowed to step up the assets to their fair market value, thereby realizing future tax benefits through higher depreciation and depletion deductions. On the negative side, certain tax deductions taken in the past by the acquired company became recaptured and had to be repaid immediately upon liquidation. For example, since Gulf used the LIFO (last in, first out) method to account for petroleum inventories, the difference between the FIFO (first in, first out) and LIFO valuations had to be treated as ordinary income and taxes paid accordingly. Also recaptured and treated as ordinary income was any depreciation in excess of the straight-line amount on real property and certain accelerated drilling costs.

[4]*Fortune*, April 2, 1984, p. 22.

thing, but when a whole industry is consolidating, it's a very different matter. One's a glass of wine with Christmas dinner; the other, a six-month binge."[5]

After the shock subsided, Gulf's response to the investors' group was one of indignation and outrage. The chairman of Gulf, James Lee, described the group led by Mr. Pickens as "corporate raiders" who were "cannibalizing" the company. Harold Hammer, the chief administrative officer of Gulf, said, "We've got to roll up our sleeves and hit him where it really smarts."[6] In the meantime, the investors' group raised its share in Gulf to 13.2%.

Mr. Pickens stated that his immediate objective was to put himself on the board of directors, where he could effect changes in Gulf policy. He said he was particularly interested in forcing Gulf to spin off its domestic oil and gas properties into a royalty trust, a device he popularized and perfected at Mesa.[7] To thwart this, Gulf sought to move its corporate charter from Pennsylvania to Delaware, where Mr. Pickens would need a majority vote of the shareholders to elect alternative directors. This move, which occurred on January 18, 1984, followed a long and acrimonious proxy battle over the reincorporation. Gulf won that battle with 53% of the vote in its favor. In that contest, Gulf was heavily supported by individual investors, most of whom were personally lobbied by Gulf executives (Exhibit 4). After winning the proxy contest, Gulf felt confident that the reincorporation would deny the investors' group, with limited capital at its disposal, its only means of access to the boardroom.

On February 22, 1984, Mr. Pickens announced a partial tender offer at $65 per share. This price was within the range that the Gulf Investors' Group estimated the royalty trust shares would trade if the proposed reorganization took place, according to its December 30 presentation to the Gulf board of directors. The offer price represented a significant premium over price levels of the recent past (Exhibit 5) and the closing price of $52⅝ on the day before. To make the offer, Mr. Pickens had to borrow $300 million from Penn Central Corp., using securities of Mesa Petroleum as collateral. Even with this capital infusion, the investors' group could only afford to purchase 13.5 million shares, which would leave it far short of a majority, with 21.3% of the stock. The Pickens group, however, hoped that this show of strength would enable it to attract further financial backing.

The motives of the Pickens group were widely impugned by those sympathetic to Gulf's management. On the day of the tender offer, for instance, a local Pittsburgh paper editorialized: "Mesa chairman T. Boone Pickens, Jr., expects primarily to cash in on Gulf's golden eggs, which are in the form of vast amounts of oil and gas. After obtaining the revenue there, he plans to slaughter the goose."[8]

The tender offer precipitated a crisis at Gulf. Seeming to sense the inevitability of the outcome. Gulf decided to seek a liquidation on its own terms. James Murdy, an executive vice president of Gulf, said in a retrospective interview:[9]

> Now all of this attention put enormous speculative pressure on our stock. We saw that, and we knew we had to do the best job for all shareholders while at the same time saving as much as possible for employees and others with a stake in Gulf. So when Mesa finally launched its unfair partial tender offer, our board was willing to consider selling the company to a strong merger partner rather than see Mesa steal the company.

[5]Ibid.

[6]*New York Times,* November 5, 1983.

[7]The principal advantage of a trust was the elimination of a second layer of taxation on distributed earnings and the tax savings from the step-up in the basis of the properties. However, some past tax deductions were recaptured in the process, and the shareholders had to pay capital gains rates on the difference between the trading value of the trust units and their basis in the corporation's stock. The arrangement worked well if the corporation had a high dividend payout ratio and stockholders had a high tax basis.

[8]*Pittsburgh Post Gazette,* February 23, 1984.

[9]*Energy Bureau Seminar,* October 3, 1984.

Having made the decision to liquidate, Gulf contacted several firms—including Allied, ARCO, Socal, Sohio, and Unocal—and invited them to Pittsburgh for an unprecedented sale.

Recent History

In 1975, Gulf lost a large portion of its reserves when Kuwait and Venezuela canceled Gulf's oil concession. In the years that followed, total reserves declined, reaching a record low in 1981. In that year, James Lee became chairman. Mr. Lee enunciated a clear strategy to reverse the decline in Gulf's competitive position. His strategy was twofold. First, he would concentrate Gulf's efforts on oil. In the past, Gulf had developed into an energy conglomerate through acquisitions of coal mines, uranium mines, and synthetic fuel plants. In the future, Gulf intended to de-emphasize these ventures, which were not notably successful. The second part of the strategy arose naturally from the first. In keeping with the renewed emphasis on oil, Mr. Lee continued to increase expenditures on exploration and development. As a result of this policy, outlays for exploration more than doubled between 1978 and 1982, and the long decline in reserves was finally arrested and reversed. He was quite explicit about his policy. In this own words, "Gulf's number one priority is to replace our domestic reserves of hydrocarbons through discoveries and acquisitions."[10]

A key phrase in this statement of purpose is "discoveries *and* acquisitions." In 1982, Gulf made an effort to acquire Cities Service. Ironically, Gulf's attempted acquisition of Cities Service involved a confrontation with Mesa Petroleum, which almost cost Mesa its corporate life. The takeover of Cities Service collapsed at the last minute, however, when the Federal Trade Commission raised several objections and Gulf withdrew its offer, causing many arbitrageurs to lose heavily.

Mr. Lee's business plan underwent a midcourse correction as a result of developments in the oil markets. Beginning in 1982 and continuing throughout 1983, the real price of oil and natural gas declined (Exhibit 6). As 1984 began, almost all experts were in agreement that, in constant dollars, the price of oil would not change for the next 10 years. Even the oil ministers of Saudi Arabia and Qatar shared this opinion.

In response to these changing fundamentals, Mr. Lee trimmed exploration expenditures significantly in 1983.[11] Even at this reduced level, however, spending for exploration in real terms equaled or exceeded that of every year before his arrival except one (Exhibit 3).

In addition to investing in discovering new sources of oil and gas, Gulf management began using the company's sizable cash flow to repurchase shares. From mid-1981 to March 1983, Gulf purchased 30 million shares of the 195 million outstanding. At that point, Mr. Lee said, "I have no philosophical problem with another bite if everything is as it is now and if our stock is as good a buy as it is now."[12]

Mr. Keller's Decision

Mr. Keller was as aware as Mr. Lee of Gulf's lackluster showing on most measures of financial performance (Exhibit 7). Indeed, Gulf's sluggish returns and weak earnings were the chief attraction, since they suggested great opportunities for improvement. The only uncertainty facing Mr. Keller on the morning of March 5 was not whether to bid but how much to bid to be sure the opportunities did not get away.

[10]Gulf Oil Corporation, Annual Report (1981), p. 3.

[11]See Exhibit 8 for a discussion of accounting policies relating to exploration and development.

[12]Quoted in *Gulf Oil Corporation Appraisal* (John S. Herold, Inc., 1983), p. 349.

EXHIBIT 1
Results of 1983 Operations, Oil and Gas Producing Activities Only (millions of dollars)

	Gulf	Socal
Revenues, oil and gas production only	$6,503	$5,742
Less: Costs		
Lifting costs		
Production	911	1,454
Wellhead taxes	792	504
Exploration expense	594	758
Depreciation, etc.	1,000	646
Other operating expenses	358	116
Income taxes[a]	1,933	1,368
Results of operations after income taxes	$ 915	$ 896

Comparison of 1983 Balance Sheets for Total Corporation (millions of dollars)

	Gulf	Socal
Current assets	$ 5,653	$ 7,328
Net properties	14,090	14,222
Investments in affiliates	608	2,319
Deferred charges and other assets	613	141
Total assets	$20,964	$24,010
Current liabilities	$ 4,756	$ 5,117
Long-term debt and capital leases	2,291	1,896
Deferred taxes	2,651	1,960
Deferred credits	—	852
Other liabilities	355	79
Minority interests	783	—
Total liabilities	10,836	9,904
Common stock	165	1,026
Paid-in capital	1,095	871
Retained earnings	8,868	12,209
Stockholders' equity	10,128	14,106
Total liabilities and stockholders' equity	$20,964	$24,010
Beta of common stock	1.15	1.15

[a]Gulf's effective marginal tax rate was approximately 50%.

EXHIBIT 2
Pro Forma Balance Sheet, Gulf and Socal Combined (millions of dollars)

	Offer Price of Socal for All Outstanding Gulf Shares[a]		
	$70/Share	$80/Share	$90/Share
Current assets	$12,751	$12,751	$12,751
Net properties	29,768	31,421	33,075
Other assets	3,901	3,901	3,903
Total assets	$46,420	$48,073	$49,727
Current liabilities	$ 9,873	$ 9,873	$ 9,873
Long-term debt and capital leases	15,761	17,414	19,068
Deferred items	5,463	5,463	5,463
Other liabilities and minority interests	1,217	1,217	1,217
Total liabilities	32,314	33,967	35,621
Stockholders' equity	14,106	14,106	14,106
Total liabilities and stockholders' equity	$46,420	$48,073	$49,727

[a]Gulf had 165.3 million shares outstanding.

EXHIBIT 3 **Exploration Cost and Reserve Data for Gulf and Socal, 1976–1983**

	Gulf							Socal						
	Exploration Cost ($ millions)			Reserve Data (millions of composite bbls)				Exploration Cost ($ millions)			Reserve Data (millions of composite bbls)			
	Expensed +	Capitalized =	Total	Begin +	Add'ns –	Prod'n =	End	Expensed +	Capitalized =	Total	Begin +	Add'ns –	Prod'n =	End
1976	$343	$ 645	$ 988	3,672	280	365	3,257[a]	$256	$ 518	$ 774	3,263	115	260	3,118
1977	457	1,175	1,632	3,257	326	338	3,333[b]	250	640	890	3,118	180	255	3,043
1978	367	905	1,272	3,333	392	334	3,392	371	792	1,163	3,043	129	252	2,920
1979	389	1,223	1,612	3,392	127	367	3,152	409	1,194	1,603	2,920	345	261	3,004
1980	561	1,524	2,085	3,152	198	342	3,008	629	1,601	2,230	3,004	246	262	2,988
1981	688	2,008	2,696	3,008	266	323	2,951	862	2,700	3,562	2,988	162	259	2,891
1982	727	1,919	2,646	2,951	314	296	2,969	939	1,851	2,790	2,891	198	257	2,832
1983	594	1,595	2,189	2,969	359	290	3,038[c]	758	1,332	2,090	2,832	240	261	2,811

[a]Reduced by 330 million bbls expropriated by Ecuador.
[b]Includes 88 million bbls acquired from Kewanee Industries, Inc.
[c]J. S. Herold estimates that 725 million bbls in West Africa are not recoverable because of expropriation, which reduces the recoverable reserves to 2,313 million bbls.

EXHIBIT 4
Results of Proxy Vote on Reincorporation Proposal

	Voting by Shares (millions)			
	For	Against	Abstain[a]	Subtotal
Individuals	71.1	9.2	12.0	92.3
Gulf Investors' Group	—	21.7	—	21.7
Institutions	16.0	23.2	12.1	51.3
Total	87.1	54.1	24.1	165.3
	(52.7%)	(32.7%)	(14.6%)	(100%)
	Percentage Voting by Category			
	For	Against	Abstain[a]	Subtotal
Individuals	77%	10%	13%	100%
Gulf Investors' Group	—	100	—	100
Institutions	31	45	24	100

[a]An abstention is essentially a vote against the proposal.

EXHIBIT 5
Trading Prices and Volumes, Gulf and Socal, 1983–1984

	Gulf		Socal	
	Price	Volume[a]	Price	Volume[a]
Aug. 5, 1983	$37⅜	16,633	$35⅝	21,473
Aug. 12	39	23,955		
Aug. 19	42⅝	49,186		
Aug. 26	41½	13,737		
Sept. 2	41½	8,942	37¼	11,452
Sept. 9	41½	23,020		
Sept. 16	41½	26,515		
Sept. 23	44½	31,475		
Sept. 30	42⅛	14,590		
Oct. 7	44⅛	39,708	35⅜	17,384
Oct. 14	47	71,629		
Oct. 21	46½	91,278		
Oct. 28	47½	19,415		
Nov. 4	44½	39,761	35⅜	18,269
Nov. 11	45⅛	26,660		
Nov. 18	42¼	56,685		
Nov. 25	43¾	43,358		
Dec. 2	45⅛	65,168	34⅛	14,356
Dec. 9	43	15,568		
Dec. 16	42¾	13,879		
Dec. 23	42⅝	5,210		
Dec. 30	43⅛	10,301		
Jan. 6, 1984	46⅝	34,790	34⅞	9,959
Jan. 13	49¼	51,756	35⅝	15,098
Jan. 20	47	23,003	35⅞	16,351
Jan. 27	53⅛	39,693	35½	15,687
Feb. 3	55½	62,309	36½	16,680
Feb. 10	57	48,409	33⅞	19,866
Feb. 17	54	70,678	35⅞	13,798
Feb. 24	62⅝	96,862	36⅝	12,775
Mar. 2	69½	175,126	35¾	20,691
Mar. 9	65⅛	153,597	34½	23,149

[a]Total volume for week in hundreds of shares. All dates shown are Fridays.

EXHIBIT 6 Selected Market Prices, 1976–1983

	S&P 500[a]	Oil Price per Composite Bbl[b]	Consumer Price Index	Avg. Stock Price, Seven Majors[c]	Gulf		Socal	
					Closing Price	Dividend/ Share	Closing Price	Dividend/ Share
1976	107.46	$ 5.76	170.5	$56.21	$29	$1.73	$21	$1.06
1977	95.10	7.22	181.5	45.92	27	1.83	19	1.18
1978	96.73	8.35	195.4	43.20	24	1.90	23	1.28
1979	105.76	10.63	217.4	51.89	35	2.06	28	1.45
1980	136.34	16.92	246.8	70.00	44	2.37	50	1.80
1981	122.74	22.88	272.4	51.55	35	2.65	43	2.20
1982	138.34	22.21	289.1	44.48	30	2.80	32	2.40
1983	164.90	22.42	298.4	53.03	43	2.85	35	2.40

[a]End of year.
[b]Composite amounts represent crude oil, natural gas liquids, and natural gas on a per barrel basis. Natural gas volumes are converted to crude oil equivalent barrels using conversion ratio of 5.7 thousand cubic feet per barrel.
[c]Exxon, Gulf, Mobil, Shell, Standard Oil California, Standard Oil Indiana, and Texaco.

EXHIBIT 7 Comparison of Gulf with Industry (Seven Major Producers), 1972–1982

	Production[a]		Earnings/ Share[b]	Return on Equity		Return on Assets	
	Oil	Gas		Gulf	Industry	Gulf	Industry
1972	5.3%	4.4%	49%	10%	14%	4.8%	6.0%
1973	5.0	4.0	56	13	15	8.0	8.5
1974	4.8	3.7	56	14	16	8.5	9.0
1975	4.6	3.6	52	10	12	5.6	6.5
1976	4.4	3.4	54	12	14	6.1	7.0
1977	4.3	3.5	48	11	14	5.3	6.0
1978	4.0	3.6	49	11	14	5.3	6.0
1979	3.9	3.5	44	16	21	7.7	9.0
1980	3.6	3.3	39	15	24	7.5	9.0
1981	3.2	3.1	38	13	20	6.0	8.0
1982	3.0	2.8	40	9	11	4.4	5.5

Note: The seven major producers are Exxon, Gulf, Mobil, Shell, Standard Oil California, Standard Oil Indiana, and Texaco.
[a]Gulf's U.S. production as percent of U.S. production of seven majors.
[b]As percent of seven-company average.

EXHIBIT 8 Summary of Accounting Policies

Exploration and Development

The most significant accounting policy in the petroleum industry relates to the method of accounting for the exploration and development of oil and gas reserves. Gulf follows the "successful efforts" concept, which requires that all exploratory drilling and equipment costs be capitalized pending determination of whether the drilling is unsuccessful or successful; if unsuccessful, these costs are expensed. All other exploratory costs, including geological and geophysical costs, are charged against income as incurred. All development drilling and equipment costs are capitalized whether successful or unsuccessful.

Depreciation and depletion expenses for all capitalized costs of oil- and gas-producing properties are determined on a unit-of-production method as the reserves are produced.

Philip Morris Companies and Kraft, Inc.

John M. Richman, the chairman and chief executive officer of Kraft, Inc., concluded his October 23, 1988, letter to shareholders as follows:

> We deeply regret the dislocation and hardships that the [restructuring] plan we contemplate will cause, and we will seek to ameliorate these hardships as much as possible. We know that our shareholders, employees, customers, suppliers and communities recognize that today's situation is not of our making. Rather it is the product of current era investment policies and financial attitudes that favor short-term financial gratification over steady, long-term growth and the need to provide a sound economy for future generations.
>
> It will take several years, but with the history and traditions of Kraft and the dedication of Kraft people, we are confident that we will rebuild Kraft to the leading position it occupies today.

The letter announced a radical restructuring of Kraft in response to a hostile tender offer by Philip Morris Companies: $90 per share in cash for all of Kraft's outstanding common stock. The offer had been announced just five days earlier, on October 18, 1988.

Kraft, Inc.

In 1987, Kraft was known for such brand names as Miracle Whip, Seven Seas, and Kraft salad dressings; Kraft mayonnaise; Velveeta cheese; Parkay and Chiffon margarines; Lender's Bagels; and Breyers ice cream. Net sales from continuing operations were $9.9 billion in 1987, an increase of 27% over 1986. Net income from continuing operations rose 11%, to $435 million. Exhibit 1 presents operating and stockholder information for Kraft from 1982 through 1987. Exhibit 2 presents balance sheet information for 1986 and 1987.

Kraft's strategy was focused on food. Its 1987 annual report stated:

> The food industry offers such diverse and rewarding opportunities that we see no purpose in running the risk of diluting our efforts or our focus with other lines of business.

This all-food strategy was in sharp contrast to its earlier diversification program. Most of the diversification occurred when Mr. Richman engineered the September 1980 merger between Kraft and Dart Industries, a $2.4 billion consumer products manufacturer. Mr. Richman, who had been promoted to chairman and CEO less than 1 year before the merger noted that the merger brought "diversification in one fell swoop to Kraft." Dart's products included Tupperware containers, Duracell batteries, and West Bend appliances. The merger was accomplished by exchanging one share of the merged company, Dart & Kraft, for each outstanding share of the two preexisting companies. Dart & Kraft was the twenty-seventh-largest company in the United States at the time of the merger. Six months later, in March 1981, Dart & Kraft acquired Hobart Corporation, the manufacturer of KitchenAid and other food related equipment, for $460 million.

Copyright © 1989 by the President and Fellows of Harvard College. Harvard Business School case 289-045.

Mr. Richman reversed direction and began pursuing the all-food strategy in 1986. Kraft spun off most of its nonfood businesses acquired in the Dart & Kraft merger into Premark International, Inc., on October 31, 1986. Each shareholder of Dart & Kraft received one share of Kraft common stock and a quarter share of Premark. Kraft, with sales of about $9.9 billion after the spin-off, retained its food businesses and Duracell batteries. Premark's share of Dart & Kraft included Tupperware and Hobart food service equipment, with combined sales of $1.8 billion.[1]

Kraft sold its last nonfood asset, Duracell, to Kohlberg, Kravis, Roberts & Co., a leveraged buyout firm, for $1.8 billion in June 1988. According to Kraft's 1987 annual report, the proceeds of the sale were to be used to repurchase shares and to repay debt obligations. In October 1987, Kraft authorized the repurchase of 10 million shares, and 6 million were repurchased under the authorization by year-end.

In 1987, Kraft was organized into three business segments: U.S. Consumer Food, U.S. Commercial Food, and International Food. In 1987, U.S. Consumer Food had sales of $4.5 billion and an operating profit of $593 million. U.S. Commercial Food, which included Kraft Foodservice, the second-largest U.S. food service distributor, had sales of $3 billion and an operating profit of $86.4 million. International Food had sales of $2.3 billion and an operating profit of $229.8 million. Exhibit 3 presents a financial summary of Kraft by business segment.

The Philip Morris $90-per-Share Tender Offer

On the evening of October 18, 1988, Philip Morris offered to purchase all Kraft common stock at $90 per share in cash. The offer represented a 50% premium over the $60.125 closing price on October 18. At $11 billion in total value the bid, if successful, would have been the second-largest acquisition ever completed, exceeded only by Chevron Corporation's $13.3 billion acquisition of Gulf Oil Corporation in 1984.[2]

Most Philip Morris sales and profits came from its Marlboro, Benson & Hedges, and Virginia Slims cigarettes. The company's tobacco sales increased by 15%, to $14.6 billion, in 1987. Philip Morris increased its domestic share of the cigarette market to 38% in 1987, from 37% in 1986, and 1987 operating profits were $3.3 billion. Nevertheless, consumption of cigarettes in the United States had been declining from its 1981 peak of 640 billion cigarettes. Estimated U.S. consumption for 1988 was 563 billion cigarettes. Increases in exports offset the decline in U.S. consumption, as new markets were entered, especially Japan and Taiwan. Overall, cigarette exports were predicted to increase by 15%, to 115 billion cigarettes in 1988.

Philip Morris had been pursuing a strategy of diversifying out of the tobacco business since 1969, when it acquired 53% of the Miller Brewing Company's common shares, the remainder of which it acquired in 1970. With brands like Miller, Lite, and Matilda Bay Wine Coolers, the brewing division generated sales of $3.1 billion in 1987. Philip Morris also purchased Seven-Up Company in May 1978 for $520 million. Its largest food acquisition by far was General Foods, which Philip Morris purchased in 1985 for $5.6 billion. Like Kraft, General Foods was based on brand-name products such as Maxwell House coffee, Birds Eye frozen foods, Jell-O, Oscar Mayer meats, Ronzoni pasta, and Post cereals. It had 1987 sales of $10 billion.

[1]KitchenAid had been sold in February 1986 for $150 million.

[2]Kraft had 119,285,155 shares outstanding and outstanding employee stock options on 2,396,808 shares. The total number of Kraft shares purchased under the offer was therefore 121,681,963.

Philip Morris's acquisitions had mixed results. See Exhibit 4 for operating and stockholder information from 1982 through 1987. Exhibit 5 presents balance sheet information for 1986 and 1987. Exhibit 6 presents the consolidated changes in financial position, and Exhibit 7 reports line-of-business information.

Philip Morris sold its Seven-Up operations in 1986 for about book value after a $50 million write-off in 1985. General Foods' operating profit declined from $624 million in 1986 to $605 million in 1987. The 1987 operating profit represented a 9.3% return on Philip Morris's $6.5 billion investment in the food industry, including additional postacquisition investments of $868 million. Speculation was that Philip Morris might use Kraft's management team to revitalize General Foods, which had been without a chief executive officer since July 1988, when Philip L. Smith left to become chairman of Pillsbury.[3] Smith, a 22-year veteran of General Foods, had been president and chief operating officer before its merger with Philip Morris.

The acquisition of Kraft would have made Philip Morris the world's largest food company, and it would have been a major step in the firm's strategy of reducing its dependence on tobacco and moving into the food business. As Hamish Maxwell, the chairman and CEO of Philip Morris, said in his October 21, 1988, letter to John Richman:

> Our goal is to have Kraft combine with Philip Morris to create the leading international food company. . . . Our intention is to keep Kraft's present businesses intact and for the company to be managed by Kraft executives, using your present headquarters and facilities.

Exhibit 8 contains excerpts from the letters between the two companies throughout the takeover contest.

Philip Morris proposed to finance the acquisition with $1.5 billion in excess cash and its available bank credit lines of up to $12 billion.

Kraft's Response

On October 23, 1988, Kraft's board of directors rejected the Philip Morris bid:

> We strongly believe the $90 takeover bid . . . undervalues Kraft, for these important reasons: first, after careful analysis, our investment banker, Goldman, Sachs & Co., has advised us that the bid is inadequate; and second, our stock has been trading above the $90 offer, a clear signal that investors see the bid as low.

Kraft's response occurred when the food industry was undergoing a major restructuring and revaluation. Grand Metropolitan PLC began a hostile tender offer for Pillsbury on October 4, 1988. Grand Met was a diversified British company that brewed and distributed beer, ale, and lager; produced and distributed alcoholic beverages; and owned and operated pubs and restaurants. Pillsbury was a diversified food and restaurant company, with popular brands such as Pillsbury Doughboy bakery items, Green Giant vegetables, and Häagen-Dazs ice cream in its food business, and Burger King in its restaurant group. Like Kraft, Pillsbury had just completed a major restructuring that focused the company on the food business. The $5.2 billion Grand Met bid was a 53% premium over the previous market price—about 25 times Pillsbury's net earnings and about four times the book value of common equity.[4] Pillsbury opposed the bid, and its outcome was uncertain.

[3]The combination also would have increased leverage with grocery stores and advertisers. In 1987, Philip Morris spent $1.5 billion and Kraft $400 million on advertising.

[4]Pillsbury's 1988 net earnings per share were $2.45, excluding unusual items, and $.81, including unusual items. The difference was due to a restructuring charge of $1.64 per share. Its 1987 net earnings per share were $2.24, excluding unusual items, and $2.10, including unusual items.

The developments at RJR Nabisco were more startling. Management, in partnership with the investment banking firm of Shearson Lehman Hutton, had proposed a $17 billion leveraged buyout of RJR Nabisco on October 20, 1988. Like Philip Morris, RJR Nabisco was a tobacco and food company, with brand names such as Winston and Salem cigarettes, Oreo cookies, Ritz crackers, Planters nuts, LifeSavers candies, Royal gelatin, and Del Monte fruit and vegetables. At $75 per share, the buyout offer was a 34% premium over the previous market price of RJR Nabisco, $55.875. The $75 offer was about 16 times RJR Nabisco's 1987 earnings per share of $4.70 and about three times the book value of common equity. Analysts speculated that a higher offer for RJR Nabisco was likely: its stock closed above the offer price.

Taken together, the Philip Morris bid for Kraft, Grand Metropolitan's bid for Pillsbury, and the RJR Nabisco leveraged buyout attempt by its management involved about $34 billion—an amount unprecedented in the history of the industry. Exhibit 9 examines this history, with statistics on mergers and acquisitions for food and beverage firms as well as a listing of transactions of more than $1 billion. Exhibit 10 contains historical stock prices and return-on-equity information for the food and tobacco industries.

Kraft proposed a restructuring plan as an alternative to the Philip Morris tender offer. For each share of common stock, shareholders would receive a cash dividend of $84 and a high-yield debt valued at $14, and they would retain their now highly leveraged equity interest. Kraft valued the postrestructuring stock at $12 per share and the total restructuring package at $110 per share.

Under the plan Kraft would sell some businesses for cash proceeds of about $2.1 billion after taxes. The businesses to be sold represented 45% of estimated 1988 revenues and 19% of estimated 1988 operating profits. Kraft would also reduce operating expenses. It would finance the $10.2 billion in dividend payments to shareholders with $6.8 billion in bank borrowings at a 12% annual interest rate and the $3 billion in debt with rates ranging from 12.5% to 14.75%. The $2.1 billion from asset sales would be used to pay down the bank debt.

The company planned to retain $904 million of existing debt at an average annual interest rate of 8.65%.

The debt received by shareholders would accrue interest at a 15.25% annual rate (paid semiannually), with no cash payments in the first 5 years. Interest would be paid in cash at the 15.25% semiannual rate after the fifth year. Exhibit 11 presents pre-bid sales and profit forecasts for Kraft through 1989. Exhibit 12 presents earnings and cash flow forecasts for the restructuring plan proposed by Kraft's management.

The Stock Market Response

The price of Kraft common stock rose $10 per share, to $102, in response to the restructuring announcement. Philip Morris criticized the restructuring plan and reiterated its offer to negotiate with Kraft, which responded that "if Philip Morris or another company truly wishes to negotiate with Kraft, a simple phone call proposing a price of more than $110 is all that is necessary." Philip Morris did not increase its bid.

Uncertainty about the market value of food assets grew as Kohlberg, Kravis, Roberts entered the bidding for RJR Nabisco, with a $20.6 billion offer on October 24, 1988.

On Thursday, October 27, Kraft's common stock closed at $94.50. On Friday, October 28, Kraft's stock rose $2, closing at $96.50. Exhibit 13 contains the closing stock prices for Kraft and Philip Morris throughout the takeover contest.

EXHIBIT 1

Condensed Operating and Stockholder Information for Kraft, 1982–1987 (millions of dollars except per share data)

Sources: Company reports and casewriter's estimates.

	1982	1983	1984	1985	1986	1987
Revenues	$7,041	$6,660	$6,831	$7,065	$7,780	$9,876
Cost of goods sold[a]	5,350	4,928	4,969	4,963	5,393	6,912
Depreciation	103	80	74	74	79	103
Delivery, sales, and administrative expenses	1,183	1,157	1,238	1,391	1,620	2,068
Interest, net	24	(8)	22	26	31	91
Other income (expense)[b]	(38)	23	43	37	37	86
Income from continuing operations before taxes	343	526	571	648	694	788
Income taxes	164	225	252	286	300	353
Income from continuing operations	179	301	319	362	394	435
Income from discontinued operations[c]	171	134	137	104	19	54
Net income	$ 350	$ 435	$ 456	$ 466	$ 413	$ 489
Earnings per share	$ 2.13	$ 2.65	$ 3.17	$ 3.24	$ 3.06	$ 3.73
Dividends per share	1.20	1.28	1.38	1.52	1.68	1.84
Closing stock price[d, e]	22.83	22.21	28.04	43.38	49.38	48.25
Price-earnings ratio[e]	11	8	9	13	16	13
Number of shares (millions)[e]	164	164	144	144	135	131
Beta[f]	.72	.55	.69	1.12	1.18	.74

[a]Cost of goods sold does not include annual depreciation.
[b]Includes the cumulative effect of a change in method of accounting for income taxes of $45 million in 1987 and a nonoperating item of –$91 million in 1982.
[c]Discontinued operations include Duracell, the sale of which was announced in 1987, and the business of Premark International, which was spun off on October 31, 1986. Also included in discontinued operations is a $41 million gain on the sale of KitchenAid in 1986.
[d]Adjusted for a 3-for-1 stock split in 1985.
[e]Year-end.
[f]Calculated by ordinary least-squares regression using daily stock price data.

EXHIBIT 2

Consolidated Balance Sheets for Kraft, 1986–1987 (millions of dollars)

Source: Company reports.

	1986	1987
Cash	$ 321.5	$ 189.0
Accounts receivable	637.6	763.6
Inventories	1,061.1	1,283.4
Investments and long-term receivables	236.2	178.3
Prepaid and deferred items	127.5	161.5
Property, plant, equipment, net	1,087.7	1,424.2
Intangibles	419.0	888.3
Net assets of discontinued operations	600.7	598.4
Total assets	$4,491.3	$5,486.7
Accounts payable	$ 492.1	$ 544.8
Short-term borrowings	596.4	645.9
Accrued compensation	148.9	151.2
Accrued advertising and promotions	113.7	132.8
Other accrued liabilities	188.4	245.4
Accrued income taxes	335.3	399.3
Current portion of long-term debt	108.5	37.2
Current liabilities	1,983.3	2,156.6
Long-term debt	237.7	895.3
Deferred income taxes	286.4	282.7
Other liabilities	185.9	253.7
Total liabilities	2,693.3	3,588.3
Shareholders' equity	2,798.0	1,898.4
Total liabilities and net worth	$4,491.3	$5,486.7

EXHIBIT 3 **Financial Summary for Kraft by Business Segment, 1983–1987 (millions of dollars)**

Source: Company reports.

	1983	1984	1985	1986	1987
U.S. Consumer Food[a]					
Sales	$3,718.0	$3,781.2	$3,911.3	$4,016.1	$4,518.9
Operating profit	388.1	446.0	527.3	545.9	593.3
Identifiable assets	1,450.9	1,615.4	1,309.1	1,807.6	2,509.3
Depreciation	54.0	50.0	37.6	36.6	47.4
Capital expenditures	58.0	71.7	63.1	93.7	151.2
Operating profits/Identifiable assets	26.75%	27.61%	40.28%	30.20%	23.64%
U.S. Commercial Food					
Sales	$1,172.7	$1,349.3	$1,421.0	$1,755.8	$3,022.0
Operating profit	na	na	61.7	79.5	86.4
Identifiable assets	na	na	291.4	558.9	914.6
Depreciation	na	na	7.6	8.0	15.3
Capital expenditures	na	na	5.2	17.6	33.7
Operating profits/Identifiable assets	na	na	21.17%	14.22%	9.45%
International Food					
Sales	$1,769.7	$1,707.2	$1,733.0	$2,007.7	$2,334.8
Operating profit	165.4	169.4	145.9	182.8	229.8
Identifiable assets	680.9	701.1	793.7	861.1	1,000.5
Depreciation	19.2	18.9	20.6	27.5	34.0
Capital expenditures	37.3	36.2	39.2	41.7	48.3
Operating profits/Identifiable assets	24.29%	24.16%	18.38%	21.23%	22.97%
Direct Selling[b]					
Sales	$ 825.1	$ 776.9	—	—	—
Operating profit	189.3	138.8	—	—	—
Identifiable assets	462.7	488.0	—	—	—
Depreciation	36.0	28.9	—	—	—
Capital expenditures	40.7	62.8	—	—	—
Operating profits/Identifiable assets	40.91%	28.44%	—	—	—
Consumer Products[c]					
Sales	$1,181.0	$1,244.8	$ 962.5	—	—
Operating profit	104.7	118.4	66.9	—	—
Identifiable assets	828.0	958.8	849.6	—	—
Depreciation	26.9	42.9	34.2	—	—
Capital expenditures	43.0	67.9	47.4	—	—
Operating profits/Identifiable assets	12.64%	12.35%	7.87%	—	—
Commercial Products[d]					
Sales	$1,047.5	$ 899.3	—	—	—
Operating profit	104.8	101.0	—	—	—
Identifiable assets	727.6	556.9	—	—	—
Depreciation	30.4	23.9	—	—	—
Capital expenditures	25.4	28.1	—	—	—
Operating profits/Identifiable assets	14.40%	18.14%	—	—	—

na = not available.

[a]Figures for 1983 and 1984 include both U.S. consumer foods and U.S. commercial foods.

[b]Includes Tupperware, which was spun off to Premark International in 1988.

[c]Includes Duracell, West Bend, Health Care, and KitchenAid. All assets except Duracell were sold or spun off to Premark International in 1986.

[d]Includes Hobart, which was spun off to Premark International in 1986.

EXHIBIT 4
Condensed Operating and Stockholder Information for Philip Morris, 1982–1987 (millions of dollars except per share data)

Sources: Company reports and casewriter's estimates.

	1982	1983	1984	1985[c]	1986	1987
Revenues	$11,586	$12,976	$13,814	$15,964	$25,409	$27,695
Cost of goods sold[a]	5,046	5,028	5,170	5,926	10,495	10,664
Excise taxes	2,615	3,510	3,676	3,815	4,728	5,416
Depreciation and amortization	281	327	375	424	655	704
Selling, administrative, and research expenses[b]	2,125	2,377	2,467	3,244	6,061	7,004
Equity in net earnings of unconsolidated subsidiaries	71	83	54	82	111	126
Interest	246	230	273	308	770	685
Other expense	44	—	300	—	—	—
Income before taxes	1,300	1,587	1,607	2,329	2,811	3,348
Income taxes	518	681	718	1,074	1,333	1,506
Net income	$ 782	$ 906	$ 889	$ 1,255	$ 1,478	$ 1,842
Earnings per share	$ 3.11	$ 3.58	$ 3.62	$ 5.24	$ 6.20	$ 7.75
Dividends per share	1.20	1.45	1.70	2.00	2.48	3.15
Closing stock price[d]	30	35.875	40.375	44.125	71.875	85.375
Price-earnings ratio[d]	9	10	11	8	11	11
Number of shares (millions)[d]	252	250	243	239	238	237
Beta[e]	1.04	.77	.94	.88	1.24	.88

[a]Cost of goods sold does not include annual depreciation.
[b]Selling, administrative, and research cost includes corporate expenses.
[c]General Foods was acquired on November 1, 1985.
[d]Year-end.
[e]Calculated by ordinary least-squares regression using daily stock price data.

EXHIBIT 5
Consolidated Balance Sheets for Philip Morris, 1986–1987 (millions of dollars)

Source: Company reports.

	1986	1987
Cash	$ 73	$ 189
Receivables	1,878	2,083
Inventories	3,836	4,154
Other current assets	127	146
Property, plant, equipment, net	6,237	6,582
Investments in unconsolidated subsidiaries and affiliates	1,067	1,244
Goodwill and other intangibles	3,988	4,052
Other assets	436	695
Total assets	$17,642	$19,145
Notes payable	$ 864	$ 691
Accounts payable	813	803
Current portion of long-term debt	103	465
Accrued liabilities	1,967	2,277
Income taxes payable	557	727
Dividends payable	178	213
Current liabilities	4,482	5,176
Long-term debt	5,945	5,222
Deferred income taxes	994	1,288
Other liabilities	566	636
Total liabilities	11,987	12,322
Stockholders' equity	5,655	6,823
Total liabilities and net worth	$17,642	$19,145

EXHIBIT 6
Consolidated Statements of Changes in Financial Position for Philip Morris, 1985–1987 (millions of dollars)

Source: Company reports.

	1985	1986	1987
Funds Provided by			
Net earnings	$ 1,255	$ 1,478	$ 1,842
Depreciation and amortization	424	655	704
Deferred income taxes	159	133	338
Equity in undistributed net earnings of unconsolidated subsidiaries and affiliates	(63)	(52)	(95)
Total funds from operations	1,775	2,214	2,789
Increase in accrued liabilities and other payments	1,467	226	505
Working capital from sales of operations	169	487	20
Currency translation adjustments affecting working capital	18	77	139
Other, net	211	210	—
Total funds provided	$ 3,640	$ 3,214	$ 3,453
Funds Used for			
Increase (decrease) in			
Cash and receivables	$ 1,005	$ (2)	$ 321
Inventories	1,174	9	318
Other current assets	74	14	19
Capital expenditures	347	678	718
Dividends declared	479	590	749
Increase in property, plant, and equipment from income tax election	—	508	—
Investment in General Foods Corp. exclusive of $718 million working capital acquired	4,864	—	—
Other, net	—	—	301
Total funds used	$ 7,943	$ 1,797	$ 2,426
Net funds provided (used)	$(4,303)	$ 1,417	$ 1,027
Financing Activities			
Increase in current notes payable	$ 149	$ 289	$ 189
Long-term debt financing	4,666	1,788	492
Reduction of long-term debt	(326)	(3,385)	(1,534)
Purchase of treasury stock	(216)	(140)	(200)
Issuance of shares	30	31	26
Funds (used for) provided from financing activities	$ 4,303	$(1,417)	$(1,027)
Increase (decrease) in working capital	$ 637	$ (494)	$ (36)
Working capital (year-end)	1,926	1,432	1,396

EXHIBIT 7 Financial Summary for Philip Morris by Business Segment, 1982–1987 (millions of dollars)

Source: Company reports.

	1982	1983	1984	1985	1986	1987
Tobacco						
Sales	$7,821.8	$9,094.9	$9,802.0	$10,539.0	$12,691.0	$14,644.0
Operating profit	1,475.7	1,647.0	2,141.0	2,441.0	2,827.0	3,273.0
Identifiable assets	5,070.7	5,114.3	5,149.0	5,622.0	5,808.0	6,467.0
Depreciation	97.7	124.7	151.0	166.0	200.0	214.0
Capital expenditures	498.0	319.9	163.0	151.0	191.0	256.0
Operating profit/ Identifiable assets	29.10%	32.20%	41.58%	43.42%	48.67%	50.61%
Food Products						
Sales	—	—	—	$ 1,632.0	$ 9,664.0	$ 9,946.0
Operating profit	—	—	—	95.0	624.0	605.0
Identifiable assets	—	—	—	7,974.0	8,629.0	9,129.0
Depreciation	—	—	—	29.0	167.0	201.0
Capital expenditures	—	—	—	71.0	395.0	402.0
Operating profit/ Identifiable assets	—	—	—	1.19%	7.23%	6.63%
Beer						
Sales	$2,935.5	$2,935.5	$2,940.0	$ 2,925.0	$ 3,054.0	$ 3,105.0
Operating profit	159.0	227.1	116.0	136.0	154.0	170.0
Identifiable assets	2,113.7	2,138.9	1,892.0	1,779.0	1,736.0	1,680.0
Depreciation	122.3	130.5	144.0	134.0	136.0	137.0
Capital expenditures	286.3	174.6	94.0	87.0	80.0	57.0
Operating profit/ Identifiable assets	7.52%	10.62%	6.13%	7.64%	8.87%	10.12%
Other[a]						
Sales	$ 822.9	$ 945.5	$1,072.0	$ 868.0	—	—
Operating profit (loss)	(2.4)	(10.9)	23.0	14.0	$ (9.0)	$ 19.0
Identifiable assets	979.4	1,007.3	1,018.0	643.0	—	—
Depreciation	—	—	—	—	—	—
Capital expenditures	—	—	—	—	—	—
Operating profit/ Identifiable assets	–.25%	–1.08%	2.26%	2.18%	—	—

[a]Includes the Seven-Up Company, which was sold in 1986.

EXHIBIT 8 Correspondence during Takeover Bid between Kraft and Philip Morris, October 1988

October 20, 1988

Mr. Hamish Maxwell
Chairman and Chief Executive Officer
Philip Morris Companies Inc.
120 Park Avenue
New York, NY 10017

Dear Hamish:

In addition to your letter requesting "negotiations" following your commencing, on Monday, a tender offer without talking to me beforehand, your lawyers and investment bankers have been barraging our advisers with similar requests. You did not see fit to discuss your takeover attempt when we were together at the Grocery Manufacturers of America meeting last Wednesday and Thursday, nor did you see fit to tell me that you were planning on filing a bizarre and baseless law suit against me and our Board of Directors on Monday.

You must have been planning your takeover bid for a long time. We intend to take our time and study the situation very carefully. We have a fiduciary duty to our shareholders and an obligation to our employees, customers, suppliers, and communities to do so. Following our study, the Board of Directors will consider the situation and determine Kraft's response. If at that time there is a purpose to be served by our meeting, we will so advise you.

Sincerely,
John M. Richman
Chairman and Chief Executive Officer
Kraft, Inc.

October 21, 1988

Mr. John M. Richman
Chairman and Chief Executive Officer
Kraft, Inc.
Kraft Court
Glenview, IL 60025

Dear John:

I understand and sympathize with your reaction to the events of this week. I would have preferred to discuss our offer with you prior to taking the actions we commenced. However, in the current legal environment in which we live, I accepted the advice to proceed as we did as a business decision. Our actions were designed to minimize uncertainties and delays in addressing the main issue—the economic benefits and other factors favoring the merger of Kraft with Philip Morris.

I hope you understand that any discussion of our interest in Kraft would have been premature and inappropriate when we saw each other last week at the Grocery Manufacturers of America meeting. At that time we had made no final decision to proceed with an offer and our Board had not yet approved our actions. In any event, I am hopeful you and we can now move forward in a positive and constructive manner.

I quite appreciate your need to study our offer carefully before responding to it. We have, however, seen press reports that Kraft may consider other possibilities including highly leveraged transactions that could encumber the company, operationally and financially, and which also might lead to the dismemberment of Kraft. From what I know of you and some public statements you have made, I feel sure that this is not the route you would prefer to take.

As we have said, our goal is to have Kraft combine with Philip Morris to create the leading international food company. I repeat that our intention is to keep Kraft's present businesses intact and for the company to be managed by Kraft executives, using your present headquarters and facilities.

I believe it to be in the best interests of your shareholders and other constituencies that we avoid a prolonged struggle that could disrupt Kraft's business without adding to the value that would be realized by your shareholders.

(continued)

EXHIBIT 8 *(Continued)*

I also believe that a meeting between us could only be helpful to you in understanding our purposes and positive thoughts concerning a combination of our two companies. . . . I want to emphasize that we are prepared to discuss all aspects of our offer.

I would be available to meet with you in Chicago at any time on short notice. I can be reached through my office if, as I hope, you see the benefits of such a meeting.

Yours sincerely,
HAMISH MAXWELL
Chairman and Chief Executive Officer
Philip Morris Companies Inc.

October 23, 1988

To: Shareholders of Kraft, Inc.

Dear Shareholder:

Kraft has an outstanding record of profitability and growth. It is a great company with great traditions, great brands, a great future, and great people who have devoted their lives to making your company what it is today.

Kraft's record of succession—an increase in shareholder value, without regard to recent events, at a compound annual rate of more than 20% over the past 5 years—has been based on a strategy of balancing significant short-term returns and continued investment for long-term growth. This strategy has been working, but—frustratingly—the stock market has long been undervaluing companies which, like Kraft, sacrifice short-term profit in order to invest in long-term growth.

Last Monday, Philip Morris Companies, seeking to take advantage of this undervaluation, announced an unsolicited tender offer for Kraft at $90 per share.

We strongly believe the $90 takeover bid also undervalues Kraft, for these important reasons: first, after careful analysis, our investment banker, Goldman, Sachs & Co., has advised us that the bid is inadequate; and second, our stock has been trading above the $90 offer, a clear signal that investors see the bid as low.

Your Board of Directors has unanimously rejected the offer, and we strongly recommend that you do not tender your Kraft shares to Philip Morris.

At the same time, both your Board and company management recognize that, as a practical matter, the Philip Morris bid makes it impossible for us to go back to the situation that existed prior to the bid. Under the circumstances, your Board believes that we should take action to maximize shareholder value rather than accept an inadequate offer. Together with Goldman, Sachs we are developing a potential recapitalization plan that we believe will have a value of significantly more than $90 per share.

The plan we are working on is intended to result in a total value estimated to be in excess of $110 per share, with a distribution in cash and securities totaling approximately $98 per share and the retention of your common stock interest, the price of which will be adjusted by the market to reflect the cash and securities distribution. Under the plan, you will receive a cash distribution and new securities, and retain your Kraft common stock. Most shareholders will have less tax to pay as a result of the distribution than if Kraft were to be acquired by Philip Morris (or anyone else) at a price that is equal to the value of the restructuring plan.

Your Board believes that this plan will enable you as a shareholder to realize present value for your shares and also continue to participate in the future of Kraft, including some exciting new product lines we have been developing.

The plan will involve the sale of some of our businesses, bank borrowings of more than $6.8 billion, and the sale of $3.0 billion of debt. We have already begun to implement some of these transactions. Goldman, Sachs has advised us that it is highly confident with respect to the placement of the debt under current market conditions. We will retain our core businesses, together with the key brands which have provided Kraft's historic strength and currently account for approximately 80% of its profitability.

(continued)

EXHIBIT 8 (*Continued*)

Because the restructured Kraft will have more than $12.4 billion in debt and require herculean efforts by our employees, the plan will replicate the structure currently in use in sponsored leveraged buyouts by providing significant equity incentives for employees in the form of stock options and an employee stock ownership plan. This very important link between employee compensation and company performance will, we believe, ensure the enormous efforts required to make the recapitalization a complete success.

We expect that the plan will be fully developed and our Board will be able to approve it in the very near future, at which time we will announce the details. Because the plan involves very significant restructuring of our businesses and financial structure, the Board also believes you should have the opportunity to vote upon it at a special meeting of shareholders.

For your further information, on Friday, October 21, there was a series of communications with Philip Morris. Philip Morris renewed their request for immediate negotiation, stating that all aspects of their offer, including price, are open for discussion. Philip Morris said that there would be real value to them if they could conclude the agreement with us over the weekend and asked for a meeting on Saturday. We responded that if Philip Morris were prepared to offer a realistic price, we would meet on Saturday. We told Philip Morris that their $90 bid is substantially below our valuation and Goldman, Sachs's valuation and that there would be no purpose served by a meeting unless Philip Morris were prepared to start the negotiations from a price substantially greater than $90. We asked Philip Morris to tell us where they stood and told Philip Morris that if they were in the range of value that we and Goldman, Sachs believe is obtainable, we would meet with them on Saturday. Philip Morris replied that they completely disagree with our opinion of their $90 price, that they believe $90 represents full value, and they would not tell us what price they are prepared to offer. Given this attitude on the part of Philip Morris, it was clear that a meeting would not have served any purpose of Kraft and its shareholders, and we so advised Philip Morris. We also advised Philip Morris that we were not foreclosing negotiations and that if they were to offer a price that reflects the full value of Kraft, we would negotiate with them.

Since we believe that the restructuring plan will create greater shareholder value and opportunity than the Philip Morris bid or any other known alternative, it is our intention to proceed with the restructuring on an exclusive basis. However, if someone comes forward with a transaction that would be more desirable than the restructuring plan, we will negotiate and your Board will give full consideration to such a transaction.

We deeply regret the dislocation and hardships that the plan we contemplate will cause, and we will seek to ameliorate these hardships as much as possible. We know that our shareholders, employees, customers, suppliers, and communities recognize that today's situation is not of our making. Rather it is the product of current era investment policies and financial attitudes that favor short-term financial gratification over steady, long-term growth and the need to provide a sound economy for future generations.

It will take several years, but with the history and traditions of Kraft and the dedication of Kraft people, we are confident that we will rebuild Kraft to the leading position it occupies today.

On behalf of the Board of Directors,
JOHN M. RICHMAN
Chairman

October 24, 1988

Calvin J. Collier, Esq.
Senior Vice President and General Counsel
Kraft, Inc.
Kraft Court
Glenview, IL 60025

Dear Mr. Collier:

In light of the announcement yesterday of Kraft, Inc.'s proposed recapitalization plan, Philip Morris believes that Kraft is required to take all necessary steps to ensure that Philip Morris is given an opportunity to analyze fully Kraft's contemplated recapitalization transaction and any other proposed transaction for the sale of Kraft or any of its assets to a third party. . . .

(continued)

EXHIBIT 8 *(Continued)*

We have a number of questions that bear on the feasibility and value to Kraft's shareholders of the announced recapitalization plan. . . .

We request that Kraft immediately supply to us specific information concerning the details of Kraft's recapitalization plan, all information concerning Kraft which may assist us in evaluating the company, and any information supplied to other third parties with respect to the sale of the company or any parts of the company.

We also request that, consistent with the responsibilities of your Board of Directors to your shareholders, Kraft not enter into, or agree to enter into, any extraordinary transaction, including a recapitalization plan, a sale of assets or securities of Kraft, or a sale of the company, or take any steps to implement any of the foregoing, until Philip Morris is given a full and fair opportunity to develop its response, and that Kraft not take any action which may diminish the value of Kraft. To that end we are today filing a motion in the Federal District Court.

Philip Morris continues to believe that, if our companies work together, a transaction can be negotiated which will achieve maximum value for Kraft's shareholders speedily and without the extraordinary disruptions to Kraft's businesses which Kraft acknowledges would be inherent in the contemplated restructuring plan.

Sincerely,
Murray H. Bring
Senior Vice President and General Counsel
Philip Morris Companies Inc.

October 25, 1988

Mr. Hamish Maxwell
Chairman and Chief Executive Officer
Philip Morris Companies Inc.
120 Park Avenue
New York, NY 10017

Dear Hamish:

I have previously advised Philip Morris of Kraft's position on your tender offer. The letter your general counsel sent to our general counsel yesterday, and the papers your lawyer filed in court yesterday, indicate that Philip Morris does not understand what Kraft is doing—or more likely, Philip Morris is pretending not to understand in order to increase its pressure tactics. Obviously it is in your interest to try to pressure Kraft and the Kraft shareholders into a transaction that benefits you at their expense. Kraft will not permit this.

Let me again make clear Kraft's position.

Kraft was not "for sale" and is not "for sale." This is no "auction" of Kraft. Philip Morris made a unilateral tender offer for Kraft. The Kraft Board of Directors rejected your tender offer. Your price is too low. Kraft has a recapitalization plan that creates far greater value for the Kraft shareholders than your inadequate offer. Kraft is submitting the recapitalization plan to Kraft shareholders for their consideration. The recapitalization will take place only if our shareholders approve it. Kraft will not pressure its shareholders, nor will Kraft permit you to stampede them. The Kraft Board is not taking action to "entrench" itself. Just the opposite, it is proceeding expeditiously to provide Kraft shareholders with a choice between your inadequate $90 bid and a better than $110 recapitalization.

As frequently happens—witness the RJR Nabisco situation—new bidders appear and old bidders raise their bids. The Kraft Board recognizes that another company or Philip Morris may offer more than $110 per share to acquire Kraft. Accordingly, the Kraft Board said that Kraft would negotiate with that company, or you, and if it, or your company, has a better transaction than the recapitalization plan, Kraft will enter into that transaction.

In other words, if Philip Morris or another company truly wishes to negotiate with Kraft, a simple phone call proposing a price of more than $110 is all that is necessary.

Please give a copy of this letter to your general counsel as our answer to his letter, and ask him to give copies to your other lawyers and financial advisers, and instruct them to stop mischaracterizing our position.

Sincerely,
John M. Richman
Chairman and Chief Executive Officer
Kraft, Inc.

EXHIBIT 9 Mergers and Acquisitions in the Food Processing and Beverage Industries, 1981–1987

Source: W. T. Grimm and Co., *Mergerstat Review*, 1981–1987.

	Number and Dollar Value of Mergers in the Food and Beverage Industry	
	Number of Transactions	Amount Paid ($ billions)
1981	88	$ 4.55
1982	83	4.96
1983	85	2.71
1984	79	7.95
1985	105	12.86
1986	127	8.43
1987	97	7.75

Mergers in the Food and Beverage Industry over $1 Billion ($ millions)

Bidder	Target	Year	Target's Sales	Amount Paid	Premium Percent	Price-Earnings Ratio	Multiple to Book
Philip Morris	General Foods	1985	$9,022.4	$5,627.5	35.2%	18.7	3.5
RJ Reynolds	Nabisco Brands	1985	5,985.0	4,906.4	31.5	16.7	4.1
Nestlé S.A.	Carnation Co.	1984	3,370.0	2,885.4	9.9	14.4	2.7
Beatrice Foods	Esmark Inc.	1984	4,120.0	2,508.6	39.5	15.7	2.5
RJ Reynolds	Heublein, Inc.	1982	2,140.0	1,302.6	36.5	13.1	2.7
Bond Corporate Holdings Ltd.	G. Heileman Brewing Co.	1987	1,173.8	1,083.6	21.6	23.0	3.2

EXHIBIT 10
Stock Price Indexes and Returns on Equity, 1982–1987

	1982	1983	1984	1985	1986	1987
Stock price index (1981 = 100)						
Kraft	144.1	148.5	200.6	321.2	397.3	409.3
Philip Morris	128.8	161.2	190.0	218.3	368.7	453.0
RJR Nabisco	114.8	144.8	192.2	220.1	357.4	337.0
Pillsbury	133.0	202.1	256.4	365.4	413.5	440.8
Food index	132.9	161.1	186.9	297.6	387.4	398.8
Tobacco index	117.7	142.4	165.7	179.2	279.7	299.0
S&P 500 index	114.7	134.5	136.4	172.3	197.6	201.5
Return on equity (ROE)						
Kraft	12.6%	14.9%	17.6%	16.2%	23.0%	25.8%
Philip Morris	21.3	22.4	21.7	26.5	26.1	27.0
RJR Nabisco	20.8	17.1	22.3	20.8	20.0	22.8
Pillsbury	16.6	15.0	17.0	17.3	16.8	13.5
Food index	14.3	17.0	17.9	18.0	12.0	12.5
Tobacco index	19.0	18.2	19.4	21.6	20.0	20.3
S&P 500 index	10.9	11.7	13.1	11.0	10.5	11.8

EXHIBIT 11
Pre-Bid Sales and Profit Forecasts for Kraft, 1988–1989 (millions of dollars)

Source: Analysts' estimates.

	1987	Est. 1988	Est. 1989
Revenues	$9,876	$11,200	$12,500
Earnings before interest and taxes	834	950	1,050
Interest, net	91	95	108
Income from continuing operations before taxes	743	855	942
Income taxes	353	333	368
Accounting change	45	—	—
Income from continuing operations	435	522	574
Income from discontinued operations[a]	54	658	—
Net income	$ 489	$ 1,180	$ 574

[a]Duracell was sold to Kohlberg, Kravis, Roberts & Co. for $1.8 billion on June 24, 1988. Duracell's 1987 after-tax income was $54 million, and Kraft's 1988 gain on its sale was $658 million.

EXHIBIT 12 Projections for Kraft's Restructuring Plan, 1989–1998 (millions of dollars)

Sources: Kraft and casewriter's estimates.

	1989	1990	1991	1992	1993	1994	1995	1996	1997	1998
Sales	$ 6,515	$ 6,804	$7,125	$7,481	$7,855	$8,248	$8,660	$9,093	$9,548	$10,025
Earnings before interest and taxes	1,280	1,487	1,671	1,755	1,842	1,935	2,031	2,133	2,239	2,351
Interest	1,380	1,270	1,310	1,286	1,278	1,257	1,212	1,155	1,086	1,010
Taxes	(39)	89	148	192	231	278	336	401	473	550
Profit (loss) after taxes from continuing operations	(61)	128	213	277	333	400	483	577	680	791
Cash flow available for capital payments[a]	2,481[b]	496	636	630	742	334	411	500	597	728
Principal payments										
Preexisting debt	111	33	57	287	100	100	100	100	16	0
Bank debt	2,370	463	579	343	642	234	311	400	581	728
Year-end book values										
Preexisting debt	793	759	703	416	316	216	116	16	0	0
Bank debt	4,430	3,968	3,389	3,046	2,404	2,170	1,859	1,459	878	150
High-yield debt	3,000	3,000	3,000	3,000	3,000	3,000	3,000	3,000	3,000	3,000
Cram-down debt	1,974	2,286	2,648	3,067	3,553	3,553	3,553	3,553	3,553	3,553
Total	$10,197	$10,013	$9,740	$9,529	$9,273	$8,939	$8,528	$8,028	$7,431	$ 6,703

[a]Cash flow available for capital payments = Net income + Depreciation, amortization, deferred taxes – Capital expenditures – Change in working capital + Net proceeds from asset sales.

[b]Includes the $2,146 million in cash proceeds from the sale of businesses in 1989.

EXHIBIT 13
Stock Prices and Market Index, October 1988

Date	Philip Morris	Kraft	S&P 500	Event
Oct. 3	$ 97.000	$ 60.000	638.710	
4	98.000	58.500	637.010	Grand Metropolitan bids for Pillsbury Company.
5	97.375	59.375	640.020	
6	96.875	59.375	641.360	
7	100.875	60.625	654.830	
10	101.125	60.750	655.320	
11	100.750	60.375	654.680	
12	98.875	59.500	645.470	
13	99.250	59.250	648.480	
14	98.625	59.500	649.230	
17	100.000	60.125	651.460	
18	95.500	88.250	658.560	Philip Morris bids $90 per share for Kraft.
19	94.000	90.375	652.970	
20	99.000	90.250	666.990	RJR Nabisco management proposes a $17 billion leveraged buyout.
21	97.375	92.000	668.920	
24	97.500	102.000	665.760	Kraft proposes its restructuring plan and Kohlberg, Kravis, Roberts announces its bid for RJR Nabisco.
25	95.875	99.000	666.090	
26	95.500	97.500	663.820	
27	95.000	94.500	654.240	
28	94.750	96.500	657.280	

John M. Case Company

In March 1985, Anthony W. Johnson was working on a proposal to purchase his employer's firm, the John M. Case Company. The Case Company, with corporate headquarters in Dover, Delaware, was a leading manufacturer of commercial desk calendars. Mr. Johnson, vice president of finance and administration, considered the company an excellent acquisition opportunity, provided the owner's asking price was acceptable and satisfactory financing for the transaction could be arranged.

Background

A few weeks earlier, John M. Case, board chairman, president, and sole owner of the company, had informed his senior management group that he intended to retire from business and was about to initiate a campaign to sell the company. For several years, his physician had been urging him to avoid all stress and strain; now Mr. Case had decided to sever his business connections and devote his time to travel and a developing interest in art history and collection.

On the basis of previous offers for the company, Mr. Case had decided to ask for $20 million, with a minimum of $16 million immediately payable in cash. He thought acquisitive corporations should find this price attractive, and he believed it would be easy to dispose of the business.

Mr. Case had assured the management group that its jobs and benefits would be well protected by the terms of any sale contract that he might negotiate. Despite his faith in Mr. Case's good intentions, Mr. Johnson had been quite apprehensive about the prospect of having his career placed in the hands of an unknown outsider. However, after some reflection. Mr. Johnson had concluded that the sale decision should be viewed as an opportunity to acquire control of a highly profitable enterprise. Purchase of the Case Company would not only ensure career continuity but also provide a chance to turn a profit in the company's equity. Mr. Johnson had realized that his personal financial resources were far too limited to allow him to bid alone for control of the company. Consequently, he had persuaded August Haffenreffer, vice president–marketing; William Wright, vice president–manufacturing; and Richard Bennink, the controller, to join him in trying to buy the company, rather than standing by while control passed to an outsider. In response to Mr. Johnson's request, Mr. Case had agreed to defer all steps to merchandise the company until he had accepted or rejected a purchase proposal from the management group, provided this proposal was submitted within six weeks.

Because of his background in finance and his role in initiating the project, Mr. Johnson had assumed primary responsibility for assessing the profit potential of the opportunity and for structuring a workable financial plan for the acquisition. Since Mr. Case had not yet solicited bids from other potential purchasers, Mr. Johnson believed that it would be most realistic to regard Mr. Case's stated sale terms as fixed and nonnegotiable.

Mr. Johnson, then, needed to determine whether he could meet the asking price and still realize a profit commensurate with the risk in this purchase. Moreover, he needed to figure out how the management group, with roughly $500,000 among them, could finance the purchase and at the same time obtain voting control of the company.

Copyright © 1990 by the President and Fellows of Harvard College. Harvard Business School case 291–008.

Thus far Mr. Johnson had managed to obtain a tentative commitment for a $6 million unsecured bank term loan, and he had persuaded Mr. Case to accept unsecured notes for the noncash portion of the purchase price. He was still faced with the problem of raising close to $10 million on an equity base of $500,000 without giving up control to outsiders.

Mr. Johnson now had three weeks in which to come up with a workable financial plan or lose the deal. He was acutely aware that his own life savings and those of his associates would ride on his judgment and ingenuity.

Description of the Company

The John M. Case Company was the leading producer of business calendars in the United States. The company was established in 1920 by Robert Case (Mr. Case's paternal grandfather) to do contract printing of commercial calendars. Mr. Case had joined the organization in 1946 upon graduation from college, and in 1951 he had inherited the company.

Under Mr. Case's leadership, primary emphasis was placed on controlled expansion in the established line of business. By 1984 the company, with an estimated 60–65% share of its market, had been for a decade the largest company in a small but lucrative industry. Operations had been profitable every year since 1932, and sales had increased every year since 1955. In 1984, the most recently completed fiscal year, earnings had amounted to $1,966,000 on sales of approximately $15.3 million. The return on average invested capital in 1984 was about 20%. Over the past 5 years, sales had increased at a 7% compound rate, while earnings, benefiting from substantial cost reductions, had more than doubled. Exhibits 1–3 present recent financial figures for the company.

Products

As noted, the Case Company's principal products were commercial desk calendars. The company designed and manufactured disposable-page and flipover-page desk calendar pads in a variety of sizes. The company also sold desk calendar bases, which were purchased from outside suppliers who manufactured to Case's specifications. In 1984 standard desk calendar pads had contributed approximately 80% of net sales and 90% of earnings before taxes. Bases accounted for 10% of sales, and miscellaneous merchandise, chiefly wall calendars, accounted for the rest.

Sales were highly seasonal. Most final consumers did not start using calendars for the forthcoming year until November or December of the current year. Consequently, about 90% of Case's total shipments typically took place between June and December, with about 60% of shipments concentrated in the third quarter and 25% in the fourth quarter. Since calendar pads were dated, any merchandise remaining in stock at the end of the selling season was subject to rapid obsolescence.

Manufacturing

The production process was relatively simple, employing widely available skills and technology. High-speed offset presses were used to print appropriate dates on paper purchased in bulk from outside suppliers; the printed sheets were then trimmed to the required sizes and stored for shipment. The entire process was highly automated and was characterized by high fixed costs, high setup costs, and low variable costs.

In spite of highly seasonal sales, the Case Company operated on level production schedules. Since the product lines were for all practical purposes undifferentiated from competing lines and the relevant production technology was well known, the capacity to sell on the basis of price, while achieving a good return on invested capital, was regarded by management as a critical success factor in the industry. Minimum production costs were therefore imperative.

Level production enabled the company to take advantage of extremely long production runs and thus to minimize down time, the investment in equipment, expensive setups, and the use of transient labor. Level production, in conjunction with the company's dominant market share, provided scale economies well beyond the reach of any competitor.

The combination of seasonal sales and level production resulted in the accumulation of large seasonal stocks. However, by concentrating the sales effort in the middle six months of the year, the Case Company was able to circumvent most of the risk usually associated with level production in a seasonal company in return for modest purchase discounts. Since customers could easily predict their needs for Case products as their budgets for the forthcoming year took shape, they were willing to place their orders well in advance of shipment. As a result, Case could manufacture against a firm backlog in the last few months of the year and thus circumvent the risk of overproducing and ending the year with large stocks of outdated finished goods.

The company maintained production facilities in nearby Wilmington, Delaware, and, through a wholly owned subsidiary, in Puerto Rico. Earnings of the Puerto Rican subsidiary, which sold all its output to the U.S. parent, were entirely exempt from U.S. taxes and until 1992 would be exempt from all Puerto Rican taxes. The tax exemption on Puerto Rican production accounted for Case's unusually low income tax rate. All Case plants and equipment were modern and excellently maintained. A major capital expenditures program, completed in 1983, had resulted in the company's having the most modern facilities in the industry. At the predicted rate of future sales growth, Mr. Wright, the chief production officer, did not anticipate any need for substantial capital expenditures for at least 5 or 6 years.

None of the company's work force was represented by labor unions.

Marketing

As its products were nondifferentiable, Case's marketing program concentrated on providing high-quality customer service and a uniformly high-quality product. Case products were sold nationwide. Geographically, the company was strongest in the Northeast, the Southwest, and the far West. Large accounts were handled by the company's five salespeople, and smaller accounts were serviced by office supply wholesalers. Roughly 10% of sales had historically gone to the federal government.

Even though the product was undifferentiated, Mr. Haffenreffer, the marketing vice president, believed that it did have some significant advantages from a marketing viewpoint. Selling costs were extremely low, as consumption of the product over the course of a year automatically generated a large replacement demand without any effort on the part of Case. About 95% of total sales generally consisted of reorders from the existing customer base, with only 5% of sales going to new customers. Historically, over 98% of the customer base annually reordered Case pads and, as needed, additional Case bases. By dealing with only one source of supply, the customer was able to take maximum advantage of discounts for volume purchases. As the product was virtually immune to malfunction and the resultant customer dissatisfaction, once Case bases had been installed, the typical buyer never had any incentive to spend time and money on a search for alternative sources. Consumption of Case products was, in addition, extremely insensitive to budget cuts, economy drives, consumer whims, and the like. The desk calendar was a small-ticket but high-priority item. It was an essential in the work routines of most of its users, and it was not expensive enough to yield a meaningful reward in savings to would-be cutters. As a dated product, the desk calendar, unlike many other office products, represented a nondeferrable purchase.

Finances

Mr. Case had been greatly influenced by his father's memories of the Great Depression, and he steadfastly refused to consider leveraging his equity in the company. Accordingly, the company operated with an all-equity capitalization. The size of the capital budget was determined by the volume of internally generated funds in conjunction with Mr. Case's decision on how much to withdraw in the form of dividends. Dividend payments had sometimes been sharply contracted to accommodate capital investment opportunities. Over the past 3 years, however, internally generated funds had been plentiful, and dividends had averaged 70% of net earnings.

Like the capital budget, the seasonal accumulation of inventories and receivables was financed from internal sources. To minimize warehousing expenses for finished goods, Case provided generous credit terms to customers who accepted early shipments. Payments for June–October shipments were not due until the end of November, although substantial discounts were offered for earlier payment. The collection period averaged 60 days. Credit experience was excellent, and generous credit terms were considered a key factor in the company's competitive success.

Although the company had not resorted to seasonal borrowing in nearly 10 years, it maintained for emergency purposes two $2 million lines of credit at major Eastern banks. Exhibit 4 shows 1984 working capital balances by month.

The Case Company's credit with suppliers was excellent. All trade obligations were promptly paid when due.

Management

The senior management team consisted of Mr. Case plus the four individuals interested in buying the company. Transfer of ownership to the latter would not occasion much change in the de facto management of the organization. Although Mr. Case continued to exercise the final authority on all major issues of policy and strategy, over the past few years he had gradually withdrawn from day-to-day affairs and now spent much of his time in Europe and Puerto Rico. As Mr. Case had relaxed his grip on the company's affairs, he had increasingly delegated the general management of the firm to Mr. Johnson.

Compensation was generous at the senior executive level. Mr. Case drew an annual salary of $400,000; his four key subordinates received an average salary of $90,000. In addition, the four senior executives received annual bonuses which aggregated 10% of earnings before taxes and bonuses.

The members of the purchasing group were all in their thirties and early forties and among them represented close to 50 years' experience in the business. A graduate of a leading school of business administration, Mr. Johnson, aged 40, had worked for 5 years in the venture capital department of a large Eastern bank and for 2 years in his own management consulting firm before joining the Case Company.

Company Prospects

The overall prospect was for continued growth at a steady, though unspectacular, pace. The rate of Case sales growth, management believed, was closely correlated with the rate of growth in the size of the domestic white-collar work force. Given expectations of a continuing shift of labor out of agricultural and blue-collar and into white-collar occupations, this suggested that the company should grow somewhat faster than the economy as a whole. Assuming no material changes in product lines or market share, management thought sales growth would average about 5–6% per year in the foreseeable future. Profit margins were expected to improve somewhat over the next few years, as volume expanded and an increasing proportion of new production was directed to the tax-exempt Puerto Rican facility.

Competition

Although the commercial desk calendar industry was profitable indeed for its leading participant, it was not, in the opinion of Case management, an attractive area for potential new competitors. At that time, the industry was divided between Case, with roughly a 60–65% share of market, and the Watts Corporation, a privately held company, with an estimated 20–25% share. Watts's strength was concentrated in the Midwest and Southeast. The remainder of industry sales was fragmented among a host of small, financially weak printing shops. Case management found it difficult to imagine how a potential competitor could arrive at an economically justifiable decision to enter their market. Price was the only conceivable basis on which a new entrant could compete, but lacking the scale economies available to Case, a new entrant would necessarily be a high-cost competitor. Mr. Haffenreffer estimated that it would take a new entrant at least 3–5 years to reach break-even, assuming no retaliatory price cuts by Case. Furthermore, entering this market would necessitate a minimum capital investment of $2–4 million plus the working capital needed to support seasonal sales. On balance, it seemed unlikely that a potential competitor would brave these obstacles in the hope of grabbing a share of a $25–30 million industry with mediocre growth prospects.

Mr. Case judged that the company's financial strength, relative cost advantages, and entrenched distribution system had served to deter Watts from trying to invade any of Case's prime market areas. Similarly, he thought Case could not take away a substantial market share from Watts without risking a price war that might seriously impair margins for a protracted period.

Unexploited Opportunities

The business plan finally approved by Mr. Case had not incorporated a diversification scheme vigorously advanced by the other members of senior management. The vice president had contended that the company could significantly boost both the rate of growth and level of earnings by using its cash flow and its production and distribution strengths to expand into related product lines. The proposal had called for expansion into other dated products, such as appointment books, planning books, and the like, imprinted with the name, logo, or other message of the customer, and into desk calendars similarly imprinted. Mr. Johnson had estimated that this project would require an initial capital investment of $200,000 and special product development and merchandising expenses of $900,000 spread over the first 2 years of the undertaking. It had been estimated that the new line should yield sales of approximately $1 million in the first full year of operation, with a growth rate of about 40% per year in years 2–4, as the line achieved nationwide distribution and recognition. A 12–15% growth rate was anticipated in subsequent years. It was thought that this type of product line would have a profit margin before taxes of about 6%. The management group believed that the proposed line could serve as a profitable first step toward developing a full line of desktop products for commercial, industrial, and government markets.

Mr. Case had rejected the proposal on several grounds. He had observed that the proposal advocated entering a riskier line of business in which none of the management group had experience. In the proposed line of business the customer could choose among a variety of competing designs, and manufacturers had to actively generate repeat sales. He had also pointed out that the project would require a substantial investment in working capital for seasonal sales, if the new line grew as predicted. Finally, he had stated, he was quite content with his present income and, at his age, unwilling to reinvest earnings in the hope of achieving a strong position in a more competitive and less profitable business than the present one.

With Mr. Case out of the picture, the management group would have the freedom to pursue its growth program. Mr. Johnson believed that over a period of years, the Case Company's growth rate could be improved significantly if earnings were reinvested in related businesses rather than disbursed as dividends. The higher growth rate would be translated into profits for management if, for instance, the faster growth allowed them to take the company public at a relatively high price-earnings ratio.

The Purchase Proposal

Mr. Johnson recognized that a successful proposal would have to blend and reconcile the interests and goals of all parties to the transaction: the seller, the buyers, and external suppliers of finance.

The management group had determined that among them they could raise at most about $500,000 for investment in Case. Raising this amount would necessitate drawing down savings accounts, refinancing home mortgages, and liquidating positions in the stock market. Mr. Johnson was prepared to commit $160,000, Mr. Haffenreffer $140,000, and Messrs. Wright and Bennink $100,000 apiece. It had been tentatively agreed that all members of the management group would buy stock at the same price. It had also been tentatively concluded that the group would not accept a proposal that left them with less than 51% of the shares. With less than 51% of the stock, the management group might not achieve the autonomy to establish corporate policy or to dispose of the company where and as it chose.

Valuation

As mentioned previously, Mr. Johnson believed that Mr. Case's asking terms of $20 million with a minimum of $16 million in cash would remain fixed, at least until the company had been shown to a number of prospective buyers. In the past year Mr. Case had held discussions with two companies that had made unsolicited bids to purchase the company. The first offer, $15 million in cash, had come from a medium-sized firm with a diversified line of office products. It had been rejected by Mr. Case on the basis of price. The second offer had come from a highly diversified, medium-sized company sporting a price-earnings ratio of more than 20 and seeking to establish a position in office products through a series of acquisitions. The final offer had come to $32 million in letter stock of the acquirer.[1] Mr. Case had found this bid extremely tempting but had been unwilling to tie up his wealth in unmarketable shares of a company with which he was not intimately familiar. The acquirer, lacking excess debt capacity and unwilling to float new stock to raise cash, had backed out of the discussions.

Mr. Johnson had, in addition, assembled financial figures on the publicly traded companies he thought most comparable to the Case Company. These data are presented in Exhibit 5.

[1]Letter stock is unregistered stock. Such stock may not be sold to the public without registration under the Securities Act of 1933, a costly and time-consuming process. Because letter stock is restricted in its transferability, it represents a relatively illiquid investment and generally sells at a discount below the price that registered stock would command in the public securities markets. When letter stock is issued in an acquisition, the acquirer generally specifies that the stock cannot be registered for a certain period of time.

Financing

In terms of the mechanics of the transaction, Mr. Johnson planned to effect the purchase through a new corporation in which the management group would buy 500,000 common shares at $1.00 per share. Given the management group's $500,000 versus the $20 million asking price, the biggest problem facing Mr. Johnson was how to fund the new company at all, not to mention the objective of keeping control in the management group. Mr. Johnson had managed to obtain tentative commitments for $10.5 million, including the management group's $500,000. Prior to submitting a purchase proposal to Mr. Case, however, he would have to line up commitments for the entire $20 million funds needed.

It was clear that the noncash component of the purchase price would have to be met by issuing notes with a market value of $4 million to Mr. Case. In order to maintain the maximum amount of flexibility and borrowing capacity for raising financing from outsiders, Mr. Johnson had proposed that Mr. Case take 4%, junior subordinated, nonamortizing notes. After some negotiation, Mr. Case had expressed his willingness to accept a $6 million nonamortizing, 4% 5-year note that would be junior to all other debt obligations of the newly formed corporation. The members of the management group, as well as the corporate acquirer, would have to endorse the note. It was agreed that covenants on the note would include: (1) no additional debt or leases except debt incurred in the acquisition of the Case Company, short-term seasonal borrowings, or debt incurred to retire the 5-year note; (2) no dividends and maintenance of at least $3 million in working capital; (3) no changes in management or increase in management compensation; and (4) no sale of Case shares by Messrs. Johnson, Haffenreffer, Wright, or Bennink as long as the 5-year note was outstanding. If the borrower should default on any terms of this note or of any other indebtedness, the junior subordinated notes would become immediately due and payable. If not promptly paid, ownership of the shares held by the management group would revert to Mr. Case. The note could be retired before maturity in whole or in part in accord with the following schedule of discounts:

Year	Percent of Face Value
1	58%
2	71
3	81
4	96
5	100

In his efforts to line up financing from outside sources, Mr. Johnson had succeeded in obtaining a tentative commitment for a $6 million term loan from a large Philadelphia bank known for its aggressive lending policies. This loan would be amortized over a maximum period of 6 years through annual installments. The rate would be two points above floating prime, and the borrower would have to maintain average compensating balances of 10% of the outstanding principal amount of the loan. The amount of $6 million was the maximum the bank would commit on a term basis. Lending officers of the bank had emphasized that any additional term indebtedness incurred in the acquisition of Case would have to be effectively subordinated to this loan. Exhibit 6 presents an abstract of the provisions that the bank term loan would bear. Exhibit 7 presents Mr. Johnson's forecast of Case's cash flows over the next 6 years.

Having negotiated the bank commitment, Mr. Johnson was still left with the problem of raising an additional $9.5 million. He thought that he would have to turn to venture capital sources to raise the rest of the funds needed. Based on his experience in venture finance, Mr. Johnson knew that a venture capitalist would expect to earn about 20–25% on funds. He also knew that most venture capitalists preferred to place their funds in the form of debt securities rather than common stock. The venture capitalist could generally exercise more effective control over investment through the covenants on a debt obligation than through the voting power on stock. Principal repayment on debt also provided a mechanism for a tax-free recovery of capital; this might not be possible with stock until the company had gone public. Mr. Johnson expected to have to pay an 8–9% coupon rate on any debt funds obtained from a venture capital source. The venture capitalist would probably attempt to realize the rest of the return by taking warrants to buy shares in the new corporation at $1.00, the same price initially paid by the management group. The venture capitalist would probably insist on having the option of exercising the warrants in either cash or Case debentures.

EXHIBIT 1
Consolidated Income Statements, 1980–1984 (thousands of dollars)

	1980	1981	1982	1983	1984
Net sales	$9,740	$10,044	$11,948	$13,970	$15,260
Cost of sales	5,836	5,648	6,994	8,304	9,298
Gross profit on sales	3,904	4,396	4,954	5,666	5,962
Selling and administrative expenses	2,216	2,072	2,470	3,022	3,274
Other income, net	40	108	70	128	120
Profit before income taxes	1,728	2,432	2,554	2,772	2,808
Federal income taxes	816	972	920	942	842
Net profit	$ 912	$ 1,460	$ 1,634	$ 1,830	$ 1,966

EXHIBIT 2 Consolidated Balance Sheet at December 31, 1984 (thousands of dollars)

Cash and marketable securities	$ 5,762	Accounts payable	$ 654
Accounts receivable	2,540	Accrued expenses	366
Inventories at lower of cost or market	588	Accrued income taxes	246
Prepaid expenses	108	Current liabilities	1,266
Current assets	8,998	Common stock ($1.00 par value)	200
Property, plant, equipment, net	2,110	Retained profits	9,716
Miscellaneous assets	74	Shareholders' equity	9,916
Total assets	$11,182	Total liabilities and shareholders' equity	$11,182

EXHIBIT 3 **Ten-Year Summary of Operations, 1975–1984 (thousands of dollars except per share data)**

	1975	1976	1977	1978	1979	1980	1981	1982	1983	1984
Net sales	$7,688	$8,356	$8,526	$8,790	$9,350	$9,740	$10,044	$11,948	$13,970	$15,260
Net profit	638	668	742	748	758	912	1,460	1,634	1,830	1,966
Dividends	600	200	280	280	440	440	480	1,220	1,374	1,480
Earnings per share	$ 3.19	$ 3.34	$ 3.71	$ 3.74	$ 3.79	$ 4.56	$ 7.30	$ 8.17	$ 9.15	$ 9.83
Net profit margin	8.3%	8.0%	8.7%	8.5%	8.1%	9.4%	14.5%	13.7%	13.1%	12.9%

EXHIBIT 4 **Monthly Working Capital Balances, 1984 (thousands of dollars)**

	Jan.	Feb.	Mar.	Apr.	May	June	July	Aug.	Sept.	Oct.	Nov.	Dec.
Cash	$5,536	$5,714	$5,396	$4,784	$4,328	$4,098	$2,354	$ 766	$2,050	$3,830	$5,734	$5,762
Accounts receivable	1,480	760	734	804	718	604	3,432	6,104	6,164	4,322	2,398	2,540
Inventories	1,124	1,666	2,210	2,752	3,294	3,838	2,754	1,670	526	588	608	588
Current liabilities	(1,186)	(1,220)	(1,242)	(1,146)	(1,422)	(1,344)	(1,072)	(1,216)	(1,174)	(1,384)	(1,340)	(1,266)
Net working capital	$6,954	$6,920	$7,098	$7,194	$6,918	$7,196	$7,468	$7,324	$7,566	$7,356	$7,400	$7,624

EXHIBIT 5 Comparative Data on Selected Companies in Related Lines of Business

	S&P Publishing Averages	S&P 425 Industrial Stocks	DeLuther[a]		Wakefield Co.[b]		Officomp[c]		Case Co.	
Trading market			OTC		OTC		OTC		—	
Current market price			$22¼		$14¾		$29¼		—	
Indicated dividend yield			5.5%		8.7%		3.7%		—	
Price-earnings ratio										
1984	14.6	9.9	8.7		7.2		10.5		—	
1983	19.6	11.8	6.4		5.0		10.2		—	
1982	14.4	10.4	10.8		11.9		13.8		—	
Price range										
1984			$24⅝–16¼		$14⅞–8⅛		$33⅛–26½		—	
1983			18½–12⅛		11½–5⅛		19¾–12⅞			
Earnings per share (E) and index (I)			(E)	(I)	(E)	(I)	(E)	(I)	(E)	(I)
1984			$ 2.48	110	$ 1.62	82	$ 2.98	177	$ 9.83	$216
1980			2.26	100	1.97	100	1.68	100	4.56	100
Sales (S) ($ 000s) and index (I)			(S)	(I)	(S)	(I)	(S)	(I)	(S)	(I)
1984			$16,427	2	$12,223	108	$18,608	160	$15,260	$157
1980			11,568	100	11,317	100	11,630	100	9,740	100
Net earnings (N) ($ 000s) and index (I)			(N)	(I)	(N)	(I)	(N)	(I)	(N)	(I)
1984			$ 1,051	117	$ 501	84	$ 1,656	178	$ 1,966	$216
1980			902	100	600	100	930	100	912	100
Net profit margins										
1984			6.4%		4.1%		8.9%		12.9%	
1980			7.8		5.3		8.0		9.4	
Profit/Net worth										
1984			16.6%		6.0%		16.9%		19.8%	
1983			14.2		5.7		15.0		19.0	
1982			15.4		8.8		14.7		19.2	
Book capitalization[d] ($ 000s)										
Long-term debt			$ 3,995	38.7%	$ 1,822	18.0%	$ 4,173	29.9%	—	—
Common stock and surplus			6,318	61.3	8,298	82.0	9,783	70.1	$ 9,916	100.0%
Total			$10,313	100.0%	$10,120	100.0%	$13,956	100.0%	$ 9,916	100.0%
Total market value ($ 000s)			$ 9,456		$ 4,573		$16,234		—	
Shares outstanding (000s)			425		310		555		200	

[a] Producer of desk-top accessories, advertising specialty calendars, office stationery.
[b] Producer of advertising specialty calendars.
[c] Producer of broad line of office paper products and desk accessories.
[d] All companies, December 31, 1984.

EXHIBIT 6 Excerpts from Summary of Loan Agreement for Bank Term Loan

Description of the Loan

Amount. $6 million.

Rate. Prime rate plus 2%, floating.[a]

Term. 6 years.

Repayment. Annual payments equal to the greater of $1 million or the sum of net profit plus amortization of goodwill and debt discounts less $200,000.

Prepayment. Permitted in whole or in part at any time without penalty. All prepayments to be applied to the outstanding principal balance of the loan in inverse order of maturity.

Compensating balances. Borrower must maintain average annual deposit balances equal to at least 10% of the outstanding principal amount of the loan.

Conditions Precedent

Prior to the making of the loan described above, borrower must have satisfied the following terms and conditions:

Incorporation. Borrower must be a duly incorporated corporation authorized to undertake this borrowing and all other transactions associated with this borrowing.

Purchase agreement. Borrower must have entered a contract to purchase 100% of the John Case Company.

Financing. Borrower must have arranged firm commitments for the financing of this transaction in a manner consistent with the terms of this loan agreement.

Equity purchase. Messrs. Johnson, Haffenreffer, Wright, and Bennink must have committed not less than $500,000 to the purchase of common stock in the newly formed corporation that will purchase the John Case Company.

Affirmative Covenants

During the life of this loan, borrower will adhere to the following terms and conditions:

Financial statements. Quarterly financial statements must be provided within 60 days of the end of the first three quarters. Audited financial statements bearing an unqualified opinion from a public accounting firm must be provided within 90 days of the end of borrower's fiscal year.

Accounting changes. Borrower will make no changes in its method of accounting.

Negative Covenants

During the life of this loan, borrower will not do any of the following without written consent of the lender:

Continuation of management. No changes in management. Aggregate compensation to Messrs. Johnson, Haffenreffer, Wright, and Bennink not to be increased by more than 5% in any year. Present compensation to serve as a base for this computation.

Negative pledge. No assets to be pledged or otherwise used as collateral for any indebtedness.

Sales of assets. No sale of a substantial portion of the assets of the borrower. Borrower will not merge with or be acquired by any other entity.

Acquisitions. Borrower will not acquire any other entity.

Capital expenditures. Not to exceed $300,000 in any one year.

Dividends. In any one year restricted to after-tax profits minus all principal repayments on outstanding indebtedness.

Working capital. Not to decline below $3 million.

Additional indebtedness. No additional debt (including leases) with a term exceeding 1 year, unless subordinated to this loan. Any short-term debt must be retired for a period of at least 30 consecutive days in every year.

Senior debt. Senior debt, including all short-term indebtedness, may not exceed $10 million plus all earnings retained in the business after Dec. 31, 1985.

Events of Default

In the event of default, this loan plus accrued interest will become immediately due and payable. The following will constitute events of default:

Failure to pay interest or principal when due.
Violation of any affirmative or negative covenant on this loan.
Bankruptcy, reorganization, receivership, liquidation.
Commission of an event of default on any other indebtedness.

[a]At the time of the case, the prime rate was 10.00%.

EXHIBIT 7 Cash Flow Forecasts, 1985–1990 (thousands of dollars)

	1985	1986	1987	1988	1989	1990
Net sales	$16,024	$16,844	$17,686	$18,570	$19,498	$20,472
Earnings before interest and taxes[a]	3,433	3,640	3,757	3,608	3,788	3,976
Interest expense[b]	1,675	1,538	1,369	908	800	800
Profit before taxes	1,758	2,102	2,388	2,700	2,988	3,176
Taxes	274	364	440	556	660	714
Profit after taxes	1,484	1,738	1,948	2,114	2,328	2,462
Add back: Noncash charges	240	260	284	300	310	340
Cash flow from operations	1,724	1,998	2,232	2,444	2,638	2,802
Less: Increase in working capital	156	162	170	180	190	200
Less: Capital expenditures	120	134	142	150	466	600
Available for debt retirement	$ 1,448	$ 1,702	$ 1,920	$ 2,114	$ 1,982	$ 2,002
Planned debt retirement						
Bank loan	$ 1,448	$ 1,702	$ 1,920	$ 930	$ 0	$ 2,002
Mr. Case's note	0	0	0	1,184	4,766[c]	0
Subordinated loan	0	0	0	0	0	0
Debt as percent of total capital	89%	80%	70%	58%	47%	35%

[a]Reflects elimination of Mr. Case's salary.

[b]9% coupon on subordinated loan of $6 million; 4% coupon on seller's note of $6 million; 12% rate on bank term loan; 10% rate on seasonal loan.

[c]Mr. Case's note is retired from cash flow and a $2.8 million new bank term loan in 1989.

Congoleum Corporation (Abridged)

In the summer of 1979, Thomas Cassidy, Arthur Nagle, and Anthony Grassi, officers of First Boston Corporation, were discussing with David Koester and John Uecker of Prudential Insurance Company the proposed terms for participation in the largest leveraged buyout (LBO) in history. The subject of these discussions was Congoleum Corporation, a diversified firm competing in resilient flooring, shipbuilding, and automotive accessories.

Messrs. Cassidy and Nagle first approached Prudential in May 1979 to solicit interest in the concept of the LBO. The participation of Prudential, the largest institutional investor in the United States, was considered crucial to the development of a deal. Prudential did express interest. On July 16, 1979, First Boston formally proposed the purchase of Congoleum by private and institutional investors at $38 per common share. The preceding trading day, Congoleum common closed at $25.375 per share. Given 12.2 million shares outstanding, this implied an aggregate premium of $154 million. The directors of Congoleum agreed to discuss this offer and to provide some confidential information necessary to value the firm.

The next step was to agree in principle to merge Congoleum into a new holding company. This included arranging the terms and commitments for financing.

Description of Congoleum Corporation

In 1978, Congoleum had earnings of $42 million on revenues of $576 million (see Exhibits 1 and 2). Its base of total assets was $323 million (see Exhibit 3). The firm was active in three product market segments (see Exhibit 4): home furnishings, shipbuilding, and automotive and industrial distribution. Congoleum had no material intersegment sales.

Home furnishings products included resilient flooring targeted to the home remodeling market, and furniture and bedding for sale to the mobile home industry. The firm was one of the four largest producers of resilient flooring. The principal elements of competition were product styling, price, product performance, and service. Because of the importance of style, Congoleum produced and sold a large number of different designs and colors and introduced many new designs each year. The process for manufacturing resilient flooring was developed and patented by Congoleum. The foreign and domestic patents covering this process were due to expire from 1980 to 1987, although most would expire by 1984. The firm successfully defended its patents against infringement by three competitors, which in one case resulted in a $35 million out-of-court settlement paid by Armstrong Cork Company in 1976. Congoleum granted royalty-bearing licenses under these patents to other manufacturers, generating royalties of $17.2 million in 1978 and $13.2 million in 1977. Research and development expenditures were approximately $5 million in both 1978 and 1977.

Congoleum's shipbuilding subsidiary, Bath Iron Works (BIW), built and refurbished naval and civilian vessels. It held an excellent reputation for quality work completed within budget and on schedule. BIW had between 10 and 15 domestic competitors, most of whom were substantially larger and had poorer performances despite government

Copyright © 1986 by the President and Fellows of Harvard College. Harvard Business School case 287-029.

support. The backlog at December 31, 1978, of $445 million included $413 million for naval ships and overhauls and $32 million for commercial ships and industrial work. This compared with a backlog of $453 million for 1977. BIW expected to fill about $225 million of its backlog in 1979. In April 1979, BIW was awarded $209 million in more naval contracts.[1] The contracts for merchant ships were fixed-price but contained escalation provisions. Naval ships were built under fixed-priced incentive contracts also containing escalation provisions. Naval contracts were subject to termination at the convenience of the government, in which case the government would pay costs incurred, termination costs, and a portion of the profit. In the last 10 years, none of BIW's contracts was terminated in this manner.

The third segment of Congoleum's business was the distribution of automotive and industrial maintenance parts. This business segment was created from Curtis Noll Corporation, which was acquired in October 1977. The products distributed were purchased from numerous suppliers. Congoleum owned patents for a code key cutter and duplicator, which it considered significant to the business of this segment. In 1978 this segment provided revenues of $115 million and operating income of $10 million (see Exhibit 4).

Officers and directors owned beneficially 3.8% of the equity of Congoleum on a fully diluted basis. A portion of these shares was represented by stock options exercisable at an average price of $13.07 (see Exhibit 5). It was planned that the chairman, vice chairman, and other officers would remain with the firm after the transaction (Exhibit 5). Byron C. Radaker, chairman and chief executive officer, and Eddy G. Nicholson, vice chairman and chief operating officer, had managed Congoleum since 1975 and were credited for the company's improved performance. This was accomplished by an internal reorganization, the divestment of less profitable businesses, and the turnaround of other businesses.

Valuation by Lazard Frères & Co.

The firm of Lazard Frères & Co. was retained by Congoleum's directors to render an opinion as to the $38 per share offer. Lazard concluded, "We are of the opinion that the proposed offer of $38 per share of Congoleum is fair to the shareholders of Congoleum from a financial point of view." This analysis was based on a comparison of Congoleum's operations with its competitors, premiums paid in other recent acquisitions (see Exhibit 6), and values obtainable on liquidation (see Exhibit 7). Lazard relied on a method of valuation based on price-earnings multiples. Other information of significance in the valuation is presented in Exhibits 8 and 9.

Description of Prudential

The Prudential Insurance Company of America was the largest institutional investor in the United States, with assets of $21 billion invested in fixed-income securities. It was regarded as the leader in privately placed investments. Of Prudential's $6 billion annual cash flow, about 60% was invested through its corporate finance department in fixed-income securities (debt securities and preferred stocks). The department's portfolio consisted of investments in more than 1,400 companies in all major industries. Loan proposals were typically analyzed by teams of three officers and approved by

[1] First Boston's offering circular noted: "Bath Iron Works does not anticipate being able to deliver any new commercial business until at least 1985 because of capacity limitations and its expectations for continued involvement in the [Navy's] FFG program."

the senior vice president in charge of the department and by the finance committee of the board of directors.

Prudential's private lending included LBOs. The term of most of its private loans typically ranged from 12 to 20 years. Loan size varied from $500,000 to $250 million. The majority of the loans carried a fixed interest rate and were unsecured. Prudential's literature stated:

> On leveraged buyouts or credits for other borrowers with higher risk characteristics, our loans may include profit participation, warrants, or convertible securities in addition to a fixed interest rate.

John T. Uecker, vice president and member of the team considering First Boston's proposal, commented on financing of leveraged buyouts:

> These investments fit with our long-term portfolio strategy. We're more risk-oriented than our competitors. But we structure the deals so that the reward is consistent with the risk we take. We always compare the terms with other buyouts we may be considering at the same time, as well as other investment alternatives we have. And we analyze the company's earnings and cash flow projections—modified by the probability of meeting them. Furthermore, we value each segment of a company on its own. Finally, we compare the returns on each type of security with those available in the market [Exhibits 10 and 11]. This is done by individual securities and then as a package. The senior debt and common stock are relatively easy to value; the junior debt is more difficult. Given the huge proportion of debt in these deals, we can view the junior notes as equity and seek an equity-type return. The alternative is to compare them to B-rated securities and look for some premium over their returns. But obtaining a high yield on junior debt is inevitably constrained by what the company can service. In these cases, we look for an equity kicker (through warrants, convertibles, and common stock) to achieve the required rate of return. In the final analysis, we're more concerned about getting an appropriate return on the total package rather than how that return gets divided up between the various securities, though we would like to see each security able to stand on its own.

About 50% of Prudential's private placement financing was proposed by investment bankers.

Description of First Boston

First Boston Corporation was a special bracket investment banking firm. Although the firm had originated no leveraged buyouts previously, it had considerable experience with aspects of the deal: private placement financing, firm valuation, acquisitions, and so forth. The three officers, Thomas L. Cassidy and Arthur Nagle, both managing directors, and Anthony Grassi, vice president, developed the proposed deal. James Harpel, president of Century Capital Corporation, originally identified Congoleum as an LBO candidate and proposed that First Boston lead the negotiations. But Century Capital remained as one of the prospective equity participants. Thomas Cassidy said:

> The ability to deal effectively with people having diverse interests is extremely important in a transaction as complex as this. It may appear relatively simple after the fact. But actually it is fragile up until closing. At the beginning the interest among the participants was understandably tentative. Our first conversations with the Pru were of a conceptual nature, and the initial reaction of Congoleum management—whose involvement was very important—was "We're open to the idea, assuming you can put together the rest of the pieces and assuming the end result is in the best interests of our stockholders. . . ." The final form of the deal evolved out of a series of negotiations. Originally it was to have been a purchase of stock; it eventually evolved into a purchase of assets. Our "strip" concept was very helpful in keeping all of the institutions together. Closing the deal requires a fair amount of corporate finance capability, ingenuity, determination, and patience.

Terms of the Proposal

Cassidy, Nagle, and Grassi proposed that a bolding company be formed to buy Congoleum for an amount equivalent to about $38 per share. The buyout actually consisted of a two-step merger and sale. First, the stock of Bath Iron Works would be purchased for $92.3 million. BIW would then be merged into the buying company. Second, the remaining net assets of Congoleum (including about $95.1 million of excess cash and the Congoleum Corporation name) would be purchased for approximately $371.3 million. The "old Congoleum" would settle its remaining liabilities and pay a liquidating dividend of $38 per share.

The purchasers would adopt the name Congoleum Corporation and proceed as a privately held firm. The assets of BIW and Congoleum would have a tax basis equal to the amounts paid for the stock and assets, respectively, plus any liabilities assumed. Accordingly, the tax basis of the new firm would exceed its present tax basis by several hundred million dollars. This increase in tax basis could result in reduced taxable income because of increased deductions for (a) the amortization of the value of patents and patent-licensing agreements, (b) depreciation, and (c) cost of goods sold due to the write-up of shipbuilding backlog and inventories. This increase in tax basis would be available only in the event of a taxable acquisition and could not be achieved by the current stockholders. Exhibit 12 describes the allocation of the purchase premium in more detail.

The proposal provided financing of $379.6 million for the purchase in the form of bank borrowings, debt securities, and preferred and common stock. The distinctive feature of prior LBOs was that debt as a percent of total capital ranged up to 80%. Since banks typically would not allow all of that to be senior financing, the layering of the claims usually was one of the more delicate points of negotiation. David Koester, senior member of Prudential's team, said:

> We wanted all the players to share the same incentives in order to reduce any intramural warfare if trouble developed. So we insisted that the institutional investors purchase "strips," or units, containing a mixture of senior notes, subordinated notes, preferred stock, and common stock. This made First Boston's job more difficult. Previously, no leveraged buyouts had been financed in this manner. First Boston did an outstanding job assembling the players for a financing of this type and size.

Also it was proposed that First Boston, Century Capital, and the management of the new firm purchase common stock. The purchase of stock by management in the new firm was typical of LBOs. In summary, the proposed amounts to be financed by each investor and type of security were as shown in Table A.

The Decision

At this stage of negotiation, the central issues under consideration were valuation and the appropriateness of the offering price of $38 per share.[2] Exhibit 13 shows the financial forecast on which the valuation of Congoleum was based. Exhibits 14–16 provide supporting material for the Exhibit 13 forecast.

[2]In the cases of First Boston, Century Capital, and Congoleum management, it was also possible to augment common stock returns with other forms of compensation, such as consulting fees, stock options, and salaries guaranteed by employment contracts. As investment banker in this transaction, First Boston would be paid a fee.

TABLE A
Sources of Acquisition Financing (millions of dollars)

Bank borrowings		$125.0
Insurance company investor "strips"		
11¼% senior notes, principal amount $115,000,000 (due 1995)	$113.6	
12¼% subordinated notes, principal amount $92,000,000 (due 2000)	89.8	
($11.00) cumulative preferred stock (322,000 shares)	26.2	
Common stock	16.5	
		246.1
First Boston and Century Capital		4.5
Congoleum management		4.0
		$379.6

EXHIBIT 1 Ten-Year Historical Financial Data, 1969–1978 (millions of dollars except per share data)

	1969	1970	1971	1972	1973	1974	1975	1976	1977	1978
Net sales	$189.9	$187.7	$250.6	$345.2	$385.7	$377.1	$395.9	$294.8	$388.6	$575.8
Royalty revenues (incl. in net sales)	—	—	—	—	4.0	5.5	7.0	10.1	13.2	17.2
Net income	7.6	7.0	12.1	23.4	22.2	.5	9.6	15.7	24.7	41.7
Earnings per share	$ .70	$ .65	$ 1.07	$ 1.67	$ 1.89	$ .05	$ .83	$ 1.36	$ 2.13	$ 3.58
Dividends per share	—	.02	.09	.13	.20	.27	.27	.33	.40	.67
Stock price										
High	17.5	11.6	24.0	30.9	24.6	14.9	9.2	12.9	14.6	26.3
Low	7.5	3.9	10.1	20.7	8.5	2.4	3.0	8.0	8.8	12.0
Working capital	$ 35.2	$ 49.0	$ 53.5	$ 69.6	$ 88.1	$ 92.8	$ 81.1	$ 76.8	$ 78.0	$110.1
Long-term debt	31.7	42.6	40.0	42.1	59.3	74.6	52.3	16.6	16.1	14.9
Net worth	58.9	59.1	73.3	99.5	116.3	113.8	120.3	132.6	153.1	187.5

Note: Congoleum acquired Curtis Noll Corporation October 31, 1977, on a purchase basis. Its performance is consolidated with Congoleum after October 31, 1977. Certain operations were discontinued in 1976. Results for 1969 to 1975 have not been adjusted for discontinued operations.

EXHIBIT 2

Historical Income Statements for Years Ending December 31, 1976–1978 (thousands of dollars except per share data)

	1976	1977	1978
Net sales	$284,735	$375,466	$558,633
Royalties[a]	10,080	13,163	17,197
Total revenues	294,815	388,629	575,830
Cost of sales	224,028	285,770	385,851
Selling and administrative expenses	37,805	55,023	108,648
Operating income	32,982	47,836	81,331
Interest expense	(2,064)	(1,734)	(1,266)
Miscellaneous income	3,821	3,538	4,281
Total other income and expense	1,757	1,804	3,015
Income from continuing operations before income taxes	34,739	49,640	84,346
Provision for income taxes	17,400	24,900	42,600
Income from continuing operations	17,339	24,740	41,746
Loss from discontinued operations	(19,500)	—	—
Patent infringement settlement	17,885	—	—
Net income	$ 15,724	$ 24,740	$ 41,746
Per Share			
Income from continuing operations	$ 1.50	$ 2.13	$ 3.58
Loss from discontinued operations	(1.69)	—	—
Patent infringement settlement	1.55	—	—
Net income	$ 1.36	$ 2.13	$ 3.58

Note: These statements reflect the addition of Curtis Noll Corporation only after October 31, 1977, the date of acquisition. The acquisition was accounted for as a purchase. Restating the results of 1977 and 1976 as if Noll were included yields the following:

	1976	1977
Total revenues	$416,000	$497,300
Income from continuing operations	19,592	27,725
Net income	17,977	27,725
Earnings per share	$ 1.56	$ 2.39

[a]Royalties are from licenses of the company's resilient flooring patents as well as license agreements for know-how. These patents expire from 1980 through 1987, although most expire by 1984.

EXHIBIT 3

Consolidated Balance Sheets at December 31, 1977–1978 (thousands of dollars)

	1977	1978
Cash and temporary investments	$ 12,369	$ 77,254
Receivables	55,053	40,424
Shipbuilding contracts in progress	18,936	24,058
Inventories	73,318	75,258[a]
Other	5,679	3,511
Current assets	165,355	220,505[b]
Property, plant, and equipment	131,621	135,627[c]
Less: Accumulated depreciation and amortization	60,472	64,850[d]
Net	71,149	70,777[e]
Goodwill	18,520	18,520
Other	11,356	13,250
Total assets	$266,380	$323,052[f]
Current maturities of long-term debt	$ 2,055	$ 460
Accounts payable	38,391	41,578
Accrued liabilities	28,928	30,102
Income taxes	17,985	38,257
Current liabilities	87,359	110,397
Long-term debt	16,067	14,949
Deferred income taxes and other liabilities	9,886	10,221
Common stock	5,859	5,859
Surplus	11,846	11,345
Retained earnings	137,256	171,229
Treasury stock	(1,893)	(948)
Net worth	153,068	187,485
Total liabilities and net worth	$266,380	$323,052

Replacement cost data:

[a]$79,518.
[b]$224,765.
[c]$282,267.
[d]$188,281.
[e]$93,986.
[f]$352,710.

EXHIBIT 4 Product Line Data, 1974–1979 (millions of dollars)

	Year Ended December 31					9 Months	
	1974	1975	1976	1977	1978	1978	1979
Revenues by segment							
Home furnishings	$143	$153	$180	$198	$225	$170	$177
Shipbuilding	107	126	115	167	211	158	181
Automotive and industrial distribution	79	85	95	105	115	86	89
	$329	$364	$390	$470	$551	$414	$447
Operating income (loss) by segment[a]							
Home furnishings	$ 22	$ 27	$ 34	$ 42	$ 58	$ 43	$ 40
Shipbuilding	(11)	1	2	10	19	13	28
Automotive and industrial distribution[b]	6	7	8	9	10	7	8
	$ 17	$ 35	$ 44	$ 61	$ 87	$ 63	$ 76
Identifiable assets by segment							
Home furnishings	$ 93	$ 93	$ 97	$ 92	$ 93	na	na
Shipbuilding	37	38	42	54	59	na	na
Automotive and industrial distribution	48	52	56	62	64	na	na
	$178	$183	$195	$208	$216	na	na

na = not available.

[a]Operating income does not include an allocation of interest income or expense, miscellaneous and other unallocable expenses, corporate office expenses, or provisions for income taxes.

[b]The pro forma amounts for the automotive and industrial distribution segment include the results of Curtis Noll Corporation.

EXHIBIT 5 Management Stock and Option Ownership in Congoleum Corporation, Autumn 1979

	Number of Shares Subject to Options and Stock Appreciation Rights	Weighted Average Exercise Price	Number of Other Shares Beneficially Owned	Total Number of Shares Beneficially Owned
Byron C. Radaker (Chairman, CEO)	47,250	$11.87	12,750	60,000
Eddy G. Nicholson (Vice Chairman, COO)	27,750	11.31	11,250	39,000
Harry F. Pearson (Executive Vice Pres.)	7,000	15.38	47,492	64,492
All directors and officers as a group	164,699	13.07	293,023	457,722

Note: Officers of Congoleum expected to assume equivalent positions in the new firm.

It was proposed that Radaker and Nicholson be allowed to purchase 7% and 5%, respectively, of the new firm's equity, subject to the right of the firm to repurchase the equity if their employment is terminated before 1984. Stock in the new venture was also reserved for other key employees.

Radaker and Nicholson would be employed under 5-year contracts, which specified a base salary, incentive compensation, and entitlements in the event of termination. Current and proposed compensation compared as follows:

	Radaker	Nicholson
1979 compensation	$370,000	$295,000
1980 compensation per contract		
Maximum	500,000	380,000
Minimum	375,000	290,000

EXHIBIT 6 Data on Comparable Leveraged Buyouts and Other Acquisitions

Company Acquired	Date	Aquisition of Stock or Assets	Premium/Price One Day Prior to Announcement	Offer as a Multiple of Net Income	Offer as a Multiple of Book Value	Senior Debt/ Total Debt	Sub. Debt/ Total Debt	Senior Debt/ Total Cap.	Sub. Debt/ Total Cap.
Houdaille Industries	10/28/78	S	93%	13.9	2.0	65.5%	34.5%	56%	29.6%
Bliss & Laughlin	8/10/79	A	23	8.7	1.7				
Carrier Corp	9/16/78	A	39	10.2	1.6				
Gardner-Denver	1/22/79	A	46	12.2	2.1				
Washington Steel	3/12/79	A	34	7.3	1.3				
Eltra Corp.	6/29/79	A	25	11.6	1.5				
Studebaker-Worthington	7/25/79	A	17	10.7	1.4				
Marathon Manufacturing . . .	8/13/79	A	13	11.4	2.1				
Congoleum		A/S	50	9.4	2.4	68.6	31.4	60.4	27.6

EXHIBIT 7 **Valuation Based on a Breakup Price Estimated by Lazard Frères for Each Component (millions of dollars except per share data)**

	1979 Estimated Results by Segment							
	Home Furnishings Segment		Bath Iron Works		Automotive and Industrial Distribution		Total Corporate Consolidated	
Operating income[a]	$56.1		$29.0		$11.9		$97.0	
Corporate office and other[b]	1.1		1.3		.7		3.1	
Pre-tax income	55.0		27.7		11.2		93.9	
Taxes (48%)	26.4		13.3		5.4		45.1	
Net income	$28.6		$14.4		$ 5.8		$48.8	
	Valuation Based on Assumed Price-Earnings Ratio							
	Low	High	Low	High	Low	High	Low	High
Assumed price-earnings ratio	9.0	10.0	5.0	6.0	10.0	11.0		
Derived valuation	$257.4	$286.0	$72.0	$86.4	$58.0	$63.8	$387.4	$436.2
Plus: Estimated excess cash on 12/31/79[c]							95.1	95.1
Less: Estimated long-term debt and current maturity of long-term debt on 12/31/79							15.6	15.6
Less: Unfunded vested pension liabilities (as of 12/31/78)							34.5	34.5
Net breakup value							$432.4	$481.2
Net breakup value per share (based on 12,201,000 shares)							$35.44	$39.43

[a]From Congoleum's internal reporting of quarterly operating income and performance report. Operating income for the Home Furnishings segment was reduced by $2.7 million attributable to the Kinder Division. This operation has been assumed to be sold for $10 million by the end of 1979.
[b]Allocated based on 1979 estimated sales (excluding $36.0 million attributable to Kinder and excluding royalty payments).
[c]Total cash at year-end estimated at $103.1 million minus $8 million. Excess cash is therefore estimated at $95.1 million.

EXHIBIT 8 **Forecast of Congoleum Operations, 1979–1981 (millions of dollars except per share data)**

	1979	1980	1981
For Year Ended December 31			
Revenues	$ 596	$ 680	$ 737
Operating income	86	97	112
Net income	45	51	60
Net income per share	$3.80	$4.35	$5.00
Dividends per share	.90	1.10	1.30
At December 31			
Cash and temporary investments	$ 93	$ 136	$ 182
Working capital	140	169	209
Long-term debt	15	14	14
Stockholders' investment	220	259	304

Note: These data are from an internal forecast by Congoleum prepared in the summer of 1978 and subsequently made available to First Boston Corp.

EXHIBIT 9 **Financial Data on Market Segment Competitors**

	Five-Year Expected Growth	P/E	β^a	LT Debt % Cap.	1979 ROE	1982–1984 Expected Div. Yield
Home furnishings						
Armstrong Cork	17.5%	5.8	1.00	18.2%	11.6%	3.2%
GAF Corp.	14.0	6.0	1.15	35.0	10.4	2.6
Shipbuilding						
Todd Shipyards	21.0	5.3	1.00	69.0	22.0	2.0
Automotive and industrial distribution						
Genuine Parts	16.0	10.4	.95	5.0	19.2	2.5
General Automotive Parts	16.0	9.6	.75	7.0	19.0	2.4
Barnes Group	12.5	5.1	.85	18.0	20.6	2.7
Congoleum	22.5	7.9	1.25	7.0	23.0	3.0

[a]The risk-free rate was assumed to be 9.5% and the market premium 8.6%.

EXHIBIT 10 **Average or Comparable Debt Yields by Quality, September 1979**

S&P Rating	Yield	Firm Name	Debt/Total Capital
AAA	9.35%	Average in category	
AA	9.54	Average in category	
A	9.78	Average in category	
BBB	10.49	Average in category	
BB	13.76	Action Industries	56.9%
	11.06	Control Data	21.1
	11.86	Sun Chemical	47.6
	10.59	Talley Industries	43.0
B	13.32	APL Corp.	57.9
	12.70	Arrow Electronics	49.7
	11.98	Charter Company	50.4
	12.46	Columbia Pictures	41.3
	12.87	Texas International Airlines	51.0
CCC	16.11	Altec Corp.	70.8
	13.32	General Host	74.4
	17.22	Grolier, Inc.	na
	14.26	LTV Corp.	73.8
	15.02	Rapid American Corp.	75.7

na = not available.

EXHIBIT 11
Average or Comparable Preferred Stock Dividend Yields by Quality, September 1979

S&P Rating	Yield	Firm Name	Debt/Total Capital
Moody's Rating			
Aaa	NR	Average in category	
Aa	9.6%	Average in category	
A	10.3	Average in category	
Baa	10.5	Average in category	
S&P Rating			
BB	10.0	Control Data	21.1%
	10.8	Evans Products	36.8
	10.0	Fairmont Foods	39.0
	11.5	Flexi-Van Corp.	64.0
B	12.1	Eastern Airlines	68.1
	11.5	Humana, Inc.	72.1
	12.5	Norin Corp.	49.5
	12.6	Petro-Lewis	67.2
CCC	18.2	Chrysler Corp.	33.8
	11.9	Continental Copper Steel	45.0
	14.0	Susquehanna Corp.	25.3
	15.0	United Brands	33.3
	14.0	Warnaco	35.0
	13.0	Wheeling Pittsburgh Steel	33.7

NR = not rated.

EXHIBIT 12
Sources and Allocation of Purchase Premium (millions of dollars)

Cost of stock ($38 × 12.2 million shares)	$463.6	
Expenses	7.0	
Purchase price		$470.6
Stockholders' investment, 12/31/78	$187.5	
Claim settlement	3.5	
Proceeds from exercise of stock options	5.0	
Estimated 1979 additions to retained earnings	37.7	
Stockholders' investment, 12/31/79	233.7	
Less: Unfunded pension liabilities	34.5	
Adjusted stockholders' investment, 12/31/79		199.2
Purchase premium		$271.4
Inventory write-up from recapture of LIFO reserve	$ 4.2	
Fixed assets	83.4	
Patents	150.0	
Goodwill	33.8	
Purchase premium		$271.4

Note: After the July 16, 1979, bid First Boston retained American Appraisal Company to render a "comfort level" opinion of the fair market value of inventories as of June 30, 1979, and the shipbuilding contract backlog and patents and patent licensing agreements at December 31, 1979. Its report concluded that the net realizable value of the inventories was $83,633,000, of the backlog was $73,500,000, and of the patents and patent licensing agreements was $174,000,000. The book value of inventories at June 30, 1979, was $50,000,000. Shipbuilding contract backlog and patents and patent licensing agreements had been carried on the books at nominal values.

EXHIBIT 13 Income and Cash Flow Forecast for Congoleum Reflecting the Terms of Proposed Leverage Buyout, 1978–1984 (millions of dollars)

	Actual	Projected						
	1978	1979	1980	1981	1982	1983	1984	Total 1980–1984
1. Operating income (Exhibit 15)	$95.5	$105.9	$111.5	$132.2	$158.7	$175.9	$ 166.1	
2. Less: Corporate expenses	7.5	8.6	4.3	5.1	5.9	6.8	7.6	
3. Less: Depreciation and amortization	6.7	7.5	35.51	36.26	37.07	37.95	21.23	
4. Earnings before interest and taxes	81.3	89.8	71.69	90.84	115.73	131.15	137.27	
5. Less: Interest expense, net[a]	(3.0)	(5.7)	42.92	40.55	37.33	34.12	29.87	
6. Profit before taxes	$84.3	$ 95.5	$28.77	$50.19	$78.40	$97.03	$107.40	
7. Less: Tax (@ 48%)		45.8	13.80	24.09	37.63	46.57	51.55	
8. Profit after taxes		$ 49.7	$14.97	$26.10	$40.77	$50.46	$ 55.85	$188.2
Adjustments								
9. Add back: Depreciation and amortization[b]			$35.51	$36.26	$37.07	$37.95	$ 21.23	$168.0
10. Less: Capital expenditures			15.0	16.2	17.5	18.9	20.4	88.0
11. Less: Investment in working capital			2.0	14.0	23.3	11.2	12.8	63.3
12. Less: Preferred dividends			3.5	3.5	3.5	3.5	3.5	17.5
13. Less: Principal repayments			17.14	24.75	24.52	36.75	24.55	127.7
14. Free cash flow (to common stock)[c]			12.84	3.91	9.02	18.06	15.83	59.7
15. Add: Dividends, interest, and principal			63.56	68.80	65.35	74.37	57.96	330.0
16. Free cash flow (to all capital)			76.40	72.71	74.37	92.43	73.79	389.7
17. Less: Bank and preexisting interest and principal			35.85	33.46	30.86	40.74	25.28	166.2
18. Free cash flow to buyout participants			$40.55	$39.25	$43.51	$51.69	$48.51	$ 223.5
19. Net working capital		$120.0	$122.0	$136.0	$159.3	170.5	$ 183.3	
20. Change in net working capital			2.0	14.0	23.3	11.2	12.8	

[a]With no leveraged buyout, Congoleum's net interest expenses were expected to be, in millions of dollars, $(2.0), $(2.0), $(2.1), $(2.1), and $(3.0) over the years 1980–1984.
[b]With no leveraged buyout, Congoleum's depreciation and amortization expenses were expected to be, in millions of dollars, $7.5, $8.3, $9.0, $9.9, and $10.9 over the years 1980–1984.
[c]Because of covenants prohibiting dividends, these free cash flows would be reinvested (presumably in cash and marketable securities), reducing financial risk and increasing the free cash flow. Does not reflect income from the reinvestment of surplus cash.

EXHIBIT 14
Assumptions for Financial Projections

Corporate Expenses
$8.6 million in 1979, growing at 8% thereafter from 1980 to 1984. A savings of $5 million annually is assumed as a result of Congoleum's being a private company.

Depreciation and Amortization
The amortization of patents was proposed as follows. Amortization of patents will be the same for book and tax purposes.

	Value ($ millions)	Remaining Life (years)
Chemical embossing process	$ 40	4
Code key cutter	40	10
Future value of U.S. royalties	30	4
Future value of foreign royalties ...	40	10
Total	$150	

Depreciation of Plant and Equipment
For tax purposes, the fixed asset base will be $200.2 million. Of this, 50% is assumed to relate to plant and will be depreciated over 20 years. The other 50%, related to equipment, will be depreciated over 7 years. All subsequent capital expenditures will be depreciated over 20 years. For book purposes, the fixed asset base will be $154.0 million. The other policies above will apply.

Interest Expense and Principal Repayments
Bank debt. Assume 14% interest on principal of $120 million. Principal is to be amortized at $16.666 million annually starting in 1980.

Senior notes. 11¼% interest on principal of $115 million, amortized at $7,636,000 per year starting on January 30, 1981.

Subordinated notes. 12¼% interest on principal of $92 million, amortized at $7,636,000 per year starting on January 30, 1989.

Covenants. Prohibit the payment of dividends on other than the preferred stock.

Taxes. The corporate income tax rate is assumed to be 48%.

Capital expenditures. Assumed to be $15 million in 1980 and increasing 8% annually thereafter.

Minimum working capital. 20% of nonroyalty sales. Net working capital immediately following the buyout is projected to be $120 million.

Required cash. Assumed to be 2.5% of nonroyalty sales.

Note. By 1980 a pattern of leveraged buyouts had emerged such that the firms were taken public again within a few years, usually when the various value-creating effects were diminished. The end of 1984 was one such horizon for Congoleum.

EXHIBIT 15 Projected Segment Revenue and Operating Income for Congoleum, 1979–1984 (millions of dollars)

	Actual	Projected					
	1978	1979	1980	1981	1982	1983	1984
Revenues							
Home furnishings, net	$207.9	$234.9	$217.9	$241.9	$273.3	$308.8	$349.0
Home furnishings royalties	17.2	20.6	24.8	29.7	35.7	42.8	21.4
Total home furnishings	225.1	255.5	242.7	271.6	309.0	351.6	370.4
Shipbuilding	211.0	230.4	247.9	279.2	345.1	345.1	345.1
Automotive, expediter	78.8	90.6	104.2	119.8	137.8	158.5	182.3
Automotive, conventional	45.0	45.0	40.0	40.0	40.0	40.0	40.0
Total automotive	123.8	135.6	144.2	159.8	177.8	198.5	222.3
Total revenues	$559.9	$621.5	$634.8	$710.6	$831.9	$895.2	$937.8
Operating Income							
Home furnishings, net	$ 43.7	$ 42.0	$ 39.2	$ 48.4	$ 57.4	$ 64.8	$ 73.3
Home furnishings royalties	17.2	20.6	24.8	29.7	35.7	42.8	21.4
Total home furnishings	60.9	62.6	64.0	78.1	93.1	107.6	94.7
Shipbuilding	21.7	31.5	33.9	38.5	47.7	47.7	47.7
Automotive, expediter	na	11.8	13.6	15.6	17.9	20.6	23.7
Automotive conventional	na	0	0	0	0	0	0
Total automotive	12.9	11.8	13.6	15.6	17.9	20.6	23.7
Total operating income	$ 95.5	$105.9	$111.5	$132.2	$158.7	$175.9	$166.1

Note: These data are from projections made by First Boston Corporation, and assume the buyout is completed. Neither depreciation nor corporate-level expenses are reflected in operating income, nor is income from the reinvestment of surplus cash.
na = not available.

EXHIBIT 16 Capital Structure and Debt Repayment Schedule for Congoleum, 1979–1984 (millions of dollars)

		Projected as of December 31				
	1979	1980	1981	1982	1983	1984
Old Debt						
1. 7½% subordinated debentures due 1983	$ 12.2	$ 12.2	$ 12.2	$ 12.2	$ 0	$ 0
2. Other long-term debt	4.24	3.77	3.32	3.11	2.86	2.61
New Debt						
3. Bank term notes	$125.0	$108.33	$91.67	$75.00	$58.34	$41.67
4. 11¼% senior notes due 1995	113.6	113.6	106.0	98.3	90.7	83.1
5. 12¼% subordinated notes due 2000	89.8	89.8	89.8	89.8	89.8	89.8
6. Preferred stock $11.00 (322,000 shares)	26.2	26.2	26.2	26.2	26.2	—
Common Stock						
7. Par value .10 (1,000,000 shares)	$ .1	$ .1	$ .1	$ .1	$ .1	$ .1
8. Paid-in surplus	24.9	24.9	24.9	24.9	24.9	24.9
Interest						
9. 7½% subordinated debentures } (assumed in acquisition)		$ .92	$ .92	$ .92	$ .92	—
10. Other long-term debt } (assumed in acquisition)		.30	.26	.23	.22	$ .20
11. Bank term notes @ 14%		17.50	15.17	12.83	10.50	8.17
12. 11¼% senior notes		12.94	12.94	12.08	11.22	10.23
13. 12¼% subordinated notes		11.27	11.27	11.27	11.27	11.27
14. Total interest payments		$42.92	$40.56	$37.33	$34.12	$29.87
15. Preferred dividend		3.54	3.54	3.54	3.54	3.54
Amortization						
16. 7½% subordinated debentures } (assumed in acquisition)	—	—	—	—	$12.20	—
17. Other long-term debt } (assumed in acquisition)	$ .46	$ .47	$ .45	$ .21	.24	$ .25[a]
18. Bank term notes		16.67	16.67	16.67	16.67	16.67
19. 11¼% senior notes		—	7.67	7.67	7.68	7.67
20. 12¼% subordinated notes		—	—	—	—	—
21. Total: Interest, principal, dividends		63.60	68.85	65.39	74.41	57.96

Note: Totals may not add exactly due to rounding.
[a]Includes anticipated repayments as well as required repayments.

RJR Nabisco

On October 20, 1988, Charles E. Hugel, chairman of RJR Nabisco, was appointed chairman of the Special Committee. The Special Committee (Exhibit 1) was formed to consider a proposal to purchase the company for $17 billion by a group (the Management Group) consisting of F. Ross Johnson, president and chief executive officer of RJR Nabisco; Edward A. Horrigan, vice chairman of RJR Nabisco and chief executive officer of RJ Reynolds Tobacco Company; and the investment banking firm of Shearson Lehman Hutton. At $75 per share, the buyout offer was 34% above the pre-offer price of $55.875. No details about the form of the offer were immediately available.[1] Within four days, Kohlberg, Kravis, Roberts & Co. (KKR), a firm specializing in leveraged buyouts, announced a competing tender offer for RJR Nabisco. The KKR bid was for $90 per share, or about $20.3 billion in total.

Company Background

RJR Nabisco began as a tobacco company in 1875 and remained primarily a tobacco company until the RJR Foods subsidiary was formed after a series of acquisitions in 1967. By 1987 the company's sales had grown to $15.8 billion (Exhibit 2), and assets stood at $16.9 billion (Exhibit 3). The tobacco business included established brand-name cigarettes such as Winston, Salem, Camel, and Vantage, and also products such as Planters nuts and LifeSavers candies. The business segment data in Exhibit 4 show that the tobacco business had sales of $6.3 billion and operating income of $1.8 billion in 1987.

The food products initially included Hawaiian Punch beverages, Chun King oriental foods, My-T-Fine puddings, Davis baking powder, Vermont Maid syrup, and Patio Mexican dinners. Del Monte, which was acquired in 1979, added canned goods and fresh bananas and pineapples. RJR Nabisco's food businesses expanded substantially with the 1985 acquisition of Nabisco Brands, Inc., which added brand names like Oreo, Fig and Fruit Newtons, and Chips Ahoy! cookies; Ritz, American Classic, and Quakers crackers; Nabisco Shredded Wheat cereal; Fleischmann's margarine; A-1 Steak Sauce; Ortega Mexican foods; and Milk-Bone dog biscuits. In 1987 the food business had sales of $9.4 billion and an operating income of $915 million.

RJR Nabisco had also entered and exited several lines of business. Sea-Land, a container-shipping company, was acquired in 1969 and divested in 1984. Heublein, Inc., a producer of alcoholic beverages and the owner of Kentucky Fried Chicken, was acquired in 1982. Kentucky Fried Chicken was sold in 1986, and the wine and spirits business of Heublein was sold in 1987. The company entered the energy business with the acquisition of American Independent Oil Company in 1970 and the U.S. subsidiaries of Burmah Oil Company in 1976. It exited the energy business by selling these assets in 1984.

[1]The directors of RJR Nabisco viewed Mr. Johnson's consideration of a buyout as material information and disclosed the buyout proposal when it was discussed by the board.

This case was prepared by Professor Richard S. Ruback.

Copyright © 1989 by the President and Fellows of Harvard College. Harvard Business School case 289-056.

Exhibit 5 contains projections for RJR Nabisco, assuming that it continued under its pre-offer operating plans. A total of nearly $10 billion in capital expenditures was projected for 1989 through 1998. The major investment in the tobacco business was extending development and test marketing of Premier, a smokeless cigarette. The company had already spent $300 million on Premier, and substantial costs would be associated with manufacturing and marketing the product. It had also approved plans to spend about $2.8 billion to modernize Nabisco's bakeries. The plans included constructing two new bakeries for $600 million each, spending $1.6 billion on the complete retrofittings of four plants, and closing five others.

The Management Group Bid

The Management Group's strategy was to sell off RJR Nabisco's food businesses and retain its tobacco business. The strategy was based on the view that the market undervalued the strong cash flow from the tobacco business and did not fully value its food businesses because of its association with tobacco. Selling RJR Nabisco's food assets and taking the tobacco business private would eliminate the undervaluation and generate substantial gains.

F. Ross Johnson had experience selling food assets. He was CEO of Standard Brands when Nabisco acquired it to form Nabisco Brands in 1981. And he was CEO of Nabisco Brands when RJ Reynolds acquired it in 1985 to form RJR Nabisco. Furthermore, the Management Group bid occurred when the food industry was undergoing a major restructuring and revaluation. Both Pillsbury and Kraft were in the midst of takeover contests.

Grand Metropolitan PLC began a hostile tender offer for Pillsbury on October 4, 1988. Grand Met was a diversified British company that brewed and distributed beer, ale, and lager; produced and distributed alcoholic beverages; and owned and operated pubs and restaurants. Pillsbury was a diversified food and restaurant company, with popular brands such as Pillsbury Doughboy bakery items, Green Giant vegetables, and Häagen-Dazs ice cream in its food business, and Burger King in its restaurant group. The $5.2 billion Grand Met bid was a 53% premium over the previous market price—about 25 times Pillsbury's net earnings and about four times the book value of common equity.[2] Pillsbury opposed the bid, and its outcome was uncertain.

Philip Morris offered to purchase all Kraft common stock at $90 per share in cash on October 18, 1988. Like RJR Nabisco, Philip Morris earned most of its profits from tobacco: its Marlboro, Benson & Hedges, and Virginia Slims cigarettes had 1987 sales of $14.6 billion and operating profits of $3.3 billion. And, also like RJR Nabisco, Philip Morris acquired most of its food assets in 1985. Philip Morris acquired General Foods, which had brand-name products such as Maxwell House coffee, Birds Eye frozen foods, Jell-O, Oscar Mayer meats, Ronzoni pasta, and Post cereals. Philip Morris also had brewing interests, with brands like Miller, Miller Lite, and Matilda Bay Wine Coolers. Kraft was known for such brand names as Miracle Whip, Seven Seas, and Kraft salad dressings; Kraft mayonnaise; Velveeta cheese; Parkay and Chiffon margarines; Lender's Bagels; and Breyers ice cream. The $11 billion Philip Morris offer for Kraft was a 50% premium over the pre-offer stock price and about 21 times Kraft's net earnings.[3]

[2]Pillsbury's 1988 net earnings per share were $2.45, excluding unusual items, and $.81, including unusual items. The difference was due to a restructuring charge of $1.64 per share. Its 1987 net earnings per share were $2.24, excluding unusual items, and $2.10, including unusual items.

[3]Kraft's forecasted 1988 net income from continuing operations was $522 million. It also had income of $658 million from the sale of its Duracell battery business to KKR in 1988.

Based on the prices bid for Pillsbury and Kraft, analysts estimated the value of RJR Nabisco's food businesses as follows (billions of dollars):

Nabisco	$ 8–9.5
Del Monte	$ 3–4
Planters	$ 1.5–2
Total	$12.5–15.5

Exhibit 6 contains projections for RJR Nabisco under the Management Group plan.

The KKR Bid

Henry Kravis, a general partner of KKR, first expressed interest in organizing a leveraged buyout of RJR Nabisco at a September 1987 dinner meeting with F. Ross Johnson. KKR had been organized in 1976 by three former executives of Bear Stearns Companies, Inc.: Jerome Kohlberg, Henry Kravis, and George Roberts. Since then, KKR had acquired more than 35 companies, paying more than $38 billion in total. KKR also completed the $6.2 billion leveraged buyout of Beatrice foods in 1986, at the time the largest completed leveraged buyout.

KKR offered to purchase up to 87% of RJR Nabisco common stock for $90 per share in cash. The remaining shares would receive securities with a value of $90 per share and terms to be negotiated by KKR and the Special Committee. KKR's $20.7 billion bid also offered $108 per share for the preferred stock of RJR Nabisco.[4] The KKR bid was conditional on approval of the merger by RJR Nabisco's board of directors.

KKR's strategy for managing RJR Nabisco contrasted sharply with the Management Group's proposal to sell all of the company's food assets. According to KKR's letter to the Special Committee:

> We do not contemplate the dismemberment of the company's operations. . . . Our present intention is to retain all of the tobacco businesses and to continue their important presence in Winston-Salem, North Carolina. We also expect to retain a significant portion of the food operations. Moreover, our financing plan does not require, nor do we intend, any presales of parts of the company.

Exhibit 7 contains projections for RJR Nabisco under the KKR operating plan.

KKR did not present specific details on financing for its offer. It had raised a $5.6 billion pool of equity capital for investments in leveraged buyouts. Also, KKR retained Morgan Stanley Group, Inc., Wasserstein, Perella & Co., Drexel Burnham Lambert Inc., and Merrill Lynch Capital Markets to assist in financing the cash portion of the buyout.

Following its bid, KKR entered into a confidentiality agreement with RJR Nabisco, giving KKR access to nonpublic material information about the company. The agreement also gave KKR the opportunity to meet with RJR Nabisco's management. Meeting them was especially important to KKR because its rival, the Management Group, had access to such information because of its position within the firm. In return for access to the information, KKR agreed not to purchase any RJR Nabisco securities, participate in a proxy contest, or advise or influence any participant in such a contest for 2 years unless it obtained approval of RJR Nabisco's board of directors.

[4]RJR Nabisco had 225,336,442 shares of common stock outstanding and outstanding employee stock options to purchase 3,628,414 common shares. There were 1,308,760 shares of preferred stock outstanding.

KKR invited the Management Group to join with it in a joint bid. However, the two parties could not agree on a joint bid and abandoned the attempt on October 26, 1987. A second attempt to form a joint bid also failed, on November 3, and later that same day the Management Group announced a revised proposal to acquire RJR Nabisco. The revised bid was for $92 per share, or $21.1 billion in total, and included $84 per share in cash and $8 per share in securities. Like the KKR bid, no details on the financing for the offer or the terms of the securities were available.

In addition to the bids by the Management Group and KKR, a third bid for RJR Nabisco by groups led by Forstmann, Little & Co. and First Boston Corporation was being considered. The Forstmann, Little group had entered into a confidentiality agreement much like KKR's agreement with RJR Nabisco.

The Auction

On November 7, the Special Committee adopted a set of rules and procedures "to determine which alternative would best serve the interests of [RJR Nabisco's] shareholders." Although not a commitment to recommend selling the company, the rules were "intended to constitute a single round of bidding. Any proposal should reflect the potential purchaser's highest offer." All bids were due by 5 P.M. on Friday, November 18. Any bid that did not conform to these rules would be considered hostile by the Special Committee.[5] The rules for bids included the following:

- Proposals should not be conditional on the sale of any assets of RJR Nabisco.
- Proposals should provide RJR Nabisco shareholders with a "substantial common-stock-related interest."
- Proposals should include details on financing arrangements, including commitment agreements and details of any noncash component of the offer.
- Proposals should be approved by the bidding firm's board of directors.

The board of directors and the Special Committee reserved the right to amend or terminate any of the rules, to terminate discussions with any bidder, and to reject any or all proposals.

The Bids

On a per share basis, KKR's bid was $75 cash, $11 for pay-in-kind preferred stock, and $6 principal amount of pay-in-kind converting debt, which KKR valued at $8.[6] The debt would convert to common stock at the end of 1 year unless the holder decided to retain it. If all debt was converted into common stock, it would represent 25% of the outstanding common stock of RJR Nabisco. The cash portion of the bid would be financed by $1.5 billion in equity, $3.5 billion in subordinated debt, and $12.4 billion in bank debt. KKR also planned on assuming the $5.2 billion of preexisting debt.

On a per share basis, the Management Group's bid was $90 cash, $6 of pay-in-kind preferred stock, and $4 of convertible preferred stock. The convertible preferred stock,

[5]RJR Nabisco had a variety of antitakeover provisions that could be used to oppose a hostile offer, including a supermajority provision (requiring a two-thirds vote of disinterested shareholders to approve a merger), a poison pill rights plan (which forces an acquiring firm to purchase preferred stock at a substantial premium), and Section 203 of Delaware Law (which prevents a merger within 3 years of acquiring 15% or more of a target firm).

[6]Pay-in-kind securities pay dividends and coupons with additional units of the security instead of cash.

as a class, could be converted into about 15% of the surviving company's equity, but it was callable by the company at any time for the face value and accumulated dividends. The cash portion of the bid would be financed by $2.5 billion in equity, $3 billion in subordinated debt, and $15 billion in bank debt. Like KKR, the Management Group planned on assuming the $5.2 billion of outstanding debt.

The First Boston group's offer involved the purchase of RJR Nabisco's tobacco business by the First Boston group and the sale of the food businesses. The food businesses would be sold for a $13 billion installment note before December 31, 1988, and a right to 80% of the net proceeds of the subsequent sale of the food business in excess of the installment note. RJR Nabisco shareholders would receive the proceeds from the sale of the food business. First Boston would purchase the tobacco business for $15.75 billion, plus warrants (valued at $2–3 per RJR Nabisco share) to acquire up to 20% of the equity of the tobacco business. On a per share basis, RJR Nabisco shareholders would receive a cash payment ranging from $98 to $110, securities valued at $5, and warrants worth $2–3. Unlike the bids by KKR and the Management Group, the First Boston proposal did not include information about its financing.

EXHIBIT 1

Composition of the Special Committee of the RJR Nabisco Board of Directors to Consider Offers for the Company

Committee Member	Biographical Sketch	Common Stock Ownership (shares)
Charles E. Hugel, Chairman	Age 60; chairman of RJR Nabisco; president and chief executive officer of Combustion Engineering, Inc.	750
John D. Macomber, Vice Chairman	Age 60; chairman of Lasertechnics; retired chairman and chief executive officer of Celanese Corporation	16,425
Martin S. Davis	Age 61; chairman and chief executive officer of Gulf and Western, Inc.	1,000
William S. Anderson	Age 69; retired chairman and chief executive officer of the executive committee of NCR Corporation	1,500
Albert L. Butler, Jr.	Age 70; president of Arista Company; chairman of RJR Nabisco's organization, compensation, and nominating committee	9,465
Investment Bankers	*Legal Counsel*	
Dillon, Read & Co.	Skadden, Arps, Slate, Meagher and Flom	
Lazard Frères, Inc.	Young, Conaway, Stargatt and Taylor	

EXHIBIT 2 Condensed Operating and Stockholder Information, 1982–1987 (millions of dollars except per share data)

Sources: Company reports and casewriter's estimates.

	1982	1983	1984	1985	1986	1987
Revenues	$7,323	$7,565	$8,200	$11,622	$15,102	$15,766
Operating Income	1,142	1,205	1,412	1,949	2,340	2,304
Interest and debt expense	180	177	166	337	565	489
Income before income taxes	1,012	1,110	1,353	1,663	1,782	1,816
Income from continuing operations	548	626	747	917	1,025	1,081
Income from discontinued operations[a]	322	255	463	84	39	128
Net income	$ 870	$ 881	$1,210	$ 1,001	$ 1,064	$ 1,209
Earnings per share	$ 3.13	$ 2.90	$ 4.11	$ 3.60	$ 3.83	$ 4.70
Dividends per share	1.14	1.22	1.30	1.41	1.51	1.76
Closing stock price[b]	20.40	24.30	28.80	31.38	49.25	45.00
Price-earnings ratio[b]	6.5	8.38	7.01	8.72	12.86	9.57
Numbers of shares (millions)[b, c]	281.5	283.2	258.4	250.6	250.4	247.4
Beta[d]	.80	.70	.74	1.21	1.24	.67

[a]Divestitures and acquisitions for 1982–1987 are as follows:
1982 Heublein acquired for $1.36 billion
1983 Energy division sold for after-tax gain of $275 million.
1984 Divestiture of transportation division completed by spinning off common stock to Sea-Land Corp. (transportation accounted for as a discontinued operation since 1983).
1985 Nabisco Brands acquired at a total cost of $4.9 billion.
1986 Kentucky Fried Chicken sold at after-tax loss of $39 million.
1987 Heublein sold for after-tax gain of $215 million.
[b]Year-end.
[c]Figures include a 2.5-for-1 stock split effective May 17, 1985.
[d]Calculated by ordinary least-squares regression using daily stock price data.

EXHIBIT 3
Consolidated Balance Sheets, 1986–1987 (millions of dollars)

Source: Company reports.

	1986	1987
Cash	$ 827	$ 1,088
Net receivables	1,675	1,745
Inventories	2,620	2,678
Other current assets	273	329
Property, plant, and equipment, net	5,343	5,847
Goodwill and other intangibles	4,603	4,525
Net assets of discontinued operations	716	—
Other assets	644	649
Total assets	$16,701	$16,861
Notes payable	$ 518	$ 442
Accounts payable	2,923	3,187
Current portion of long-term debt	423	162
Income taxes payable	202	332
Current liabilities	4,066	4,123
Long-term debt	4,833	3,884
Deferred income taxes	751	846
Redeemable preferred stock	291	173
Other liabilities	1,448	1,797
Total liabilities	11,389	10,823
Stockholders' equity	5,312	6,038
Total liabilities and net worth	$16,701	$16,861

EXHIBIT 4 **Financial Summary by Business Segment, 1982–1987 (millions of dollars)**

Source: Company reports.

	1982	1983	1984	1985	1986	1987
Tobacco						
Sales	$4,822	$4,807	$5,178	$5,422	$5,866	$6,346
Operating profit	1,187	1,150	1,305	1,483	1,659	1,821
Identifiable assets	3,219	3,378	3,812	4,496	4,822	5,208
Depreciation	81	78	108	146	205	244
Capital expenditures	238	383	527	647	613	433
Restructuring expense	—	—	—	—	—	(261)
Operating profit/Identifiable assets	36.9%	34.0%	34.2%	33.0%	34.0%	35.0%
Food Products						
Sales	$2,501	$2,758	$3,022	$6,200	$9,236	$9,420
Operating profit	21	129	181	549	820	915
Identifiable assets	1,710	1,761	2,211	9,598	9,822	10,117
Depreciation	51	56	68	195	376	380
Capital expenditures	84	94	86	279	344	445
Restructuring expense	—	—	—	—	—	18
Operating profit/Identifiable assets	1.2%	7.3%	8.2%	6.0%	8.0%	9.0%
Spirits and Wines						
Sales	$ 392	$ 746	$ 703	$ 766	$ 876	—
Operating profit	53	113	122	131	138	—
Identifiable assets	1,084	740	815	895	991	—
Depreciation	14	24	22	24	30	—
Capital expenditures	11	13	13	26	25	—
Restructuring expense	—	—	—	—	—	—
Operating profit/Identifiable assets	4.9%	15.3%	15.0%	14.6%	14.0%	—
Other (Including Corporate)[a]						
Sales	—	—	—	—	—	—
Operating profit (loss)	$ (66)	$ (74)	$ (74)	($ 83)	$ (139)	$ (182)
Identifiable assets	3,106	3,197	2,257	1,684	1,319	1,536
Depreciation	11	16	16	13	24	28
Capital expenditures	16	15	29	20	65	58
Restructuring expense	—	—	—	—	—	(7)
Operating profit/Identifiable assets	–2.1%	–2.3%	–3.3%	–5.0%	–10.5%	–11.9%

[a]Includes earnings on cash and short-term investments and miscellaneous discontinued operations.

EXHIBIT 5 Cash Flow Projections under Pre-Bid Strategy, 1988–1998 (millions of dollars)

	1988	1989	1990	1991	1992	1993	1994	1995	1996	1997	1998
Tobacco sales	$ 7,061	$ 7,650	$ 8,293	$ 8,893	$ 9,731	$10,540	$11,418	$12,368	$13,397	$14,514	$15,723
Food sales	9,889	10,438	11,383	12,092	12,847	13,651	14,507	15,420	16,393	17,428	18,533
Total	16,950	18,088	19,676	21,075	22,578	24,191	25,925	27,788	29,790	31,942	34,256
Operating income (expense)											
Tobacco	1,924	2,022	2,360	2,786	3,071	3,386	3,733	4,115	4,534	4,998	5,508
Food	1,079	1,163	1,255	1,348	1,459	1,581	1,713	1,855	2,011	2,178	2,361
Corporate	(350)	(287)	(279)	(296)	(314)	(333)	(353)	(374)	(396)	(420)	(445)
Total	2,653	2,898	3,336	3,838	4,216	4,634	5,093	5,596	6,149	6,756	7,424
Interest expense	551	582	662	693	690	658	594	458	410	259	–21
Net income	1,360	1,498	1,730	2,023	2,259	2,536	2,858	3,251	3,625	4,094	4,625
Depreciation, amortization, deferred taxes	730	807	791	819	849	866	867	867	867	867	861
Capital expenditures	1,142	1,708	1,462	1,345	930	738	735	735	735	735	735
Change in working capital	—	80	111	98	105	113	121	130	140	151	162
Cash flow available for capital payments[a]	—	$ 517	$ 948	$ 1,399	$ 2,073	$ 2,551	$ 2,869	$ 3,253	$ 3,617	$ 4,075	$ 4,589

[a]Cash flow available for capital payments = Net income + Depreciation, amortization, deferred taxes – Capital expenditures – Change in working capital.

EXHIBIT 6 Cash Flow and Capital Structure Projections under the Management Group Strategy, 1989–1998 (millions of dollars)

	1989	1990	1991	1992	1993	1994	1995	1996	1997	1998
Operating Information										
Sales	$ 7,650	$ 8,293	$8,983	$9,731	$10,540	$11,418	$12,368	$13,397	$14,514	$15,723
Operating income	1,917	2,385	2,814	3,266	3,589	3,945	4,337	4,768	5,243	5,766
Interest expense	2,792	1,353	1,286	1,183	1,037	850	624	351	0	0
Amortization[a]	388	388	388	388	388	388	388	388	388	388
After-tax income	(965)	293	621	987	1,297	1,655	2,063	2,527	3,073	3,418
Depreciation, amortization, deferred taxes	777	725	726	735	749	754	758	763	769	774
Capital expenditures	432	381	380	389	396	402	412	422	432	442
Change in working capital	41	45	48	52	57	61	67	72	78	85
Net proceeds from asset sales	12,680	0	0	0	0	0	0	0	0	0
Cash flow available for capital payments[b]	$12,018	$ 593	$ 919	$1,282	$ 1,594	$ 1,946	$ 2,344	$ 2,797	$ 3,332	$ 3,666
Capital Structure										
Principal payments										
Assumed debt	$ 310	$ 375	$ 721	$ 816	$ 400	$ 728	$ 1,854	$ 0	$ 0	$ 0
Bank debt	11,708	218	198	466	1,194	1,217	0	0	0	0
Subordinated debt	0	0	0	0	0	0	490	2,510	0	0
Preferred stock	0	0	0	0	0	0	0	287	3,332	3,327
Convertible preferred stock	0	0	0	0	0	0	0	0	0	339
Total	$12,018	$ 593	$ 919	$1,282	$ 1,594	$ 1,946	$ 2,344	$ 2,797	$ 3,332	$ 3,666
Year-end book values										
Assumed debt	4,894	4,519	3,798	2,982	2,582	1,854	0	0	0	0
Bank debt	3,292	3,075	2,877	2,411	1,217	0	0	0	0	0
Subordinated debt	3,000	3,000	3,000	3,000	3,000	3,000	2,510	0	0	0
Total	$11,186	$10,594	$9,675	$8,393	$ 6,799	$ 4,854	$ 2,510	$ 0	$ 0	$ 0
Preferred stock	1,632	1,938	2,303	2,736	3,250	3,861	4,587	5,162	2,801	0
Convertible preferred stock	1,035	1,229	1,460	1,735	2,061	2,448	2,909	3,455	4,105	4,538
Common stock	1,535	1,828	2,449	3,436	4,733	6,388	8,451	10,978	14,051	17,469
Total	$ 4,202	$ 4,995	$6,212	$7,907	$10,044	$12,697	$15,947	$19,595	$20,957	$22,007

Note: Figures may not add exactly because of rounding.

[a]The amortization of goodwill of $338 million per year is from the proposed acquisition of RJR Nabisco at $22.9 billion, which had the book value of $7.4 billion at the end of 1988. The difference between the purchase price and book value is amortized over 40 years using the straight-line method.

[b]Cash flow available for capital payments = Net income + Depreciation, amortization, deferred taxes – Capital expenditures – Change in working capital + Net proceeds from asset sales.

EXHIBIT 7 Cash Flow and Capital Structure Projections under KKR's Strategy, 1989–1998 (millions of dollars)

	1989	1990	1991	1992	1993	1994	1995	1996	1997	1998
Operating Information										
Tobacco sales	$ 7,650	$ 8,293	$ 8,983	$ 9,731	$10,540	$11,418	$12,368	$13,397	$14,514	$15,723
Food sales	8,540	6,930	7,485	8,084	8,730	9,428	10,183	10,997	11,877	12,827
Total	16,190	15,223	16,468	17,815	19,270	20,846	22,551	24,394	26,391	28,550
Operating income (expense)										
Tobacco	2,022	2,360	2,786	3,071	3,386	3,733	4,115	4,534	4,998	5,508
Food	1,060	1,026	1,191	1,245	1,307	1,367	1,430	1,494	1,561	1,630
Corporate	(219)	(158)	(167)	(176)	(185)	(194)	(203)	(213)	(224)	(235)
Total	2,862	3,228	3,811	4,140	4,508	4,906	5,341	5,815	6,335	6,902
Interest expense	2,754	2,341	1,997	1,888	1,321	1,088	806	487	21	0
Amortization[a]	388	388	388	388	388	388	388	388	388	388
After-tax income	(281)	233	845	1,134	1,751	2,168	2,641	3,164	3,814	4,203
Depreciation, amortization, deferred taxes	1,159	991	899	907	920	924	928	933	939	945
Capital expenditures	774	556	555	572	586	598	618	638	658	678
Change in working capital	79	84	87	94	102	110	119	129	140	151
Noncash interest expense	206	237	312	366	0	0	0	0	0	0
Net proceeds from asset sales	3,500	2,700	0	0	0	0	0	0	0	0
Cash flow available for capital payments[b]	$ 3,732	$ 3,521	$ 1,414	$ 1,740	$ 1,983	$ 2,383	$ 2,832	$ 3,330	$ 3,956	$ 4,319
Capital Structure										
Principal payments										
Assumed debt	$ 310	$ 375	$ 721	$ 816	$ 400	$ 400	$ 2,182	$ 0	$ 0	$ 0
Bank debt	3,422	3,146	693	924	1,583	1,983	629	0	0	0
Subordinated debt	0	0	0	0	0	0	21	3,330	149	0
Preferred stock	0	0	0	0	0	0	0	0	3,806	4,319
Total	$ 3,732	$ 3,521	$ 1,414	$ 1,740	$ 1,983	$ 2,383	$ 2,832	$ 3,330	$ 3,956	$ 4,319
Year-end book values										
Assumed debt	4,894	4,519	3,798	2,982	2,582	2,182	0	0	0	0
Bank debt	8,958	5,812	5,119	4,195	2,612	629	0	0	0	0
Subordinated debt	3,500	3,500	3,500	3,500	3,500	3,500	3,470	149	0	0
Converting debt[c]	1,580	1,817	2,129	2,495	0	0	0	0	0	0
Total	18,932	15,648	14,546	13,172	8,694	6,311	3,470	149	0	0
Preferred stock	2,896	3,331	3,958	4,702	5,586	6,636	7,883	9,365	7,320	4,377
Common stock	1,219	1,452	2,297	3,430	7,676	9,844	12,485	15,648	19,463	23,666
Total	$ 4,115	$ 4,783	$ 6,255	$ 8,132	$13,262	$16,480	$20,368	$25,013	$26,783	$28,043

Note: Figures may not add exactly because of rounding.

[a]The amortization of goodwill of $338 million per year is from the proposed acquisition of RJR Nabisco at $22.9 billion, which had the book value of $7.4 billion at the end of 1988. The difference between the purchase price and the book value is amortized ever 40 years using the straight-line method.

[b]Cash flow available for capital payments = Net income + Depreciation, amortization, deferred taxes – Capital expenditures – Change in working capital + Noncash interest expense + Net proceeds from asset sales.

[c]Assumes converting to equity in 1993.

Laura Martin: Real Options and the Cable Industry

On May 4, 1999, Laura Martin paced in the Rainbow Room of the Rockefeller Center in New York City as she prepared for her presentation at the Credit Suisse First Boston (CSFB) 1999 Broadband conference. She had assembled a panel of four leading figures from the U.S. cable industry to address a group of 400 institutional money managers on the state of the industry. On her panel were the CFO of Adelphia Communications, the CEO of AT&T's Cable Operations, the Vice Chairman of Comcast Corporation, and the CEO of Cox Communications. As the equity research analyst for cable stocks at CSFB, a global investment banking firm, Martin realized that this meeting afforded her a unique opportunity to demonstrate her knowledge of the drivers of value in the cable industry. The stakes were even higher as she had chosen to unveil a new approach to valuing cable stocks at this panel. This "real options" valuation metric would be new to both the panel and the audience, and Martin wondered if they would appreciate a new way to think about their industry—or if they would simply dismiss it.

The cable industry historically generated revenues exclusively from providing analog video. Rapid advances in digital and compression technologies were now creating new potential sources of revenue including digital video, cable telephony, and high-speed Internet access. Additionally, the industry, once the domain of family-owned local operators, was consolidating quickly and the boundaries between the cable industry and other media industries were quickly dissolving.

Martin had observed these changes as a sell-side analyst for CSFB covering the cable industry for the last five years. During that time, she had tried to differentiate herself from her competitors through an emphasis on more advanced valuation techniques. While most of her competitors were content with metrics such as Earnings Before Interest, Taxes, Depreciation, and Amortization (EBITDA) multiples, Martin had chosen to emphasize discounted cash flow analyses and Economic Value Added analyses. Recently, her attention had shifted to real options analysis as she felt other valuation metrics neglected an important aspect of the cable valuation puzzle. She had chosen this conference as the moment to unveil the implications of real options analysis to the companies she evaluated and the money managers she served as clients.

As she prepared to present her findings, she reviewed the details of her analyses and considered how she could best ensure the acceptance of her ideas. Was she correct in thinking of the unused capacity as a real option? Were the inputs to her analysis correct? Most importantly, how could she overcome the resistance to complex valuation metrics in an industry that still emphasized EBITDA multiples—a valuation metric she dismissed as primitive?

Professors Mihir A. Desai and Peter Tufano prepared this case with the assistance of Joshua Musher, Research Associate, as the basis for class discussion rather than to illustrate either effective or ineffective handling of an administrative situation.

Copyright © 2000 by the President and Fellows of Harvard College. To order copies or request permission to reproduce materials, call 1-800-545-7685, write Harvard Business School Publishing, Boston, MA 02163, or go to http://www.hbsp.harvard.edu. No part of this publication may be reproduced, stored in a retrieval system, used in a spreadsheet, or transmitted in any form or by any means—electronic, mechanical, photocopying, recording, or otherwise—without the permission of Harvard Business School.

Laura Martin and the Equity Research Industry

After graduating from Harvard Business School in 1983, Martin spent seven years as an investment banker at Drexel Burnham Lambert, four years as a "buy-side" analyst at Capital Research and Management, and the last five years as a "sell-side" equity analyst at CSFB.

A "buy-side" analyst typically worked for a money management firm. In her capacity as a buy-side analyst, Martin both managed a portfolio of equities and provided her portfolio manager colleagues with stock recommendations for the industries she covered. Research produced by buy-side analysts was solely for the firm that employed the analyst, and was not distributed widely. In contrast, a "sell-side" analyst worked for a broker-dealer that distributed or sold the research to their buy-side clients. CSFB employed 265 equity analysts worldwide who covered eighty-five industries, and another five analysts who covered broad trends in the equity markets.

Martin's primary motivation in moving to the sell-side from the buy-side was to take advantage of the depth of analysis conducted on the sell-side. Martin commented, "On the buy-side I covered five industries and 150 stocks. On the sell-side, I only cover 15 large capitalization stocks and I focus on two industries. In addition, while firms on the buy side typically have a specific investment style, on the sell-side I serve clients with all types of money management disciplines. This requires me to tailor my analysis and recommendations to each client's needs."[1]

Martin considered three constituencies central to her work as a sell-side analyst—the companies she covered, the buy-side firms she advised, and internal CSFB constituencies. Martin estimated that she spent approximately 40% of her time analyzing the firms she covered, 35% communicating that analysis to buy-side clients, and 25% on internal CSFB activities.

- Martin visited each of the companies she covered at least once a year. During those meetings, Martin would typically meet with many company representatives including the CEO, CFO, operating division chiefs (marketing, sales, technology, production, etc.), and the head of investor relations. These visits typically lasted one day. In addition, many companies sponsored one-day investor conferences each year that Martin would attend along with 100 other buy-side and sell-side representatives. Also, Martin spoke with company representatives by phone at least every quarter. Finally, Martin interacted with company representatives at industry shows and at conferences.
- Martin regularly communicated via fax, voice mail, or email with approximately 900 individuals employed by the largest institutional money managers in the world, predominantly in the United States. Because CSFB did not have retail operations, Martin did not call on non-institutional clients. Martin believed that she saw or visited approximately 250 of those accounts annually. For the remainder, she would field inquiries over the phone. Martin emphasized that communicating with clients was her mainstay. "I get paid to talk. On the buy-side, you get paid to outperform your index. You don't have to talk to anyone. The sell-side is more about communicating the results of your analysis, either in print or verbally. I publish 1,000 pages

[1]Money managers typically tailored their funds according to particular investment strategies or styles. For example, managers might favor stocks with high expected earnings growth, or "growth" stocks. Alternatively, other managers might favor neglected stocks that were considered relatively cheap, or "value" stocks.

each year[2] and I use a variety of communication technologies, including blast faxes, blast voicemails and blast emails, to reach my institutional clients." Her reports were typically filled with valuation analyses that supported a target price for a given stock, earnings estimates for that stock, and her investment recommendation (buy, sell, or hold).[3]

- Martin considered her relationships with internal CSFB constituencies to be the third important dimension of her job. These internal constituencies were the institutional sales force, the trading desk, and the investment banking arm of CSFB. The sales force was an important conduit between Martin and her buy-side clients. When Martin had an important idea to share about any of her companies, she would communicate it on CSFB's 7:30 AM daily research call. CSFB's sales force would make thirty to forty calls each to interested clients, rapidly disseminating her message to hundreds of buy-side clients prior to the market opening. Martin also interacted with CSFB's trading desk frequently. CSFB acted as an agent and principal in trading activity; if there was unusual behavior in one of Martin's stocks, a trader might call Martin to ask her to follow up with the company or discuss rumors that might be affecting the stock. Investment banking was Martin's third internal constituency and an important CSFB profit center. If any of Martin's companies issued equity, Martin was expected to answer questions regarding valuation and the overall business for any clients that were considering participating in the deal. In merger and acquisition activity, Martin was sometimes asked for expert advice about how the market would react to specific deal structures or pricing.

According to Bloomberg, 29 equity research analysts covered the broadcasting/cable industry.[4] Martin sought to differentiate herself from other equity research analysts through the depth of her analyses and the use of novel valuation techniques.

[2]Each written report contained a lengthy disclaimer by CSFB, which we reproduce here at their request: "This report is provided to you solely for informational purposes and does not constitute an offer or solicitation of an offer, or any advice or recommendation, to purchase any securities or other financial instruments and may not be construed as such. This report may not be reproduced or redistributed to any other person, in whole or in part, without the prior written consent of the distributor listed below. The information set forth herein has been obtained or derived from sources believed by Credit Suisse First Boston Corporation and its affiliates ("CSFB" or "the firm") to be reliable, but CSFB does not make any representation or warranty, express or implied, as to its accuracy or completeness. Past performance should not be taken as an indication or guarantee of future performance, and no representation or warranty, express or implied, is made regarding future performance. Opinions and estimates may be changed without notice. The firm, or one or more of its partners or employees, from time to time may have long or short positions in, or buy and sell and make markets in, any of the financial instruments referred to herein. If CSFB makes a market in any security, there can be no assurance that CSFB will continue to do so. Additional information is available upon request. CSFB may have issued other reports that are inconsistent with, and reach different conclusions from, the information presented herein. Those reports reflect the different assumptions, views and analytical methods of the analysts who prepared them. This report is being distributed in the United States by CSFB, and in Canada by Credit Suisse First Boston Canada, Inc. ("CSFBSC") with CSFB as mailing/delivery agent. In jurisdictions where CSFB is not registered or licensed to trade in securities, any trade will be made only in accordance with applicable securities legislation which will vary from jurisdiction to jurisdiction and may require that the trade be made in accordance with applicable exemptions from registration or licensing requirements. CSFBSC has approved the distribution of this memorandum. Any U.S. customer wishing to effect a transaction in any security should do so only by contacting a representative at Credit Suisse First Boston Corporation, Eleven Madison Avenue, New York, NY 10010 (212) 325-2000."

[3]According to a Zacks Investment Research study, 67.5% of all analyst recommendations were buys, 1.4% sells, and 31.1% holds. Jeffrey M. Laderman, "Wall Street's Spin Game," *Business Week,* October 5, 1998.

[4]According to Nelson Information Services, there were 3,724 full-time equity analysts. Laderman, ibid.

Among the analysts who covered the industry, Martin suggested that "everyone carves out different niches. I compete on intellectual leadership and depth of analysis. I have competitors who position themselves as detail folks who publish loads of details while others are relationship types who call every CEO every month." With respect to valuation, virtually all leading analysts reported valuation in terms of EBITDA multiples, with a quarter also reporting multiples of price-to-free-cash flow, and about a quarter reporting discounted cash flow analyses.

Martin believed that there were two primary drivers to her compensation: her annual ranking in *Institutional Investor* magazine and revenues linked to corporate finance deals. While there was not an explicit formula linking her compensation to these metrics, Martin felt that compensation was quite sensitive to both measures. Each year, *Institutional Investor* polled investors to create an "All-America Research Team." Voters were asked to rank five attributes of all sell-side analysts. In 1999, these attributes were ranked as follows: (1) industry knowledge (8.09 out of 10), (2) written reports (7.26 rating), (3) stock selection (7.20 rating), (4) earnings estimates (6.83 rating), and (5) special services including company visits and conferences (6.70 rating). Martin concurred with the survey's emphasis on industry knowledge and the downplaying of stock selection and earnings estimates. Martin also added that for high ratings, "accessibility is extremely important. I have to basically be available 24 hours a day." Martin was ranked in both industry categories that she covered.

Valuation in the Cable Industry: Cox Communications

Cable television began in the early 1950s in the United States when entrepreneurs established "community antenna television" (CATV) systems in rural areas where over-the-air broadcast reception was poor. By 1955, there were 400 CATV systems with 150,000 subscribers. Cable entrepreneurs subsequently expanded into suburban systems and urban areas. By 1978, cable wires passed a total of 26.8 million households (representing 34% of total U.S. television households) and there were 14.2 million basic cable subscribers paying an average of $7.13 per month for an average of eight channels. By 1999, according to the MPAA, there were 97 million homes passed by cable wires (representing 97% of households) and 69 million cable subscribers paying an average of $38 per month for 45 channels.[5]

In December 1998, Cox was the fifth largest multiple system operator (MSO) of cable systems in the U.S. with 3.78 million basic cable subscribers in its consolidated cable systems which passed 5.97 million homes. The corresponding 63% penetration rate was the highest penetration rate among the five largest MSOs. Cox's cable systems were tightly clustered with approximately 80% of its total subscribers in its ten largest clusters. In addition to its cable assets, Cox held stakes in cable programming services and in technology and telephony companies. In valuing a company such as Cox, Martin separately valued each of the companies held and then aggregated the implied equity values with the value of the cable business. Historical financials for Cox Communications are presented in Exhibit 1. Exhibit 2 provides summary financials for several comparable cable companies.

According to Martin, the cable industry was on the cusp of dramatic changes. Historically, cable companies delivered only analog video signals to homes that paid for the service (cable subscribers). Technological change had created three new potential revenue sources, all based on digital technology: digital video, high-speed data, and cable

[5]For industry history, see Sally Bedell Smith's *In All His Glory: The Life of William S. Paley*, New York: Simon & Schuster, 1990.

telephone. As a result of these new potential profit centers, Martin forecast three changes in fundamentals that would become key value drivers for the cable business in the future:

1. *Revenue growth would accelerate and diversify:* From 1998 to 2003, Martin projected that revenue would grow at a compound annual growth rate (CAGR) of 14.2%. The mix of revenue would shift from nearly 100% analog video revenue in 1998 to an equal division between analog and digital product revenues over the 5-year period. (See Exhibit 3.)
2. *Capital spending would slow and the nature of investments would change:* While upgrading the existing cable plant and maintenance capital constituted the majority of capital spending in 1998 and was expected to increase for the following two years, further capital spending would substantially decrease. What spending remained would be directed toward the new technologies. Consequently, overall capital spending, excluding acquisitions, would diminish at an average CAGR of –6.5%. Martin believed that the shift from non-revenue linked (plant upgrades) to revenue linked (new technologies) capital expenditures implied falling risk for investors.
3. *The digital revenue streams would yield higher returns on invested capital:* According to Martin, the shift in capital spending toward new technologies would generate considerably higher returns on invested capital (ROIC).[6] Martin estimated that marginal ROICs (excluding the cost of upgrading the cable plant) were 45% to 65%, compared to a 1998E ROIC of approximately 5% for Cox. (See Exhibit 4.)

Martin also believed that the industry structure of cable was changing. Historically, the cable industry had been the domain of family-owned local operators. Aggressive consolidation within the cable industry and acquisitions of cable companies by non-cable companies (a trend labeled "convergence") implied that the boundaries between the cable industry and other industries (telephone, Internet, etc.) were dissolving.

While there were investment risks to the sector and to Cox—including regulatory changes, the difficulty in creating scale economies, and the super-voting power of the Cox family[7]—Martin believed that the changing industry structure would drive price appreciation in the cable sector and for Cox. Martin believed that, in equity research, "unless you can quantify it, you don't get credit for it." Martin employed several methodologies to translate the new fundamentals and industry structure into valuation metrics for the cable stocks, and estimate the potential price appreciation of Cox.

ROIC Target Price Analysis: Historically, cable valuations had closely tracked ROIC according to Martin. Using regression analysis, Martin analyzed the relationship between ROIC and the valuation of cable and entertainment companies as defined by the ratio of enterprise value to average invested capital.[8] (See Exhibit 5.) Martin projected that Cox would improve its ROIC by 0.8%, or 80 basis points, in 1999. Martin then used the regression line to estimate the target enterprise value to average invested capital multiple.[9] Adjusting for non-consolidated assets, other assets, cash and option proceeds, and debt, Martin then inferred a target price for Cox by year-end 1999 of $50. This ROIC "Target Price" Analysis indicated to Martin that Cox had significant upside potential relative to its current stock price of $37.50.

[6]Martin calculated ROIC by dividing net operating profit after taxes by the average invested capital for the period. Invested capital is the sum of fixed assets and net working capital.

[7]Cox Enterprises, owned by the Cox family, controlled 76% of the vote of Cox, mostly through a class of supervoting stock that had ten votes per share.

[8]Regression analysis is performed to determine the statistical relationship between variables of interest.

[9]Enterprise value was calculated by summing the market capitalization of the equity with book value of debt. Invested capital was the sum of fixed assets and net working capital.

EBITDA Multiples Analysis: Martin also framed her target price in the language of EBITDA multiples, a common metric in the cable business. Exhibit 6 compares how Cox currently traded as a multiple of EBITDA relative to how it would trade if Martin's target price of $50 and her projections for EBITDA were realized. According to this analysis, Cox currently traded at 13.3X EBITDA and Martin's target price would translate into a 20.9X EBITDA multiple for 1999. While these analyses were a mainstay in the cable industry, Martin didn't think they "asked the right questions. They're not predictive; they really just reflect the past. Finally, they don't account adequately for the dynamics of balance sheet items which are vital to a capital intensive industry like cable."

Discounted Cash Flow Analysis: Martin's preferred method of valuing companies was the discounted cash flow (DCF) method employed in Exhibit 7. Martin preferred the DCF method as she felt "that it forces me to ask better questions." In particular, Martin felt that the explicit treatment of capital spending and depreciation was important for valuing cable companies and that the DCF analysis forced her to think through the dynamics of EBITDA growth for the company. Martin forecasted ten years of EBITDA growth rates for the company and industry, changes in the competitive and regulatory environments, technological shifts, emerging industry structures and value drivers, and other factors that would affect long-term growth. She typically tried to be conservative in her estimates. Similarly, Martin forecast ten years of capital spending and depreciation to arrive at an unlevered "free cash flow" (or cash flow available for all capital providers) for each year through 2008. Using a terminal multiple of 13 times EBITDA and a weighted average cost of capital (WACC) of 9.3%,[10] the DCF analysis implied that Cox's stock was worth $54.29. Again, this represented substantial appreciation relative to the current stock price.

Other methods: In addition, Martin reported two other valuation measures. In her *private market valuation analysis,* she took into account the takeover or control premium for Cox's holdings of non-public assets. In a takeover, these assets might sell for considerably more than their public market value. The private market analysis also provided valuations of all non-consolidated assets. Based on this analysis, she calculated a theoretical value of Cox of about $51. In her *competitive advantage period analysis,* she calculated how long Cox could sustain returns above its cost of capital. She estimated that Cox could sustain a 15-year period of above-market returns, implying a theoretical value well above the current price of $37.50.

Real Options Valuation Analysis

While Martin felt that discounted cash flow analysis was a significantly better valuation tool than EBITDA multiples, she perceived several shortcomings in the new digital world of the cable industry. In particular, Martin noted that the previous analysis did not include the value from unused bandwidth capacity.

Cable companies were upgrading their cable infrastructure to have 750 megahertz (MHz) of bandwidth capacity by replacing coaxial cable with fiber optic cables.[11]

[10]Martin calculated Cox's cost of equity (10.5%) as the 10-year risk-free rate of 5.12% plus the product of Cox's beta of 1.07 times an estimated risk premium of 4.98%. Martin calculated Cox's after-tax cost of debt as 3.65% by assuming that Cox could borrow at 86 basis points above the risk-free rate and that Cox faced a tax rate of 39%. Finally, Martin employed a debt-to-total capital ratio of 18% in arriving at a WACC of 9.3%.

[11]Martin estimated that 66% of Cox's plant would be upgraded to 750MHz and an additional 15% to 550 MHz by June 1999. Martin estimated this to cost $280 per home passed, $40 of which Martin associated with the extra capacity of the stealth tier.

(Coaxial cable remained in the ground for the last mile to the home as coaxial cable had enormous bandwidth over short distances.) Of the 750 MHz of capacity in an upgraded cable plant, 550 MHz was typically devoted to analog video and another 98 MHz was dedicated to digital services, network control, telephony and Internet services. The remaining 102 MHz, comprised of seventeen 6 MHz channels, was "dark" or "unlit" and was essentially unused. (See Exhibit 8.)

Martin considered the DCF valuation unsatisfactory for these unused channels because "companies are being hit for 100% of the capital spending but we're only counting the visible revenue streams from existing services. That unused capacity could be used for a bunch of new interactive services or services that don't even exist today which we're not giving these companies credit for." For example, technologies under development would allow for video streaming, interactive games, and the implementation of local intranets. Martin called the 102 MHz of unused capacity the "stealth tier" as the revenue streams were invisible but, in her estimation, not valueless.[12] Given that Cox's stock price was below the DCF valuation and the DCF valuation did not incorporate the value of the stealth tier, Martin reasoned that the stealth tier was actually being ignored by the market.

Martin turned to real options to value the stealth tier. While familiar with financial options, she had recently read several articles and a book that described the use of financial option-pricing methodologies in broader settings.[13] According to Martin, the stealth tier represented a real option for cable companies such as Cox as they could potentially "light up" the stealth tier as new, currently immature or unknown interactive services were developed. For Martin, the contingent nature of the investment decision and the uncertainty surrounding the ultimate revenue streams made the stealth tier ideal for valuation through real options analysis. Just as financial options give holders the right, but not obligation, to buy securities, this real option gave each upgraded cable company the right, but not the obligation, to obtain revenues from the stealth tier, depending on market conditions. Real options analyses had been used in several industry settings including natural resources extraction and pharmaceutical research. In both cases, managers had rights to pursue investment projects, such as extraction or drug development, without obligations to pursue them.

Financial options were valued using a wide variety of methods, the best known being the Black-Scholes model used to value simple European-style equity options.[14] In order to conduct a real options valuation of the stealth tier, Martin realized that she needed analogous inputs to the inputs used for valuing financial options. Martin considered that the best approach was to value the option of *each* channel of the stealth tier *per* home passed.

- As a proxy for the present value of each channel on the stealth tier, Martin used the average current market value per home passed for a typical cable company of $2,500. She divided $2,500 by the 108 lit channels currently being employed to yield a current value of a channel per home passed of $23.15.
- For the strike price of the option, Martin had to calculate the cost to light up one of the seventeen channels of the stealth tier. The technological costs of actually lighting

[12]The B-2 Stealth Bomber was deployed by the U.S. Air Force as a long-range bomber that employs a technology allowing it to go undetected by enemy radar.

[13]M. Amram and N. Kulatilaka, *Real Options: Managing Strategic Investment in an Uncertain World* (Boston: Harvard Business School Press, 1999).

[14]F. Black and M. Scholes, "The Pricing of Options and Corporate Liabilities," *Journal of Political Economy;* 81 (May–June 1973): 637–659. While European-style options are exercisable only at maturity, American-style options are exercisable anytime prior to maturity.

up the fiber were minimal, probably close to zero. It therefore seemed intuitive to use stealth tier channels for existing applications such as additional analog video channels, and switch over to the new high margin applications when they became available. However, turning off analog channels in the cable industry was typically very costly in terms of customer satisfaction, but this cost was difficult to estimate.[15]

Consequently, Martin thought she might want to consider the higher opportunity cost of not lighting up the fiber immediately. To estimate these forgone profits, Martin began with the current revenue stream per subscriber of approximately $36 per month or $432 per year. A 61% penetration rate implied $263 of annual revenue, or $2.44 ($263/108 channels) per channel. Using a typical cable industry margin of 50%, this translated into $1.22 of forgone annual profit per channel per home passed.

- Martin derived an implied volatility from a traded at-the-money call option on the Cox stock to estimate the relevant volatility for the real option. A one-month call option traded in the market was priced to imply a volatility 50% per year.
- Martin used the life of the cable plant, widely regarded to be 10 years, as the term to maturity.
- For an interest rate, Martin collected information on U.S. Treasury securities. (See Exhibit 9.)

These inputs were employed by Martin to estimate an option value of $22.45. (See Exhibit 10.) Martin multiplied this result by the number of channels in the stealth tier to arrive at a total value of $381.65. Martin acknowledged, "the seventeen channels should be worth more than just the sum, but I'd prefer to understate the value just to make sure that clients accept the number. It's important to be conservative so that clients don't get lost quibbling with assumptions since my primary goal is to get my clients to consider whether DCF is enough." After netting out the $40 of incremental capital costs Martin associated with installing the stealth tier, corresponding to the premium that the cable company paid for the option, Martin arrived at a net value of the stealth tier per home passed of $341.65. This figure represented an additional 14% premium to the current market valuation per home passed.

Conclusion

While concerned with the individual inputs, Martin was more concerned about the overall message for her clients. Martin noted, "80% of my clients have never heard of this stuff and are still using EBITDA multiples. What I would like to convey is that current valuation methodologies, even DCF, don't give any value to the stealth tier." More generally, Martin was convinced of the value in using real options analysis: "With the New Economy, real options go much further in capturing the nature of investment opportunities. I really believe that real options analysis makes you view companies differently and, as a result, you ask better questions about a company's strategic position and long-term value drivers. For me, the primary goal of all the valuation work that I do is about asking the right question." Having concluded her presentation, Martin turned to the task of selling her analysis, and its implications, to her client base.

[15]For example, one industry executive on Martin's panel told the story of how his company had used an extra channel to show live programming using a camera pointed at a garbage dumpster. When the cable company replaced this with a legitimate cable channel, the executive complained of receiving irate mail from viewers and bad press for canceling "the garbage channel."

EXHIBIT 1 Cox Communications Historical Financials, 1993–1998

Source: Cox Communications Annual Reports

	1993	1994	1995	1996	1997	1998
Selected Balance Sheet Items ($Mil.)						
Gross Property, Plant, and Equipment	$1,104.5	$1,234.9	$2,081.5	$2,343.0	$2,840.9	$ 3,702.3
Accumulated Depreciation	516.0	570.7	867.6	811.2	861.9	1,050.1
Net Property, Plant, and Equipment	588.5	664.3	1,213.9	1,531.8	1,979.1	2,652.2
Investments at Equity	265.8	534.6	647.2	713.5	795.2	90.7
Other Investments	27.1	34.4	554.0	505.6	854.0	5,890.4
Intangibles	565.9	542.7	2,775.9	2,729.0	2,458.7	3,959.9
Other Assets	34.6	53.5	207.2	139.8	93.2	88.3
Total Assets	1,527.4	1,874.7	5,555.3	5,784.6	6,556.6	12,878.1
Long-Term Debt	595.6	787.8	2,575.3	2,881.0	3,141.2	3,885.3
Deferred Taxes	100.1	97.1	288.0	294.5	721.6	2,886.6
Other Liabilities	37.2	56.1	147.7	117.0	110.9	227.2
Preferred Stock	0.0	0.0	0.0	0.0	0.0	2.4
Common Stock	0.0	0.0	270.2	270.3	271.1	277.4
Capital Surplus	581.0	670.5	1,739.4	1,742.1	1,790.8	2,152.3
Retained Earnings	135.6	164.3	322.4	248.9	295.4	2,944.5
Total Equity	716.6	834.8	2,332.0	2,261.3	2,357.3	5,376.6
TOTAL LIABILITIES AND EQUITY	1,527.4	1,874.7	5,555.3	5,784.6	6,556.6	12,878.1

	1993	1994	1995	1996	1997	1998
Income Statement ($ Mil.)						
Sales	$ 708.0	$ 736.3	$1,286.2	$1,460.3	$1,610.4	$ 1,716.8
Operating Income Before Depreciation	295.6	268.5	498.4	556.9	609.8	659.1
Depreciation, Depletion & Amortization	116.0	128.8	267.3	335.2	404.5	457.7
Operating Profit	179.7	139.8	231.1	221.7	205.3	201.4
Interest Expense	12.9	46.1	146.5	189.3	202.1	223.3
Non-Operating Income/Expense	–23.7	–41.3	–64.6	–115.7	–400.5	–534.1
Special Items	0.0	0.0	183.7	54.7	207.4	2,649.5
Pretax Income	143.1	52.3	203.7	–28.5	–190.0	2,093.5
Total Income Taxes	66.0	25.8	99.9	23.0	–53.5	822.8
Income Before Extraordinary Items & Discontinued Operations	77.1	26.6	103.8	–51.6	–136.5	1,270.7
Extraordinary Items	20.7	0.0	0.0	0.0	0.0	0.0
Discontinued Operations	0.0	0.0	0.0	0.0	0.0	0.0
Net Income	97.8	26.6	103.8	–51.6	–136.5	1,270.7

EXHIBIT 2 Summary Financials for Selected Comparable Companies, December 31, 1998 ($ millions)

Source: Bloomberg, Credit Suisse First Boston, and casewriter estimates. The information is being provided for educational purposes only, and CSFB has not undertaken any review of the suitability of the information or any recommendations contained therein for the recipients of this publication.

	Adelphia[a]	Comcast	Cox	Time Warner[b]	Media One
Current Price (4/26/99)	$67.88	$66.00	$37.50	$74.82	$78.82
Fully Diluted Shares Outstanding (millions)	131.4	400.0	565.2	1,379.0	663.8
Market Capitalization (4/26/99)	$8,919	$26,400	$21,195	$103,177	$52,321
Total Debt	$3,527	$5,578	$3,920	$10,944	$5,422
Preferred Stock	$648	$0	$0	$575	$1,100
Cash & Option Proceeds	($229)	($982)	($31)	($640)	($915)
Adjusted Enterprise Value	$16,903	$30,882	$25,254	$120,615	$58,457
Non-Cable Consolidated Assets	($999)	($5,914)	($400)	($60,000)	$0
Non-Consolidated Assets	($697)	($7,419)	($11,600)	($20,000)	($31,950)
Implied Cable Value	$15,207	$17,549	$13,254	$40,615	$26,508
Homes Passed (millions)	7.5	7.4	5.9	17.5	7.8
Current Market Value Per Home Passed	$2,041	$2,371	$2,246	$2,320	$3,400
Implied Cable Value + Non-Cable Consolidated Assets	$16,206	$23,463	$13,654	$100,615	$26,508
Adjusted 1999E EBITDA	$1,293	$1,583	$800	$4,816	$1,260
Implied Cable Value + Non-Cable Consolidated Assets /1999E Adj. EBITDA	12.5	14.8	17.1	20.9	21.1
Other Financial Data					
Equity Beta	0.75	1.08	1.07	0.88	1.08
Historic Equity Volatility	57%	51%	47%	44%	NA
Implied Volatility from Options	66%	59%	50%	41%	NA

[a]Pro forma estimates include announced FrontierVision Partners, Century Communications, and Harron Communications acquisitions, which were expected to close in the second half of 1999.

[b]Includes 100% of Time Warner Enterprises.

EXHIBIT 3
Forecasted Revenue and Subscriber Growth for Cox Communications, 1998–2003

Source: Credit Suisse First Boston estimates, published in Laura Martin, *Cox Communications* (Oct. 12, 1999, Credit Suisse First Boston Corporation). The information is being provided for educational purposes only, and CSFB has not undertaken any review of the suitability of the information or any recommendations contained therein for the recipients of this publication.

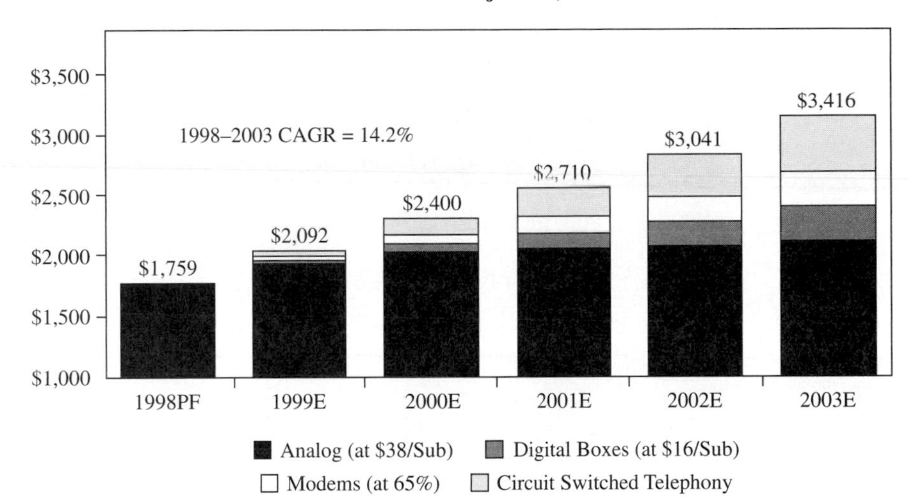

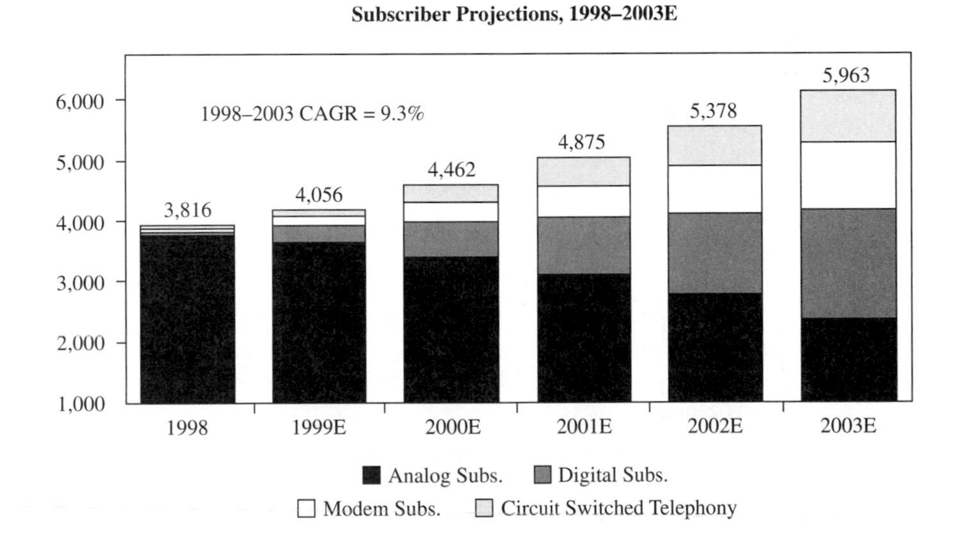

EXHIBIT 4
Forecast ROICs for New Investments by Cox Communications

Source: Credit Suisse First Boston estimates, published in Laura Martin, *Cox Communications* (Oct. 12, 1999, Credit Suisse First Boston Corporation). The information is being provided for educational purposes only, and CSFB has not undertaken any review of the suitability of the information or any recommendations contained therein for the recipients of this publication.

Marginal returns on invested capital for new products such as compression boxes, modems, and wireline telephone appear to be significantly higher than the cost of capital. However, total returns on capital (including infrastructure upgrade) will depend on the level of consumer demand, consumer price sensitivity, and new product profit margins, each of which is unknown today.

Digital compression boxes Returns are enhanced because digital box costs plus an 11.25% return are legislatively allowed to be recovered over the entire subscriber base over a five-year period.

Marginal ROIC on a Digital Compression Box

Average Cost of Compression Box to Cable Operator	$350
Annual Income:	
Recovery of Box Cost ($6.50/month × 100% profit)	$ 78
Incremental Revenue ($14/month × 50% profit)	$ 84
Annual Income	$162
ROIC/Box	46%

Cable modems Assumes a monthly fee to cable modem subscribers of $40 at a 50% margin.

Marginal ROIC on a Cable Modem

Cost of Modem to Cable Operator	$400
Annual Revenue/Subscriber ($40/month)	$480
Assumed Profit Margin	50%
Profit Per Modem	$240
ROIC/Modem	60%

Wireline telephone Based on Cox Communications' experience in Orange County, California, with a typical monthly bill for telephone customers of $55 at a 56% profit margin.

Marginal ROIC on Wireline Telephone

Marginal Cost to Cable Operator	$825
Average Revenue Per Customer[a]	$660
Direct Costs[b]	132
Employees	60
Customer Service	12
Marketing	24
Other	60
Profit Per Telephone Customer Per Year	372
ROIC/Telephone	45%

[a]Includes primary lines, 30% additional lines, access 22, voice mail ports, interconnect trunks, 411, etc.
[b]Includes billing, property taxes, bad debts, powering, etc.

EXHIBIT 5
ROIC Target Price Analysis for Cox Communication

Source: Credit Suisse First Boston estimates, published in Laura Martin, *Cox Communications* (Oct. 12, 1999, Credit Suisse First Boston Corporation). The information is being provided for educational purposes only, and CSFB has not undertaken any review of the suitability of the information or any recommendations contained therein for the recipients of this publication.

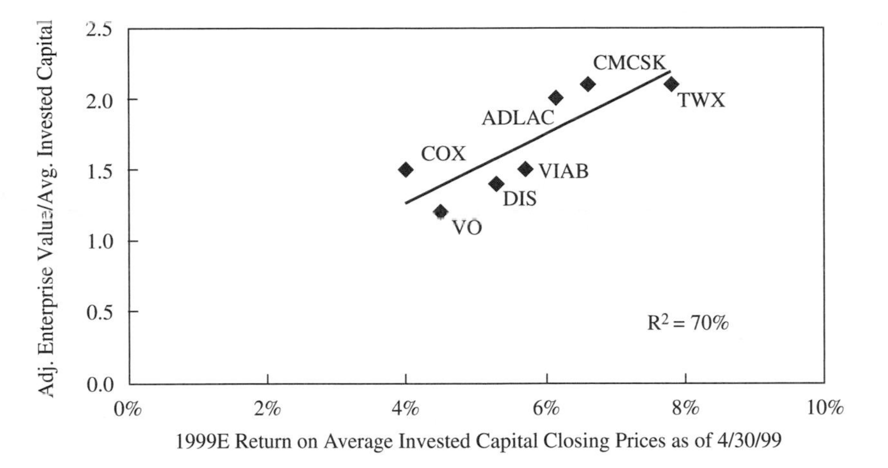

Based on Multiple of Invested Capital	1999E
Target multiple—1999E	1.594
Average Invested capital	$12,136
Implied enterprise value	$19,345
Plus: Nonconsolidated assets	$12,292
Plus: Other assets	$ 400
Plus: Cash & option proceeds at year end	$ 23
Less: Debt at year end	$(3,800)
Implied equity value	$28,260
Shares outstanding (millions)	565.2
Target price	$ 50.00
Current price	$ 37.50
(Target-current)/target	25%
(Target-current)/current	33%

EXHIBIT 6 EBITDA Multiple Analysis for Cox Communications, 1999–2000

Source: Credit Suisse First Boston estimates, published in Laura Martin, *Cox Communications* (Oct. 12, 1999, Credit Suisse First Boston Corporation). The information is being provided for educational purposes only, and CSFB has not undertaken any review of the suitability of the information or any recommendations contained therein for the recipients of this publication.

Based on Enterprise Value EBITDA Year Ended 12/31:	1999E	2000E	Target Price of 2000E EBITDA	Discount from Target Price	Price Appreciation to Target Price
Current share price (4/26/99)	$37.50	$37.50	$50.00	25%	33%
Shares outstanding at year end	565.2	565.2	565.2		
Market capitalization	$21,195	$21,195	$ 28,260		
Plus: Debt at year end	$ 4,090	$ 3,800	$ 3,800		
Less: Non-consolidated assets	(11,600)	(12,292)	(12,292)		
Less: Other assets (see PMV)	(400)	(400)	(400)		
Less: Cash at year end	(31)	(23)	(23)		
Implied cable value	13,254	12,280	19,345		
EBITDA	$ 800	$ 924	$ 924		
Implied cable value/EBITDA	16.6	13.3	20.9		

EXHIBIT 7 Discounted Cash Flow Analysis for Cox Communications ($ and shares in millions, except per share data)

Source: Credit Suisse First Boston estimates, published in Laura Martin, *Cox Communications* (Oct. 12, 1999, Credit Suisse First Boston Corporation). The information is being provided for educational purposes only, and CSFB has not undertaken any review of the suitability of the information or any recommendations contained therein for the recipients of this publication.

	1998	1999E	2000E	2001E	2002E	2003E	2004E	2005E	2006E	2007E	2008E	CAGR 99-08
Total EBITDA	$659	$800	$924	$1,047	$1,214	$1,408	$1,634	$1,895	$2,198	$2,550	$ 2,958	16%
Less: Depreciation & Amortization	($458)	($607)	($680)	($674)	($644)	($616)	($591)	($569)	($549)	($531)	($515)	–2%
Earnings Before Interest and Taxes	$201	$193	$244	$372	$570	$792	$1,042	$1,326	$1,649	$2,019	$ 2,443	33%
Less: Taxes (EBIT + Amortization at 35%)	($100)	($104)	($123)	($168)	($237)	($315)	($402)	($502)	($615)	($744)	($893)	27%
Plus: Depreciation & Amortization	$458	$607	$680	$674	$644	$616	$591	$569	$549	$531	$515	–2%
Less: Capital Spending & Investments	($978)	($1,040)	($750)	($587)	($517)	($261)	($261)	($261)	($261)	($261)	($261)	–14%
Unlevered Free Cash Flow	($419)	($344)	$51	$292	$460	$833	$970	$1,133	$1,323	$1,545	$ 1,804	
Terminal Value (TV) of 2008E Total EBITDA											$38,454	

Equity Valuation Analysis	Value	% DCF
PV of Unlevered Cash Flow	$4,456	15%
PV of Terminal Value Discounted to 1999 @ WACC	$17,316	56%
– Long-term Debt at 12/31/99E	($3,800)	–12%
+ Cash at 12/31/99E	$23	0%
+ Non-Consolidated Assets, Private Market Value[a]	$12,292	40%
+ Other Assets, Private Market Value[a]	$400	1%
Discounted Cash Flow Value (DCF)	$30,687	100%
Shares Outstanding @ 9/30/99	565.2	
Discounted Cash Flow Value/Share	**$54.29**	
Current Share Price (4/26/99)	$37.50	
Discount to DCF Value = (DCF-Current Price)/DCF	31%	
Price Appreciation to DCF = (DCF-Current Price)/Current Price	45%	
Assumptions:		
Discount Rate, Weighted Average Cost of Capital	9.3%	
Terminal Multiple	13.0	

[a]The Private Market Value took into account the takeover or control premium for Cox's holdings of non-public assets. In a takeover, these assets might sell for considerably more than their public market value.

EXHIBIT 8 "Stealth Tier" Analysis of 750 MHz Cable Plant Usage

Source: Credit Suisse First Boston estimates, published in Laura Martin, *Cox Communications* (Oct. 12, 1999, Credit Suisse First Boston Corporation). The information is being provided for educational purposes only, and CSFB has not undertaken any review of the suitability of the information or any recommendations contained therein for the recipients of this publication.

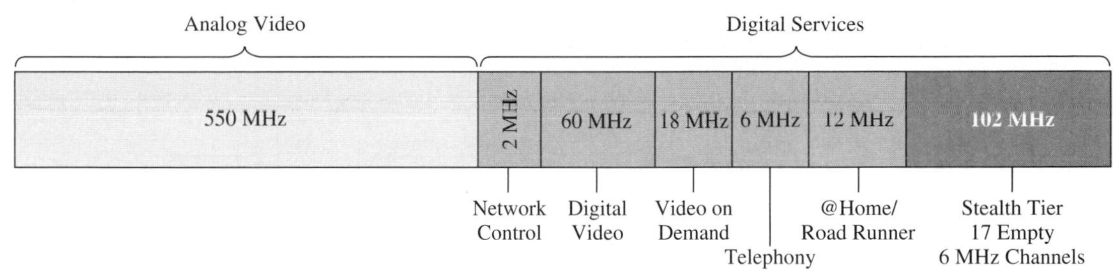

EXHIBIT 9
U.S. Treasury Interest Rates as of May 1, 1999

Source: Bloomberg. All yields are quoted on a bond-equivalent-yield basis.

Term	Rate
3-Month	4.560%
6-Month	4.657%
1 Year	4.779%
2 Year	5.066%
5 Year	5.219%
10 Year	5.359%

EXHIBIT 10
Black-Scholes Valuation for Stealth Tier

Source: Credit Suisse First Boston estimates, published in Laura Martin, *Cox Communications* (Oct. 12, 1999, Credit Suisse First Boston Corporation). The information is being provided for educational purposes only, and CSFB has not undertaken any review of the suitability of the information or any recommendations contained therein for the recipients of this publication.

PV of Potential Project/Home Passed (S)	$23.15
Investment Cost (X)	$1.22
Time to Maturity (T, years)	10
Risk Free Rate (r_f)—	5.25%
Volatility (σ)	50%
Call Option Value/Home Passed	**$22.45**
Times: Number of Empty 6 MHz Channels on the Stealth Tier	17
Asset Value of the Stealth Tier	$381.65
Less: Current Investment/Home Passed	$40.00
Value of the Stealth Tier/Home Passed	$341.65
Current Market Valuation/Home Passed	$2,500
Stealth Tier/Current Valuation	14%

Arundel Partners: The Sequel Project

In April 1992, David A. Davis, a movie industry analyst at Paul Kagan Associates, Inc. in Los Angeles, was asked to look at and comment on an unusual business idea. The idea was to create an investment group, Arundel Partners, that would purchase the sequel rights associated with films produced by one or more major U.S. movie studios. As owner of the rights, Arundel would judge the success of a movie and then decide whether or not to produce a second film based on the story or characters of the first.

The proposal was innovative in several respects. First, Arundel would purchase sequel rights before the first films were even made, let alone released. Second, the investor group would not make artistic judgments or attempt to select the rights for particular movies based on predictions of a possible sequel's success. Instead, Arundel would contract to purchase *all* of the sequel rights for a studio's entire production during a specified period (1–2 years) or, alternatively, for a specified number of major films (15–30). Third, Arundel's advance cash payments for the rights, at an agreed-upon price per film, would help finance production of the initial films.

The idea was intended to capitalize on a few specific characteristics of the movie industry. Producing and distributing motion pictures was a risky business, and predicting the success of any one film was extremely difficult, if not altogether impossible. Moreover, studios' production decisions were driven by both creative and business considerations, which often conflicted. The combination of uncertainty and conflict sometimes strained the financial resources of even the largest studios. Arundel could expect to avoid the conflict between art and commerce and, at the same time, escape (for a price) much of the risk associated with the unpredictability of moviegoers' tastes. The idea was expected to appeal to studios because Arundel would offer cash when it was needed most, during an initial film's production. Since Arundel would seek to purchase the rights to many films, the total payments by Arundel could be substantial and would help reduce individual studio borrowing.

Whether Arundel could expect to make money depended heavily on how much it had to pay to purchase a portfolio of sequel rights. In 1992 the major studios did not usually sell sequel rights, nor did they explicitly assign them a value when deciding to put a project into production. However, casual inquiries suggested that studios would find the idea tempting at a price of $2 million or more per movie. At prices below $1 million per movie, they probably would not even discuss it. Paul Kagan Associates, Inc. had expertise in analyzing the film business, and it had assembled certain proprietary data on industry cash flows. Hence, Mr. Davis was asked how much the sequel rights were worth.

The Movie Business

To reach the public, a movie went through three stages: production, distribution, and exhibition. Production involved creating the film negative. Distribution consisted of advertising the film, making prints, shipping prints to theaters, reproducing the film

This case was prepared by William A. Teichner, Charles M. Williams Fellow, under the supervision of Professor Timothy A. Luehrman.

Copyright © 1992 by the President and Fellows of Harvard College. Harvard Business School case 292–140.

onto videocassettes, and licensing the film to pay and nonpay television and other outlets. Finally, exhibition traditionally consisted of projecting films in theaters, but it increasingly included other viewing media, such as home video.

In 1992 the major movie companies (and ultimate parent companies, if different) involved in U.S. production and distribution were MCA Universal (Matsushita Electric Industrial Co., Ltd.); Metro-Goldwyn-Mayer, Inc. (Credit Lyonnais Bank Nederland N.V.); Orion Pictures Corp.; Paramount Pictures Corp. (Paramount Communications, Inc.); Sony Pictures Entertainment, Inc. (Sony Corp.);[1] The Walt Disney Company;[2] Twentieth Century Fox Film Corp. (The News Corporation, Ltd.); and Warner Brothers, Inc. (Time Warner, Inc.).

These companies, or studios, were all engaged in both production and distribution, and in some cases, exhibition as well. Several of the parent companies or their subsidiaries owned movie theater chains, pay TV channels, and/or TV stations.

In 1991 the major studios and smaller distributors released 150 and 274 films, respectively, in the United States. While the major studios distributed just 35% of all films released in the United States, they accounted for 93% of all revenues received from U.S. movie theaters. These revenues were known as film rentals because the distributor essentially rented prints of the film to theaters for a specified period of time. The top U.S. rental film of 1991, Tri-Star's *Terminator 2,* represented approximately 5% of total U.S. industry rentals. The top five films accounted for 16% of total rentals and the top ten films accounted for 26%. The industry's market share leader (in rentals) changed from year to year according to which studio's releases were most successful. Exhibit 1 presents selected data from 1980–1991 for U.S. film distributors.

Production

Most movies were based on existing literary properties, and producers who planned to adapt a property into a movie normally had to acquire its film rights.[3] Sometimes, literary agents introduced properties to producers. Other times, large talent agencies presented producers with packages consisting of a script, director, and principal actors. Producers sometimes discovered or created properties on their own. Producers frequently purchased options on the film rights to literary properties. However, most such options were never exercised—the likelihood that a movie would be made from an optioned property was very small.

Production costs were incurred in each of three primary stages: preproduction, principal photography, and postproduction. Costs for preproduction included expenditures for script development, set design, casting of actors, film crew selection, costume design, location scouting, and budget planning. The costs associated with principal photography included fixed salaries of actors, directors, and other personnel.[4] They also included rent, wages, and other expenses for soundstages, set construction, lighting, transportation (for location shooting), costume making, special effects, and miscellaneous items. Finally, postproduction costs consisted of expenses for film editing, the

[1]Sony Pictures owned Columbia Pictures and Tri-Star Pictures. Both were involved in production and distribution.

[2]The Walt Disney Company owned three film studios: Walt Disney, Touchstone, and Hollywood Pictures, and distributed its films through Buena Vista Pictures Distribution, Inc., a wholly owned subsidiary.

[3]The term *producer* was used in a variety of ways in the motion picture industry. Here, it refers to the individuals or companies that owned the rights to produce a film.

[4]It also included the costs of line producers who were hired by the financiers or producers of a movie. Line producers managed the day-to-day physical production of the movie, from pre- to postproduction. They also oversaw production costs and hired and fired personnel. Their screen credits included executive producer, producer, and associate producer.

laying down of sound effects and music, and the addition of titles and credits. On average, the entire production cycle required 1 year from the time a project was put into production until the finished film was released to theaters.[5]

The total cost of production, including fixed expenses for story acquisition, was called the negative cost, the cost to create the film's completed negative, from which positive prints could be made.[6] The negative cost excluded advertising and other distribution expenses. While the negative cost included fixed salaries to actors and others, it did not include future compensation that was linked to either the film's revenues or its earnings. Exhibit 2 presents a breakdown of items normally included in a film's negative cost.

In 1991 the average negative cost, excluding interest, for a major new movie was approximately $20 million. This cost had to be financed somehow. Some producers (such as wealthy individuals, producer partnerships, and movie studios) financed their own projects. In some cases, the rights to certain revenues, such as from the home video or non-U.S. theater markets, were presold to raise cash for production. In other cases, independent producers obtained financing from major studios. When a studio financed an independent production, it frequently supplied personnel, facilities, supervision, and equipment.

It was very common for a project to be rejected by one or more studios before it finally received financial support. Furthermore, studios often backed out of projects after investing initial time or money but before beginning principal photography.

Distribution

Typically, the studio that produced or financed a particular movie also distributed it. When producers financed negative costs without help from studios, they often engaged studios simply to pick up, or distribute, their films once they were completed. In their capacity as film distributors, the studios managed the circulation of movies to theaters, the licensing of films to pay and nonpay TV, and the duplication and distribution of videocassettes. They handled advertising, publicity, and promotion for the films they distributed, and they also collected proceeds from theaters and ancillary revenue sources.

The traditional contract between the distributor and the producer allowed the distributor to charge distribution expenses and distribution fees, which were deducted from the revenue the distributor collected from theaters and ancillary markets. Distribution expenses included the direct costs of distributing the film; distribution fees were charged to cover the distributor's overhead and profit.

Distribution Expenses

These expenses primarily represented the costs of advertising in newspapers and on television, of making prints of the film for theaters, and of duplicating videocassettes. Advertising costs were ordinarily the largest single distribution expense by a wide margin and occasionally exceeded a film's negative cost. They varied with the length of time a movie played in theaters. In 1991 the average U.S. advertising cost for a major film was $10 million. The cost of prints and videocassette duplication varied with the number of theaters in which a movie played and the number of videocassettes sold, respectively. Other smaller distribution expenses were shipping costs, insurance costs, and miscellaneous fees, duties, and taxes.

[5]While it took about a year to complete most production, a script might hibernate in preproduction development for several months or even years before the beginning of principal photography if a producer could not easily arrange financing or if a studio was not very interested in the project.

[6]Interest charges on loans to finance production were sometimes included in negative costs. Here, interest charges are excluded from negative costs.

Distribution Fees

Distributors traditionally charged a fixed percentage of the proceeds they received from the various theatrical and ancillary markets to cover their overhead and profit. Because distribution fees were often calculated as a fixed percentage, they could be more or less than the overhead expenses actually incurred by the distributor.[7] In its role as a distributor, the studio generally charged lower fees when an independent producer (rather than the studio) financed the negative. In addition, fees varied by ancillary market and country. For example, fees were usually higher on non-U.S. proceeds than on U.S. proceeds.

For independently financed films distributed by a studio, a common distribution fee was 22.5% of U.S. rentals and 32.5% of most non-U.S. rentals. However, if the movie was financed by the studio, the fee was generally 30% of U.S. rentals and 40% of most non-U.S. rentals.[8] Fees on home video and pay television revenues were often the same as those on theater rentals. U.S. network TV fees were sometimes several percentage points lower, while U.S. syndicated TV and non-U.S. TV fees were several percentage points higher.

Exhibition

Exhibition usually referred to projection of movies in theaters, but defined broadly, it encompassed ancillary markets as well. Films were released to the various markets in stages that spanned 7 or more years from the date of initial release. U.S. films were typically released first to U.S. movie theaters, about 1 year after going into production. Revenues from ticket sales in movie theaters were known as gross box office proceeds. During 1991, for each dollar of gross box office proceeds, about 50¢ were remitted to the distributor as film rentals.[9]

Films were released to non-U.S. theaters about two months after their release in the United States. About eight months after theatrical release, videocassettes were sold in the United States; they were sold soon thereafter in non-U.S. markets. Movies normally appeared on pay TV in the beginning of the second year after release and shortly afterwards on non-U.S. pay TV. In the third year, films aired on U.S. networks and non-U.S. TV. Finally, films might be licensed to independent television stations around the world 6 to 8 years after their theatrical release. Exhibit 3 illustrates the sequence of releases to various markets.

Calculation of Net Profits

After distribution expenses, distribution fees, the negative cost, and any other expenses were subtracted from all revenue, what remained were net profits.

For an independently financed film distributed by a studio, the studio collected proceeds from the various revenue sources, subtracted distribution expenses and fees, and remitted the balance to the producer.[10] After subtracting the cost of the film's negative,

[7]The distribution fee percentage was sometimes lowered once certain predetermined dollar amounts were reached.

[8]Under both scenarios, fees on U.K. and Canadian rentals were typically lower than for other countries. In addition, distribution fees were generally lower when independent producers helped finance distribution expenses.

[9]A common arrangement between the distributor and the theater exhibitor provided that the distributor would receive the greater of: (1) 70% of the gross box office proceeds in the first two weeks (60% for the following two; 50% for the next two; 40% for the next two; and 35% for the remainder of the run) or (2) 90% of the gross box office proceeds after subtracting out a reasonable, predetermined amount of cash to cover the costs of operating the theater.

[10]Occasionally, a major actor's contract specified that he or she would receive a percentage of the film's revenues. In that case, these gross participations were often paid out of the distributor's proceeds before fees and expenses.

the independent producer was left with the film's net profits.[11] See Exhibit 2 for the calculation of net profits for a typical movie.

For movies financed by a studio, the studio—rather than the producer—subtracted out the negative cost. Again, what remained was the film's net profits. For taking on the risk of financing the film, the studio often kept 50% or more of the net profits and remitted what was left to the producer. If there were zero or negative net profits, the studio remitted nothing and bore any loss itself.

Sequels and Arundel Partners

More than 60 films produced since 1970 had one or more sequels. Not all commercially successful first films were followed by sequels, but practically all sequels followed successful films. Many of the most profitable movies of the past 20 years spawned one or more sequels. These included, for example, *Airport, Back to the Future, Beverly Hills Cop, Friday the 13th, Ghostbusters, The Godfather, Jaws, Police Academy, Raiders of the Lost Ark, Rocky, Star Trek, Star Wars, Superman, Teenage Mutant Ninja Turtles,* and *Terminator.* The long-running James Bond film series, which began in 1962 with *Dr. No,* included 16 sequels.

Sequels were based on characters or situations portrayed in the initial movies. Scripts for sequels were usually written after the first film's release and, in some cases, were worked on by individuals other than those who had created the original. The median release date for a sequel was 3 years after the first film's release; most sequels were released within 1 to 5 years.

The average negative cost for a sequel was higher than for the first film. For sequels made after 1970, the inflation-adjusted negative cost was about 120% of the first film's negative cost, according to one estimate. This was partly because the commercial success of the first film enhanced the bargaining power of key creative talent, who demanded higher compensation for the sequel.

A similar analysis showed that the average sequel produced only 70% of the inflation-adjusted (real) rentals that the initial film had earned. Exhibit 4 displays comparative inflation-adjusted cost and revenue data for a sample of first films and their sequels. Exhibit 5 shows rental data for a small number of films that spawned more than one sequel. For most such film series, rentals declined with each additional installment in the series.

The Sequel Project

Arundel Partners would be interested in purchasing the sequel rights for one or more studios' entire production over an extended period of not less than 1 year. If a particular film was a hit and Arundel thought a sequel would be profitable, it would exercise its rights by producing the sequel itself or hiring professionals to do so. Alternatively, it could sell the rights to the highest bidder. Inevitably, most first films would not justify sequels; for those films, the sequel rights would simply not be exercised. As a practical matter, for most movies, it would be very clear after their first few weeks in U.S. theaters whether or not a sequel would be economical.

[11] Sometimes creative talent received net profit participations, or percentages of any positive net profits the film made. The arrangement described in the text, wherein fees were deducted by the distributor, was fairly standard in the industry and was called a distribution fee deal or net deal. In the 1980s, two other kinds of deals became common. These were the gross percentage deal and adjusted gross percentage deal. In the gross percentage deal, the producer received a fixed percentage of the film's proceeds received by the distributor. In the adjusted gross percentage deal, the producer received a fixed percentage of the distributor's proceeds after certain items were first subtracted.

It would be critically important to Arundel that a number of films and a price per film be agreed upon *before* either Arundel or the studio knew which films would be produced. Once production started, the studio would gradually, but inevitably, form an opinion about the movie, and Arundel would not want to have to bargain over individual projects about which it knew less than the studio.

Otherwise, many details of a potential contract between Arundel and the prospective studio still needed to be worked out. For example, in addition to the price of the rights, a satisfactory method of payment had to be agreed upon. The simplest approach would be for Arundel to make payments to an escrow account when a first film went into production. These payments could then be disbursed to a studio as the movie progressed through production. Certain films might have to be excluded from the arrangement if the studio itself did not already own their sequel rights. To keep the studio committed to the success of possible sequels, it would probably be desirable to have the studio retain an interest in the revenues or the net profits of the sequel, or to have rights for subsequent sequels—that is, third, fourth, and other future films—revert to the studio.

For tax purposes, it might be desirable to fix an expiration date for the sequel rights, perhaps 3 years from the first film's release, by which time Arundel would have to declare its intentions or forfeit the rights. This would allow Arundel enough time to make a decision about making a sequel and enable it to write off more quickly its investment in rights it chose not to exercise. If the studio were interested, Arundel could grant it a right of first refusal on any rights it planned to sell. The contract also could provide that Arundel would use the original studio for distribution, assuming its distribution fees and expenses were competitive.

Available Movie Data

The value of the sequel rights depended heavily on the statistical distribution that characterized the returns earned by first films. Actual data on realized returns for a large sample of first films were not publicly available, although rough estimates could be made for hundreds of films based on public information. Further, Paul Kagan Associates, Inc. had assembled a proprietary database on which even more reliable estimates could be based for an even larger sample of recent movies.

Estimates of the financial performance of all first films released by six major studios during 1989 are presented in Exhibit 6.[12] These estimates were used to compute the discounted cash flows presented in Exhibit 7, under the assumptions described in the Appendix. The discounted costs and revenues were used to compute simple 1-year returns for each film. As Exhibit 7 shows, returns were highly variable, ranging from 1,224% for Tri-Star's *Look Who's Talking* to –91% for Paramount's *We're No Angels*.

Exhibit 6 and 7 also estimate costs, revenues, and 1-year returns for hypothetical sequels for each first film, according to the assumptions outlined in the Appendix. Essentially, these figures are projections of how a sequel would perform, assuming it were made and assuming it were "typical." For example, Warner Brothers' *Batman* was expected to result in a successful sequel, with a projected return of 225%. Not surprisingly, however, most movies' hypothetical sequels performed poorly and undoubtedly would not be produced. Exhibit 8 presents histograms of the one-year returns tabulated in Exhibit 7 for first films and sequels. Exhibit 9 summarizes some characteristics of the distribution of hypothetical sequel returns for a sample of first films released in 1987 and 1988 that had negative costs of at least $14 million.

Because Arundel's tax situation might be exceedingly complex, David Davis was asked to estimate the value of the sequel rights on a pretax basis. He had access to data such as that in Exhibits 6–9, as well as the larger, more detailed dataset at Paul Kagan

[12]Exhibits 6–9 exclude releases from Orion and Metro-Goldwyn-Mayer, both of which were experiencing severe financial problems in 1992. Orion was in Chapter 11 bankruptcy proceedings in April 1992.

Associates. There were two obvious ways to begin analyzing the data. One was to use the projected financial performances of all the 1989 hypothetical sequels to decide which ones should be produced. It would then be possible to estimate how much money they would make in total, and hence, how much per 1989 first film. The other approach would be to apply a simple option pricing model to the parameters of the distribution of sequel returns or sequel net present values and so estimate directly the value of sequel rights for a random film in the available sample. Each approach would require some simplifying assumptions. Davis wondered what biases might be generated by the various assumptions, which methodology would give the more useful result, and whether either result was reliable enough to justify an investment of millions of dollars.

EXHIBIT 1 Selected Motion Picture Industry Data, 1980–1991

Sources: Goldman Sachs Investment Research, *Movie Industry Update 1992;* MPAA, *1991 U.S. Economic Review,* and industry sources.

North American Theatrical Film Rental Shares of Major Film Distributors[a,b]

	Sony[c]	20th Century Fox	Metro-Goldwyn-Mayer	Paramount	MCA Universal	Warner Brothers	Buena Vista[d]	Orion	Total Majors
1980	14%	16%	7%	16%	20%	14%	4%	2%	93%
1981	13	13	9	15	14	18	3	1	86
1982	10	14	11	14	30	10	4	3	96
1983	14	21	10	14	13	17	3	4	96
1984	21	10	7	21	8	19	4	5	95
1985	20	11	9	10	16	18	3	5	92
1986	16	8	4	22	9	12	10	7	88
1987	9	9	4	20	8	13	14	10	87
1988	10	12	10	15	10	11	19	7	94
1989	16	7	6	14	17	17	14	4	95
1990	14	13	3	15	13	13	16	6	93
1991	20	12	2	12	11	14	14	9	93

	Number of Films Released in the U.S. by Major and Independent Distributors[e]		Aggregate Box Office Data		
	Major Releases	Independent Releases	U.S. and Canada Gross Box Office (millions)	U.S. Rentals[f] (millions)	U.S. Average Theater Ticket Price
1980	134	NA	$2,749	$1,235	$2.69
1981	145	NA	2,967	1,335	2.78
1982	150	211	3,453	1,555	2.94
1983	166	230	3,766	1,700	3.15
1984	152	256	4,031	1,800	3.36
1985	138	251	3,749	1,635	3.55
1986	133	286	3,778	1,650	3.71
1987	122	365	4,253	1,830	3.91
1988	153	319	4,458	1,920	4.11
1989	157	292	5,033	2,165	4.45
1990	158	221	5,022	2,260	4.75
1991	150	274	4,803	2,160	4.89

[a]Several companies have undergone various transformations since 1980. The chart shows the company's current name.
[b]Includes rereleases of films that were first released in earlier years.
[c]Includes films distributed by Columbia and Tri-Star. Tri-Star began operations in 1984.
[d]Buena Vista distributes films by The Walt Disney Company; data include films produced by the Disney, Touchstone, and Hollywood Pictures studios.
[e]Excludes rereleases of films first issued in prior years.
[f]Excludes independent films.

EXHIBIT 2
Revenue and Cost Estimates for Typical Film Distributed by a Major Studio[a,b] (millions of 1991 dollars)

			Percent of U.S. Theatrical Rentals	Percent of Total Revenue
Revenue Collected by Distributor				
U.S. theater rentals	$10.0		100%	22%
Non-U.S. theater rentals	9.0		90	19
Worldwide home video	15.0		150	32
Worldwide pay TV	5.5		55	12
Worldwide TV[c]	7.0		70	15
Total		$46.5	465%	100%
Distribution Fees				
Worldwide theater	$ 5.0		50%	11%
Worldwide home video	4.0		40	9
Worldwide pay TV	1.5		15	3
Worldwide TV	2.0		20	4
Total		$12.5	125%	27%
Distribution Expenses				
Worldwide theater	$12.0		120%	26%
Worldwide home video	3.5		35	8
Worldwide pay TV	—		—	—
Worldwide TV	—		—	—
Total		$15.5	155%	33%
Negative Cost[d]				
Story rights/script development	$0.5			
Actors/director	6.0			
Production management	1.0			
Production crew	1.0			
Set design/construction	2.0			
Transportation/locations	1.5			
Wardrobe/makeup/hair	0.5			
Extras/props	0.5			
Lighting	0.3			
Special effects	0.3			
Other principal photography	1.0			
Film editing	0.7			
Music	0.4			
Other postproduction	0.8			
All other	1.5			
Total negative cost		$18.0		
Pretax net profits[e]		$ 0.5		

[a]The figures represent estimates of a typical film, not the average film.
[b]Fee structure assumes film is independently financed.
[c]In this chart, worldwide TV includes U.S. network, U.S. syndicated, and non-U.S. television.
[d]The negative cost breakdown is shown for illustrative purposes only and provides one possible breakdown of a film's cost.
[e]Excludes interest charges. Assumes no gross participation.

EXHIBIT 3 Typical Beginning Dates for Film Production and Release

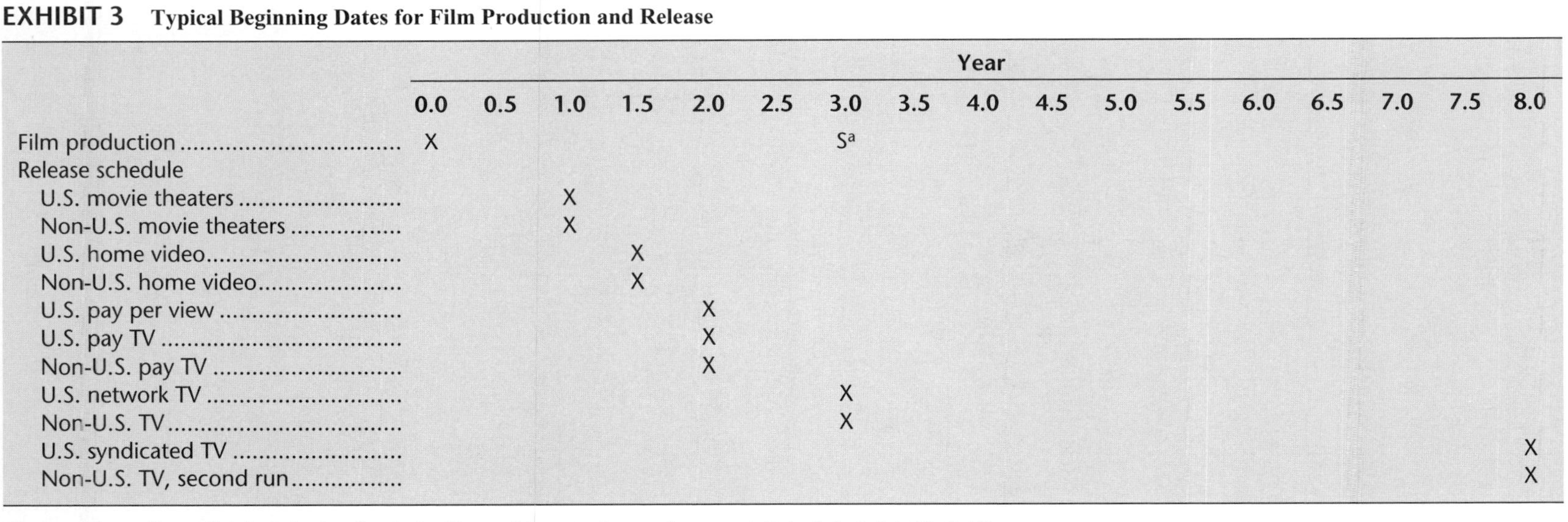

	Year																
	0.0	0.5	1.0	1.5	2.0	2.5	3.0	3.5	4.0	4.5	5.0	5.5	6.0	6.5	7.0	7.5	8.0
Film production	X						S[a]										
Release schedule																	
U.S. movie theaters			X														
Non-U.S. movie theaters			X														
U.S. home video				X													
Non-U.S. home video				X													
U.S. pay per view					X												
U.S. pay TV					X												
Non-U.S. pay TV					X												
U.S. network TV							X										
Non-U.S. TV							X										
U.S. syndicated TV																	X
Non-U.S. TV, second run																	X

[a] S = A possible sequel's most likely beginning date of production. The rest of the pattern for a sequel was expected to be similar to that of the first film.

EXHIBIT 4
Comparative Cost and Revenue Data of First Films and Their Sequels

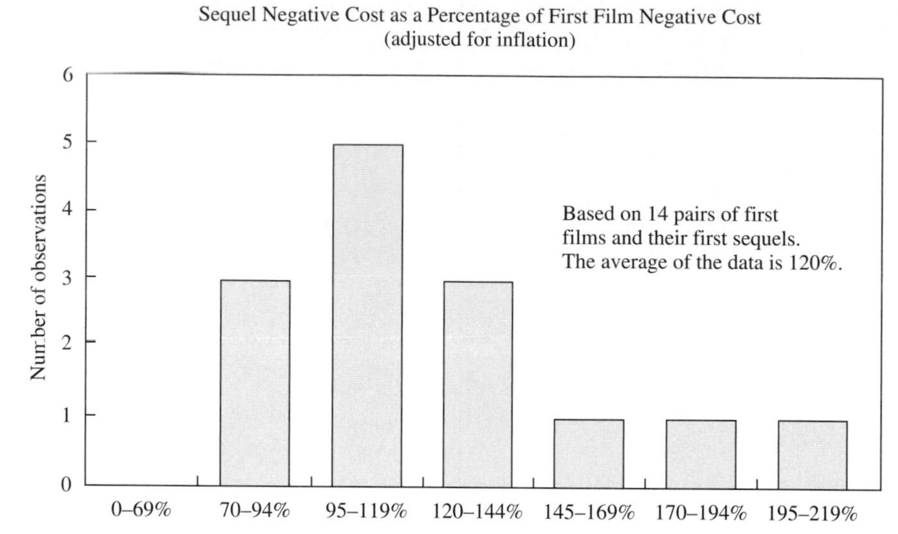

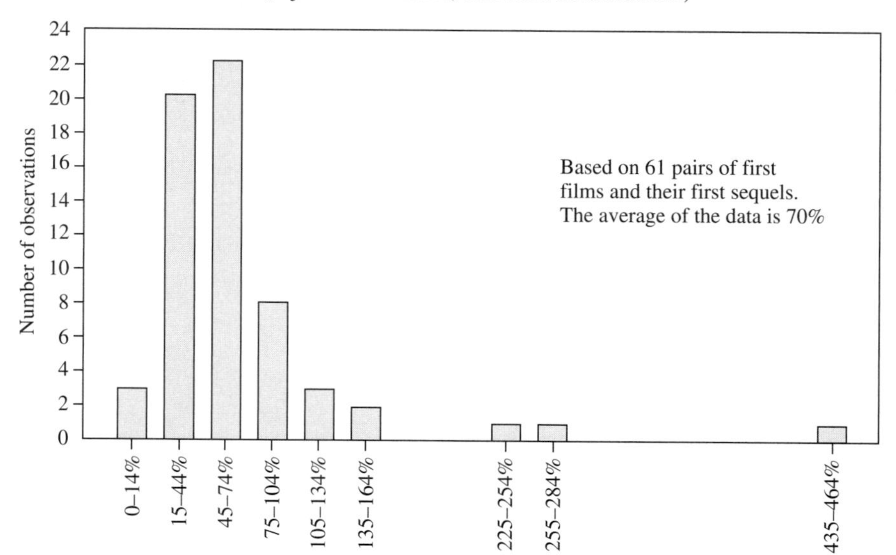

EXHIBIT 5
U.S. Theater Rental Data for Several Films Having More Than One Sequel

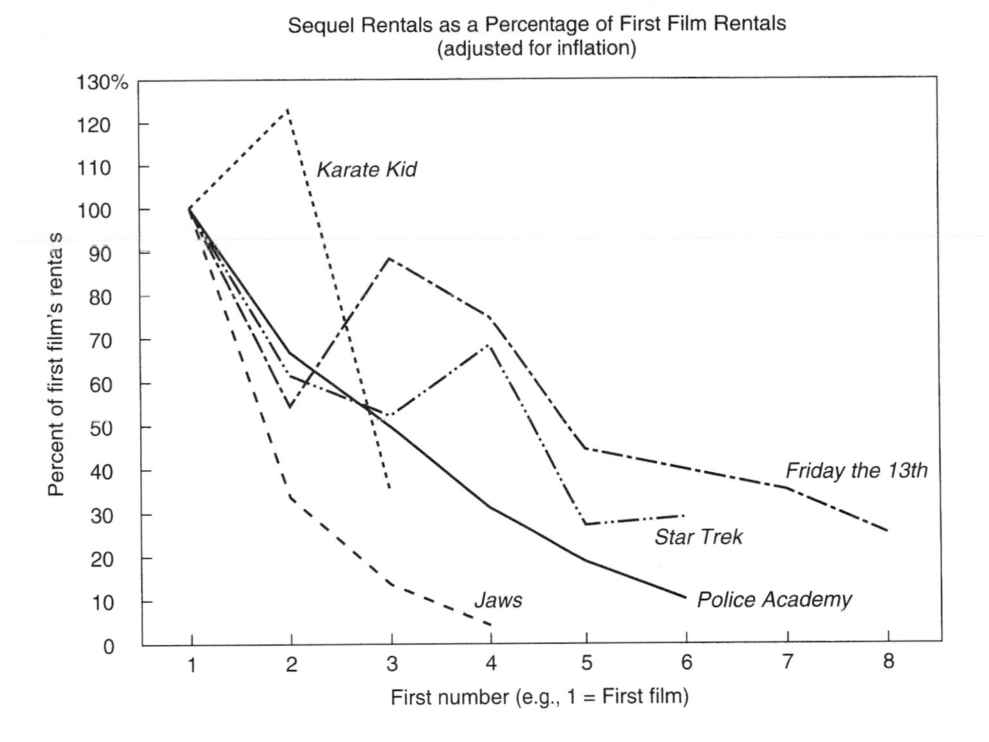

EXHIBIT 6 Estimated Revenues and Costs for Films Released in 1989 by Six Major Studios and Their Hypothetical Sequels[a] (millions of dollars)

Studio/Movie Title	First Film					Hypothetical Sequel				
	U.S. Theater Rentals	Other Revenue	Distribution Fees	Distribution Expense	Negative Cost	U.S. Theater Rentals	Other Revenue	Distribution Fees	Distribution Expense	Negative Cost
MCA Universal										
1 *Parenthood*	$55.0	$146.1	$53.6	$43.1	$22.0	$38.5	$106.1	$38.5	$32.6	$26.4
2 *Born on the Fourth of July*	40.5	110.9	40.3	33.1	19.8	28.4	81.4	29.2	26.0	23.7
3 *Field of Dreams*	33.6	94.1	34.0	31.6	17.6	23.5	69.7	24.8	22.9	21.1
4 *Uncle Buck*	33.3	93.6	33.8	30.2	16.5	23.3	69.3	24.7	22.8	19.8
5 *Sea of Love*	31.5	89.0	32.1	32.0	27.5	22.0	66.1	23.5	22.0	33.0
6 *Always*	22.0	66.1	23.4	28.0	34.1	15.4	50.1	17.4	17.7	40.9
7 *K-9*	20.5	62.3	22.0	20.9	13.2	14.3	47.5	16.4	17.0	15.8
8 *The 'Burbs*	19.0	58.9	20.7	22.9	18.7	13.3	45.0	15.5	16.4	22.4
9 *The Dream Team*	15.8	51.1	17.8	19.0	16.5	11.1	39.6	13.5	14.9	19.8
10 *Do the Right Thing*	14.6	48.2	16.7	14.6	7.7	10.2	37.6	12.7	14.4	9.2
11 *Dad*	11.9	41.5	14.2	20.0	20.9	8.3	32.9	11.0	13.1	25.0
12 *Shocker*	8.3	32.7	10.9	14.6	6.6	5.8	26.7	8.6	11.5	7.9
13 *The Wizard*	5.5	26.1	8.4	9.5	8.8	3.9	22.1	6.9	10.3	10.5
14 *Renegades*	4.6	23.9	7.6	13.1	13.2	3.2	20.6	6.3	9.9	15.8
Paramount Pictures										
15 *Harlem Nights*	$36.3	$100.8	$36.5	$41.7	$33.0	$25.4	$ 74.4	$26.6	$24.1	$39.5
16 *Pet Sematary*	29.1	83.2	29.9	27.1	12.1	20.3	62.0	21.9	20.9	14.5
17 *Black Rain*	27.5	79.4	28.5	31.6	33.0	19.3	59.4	20.9	20.2	39.5
18 *Major League*	23.7	70.1	25.0	26.1	13.2	16.6	52.9	18.5	18.4	15.8
19 *Cousins*	11.0	39.4	13.4	14.4	14.3	7.7	31.4	10.4	12.8	17.1
20 *We're No Angels*	5.5	26.1	8.4	19.9	24.2	3.9	22.1	6.9	10.3	29.0
21 *Let it Ride*	2.3	18.3	5.5	10.8	19.8	1.6	16.7	4.8	8.8	23.7
22 *Shirley Valentine*	2.3	18.3	5.5	5.6	8.8	1.6	16.7	4.8	8.8	10.5
23 *Fat Man and Little Boy*	1.5	16.5	4.8	9.2	20.9	1.1	15.3	4.3	8.5	25.0
24 *The Experts*	0.0	12.7	3.4	0.8	13.2	0.0	12.7	3.4	7.8	15.8
Sony Pictures Entertainment[b]										
25 *Look Who's Talking* (TS)	$75.8	$196.5	$72.6	$51.7	$11.0	$53.1	$141.4	$51.8	$41.9	$13.2
26 *When Harry Met Sally* (C)	46.1	124.5	45.4	38.1	20.9	32.3	91.0	32.8	28.5	25.0
27 *Steel Magnolias* (TS)	44.0	119.4	43.5	35.9	24.2	30.8	87.4	31.5	27.6	29.0
28 *See No Evil; Hear No Evil* (TS)	22.5	67.1	23.8	23.1	19.8	15.7	50.8	17.7	17.9	23.7
29 *The Bear* (TS)	14.9	48.7	16.9	22.5	23.1	10.4	37.9	12.8	14.5	27.7
30 *Glory* (TS)	14.3	47.4	16.4	14.5	23.1	10.0	37.0	12.5	14.2	27.7
31 *Look Up* (TS)	8.8	34.1	11.4	16.1	18.7	6.2	27.7	9.0	11.8	22.4
32 *Casualties of War* (C)	8.1	32.5	10.8	17.1	27.5	5.7	26.6	8.6	11.5	33.0
33 *Chances Are* (TS)	7.2	30.1	9.9	15.4	19.8	5.0	24.9	7.9	11.0	23.7

EXHIBIT 6 *(continued)*

Studio/Movie Title	First Film: U.S. Theater Rentals	First Film: Other Revenue	First Film: Distribution Fees	First Film: Distribution Expense	First Film: Negative Cost	Hypothetical Sequel: U.S. Theater Rentals	Hypothetical Sequel: Other Revenue	Hypothetical Sequel: Distribution Fees	Hypothetical Sequel: Distribution Expense	Hypothetical Sequel: Negative Cost
34 *Family Business* (TS)	$ 6.6	$ 28.7	$ 9.4	$ 16.5	$19.8	$ 4.6	$ 23.9	$ 7.6	$10.8	$23.7
35 *She's Out of Control* (C)	5.7	26.6	8.6	12.2	16.5	4.0	22.4	7.0	10.4	19.8
36 *Who's Harry Crumb?* (TS)	5.0	24.7	7.9	13.2	15.4	3.5	21.1	6.5	10.0	18.5
37 *Adventures of Baron Munchausen* (C)	4.3	23.1	7.3	7.8	57.1	3.0	20.0	6.1	9.7	68.5
38 *True Believer* (C)	4.1	22.6	7.1	12.8	15.4	2.9	19.6	6.0	9.6	18.5
39 *Troop Beverly Hills* (C)	4.0	22.3	7.0	11.5	19.8	2.8	19.5	5.9	9.6	23.7
40 *Tap* (TS)	3.9	22.1	6.9	11.4	16.5	2.7	19.3	5.8	9.5	19.8
41 *Deepstar Six* (TS)	3.4	21.0	6.5	10.0	8.8	2.4	18.5	5.5	9.3	10.5
42 *Johnny Handsome* (TS)	2.9	19.7	6.0	9.7	22.0	2.0	17.6	5.2	9.1	26.4
43 *Music Box* (TS)	2.8	19.4	5.9	8.4	19.8	1.9	17.4	5.1	9.0	23.7
44 *Immediate Family* (C)	2.3	18.3	5.5	12.1	15.4	1.6	16.7	4.8	8.8	18.5
45 *Listen to Me* (C)	2.0	17.5	5.2	12.0	16.5	1.4	16.1	4.6	8.7	19.8
46 *Physical Evidence* (C)	1.7	16.7	4.9	9.2	18.7	1.2	15.5	4.4	8.5	22.4
47 *Old Gringo* (C)	1.5	16.5	4.8	6.6	37.3	1.1	15.3	4.3	8.5	44.8
48 *Loverboy* (TS)	1.5	16.5	4.8	10.5	11.0	1.1	15.3	4.3	8.5	13.2
49 *Sing* (TS)	1.0	15.1	4.3	9.0	15.4	0.7	14.4	4.0	8.2	18.5
50 *Winter People* (C)	0.8	14.6	4.1	6.3	17.6	0.5	14.0	3.8	8.1	21.1
51 *Welcome Home* (C)	0.4	13.8	3.8	4.9	15.4	0.3	13.5	3.6	8.0	18.5
52 *Adventures of Milo and Otis* (C)	0.1	13.0	3.5	6.0	8.8	0.1	12.9	3.4	7.8	10.5
53 *The Big Picture* (C)	0.1	13.0	3.5	0.8	8.8	0.1	12.9	3.4	7.8	10.5
54 *Slaves of New York* (TS)	0.1	13.0	3.5	1.5	6.6	0.1	12.9	3.4	7.8	7.9
55 *Eat a Bowl of Tea* (C)	0.1	13.0	3.5	0.8	2.2	0.1	12.9	3.4	7.8	2.6
56 *To Kill a Priest* (C)	0.0	12.7	3.4	0.8	11.0	0.0	12.7	3.4	7.8	13.2
57 *Me and Him* (C)	0.0	12.7	3.4	0.8	8.8	0.0	12.7	3.4	7.8	10.5
58 *Bloodhounds of Broadway* (C)	0.0	12.7	3.4	0.8	3.3	0.0	12.7	3.4	7.8	4.0
Twentieth Century Fox										
59 *The War of the Roses*	$ 45.6	$123.2	$ 44.9	$ 39.1	$27.5	$ 31.9	$ 90.0	$ 32.5	$28.3	$33.0
60 *The Abyss*	31.6	89.3	32.2	37.2	49.4	22.1	66.3	23.5	22.0	59.3
61 *Weekend at Bernie's*	15.4	50.1	17.4	16.3	11.0	10.8	38.9	13.2	14.7	13.2
62 *Say Anything*	9.8	36.5	12.3	15.2	14.3	6.9	29.4	9.6	12.2	17.1
63 *Skin Deep*	9.4	35.4	11.9	15.0	11.0	6.5	28.6	9.3	12.0	13.2
64 *The Fabulous Baker Boys*	8.8	34.1	11.4	16.1	14.3	6.2	27.7	9.0	11.8	17.1
65 *Millennium*	2.6	19.1	5.8	7.1	16.5	1.8	17.2	5.0	9.0	19.8
66 *Worth Winning*	1.7	16.7	4.9	10.5	14.3	1.2	15.5	4.4	8.5	17.1

EXHIBIT 6 *(continued)*

Studio/Movie Title	First Film					Hypothetical Sequel				
	U.S. Theater Rentals	Other Revenue	Distribution Fees	Distribution Expense	Negative Cost	U.S. Theater Rentals	Other Revenue	Distribution Fees	Distribution Expense	Negative Cost
67 *Gleaming the Cube*	$ 1.2	$ 15.7	$ 4.5	$ 6.5	$12.1	$ 0.8	$ 14.8	$ 4.1	$ 8.3	$14.5
68 *How I Got into College* ..	0.6	14.1	3.9	8.8	13.2	0.4	13.7	3.7	8.0	15.8
69 *When the Whales Came* .	0.0	12.7	3.4	1.4	4.4	0.0	12.7	3.4	7.8	5.3
Warner Brothers										
70 *Batman*	$165.6	$414.2	$154.5	$102.0	$54.9	$115.9	$293.7	$109.2	$82.3	$65.9
71 *Driving Miss Daisy*	55.6	147.4	54.1	43.3	8.8	38.9	107.0	38.9	32.8	10.5
72 *Tango & Cash*	33.1	93.0	33.6	40.4	60.4	23.2	68.9	24.5	22.7	72.5
73 *Lean on Me*	15.8	51.1	17.8	17.7	16.5	11.1	39.6	13.5	14.9	19.8
74 *Her Alibi*	10.1	37.3	12.6	16.6	22.0	7.1	29.9	9.8	12.4	26.4
75 *Next of Kin*	7.7	31.4	10.4	14.3	13.2	5.4	25.8	8.3	11.3	15.8
76 *Pink Cadillac*	7.5	30.9	10.2	16.8	20.9	5.2	25.4	8.1	11.2	25.0
77 *Young Einstein*	6.6	28.7	9.4	11.3	4.4	4.6	23.9	7.6	10.8	5.3
78 *Dead-Bang*	3.9	22.1	6.9	11.4	15.4	2.7	19.3	5.8	9.5	18.5
79 *Dead Calm*	3.6	21.5	6.7	10.1	9.9	2.5	18.9	5.7	9.4	11.9
80 *Second Sight*	2.8	19.4	5.9	9.7	11.0	1.9	17.4	5.1	9.0	13.2
81 *See You in the Morning* ..	2.4	18.6	5.6	9.6	18.7	1.7	16.8	4.9	8.9	22.4
82 *In Country*	1.8	17.0	5.0	9.3	19.8	1.2	15.7	4.5	8.6	23.7
83 *Cookie*	1.1	15.4	4.4	5.1	14.3	0.8	14.6	4.1	8.3	17.1
84 *How to Get Ahead in Advertising*	0.2	13.3	3.6	0.9	5.5	0.2	13.1	3.5	7.9	6.6
85 *Powwow Highway*	0.1	13.0	3.5	0.8	4.4	0.1	12.9	3.4	7.8	5.3
86 *Bert Rigby, You're a Fool* .	0.0	12.7	3.4	1.4	14.3	0.0	12.7	3.4	7.8	17.1
87 *Penn & Teller Get Killed* .	0.0	12.7	3.4	0.8	8.8	0.0	12.7	3.4	7.8	10.5
88 *Checking Out*	0.0	12.7	3.4	0.8	5.5	0.0	12.7	3.4	7.8	6.6
The Walt Disney Company										
89 *Honey, I Shrunk the Kids* (W)	$ 80.0	$206.7	$ 76.4	$ 58.6	$24.2	$ 56.0	$148.5	$ 54.5	$43.8	$29.0
90 *Dead Poets Society* (T) ..	53.3	141.8	52.0	46.2	22.0	37.3	103.1	37.4	31.8	26.4
91 *The Little Mermaid* (W) ..	44.2	120.0	43.7	38.6	22.0	31.0	87.8	31.6	27.7	26.4
92 *Turner & Hootch* (T)	38.8	106.9	38.8	32.5	19.8	27.2	78.6	28.2	25.3	23.7
93 *Three Fugitives* (T)	20.4	62.1	21.9	22.2	18.7	14.3	47.3	16.4	17.0	22.4
94 *An Innocent Man* (T) ...	11.6	40.7	13.9	17.2	18.7	8.1	32.3	10.7	13.0	22.4
95 *Blaze* (T)	9.9	36.7	12.4	17.8	19.8	6.9	29.5	9.7	12.3	23.7
96 *New York Stories* (T)	5.2	25.3	8.1	10.7	20.9	3.6	21.5	6.7	10.1	25.0
97 *Gross Anatomy* (T)	5.1	25.0	8.0	13.2	13.2	3.5	21.3	6.6	10.1	15.8
98 *Disorganized Crime* (T) ..	4.4	23.4	7.4	11.7	12.1	3.1	20.2	6.2	9.8	14.5
99 *Cheetah* (W)	4.4	23.4	7.4	10.4	7.7	3.1	20.2	6.2	9.8	9.2
Averages	$ 14.9	$ 48.8	$ 16.9	$ 17.4	$17.6	$ 10.4	$ 38.0	$ 12.9	$14.5	$21.2

[a]Metro-Goldwyn-Mayer and Orion are excluded. Fees assume films were financed by an independent producer. Costs exclude gross participations and interest charges.
[b]C = Columbia Pictures; TS = Tri-Star; W = Walt Disney; T = Touchstone.

EXHIBIT 7 Estimated Expected Present Values and 1-Year Holding Period Returns Based on Data in Exhibit 6 (millions of dollars)

	First Film			Hypothetical Sequel		
Studio/Movie or Title	PV of Net Inflows at Year 1[a]	PV of Negative Cost at Year 0	1-Year Return[b]	PV of Net Inflows at Year 4[a]	PV of Negative Cost at Year 3	1-Year Return[b]
MCA Universal						
1 *Parenthood*	$100.1	$21.5	$ 3.65	$ 76.8	$28.2	$1.72
2 *Born on the Fourth of July*	74.5	19.4	2.85	56.8	25.4	1.24
3 *Field of Dreams*	59.1	17.2	2.44	47.3	22.6	1.10
4 *Uncle Buck*	60.0	16.1	2.72	47.0	21.2	1.22
5 *Sea of Love*	53.5	26.9	0.99	44.4	35.3	0.26
6 *Always*	34.3	33.3	0.03	31.4	43.7	(0.28)
7 *K-9*	37.8	12.9	1.93	29.3	16.9	0.73
8 *The 'Burbs*	32.2	18.3	0.76	27.3	24.0	0.14
9 *The Dream Team*	28.4	16.1	0.76	22.9	21.2	0.08
10 *Do the Right Thing*	30.0	7.5	2.98	21.2	9.9	1.15
11 *Dad*	17.7	20.4	(0.13)	17.4	26.8	(0.35)
12 *Shocker*	14.3	6.5	1.22	12.4	8.5	0.47
13 *The Wizard*	12.7	8.6	0.48	8.7	11.3	(0.23)
14 *Renegades*	6.9	12.9	(0.46)	7.4	16.9	(0.56)
Paramount Pictures						
15 *Harlem Nights*	$ 55.4	$32.3	0.72	$ 51.1	$42.3	0.21
16 *Pet Sematary*	52.6	11.8	3.45	41.1	15.5	1.65
17 *Black Rain*	44.1	32.3	0.37	39.0	42.3	(0.08)
18 *Major League*	40.3	12.9	2.12	33.7	16.9	0.99
19 *Cousins*	21.2	14.0	0.52	16.2	18.3	(0.11)
20 *We're No Angels*	2.1	23.7	(0.91)	8.7	31.0	(0.72)
21 *Let It Ride*	3.6	19.4	(0.82)	4.3	25.4	(0.83)
22 *Shirley Valentine*	8.9	8.6	0.04	4.3	11.3	(0.62)
23 *Fat Man and Little Boy*	3.3	20.4	(0.84)	3.2	26.8	(0.88)
24 *The Experts*	8.2	12.9	(0.36)	1.1	16.9	(0.94)
Sony Pictures Entertainment[c]						
25 *Look Who's Talking* (TS)	$142.3	$10.8	12.24	$105.5	$14.1	6.48
26 *When Harry Met Sally* (C)	83.3	20.4	3.08	64.6	26.8	1.41
27 *Steel Magnolias* (TS)	80.4	23.7	2.40	61.7	31.0	0.99
28 *See No Evil; Hear No Evil* (TS)	40.5	19.4	1.09	32.0	25.4	0.26
29 *The Bear* (TS)	22.4	22.6	(0.01)	21.5	29.6	(0.27)
30 *Glory* (TS)	29.3	22.6	0.30	20.8	29.6	(0.30)
31 *Look Up* (TS)	14.1	18.3	(0.23)	13.2	24.0	(0.45)
32 *Casualties of War* (C)	11.4	26.9	(0.57)	12.3	35.3	(0.65)
33 *Chances Are* (TS)	10.8	19.4	(0.44)	10.9	25.4	(0.57)
34 *Family Business* (TS)	8.3	19.4	(0.57)	10.2	25.4	(0.60)
35 *She's Out of Control* (C)	10.5	16.1	(0.35)	9.0	21.2	(0.58)
36 *Who's Harry Crumb?* (TS)	7.6	15.1	(0.49)	7.9	19.7	(0.60)
37 *Adventures of Baron Munchausen* (C)	11.6	55.9	(0.79)	7.0	73.4	(0.90)
38 *True Believer* (C)	5.8	15.1	(0.61)	6.7	19.7	(0.66)
39 *Troop Beverly Hills* (C)	6.9	19.4	(0.64)	6.5	25.4	(0.74)
40 *Tap* (TS)	6.7	16.1	(0.58)	6.4	21.2	(0.70)
41 *Deepstar Six* (TS)	7.1	8.6	(0.17)	5.8	11.3	(0.49)
42 *Johnny Handsome* (TS)	6.0	21.5	(0.72)	5.0	28.2	(0.82)
43 *Music Box* (TS)	7.1	19.4	(0.63)	4.9	25.4	(0.81)
44 *Immediate Family* (C)	2.2	15.1	(0.85)	4.3	19.7	(0.78)
45 *Listen to Me* (C)	1.6	16.1	(0.90)	3.8	21.2	(0.82)
46 *Physical Evidence* (C)	3.6	18.3	(0.80)	3.4	24.0	(0.86)
47 *Old Gringo* (C)	6.0	36.6	(0.84)	3.2	48.0	(0.93)
48 *Loverboy* (TS)	2.0	10.8	(0.81)	3.2	14.1	(0.77)
49 *Sing* (TS)	2.2	15.1	(0.85)	2.4	19.7	(0.88)
50 *Winter People* (C)	4.4	17.2	(0.74)	2.1	22.6	(0.91)
51 *Welcome Home* (C)	5.1	15.1	(0.66)	1.7	19.7	(0.91)
52 *Adventures of Milo and Otis* (C)	3.1	8.6	(0.64)	1.2	11.3	(0.89)
53 *The Big Picture* (C)	8.4	8.6	(0.02)	1.2	11.3	(0.89)
54 *Slaves of New York* (TS)	7.8	6.5	0.20	1.12	8.5	(0.85)
55 *Eat a Bowl of Tea* (C)	8.4	2.2	2.92	1.2	2.8	(0.56)
56 *To Kill a Priest* (C)	8.2	10.8	(0.24)	1.1	14.1	(0.92)

(continued)

EXHIBIT 7 (continued)

Studio/Movie or Title	First Film: PV of Net Inflows at Year 1[a]	First Film: PV of Negative Cost at Year 0	First Film: 1-Year Return[b]	Hypothetical Sequel: PV of Net Inflows at Year 4[a]	Hypothetical Sequel: PV of Negative Cost at Year 3	Hypothetical Sequel: 1-Year Return[b]
57 *Me and Him* (C)	$ 8.2	$ 8.6	$(0.05)	$ 1.1	$11.3	$(0.90)
58 *Bloodhounds of Broadway* (C)	8.2	3.2	1.54	1.1	4.2	(0.74)
Twentieth Century Fox						
59 *The War of the Roses*	$ 80.8	$26.9	$ 2.01	$ 63.8	$35.3	$ 0.81
60 *The Abyss*	48.4	48.4	0.00	44.6	63.5	(0.30)
61 *Weekend at Bernie's*	30.2	10.8	1.81	22.3	14.1	0.58
62 *Say Anything*	17.5	14.0	0.25	14.6	18.3	(0.21)
63 *Skin Deep*	16.6	10.8	0.54	14.0	14.1	(0.01)
64 *The Fabulous Baker Boys*	14.1	14.0	0.01	13.2	18.3	(0.28)
65 *Millennium*	8.2	16.1	(0.49)	4.7	21.2	(0.78)
66 *Worth Winning*	2.2	14.0	(0.84)	3.4	18.3	(0.82)
67 *Gleaming the Cube*	5.3	11.8	(0.55)	2.7	15.5	(0.82)
68 *How I Got into College*	1.3	12.9	(0.90)	1.8	16.9	(0.89)
69 *When the Whales Came*	7.5	4.3	0.75	1.1	5.6	(0.81)
Warner Brothers						
70 *Batman*	$311.5	$53.8	$ 4.80	$229.1	$70.5	$ 2.25
71 *Driving Miss Daisy*	101.2	8.6	10.76	77.6	11.3	5.87
72 *Tango & Cash*	48.9	59.1	(0.17)	46.7	77.6	(0.40)
73 *Lean on Me*	29.8	16.1	0.85	22.9	21.2	0.08
74 *Her Alibi*	16.8	21.5	(0.22)	15.0	28.2	(0.47)
75 *Next of Kin*	13.2	12.9	0.02	11.7	16.9	(0.31)
76 *Pink Cadillac*	10.1	20.4	(0.51)	11.4	26.8	(0.58)
77 *Young Einstein*	13.6	4.3	2.17	10.2	5.6	0.80
78 *Dead-Bang*	6.7	15.1	(0.55)	6.4	19.7	(0.68)
79 *Dead Calm*	7.6	9.7	(0.22)	6.1	12.7	(0.52)
80 *Second Sight*	5.8	10.8	(0.46)	4.9	14.1	(0.65)
81 *See You in the Morning*	5.1	18.3	(0.72)	4.4	24.0	(0.82)
82 *In Country*	3.8	19.4	(0.80)	3.5	25.4	(0.86)
83 *Cookie*	6.4	14.0	(0.54)	2.6	18.3	(0.86)
84 *How to Get Ahead in Advertising*	8.6	5.4	0.61	1.4	7.1	(0.80)
85 *Powwow Highway*	8.4	4.3	0.96	1.2	5.6	(0.78)
86 *Bert Rigby, You're a Fool*	7.5	14.0	(0.46)	1.1	18.3	(0.94)
87 *Penn & Teller Get Killed*	8.2	8.6	(0.05)	1.1	11.3	(0.90)
88 *Checking Out*	8.2	5.4	0.53	1.1	7.1	(0.85)
The Walt Disney Company						
89 *Honey, I Shrunk the Kids* (W)	$145.5	$23.7	$ 5.15	$111.2	$31.0	$ 2.58
90 *Dead Poets Society* (T)	92.5	21.5	3.30	74.4	28.2	1.64
91 *The Little Mermaid* (W)	78.1	21.5	2.63	62.0	28.2	1.20
92 *Turner & Hootch* (T)	71.2	19.4	2.68	54.6	25.4	1.15
93 *Three Fugitives* (T)	36.3	18.3	0.98	29.1	24.0	0.21
94 *An Innocent Man* (T)	19.7	18.3	0.08	17.0	24.0	(0.29)
95 *Blaze* (T)	15.0	19.4	(0.22)	14.7	25.4	(0.42)
96 *New York Stories* (T)	10.7	20.4	(0.47)	8.2	26.8	(0.69)
97 *Gross Anatomy* (T)	7.8	12.9	(0.39)	8.1	16.9	(0.52)
98 *Disorganized Crime* (T)	7.8	11.8	(0.34)	7.1	15.5	(0.54)
99 *Cheetah* (W)	9.2	7.5	0.22	7.1	9.9	(0.28)
Average	$ 27.7	$17.3	$ 0.67	$ 21.6	$22.6	$(0.08)
Median	$ 10.5	$16.1	$(0.02)	$ 8.7	$21.2	$(0.54)
Standard deviation	$ 41.4	$10.1	$ 2.07	$ 31.5	$13.3	$ 1.21
Interquartile range	$ 6.9 to $ 34.3	$10.8 to $20.4	$(0.55) to $ 0.99	$ 3.4 to $ 29.1	$14.1 to $26.8	$(0.82) to $ 0.21

[a]Net inflows consist of all revenues minus associated distribution fees and expenses.
[b]One-year return is defined as: (PV of net inflows – PV of negative cost) ÷ (PV of negative cost).
[c]C = Columbia Pictures; TS = Tri-Star; W = Walt Disney; T = Touchstone.

EXHIBIT 8
Histograms of 1-Year Returns for First Films and Hypothetical Sequels (based on data calculated in Exhibit 7)

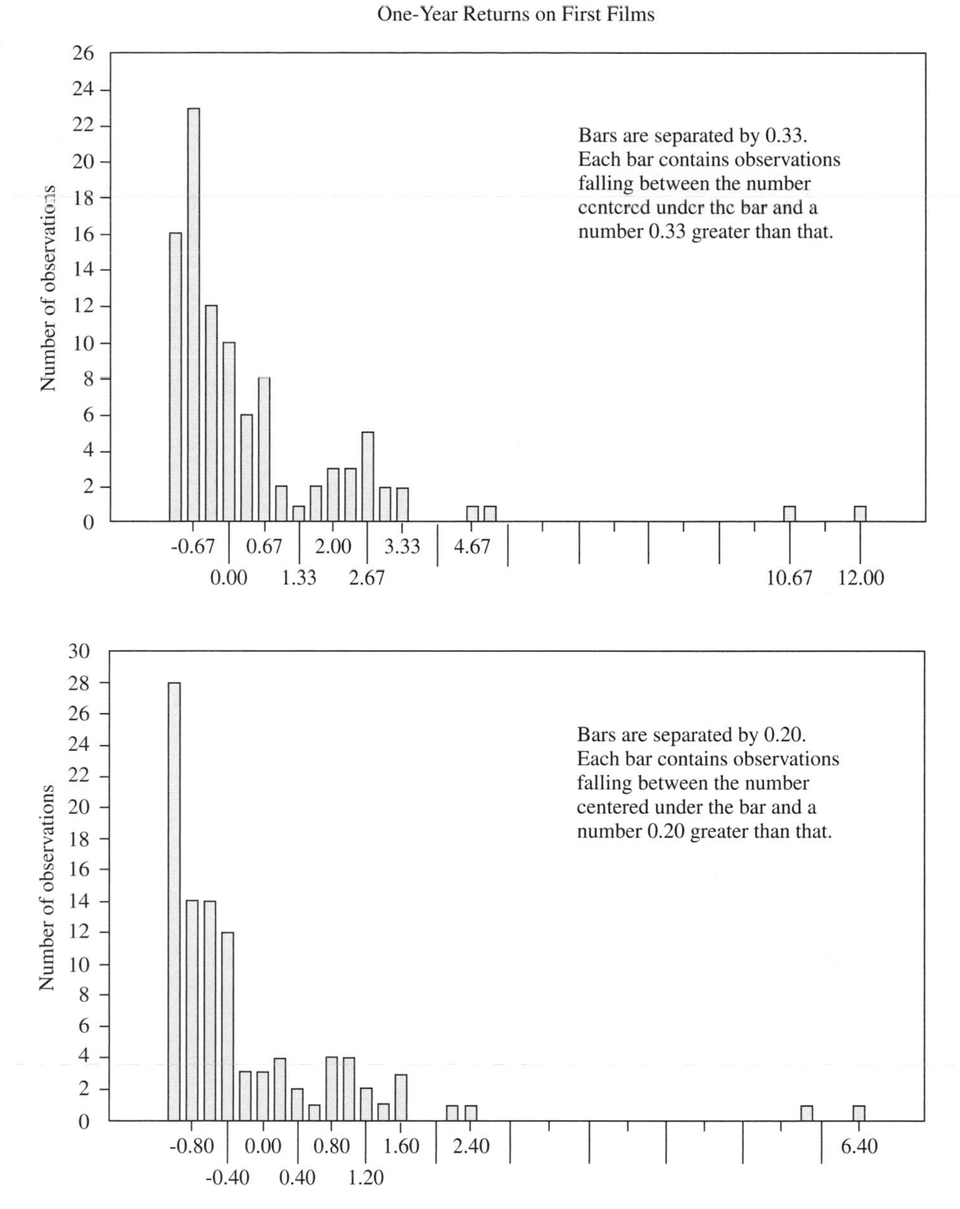

EXHIBIT 9 Summary Statistics for Samples of Films Released in 1987 and 1988[a] (millions of dollars)

1987 Data

	First Film					Hypothetical Sequel				
	U.S. Theater Rentals	Other Revenue	Distribution Fees	Distribution Expense	Negative Cost	U.S. Theater Rentals	Other Revenue	Distribution Fees	Distribution Expense	Negative Cost
Average (in 1991 dollars)	$21.3	$64.4	$22.8	$21.5	$26.3	$14.9	$ 48.9	$17.0	$17.4	$31.6

	First Film			Hypothetical Sequel		
	PV of Net Inflows at Year 1	PV of Negative Cost at Year 0	1-Year Return[a]	PV of Net Inflows at Year 4	PV of Negative Cost at Year 3	1-Year Return[a]
Average	$39.4	$25.8	$0.71	$30.4	$33.8	$0.01
Median	$30.9	$22.3	0.04	$24.0	$29.3	(0.39)
Standard deviation	$38.4	$ 9.4	2.05	$29.4	$12.3	1.20
Interquartile range	$11.1 to $52.1	$18.8 to $29.3	$(0.60) to $ 1.22	$ 8.8 to $40.2	$24.6 to $38.5	$(0.75) to 0.31

1988 Data

	First Film					Hypothetical Sequel				
	U.S. Theater Rentals	Other Revenue	Distribution Fees	Distribution Expense	Negative Cost	U.S. Theater Rentals	Other Revenue	Distribution Fees	Distribution Expense	Negative Cost
Average (in 1991 dollars)	$19.7	$60.5	$21.3	$20.5	$24.4	$13.8	$46.1	$15.9	$16.7	$29.2

	First Film			Hypothetical Sequel		
	PV of Net Inflows at Year 1	PV of Negative Cost at Year 0	1-Year Return[a]	PV of Net Inflows at Year 4	PV of Negative Cost at Year 3	1-Year Return[a]
Average	$36.4	$23.8	$0.48	$28.2	$31.3	$(0.13)
Median	$22.4	$20.3	0.01	$17.5	$26.6	(0.40)
Standard deviation	$38.2	$11.4	1.37	$29.3	$14.9	0.80
Interquartile range	$ 9.3 to $42.1	$16.9 to $24.8	$(0.48) to $0.93	$ 7.5 to $32.5	$22.2 to $32.5	$(0.69) to $ 0.14

[a]One-year return is defined as: (PV of net inflows – PV of negative cost) ÷ (PV of negative cost).

Appendix

This appendix describes how the estimates of first films' and hypothetical sequels' financial performance were produced for Exhibits 6 and 7. (Exhibit 9 is exactly analogous.)

Description of Exhibit 6: Revenues and Costs In 1991 Dollars

Exhibit 6 presents estimates for the major categories of revenues and costs for first films released by six major studios in 1989, and corresponding estimates for a hypothetical sequel based on each. These are estimates of how each film would perform if independently financed (Arundel would finance its own productions). Figures in Exhibit 6 are based on film-by-film estimates of negative costs, U.S. rentals, and U.S. print and advertising costs published by the trade periodical *Variety* between 1990 and 1992. Estimates of ancillary market revenues, distribution fees, and distribution expenses are based on expected relationships between each of these variables and one or more items of the *Variety* data. All items in Exhibit 6 are expressed in 1991 dollars to facilitate the use of expected relationships between real variables, as derived from various datasets.

Revenues for each of the ten ancillary markets listed in Exhibit 3 are projected from estimated U.S. rentals according to relationships derived from a large sample of films. Distribution fees are computed as a fixed percentage of the revenue from each source, assuming independent financing. Distribution expenses for the U.S. theatrical run are grossed up from *Variety*'s estimates of U.S. print and advertising costs; distribution expenses for other, ancillary markets are based on expected relationships between a given market and its associated expenses. Negative costs are equal to *Variety*'s estimates, inflated to 1991 dollars.

Estimates of the performance of a hypothetical sequel for each first film were developed similarly. The sequel's estimated negative cost and U.S. theater rentals are 120% and 70%, respectively, of the corresponding items for the first film, per Exhibit 4. However, ancillary market revenues and distribution fees and expenses are not 70% of the corresponding figures for first films, but only because the underlying relationship between ancillary revenues and U.S. theater rentals is not a fixed percentage.

Description of Exhibit 7: Discounted Values and the Distribution of Returns

Exhibit 7 uses data from Exhibit 6 to compute nominal cash flows, distribute them over time, discount them, and estimate 1-year returns. In effect, Exhibit 7 treats film production as a 1-year investment. For both first films and sequels, the producer invests the present value of the negative cost; 1 year later, he or she receives the discounted value of all future net cash flows.

Films' future net cash flows consist of all ancillary revenues minus associated distribution fees and expenses, each inflated to nominal dollars (at 1.5% semiannually) and arrayed in time according to Exhibit 3. Negative costs are spread evenly over the year in which production occurs, and are partly inflated. Nominal negative costs are discounted (at 6% semiannually) to the point at which the production decision is made. Future net cash flows are discounted to a point 1 year later, at the assumed U.S. theatrical release date. The return on this 1-year investment is computed simply as net cash flow minus cost, divided by cost. Sample statistics in Exhibit 7 are based on the sample of 99 films and corresponding sequels.

Capital Projects as Real Options: An Introduction

This note introduces an approach to capital budgeting that relies on option pricing theory to analyze and evaluate capital projects. The approach is intended to supplement, not replace, capital budgeting analyses and investment criteria based on standard discounted cash flow (DCF) methodologies. For a wide range of corporate investments, insights from an options-based analysis can improve estimates of project value and, perhaps more important, enhance project management.

Motivation

Why treat a corporate investment proposal as a call option, as suggested here, rather than as a bond or an unlevered equity? The latter are easier to understand and value, and the associated analyses are easier to communicate and defend within a large organization. However, many corporate investment proposals, particularly "strategic" ones, bear a stronger resemblance to a call option than to a stock or a bond. Ignoring the optionlike features of such projects can lead to poor decisions. The most likely mistakes are (1) failing to invest in a valuable project because imbedded options are overlooked—this will make the corporation appear shortsighted; and (2) not getting the timing right, that is, committing funds earlier or later than would be ideal.

Asset-in-Place versus Options

Standard DCF valuation methodologies treat projects as follows: managers make a decision to invest (or not) and then wait to see what happens (see Figure I). For some projects this is an adequate representation of reality, but for others, it is backwards. Sometimes managers can wait and see what happens (at least some uncertainty is resolved) and *then* make a decision to invest or not (see Figure II). These two are obviously quite different. The latter is an option and the former is not. An efficient capital market would not place the same value on both, and neither should a corporation.

A great many corporate investment proposals are complex and fit neither of these examples exactly. More often, they contain elements of both. An R&D program, for example, may create both a cash-producing new product and opportunities for further R&D aimed at yet more new products. Investing in a new market may lead to both immediate cash flow and future expansion opportunities. Creating a brand identity may simultaneously create future brand-extension possibilities. Replacing a first-generation technology with a second makes it possible eventually to replace the second with a third, and so forth. All of these examples contain both *assets-in-place* (cash-producing assets that can be evaluated with DCF methodologies) and *growth options* (opportunities to make future investments, which require an option-pricing methodology). Growth options and a few other decision opportunities are known, collectively, as "real" options to distinguish them from "financial" options such as exchange-traded puts and calls. Projects with high option content are likely to be misevaluated by DCF techniques: either the options will be

This note was prepared by Professor Timothy A. Luehrman.

Copyright © 1994 by the President and Fellows of Harvard College. Harvard Business School case 295–074.

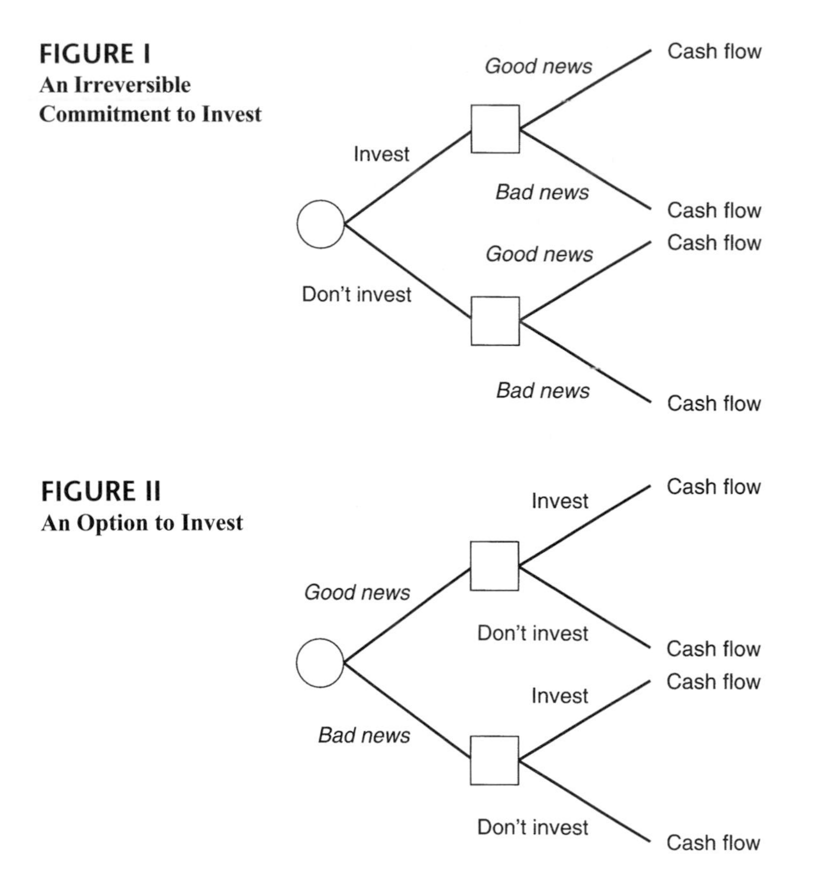

FIGURE I
An Irreversible Commitment to Invest

FIGURE II
An Option to Invest

ignored (resulting in undervaluation and under-investment), or they will be poorly approximated (resulting in either under- or over-investment in addition to poor timing and management).

A sensible solution is to separate a project's assets-in-place from its growth options and to analyze each part accordingly. Unfortunately, this is often difficult, first because a neat separation may not be possible, and second, because estimating the option valuation for a capital project is usually a difficult analytical task. This note is aimed at the second problem. It explains (1) how to set up a mapping between the simplified project and a call option; (2) how to perform an option valuation and relate it to a DCF valuation; and (3) how to extract some managerial insights from the option-pricing framework.

Preliminaries

As a starting point, this note presumes a working knowledge of basic option pricing and basic capital budgeting (see Figure III). Readers should be acquainted with puts and calls, position diagrams, determinants of call option value, option deltas, and comparative statics. This body of material is covered in most graduate-level corporate finance texts.[1] Readers also need to be familiar with incremental cash flows, time value, opportunity cost, value additivity, net present value, and the NPV rule.[2]

[1]See, for example, Brealey and Myers, *Principles of Corporate Finance,* 4th ed. (New York: McGraw-Hill, Inc., 1991), chapter 20, pp. 483–510.

[2]Ibid. Chapters 2–6 pp. 11–128.

FIGURE III
Preliminaries

	Basic Option Pricing	Basic Capital Budgeting
To get started analyzing corporate projects as real options, you need to know:	Basic definitions Position diagrams Determinants of value Comparative statics Put-call parity Complications: Dividends Early exercise	Incremental cash flows Opportunity cost Basic discounting: Time value Risk NPV rule

FIGURE IV
Mapping Project Characteristics onto Call Option Variables

Project	Variable	Call Option
Expenditures required to acquire the assets	X	Exercise price
Value of the operating assets to be acquired	S	Stock price
Length of time decision may be deferred	t	Time of expiration
Riskiness of the underlying operating assets	σ^2	Variance of returns on stock
Time value of money	r	Risk-free rate of return

From this knowledge base, it is possible to construct a mapping between a corporate investment project and a call option and to see the relationship between a project's NPV and the value of an analogous call option.

Projects as Call Options

An opportunity to invest in a corporate project bears an obvious similarity to an option to invest in a corporation's stock. Both involve the right, but not the obligation, to acquire an asset by paying a certain sum of money on or before a certain time. The right to buy the stock is known as a call option. European calls are exercisable only at expiration, whereas an American call may be exercised at any time prior to expiration. Obviously, an American call must be at least as valuable as an otherwise-identical European call. The Black-Scholes option pricing model gives the value of a European call on a tradable stock that pays no dividends as a function of five variables: the stock price, S; the exercise price, X; the time to expiration, t; the risk-free rate of return, r; and the standard deviation of returns on the stock, σ.

By establishing a mapping between project characteristics and the determinants of call-option value, a corporate project can be valued in the same way (see Figure IV). Most projects involve making an expenditure to buy or build a productive asset. This is analogous to exercising an option: the amount expended is the exercise price (X), and the value of the asset built or acquired is the stock price (S). The length of time the company can wait without losing the opportunity is the time to expiration (t), and the riskiness of the project is reflected in the standard deviation of returns on the asset (σ). Time value is still given by the risk-free rate (r).

FIGURE V
Expressing NPV as a Quotient Rather Than a Difference

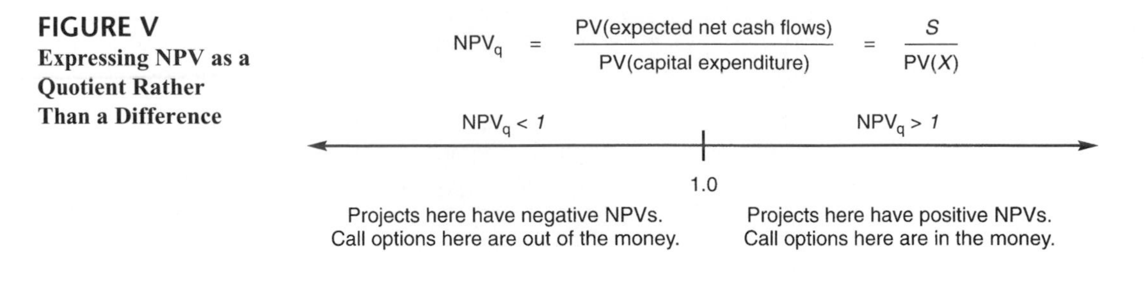

Relating DCF Valuation to Option Valuation

To see how option valuation is related to traditional DCF-based capital budgeting, begin by considering the typical project's NPV. NPV is simply a measure of the difference between how much an asset is worth and what it costs. When it is worth more than it costs, the project has a positive NPV and the corporation goes ahead and invests. Put another way, NPV = PV(expected net cash flows) - PV(capital expenditure), and the decision rule is "invest if NPV > 0."

Notice that NPV can be expressed as a quotient rather than a difference: Define $NPV_q \equiv$ PV(expected net cash flows) ÷ PV (capital expenditure). And similarly, the decision rule can be restated as "invest if $NPV_q > 1$." Figure V shows a line on which projects can be arrayed according to NPV_q. Those for which $NPV_q > 1$ are accepted; those for which $NPV_q < 1$ are rejected.

Figure V can be used in the same way to decide whether to exercise a call option *at expiration.* A call option should be exercised if, at expiration, the stock price exceeds the exercise price (the call is "in the money"). Here, the stock price, *S,* corresponds to PV(expected net cash flows) and the exercise price, *X,* corresponds to PV(capital expenditure). Thus, for a call option, $NPV_q = S/PV(X)$. If this quotient exceeds 1, the option should be exercised. If $NPV_q < 1$, the option is "out of the money" and should not be exercised. In effect, the traditional approach to deciding whether to invest in a project is identical to deciding whether to exercise a call option at expiration. Notice that NPV_q combines four of the five determinants of option value: *S; X; r;* and *t.*[3] Note further that call option value is an increasing function of NPV_q: the higher NPV_q, the higher the call value.

When a decision cannot be delayed, the call option and the project can *both* be evaluated using simple DCF tools and rules—reality is pretty well represented by Figure I. But when the decision can be delayed, the project is like an option that has not yet expired—reality is better represented by Figure II. In this case, NPV_q still matters, but so does the riskiness of the project, which is reflected in the remaining option-pricing variable, σ.

The variability, per unit of time, of returns on the project is measured by the variance of returns, σ^2. Multiplying the variance per unit of time by the amount of time remaining gives cumulative variance, $\sigma^2 t$. Cumulative variance is a measure of how much things could change before time runs out and a decision must be made. The more cumulative variance, the more valuable the option. It may be helpful to think of a collection of balls, each with a number on it, that has been placed in an urn. Variance is the amount of variability in the set of numbers written on the balls, and *t* is the number of draws to be made from the urn. Cumulative variance is simply the variance for each draw times the number of draws.

[3]The variables *r* and *t* come into NPV_q because *X* is being discounted to present value. In the Black-Scholes model, discounting is performed on a continuously compounded basis, so the present value of *X* is actually given by $X(e^{-rt})$. Note, though, that at expiration, $t = 0$, therefore the present value of *X* is simply *X* and NPV_q is simply S/X as stated in the text. Prior to expiration, however, $X(e^{-rt}) < X$ so, all else equal, $NPV_q > S/X$.

FIGURE VI
Pricing Call Options: NPV_q and Cumulative Variance

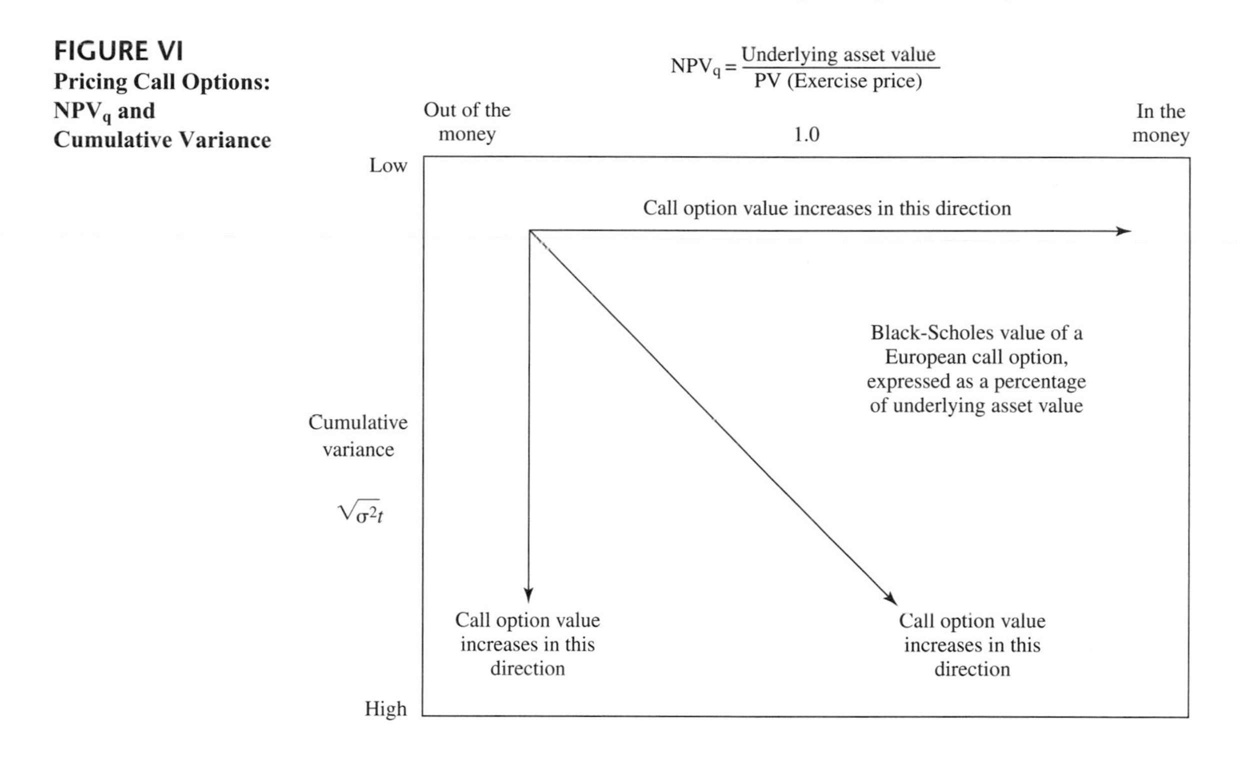

Cumulative variance and NPV_q together are sufficient to value a European call option. Figure VI expands Figure V to include an extra dimension for $\sigma\sqrt{t}$, which is simply the square root of cumulative variance. Options (or projects) for which either σ or t is zero have no cumulative variance and can be evaluated with standard discounted cash flow techniques, that is, with NPV or NPV_q alone. When both σ and t are nonzero, however, a DCF analysis will certainly give the wrong value and may lead to the wrong exercise (or investment) decision: in other words, Figure VI should be used rather than Figure V.

The Black-Scholes model, with values for the five variables as inputs, will give a dollar value for a European call option. Some financial calculators and spreadsheet applications come preprogrammed with the Black-Scholes formula. Alternatively, Exhibit 1 tabulates European call option value as a percentage of the underlying asset value *(S)* for combinations of NPV_q and $\sigma\sqrt{t}$. The value of a European call can simply be looked up, without a formula or a computer.

To illustrate, consider a simple project that requires an investment of \$100, in return for which the company would receive an asset that is currently worth \$90. However, the asset is risky and its value is likely to change; returns on the asset have a standard deviation of about 40% per year. Moreover, the company can wait for up to 3 years before deciding to invest. Finally, suppose the risk-free rate is 5%. Viewed conventionally, this project's NPV is \$90 – \$100 = –\$10. Clearly though, having the opportunity to wait 3 years and see what happens is valuable. In effect, the company owns a 3-year European call with an exercise price of \$100 on underlying assets worth \$90. NPV_q for this option is $\$90 \div [\$100/(1.05)^3] = 1.04$.[4] Cumulative variance is 0.40 times $\sqrt{3}$, or 0.69. Exhibit 1 shows that an option with these characteristics is worth 28.4% of the value of the underlying asset, or .284(\$90) = \$25.56.

[4]The difference between discrete and continuous compounding to compute the present value of *X* is negligible in this case.

Managerial Decisions: Optimal Exercise

The simple project just examined had an NPV of –$10 but an option value of more than $25. Are these contradictory? What should the company do? In fact, the NPV and the option value do not contradict one another. The company should not invest in the project now. If it does, it will both forfeit the option and waste $10. But neither should it discard the project. It should wait, watch, and actively cultivate the project over the next 3 years. Although NPV < 0, the project is very promising because $NPV_q > 1$. That is to say, although $X > S$, these two variables are relatively close to one another because $S > PV(X)$. They are separated only by time value. Over time, we expect the market value of the asset, *S,* to increase at some rate greater than *r* (no one would be willing to hold the asset otherwise).[5] By the end of 3 years, there is a good chance that the NPV will exceed zero and the option will be exercised. In any event, at expiration, the option will be worth the greater of zero or $S - X$. In the meantime, the option on the project really is worth $25, not –$10, provided the company does not exercise it (invest) now.

The difference between NPV and NPV_q contains a useful managerial insight. As time runs out, these two must converge to some agreement: at expiration, they will be either greater than 0 and 1, respectively, or less than these values. But prior to expiration, NPV_q may be positive even when NPV is negative (just as in the preceding example). Figure VII shows this diagrammatically. All options that fall in the right half of Figure VII have $NPV_q > 1$. But not all of these are in the money; that is, the NPV of an "exercise-now" strategy is positive for some and negative for others. The locus of points that corresponds to NPV(exercise now) = 0 is a curve that starts at the top,

FIGURE VII
Mapping Projects into Call-Option Space

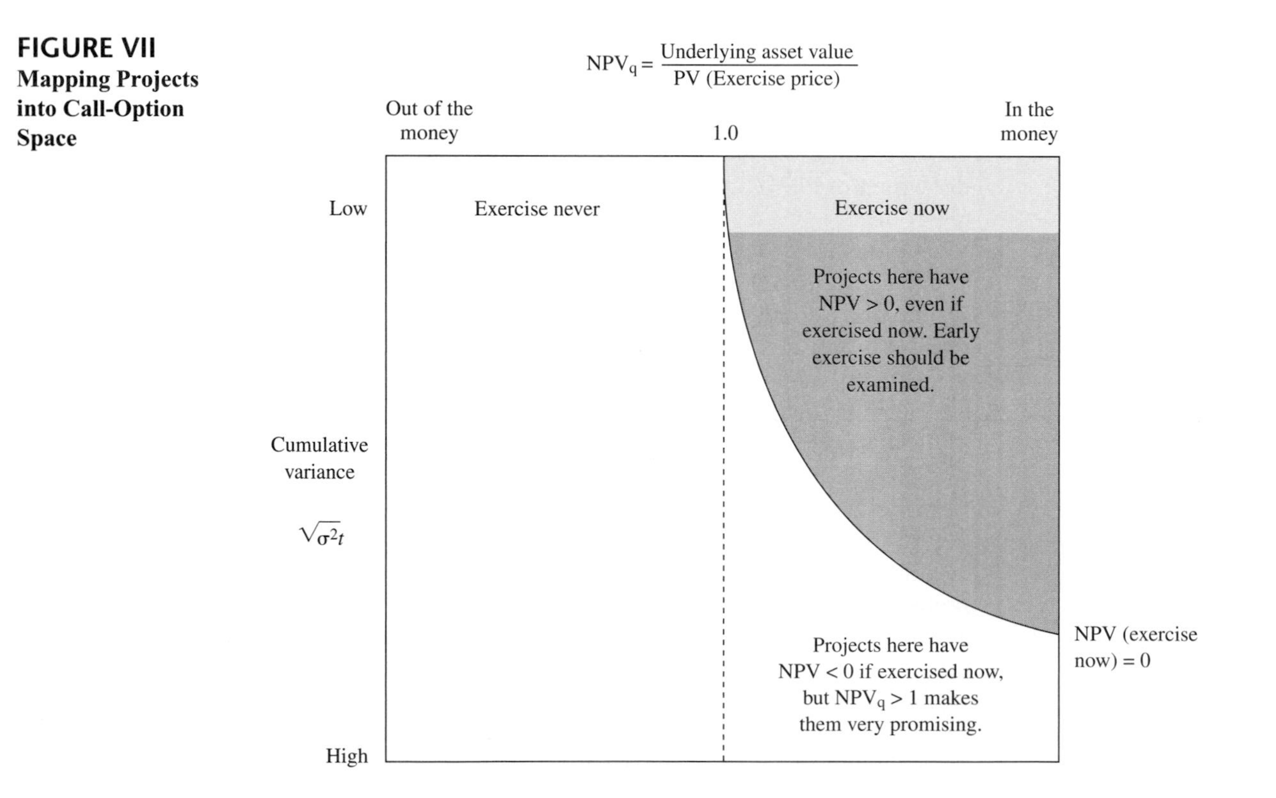

[5]This argument assumes that the asset is like a stock that pays no dividends. The exception to this case is quite important and is treated below.

where cumulative variance is zero and $NPV_q = 1$, and runs down and to the right.[6] Options that fall above this curve have both NPV > 0 and $NPV_q > 1$; they are in the money. Those below the curve have $NPV_q > 1$ but NPV < 0; they are out of the money.

We can now generate three different managerial prescriptions for options with $NPV_q > 1$, each corresponding to a different region in the right half of Figure VII. At the very top right (light shading) are options with no cumulative variance—either time has run out or there is no variance. These options are in the money (NPV > 0) and should be exercised immediately—there is no value in waiting.

Just below these (darker shading) are options that are in the money, but for which there is still some cumulative variance. The company should wait, if possible, to exercise these options. Early exercise may be desirable when the underlying asset is "wasting." If, for example, its value is subject to erosion due to competitors' actions, or if it is already paying out cash, then it is analogous to a dividend-paying stock. Holders of American call options on a dividend-paying stock sometimes will find it optimal to exercise early, prior to expiration. This is a way to capture the cash being paid out or prevent the value erosion. However, by exercising early, the holder of an American call option foregoes the interest on the exercise price. Hence, a tradeoff must be evaluated in order to determine the better course of action. The distinction between American and European calls is very important for real options. Real options typically can be exercised early, and often, the value of the underlying asset is subject to erosion by competitors' actions or technical or demographic changes.[7]

Finally, at the bottom of the right half of Figure VII (no shading) are options like the simple example presented above; they are very promising because $NPV_q > 1$ even though NPV < 0. If, as time runs out, neither S nor X changes, then NPV_q will fall and these options will expire unexercised. But among a large sample of such projects, we should expect many to end up in the money, especially if they receive active attention and management.

A Stylized Map: The "Tomato Garden"

Pushing the logic of Figure VII a bit further, we can divide the call-option space roughly into six regions, each corresponding to a different managerial prescription as shown in Figure VIII. The right side of Figure VIII is divided into regions I, II, and III, in all of which $NPV_q > 1$. These correspond to the three regions in the right half of Figure VII just described. The left half of Figure VIII is divided symmetrically, into regions IV, V, and VI, in all of which $NPV_q < 1$. In region VI at the top, cumulative variance is zero, so these options are never exercised. Region V contains relatively unpromising options. For them, NPV_q and/or $\sigma\sqrt{t}$ is low. Not many of these projects will make it, regardless of the attention they may receive. In region IV are options for which either NPV_q or $\sigma\sqrt{t}$ is reasonably high, but the other is low. These projects require active development to end up in the money. In general, projects will tend to move upward in Figure VIII as time passes, because time runs out and uncertainty is resolved. Managers have two jobs: (1) to try to move projects to the right before time runs out, and (2) to avoid making mistakes in their exercise (investment) decisions in the meantime.

[6] The location of this curve varies with r and σ. The curve is located by holding r and σ constant as t varies, and solving for the NPV_q that corresponds to NPV = 0. Note that in the extreme case of $r = 0$, the curve is a vertical line passing through $NPV_q = 1$. As r increases, the slope of the curve decreases, bending to the right, as shown in Figure VII.

[7] For more on American calls and dividend-paying stocks, see Brealey and Myers, *Principles of Corporate Finance,* 4th ed. (New York: McGraw-Hill, Inc., 1991), chapter 21, pp. 526–529.

FIGURE VIII
A Stylized Mapping of Projects into Call-Option Space

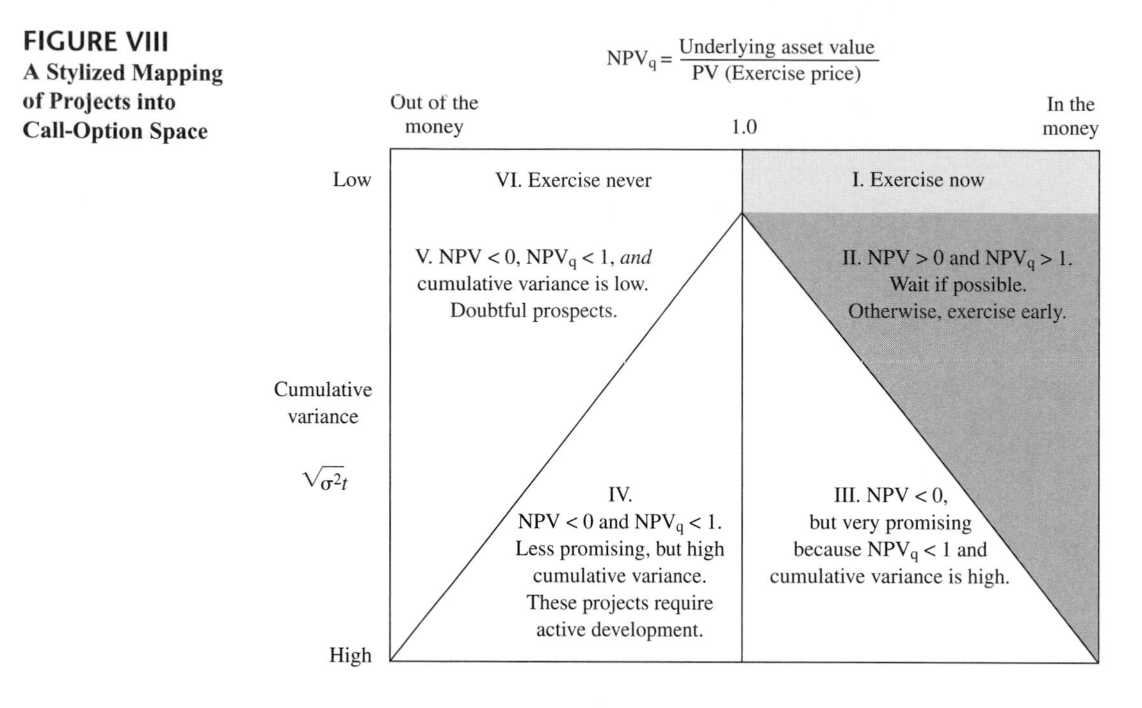

The analogy of a tomato garden located in an unpredictable climate may be a helpful memory cue. Managers are the gardeners; they do the cultivating and eventually decide which tomatoes to pick. At one extreme are perfect, ripe tomatoes (region I of Figure VIII), which should be picked and eaten immediately. At the other extreme are rotten tomatoes (region VI), which should never be picked. In between are many different tomatoes with varying prospects. Those in region II are edible and could be picked, but they would improve with more time on the vine. The gardener will pick them early only if competitors (e.g., squirrels) are likely to get them otherwise. Tomatoes in region III are not edible and should not be picked regardless of competitors. Over time, however, many in region III will ripen and eventually be picked. Region IV contains fruit that is less promising and may not ripen before the season is over. Nevertheless, with more sun or water, fewer weeds, or just good luck, some of these tomatoes may become edible. Finally, region V contains late blossoms and small green tomatoes that have not much chance of growing and ripening before the season ends.

Practical Issues

Using option pricing models to analyze capital projects presents some practical problems. Comparatively few of these have completely satisfactory solutions; on the other hand, some insight is gained just from formulating and articulating the problems. Still more, perhaps, is available from approximations. To interpret an analysis, it helps to remain aware of whether it represents an exact answer to an approximated (simplified) problem, or an approximate answer to an exact problem. Either may be useful.

Simplifying Complex Projects

Real corporate projects, especially long-horizon ones, are complex. They are most often combinations of assets-in-place and options. Further, the options are nested: that is, managers face a *sequence* of serially dependent choices. It helps to simplify such problems, not only for formal analytical purposes, but also to make them understandable and discussible within the group of responsible managers. Further, an unsimplified problem may be unique (and practically insoluble), whereas a simplified problem may fit into a larger class of problems, which will provide hints or boundaries for a solution.

Most real option problems can either be abstracted as fairly simple call options, or broken into pieces, each one of which is a fairly simple call option. A useful guide in simplifying is to search for the primary uncertainty against which managers select. That is, by waiting and watching, what is the main thing a manger learns, and how will he or she exploit the learning? Some projects have optionlike characteristics (e.g., the project is risky and managers clearly have a choice about whether to undertake it), but as long as the company does nothing, it learns nothing. For such projects, a DCF approach may be appropriate; in effect, the company has to make the investment in order to resolve the uncertainty (such projects resemble Figure A). However, for many other projects, the resolution of a small set of uncertainties determines the outcome, and at least some can be resolved without making the entire investment. Such projects resemble Figure II, and identifying the key uncertainties is the first step toward a useful simplification.

Another useful approach is to construct simplifications such that the simplified project is both priceable and either dominating or dominated, compared to the real project. A dominated project is one that is clearly less valuable than the real project. If it also can be priced, then its value provides a lower bound for the project value. For example, a simple European call is clearly dominated by a (more realistic) American call on an asset exposed to erosion by competitors' investments. Dominating simplifications similarly provide an upper bound for project value. Sometimes it is possible to construct and compute both upper and lower bounds.

Estimating Volatility

The option-pricing input managers are least accustomed to estimating is variance, or standard deviation. For a real option, σ cannot be looked up in a table or newspaper, and most people do not have highly developed intuition about, for example, the annual variance of returns on assets associated with entering a new market. Nevertheless, estimating σ is not a completely hopeless task. There are at least three reasonable approaches:

1. *Take a guess.* Systematic risk (β) and total risk (σ) are positively correlated in large samples of operating assets; those with high asset betas are likelier to have higher standard deviations. What is a high standard deviation? Returns on broad-based U.S. stock market indices had a standard deviation of about 20% per year for much of 1986–1994, with exceptions (upward spikes) associated with events like the 1987 market crash and the 1990–1991 Persian Gulf crisis. Individual projects will have higher volatilities than a diversified portfolio of the same projects. Volatility of 20–30% per year is not remarkably high for a single project.
2. *Gather some data.* Volatility can be estimated for some businesses using historical data on investment returns in certain industries. Alternatively, implied volatilities can be computed from quoted option prices for a very large number of traded equities. The length, breadth, and quality of such data have improved greatly in recent years and should continue to do so. These data do require some adjustment, however. Equity returns are levered and are therefore more volatile than underlying asset returns.
3. *Simulate σ.* Spreadsheet-based projections of a project's future cash flows, together with Monte Carlo simulation techniques, can be used to synthesize a probability

distribution for project returns. Inputs include estimated volatilities for specific items, such as commodity prices or exchange rates. Using these inputs, a computer simulates the project and, in the process, synthesizes a probability distribution for desired output variables, such as project returns. From the synthesized probability distribution, σ can be estimated.[8] Simulation software for desktop computers is commercially available and designed to work as an add-in with popular spreadsheet applications.

Some insight is available from Figure VIII even without precise estimates of σ. Simply knowing whether cumulative variance is high or low is enough to locate a project in one part or another of Figure VIII and, with some knowledge of NPV_q, to suggest a managerial course of action.

Checking Models and Distributions

All formal option pricing models, including Black-Scholes, assume that the riskiness of an asset can be expressed as a probability distribution for returns (or prices or payouts) for the asset. Some of the assumed distributions are elegantly simple, such as the lognormal distribution assumed by Black-Scholes. But corporate data for some real projects are inelegant and may be inconsistent with, for example, a lognormal distribution. One approach to this problem is to figure out in which direction a simplified distribution biases the analysis and then interpret the output accordingly, as an upper or lower bound for the actual project's value. Another is to choose a model, if one exists, based on a more appropriate distribution. Many models have been constructed and solved, though most are mathematically sophisticated and unwieldy for use with real options.[9]

More fundamental than the particular distribution assumed by a given model is the type of world being modeled. The Black-Scholes world, for example, is one in which underlying assets are securities that are traded continuously. Real options involve underlying assets that are not traded continuously or, in some cases, not traded at all. For such assets, the five variables (six, if dividends are allowed) of the Black-Scholes model are not sufficient to characterize and price a call option. Whether one model or another remains useful as a way to price a simplified version of the project is a judgment the analyst must make. One alternative to such modeling is brute force, in the form of computing power. High-speed computers and advanced spreadsheet software make it possible to simulate some projects as a complicated decision tree. Decision-tree analysis is not, formally speaking, option pricing, but if well executed, it provides a better treatment of uncertainty and of managers' scope for decision making than conventional DCF analysis alone.

Interpreting Results

To execute a useful analysis, simplification is essential. To interpret the results, some sophistication is equally essential. This typically involves layering complexity back into the problem, in the form of sensitivity analyses and the conditioning or qualifying of inferences. To arrive at Figure VIII, we first took a complicated project and simplified it

[8]Skillful simulation requires knowledge of probability and statistics, including the forms of distributions, elementary sampling theory, differences between time series and cross-sectional analyses, and so forth. A useful reference is Kelton and Law, *Simulation Modeling and Analysis* (New York: McGraw-Hill, Inc., 1991).

[9]A bibliography of sophisticated models is given in Merton, *Continuous-Time Finance* (Cambridge, Mass.: Basil Blackwell, Inc., 1990). A more narrowly focused reference is Wilmott, Dewynne, and Howison, *Option Pricing: Mathematical Models and Computation* (Oxford: Oxford Financial Press, 1993).

enough to regard it as a European call option. Then, drawing on an understanding of option pricing and capital budgeting, we further simplified the analysis by combining five variables into two. But now, after valuing a project and locating it in Figure VIII, we should put some of the complexity back in and begin looking at sensitivity analyses. This will help us understand which of a project's characteristics cause it to fall where it does on the map. For example, in region III, is cumulative variance high primarily because of σ or t? Which of the elements of NPV_q is most readily managed—net cash inflows *(S)* or capital expenditures *(X)?* And so forth. The process is iterative. The results of one analysis suggest a further one until the process converges on an understanding, in both financial and managerial terms, of the project.

EXHIBIT 1 Option-Pricing Table: Black-Scholes Value of a European Call Option, Expressed as a Percentage of Underlying Asset Value

Source: The format of the table was adapted from Brealy and Myers, *Principles of Corporate Finance,* 4th edition (New York: McGraw-Hill, Inc., 1991), Appendix Table 6, pp. AP12–13.

Cumulative variance: s[sqrt(t)]	NPV$_q$ = (Underlying asset value)/PV(Exercise price)																																			
	0.30	0.35	0.40	0.45	0.50	0.55	0.60	0.65	0.70	0.75	0.80	0.82	0.84	0.86	0.88	0.90	0.92	0.94	0.96	0.98	1.00	1.02	1.04	1.06	1.08	1.10	1.12	1.14	1.16	1.18	1.20	1.25	1.30	1.35	1.40	1.45	1.50	1.75	2.00	2.50	
0.05	0.0	0.0	0.0	0.0	0.0	0.0	0.0	0.0	0.0	0.0	0.0	0.0	0.0	0.0	0.0	0.0	0.1	0.3	0.6	1.2	2.0	3.1	4.5	6.0	7.5	9.1	10.7	12.3	13.8	15.3	16.7	20.0	23.1	25.9	28.6	31.0	33.3	42.9	50.0	60.0	0.05
0.10	0.0	0.0	0.0	0.0	0.0	0.0	0.0	0.0	0.0	0.0	0.0	0.1	0.2	0.3	0.5	0.8	1.2	1.7	2.3	3.1	4.0	5.0	6.1	7.3	8.6	10.0	11.3	12.7	14.1	15.4	16.8	20.0	23.1	25.9	28.6	31.0	33.3	42.9	50.0	60.0	0.10
0.15	0.0	0.0	0.0	0.0	0.0	0.0	0.0	0.0	0.1	0.2	0.5	0.7	1.0	1.3	1.7	2.2	2.8	3.5	4.2	5.1	6.0	7.0	8.0	9.1	10.2	11.4	12.6	13.8	15.0	16.2	17.4	20.4	23.3	26.0	28.6	31.1	33.3	42.9	50.0	60.0	0.15
0.20	0.0	0.0	0.0	0.0	0.0	0.0	0.0	0.1	0.4	0.8	1.5	1.9	2.3	2.8	3.4	4.0	4.7	5.4	6.2	7.1	8.0	8.9	9.9	10.9	11.9	13.0	14.1	15.2	16.3	17.4	18.5	21.2	23.9	26.4	28.9	31.2	33.5	42.9	50.0	60.0	0.20
0.25	0.0	0.0	0.0	0.0	0.0	0.1	0.2	0.5	1.0	1.8	2.8	3.3	3.9	4.5	5.2	5.9	6.6	7.4	8.2	9.1	9.9	10.9	11.8	12.8	13.7	14.7	15.7	16.7	17.7	18.7	19.8	22.3	24.7	27.1	29.4	31.7	33.8	42.9	50.0	60.0	0.25
0.30	0.0	0.0	0.0	0.1	0.1	0.3	0.7	1.2	2.0	3.1	4.4	5.0	5.7	6.3	7.0	7.8	8.6	9.4	10.2	11.1	11.9	12.8	13.7	14.6	15.6	16.5	17.4	18.4	19.3	20.3	21.2	23.5	25.8	28.1	30.2	32.3	34.3	43.1	50.1	60.0	0.30
0.35	0.0	0.0	0.1	0.2	0.4	0.8	1.4	2.3	3.3	4.6	6.2	6.8	7.5	8.2	9.0	9.8	10.6	11.4	12.2	13.0	13.9	14.8	15.6	16.5	17.4	18.3	19.2	20.1	21.0	21.9	22.7	24.9	27.1	29.2	31.2	33.2	35.1	43.5	50.2	60.0	0.35
0.40	0.0	0.1	0.2	0.5	0.9	1.6	2.4	3.5	4.8	6.3	8.0	8.7	9.4	10.2	11.0	11.7	12.5	13.4	14.2	15.0	15.9	16.7	17.5	18.4	19.2	20.1	20.9	21.8	22.6	23.5	24.3	26.4	28.4	30.4	32.3	34.2	36.0	44.0	50.5	60.1	0.40
0.45	0.1	0.2	0.5	1.0	1.7	2.6	3.7	5.0	6.5	8.1	9.9	10.6	11.4	12.2	12.9	13.7	14.5	15.3	16.2	17.0	17.8	18.6	19.4	20.3	21.1	21.9	22.7	23.5	24.3	25.1	25.9	27.9	29.8	31.7	33.5	35.3	37.0	44.5	50.8	60.2	0.45
0.50	0.2	0.5	1.0	1.7	2.6	3.7	5.1	6.6	8.2	10.0	11.8	12.6	13.4	14.2	14.9	15.7	16.5	17.3	18.1	18.9	19.7	20.5	21.3	22.1	22.9	23.7	24.5	25.3	26.1	26.8	27.5	29.5	31.3	33.1	34.8	36.4	38.1	45.3	51.3	60.4	0.50
0.55	0.5	1.0	1.7	2.6	3.8	5.1	6.6	8.3	10.0	11.9	13.8	14.6	15.4	16.1	16.9	17.7	18.5	19.3	20.1	20.9	21.7	22.4	23.2	24.0	24.8	25.5	26.3	27.0	27.8	28.5	29.2	31.0	32.8	34.5	36.1	37.7	39.2	46.1	51.9	60.7	0.55
0.60	0.9	1.6	2.5	3.7	5.1	6.6	8.3	10.1	11.9	13.8	15.8	16.6	17.4	18.1	18.9	19.7	20.5	21.3	22.0	22.8	23.6	24.3	25.1	25.8	26.6	27.3	28.1	28.8	29.5	30.2	30.9	32.6	34.3	35.9	37.5	39.0	40.4	47.0	52.5	61.0	0.60
0.65	1.4	2.4	3.6	4.9	6.5	8.2	10.0	11.9	13.8	15.8	17.8	18.6	19.3	20.1	20.9	21.7	22.5	23.2	24.0	24.7	25.5	26.2	27.0	27.7	28.4	29.1	29.8	30.5	31.2	31.9	32.5	34.2	35.8	37.4	38.9	40.3	41.7	48.0	53.3	61.4	0.65
0.70	2.1	3.3	4.7	6.3	8.1	9.9	11.9	13.8	15.8	17.8	19.8	20.6	21.3	22.1	22.9	23.6	24.4	25.2	25.9	26.6	27.4	28.1	28.8	29.5	30.2	30.9	31.6	32.3	32.9	33.6	34.2	35.8	37.3	38.8	40.3	41.6	43.0	49.0	54.0	61.9	0.70
0.75	3.0	4.4	6.1	7.9	9.8	11.7	13.7	15.8	17.8	19.8	21.8	22.5	23.3	24.1	24.8	25.6	26.3	27.1	27.8	28.5	29.2	29.9	30.6	31.3	32.0	32.7	33.3	34.0	34.6	35.3	35.9	37.4	38.9	40.3	41.7	43.0	44.3	50.0	54.9	62.4	0.75
0.80	4.0	5.7	7.5	9.5	11.5	13.6	15.7	17.7	19.8	21.8	23.7	24.5	25.3	26.0	26.8	27.5	28.3	29.0	29.7	30.4	31.1	31.8	32.4	33.1	33.8	34.4	35.1	35.7	36.3	36.9	37.5	39.0	40.4	41.8	43.1	44.4	45.6	51.1	55.8	63.0	0.80
0.85	5.1	7.1	9.1	11.2	13.3	15.5	17.6	19.7	21.8	23.8	25.7	26.5	27.2	28.0	28.7	29.4	30.2	30.9	31.6	32.2	32.9	33.6	34.2	34.9	35.5	36.2	36.8	37.4	38.0	38.6	39.2	40.6	41.9	43.3	44.5	45.8	46.9	52.2	56.7	63.6	0.85
0.90	6.4	8.5	10.7	13.0	15.2	17.4	19.6	21.7	23.8	25.8	27.7	28.4	29.2	29.9	30.6	31.3	32.0	32.7	33.4	34.1	34.7	35.4	36.0	36.6	37.3	37.9	38.5	39.1	39.6	40.2	40.3	42.1	43.5	44.7	46.0	47.1	48.3	53.3	57.6	64.3	0.90
0.95	7.8	10.1	12.5	14.8	17.1	19.4	21.6	23.7	25.7	27.7	29.6	30.4	31.1	31.8	32.5	33.2	33.9	34.6	35.2	35.9	36.5	37.2	37.8	38.4	39.0	39.6	40.1	40.7	41.3	41.8	42.4	43.7	45.0	46.2	47.4	48.5	49.6	54.5	58.6	65.0	0.95
1.00	9.3	11.8	14.3	16.7	19.1	21.4	23.6	25.7	27.7	29.7	31.6	32.3	33.0	33.7	34.4	35.1	35.7	36.4	37.0	37.7	38.3	38.9	39.5	40.1	40.7	41.2	41.8	42.4	42.9	43.4	44.0	45.2	46.5	47.6	48.8	49.9	50.9	55.6	59.5	65.7	1.00
1.05	10.9	13.6	16.1	18.6	21.0	23.3	25.6	27.7	29.7	31.6	33.5	34.2	34.9	35.6	36.2	36.9	37.6	38.2	38.8	39.4	40.0	40.6	41.2	41.8	42.4	42.9	43.5	44.0	44.5	45.0	45.5	46.8	48.0	49.1	50.2	51.2	52.2	56.7	60.5	66.5	1.05
1.10	12.6	15.4	18.0	20.6	23.0	25.3	27.5	29.6	31.6	33.5	35.4	36.1	36.7	37.4	38.1	38.7	39.3	40.0	40.6	41.2	41.8	42.3	42.9	43.5	44.0	44.5	45.1	45.6	46.1	46.6	47.1	48.3	49.4	50.5	51.6	52.6	53.5	57.9	61.5	67.2	1.10
1.15	14.4	17.2	20.0	22.5	25.0	27.3	29.5	31.6	33.6	35.4	37.2	37.9	38.6	39.2	39.9	40.5	41.1	41.7	42.3	42.9	43.5	44.0	44.6	45.1	45.6	46.2	46.7	47.2	47.7	48.2	48.6	49.8	50.9	51.9	52.9	53.9	54.9	59.0	62.5	68.0	1.15
1.20	16.2	19.1	21.9	24.5	27.0	29.3	31.5	33.6	35.5	37.3	39.1	39.7	40.4	41.0	41.7	42.3	42.9	43.5	44.0	44.6	45.1	45.7	46.2	46.7	47.3	47.8	48.3	48.7	49.2	49.7	50.1	51.3	52.3	53.3	54.3	55.2	56.1	60.2	63.5	68.8	1.20
1.25	18.1	21.1	23.9	26.5	29.0	31.3	33.5	35.5	37.4	39.2	40.9	41.5	42.2	42.8	43.4	44.0	44.6	45.2	45.7	46.3	46.8	47.3	47.8	48.4	48.8	49.3	49.8	50.3	50.7	51.2	51.6	52.7	53.7	54.7	55.7	56.6	57.4	61.3	64.5	69.6	1.25
1.30	20.0	23.0	25.9	28.5	31.0	33.3	35.4	37.4	39.3	41.0	42.7	43.3	43.9	44.5	45.1	45.7	46.3	46.8	47.4	47.9	48.4	48.9	49.4	49.9	50.4	50.9	51.3	51.8	52.2	52.7	53.1	54.1	55.1	56.1	57.0	57.9	58.7	62.4	65.5	70.4	1.30
1.35	21.9	25.0	27.9	30.5	33.0	35.2	37.3	39.3	41.1	42.8	44.4	45.1	45.7	46.3	46.8	47.4	47.9	48.5	49.0	49.5	50.0	50.5	51.0	51.5	52.0	52.4	52.9	53.3	53.7	54.1	54.6	55.6	56.5	57.4	58.3	59.1	59.9	63.5	66.5	71.1	1.35
1.40	23.9	27.0	29.9	32.5	34.9	37.1	39.2	41.1	42.9	44.6	46.2	46.8	47.4	47.9	48.5	49.0	49.6	50.1	50.6	51.1	51.6	52.1	52.6	53.0	53.5	53.9	54.3	54.8	55.2	55.6	56.0	56.9	57.9	58.7	59.6	60.4	61.2	64.6	67.5	71.9	1.40
1.45	25.8	29.0	31.9	34.5	36.9	39.1	41.1	43.0	44.7	46.4	47.9	48.5	49.0	49.6	50.1	50.7	51.2	51.7	52.2	52.7	53.2	53.6	54.1	54.5	55.0	55.4	55.8	56.2	56.6	57.0	57.4	58.3	59.2	60.0	60.9	61.6	62.4	65.7	68.4	72.7	1.45
1.50	27.8	31.0	33.8	36.4	38.8	40.9	42.9	44.8	46.5	48.1	49.6	50.1	50.7	51.2	51.8	52.3	52.8	53.3	53.7	54.2	54.7	55.1	55.6	56.0	56.4	56.8	57.2	57.6	58.0	58.4	58.8	59.7	60.5	61.3	62.1	62.9	63.6	66.8	69.4	73.5	1.50
1.55	29.8	33.0	35.8	38.4	40.7	42.8	44.8	46.6	48.2	49.8	51.2	51.8	52.3	52.8	53.3	53.8	54.3	54.8	55.3	55.7	56.2	56.6	57.0	57.4	57.8	58.2	58.6	59.0	59.4	59.7	60.1	61.0	61.8	62.6	63.3	64.1	64.7	67.8	70.3	74.3	1.55
1.60	31.8	35.0	37.8	40.3	42.6	44.6	46.5	48.3	49.9	51.4	52.8	53.4	53.9	54.4	54.9	55.4	55.9	56.3	56.8	57.2	57.6	58.0	58.5	58.9	59.2	59.6	60.0	60.4	60.7	61.1	61.4	62.3	63.1	63.8	64.5	65.2	65.9	68.8	71.3	75.1	1.60
1.65	33.8	36.9	39.7	42.2	44.4	46.4	48.3	50.0	51.6	53.1	54.4	54.9	55.4	55.9	56.4	56.9	57.3	57.8	58.2	58.6	59.1	59.5	59.9	60.2	60.6	61.0	61.4	61.7	62.1	62.4	62.7	63.5	64.3	65.0	65.7	66.4	67.0	69.9	72.2	75.9	1.65
1.70	35.8	38.9	41.6	44.0	46.2	48.2	50.0	51.7	53.2	54.7	56.0	56.5	57.0	57.5	57.9	58.4	58.8	59.2	59.7	60.1	60.5	60.9	61.2	61.6	62.0	62.3	62.7	63.0	63.4	63.7	64.0	64.8	65.5	66.2	66.9	67.5	68.2	70.9	73.1	76.6	1.70
1.75	37.7	40.8	43.5	45.9	48.0	50.0	51.7	53.4	54.8	56.2	57.5	58.0	58.5	58.9	59.4	59.8	60.2	60.7	61.1	61.5	61.8	62.2	62.6	62.9	63.3	63.6	64.0	64.3	64.6	64.9	65.3	66.0	66.7	67.4	68.0	68.7	69.2	71.9	74.0	77.4	1.75
2.00	47.3	50.1	52.5	54.6	56.5	58.2	59.7	61.1	62.4	63.6	64.6	65.0	65.4	65.8	66.2	66.6	66.9	67.3	67.6	67.9	68.3	68.6	68.9	69.2	69.5	69.8	70.0	70.3	70.6	70.8	71.1	71.7	72.3	72.9	73.4	73.9	74.4	76.5	78.3	81.0	2.00
2.25	56.1	58.6	60.7	62.5	64.1	65.6	66.8	68.0	69.1	70.0	70.9	71.3	71.6	71.9	72.2	72.5	72.8	73.1	73.4	73.7	73.9	74.2	74.4	74.7	74.9	75.2	75.4	75.6	75.8	76.0	76.3	76.8	77.2	77.7	78.1	78.5	78.9	80.6	82.1	84.3	2.25
2.50	64.0	66.1	67.9	69.4	70.8	72.0	73.1	74.0	74.9	75.7	76.4	76.7	77.0	77.2	77.5	77.7	78.0	78.2	78.4	78.7	78.9	79.1	79.3	79.5	79.7	79.9	80.0	80.2	80.4	80.6	80.7	81.1	81.5	81.9	82.2	82.6	82.9	84.3	85.4	87.2	2.50
2.75	70.9	72.7	74.2	75.4	76.6	77.5	78.4	79.2	79.9	80.5	81.1	81.4	81.6	81.8	82.0	82.2	82.4	82.6	82.7	82.9	83.1	83.3	83.4	83.6	83.7	83.9	84.0	84.2	84.3	84.4	84.6	84.9	85.2	85.5	85.8	86.0	86.3	87.4	88.3	89.7	2.75
3.00	76.9	78.3	79.5	80.5	81.4	82.2	82.9	83.5	84.1	84.6	85.1	85.3	85.4	85.6	85.8	85.9	86.1	86.2	86.4	86.5	86.6	86.8	86.9	87.0	87.1	87.3	87.4	87.5	87.6	87.7	87.8	88.1	88.3	88.5	88.8	89.0	89.2	90.0	90.7	91.8	3.00
3.50	86.0	86.9	87.6	88.3	88.8	89.3	89.7	90.1	90.5	90.8	91.1	91.2	91.3	91.4	91.5	91.6	91.6	91.7	91.8	91.9	92.0	92.1	92.1	92.2	92.3	92.4	92.4	92.5	92.6	92.6	92.7	92.8	93.0	93.1	93.3	93.4	93.5	94.0	94.4	95.1	3.50
4.00	92.0	92.5	92.9	93.3	93.6	93.9	94.2	94.4	94.6	94.8	94.9	95.0	95.0	95.1	95.2	95.2	95.3	95.3	95.4	95.4	95.4	95.5	95.5	95.6	95.6	95.7	95.7	95.7	95.8	95.8	95.8	95.9	96.0	96.1	96.2	96.2	96.3	96.6	96.8	97.2	4.00
4.50	95.7	96.0	96.2	96.4	96.6	96.7	96.9	97.0	97.1	97.2	97.3	97.3	97.3	97.4	97.4	97.4	97.5	97.5	97.5	97.5	97.6	97.6	97.6	97.6	97.6	97.7	97.7	97.7	97.7	97.8	97.8	97.8	97.9	97.9	97.9	98.0	98.0	98.2	98.3	98.5	4.50
5.00	97.8	97.9	98.1	98.2	98.3	98.3	98.4	98.5	98.5	98.6	98.6	98.6	98.6	98.7	98.7	98.7	98.7	98.7	98.7	98.7	98.8	98.8	98.8	98.8	98.8	98.8	98.8	98.8	98.8	98.9	98.9	98.9	98.9	98.9	99.0	99.0	99.0	99.1	99.1	99.2	5.00
6.00	99.5	99.5	99.6	99.6	99.6	99.6	99.7	99.7	99.7	99.7	99.7	99.7	99.7	99.7	99.7	99.7	99.7	99.7	99.7	99.7	99.7	99.7	99.7	99.7	99.7	99.7	99.7	99.7	99.7	99.8	99.8	99.8	99.8	99.8	99.8	99.8	99.8	99.8	99.8	99.8	6.00

Note: Values in the table represent percentages of underlying asset values: e.g., 39.3 denotes a call option worth 39.3% of the underlying asset value.
Values in the table were computed from the Black-Scholes option pricing model.

Part 4

Review and Synthesis

Pharmacyclics: Financing Research and Development

Dr. Richard Miller, the president and CEO at Pharmacyclics (PCYC), was considering whether to sell $60 million of equity. Pacific Growth Equities, a placement agent Miller had used in the past, indicated that there was a demand for a private placement of PCYC shares from four financial institutions that had received small allocations of PCYC stock in its last public offering. The four institutions wanted to increase their positions significantly by buying more equity at or near the prevailing market price. On Friday, February 25, 2000, PCYC closed at $78.75.

PCYC focused on improving existing treatments of cancer, atherosclerosis, and retinal disease. By 1999, it had developed four new drugs that were in some phase of the Food and Drug Administration's (FDA) approval process. Because of the expense of that process, smaller pharmaceutical companies such as PCYC often licensed their compounds to larger companies that had the resources to bring drugs to market. Although it had licensed its ophthalmology drugs, PCYC wanted to retain all of the rights to its most promising oncology drug, Xcytrin, which was in the most expensive phase of the FDA approval process, Phase III. In September 1999, a seasoned equity offering (SEO) had strengthened the firm's cash position to fund the cost of the Phase III clinical trial of Xcytrin. Although PCYC did not need to sell the $60 million of equity to fund the ongoing trial, the funding would provide additional flexibility and the resources to develop its atherosclerosis drugs without licensing them.

Cancer Treatment

The standard treatment options for cancer were surgery, radiation, chemotherapy, hormone therapy, and immunotherapy. Surgery was the oldest form of cancer treatment and still offered the best prospect of a complete cure for many types of cancer. The American Cancer Society estimated that 60 percent of those diagnosed with cancer have some type of operation. Radiation therapy used x-rays or gamma rays to destroy tumors. Chemotherapy referred generally to the use of medicine to kill cancer cells. Unlike surgery or radiation therapy, systemic chemotherapy could treat cancer that had spread throughout the body, known as metastatic cancer. Hormone therapy slowed the growth or killed hormone-sensitive tumors. Finally, immunotherapy enhanced the immune response to cancer cells.

The appropriate choice of therapy depended on the size, location, and spread of the tumor. In 1999, approximately 3,000 radiation oncologists administered radiation therapy to over 700,000 cancer patients at a cost of $10,000 to $25,000 for the course of treatment, while more than 350,000 patients received some form of chemotherapy.[1] Of

[1]Source: Pharmacyclics 10-K, 1999.

Professor Malcolm Baker, Professor Richard Ruback, and Research Associate Aldo Sesia prepared this case. HBS cases are developed solely as the basis for class discussion. Cases are not intended to serve as endorsements, sources of primary data, or illustrations of effective or ineffective management.

Copyright © 2001 President and Fellows of Harvard College. To order copies or request permission to reproduce materials, call 1-800-545-7685, write Harvard Business School Publishing, Boston, MA 02163, or go to http://www.hbsp.harvard.edu. No part of this publication may be reproduced, stored in a retrieval system, used in a spreadsheet, or transmitted in any form or by any means—electronic, mechanical, photocopying, recording, or otherwise—without the permission of Harvard Business School.

the radiation treatments, approximately 170,000 were for brain metastases.[2] In addition to the standard treatment options, some cancer patients chose alternative and complementary therapies, or very new or unproven approaches to treatment. For example, photodynamic therapy was a new treatment, recently approved by the FDA.

Before a new pharmaceutical product could be marketed, the FDA required pre-clinical laboratory and animal tests, three phases of human trials to establish the safety and efficacy of a drug for its proposed use, and the submission of the results of these trials for final approval by the FDA. In Phase I, the drug was given to a small number of healthy volunteers to test for safety. In Phase II, a larger number of patients were tested to determine if the drug was effective in treating a certain condition and to measure potential side effects. Finally, in Phase III, a large number of patients were tested for safety and efficacy. Exhibit 1 summarizes the FDA approval process.

Oncology drugs could be developed more rapidly than other pharmaceuticals. Because of the immediacy and life-threatening nature of cancer and AIDS, the FDA had created a "fast-track" approval process in 1992 for these illnesses.[3] In addition, the short life expectancy of trial subjects with terminal illnesses made proving the efficacy of a drug in clinical trials much faster and simpler for oncology drugs. Taking these factors into account, Miller estimated the cost to PCYC of developing an oncology compound at around $100 million.

While clinical trials were designed around a particular diagnosis, physicians could prescribe drugs for "off-label" uses following FDA approval. Reimbursement was sometimes more difficult, but physicians were free to prescribe approved drugs for any indication. For example, Taxol, a drug developed by Bristol Myers Squibb, was initially approved for the treatment of recurrent ovarian cancer. Because preliminary data suggested promise in treating breast and lung cancer, the drug was immediately used for these more common diagnoses.

Pharmacyclics

Pharmacyclics was a pharmaceutical company focused on improving existing treatments of cancer, atherosclerosis, and retinal disease. Miller and Dr. Jonathan Sessler, a professor at the University of Texas (UT), started the company in 1991. Sessler, a patient of Miller's at that time, had figured out how to synthesize compounds that were selectively attracted to cancer cells.

Early rounds of funding allowed PCYC to obtain patents on these compounds from UT and start the company. Initially, Miller invested some of his own money. As detailed in the funding history contained in Exhibit 2, the firm raised a total of $2.7M in convertible preferred stock from venture capitalists Asset Management, Kleiner, Perkins, Caufield & Byers, and Venrock Associates by April 1992.[4] With this money, PCYC hired three scientists from Sessler's lab, leased lab space, and began the preclinical studies. Their aim was to start the Phase I human trials within 18 months.

The next round of financing coincided with the beginning of the first Phase I trials of the first oncology drug, Xcytrin. In December 1992, the firm raised $7.7M from four venture firms, the original three and Mayfield. The company raised a third round of $7.6M in June 1994 and a final mezzanine round of $5.6M in July 1995. In October of that year, PCYC completed an initial public offering (IPO), raising $26M at $12 per share. The Phase II trial began in June 1996. In November 1996, PCYC raised $8.1M

[2]Source: Adams, Harkness & Hill, Inc., November 29, 1999.

[3]A 50% reduction in approval time was anticipated at the time of the FDA change.

[4]Source: VentureOne.

at $14 per share in another private placement. This was followed by a private placement in February 1997 which yielded an additional $16.3M at $19 per share. Miller preferred these private placements, typically executed in less than ten days, because they offered more money without requiring a road show, a prospectus, or a discount from the market price. In February 1998, however, the company raised $40.8M at $21.75 per share in a seasoned equity offering. PCYC started a 425-patient Phase III trial soon after in September 1998.

Pharmacyclics had raised a total of $117M and spent $73M on research and development from the time the company was founded in 1991 through June 1999. By then, Xcytrin was in Phase III clinical trials. None of its products had been approved and no significant revenue had been recorded. Exhibits 3 and 4 contain the company's Income Statement and Balance Sheet.

In September 1999, PCYC completed a second seasoned equity offering, raising $96M at $38.75 per share.[5] Exhibit 5 contains excerpts from the company announcement of this SEO. Since then its stock price had risen rapidly. The PCYC stock price at the end of February was almost double the 1999 close and nearly seven times the IPO price. Exhibit 6 provides a complete stock price history of the firm and the corresponding performance of the S&P 500 index of biotechnology shares. The rise in biotechnology valuations could be attributed in part to excitement surrounding the sequencing of the human genome.[6]

The company's strategy had been to obtain funds to meet the anticipated funding need of each stage, and to conserve cash to complete development stages before seeking additional funding. To conserve cash, PCYC contracted out much of its research and development, including the completion of particular experiments. It also outsourced the manufacture of the compounds used in testing. Miller believed that funding later would keep the share price rising and that funding less would limit dilution, a key to adding value and motivating employees. Running out of cash before milestones were met, however, would threaten the company's survival. Miller recognized that the financial climate tended to change over time and that timing was key. Despite his preference for funding later, he believed in taking advantage of pricing opportunities as they occurred.

The Product Portfolio

As of June 1999, PCYC had four drugs in the pipeline. The four patented molecules, called texaphyrins, were designed to accumulate in tumors of cancer patients (Xcytrin and Lutrin), diseased blood vessels associated with atherosclerosis (Antrin), and small growths in the retina (Optrin). The compounds, which contain a metal atom, destroy diseased tissue when exposed to energy from radiation therapy, chemicals from chemotherapy, and light from photodynamic therapy. By focusing the power of existing therapies, texaphyrins minimize the damage to healthy cells. By June 1999, the four drugs were being tested for 17 targeted diseases. PCYC was sponsoring the testing for five diseases, the National Cancer Institute (NCI) for eleven, and Alcon for one.[7] Exhibit 7 summarizes PCYC products and their development status and Exhibit 8 summarizes the timing of the five sets of PCYC clinical trials.

[5]PCYC sold 2,645,000 shares including an overallotment of 345,000 shares.

[6]"Biodegradable: One Fund Manager Sees a Bubble for Boom-and-Bust Biotech Stocks," *Barrons*, February 21, 2000.

[7]In December 1997, Pharmacyclics and Alcon, a wholly owned subsidiary of Nestlé, entered into an evaluation and license agreement to commercialize Optrin for ophthalmology indications. Under the terms of the agreement, Alcon was to conduct the clinical trials and bear all costs for worldwide development and drug registration. Pharmacyclics was to receive milestone payments during development and a royalty on any product sales.

The four drugs were designed to be easy to administer and to complement existing therapies. An industry analyst at Adams, Harkness & Hill (AHH) believed these two factors would allow the drugs to be easily incorporated into standard practice if approved by the FDA. She compared Xcytrin to Amgen's $1 billion drug, Neupogen, which was designed to prevent a side effect of chemotherapy.

- **Xcytrin.** The destructive effect of conventional radiation and chemotherapy was not limited to tumor cells. Xcytrin was developed to improve the effectiveness of radiation and chemotherapy treatment. The drug, when injected into the blood stream, accumulated around tumor cells. In pre-clinical animal trials, Xcytrin doubled the effectiveness of subsequent radiation. Phase I-II trials, and early data on a Phase III trial, showed similar promise for patients with brain metastases. PCYC also had clinical trials under way for patients with primary brain cancer, pancreatic cancer, pediatric glioma, and prostate and lung cancer.

  Xcytrin was PCYC's most promising product in terms of both the probability of near-term approval and profitability. Analysts estimated the likelihood of FDA approval at better than 50% and expected Xcytrin to gain approval late in FY02. Assuming approval, Xcytrin was expected to be used in 2% of the 170,000 radiation treatments for brain metastases in the United States in FY02. Its use was expected to grow to 17% of those treatments in FY03, 26% in FY04, and reach its peak use of 40% in FY05. The expected cost per treatment course was $10,000, which was in line with similar oncology drugs, such as Taxol at $10,000, Rituxan at $12,000, and Herceptin at $17,000. Patent life was expected to be about 10 years after FDA approval. Cost of goods sold was estimated at $2,000 per treatment. As Exhibit 9 details, building a domestic selling and marketing team would require $15 million in FY01, growing to over $60 million in FY04. Working capital requirements and capital investments were not anticipated to be significant.

  Analysts expected that PCYC would engage a marketing partner for its sales outside the United States. The number of radiation treatments conducted outside the United States was about equal to the number conducted in the United States. Xcytrin was expected to be adopted more slowly outside of the United States, with 5% in FY03, 15% in FY04, and reaching a peak use of 25% in FY05. PCYC would realize profits equal to 30% of the revenues outside of the United States.
- **Lutrin.** While radiation and chemotherapy were widely used cancer treatments, photodynamic therapy (PDT) was comparatively new. Lutrin was developed to improve the effectiveness of PDT. The ideal dosage of Lutrin had not yet been established in Phase II trials, and the drug was entering a Phase IIb trial as a result. Earlier trials were under way for esophageal and cervical cancer. As long as the use of PDT remained modest, Lutrin would not be a blockbuster drug. If Lutrin received FDA approval, Lutrin's expected contribution to pre-tax income would be about $3 million in FY02, $9 million in FY03, and $20 million in FY04.
- **Optrin and Antrin.** Photodynamic therapy was also used in the treatment of age-related macular degeneration (AMD) and for photoangioplasty. PDT had yet to replace laser surgery and standard angioplasty in the treatment of these diseases. However, the potential market was large, with 200,000 new AMD diagnoses and 1.2 million angioplasties and stents per year.[8] AHH's analyst thought it was too early to tell whether Optrin and Antrin would produce revenue.

Many biopharmaceutical companies were competing with PCYC in these markets. Sanofi, OXiGENE, Allos Therapeutics, and Vion all had developed radiation en-

[8]Source: Adams, Harkness & Hill, Inc., November 29, 1999.

hancers. Lutrin, Optrin, and Antrin also faced competition, but AHH's analyst thought that the PCYC products had significant advantages.

The Private Placement

Dr. Miller had to decide whether PCYC should proceed with the private placement now or wait until the Phase III clinical trial for Xcytrin was complete.

The decision depended on two factors. The first was funding needs. In the past, Miller had delayed funding whenever possible. The rule had been "fund later, fund less, but never run out of cash." By delaying funding, Miller and the other insiders had retained a larger fraction of the firm. In this case, however, funding would provide a cushion for the completion of the Phase III Xcytrin trial, and could also be used to push the development of Antrin forward without bringing on a partner. Exhibit 9 shows the projected research and development costs and the selling, general, and administrative expenses.

The second factor was valuation. PCYC stock was at an all time high and in the past, Miller had tried to take advantage of pricing opportunities as they occurred. Miller felt, however, that the market price incorporated a substantial probability that Xcytrin would not successfully complete the FDA approval process. Exhibit 10 summarizes recent news developments since the AHH forecasts were made. Exhibits 11A and 11B contain betas and other financial information for PCYC and comparable firms. Exhibit 11C contains information on bond yields.

EXHIBIT 1 **Compound Success Rates by Stage**

Source: PhRMA, based on data from Center for the Study of Drug Development, Tuft University, 1995.

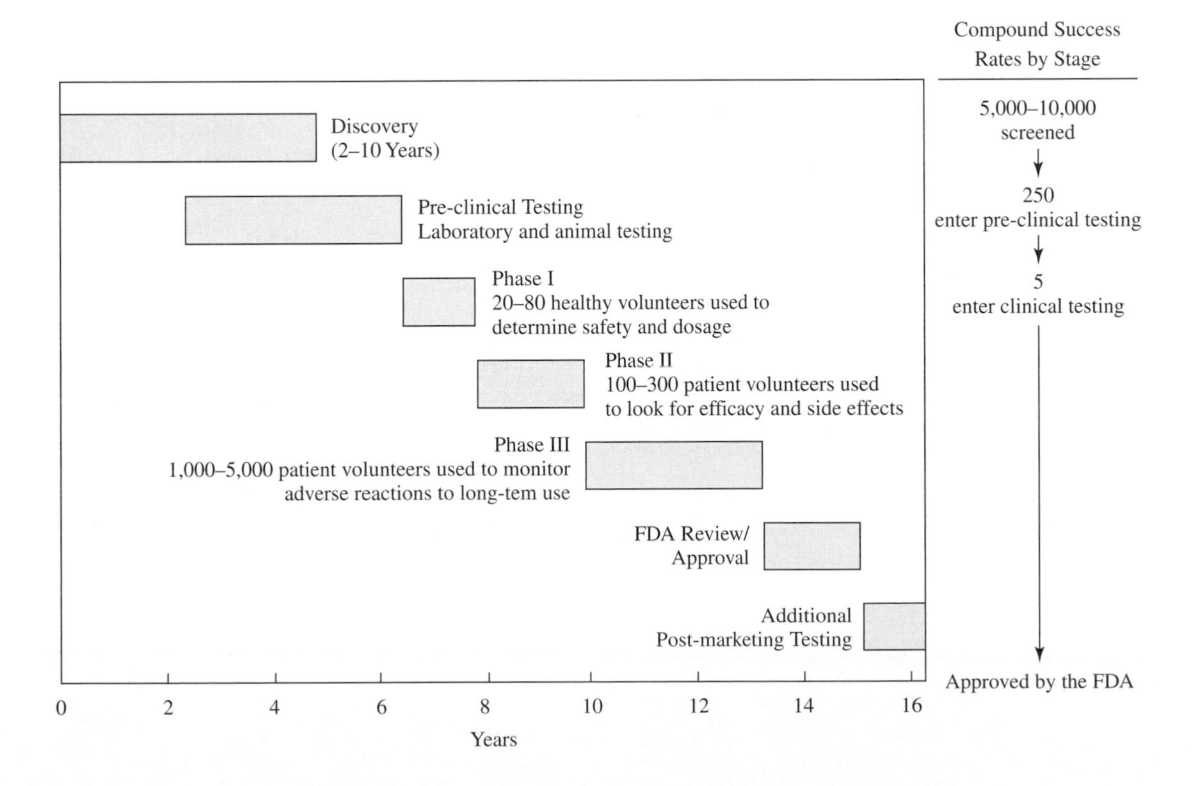

EXHIBIT 2
Pharmacyclics Financing History

Source: Pharmacyclics 10-K, 1999 and SEO press release.

Fiscal Year[a]	Transaction Type	Shares Issued	Average Share Price	Funding Raised ($000)
Insider Financing				
91	Equity	400,000	.02	6
92	Equity	97,111	.02	2
93	Equity	49,000	.06	3
94	Option Exercised	324,188	.12	38
95	Option Exercised	38,403	.24	9
96	Option Exercised	100,301	9.46	208
97	Option Exercised	110,840	3.77	417
98	Option/Purchase Rights Exercised	99,305	7.38	733
99	Option Exercised	88,918	6.28	558
Private Financing				
92	Convertible Preferred Stock	2,040,784	1.32	2,667
93	Convertible Preferred Stock	1,580,095	4.88	7,674
94	Convertible Preferred Stock	886,960	8.63	7,623
95	Warrants Issued	—	—	49
96	Convertible Preferred Stock	649,132	8.63	5,601
97	Common Stock	1,442,190	16.93	24,420
98	Common Stock (Warrants Exercised)	80,033	—	—
99	Common Stock (Warrants Exercised)	45,661	—	—
Public Financing				
96	IPO—Common Stock	2,383,450	12.00	26,042
98	SEO—Common Stock	2,012,500	21.75	40,796
00	SEO—Common Stock September 1999	2,645,000	38.75	96,200
Totals[b]		15,073,871	—	213,046

[a]PCYC's fiscal year runs from July 1 to June 30.
[b]Funding raised excludes stock compensation expense of $331K.

EXHIBIT 3 Pharmacyclics Income Statements 1991–2000 (thousands of dollars)

Source: Pharmacyclics Second Quarter 2000 10Q, 1999 10K, and October-23-5 Pre IPO Prospectus.

	Fiscal Year Ending June 30								
	2000[a]	1999	1998	1997	1996	1995	1994	1993	1992
Licence & Grant Revenue	1,000	750	2,700	25	301	79	3,000	0	0
Contract Revenue	303	1,291	831	0	0	0	0	0	0
Total Revenue	**1,303**	**2,041**	**3,531**	**25**	**301**	**79**	**3,000**	**0**	**0**
Research & Development	10,967	21,889	13,973	9,632	7,641	9,330	6,909	3,161	487
General & Administrative	1,934	2,762	1,987	1,905	1,515	996	1,042	559	58
Total Operating Expense	**12,901**	**24,651**	**15,960**	**11,537**	**9,156**	**10,326**	**7,951**	**3,720**	**545**
Loss from Operations	**(11,598)**	**(22,610)**	**(12,429)**	**(11,512)**	**(8,855)**	**(10,247)**	**(4,951)**	**(3,720)**	**(545)**
Interest Income	2,557	3,398	2,826	1,480	940	187	164		
Interest Expense	(8)	(34)	(72)	(226)	(320)	(419)	(253)		
Interest Net	**2,549**	**3,364**	**2,754**	**1,254**	**620**	**(232)**	**(89)**	**140**	**22**
Loss Before Income Tax	(9,049)	(19,246)	(9,675)	(10,258)	(8,235)	(10,479)	(5,040)	(3,580)	(523)
Provision for Income Taxes	0	0	0	0	0	0	(101)	0	0
Net Profit (Loss)	**(9,049)**	**(19,246)**	**(9,675)**	**(10,258)**	**(8,235)**	**(10,479)**	**(5,141)**	**(3,580)**	**(523)**

[a]Year-to-date through the second quarter ending December 31, 1999.

EXHIBIT 4 Pharmacyclics Balance Sheets 1991–2000 (thousands of dollars)

Source: Pharmacyclics Second Quarter 2000 10Q, 1999 10K, and October-23-95 Pre IPO Prospectus.

	Fiscal Year Ending June 30								
	2000[a]	1999	1998	1997	1996	1995	1994	1993	1992
Cash & cash equivalents[b]	61,164	3,930	13,456	15,869	13,950	376	8,690		
Short-term investments[c]	45,329	42,475	23,189	14,958	8,053	0	0		
Accounts receivable	70	309	166	0	0	0	0		
Prepaid expenses	2,592	463	166	216	241	164	65		
Long-term investments[d]	28,893	5,067	33,736	6,103	0	0	0		
Property and equipment, net	2,829	3,228	2,253	2,504	2,622	2,850	3,242		
Other assets	85	85	53	57	149	149	53		
Total Assets	**140,962**	**55,557**	**73,019**	**39,707**	**25,015**	**3,539**	**12,050**	**6,880**	**2,157**
Accounts payable	2,738	4,563	3,377	1,323	753	689	642		
Accrued liabilities	487	747	432	311	300	257	148		
Notes payable	0	0	0	0	0	2,000	0		
Current portion of capital leases	150	216	255	768	917	749	590		
Capital lease obligations	14	59	275	530	941	1,429	1,880		
Deferred rent	42	15	39	79	113	67	21		
Total Liabilities	**3,431**	**5,600**	**4,378**	**3,011**	**3,024**	**5,191**	**3,281**	**631**	**5**
Common stock at par	2	1	1	1	1	0	0		
Additional paid-in capital	214,013	117,178	116,531	74,911	49,948	18,071	18,013		
Accumulated other income (loss)	(298)	(85)	0	0	0	0	0		
Development deficit	(76,186)	(67,137)	(47,891)	(38,216)	(27,958)	(19,723)	(9,244)	(4,103)	(523)
Total Stockholders' Equity	**137,531**	**49,957**	**68,641**	**36,696**	**21,991**	**(1,652)**	**8,769**	**6,249**	**2,152**

[a]Balances at close of second quarter 2000 ending December 31, 1999.
[b]Includes cash in banks and money market investments.
[c]Includes corporate, state, or political subdivision debt maturing within one year.
[d]Includes corporate, state, or political subdivision debt maturing at various dates through 2001.

EXHIBIT 5
Excerpts from Company Press Release— September 24, 1999

Source: Pharmacyclics press release.

SUNNYVALE, Calif.—September 24, 1999—Pharmacyclics, Inc. (NNM:PCYC) announced today that it commenced its public offering of 2,300,000 shares of its common stock at a price of $38.75 per share, which will result in net proceeds to the company of approximately $83.6 million. All of the shares are being sold by the company.

Pharmacyclics intends to use the funds from the offering for research and development activities, including clinical trails, process development and manufacturing support and for general corporate purposes, including working capital. Proceeds may also be used to acquire or invest in complementary businesses, products or technologies.

EXHIBIT 6
Historical Stock Performance Pharmacyclics and the S&P 500 Biotech Index

Source: Datastream.

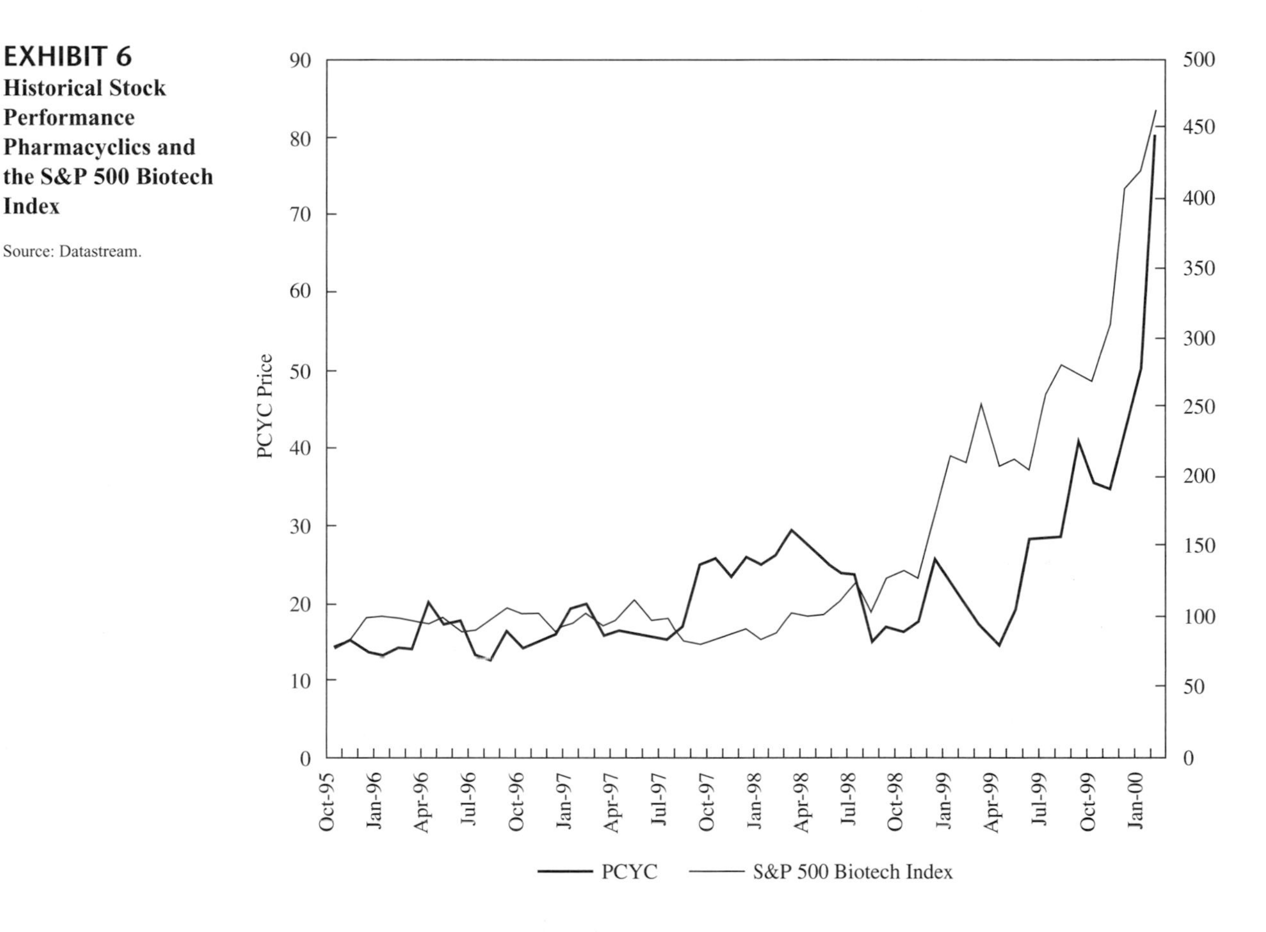

EXHIBIT 7 Pharmacyclics Product Portfolio

Source: Pharmacyclics company reports.

<table>
<tr><th rowspan="2">Product</th><th rowspan="2">Targeted Disease</th><th colspan="6">Development Status</th></tr>
<tr><th>PC (a)</th><th>IND (b)</th><th>PH1 (c)</th><th>PH2 (d)</th><th>PH3 (e)</th><th>NDA (f)</th></tr>
<tr><td colspan="8">Cancer Therapy</td></tr>
<tr><td>XCYTRIN Radiation Enhancer</td><td>Brain Metastases</td><td colspan="5">PCYC</td><td></td></tr>
<tr><td></td><td>Primary Brain</td><td colspan="3">NCI (g)</td><td></td><td></td><td></td></tr>
<tr><td></td><td>Pancreatic</td><td colspan="3">NCI</td><td></td><td></td><td></td></tr>
<tr><td></td><td>Lung</td><td colspan="3">NCI</td><td></td><td></td><td></td></tr>
<tr><td></td><td>Prostate</td><td colspan="2">NCI</td><td></td><td></td><td></td><td></td></tr>
<tr><td></td><td>Pediatric</td><td colspan="3">NCI</td><td></td><td></td><td></td></tr>
<tr><td>XCYTRIN Chemotherapy Enhancer</td><td>Variety of cancers</td><td>PCYC</td><td></td><td></td><td></td><td></td><td></td></tr>
<tr><td>LUTRIN Photosensitizer</td><td>Breast</td><td colspan="4">PCYC</td><td></td><td></td></tr>
<tr><td></td><td>Cervical</td><td colspan="2">NCI</td><td></td><td></td><td></td><td></td></tr>
<tr><td></td><td>Esophageal</td><td colspan="2">NCI</td><td></td><td></td><td></td><td></td></tr>
<tr><td></td><td>Lung</td><td colspan="2">NCI</td><td></td><td></td><td></td><td></td></tr>
<tr><td></td><td>Head and Neck</td><td colspan="2">NCI</td><td></td><td></td><td></td><td></td></tr>
<tr><td></td><td>Ovarian</td><td colspan="2">NCI</td><td></td><td></td><td></td><td></td></tr>
<tr><td></td><td>Prostate</td><td colspan="3">NCI</td><td></td><td></td><td></td></tr>
<tr><td colspan="8">Atherosclerosis Therapy</td></tr>
<tr><td>ANTRIN Photosensitizer</td><td>Peripheral Artery</td><td colspan="4">PCYC</td><td></td><td></td></tr>
<tr><td></td><td>Coronary Artery</td><td colspan="3">PCYC</td><td></td><td></td><td></td></tr>
<tr><td colspan="8">Macular Degeneration</td></tr>
<tr><td>OPTRIN Photosensitizer</td><td>Retina Degeneration</td><td colspan="4">Alcon</td><td></td><td></td></tr>
</table>

[a]Pre-Clinical: Test animal models for safety and efficacy prior to human trials.
[b]Investigational New Drug Application: Request approval from the FDA for human trials.
[c]Phase 1: Conduct initial human clinical trials to determine safety and efficacy.
[d]Phase 2: Obtain preliminary data on drug effectiveness, short-term side effects, and risks for a particular indication(s) in patients with the disease or condition.
[e]Phase 3: Expanded controlled and uncontrolled trials after Phase 2 studies suggest drug effectiveness.
[f]New Drug Application: Request commercial approval of drug from the FDA.
[g]National Cancer Institute.

EXHIBIT 8 Pharmacyclics Clinical Trials

Source: Pharmacyclics company reports.

		Phase I		Phase II		Phase III	
Product	**Diagnosis**	**Start**	**End**	**Start**	**End**	**Start**	**End**
Xcytrin	Brain Metastases	12/94	2/97	6/96	9/98	9/98	Ongoing
Lutrin	Breast	1/96	1/97	7/97	5/99		
Antrin	Peripheral Artery	8/98	8/99				
	Coronary Artery	4/99	Ongoing				

EXHIBIT 9 Pharmacyclics Projected Operating Expenses (millions of dollars)

Source: Adams, Harkness & Hill, Inc., November 29, 1999.

	Fiscal Year Ending June 30				
	2000	**2001**	**2002**	**2003**	**2004**
R&D Expense	27.5	42.5	38.0	44.0	54.5
SG&A	5.0	15.0	35.0	53.0	62.0
Total Operating Expenses	32.5	57.5	73.0	97.0	116.5

EXHIBIT 10 Pharmacyclics News Announcements December 1, 1999, to February 25, 2000

Source: Company press release, Dow Jones News Service, Investor's Business Daily.

Date	Source	Announcement	Next Day Close	Previous Close
2-16-00	Investor's Business Daily	PCYC is listed as a "hot stock to watch"	$83.00	$62.75
2-03-00	Company Press Release	**Second quarter results:** PCYC loses 36 cents a share versus 35 cents a year earlier and revenue increases $.9M, or 433%, with a milestone payment from Alcon	$67.00	$54.50
1-19-00		No news on PCYC	$60.00	$40.38
1-10-00	Company Press Release	PCYC receives milestone payment from Alcon	$43.00	$40.88
12-31-99	Dow Jones Business News	CEO Miller refutes a Stanford University researcher's report that Xcytrin is ineffective	$39.00	$37.06

EXHIBIT 11A Betas for Pharmaceutical Companies

Company	Equity Beta[a]	Equity Market Value[b]	Interest Bearing Debt[c]	EBITDA[d]	Leverage Ratio 1996–2000[e]
American Home Products	.53	51,179	3,669	3,760	7.2%
Bristol Myers Squibb	.86	127,144	1,342	6,531	1.1%
Johnson & Johnson	1.03	129,588	2,450	7,370	1.9%
Lilly (Eli) & Co.	.75	72,501	2,812	3,713	3.9%
Merck & Co.	.93	156,486	3,144	8,683	2.0%
Pfizer Inc.	.87	124,789	525	5,325	0.4%
Pharmacia & Upjohn Inc.	.65	23,385	332	1,651	1.4%
Schering-Plough	1.13	62,376	6	2,959	0.0%
Warner-Lambert Co.	.76	70,634	1,250	3,032	1.8%

EXHIBIT 11B Beta for Pharmacyclics and Competitors

Source: Compustat.

Company	Equity Beta[a]	Equity Market Value[b]	Interest Bearing Debt[c]	EBITDA[d]	Leverage Ratio 1996–2000[e]
Cell Therapeutics	.43	109	2	–36	2.1%
Elan Corporation	.39	7,939	1,549	394	19.7%
Mallinckrodt	.96	2,572	743	457	28.8%
OXiGENE	1.34	176	0	–12	0.0%
Pharmacyclics	.97	348	0	–22	0.0%
QLT	1.31	3,810	0	–29	0.0%

[a]Beta as of February 2000 estimated using monthly stock returns during the five fiscal years prior to February 2000.
[b]Market value of equity at company's fiscal year end prior to February 2000.
[c]Long-term debt in millions at company's fiscal year end prior to February 2000.
[d]Earnings before interest, taxes, and depreciation at company's fiscal year end prior to February 2000.
[e]Average ratio of long-term debt to the market value of equity plus long-term debt for the five fiscal years prior to February 2000.

EXHIBIT 11C Corporate and Government Bond Rates as of February 28, 2000

Source: Datastream.

Government Bond Yields	
Maturity	**Rate (%)**
3 months	5.82
6 months	6.03
1 year	6.21
3 years	6.58
5 years	6.58
10 years	6.55
30 years	6.19

Corporate Bonds (10-Year Maturity)	
Maturity	**Rate (%)**
AAA	7.28
AA	7.38
A	7.49
BBB	7.85
BB	9.07
B	10.04

Valuing Project Achieve

Stacey Boyd, president and CEO of Project Achieve, returned to her office on the afternoon of June 7, 1999, to the usual deluge of email. Several of the messages concerned her current efforts to raise additional financing for the business. Prior to this round of financing, Project Achieve had relied on self-financing and an interim financing from angel investors. Boyd was now in discussions with several potential investors, including Daniel Eliot, an individual who had already provided some financing, a group of venture capitalists, and Jostens, a school supply company. Boyd recognized that her decisions on financing would have a critical impact on the future of Project Achieve. Each of the potential investors had a different interest in the business, and she had to weigh carefully how future financing would affect control of the business and its direction. Boyd's discussions with the potential investors had also made clear to her that they had widely varying views about the value of Project Achieve. Boyd recognized that she needed to construct a convincing case for the valuation of the business before proceeding with the detailed negotiations on financing.

Project Achieve Background

In March 1998, Boyd and HBS classmate Mandy Lee founded Project Achieve (see Exhibit 1 for profiles of Boyd and Lee). At the time, Boyd was beginning to wind down as the principal and founder of a charter school, the Academy of the Pacific Rim, in Boston.[1] During her time as a principal and a teacher, Boyd had been surprised by the enormous load of administrative tasks facing principals and teachers, the difficulty in tracking school and student progress and the antiquated information management systems found in most schools. Unsatisfied with the existing products in the marketplace, she developed a homegrown database that allowed her to manage the myriad information regarding students, teachers, and the curriculum that every principal struggles with. At the conclusion of the 1998 school year, she decided to leave her charter school and dedicate herself to developing commercialized and scaleable software that would become Achieve.

Boyd was also drawn by what she considered a sizable opportunity. In the United States, over 16,000 school districts comprising 112,000 K–12 schools enrolled an estimated 53 million students during the 1998–1999 school year. While per student spending was among the highest in the world, disappointment over educational outcomes had spurred an increased call for accountability of public schools through the implementation of educational standards. Numerous efforts were under way to create state or nationwide guidelines for the scope and depth of material covered at different stages of a

[1]The charter school movement grew out of the desire to allow concerned community members the ability to create publicly funded schools that were not encumbered by the regulations that governed most of public education in the United States. A group of individuals created a "charter" articulating a mission for a school, sought state approval, and then began attracting parents and students to the school.

Professor Mihir Desai and Research Associate Kathleen Luchs prepared this case as the basis for class discussion rather than to illustrate either effective or ineffective handling of an administrative situation.

Copyright © 2001 by the President and Fellows of Harvard College. To order copies or request permission to reproduce materials, call 1-800-545-7685, write Harvard Business School Publishing, Boston, MA 02163, or go to http://www.hbsp.harvard.edu. No part of this publication may be reproduced, stored in a retrieval system, used in a spreadsheet, or transmitted in any form or by any means—electronic, mechanical, photocopying, recording, or otherwise—without the permission of Harvard Business School.

student's career. Boyd's vision was to design an information management system for schools that would allow coordination of teaching materials to further standards and also allow for greater monitoring of students and teachers.

At the same time that the calls for standards and accountability were increasing, technology was spreading through American classrooms and schools. The percentage of classrooms connected to the Internet had advanced significantly from 3% in 1995 to 57% in 1999 and was expected to be 95% by 2002. Moreover, technology spending in public schools had increased at a 12.5% annual rate during the nineties, resulting in $5.4 billion of technology spending in 1998–1999. Despite this strong growth, technology spending was still only 1.5% of total expenditures in schools, far below the share of expenditures on technology for many other industries.

The Testing of Project Achieve

Beginning in the spring of 1998, Boyd began speaking at education conferences on school information management systems and their role in promoting accountability. Surprised by the apparent vacuum in this field, Boyd began seeking pilot schools which would adopt a system that combined administrative and curricular functionality. The product was christened Achieve and Boyd began working with software developers to create a standardized product. In seeking pilot schools, Boyd received over one hundred applications. Boyd selected 16 schools and tried to create a set with as much diversity as possible. In particular, Boyd wanted a mix of school types (private, public, and charter) as well as geographic dispersion. Through the school year, Boyd and her team continued to monitor their progress and used ideas from them in developing and refining the Achieve product. While Boyd had a technology director in-house, much of the product development was currently outsourced creating the largest expense for the company. In December of 1998, Boyd also decided that moving Project Achieve to San Francisco would be in the best interest of the company.

By June 1999, Boyd felt that Project Achieve had made significant advances in staffing, product development, and the creation of a viable business model. On the staffing front, the move to San Francisco resulted in the hiring of two key employees—Melissa Williams and Bala Ganesh (see Exhibit 1)—that rounded out the product marketing and development effort. Recruitment was still a major drain on Boyd's time, as the labor market in San Francisco proved extremely tight. Feedback from the pilot schools and the addition of Williams and Ganesh had resulted in a considerably revamped product. In particular, Achieve was transformed into an entirely Web-based information management system that would be remote hosted. Boyd and her team chose to move to this architecture to reduce the hardware costs for schools and to take advantage of the scalability provided by the Web. Full security would be ensured and parents, teachers, and administrators would be able to access the system from work or home.

The Competition

The school MIS market was a highly fragmented and competitive market. Boyd believed that, to date, no competitor offered as comprehensive an administrative and educational system as Achieve. According to Boyd, National Computer Systems offered similar functionality to Achieve by combining two separate products, its Schools Administrative Student Information software (SASI) for student data and ABACUS for curriculum planning. These products lacked Achieve's integrated Web-based design and were priced much higher. NCS also offered two older DOS-based systems, with installed user bases of 5,000 schools for the *Orisis* system, and 8,000 schools for *The*

School System. Another competitor, Power School, offered a system based on the Apple G3 platform and provided primarily administrative functions. Boyd also surmised that Campus America, which sold the IMSeries, had similar functionality to Achieve, but lacked a user-friendly interface and was not easily customized. Although the IMSeries had been marketed for many years, Boyd estimated its installed base at approximately 125 schools. Chancery Software, through its *Mac-School* and *Win-School* products, had an administrative package, but did not have a combined product, according to Boyd. She estimated Chancery's installed base at approximately 6,000 schools.

Boyd felt that none of Achieve's competitors approached the education information management industry from the "enterprise software" perspective focusing on organizational and educational change. Furthermore, most of the larger competitors maintained direct sales forces, which Boyd hoped to bypass. Achieve's primary advantage, according to Boyd, was that none of the competitors' management information packages were fully Web-based. Boyd sensed that this feature would be critical in enabling schools to leapfrog outdated technology. Despite her confidence regarding the relative advantages of Achieve, Boyd sensed that a relatively limited window would be open until the competitors would catch up. Exhibit 2 summarizes Project Achieve's assessment of the competitive landscape.

Boyd also collected detailed information on public education companies that is summarized in Exhibit 3. For those public companies, Boyd also obtained their monthly returns for the last five years along with the market returns as presented in Exhibit 4. In looking for comparable private education companies, Boyd obtained information contained in Exhibit 5 for their financing histories. Finally, Boyd informed herself about current interest rates, given in Exhibit 6. Boyd felt confident that her analysis of comparable companies, along with Project Achieve's marketing plan, would enable her to make a convincing case on the value of Project Achieve to potential investors.

Marketing Plan

By June 1999, the company had decided on its marketing plan. The full Achieve line consisted of eleven modules, summarized in Exhibit 7. The eight administrative modules of the product, called Achieve Express, would be provided free to carefully targeted schools. This giveaway of Achieve Express would allow Achieve to avoid the significant cost of creating a sales force and would ensure the rapid acceptance of the product. Revenues would be generated by selling products and services to the schools using Achieve Express, including the selling of the three modules excluded from the giveaway version, called Achieve Logic. Creating paying customers was therefore a two-stage process: a school first had to become users of the free Achieve Express, and then the school had to buy Achieve Logic and/or other products or services to enhance the capabilities of Achieve Express. Boyd therefore devoted considerable effort to selecting the schools offered the giveaway product, since the schools which became users of Achieve Express would constitute the market for the revenue generating products of the business.

Boyd and her team completed a state-by-state survey of educational resources, identifying the numbers of schools, districts, students, and teachers in each state, the number of schools and classrooms with Internet access, as well as the money spent on educational technology by each state. She then selected a group of target states, and specific school districts within those states, in which to launch Project Achieve. Project Achieve's main marketing effort would be based on aggressive campaigns targeted at state governors and consortia of private or charter schools. A secondary marketing effort would be directed at enrolling schools in the target states through press campaigns, educational associations, and partner agreements. This detailed analysis resulted in her projections of targeting 3,990 schools in 1999–2000, 3,226 schools in 2000–2001, and

2,438 schools in each of the subsequent three years. Thereafter, Boyd assumed that she would continue to target a similar number of schools in other states and that the overall number of target schools would increase at a conservative rate of 2%.

Since the initial product would be provided free, Boyd anticipated that among the specially targeted schools there would be a high conversion rate, with 65% of the schools initially committing to becoming users of Achieve Express. Among those schools committing to become users of Achieve Express, Boyd forecast that 20% would become users and also subscribers to the complete package, Achieve Logic. As such, there would be two classes of users—those schools committing to use Achieve Express and those subscribing to the whole suite of modules known as Achieve Logic subscribers.

Among the schools which only became users of the free Achieve Express product, Boyd estimated that half would remain users for only two years, while half would remain long-term users of Achieve Express. Project Achieve would provide technical support to the Achieve Express user schools, free of charge. This support would be provided mainly via Project Achieve's website, but telephone support would also be available. Boyd anticipated that the annual cost per school for technical support for Achieve Express would average $250.

Additional products would also be offered to all the schools using Achieve Express, even if they did not purchase the complete Achieve Logic. These products included Reports, which provided detailed analyses, Dashboard, which provided enhanced reporting capabilities, and a Data Analysis Service for school districts, which aggregated individual school data. Additionally, Boyd anticipated that she could sell advertising slots on the company's website. Boyd and her team worked out detailed forecasts for each of the company's other products, and also for the anticipated revenues from Web advertising. Overall, she expected that each Achieve Express and Achieve Logic school would provide $500 in annual revenues from other products and services that the company could sell to them. For those Achieve Express users that dropped after two years, Boyd assumed that they were complete non-users and would not contribute any ancillary revenue streams.

Achieve Logic Subscribers

The schools which became users of the give-away Achieve Express would comprise the market for Project Achieve's revenue-generating products and services. The most important product would be the complete Achieve package, Achieve Logic. Achieve Logic included the three modules—Student Monitoring, Lesson Plans, and Linked Grading—not included in the giveaway version. These additional modules would provide schools with a complete and integrated information management system, covering both administrative and academic functions. Among the 20% of Achieve Express users that became Achieve Logic subscribers, Boyd expected that 25% would drop their subscription after two years and no longer use Achieve Express, and that 75% would become long-term users and subscribers.

Schools buying the Achieve Logic package would pay an up-front installation fee and an annual per student subscription fee, based on numbers of students per school. For a typical school, the net installation fee would be $5,000 and the ongoing subscription fee would be $9,600. Schools which bought Achieve Logic would also receive much higher levels of support, including support and guidance in implementing the complete system, and ongoing technical support resulting in a cost to Project Achieve of $1,500 per year per school. Finally, the base of long-term Achieve Logic subscribers would also contribute $500 in ancillary revenue streams annually.

Overhead Costs

Project Achieve's overhead costs included marketing and sales costs, the costs of remote hosting to support Achieve Express and Achieve Logic, research and development for the next version of Achieve, and headquarters costs. Each of these cost items had been built up from detailed analyses of the separate line items and Table A summarizes the costs, aside from those factored in the marketing plan, for 1999–2000. Boyd anticipated that total costs would increase 20% a year over the following four years and wanted to incorporate those costs into her valuation effort.

While Boyd realized that some of these costs would fluctuate with the number of schools, she considered the 20% increases for the four years after 1999–2000 a realistic estimate of how her costs would increase over the near term. Boyd assumed that after the fifth year, overhead costs would rise in line with her subscription base.

Discussions with Investors

Boyd considered the marketing plan and forecasts assembled by her team as a viable plan. However, she knew that potential investors would want to see how that plan corresponded to a valuation of Project Achieve for a proposed investment. Additionally, Boyd sensed that potential investors would question how robust the plan was to changes in assumptions and she wanted to be prepared to discuss alternative scenarios and their implications for valuation. Indeed, previous discussions with investors had yielded a dizzying array of valuation alternatives. Finally, Boyd also had to take into account the $1 million loss incurred to date by Project Achieve.

Beginning in late 1998, Boyd sought funding from a variety of angel investors who cumulatively provided $544,000 in the months prior to April 1999. These financings were tied together in a Series A financing that was priced at $6.48 a share. The remaining capitalization of the company consisted of 1,000,000 common shares distributed among the founders and an option pool for employees of 235,000 shares. In contrast, her efforts to raise additional amounts had yielded an offer to invest at a valuation of $2 million which Boyd had immediately rejected. As weeks passed and Project Achieve burned through its remaining cash, Boyd was entertaining an offer from Daniel Eliot to invest $5 million at $5.00 a share and from Jostens to invest $2 million at $6.48 a share, the same terms of the angel round. Boyd struggled to reconcile these offers with the valuation stemming from her detailed analysis and sought more ammunition for further conversations with Eliot and Jostens.

TABLE A
Project Achieve Estimated Overhead Costs 1999–2000

Marketing and Sales	$2,003,100
Remote Hosting	$1,380,000
R & D	$1,786,000
HQ	$1,355,726
	$6,524,826

EXHIBIT 1
Key Personnel in June 1999

Source: Company documents.

Stacey Boyd, President and Chief Executive Officer Stacey Boyd is ACHIEVE™'s architect and designer. In 1996, during her last year of business school, she founded the Academy of the Pacific Rim, a charter school in Boston now serving 150 students with a staff of fifteen, and served as the school's principal during its first year of operation. Under her leadership, the Academy was written up in the *Wall Street Journal, WIRED* magazine, the *Weekly Standard,* the *Boston Globe,* and the *Boston Herald.* Prior to founding the Academy, she worked for the Edison Project on its public school partnership team doing school design work and marketing. She has also taught in Japan. She has her Bachelor of Arts from Hamilton College, her Master in Public Policy from the John F. Kennedy School of Government at Harvard University, and her Master in Business Administration from the Harvard Business School.

Mandy Lee, Chief Operating Officer Mandy Lee was most recently a principal at the Parthenon Group in Boston where she worked with several clients in the education industry. Prior to Parthenon, she worked at Bain and Co. as a senior associate consultant. For the Carnegie Foundation for Advancement in Teaching, she analyzed corporate involvement in U.S. education reform. She has her Bachelor of Arts from Princeton University and her Master in Business Administration from Harvard Business School.

Melissa Williams, Director of Product Marketing Melissa has in-depth experience in software development, product management, and marketing. She was most recently at Evolve Software where she managed the company's first suite of products from inception to launch. Prior to Evolve, she worked as a management consultant, helping several large software companies shorten their product development lifecycles. She has a Bachelor of Science in Systems Engineering from the University of Virginia and a Master in Business Administration from Harvard Business School.

Bala Ganesh, Director of Engineering Bala is responsible for the development of Achieve Express. He has been involved in the implementation and management of enterprise-class customer relationship management applications for various customers of Diffusion Software and Chordiant Software. He was a member of the initial consulting team at Remedy Corporation, and was involved in designing, developing, and implementing a wide range of applications using their state-of-the-art adaptable technology. He has lived and worked throughout the United States. He has a Bachelor of Engineering from University of Madras, India, and a Master in Industrial Management from the India Institute of Technology, Madras, India.

EXHIBIT 2
Project Achieve's Assessment of the Competition

Source: Company documents.

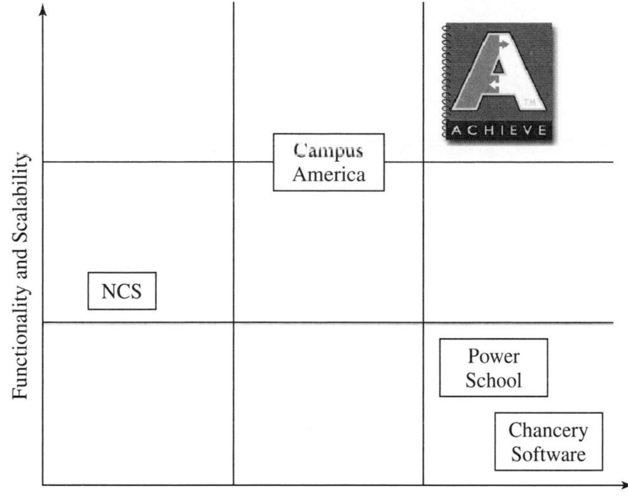

Product Price Comparison

	NCS	Power School	Campus America	Chancery Software
Price (Year One)[a]	$53,500	$18,200	$28,100	$13,200
Price (Year Two)[a]	7,000	2,500	2,500	0

[a]Prices based on average school size of 650 students.

EXHIBIT 3 Selected Comparable Public Companies

Source: SDC, *Compustat.*

Company	Business Description	IPO Date	May 1999 Market Capitalization $Millions	1998 Debt $Millions	1998 Sales $Millions	1998 Net Income $Millions
Advantage Learning Systems	Provides learning information systems to grades K–12, consisting of computer software and related training designed to improve students' academic performance by increasing the quality, quantity, and timeliness of performance data.	09/25/97	754.01	0.00	54.76	12.73
Click2learn.Com	Provider of online learning solutions designed to enable customers to create, distribute, and manage learning applications throughout an enterprise.	06/12/98	57.71	0.00	33.35	–5.16
Educational Insights	Develops and markets supplemental educational materials, such as electronic games and learning aids, activity books, science and nature kits, board games, and other materials for use in school and at home.	04/15/94	13.20	0.93	39.54	–2.28
Infonautics Corporation	Information services company and provider of online information. Properties include Electric Library, Company Sleuth, Sports Sleuth, Job Sleuth, Encyclopedia.com, and Researchpaper.com.	04/29/96	71.79	0.05	14.93	–17.45
Learn2.Com	Creates and distributes online advanced learning and training. Its products allow interactive multimedia and animated courseware to be accessed instantly on the Web.	05/18/94	184.60	0.05	1.57	–10.96
National Computer Systems	Provides services, software, and systems for the collection, management, and interpretation of data to two broad markets: Education and Large Scale Data Management.	pre-1980	988.69	19.00	406.02	25.18
Scholastic Corporation	Publisher and distributor of children's books, K–12 textbooks, classroom materials and magazines, instructional technology, and entertainment products such as TV programming, videos, movies, and Internet services.	02/24/92	798.94	254.50	1,058.40	23.60
Sylvan Learning Systems	Provides educational services to families and schools through Learning Centers, Contract Educational Services, English Language Instruction, and International Universities.	12/09/93	1,394.25	12.50	440.33	35.71
Vcampus Corporation	Provides interactive and on-demand educational courseware for the online education and training market through the World Wide Web.	11/26/96	20.85	1.94	14.68	–19.81

EXHIBIT 4 Selected Comparable Companies' Monthly Returns

Source: *Compustat*

	S&P Industrials Ltd.	Advantage Learning Sys Inc.	Click2learn.com Inc.	Educational Insights Inc.	Infonautics Corp.—CLA	Learn2.com Inc.	National Computer Sys Inc.	Scholastic Corp.	Sylvan Learning Systems Inc.	Vcampus Corp.
Jun94	−2.40%	NA	NA	−10.80%	NA	NA	−7.10%	5.60%	0.50%	NA
Jul94	3.40%	NA	NA	−3.00%	NA	NA	8.50%	16.90%	4.30%	NA
Aug94	4.00%	NA	NA	−25.00%	NA	NA	2.70%	2.00%	13.80%	NA
Sep94	−2.50%	NA	NA	10.40%	NA	NA	4.80%	8.30%	−6.80%	NA
Oct94	2.30%	NA	NA	1.90%	NA	NA	6.40%	−6.40%	4.30%	NA
Nov94	−3.70%	NA	NA	−29.60%	NA	−19.50%	5.20%	3.00%	15.30%	NA
Dec94	1.66%	NA	NA	13.16%	NA	−36.36%	5.17%	8.51%	−4.81%	NA
Jan95	1.46%	NA	NA	−6.98%	NA	42.86%	2.23%	−0.98%	−3.80%	NA
Feb95	4.06%	NA	NA	45.00%	NA	−3.33%	1.61%	0.00%	−6.57%	NA
Mar95	3.79%	NA	NA	−15.52%	NA	13.79%	6.35%	7.92%	0.00%	NA
Apr95	2.90%	NA	NA	−14.29%	NA	4.55%	0.54%	2.75%	−2.12%	NA
May95	3.48%	NA	NA	4.76%	NA	1.45%	5.97%	−1.34%	5.04%	NA
Jun95	2.86%	NA	NA	9.09%	NA	62.86%	7.04%	−1.81%	17.82%	NA
Jul95	3.43%	NA	NA	10.42%	NA	19.30%	9.68%	21.20%	39.52%	NA
Aug95	−0.86%	NA	NA	−22.64%	NA	4.41%	1.80%	−6.84%	−5.00%	NA
Sep95	3.62%	NA	NA	2.44%	NA	18.31%	−2.95%	2.45%	11.40%	NA
Oct95	−0.20%	NA	NA	−14.29%	NA	−29.76%	5.32%	−1.59%	−24.41%	NA
Nov95	4.20%	NA	NA	−22.22%	NA	17.80%	−11.63%	12.15%	0.00%	NA
Dec95	1.51%	NA	NA	−21.43%	NA	−19.42%	10.53%	12.27%	23.95%	NA
Jan96	3.46%	NA	NA	63.64%	NA	−19.64%	−9.69%	−6.11%	12.61%	NA
Feb96	1.27%	NA	NA	−16.67%	NA	−2.22%	7.28%	−4.45%	−7.84%	NA
Mar96	1.27%	NA	NA	−10.00%	NA	−7.95%	−2.47%	−1.43%	15.79%	NA
Apr96	2.16%	NA	NA	0.00%	NA	−14.81%	2.99%	−4.73%	8.39%	NA
May96	2.90%	NA	NA	5.54%	−5.66%	44.93%	7.41%	−4.96%	0.00%	NA
Jun96	−0.08%	NA	NA	−15.78%	−36.00%	3.00%	11.49%	−0.40%	−2.58%	NA
Jul96	−4.68%	NA	NA	−16.67%	−32.81%	−38.83%	−11.48%	5.24%	−11.26%	NA
Aug96	1.86%	NA	NA	10.00%	6.98%	−9.52%	−5.27%	3.83%	9.70%	NA
Sep96	5.71%	NA	NA	−4.55%	−26.09%	−10.53%	0.00%	7.01%	11.57%	NA
Oct96	1.82%	NA	NA	−19.05%	−8.82%	−19.61%	1.68%	1.03%	3.05%	NA
Nov96	7.46%	NA	NA	29.41%	3.23%	−4.88%	4.88%	1.71%	−7.25%	NA
Dec96	−1.72%	NA	NA	−18.18%	−6.25%	−23.08%	10.47%	−9.73%	9.09%	3.92%
Jan97	6.19%	NA	NA	11.11%	−16.67%	13.33%	7.75%	−12.27%	3.51%	15.09%
Feb97	0.28%	NA	NA	−20.00%	−20.00%	−16.92%	−4.17%	−44.07%	15.68%	−11.48%

(continued)

EXHIBIT 4 *(Continued)*

	S&P Industrials Ltd.	Advantage Learning Sys Inc.	Click2learn.com Inc.	Educational Insights Inc.	Infonautics Corp.—CLA	Learn2.com Inc.	National Computer Sys Inc.	Scholastic Corp.	Sylvan Learning Systems Inc.	Vcampus Corp.
Mar97	–3.60%	NA	NA	3.10%	–25.00%	–11.50%	1.28%	–14.39%	–27.47%	–11.11%
Apr97	6.04%	NA	NA	–3.01%	0.00%	–24.00%	2.38%	–11.50%	21.72%	–16.67%
May97	6.44%	NA	NA	0.00%	–3.36%	–18.44%	–0.50%	19.00%	19.09%	15.00%
Jun97	4.36%	NA	NA	–12.50%	106.95%	35.52%	0.50%	17.65%	–5.23%	6.52%
Jul97	7.40%	NA	NA	7.14%	–33.33%	–4.76%	5.80%	0.71%	14.70%	12.24%
Aug97	–5.36%	NA	NA	3.31%	–10.00%	22.48%	3.29%	–2.84%	–4.17%	18.18%
Sep97	4.98%	NA	NA	32.27%	22.22%	–18.35%	19.09%	15.33%	17.39%	51.54%
Oct97	–3.77%	0.00%	NA	–23.15%	–2.29%	–20.00%	8.29%	2.53%	–3.99%	–12.69%
Nov97	4.71%	–9.90%	NA	20.62%	–2.31%	3.10%	7.42%	–5.71%	–3.26%	–25.58%
Dec97	0.79%	–6.04%	NA	–9.22%	–23.81%	–18.19%	–3.95%	–1.80%	–4.30%	3.13%
Jan98	2.25%	24.55%	NA	–23.19%	–3.15%	–3.68%	–3.18%	–6.67%	1.28%	–21.21%
Feb98	6.97%	0.47%	NA	20.77%	3.25%	–5.78%	–2.84%	13.21%	15.98%	8.65%
Mar98	4.89%	28.51%	NA	0.00%	146.85%	4.11%	16.43%	6.62%	2.87%	–29.20%
Apr98	1.09%	–8.37%	NA	6.25%	–4.42%	331.30%	13.10%	–11.83%	4.77%	8.75%
May98	–1.58%	–14.29%	NA	–5.88%	–28.48%	–36.36%	11.11%	7.38%	–7.34%	–20.69%
Jun98	4.09%	1.39%	NA	0.00%	0.00%	–5.01%	–3.00%	–0.31%	7.38%	–20.29%
Jul98	–1.11%	26.48%	2.07%	–23.45%	–14.81%	–0.75%	–0.82%	5.09%	–13.36%	1.82%
Aug98	–13.08%	–16.97%	–33.78%	2.02%	–32.59%	–51.52%	–7.29%	–7.53%	–24.67%	–14.29%
Sep98	7.29%	32.17%	4.08%	12.04%	9.65%	48.45%	–1.69%	9.68%	9.36%	–18.75%
Oct98	7.81%	21.05%	–4.91%	–14.29%	–35.29%	–21.05%	35.09%	–7.20%	32.09%	–23.08%
Nov98	6.13%	20.11%	–1.02%	33.33%	313.67%	49.32%	–5.08%	20.76%	–5.87%	93.33%
Dec98	6.66%	19.00%	–27.08%	–15.60%	–20.89%	–24.11%	17.41%	12.60%	4.95%	–18.10%
Jan99	4.96%	2.09%	8.57%	11.08%	1.38%	3.54%	12.70%	5.59%	3.08%	–17.90%
Feb99	–3.98%	12.11%	–11.83%	20.00%	–8.90%	0.00%	3.38%	–13.02%	5.76%	–30.77%
Mar99	4.24%	–17.44%	11.94%	–18.04%	–6.76%	115.93%	–16.26%	–0.76%	–17.67%	18.52%
Apr99	3.02%	–15.09%	–12.01%	1.68%	61.29%	9.46%	–23.36%	–3.26%	–8.22%	–18.75%
May99	–1.95%	–15.64%	0.00%	0.00%	–1.50%	–8.65%	14.29%	2.58%	8.46%	50.00%

EXHIBIT 5 **Financing History of Selected Comparable Private Companies**

Source: SDC—VentureXpert

Company	Business Description	Date of Founding	Website	Dates of Financing	Amount of Financing	Investors
Blackboard, Inc	Develops technologies for teaching and learning on the Internet. The Company creates software tools for hosting virtual campuses, university intranets, and corporate training environments.	1997	*www.blackboard.com*	09/29/1998 06/08/1999	3,100 12,500	Aurora Capital Partners Aurora Funds, Inc. Carlyle Group, The Internet Capital Group Merrill Lynch Capital Partners Novak Biddle Venture Partners, L.P. Undisclosed Venture Firm
Classroom Connect	Provides Internet resources, curriculum, and training for educators and students in kindergarten through 12th grade classes.	1994	*www.classroomconnect.com*	09/01/1998 round in process	15,000 31,000	Brentwood Venture Capital Cambria Group, The Hillman Company Intel Corp. Media Technology Ventures MediaOne Group, Inc. U.S. Trust Private Equity Waller Capital Corp.
Family Education Network	Provides educational services via the Internet that connect parents, children, and educators. The website contains national programming, shared practices, community discussions, e-commerce, and a search engine for family/education topics	1990	*www.familyeducation.com*	04/27/99	51,000	America Online, Inc. DLJ Capital Intel Corp. Morningside Group Sprout Group
Lightspan Partnership	Provides interactive educational digital video products to schools and private homes. The Company is delivering a new generation of educational programming for digital video devices, including video-capable Windows and the Sony Playstation.	1993	*www.lightspan.com*	12/01/1993 02/07/1995 06/07/1995 09/20/1996 03/19/1997 06/24/1997 03/10/1998	7,000 17,500 17,500 20,000 5,000 28,767 20,600	Accel Partners Comcast Interactive Capital Group Ignite Group JAFCO America Ventures, Inc. Kleiner Perkins Caufield & Byers Liberty Media Group Microsoft Nassau Capital, L.L.C. Sony Corporation Tribune Ventures

EXHIBIT 6
U.S. Treasury Interest Rates for Selected Maturates on June 7, 1999

Source: *http://www.bog.frb.fed.us/releases/H15/19990607/*

Three Months	4.77
Six Months	4.97
One Year	5.09
Ten Years	5.78
Twenty Years	6.27
Thirty Years	5.94

EXHIBIT 7
Project Achieve Product Description

Source: Company Documents

The ACHIEVE Product Line

The ACHIEVE suite of products is designed to provide schools with a comprehensive information management system capable of streamlining and automating administrative, instructional, and communication processes. The ACHIEVE product is a powerful and easy-to-use system that offers fully integrated curriculum management functionality in addition to information tracking and communications capabilities. ACHIEVE Express offers information tracking and communications modules through a very similar user interface. ACHIEVE Express is most often used in the marketing process to introduce schools to the capabilities of a sophisticated information management system specifically designed for the school environment, and the Company expects it will prove valuable in building demand for the core ACHIEVE product. ACHIEVE Dashboard works in conjunction with ACHIEVE and ACHIEVE Express, providing enhanced data analysis and reporting functions. All ACHIEVE products are fully Web-based and can be accessed through standard Web browsers.

ACHIEVE

ACHIEVE provides schools the capability to effectively and efficiently complete such important functions as creating focused, standards-based lesson plans, sharing information about teaching methodologies, students and educational trends, linking lessons and grades to state standards, and identifying performance trends. ACHIEVE also provides parents with the ability to monitor their child's lessons and performance without the need for direct contact with teachers and administrators. In addition, ACHIEVE automates many standard administrative functions, saving schools time and money. ACHIEVE's latest version, 2.0, which is currently being sold for installation, includes eleven modules that offer the user powerful capabilities combined with a user-friendly interface. Many of the modules can be customized through the addition of check-boxes and drop-down menus.

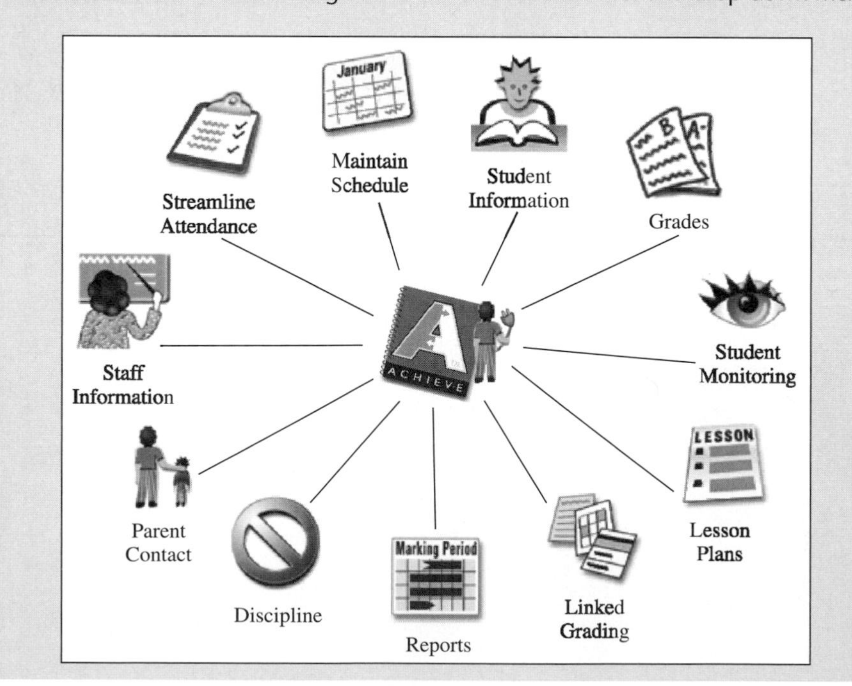

Lesson Plans: Enables teachers to create standards-based lesson plans with ease. This module links lesson plans to school (or district/state) standards and monitors how frequently each standard has been covered. Teachers can access and contribute to the school's archived lessons and curriculum, creating and improving upon shared institutional knowledge.

Linked Grading: Helps teachers keep track of what standards students have mastered. With this module, teachers can easily pinpoint trouble areas for individuals or groups and identify strategies for helping students master difficult standards. Teachers are given the ability to create assessments that address specific content and skill standards.

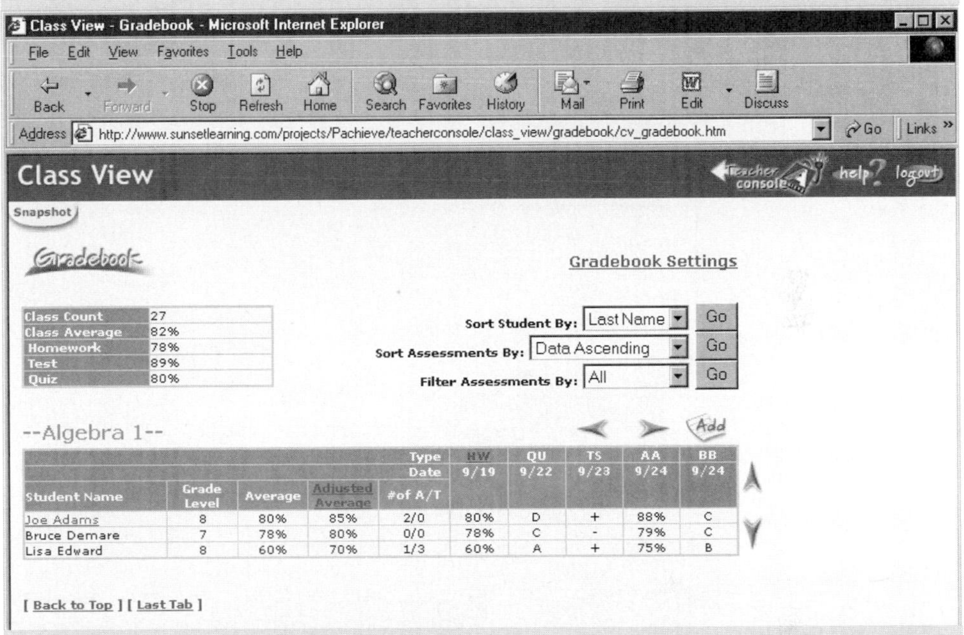

Class View - Gradebook - Microsoft Internet Explorer

File Edit View Favorites Tools Help

Back Forward Stop Refresh Home Search Favorites History Mail Print Edit Discuss

Address http://www.sunsetlearning.com/projects/Pachieve/teacherconsole/class_view/gradebook/cv_gradebook.htm Go Links »

Class View

Teacher console help? logout

Snapshot

Gradebook

Gradebook Settings

Class Count	27
Class Average	82%
Homework	78%
Test	89%
Quiz	80%

Sort Student By: Last Name Go

Sort Assessments By: Data Ascending Go

Filter Assessments By: All Go

--Algebra 1--

Add

				Type	HW	QU	TS	AA	BB
				Date	9/19	9/22	9/23	9/24	9/24
Student Name	Grade Level	Average	Adjusted Average	#of A/T					
Joe Adams	8	80%	85%	2/0	80%	D	+	88%	C
Bruce Demare	7	78%	80%	0/0	78%	C	-	79%	C
Lisa Edward	8	60%	70%	1/3	60%	A	+	75%	B

[Back to Top] [Last Tab]

Screenshot—Electronic Gradebook

Grades: Calculates grades automatically, allowing teachers to spend more time on other activities. Grades are recorded via electronic gradebooks to evaluate students' ongoing progress and allow for early intervention. Attendance data and discipline records are automatically linked with the gradebook.

Student Monitoring: Allows information about students to be shared effortlessly. This module provides instant access to all teachers' thoughts and strategies for a particular student, eliminating the need for lengthy staff meetings. Information about each student is archived in a database, which saves teachers and staff valuable classroom time by providing quick and convenient access to student information.

Streamline Attendance: Streamlines the attendance taking process, creating more classroom teaching time. This module captures on-line real-time attendance, by day or by class, eliminating the need for scanner forms or dual entry of data. Attendance data is automatically linked with other school information, such as discipline and grades, and can be aggregated and submitted at the school, district, and state levels.

Discipline: With this module, teachers can document discipline incidents quickly. All discipline incidents are logged directly into ACHIEVE, immediately informing administrators and eliminating the need to fill out additional forms. By capturing information on discipline incidents, teachers can access and contribute information on successful and unsuccessful strategies used in solving discipline problems.

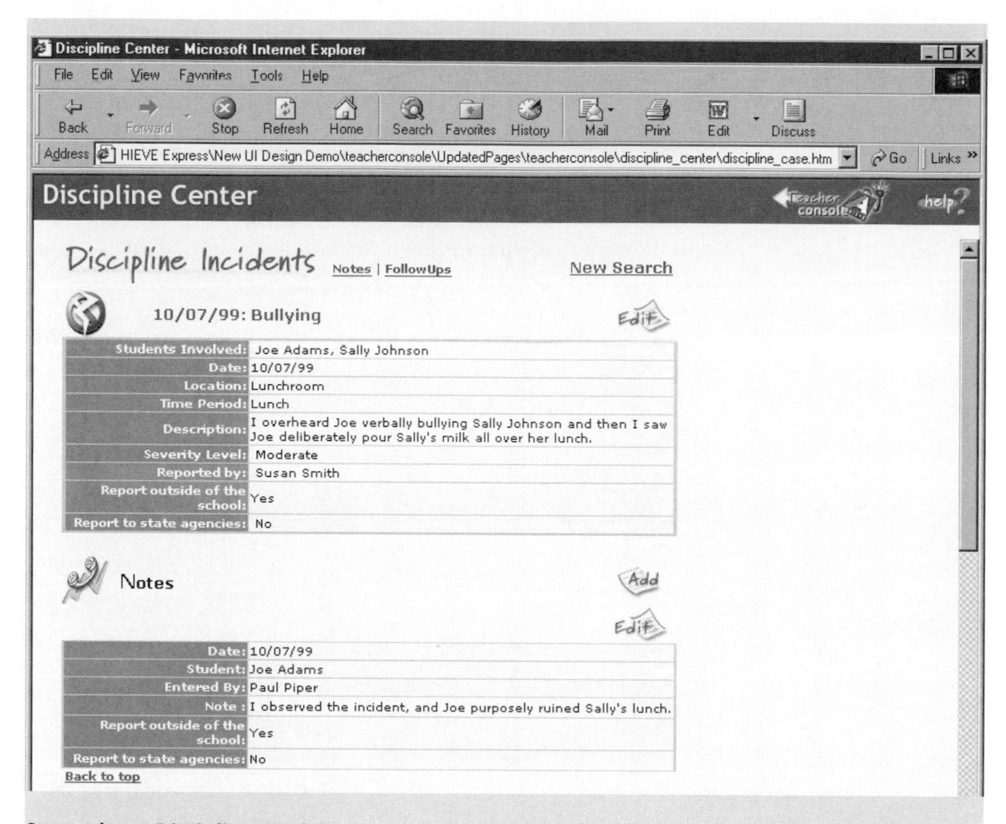

Screenshot—Discipline Module

Parent Contact: Records all parent contact details, improving the quality of time conversing with parents. Schools can log all phone conversations with each parent in order to track recent conversations. Enables schools to provide parents with timely information, alerting them to the academic and disciplinary needs of their student.

Student Information: Allows principals and teachers to find student information quickly, providing more time for strategizing about improving individual student performance. With this module, information known about a student, such as parent contact information, schedule, grades, and attendance history, is easily obtainable from a single place.

Staff Information: Provides quick access to information about staff members. All information about staff, backgrounds, degrees, and contact information can be easily consolidated.

Maintain Schedule: Enables easy access to students, teachers, and staff by storing schedule information. Administrators and staff can access scheduling information about special circumstances at school, such as assemblies and ongoing projects, and easily locate students, teachers, and staff in emergency situations. Teachers can easily identify meeting times with one another when creating interdisciplinary units.

Reports: Allows for increased accountability and constant monitoring. Parents can be easily informed about academic progress, future course objectives, and behavioral progress. Administrators can access school-wide statistics on items such as homework quality and test scores, and gather information on standards-based performance.

While each of the modules independently has important singular functionality, the real power of ACHIEVE is the ability to simultaneously pull all of the information together. Within seconds, a teacher or administrator can access vast amounts of student data to make timely and informed decisions for selecting approaches to teaching, addressing parent concerns, and creating solutions for student problems.

Student Information

Snapshot | Grades | Discipline | Attendance | Homework | General | Family | Emergency | Schedule | Transportation | Health

--Joe Adams--

Snapshot

Family Information | Emergency Contacts | Attendance | Discipline | Grades

Family Information

Contact Name:	Patty Adams
Relation:	Mother
Phone#:	(415) 625-0408(work); (415) 985-0111(home)
Best time to call:	After 6pm
E-mail address:	padams@yahoo.com

Contact Name:	Paul Smith
Relation:	Stepfather
Phone#:	(415) 555-3456(work)
E-mail address:	psmith@yahoo.com

Back to top

Emergency Contact

Contact Name:	Patty Adams
Relation:	Mother
Phone#:	(415) 625-0408(work); (415) 985-0111(home)
E-mail address:	padams@yahoo.com

Contact Name:	Jean Adams
Relation:	Grandmother
Phone#:	(415) 555-1234(home)
E-mail address:	
E-mail address:	

Back to top

Attendance

	Semester 1	Semester 2	Total
Absences:	4	2	6
Tardies:	4	1	5
Last 2 weeks:	10/08/99 10/09/99 10/10/99	History1 Literary Forms Science1	Tardy Absent Absent

Back to top

Discipline

	Semester 1	Semester 2	Total
Discipline Incidents:	1	1	2
Last 2 weeks:	10/07/99	Bullying	

Back to top

Grades

	Semester 1		Semester 2		Final	
Literary Forms	88	B	92	A	90	A
Science I	87	B	88	B	88	B
Algebra I	92	A	96	A	94	A
Art 3	80	B	84	B	82	B
History I	78	C	75	C	76	c

Back to top

Seagate Technology Buyout

In early November 1999, Stephen Luczo, president and chief executive officer of Seagate Technology, Inc. ("Seagate"), met with representatives of the private equity firm Silver Lake Partners L.P. to discuss a major restructuring proposal. Seagate was one of the world's largest manufacturers of computer disk drives and related data storage devices, with approximately $6.5 billion in annual revenues. The restructuring contemplated a leveraged buyout of Seagate's disk drive operations, followed by the tax-free acquisition of Seagate's remaining assets by VERITAS Software Corporation, an independent manufacturer of storage management software. Besides the disk drive operations, Seagate's main asset was a significant ($21 billion) stake in VERITAS's common stock.

Management and Silver Lake believed the two-step transaction could generate significant wealth gains for Seagate shareholders. The need to take some action had become increasingly apparent since late summer, when, following a major run up in VERITAS's stock price, the market value of Seagate's VERITAS stake had come to substantially exceed Seagate's *entire* market capitalization. Management attributed this "value gap" to two factors. First, the company would incur a significant tax liability if it attempted to monetize its VERITAS stake by selling the shares, and this liability was capitalized in Seagate's stock price. Second, the company's core disk drive operations were not receiving full value in the stock market, which currently favored Internet businesses and companies that manufactured cheaper data storage hardware. The proposed transaction was designed to allow Seagate shareholders to realize full value for the company, by distributing the VERITAS stock tax free, and by selling the disk drive operations at fair market value.

The transaction raised a number of thorny issues, however. First was the question of how much the investors should pay to acquire Seagate's disk drive operations. Since Seagate was a public company, Luczo and the other company directors had a fiduciary duty to obtain a fair price for their shareholders in the sale. However, Silver Lake and its co-investors had to earn a rate of return on their investment that would adequately compensate them for the risks they would incur, and Luczo and other key senior Seagate executives would continue to manage the disk drive business.[1]

A second issue was how the buyout should be financed, since this would directly determine the capital structure of the new Seagate. This was a pioneering transaction in the emerging area of technology buyouts, and traditional buyout financial structures might not be appropriate.

[1]As the only member of management on Seagate's board of directors, in order to avoid any conflicts of interest, Luczo was excluded from all board deliberations, and from the final vote that approved the transactions described in the case. The entire process was coordinated and supervised by the Co-Chairmen of Seagate's board, Gary Filler and Lawrence Perlman, neither of whom were members of management or investors in the buyout.

Professors Gregor Andrade, Stuart Gilson, and Todd Pulvino prepared this case. The case draws on research by George Taylor (HBS Class of 2000) as reported in his paper, "The Emergence of Technology Buyouts" and on discussions with Cindy Shaw of Salomon Smith Barney. HBS cases are developed solely as the basis for class discussion. Cases are not intended to serve as endorsements, sources of primary data, or illustrations of effective or ineffective management.

Copyright © 2001 President and Fellows of Harvard College. To order copies or request permission to reproduce materials, call 1-800-545-7685, write Harvard Business School Publishing, Boston, MA 02163, or go to http://www.hbsp.harvard.edu. No part of this publication may be reproduced, stored in a retrieval system, used in a spreadsheet, or transmitted in any form or by any means—electronic, mechanical, photocopying, recording, or otherwise—without the permission of Harvard Business School.

Third, the deal had to address the needs and a concerns of VERITAS, as an essential participant in the transaction. The terms of the second-stage merger therefore had to be attractive to VERITAS shareholders as well. Without their consent, the restructuring could not be done.

Finally, Seagate's board had considered several alternative options for addressing the company's low stock price. These included repurchasing Seagate stock and selling off part of the VERITAS stake, undertaking a tax-free spin-off of either the disk drive business or the entire VERITAS stake, and selling Seagate as a whole. The Silver Lake transaction had to be approved by both Seagate and VERITAS shareholders, so it was necessary to show that the transaction dominated these alternative restructuring options.

Negotiations among Silver Lake, Seagate, VERITAS, and their advisors continued through March 2000. The transaction was extremely complicated, and there was no guarantee that deal terms could be found that would be acceptable to all parties.

The Disk Drive Industry

Hard disk drives were the most common medium for storing electronic information and data, thus making them the largest sector of the information storage industry. Disk drives were integrated into various products, largely classified into three main markets:

- **Desktop:** The desktop market included all desktop personal computers, targeted for either home or business use. For the most part, performance attributes (speed, capacity, etc.) and quality were standardized across disk drive manufacturers. Furthermore, there was little disk drive brand awareness at the PC consumer level. As a result, disk drives had become commodities and manufacturers competed largely on price. Gross margins in the desktop sector were around 10–15%.
- **Enterprise:** The enterprise market included high performance workstations, servers, minicomputers, mainframes, and redundant arrays of inexpensive drive (RAID) subsystems. Because most applications and software that ran on enterprise systems were highly computation- and data-intensive (such as CAD/CAM, scientific applications, and corporate-wide accounting and payroll systems), manufacturers of these disk drive products emphasized performance and reliability, as well as price, as key selling points. The enterprise market was characterized by higher value-added products than those in the desktop market, with higher average gross margins of 20–25%.
- **Mobile:** The mobile market included laptop computers, hand-held computers, and personal digital assistants. Mobile disk drives differed from desktop drives in that they were smaller, and were made from more durable materials. Profit margins were higher than in the desktop segment, as products competed on not only price, but also durability and power consumption. In the long run, however, analysts expected the markets for mobile and desktop drives to converge.

Table A summarizes worldwide market shares for the major disk drive manufacturers.[2] Six firms accounted for 95% of all sales. Competition was intense, with manufacturers fighting for a limited number of major customers. These customers would normally do business with only two or three disk drive suppliers at a time. At the beginning of each new product cycle, which usually lasted from 6 to 12 months, customers would pre-select

[2]Seagate and most other major independent disk drive manufacturers competed with some of their own customers, including IBM, Fujitsu, and Samsung. These companies could either purchase disk drives from third parties or manufacture the drives in-house.

TABLE A
Market Share in the Worldwide Disk Drive Industry, 1999

Source: "Disk Drive Quarterly Report" (March 2000) by Salomon Smith Barney.

	Total Market[a]	Enterprise	Desktop
Number of units shipped			
Seagate	21.1%	41.0%	21.1%
Quantum	17.1	7.2	20.5
IBM	14.0	34.6	6.1
Maxtor	13.3	b	17.7
Fujitsu	12.3	8.8	12.4
Western Digital	11.1	3.8	14.6
Samsung	5.9	b	7.5
Total sales ($millions)	$25,273	$7,438	$14,627

[a]Includes mobile.
[b]Amount is not material.

their suppliers for that cycle, based on pre-announced performance and reliability requirements. Therefore, if a disk drive manufacturer did not have new products ready to submit to customers for testing at the time of pre-selection, they could miss up to a year's worth of sales and risk damaging key sales relationships.

In the late 1990s, the disk drive industry had benefited from increasing worldwide demand for electronic data storage, but had also experienced fierce price competition. Exhibit 1 shows that since 1997, while the number of disk drive units sold had grown at rates in the upper teens, prices had dropped dramatically, causing overall revenues to decline. Industry experts did not expect this situation to change. Through the medium-term at least, revenue growth was expected to lag far behind unit growth. As a result, disk drive manufacturers sought new avenues for growing revenues. Two areas in particular appeared promising:

Storage Networking

With the rapid expansion in Internet use and e-mail, as well as the increasingly data-intensive nature of audio and video-based applications, the amount of data stored was, for the foreseeable future, expected to double every year. As a result, there was increasing demand for larger and more efficient data access and storage solutions. Two new storage architectures appeared to be particularly promising in meeting this demand: Storage Area Networks (SAN) and Network Attached Storage (NAS). Both technologies combined arrays of disk drives with sophisticated networking equipment and software, providing disk drive manufacturers the means to differentiate their products.

Consumer Electronics Market

Newly developed consumer electronics appliances, requiring storage of large amounts of data, represented a rapidly expanding source of demand for desktop disk drives. Most applications were video-related, such as digital recorders (e.g., Tivo) and video games (e.g., Microsoft's Xbox). While small relative to the traditional disk drive market (analysts projected 2000 sales of $0.5 billion vs. more than $26 billion in the mainstream market), this segment was expected to grow over 50% annually over the next three years.

While these areas appeared promising, it was difficult to assess their likely impact on disk drive manufacturers' bottom lines. In consumer electronics, all major disk drive suppliers intended to compete vigorously. Therefore, it was possible that the business would experience the same fierce competition as the traditional disk drive business. As for storage networking, disk drive producers would be competing against large established manufacturers of hardware and software, such as IBM, Sun Microsystems, Dell, Compaq, and EMC.

Seagate Technology

Seagate was founded in 1979 by a group of five technology entrepreneurs and executives, whose collective experience included playing a key role in the early development of hard disk drives.[3] By 2000, Seagate was the leader in the worldwide disk drive industry, with total annual revenues of nearly $7 billion and a market share of 21%. The company designed, manufactured, and marketed a broad line of disk drives for use in computer systems for desktop PCs, workstations and servers, and supercomputers. For the fiscal year ending June 1999, 39% of Seagate's sales came from desktop drives and 51% came from enterprise systems. Tape drives and software contributed the remaining 10%.

Seagate sold its products both to original equipment manufacturers (OEMs) for use in their own computer systems, and through distributors, dealers, and retailers. Sales to OEMs accounted for 65% of Seagate's total disk drive revenues. Drives were produced almost entirely offshore, taking advantage of low-cost labor. In 1997, approximately 80% of Seagate's 111,000 employees were located in Asia.

Seagate was the only major independent disk drive manufacturer to be fully vertically integrated. In addition to assembling disk drives, Seagate designed and manufactured most of the key components.[4] Although this necessitated higher R&D and capital expenses than those incurred by its competitors (see Exhibits 2 and 3), management believed that vertical integration gave the company some important competitive advantages.

First, having control over critical enabling technologies—by developing them in-house—meant that Seagate would not have to depend on independent suppliers to develop those technologies. This eliminated the risk that in an economic downturn, these suppliers might cut back on R&D, reducing Seagate's ability to offer cutting-edge technologies in its products.

A second benefit of being vertically integrated was that it gave the company more control over the manufacturing process, allowing it to ramp up production more quickly in response to unexpected surges in demand. Such ramp-ups could also be achieved at a higher yield (fewer defects coming off the line). When Luczo became COO in 1997, Seagate required 12 weeks to ramp up production to 80% of increased target output, and it was recognizing $200 million every quarter in scrap (defective components or products that were either destroyed or sent back to manufacturing to be repaired). The ability to ramp up quickly was becoming increasingly important in the disk drive industry, given the sharp decline in product life cycles, and the increasing consolidation of the industry's customers.[5]

Finally, management believed that vertical integration allowed the company to maintain lower inventories of disk drive components, since it did not have to worry whether suppliers would be able to provide it with the components during a sudden increase in demand.

[3]The founders were Finis Conner, Syed Iftkar, Doug Mahon, Tom Mitchell, and Alan Shugart.

[4]The technical performance of a disk drive depended on numerous factors. Among the most important were the disk media (the material comprising the part of the drive that actually spins, and that affects how much information can be stored), the head (essentially the stylus that reads the information contained on the media), and the spindle (on which the disk spins).

[5]With fewer customers, represented by such large firms as Dell Computer and IBM, disk drive manufacturers could no longer afford to be late to market with a new product, or come out with an inferior product. In addition, shorter product cycles meant that drive manufacturers had little time to redesign their products to match better products made by the competition, since by the time the redesign was complete, the current generation of products would already be technologically obsolete.

Most financial analysts who covered the disk drive industry disagreed with Seagate's views on vertical integration, however. They argued that vertically integrated firms had substantially higher fixed costs, which would hurt them in a downturn. In apparent support of this view, in recent years technology firms like Hewlett-Packard, Cisco, and IBM had increasingly outsourced the manufacture of computer hardware to specialized contract equipment manufacturers, such as Solectron. In theory, these entities could achieve substantial economies of scale by serving the computer industry's combined manufacturing needs.

Historically, the financial performance of Seagate and the rest of the disk drive industry had been extremely volatile (Exhibit 2). During slowdowns in PC sales in the mid 1980s, early 1990s, and again in 1997–98, computer manufacturers severely cut back on disk drive purchases. Because of long manufacturing lead times, hard disk producers often ended up with excess capacity and inventory, resulting in price cuts and sharp profit declines.

Always known as an efficient, low-cost producer, Seagate fared better than most—it was the only independent disk drive manufacturer to remain profitable in 1992–93 and again in 1999. A key reason for the company's cost advantage was that, unlike most of its competitors, it maintained a mix of products in both high end *and* low end markets. The latter included, for example, hard disk drives for PCs. Although the company earned relatively low margins for these products, serving these less glamorous markets on a large scale produced significant scale economies that translated into lower costs for Seagate's other businesses as well.

In 1996 and early 1997, Seagate's business experienced a downturn with the rest of the industry, and it launched a broad restructuring effort.[6] Beginning in 1997, Seagate closed or sold selected manufacturing operations in Ireland, Scotland, Malaysia, Mexico, and the Philippines. It exited from the mobile disk drive segment, discontinued a number of product lines, and cut back expenditures on new production facilities. As a result of these initiatives, by late 1999 the company's employee headcount had declined by over 20%. An additional casualty was Seagate's co-founder and CEO, Alan Shugart, who was ousted by the board and replaced by Stephen Luczo in July 1998.

Luczo and his management team viewed the primary challenge facing Seagate as one of consolidating and expanding the firm's leadership position, not only in hard disk drives, but in general data storage applications.[7] This meant diversifying away from traditional disk drive segments into faster growing and higher margin businesses. The company had already begun supplying WebTV with disk drives, and other consumer electronics applications were being developed. In addition, Seagate began to target network-based storage applications. In January 2000, Seagate made its first major foray into storage networking with the acquisition of privately held XIOtech Corp, a provider of SAN technology.

Analysts also expected that Seagate would re-enter the mobile disk drive segment. Currently, there were no independent mobile drive suppliers in the market. However, most computer manufacturers liked to deal with at least two disk drive suppliers, and preferably none that were competitors in the consumer market. Industry analysts believed that a reputable independent supplier could quickly gain significant share in the

[6]Seagate's problems were exacerbated, or possibly even primarily caused, by an earlier decision in 1996 to focus on the development and manufacture of high performance, but expensive, dual processor drives. Soon after this decision had been taken, IBM introduced a competing single drive device that, while less sophisticated than Seagate's product, was much cheaper and sufficiently powerful to attract a significant number of customers from Seagate. Seagate management estimated that the company lost almost $1 billion in revenue to IBM as a result.

[7]*Financial Times,* May 3, 2000.

mobile segment. Because of the higher margins, and the technological proximity and customer overlap between the mobile and desktop drive segments, this would be a potentially attractive area for future growth in Seagate's business.

Seagate's future business expansion required it to make significant capital investments, however. When Luczo took over as CEO, he felt that the company had been seriously under-investing in technology, and correcting this would require large outlays on R&D and improvements in manufacturing capacity. The company estimated that expenditures on R&D and capital could be increased by no less than $1–$2 million, a year.

With disk drive producers already out of favor in the stock market, obtaining capital for long-term projects from public financial markets could prove to be difficult. By going private, Seagate might be able to aggressively pursue investments that had longer-term payoffs. Roger McNamee, a co-founder of Silver Lake Partners, said that once Seagate was taken private, it would "invest like crazy" in new product development and manufacturing facilities to support the growth of Seagate's core disk drive business.[8]

Background of the Buyout Transaction

In May 1999, Seagate Technology sold its Network & Storage Management Group (NSMG) to VERITAS Software. In exchange, Seagate received approximately 155 million shares of VERITAS stock, making it VERITAS's largest stockholder with an ownership stake over 40%.[9]

In the six months following the transaction, VERITAS's stock price increased by more than 200%. In contrast, over the same period, Seagate's stock price increased by 25%. Seagate's board was concerned that the market was not recognizing the full potential value of the company's VERITAS stake. At times, the value of Seagate's stake in VERITAS exceeded the entire market value of Seagate's equity. (See Exhibit 4 for a stock price history of Seagate and VERITAS, and Exhibit 5 for selected financial information about VERITAS.) The market appeared to be assigning no value—even a *negative* value—to Seagate's disk drive business, despite its large size and market-leading position.

Management realized it had to act quickly to address the situation. The company had been receiving numerous inquiries from concerned stockholders. And it was becoming more difficult to provide proper incentives to employees. Although Seagate's employees held significant amounts of stock options and restricted stock in the company, the increasing market value of the VERITAS stake meant that Seagate's stock price was becoming increasingly tied to VERITAS's stock price—and less to the performance of Seagate's core disk drive business.

As a result, senior management began to consider ways to increase the stock price and unlock the value that it saw in the VERITAS stake and disk drive operations. The company sold some VERITAS shares and repurchased its own shares in the open market. However, both actions proved ineffective. Seagate's ability to sell off its VERITAS stake was limited by prior agreement with VERITAS (which feared that such sales would depress its own stock price), and the fact that such sales were taxable. Repurchasing Seagate stock had little impact on the stock price.

In late October, the board of directors authorized Luczo to engage Morgan Stanley to advise the company on its options for increasing Seagate's stock price. A major consideration in any analysis of Seagate's options was the potentially huge tax liability that

[8]*Financial Times,* March 31, 2000.

[9]The number of shares reported in the case has been adjusted for stock splits and stock dividends.

would be created—at both the corporate and personal levels—if Seagate simply sold its VERITAS shares, or distributed those shares to Seagate shareholders.[10]

In early November, Morgan Stanley arranged a meeting between Luczo and representatives of Silver Lake Partners, a successful private equity firm that had extensive experience investing in technology businesses. After several months of discussion and analysis, the Silver Lake group, led by James Davidson, Glenn Hutchins, David Roux, and Integral Capital Partners, produced a proposal that would necessitate Seagate separating its disk drive operations from its VERITAS stake without triggering the punitive tax liability.

The proposal was a complicated two-stage transaction (see Exhibit 6). In the first stage, Seagate would sell all of its disk drive manufacturing assets, including approximately $765 million of cash, to a newly formed company ("Suez Acquisition Company") controlled by Silver Lake. The purchase price would be financed with a combination of equity (put up by Silver Lake and a group of other private equity investors[11]) and a significant but as yet undetermined amount of debt. Thus Silver Lake proposed to take Seagate's disk drive business private in a leveraged buyout (LBO).

In the second stage of the transaction, the remaining Seagate shell corporation, whose assets would then consist of 128,059,966 VERITAS shares, a few miscellaneous equity investments, and proceeds from the Seagate buyout, would be merged with VERITAS through a tax-free stock swap.[12] Under terms of the agreement, each share of Seagate stock would be exchanged for a combination of cash and VERITAS shares.[13] VERITAS executives indicated they would be interested in acquiring the Seagate shell corporation in exchange for 109,330,300 VERITAS shares. Provided the merger qualified as a "reorganization" under Section 368(a) of the Internal Revenue Code, no corporate or personal tax liability would be created by the deal.

Silver Lake had great confidence in the abilities of Seagate's current management team. On average, Seagate's top executives had over 10 years of experience in the disk drive industry. Therefore as an important condition of the deal, the six top managers, including Luczo and Charles Pope, Seagate's chief financial officer, had to continue in these roles, and convert a portion of their Seagate equity into new equity and deferred compensation of the company that would operate the disk drive business.

The Buyout Market

The term "buyout" refers to the purchase, typically by a group of private investors, of a controlling stake in a company's equity. The traditional buyout model involved a group of investors purchasing a company or a division of a larger company, employing a small amount of equity (the investor's own capital), and financing most of the purchase

[10]Because Seagate owned less than 80% of VERITAS's voting stock, a distribution of the 128 million VERITAS shares to Seagate shareholders would be treated like a sale of the shares. Therefore, Seagate would have to pay corporate income tax on the gain, i.e., the difference between the current value of those shares distributed and their tax basis. In addition, Seagate shareholders would have to pay ordinary income taxes on the VERITAS shares they received, as if they were a dividend. If instead Seagate sold the VERITAS shares, and distributed the cash to shareholders, the tax treatment would be the same (tax on the gain, shareholder taxes on the dividend).

[11]Silver Lake would be the controlling shareholder of Suez Acquisition Company. The remainder of the equity investment in the buyout entity would be made by Texas Pacific Group, August Capital, Chase Capital Partners, and Goldman Sachs.

[12]Transactions where some of a company's assets are sold and the remaining shell is merged with another company are sometimes referred to as "downstairs mergers."

[13]Seagate shareholders would be immediately taxed on the cash portion of the distribution. Taxes on the equity portion, i.e., the VERITAS shares, would be deferred until the VERITAS shares were sold.

price with debt backed by the company's assets. Because the resulting capital structures were often highly leveraged, these transactions were commonly called leveraged buyouts (LBOs). Investment returns from buyouts came from business efficiency improvements, improved management incentives, and increased interest tax shields (when the buyout is financed with debt). In addition, in some cases buyouts provided an opportunity to purchase undervalued assets at a favorable price.

Buyouts had their origin in the 1970s and grew to prominence in the 1980s. As buyout deals became larger, eventually it seemed like every company in America was a potential target. The $30 billion purchase of RJR Nabisco in April 1989, led by the private equity investment firm Kohlberg, Kravis, and Roberts, is the largest buyout in history. This transaction spawned the *New York Times* best selling book and movie *Barbarians at the Gate,* epitomizing the degree to which the buyout craze captured the fascination of not only Wall Street investment bankers, but also the American public.

The growth of the buyout market in the 1980s was fueled in large part by the increasing availability of high-yield bond financing.[14] High yield bonds allowed buyout specialists to borrow heavily against the assets of their target companies, and pursue ever-larger deals. Exhibit 7 displays common capital structures for LBOs over the last twenty years. By the late 1980s, when the frequency and size of LBO activity peaked, the average transaction had a debt-to-total capitalization ratio of 92%.[15]

In a typical LBO, financial leverage was highest right after the deal closed, and then declined over time as cash flows from asset sales and operations were used to pay down the debt. To support the high levels of debt, LBO firms typically targeted companies that operated in mature industries, generated stable and predictable cash flows, and had significant tangible assets that could be used as collateral.

Investors' fascination with LBOs faded in the early 1990s when some of the 1980s LBOs failed spectacularly, generating large losses for both debt and equity investors. Although LBOs resurfaced in the mid-1990s, they were much smaller, and generally exhibited more conservative capital structures than those of the 1980s.

Emergence of Technology Buyouts

In the 1980s and early 1990s, LBO firms tended to avoid technology businesses where the combination of rapid growth, short product cycles, and substantial demand uncertainty made cash flows extremely hard to predict. The lack of tangible assets in many technology businesses further reduced their attractiveness to LBO specialists. These attitudes began to change in the late 1990s, however. Many investors and industry insiders believed that certain segments of the technology sector had begun to exhibit the maturity and stability typical of traditional LBO candidates. In addition, based on then-current stock market valuation multiples, entire segments of the technology sector were trading at all time lows. And the high-yield debt market had significantly rebounded, making large amounts of financing available for new deals.

In the wake of these developments, there began to emerge a new class of private equity investors, who had expertise in both LBOs and technology businesses. Major private equity firms like Silver Lake Partners, Texas Pacific Group, and Hicks Muse Tate & Furst raised billions of dollars to invest in technology buyouts.

[14]High-yield bonds, also known as "junk bonds," are corporate bonds, which carry ratings below investment grade (i.e., BB or lower). They are considered highly speculative, with significant default risk. As a result, they pay much higher interest than investment grade bonds.

[15]In contrast, historically the average publicly traded corporation in the United States has held a 20% to 35% debt-to-total market capital ratio (Source: Ronald Masulis, 1988, "The Debt/Equity Choice," pages 8–9, Ballinger Publishing).

Against this backdrop, Silver Lake began to investigate the possibility of acquiring Seagate's disk drive operations. Due to Seagate's size, market capitalization, and industry-leading position, the proposed buyout had the potential to become a landmark transaction, similar in stature to the RJR Nabisco deal in 1989.

The characteristics of the disk drive business, which Luczo would describe as "the extreme sport of technology,"[16] did not make it an easy place to do LBOs, however. Price competition was intense, product life cycles were extremely short (often under six months), and the technological sophistication of disk drives required large expenditures on R&D. R&D was the lifeblood of the business, as being the first to introduce a new product or innovation generally made the difference between making or losing money. In addition, to win business, a disk drive manufacturer had to be able to produce an order to a customer's specifications quickly and on a large scale. This required significant investment in manufacturing capacity. Like the expenditures on R&D, this investment would use up scarce cash and make it more difficult to support a relatively high debt load, as found in traditional LBO structures.

In addition to all this, Seagate's disk drive business was highly vertically integrated, which also required significant investment in R&D and capital equipment. Thus Seagate appeared to be particularly unsuited for an LBO.

Seagate's disk drive business had a number of characteristics that might allow it to do well as an LBO, however. Management believed that being vertically integrated gave the company a strong competitive advantage, allowing it to respond more quickly to changes in technology and customer demands, and avoid costly supply chain disruptions. And high R&D and capital expenditures, while using up cash, could also give the company a competitive advantage, by deterring new entry by smaller, less well-capitalized competitors.

The Silver Lake team was also extremely optimistic about the disk drive industry's prospects. For the last two years the firm had come to the view that data storage was going to be the wave of the future in technology. Disk drives were the key technological component in a growing number of hardware products, including workstations and related technologies that managed and processed data. As Glenn Hutchins, one of Silver Lake's principals, would say: "If there's going to be an information superhighway, we're going to need plenty of parking lots."

Closing the Deal

Silver Lake's proposal offered a potentially attractive solution to Seagate's difficulties. However, the buyout group still had to determine how much to pay for the disk drive operations and how to finance the deal. As part of this process, the group intensively analyzed Seagate's historical financial performance and that of its competitors (Exhibits 2 and 3). In addition, it developed detailed financial projections for Seagate following the buyout and merger (Exhibit 8).[17]

Despite continued competitive pressure in its traditional disk drive segments, revenues and profits were expected to grow as Seagate re-entered the mobile disk drive segment and capitalized on its foray into SAN and NAS storage networking. Capital expenditures were projected to continue rising through 2003 as Seagate invested in

[16] *Financial Times,* May 3, 2000.

[17] The projections in Exhibit 8 are based on publicly disclosed projections of revenues, gross margins, and EBITA from Seagate SEC filings, and case writer estimates of depreciation and capital expenditures.

these new opportunities, but were projected to drop thereafter. Net noncash operating working capital used in the disk drive business had historically been about zero.[18]

These base case projections represented a "best guess" concerning performance, and thus summarized expectations for the future. However, to assess the sensitivity of the valuation to the underlying growth assumptions, both "upside" and "downside" projections were generated. Excerpts from the valuation performed by Seagate's financial advisor, Morgan Stanley, are shown in Exhibit 9.

Another decision that the buyout team had to make involved the capital structure of the new entity. In order to maximize the return on their equity investments, LBOs had traditionally employed large amounts of debt and maintained small cash balances. Given the volatility of disk drive profits, a prudent capital structure for this transaction would be more conservative (i.e., less leveraged) than that of traditional LBOs. The challenge was to weigh the possible benefits of higher debt against the potential costs. Seagate's access to future financing would probably be enhanced if it were able to maintain an investment grade rating of BBB or better throughout the projection period. Therefore, credit rating agencies' assessment of Seagate's debt post-buyout would no doubt be an important consideration in the buyout team's analysis.

Exhibit 10 contains information on long-term interest rates for different credit ratings, as of March 2000. Exhibit 11 reports median coverage and leverage ratios, by S&P debt rating, for a large sample of industrial issuers. However S&P explicitly points out "financial ratios are viewed in the context of a firm's business risk. A company . . . with more predictable cash flows can afford to undertake added financial risk while maintaining the same credit rating."[19] Conversely, companies with above average business risk and less predictable cash flows would need higher coverage and lower leverage than the figures reported in Exhibit 11 to attain a given rating.

A final consideration was that the buyout could not proceed unless VERITAS shareholders approved the second-stage merger. Therefore it would be necessary to offer them a sufficiently attractive return for acquiring the remaining assets of Seagate (mainly 128 million VERITAS shares) after the disk drive business had been sold.

[18]Net noncash operating working capital is defined as (Accounts Receivable + Inventories + Other Current Assets) – (Accounts Payable + Accrued Employee Compensation + Accrued Expenses).

[19]Source: *Standard & Poor's 2000 Ratings Criteria.*

EXHIBIT 1 Worldwide Hard Disk Drive Industry Historical Performance and Projections, 1991–2003E

Source: *Computer Industry Abstracts* (various issues) and "Disk Drive Quarterly Report" (June 1999) by Salomon Smith Barney.

	1991	1992	1993	1994	1995	1996	1997	1998	1999	2000E	2001E	2002E	2003E
Total Sales (000s of units)	33.1	38.4	51.8	69.0	90.0	106.8	129.3	143.6	165.9	187.8	212.5	238.1	268.2
Y/Y % Change		*16.0%*	*34.9%*	*33.2%*	*30.4%*	*18.7%*	*21.0%*	*11.1%*	*15.5%*	*13.2%*	*13.1%*	*12.1%*	*12.6%*
Total Revenues (millions of $)	$24,300	$26,200	$21,730	$22,966	$22,991	$27,596	$27,340	$25,483	$25,273	$26,640	$28,409	$30,450	$32,699
Y/Y % Change		*7.8%*	*–17.1%*	*5.7%*	*0.1%*	*20.0%*	*–0.9%*	*–6.8%*	*–0.8%*	*5.4%*	*6.6%*	*7.2%*	*7.4%*

EXHIBIT 2 Historical Operating Performance and Capitalization Ratios for Seagate Technology and U.S. Disk Drive Industry (1981 to 1999)

Source: Casewriters' estimates based on data compiled from Compustat.

	1981	1982	1983	1984	1985	1986	1987	1988	1989	1990	1991	1992	1993	1994	1995	1996	1997	1998	1999
Seagate																			
Sales	9.79	40.45	110.41	343.90	214.65	459.84	958.07	1,265.97	1,371.57	2,413.18	2,676.98	2,875.27	3,043.60	3,500.10	4,539.57	8,588.35	8,940.02	6,819.00	6,802.00
% Growth		*313.2%*	*173.0%*	*211.5%*	*–37.6%*	*114.2%*	*108.3%*	*32.1%*	*8.3%*	*75.9%*	*10.9%*	*7.4%*	*5.9%*	*15.0%*	*29.7%*	*89.2%*	*4.1%*	*–23.7%*	*–0.2%*
EBITDA	0.87	10.70	18.82	63.51	0.07	58.34	208.24	150.77	90.97	297.24	255.57	309.04	439.05	449.17	629.85	1,004.53	1,521.03	451.00	1,011.00
% Sales	*8.9%*	*26.5%*	*17.0%*	*18.5%*	*0.0%*	*12.7%*	*21.7%*	*11.9%*	*6.6%*	*12.3%*	*9.5%*	*10.7%*	*14.4%*	*12.8%*	*13.9%*	*11.7%*	*17.0%*	*6.6%*	*14.9%*
EBIT	0.65	9.89	16.16	55.72	–12.01	39.18	180.63	100.40	12.96	179.32	117.31	139.91	284.03	310.96	442.98	627.38	1,019.83	–138.00	398.00
% Sales	*6.6%*	*24.4%*	*14.6%*	*16.2%*	*–5.6%*	*8.5%*	*18.9%*	*7.9%*	*0.9%*	*7.4%*	*4.4%*	*4.9%*	*9.3%*	*8.9%*	*9.8%*	*7.3%*	*11.4%*	*–2.0%*	*5.9%*
Assets	9.47	43.47	157.25	214.72	275.23	305.08	814.12	1,093.95	1,076.77	1,851.46	1,880.06	1,816.60	2,031.19	2,877.53	3,361.26	5,239.64	6,722.88	5,645.00	7,072.00
Depreciation & Amortization	0.22	0.81	2.65	7.80	12.08	19.17	27.60	50.37	78.02	117.91	138.26	169.13	155.02	138.21	186.86	377.15	501.20	589.00	613.00
CAPX	2.45	5.04	38.83	42.66	31.22	38.68	78.40	284.41	78.09	102.38	90.87	90.66	173.57	197.68	353.43	906.94	890.46	709.00	603.00
Debt/Book Assets	19%	1%	5%	5%	13%	5%	37%	28%	29%	31%	23%	18%	14%	19%	16%	15%	10%	12%	10%
Debt/Mkt. Assets	NA	0%	1%	2%	9%	2%	14%	20%	24%	28%	27%	16%	14%	18%	12%	11%	6%	8%	8%
(Debt-Cash)/Book Assets	18%	–27%	–10%	–2%	11%	–10%	–11%	20%	11%	17%	9%	–10%	–17%	–27%	–21%	–7%	–24%	–20%	–13%
(Debt-Cash)/Market Assets	NA	–6%	–2%	–1%	7%	–5%	–4%	14%	9%	15%	11%	–9%	–17%	–26%	–15%	–5%	–13%	–13%	–10%
EBITDA Interest Coverage	10.12	57.84	47.05	73.51	0.04	20.26	41.01	6.88	3.77	6.10	6.01	9.09	18.67	17.05	19.11	17.99	43.66	8.84	20.25
EBIT Interest Coverage	7.56	53.46	40.40	64.49	–6.84	13.61	35.57	4.58	0.54	3.68	2.76	4.11	12.08	11.81	13.44	11.24	29.27	–2.71	8.29
Disk Drive Industry Medians																			
EBITDA as % of Sales	8.9%	6.2%	7.3%	0.7%	–4.4%	8.6%	7.8%	6.2%	7.3%	9.6%	8.6%	8.9%	3.9%	2.5%	4.7%	7.0%	9.3%	5.6%	6.1%
EBIT as % of Sales	5.4%	3.2%	3.4%	–3.5%	–10.3%	5.3%	4.5%	2.3%	5.3%	5.9%	4.3%	5.9%	–0.3%	–2.4%	1.9%	3.9%	7.5%	–1.4%	1.1%
Debt/Book Assets	19%	9%	5%	12%	19%	13%	16%	12%	13%	10%	13%	16%	19%	12%	10%	13%	6%	14%	9%
Debt/Mkt. Assets	7%	4%	1%	5%	7%	5%	7%	8%	8%	9%	8%	16%	13%	7%	3%	4%	1%	7%	4%
(Debt-Cash)/Book Assets	9%	–5%	–12%	–6%	–5%	–7%	–11%	0%	–5%	–7%	2%	–1%	–9%	–4%	–8%	–5%	–21%	–9%	–23%
(Debt-Cash)/Mkt Assets	0%	–2%	–6%	–2%	–3%	–4%	–4%	–3%	–2%	–4%	–1%	–3%	–3%	–2%	–3%	–5%	–8%	–5%	–5%
EBITDA Interest Coverage	3.31	3.46	4.12	–1.58	–3.19	6.20	6.37	8.15	5.74	6.03	4.06	9.00	4.38	5.58	3.59	7.06	13.00	4.20	–0.09
EBIT Interest Coverage	2.19	1.42	2.34	–3.37	–7.57	2.25	1.94	4.58	2.71	3.30	1.55	4.31	–0.05	0.37	1.84	5.04	8.52	–2.04	–2.91

EXHIBIT 3 Summary Financial Data on Publicly Traded Hard Disk Drive Manufacturers

Source: Data compiled from Compustat and SEC Filings.

	Seagate Technology			Quantum HDD[a]			Western Digital			Maxtor		
	Jun97	Jun98	Jun99	Mar97	Mar98	Mar99	Jun97	Jun98	Jun99	Dec96	Dec97	Dec98
Income Statement ($ million)												
Sales	$8,940	$6,819	$6,802	$4,591	$4,615	$3,599	$4,178	$3,542	$2,767	$799	$1,424	$2,409
Cost of Goods Sold	6,918	5,830	5,250	4,093	4,242	3,308	3,464	3,187	2,562	842	1,287	2,034
Gross Margin	2,022	989	1,552	498	373	291	714	355	205	–43	137	375
EBITDA	1,521	451	1,011	146	–6	–61	365	–41	–188	–191	–32	134
Depreciation + Amortization	501	589	613	109	68	71	63	107	131	47	66	74
Operating Profit	1,020	–138	398	37	–74	–133	302	–148	–319	–238	–97	60
Interest Expense	35	51	48	20	11	9	0	12	33	18	37	29
Net Income	658	–530	1,176	41	–53	–153	268	–290	–493	–256	–110	31
Capital Expenditures	890	709	603	164	119	82	156	199	107	54	82	95
Balance Sheet ($ million)												
Cash and Equivalents	$2,284	$1,827	$1,623	NA	$325	$524	$208	$460	$226	$31	$33	$258
Net Receivables	1,041	799	872	NA	586	392	546	369	273	89	248	318
Inventories	808	508	451	NA	212	148	224	187	144	81	155	153
Net Property, Plant, and Equipment	1,787	1,669	1,687	NA	228	199	248	347	238	92	99	108
TOTAL ASSETS	6,723	5,645	7,072	NA	1,646	1,470	1,307	1,443	1,022	315	555	863
Accounts Payable	883	577	714	NA	401	342	418	330	336	110	207	428
Short-term Debt	1	1	1	NA	0	0	0	0	10	204	245	5
Long-term Debt	702	704	703	NA	109	115	0	519	534	229	224	145
Shareholders' Equity	3,476	2,937	3,563	NA	906	791	620	318	–154	–327	–221	169
Net Working Capital[b]	2,717	2,241	1,773	NA	739	709	364	464	72	93	440	170
Capital Market Information ($ million)												
Year-end Market Equity Capitalization	$5,861	$5,844	$8,620	NA	NA	NA	$2,716	$1,043	$589	NA	NA	$1,320
Equity Betas[c]			1.2			0.8			0.6			1.0
Total Book Debt (3/10/00)			704			110			236			114
Debt Rating			BBB			B2			B2			B1
Stock Price (3/10/00)—$/share			64.25			8.875			5.1875			11.625
Shares Outstanding (3/10/00)—millions			227.2			82.6			129.1			113.2

[a]Quantum HDD was floated in August 1999 as a separately traded subsidiary of Quantum Corporation, containing just the hard disk drive operations. As a result, there is no information on historical stock prices or market capitalization, prior to that date.

[b]Net Working Capital = Total Current Assets – Total Current Liabilities (excluding Short-term Debt).

[c]Equity betas estimated using daily returns over the six-month period from 9/1/99 to 3/1/00.

EXHIBIT 4
Stock Market Valuation of Seagate and VERITAS Stake

Source: Casewriters' estimates based on stock prices compiled from Yahoo.

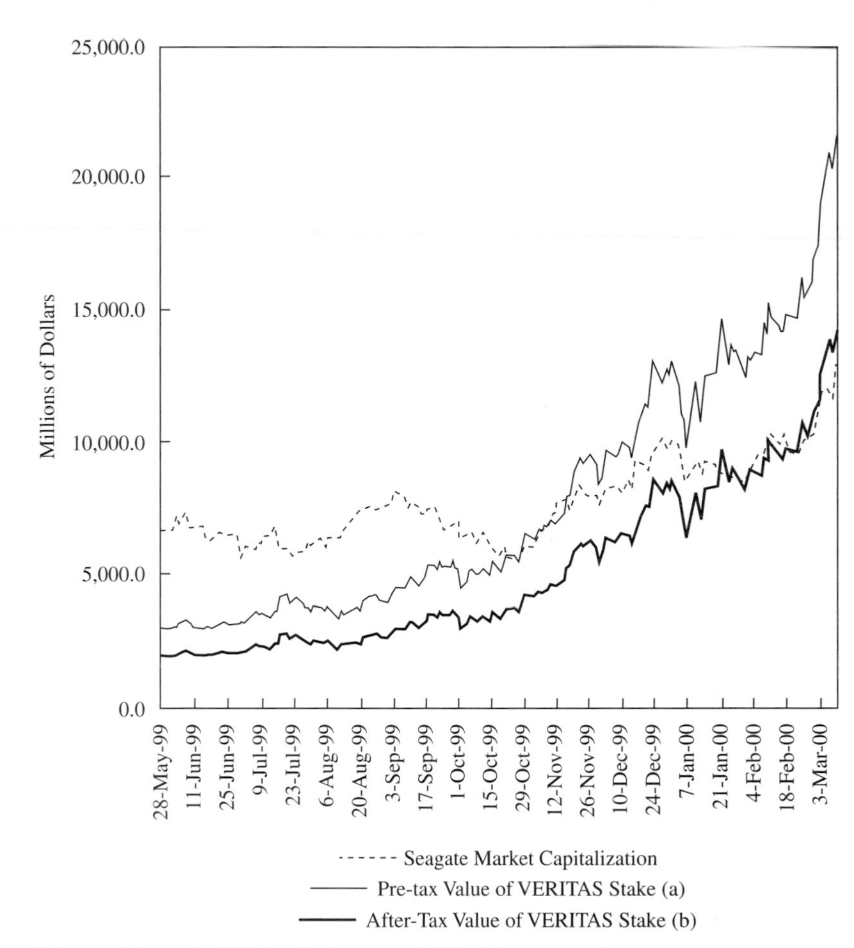

[a](Number of shares of VERITAS held by Seagate) × (VERITAS closing stock price).

[b]Assumes Seagate sells its entire VERITAS stake at the pretax value, and pays a 34% corporate tax on the full proceeds. Ignores any personal taxes paid by Seagate shareholders on any proceeds distributed by Seagate.

EXHIBIT 5
Summary Financial Data on VERITAS Software

Source: Compustat and SEC Filings.

	VERITAS Software		
	Dec96	**Dec97**	**Dec98**
Balance Sheet ($ Million)			
Cash and Equivalents	$67.6	$151.3	$278.2
Net Receivables	16.0	30.3	52.7
Inventories	NA	NA	NA
Net Property, Plant, and Equipment	7.0	10.1	26.5
TOTAL ASSETS	94.5	241.9	349.1
Accounts Payable	1.8	1.6	5.0
Short-term Debt	0.1	0.0	0.0
Long-term Debt	0.5	100.0	100.0
Shareholders' Equity	75.0	104.2	169.9
Stock Market Information			
Total Book Debt (3/10/00)—$ Millions			451
Equity Beta[a]			1.81
Stock Price (3/10/00)—$/Share			168.69
Shares Outstanding (3/10/00)—Millions			393.6

[a]Equity beta estimated using daily returns over the six-month period from 9/1/99 to 3/1/00.

EXHIBIT 6
Key Features of Proposed Transaction between Seagate Technology and VERITAS

Source: VERITAS and Seagate Joint Proxy Statement/Prospectus dated October 23, 2000, and casewriter adjustments.

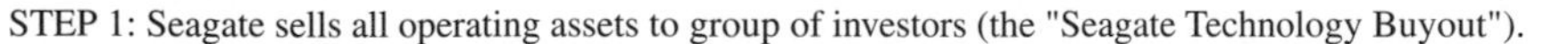
STEP 1: Seagate sells all operating assets to group of investors (the "Seagate Technology Buyout").

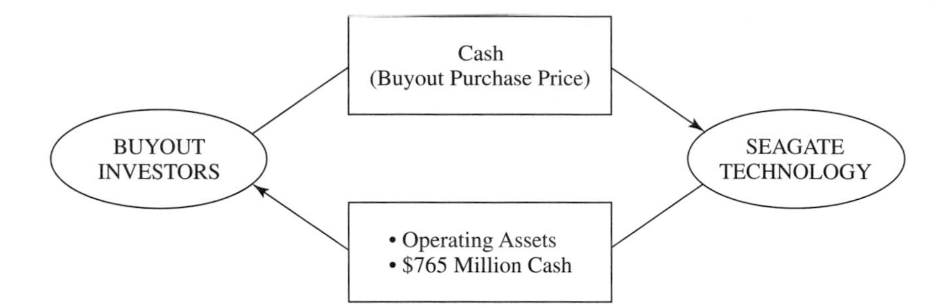

STEP 2: Seagate exchanges existing equity stake in VERITAS for new VERITAS shares. The remaining Seagate assets are distributed to shareholders.

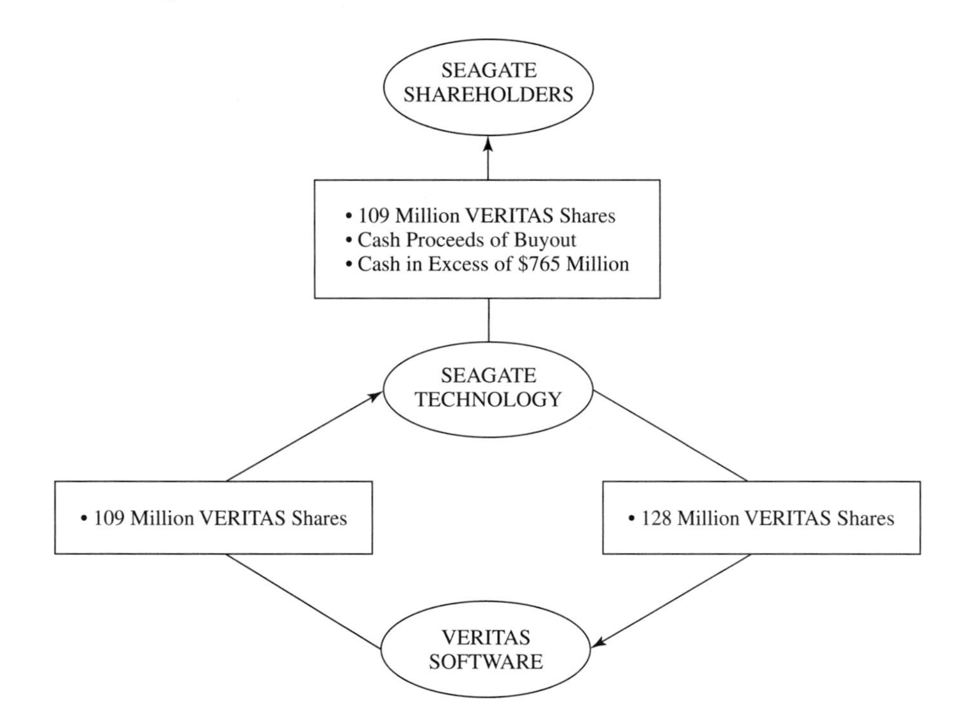

EXHIBIT 7 Capitalization Structure for LBO Transactions (1980–1999)

Source: Reproduced from "The Emergence of Technology Buyouts," an HBS student project by George Taylor. Original data from Chase Securities, Inc. and Thomas H. Lee Company Research.

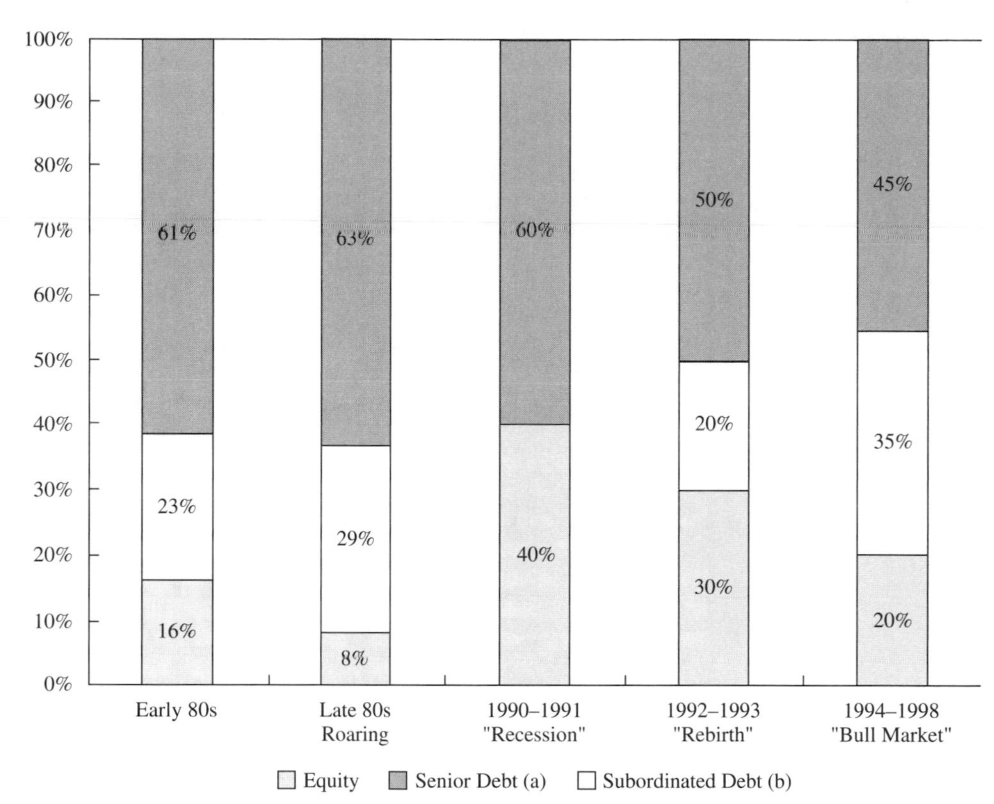

(a)Senior debt is defined as all debt instruments, which have first priority in a liquidation or bankruptcy.
(b)Subordinated debt is defined as all debt instruments that have lower priority than senior debt in liquidation.

EXHIBIT 8 Projeced Operating Performance of Seagate Disk Drive Business

Source: Casewriters' estimates based on revenues and EBITA projections contained in SEC filings.

	Year Ending June 30,						
	2000	2001	2002	2003	2004	2005	2006
Base Case ($ million)							
Revenues	$6,619	$7,417	$8,564	$9,504	$10,416	$11,359	$12,350
Gross Margin	1,264	1,409	1,696	2,043	2,312	2,624	3,026
EBITA	141	189	316	449	499	614	724
Depreciation	625	626	642	666	708	726	729
Capital Expenditures	627	690	720	795	700	725	750
Upside Case ($ million)							
Revenues	$6,619	$8,185	$10,146	$11,283	$12,626	$13,961	$15,404
EBITA	141	365	689	783	867	1,000	1,167
Downside Case ($ million)[a]							
Revenues	$6,619	$7,393	$7,797	$8,310	$8,801	$9,269	$9,759
EBITA	141	189	322	363	378	403	407

[a]The "downside case" is based on the "buyer case" described in the first VERITAS and Seagate Joint Proxy Statement/Prospectus filed with the SEC in May 2000.

EXHIBIT 9
Morgan Stanley Fairness Opinion

Source: Seagate Technology, Inc., SEC Filings. Form 13E3, filed on May 19, 2000.

Under an engagement letter dated February 10, 2000, Seagate retained Morgan Stanley to provide it with financial advisory services in connection with a possible strategic business combination, restructuring or other transaction.

In connection with rendering its opinions, Morgan Stanley, among other things:

—reviewed certain publicly available financial statements and other information concerning Seagate;
—reviewed certain internal financial statements and other financial and operating data concerning Seagate prepared by the management of Seagate;
—reviewed certain financial projections prepared by the management of Seagate;
—discussed with senior executives of Seagate the past and current operations and financial condition and the prospects of Seagate.

Morgan Stanley also reviewed for illustrative purposes estimated ranges of values for Seagate's operation businesses derived using various methodologies, including a comparable companies analysis, (. . .) a discounted cash flow analysis, and a hypothetical "sum-of-the-parts" analysis of Seagate's disc drives, tapes, information management, and storage area network segments.

As part of this review, Morgan Stanley analyzed the two cases developed by Seagate management, as well as a third case developed by Morgan Stanley as a sensitivity case, which reflected Seagate management's base case but assumed that gross margins for the desktop segment of Seagate's disk drive business remained constant for years 2000 through 2008. For each of these analyses, Morgan Stanley calculated an implied value for Seagate's operation assets (. . .). The discounted cash flow analysis (was) based upon multiples of calendar year 2006 EBITA ranging from 6.0x to 9.0x and a discount rate of 15%.

EXHIBIT 10 Market Interest Rates (March 2000)

Source: Standard & Poor's Datastream.

Corporate Long-Term Bonds						Government Securities		
AAA	AA	A	BBB	BB	B	3 Month	6 Month	30 Year
7.01%	7.14%	7.31%	7.72%	9.18%	10.44%	5.88%	6.15%	5.84%

EXHIBIT 11 S&P Key Industrial Financial Ratios by Long-Term Debt Rating

Source: Standard & Poor's Credit Week, September 2000.

	Three-Year Medians—1997 to 1999						
	AAA	AA	A	BBB	BB	B	CCC
EBIT Interest Coverage	17.5x	10.8x	6.8x	3.9x	2.3x	1.0x	0.2x
Total Debt as % of Market Cap.[a]	3.7%	9.2%	16.4%	30.4%	47.5%	59.3%	74.3%

[a]Defined as the ratio of Total Debt (long term and short term) to Total Market Capitalization (the sum of total debt, minority interest, preferred equity, and year-end market value of equity).

Friendly Cards, Inc.

In early 1988, Wendy Beaumont, president of Friendly Cards, Inc., met with Amy McConville, a friend and financial consultant. They had been discussing the future of Friendly in relation to the research Ms. McConville had been doing on the firm. (Exhibits 1 and 2 show the company's income statements, balance sheets, and financial projections.) Mrs. Beaumont commented:

> Money is tight and, quite frankly, the cost of financing growth is now so high that I wish we could sit still for a year. But we really can't do that. You know the record and you saw our growth for last year. We're projecting a 20% increase in sales and an even larger increase in earnings for next year. I hope you can come up with some suggestions concerning the financing of our expansion, so we can talk about them on Friday morning.

Industry Background Data

In 1988 the greeting card industry consisted of over 100 companies; the "Big Three" (see Exhibit 3) dominated the scene with an overwhelming market share. Of these three, two were publicly owned (American Greetings and Gibson), and one was private (Hallmark). (See Exhibit 5 for financial data on American Greetings and Gibson.)

The rest of the industry was made up predominantly of small firms, many of which were privately owned and family controlled. Growth, however, was most prominent in the larger firms, which had larger, more diversified product lines and more efficient national distribution channels. Smaller companies were often crippled by the expense of setting up a large sales system, of producing a full line and constantly reviewing it, and of designing and preparing new cards. As a result, the total number of firms in the industry had declined by about 15% each decade since 1954. Most of this decline occurred among companies of less than 50 employees.

In order to compete successfully, all firms had to deal effectively with high fixed costs. Companies ran large inventory costs because of the necessity of keeping stock for reorders. Production was costly and long lead times prevented rerunning successful designs. In addition, many retailers could return unsold or soiled cards to the manufacturer for full refund or credit.

Because of these high fixed costs and the overall competitiveness of the industry, distribution costs were very important to overall firm profitability. The large companies used their own sales forces to sell directly to various outlets. Often companies would try to increase sales by expanding the distribution network. Sales trends within the industry were often characterized (especially in the case of smaller companies) by seasonal peaks, as most of the actual sales occurred in a short period of time even though cards were in production all year. As an example, 32% of industry dollar sales occurred at Christmas, with Valentine's Day (7% of sales), Mother's Day (5%), and Father's Day (2%) being other examples in which the selling season was short but the revenues were large. Within the industry, companies were placing an increasing emphasis on a larger variety of cards and on the rapid replacement of slow sellers to encourage more impulse buying of everyday cards. This had been successful to the extent that in 1969, 40% of card volume was represented by everyday sales, and in 1987, this figure was above 50%.

Copyright © 1993 by the President and Fellows of Harvard College. Harvard Business School case 293–135.

Within the industry, trends included a conscious move away from sole reliance on greeting card sales. Hallmark, for example, also marketed glassware, jewelry, candles, silverware, and giftbooks; American Greetings diversified into gift wrap and stationery goods, such as playing cards, giftbooks, and college study guides.

Friendly Cards, Inc.

In 1978, Wendy Beaumont founded Beaumont Greeting Card Company in New York City with $15,000. Shortly thereafter, she acquired the bankrupt Lithograph Publishing Company of Reading, Connecticut and moved all operations to the new plant. A year later, the renamed firm, Friendly Cards, Inc., went public through a stock offering at $3 per share.

In the years that followed, Friendly expanded rapidly through internal growth and acquisitions. Glitter Greetings of Lansing, Michigan, a firm that primarily sold cards to supermarkets, became a wholly owned subsidiary in a deal involving both cash and stock. In 1986, Friendly acquired Edwards & Company (Long Beach, New York) for cash. Edwards was a small company that sold juvenile valentines through a distribution system that included chain, drug, variety, and discount stores as well as wholesalers, rack jobbers, and supermarkets. Still another market was opened with the acquisition of a California firm, again by means of cash and stock. The California firm was renamed Friendly Artists and provided the company with distribution on the West Coast as well as an operation specializing in direct sales of packaged personalized Christmas cards to the retailer.

Friendly Cards' Operations

Unlike most small companies, Friendly manufactured a full line of greeting cards, with 1,200 designs in its 1988 line. Approximately 30% of dollar sales were accounted for by Christmas sales and 25% by valentines, with the remainder made up of everyday and spring holiday cards. Twenty-five percent of total sales were of packaged boxes of cards, which were either "title" cards (i.e., Brother's Birthday) or assortments. The sale of packaged boxes helped to cut costs because the manufacturer did not have to supervise racks and take reorders of individual cards in every outlet. Returns expense was also low because once the package was sold to a store, it was generally not returnable. In addition, the giants of the industry were not as active in packaged sales, concentrating more heavily on the sale of individual cards.

None of Friendly's designs were higher fashion studio cards. Friendly sold primarily to the over-40-year-old market. Ms. Beaumont characterized a large part of her market as cost conscious. She felt that most of the purchasers of her cards would not spend the time or the money to select *the* perfect card for each occasion but would prefer to have the less expensive, more convenient packages at home whenever a card was needed.

The designing, printing, and packaging of all cards and giftwrap were done at the 250-employee plant in Reading. The plant was operating at capacity, but much of the printing work could be done by outside printers if necessary.

Friendly Cards' Distribution Method

Distribution itself was not a large expense at Friendly. The 25-person company sales force (one-third of which worked on a full-commission basis) sold either directly to the central buyers for such stores as Kmart Corp., Wal-Mart, and Bradlees or to rack jobbers and wholesalers. This system, however, was a prime factor in the low margins earned by

Friendly, for there were often two intermediaries between the manufacturer and the ultimate customer. As a reflection of this, Ms. Beaumont estimated that dollar sales of her cards at the retail level were three times the sales figures shown in her income statement.

Operations at Friendly were closely supervised. Management included three production and shipping managers, one art director, and a sales manager and an assistant to the president. Besides Ms. Beaumont, there were nine officers, six of whom were also directors.

Financial Problems

According to Ms. Beaumont, Friendly had never been without financing problems. The business was capital intensive, and Ms. Beaumont attributed much of her success to the company's good relations with its banks and suppliers. Its line of credit with nearby banks totaled $6.25 million. The company borrowed at 2½% above the prime rate, with the current prime rate being 8.5%. Because of the seasonal nature of the industry, Ms. Beaumont estimated that the company's peak needs for bank and trade credit (which amounted to over $9.0 million at the end of 1987) occurred in December and January. She also stated that the company's low-borrowing point following each selling season occurred in April, at which point bank and trade credit was reduced to about 50% of peak needs.

Although the company had a good relationship with its banks, Ms. Beaumont had been urged to seek additional equity capital. Friendly's bankers felt uneasy about the extent to which the company was depending on debt capital to finance its operations. Early in 1988, they suggested that their willingness to finance the company through an enormous sales expansion in 1986 was based on an expectation that sales growth would thereafter slow substantially. Under these expected circumstances, growth in the equity account through earnings retentions would have rapidly reduced the firm's liabilities/equity ratio to the 1985 level, a point substantially below the lofty 5.2 to 1 reached in 1986 (Exhibit 2). Given the firm's performance in 1987 and Ms. Beaumont's sales projections (Exhibits 1 and 2), however, a return to the 1985 level in Friendly's liabilities/equity ratio was at best still several years away. Friendly's bankers, therefore, insisted that the firm take some action before its peak borrowing season to make sure that the company would stay safely within two restrictions that the bankers planned to impose on future loans to Friendly. These two restrictions, which would apply at the end of 1988, were as follows:

1. The bank loans outstanding at any time could not exceed 85% of Friendly's accounts receivable.
2. Friendly's total liabilities could not exceed three times the book value of the company's net worth.

For planning purposes, Ms. Beaumont had decided to retain some margin of safety by holding Friendly's ratio of all interest-bearing debt/equity to a maximum of 2 to 1.

Decisions Confronting Friendly Cards

Ms. McConville was familiar with the background information on the greeting card industry and on Friendly Cards. Ms. Beaumont had also referred three other questions to Ms. McConville:

1. Should Friendly invest in equipment to enable the company to make rather than to buy its envelopes?

2. Should Friendly Cards acquire Creative Designs, Inc., a small midwestern manufacturer of studio cards?
3. Should Friendly go to the market to raise additional equity capital in order to relieve the pressure on its financial position?

Envelope Machine Proposal

The cost of envelopes was one of the largest components of total costs. Friendly was still purchasing its entire supply of envelopes. During 1987, it had spent $1.5 million to purchase the 100 million envelopes used by the company that year. Ms. Beaumont estimated that she could buy equipment for $500,000 that, when operated at full capacity, would enable her to manufacture all the envelopes she had used in 1987. She estimated that the envelope-making equipment would have an economic life of about 8 years.

Ms. Beaumont estimated that the people required to run the envelope-making operation would have an annual cost of $91,000. These and other expenses are shown in Exhibit 4. From these data, Ms. McConville calculated that the envelope machine project would generate a positive cash flow annually for an 8-year period, disregarding working capital and financing requirements.

The additional warehouse space included in Exhibit 4 would be needed because, if the machine was purchased, the company would be producing envelopes at a level rate substantially in excess of shipments during the spring and summer months so as to build the large inventories needed to meet year-end shipping schedules. If she started manufacturing her own envelopes, Ms. Beaumont anticipated that her average net working capital requirement would immediately increase by $200,000 and remain at that level during the life of the machine.

Possible Acquisition of Creative Designs, Inc.

Ms. Beaumont had also been investigating a possible acquisition candidate, Creative Designs, Inc. (CD), a small midwestern manufacturer of studio cards. Creative Designs was privately owned and had sales of about $5 million in 1987 (Exhibit 6). Ms. Beaumont had spent considerable time over a four-month period examining the details of CD's operations. She had become convinced that under her management, CD could almost immediately reduce its cost of goods sold by 5%, or $154,000 at current sales levels. She also anticipated that by eliminating duplication, she could reduce CD's other expenses by 10% (or $155,000). She estimated that if Friendly acquired CD in early 1988, CD's sales would remain flat during the year of ownership change, but beyond 1988, the company would achieve sales increases of about 6% per year. What particularly interested Ms. Beaumont about the potential acquisition was the strength of CD's balance sheet (Exhibit 7). She felt CD's suppliers would be willing to go a good deal further in providing trade credit than they had in the past, and she knew that the company had unused bank credit lines. In her discussion with the three present owners of CD, all of whom were approaching retirement age, Ms. Beaumont concluded that the company could be acquired for 11 times its 1987 earnings. The principals were willing to take Friendly common stock valued at $9.50 a share, which would give them a total of 198,000 shares. A check with her public accounting firm convinced Ms. Beaumont that the exchange of securities would be a tax-free exchange. The acquisition would be treated as a "pooling of interests" for accounting purposes, so that the balance sheet for the resulting firm would simply be the sum of the two companies' statements.

Ms. Beaumont had asked Ms. McConville for a recommendation as to whether she should acquire Creative Designs on these terms. Ms. McConville knew that she would have to consider the impact of the acquisition on the earnings position of Friendly, and also the implications of the acquisition for Friendly's financial position.

Possible Sale of New Common Stock

In order to sustain the projected rapid growth for the next several years and in view of Friendly's extremely tight financial position (Exhibits 1 and 2), Ms. Beaumont was aware that she might have to raise additional equity capital. Ms. McConville knew that Ms. Beaumont would be most reluctant to accept a policy recommendation that would force her to curtail the growth in sales projected in Exhibit 1. As already indicated, Ms. Beaumont believed that if potential increases in orders from new or existing customers were turned down, it would be very difficult and perhaps impossible to retain these customers in subsequent years. Ms. Beaumont was also concerned that restrictions on the acceptance of new orders would be demoralizing to the company's sales force and perhaps would cause some of the most valuable sales representatives to shift to a competing firm.

Ms. McConville was also troubled by the fact that this was a most difficult and expensive time for any company to raise new equity capital, especially for a small company like Friendly with unseasoned securities.

Friendly Cards' stock was traded in the over-the-counter market. Volume was light, averaging about 3,000 shares a week. Due to extremely light trading volume in the stock of Friendly Cards, Inc., it was difficult to compute a β value for the stock of this company directly from stock price data. During the past two months, the stock price had held at about $9.50. During 1986 and 1987, the price of the stock had ranged from a low of $9.50 to a high of $15 per share. Ms. Beaumont owned about 55% of the stock currently outstanding. Another 20% was owned by employees and officers of the company. About 25% of the outstanding stock was owned by the public.

Ms. McConville knew that Ms. Beaumont had recently received an offer from a group of West Coat investors who had a long-term interest in the company. They had offered to buy 200,000 shares of Friendly's common stock at $8 per share. If this offer was accepted, Friendly would have to pay a finder's fee of $80,000, or 10,000 shares, to the individual who had brought this offer to Ms. Beaumont's attention.

In considering this offer, Ms. McConville approached Samuel Hexter, a friend of hers and a partner in the Boston office of the investment banking firm of Stoddard, White & Driscoll, to inquire about the feasibility of a public offering of Friendly stock. Mr. Hexter was not encouraging. He commented:

> Now is a tough time to raise equity money, especially for a small company like Friendly. The October stock market crash was a killer. The Dow Jones index of industrial stocks has fallen from 2596 in September 1987 to under 2000 right now, and there's no telling what will happen tomorrow. This is a bad time for a small company to raise money. I hate to say so, but I don't see how we could possibly take Friendly's stock to the market at more than $8 a share. Frankly, I am uncertain how many shares we could sell even at a price as low as $8.

This conversation confirmed Ms. McConville's initial impression that the only realistic prospect for raising new capital was to accept the offer of the West Coast group.

EXHIBIT 1 Consolidated Income Statements, 1985–1987, and Projected Income Statements, 1988–1990[a] (years ending December 31; in thousands of dollars except per share data)

Source: Annual reports and management projections.

	Actual Data			Projected Data			
	1985	1986	1987	1988	1989	1990	
Net sales	$8,055	$12,765[b]	$16,253	$19,500	$23,250	$28,000	
Cost of goods sold	5,690	8,785	10,540	12,675	15,112	18,200	(65% of proj. sales)
Gross profit on sales	$2,365	$ 3,980	$ 5,713	$ 6,825	$ 8,138	$ 9,800	(35% of proj. sales)
Expenses							
Selling, delivery, and warehousing	$1,015	$ 1,793	$ 2,373	$ 2,828	$ 3,371	$ 4,060	(14.5% of proj. sales)
General and administrative	547	945	1,125	1,365	1,628	1,960	(7.0% of proj. sales)
Total expenses	$1,562	$ 2,738	$ 3,498	$ 4,193	$ 4,999	$ 6,020	
Earnings before interest and taxes	803	1,243	2,215	2,633	3,139	3,780	
Interest	495	605	950	1,075[d]	1,188[d]	1,320[d]	
Income before federal income taxes	$ 308	$ 638	$ 1,265	$ 1,558	$ 1,951	$ 2,460	
Provision for federal income taxes	113	225	481	592	742	935	(38% of proj. PBT)
Net income	$ 195	$ 413	$ 784	$ 966	$ 1,209	$ 1,525	
Shares outstanding (000)	534	550	580	580	580	580	
Earnings per share (in dollars)	.37	.75[c]	1.35	1.67	2.08	2.63	

[a]Net sales and net income for 1982–1984 were as follows:

	Net Sales (millions)	Net Income (thousands)
1982	$5.5	$ 53
1983	6.3	105
1984	7.0	148

[b]$1.5 million of 1986 sales were from the Edwards acquisition.

[c]0.16 was from the Edwards acquisition.

[d]Additional financing required beyond 1987 is assumed to carry an interest cost equal to the prime rate of 8½% plus 2½%.

EXHIBIT 2 **Consolidated Balance Sheets, 1985–1987, and Projected Balance Sheets, 1988–1990 (years ending December 31; thousands of dollars)**

	Actual Data			Projected Data			
	1985	1986	1987	1988	1989	1990	
Assets							
Cash	$ 200	$ 370	$ 240	$ 250	$ 250	$ 250	
Notes and accounts receivable	2,920	5,883	7,013	8,385	9,998	12,040	(43% of proj. sales)
Inventory	2,500	3,708	5,588	6,630	7,905	9,520	(34% of proj. sales)
Prepaid expenses	43	117	192	195	232	280	(1% of proj. sales)
Total current assets	$5,663	$10,078	$13,033	$15,460	$18,385	$ 22,090	
Net fixed assets	903	2,208	2,433	2,925	3,488	4,200	(15% of proj. sales)
Other assets	184	907	892	905	905	905	
Total assets	$6,750	$13,193	$16,358	$19,290	$22,778	$ 27,195	
Liabilities							
Bank loans	$2,323	$ 4,350	$ 6,070	$ 7,586[a]	$ 9,321[a]	$ 11,404[a]	
Accounts and trade notes payable	1,503	2,748	3,057	3,705	4,417	5,320	(19% of proj. sales)
Accrued expenses and other items	332	683	1,231	1,462	1,744	2,100	(7.5% of proj. sales)
Current portion of long-term debt	117	350	433	450	450	450	
Other	0	187	246	250	250	250	
Total current liabilities	$4,275	$ 8,318	$11,037	$13,453	$16,182	$ 19,524	
Long-term debt	787	2,752	2,458	2,008	1,558	1,108	
Total liabilities	$5,062	$11,070	$13,495	$15,461	$17,740	$ 20,632	
Common stock ($0.10 par value)	53	55	58	58	58	58	
Paid-in capital	740	763	815	815	815	815	
Retained earnings	895	1,305	1,990	2,956	4,165	5,690	
Total liabilities and net worth	$6,750	$13,193	$16,358	$19,290	$22,778	$ 27,195	
Ratio Data							
Bank loan/receivables	80	.74	.87	.90	.93	.95	
Liabilities/equity	3.00	5.22	4.72	4.04	3.52	3.11	
Interest-bearing debt/equity	1.91	3.51	3.13	2.62	2.25	1.98	

[a]For convenience in forecasting, additional financing required beyond 1987 is assumed to be borrowed from banks. Due to loan covenant tests, this might not be possible.

EXHIBIT 3
Greeting Card Industry Data, 1987

Company	Sales[a] (in millions)	Income after Taxes (in millions)	Earnings per share (in dollars)	Stock Price/ Earnings Ratio
Hallmark	$2,000	NA	NA	NA
American Greetings	1,174	$33.4	$1.04	13[a]
Gibson Greetings	359	24.1	1.53	8[a]
Friendly Cards	16	.8	1.35	7[a]

[a]Sales include all products of these companies, but they consist primarily of greeting cards.

EXHIBIT 4
Estimated Annual Savings from Operation of Envelope Machine, Years 1 through 8 (thousands of dollars)

Savings: Outlays for envelopes purchased in 1987	$1,500
Incremental expenses from manufacturing envelopes:	
Materials	$ 902
Warehouse	94
Labor	91
Depreciation	62
Total expenses	$1,149
Increase in profits before taxes	351
Increase in income taxes @ .38	133
Increase in profit after taxes	$ 218

EXHIBIT 5 Financial Data on Large Publicly Traded Greeting Card Firms

	American Greetings			Gibson Greetings		
	1985	1986	1987	1985	1986	1987
Sales (millions)	$1,012	$1,102	$1,174	$330	$323	$359
Net income (millions)	74.2	63.4	33.4	31.5	22.6	24.1
EPS	2.32	1.97	1.04	1.99	1.43	1.53
Closing stock price	32⅝	26¼	14	19⅝	16	12⅝
Total debt (millions)	168	271	341	85	75	75
Net worth (millions)	483	524	539	119	138	154
Beta[a]			1.07			.93
Interest coverage	8.1×	5.1×	2.7×	8.3×	8.2×	9.0×

[a]Based on previous 5 years.

	1988 Interest Rates
Treasury bills	6.1%
Long-term government bond	8.4%
AAA corporate bond	8.7%
Corporate bond (similar in quality to Friendly Cards at current time)	11.5%

EXHIBIT 6 **Income Statements for Creative Designs, Inc.; Actual, 1985–1987, and Projected, 1988–1990[a] (years ending December 31; thousands of dollars)**

	Actual Data			Projected Data		
	1985	1986	1987	1988	1989	1990
Net sales	$4,175	$4,575	$5,000	$5,000[a]	$5,300[a]	$5,618[a]
Cost of goods sold[b]	2,532	2,770	3,075			
Gross profit on sales	$1,643	$1,805	$1,925			
Expenses						
Selling, delivery, and warehousing	$1,050	$1,180	$1,200			
General and administrative	280	300	350			
Total expenses	$1,330	$1,480	$1,550			
Earnings before interest and taxes	$ 313	$ 325	$ 375			
Interest	75	95	100			
Income before federal income taxes	$ 238	$ 230	$ 275			
Provision for federal income taxes	95	85	104			
Net Income	$ 143	$ 145	$ 171			
Dividends	80	80	96			
Retained earnings	$ 63	$ 65	$ 75			

[a]Projection made by Ms. Beaumont.
[b]The bulk of the depreciation expense for Creative Designs was included in the cost-of-goods-sold expense category.

EXHIBIT 7
Balance Sheets of Creative Designs, Inc. 1985–1987 (years ending December 31; thousands of dollars)

	1985	1986	1987
Assets			
Cash	$ 68	$ 58	$ 88
Notes and accounts receivable	1,360	1,533	1,600
Inventory	1,338	1,550	1,500
Prepaid expenses	32	54	62
Total current assets	$2,798	$3,195	$3,250
Net fixed assets[a]	1,090	1,225	1,250
Total assets	$3,888	$4,420	$4,500
Liabilities			
Bank loans	$ 0	$ 125	$ 250
Accounts payable	440	550	500
Current portion of long-term debt	38	50	50
Other	427	470	450
Total current liabilities	$ 905	$1,195	$1,250
Long-term debt	873	1,050	1,000
Total liabilities	$1,778	$2,245	$2,250
Common stock	100	100	100
Paid-in capital	300	300	300
Retained earnings	1,710	1,775	1,850
Total liabilities and net worth	$3,888	$4,420	$4,500
	Ratio Data		
Bank loan/receivables	0	.08	.16
Total liabilities/equity	.84	1.03	1.00
Interest-bearing debt/equity	.43	.56	.58

[a]Reconciliation of net fixed assets:

	1985	1986	1987
Net fixed assets at beginning of year	$1,050	$1,090	$1,225
(+) Capital spending	190	297	190
(–) Depreciation expense	(150)	(162)	(165)
Net fixed assets at end of year	$1,090	$1,225	$1,250

Pinkerton's (A)

Late one afternoon in November 1987, Tom Wathen, sole owner and CEO of California Plant Protection (CPP), sat in his office staring at two financing plans. Wathen was trying to decide whether or not he should increase his $85 million bid to purchase Pinkerton's—the legendary security guard firm—from its current owner, American Brands.

On the previous day, Wathen had been told by Morgan Stanley, American Brands' investment banker, that his bid of $85 million had been rejected and that nothing less than $100 million would be accepted. While Wathen was elated at still being in the deal, he had a problem. CPP's board of directors had reluctantly approved the earlier $85 million bid and was sure to balk at a $100 million bid. Wathen desperately wanted to buy Pinkerton's, but he was not sure how much it was worth or how to finance it. Wathen knew he had to act now or miss this unprecedented growth opportunity and probably his last chance to be one of the industry's biggest players.

The Security Guard Industry

The security guard industry had two segments: (1) proprietary guards and (2) contract guards. While both types of guards performed similar services, a proprietary guard was an employee on the payroll of a nonsecurity firm. Contract guards were "rented" from specialist suppliers like Pinkerton's, CPP, Wackenhut, and Baker Industries. The historical growth of the contract guard segment of the industry was due in part to companies concluding that they gained operating flexibility by contracting out their security needs as opposed to managing their own security operations. By late 1987, security guard services was a $10 billion industry growing at 6% a year. But the industry was also mature, fragmented, and price competitive. As a result, there was an ongoing trend toward consolidation at the expense of smaller, local guard companies, whose employees were often imperfectly screened and poorly trained.

Pinkerton's

The security guard industry began in 1850 when Allan Pinkerton founded the Pinkerton's Detective Agency. The firm gained fame in the nineteenth century with its pursuit of such outlaws as Butch Cassidy and the Sundance Kid. In the film portrayal of that pair, Paul Newman repeatedly asks Robert Redford, "Who are those guys?" The "guys" were Pinkerton's men and women.

Pinkerton ran his firm until he died in 1884. The company was then headed by four generations of Pinkertons until the family's reign ended in 1967 with the death of Robert Pinkerton. American Brands, the $5 billion consumer goods company, with brand names such as Lucky Strike cigarettes, Jim Beam bourbon, Master Lock padlocks, and Titleist golf balls, purchased Pinkerton's for $162 million in 1982. American Brands made the acquisition in order to expand the service side of its business and because it saw the

This case was prepared by Adam S. Berger (MBA 1991) under the supervision of Professor Scott P. Mason.

Copyright © 1991 by the President and Fellows of Harvard College. Harvard Business School case 291–051.

Pinkerton's brand name as a great addition to "a company of great brand names." The Pinkerton family sold the company to American Brands because they felt the industry was becoming extremely price competitive and that, as a result, the company needed a strong parent to compete and grow. In 1987, Pinkerton's was among the largest security guard firms in the United States, with sales of over $400 million; 150 offices in the United States, Canada, and the United Kingdom; and a particular strength in the eastern United States. Exhibit 1 gives selected financial data for Pinkerton's.

California Plant Protection

When Wathen bought CPP in 1963, the firm had 18 employees and revenues of $163,000. By 1987, Wathen had built CPP into a $250 million security guard company with 20,000 employees and 125 offices in 38 states and Canada. Exhibit 2 gives selected financial data for CPP. Wathen built CPP with his consummate marketing skills and the strategy of differentiating the firm with employee screening and continual training. CPP's expansion was aided by the explosive growth of California's economy and by the failure of the bigger, more established East Coast security guard firms to enter the West Coast aggressively.

While Wathen was the sole owner of CPP, he had a board of directors that he used as advisors. The board had three members: Albert Berger, James Hall, and Gerald Murphy. Berger was an entrepreneur, COO of an electrical connector firm, and a CPP director since 1975. Hall was an attorney, a former vice president of MCA, the former California secretary of health, education and welfare, and a CPP director since 1976. Murphy was president of ERLY Industries, a director of several companies, and a CPP director since 1975.

CPP's Acquisition of Pinkerton's

Wathen wanted to buy Pinkerton's for several reasons. First, he had always had the goal of creating the largest firm in the security guard industry. The acquisition of Pinkerton's would put him in a virtual tie with Baker Industries, a subsidiary of Borg Warner, and the largest provider of contract guard services. Second, Wathen had been convinced for some time that American Brands was mismanaging Pinkerton's and destroying a great brand name with its pricing strategy.

In October 1987, American Brands announced its decision to sell Pinkerton's because of its poor fit with Brands' long-range business strategy. Upon this announcement, Jerry Brown, CPP's secretary and general counsel, recalls, "Tom [Wathen] called me in, and from that moment I knew he was going to do whatever it took to buy Pinkerton's. Tom was always hung up on being the largest, and on Pinkerton's name."

Morgan Stanley, an investment bank, was to represent American Brands in the sale, and the bidding promised to be hotly contested. A task force of senior managers was quickly formed to prepare CPP's bid, which it knew, given the time pressures of the sale, would not have the benefit of adequate preparation.

The task force believed there were three ways CPP could create value by acquiring Pinkerton's. The most obvious source of value would come from the consolidation of the operations of CPP and Pinkerton's. This would eliminate common overhead expenses such as corporate headquarters, support staff, and redundant offices. Second, the task force believed that significant improvements could be made in the management of Pinkerton's net working capital.

The third source of value, and possibly a unique insight by Wathen and the CPP task force, was Pinkerton's pricing strategy. American Brands had instituted a strategy of low price and high market share at Pinkerton's in 1985. While the strategy had been successful in attracting new customers, it adversely affected profitability.

Wathen and the CPP task force planned to capitalize on the strength of the Pinkerton brand name by charging a premium price for services. The new pricing strategy would result in the loss of price-sensitive customers. Pinkerton's revenues would shrink, in a smooth fashion, to 70% of its 1987 level by the end of 1990, and would then grow at 5% per year thereafter. However, the new pricing strategy seemed likely to improve Pinkerton's gross profit margins from 8.5% in 1988 to 9.0% in 1989, 9.5% in 1990, and 10.25% thereafter. The task force further expected the new strategy to produce higher margins for CPP, increasing the operating profit from CPP's own projected business by $1.2 million in 1989, $1.5 million in 1990, $2,0 million in 1991, and $3 million in 1992. This increase in CPP's projected operating profit was expected to grow at 5% a year, in line with sales, beyond 1992. (Exhibit 3 gives a 5-year forecast of CPP's net income and cash flow assuming Pinkerton's is *not* acquired.) However, the task force realized there was a distinct possibility that the new pricing strategy might have little or no impact on CPP's projected operating profits and that Pinkerton's gross margins might improve to only 8.5% in 1988, 8.75% in 1989, 9% in 1990, and 9.5% thereafter.

The task force was confident that, as a result of eliminating common overhead, Pinkerton's operating expenses, as a percentage of sales, could be reduced to 6% in 1988, 5.9% in 1989, and 5.8% in 1990 and beyond. The task force was also confident that Pinkerton's net plant and equipment could be reduced to 4% of sales and could be kept there for the foreseeable future.

The task force was somewhat less confident in its estimate of improvements in the management of Pinkerton's net working capital. This was due to concerns over the ability of CPP's accounting department to handle a much larger and more geographically diverse operation. The task force expected that Pinkerton's net working capital, as a percentage of sales, could be reduced to 8.6% in 1988, 7.4% in 1989, and 6.2% thereafter. However, if CPP's accounting department experienced difficulties in integrating the two firms' operations, Pinkerton's net working capital would remain at 9.5% of sales.

The acquisition of Pinkerton's by CPP was not universally popular. Most of the investment banks and lenders contacted by CPP expressed negative feelings about the potential acquisition, citing inadequate cash flow and weak market conditions following the dramatic dislocation of the stock market in the previous month. However, a representative of Sutro & Company, a prominent West Coast investment bank, indicated that he was "highly confident" he could get financing for the acquisition from either Manufacturers Hanover Trust Corporation or General Electric Credit Corporation.

In addition, Wathen had some problems with CPP's board of directors. For example, Berger thought there would be obvious synergies in merging the two businesses, but he believed that CPP did not have enough management depth to run the combined firms. According to Berger, there was no COO, no CFO, no marketing manager, and nobody to handle the day-to-day details of operating a $650 million firm. The last thing CPP needed was growth, Berger argued. He felt that the field people could handle a larger firm but the corporate management could not.

Nonetheless, the task force pressed on with its analysis of Pinkerton's. In addition to current financial market conditions, the analysis took special notice of Wackenhut, the only publicly traded security guard firm. (See Exhibits 4 and 5.) Only 12 days after receiving the details of the sale from Morgan Stanley, and with the reluctant approval of his board, Wathen bid $85 million for Pinkerton's.

Wathen did not receive a response to his bid for two weeks. Through his own network, Wathen knew another firm had bid more than CPP and that Morgan Stanley was negotiating with that firm. Wathen was disappointed that he might miss his last opportunity to be one of the biggest in the business. When Morgan Stanley finally called and told Wathen that his $85 million bid was too low and that nothing less than $100 million would be accepted, Wathen was elated that he had another chance to buy Pinkerton's. But he suspected the reason Morgan Stanley had finally called him was that the other buyer had been unable to finance its higher bid.

Financing a $100 Million Bid

In a last ditch effort to improve his bid for Pinkerton's, Wathen asked his investment banker to determine the options for financing a $100 million bid. The banker responded with only two alternatives. The first alternative came from an investment firm that would provide both debt and equity financing. The debt, in the amount of $75 million, would have a 7-year maturity and an 11½% interest rate. The loan principal would not be amortized prior to maturity, at which time the entire $75 million would come due. Finally, this debt would be a senior obligation and would be backed by all the assets of the newly combined firm. The equity, in the amount of $25 million, would be provided for 45% of the equity in the newly combined firm.

The second alternative was a 100% debt financing offered by a bank. The bank would lend $100 million at the rate of 13½% a year. The loan principal would be amortized at the rate of $5 million a year for 6 years, with a final payment of $70 million at the end of the seventh year. This loan would be collateralized by all of the assets of the newly combined firm.

Under either financing alternative, Wathen was very concerned about the required debt service. The newly combined firm's nonpublic, as well as high-leverage, status could make any cash flow problems over the next 5 years highly problematic. The task force also reminded Wathen that a $100 million purchase price would result in the creation of goodwill on his balance sheet that would have to be amortized at the rate of $5 million per year for the next 10 years.[1]

Wathen sat in his office and prepared to make the biggest decision of his career. As an entrepreneur and an experienced security guard executive, Wathen was sure Pinkerton's was a good buy. However, he had routinely relied on his board and other advisers for financial advice. His board had reluctantly approved his earlier bid of $85 million and was sure to balk at a $100 million bid. How could he justify a $100 million bid for Pinkerton, particularly in light of his earlier bid of $85 million? And if he was successful in convincing the board, how was he going to finance the acquisition?

[1]Amortization of goodwill had to be expensed for financial reporting purposes and could not be expensed for tax purposes. The current corporate tax rate was 34%.

EXHIBIT 1 **Selected Pinkerton's Financial Data (millions of dollars)**

	1983	1984	1985	1986	1987(E)
Income from services	$296.4	$307.7	$312.4	$367.7	$408.3
Cost of services provided	264.5	275.4	286.3	342.5	381.7
Gross profit	31.9	32.3	26.1	25.2	26.6
Operating expenses	15.5	17.1	24.9	24.5	27.0
Operating profit	$ 16.4	$ 15.2	$ 1.2	$ 0.7	$ -0.4
Cash	$ 3.8	$ 2.7	$ 2.3	$ 0.0	$ 1.1
Accounts receivable, net	48.7	51.0	55.0	62.8	67.3
Other current assets	0.0	0.0	0.6	0.6	1.0
Total current assets	52.5	53.7	57.9	$ 63.4	69.4
Net property, plant, and equipment	11.0	11.3	13.1	15.1	17.6
Total assets	$ 63.5	$ 65.0	$ 71.0	$ 78.5	$ 87.0
Accounts payable	$ 0.4	$ 1.0	$ 2.4	$ 4.7	$ 3.4
Accrued expenses and other current liabilities	29.3	29.1	25.6	22.6	27.2
Total current liabilities	$ 29.7	$ 30.1	$ 28.0	$ 27.3	$ 30.6

EXHIBIT 2
Selected CPP Financial Data (millions of dollars)

	Year Ending 12/31/86	Year Ending 12/31/87(E)
Income from services	$243.6	$251.5
Cost of services provided	221.9	229.4
Gross profit	21.7	22.1
Operating expenses	16.1	14.5
Operating profit	5.6	7.6
Interest expense, net	0.7	0.4
Amortization of goodwill	0.3	0.3
Income before tax	4.6	6.9
Taxes	2.4	2.9
Net income	$ 2.2	$ 4.0
Cash	$ 1.0	$ 1.2
Accounts receivable, net	33.8	34.0
Other current assets	8.3	13.4
Total current assets	$ 43.1	$ 48.6
Notes receivable	$ 2.4	$ 2.4
Goodwill	1.8	1.5
Net property, plant, and equipment	1.8	2.6
Total assets	$ 49.1	$ 55.1
Notes payable	$ 1.0	$ 1.6
Current portion of long-term debt	1.0	1.1
Accounts payable	2.7	2.1
Accrued expenses and other current liabilities	26.5	30.4
Total current liabilities	$ 31.2	$ 35.2
Long-term debt, less current portion	$ 3.1	$ 2.0
Shareholders' equity	14.7	18.0
Total liabilities and equities	$ 49.0	$ 55.2

EXHIBIT 3

Five-Year Forecast of CPP Income and Cash Flow (millions of dollars)[a]

	1988	1989	1990	1991	1992
Net income	$4.1	$4.3	$4.6	$4.8	$5.0
Plus amortization of goodwill	0.3	0.3	0.3	0.3	0.3
Less change in net property, plant, and equipment	0.1	0.1	0.1	0.1	0.1
Less change in net working capital	1.2	0.7	0.7	0.7	0.8
Less amortization of long-term debt	1.1	1.0	1.0	0.0	0.0
Total cash flow	$2.0	$2.8	$3.1	$4.3	$4.4

[a]Under the assumption CPP does not acquire Pinkerton's.

EXHIBIT 4

Wackenhut 1987 Financial Data (millions of dollars except share data)[a]

Sales	$382.0	Debt	$ 10.6
Earnings	5.7	Assets	130.4
Earnings per share	1.47	Stock price ($)	18.00
Book equity	39.7	Beta	0.89
Shares outstanding (millions)	3.9		

[a]Wackenhut Corporation provides guard and investigative services to industry and government.

EXHIBIT 5

Selected Capital Markets Information as of November 1987

3-month Treasury bill rate	5.78%
30-year Treasury bond rate	8.58
Corporate bond yields	
AAA	9.38%
AA	9.68
A	9.99
BBB	10.58

Vodafone AirTouch's Bid for Mannesmann

On December 17, 1999, the board of Vodafone AirTouch convened to review the company's decision to launch a formal hostile bid[a] for Mannesmann, the German telecommunications company. Several days prior, Mannesmann had rejected a friendly offer from Vodafone. At stake for Vodafone and Mannesmann was the dominance of the European and world telecommunications market. In the rapidly growing and consolidating telecommunications industry, the two companies were competing to be one of the top four to five operators in the world. If Vodafone AirTouch succeeded in acquiring Mannesmann, the resulting company would be the global leader in the industry, with operations in 25 countries and 42 million equity subscribers.[b]

However, this was not going to be easy. If successful, Vodafone's hostile bid for Mannesmann would be the largest hostile takeover in the world, as well as the first ever successful foreign hostile takeover in Germany. Besides, Vodafone and Mannesmann had reached very different determinations of Mannesmann's value. Vodafone AirTouch's initial offer valued Mannesmann at €138 billion, i.e., €266 per share based on prices on December 17. This price was a premium of 14% over the Mannesmann price that day and a premium of 72.2% over Mannesmann's closing price on October 18.[c] Mannesmann rejected this offer, which stipulated an exchange of 53.7 Vodafone shares for every Mannesmann share, on the grounds that it was inadequate. Mannesmann claimed, instead, that its value was close to €350 per share. This was despite the fact that Mannesmann had offered shares at around €157.8 only a few weeks earlier in connection with its latest acquisition.

The Global Cellular Industry

The telecommunications industry was broadly defined to include the transmission of a wide range of information, from traditional phone-to-phone communications to broadband media, particularly terrestrial cable systems and data communications. The

[a]A takeover was called hostile if it was done against the wishes of current management and the board of directors. If the price was high enough, the shareholders might vote to accept the offer even if management resisted.

[b]Vodafone had partial equity stakes in many telecommunications firms around the world. Vodafone's share of the total subscriber base of all companies with which it was affiliated was calculated based on its equity stake in these companies. These subscribers, attributable to Vodafone, were referred to as "equity subscribers" or "proportionate subscribers."

[c]October 18, 1999, was the day prior to the speculation regarding a possible transaction between Mannesmann and Orange PLC, a U.K. telecommunications firm.

Professor Simi Kedia prepared this case. This case was developed from published sources. HBS cases are developed solely as the basis for class discussion. Cases are not intended to serve as endorsements, sources of primary data, or illustrations of effective or ineffective management.

Copyright © 2001 President and Fellows of Harvard College. To order copies or request permission to reproduce materials, call 1-800-545-7685, write Harvard Business School Publishing, Boston, MA 02163, or go to http://www.hbsp.harvard.edu. No part of this publication may be reproduced, stored in a retrieval system, used in a spreadsheet, or transmitted in any form or by any means—electronic, mechanical, photocopying, recording, or otherwise—without the permission of Harvard Business School.

industry had grown rapidly and in 1998 had global revenues of over U.S. $1 trillion, accounting for 4% to 5% of global GDP. The industry was forecast to grow at 29% per annum in the near future.[1] Within the telecommunications industry, the fastest growth had been in the wireless or mobile segment that experienced a compound annual growth rate (CAGR) of 52% from 1990 to 1999.[2] Worldwide mobile customers were expected to increase from 10 million in 1990 to 500 million by the end of 1999.[3] With world population of 6 billion, the penetration rate in 1999 was a mere 8%. Penetration rates were expected to increase rapidly in the coming decade.[4]

Along with voice traffic, increased demand for data transfer was expected to be a big growth driver in the wireless business. In 1999, data traffic on mobile networks was less than 2% and was forecast to increase to 45% by 2003.[5] Evidence of the importance of data was already available in NTT DoCoMo's incredibly successful launch of its mobile Internet service, "i-mode." I-mode had acquired more than 2 million subscribers in the first 8 months and reported average revenue per user (ARPU) that was 20% to 25% above traditional levels.[6] To capture the potential of data, new technologies with enhanced data capabilities were to be deployed in the near future.[d] Licenses for next generation technologies (3G) were going to be auctioned in 2000 in most European markets and bidding was expected to be aggressive.[7] There was expected to be significant capital expenditure in the deployment of the new technology. DoCoMo alone was anticipating spending $7.6 billion for its 3G network to be opened in spring 2001.[8]

With the development of new technology, mobile operators had the opportunity to become wireless Internet portals. Size and global scale were critical in attracting the best global content providers on the best terms. With the U.S. a leader in Internet usage, Europe a leader in mobile usage, and Japan a leader in wireless data usage, it was becoming increasingly important for telecommunications operators to establish a global presence in all three markets.[9] An extensive global footprint allowed an operator to be the partner of choice for multinational companies and for consumers who increasingly valued seamless global communication. In addition, size allowed purchasing economies for infrastructure, IT, and handset procurement, and resulted in a significant reduction in the cost of network operations. The importance of establishing an extensive footprint had spurred rapid consolidation in the industry. (See Exhibit 1 for the major operators.) Industry merger activity reached record levels in 1999 of approximately U.S. $1.2 trillion.[10]

Western Europe, with a population of 400 million, was the world's single largest market for mobile communications with the highest number of subscribers followed by the U.S. and Japan.[11] (See Exhibit 2 for wireless markets.) Western Europe had enjoyed a CAGR in number of subscribers of 58% from 1995 to 1998 and was expected to continue to enjoy such numbers in the near future.[12] This spectacular growth was attributed to the adoption of a common technological standard, Global System for Mobile (GSM) communications, as well as to the deregulation of the mobile market in most European countries. The largest European wireless markets were those of Germany, U.K., France, Spain, and Italy, representing 94 to 100 million mobile users, approximately 70% of all mobile users in Europe.[13] Increases in penetration rates in these markets were expected to drive future growth in subscribers.

In contrast to Europe, the U.S. wireless market not only was fragmented with 3,500 mobile licensees as of December 1999 (more than the rest of the world put together) but also had a variety of incompatible operating technologies.[14] This complexity was

[d]Intermediate technology (2.5 G) options consisted of General Packet Radio Service (GPRS) and Enhanced Data rates for Global Evolution (EDGE). Third generation (3G) technology Universal Mobile Telephone System (UMTS) would open up new radio spectrum and carry data traffic at much faster speeds.

often cited for the slow growth of wireless in the U.S. with penetration levels of only 30% and a CAGR of 24% over 1995 to 1999.[15] The Asia-Pacific market, on the other hand, was heterogeneous. It consisted of developed countries like Japan and Australia with rapidly increasing penetration rates. There were also countries like China and India where mobile telephony was seen as part of infrastructure modernization and hailed as a complete alternative to fixed line.[16]

Vodafone AirTouch

Vodafone AirTouch, based in the U.K., was one of the world's leading international mobile telecommunications companies. One of the first mobile licensees in the U.K. (see Exhibit 3 for the U.K. market), the company began offering mobile services in 1986 and by 1999 had grown to be the largest mobile company in the world.[17] With operations in 24 countries, Vodafone AirTouch had 31 million equity subscribers and a population footprint[e] of 960 million people.[18] (See Exhibit 4 for Vodafone AirTouch's holdings.) Offering a full range of services including cellular, broadband, paging, and other communications, Vodafone accounted for 7% of the FTSE 100 index.[19]

To reap economies of scale and pave the way for standardization in technology, Vodafone AirTouch increased its size and global reach. It expanded outside the U.K. into other European countries in 1988, and outside Europe in 1993.[20] In 1999 Vodafone focused on the important U.S. market. It acquired AirTouch Communications in January 1999 and changed its name to Vodafone AirTouch.[21] In September 1999, it combined its wireless assets with those of Bell Atlantic Corporation in a joint venture. This joint venture, 55% owned by Bell Atlantic and 45% owned by Vodafone AirTouch, was to be managed by Bell Atlantic.[22] By December 1999, the Vodafone AirTouch/Bell Atlantic alliance was the largest wireless operator in the U.S. with an estimated market share of 33%.[23] However, Europe was still the most important region for Vodafone AirTouch and accounted for 62% of its equity subscribers.[24]

As it expanded, Vodafone's strategy had been to focus exclusively on mobile telecommunications, rather than combining mobile and fixed networks as was more common. This strategy reflected the company's strong conviction that mobile would continue to be the fastest growing segment of the telecommunications industry.[25] In fact, Vodafone AirTouch's wireless strategy was very successful and rewarded its shareholders handsomely. (See Exhibit 9.) Sales and operating profits of continuing operations were up 34% and 17% for the six months ended September 1999, over a similar period in the prior year. (See Exhibit 5 for financials.)[26]

Mannesmann AG

Mannesmann, formed in 1890 as a producer of seamless steel tubes, entered the telecommunications industry in 1990 by establishing and operating D2, the first private mobile phone network in Germany. Mannesmann quickly became one of Europe's largest telecommunications companies, although it continued to be a leading global supplier in the fields of hydraulics, materials handling, plastics technology, and steel tubes.[27] (See Exhibit 6 for lines of business.) The engineering and automotive businesses employed 78% of employees and accounted for 69% of sales[28] but, due to the rapid growth and success of its telecommunications business, these subsidiaries contributed only 8 to 10% to total enterprise value.[29] Mannesmann had initiated a program

[e]A population footprint was the total population of areas served by Vodafone and its affiliates.

to rebalance its portfolio of assets and had announced its intention to spin off its engineering and automotive activities as a separate industrial group by 2001.[30]

In contrast to Vodafone, Mannesmann pursued an integrated telecommunications strategy focused on the European market.[31] In keeping with its European focus, Mannesmann had not established any operations in the markets of the U.S. and Japan. By 1999, however, Mannesmann had gained a leading position in four of the largest European mobile markets. Its subsidiaries, D2 and Omnitel Pronto Italia (OPI), had 8 and 9 million subscribers and were the number one and two operators in Germany and Italy, respectively.[32] In the U.K., Mannesmann's fully owned subsidiary, Orange PLC, was the third largest and fastest growing U.K. operator with 3.5 million subscribers.[33] Mannesmann also held a 12% stake in the second largest wireless operator in France.[34] In 1999, Mannesmann was the second largest company on the DAX share index and reported a proportionate telecommunications EBITDA[f] of €2.2 billion, up by 70%.[35] This was reflected in its stock price performance. (See Exhibit 7 for summary financials, and Exhibit 9 for stock price.) Mannesmann's strategy to be a single supplier of fixed lines, wireless, and Internet activities was based on a belief that integrated products best satisfied customer demand and increased average revenue per user (ARPU).[36] Mannesmann entered the fixed line market in Germany through Mannesmann Arcor, in Italy though Infostrada (majority stake acquired in 1999), in France through Cegetel, and in Austria through tele-ring. Mannesmann was also the number three Internet service provider (ISP) in Europe with 2.6 million Internet customers and a leading portal operation in Europe. A downside of providing integrated services was not only that Mannesmann would require significant capital investment for its fixed line operations but also that it would face significant challenges from the likes of British Telecom (BT), Deutsche Telekom (DT), and France Telecom.

The last prong of Mannesmann's strategy was the belief that control[g] was an essential element for success. Control facilitated network connectivity and systems compatibility and enabled maximization of value inherent in a customer base.[37]

Mannesmann's Acquisition of Orange PLC

Vodafone AirTouch and Mannesmann had been indirect partners through their stakes in Cegetel, D2, OPI, and Mannesmann Arcor. Therefore, when in late January 1999 media speculation focused on Mannesmann as a possible takeover target, Dr. Klaus Esser, CEO of Mannemann, telephoned Chris Gent, CEO of Vodafone AirTouch, to inquire about his intentions in this regard.[38] Esser was reassured that Vodafone AirTouch would discuss any such intentions with him first. Gent offered further reassurances in February in response to continued media speculation.[39] Meanwhile, the two firms were involved in discussions regarding their partnership interests and opportunities for further cooperation. The last such reported meeting was held on October 18, 1999.[40]

On October 19, the press reported Mannesmann's interest in acquiring Orange PLC, Vodafone AirTouch's rival in the U.K. market. Orange, formed in 1994, was the third largest wireless operator in the U.K. with a market share of 18%.[41] It also held a 17.45% interest in Connect Austria Gmbh (Austria's third mobile network); a 45.5% interest in Orange Communications SA (which won the third Swiss mobile license); and a 50% interest in KPN Orange Belgium NV (the third Belgian mobile license).[42] Orange was the

[f]Proportionate EBITDA was Mannesmann's share of the total EBITDA of all firms in which it had equity stakes.

[g]Control of an alliance was possible if the firm had a majority of votes. This was achieved through majority ownership in the alliance.

last major operator in the U.K. market which was not part of an international telecommunications group.[43] In August 1999, DT had acquired One2One for around €14 billion.[44] (See Exhibit 8 for mobile deals and Exhibit 3 for U.K. wireless operators.)

Upon learning of the offer, Gent contacted Esser "to discuss a more constructive route for the two companies to follow."[45] On October 20, Esser cancelled the meeting as he had already signed an agreement with Orange. The agreement specified that Mannesmann would pay £6.40 in cash and 0.0965 newly issued Mannesmann shares for every Orange share.[46] This valued Orange at £20 (€31) billion, a premium of 17% over the then-prevailing value of Orange. On October 18, prior to its announcement of the Orange acquisition, Mannesmann's share price was at €154.1, but by October 22, it had dropped 8% to a low of €141.3.[47]

As a result of Mannesmann's acquisition of Orange, Hutchison Whampoa, a diversified investment company based in Hong Kong, which owned 44.82% of Orange, acquired a 10.1% stake in Mannesmann and a seat on its supervisory board.[48] As part of the deal, Hutchison Whampoa was committed not to dispose of its block of shares for a period of 18 months, unless the Mannesmann board recommended the offer or unless there had been a change of control.[49]

Vodafone AirTouch's Response

Mannesmann's offer for Orange was a disappointment to Vodafone AirTouch, which had assumed that it would be the suitor of choice given their partnership interests. The frustration was compounded as Mannesmann's offer for Orange came after Vodafone AirTouch had sold its stake in E-Plus, its other German interest, to France Telecom.[50] This meant that Vodafone AirTouch was not in a position to reorient itself in the German market by acquiring a controlling interest in E-plus. Moreover, the souring of its relationship with Mannesmann potentially foiled Vodafone AirTouch's ambitions in the key markets of France and Italy.

On October 22, Gent contacted Goldman Sachs and Warburg Dillon Read to act as Vodafone AirTouch's financial advisors in connection with a potential acquisition of Mannesmann.[51] Vodafone AirTouch tried hard to hire a German bank to give the bid a German supporter. Deutschebank faced a conflict of interest but no other German bank with an advisory arm agreed.[52] On November 14, Gent wrote a letter to Esser setting forth the strategic case for combining the two companies and offering to pay 43.7 Vodafone AirTouch shares for each Mannesmann share. Esser rejected the offer on the grounds that it was inadequate.[53] On November 15, Mannesmann filed an application with the U.K. High Court seeking an injunction to restrain Goldman Sachs from acting on Vodafone AirTouch's behalf. Mannesmann claimed that Goldman Sachs had a conflict of interest because of its prior involvement in matters affecting Mannesmann. On November 18, the U.K. High Court dismissed the injunction application.[54]

On November 19, Vodafone AirTouch announced an amended offer at an exchange ratio of 53.7 Vodafone AirTouch shares for each Mannesmann share.[55] The 27.8 billion new Vodafone AirTouch shares to be issued would give 47.2% of the combined company to Mannesmann shareholders and valued Mannesmann at around €232 a share, a 20% premium over prices that day.[56] Vodafone AirTouch stated its intention of continuing with the proposed spin-off of the engineering and automotive assets of Mannesmann and, in order to gain regulatory approval, further proposed to spin off Orange to shareholders.[57]

The same day, Mannesmann's board advised shareholders to reject Vodafone AirTouch's offer on the grounds that it was inadequate.[58] In response, Esser stressed Mannesmann's superior strategy of integrated products and claimed that it was worth €350 a share.[59] He pointed out that, of the world's 10 largest telecommunications firms, only

Vodafone AirTouch did not own fixed line operations.[h] He said that it was of particular concern that Vodafone AirTouch's partners in the important markets of the U.S. (Bell Atlantic) and Japan (BT and AT&T) were substantial operators with global ambitions who continued to promote fixed-mobile services under their own competing brands.[60]

Vodafone AirTouch's response was one of disbelief: "Since we announced our intention to make an offer, Mannesmann's management has placed ever increasing valuations. . . . In the second week of December they valued Mannesmann at over €350 per share, while less than six weeks prior to that they were prepared to issue 117 million shares at €157.8 per share to fund the acquisition of Orange. This is less than half of what Mannesmann now says is fair value for the company."[61] On November 22, 1999, Mannesmann's offer for Orange became wholly unconditional.[i]

Gent's Decision

The Mannesmann board's rejection of Vodafone AirTouch's offer meant that, to acquire Mannesmann, Gent would have to convince Mannesmann's shareholders that a combination of Vodafone AirTouch and Mannesmann was in a better position to capitalize on new opportunities in wireless and data than a combination of Orange and Mannesmann.

As Vodafone AirTouch was much bigger than Orange, there was little doubt that Vodafone-Mannesmann would be a more powerful entity than Mannesmann-Orange. Together, Vodafone AirTouch and Mannesmann could be the leading European and world telecommunications group. With combined sales of €13 billion, it would have operations in 25 countries, and 42 million equity subscribers, 70% of which could be controlled.[62] In contrast Mannesmann-Orange would have combined sales of €5.7 billion and a presence in 7 countries with 14 million equity subscribers.[63]

For Mannesmann, the attraction of Orange was its spectacular growth—it had a CAGR of 115% over 1994–1998 in comparison to Vodafone AirTouch's 46.1%. Orange, the first to aggressively market mobile data services, was poised to launch its own free ISP in late 1999. In contrast, Vodafone AirTouch had not been vocal about its mobile data strategy, and it was only recently that it had announced plans for developing a single global Internet platform.[64]

The combination of Vodafone AirTouch and Mannesmann, however, would also give rise to significant synergies. The Vodafone board estimated that synergies from the voice business were around £500 million on a proportionate after-tax basis in 2003, and £600 million in 2004.[65] In 2003, revenue enhancement, cost savings, and savings on capital expenditure accounted for around 20%, 40%, and 40% of these savings. In 2004, synergies from revenue enhancement would increase to 25%, while those from capital expenditure would decrease to 35% of estimated synergies.[66] The Vodafone board estimates did not include any potential synergies from the data business, i.e., from creating a global platform for data and the Internet. These synergies were difficult to estimate, as they related to revenues from services not yet offered and capital expenditure savings on a 3G network not yet produced. Goldman Sachs' estimates of total synergies (voice and data) are shown in Exhibit 10. Goldman Sachs assumed that the revenue and cost synergies would grow at 4% in perpetuity while capital expenditure synergies associated with 3G would not be perpetual but would end in 2006.[67] Lehman Brothers equity analysts[j] had increased the Vodafone board estimates by 20% to account for these uncertain synergies from the data business.

[h]The ten telecommunications firms considered were AT&T, Bell Atlantic/GTE, BT, Deutsche Telekom, France Telecom, Mannesmann, MCI Worldcom, NTT/DoCoMo, SBC, and Vodafone.

[i]An offer goes unconditional when all conditions put forth for its successful completion are met.

[j]Lehman Brothers was not advising Vodafone AirTouch or Mannesmann with regard to the acquisition.

Though the global scale of the firm and the resulting synergies made a compelling case, it was unclear how far Vodafone Airtouch should go in its quest to acquire Mannesmann. This decision was complicated by disagreement among the analysts as to the correct valuation of Mannesmann. Though Julius Baar, a German investment bank, valued Mannesmann between €250 and €350 a share, most other analysts valued Mannesmann between €174 and €250 per share. (See Exhibits 11 and 12 for valuations, and Exhibit 14 for exchange rates.)

If the Vodafone AirTouch bid was unsuccessful, the fate of the two firms would be at stake. A failed bid would make Mannesmann a direct competitor in the U.K. and negatively impact joint holdings in Germany, Italy, and France. It might also make both Mannesmann and Vodafone AirTouch potential takeover targets of companies such as MCI Worldcom, SBC, Bell Atlantic, and NTT DoCoMo. Such a takeover would destroy the prospect of a European telecommunications champion.

Complicating Gent's problems was the German corporate governance system, which was markedly different from the Anglo-Saxon one and made it difficult for a hostile takeover to succeed. In Germany, law dictated the division of the board into a supervisory and a management board, each with distinct functions. The task of the supervisory board was primarily to appoint and dismiss the members of the management board. In corporations with more than 2,000 workers, the supervisory board consisted of 20 members—ten represented the shareholders, seven the workforce of the corporation, and three the trade unions. In case of a deadlock, the chairman of the supervisory board, who was elected by the shareholders, could cast the deciding vote. The management board was concerned with the day to day operations of the firm and was headed by the CEO, who was usually not a member of the supervisory board. The members of the management board were appointed for a term of up to five years, with reappointment permissible and usual. Members of a management board could be dismissed by the supervisory board through a simple majority but only for compelling reasons,[k] giving management some security and independence.

The principal of codetermination, where worker representatives held half the seats on the supervisory board, implied that unlike in the U.K. and U.S., takeovers which increase shareholder value would not necessarily be approved by the board. Despite Vodafone AirTouch's announcement that it was committed to fully protecting the rights of Mannesmann's present employees, IG Metall Union, which elected the 10 worker representatives on the supervisory board, had opposed the merger.[68]

The principal of codetermination affected other dimensions as well. Whereas in the U.S. and U.K. board members focused on "shareholders" and were keenly aware of their fiduciary duty to maximize shareholder value, many in Germany viewed their duty as maximization of value for all "stakeholders." CEOs of Anglo Saxon firms received incentives to maximize shareholder value by receiving a substantial part of their compensation in stock and stock options. In contrast, German CEOs were given little or no stock or stock options.[69] Gent owned 443 thousand options with a weighted average exercise price of £4.25 on March 31, 1999, and had exercised options worth $6.3 million in the year before.[l] In contrast, Esser owned no options and only a handful of shares.[70] Further, on account of these stock options and due to pre-negotiated golden

[k]Reasons for which the management board could be dismissed consisted of a serious neglect of duty, inability to conduct business in an orderly manner, or the withdrawal of confidence by the general shareholder's meeting.

[l]Vodafone Group Annual Report, March 31, 1999. Other than 133 thousand options granted at the exercise price of 7.8 in the year ended March 31, 1999, all other options were in the money in December 1999.

parachutes,[m] U.S. and U.K. CEOs sometimes profited handsomely when their companies were acquired. No such benefits accrued to German CEOs.[n]

A corporate raider could gain control of the supervisory board if it acquired control of the shareholder vote. However, for this it would need to acquire 75% of the votes of the corporation.[o] Given the German shareholding structure, this was unlikely to be easy. Typically, large German firms had at least one large shareholder with a stake of 25% or more.[p] Furthermore, cross-shareholdings were common where large shareholders tended to be other non-financial German firms.[71] Fortunately for Gent, Mannesmann's major shareholdings were not typical of a German firm.[q] Mannesmann's major shareholders were large institutional investors based in the U.S. or U.K., and there were few cross-shareholdings. (See Exhibit 13 for Mannesmann's shareholder structure.) By one estimate, 40% of Mannesmann shareholders were also shareholders of Vodafone AirTouch.[72]

Another major obstacle was the voting restriction in Mannesmann's articles of association. By this statute, no shareholder was entitled to vote in excess of 5% of the outstanding capital stock of Mannesmann. This meant that regardless of the number of shares acquired by Vodafone AirTouch, its vote could not exceed 5%. However, this restriction was to be rescinded on June 1, 2000, pursuant to the new German Law Regarding Control and Transparency in Business Enterprises. Even if Vodafone AirTouch acquired 75% of the firm, it might have to wait until June 2000 to replace the supervisory board and take control of Mannesmann's management.

There was also concern regarding the response to the hostile takeover in Germany and the ensuing debate in Europe. Vodafone AirTouch's bid for Mannesmann at €138 billion was one of the few foreign hostile bids in Germany and the largest one. The public response in Germany had been quite negative. Chancellor Schroeder stated that "hostile takeovers destroy corporate culture," while on the other side, Prime Minister Tony Blair said, "We live in a European market today where European companies are taking over other European companies."[73] There were, however, some champions of market forces in Germany; Esser himself had stated that he would leave the decision to the shareholders rather than retreating into "Fortress Germany."[74] Similar views were held by two outside directors of Mannesmann—Jurgen Schrempp, CEO of Daimler Chrysler, and Henning Schulte-Noelle, head of Allianz insurance group.[75] Whether the German

[m]A golden parachute was a contract which provided benefits to a top executive in the event that a takeover of the company resulted in his losing his job. The benefits consisted of severance pay, stock options, or a bonus.

[n]Sam Ginn was paid $150 million when he sold AirTouch to Vodafone, and Hans Snook, CEO of Orange, made $70 million when he sold Orange to Mannesmann. "In Vodafone Battle, Esser Was Flying with No Parachute," *Wall Street Journal Europe,* February 7, 2000.

[o]Under German Law and Mannesmann's article of association, most corporate actions could be taken with the approval of a majority of Mannesmann's outstanding share capital present and voting. However, a number of actions requiring the consummation of the offer could only be taken with the approval of 75% of the outstanding share capital present and voting. Such actions included causing Mannesmann to enter into mergers, consolidations, or spin-offs and causing it to enter into agreements that concerned the structure of Mannesmann.

[p]A study by Franks and Mayer in 1992 found that nearly 90% of the largest 200 companies in Germany at the end of 1980's had at least one shareholder with an ownership stake of at least 25%. In contrast, they found that two-thirds of the largest 200 firms in the U.K. had no single shareholder with a holding of more than 10%.

[q]Typically, banks also had an important role to play in the success of takeover bids in Germany, and this influence was exercised through many channels. Banks owned equity in the firm and often were members of the supervisory board; therefore their consent could affect the outcome. The more important channel of influence was their ability to vote on behalf of shareholders who had deposited their shares with the banks. However, Mannesmann's unusual shareholding significantly reduced the role of banks.

government would demonstrate its willingness to embrace global capitalism by keeping out of this battle was important for Europe's vision of a single borderless market.

Gent would need to review the strategic case underlying the combination of Vodafone AirTouch and Mannesmann, the correct price to pay for Mannesmann, and the probability of success of an unprecedented and historic hostile takeover bid in Germany. His recommendation would be crucial to the future course of action charted by the Vodafone AirTouch board.

EXHIBIT 1 Major Global Mobile Operators, June 1999

Source: WestLB Panmure Research, November 1999; case writer's estimates.

Company	Country of Incorporation	Number of Customers as of June 99 (000s)	Global Rank by Number of Subscribers	CAGR in # of Subscribers 94–98 (%)
Vodafone	U.K.	29,242	1	46.1
DoCoMo	Japan	25,067	2	78.6
TIM	Italy	17,679	3	57.3
Deutsche Telecom	Germany	15,732	4	55.5
Mannesmann	Germany	9,658	7	86.7
Orange	U.K.	3,500	19	115.5

EXHIBIT 2 Major Global Markets, September 1999

Source: Dresdner Kleinwort Benson Research, December 10, 1999; West LB Panmure Research, November 1999; and case writer's estimates.

Country	Mobile Subscribers (000s)	Penetration (%)	CAGR (95–99)	Company	Market Share[a] (%)	Major Shareholders
W. Europe	132,000	34.0	58			
U.K.	19,289	33.2	44	Vodafone	35	Vodafone (100%)
				Cellnet	30	British Telecom (BT) (100%)
				Orange	18	Hutchison Whampoa (45%)
				One-2-One	17	Deutsche Telekom (100%)
Germany	19,421	23.8	58	D2	41	Vodafone (35%), Mannesmann (65%)
				D1	40	Deutsche Telekom (100%)
				E-Plus	16	Bell South (22.5%), Vodafone (17%)
France	15,955	27.1	88	Itineris	49	France Telecom (100%)
				SFR	36	Vivendi (35%), BT (21%), Mannesmann (12%), Vodafone (20%)
Italy	27,028	47.6	64	TIM900	64	Telecom Italia (52%), Bell Atlantic (23)
				OPI	33	Vodafone (22%), Mannesmann (55%)
Spain	12,185	31.1	95	Telefonica	63	
				Airtel	33	Vodafone (22%), BT (23%)
U.S.	80,750	30.4	24.3	Alliance	33	Vodafone (45%), Bell Atlantic (55%)
				AT&T	13	
Asia	150,000	4.7	64			
Japan	46,288	37.3	59	NTT DoCoMo	57	NTT (100%)
				Digital phone	10	Vodafone various, Japan Telecom
E. Europe	13,380	6.8	100			
M. East	10,650	11.4	80			
Africa	5,405	1.3	100			

[a]These numbers are as of December 1999.

EXHIBIT 3 Wireless Players in the U.K. Market, September 1999

Source: Morgan Stanley Dean Witter, December 13,1999; ABN-AMRO research, November 8, 1999; case writer's estimates.

	Vodafone	Cellnet	Orange	One2One
Market Share based on number of subscribers	35%	30.4%	18%	16.6%
1999E U.K. Revenues (billion £)	3	2.4	1.4	1.14
1999E EBITDA Margin	34%	12.8%	18%	14%
1999E EBIT Margin	—	2.7%	8%	5%
EV/EBITDA[a]	30	23	77.5	57
European Average EV/EBITDA[b]	21.9			
European Median EV/EBITDA	21			

[a]EV was the enterprise value, i.e., market value of equity and debt. The EV/EBITDA multiples for Orange and One2One use the acquired price to estimate the enterprise value while those of Vodafone and Cellnet were based on analyst estimates.
[b]The European average includes valuations of fixed line operators, which were lower than wireless operators.

EXHIBIT 4 Summary of Vodafone AirTouch Holdings around the World, September 1999

Source: WestLB Panmure, Dresdner Kleinwort Benson Research, Goldman Sachs Research, and case writer's estimates.

Company	No. of Countries	No. of Controlled Countries	Enterprise Subscribers	Controlled Subscribers
Europe	14	7	43,158	12,694
United States	1	0	25,000	—
Asia	6	2	12,110	1,593
Africa and Middle East	3	1	2,686	244

EXHIBIT 5 Selected Items from Consolidated Financial Statements for Vodafone AirTouch (£ million)

Source: Vodafone AirTouch prospectus. Financial statements are in accordance with U.K. GAAP.

	6 Months Ending September 1999[a]	Year Ended 31 March		
		1999	1998	1997
Turnover (Revenues)	4,208	3,360	2,470.8	1,749
Total Group Operating Profit	253[b]	962.6	686.4	538.9
Net Profits (loss)	(455)	636.7	418.8	363.8
Total Fixed Assets[c]	48,483	2,852.1	1,911.5	1,926.6
Total Current Assets	2,247	791.5	590.8	495.2
Liabilities due within one year	7,700	1,529.9	1,426.4	1,013.2
Liabilities due after one year	2,036	1,189.4	696.4	580
Capital and Reserves[d]	40,994	924.3	379.5	828.6

[a]Pro forma profit and loss under the assumption that Vodafone AirTouch merger took place on April 1, 1999.
[b]Total operating profit before goodwill was £1.4 billion. Amortization of goodwill was £1.2 billion.
[c]The goodwill arising from the merger of Vodafone with AirTouch was estimated to be £40.9 billion.
[d]Total equity shareholders' funds increased on account of the issue of new share capital of £39 billion in relation to Vodafone's merger with AirTouch.

EXHIBIT 6 Mannesmann and Its Businesses

Source: Mannesmann company information, 1999. Adapted by case writer.

	Country	Stake	Products	Sales 1998 (εm)	Employees 1998
Engineering					
Rexroth	Germany	100	Motion Control Equipment	2,547	20,927
Dematic	Germany	100	Cranes & Handling Equipment	1,989	12,907
Demag KraussMalfee	Germany	100	Plastic Machinery and Compressors	2,132	11,265
Automotive					
VDO	Germany	100	Engineering Auto Manufacturers	3,338	23,036
Sachs	Germany	100	Power Train & Chassis	2,150	19,860
Tubes	Germany	100	Seamless Welded Steel Tubes	2,338	13,084
Wireline Telecommunications					
Arcor	Germany	70.1		939	6,554
Infostrada	Italy	100		188	
Cegetel	France	15		156	
tele-ring	Austria	53.8			
Wireless Telecommunications					
Mobilfunk (D2)	Germany	65.2		3,731	6,711
Omnitel	Italy	55.2		2,332	
SFR	France	12		2,658	
Orange[a]	U.K.	100		1,731	6,144

[a]Consolidated results for Orange PLC, acquired by Mannesmann in October 1999.

EXHIBIT 7 Selected Items from Consolidated Financial Statements for Mannesmann (ε millions)

Source: Vodafone AirTouch prospectus; Mannesmann company reports, 1999; ABN-AMRO, November 8, 1999. Prepared in accordance with German GAAP.

	Year Ended December 31,		
	1998	1997	1996
Total Sales	19,065	19,989	18,115
EBITDA	3,125	2,204	1,992
EBIT	1,469	894	954
Net Profit (loss)	239	189	584
Intangible Assets	2,816	2,003	997
Tangible Assets	4,902	4,689	3,809
Trade Creditors	1,452	1,696	1,428
Amounts Owned to Credit Institutions	1,803	1,361	617
Other Liabilities[a]	7,734	7,514	6,314
Shareholder's Equity	6,360	4,498	3,942

[a]Includes provisions for pension liabilities and other liabilities.

EXHIBIT 8 European and U.S. Mobile Transactions in 1999

Source: WestLB Panmure research, November 1999; case writer's estimates.

Date	Name	Stake Acquired (%)	Equity POPS[a] (m)	Equity Subscribers (m)	EV/ Sub[c](ε)	EV/ POP[c](ε)
European Mobile Transactions (Acquirer-Target)						
Jun	Bouygues - Bouyges Tel	20	11.6	1.9	932	153
Jul	BT-BT Cellnet	40	4.6	2.08	2,813	1,272
Aug	Deutsche Telekom—One2One	100	58.1	2.98	4,745	243
Oct	France Tel—E Plus	17.3	14.1	0.51	5,157	187
Oct	France Tel—E Plus	60.1	49.3	1.77	5,989	215
Oct	Tele Danmark—Netcom	19.6	0.8	0.15	2,800	525
Oct	Mannesmann—Orange	100	58.1	3.5	8,857	533
Mar	Mannesmann—Omnitel	23.5	13.5	1.6	3,538	419
Mean					4,354	443
Mean for controlling deals[b]					6,530	330
U.S. Mobile Transactions (Acquirer-Target)						
Jun	Vodafone—AirTouch	100	211.8	14.2	5,620	377
Mar	AT&T—Vanguard	100	9.7	0.7	2,629	190
Mar	SBC—Comcast	100	8.6	0.75	2,413	210
Apr	GTE—Ameritech	100	11.0	1.7	2,018	312
Jun	Hutchison—Voicestream	30	17.6	0.55	2,236	70
Jun	Voicestream—Omnipoint	100	26.4	0.59	2,085	47
Jul	Vodafone—Comnet	100	7.6	0.34	4,206	188
Sep	Voicestream—Aerial	100	25.4	0.35	5,480	76
Oct	Worldcom—Sprint	100	220.0	4.0	12,100	220
Mean					4,310	188
Mean for controlling deals[b]					4,569	203

[a]Equity POPS is a pro-rata value, which reflects the firm's share of the population served by the target firm, based on the equity stake acquired.
[b]Controlling deals were deals in which a majority stake was acquired.
[c]The EV/Subscriber multiple was obtained by dividing enterprise value by the equity subscribers, while the EV/POP multiple was the enterprise value divided by equity POPS of the firm.

EXHIBIT 9
Vodafone, Mannesmann, and FTSE Western European Index[a] Returns

Source: Datastream.

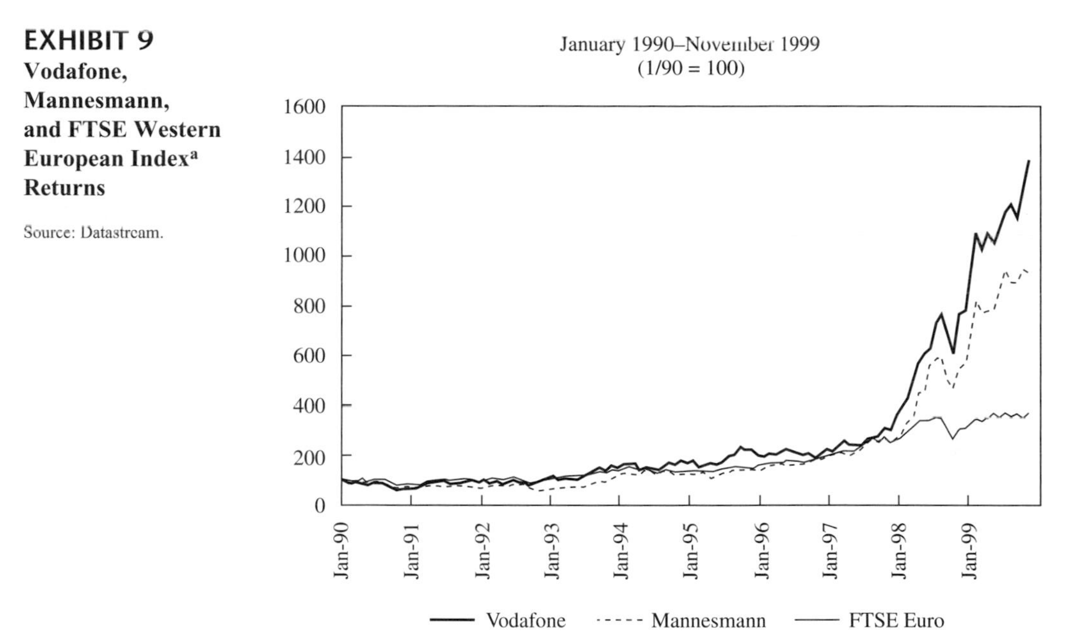

[a]The FTSE West European Index is composed of twelve countries from Western Europe, including the U.K. and Germany.

EXHIBIT 10 Estimation of Synergies from Vodafone AirTouch's Acquisitions of Mannesmann (£ m)

Source: Goldman Sachs Research, "Vodafone Airtouch: Telecom Wireless," February 28, 2000.

	Year End March							Synergy as % of Combined Firm in 2004[c]
	2000E	2001E	2002E	2003E	2004E	2005E	2006E	
Revenue Synergy	0	50	153	469	656	977	1,221	1.7%
Cost Associated with Revenue Synergy	0	(40)	(107)	(281)	(328)	(488)	(610)	
Cost Synergy	0	80	200	500	656	732	879	
Total Operating Profit Impact	0	90	246	688	984	1,221	1,489	5.7%
Savings in Capital Expenditures	0	60	147	360	420	469	506	7.8%
Assumptions								
WACC[a]	7.6%							
Perpetuity Growth[b]	4%							
Tax Rate	35%							

[a]The WACC assumed a Nominal Sterling (£) risk-free rate of 5.5%, a market risk premium of 2%, cost of debt of 7%, gearing (ratio of debt to total market value of the firm) at 5%, and corresponding equity beta for Vodafone of 1.1.
[b]The estimated inflation in the U.K. was 2.5%.
[c]The expected synergies in 2004 as a percentage of the respective categories, i.e., revenues, operating profits, and capital expenditures for the combined firm in 2004.

EXHIBIT 11A Value of Vodafone AirTouch and Mannesmann (£ m)

Source: Goldman Sachs Research "Vodafone Airtouch: Telecom Wireless," February 28, 2000, and case writer's estimates.

Year Ending March	2000E	2001E	2002E	2003E	2004E	2005E
Vodafone AirTouch						
Proportionate EBITDA[a]	3,925	5,191	6,747	8,497	10,653	13,044
Taxes Paid[b]	861	1,188	1,594	2,042	2,559	3,138
Capital Expenditure[c]	3,505	3,945	4,169	4,265	4,324	4,534
Free Cash Flows	(441)	58	984	2,189	3,770	5,372
Terminal Value						155,200
Enterprise Value	116,361					
Mannesmann's Telecommunications Business (not including Orange)						
Proportionate Telecommunications EBITDA[a]	1,565	2,101	2,923	3,908	4,822	5,905
Taxes Paid[b]	343	481	690	939	1,158	1,420
Capital Expenditures[c]	1,125	1,145	1,192	1,324	1,342	1,256
Free Cash Flows	96	474	1,041	1,645	2,322	3,228
Terminal Value						93,261
Value of Telecommunications Business	71,387					
Assumptions						
1. WACC = 7.6%						
2. Terminal Value Growth Rate = 4%						

[a]Proportionate EBITDA is a pro-rata consolidation which reflects the firm's share of EBITDA in both its consolidated and unconsolidated entities. Proportionate EBITDA is not a recognized presentation under either U.K. or German GAAP. The EBITDA for Mannesmann's telecommunications business does not include Orange PLC.

[b]The taxes paid were estimated after deducting depreciation but before any interest payments.

[c]The estimated depreciation was assumed to be approximately equal to capital expenditure in 2005.

EXHIBIT 11B Equity Valuation of Vodafone and Mannesmann (£ m)

Source: Goldman Sachs Research, February 28, 2000; Lehman Brothers Research, 1999; Dresdner Kleinwort Benson Research, December 10, 1999; case writer's estimates.

	Vodafone AirTouch	Mannesmann
Value of Telecommunications Business	116,361	71,387
Value of Orange PLC[a]		17,730
Value of Industrials[b]		7,405
Total Enterprise Value (EV)	116,361	96,522
Value of Proportionate Net Debt	8,000	16,250
Value of Equity (£)	108,361	80,272
Value of Equity (€)[c]	173,377	128,434

[a]The value of Orange was based on an EBITDA estimate of £598 for 2000 and Vodafone's EV/EBITDA multiple of 29.6.

[b]The value of Mannesmann's non-telecommunications industrial assets was based on the EBITDA estimate of £903 for 2000 and an EV/EBITDA multiple of 8.2.

[c]The £ value was converted to € at the spot exchange rate on December 17, 1999, of €1.6 = 1£.

EXHIBIT 12 **Equity Valuations of Mannesmann and Vodafone AirTouch (Billions €)**

Source: Equity Analyst Reports dated November 1999 and December 1999.

Date	Analyst	Mannesmann	Vodafone AirTouch	Valuation Methodology
Nov 99	Credit Suisse First Boston	90	143	Sum of Parts, DCF, EV/EBITA
Dec 99	Dresdner Kleinwort Benson	131	178	Sum of Parts, DCF, EV/EBITDA
Dec 99	Exhibit 11	128	173	DCF on Proportionate Cash Flows
Dec 99	Julius Bär	129–181		Sum of Parts, DCF, M&A premium, and Conglomerate Discount
Nov 99	Commerzbank	122		Sum of Parts, DCF, EV/EBITDA
Nov 18	Market Prices	108	138	
Dec 17	Market Prices	121	154	

Note: Equity valuations were made under the assumption of full acceptance of Mannesmann's offer for Orange. Mannesmann had 517.9 million and Vodafone AirTouch had 31,105 million shares outstanding. Sum of Parts methodology valued each affiliate using DCF or multiples and added proportionate values based on equity stake to obtain the value of the group. DCF on proportionate cash flows first estimated proportionate cash flows of the group (based on equity stakes held in affiliates), which were then discounted.

EXHIBIT 13A
Largest Shareholders of Mannesmann as of December 1999

Source: SG Securities, affiliated with the Societe Generale Group, December 1999, and case writer's estimates.

Major Shareholders	Country	Holding (%)
Hutchison Whampoa	Hong Kong	10.1
Capital Group	U.S.	3.0
Templeton	U.K./Hong Kong	1.8
Janus	U.S.	1.7
Deutsche FM	Germany/U.S./U.K.	1.2

EXHIBIT 13B
Geographic Distribution of Mannesmann's Shareholders, October 1999

Source: Dresdner Kleinwort Benson Research, December 10, 1999. Adapted by case writer.

Areas	Category	Holdings (%)
Germany	Retail	12
	Institutional	16
	Mannesmann Employees	4
U.K.		18
Rest of Europe		13
U.S.		25
Rest of the World	Hutchison Whampoa	10
	Others	2

EXHIBIT 14 Share Prices and Exchange Rates, October 1999–December 1999

Source: Datastream. Adapted by case writer.

Date	Mannesmann	Vodafone	£ Value of 1ε		Date	Mannesmann	Vodafone	£ Value of 1ε
10/19/1999	153	2.74	0.6467	Press reports Mannesmann's interest in Orange PLC	11/23/1999	181.5	2.73	0.6329
10/20/1999	158.6	2.57	0.6465	Mannesmann makes deal with Orange	11/24/1999	187.5	2.79	0.6322
10/21/1999	145.35	2.70	0.645		11/25/1999	202.8	3.00	0.6313
10/22/1999	141.3	2.69	0.6428		11/26/1999	202	2.98	0.6301
10/25/1999	143	2.64	0.6422		11/29/1999	204.95	2.95	0.6287
10/26/1999	147.5	2.73	0.6402		11/30/1999	206.4	2.95	0.6322
10/27/1999	145.5	2.72	0.6392		12/01/1999	215.7	3.02	0.631
10/28/1999	148.5	2.69	0.6413		12/02/1999	220.6	3.00	0.6276
10/29/1999	149.5	2.83	0.6406		12/03/1999	226	3.05	0.6253
11/01/1999	146.5	3.00	0.639		12/06/1999	234.5	3.18	0.6321
11/02/1999	144.75	2.89	0.6372		12/07/1999	238.6	3.26	0.6298
11/03/1999	146	2.95	0.6374		12/08/1999	231	3.12	0.6303
11/04/1999	147.9	3.01	0.6373		12/09/1999	234.5	3.14	0.6268
11/05/1999	159.95	3.17	0.6412		12/10/1999	229.8	3.11	0.6264
11/08/1999	165.25	3.18	0.6413		12/13/1999	224	3.04	0.6231
11/09/1999	162.6	3.22	0.6415		12/14/1999	229	3.08	0.6226
11/10/1999	175.2	3.20	0.6419		12/15/1999	221	2.99	0.6241
11/11/1999	178.9	3.17	0.6413		12/16/1999	227	3.06	0.6313
11/12/1999	185	2.96	0.6394	Vodafone's first bid for Mannesmann	12/17/1999	234	3.11	0.6274
11/15/1999	201.5	2.92	0.6362					
11/16/1999	206.2	2.71	0.6371					
11/17/1999	195.8	2.77	0.6396					
11/18/1999	208.7	2.83	0.6381					
11/19/1999	194	2.75	0.6365	Vodafone's amended offer for Mannesmann				
11/22/1999	186.5	2.75	0.6371	Mannesmann's offer for Orange PLC becomes unconditional				

Endnotes

[1]"Mobile Data Handbook," Merrill Lynch, September 24, 1999.

[2]West LB Panmure Research, November 1999.

[3]Ibid.

[4]Ibid.

[5]"Mobile Data Handbook," Merrill Lynch, September 24, 1999.

[6]"The Company That Got Japan to Log On," *Business Week,* July 12, 1999.

[7]West LB Panmure Research, November 1999.

[8]"The Company That Got Japan to Log On," *Business Week,* July 12, 1999.

[9]West LB Panmure Research, November 1999.

[10]Ibid.

[11]Dresdner Kleinwort Benson Research, December 10, 1999; West LB Panmure Research, November 1999; and case writer's estimates.

[12]Ibid.

[13]Dresdner Kleinwort Benson Research, December 10, 1999; West LB Panmure Research, November 1999; and case writer's estimates.

[14]West LB Panmure Research, November 1999.

[15]Dresdner Kleinwort Benson Research, December 10, 1999; West LB Panmure Research, November 1999; and case writer's estimates.

[16]West LB Panmure Research, November 1999.

[17]Vodafone AirTouch, Offer for Mannesmann AG, December 23, 1999.

[18]West LB Panmure Research, November 1999; Dresdner Kleinwort Benson Research, December 10, 1999.

[19]West LB Panmure Research, November 1999.

[20]Vodafone AirTouch, Offer for Mannesmann AG, December 23, 1999.

[21]Ibid.

[22]West LB Panmure Research, November 1999.

[23]Dresdner Kleinwort Benson Research, December 10, 1999; West LB Panmure Research, November 1999; and case writer's estimates.

[24]Goldman Sachs Research, July 14, 1999.

[25]Vodafone AirTouch, Offer for Mannesmann AG, December 23, 1999.

[26]Ibid.

[27]Mannesmann company information, 1999.

[28]Credit Suisse First Boston Research, November 24, 1999.

[29]Ibid.

[30]Vodafone AirTouch, Offer for Mannesmann AG, December 23, 1999.

[31]Letter from Klaus Esser, CEO of Mannesmann, to shareholders dated January 14, 2000.

[32]Mannesmann AG Press Release, February 21, 2000.

[33]Vodafone AirTouch, Offer for Mannesmann AG, December 23, 1999.

[34]Dresdner Kleinwort Benson Research, December 10, 1999; West LB Panmure Research, November 1999; and case writer's estimates.

[35]Letter from Klaus Esser, CEO of Mannesmann, to shareholders dated January 14, 2000.

[36]Ibid.

[37]Ibid.

[38]Vodafone AirTouch, Offer for Mannesmann AG, December 23, 1999.

[39]Ibid.

[40]Ibid, p. 47.

[41]HSBS Research, October 4, 1999.

[42]Vodafone AirTouch, Offer for Mannesmann AG, December 23, 1999.

[43]HSBS Research, October 4, 1999.

[44]West LB Panmure Research, November 1999.

[45]Vodafone AirTouch, Offer for Mannesmann AG, December 23, 1999, p. 47.

[46]Ibid.

[47]DataStream.

[48]Vodafone AirTouch, Offer for Mannesmann AG, December 23, 1999.

[49]Ibid.

[50]West LB Panmure Research, November 1999.

[51]Vodafone AirTouch, Offer for Mannesmann AG, December 23, 1999.

[52]"The Bid That Couldn't Fail," *Euromoney,* March 2000.

[53]Vodafone AirTouch, Offer for Mannesmann AG, December 23, 1999.

[54]Ibid.

[55]Ibid.

[56]Datastream.

[57]Vodafone AirTouch, Offer for Mannesmann AG, December 23, 1999.

[58]Ibid.

[59]Letter from Klaus Esser, CEO of Mannesmann, to shareholders dated January 14, 2000.

[60]Ibid.

[61]Vodafone AirTouch press release, December 8, 1999.

[62]West LB Panmure Research, November 1999.

[63]Ibid.

[64]Vodafone AirTouch press release, January 11, 2000.

[65]Vodafone AirTouch press release, November 16, 1999.

[66]Ibid.

[67]Goldman Sachs Research, February 2000.

[68]Vodafone AirTouch, Offer for Mannesmann AG, December 23, 1999.

[69]*Wall Street Journal Europe,* February 7, 2000.

[70]Ibid.

[71]*Banks, Finance and Investment in Germany,* by Jeremy Edwards and Klaus Fischer, Cambridge University Press, 1993.

[72]*Financial Times,* December 2, 1999.

[73]*Wall Street Journal,* December 30, 1999.

[74]"Will Fortress Germany Prevail?" *Fortune Magazine,* December 20, 1999.

[75]Ibid.

Index of Cases